# The **Rough Guide** to

written and researched by

**David Cleary, Dilwyn Jenkins and Oliver Marshall**

www.roughguides.com

# Contents

**Brazilian food and drink** colour section following p.264

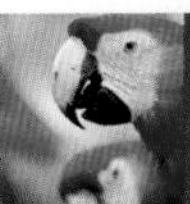

**Amazon flora and fauna** colour section following p.408

◄◄ Colonial-style architecture, Olinda, Pernambuco ◄ Catedral Metropolitana Nossa Senhora Aparecida, Brasília

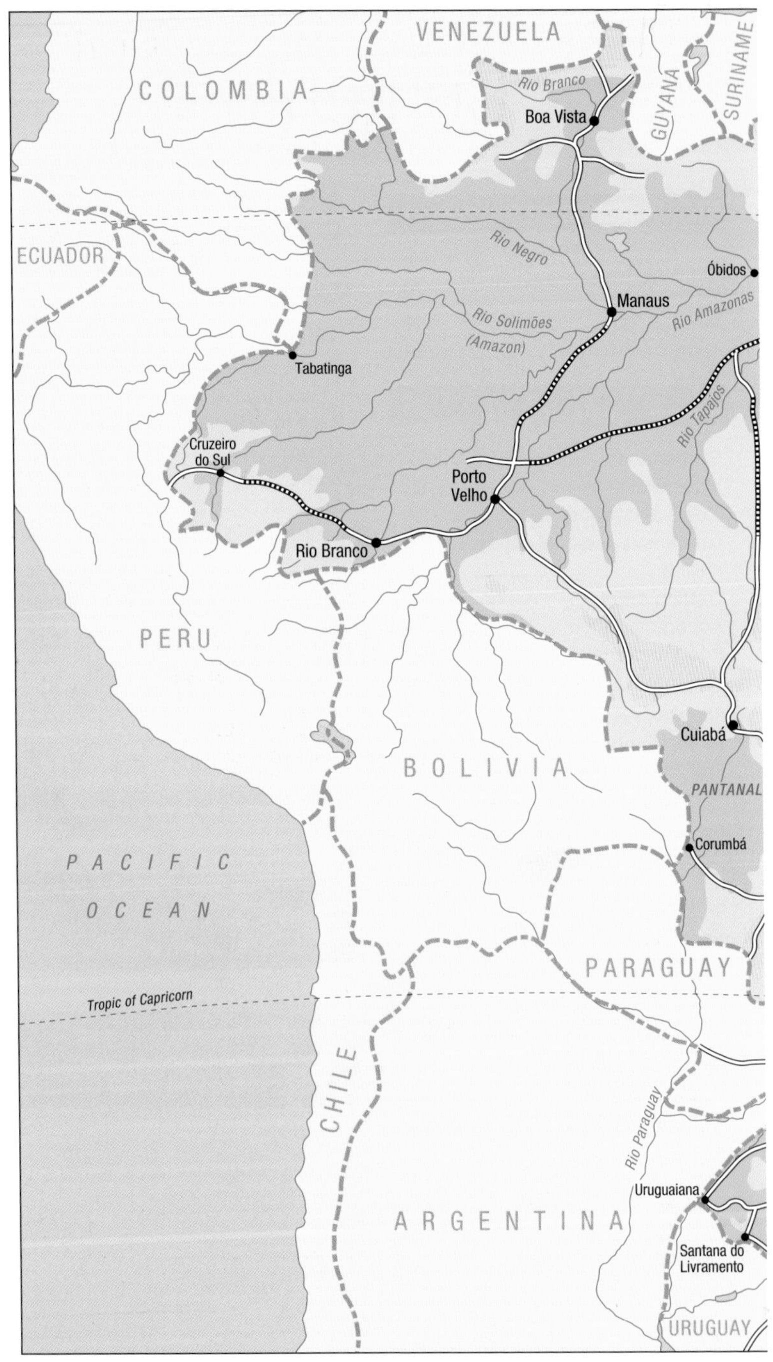
VENEZUELA
COLOMBIA
GUYANA
SURINAME
Rio Branco
Boa Vista
ECUADOR
Rio Negro
Óbidos
Manaus
Rio Amazonas
Rio Solimões
(Amazon)
Tabatinga
Rio Tapajós
Cruzeiro
do Sul
Porto
Velho
Rio Branco
PERU
Cuiabá
BOLIVIA
PANTANAL
Corumbá
PACIFIC
OCEAN
PARAGUAY
Tropic of Capricorn
CHILE
Rio Paraguay
Uruguaiana
ARGENTINA
Santana do
Livramento
URUGUAY

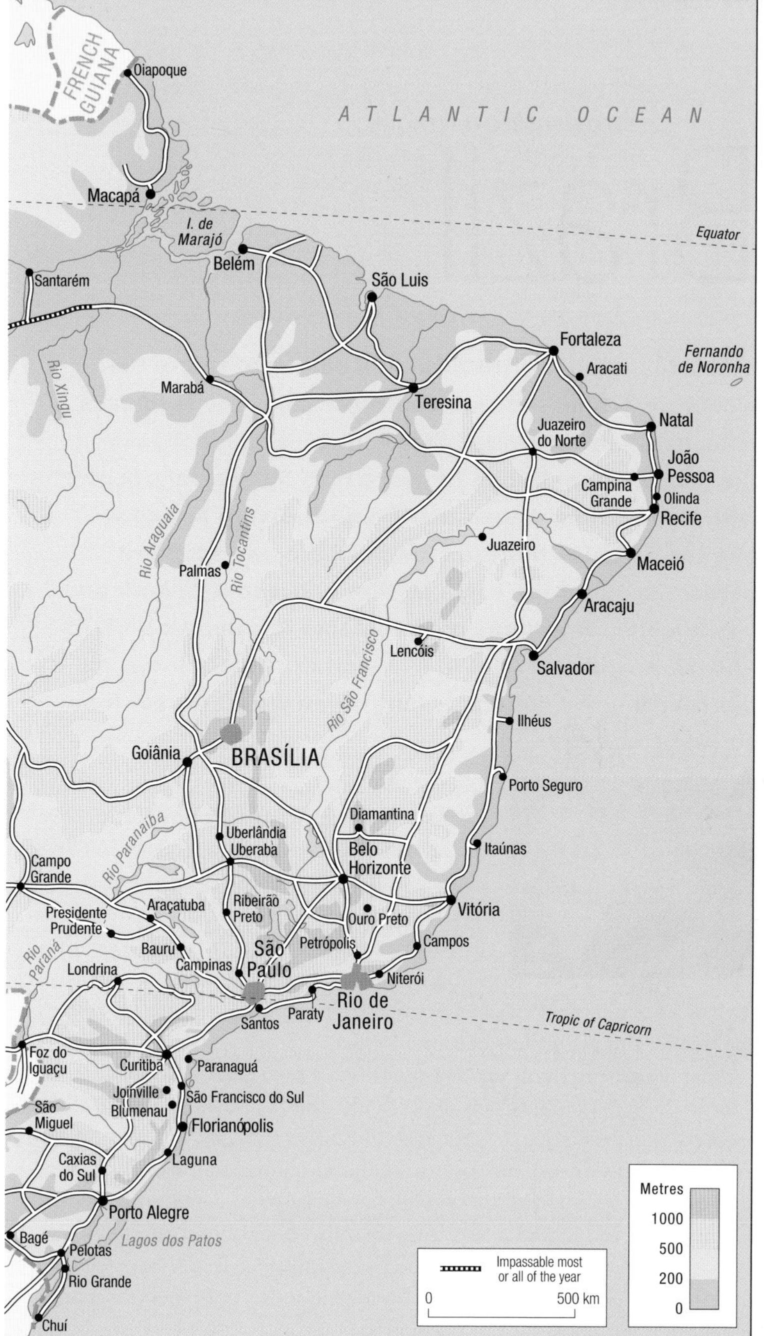
ATLANTIC OCEAN
FRENCH GUIANA
Oiapoque
Macapá
Equator
I. de Marajó
Belém
Santarém
São Luis
Fortaleza
Aracati
Fernando de Noronha
Rio Xingu
Marabá
Teresina
Natal
Juazeiro do Norte
João Pessoa
Campina Grande
Olinda
Recife
Rio Araguaia
Rio Tocantins
Juazeiro
Maceió
Palmas
Aracaju
Lençóis
Rio São Francisco
Salvador
Ilhéus
Goiânia
BRASÍLIA
Porto Seguro
Rio Paranaíba
Diamantina
Uberlândia
Uberaba
Itaúnas
Campo Grande
Belo Horizonte
Presidente Prudente
Araçatuba
Ribeirão Preto
Ouro Preto
Vitória
Rio Paraná
Bauru
Petrópolis
São Paulo
Campos
Londrina
Campinas
Niterói
Santos
Paraty
Rio de Janeiro
Tropic of Capricorn
Foz do Iguaçu
Curitiba
Paranaguá
Joinville
São Francisco do Sul
Blumenau
São Miguel
Florianópolis
Caxias do Sul
Laguna
Porto Alegre
Bagé
Lagos dos Patos
Pelotas
Rio Grande
Chuí
Impassable most or all of the year
0
500 km
Metres
1000
500
200
0

# Introduction to Brazil

**Brazilians often say they live in a continent rather than a country. It's an excusable exaggeration. The landmass is bigger than the United States if you exclude Alaska; the journey from Recife in the east to the western border with Peru is longer than that from London to Moscow, and the distance between the northern and southern borders is about the same as that between New York and Los Angeles. Brazil has no mountains to compare with its Andean neighbours, but in every other respect it has all the scenic – and cultural – variety you would expect from so vast a country.**

Despite the immense expanses of the interior, roughly two-thirds of Brazil's **population** live on or near the coast and well over half live in cities – even in the Amazon. In Rio and São Paulo, Brazil has two of the world's great metropolises, and ten other cities have over a million inhabitants. Yet Brazil still thinks of itself as a frontier country, and certainly the deeper into the interior you go, the thinner the population becomes.

Other South Americans regard Brazilians as a **race** apart, and language has a lot to do with it – Brazilians understand Spanish, just about, but Spanish-speakers won't understand Portuguese. Brazilians also look different. In the extreme south German and eastern European immigration has left distinctive traces; São Paulo has the world's largest Japanese community outside Japan; slavery lies behind a large Afro-Brazilian population concentrated in Rio, Salvador and São Luís; while the Indian influence is still very visible in the Amazon. Italian and Portuguese immigration has been so great that its influence is felt across the entire country.

▲ Sunset over the Pantanal

## Fact file

• By far the **largest country** in South America, Brazil covers nearly half the continent and is only slightly smaller than the US, with an area of just over 8.5 million square kilometres. It shares a **frontier** with every South American country except Chile and Ecuador.

• Brazil has around 200 million **inhabitants**, making it the fifth most populous country in the world.

• Almost ninety percent of Brazil's **electricity** is generated from hydropower, about six percent from fossil fuels and six percent from nuclear power. Brazil is becoming an important **oil** exporter, with new reserves recently discovered offshore from Rio.

• Brazilian **exports** consist mainly of manufactured products (including automobiles, machinery and footwear), minerals and foodstuffs as varied as coffee, beef and orange juice. But only thirteen percent of GDP comes from exports: Brazil's growing **domestic economy** is the powerhouse of its development.

Brazil is a land of profound **economic** contradictions. Rapid post-war industrialization made it one of the world's ten largest economies by the 1990s and it is misleading to think of Brazil as a developing country; it is quickly becoming the world's leading agricultural exporter and has several home-grown multinationals competing successfully in world markets. The last decade has seen millions of Brazilians haul their way into the country's expanding middle class, and across-the-board improvements in social indicators like life expectancy and basic education. But yawning social divides are still a fact of life in Brazil. The cities are dotted with *favelas*, shantytowns that crowd around the skyscrapers, and there are wide **regional differences**, too: Brazilians talk of a "Switzerland" in the South, centred on the Rio–São Paulo axis, and an "India" above it, and although this is a simplification the level of economic development does fall the further north or east you go. Brazil has enormous natural resources but their exploitation has benefited fewer than it should. Institutionalized corruption, a bloated and inefficient public sector and the reluctance of the country's middle class to do anything that might jeopardize its comfortable lifestyle are a big part of the problem. Levels of violence that would be considered a public emergency in most countries are fatalistically accepted in Brazil – an average of seventeen murders per day in the city of Rio de Janeiro, for example.

## Carnaval

**Carnaval** plunges Brazil into the most serious partying in the world. Mardi Gras in New Orleans or Notting Hill in London are not even close; nothing approaches the sheer scale and spectacle of Carnaval in Rio, Salvador and Olinda, just outside Recife. But Carnaval also speaks to the streak of melancholy that is the other side of the stereotype of fun-loving Brazil.

Part of the reason is Carnaval's **origins** at the time when Brazil was still the largest slaveholding country in the Americas. The celebrations just before Lent acquired a kind of "world turned upside down" character, with slaveowners ceremonially serving their slaves food and allowing them time off work – giving a particularly double-edged feel to Carnaval as servitude reasserted itself come Ash Wedneday. Brazil has come a long way since then, but the traditional freedom to transgress that comes with Carnaval gives its partying an edge that deepens in the small hours, as alcohol and crowds generate their usual tensions – the already high murder rate hits its peak over the festival and traffic deaths are also at their annual high. There is a big difference between day and night. Carnaval during the **day** is for families, and you can relax along with the Pierrots, masks and brass bands that ply the streets and squares: if you travel with children they will remember a good Carnaval for the rest of their lives. Carnaval at **night** is memorably spectacular in Rio (see pp.123–127) and the biggest street party you will ever see in Salvador and Olinda, but it's best to keep your wits about you and your head clear. See p.54 and the relevant sections of the guide for more information.

▲ View across Rio's Lagoa towards Ipanema and Leblon

These difficulties, however, don't overshadow everyday life in Brazil, and violence rarely affects tourists. It's fair to say that nowhere in the world do people enjoy themselves more – most famously in the annual orgiastic celebrations of **Carnaval**, but reflected, too, in the lively year-round nightlife that you'll find in any decent-sized town. This national hedonism also manifests itself in Brazil's highly developed **beach culture**, superb **music** and dancing, rich regional **cuisines** and the most relaxed and tolerant attitude to **sexuality** – gay and straight – that you'll find anywhere in South America.

# Where to go

The most heavily populated part of the country is the Southeast, where the three largest cities – **São Paulo**, **Rio de Janeiro** and **Belo Horizonte** – form a triangle around which the economy pivots. All are worth visiting but **Rio**, which really is as beautiful as it seems in pictures, is the one essential destination. The **South**, encompassing the states of Paraná, Santa Catarina and Rio Grande do Sul, is the most economically advanced part of the country and includes much of the enormous **Paraná** river system. The spectacular **Iguaçu Falls** on the border with Argentina is one of the great natural wonders of South America.

▲ Candomblé priest and child, Salvador

Central Brazil is dominated by an enormous plateau of savanna and rock escarpments, the **Planalto Central**. In the middle stands **Brasília**, the country's space-age capital, built from scratch in the late 1950s and still developing today. The capital is the gateway to a vast interior, **Mato Grosso**, only fully charted and settled over the last fifty years; it includes the **Pantanal,** the largest wetlands in the world and the richest wildlife reserve anywhere in the Americas. North and west Mato Grosso shades into the **Amazon**, the world's largest river basin and a mosaic of jungle, rivers, savanna and marshland that also contains two major cities – **Belém**, at the mouth of the Amazon itself, and **Manaus**, some 1600km upstream. The tributaries of the Amazon, rivers like the Tapajós, the Xingú, the Negro, the Araguaia or the Tocantins, are virtually unknown outside Brazil, but each is a huge river system in its own right.

The other major sub-region of Brazil is the **Northeast**, the part of the country that curves out into the Atlantic Ocean. This was the first part of Brazil to be settled by the Portuguese and colonial remains are thicker on the ground here than anywhere else in the country – notably in the cities of **Salvador** and **São Luís** and the lovely town of **Olinda**. It's a region of dramatic contrasts: a lush tropical coastline with the best beaches in Brazil quickly gives way to the *sertão*, a semi-arid interior plagued by drought and grinding poverty. All the major cities of the Northeast are on the coast; the two largest are sprawling **Recife** and

**Salvador**, Brazil's most heavily Afro-Brazilian city and a fascinating place to visit. The coast of the Northeast is developing rapidly these days, taking advantage of proximity to Europe to attract package tourists and holiday-home buyers. But it is big enough for it still to be possible to get away from it all.



# When to go

Brazil splits into four distinct **climatic** regions. The coldest part – in fact the only part of Brazil that ever gets really cold – is the **South and Southeast**, the region roughly from central Minas Gerais to Rio Grande do Sul that includes Belo Horizonte, São Paulo and Porto Alegre. Here, there's a distinct winter between June and September, with occasional cold, wind and rain. Although Brazilians complain, it's all fairly mild to anyone coming from the US or UK. Temperatures rarely hit freezing overnight, and when they do it's featured on the TV news. The coldest part is the interior of Rio Grande do Sul, in the extreme south of the country, but even here there are many warm, bright days in winter, and the summer (Dec–March) is hot. Only in Santa Catarina's central highlands does it (very occasionally) snow.

▲ Fernando de Noronha archipelago, off the Northeast's gorgeous coastline

▲ The mighty Iguaçu Falls border Brazil and Argentina

The **coastal climate** is exceptionally good. Brazil has been called a "crab civilization" because most of its population lives on or near the coast – and with good reason. Seven thousand kilometres of coastline, from Paraná to near the equator, bask under a warm tropical climate. There is a "winter", when there are cloudy days and sometimes the temperature dips below 25°C (77°F), and a rainy season, when tropical downpours are severe enough to kill dozens every year in flash floods and landslides. In Rio and points south, **the rains** last from October through to January, but they come much earlier in the Northeast, lasting about three months from April in Fortaleza and Salvador, and from May in Recife. Even in winter or the rainy season, the weather will be sunny much of the time, with rain usually falling in intense but short bursts.

The **Northeast** is too hot to have a winter. Nowhere is the average monthly temperature below 25°C (77°F) and the interior, semi-arid at the best of times, often soars beyond that – regularly to as much as 40°C (104°F). Rain is sparse and irregular, although violent. **Amazônia** is stereotyped as steamy jungle with constant rainfall, but much of the region has a distinct dry season – apparently getting longer every year in the most deforested areas. Belém is closest to the image of a humid tropical city: it rains there an awful lot from January to May, and merely quite a lot for the rest of the year. Manaus and central Amazônia, in contrast, have a marked dry season from July to October.

## Average temperatures and rainfall

| | Jan | Mar | May | Jul | Sep | Nov |
|---|---|---|---|---|---|---|
| **Belém** | | | | | | |
| Max/min (°C) | 31/23 | 30/23 | 31/23 | 32/22 | 32/22 | 32/22 |
| Max/min (°F) | 88/73 | 86/73 | 88/73 | 90/71 | 90/72 | 90/72 |
| Rainy days | 24 | 25 | 24 | 14 | 13 | 11 |
| **Belo Horizonte** | | | | | | |
| Max/min (°C) | 27/18 | 27/17 | 25/12 | 24/10 | 27/14 | 27/17 |
| Max/min (°F) | 81/64 | 81/63 | 77/54 | 75/50 | 81/57 | 81/63 |
| Rainy days | 15 | 9 | 4 | 2 | 2 | 12 |
| **Brasília** | | | | | | |
| Max/min (°C) | 27/18 | 28/18 | 27/15 | 26/13 | 30/16 | 27/18 |
| Max/min (°F) | 81/64 | 82/64 | 81/59 | 79/55 | 86/61 | 81/64 |
| Rainy days | 19 | 15 | 3 | 0 | 4 | 15 |
| **Manaus** | | | | | | |
| Max/min (°C) | 30/23 | 30/23 | 31/24 | 32/23 | 33/24 | 32/24 |
| Max/min (°F) | 86/73 | 86/73 | 88/75 | 90/73 | 91/75 | 90/73 |
| Rainy days | 20 | 21 | 18 | 12 | 7 | 12 |
| **Porto Alegre** | | | | | | |
| Max/min (°C) | 31/20 | 29/19 | 22/13 | 20/10 | 22/13 | 27/17 |
| Max/min (°F) | 88/68 | 84/66 | 72/55 | 68/50 | 72/55 | 81/63 |
| Rainy days | 9 | 10 | 6 | 8 | 11 | 8 |
| **Recife** | | | | | | |
| Max/min (°C) | 30/25 | 30/24 | 29/23 | 27/21 | 28/22 | 30/24 |
| Max/min (°F) | 86/77 | 88/75 | 84/73 | 81/70 | 82/72 | 86/75 |
| Rainy days | 7 | 10 | 17 | 17 | 7 | 4 |
| **Rio de Janiero** | | | | | | |
| Max/min (°C) | 30/23 | 27/23 | 26/20 | 25/18 | 25/19 | 28/20 |
| Max/min (°F) | 86/73 | 81/73 | 79/68 | 77/64 | 77/66 | 82/68 |
| Rainy days | 13 | 9 | 6 | 5 | 5 | 10 |
| **Salvador** | | | | | | |
| Max/min (°C) | 29/23 | 29/24 | 27/22 | 26/21 | 27/21 | 28/23 |
| Max/min (°F) | 84/73 | 84/75 | 81/72 | 79/70 | 81/70 | 82/73 |
| Rainy days | 6 | 17 | 22 | 18 | 10 | 9 |
| **São Paulo** | | | | | | |
| Max/min (°C) | 28/18 | 27/17 | 23/13 | 21/10 | 25/13 | 25/15 |
| Max/min (°F) | 82/64 | 81/63 | 73/55 | 70/50 | 77/55 | 77/59 |
| Rainy days | 15 | 12 | 3 | 4 | 5 | 11 |

# 32 things not to miss

*It's not possible to see everything Brazil has to offer in one trip – and we don't suggest you try. What follows is a selective taste of the country's highlights: vibrant cities, world-class festivals, natural wonders and stunning architecture. They're arranged in five colour-coded categories, which you can browse through to find the very best things to see and experience. All highlights have a page reference to take you straight into the Guide, where you can find out more.*

**01 Views from the Corcovado, Rio** Page **94** • Ascend the Corcovado mountain – where the image of Christ the Redeemer stands – for breathtaking views taking in the whole of Rio and Guanabara Bay.

**02 Capoeira** Page **244** • Step into a *capoeira* school, where you can watch the dance-like sparring of this distinctive martial art for free.

**03 Markets** Page **564** • Walk through any market in Brazil to get a sense of the country's natural abundance. São Paulo's Mercado Municipal, crammed with produce from all over Brazil, is particularly impressive.

**04 The Pantanal** Page **519** • You'll be hard-pressed to not spot wildlife in the world's biggest inland swamp.

**05 Theatro Municipal, Rio** Page **91** • If you can't catch a show inside Rio's sumptuous belle époque theatre, be sure to stop for lunch or a drink in its lavish, Assyrian-inspired café.

**06 Reggae bands** Page **354** • Keep your ears open for infectious reggae beats throughout the Northeast, whether in atmospheric bars or on the street.

**07 Avenida Paulista, São Paulo** Page **570** • Get a sense of the city's impressive modern face through its major thoroughfare, lined with skyscrapers and opulent mansions.

**08 Fazendas** Page **594** • Visit these impressive rural estates, relics of São Paulo's coffee-producing boom. The *Fazenda Pinhal*, near São Carlos, is among the best preserved.

**09 Trekking in the Chapada Diamantina** Page **271** • Explore the dramatic terrain of this enormous national park, which includes mesas, forest, river beaches, waterfalls and a kilometre-long grotto.

**10 Olinda** Page **306** • The cobbled streets of the city's historic centre offer up countless examples of beautiful colonial architecture.

**11 Churrascarias** Page **51** • Sample grilled meats – numerous cuts of beef, plus pork, lamb, chicken, duck and more – at these typical gaúcho barbecue houses.

**12 Pedra Azul** Page **226** • This massive stone mountain is renowned for the shade of blue it seems to turn at dawn and at sunset.

**13 Candomblé celebrations** Page **253** • Usually identifiable by their white dress, followers of this popular Afro-Brazilian religious cult worship together in exuberant dance ceremonies as well as at fiestas.

**14 Parque Nacional Chapada dos Veadeiros** Page **486** • Head just a few hours north of Brasília to take in this spectacular wilderness area, dotted with striking geological formations, caves, waterfalls and hiking trails.

**15 Paraty** Page **143** • This picturesque spot remains one of Brazil's best-preserved colonial towns, and it's a great base from which to explore the surrounding Costa Verde.

**16** **Florianópolis beaches** Page **656** • Head to the island capital of Santa Catarina state, where kilometres of beaches include treacherous surfing spots and calm waters for safe swimming.

**17** **Ouro Preto** Page **183** • Some truly remarkable Baroque churches are tucked away in the steep, narrow streets of this charming town.

**18 Northeast beaches** Page **347** • North of Salvador the coastline is stunning, with waters good for surfing or sailing in a traditional *jangada*, as well as fine white sand dunes, seen here near Fortaleza.

**19 Parque Nacional da Tijuca** Page **111** • This impressive expanse of Mata Atlântica is criss-crossed by shaded trails and features refreshing waterfalls and spectacular views across Rio.

**20 Museu de Arte Contemporânea, Niterói** Page **131** • Take a short ferry ride from Rio and spend some time at this spaceship-like museum, one of Oscar Niemeyer's architectural masterpieces.

**21 Brazilian architecture** Pages **131** & **465** • Whether it looks like a futuristic dream or a modern-day nightmare, Brazil's contemporary architecture is often otherworldly.

**22 Ilhabela** Page **600** • A playground for São Paulo's rich, this island boasts some of the area's most beautiful beaches, thanks to strictly enforced environmental protection laws.

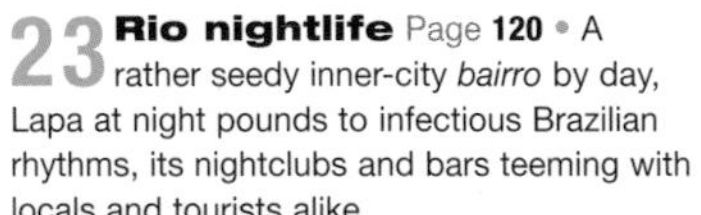

**23 Rio nightlife** Page **120** • A rather seedy inner-city *bairro* by day, Lapa at night pounds to infectious Brazilian rhythms, its nightclubs and bars teeming with locals and tourists alike.

**24 The Jesuit missions** Page **701** • Admire the striking ruins of São Miguel in Brazil or combine a visit with other Jesuit missions in what is now Argentina and Paraguay.

**25 River journeys** Page **368** • Take a slow boat along the Amazon for close-up views of the mighty river and its wildlife.

**26 Colonial Rio** Page **101** • There are more colonial churches in Rio than anywhere else in Brazil – the pretty Igreja de Nossa Senhora da Glória do Outeiro is perhaps the city's finest.

**27 The Aquário Natural** Page **511** • Snorkel among some thirty-odd species of fish in the crystalline waters of this marine sanctuary, or spy on them from above in a glass-bottomed boat.

28 **Visiting Rio's beaches** Page **97** • On weekends you can hang with locals who escape to Rio's sands to play sports, catch up on gossip or simply people-watch.

29 **Brazilian Baroque art** Page **197** • Within this style, Aleijadinho's sculptures are remarkable, none more so than the Passion figures in Congonhas.

**30** **Iguaçu Falls** Page **646** • The power and beauty of the falls is quite simply astonishing, only rivalled by the tranquillity of the Mata Atlântica behind.

**31** **Carnaval** Page **54** • For a memorable experience, take in the most important of Brazil's festivals, celebrated in notably grand style in Rio, Salvador and Olinda.

**32** **Teatro Amazonas** Page **412** • If you can't attend one of the regular concerts, be sure to take a guided tour of this remarkable opera house, painstakingly built from materials brought from Europe.

# Basics

# Basics

# Getting there



**Unless you're entering Brazil overland from a neighbouring country, you'll almost certainly arrive by air. Airfares always depend on the season: specific dates vary between airlines, but high season is generally July and August, then again mid-December to Christmas Day; low season is any other time. Fares don't normally rise over Carnaval (Feb–March), but getting a seat at this time can be difficult. Airline competition is fierce, however, and offers are often available.**

The internet is rapidly making specialist travel agents less of an essential first stop, but you may want to use one if you prefer to book your first few days' accommodation before you arrive or you're looking for a tailor-made package. Apart from discounted tickets, it's worth checking fares **directly with the airlines** that fly to Brazil; they frequently offer competitive fares, especially during low season, although these may carry certain restrictions such as having to spend at least seven days abroad (maximum stay three months).

If you plan to do a fair amount of travelling within Brazil, think about buying a TAM **air pass** with your main ticket, available whether or not you fly your international legs on TAM – though the price will be higher if you arrive with a different airline. Depending on your itinerary, it can save you a lot of money, but can only be bought outside South America. See p.42 for details of the various options.

## From the US and Canada

There are numerous gateways to Brazil in the **US and Canada**; direct flights leave from Atlanta, Chicago, Dallas, Houston, Los Angeles, Miami, Newark, New York, Orlando, Washington and Toronto. TAM is the only Brazilian carrier serving the US at present, while the North American airlines are American, Air Canada, Continental, Delta and United; Japan Airlines and Korean Air also carry passengers between the US and Brazil. Most flights go to either **Rio** or **São Paulo**; if you want to fly anywhere else, your options are limited to TAM from Miami to Manaus, Belém, Recife, Belo Horizonte and Salvador; **American**, also from Miami, to Belo Horizonte; and Delta from Atlanta to Fortaleza, Manaus and Recife, although Copa will fly you to Manaus via Panama if you want to focus your trip on the Amazon. If your ultimate destination is somewhere other than these cities, it is usually best to connect in Rio or São Paulo.

Excursion-fare ticket **prices** vary depending on your length of stay in Brazil: count on spending at least US$150 more for a ticket valid for up to three months than a ticket for up to one month. Fares to Rio and São Paulo are almost always the same. Excursion fares are around US$1000 out of New York, US$900 out of Miami; for unrestricted fares, add at least US$400.

It's worth going to some trouble to **avoid São Paulo's Guarulhos airport**, where queues can be nightmarish and the airport layout is extraordinarily confusing. Even if you have what on paper looks like a direct flight to Rio, make sure that it doesn't stop at São Paulo on the way, where you will almost always have to deplane and hang around for a weary couple of hours, or even change planes to Rio – take care with TAM on this, since they are ruthless about shunting international passengers onto domestic connections in São Paulo even if your ticket is to Rio.

### Flights via other countries

For slightly cheaper fares (but longer flight times), or if you're tempted to break your journey, it's worth checking out what the national airlines of Brazil's South American neighbours have to offer. **Aerolíneas Argentinas**, for instance, flies to Rio and São Paulo from Miami and New York via Buenos Aires. Others routings worth investigating include travelling via Bogotá with **Avianca**, Panama with **Copa Airlines**, Lima with **LAN Peru** and Santiago with **LAN Chile**. If you can get yourself to Lima, Santiago, Buenos Aires, or Santa Cruz in Bolivia, the Brazilian no-frills airline Gol has cheap onward fares to Rio and São Paulo. If you do route yourself via another South American country, however, you may need a vaccination certificate for yellow fever.

If you plan on travelling in other South American countries besides Brazil, the **TAM South American Airpass** is a good-value option (see p.42).

## From the UK and Ireland

There are plenty of choices of carrier to Brazil **from the UK**, with São Paulo and Rio being the usual points of arrival. If your ultimate destination is neither of these cities, it is usually best to connect in Rio, or connect with a flight on the continent, where your options are TAM to Recife from Paris, or TAP via Lisbon to Recife, Salvador, Fortaleza, Natal, Belo Horizonte and Brasília. If you only want to go to the Amazon, Manaus via Miami with TAM is your best bet, but it's unlikely to be cheaper or quicker than a flight to Rio or São Paulo and then a connection north.

British Airways and TAM operate **direct flights** to Brazil from the UK; despite BA having newer planes and a much higher level of service, their official fares are usually very similar, starting at around £700 return **to Rio or São Paulo** in low season, £900 high season (July, Aug & Dec 14–25). With these tickets, return dates are in theory fixed, but once in Brazil both airlines will allow you to change the date (within 30 days) for a fee of around £75. You can usually get the same tickets through websites and **specialist travel agencies** at reduced prices; fares are sometimes as little as £500 in low season, rising to around

### Six steps to a better kind of travel

At Rough Guides we are passionately committed to travel. We feel strongly that only through travelling do we truly come to understand the world we live in and the people we share it with – plus tourism has brought a great deal of **benefit** to developing economies around the world over the last few decades. But the extraordinary growth in tourism has also damaged some places irreparably, and of course **climate change** is exacerbated by most forms of transport, especially flying. This means that now more than ever it's important to **travel thoughtfully** and **responsibly**, with respect for the cultures you're visiting – not only to derive the most benefit from your trip but also to preserve the best bits of the planet for everyone to enjoy. At Rough Guides we feel there are six main areas in which you can make a difference:

- Consider what you're contributing to the **local economy**, and how much the services you use do the same, whether it's through employing local workers and guides or sourcing locally grown produce and local services.
- Consider the **environment** on holiday as well as at home. Water is scarce in many developing destinations, and the biodiversity of local flora and fauna can be adversely affected by tourism. Try to patronize businesses that take account of this.
- Travel with a purpose, not just to tick off experiences. Consider **spending longer** in a place, and getting to know it and its people.
- Give thought to how often you **fly**. Try to avoid short hops by air and more harmful night flights.
- Consider **alternatives to flying**, travelling instead by bus, train, boat and even by bike or on foot where possible.
- Make your trips **"climate neutral"** via a reputable carbon offset scheme. All Rough Guide flights are offset, and every year we donate money to a variety of charities devoted to combating the effects of climate change.

£800 for high-season departures. The **cheapest fares**, however, are often offered on **routes via Europe** – with Air France via Paris, TAP via Lisbon, Iberia via Madrid or Lufthansa via Frankfurt, all to both Rio and São Paulo. Other inexpensive options to São Paulo include Alitalia via Milan, KLM via Amsterdam and Swiss Airlines via Zurich. Prices tend to be the same whether you begin your journey in London or at one of the UK's **regional airports**.

As Brazil is such a large country, an **open-jaw ticket** – flying into one city and leaving from another – may, according to your itinerary, make sense. Rio and São Paulo offer most airline possibilities, but flying with TAP broadens your options, including also Belo Horizonte, Brasília, Fortaleza, Natal, Recife and Salvador.

There are no direct flights **from Ireland** to Brazil: connect via London or other European capitals. The best deals are available from budget or student travel agents in Ireland, but it's also worth contacting specialist agents in England for cheap fares, an unusual route or a package.

### Other ticket options

Several airlines offer **stopovers** to or from Brazil at no extra cost. Apart from the airlines with European transit points already mentioned, stopover possibilities most commonly involve the **US**. United Airlines via Washington or Chicago is generally the least expensive option (around £550 low season, £800 high season) with good deals also sometimes available with American Airlines via Miami, Continental via Newark or Houston, Delta via Atlanta or Air Canada via Toronto.

Combining Brazil with a longer trip in the southern hemisphere, or putting together a **Round-the-World (RTW) ticket**, is possible but expensive. The most popular ticket option is a one-way to Sydney via Brazil and Argentina and a separate ticket back to London via Southeast Asia or North America. Another possibility is onward to Johannesburg from São Paulo on South African Airways.

## From Australia, New Zealand and South Africa

The best deals and fastest routing to Brazil **from Australasia** are offered by Aerolíneas Argentinas and LAN Chile. There are fewer options flying via the US, flights take longer and the tickets are more expensive. Round-the-World fares that include South America tend to cost more than other RTW options, but can be worthwhile if you have the time to make the most of a few stopovers.

From **Australia**, flights to South America leave from Sydney. The most direct route is with Aerolíneas Argentinas, which flies via Auckland to Buenos Aires, from where there are good connections direct to Florianópolis, Porto Alegre, Rio and São Paulo. LAN Chile has a weekly direct flight via Auckland to Santiago, with connections to Rio or São Paulo. More long-winded, there are twice-weekly connections via Papeete and Easter Island with Air New Zealand and LAN Chile to Santiago. Travelling through the US, United Airlines, American Airlines or Delta can fly you to São Paulo or Rio via either Los Angeles or San Francisco and Atlanta or Miami. From

**New Zealand**, you can pick up one of the United, Aerolíneas Argentinas or Air New Zealand/LAN Chile flights in Auckland.

In general, **fares** depend on the duration of stay, rather than the season – cut-off points when flying via Chile and Argentina are 35 days, 45 days, 90 days, 6 months and 1 year; flying via the US they are 21 days, 45 days and 180 days – but bear in mind that availability is a problem during Christmas and Carnaval (Dec–March). On the more direct routes with Aerolíneas Argentinas you should be able to get a return fare for A$2400/NZ$2600. Flying via Santiago with LAN Chile, you can expect to pay around A$3100/NZ$3300, while fares via the US will be at least A$3500/NZ$3700.

An **open-jaw ticket** can work out to be a convenient option. Flying into Rio and out of São Paulo (or vice versa) on Aerolíneas Argentinas or LAN Chile, for example, won't cost you any more than a straight through-fare to Rio.

From **South Africa**, Brazil can be reached directly from Johannesburg with South African Airlines to São Paulo. For indirect flights, your best option is Malaysian Airlines from Johannesburg and Cape Town to Buenos Aires and a separate onward ticket to a Brazilian destination. Also worth investigating are flights with TAAG Angolan Airlines from Johannesburg to Rio via Luanda.

## Airlines

**Aerolíneas Argentinas** ⓦwww.aerolineas.com
**Air Canada** ⓦwww.aircanada.com
**Air France** ⓦwww.airfrance.com
**Alitalia** ⓦwww.alitalia.com
**American Airlines** ⓦwww.aa.com
**Avianca** ⓦwww.avianca.com
**British Airways** ⓦwww.britishairways.com
**Continental Airlines** ⓦwww.continental.com
**Copa Airlines** ⓦwww.copaair.com
**Delta** ⓦwww.delta.com
**Iberia** ⓦwww.iberia.com
**JAL (Japan Air Lines)** ⓦwww.jal.com
**KLM (Royal Dutch Airlines)** ⓦwww.klm.com
**Korean Air** ⓦwww.koreanair.com
**LAN Chile** ⓦwww.lan.com
**Lufthansa** ⓦwww.lufthansa.com
**Malaysia Airlines** ⓦwww.mayalysiaairlines.com
**South African Airways** ⓦwww.flysaa.com
**Swiss** ⓦwww.swiss.com
**TAM** ⓦwww.tam.com.br
**TAP (Air Portugal)** ⓦwww.flytap.com
**United Airlines** ⓦwww.united.com

## Packages and tours

If your trip is short, and if your plan is simply to visit Rio for two weeks, then **package holidays** (flight and accommodation included) can be very good value. A week in a three-star hotel in Copacabana can cost less than £700, and for an extra £400 you can add on a week's tour taking in three or four key places such as Manaus, Salvador and Iguaçu. These packages can be found in brochures at any travel agent, such as Kuoni and Thomas Cook, and through some of the specialists listed here. If you want to go for Carnaval, you'll need to book months in advance and be prepared to pay more.

More varied **tours** are offered by many specialist operators and upmarket package companies, who can plan itineraries to meet individual requirements, including organizing hotels and transportation within Brazil.

Package tours from Australia and New Zealand are few and far between, but while they may seem a little expensive, can be well worth it, especially if your time is limited. Specialist travel agents and operators such as Adventure Associates offer a range of Brazilian itineraries, from the full package experience to shorter **add-on tours** that give you the flexibility of combining independent travel with, say, an Amazon cruise.

## Specialist agents and operators

**African American Travel Agency** US ⓣ1-215/473-6495, ⓦwww.africanamericantravelagency.com. Tours that focus on the legacy of Africa in Brazil, in particular Bahia.

**Brazil Nuts** US ⓣ1-800/553-9959, ⓦwww.brazilnuts.com. Tours that promise to take you off the beaten track to experience Brazil's cities, the Amazon basin and the Pantanal.

**Brazil Tours** UK ⓣ0870/442 4241, ⓦwww.braziltours.co.uk. Flight agents and tour operators to Brazil and elsewhere in South America.

**Festival Tours** US ⓣ1-800/225-0117, ⓦwww.festivaltours.com. An all-encompassing tour operator to Latin America focusing on main tourist sights.

**Journey Latin America** UK ⓣ020/8747 3108, ⓦwww.journeylatinamerica.co.uk. Flight agents and tour operators offering guided tours of Brazil as well as larger-scale overland options, which also take in Paraguay, Bolivia and Peru, or Chile and Argentina.

**Last Frontiers** UK ⓣ01296/653 000, ⓦwww.lastfrontiers.com. Tailor-made itineraries to Brazil with a strong wildlife slant. Friendly and knowledgeable staff will point you towards small hotels in destinations throughout the country and occasionally organize small groups to attend *rodeios* or to learn to play polo.

**Lost World Adventures** US ⓣ1-800/999-0558, ⓦwww.lostworldadventures.com. Customized individual and group tours to Brazil, including Amazon River excursions, and multi-country tours.

**Solar Tours** US ⓣ202/861-5864, ⓦwww.solartours.com. A big operator throughout Latin America, offering cruises, city tours, jungle trips and Carnaval specials.

**South America Travel Centre** Australia ⓣ1800/655-051 or 03/9642-5353, ⓦwww.satc.com.au. Specializes in tailor-made trips to Brazil.

**South American Adventure Travel** Australia ⓣ07/3854-1022. Independent and group travel specialists.

**South American Experience** UK ⓣ0845/277 3366. One of the more experienced British travel agents specializing in South America, offering flights, tours and tailor-made packages.

**Steamond Travel** UK ⓣ020/7730 8646, ⓦwww.easyticket.com. Flight agents and tour operators for Brazil and Latin America.

**Veloso Tours** UK ⓣ020/8762 0616, ⓦwww.veloso.com. Latin American flight specialist and tour operator with a range of Brazilian options including Rio de Janeiro, the Northeast and the Amazon.

# Visas and entry requirements

**Citizens of most EU countries, New Zealand and South Africa only need a valid passport and either a return or onward ticket, or evidence of funds to pay for one, to enter Brazil. You fill in an entry form on arrival and get a tourist visa allowing you to stay for ninety days. Australian, US and Canadian citizens need visas in advance, available from Brazilian consulates abroad; a return or onward ticket is usually a requirement. You'll also need to submit a passport photo with your visa application and pay a processing fee (consulates in the US only accept postal money orders, while consulates in other countries may accept bank or personal cheques). Fees vary according to nationality, with US citizens currently paying US$130, Canadians C$117 and Australians A$63.**

Try not to lose the **carbon copy of the entry form** the police hand you back at passport control; you are meant to return it when you leave Brazil, but you are no longer fined if you don't. EU, New Zealand and South African citizens can extend a tourist permit for an additional ninety days if you apply at least fifteen days before your initial one expires, but it will only be extended once; if you want to stay longer, you'll have to leave the country and re-enter. There's nothing in the rulebook to stop you re-entering immediately, but it's advisable to wait at least a day. You'll be fined if you overstay your tourist permit or visa. A US$10 charge, payable in Brazilian currency, is made on tourist permit and visa extensions.

## Consulates

Foreign countries are represented at **embassy level** in Brasília, and most also maintain **consulates** in Rio and São Paulo. Elsewhere, consulates, vice-consulates or honorary consulates are found in many major cities, from Manaus to Porto Alegre. Levels of service vary depending on the nature of the particular post, but at the very least you can count on some immediate advice. Addresses and telephone numbers of embassies and consulates can be found in the "Listings" section of the cities in the Guide. Where their country doesn't have a representative, in an emergency a Commonwealth national can seek help at a British mission, and a European Union citizen at another EU mission.

### Brazilian embassies and consulates abroad

**Australia** Embassy and consulate: 19 Forster Crescent, Yarralumla, Canberra, ACT 2600 ⓣ02/6273-2372, ⓦwww.brazil.org.au; consulate: 31 Market St, Sydney ⓣ02/9267-4414, ⓦwww.brazilsydney.org.

**Canada** Embassy and consulate: 450 Wilbroad St, Ottawa, ON K1V 6M8 ⓣ1-613/237-1090, ⓦwww.brasembottawa.org; consulates also in: Montréal ⓣ1-514/499-0968, ⓦwww.consbrasmontreal.org; Toronto ⓣ1-416/922-2503, ⓦwww.consbrastoronto.org; and Vancouver ⓣ1-604/696-5311, ⓦwww.consbrasvancouver.org.

**Ireland** Embassy and consulate: HSBC House, 41–54 Harcourt Centre, Harcourt St, Dublin 2 ⓣ01/475 6000, ⓦwww.brazil.ie.

**New Zealand** Embassy and consulate: 10 Brandon St – Level 9, PO Box 5032, Wellington ⓣ04/473-3516, ⓦwww.brazil.org.nz.

**South Africa** Embassy and consulate: Block C, 1st Floor, Hatfield Office Park, 1267 Pretorius St, Hatfield, Pretoria ⓣ012/426-9400, ⓦwww.brazilianembassy.org.za; consulate: 2nd Floor, Safmarine House, 22 Riebeeck St, PO Box 7958, Roggebaai 8012, Cape Town ⓣ021/421-4040.

**UK** Embassy: 32 Green St, London W1Y 4AT ⓣ020/7499 0877; consulate: 6 St Alban's St, London SW1Y 4SQ ⓣ020/7930 9055, ⓦwww.brazil.org.uk.

**US** Embassy: 3006 Massachusetts Ave NW, Washington DC 20008 ⓣ1-202/238-2700, ⓦwww.brasilemb.org; consulates in Atlanta ⓣ1-404/949-2400; Boston ⓣ1-617/542-4000; Chicago ⓣ1-312/464-0244; Houston ⓣ1-713/961-3063; Los Angeles ⓣ1-323/651-2664;

Miami ☎1-305/285-6200; New York ☎1-917/777-7777; San Francisco ☎1-415/981-8170; and Washington ☎1-202/238-2828.

### Longer stays: academic visits

**Academic visitors and researchers** making a short trip or attending a conference are best advised to enter on a tourist visa, which cuts down on the bureaucracy. If you're staying for a longer period, or intend to do extended research, you need to get a special visa, known as a "**Temporário**", before you leave home. The requirements change constantly, so check at your nearest Brazilian consulate, and plan ahead, because the process can easily take six months or longer. As a minimum, you'll need to present a letter from a Brazilian institution of higher education saying it approves your research and will host you during your stay in Brazil. Visas are issued for six months, a year or two years; if in any doubt about exactly how long you're going to stay, apply for the two-year visa. One-year visas can be extended for a further year inside Brazil, but only after months of chasing up the police, and often involving a trip to the Ministry of Justice in Brasília.

On arrival on a Temporário you must **register** within thirty days at the *seção dos estrangeiros* office in the federal police station nearest to where you are based. You'll need to fill out forms, supply an authenticated photocopy of your passport, pay a registration fee and provide some passport photographs. Several weeks later, you'll be issued with an identity card; you can expect registering and getting the card to take at least a day of mindless drudgery and sitting in lines, but it has to be done. If your work involves taking samples out of Brazil, a whole new bureaucratic ballgame begins; you will need to get in touch well in advance with the Brazilian embassy in your home country and with your sponsoring Brazilian institution. New rules meant to deter bio-piracy mean that exporting plant materials from Brazil is now almost impossible.

If you are moving to Brazil to work or because you have a Brazilian spouse, Brazilian consulates will advise you on what documentation you need.

# Costs and money

**The cost of living in Brazil is low outside the main tourist spots, and even within them shopping around can lower costs a lot. Europeans will mostly think Brazil cheap, North Americans a little less so but still comparing favourably with the US for most things. Particularly reasonable are hotels (except in Rio), foodstuffs (including eating out) and bus travel, while most museums are free. The exception is internal plane tickets, which a near-monopoly between TAM and Gol make expensive, unless you have an airpass. Other relatively expensive things are sunblock, good-quality clothing, cameras and anything to do with computers (except internet cafés, which are very cheap).**

On the whole, Brazil is very much a viable destination for the budget traveller. The cheapness of food and budget hotels – and the fact that the best attractions, such as the beaches, are free – still make it possible to have an enjoyable time on a **budget** of less than R$125 a day. Staying in good hotels, travelling by comfortable buses or planes and not stinting on the extras is likely to cost you around R$400 a day.

The Brazilian **currency** is the *real* (pronounced "hey-al"); its plural is *reís* (pronounced "hey-ice"), written R$. The *real* is made up of one hundred *centavos*, written ¢.

## Surviving an assalto

Every year, a number of tourists are killed simply because they did not know how to react to an armed hold-up or **assalto**. The simplest *assalto* happens on the street; just hand over your wallet and you're done. If in a car, and someone taps on the window with a gun, they want your wallet – hand it out through the window. If they want the car, they will signal you out of it; get out immediately and do not delay to pick up anything. If you try to drive off at speed, there's a good chance they will shoot. If in a restaurant or sitting down, make no sudden movements and do not stand up, even if only to get your wallet out – wriggle instead.

The rather pleasing notes, themed after Brazilian wildlife and all the same size but different colours, are for 2, 5, 10, 20, 50 and 100 *reís*; coins are 1, 5, 10, 25, 50 *centavos* and the 1 *real*. You will occasionally see a tattered R$1 note but these are being phased out, although they are legal tender. Throughout the Guide, all prices are given in Brazilian *reís* unless otherwise noted. However, US dollars and euros are easy enough to change in banks and exchange offices anywhere, and are also readily accepted by luxury hotels, tour companies and souvenir shops in the big cities.

Changing money in Brazil is simple; just take your bank or credit card with PIN (Personal Identification Number, which you must set up with your bank before your trip), and use **ATMs** – they are now ubiquitous in Brazil, to be found in most supermarkets, many pharmacies and all airports, as well as banks. Only Visa cards can be used to withdraw cash advances at the ATMs of Banco do Brasil and Banco Bradesco; only MasterCard at HSBC, Itaú and Banco Mercantil. Increasing numbers of Brazilian banks are linking their cash dispensers to the Cirrus and Maestro networks; the most reliable and widespread is the Banco 24 Horas network and HSBC. One important thing to note is that for security reasons most bank ATMs stop dispensing cash after 8pm, although Banco 24 Horas in large supermarkets will dispense until 10pm. Airport ATMs are the only ones that dispense cash all hours.

The main **credit cards** are widely accepted by shops, hotels and restaurants throughout Brazil, even in rural areas. MasterCard and Visa are the most prevalent, with Diners Club and American Express also widespread. It's a good idea to inform your credit-card issuer about your trip before you leave so that the card isn't stopped for uncharacteristic use.

Given the ease of using plastic, **traveller's cheques** are not recommended, unless you want a small emergency reserve. Only the head offices of major **banks** (Banco do Brasil, HSBC, Banco Itaú, Banespa) will have an exchange department (ask for *câmbio*); whether changing cash or traveller's cheques, you'll need your passport. You can also change cash and traveller's cheques in smart hotels and in some large travel agencies. Airport banks are open seven days a week, others only Monday to Friday.

**Exchange rates** were stable in the US$1.80–2.20 range for years but rose against the dollar with the financial crisis of late 2008, making Brazil cheaper for North Americans but more expensive for Europeans, especially Britons. But since Brazil's newfound economic stability means it is now well placed to weather crises, exchange-rate turbulence is unlikely to be a feature of your stay. You will see two rates quoted in hotels: the *oficial*, or interbank rate, which you will be able to get in a *casa de câmbio*, an exchange counter in a travel agency or specialized exchange dealer (although these are now thin on the ground), and the *turismo*, a few cents less – more in hotels, where they bank on the ignorance of the clientele. Rates out of ATMs are usually the *oficial*, making plastic an even better option.

# Crime and personal safety

**Brazil has a reputation as a rather dangerous place, and while it's not entirely undeserved, it is often overblown and you should not let fear overshadow your stay. If you take the precautions outlined below, you are extremely unlikely to come to any harm – although you might still have something stolen somewhere along the way. The tips in this section apply everywhere, but be particularly alert in Rio, Salvador and Recife.**

Criminals know that any injury to a foreign tourist is going to mean a heavy clampdown, which in turn means no pickings for a while. So unless you resist during an incident, nothing is likely to happen to you. That said, having a knife or a gun held on you is something of a shock: it's very difficult to think rationally. But if you are unlucky enough to be the victim of an *assalto* (a hold-up), try to remember that it's your possessions rather than you that are the target. Your money and anything you're carrying will be snatched, your watch will get pulled off your wrist, but within a couple of seconds it will be over. On no account resist: it isn't worth the risk.

## Taking precautions

As a rule, *assaltos* are most common in the larger cities, and are rare in the countryside and towns. Most *assaltos* take place at night, in backstreets with few people around, so stick to busy, well-lit streets; in a city, it's always a lot safer to take a taxi than walk. Also, prepare for the worst by locking your money and passport in the hotel safe – the one in your room is more secure than the one at reception. If you must carry them, make sure they're in a **moneybelt** or a **concealed internal pocket**. Do not carry your valuables in a pouch hanging from your neck. Only take along as much money as you'll need for the day, but do take at least some money, as the average *assaltante* won't believe a gringo could be out of money, and might get rough. Don't wear an expensive watch or jewellery: if you need a watch you can always buy a cheap plastic digital one on a street corner. And keep wallets and purses out of sight – pockets with buttons or zips are best.

You need to take special care when carrying a laptop – around business-oriented airports, like Congonhas in São Paulo and Santos Dumont in Rio, laptop stealing has become epidemic. Scouts wait at exits and phone ahead to thieves on motorbikes, who pull alongside your taxi when it is stuck in traffic and tap on the window with a revolver. Conceal laptops inside bags that do not look like computer bags, and try to avoid looking like a businessperson even if you are one.

More common than an *assalto* is a simple theft, a **furto**. Brand-new, designer-label bags are an obvious target, so go for the downmarket look. You're at your most vulnerable when travelling and though the luggage compartments of buses are pretty safe – remember to get a baggage check from the person putting them in and don't throw it away – the overhead racks inside are less safe; keep an eye on things you stash there, especially on night journeys. On a city beach, never leave things unattended while you take a dip: any beachside bar will stow things for you. Most hotels (even the cheaper ones) will have a safe, a *caixa*, and unless you have serious doubts about the place you should lock away your most valuable things: the better the hotel, the more secure it's likely to be. In cheaper hotels, where rooms are shared, the risks are obviously greater – some people take along a small padlock for extra security and many wardrobes in cheaper hotels have latches fitted for this very purpose. Finally, take care at Carnaval as it's a notorious time for pickpockets and thieves.

At international **airports**, particularly Rio and São Paulo, certain scams operate; for instance, well-dressed and official-looking men target tourists arriving off international flights in the arrivals lounge, identify themselves as policemen, often flashing a card, and tell the tourists to go with them. The tourists are then pushed into a car outside and robbed. If anyone, no matter how polite or well dressed they are, or how good their English is, identifies themselves as a policeman to you, be instantly on your guard – real policemen generally leave foreigners well alone. They won't try anything actually inside a terminal building, so go to any airline desk or grab one of the security guards, and on no account leave the terminal building with them or leave any luggage in their hands.

## The police

If you are robbed or held up, it's not necessarily a good idea to go to the **police**. Except with something like a theft from a hotel room, they're very unlikely to be able to do anything, and reporting something can take hours even without the language barrier. You may have to do it for insurance purposes, when you'll need a local police report: this could take an entire, and very frustrating, day to get, so think first about how badly you want to be reimbursed. If your passport is stolen, go to your consulate and they'll smooth the path.

If you have to deal with the police, there are various kinds. The best are usually the **Polícia de Turismo**, or tourist police, who are used to tourists and their problems and often speak some English, but they're thin on the ground outside Rio. In a city, their number should be displayed on or near the desk of all hotels. The most efficient police by far are the **Polícia Federal**, the Brazilian equivalent of the American FBI, who deal with visas and their extension; they have offices at frontier posts, airports and ports and in state capitals. The ones you see on every street corner are the **Polícia Militar**, with blue or green uniforms and caps. They look mean – and very often are – but, apart from at highway road blocks, they generally leave gringos alone. There is also a plain-clothes **Polícia Civil**, to whom thefts are reported if there is no tourist police post around – they are overworked, underpaid and extremely slow. If you decide to go to the police in a city where there is a consulate, get in touch with the consulate first and do as they tell you.

## Drugs

The drug wars in the *favelas* that you will have heard about and may well see on local TV during your stay are very localized and unlikely to have any impact on foreign tourists. But you should be extremely careful about using drugs in Brazil. **Marijuana** – *maconha* – is common, but you are in trouble if the police find any on you. You'll be able to bribe your way out of it, but it will cost you the daily withdrawal limit on whatever plastic you have. Foreigners sometimes get targeted for a shakedown and have drugs planted on them – the area around the Bolivian border has a bad reputation for this – in order to get a bribe out of them. If this happens to you, deny everything, refuse to pay and insist on seeing a superior officer and telephoning the nearest consulate – though this approach is only for the patient.

**Cocaine** is not as common as you might think, as most of it simply passes through Brazil from Bolivia or Colombia bound for Europe. Nevertheless, the home market has grown in recent years, controlled by young and vicious gang-leaders from the *favelas* of the major cities.

Be careful about taking anything illegal on buses: they are sometimes stopped and searched at state lines. The stupidest thing you could do would be to take anything illegal anywhere near Bolivia, as buses heading to or from that direction get vigorously searched by the *federais*. Much the same can be said of smuggling along the rivers into Peru and Colombia: don't even think about it.

# Health

**There are no compulsory vaccinations required to enter the country from Europe or North America (although you may need a yellow fever certificate entering from another South American country), but certain precautions should be taken, especially if you're staying for any length of time or visiting more remote regions. Taking out travel insurance is vital (see p.58), and you should be especially aware of HIV and dengue fever, a significant problem in Rio during the Brazilian summer (Dec–April). But you should not let health issues make you unduly paranoid – if you need it, good medical care is available cheaply for all but the most serious of problems.**

## Pharmacies and medical treatment

Most standard drugs are available in **pharmacies** (*farmácias*), which you'll find everywhere – no prescriptions are necessary. A pharmacy will also give injections (unless you've already had one, you'll need a tetanus jab if you get bitten by a dog) and free medical advice, and they're a good first line of defence if you fall ill.

If you are unlucky enough to need **medical treatment** in Brazil, forget about the public hospitals – as a foreigner, you have virtually no chance of getting a bed unless you have an infectious disease, and the level of health care offered by most is appalling. You can get good medical and dental care privately: North Americans will think it fairly inexpensive, Europeans used to state-subsidized health care will not. A doctor's visit will cost on average US$40–75; drugs are relatively cheap. Hotels in big cities will have lists of English-speaking **doctors**; ask for a *médico*. Outside the larger centres, you will probably have to try out your Portuguese. Any Brazilian doctor will also understand – although not necessarily speak – Spanish.

## Food and water

Many diseases are directly or indirectly related to impure **water** and contaminated **food**, and care should be taken in choosing what to eat and drink.

You should, of course, take particular care with seafood, especially **shellfish** – don't eat anything that's at all suspicious. Fruit and salad ingredients should be washed in bottled or purified water or, preferably, peeled. Ultimately, you are going to run some risks with food, so if you're going to enjoy your stay to the full, you can't be too paranoid.

Even in the most remote towns and villages **mineral water** (*água mineral*), either sparkling (*com gás*) or still (*sem gás*), is easily available and cheap. To avoid dehydration be sure to drink plenty of non-alcoholic liquids, always carry a bottle of water on long trips, and check that the seal on any bottled water you use is intact.

As with food, it's difficult to be on guard all the time whilst drinking; fruit juices are often diluted with water, and ice is rarely made with filtered water outside a smart hotel. It is not realistic to restrict all water intake to mineral water, but if you are sensible you can at least minimize risk.

## Chagas' disease

A serious disease you should guard against is **Chagas' disease**, which is endemic in parts of the **Northeast** and **the Amazon**. Although it is difficult to catch, it can lead to serious heart and kidney problems that appear up to twenty years after infection. The disease is carried in the faeces of beetles that live in the cracks of adobe walls, so if sleeping in an adobe hut, make sure nothing can crawl into your hammock; either use a mosquito net or sling the hammock as far from walls as you can. The beetle bites and then defecates next to the spot: scratching of the bite will rub in the infected faeces, so before scratching a bite that you know wasn't caused by a mosquito, **bathe it in alcohol**. If you are infected, you will have a fever for a few days that will then clear up as if nothing untoward happened. Though the disease can be treated in its early stages, it becomes incurable once established. If you travel through a Chagas area and get an undiagnosed fever, have a blood test as soon as possible afterwards.

## Dengue fever

**Dengue fever**, a viral disease transmitted by mosquito bites, is increasingly common in all Brazilian cities save the extreme south of the country. Rio has been particularly badly affected in recent years, as the spectacular incompetence of its city government has allowed the mosquito problem to get out of hand. It is highly seasonal, peaking in the southern hemisphere summer (Dec–April). The symptoms are debilitating rather than dangerous: light but persistent fever, tiredness, muscle and joint pains, especially in the fingers, and nausea and vomiting. It is easily treatable, but you will feel pretty grim for a week or so. It is much more widespread than any other disease in urban areas, and is currently the focus of much educational and preventive work by the Brazilian government. The same precautions against mosquito bites outlined in the section on malaria above apply here. The difference is that the dengue mosquito comes out during the day rather than at night. Be cautious in urban environments around anything that could act as a water retainer and thus as a mosquito breeding ground: drainage channels, old oil drums and tyres, abandoned lots, swampy areas in general.

There is one dangerous form of dengue, **hemorraghic dengue**, which kills hundreds of people a year in Brazil. Tourists tend not to get it, since you almost always need to have had a previous attack of dengue to be vulnerable to it. It is particularly dangerous to children. The body's immune system is provoked to attack itself by the dengue virus, resulting in internal bleeding that can quickly get out of hand. If dengue-like symptoms are accompanied by bleeding from the nose and ears or highly bloodshot eyes, get yourself to a private hospital fast. Even if you are unlucky enough to get it, in the vast majority of cases getting timely treatment will mean a few days in hospital is all that's needed for complete recovery. You will feel very weak and should take things easy for a couple of weeks after you leave hospital, however.

## Diarrhoea, dysentery and giardia

**Diarrhoea** is something everybody gets at some stage, and there's little to be done except drink a lot (but not alcohol) and bide your time. You should also replace salts either by taking oral rehydration salts or by mixing a teaspoon of salt and eight of sugar in a litre of purified water. You can minimize the risk by being sensible about what you eat, and by not drinking tap water anywhere. This isn't difficult, given the extreme cheapness and universal availability of soft drinks and *água mineral*, while Brazilians are great believers in herbal teas, which often help alleviate cramps.

If your diarrhoea contains blood or mucus, the cause may be dysentery or giardia. With a fever, it could well be caused by **bacillic dysentery** and may clear up without treatment. If you're sure you need it, a course of antibiotics such as tetracyclin or ampicillin (travel with a supply if you are going off the beaten track for a while) should sort you out, but they also destroy "gut flora" that help protect you. Similar symptoms without fever indicate **amoebic dysentery**, which is much more serious, and can damage your gut if untreated. The usual cure is a course of metronidazole (Flagyl), an antibiotic that may itself make you feel ill, and should not be taken with alcohol. Similar symptoms, plus rotten-egg belches and farts, indicate **giardia**, for which the treatment is again metronidazole. If you suspect you have any of these, seek medical help, and only start on the metronidazole (750mg three times daily for a week for adults) if there is definitely blood in your diarrhoea and it is impossible to see a doctor.

## Hepatitis A

Wherever you go, protection against **hepatitis A** is a sensible precaution. The disease is transmitted through contaminated water and food, resulting in fever and diarrhoea, and it can also cause liver damage. Gammaglobulin injections, one before you go and boosters every six months, are the standard protection.

If you plan to spend much time in Amazônia or the Northeast, or if you know that you will be travelling rough, it's well worth protecting yourself. If you have had jaundice, you may well have immunity and should have a blood test to see if you need the injections. A newer vaccine – Havrix – is very effective and lasts for up to ten years.

## HIV and AIDS

Brazil has a relatively high number of people with **AIDS and HIV**. There are many reasons for this: a scandalous lack of screening of either blood donors or supplies in the 1980s; the level of gay sex between Brazilian men, among whom bisexuality is common; the popularity of anal sex, not least among heterosexual couples; and the sharing of needles among drug users in large cities. But Brazil has been a world leader in dealing with the epidemic. It faced down international drug companies in the late 1990s with the threat that they would independently manufacture AIDS drugs – with the result that all HIV-positive Brazilians now receive free anti-retroviral medicines in a programme that has become a global model for developing countries. Brazil also has some of the funniest and most imaginative safe-sex campaigns anywhere, particularly in evidence during Carnaval.

A straightforward understanding of the disease and how it is transmitted is the best defence. Firstly, HIV is not evenly distributed throughout Brazil. A majority of HIV carriers are concentrated in the big cities. As anywhere else, sex with a prostitute is a high-risk activity. The situation with blood and blood products has now improved enormously, but in remoter parts of the country, especially the Amazon, make sure that if you have an injection it is with a needle you see being removed from its packaging. Finally, **use a condom**. Only a tiny minority of sexually active Brazilian men carry them as a matter of course. They are widely available in pharmacies, where you should ask for a *camisinha*.

## Malaria

**Malaria** is endemic in **northern Brazil**, and anyone intending to travel in Amazônia should take precautions very seriously. You are safe if you are only visiting cities and towns, where intensive campaigns keep malarial mosquitoes at a distance, and if your visit will be restricted to Manaus, Santarém and Belém you can forego prophylaxis. Mosquitoes are also not a problem on river journeys, since the breezes keep them off, and they are much less common in black-water river systems – such as the River Negro, where jungle lodges around Manaus are concentrated – where malaria is rare.

If you will be sleeping in a rural area anywhere else in the Amazon, however, it is a good idea to take precautions. In recent years, rates have climbed as mosquitoes have become more resistant to insecticides and drugs, and a few unwary tourists die avoidably every year. Southern Pará state and much of rural Rondônia state are the riskiest areas for malaria. However, with simple precautions you can minimize the chances of getting it even in highly malarial areas, and, properly treated, a dose of malaria should be no worse than a severe bout of flu. But make no mistake – unless you follow the **precautions** outlined here, and take malaria prophylaxis when appropriate, malaria can kill.

There are two kinds of malaria in Brazil: **falciparum**, which is more serious but less common, and **vivax**. Both are transmitted by anopheles mosquitoes, which are most active at sunrise and for an hour or so before sunset. Even in very malarial areas, only around five percent of anopheles are infected with malarial parasites, so the more you minimize mosquito bites, the less likely you are to catch it. Use **insect repellent**: the most commonly used in Brazil is **Autan**, often in combination with Johnson's Baby Oil to minimize skin irritation. The most effective mosquito repellents – worth looking out for before you leave home – contain **DEET** (diethyl toluamide). DEET is strong stuff, so follow the manufacturers' instructions, particularly with use on children. If you have sensitive skin, a natural alternative is citronella or, in the UK, Mosi-guard Natural, made from a blend of eucalyptus oils (though still use DEET on clothes and nets). Wear long-sleeved shirts and trousers, shoes and socks during the times of day when mosquitoes are most active. Sleep under a sheet and, crucially, use a **mosquito net**. Nets for hammocks (*mosqueteiro para rede*) are reasonable and easily available in Amazonian cities and towns. Mosquito coils also help keep the insects at bay.

When taking **preventive tablets** it's important to keep a routine and cover the period before and after your trip with doses. Doctors can advise on which kind to take. As resistance to chloroquin-based drugs increases, mefloquin, which goes under the brand name of Lariam, has become the recommended prophylactic for most travellers to Brazil. This has very strong side effects, and its use is controversial. The website Ⓦwww.cdc.gov/travel/regionalmalaria is a useful resource, giving advice on risk areas in Brazil and the best methods of protection.

Malaria has an incubation period of around two weeks. The first **signs of malaria** are remarkably similar to flu – muscle pains, weakness and pain in the joints, which will last for a day or two before the onset of malaria fever proper – and may take months to appear: if you suspect anything go to a hospital or clinic immediately. You need immediate treatment and a blood test to identify the strain. **Malaria treatment** is one public-health area where Brazil can take some credit. Dotted in malarial parts of the Amazon are small malaria control posts and **clinics**, run by the anti-malaria agency SUCAM – ask for the *posto da SUCAM*. They may not look like much, but the people who staff them are very experienced and know their local strains better than any city specialist. Treatment in a *posto* is free, and if you do catch malaria you should get yourself taken to one as quickly as possible; don't shiver in your hammock and wait for it to pass. It often does, but it can also kill. If in a city and you get the same symptoms (a fever and the shakes), make sure you get a blood test right away; you'll get your results in a few hours, and quick diagnosis is vital. Remember that the incubation period means that the symptoms may only appear after you return home – make sure to tell your doctor where you've been if you get a fever shortly after your return home.

Malaria is a much more serious issue for a **child**. We specifically recommend avoiding the state of Rondônia other than Porto Velho, rural Acre and Amapá and southern Pará if you are travelling with children.

## Yellow fever

Getting a **yellow fever vaccination**, which offers protection for ten years, is recommended if you're going to **Amazônia, Goiás or Mato Grosso**. This viral disease is transmitted by mosquitoes and can be fatal, but is extremely rare even in places where it is endemic. Symptoms include headache, fever, abdominal pain and vomiting, and though victims may appear to recover, without medical help they may suffer from bleeding, shock and kidney and liver failure. While you're waiting for help, it is important to keep the fever as low as possible and prevent dehydration.

## In the Amazon

Given the remoteness of many parts of the Amazon and the prevalence of insects and snakes, health care takes on a special significance. If you are trekking through forest or savanna, long trousers are a good idea, and it is vital to wear good boots that protect your ankles from snake bites, chiggers (mites) and scorpions. You should never trek alone.

**Snakes** are timid and, unless you're unlucky, only attack if you step on them. Many of the most poisonous snakes are tiny, easily able to snuggle inside a shoe or a rucksack pocket. Always shake out your hammock and clothes, keep rucksack pockets tightly closed and take special care when it rains, as snakes, scorpions and other nasty beasties quite sensibly head for shelter in huts. If you do get bitten by a snake, try to kill it for identification – but only if this can easily be done. Use a shoelace or a torn piece of shirt wound round the limb with a stick as a tourniquet, which you should repeatedly tighten for twenty seconds and then release for a minute, to slow down the action of the poison. Contrary to popular belief, cutting yourself and sucking out blood will do you more harm than good. It goes without saying that you should get yourself to a doctor as soon as possible. If you are well off the beaten track, health posts in the nearest town may have serum, but you must know the type of snake involved.

Due to the humidity, any **cut** or **wound** gets infected very easily. Always clean cuts or bites with alcohol or purified water before dressing. As a general rule, leave all insects alone and never handle them. Even the smallest ants, caterpillars and bees can give you nasty stings and bites, and scorpions, large soldier ants and some species of bee will give you a fever for a day or two as well.

# Getting around

**Local travel in Brazil is always easy. Public transport outside of the Amazon is generally by bus or plane, though there are a few passenger trains, too. However you travel, services will be crowded, plentiful and, apart from planes, fairly cheap. Car rental is possible, but driving in Brazil is not for the faint-hearted. Hitchhiking, over any distance, is not recommended.**

## By plane

It's hardly surprising that a country the size of Brazil relies on **air travel** a good deal; in some parts of Amazônia, air links are more important than roads and rivers. Any town has at least an airstrip, and all cities have airports, usually some distance from the city but not always: Santos Dumont in Rio, Congonhas in São Paulo and Guararapes in Recife are all pretty central. The airports of Brasília, Congonhas and, above all, Guarulhos in São Paulo are chronically crowded, with long check-in lines. If flying internationally from Guarulhos, add at least an extra hour to account for the phenomenal queues to get through passport control, and don't be surprised, on arrival, for it to take an hour or more to clear customs and immigration. If travelling with children, go straight to the front of the lines: families, pregnant women and seniors have priority.

### Air passes

When buying your international ticket, you should consider the possibility of adding an **air pass**, though note that the emergence of budget airlines in the country means that they now only make sense if you're planning a series of long-haul trips – from the South to the Amazon and back via the Northeast, for example.

If Brazil is only one stop on a longer trip, consider the **Mercosur Airpass**, which covers eight airlines of Argentina, Brazil, Chile, Paraguay and Uruguay. The regulations are fairly complicated but the passes basically allow two stopovers per country (plus point of origin) up to a maximum of eight, although an extra stopover is allowed to give you use of both the Argentine and Brazilian airports at Iguaçu Falls. The route must include at least two countries, and the price of a pass is based on the number of miles flown, which always works out costing far less than purchasing regular tickets. Prices may be affected by the time of year that you travel.

If Brazil is your only destination, the **TAM Air Pass** can be a huge moneysaver. It is valid for thirty days from the first flight and costs US$530 for four flights if bought together with a TAM international flight, US$700 if you fly with another carrier. Additional flights are around US$150 each, much cheaper than you are likely to pay if you book a flight yourself within Brazil.

Lastly, if you have an air pass and change the time or date of your flight, always remember to **cancel the original flight**. If you don't, the computer flags you as a no-show, and all your other air-pass reservations will also be cancelled.

### Budget airlines

A recent phenomenon in Brazil is the appearance of budget airlines, of which the biggest is **GOL** (Ⓦwww.voegol.com.br); others include

**Webjet** (@www.webjet.com.br) and **Azul** (@www.voeazul.com.br), which started operating in 2009. GOL has an extensive network, cheap seats, is efficient and usually much better value than TAM – though, irritatingly, American Express is the only foreign credit-card that's accepted on its website. In Brazilian holiday periods (July, around Xmas, and Carnaval) flights are often booked up and you need to book as far in advance as you can. Outside these times, if you can be a little flexible on dates and if the TAM airpass does not meet your needs, your cheapest strategy would be to book tickets with Gol after arriving in Brazil at a Gol desk in an airport.

Flying to the Northeast or Amazônia from the South can be tiresome, as many of these long-distance routes are no more than glorified bus runs, stopping everywhere before heading north. In planning your itinerary, it's a good idea to check carefully how many times a plane stops – for example, between São Paulo and Fortaleza, a flight may stop as many as four times or as few as once.

There are **safety issues** to consider when flying in the Amazon, where investigations following a recent series of crashes revealed serious problems in a number of regional airlines, notably **Rico**. Where possible, stick to Gol and TAM when flying around the Amazon. In many parts of Amazônia, air travel in small planes, or **aerotaxis**, is very common – the regional word for these flights is *teco-teco*. Before taking one, you should be aware that the airstrips are often dangerous, the planes routinely fly overloaded and are not reliably maintained, and no checks are made on the qualifications of pilots – some don't have any.

### Fares

Prices are reasonable in the South and Northeast but climb steeply as soon as the Amazon is involved, where a return flight from Rio or São Paulo can often be scarily similar to the cost of a flight to Miami. It's always much cheaper to buy internal tickets linked to your international flights if you plan on heading to the Amazon from Rio or São Paulo. If you are flying outside holiday periods in Brazil (July & Dec–March) and you're not heading to the Amazon, you will probably get a cheaper deal buying a ticket in Brazil after you arrive.

## By train

You probably won't be taking many **trains** in Brazil. Although there's an extensive rail network, most of it is for cargo only, and even where there are passenger trains they're almost invariably slower and less convenient than the buses. Exceptions are the *metrô* rail systems in Porto Alegre, Rio, São Paulo and Brasília and a few **tourist journeys** worth making for themselves, especially in the South and Minas Gerais.

## By bus

The **bus system** in Brazil is excellent and makes travelling around the country easy, comfortable and economical, despite the distances involved. Inter-city buses leave from a station called a **rodoviária**, usually built on city outskirts.

Buses are operated by hundreds of private companies, but **prices** are standardized, even when more than one firm plies the same route, and are reasonable: Rio to São Paulo is around R$80, to Belo Horizonte R$75, to Foz do Iguaçu R$200 and to Salvador R$240, while São Paulo to Brasília is around R$150. Long-distance buses are comfortable enough to sleep in, and have on-board toilets (which can get smelly on long journeys): the lower your seat number, the further away from them you'll be. Buses stop every two or three hours at well-supplied *postos*, but as prices at these are relatively high it's not a bad idea to bring along water and some food. Some bus companies will supply meal vouchers for use at the *postos* on long journeys.

There are luxury buses, too, called **leitos**, which do overnight runs between the major cities – worth taking once for the experience, with fully reclining seats in curtained partitions, freshly ironed sheets and an attendant plying insomniacs with coffee and conversation. They cost about a third of the price of an air ticket, and twice as much as a normal long-distance bus; they're also less frequent and need to be booked a few days in advance. No matter what kind of bus, it's a good idea to have a light sweater or blanket during night journeys, as the air conditioning is often uncomfortably cold.

Going any distance, it's best to **buy your ticket** at least a day in advance, from the *rodoviária* or, in some cities, from travel

## Timetables

Although plane and bus **timetables** are kept to whenever possible, in the less developed parts of the country – most notably Amazônia but also the interior of the Northeast – delays often happen. Brazilians are very flexible in their attitude to time, and if ever there was a country where patience will stand you in good stead it's Brazil. Turn up at the arranged time, but don't be surprised at all if you're kept waiting. (Waiting times are especially long if you have to deal with any part of the state bureaucracy, like extending a visa.) There is no way around this; just take a good book.

agents. An exception is the Rio–São Paulo route, where a shuttle service means you can always turn up without a ticket and never have to wait more than fifteen minutes. Numbered seats are provided on all routes: if you want a window, ask for *janela*. If you cross a state line, you will get a small form with the ticket, which asks for the number of your seat (*poltrona*), the number of your ticket (*passagem*), the number of your passport (*identidade*) and your destination (*destino*). You have to fill it in and give it to the driver before you'll be let on board. Buses have **luggage** compartments, which are safe: you check pieces at the side of the bus and get a ticket for them. Keep an eye on your hand luggage, and take anything valuable with you when you get off for a halt.

## By car

**Driving** standards in Brazil hover between abysmal and appalling. The country has one of the highest death tolls from driving-related accidents in the world, and on any journey you can see why, with thundering trucks and drivers treating the road as if it were a Grand Prix racetrack. Fortunately, inter-city bus drivers are the exception to the rule: they are usually very good, and their buses usually have devices fitted that make it impossible for them to exceed the speed limit. Electronic speed traps are widely used everywhere, and if you get caught by one in a rental car, the fine will simply be added to your credit card. Since 2008, a zero-tolerance law has made it strictly illegal to drive after consuming any amount of alcohol, a response to the enormous death toll caused by drunk drivers. Offenders risk severe punishments if tests detect any alcohol in their blood – expect at least a hefty fine and the threat of imprisonment.

**Road quality** varies according to region: the South and Southeast have a good paved network; the Northeast has a good network on the coast but is poor in the interior; and roads in Amazônia are by far the worst, with even major highways closed for weeks or months at a time as they are washed away by the rains. Most cities are fairly well signposted, so getting out of town shouldn't be too difficult; if city traffic is daunting, try to arrange to collect your car on a Sunday when traffic is light. If at all possible, avoid driving at night because potholes (even on main roads) and *lombadas* (speed bumps) may not be obvious, and breaking down after dark could be dangerous. Outside the big cities, Brazilian roads are deathtraps at night; poorly lit, in bad condition and lightly policed. Especially worth avoiding at night are the **Via Dutra**, linking Rio and São Paulo, because of the huge numbers of trucks and the treacherous ascent and descent of the Serra do Mar, and the **Belém–Brasília highway**, whose potholes and uneven asphalt make it difficult enough to drive even in daylight. Where possible, avoid driving after dark in the Mato Grosso and Amazon regions as well; though rare, armed roadside robberies have been known to happen there.

An **international driving licence** is useful: although foreign licences are accepted for visits of up to six months, you may have a hard time convincing a police officer of this. Outside of the towns and cities, service stations can be few and far between, so keep a careful eye on the fuel gauge. Service stations sell both petrol (*gasolina*) and ethanol (*álcool*), with new cars (including rentals) usually capable of running on either fuel. *Álcool* is considerably cheaper than *gasolina*, and there's no longer a noticeable difference in terms of performance.

Service stations in rural areas do not always accept international credit cards, so make sure you have sufficient cash on a long trip. In urban areas, plastic is universally accepted at petrol stations, although a common scam is to charge around twenty percent more per litre when payment is made by credit card rather than cash: always check in advance whether there is a price difference if you intend to pay by credit card.

**Parking**, especially in the cities, can be tricky due to security and finding a space, and it's worth paying extra for a hotel with some kind of lock-up garage. A universal feature of city driving in Brazil is the *flanelinha*, named for the flannel that informal parking attendants wave at approaching cars; these attendants will help you into and out of parking spaces and guard your car, in return for a *real* or two. Brazilians will go to almost any lengths to avoid paying them, but they're making a living and providing a service, so do the decent thing. In any event, never leave anything valuable inside the car.

Driving in Brazil is very different from northern Europe and the US. Do not expect Brazilians to pay much attention to lane markings, use indicators or worry about cutting you off or overtaking you on the inside. Use your rear and wing mirrors constantly when city driving. At night, you should cautiously roll through red lights in city centres or deserted-looking streets, to avoid *assaltantes*. And a crucial thing to know is that **flashing lights** from an oncoming car mean "I'm coming through – get out of the way" and NOT "please go ahead", as in the UK and US. It sounds intimidating, and it is for the first couple of days, but it is surprising how quickly you get used to it.

## Renting a car

**Renting a car** in Brazil is straightforward. Of the big-name international companies, Hertz and Avis are the most widely represented, with Budget and Dollar increasing their representation. There are also plenty of reliable Brazilian alternatives, such as Unidas, Interlocadora and Localiza. Car-rental offices (*locadoras*) can be found at every airport and in most towns regardless of size, although you will pay slightly more for airport pick-up and drop-off. Almost all cars in Brazil have manual gears; automatics are rare.

**Rates** start from around R$120 a day for a compact car (Fiat Punto or similar) including unlimited mileage; a basic air-conditioned model will start at around R$140, also including unlimited mileage. Four-wheel-drive vehicles are rare and extremely expensive. Prices don't always include **insurance** – a comprehensive policy will cost an additional R$25 per day or so with a deductible of R$500. If you have a US credit card, you may find that it can be used to cover the additional liability – check before leaving home. In any case, a credit card is essential for making a deposit when renting a car. It's not a bad idea to reserve a car before you arrive in Brazil, as you can be sure to get the best available rate.

As you would anywhere, carefully check the condition of the car before accepting it and pay special attention to the state of the tyres (including the spare), and make sure there's a jack, warning triangle and fire extinguisher: the police will check for these if you get pulled over. All cars have front and back seatbelts; their use is compulsory, and stiff on-the-spot fines are imposed on drivers and front-seat passengers found not to be wearing them.

### Car-rental agencies

**Avis** US ⓣ1-800/331-1084, Canada ⓣ1-800/272-5871, UK ⓣ0870/606 0100, Republic of Ireland ⓣ01/605 7500, Australia ⓣ13 63 33 or 02/9353-9000, New Zealand ⓣ09/526-2847 or 0800/655-111; ⓦwww.avis.com.

**Budget** US ⓣ1-800/527-0700, Canada ⓣ1-800/268-8900, UK ⓣ0800/181181, Republic of Ireland ⓣ0906/627711, Australia ⓣ1300/362-848, New Zealand ⓣ09/976-2222; ⓦwww.budget.com.

**Dollar** US & Canada ⓣ1-800/800-3665, UK ⓣ0808/234 7524, Republic of Ireland ⓣ1800/515800; ⓦwww.dollar.com.

**Hertz** US ⓣ1-800/654-3001, Canada ⓣ1-800/263-0600, UK ⓣ0870/844 8844, Republic of Ireland ⓣ01/676 7476, Australia ⓣ13 30 39 or 03/9698-2555, New Zealand ⓣ0800/654-321; ⓦwww.hertz.com.

**Interlocadora** Brazil ⓣ0800/138-000, ⓦwww.interlocadora.com.br.

**Localiza** Brazil ⓣ0800/992-000, ⓦwww.localiza.com.br.

**Unidas** Brazil ⓣ0800/121-121, ⓦwww.unidas.com.br.

## Amazon riverboats

In Amazônia, rivers have been the main highways for centuries, and the Amazon itself is navigable to ocean-going ships as far west as Iquitos in Peru, nearly 3000km upstream from Belém.

In all the large riverside cities of the Amazon – notably Belém, Manaus and Santarém – there are *hidroviárias*, ferry terminals for waterborne bus services. **Amazon river travel** is slow and can be tough going, but it's a fascinating experience. On bigger boats, there are a number of classes; in general, it's better to avoid *cabine*, where you swelter in a cabin, and choose *primeiro* (first class) instead, sleeping in a hammock on deck. *Segundo* (second class) is usually hammock space in the lower deck or engine room. Wooden boats are much more comfortable than metal, but usually slower. Take plenty of provisions, and expect to practise your Portuguese.

The **range of boat transport** in the Amazon runs from luxury tourist boats and large three-level riverboats to smaller one- or two-level boats (the latter normally confining their routes to main tributaries and local runs) and covered launches operated by tour companies. The most popular route is the **Belém–Manaus trip**, which takes four to six days.

### Taxis

There are enormous numbers of **taxis** in Brazilian cities, and they're very cheap, especially if there are two or more passengers. City cabs are metered, and have two rates: 1 is cheaper, 2 more expensive. The rate the taxi is using is indicated on the taximeter, after the fare. Rate 2 is automatic on trips to and from airports and bus stations in big cities, after 8pm, and all day Sunday and public holidays. Many cities give taxi drivers a Christmas bonus by allowing them to charge Rate 2 for the whole of December. Occasionally, drivers will refer to a sheet and revise the fare slightly upwards – they are not ripping you off, but referring to price updating tables that fill the gap until taximeters can be readjusted to reflect the official annual increases.

Taxis in small towns and rural areas do not often have meters, so it's best to agree on the fare in advance – they'll be more expensive than in the cities. Most airports and some bus stations are covered by taxi cooperatives, which operate under a slightly different system: attendants give you a coupon with fares to various destinations printed on it – you pay either at a kiosk in advance, or the driver. These are more expensive than regular taxis, but they're reliable and often more comfortable. Tipping is not obligatory, but appreciated.

## By ferry and boat

**Water travel and ferries** are also important forms of transport in parts of Brazil. Specific details are included in the relevant sections of the Guide, but look out for the ferry to Niterói, without which no journey to **Rio** would be complete; **Salvador**, where there are regular services to islands and towns in the huge bay on which the city is built; in the **South** between the islands of the Bay of Paranaguá; and most of all in **Amazônia**.

# Accommodation

**Accommodation in Brazil covers the full range, from hostels and basic lodgings clustered around bus stations to luxury resort hotels. You can sometimes find places to sleep for as little as R$20 a night, but, more realistically, a clean double room in a basic option will set you back upwards of R$30–45. A good, comfortable hotel varies according to the city – Rio being considerably more expensive – but R$100–150 a night will get you better accommodation than you'd expect for that price in Europe or the US. As is so often the case, single travellers get a bad deal, usually paying almost as much as the cost of a double room. In whatever category of place you stay, in tourist spots – both large and small – over New Year and Carnaval you'll be expected to book a room for a minimum of four or five days.**

## Hotels

**Hotels** proper run from dives to luxury apartments. There is a Brazilian **classification system**, from one to five stars, but the absence of stars doesn't necessarily mean a bad hotel: they depend on bureaucratic requirements such as the width of lift shafts and kitchen floor space as much as on the standard of accommodation – many perfectly good hotels don't have stars.

Hotels offer a range of different rooms, with significant price differences: a **quarto** is a room without a bathroom, an **apartamento** is a room with a shower (Brazilians don't use baths); an *apartamento de luxo* is normally just an *apartamento* with a fridge full of (marked-up) drinks; a **casal** is a double room; and a **solteiro** a single. In a starred hotel, an *apartamento* upwards would come with telephone, air conditioning (*ar condicionado*) and cable TV; a *ventilador* is a fan. Even cheaper hotels now have wi-fi (*sem fio*) in the lobby at least, and three-star hotels upwards have wi-fi and/or cable (*cabo*) in rooms as standard, although you will often have to pay a surcharge.

**Rates** for rooms vary tremendously between different parts of Brazil, but start at around R$25 in a one-star hotel, around R$60 in a two-star hotel, and around R$80 in a three-star place. Generally speaking, for R$60–80 a night you could expect to stay in a reasonable mid-range hotel, with bathroom and air conditioning. Many hotels in this bracket are excellent value for the standard of accommodation they offer – but expect to pay more in major cities such as Rio and São Paulo. During the off season, most hotels in tourist areas offer hefty **discounts**, usually around 25–35 percent.

Most hotels – although not all – will add a ten percent **service charge** to your bill, the *taxa de serviço*: those that don't will have a sign at the desk saying "*Nós não cobramos taxa de serviço*", and it's very bad form to leave the hotel without tipping the receptionist. The price will usually include a breakfast buffet with fruit, cheese, ham,

### Accommodation price codes

In this guide, accommodation has been categorized according to the price codes outlined below. These categories represent the minimum you can expect to pay for a **double room in high season** – though note that many of the budget places will also have more expensive rooms. Rates for hostels and basic hotels where guests are charged **per person** are given in R$.

1. R$40 and under
2. R$41–70
3. R$71–120
4. R$121–180
5. R$181–260
6. R$261–350
7. R$351–500
8. R$501–700
9. R$701 and over

bread, cakes and coffee but no other meals, although there will often be a restaurant on-site. Hotels usually have a **safe deposit box**, a *caixa*, which is worth asking about when you check in; they are free for you to use and, although they're not invulnerable, anything left in a *caixa* is safer than on your person or unguarded in your room. Many hotels also offer a safe deposit box in your room, which is the safest option of all.

Finally, a **motel**, as you'll gather from the various names and decor, is strictly for couples. This is not to say that it's not possible to stay in one if you can't find anything else – since they're used by locals, they're rarely too expensive – but you should be aware that most of the other rooms will be rented by the hour.

## Pensões, postos and pousadas

In a slightly higher price range are the small, family-run hotels, called either a **pensão** (*pensões* in the plural) or a *hotel familiar*. These vary a great deal: some are no more appealing than a *dormitório*, while others are friendlier and better value than many hotels and can be places of considerable character and luxury. *Pensões* tend to be better in small towns than in large cities, but are also usefully thick on the ground in some of the main tourist towns. In southern Brazil, many of the **postos**, highway service stations on town outskirts, have cheap rooms and showers, and are usually well kept and clean.

You will also come across the **pousada**, which can just be another name for a *pensão*, but can also be a small hotel, running up to luxury class but usually less expensive than a hotel proper. In some small towns – such as Ouro Preto and Paraty – *pousadas* form the bulk of mid- and upper-level accommodation options. In the Amazon and Mato Grosso in particular, *pousadas* tend to be purpose-built *fazenda* lodges geared towards the growing ecotourist markets.

## Dormitories and hostels

At the bottom end of the scale, in terms of both quality and price, are **dormitórios**, small and very basic (to put it mildly) hotels, situated close to bus stations and in the poorer parts of town. They are extremely cheap (just a few dollars a night), but usually unsavoury and sometimes downright dangerous. They should be avoided unless you have no choice.

You could stay for not much more, in far better conditions, in a **youth hostel**, an *albergue de juventude*, also sometimes called a *casa de estudante*, where the cost per person is between R$20 and R$35 a night. There's an extensive network of these hostels, with at least one in every state capital, and they are very well maintained, often in restored buildings. It helps to have an IYHF card (available from your national youth hostel associations) with a recent photograph – you're not usually asked for one, but every so often you'll find an *albergue* that refuses entry unless it's produced. The Federação Brasileira dos Albergues de Juventude in Rio publishes an excellent illustrated guide to Brazil's official hostels – and there's a growing number of hostels that aren't affiliated with the IYHF, many of which are very good.

### Addresses

Trying to find an address can be confusing: streets often have two names, numbers don't always follow a logical sequence, and parts of the address are often abbreviated (Brasília is a special case – see p.458). The street name and number will often have a floor (*andar*), apartment or room (*sala;* "s" for short) number tacked on: thus R. Afonso Pena 111-3° s.234 means third floor, room 234 at 111 Rua Alfonso Pena. You may also come across *Ed.* (*edifício*, or building) or *s/n* (*sem número*, no number), very common in rural areas and small towns. All addresses in Brazil also have an eight-digit postcode, or *CEP*, often followed by two capital letters for the state; leaving it out causes delay in delivery. So a full address might read:

Rua do Sol 132-3° andar, s.12
65000-100 São Luís – MA

Demand for places far outstrips supply at certain times of year – July, and December to Carnaval – but if you travel with a **hammock** you can often hook it up in a corridor or patio. A major advantage that hostels have is to throw you together with young Brazilians, the main users of the network.

## Camping

There are a fair number of **campsites** in Brazil and almost all of them are on the coast near the bigger beaches – mostly, they're near cities rather than in out-of-the-way places. They will usually have basic facilities – running water and toilets, perhaps a simple restaurant – and are popular with young Argentines and Brazilians. A few fancier sites are designed for people with camper vans or big tents in the back of their cars. Having your own tent, or hiring one, is also particularly useful in ecotourist regions such as the Amazon and the Pantanal, where it can really open up the wilderness to you. In all cases, however, the problem is **security**, partly of your person, but more significantly of your possessions, which can never really be made safe. Great caution should be exercised before camping off-site – only do so if you're part of a group and you've received assurances locally as to safety.

# Food and drink

**It's hard to generalize about Brazilian food, largely because there is no single national cuisine but numerous very distinct regional ones. Nature dealt Brazil a full hand for these: there's an abundant variety of fruit, vegetables and spices – as you can see for yourself walking through any food market.**

There are five main **regional cuisines**: *comida mineira* from Minas Gerais, based on pork, vegetables (especially *couve*, collard greens) and *tutu*, a kind of refried bean cooked with manioc flour and used as a thick sauce; *comida baiana* from the Salvador coast, the most exotic to gringo palates, using fresh fish and shellfish, hot peppers, palm oil, coconut milk and fresh coriander; *comida do sertão* from the interior of the Northeast, which relies on rehydrated, dried or salted meat and the fruit, beans and tubers of the region; *comida gaúcha* from Rio Grande do Sul, the most carnivorous diet in the world, revolving around every imaginable kind of meat grilled over charcoal; and *comida amazônica*, based on river fish, manioc sauces and the many fruits and palm products of northern Brazil. *Comida do sertão* is rarely served outside its homeland, but you'll find restaurants serving the others throughout Brazil, although – naturally – they're at their best in their region of origin.

Alongside the regional restaurants, there is a **standard fare** available everywhere that can soon get dull unless you cast around: steak (*bife*) or chicken (*frango*), served with *arroz e feijão* (rice and beans), and often with salad, fries and *farinha*, dried manioc (cassava) flour that you sprinkle over everything. *Farofa* is toasted *farinha*, and usually comes with onions and bits of bacon mixed in. In cheaper restaurants, all this would come on a single large plate: look for the words "*prato feito*", "*prato comercial*" or "*refeição completa*" if you want to fill up without spending too much.

**Feijoada** is the closest Brazil comes to a national dish. It is a stew of pork leftovers (ear, pizzle and other unmentionables that fortunately can be fished out), sausage, smoked ribs and beef jerky cooked slowly for hours with black beans and garlic until mouthwateringly tender, served garnished with slices of orange and pork crackling and accompanied by shots of *cachaça* rum. It is a national ritual for Saturday lunch, when restaurants serve *feijoada* all day.

Some of the **fruit** is familiar – *manga* (mango), *maracujá* (passion fruit), *limão* (lime) – but most of it has only Brazilian names: *jaboticaba*, *fruta do conde*, *sapoti* and *jaca*. The most exotic fruits are Amazonian: try *bacuri*, *açaí* – increasingly seen in Europe and the US as a health food or juice – and the extraordinary *cupuaçú*, the most delicious of all. These all serve as the basis for juices and **ice cream** (*sorvete*), which can be excellent; keep an eye out for *sorvetarias*, ice-cream parlours.

For a list of common **menu** terms, see p.776.

## Snacks and street food

On every street corner in Brazil you will find a **lanchonete**, a mixture of café and bar that sells beer and rum, snacks, cigarettes, soft drinks, coffee and sometimes small meals. **Bakeries** – *padarias* – often have a *lanchonete* attached, and they're good places for cheap snacks: an *empada* or *empadinha* is a small pie, which has various fillings – *carne* (meat), *palmito* (palm heart) and *camarão* (shrimp) being the best; a *pastel* is a fried, filled pasty; an *esfiha* is a savoury pastry stuffed with spiced meat; and a *coxinha* is spiced chicken rolled in manioc dough and then fried. In central Brazil, try *pão de queijo*, a savoury cheese snack that goes perfectly with coffee; in the Amazon, keep an eye out for a *tapioquinha*, a tapioca pancake folded with cheese, ham or whatever else you want to start the day with. All these savoury snacks fall under the generic heading *salgados*.

If you haven't had **breakfast** (*café da manha*) at your hotel, then a bakery/*lanchonete* is a good place to head for; and for a more substantial meal *lanchonetes* will generally serve a *prato comercial*, too. In both *lanchonetes* and *padarias* you usually pay first at the till, and then take your ticket to the counter to get what you want. You'll find a growing number of **fast food** outlets in cities. Menus in them are easy to understand because they are in mangled but recognizable English, albeit with Brazilian pronunciation. A hamburger is a *X-burger* (pronounced "*sheezboorga*"), a hot dog is *cachorro quente*; a *baurú* is a club sandwich with steak and egg; a *mixto quente* a toasted cheese and ham sandwich.

Food sold by **street vendors** should be treated with caution, but not dismissed out of hand. You can practically see amoebas crawling over some of the food you see on sale in the streets, but plenty of vendors have proper stalls and can be very professional, with a loyal clientele of office workers and locals. Some of the food they sell has the advantage of being cooked a long time, which reduces the chance of picking anything up, and in some places – Salvador and Belém especially – you can get good food cheaply in the street; just choose your vendor sensibly. In Salvador, try *acarajé*, only available from street vendors – a delicious fried bean mix with shrimp and hot pepper; and in Belém go for *maniçoba*, spiced sausage with chicory leaves, *pato no tucupi*, duck stewed in manioc sauce, or *tacacá*, shrimp stewed in manioc sauce.

## Restaurants

**Restaurants** – *restaurantes* – are ubiquitous, portions are very large and prices extremely reasonable. A *prato comercial* is around R$10, while a good full meal can usually be had for about R$35, even in expensive-looking restaurants. Cheaper places, though, tend only to be open for lunch. One of the best options offered by many restaurants, typically at lunchtime only, is self-service *comida por kilo*, where a wide choice of food is priced according to the weight of the food on your plate. Specialist restaurants to look out for include a *rodizio*, where you pay a fixed charge and eat as much as you want; most *churrascarias* – restaurants specializing in charcoal-grilled meat of all kinds, especially beef – operate this system, too, bringing a constant supply of meat on huge spits to the tables.

Many restaurants will present unsolicited food the moment you sit down – the **couvert**, which can consist of anything from a couple of bits of raw carrot and an olive to quite an elaborate and substantial plate. Although the price is generally modest, it still has to be paid for. If you don't want it, ask the waiter to take it away.

Brazil also has a large variety of **ethnic restaurants**, thanks to the generations of Portuguese, Arabs, Italians, Japanese, German and other immigrants who have made the country their home. The widest selection is in São Paulo, with the best Italian, Lebanese and Japanese food in Brazil, but anywhere of any size will have good ethnic restaurants, often in surprising places: Belém, for example, has several excellent Japanese restaurants, thanks to a Japanese colony founded fifty years ago in the interior. Ethnic food may be marginally more expensive than Brazilian, but it's never exorbitant.

While the bill normally comes with a ten percent service charge, you should still tip, as waiters rely more on tips than on their very low wages.

## Vegetarian food

Being a **vegetarian** – or at least a strict one – is no easy matter in Brazil. If you eat fish, there's no problem, especially in the Northeast and Amazônia, where seafood forms the basis of many meals. You can usually get a fair choice of vegetarian food at a *comida por kilo* restaurant, which offers a range of salads and vegetables, as well as rice, manioc and potatoes. However, they are often only open during the day, as are the occasional vegetarian restaurants (usually described as *Restaurante Natural*) that can be found in the larger cities. Otherwise, you're up against one of the world's most carnivorous cultures. In the South and centre-west, *churrasco* rules – served at restaurants where you eat as many different cuts of meat as you can manage, and where requests for meals without meat are greeted with astonishment. At most restaurants – even *churrascarias* – huge salads are available but, if you're a vegan, always enquire whether eggs or cheese are included. If you get fed up with rice, beans and salad, there are always pizzerias around.

## Hot drinks and soft drinks

**Coffee** is the great national drink, served strong, hot and sweet in small cups and drunk quickly. However, coffee is often a great disappointment in Brazil: most of the good stuff is exported, and what's available tends to come so stiff with sugar that it's almost undrinkable unless you order an *expresso*. By far the best coffee is found in São Paulo and points south. You are never far from a *cafézinho* (as these small cups of coffee are known; *café* refers to coffee in its raw state). The best way to start your day is with *café com leite*, hot milk with coffee added to taste. Decaffeinated coffee is almost impossible to find in restaurants, and difficult even in delicatessens.

**Tea** (*chá*) is surprisingly good. Try *chá mate*, a strong green tea with a noticeable caffeine hit, or one of the wide variety of herbal teas, most notably that made from *guaraná* (see below). One highly recommended way to drink tea is using the *chimarrão*, very common in Rio Grande do Sul: a gourd filled with *chá mate* and boiling water, sucked through a silver straw. You will need some practice to avoid burning your lips, but once you get used to it, it is a wonderfully refreshing way to take tea.

The great variety of **fruit** in Brazil is put to excellent use in *sucos*: fruit is popped into a liquidizer with sugar and crushed ice to make a delicious drink. Made with milk rather than water it becomes a *vitamina*. Most *lanchonetes* and bars sell *sucos* and *vitaminas*, but for the full variety you should visit a specialist *casa de sucos*, which are found in most town centres. Widely available, and the best option to quench a thirst, are *suco de maracujá* (passion fruit) and *suco de limão* (lime). In the North and Northeast, try *graviola*, *bacuri* and *cupuaçu*. Sugar will always be added to a *suco* unless you ask for it *sem açúcar* or *natural*; some, notably *maracujá* and *limão*, are undrinkable without it.

**Soft drinks** are the regular products of corporate capitalism and all the usual brands are available. Outshining them all, though, is a local variety, *guaraná*, a fizzy and very sweet drink made out of Amazonian berries. An energy-loaded powder is made from the same berries and sold in health stores in the developed world – basically, the effect is like a smooth release of caffeine without the jitters.

## Alcoholic drinks

**Beer** is mainly of the lager type. Brazilians drink it ice-cold, and it comes mostly in 600ml bottles or cans: ask for a *cerveja*. Many places only serve beer on draught – called *chopp*. The best brands are the regional beers of Pará and Maranhão, Cerma and Cerpa, the latter available in good restaurants nationwide and called a *cerpinha*. The best nationally available beers are Antárctica, Bohêmia and Brahma. **Wine** (*vinho*) is mostly mediocre and sweet, though some of the wines produced in areas of Italian settlement in the South are pretty good, while sparkling wines can be excellent. The most reliable, widely available Brazilian label is Miolo, a smallish producer whose wines are found in good supermarkets throughout Brazil. Keep an eye out for the wines of the Casa Valduga and Don Laurindo, as well as the truly outstanding Villa Francioni label, a fragrant white produced near São Joaquim in the highlands of Santa Catarina. Commercial wine production has recently started in Bahia's São Francisco valley, with some surprisingly good results: the Miolo Shiraz can be found in many supermarkets. Despite the undoubted improvement in the quality of Brazilian wines in recent years, however, imported wines from Chile and Argentina (or Europe) remain more reliable and can be cheaper than the best that Brazil produces.

As for **spirits**, you can buy **Scotch** (*uisque*), either *nacional*, made up from imported whisky essence and not worth drinking, or *internacional*, imported and extremely expensive. Far better to stick to what Brazilians drink, *cachaça* (also called *pinga* or in Rio, *paraty*), sugar-cane rum. The best *cachaça* is produced in stills on country farms; it is called *cachaça da terra* and, when produced with care, has a smoothness and taste the larger commercially produced brands lack; look out for *cachaça* from Minas Gerais particularly. Alternatively, there are scores of brands of rum: some of the commonest ones are Velho Barreiro, Pitu and 51, but they are best drunk mixed in a *caipirinha* (see below) than neat.

Brazilians drink *cachaça* either neat or mixed with fruit juice. Taken neat it's very fiery, but in a cocktail it can be delicious. By far the best way to drink it is in a **caipirinha**, along with football and music one of Brazil's great gifts to world civilization – rum mixed with fresh lime, sugar and crushed ice: it may not sound like much, but it is the best cocktail you're ever likely to drink. Be sure to stir it regularly while drinking, and treat it with healthy respect – it is much more powerful than it tastes. Variants are the *caipirosca* or *caipiríssima*, the same made with vodka. Waiters will often assume foreigners want vodka, so make sure you say *caipirinha de cachaça*. You can also get *batidas*, *cachaça* mixed with fruit juice and ice, which flow like water during Carnaval: they also pack quite a punch, despite tasting like a soft drink.

There are no **licensing laws** in Brazil, so you can get a drink at any time of day or night – though driving after consuming even a small amount of alcohol is strictly forbidden.

# The media

**As in the US, Brazil has a regional press rather than a national one. Even the top Rio and São Paulo papers are a little parochial; elsewhere, newspapers are at best mediocre but are always valuable for listings of local events. Brazil also boasts a lurid but entertaining yellow press, specializing in gruesome murders, political scandals and football.**

## Newspapers and magazines

The top **newspapers** are the slightly left-of-centre *Folha de São Paulo* and the Rio-based, right-of-centre *O Globo*, usually available, a day late, in large cities throughout the country. Both are independent and have extensive international news, cultural coverage and entertainment listings, but are respectable rather than exciting. Even stodgier but reasonable is the right-wing *Estado de São Paulo*, while the *Gazeta Mercantil* and *Valor Econômico* are high-quality equivalents of the *Financial Times* or *Wall Street Journal*. The most enjoyable of the yellow press is Rio's *Última Hora*, especially good for beginners in Portuguese, with a limited vocabulary and lots of pictures, but all major cities have similar local tabloids.

There are also two good weekly current-affairs **magazines**: *Veja* and *Isto É*. They are expensive, around US$5, since their readership is exclusively middle class. You will find Brazilian editions of most major fashion and women's magazines. The weekly *Placar* is essential for anyone wanting to get to serious grips with Brazilian football. *Vogue Brasil*, edited in São Paulo and published by Condé Nast, is a quality magazine offering great insight into the style of the Brazilian elite, while *Plástica* is a glossy monthly magazine that sheds light on Brazil's apparent obsession with plastic surgery.

Apart from in airports, Rio and São Paulo, where you can find the *International Herald Tribune* and the *Economist*, **English-language newspapers** and magazines are very difficult to find in Brazil. The exceptions are *Time* and *Newsweek*, which are widely available in newspaper kiosks in big cities, albeit often weeks old.

## Radio

**Radio** is always worth listening to if only for the music. FM stations abound everywhere, and you should always be able to find a station that plays local music. Shortwave reception for the BBC World Service is good in Brazil.

### Television

Brazilian **TV** is ghastly, the worst you are ever likely to see, and therefore compulsive viewing even if you don't understand a word of Portuguese. There are several national channels, of which the most dominant is TV Globo, the centrepiece of the Globo empire, Latin America's largest media conglomerate. The empire was built up by Brazil's answer to Rupert Murdoch, Roberto Marinho, who died in 2003. One of the most powerful men in Brazil, Marinho was very cosy with the military regime and prone to use his papers and TV channels as platforms for his ultra-conservative views. The other major national channels are Manchete, TV Bandeirantes, SBT and Record.

The channels are dominated by **telenovelas**, glossy soap operas that have massive audiences in the evenings. **Football coverage** is also worth paying attention to, a gabbling, incomprehensible stream of commentary, punctuated by remarkably elongated shouts of "Gooooool" whenever anyone scores – which is often, Brazilian defenses being what they are. However, there are a few genuine highlights, notably **Jô Soares**, the funniest and cleverest of Brazilian comedians, who hosts a very civilized late-night chat show on Globo every weekday.

### Internet

Brazilian has the highest number of computers with internet access in South America and all things online are highly developed, with internet cafés on every corner, and much of what used to be tediously queued up for – banking, cinema-going, buying plane tickets – now done online as a matter of course.

# Festivals

**Carnaval is the most important festival in Brazil, but there are other parties, too, from saints' days to celebrations based around elections or the World Cup.**

### Carnaval

When **Carnaval** comes, the country gets down to some of the most serious partying in the world. A Caribbean carnival might prepare you a little, but what happens in Brazil is more spectacular, goes on longer and is on a far larger scale. Every place in Brazil, large or small, has some form of Carnaval, and in three places especially – Rio, Salvador and Olinda, just outside Recife – Carnaval has become a mass event, involving seemingly the entire populations of the cities and drawing visitors from all over the world.

When exactly Carnaval begins depends on the ecclesiastical calendar: it starts at midnight of the Friday before Ash Wednesday and ends on the Wednesday night, though effectively people start partying on Friday afternoon – over four days of continuous, determined celebration. It usually happens in the middle of February, although very occasionally it can be early March. But in effect, the entire period from Christmas is a kind of run-up to Carnaval. People start working on costumes, songs are composed and rehearsals staged in school playgrounds and backyards, so that Carnaval comes as a culmination rather than a sudden burst of excitement and colour.

#### Carnaval dates

**2010** Feb 13–16
**2011** March 5–8
**2012** Feb 18–21
**2013** Feb 9–12
**2014** March 1–4

### A Carnaval warning

Wherever you go at Carnaval, take care of your possessions: it is high season for **pickpockets and thieves**. Warnings about specific places are given in the text, but the basic advice is if you don't need it, don't take it with you.

During the couple of weekends immediately before Carnaval proper, there are carnival balls (*bailes carnavalescos*), which get pretty wild. Don't expect to find many things open or to get much done in the week before Carnaval, or the week after it, when the country takes a few days off to shake off its enormous collective hangover. During Carnaval itself, stores open briefly on Monday and Tuesday mornings, but banks and offices stay closed. Domestic airlines, local and inter-city buses run a Sunday service during the period.

The most familiar and most spectacular Carnaval is in **Rio**, dominated by samba and the parade of samba schools down the enormous concrete expanse of the gloriously named Sambódromo. One of the world's great sights, and televised live to the whole country, Rio's Carnaval has its critics. It is certainly less participatory than Olinda or Salvador, with people crammed into grandstands watching, rather than down following the schools.

**Salvador** is, in many ways, the antithesis of Rio, with several focuses around the old city centre: the parade is only one of a number of things going on, and people follow parading schools and the *trio elétrico*, groups playing on top of trucks wired for sound. Samba is only one of several types of music being played; indeed, if it's music you're interested in, Salvador is the best place to hear and see it.

**Olinda**, in a magical colonial setting just outside Recife, has a character all its own, less frantic than Rio and Salvador; musically, it's dominated by *frevo*, the fast, whirling beat of Pernambuco, and is in some ways the most distinctive visually, with its *bonecos*, large papier-mâché figures that are the centrepiece of the Olinda street parades.

Some places you would expect to be large enough to have an impressive Carnaval are in fact notoriously bad at it: cities in this category are São Paulo, Brasília and Belo Horizonte. On the other hand, there are also places that have much better Carnavals than you would imagine: the one in **Belém** is very distinctive, with the Amazonian food and rhythms of the *carimbó*, and **Fortaleza** also has a good reputation. The South, usually written off by most people as far as Carnaval is concerned, has major events in Florianópolis, primarily aimed at attracting Argentine and São Paulo tourists, and the smaller but more distinctive Carnaval in Laguna. For full details of the events, music and happenings at each of the main Carnavals, see under the relevant sections of the Guide.

## Other festivals

The third week in June has **festas juninas**, geared mainly towards children, who dress up in straw hats and checked shirts and release paper balloons with candles attached (to provide the hot air), causing anything from a fright to a major conflagration when they land.

Elections and the World Cup are usually excuses for impromptu celebrations, while official celebrations, with military parades and patriotic speeches, take place on September 7 (Independence Day) and November 15, the anniversary of the declaration of the Republic.

In towns and rural areas, you may well stumble across a **dia de festa**, the day of the local patron saint, a very simple event in which the image of the saint is paraded through the town, with a band and firecrackers, a thanksgiving Mass is celebrated, and then everyone turns to the secular pleasures of the fair, the market and the bottle. In **Belém**, this tradition reaches its zenith in the annual Cirio on the second Sunday of October (see p.381), when crowds of over a million follow the procession of the image of Nossa Senhora de Nazaré, but most *festas* are small-scale, small-town events.

In recent years, many towns have created new festivals, usually glorified **industrial fairs** or **agricultural shows**. Often these events are named after the local area's most important product, such as the Festa Nacional do Frango e do Peru (chickens and turkeys) in Chapecó (see p.678). Occasionally, these local government creations can be worth attending as some promote local popular culture as well as industry. One of the best is Pomerode's annual **Festa Pomerana** (see p.668), which takes place in the first half of January and has done much to encourage the promotion of local German traditions.

# Football

**Going to a football match in Brazil is something even those bored by the game will enjoy as spectacle: the stadiums are sights in themselves and big matches are watched behind a screen of tickertape and waving flags, huge banners, massed drums, fireworks and firecrackers, to the chants, roars and whistling of the world's most passionate football supporters.**

Brazil's major teams are concentrated in Rio and São Paulo. In Rio, Flamengo is the best-supported team in the country, and its distinctive shirt of red and black hoops is seen everywhere. Its clashes with perennial Rio rival Fluminense (maroon, green and white stripes) is one of the most intense matches in Brazilian club football, rivalled only by the games between São Paulo's two leading teams, São Paulo (white with red and black hoops) and Coríntians (white). In Rio, Botafogo (black and white stripes with the famous white-star badge) and Vasco (white with black diagonal stripe) vie with Fla-Flu for dominance, while Palmeiras (green) and Santos (white) make up the big four in São Paulo. The only teams that consistently live with the best of Rio and São Paulo are Internacional (red) and Grêmio (blue, white and black stripes) from Porto Alegre, and Atlético Mineiro (white) and Cruzeiro (dark blue) from Belo Horizonte.

Brazilian stadiums tend to be enormous, concrete, and with a few exceptions rather dingy and lacking in character: they are rarely full save for *clássicos*, matches between major teams, and rely on the supporters rather than their architecture for colour and feeling. Most pitches are separated from supporters by a wide running track and sometimes even a moat, which puts the play further from the terraces than British fans will be used to. But some stadiums are worth going out of your way for: the Maracanã in Rio, it goes without saying, but also the beautiful Art Deco Pacaembú in São Paulo. No football fan should visit Rio without leaving a morning for the excellent tour of the Maracanã (see p.96), or miss the superb new Museu de Futbol when in São Paulo (see p.569).

Tickets are very cheap by European standards; good seats at a *clássico* will cost no more than R$50, but an ordinary match will be half that or less – the issue is availability rather than price. For *clássicos*, hotels often have packages that include transport, tickets and a guide for around R$100 all in, an expensive way of doing it but often the only practical option if you can't get a ticket a few days in advance. For ordinary matches, you can almost always turn up half an hour beforehand and look for the *bilheteria*, the ticket office, which usually only takes cash. All stadiums are two-deckers, most are now all-seaters but a few still have terracing on the lower deck: upper-deck seats are *arquibancada*, lower-deck *geral*. There is not as much of a problem with crowd violence in Brazil as in many European countries, but don't wear a Brazilian club shirt just to be on the safe side: non-Brazilian shirts are no problem (except for Argentinian ones – the two countries don't get on well in footballing terms), and Brazilian fans are extremely friendly to foreigners. December is the off season; otherwise, a mixture of state and national championships ensures constant football.

For more detail on football history and culture in Brazil, see p.766.

# Travelling with children

**Travelling with children is relatively easy in Brazil. They are made to feel welcome in hotels and restaurants in a way that's not always so in Europe or North America. In fact, it is also more secure: even thieves and assaltantes seem to respect families with children and leave them alone.**

**Travelling around** Brazil takes time, so try not to be too ambitious in terms of how much you aim to cover. Because of frequent scheduled stops and unscheduled delays it can take all day to fly from one part of the country to another. Long bus journeys are scheduled overnight and can be exhausting. Children pay full **fare** on buses if they take up a seat, ten percent on planes if under 2 years old, half-fare between 2 and 12, and full fare thereafter. Newer **airports** have a **nursery** (*berçário*) where you can change or nurse your baby and where an attendant will run your baby a bath, great on a hot day or if your plane's delayed. If you plan on **renting a car**, bring your own child or **baby seat** as rental companies never supply them and they are very expensive in Brazil. Cars are fitted with three-point shoulder seatbelts in the front, but many only have lap seatbelts in the back.

In **hotels**, kids are generally free up to the age of 5, and rooms often include both a double and a single bed; a baby's cot may be available, but don't count on it. It's rare that a room will sleep more than three, but larger hotels sometimes have rooms with an interlinking door. Hotels will sometimes offer discounts, especially if children share rooms and even beds with siblings or parents; the lower- to mid-range hotels are probably the most flexible in this regard. If you're planning on staying more than a few days in a city, you may find it cheaper and more convenient to stay in an **apartment-hotel**, which will sleep several people and comes with basic cooking facilities. Baths are rare in Brazil, so get your kids used to **showers** before leaving home. Occasionally, a hotel will provide a plastic baby bath, but bring along a travel plug, as shower pans are often just about deep enough to create a bath.

Many of the mid- and upper-range hotels have TV lounges, TVs in rooms, swimming pools, gardens and even games rooms, which are often useful in **entertaining** kids. Most large towns also have cinemas, the best often being the new multiplexes found in shopping centres.

**Food** shouldn't be a problem as, even if your kids aren't adventurous eaters, familiar dishes are always available and there's also the ubiquitous *comida por kilo* option. Portions tend to be huge, often sufficient for two large appetites, and it's perfectly acceptable to request additional plates and cutlery. Most hotels and restaurants provide high chairs (*cadeira alta*) as well. Commercial **baby food** is sold in Brazilian supermarkets. Remember to avoid tap water and use only mineral water when preparing formula and washing out bottles. Mid-range hotels and upwards have a **minibar** (*frigobar*) in the rooms where you can store bottles and baby food, but where there isn't one you will be able to store things in the hotel's refrigerator. A small cooler box or insulated bag is a good idea and, while ice compartments of *frigobars* are useless, you can always place your freezer blocks in the hotel's freezer (*congelador*).

In general, Brazilian infants don't use disposable **nappies/diapers** (*fraldas*), due to the cost, around R$12 for twenty – very expensive for most Brazilians. As brands such as Pampers are sold in pharmacies and supermarkets, it's worth only bringing a minimum with you until you can make it to a shop.

**Health** shouldn't be a problem, but before planning your itinerary check which areas entail taking **anti-malarial tablets** (the state of Rondônia other than Porto Velho, rural Acre and Amapá and southern Pará is rife with malaria and should be avoided), and make enquiries as to whether the **vaccines** recommended or required in some parts of Brazil (in particular the Amazon) are likely to have any unpleasant side effects for babies or young children. For most of Brazil, the only likely problem will be the strength of the tropical sun and the viciousness of the mosquitoes: bring plenty of **sunscreen** (at least factor 20 for babies and factor 15 for young children) and an easy-to-apply **non-toxic insect repellent**.

# Travel essentials

## Electricity

Electricity supplies vary – sometimes 110V and sometimes 220V – so check before plugging anything in. Plugs have two round pins, as in continental Europe.

## Gay and lesbian travel

Gay life in Brazil thrives, especially in the large cities, Rio in particular being one of the great gay cities of the world. In general, the scene benefits from Brazil's hedonistically relaxed attitudes towards sexuality in general, and the divide between gay and straight nightlife is often very blurred.

Attitudes vary from region to region. The two most popular gay destinations are Rio and Salvador. Rural areas and small towns, especially in Minas Gerais, the Northeast and the South, are conservative; the medium-sized and larger cities less so. A useful **resource** to consult before your trip is ⓦwww.guiagaybrasil.com.br; although the text is in Portuguese, there are enough English indicators to allow non-Portuguese speakers to navigate easily through it and benefit from the listings and tips.

## Insurance

Prior to travelling, you should take out an insurance policy to cover against theft, loss and illness or injury. Before paying for a new policy, however, it's worth checking whether you already have some degree of coverage – credit-card companies, home-insurance policies and private medical plans sometimes cover you and your belongings when you're abroad. Most travel agents, tour operators, banks and insurance brokers will be able to help you. Remember that when securing baggage insurance, make sure that the per-article limit – typically under £500 equivalent – will cover your most valuable possession.

## Laundry

Even the humblest hotel has a *lavadeira*, who will wash and iron your clothes. Agree on a price beforehand, but don't be too hard – livelihoods are at stake. Larger hotels have set prices for laundry services – usually, surprisingly expensive. Very common in larger cities are *lavandarías*, which operate a very useful *por peso* system – the clothes are weighed at the entrance, you pay per kilo, and pick them up washed and folded the next day for a couple of dollars per kilo. Ironing (*passar*) costs a little more.

## Mail

A **post office** is called a *correio*, identifiable by their bright yellow postboxes and signs. An imposing *Correios e Telégrafos* building will always be found in the centre of a city of any size, but there are also small offices and kiosks scattered around that only deal with mail. Queues are often a problem, but you can save time by using one of their franking machines for stamps; the lines move much more quickly. **Stamps** (*selos*) are most commonly available in two varieties, either for mailing within Brazil or abroad. A foreign postage stamp costs around R$1.70 for either a postcard or a letter up to 10g. It is expensive to send parcels abroad.

Mail within Brazil takes three or four days, longer in the North and Northeast, while **airmail** letters to Europe and North America usually take about a week. **Surface mail** takes about a month to North America, and two to Europe. Although the postal system is generally very reliable, it is not advisable to send valuables through the mail.

## Maps

We've provided **maps** of all the major towns and cities and various other regions. More detailed maps are surprisingly hard to get hold of outside Brazil and are rarely very good: there are plenty of maps of South America, but the only widely available one that is specifically of Brazil is the *Bartholomew Brazil & Bolivia* (1:5,000,000), which is not very easy to read. Much better are the six regional maps in the *Mapa Rodoviário Touring* series (1:2,500,000), which clearly mark all the major routes, although these, even in Brazil, are difficult to find.

A useful compendium of **city maps** and **main road networks** is published by Guias Quatro Rodas, a Brazilian motoring organization, which also has maps to Rio, São Paulo and other cities, states and regions. These are easy to find in bookstores, newsagents and magazine stalls. Very clear 1:960,000 maps of individual states are published by On Line Editora, and are usually available in Brazilian bookstores and newspaper kiosks; topographical and hiking maps are difficult to come by, though very occasionally they are available from municipal tourist offices or national parks in Brazil, or from local trekking equipment shops or tour operators.

## Opening hours and public holidays

Basic hours for most stores and businesses are from Monday to Friday 9am to 6pm and Saturday 9am to noon, with an extended lunch hour from around noon to 2pm. Shops in malls stay open until late Saturday night. Banks open at 10am, and stay open all day, but usually stop changing money at either 2pm or 3pm; except for those at major airports, they're closed at weekends and on public holidays. Museums and monuments more or less follow office hours but many are closed on Monday.

## Phones

Phones are operated by **phonecards** (*cartão telefônico*), which are on sale everywhere – from newspaper stands, street sellers' trays and most cafés. For local calls,

### Brazilian public holidays

There are plenty of local and state holidays, but on the following **national holidays** just about everything in the country will be closed:

**January 1** New Year's Day

**Carnaval** The four days leading up to Ash Wednesday

**Good Friday**

**April 21** Tiradentes Day (a martyr of the struggle for independence)

**May 1** Labour Day

**Corpus Christi**

**September 7** Independence Day

**October 12** Nossa Senhora Aparecida

**November 2** Dia dos Finados (Day of the Dead)

**November 15** Proclamation of the Republic

**December 25** Christmas Day

a 5-*real* card will last for several conversations; for long-distance or international calls, higher-value phonecards come in 10, 20, 50 or 100 *real* denominations. Calls to the US or Europe cost about US$1.50 per minute. Before dialling direct, lift the phone from the hook, insert the phonecard and listen for a dialling tone. Note that long-distance calls are cheaper after 8pm.

The **dialling tone** is a single continuous note, **engaged** is rapid pips, and the **ringing tone** is regular peals, as in the US. The phone system in Brazil is continually overloaded. If you get an engaged tone, keep trying – nine times out of ten, the phone is not actually engaged and you get through after seven or eight attempts. The smaller the place, the more often you need to try.

Long-distance and international calls can also be made from a *posto telefônico*, which all operate in the same way: you ask at the counter for a *chave*, are given a numbered key, go to the booth, insert the key and turn it to the right, and can then make up to three completed calls. You are billed when you return the key. To make a call between cities, you need to dial the trunk code, the *código* DDD (pronounced "daydayday"), listed at the front of phone directories. For international calls, ask for *chamada internacional*; a reverse-charge call is a *chamada a cobrar*. Reversing the charges costs about twice as much as paying locally, and it is much cheaper to use a telephone charge-card from home. Except in the most remote parts of Amazônia and the Northeast, everything from a small town upwards has a *posto*, though note that outside large cities they shut at 10pm.

### Long-distance telephone access codes

The privatization of Brazil's telephone system has led to a proliferation of new telephone companies and increased competition. Before making a national or international call you must now select the telephone company you wish to use by inserting a **two-digit code** between the zero and the area code or country code of the number you are calling. To call Rio, for example, from anywhere else in the country, you would dial zero + phone company code + city code followed by the seven-digit number. For local calls, you simply dial the seven- or eight-digit number.

As different phone companies predominate in different areas of the country, pay phones will display which company code should be used from that particular phone, or the hotel receptionist will let you know the correct code to be used if calling from your hotel. The commonest codes are 21, 23 and 14. If you want to reverse the charges, dial 90 and then the number with company code as above. To reverse the charges on an international call, dial 00080 followed by the country code. As ever, the simplest option to make international calls is a phonecard bought before you leave.

## Time

Most of Brazil is three hours behind GMT, but the states of Amazonas, Acre, Rondônia, Mato Grosso and Mato Grosso do Sul are four hours behind – that includes the cities of Manaus, Corumbá, Rio Branco, Porto Velho, Cuiabá and Campo Grande.

### Calling home from abroad

Note that the initial zero is omitted from the area code when dialling the UK, Ireland, Australia and New Zealand from abroad.

**US and Canada** international access code + 1 + area code.

**UK** international access code + 44 + city code.

**Republic of Ireland** international access code + 353 + city code.

**Australia** international access code + 61 + city code.

**New Zealand** international access code + 64 + city code.

**South Africa** international access code + 27 + city code.

## Tipping

Bills usually come with ten percent *taxa de serviço* included, in which case you don't have to tip – ten percent is about right if it is not included. Waiters and some hotel employees depend on tips. You don't have to tip taxi drivers (though they won't say no), but you are expected to tip barbers, hairdressers, shoeshine kids, self-appointed guides and porters. It's useful to keep change handy for them – and for beggars.

## Tourist information

You'll find tourist information fairly easy to come by once in Brazil, and there are some sources to be tapped before you leave home. Brazil's embassies or larger consulates (see p.33) have tourist sections, where you can pick up brochure information and advice.

Popular destinations such as Rio, Salvador, the Northeast beach resorts, and towns throughout the South have efficient and helpful **tourist offices**, but anywhere off the beaten track has nothing at all – only Manaus, Belém and Porto Velho have offices in the Amazon region, for example.

Most **state capitals** have tourist information offices, which are announced by signs saying "**Informações Turísticas**". Many of these provide free city maps and booklets, but they are usually all in Portuguese. As a rule, only the airport tourist offices have **hotel-booking services**, and none of them is very good on advising about budget accommodation. Tourist offices are run by the different state and municipal governments, so you have to learn a new acronym every time you cross a state line. In Rio, for example, you'll find TurisRio, which advises on the state, and Riotur, which provides information on the city. There's also **EMBRATUR**, the national tourist organization, but it doesn't have direct dealings with the general public apart from its excellent website, ⓦwww.embratur.gov.br.

### Tourist offices and government sites

**Australian Department of Foreign Affairs** ⓦwww.dfat.gov.au, ⓦwww.smartraveller.gov.au
**Brazilian Ministry of Tourism** ⓦwww.braziltour.com/site/en
**Brazilian Tourist Office** ⓦwww.braziltourism.org.uk
**British Foreign & Commonwealth Office** ⓦwww.fco.gov.uk
**Canadian Department of Foreign Affairs** ⓦwww.dfait-maeci.gc.ca
**EMBRATUR** ⓦwww.embratur.gov.br
**Irish Department of Foreign Affairs** ⓦwww.foreignaffairs.gov.ie
**New Zealand Ministry of Foreign Affairs** ⓦwww.mft.govt.nz
**South Africa Department of Environmental Affairs and Tourism** ⓦwww.environment.gov.za
**US State Department** ⓦwww.travel.state.gov

## Travellers with disabilities

Travelling in Brazil for people with disabilities is likely to be difficult if special facilities are required. For example, access even to recently constructed buildings may be impossible, as lifts are often too narrow to accept wheelchairs or there may be no lift at all. In general, though, you'll find that hotel and restaurant staff are helpful and will do their utmost to be of assistance to try to make up for the deficiencies in access and facilities.

**Buses** in cities are really only suitable for the agile; **taxis**, however, are plentiful, and most can accommodate wheelchairs. Long-distance buses are generally quite comfortable, with the special *leito* services offering fully reclining seats. Internal **airlines** are helpful, and wheelchairs are available at all the main airports.

# Guide

# Guide

# Rio de Janeiro

VENEZUELA
COLOMBIA
GUYANA
SURINAME
FRENCH GUIANA
PERU
BOLIVIA
PARAGUAY
CHILE
ARGENTINA
URUGUAY
N
1 2 3 4 5 6 7 8 9
0 1000 km

CHAPTER 1

# Highlights

* **The Corcovado** Its giant statue of Christ with outstretched arms is Rio's most famous image, and it has the best views across the city. See p.94
* **Igreja de Nossa Senhora da Glória do Outeiro** One of the smallest of Rio's colonial churches, but certainly the most beautiful. See p.101
* **Ipanema beach** The beach for people watching. See p.106
* **Instituto Moreira Salles** This splendid modernist house hosts noteworthy exhibits of nineteenth-century Brazilian art and photography. See p.108
* **Parque Nacional da Tijuca** With trails and a wealth of flora and fauna, this fine city park offers spectacular views of Rio. See p.111
* **Lapa nightlife** Samba, *forró* and other Brazilian rhythms pound out of the bars and nightclubs of this central Bohemian district. See p.120
* **Museu de Arte Contemporânea** One of Oscar Niemeyer's most stunning creations; on a fine day, its views across the bay to Rio are dazzling. See p.131
* **Paraty** Among the prettiest and best-preserved colonial towns in Brazil, Paraty is also a great base to explore the Costa Verde's islands and beaches. See p.143

▲ Christ the Redeemer, the Corcovado

# Rio de Janeiro



The citizens of the fourteen-million-strong city of **Rio de Janeiro** call it the Cidade Marvilhosa – and there can't be much argument about that. Although riven by inequality, Rio has great style. Its international renown is bolstered by a series of symbols that rank as some of the greatest landmarks in the world: the **Corcovado** mountain supporting the great statue of Christ the Redeemer; the rounded incline of the **Sugar Loaf** mountain, standing at the entrance to the bay; and the famous sweeps of **Copacabana** and **Ipanema** beaches, probably the most notable lengths of sand on the planet. It's a setting enhanced annually by the frenetic sensuality of **Carnaval**, an explosive celebration that – for many people – sums up Rio and its citizens, the **cariocas**. The major downside in a city given over to conspicuous consumption is the rapacious development that has engulfed Rio. As the rural poor, escaping drought and poverty in other regions of Brazil, swell Rio's population, the city has been squeezed like a toothpaste tube between mountains and sea, pushing its human contents ever further out along the coast. Over the decades, much of the city's rich architectural heritage has been whittled away, along with the destruction of much of its natural environment.

The **state of Rio de Janeiro**, surrounding the city, is a fairly recent phenomenon, established in 1975 as a result of the amalgamation of Guanabara state and Rio city, the former federal capital. Fairly small by Brazilian standards, the state is both beautiful and accessible, with easy trips either northeast along the **Costa do Sol** or southwest along the **Costa Verde**, taking in unspoilt beaches, washed by a relatively unpolluted ocean. **Inland** routes make a welcome change from the sands, especially the trip to **Petrópolis**, a nineteenth-century mountain retreat for Rio's rich.

The **best time to visit** both city and state, at least as far as the **climate** goes, is between May and August, when the region is cooled by trade winds, the temperature remains at around 22–32°C and the sky tends to be clear. Between December and March (the rainy season), it's more humid, with the temperature hovering around 40°C; but even then it's rarely as oppressive as it is in northern Brazil, and there's a chance of blue sky for at least part of the day.

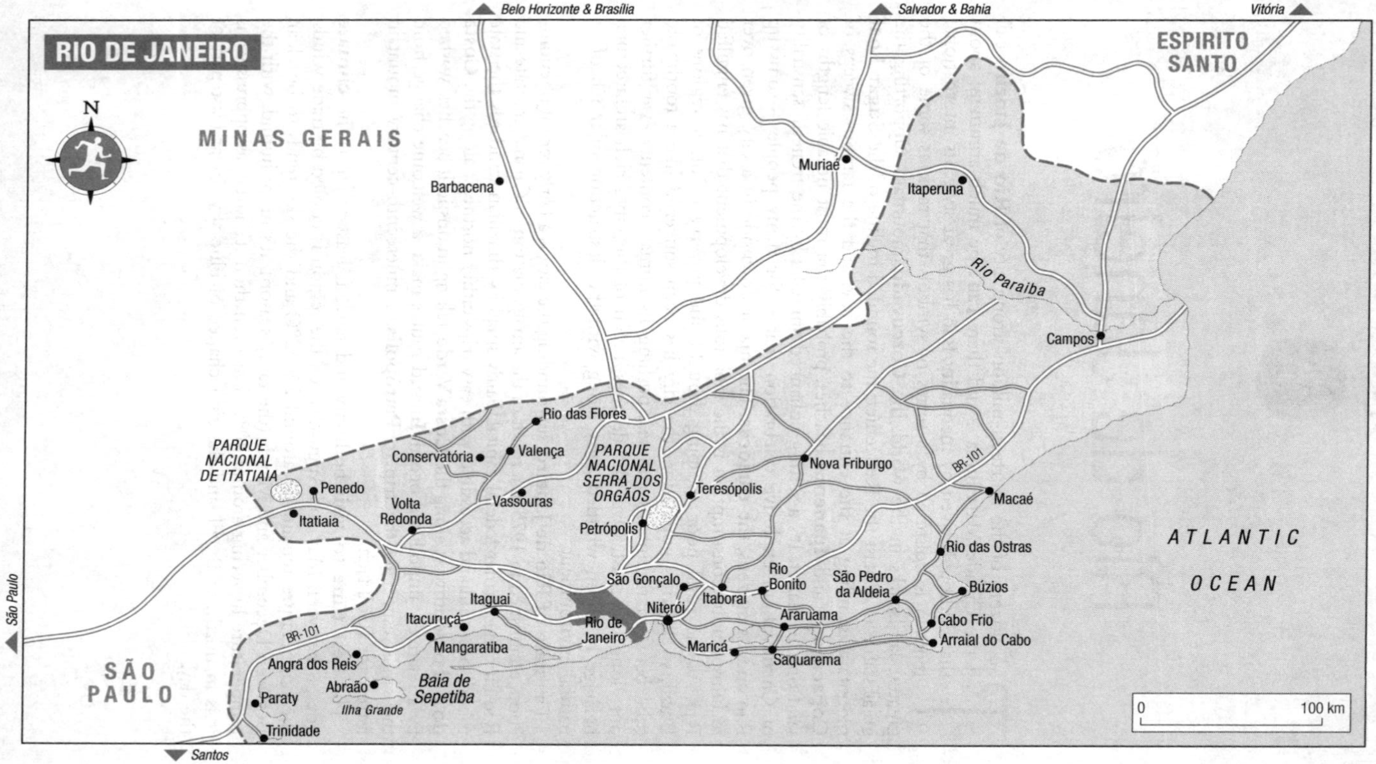

RIO DE JANEIRO
N
MINAS GERAIS
Belo Horizonte & Brasília
Salvador & Bahia
Vitória
ESPIRITO SANTO
Muriaé
Itaperuna
Barbacena
Rio Paraiba
Campos
Rio das Flores
Valença
Conservatória
PARQUE NACIONAL SERRA DOS ORGÃOS
Nova Friburgo
BR-101
PARQUE NACIONAL DE ITATIAIA
Penedo
Vassouras
Teresópolis
Macaé
Itatiaia
Volta Redonda
Petrópolis
ATLANTIC
Rio das Ostras
São Gonçalo
Rio Bonito
São Pedro da Aldeia
Búzios
OCEAN
Itaguai
Niterói
Itaboraí
Araruama
Cabo Frio
Itacuruçá
Rio de Janeiro
Arraial do Cabo
São Paulo
BR-101
Mangaratiba
Maricá
Saquarema
SÃO PAULO
Angra dos Reis
Abraão
Baia de Sepetiba
Paraty
Ilha Grande
Trinidade
Santos
0
100 km

# Rio de Janeiro city



Sitting on the southern shore of the magnificent Guanabara Bay, **RIO DE JANEIRO** has, without a shadow of a doubt, one of the most stunning settings in the world. Extending for 20km along an alluvial strip, between an azure sea and forest-clad mountains, the city's streets and buildings have been moulded around the foothills of the mountain range that provides its backdrop, while out in the bay there are many rocky islands fringed with white sand. The aerial views over Rio are breathtaking, and even the concrete skyscrapers that dominate the city's skyline add to the attraction. As the former capital of Brazil and now its second largest city, Rio has a remarkable architectural heritage, some of the country's best museums and galleries, superb restaurants and a vibrant nightlife – in addition to its legendary beaches. With so much to see and do, Rio can easily occupy a week and you may well find it difficult to drag yourself away.

## Some history

Over five hundred years, Rio has transformed from a fortified outpost on the rim of an unknown continent into one of the world's great cities. Its recorded past is tied exclusively to the legacy of the colonialism on which it was founded. No lasting vestige survives of the civilization of the **Tamoios** people, who inhabited the land before the Europeans arrived, and the city's history effectively begins on January 1, 1502, when a **Portuguese** captain, André Gonçalves, steered his craft into Guanabara Bay, thinking he was heading into the mouth of a great river (Rio de Janeiro means the "River of January"). In 1555, the French, keen to stake a claim on the New World, established a garrison near Sugar Loaf mountain. Not until 1567 were they expelled by the Portuguese, who soon after gave the settlement around the Morro do Castelo – in front of where Santos Dumont airport now stands – its official name, São Sebastião de Rio de Janeiro, after the infant king of Portugal.

With Bahia the centre of the new Portuguese colony, progress in Rio was slow, and only in the 1690s, when **gold** was discovered in neighbouring Minas Gerais, did the city's fortunes look up, as it became the control and taxation centre for the gold trade. During the seventeenth century, the **sugar cane** economy brought new wealth, but despite being a prosperous entrepôt, the city remained poorly developed. However, Rio's strategic importance grew as a result of the struggle with the Spanish over territories to the south, and in 1763 the city replaced Bahia (Salvador) as Brazil's capital.

By the eighteenth century, the majority of Rio's inhabitants were **African** slaves. Miscegenation became commonplace: even the Catholic Church tolerated procreation between the races, on the grounds that it supplied more souls to be saved. As a result, virtually nothing in Rio remained untouched by African customs, beliefs and behaviour – a state of affairs that clearly influences today's city, with its mixture of Afro-Brazilian music, spiritualist cults and cuisine.

In March 1808, having fled before the advance of Napoleon Bonaparte's forces during the Peninsular War, **Dom João VI** of Portugal arrived in Rio, bringing with him an astounding ten thousand nobles, ministers, priests and servants of the royal court. So enamoured of Brazil was he that after Napoleon's defeat in 1815 he declined to return to Portugal proclaiming Rio, instead of Lisbon, as the capital of the greatest **colonial empire** of the age. During Dom João's reign, the Enlightenment came to Rio, the city's streets were paved and lit, and it acquired

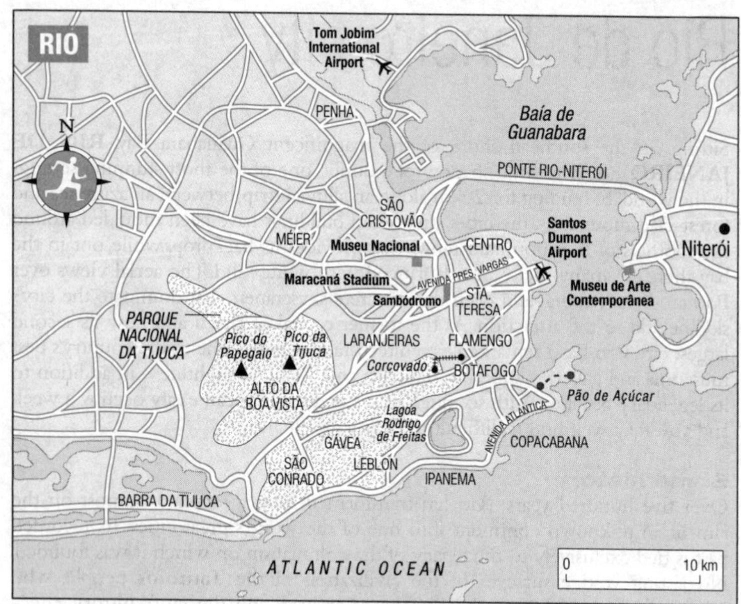


a new prosperity centred on **coffee production**. Royal patronage allowed the arts and sciences to flourish. Yet behind the imperial gloss, Rio was still mostly a slum of dark, airless habitations, intermittently scourged by outbreaks of yellow fever, its economy completely reliant upon human **slavery**.

However, by the late nineteenth century, Rio had started to develop as a modern city: trams and trains replaced sedans, the first sewerage system was inaugurated in 1864, a telegraph link was established between Rio and London, and a tunnel was excavated that opened the way to Copacabana, as people left the crowded centre and looked for new living space. Rio went through a period of **urban reconstruction**, all but destroying the last vestiges of its colonial design. The city was torn apart by a period of frenzied building between 1900 and 1910, its monumental splendour modelled on the *belle époque* of Paris with new public buildings, grand avenues, libraries and parks embellishing the city.

During the 1930s and 40s, Rio enjoyed international renown, buttressed by Hollywood images presented by the likes of **Carmen Miranda** and the patronage of the first-generation jet-set. As the nation's commercial centre, a new wave of modernization swept the city. Even the removal of the country's political administration to the new federal capital of Brasília in 1960 and the economic supremacy of São Paulo did nothing to discourage the developers. Today, with the centre rebuilt many times since colonial times, the interest of most visitors lies not in Rio's architectural heritage but firmly in the **beaches** to the south of the city centre, in an area called the Zona Sul. For more than seventy years, these strips of sand have been Rio's heart and soul, providing a constant source of recreation and income for *cariocas*. In stark contrast, Rio's **favelas** (see box, p.110), clinging precariously to the hillsides of the Zona Sul and across large expanses of the Zona Norte, show another side to the city, saying much about the divisions within it. Although not exclusive to the capital, these slums seem all the more harsh in Rio because of the abundance and beauty that lie right next to them.

# Orientation

Many people visiting Rio simply scramble their way to Copacabana or Ipanema and go no further, except on an occasional foray by guided tour. The beaches, though, are only one facet of Rio. The city is divided into three parts – centre (Centro), north (Norte) and south (Sul) – and the various *bairros* (neighbourhoods) have retained their individuality and characteristic atmosphere.

## Centro

**Centro** is the commercial and historic centre of Rio, and, though the elegance of its colonial and Neoclassical architecture has become overshadowed by the towering office buildings, it has by no means yet been swamped. The area is laid out in an effective grid, cut by two main arteries at right angles to each other: **Avenida Presidente Vargas** and **Avenida Rio Branco**. Presidente Vargas runs west from the waterfront and the Candelária church to Dom Pedro II **train station** and on to the **Sambódromo**, where the Carnaval procession takes place. Rio Branco crosses it in front of the Candelária church, running from **Praça Mauá** in the dockland area, south through **Praça Mahatma Gandhi** to **Avenida Beira Mar**. On the west side of Rio Branco, **Largo da Carioca** provides access to the hilly suburb of **Santa Teresa**, whose leafy streets wind their way upwards and westwards towards the Corcovado. Just south of Centro, at the foot of the slope on which Santa Teresa is built, lies **Lapa**, an inner-city residential and commercial district, its past grandeur reflected in the faded elegance of the **Passeio Público** park.

On the east side of Rio Branco, **Rua da Assembléia** runs into **Praça XV de Novembro** – the square near the water where you'll find the station for **ferries** and hydrofoils to **Niterói** (across the bay) and **Ilha de Paquetá** (to the north).

Both Rio Branco and Praça XV de Novembro are good places to catch a bus to the southern beaches of the Zona Sul – any bus with the name of a distant beach, such as Leblon, passes along the coastline, or parallel to it.

## Zona Norte

The northernmost part of Rio, the **Zona Norte**, contains the city's industrial areas – large expanses of *favelas* and other working-class residential *bairros* with little in the way of historic interest or natural beauty. However, the **Museu Nacional** in

### Staying safe

Although it sometimes seems that one half of Rio is constantly being robbed by the other, don't let paranoia ruin your stay. It's true that there is quite a lot of petty theft in Rio – pockets are picked and bags and cameras swiped – but use a little common sense and you're unlikely to encounter problems. Most of the real violence affecting Rio is drug related and concentrated in the *favelas*. In addition, there are certain areas that should be avoided.

In **Centro**, contrary to popular belief, Sunday is not the best time to stroll around – the streets are usually empty, which means you can be more easily identified, stalked and robbed. The area around **Praça Mauá**, just to the north of Centro, should be avoided after nightfall, and even during the day care should be taken. In the Zona Sul's **Parque do Flamengo** it's also inadvisable to wander unaccompanied after nightfall. Similarly, tourists who choose to walk between **Cosme Velho** and the **Corcovado** have been subject to robbery and assault – both of which can be best avoided by taking the train. **Copacabana**'s record has improved since the authorities started to floodlight the beach at night, but it's still not a good idea to remain on the sand after sunset.

the Quinta da Boa Vista park is a splendid collection well worth making time for. This apart, you're not likely to go much further north than Praça Mauá, exceptions being trips to and from the international airport, the inter-city bus terminal, the **Feira Nordestina** and the **Maracanã Stadium**, Brazil's footballing Mecca.



### Zona Sul

The **Zona Sul**, the name used to cover everything south of the city centre, though generally taken to mean just the *bairros* shouldering the coastline, has much more to attract you than the Zona Norte. Following Avenida Beira Mar south from Centro, the zone is heralded by the **Parque do Flamengo**, an extensive area of reclaimed land transformed into a public recreation area and beach. First up is the *bairro* of **Glória**, where the beautiful whitewashed church of Nossa Senhora da Glória do Outeiro, high on a wooded hill, makes an unmistakeable landmark. Beyond, Beira Mar becomes Avenida Praia do Flamengo, which leads into the *bairros* of **Catete** and **Flamengo** – together with Glória, areas with many cheap hotels. On the other side of Flamengo is the **Largo do Machado**, from where you can reach the *bairros* of **Laranjeiras** and **Cosme Velho**, to the west. The latter is the site of the **Corcovado** and the famous hilltop statue of Christ the Redeemer.

Further south, the bay of **Botafogo** is overshadowed by **Sugar Loaf** mountain, looming above the *bairro* of **Urca**. From Botafogo, the **Pasmado Tunnel** leads to **Leme**, a small *bairro* whose 3km of beach, bordered by **Avenida Atlântica**, sweep around to **Copacabana**. Much less classy than it once was, Copacabana has lost ground to its western neighbours, **Ipanema** and **Leblon**, which provide another 4km of sand and surf. These areas are the most chic of the residential *bairros*, with restaurants and shops sitting amidst the apartments of Rio's more prosperous citizens.

Ipanema and Leblon are situated on a thin strip of land, only a few hundred metres wide, between the Atlantic Ocean and **Lagoa Rodrigo de Freitas**, a lake tucked beneath the green hills of **Parque Nacional da Tijuca**. The **Jardim Botânico** and **Jockey Club** racecourse are on the north side of the lake, and the *bairro* of **Gávea** lies just to the west. Further south, through Gávea, the Auto Estrada Lagoa–Barra leads into **São Conrado** and its southern neighbour, **Barra da Tijuca**, the new ghetto of Rio's middle classes. São Conrado, in particular, shows up the great contradictions in Brazilian society: overlooking the exclusive Gávea Golf Club and the prosperous residences that surround it is the **Favela Roçinha**, a shantytown clinging to the mountainside and home to some 200,000 people.

## Arrival and information

You're most likely to fly into Rio or arrive by bus, as the city's train station is now only used for commuter services. Be warned that opportunistic thieves are active at all points of arrival, so don't leave baggage unattended or valuables exposed.

### By air

Rio is served by two airports. The Tom Jobim **international airport** (☎21/3398-4526) – usually referred to by its old name, **Galeão** – lies 20km north of the city. Apart from international flights, this airport also serves destinations throughout Brazil. In the arrivals hall, you'll find **tourist information** desks – Riotur and TurisRio – which supply basic information about the city and state. **Changing money** is not a problem as there are bank branches and ATMs in the arrivals hall and on the airport's third floor.

To reach a hotel in Centro, the cheapest option is to take an air-conditioned **executivo bus** (R$4) to Santos Dumont airport. For a Zona Sul hotel, there's an **executivo bus service** (R$6.50) along the coast to Flamengo, Copacabana, Ipanema and Leblon. Both services run roughly every 45 minutes between 5.20am and 11pm. Outside these hours, a **taxi** ride is the only alternative. Buy a ticket at the taxi desks, near the arrivals gate, and give it to the driver at the taxi rank; a ticket to Centro or Flamengo costs R$60 and to Botafogo, Copacabana or Ipanema R$80. Unless you're familiar with the city, it's best not to take the ordinary taxis – the driver may not know where your hotel is and you're likely to end up being overcharged. Above all, don't risk accepting a lift from one of the unofficial drivers hanging about in the airport. The ride takes about fifteen minutes into the centre or approximately half an hour to Zona Sul, unless you hit rush hour.

**Heading out** to the international airport, ask your hotel to arrange for a fixed-fare taxi to pick you up, or take the **executivo bus** – allow at least an hour from the beaches. Inside Galeão, departure desks are split into three sections: internal Brazilian flights from Sector A; sectors B and C for international flights. Duty-free shops only accept US currency or credit cards – not Brazilian *reís*.

**Santos Dumont** airport (Ⓣ21/3814-7070) at the north end of the Parque do Flamengo in the city centre mainly handles the shuttle services to and from São Paulo. Ordinary **taxis** (yellow with a blue stripe) are readily available from outside the terminal – the fare should cost around R$35 to Copacabana. A less stressful option is to purchase a voucher from one of the radio-taxi stands within the terminal. You'll be directed to your cab and will be charged a flat rate of R$45 to Copacabana or R$55 to Ipanema. Alternatively, cross the road and catch an ordinary bus from Avenida Marechal Câmara, which you can reach by taking the pedestrian walkway in front of the airport terminal: #438 to Ipanema and Leblon via Botafogo; #442 to Urca; #472 to Leme. For Copacabana, #484 goes from Avenida General Justo, over which the walkway also crosses.

## By bus

All major inter-city bus services arrive at the **Rodoviária Novo Rio** (Ⓣ21/3213-1800), 3km north of Centro in the São Cristovão *bairro*, close to the city's dockside at the corner of Avenida Rodrigues Alves and Avenida Francisco Bicalho. International buses from Santiago, Buenos Aires, Montevideo and Asunción, among others, use this terminus, too. The *rodoviária* has two sides, one for departures, the other for arrivals: once through the gate at arrivals, either purchase a voucher for a taxi (about R$15 to Centro, R$30 to Copacabana or R$35 to Ipanema), catch an *executivo* bus along the coast towards Copacabana, Ipanema and Leblon (R$4; every half-hour), or cross the road to the ordinary bus terminal in Praça Hermes. Alternatively, go to platform 60, where you can catch the Itegração Expressa bus (#406A; R$3.50) to Largo do Machado *metrô* station, from where you can transfer to a train towards Copacabana. The **tourist office** desk (daily 8am–8pm) is located at the bottom of the stairs, in front of the main exit – they'll give you a map and advise which buses to catch. There are spotlessly clean showers at the *rodoviária* (R$8, towel included).

**Leaving Rio** by bus, it's best to book two days in advance for popular in-state destinations such as Búzios or Paraty, whose buses fill up at weekends and travelling out of the state; the same goes for travelling anywhere immediately before or after Carnaval. Most **tickets** can be bought from travel agents all over the city, while inside the main *rodoviária* you'll find the ticket offices of the various bus companies. You can reach the *rodoviária* on bus #104 from Centro, #127 or #128 from Copacabana, and #456, #171 or #172 from Flamengo.

## Information

There are two official **tourist agencies** in the city, neither of them particularly useful. Information about the city of Rio is from **Riotur** (Ⓦwww.riotur.com.br), which distributes maps and brochures and has an English-speaking telephone information service, Alô Rio (Mon–Fri 9am–6pm; Ⓣ0800/285-0555). Riotur's main office is on the ninth floor of Rua da Assembléia 10 in Centro (Mon–Fri 9am–6pm; Ⓣ21/2217-7552), and it also has a branch in Copacabana at Av. Princesa Isabel 183 (Mon–Fri 9am–6pm; Ⓣ21/2541-7522). Most of Riotur's information can also be picked up at their booths at Rodoviária Novo Rio (daily 8am–8pm) and Galeão international airport (daily 6am–midnight). Basic information about other parts of the state of Rio is available from **TurisRio** (Ⓦwww.turisrio.rj.gov.br), located at Rua da Ajuda 5 in Centro (Mon–Fri 9am–6pm; Ⓣ0800/282-2007).

# Getting around

Rio's **public transport** system is fairly inexpensive and effective: most places can be easily reached by *metrô*, bus or taxi, or a combination of these. Bus services for getting about the state are also excellent, but you might want to rent a car – though driving in the city itself is not recommended unless you have nerves of steel.

### The metrô

The most comfortable way to travel is by using Rio's **metrô** system, in operation since 1979. It's limited to just two lines, which run from Monday to Saturday, 5am to midnight, and Sunday and public holidays 7am to 11pm: **Linha 1** runs from central Copacabana (Cantagalo station), north through Centro and then out to the Sãens Pena station in the *bairro* of Maracanã; **Linha 2** comes in from Maria de Graça, to the north of the city, via the Maracanã stadium, and meets Linha 1 at Central, by Dom Pedro II train station. The system is well designed and efficient, the stations bright, cool, clean and secure, and the trains gently air-conditioned, which is a relief if you've just descended from the scorching world above.

A single ticket (*unitário*) costs R$2.60. You can also buy a combined bus/*metrô* ticket (*integrado*) to Barra for R$3. Linha 1 is being extended to Ipanema but completion of the much-delayed project is still a few years off; in the meantime, buses connect Copacabana's Cantagalo station, with Praça General Osório in Ipanema.

### Organized tours

**Organized tours** highlighting different aspects of Rio are well worth considering. Carlos Roquette (Ⓣ21/3322-4872, Ⓦwww.culturalrio.com.br; R$100 per person) has been leading historical and cultural tours of the city for years, and while his mainstays are "Colonial Rio", "Imperial Rio", "Belle Époque Rio" and "Art Deco Rio", he also designs tours to meet the particular interests of individuals or groups – not the least of which are explorations of homosexual life, past and present, in the city's varied *bairros*. Also highly recommended are Marcel Armstrong's "Favela Tour" (see p.110), as well as "Rio Hiking" (see p.113), which concentrates on Rio's green spaces but also takes visitors to Lapas' bars.

## Some useful bus routes

**From Avenida Rio Branco**: #119, #121, #123, #127, #173 and #177 to Copacabana; #128 (via Copacabana), #132 (via Flamengo) and #172 (via "Jóquei Clube") to Leblon.

**From Praça XV do Novembro**: #119, #154, #413, #415 to Copacabana; #154 and #474 to Ipanema.

**From Avenida Beira Mar, in Lapa, near the Praça Deodoro**: #158 (via "Jóquei Clube"), #170, #172 (via Jardim Botânico), #174 (via Praia do Botafogo), #438, #464, #571 and #572 to Leblon; #472 to Leme; #104 to Jardim Botânico.

**From Copacabana**: #455 to Centro; #464 to Maracanã.

**From Urca**: #511 (via "Jóquei Clube") and #512 (via Copacabana) to Leblon.

**From the Menezes Cortes terminal, adjacent to Praça XV de Novembro**: air-conditioned buses along the coast to Barra de Guaratiba, south of Rio; on the return journey, these buses are marked "Castelo", the name of the area near Praça XV.

**From Rodoviária Novo Rio**: #104 to Centro, #127 or #128 to Copacabana, and #456, #171 or #172 to Flamengo.

**Parque do Flamengo**: any bus marked "via Aterro" passes along the length of the Parque do Flamengo without stopping.

Between Centro and the Zona Sul, most buses run along the coast as far as Botafogo; those for Copacabana continue around the bay, past the Rio Sul shopping centre, and through the Pasmado Tunnel; those for Leblon, via the "Jóquei Clube", turn right at Botafogo and travel along Avenida São Clemente.

### Buses

While some people avoid using the **city buses** because they're badly driven and prone to petty theft, it's worth mastering the system: with hundreds of routes and thousands of buses, you never have to wait more than a few moments for one, they run till midnight and it's not that easy to get lost.

**Numbers** and **destinations** are clearly marked on the front of buses, and there are also plaques at the front and by the entrance detailing the route. You get on at the front, pay the seated conductor (the price is on a card behind his head) and then push through the turnstile and find yourself a seat. Buses are jam-packed at **rush hour** (around 7–9am and 5–7pm), so if your journey is short, start working your way to the front of the bus as soon as you're through the turnstile; you alight at the back. If the bus reaches the stop before you reach the front, haul on the bell and the driver will wait. In the beach areas of the Zona Sul, especially along the coast, **bus stops** are not always marked. Stick your arm out to flag the bus down, or look for groups of people by the roadside facing the oncoming traffic, as this indicates a bus stop.

As a precaution against **being robbed** on the bus, don't leave wallets or money in easily accessible pockets and don't flash cameras around. Have your fare ready so that you can pass through the turnstile immediately – pickpockets operate at the rear of the bus, by the entrance, so that they can make a quick escape – and make sure that you carry any items in front of you as you pass through the turnstile. Special care should be taken on buses known to carry mostly tourists (such as those to Sugar Loaf mountain) and that are consequently considered easy targets by thieves.

### Taxis

Taxis in Rio come in two varieties: **yellow** ones with a blue stripe that cruise the streets, and the larger, newer, air-conditioned **radio cabs**, which are white with a red-and-yellow stripe and are ordered by phone. Both have meters, and unless you've pre-paid at the airport, you should insist that they are activated. The flag, or *bandeira*, over the meter denotes the tariff.

Generally speaking, Rio's taxi services are reasonably priced (Centro to Ipanema costs around R$25, Botafogo to Copacabana around R$20) and it is not in the cabbies' interest to alienate tourists by ripping them off; the only time to avoid ordinary (yellow and blue) taxis is when you're coming into town from an airport. However, late at night, drivers often quote a fixed price that can be up to three times the normal fare. Radio cabs are thirty percent more expensive than the regular taxis, but they are reliable: companies include Coopertramo (Ⓣ21/2560-2022) and Transcoopass (Ⓣ21/2560-6891).

### Ferries and hydrofoils

From Praça XV de Novembro, **ferries** transport passengers across Guanabara Bay to Niterói (Mon–Sat every 15min 6am–11pm, hourly thereafter; 20min; R$2.50) and Paquetá Island (9 daily 5.15am–11pm; 1hr 10min; R$9 return, R$17 on weekends), a popular day-trip destination to the north. The ferries are cheap and the view of Rio they afford, especially at sunset, is well worth the effort. There's also a **hydrofoil** service to Niterói (Mon–Sat every 20min 7am–8.30pm; 10min; R$5).

### Trams

Rio's last remaining **trams**, the *bondes* (pronounced "bonjis"), climb from near Largo da Carioca, across the eighteenth-century Aqueduto da Carioca, to the inner suburb of Santa Teresa and on to Dois Irmãos. Two lines run every fifteen

▲ Tram, Santa Teresa

minutes between 5am and midnight: the one for Dois Irmãos permits you to see more of Santa Teresa; the other line terminates at Largo do Guimarães. Both still serve their original purpose of transporting locals. The views of Rio from them are excellent, but beware of the young men who sometimes attempt to relieve you of your possessions. The best times to ride the tram are mid-morning and mid-afternoon when it's less crowded and, consequently, less chaotic. The tram station is downtown, behind the monumentally ugly Petrobrás building and adjacent to the Nova Catedral. Waiting passengers stand in eight lines, one for every row of seats on the tram; the fare is just 60¢, which you pay at the station turnstile going up to Santa Teresa and on board going down.

On Saturdays at 10am, a special tram service, the **Bonde Turístico Especial**, runs for tourists (R$5). This goes way beyond the normal Dois Irmãos terminal, leaving the built-up area of Santa Teresa and entering the edge of the Floresta da Tijuca, which is a good starting-point for a stroll.

### Driving in Rio

Rio's road system is characterized by a confusion of one-way streets, tunnels, access roads and flyovers, and **parking** is either difficult or impossible. **Lane markings**, apart from lending a little colouring to the asphalt, serve no apparent practical purpose, **overtaking** on the right appears to be mandatory and, between 10pm and 6am, to avoid an armed hold-up, you merely have to slow down as you approach a red **traffic light**. If you do rent a car, you're well advised to only use it to venture out of the city – to avoid the worst of Rio driving, consider collecting it on a Sunday morning when traffic is at its lightest. Car-rental agencies are listed on p.129.

## Accommodation

Although there's usually no shortage of **accommodation** in Rio, there are considerable seasonal variations in terms of demand and prices. **High season** is from December to February, when advanced reservations are recommended. If you arrive at this time without a booking, either make one through a tourist office or leave your luggage in the *guarda volumes* (baggage offices) at the *rodoviária* or Santos Dumont airport while you look; there's no point lugging heavy bags around Rio's hot thoroughfares. During **Carnaval**, prices soar, accommodation becomes hard to find and most hotels and hostels only accept bookings for a minimum of four nights' stay. During low season, most hotels decrease their prices by between thirty and fifty percent.

For much of the year, there's keen competition for guests and you should be able to find a decent double room, usually with air conditioning, for around R$150. The highest concentrations of budget places are in Glória, Catete and Flamengo, but reasonably priced accommodation can be found just about anywhere. With just a few exceptions, only luxury-class hotels have pools, which is especially frustrating during periods when the beaches are unsafe due to pollution or strong waves.

There are now numerous and very good **hostels** in Botafogo, Copacabana and Ipanema. These usually charge around R$45 per person, but during Carnaval their rates triple. In the Bohemian neighbourhood of Santa Teresa, there's an excellent bed-and-breakfast network (see p.78) – a contrast to Rio's generally uninteresting hotel options. For **apartments**, try Rio Apartments (Ⓣ21/2247-6221, Ⓦwww.rioapartments.com), which manages apartments in Copacabana and Ipanema; expect to pay from R$200 a day for a studio or one-bedroom unit.

The Mercure chain of apartment hotels (Ⓦwww.accorhoteis.com.br/mercure) has a good range of properties, all with pools, in Botafogo, Arpoador, Ipanema and Leblon; one-bedroom apartments start at around R$260 per day, depending on location. In Copacabana, Edifício Jucati at Rua Tenente Marones de Gusmão 85 (Ⓣ21/2547-5422, Ⓦwww.edificiojucati.com.br) offers studio apartments for R$120 per night for two people.



## Centro, Lapa and Santa Teresa

Most of the many cheap *pensões* and hotels in **Centro** and **Lapa** are inhabited by full-time residents, usually single men, who are working in Rio, but if you want to stay near Lapa's clubs and bars, there are a number of good hotel options. Behind Lapa is **Santa Teresa**, which, despite its leafy aspect and spirited nightlife, has only one hotel – although its numerous B&Bs (see box below) offer some of the most pleasant accommodation in Rio.

The places listed below are marked on the map on pp.84–85.

**Arcos Rio Palace** Av. Mem de Sá 117, Lapa Ⓣ21/2242-8116, Ⓦwww.arcosriopalacehotel.com.br. Rooms at this busy, comfortable, well-equipped hotel are both secure and inexpensive. Ideally situated for enjoying Lapa's nightlife. ❸

**Belas Artes** Av. Visconde do Rio Branco 52, Centro Ⓣ21/2252-6336, Ⓦwww.hotelbelasartes.com.br. This small and perfectly respectable city-centre hotel has simply furnished but impeccably clean rooms. ❸

**Casa Áurea** Rua Áurea 80, Santa Teresa Ⓣ21/2242-5830. In a charming house dating to 1871, this slightly overpriced *pousada* has twelve simple rooms, some with private bathrooms and a/c. Breakfast is served in the attractive courtyard garden, with the friendly, multilingual owner always on hand for local advice. ❺

**Formule 1** Rua Silva Jardim 32, Centro Ⓣ21/3511-8504, Ⓦwww.hotelformule1.com. By Praça Tiradentes, on the edge of Lapa. A large, efficient, completely impersonal, budget hotel that's ideal for those seeking inexpensive no-frills rooms (though all have a/c and a private bathroom). ❹

**Guanabara Palace** Av. Presidente Vargas 392, Centro Ⓣ21/2195-6000, Ⓦwww.windsorhoteis.com. Expense-account visitors stay at this lone luxury hotel in the city centre. Although utterly soulless, it's good value, with spacious guest rooms, a comfortable lounge, a business centre and the added bonus of a pool. ❻

**Ibis Rio Santos Dumont** Av. Marechal Câmara 280, Centro Ⓣ21/3506-4500, Ⓦwww.ibishotel.com. Located just 200m from Santos Dumont airport, and ideal for a late arrival or early departure. Like most Ibis hotels in Brazil, the 330 rooms here are compact yet very comfortable, and offer excellent value. ❺

**Santa Teresa** Rua Almirante Alexandrino 660, Santa Teresa Ⓣ21/2222-2755, Ⓦwww.santateresahotel.com. Long a down-at-heel hostel, this imposing 1860s building has been transformed into one of Rio's most beautiful hotels. The guest and communal rooms are decorated in

### Bed and breakfast in Santa Teresa

Given Rio's long association with glamour and international tourism, the city's hotels and hostels are in general remarkably disappointing. One refreshing development has been the emergence of a **B&B** network in Santa Teresa, offering considerable comfort and opportunities to meet local residents.

The members of *Cama e Café* group are a fascinating cross-section of the Santa Teresa community. **Hosts** tend to be either artists or professionals and include economists, sculptors, university professors and even circus-arts trainers. Almost all speak English and they're tremendous sources of local knowledge and advice. The hundred or so hosts and their properties have been carefully vetted and graded by *Cama e Café* staff according to style and levels of comfort. Double rooms range from R$95 to R$195 per night, and every effort is made to match guests to suitable hosts. For information, contact *Cama e Café*, Rua Progresso 67, Santa Teresa (Ⓣ21/2221-7635, Ⓦwww.camaecafe.com).

natural colours, using a mix of fibres and woods to convey a modern Brazilian look. Many of the rooms have spectacular views of downtown and the bay, as does the infinity pool. Aimed at both business and leisure visitors, rates remain the same throughout the year. ❽–❾



## Glória, Catete, Flamengo and Botafogo

**Glória** is not entirely without its share of prostitution, but the *bairro* is not a dangerous area and has a slightly faded grandeur that's worth getting to know. **Catete** and **Flamengo**, centred on the Largo do Machado and once the chic residential *bairros* of the middle classes, are well served by hotels – all a good bit cheaper than similar ones at Copacabana and, like Glória, conveniently located between the centre and the beach zone, with buses, taxis and the *metrô* providing easy access. For some reason, **Botafogo** offers few hotel possibilities, but there are a couple of options in this attractive neighbourhood.

Unless otherwise stated, the places listed below are marked on the map on p.102.

**Caesar Business Botafogo** Rua da Passagem 39, Botafogo ⓣ21/2131-1212, ⓦwww.caesarbusiness.com. See map, pp.98–99. Oriented to business travellers, this 110-room hotel offers large, comfortable rooms (ask for one with a view towards the Corcovado), an outdoor pool and a reasonable restaurant. ❽

**El Misti Hostel** Praia de Botafogo, Casa 9, Botafogo ⓣ21/2226-0991, ⓦwwwelmistihostel.com. See map, pp.98–99. A pretty nineteenth-century house offering rather cramped, shared dorms (R$30) and private rooms. A varied buffet breakfast is included, and excellent but inexpensive meals are offered on weekend evenings. *El Misti* is located on an alleyway with a couple of other hostels, including, at Casa 3, the *Alpha Hostel* (ⓣ21/2286-7799, ⓦwww.alphahosetel.com). ❸

**Flórida** Rua Ferreira Viana 81, Flamengo ⓣ21/2195-6800, ⓦwww.windsorhoteis.com. A highly recommended and long-established hotel that retains a traditional atmosphere and offers spacious rooms, the nicest of which overlook the gardens of neighbouring Palácio do Catete. Amenities include a rooftop pool, a good restaurant and a business centre with free internet. ❺

**Glória** Rua do Russel 632, Glória ⓣ21/2555-7272, ⓦwww.hotelgloriario.com.br. Built in the 1920s, this is one of Rio's most traditional hotels – strong on style and atmosphere and well located for both downtown and the Zona Sul. Most rooms are spacious and offer fantastic views, though some are in serious need of updating. There are two excellent pools, a spa and fitness centre. Rates vary enormously, with heavy discounts often available outside of high season if you book direct. ❼

**Golden Park Hotel** Rua do Russel 374, Glória ⓣ21/2556-8150, ⓦwww.hotelgoldenparkrio.com.br. This medium-sized hotel has modern facilities and a small rooftop pool. Rooms are fairly basic but comfortable – be sure to request one in the front, where you'll get more light and have a park view. ❺

**Imperial** Rua do Catete 186, Catete ⓣ21/2556-5212, ⓦwww.imperialhotel.com.br. Spacious, modern rooms are housed in a distinguished-looking 1880s building well located near the *metrô* and the park. Parking is available, and there's also a decent-sized pool, unusual for a hotel in this price category. ❹

**Inglês** Rua Silveira Martins 20, Catete ⓣ21/2558-3052, ⓦwww.hotelingles.com.br. This small, long-established and well-maintained hotel is one of the best places to stay in Catete. The spacious rooms, all with bathrooms, have a/c, TV and *frigobar*. ❹

**The Maze Inn** Rua Tavares Bastos 414, Casa 66, Catete ⓣ21/2558-5547, ⓦwww.jazzrio.info. The location could hardly be more unusual: in a *favela* overlooking Catete. Owned and run by a British former journalist, the guesthouse offers simple double rooms and one-bedroom apartments, a kitchen for the use of guests and a terrace with panoramic views of Guanabara Bay. With a police station next door and protective locals, there are no special safety issues – indeed, the regular jazz sessions here attract Zona Sul residents who normally wouldn't dream of entering a *favela*. ❹

**Monterrey** Rua Artur Bernardes 39, Catete ⓣ21/2265-9899. At this safe and quiet budget option, rooms have a/c (8pm–8am) and breakfast is brought to you in the morning. ❸

**Regina** Rua Ferreira Viana 29, Flamengo ⓣ21/3289-9999, ⓦwww.hotelregina.com.br. Rooms are on the small side but they are well looked after and feature all the basics: comfortable beds, minibars and a/c. With pleasant public areas, a friendly staff and an excellent location one block from the beach, this is a highly recommended spot. ❹

**Vila Carioca Hostel** Rua Estácio Coimbra 84, Botafogo ⓣ21/2535-3224, ⓦwww.vilacarioca.com.br. See map, pp.98–99. Not as raucous as some hostels but extremely friendly, with attractive lounge and terrace-garden for relaxing. Located on a quiet, safe street a block from the *metrô*. Dorms R$35. Rates include breakfast. ❸



## Copacabana and Leme

**Copacabana**'s street life and general raucousness help to make it the kind of place you either love or hate. And while the area has certainly seen better days, it still has by far the greatest concentration of places to stay in the city, ranging from hostels to luxury hotels. **Leme** – really a continuation of Copacabana – is less frenetic due to its location at the far end of the stretch of beach in the opposite direction of Ipanema.

The places listed below are marked on the map on p.106.

**Acapulco Copacabana** Rua Gustavo Sampaio 854, Leme ⓣ21/2275-0022, ⓦwww.acapulcohotel.com.br. This comfortable, highly recommended hotel is in a quiet location near the beach, a couple of minutes' walk from the Cardeal Arcoverde *metrô* station. Rooms are modern, reasonably spacious and well decorated; some of the balconies just about offer a beach view, and the staff are very helpful. ❻

**Apa Hotel** Rua República do Peru 305, Copacabana ⓣ21/2548-8112, ⓦwww.apahotel.com.br. A dreary looking but perfectly respectable hotel with simple, clean rooms (all with a/c and balconies) in a central area of Copacabana. The rooms that sleep four are excellent value. ❺

**Atlantis Copacabana** Rua Bulhões de Carvalho 61, Copacabana ⓣ21/2521-1142, ⓦwww.atlantishotel.com.br. In a quiet location just one block from Ipanema, this hotel offers compact but clean rooms and an extremely helpful staff. The small rooftop pool (not a typical feature of similar budget hotels in Rio) has great views. ❺

**Biarritz** Rua Aires Saldanha 54, Copacabana ⓣ21/2522-0542, ⓦwww.hotelbiarritz.hd1.com.br. One block back from Av. Atlântica and the beach, this basic but clean and friendly place is located in a quiet side-street. ❸

**Che Lagarto Hostel** Rua Santa Clara 304, ⓣ21/2257-3133, ⓦwww.chelagarto.com. Located in central Copacabana some five blocks from the beach, this relaxed but friendly hostel, one of *Che Largarto*'s three Rio hostels, has four- to eight-bed dorms (R$35) and en-suite doubles. A similar property is nearby at Rua Anita Garibaldi 87 (ⓣ21/2256-2776) and another is located in Ipanema (see opposite). ❹

**Copacabana Palace** Av. Atlântica 1702, Copacabana ⓣ21/2548-7070, ⓦwww.copacabanapalace.com.br. Anyone who's anyone has stayed in this gloriously maintained Art-Deco landmark, which, despite Copacabana's general decline, remains a great experience. Although every possible facility is on offer, there's a curious lack of communal areas, apart from the large pool in a central courtyard. All in all, this is a great place to relax if you can afford to do so. ❾

**Copa Linda** Av. N.S. de Copacabana 956, Copacabana ⓣ21/2267-3399. This hotel, above a row of shops, provides good, no-frills accommodation, although many rooms are small. ❸

**Debret** Av. Atlântica 3564, Copacabana ⓣ21/2522-0132, ⓦwww.debret.com. A firm favourite among European independent travellers, though the overpriced rooms are small and long overdue for refurbishing. Despite the address, few rooms have ocean views. ❻

**Excelsior Copacabana** Av. Atlântica 1800, Copacabana ⓣ21/3259-5323, ⓦwww.windsorhoteis.com. A reasonable upper-end choice in the middle of Copacabana's beachfront. Rooms are well equipped, and the rooftop pool has spectacular views. One of the oldest hotels on the *avenida* (opened in 1950), it tries to maintain the atmosphere of a bygone age. ❽

**Martinique Copa** Rua Sá Ferreira 30, Copacabana ⓣ21/2195-5200, ⓦwww.windsorhoteis.com. Popular hotel located near the quiet, western end of Copacabana, close to the Forte de Copacabana. Modern rooms have large, exceptionally comfortable beds, and there's a small rooftop pool. ❻

**Ouro Verde** Av. Atlântica 1456, Copacabana ⓣ21/2543-4123, ⓦwww.dayrell.com.br. Viewed from the outside, this 1950s hotel looks nothing special; inside, however, it's discreetly elegant, with spacious and well-kept rooms (go for the more expensive ones with sea views) and excellent service. Its regular guests consider it the only place to stay in Rio. ❻

**Portinari Design** Rua Francisco Sá 17, Copacabana ⓣ21/3222-8800, ⓦwww.hotelportinari.com.br. One of the few hotels in Rio that dares to be a bit different. Each floor has been conceived by a different Brazilian designer, with some much more successful than others. Decor differs in terms of colour, tone and texture, but all the rooms are well equipped, if on the small side. Located less than a block from the beach. 7

**Praia Leme** Av. Atlântica 866, Leme ⓣ21/2275-3322. This cosy two-storey hotel offers the best value for a beachfront location. Due to its popularity, advance reservations are highly recommended. 5

**Rio Othon Palace** Av. Atlântica 3264, Copacabana ⓣ21/2525-1500, ⓦwww.othon.com.br. With almost 600 guest rooms, this is a favourite of tour groups. The hotel has all the facilities you'd expect of a place this size and price, including several bars and restaurants, a rooftop pool and a business centre. Like much of the rest of the hotel, the spacious rooms are in need of renovation, but they're perfectly comfortable; those facing the front have marvellous ocean views. 9

**Santa Clara** Rua Décio Vilares 316, Copacabana ⓣ21/2256-2650, ⓦwww.hotelsantaclara.com.br. This small, simple but well-maintained hotel offers attentive service and good value. Located in a tranquil spot five blocks from the beach and close to the Túnel Velho leading to Botafogo's restaurants and museums. 5

**Toledo** Rua Domingos Ferreira 71, Copacabana ⓣ21/2257-1995, ⓦwww.hoteisgandara.com.br. Small but adequate rooms (including singles and some that sleep three people) halfway down Copacabana, just one block from the beach. 5

## Ipanema, Leblon and Gávea

**Ipanema**'s safe streets and fashionable beach, along with its good shopping and dining options, make the *bairro* an attractive place to stay, and despite being one of Rio's more upscale areas, it has a pretty good range of accommodation. Just beyond Ipanema lies **Leblon**, an exclusive residential neighbourhood with fewer options but some excellent eating and nightlife possibilities. Back from the beaches, **Gávea** is a quiet, exclusive *bairro*, the hillside properties offering amazing views.

The places listed below are marked on the map on pp.98–99.

**Arpoador Inn** Rua Francisco Otaviano 177, Arpoador ⓣ21/2523-0060, ⓦwww.arpoadorinn.com.br. In a peaceful location on the edge of Ipanema (bordering Copacabana) right on the beach, this popular hotel is reasonably priced for the area; because room rates don't change much during the year, however, in low season the basic accommodations may seem overpriced. Sea-view rooms cost double. 6

**Caesar Park** Av. Vieira Souto 460, Ipanema ⓣ21/2525-2525, ⓦwww.caesarpark-rio.com.br. One of Rio's finest hotels, the *Caesar Park* features every modern luxury that its celebrity guests would expect. Even the most basic of rooms are vast, with elegant furniture and huge beds. The rooftop restaurant and pool have superb views, and the hotel provides security and lifeguards on the beach fronting the property. 9

**Che Lagarto Hostel** Rua Paul Redfern 48, Ipanema ⓣ21/2512-8076, ⓦwww.chelagarto.com. The best of Rio's *Che Lagarto* hostels is in a good location just a couple of blocks from the beach and a short walk to the bars and nightlife of both Ipanema and Leblon. Excellent facilities include laundry, a kitchen and internet access, the staff are helpful, and there's a bar offering occasional live music. R$40 in a four-bed dorm. 5

**Fasano** Rua Viera Souto 80, Ipanema ⓣ21/3202-4000, ⓦwww.fasano.com.br. Ultra stylish – with prices to match – this Philippe Starck–designed hotel is *the* place to stay for visiting rock stars, supermodels and the like. Rooms are on the small side, but their breathtaking ocean views, modern tropical-hardwood furnishings and cutting-edge technology make them stand out. The rooftop coffee shop and infinity pool and the hotel's trendy bar are ideal celebrity-spotting hangouts. 9

**Hostel Harmonia** Rua Barão da Torre 177, Casa 18, Ipanema ⓣ21/2523-4904, ⓦwww.hostelharmonia.com. With a great location near excellent bars, restaurants and the beach, this is one of Rio's most popular hostels – despite the dorms (R$45; sleeping two to six people) being extremely cramped, the atmosphere impersonal and the facilities standard.

**Hostel Ipanema** Rua Barão da Torre 177, Casa 14, Ipanema ⓣ21/2247-7269, ⓦwww.hostelipanema.com. A welcoming and relaxed spot three blocks from the beach, in the same very safe courtyard in which the *Hostel Harmonia* is located. Internet access and laundry facilities are offered, and there are bikes for rent. The hostel's owner also runs Rio's most reliable hang-gliding operation (see box, p.108) and gives discounts to hostel guests. R$45 in three- to six-bed dorms. Airport pick-up can be arranged.

**Ipanema Inn** Rua Maria Quitéria 29, Ipanema ⓣ21/2523-6092, ⓦwww.ipanemainn.com.br. This excellent-value and very popular hotel is just a block from the beach and in one of the most fashionable parts of Ipanema. Comfortable rooms, while small, can squeeze in an extra (fold-out) bed. 6

**Ipanema Plaza** Rua Farme de Amoedo 34, Ipanema ⓣ21/3687-2000, ⓦwww.ipanemaplazahotel.com. The luxurious *Ipanema Plaza* (part of the Dutch-owned Golden Tulip chain) is small enough that it provides individual attention. Rooms and suites are all tastefully furnished with natural wood and beige tones, and there's a small rooftop pool with wonderful beach views. Popular with gay visitors due to its proximity to the beach's gay strip. 8

**La Maison** Rua Sérgio Porto 58, Gávea ⓣ21/3205-3585, ⓦwww.lamaisonrio.com. Chic, tranquil, five-room luxury *pousada*, perfect for those wanting to escape the frenzy of the city. From virtually every angle of the property there are breathtaking views towards either Lagoa, the beaches, the Tijuca forest or Corcovado. 8

**Lemon Spirit** Rua Cupertino Durão 56, Leblon ⓣ21/2294-1853, ⓦwww.lemonspirit.com. It's difficult to believe that there's a hostel in the heart of Leblon, just one block from the beach and in one of the oldest buildings in this exclusive *bairro*. All rooms are a/c, there's a guest kitchen and a nice patio. Dorms R$45. 4

**Marina Palace** Rua Delfim Moreira 630, Leblon ⓣ21/2172-1000, ⓦwww.hotelmarina.com.br. Beachside *Marina Palace* is the largest of Leblon's hotels and offers amenities you might expect, such as a business centre and both a restaurant and a (curiously little) pool with great views. The rooms are on the small side, but suites are also available. 7

**São Marco** Rua Visconde de Pirajá 524, Ipanema ⓣ21/2540-5032, ⓦwww.sanmarcohotel.net. A good deal for its location, on the main shopping street just a few minutes from the beach. The small rooms (and tiny bathrooms) were recently refurbished, but there's rather a lot of street noise. 5

**South American Copacabana** Rua Francisco Sá 90, Arpoador ⓣ21/2227-9161, ⓦwww.southamericanhotel.com.br. A few blocks' walk to Copacabana and Ipanema beaches, this excellent-value hotel offers bright, larger than average rooms, IKEA-style modern furnishings, a good buffet breakfast and a small rooftop pool. 6

**Yaya** Rua Farme de Amoedo 135, Ipanema ⓣ21/3813-3912, ⓦwww.yayario.com. A notch up from a youth hostel in terms of facilities, this friendly B&B offers eight single, double and triple rooms, all with a/c and private bathroom. The website makes the accommodation seem more stylish than the reality, but while simple, it's perfectly comfortable and can honestly boast a central Ipanema location. 4

# Centro

Much of historical Rio is concentrated in **Centro**, with pockets of interest, too, in the neighbouring **Saúde** and **Lapa** quarters of the city. You'll find you can tour the centre fairly easily on foot, but bear in mind that lots of the old historical squares, streets and buildings disappeared in the twentieth century under a torrent of redevelopment, and fighting your way through the traffic – the reason many of the streets were widened in the first place – can be quite a daunting prospect.

However, while much of what remains is decidedly low-key, there are enough churches and interesting museums to keep anybody happy for a day or two. The cultural influences that have shaped the city – the austere Catholicism of the city's European founders, the squalor of colonialism and the grandiose design of the Enlightenment – are all reflected in the surviving churches, streets and squares.

## Praça XV de Novembro and around

Once the hub of Rio's social and political life, **Praça XV de Novembro** takes its name from the day (Nov 15) in 1899 when Marechal Deodoro da Fonsceca, the first president, proclaimed the Republic of Brazil. One of Rio's oldest **markets** is held here on Thursdays and Fridays (8am–6pm): the stalls are packed with typical foods, handicrafts and ceramics, and there are paintings and prints, as well as a brisk trade in stamps and coins.

## The Paço Imperial

The *praça* was originally called the Largo do Paço, a name that survives in the imposing **Paço Imperial** (Tues–Sun noon–6pm; ⓣ21/2533-4207). Built in 1743, though tinkered with over the years, until 1791 the building served as the palace of Portugal's colonial governors in Rio. It was here, in 1808, that the Portuguese monarch, Dom João VI, established his Brazilian court (later shifting to the Palácio da Quinta da Boa Vista, now the Museu Nacional), and the building continued to be used for royal receptions and special occasions: on May 13, 1888, Princess Isabel proclaimed the end of slavery in Brazil from here. Today, the Paço Imperial hosts installations and other modern-art exhibitions. On the ground floor, there's a café and a restaurant.

## Arco de Teles

On the northern side of the square, the **Arco de Teles** was named after the judge and landowner Francisco Teles de Meneza, who ordered its construction upon the site of the old *pelourinho* (pillory) around 1755. Though more of an arcade than an arch, the *arco* links the Travessa do Comércio to the Rua Ouvidor. More engaging than the building itself is its social history, and that of its immediate vicinity. Families belonging to Rio's wealthy classes lived in the luxurious apartments above street level, while the street below was traditionally a refuge for "beggars and rogues of the worst type; lepers, thieves, murderers, prostitutes and hoodlums" – according to Brasil Gerson in his 1954 book *História das ruas do Rio de Janeiro*. In the late eighteenth and early nineteenth centuries, one of the leprous local inhabitants, **Bárbara dos Prazeres**, achieved notoriety as a folk devil: it was a common belief that the blood of a dead dog or cat applied to the body provided a cure for leprosy, and Bárbara is supposed to have earned her reputation around the Arco de Teles by attempting to enhance the efficacy of this cure by stealing newborn babies and sucking their blood. Behind the Arco de Teles is the **Beco de Teles**, a narrow cobblestoned alley with some charming nineteenth-century buildings.

## Igreja de Nossa Senhora do Carmo da Antigá Sé

At the back of Praça XV de Novembro, on the corner where Rua Sete de Setembro meets Rua Primero de Março, you'll find the **Igreja de Nossa Senhora do Carmo da Antigá Sé** (Mon–Fri 9am–5pm), which served, until 1980, as Rio's cathedral. Construction started in 1749 and, to all intents and purposes, continued right into the twentieth century as structural collapse and financial difficulties necessitated several restorations and delays: the present tower, for example, was built as late as 1905 by the Italian architect Rebecchi. Inside, the high altar is detailed in silver and boasts a beautiful work by the painter Antônio Parreires, representing Nossa Senhora do Carmo seated amongst the clouds and surrounded by the sainted founders of the Carmelite Order. Below, in the **crypt**, are the supposed mortal remains of Pedro Alvares Cabral, Portuguese discoverer of Brazil. In actual fact, he was almost certainly laid to rest in Santarém in Portugal.

## Museu Naval e Oceanográfico and around

Close to Praça XV de Novembro, at Rua Dom Manuel 15, the **Museu Naval e Oceanográfico** (daily noon–4.30pm) is housed in what was originally the naval headquarters. The collection charts Brazil's naval history and includes pieces such as sixteenth-century nautical charts, scale replicas of European galleons, paintings depicting scenes from the Brazil–Paraguay War and exhibits of twentieth-century naval hardware. Above all, the collections provide an insight into the colonial nature of Brazilian history, demonstrating that Brazilian naval engagements were determined by the interests of the Portuguese Empire until the nineteenth century;

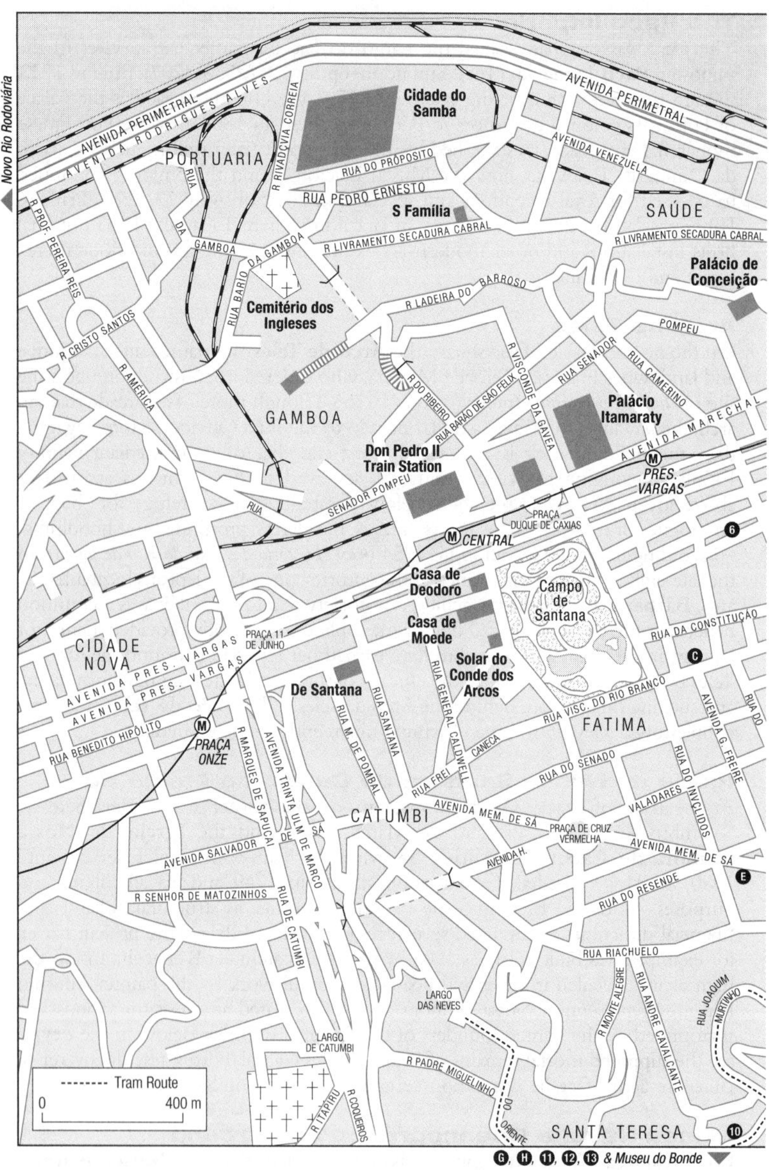


as a primarily slave-based plantation economy until 1888, Brazil's military hardware came from the foundries of industrialized Europe.

Even if you normally have no great interest in naval history, follow the bayside Avenida Alfredo Agache north a couple blocks to the **Espaço Cultural da Marinha** (Tues–Sun noon–5pm). This long dockside building was once used as the port's main customs wharf, but today houses a lengthy exhibition hall, the pride of place given to the painstakingly restored, gold-leaf-adorned **Galiota**

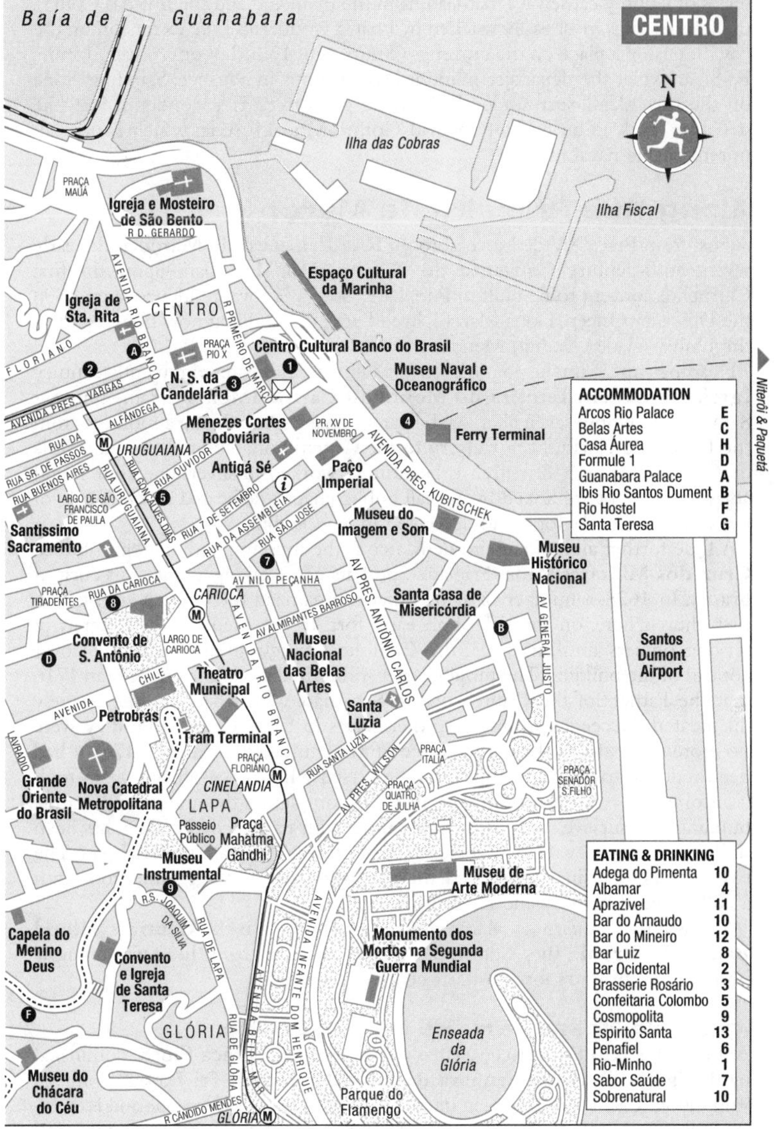


**Dom João VI**. Some 24m long and 3.6m wide, the oar-powered boat was built in Salvador in 1807, from where it was transported to Rio in 1817. Until 1920, it was used to ferry members of the royal family and visiting heads of state from their ships anchored off shore. From the docks here you can reach the small **Ilha Fiscal** (Thurs–Sun noon–5.30pm), where, in the 1880s, a customs collection centre was built. It was here also that the last grand Imperial ball was held, just days before the collapse of the monarchy in November 1889. Connected by a series of lengthy causeways that lead from the mainland and the Ilha das Cobras, the Ilha Fiscal is most easily reached by boat, a wonderful little excursion on the bay. To ensure a place on the crossings (Thurs–Sun 1pm, 2.30pm & 4pm; 15min; R$8), arrive at the departure point at least an hour in advance. Standing alone on the tiny island, surrounded by swaying palm trees, is a wonderful fort-like structure, built in an ornately hybrid Gothic-Moorish style, which is now an unremarkable naval museum.

## Along Rua Primeiro de Março

Across from Praça XV de Novembro on **Rua Primeiro de Março**, is the early seventeenth-century **Convento do Carmo** (Mon–Fri 10am–5pm), the first Carmelite convent to be built in Rio. Later used as a royal residence (after 1808 the Dowager Queen, Dona Maria I, lived here), the building now houses part of the Universidade Cândido Mendes.

Heading up Primeiro de Março you'll pass the late eighteenth-century **Igreja da Ordem Terceira do Monte do Carmo** (Mon–Fri 8am–4pm, Sat 8am–noon), whose seven altars each bear an image symbolizing a moment from the Passion of Christ, from Calvary to the Crucifixion, sculpted by Pedro Luiz da Cunha. The high altar itself is beautifully worked in silver. The church and adjacent convent are linked by a small public chapel, dedicated to Our Lady of the Cape of Good Hope, and decorated in *azulejo* tiling.

A little further along Primeiro de Março is the museum and church of **Santa Cruz dos Militares** (Mon–Fri 9am–3pm), its name giving a hint of its curious history. In 1628, a number of army officers organized the construction of the first church here, on the site of an early fort. It was used for the funerals of serving officers until, in 1703, the Catholic Church attempted to take over control of the building. The proposal met stiff resistance, and it was only in 1716 that the Fathers of the Church of São Sebastião, which had become severely dilapidated, succeeded in installing themselves in Santa Cruz. Sadly, they were no more successful in the maintenance of this church either, and by 1760 it had been reduced to a state of ruin – only reversed when army officers again took control of the reconstruction work in 1780, completing the granite and marble building that survives today. Inside, the nave, with its stuccoed ceiling, has been skilfully decorated with plaster relief images from Portugal's imperial past. The two owners long since reconciled, there's a **museum** on the ground floor with a collection of military and religious relics.

Across Rua Primeiro de Março from these churches is the **Centro Cultural Banco do Brasil** (Tues–Sun noon–10pm), a former bank headquarters now housing one of Rio's foremost arts centres (see p.123).

### Igreja de Nossa Senhora da Candelária

At the end of Rua Primeiro de Março you emerge onto **Praça Pio X**, dominated by the **Igreja de Nossa Senhora da Candelária** (Mon–Fri 7.30am–4pm, Sat 8am–noon & Sun 9am–1pm), an interesting combination of Baroque and Renaissance features resulting from the financial difficulties that delayed the completion of the building for more than a century after its foundation in 1775. Inside, the altars, walls and supporting columns are sculpted from variously coloured marble, while high above, the eight pictures in the dome represent the three theological virtues (Faith, Hope and Charity), the cardinal virtues (Prudence, Justice, Strength and Temperance) and the Virgin Mary – all of them late nineteenth-century work of the Brazilian artist João Zeferino da Costa. There's more grand decoration in the two pulpits, luxuriously worked in bronze and supported by large white angels sculpted in marble.

### Avenida Presidente Vargas

Until 1943, the Igreja da Candelária was hemmed in by other buildings, but it was appointed its own space when the **Avenida Presidente Vargas** was constructed, opening up new vistas. The avenue was inaugurated with a military parade in 1944, watched by Vargas himself in the year before he was deposed by a quiet coup. Today, it's Rio's widest avenue, running west for almost 3km and comprising fourteen lanes of traffic.

### Igreja e Mosteiro de São Bento

Heading north, on the continuation of Rua Primeiro de Março, the Ladeira de São Bento leads to the **Igreja e Mosteiro de São Bento** (daily 7–11am & 2–6pm; open also for Mass with Gregorian chant Sun 10am), in the *bairro* of **Saúde**, a seedy and run-down part of the city you'd do best to avoid, especially at night. The monastery was founded by Benedictine monks who arrived in Rio in 1586 by way of Bahia; building started in 1633, finishing nine years later. The facade displays a pleasing architectural simplicity, its twin towers culminating in pyramid-shaped spires, while the interior is richly adorned. Images of saints cover the altars, and there are statues representing various popes and bishops, work executed by the deft hand of Mestre Valentim. Panels and paintings from the late seventeenth century are particularly valuable examples of colonial art.

### Largo Santa Rita

Heading along Rua Dom Gerardo from the monastery leads you to the north end of Avenida Rio Branco, on the west side of which (off Visconde de Inhaúma) is **Largo Santa Rita** and its church, the **Igreja da Santa Rita** (Mon–Sun 8–11.30am & 2.30–5pm). Built on land previously used as a burial ground for slaves, the structure dates from 1721, its bell tower tucked to one side giving it a lopsided look. It's not one of Rio's more attractive churches, but the interior stonework is a fine example of Rococo style; additionally, it's magnificently decorated with a series of panels, three on the high altar and eight on the ceiling, painted by Ananias Correia do Amaral and depicting scenes from the life of Santa Rita.

## Rua Uruguaiana and around

In the streets between **Rua Uruguaiana** and Rua Primeiro de Março lies the most interesting concentration of stores in Rio, in the area known as **Saara**. Traditionally the cheapest place to shop, it was originally peopled by Jewish and Arab merchants, who moved into the area after a ban prohibiting their residence within the city limits was lifted in the eighteenth century; in recent years, a new wave of Jewish and Arab business-owners – along with, most recently, Chinese and Koreans – has moved here. The maze of narrow streets is lined with stalls selling trinkets and stores offering everything from basic beachware and handicraft items to expensive jewellery; additionally, the throngs of street traders and folk musicians make it a lively place to visit. Particularly good buys here include sports equipment, musical instruments, CDs and tapes.

Halfway down Rua Uruguaiana is **Largo de São Francisco de Paula**, whose church, the **Igreja de São Francisco de Paula** (Mon–Fri 9am–1pm), has hosted some significant moments in Brazil's history: behind the monumental carved wooden entrance door the Te Deum was sung in 1816 to celebrate Brazil's promotion from colony to kingdom; in 1831, the Mass celebrating the "swearing-in" of the Brazilian Constitution was performed here. The meticulous decoration of the chapel of Nossa Senhora da Vitória, on the right as you enter, is attributed to Mestre Valentim, who spent thirty years working here, while the paintings on the walls were created by a slave called Manoel da Cunha. With the consent of his owner, Manoel travelled to Europe as the assistant of the artist João de Souza, and on his return bought his own freedom with money earned from the sale of his artwork.

Across from the church, the **Real Gabinete Português de Leitura** (Mon–Fri 9am–6pm; ⓣ21/2221-3138, ⓦwww.realgabinete.com.br) is a library dedicated to Portugal and Portuguese literature. The building was completed in 1887 and is immediately identifiable by its magnificently ornate facade, styled after fifteenth-century Portuguese architecture. The reading room is lit by a red, white and blue stained-glass skylight and contains many of the library's 350,000 volumes. Amongst the rarest is the 1572 first edition of *Os Lusíados*, the Portuguese national epic poem by Luís de Camões, based on Vasco da Gama's voyage of exploration, which is occasionally on view.



### Largo da Carioca

From Largo de São Francisco de Paula, Rua Ramalho Ortigão leads the short distance to **Rua Carioca**. On the way, you can stop for a well-earned beer in Rio's oldest *cervejaria*, the *Bar Luiz* at no. 39. It's been here since 1887, changing its original name – the *Bar Adolfo* – following World War II, for obvious reasons. The place was once a favourite watering-hole for Rio's bohemian and intellectual groups and, though it's a little faded these days, it's still a bustling, enjoyable spot. The wonderful Art-Nouveau *Confeitaria Colombo* is just one block from here at Rua Gonçalves Dias 32 (see p.113).

**Largo da Carioca** itself has undergone considerable transformation since the turn of the nineteenth century, many of its buildings demolished to allow widening of the square and the improving of nearby roads. Today, street traders selling leather goods dominate the centre of the square, while a couple of things of interest remain, most notably the **Igreja e Convento de Santo Antônio** (Mon–Fri 8am–7pm, Sat 8–11am & 4–6pm, Sun 9–11am), standing above the *largo*, and known as St Anthony of the Rich (to differentiate it from St Anthony of the Poor, which is located elsewhere in the city). A tranquil, cloistered refuge, built between 1608 and 1620, this is the oldest church in Rio and was founded by Franciscan monks who arrived in Brazil in 1592. A popular saint in Brazil, St Anthony's help was sought during the French invasion of 1710: he was made a captain in the Brazilian army and in a startling lack of progress through the ranks it was 1814 before he was promoted to lieutenant-colonel, retiring from service in 1914! Also curious is the tomb of **Wild Jock of Skelater** that lies in the crypt. A Scottish mercenary who entered the service of the Portuguese Crown during the Napoleonic Wars, he was later appointed commander-in-chief of the Portuguese army in Brazil.

This aside, the interior of the church boasts a beautiful sacristy, constructed from Portuguese marble and decorated in *azulejos* depicting the miracles performed by St Anthony. There is rich wooden ornamentation throughout, carved from jacaranda, including the great chest in the sacristy. The image of Christ, adorned with a crown of thorns, came from Portugal in 1678 – a remarkable work of great skill.

## West from Praça Tiradentes

Leave Largo da Carioca by turning left along Rua Carioca, and you're soon in **Praça Tiradentes**, named after the leader of the so-called Minas Conspiracy of 1789, a plot hatched in the state of Minas Gerais to overthrow the Portuguese regime (see p.188). In the square stands the **Teatro João Caetano**, named after João Caetano dos Santos, who based his drama company in the theatre from 1840. He also notches up a bust that stands in the square, a reward for producing shows starring such theatrical luminaries as Sarah Bernhardt. In the second-storey hall of the theatre hang two large panels painted in 1930 by Emiliano di Cavalcanti (one of Brazil's great modernist artists), which, with strong tropical colours, explore the themes of Carnaval and popular religion.



### Campo de Santana and around

Three blocks west of Praça Tiradentes, along Rua Visconde do Rio Branco, the **Praça da República** lies in the **Campo de Santana**. Until the beginning of the seventeenth century this area was outside the city limits, which extended only as far as Rua Uruguaiana. Its sandy and swampy soils made it unsuitable for cultivation and the only building here was the chapel of St Domingo, sited in the area now covered by Avenida Presidente Vargas and used by the Fraternity of St Anne to celebrate the festivals of their patron saint – hence the name, Campo de Santana (Field of St Anne).

By the end of the eighteenth century, the city had spread to surround the Campo de Santana, and in 1811 an army barracks was built, the soldiers using the square as a parade ground. It was here that Dom Pedro I proclaimed Brazil's independence from the Portuguese Crown in 1822, and after 1889 the lower half of the square became known as Praça da República. The first president of the new republic, Deodoro da Fonsceca, lived at no. 197. At the start of the twentieth century, the square was landscaped, and today it's a pleasant place for a walk, with lots of trees and small lakes ruled by swans. The **Parque João Furtado** sits in the centre and is worth visiting in the evening, when small, furry shapes can be seen scuttling about in the gloom – agoutis, happily, not rats.

Directly across Avenida Presidente Vargas is the Praça Duque de Caxias and the **Panteão Nacional**, on top of which stands the equestrian statue of the Duque de Caxias, military patron and general in the Paraguayan War – his remains lie below in the Pantheon. Nearby, the **Dom Pedro II train station** – known more commonly as the Central do Brasil – is an unmistakeable landmark, its tower rising 110m into the sky and supporting clock-faces measuring 7.5m by 5.5m. Just beyond the station, at Av. Marechal Floriano 196, the **Palácio do Itamaraty** is one of Rio's best examples of Neoclassical architecture. Completed in 1853 as the pied-à-terre of the great landowner Baron of Itamaraty, it was bought by the government and became home to a number of the republic's presidents. The *palácio* now houses the **Museu Histórico e Diplomático do Itamaraty** (Mon, Wed & Fri guided visits 2pm, 3pm & 4pm), a repository of documents, books and maps relating to Brazil's diplomatic history, its collections primarily of interest to serious researchers (archives open for consultation only by appointment Mon–Fri 1–5pm; ⓣ21/2253-2828). Of perhaps wider interest is the section of the building that has been painstakingly restored with period furnishings to show how the upper classes lived in the nineteenth century.

North of Itamaraty is the extremely seedy port area Gamboa, one of the oldest parts of Rio and home to its first *favela*. Right alongside is the strangely beautiful **Cemitério dos Ingleses**, or English Cemetery (Rua da Gamboa 181; Mon–Fri 8am–4pm, Sat & Sun 8am–12.30pm); it's the oldest Protestant burial site in the country, dating from 1809, when the British community was given permission to establish a cemetery and Anglican church in Rio – essential if English merchants were to be attracted to the newly independent Brazil. Still in use today, the cemetery is set in a dramatic hillside location looking down to Guanabara Bay. The inscriptions on many of the stones make poignant reading, recalling the days when early death was almost expected.

There's long been talk about developing the dockside area in front of the cemetery, but until recently little has been done apart from turning some of the *armazéms* (warehouses) into temporary centres for performing-arts events. The one enduring project has been the **Cidade do Samba** (Tues–Sat 10am–5pm; R$10; ⓣ21/2213-2503, ⓦwww.cidadedosambarj.com.br), a vast complex where Rio's fourteen top samba schools practice and make their floats for Carnaval. For much of the year, there's little activity in the workshops, but at the very least you'll be able to inspect the previous year's floats. As Carnaval nears, activity increases and you'll be able to snatch a preview of the big event ahead. Every week, a spectacular show is held, featuring some of Rio's best samba groups and singers and a parade that is a small version of the annual Sambódromo extravaganza (Thurs 8pm; R$150 including buffet dinner). Getting to the Cidade do Samba involves either a rather grim five-minute walk along Avenida Rodrigues Alves from Praça Mauá or the Rodoviária Novo Rio or, safer, a short taxi ride: ask for the entrance across from Armazém 11.



## Nova Catedral Metropolitana and Cinelândia

South of Largo da Carioca, the unmistakeable shape of the **Nova Catedral Metropolitana** (daily 7.30am–6pm) rises up like some futuristic teepee. Built between 1964 and 1976, it's an impressive piece of engineering, whatever you think of the architecture: the Morro de Santo Antônio was levelled to make way for the cathedral's construction, and the thousands of tons of resulting soil were used for the land-reclamation project that gave rise to the Parque do Flamengo (see p.103). The cathedral is 83m high with a diameter of 104m and a capacity of 20,000 people. Inside, it feels vast, a remarkable sense of space enhanced by the absence of supporting columns. Filtering the sunlight, four huge stained-glass windows dominate, each measuring 20m by 60m and corresponding to a symbolic colour scheme – ecclesiastical green, saintly red, Catholic blue and apostolic yellow. From outside, you'll be able to see the mid-eighteenth-century **Aqueduto da Carioca** (often called the Arcos da Lapa), which since 1896 has carried trams up to Santa Teresa, the beautiful *bairro* on the hill opposite (see p.93); the tram terminal is between the cathedral and the Largo da Carioca, behind what is certainly the ugliest building in Rio, the glass, steel and concrete hulk that is the headquarters of Petrobrás, the state oil company.

▲ Nova Catedral Metropolitana

Along Avenida República de Chile, and right down **Avenida Rio Branco**, you'll come to Praça Floriano and the area known as **Cinelândia**, named after long-gone movie houses built in the 1930s. Old photos of Avenida Rio Branco, originally named Avenida Central, show its entire length bordered by Neoclassical-style buildings of no more than three storeys high, its pavements lined with trees, and with a promenade that ran right down the centre. Nowadays, however, the once-graceful avenue has been marred by ugly office buildings and traffic pollution.

### Praça Floriano

The **Praça Floriano** is the one section of Avenida Rio Branco that still impresses. Several sidewalk cafés on the western side of the square serve as popular central meeting-points in the evening, when the surrounding buildings are illuminated and at their most elegant. In the centre of the *praça* is a bust of **Getúlio Vargas**, still anonymously decorated with flowers on the anniversary of the ex-dictator's birthday, March 19. At the north end, the **Theatro Municipal** (Ⓦwww.theatromunicipal.rj.gov.br), opened in 1909 and a dramatic example of Neoclassical architecture, was modelled on the Paris Opéra – all granite, marble and bronze, with a foyer decorated in the white and gold characteristic of Louis XV style. Since opening, the theatre has been Brazil's most prestigious artistic venue, hosting visiting Brazilian and foreign orchestras, opera and theatre companies and singers. Tours are available; enquire at the box office at the back of the building. The theatre has a decent restaurant and bar, the *Café do Teatro* (Mon–Fri 11am–4pm), which is richly adorned with elaborate Assyrian-inspired mosaics.

On the opposite side of the road, the **Museu Nacional das Belas Artes** (Tues–Fri 10am–6pm, Sat, Sun & public holidays noon–5pm; R$4, Sun free; Ⓣ21/2240-0068, Ⓦwww.mnba.gov.br) is a grandiose Neoclassical pile built in 1908 as the Escola Nacional das Belas Artes, with the museum created in 1937. The modest European collection includes works by Boudin, Tournay and Franz Post amongst many others, but it's the **Brazilian collection** that's of most interest. Organized in chronological order, each room shows the various stages in the development of Brazilian painting as well as the influences imported from Europe: the years of diversification (1919–28); the movement into modernism (1921–49); and the consolidation of modern forms between 1928 and 1967, especially in the works of Cândido Portinari, Djanira and Francisco Rebolo.

The last building of note on the *praça* is the **Biblioteca Nacional** (Mon–Fri 9am–10pm, Sat 9am–5pm; Ⓣ21/2220-9433, Ⓦwww.bn.br), whose stairway was decoratively painted by some of the most important artists of the nineteenth century, including Modesto Brocas, Eliseu Visconti, Rodolfo Amoedo and Henrique Bernadelli. If you speak Portuguese and want to use the library, the staff are very obliging.

## Lapa

Continuing south from Cinelândia, Avenida Rio Branco passes Praça Mahatma Gandhi, which borders the **Passeio Público** park (daily 7.30am–9pm), well into the Lapa *bairro*. Beautifully maintained, the park is an oasis away from the hustle and bustle of the city. Opened in 1783, it was designed in part by Mestre Valentim da Fonseca e Silva, Brazil's most important late eighteenth-century sculptor, its trees providing shade for busts commemorating famous figures from the city's history, including Mestre Valentim himself.

The rest of **Lapa** has much the same faded charm as the park – attractive enough to merit exploring. Lapa is an old *bairro*; Brasil Gerson, writing in his *História das ruas do Rio de Janeiro*, noted that it was traditionally known as an "area of 'cabarets' and bawdy houses, the haunt of scoundrels, of gamblers, swashbucklers and inverteds and the 'trottoir' of poor, fallen women" – evidently a place to rush to, or avoid, depending upon your taste in entertainment. Until the mid-seventeenth century, Lapa was a beach, known as the "Spanish Sands", but development and land reclamation assisted its slide into shabby grandeur. More recently, things have been looking up with the area blossoming into one of Rio's liveliest spots for nightlife (see p.120).

From Lapa you can walk down to the Avenida Beira Mar, where the **Monumento dos Mortos na Segunda Guerra Mundial** (Monument to the Dead of World War II; Tues–Sun 10am–4pm) is a clearly visible landmark. Next to the monument, at the north end of the Parque do Flamengo (see p.103), is the glass-and-concrete **Museu de Arte Moderna** (Tues–Fri noon–5.30pm, Sat & Sun noon–6.30pm; R$5; Ⓣ21/2240-4944, Ⓦwww.mamrio.com.br), designed by the Brazilian architect and urbanist Affonso Reidy and inaugurated in 1958. The museum's collection was devastated by a fire in 1978 and only reopened in 1990 following the building's restoration. The permanent collection is still small and, despite boasting some of the great names of twentieth-century Brazilian art, extremely weak, though visiting exhibitions are occasionally worth checking out.

## Northeast to the Museu Histórico Nacional

Heading northeast from the Passeio Público, along Rua Santa Luzia, you pass the **Igreja de Santa Luzia** in the Praça da Academia, an attractive eighteenth-century church whose predecessor stood on the seashore – hard to believe today, as it's overwhelmed by surrounding office buildings. On December 13 each year, devotees enter the "room of miracles" at the back of the church and bathe their eyes in water from the white marble font – reputedly a miraculous cure for eye defects.

Rua Santa Luzia intersects with the busy Avenida Presidente Antônio Carlos, on which you'll find the imposing **Fazenda Federal**, the Federal Treasury building. Directly across the road from here, the **Santa Casa de Misericórdia**, a large colonial structure dating from 1582, was built by the Sisterhood of Misericordia, a nursing order dedicated to caring for the sick and providing asylum to orphans and invalids. It was here in 1849 that, for the first time in Rio, a case of yellow fever was diagnosed, and from 1856 to 1916 the building was used as Rio's Faculty of Medicine. The Santa Casa is not open to the public, but you can visit its **Museu da Farmácia** (Mon–Fri 8am–noon & 1–5pm) for its curious collection of pharmacological implements. Also attached to the Santa Casa is the **Igreja de Nossa Senhora de Bonsucesso** (Mon–Fri 9am–5pm), which contains finely detailed altars, a collection of Bohemian crystal and an eighteenth-century organ.

### Museu Histórico Nacional

The nearby **Museu Histórico Nacional** (Tues–Fri 10am–5.30pm, Sat, Sun & public holidays 2–6pm; R$6; Ⓣ21/2550-9255, Ⓦwww.museuhistoriconacional.com.br) is uncomfortably located in the shadow of the Presidente Kubitschek flyover that runs into Parque do Flamengo. Built in 1762 as an arsenal, it later served as a military prison where escaped slaves were detained. In 1922, the building was converted into an exhibition centre for the centenary celebrations of Brazil's independence from Portugal and has remained a museum ever since.

The large **collection** contains some pieces of great value – from furniture to nineteenth-century firearms and locomotives – and after decades of neglect, the museum has been successfully reorganized; indeed, the displays on the second floor, a documentation of Brazilian history since 1500, make it a must. Artefacts, charts and written explanations trace the country's development from the moment of discovery to the proclamation of the Republic in 1889 – a fascinating insight into the nature of imperial conquest and subsequent colonial culture. Clearly demonstrated, for example, is the structure of sixteenth-century Brazilian society, including the system of *sesmarias*, or royal land grants of enormous dimensions, which provided the basis for the highly unequal system of land tenure that endures today. Through the use of scale models and imaginatively arranged displays, the agrarian and cyclical nature of Brazil's economic history is explained, too, organized around a slave-labour plantation system that produced – at different times – sugar cane, cattle, cotton, rubber and coffee. The story continues into the eighteenth and nineteenth centuries, following the impact of England's Industrial Revolution, the spread of new ideas after the French Revolution and the transition from slavery to free labour and the importance of immigration. More recent twentieth-century developments are taken up by the Museu da República (see p.101).

# Santa Teresa and the Corcovado

Before you hit the beaches of the Zona Sul, two of the most pleasant city excursions are to *bairros* to the southwest of Centro. **Santa Teresa** offers an excellent respite from the steamy hubbub of the city's main thoroughfares, while visiting Rio without making the tourist pilgrimage up the **Corcovado** is nigh on unthinkable.

## Santa Teresa

**Santa Teresa**, a leafy *bairro* of labyrinthine, cobbled streets and steps (*ladeiras*), and with stupendous vistas of the city and bay below, makes a refreshing contrast to the city centre. Although it clings to the side of a hill, Santa Teresa is no *favela*: it's a slightly dishevelled residential area dominated by the nineteenth-century mansions and walled gardens of a prosperous community that still enjoys something of a bohemian reputation, with many artists choosing to live and work here.

There is not a great deal of traffic on the roads in Santa Teresa, which are dominated instead by ageing **trams** (*bondes*) hauling their human loads up and down the hill – a bone-rattling trip that's highly recommended. Trams run up here from Centro, from the terminal behind the massive Petrobrás building, and take you across the mid-eighteenth-century **Arcos da Lapa**, a monumental Roman-style aqueduct, high over Lapa, and past the Carmelite Convento e Igreja Santa Teresa, which marks the spot where a French force was defeated by the city's inhabitants in 1710. As you climb, Guanabara Bay drifts in and out of view between the trees that line the streets. On your right, you'll pass the **Bar do Arnaudo**, a traditional meeting-place of artists and intellectuals (see p.115); when the tram reaches the terminus at the top, you can stay on (and pay again) to descend to the bar for something to eat. Moments from here, at Largo dos Guimarães, is the **Museu do Bonde** (daily 9am–4.30pm), which is worth a visit even if you're not especially interested in transport. The small and attractively displayed collection includes an old tram, photo displays and memorabilia documenting the history of trams in Rio from their nineteenth-century introduction; it's curious to see how this means of public transport enabled the city to expand so rapidly along the coast. From the museum, it's an easy and enjoyable ten-minute walk downhill to the **Museu Chácara do Céu** (Rua Murtinho Nobre 93; daily except Tues noon–5pm; R$2, free Wed; ⓣ21/2507-1932, ⓦwww.museuscastromaya.com.br), located in a modernist stone building erected in 1957. The museum made headline news during the 2006 Carnaval when it was raided in broad daylight by armed thieves, who took four paintings by Matisse, Monet, Picasso and Dalí valued at US$50 million before melting into the crowd outside. Despite these important losses, it certainly remains one of Rio's better museums, holding a good, eclectic European collection as well as works by Cândido Portinari and Emiliano di Cavalcanti. In the upper hall, two screens depict the life of Krishna, and there are twin seventh-century iron-sculptured horses from the Imperial Palace in Beijing as well; on the second floor, look for artwork by Brazilian painters Heitor dos Prazeres and Djanira.

A pathway links the museum to the **Parque das Ruínas** (Wed–Fri & Sat 10am–10pm, Sun 10am–5pm), an attractive public garden containing the ruins of a mansion that was once home to Laurinda Santos Lobo, a Brazilian heiress around whom artists and intellectuals gathered in the first half of the twentieth century. After her death in 1946, the mansion was allowed to fall into disrepair, but in the 1990s it was partially renovated as a cultural centre and today houses art exhibitions. A pleasant café and a small stage where jazz concerts are held most Thursday evenings are on-site as well.

## The Corcovado

The most famous of all images of Rio is that of the vast statue of Christ the Redeemer (Cristo Redentor) gazing across the bay from the **Corcovado** (hunchback) hill, arms outstretched in welcome, or as if preparing for a dive into the waters below. The Art Deco **statue** (daily 9am–7pm), 30m high and weighing over 1000 metric tons, was scheduled to be completed in 1922 as part of Brazil's centenary independence celebrations, but this symbol of Rio wasn't, in fact, finished until 1931. The French sculptor Paul Landowski was responsible for the head and hands, while the engineers Heitor Silva Costa and Pedro Viana constructed the rest.

In clear weather, fear no anticlimax: climbing to the statue is a stunning experience by day, and nothing short of miraculous in the early evening. In daylight, the whole of Rio and Guanabara Bay is laid out before you; after sunset, the floodlit statue can be seen from everywhere in the Zona Sul, seemingly suspended in the darkness that surrounds it and often shrouded in eerie cloud. Up on the platform at the base of the statue, the effect of the clouds, and the thousands of tiny winged insects clustering round the spotlights, help give the impression that the statue is careering through space out into the blackness that lies beyond the arc of the lights – dramatic, and not a little hypnotic.

The **view** from the statue can be very helpful for **orientation** if you've just arrived in Rio. On a clear day, you can see as far as the outlying districts of the Zona Norte, while on the south side of the viewing platform you're directly over the Lagoa Rodrigo de Freitas, with Ipanema on the left and Leblon on the right. On the near side of the lake, Rua São Clemente is visible, curving its way through Botafogo, towards the Jardim Botânico and the racecourse, and on your left, the small *bairro* of Lagoa can be seen tucked in beneath the Morro dos Cabritos, on the other side of which is Copacabana.

Back down at the bottom of the statue, if you have the time and inclination, a five-minute walk uphill from the cog-train station on Rua Cosme Velho will take you to the **Museu Internacional de Arte Naïf** (Tues–Fri 10am–6pm, Sat & Sun, public holidays noon–6pm; R$5; ⓣ21/2205-8612, ⓦwww.museunaif.com.br), which boasts the world's largest naive-art collection; although most of the work displayed is by Brazilian artists, the museum features paintings from

## Getting to the Corcovado

All major hotels organize **excursions** to the Corcovado. Alternatively, the easiest way to get there by yourself is to take a **taxi** – about R$40 from the Zona Sul, a little more from Centro. **Buses** run to the *bairro* of Cosme Velho – take the #422 or #497 from Largo do Machado, the #583 from Leblon or the #584 from Copacabana – and stop at the **Estação Cosme Velho**, at Rua Cosme Velho 513. From here you take a cog-train (every 30min 8.30am–6.30pm; R$45 return, which also entitles you to half-price admission at the Museu Internacional de Arte Naïf; Ⓦwww.corcovado.com.br), a twenty-minute ride to the top, from where there's an escalator leading to the viewing platform. You can also **drive** up to a car park near the top if you wish, but if you want to **walk**, go in a group, as reports of assaults and robberies are frequent. However you choose to get there, keep an eye on the weather before setting out: what ought to be one of Rio's highlights can turn into a great disappointment if the Corcovado is shrouded in clouds.

across the globe. Across the road, a short distance further uphill, you'll reach the much-photographed **Largo do Boticário**, named after the nineteenth-century apothecary to the royal family (Joaquim Luiz da Silva Santo) who lived here. With its pebbled streets and fountain set in the small courtyard, this is a particularly picturesque little corner of Rio. However, as old as the *largo* might appear to be, the original mid-nineteenth-century houses were demolished in the 1920s and replaced by colourful Neocolonial-style homes, some with fronts decorated with *azulejos*.

# Zona Norte

The parts of the **Zona Norte** you'll have seen on the way in from the transport terminals aren't very enticing, and they're a fair reflection of the general tenor of northern Rio. Most of the area between the international airport and the city centre is given over to vast *favelas* and other low-income housing, but there are a few places nearer the centre that are worth making the effort to visit – especially the **Museu Nacional** in the Quinta da Boa Vista, west of the city centre, accessible by *metrô* (get off at Estação São Cristovão) or by buses #472, #474 or #475 from Copacabana or Flamengo or #262 from Praça Mauá.

## Quinta da Boa Vista

The area covered by the **Quinta da Boa Vista** (daily 9am–6pm) was once incorporated in a *sesmaria* held by the Society of Jesus in the sixteenth and seventeenth centuries. The Jesuits used the area as a sugar plantation, though it later became the *chácara* (country seat) of the royal family when the Portuguese merchant Elias Antônio Lopes presented the Palácio de São Cristovão (today the Museu Nacional) and surrounding lands to Dom João VI in 1808. The park, with its wide-open expanses of greenery, tree-lined avenues, lakes, sports areas and games tables, is an excellent place for a stroll, though the weekends can get very crowded. You may as well make a day of it and see all the sights while you're here.

### Museu Nacional

In the centre of the park, on a small hill, stands the imposing Neoclassical structure of the **Museu Nacional** (Tues–Sun 10am–4pm; R$6; Ⓣ21/2568-8262, Ⓦwww.museunacional.ufrj.br), the oldest scientific institution in Brazil and certainly one of the most important, containing extensive archeological, zoological and botanic collections, an excellent ethnological section and a good display of artefacts dating from classical antiquity – altogether, an estimated one million pieces are exhibited in 22 rooms.

The **archeological** section deals with the human history of Latin America, displaying Peruvian ceramics, the craftsmanship of the ancient Aztec, Mayan and Toltec civilizations of Mexico and mummies excavated in the Chiu-Chiu region of Chile. In the Brazilian room, exhibits of Tupi-Guaraní and Marajó ceramics lead on to the indigenous **ethnographical** section, uniting pieces collected from the numerous tribes that once populated Brazil. The genocidal policies of Brazil's European settlers, together with the ravages of disease, reduced the indigenous population from an estimated six million in 1500 to the present-day total of less than two hundred thousand. The **ethnological** section has a room dedicated to Brazilian folklore, centred on an exhibition of the ancient Afro- and Indo-Brazilian cults – such as *macumba*, *candomblé* and *umbanda* – that still play an important role in modern Brazilian society.

On a different tack, the mineral collection's star exhibit is the **Bendigo Meteorite**, which fell to earth in 1888 (for sign-seekers, the year slavery was abolished) in the state of Bahia. Its original weight of 5360kg makes it the heaviest metallic mass known to have fallen through the Earth's atmosphere. Beyond the rich native finds, you'll also come across Etruscan pottery, Greco-Roman ceramics, Egyptian sarcophagi and prehistoric remains – all in all, a good half-day's worth of exploring.

### Museu da Fauna, Jardim Zoólogico and the Feira Nordestina

The **Museu da Fauna** (Tues–Sun 9am–4.30pm), also in the Quinta da Boa Vista, has organized a collection of stuffed birds, mammals and reptiles from throughout Brazil that is worth a passing look on the way to the nearby **Jardim Zoólogico** (daily 9am–4.30pm; R$5). Founded in 1888, the zoo was a run-down and dirty place for decades; in recent years, however, it has been transformed – the animals look happier and the grounds are now kept scrupulously clean by zealous functionaries – but it's still basically an old-fashioned site where animals are kept in small cages. That said, the zoo serves an important scientific role in Brazil, managing some prominent breeding programmes for endangered native fauna.

The **Feira Nordestina**, held daily in the Campo de São Cristovão, close to the Quinta da Boa Vista (Mon–Thurs 10am–4pm, non-stop Fri 10am to Sun 10pm; Ⓦwww.feiradesaocristovao.com.br), is the best of Rio's regular **markets**. Its roots extend back to the late nineteenth century and the first large-scale migration of impoverished Northeasterners to Rio, but since 2003 it has been held in a vast, purpose-built stadium. A replica of the great Northeastern markets, it comprises **seven hundred stalls** (many of which are run by people in traditional costume) selling typical handicrafts, caged birds, food and drink, while music from the parched Northeastern backlands fills the air. Best buys are beautifully worked hammocks, leather bags and hats, *literatura de cordel* (illustrated folk-literature pamphlets), herbal medicines and spices. Weekends are the best days to go along with migrants enjoying their day off and listening to live music in the evenings. To get there, take any bus marked "São Cristovão" – #469 from Leblon, #461 from Ipanema, #462 or #463 from Copacabana.

## The Maracanã

To the west of Quinta da Boa Vista, a short walk across the rail line, over the Viaduto São Cristovão, stands the **Maracanã** or, more formally, the Estádio

## Getting to the Maracanã and seeing a game

The best way to reach the Maracanã is by **taxi**, but if you come by **metrô** (line 2) get off at the Maracanã station and walk southeast, along Avenida Osvaldo Aranha. By **bus**, catch the #464 from Leblon (Ataúlfo Paiva) via Ipanema (on Visconde de Pirajá), Copacabana (Av. N.S. de Copacabana) and Flamengo (Praia do Flamengo).

The stadium's **entrance** is on Rua Prof Eurico Rabelo, Gate 18. Arrive in plenty of time (at least a couple of hours before kick-off – 5pm – for big games) and buy your entrance card at any of the **ticket offices** set in the perimeter wall – a ticket for the *gerais* (lower terracing) costs about R$20, the *arquibancadas* (all-seated upper terracing) R$40–100; then go round to the entrance and pass your card through a machine at the turnstile. Things get frantic around the ticket offices before big games and if you're not there early enough you may get stranded outside, as the kiosk attendants leave their positions as soon as the starting whistle blows so as not to miss an early goal. After the game, it's a bit tedious getting back into town, as transport is packed. Be sure to watch your belongings in the thick crowds.



Jornalista Mário Filho. Built in 1950 for the World Cup, it's the biggest stadium of its kind in the world, holding nearly 200,000 people – in the final match of the tournament, 199,854 spectators turned up here to watch Brazil lose 1–0 to Uruguay. Well over 100,000 fans attend local derbies, such as the Flamengo v Fluminense fixture, and during November and December games are played here three times a week, as many of Rio's teams have followings that exceed the capacity of their own stadiums.

Attending a **game** is one of the most extraordinary experiences Rio has to offer, even if you don't like football, and it's worth going just for the theatrical spectacle. The stadium looks like a futuristic colosseum, its upper stand (the *arquibancadas*) rising almost vertically from the playing surface. Great silken banners wave across the stand, shrouded by the smoke from fireworks, while support for each team is proclaimed by the insistent rhythm of massed samba drums that drive the game along. *Carioca* supporters are animated to say the least, often near hysterical, but their love of the game is infectious.

The Maracanã is open for **guided tours**, too (daily 9am–5pm, match days 8–11am; R$30; ⓣ21/2299-2941). You'll be shown through the interesting **Museu dos Esportes**, with its extensive collection of Brazilian sporting memorabilia, and get to see the view from the presidential box (reached by lift), wander through the changing rooms and have a chance to tread on the hallowed turf itself.

# Zona Sul

From Rio's Bay of Guanabara to the Bay of Sepetiba, to the west, there are approximately 90km of sandy **beaches**, including one of the world's most famous – Copacabana. Rio's identity is closely linked to its beaches, which shape the social life of all the city's inhabitants, who use them for recreation and inspiration. For many, they provide a source of livelihood, and a sizeable service industry has developed around them, providing for the needs of those who regard the beach as a social environment.

Rio's sophisticated **beach culture** is entirely a product of the twentieth century. The 1930s saw the city's international reputation emerge, and "flying down to Rio" became an enduring cliché, celebrated in music, film and literature.

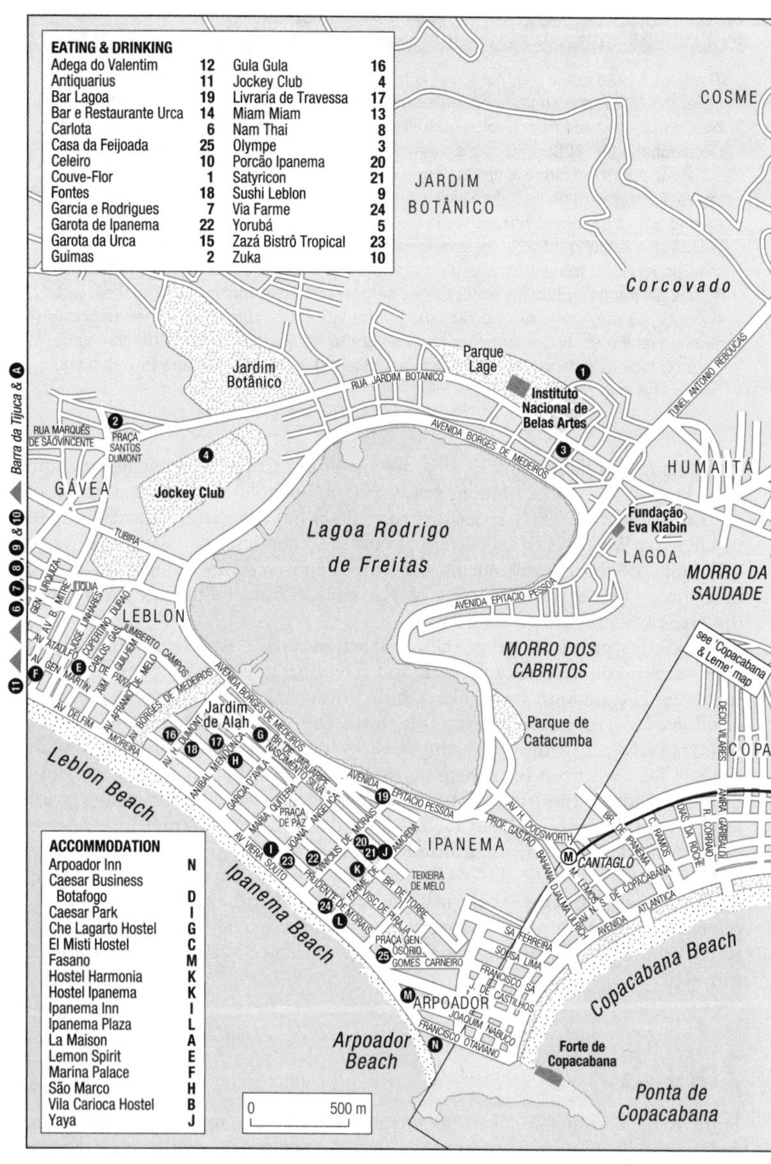


The most renowned of the beaches, **Copacabana**, was originally an isolated area, cut off from the city by mountains until 1892 when the Túnel Velho link with Botafogo was inaugurated. The open sea soon attracted beachgoers, though Copacabana remained sparsely populated until the splendid Neoclassically styled *Copacabana Palace Hotel* opened its doors in 1923, its famous guests publicizing the beach and alerting enterprising souls to the commercial potential of the area.

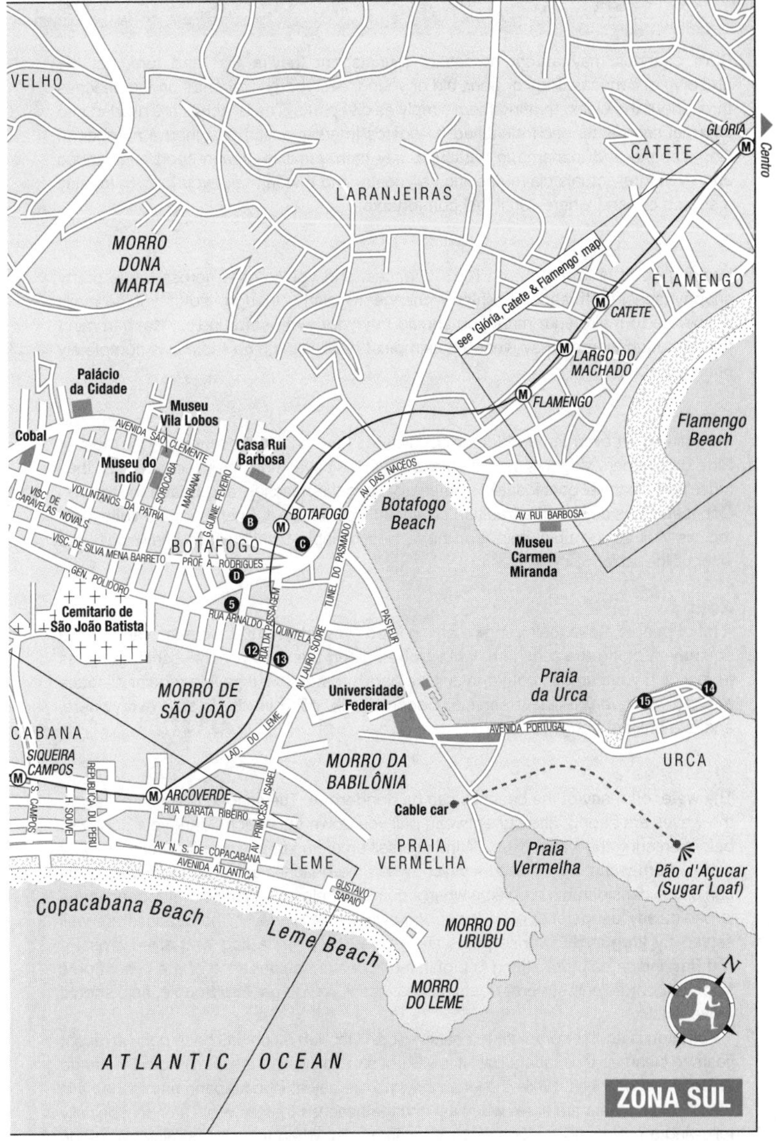


Rapid growth followed and a landfill project was undertaken, along which the two-lane **Avenida Atlântica** now runs.

Prior to Copacabana's rise, it was the beaches of **Guanabara Bay** – Flamengo, Botafogo and Urca – that were the most sought after. Today, the most fashionable beaches are those of **Ipanema** and **Leblon**, residential areas where the young, wealthy and beautiful top up their tans.

## On the beach

Rio's beaches may attract hordes of tourists but they're first and foremost the preserve of *cariocas*. Rich or poor, old or young, everybody descends on the beaches throughout the week, treating them simply as city parks. The beaches are divided into informal segments, each identified by *postos* (marker posts) assigned a number. In Copacabana and Ipanema in particular, gay men, families, beach-sport aficionados and even intellectuals claim specific segments, and it won't take you long to identify a stretch of sand where you'll feel comfortable.

### Beach fashion

Looking good is important on Rio's beaches, and you'll come across some pretty snappy seaside threads. Fashions change regularly, though, so if you're really desperate to make your mark you should buy your **swimsuits** in Rio. Keep in mind that although women may wear the skimpiest of bikinis, going topless is completely unacceptable.

### Beach sports

Maintaining an even tan and tight musculature is the principal occupation for most of Rio's beachgoers. Joggers swarm up and down the pavements, bronzed types flex their muscles on parallel bars located at intervals along the beaches, and **beach football** on Copacabana is as strong a tradition as legend would have it. There's lots of **volleyball**, too, as well as the ubiquitous **batball**, a kind of table tennis with a heavy ball, and without the table.

### Eating

A lot of people make their living by plying **food** – sweets, nuts, ice cream – and beach equipment along the seashore, while dotted along the sand are makeshift canopies from which you can buy cold drinks. Like bars, most of these have a regular clientele and deliver a very efficient service. Coconut milk, *côco verde*, is sold everywhere, and is a brilliant hangover cure.

### Staying safe

The water off many of the beaches can be **dangerous**. The seabed falls sharply away, the waves are strong, and currents can pull you down the beach. Mark your spot well before entering the water, or you'll find yourself emerging from a paddle twenty or thirty metres from where you started – which, when the beaches are packed at weekends, can cause considerable problems when it comes to relocating your towel. Copacabana is particularly dangerous, even for strong swimmers. However, the beaches are well served by **lifeguards**, whose posts are marked by a white flag with a red cross; a **red flag** indicates that bathing is prohibited. Constant surveillance of the beachfronts from helicopters and support boats means that, if you do get into trouble, help should arrive quickly.

**Pollution** is another problem to bear in mind. Although much has been done in recent years to clean up Guanabara Bay, it is still not safe to swim in the water from Flamengo or Botafogo beaches. While the water beyond the bay at Copacabana and Ipanema is usually clean, there are times when it – and the beaches themselves – aren't, especially following a prolonged period of heavy summer rain, when the city's strained drainage system overflows with raw sewage.

Natural dangers aside, the beaches hold other unwelcome surprises. Giving your passport, money and **valuables** the chance of a suntan, rather than leaving them in the hotel safe, is madness. Take only the clothes and money you'll need – it's quite acceptable to use public transport while dressed for the beach.

## Glória, Catete and Flamengo

The nearest beach to the city centre is at Flamengo, and although it's not the best in Rio you might end up using it more than you think, since the neighbouring *bairros*, Catete and Glória, are useful and cheap **places to stay** (see p.79). The streets away from the beach – especially around Largo do Machado and along Rua do Catete – are full of inexpensive hotels, and there's a pleasant atmosphere to this part of town. Until the 1950s, Flamengo and Catete were the principal residential zones of Rio's wealthier middle classes, and although the mantle has now passed to Ipanema and Leblon, the *bairros* still have a relaxed appeal. Busy during the day, the tree-lined streets come alive at night with residents eating in the local restaurants; and though the nightlife is nothing special, it's tranquil enough to encourage sitting out on the pavement at the bars, beneath the palm trees and apartment buildings.

### Glória

Across from the **Glória** *metrô* station, on top of the Morro da Glória, stands the early eighteenth-century **Igreja de Nossa Senhora da Glória do Outeiro** (Mon–Fri 9am–5pm, Sat & Sun 9am–2pm), notable for its innovative octagonal ground-plan and domed roof, the latter decked with excellent seventeenth-century blue-and-white *azulejos* tiles and nineteenth-century marble masonry. Painstakingly renovated, the church, quite simply the prettiest in Rio, is an absolute gem, easily worth a quick detour. Behind it you'll find the **Museu da Imperial Irmandade de Nossa Senhora da Glória** (Mon–Fri 9am–5pm, Sat & Sun 9am–1pm), which has a small collection of religious relics, *ex votos* and the personal possessions of Empress Tereza Cristina.

### Catete

On the Rua do Catete, adjacent to the **Catete** *metrô* station, the Palácio do Catete is home to the **Museu da República** (Tues, Thurs & Fri noon–5pm, Wed 2–5pm, Sat & Sun 2–6pm; R$6, free Wed & Sun; ⓣ21/3235-2650, ⓦwww.museudarepublica.org.br;). The palace was used as the presidential residence

▲ Igreja de Nossa Senhora da Glória do Outeiro

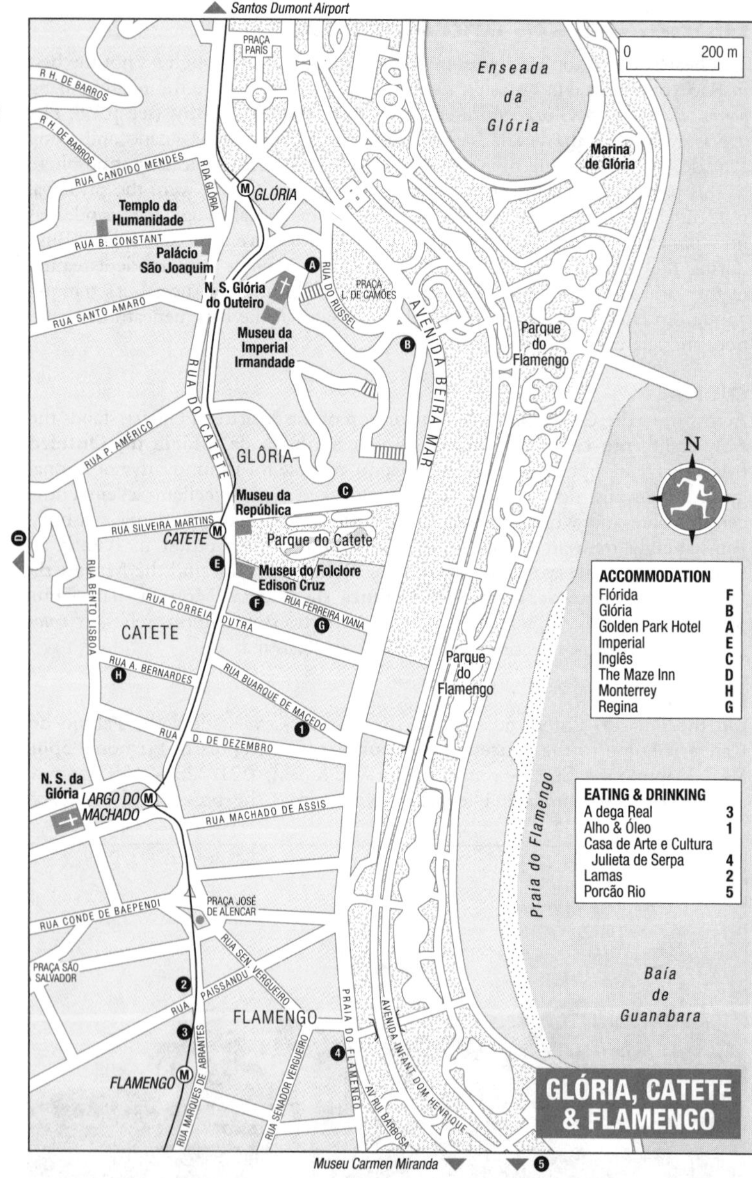


from 1897 until 1960, and it was here, in 1954, that Getúlio Vargas turned his gun on himself and took his own life. The building was erected in the 1860s as the Rio home of a wealthy coffee-*fazenda* owner. As a historical museum, the *palácio* continues where the Museu Histórico Nacional (see p.92) leaves off, with the establishment of the first Republic in 1888. The collection features both period furnishings and presidential memorabilia – including Vargas's bloodied pyjamas – though it's the opulent marble and stained glass of the building itself that make a visit so worthwhile. The grounds include a new exhibition space, theatre and art gallery, which means there is often something happening here at night, while the floodlit gardens make it a beautiful venue. The restaurant, in a glassed-in, turn-of-the-twentieth-century terrace overlooking the gardens, is only open at lunchtime and boasts an excellent salad buffet.

Divided between two buildings, one inside the palace grounds and the other in an adjacent house, the **Museu de Folclore Edison Cruz** (Tues–Fri 11am–6pm, Sat & Sun 3–6pm) is a fascinating collection that unites pieces from all over Brazil – leatherwork, musical instruments, ceramics, toys, Afro-Brazilian religious paraphernalia, photographs and *ex votos*. Behind the palace lies the **Parque do Catete** (daily 9am–6pm), whose birdlife, towering palms and quiet walking trails are good for a quick break. This is a pleasant place to take small children as it has a pond with ducks and other waterfowl, a playground, and tricycles and other toys.

### Flamengo

Following Avenida Beira Mar away from Centro you enter the **Parque do Flamengo**, the biggest land-reclamation project in Brazil, designed by the great Brazilian landscape architect and gardener Roberto Burle Marx, and completed in 1960. Sweeping round as far as Botafogo Bay, it comprises 1.2 square kilometres of prime seafront. You'll pass through the park many times by bus as you travel between Centro and the beach zone, and it's popular with local residents who use it mostly for sports – there are countless tennis courts and football pitches.

The **beach** at Flamengo runs along the park for about a kilometre and offers views across the bay to Niterói. Unfortunately, it's not a place for swimming as the water here is polluted. Instead, you might want to take a look at the quirky **Museu Carmen Miranda** (Tues–Fri 11am–5pm, Sat & Sun 2–5pm), located in a curious concrete bunker-like building in front of Av. Rui Barbosa 560, at the southern end of the park. Born in Portugal, Carmen Miranda made it big in Hollywood in the 1940s and became the patron saint of Rio's Carnaval transvestites. The museum contains a wonderful collection of kitsch memorabilia, including posters, some of the star's costumes – most notably her famed fruit-laden hats – and jewellery.

## Botafogo

**Botafogo** curves around the 800m between Flamengo and Rio's yacht club. Its name derives, reputedly, from the first white Portuguese settler who lived in the area, one João Pereira de Souza Botafogo. The bay is dominated by the yachts and boats moored near the club, and again the beach doesn't have much to recommend it to bathers due to the pollution of the bay. In many of Botafogo's streets there still stand mansions built in the nineteenth century when the area was Rio's outermost suburb and preserve of the city's rich. Most of these remaining distinguished buildings have been converted for use as offices or to house museums.

### Museu Casa de Rui Barbosa

Along Avenida São Clemente from the Botafogo *metrô* station is the **Museu Casa de Rui Barbosa** at no. 134 (Tues–Fri 10am–5pm, Sat & Sun 2–6pm; ⓣ21/3289-4600, ⓦwww.casaruibarbosa.gov.br), set amidst a lush garden with well-kept paths and borders. Built in 1850, it became the home of Rui Barbosa, jurist, statesman and author, in 1893. Born in Bahia state, Barbosa (1849–1923) studied law and, later, as a journalist and a liberal critic of the monarchy, founded the newspaper *A Imprensa*. He became senator of Bahia, and in 1905, and again in 1909, made unsuccessful attempts to be elected the country's president.

The museum is basically a collection of Barbosa's possessions – beautiful Dutch and English furniture, Chinese and Japanese porcelain, and a library of 35,000 volumes, amongst which are two hundred works penned by the man himself. Barbosa conferred a title on each room in the house – the Sala Bahia, Sala Questão Religiosa, Sala Habeas Corpus, Sala Código Civil – all of them identified with some part of his life.

### Museu Villa-Lobos and Museu do Índio

On Rua Sorocaba, a turning off Avenida São Clemente, is the **Museu Villa-Lobos** at no. 200 (Mon–Fri 10am–5.30pm; ⓣ21/2266-3894, ⓦwww.museuvillalobos.org.br). Established in 1960 to celebrate the work of the great Brazilian composer, Heitor Villa-Lobos (1887–1959), it's largely a display of his personal possessions and original music scores, but you can also buy CDs of his music here.

Botafogo's other museum, the **Museu do Índio** (Tues–Fri 9am–5.30pm, Sat & Sun 1–5pm; ⓣ21/2286-8899, ⓦwww.museudoindio.org.br), lies on the next street along, at Rua das Palmeiras 55. Housed in a mansion dating from 1880, the museum boasts a broad and interesting collection, including utensils, musical instruments, tribal costumes and ritual devices from many of Brazil's dwindling indigenous peoples. There's a good photographic exhibition, too, and an accessible anthropological explanation of the rituals and institutions of some of the tribes. Perhaps most interesting of all are the full-size shelters of different tribes that are erected on a temporary basis in the museum's grounds. The attached shop is excellent, selling a quality range of carefully sourced original artefacts at reasonable prices.

## Urca and Sugar Loaf mountain

The best bet for swimming this close to the centre is around **Urca**. There are small beaches on each side of the promontory on which this small, wealthy *bairro* stands, its name an acronym of the company that undertook its construction – Urbanizador Construção. Facing Botafogo, the **Praia da Urca**, only 100m long, is frequented almost exclusively by local inhabitants, while in front of the cable-car station, beneath the Sugar Loaf mountain, **Praia Vermelha** is a cove sheltered from the South Atlantic, whose relatively gentle waters are popular with swimmers.

You should come to Urca at least once during your stay to visit the **Pão de Açúcar**, which rises where Guanabara Bay meets the Atlantic Ocean. In Portuguese, the name means "**Sugar Loaf**", referring to the ceramic or metal mould used during the refining of sugar cane. Liquid sugar-cane juice was poured into the mould and removed when the sugar had set, producing a shape reminiscent of the mountain. The name may also come from the native Tamoyan Indian word *Pau-nh-Açuquá*, meaning "high, pointed or isolated hill" – a more apt description. The first recorded non-indigenous ascent to the summit was made in 1817 by an English nanny, Henrietta Carstairs. Today, mountaineers scaling the smooth, precipitous slopes are a common sight, but there's a cable-car ride to the summit for the less adventurous.

The **cable-car** system has been in place since 1912, though the present system, which can carry 1360 passengers every hour, was installed in the early 1970s (daily 8am–9pm, every 20min; R$44; ⓦwww.bondinho.com.br). The base station is in Praça General Tibúrcio, which can be reached by buses marked "Urca" or "Praia Vermelha" from Centro, #107 from Centro, Catete and Flamengo, or #511 and #512 from Zona Sul (returning to

Copacabana takes 1hr 30min, as the bus first passes through Botafogo, Leblon and Ipanema). The 1.4-kilometre journey is made in two stages, first to the summit of **Morro da Urca** (220m), where there is a theatre, restaurant and shops, and then on to the top of Pão de Açúcar itself (396m). The cable cars have glass walls, and the view from the top is as glorious as you could wish. Facing inland, you can see right over the city, from Centro and the Santos Dumont airport all the way through Flamengo and Botafogo; face Praia Vermelha and the cable-car terminal, and to the left you'll see the sweep of Copacabana and on into Ipanema, while back from the coast the mountains around which Rio was built rise to the Parque Nacional da Tijuca. Try to avoid the busy times between 10am and 3pm: the ride is best at sunset on a clear day, when the lights of the city are starting to twinkle. Leading down from the summit is a series of wooded trails along which you'll encounter curious small marmosets, and it's easy – and safe – to get away from the crowds.

## Leme and Copacabana

**Leme** and **Copacabana** are different stretches of the same four-kilometre-long beach: **Leme** extends for 1km, between the Morro do Leme and Avenida Princesa Isabel, by the luxury hotel *Le Meridien*, from where **Copacabana** runs for a further 3km to the Forte de Copacabana. The fort (Tues–Sun 10am–5pm; R$4; Ⓦwww.fortedecopacabana.com), built to protect the entrance to Guanabara Bay, is open to the public and worth visiting for the impressive views towards Copacabana beach, rather than for the military hardware on display in the **Museu Histórico do Exército**; there's also a branch of the excellent *Confeitaria Colombo* (see p.113), popular with tourists and elderly wives of officers, which serves light meals, cold drinks, tea and cakes. Leme beach is slightly less packed than Copacabana and tends to attract families – avoid walking through the Túnel Novo from Botafogo, as it's a favourite place for tourists to be relieved of their wallets. Copacabana is amazing, the over-the-top atmosphere apparent even in the mosaic pavements, designed by Burle Marx to represent images of rolling waves. The seafront is backed by a line of prestigious, high-rise hotels and luxury apartments that have sprung up since the 1940s, while a steady stream of noisy traffic patrols the two-lane **Avenida Atlântica**. Some fine examples of Art Deco architecture are scattered around the *bairro*, none more impressive than the *Copacabana Palace Hotel* on Avenida Atlântica, built in 1923 and considered one of Rio's best hotels (see p.80). Families, friends and couples cover the sand – at weekends, it's no easy matter to find space – the bars and restaurants along the avenue pulsate, and the busy **Avenida Nossa Senhora de Copacabana** is lined with assorted stores, which – like the *bairro* in general – are in a state of decline, being pushed aside by the boutiques of trendy Ipanema and the shopping malls of the Zona Sul.

Copacabana is dominated to the east by Sugar Loaf mountain and circled by a line of hills that stretch out into the bay. A popular residential area, the *bairro*'s expansion has been restricted by the Morro de São João, which separates it from Botafogo and the Morro dos Cabritos, which forms a natural barrier to the west. Consequently, it's one of the world's most densely populated areas as well as a frenzy of sensual activity. Some say that Copacabana is past its prime, and certainly it's not as exclusive as it once was. Even so, it's still an enjoyable place to sit and watch the world go by, and at night on the floodlit beach, football is played into the early hours.

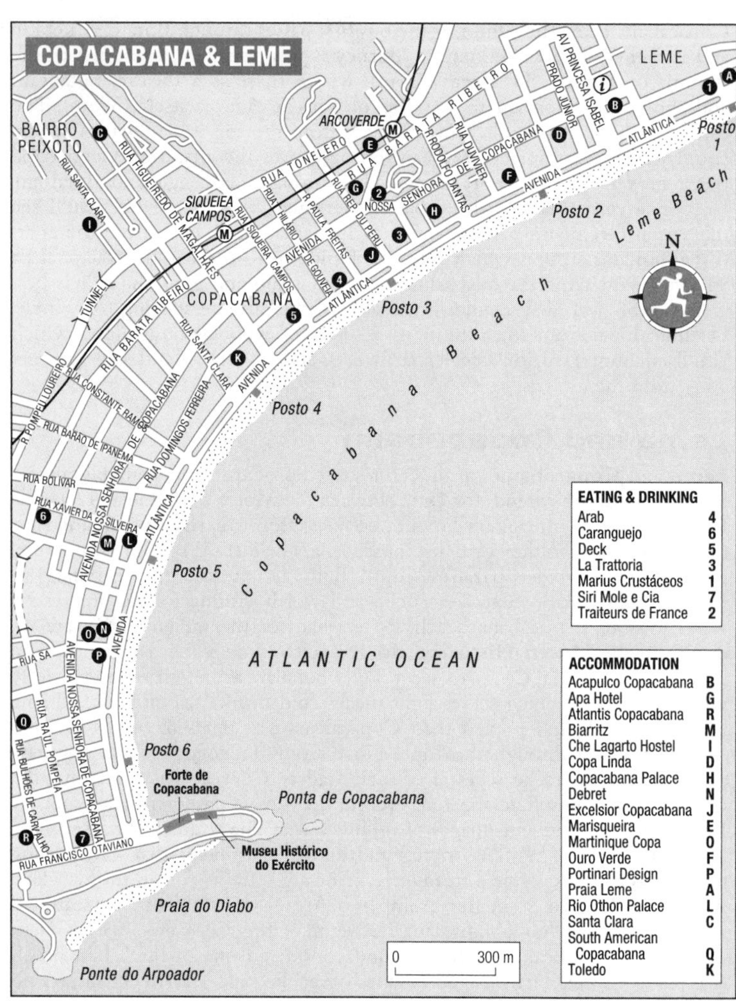


Of course, Copacabana hasn't always been as it is today, and traces remain of the former fishing community that dominated the area until the first decades of the twentieth century. Each morning before dawn, the boats of the *colônia de pescadores* (the descendants of the fishermen) set sail from the Forte de Copacabana, returning to the beach by 8am to sell their fish across from the *Sofitel* hotel.

## Arpoador, Ipanema and Leblon

On the other side of the point from Forte de Copacabana, the lively waters off the **Praia do Arpoador** are popular with families and the elderly as the ocean here is slightly calmer than at **Ipanema**, which is a couple of kilometres away (**Leblon** lies thereafter). Much more tranquil than Copacabana, the beaches in these areas are stupendous, while the only bar/restaurant on the beachfront is *Caneco*, at the far end of Leblon – a good spot to aim for anyway, as you'll enjoy a fine view towards Ipanema from here. As with Copacabana, Ipanema's beach is unofficially divided according to the supposed interest of its users. Thus, the stretch of sand east from Rua Farme de Amoedo to Rua Teixeira de Melo around *posto 8* is where gay men are concentrated, while the nearby *posto 9* is where artists and intellectuals ponder life. On Sunday, the seafront roads – Avenida Vieira Souto in Ipanema and Avenida Delfim in Leblon – are closed to traffic, given over to strollers, skateboarders and rollerbladers.

Since the 1960s, Ipanema has developed a reputation as a fashion centre second to none in Latin America. Although many in São Paulo would dispute this, certainly the *bairro* is packed with *bijou* boutiques flogging the very best Brazilian names in fine threads. If you do go shopping here, go on a Friday and take in the large **food and flower market** on the Praça de Paz. For quality clothes, however, prices are quite high compared with their European or North American equivalents.

## Lagoa

Back from Ipanema's plush beaches lies the Lagoa Rodrigo de Freitas, always referred to simply as Lagoa. A lagoon linked to the ocean by a narrow canal that passes through Ipanema's Jardim de Allah, Lagoa is fringed by apartment buildings where some of Rio's most seriously rich and status-conscious have chosen to live since the 1920s. One of the few remaining original homes now contains the **Fundação Eva Klabin** (guided visits Wed–Sun 2.30pm & 4pm; ⓣ21/2523-3471, ⓦwww.evaklabin.org.br), a cultural centre at Avenida Epitácio Pessoa 2480. Built in 1931, the house is typical of the resort-style Norman architecture popular at the time and became the family residence of Eva Klabin, a wealthy art collector of Lithuanian origin. The wide-ranging collection of Egyptian, classical Greek and Roman, Italian, French and Flemish works of art is beautifully displayed in elegant, wood-panelled rooms, and classical music recitals are regularly held here. All this seems utterly at odds with the lifestyle of the Zona Sul but serves as a reminder of the Brazilian elite's traditional cultural affinity with all things European.

Until recently, the lagoon's water was badly polluted, but a programme to clean it up has been remarkably successful and its mangrove swamps are now steadily recovering. The shore surrounding the lagoon forms the Parque Tom Jobim (named in memory of Rio's famed bossa-nova composer who died in 1994), and the area comes alive each Sunday as people walk, rollerblade, jog or cycle along the 7.5-kilometre perimeter pathway, or just gaze at the passers-by. Summer evenings are especially popular when, on the west side of the lagoon in the area known as the Parque dos Patins (Skaters' Park), there are food stalls, live music and *forró* dancing.

The steep slopes behind the area's apartment buildings are still well forested, and in 1979 a *favela* was cleared away and the **Parque da Catacumba** (daily 8am–7pm) developed in its place on one of the more accessible hills, by the southeast corner of the lagoon on Avenida Epitácio Pessoa. It's a wonderful, shaded place to relax, and the dense tropical vegetation forms an excellent backdrop for one of Brazil's few **sculpture parks**.

## Jardim Botânico and Gávea

To the northwest of the Lagoa lies the *bairro* of **Jardim Botânico**, whose **Parque Lage** (daily 8am–5pm), designed by the English landscape gardener John Tyndale in the early 1840s, consists of 137 hectares of foliage, including pristine Atlantic forest on the slopes of the Corcovado, with a labyrinthine path network and

### Hang-gliding above Rio

For a bird's-eye view of Rio's beaches and forest, take off with an experienced pilot on a tandem **hang-glider** flight from the Pedra Bonita ramp on the western edge of the Parque Nacional da Tijuca (see p.111), 520m above the beach at São Conrado. Depending on conditions, flights last between ten and thirty minutes, flying alongside the mountains and over the forest and ocean before landing on the beach at São Conrado.

The most experienced operator, Just Fly (T21/2268-0565 or 9985-7540, Wwww.justfly.com.br), offers flights daily (usually 10am–3pm) when weather permits, which includes pick-up and drop-off from your hotel. If reserving by phone or in person, mention the Rough Guide and you'll receive a ten percent discount on the standard price of R$240.

seven small lakes. A little further along the Rua Jardim Botânico, at no. 1008, is the **Jardim Botânico** itself (daily 8am–5pm; R$5; Wwww.jbrj.gov.br). Over half of it is natural forest, while the rest is laid out in impressive avenues lined with immense imperial palms that date from the garden's inauguration in 1808. Dom João used the gardens to introduce foreign plants into Brazil – tea, cloves, cinnamon and pineapple among them – and they were opened to the public in 1890. One of the world's finest botanic gardens, there are now five thousand plant species, amongst which live monkeys, parrots and other assorted wildlife. There are also a number of sculptures to be seen throughout the garden, notably the *Ninfa do Eco* and *Caçador Narciso* (1783) by Mestre Valentim, the first two metal sculptures cast in Brazil.

## Gávea and the Jockey Club

On the **Gávea** side of Lagoa, the **Jockey Club**, also known as the Hipódromo da Gávea, can be reached on any bus marked "via Jóquei" – get off at Praça Santos Dumont at the end of Rua Jardim Botânico. Racing in Rio was introduced by the British and dates back to 1825, though the Hipódromo wasn't built until 1926. Today, **races** take place four times a week (Mon 6.30–11.30pm, Fri 4–9.30pm, Sat & Sun 2–8pm), with the international Grande Prêmio Brazil taking place on the first Sunday of August. A night at the races is great fun, especially during the floodlit evening races, when the air is balmy and you can eat or sip a drink as you watch the action, and visitors can get into the palatial members' stand for just a few *reís* (no one in shorts is admitted). On alternate weekends, part of the club is taken over by the **Babilônia Feira Hype** (2–10pm; R$5; Wwww.babiloniahype.com.br), featuring a good selection of handicrafts as well as clothes and jewellery by young designers hoping to get noticed.

About 3km northwest of the Jockey Club, the **Instituto Moreira Salles**, at Rua Marquês de São Vicente 476 (Tues–Sun 1–8pm; T21/3284-7400, Wwww.ims.com.br), is one of Rio's most beautiful private cultural centres. Located in the former home of the Moreira Salles family (the owners of Unibanco, one of the country's most important banks), the house, built in 1951, is one of the finest examples of modernist residential architecture in Brazil. Designed by the Brazilian architect Olavo Redig de Campos – with gardens landscaped by Roberto Burle Marx, who also contributed a tile mural alongside the terrace, the building has been open to the public since 1999. Important exhibitions of nineteenth- and twentieth-century painting and photography are staged and there's a tearoom that serves light lunches, cakes and ice creams, and a good, but expensive (R$45 per person), high tea. It's a good half-hour walk to the *Instituto* from the Jockey Club; alternatively, you can take bus #170 from Centro (Av. Rio Branco), Botafogo, Humaitá or Jardim Botânico, or #174 from Copacabana, Ipanema or Leblon.

Also in Gávea is the **Parque da Cidade** (daily 8am–5pm) and **Museu Histórico da Cidade** (Tues–Sun 11–5pm), at the end of Estrada de Santa Marinha: buses #591, #593 or #594 from Copacabana, #179 or #178 from Centro. The museum is housed within a two-storey nineteenth-century mansion once owned by the Marquês de São Vicente, and the entire collection is related to the history of Rio from its founding until the end of the Old Republic in 1930. The exhibits – paintings, weapons, porcelain, medals and the like – are arranged in chronological order; the first salon deals with the city's foundation, the rest with the colonial period.

## The coast west of Leblon

Back on the coast, to the west of Leblon, lies kilometre after kilometre of white sand. **Praia do Vidigal**, tucked under the Morro Dois Irmãos, is only about 500m long, and used to be the preserve of the inhabitants of the **Favela do Vidigal** – one of the biggest shantytowns in Rio – until they lost their beach with the construction of the *Rio Sheraton Hotel*.

West again, the beautiful beach at **São Conrado**, dominated by apartment buildings and high-rise hotels, is becoming ever trendier: frequented by the famous and packed with hang-gliders and surfers at weekends, it's an area where the upper classes flaunt their wealth without shame, though some are uncomfortable with the encroachment of nearby *favelas*. Above São Conrado, on the slopes between the Tijuca mountains and the peak of Pedra dos Dois Irmãos, sits **Favela Roçinha** (see box, p.110) – misleadingly picturesque and glistening in the tropical sun. Some 200,000 Brazilians live here, where a salary of around R$400 a month is about as much as an entire family can expect. **Bus** #500 from Urca will take you to São Conrado via avenidas Atlântica (Copacabana), Vieira Souto (Ipanema) and Delfim Moreira (Leblon).

The last area within the city limits is **Barra da Tijuca**, where property developers have been building massive apartment buildings and shopping malls at breakneck speed – though the clean waters and white sands that run for over 16km remain popular at weekends with the beach-party-and-barbecue set. You can reach Barra da Tijuca by **bus** from Copacabana (#553), or from Botafogo *metrô* station (#524).

### Sítio Roberto Burle Marx

Some 25km along the coast from Barra da Tijuca is the quiet and unremarkable village of Guaratiba. The countryside around the village is popular amongst *cariocas* seeking a discreet retreat, and it was here in 1949 that the influential landscape gardener **Roberto Burle Marx** (1909–94) bought a forty-hectare former coffee plantation, the Sítio, and converted it into a nursery for the plants he collected on his travels around the country. In 1973, Burle Marx moved permanently to the Sítio, living there until his death.

Today, the Sítio is used as a botany research and teaching centre, and **tours** of the property and grounds are given to the public, though only in Portuguese (daily 9.30am & 1.30pm; 1hr 30min; R$7; book in advance on ⓣ21/2410-1412). Burle Marx was not only a collector of plants but also of Brazilian folk art and Peruvian ceramics – his vast collection is on display along with his own paintings and textiles inside the house. A small chapel, dating from 1610, and the Sítio's original colonial-era farmhouse are also on the grounds. Just across the road from the Sítio's front gates, the *Restaurante do Cesar* (daily 11.30am–6.30pm; weekend reservations essential; ⓣ21/2410-1202) serves excellent local seafood and is owned by Burle Marx's favourite cook; a full meal for two will cost around R$60.

## Rio's favelas

In a low-wage economy, and with minimal social services, life is extremely difficult for the majority of Brazilians. During the last forty years, the rural poor have descended upon urban centres in search of a livelihood – often unable to find accommodation, or pay rent, they have established shantytowns, or **favelas**, on any available empty space, which in Rio usually means the slopes of the hills around which the city has grown.

*Favelas* start off as huddles of cardboard boxes and plastic sheeting, and slowly expand and transform: metal sheeting and bricks provide more solid shelters of often two or more storeys. Clinging to the sides of Rio's hills, and glistening in the sun, they can from a distance appear not unlike a medieval Spanish hamlet, perched secure atop a mountain. It is, however, a spurious beauty. The *favelas* are creations of need, and their inhabitants are engaged in an immense daily struggle for survival, worsened by the prospect of landslides caused by heavy rains, which could tear their dwellings from their tenuous hold on precipitous inclines.

Life for some of Rio's *favela* dwellers is slowly changing for the better, however. Bound together by their shared poverty and exclusion from effective citizenship, the *favelados* display a great resourcefulness and cooperative strength. **Self-help initiatives** – some of which are based around the *escolas de samba* (see p.124) that are mainly *favela*-based – have emerged, and the authorities are finally recognizing the legitimacy of *favelas* by promoting "*favela-bairro*" projects aimed at fully integrating them into city life. Private enterprise, too, is taking an interest as it becomes alert to the fact that the quarter of the city's population that live in *favelas* represents a vast, untapped market.

### Favela tours

Wandering into a *favela* does not, as many middle-class *cariocas* would have you believe, guarantee being robbed or murdered. **Law and order** is essentially in the hands of highly organized drugs gangs, but it's simply not in their interest to create trouble for visitors, as this would only attract the attention of the police who normally stay clear of *favelas*. Alone, you're liable to get lost and, as in any isolated spot, may run into opportunistic thieves, but if accompanied by a *favela* resident you'll be perfectly safe and received with friendly curiosity. For the majority of people, however, the best option is to take a **tour**, with the most insightful and longest-established run by Marcelo Armstrong. Marcelo, who speaks excellent English, is widely known and respected in the *favelas* that are visited and has made a point of getting community approval. It is strongly advised to make your own arrangements with Marcelo rather than through a travel agent or hotel front desk, where you may end up with an inferior tour and be charged too much – some operators treat the *favelas* rather as they might an African game park, ferrying groups in open-topped camouflaged jeeps. But if you're worried about voyeurism, you shouldn't be: residents want outsiders to understand that *favelas* are not in fact terrifying and lawless ghettos, but inhabited by people as decent as anywhere else, eager to improve the local quality of life.

Marcelo's highly responsible tours usually take in two *favelas*: Roçinha, Rio's largest, with around 200,000 inhabitants, and Vila Canoas, much smaller, with some 3000 residents. Twice a day (9am & 2pm; R$65, part of which is donated to community projects in the *favelas*), tourists are picked up from their hotels or pre-arranged spots in the Zona Sul for the two-hour tour, which stops at lookout points, a day-care centre, a bar and other places of interest. Marcelo offers a fascinating commentary, pointing out the achievements of *favelas* and their inhabitants without romanticizing their lives. To reserve a place on a tour, call Marcelo on ⓣ21/3322-2727, mobile 9989-0074 or 9772-1133, or for more information, check out ⓦwww.favelatour.com.br.

To get to the Sítio, take **bus** #387 ("Marambaia–Passeio") from the Passeio Público in Centro, which passes through Copacabana, Ipanema and Barra da Tijuca, and will leave you right outside the Sítio's entrance gate – allow an hour and a half from Centro. Alternatively, the air-conditioned "Santa Cruz–Via Barra" or "Campo Grande–Via Barra" buses follow the same route but will leave you at the Ipiranga petrol station in Guaratiba, from where you should ask for directions; the Sítio is a fifteen-minute walk away.

## Parque Nacional da Tijuca and Alta da Boa Vista

When the Portuguese arrived, the area that is now the city of Rio was covered by dense green tropical forest. As the city grew, the trees were felled and the timber used in construction or for charcoal. However, if you look up from the streets of Zona Sul today, the mountains running southwest from the Corcovado are still covered with exuberant forest, the periphery of the **Parque Nacional da Tijuca** (daily 8am–5pm), which covers an area of approximately 120 square kilometres.

In the seventeenth century, the forests of Tijuca were cut down for their valuable hardwood and the trees replaced by sugar cane and, later, coffee plantations and small-scale agriculture. In the early nineteenth century, the city authorities became alarmed by a shortage of pure water and by landslides from the Tijuca slopes, and in 1857, a **reafforestation project** was initiated: by 1870, over 100,000 trees had been planted and the forest was reborn. Most of the seeds and cuttings that were planted were native to the region, and today the park serves as a remarkable example of the potential for the regeneration of the Mata Atlântica.

Following on from the success of the forest, fauna have gradually been reintroduced to the extent that it is once again the home of insects and reptiles, ocelots, howler monkeys, agoutis, three-toed sloths and other animals. Most successful of all has been the return of **birdlife**, making Tijuca a paradise for birdwatchers. At the same time, however, overstretched park rangers have been struggling to keep residents of the eight neighbouring *favelas* from hunting wildlife for food or for trade.

### Routes into the park

Tijuca offers lots of walks and some excellent views of Rio, and though areas of it have been burnt by forest fires it remains an appealing place to get away from the city for a few hours. Buses don't enter the park, so a **car** is useful if you plan to do an extensive tour: you can enter via Cosme Velho *bairro*, near the **Entrada dos Caboclos** (areas of the park are used as *terrenos*, places where *candomblé* and *umbanda* ritual ceremonies are performed: *caboclos* is the collective name for the spirits involved in these cults), and follow Estrada Heitor da Silva Costa. An alternative entrance is at Rua Leão Pacheco, which runs up the side of the Jardim Botânico (off Rua Jardim Botânico) and leads to the **Entrada dos Macacos** and on to the **Vista Chinesa**, above the Museu Histórico da Cidade in Gávea. From here there's a marvellous view of Guanabara Bay and the Zona Sul. Both of these entrances lead to different roads that run through the park, but they converge eventually in the *bairro* of **Alta da Boa Vista**. If you're intent upon **walking**, you should be warned that even the shorter trip from the Entrada dos Macacos will mean a hot, dehydrating climb for more than 20km.

If you don't have your own transport, it's much easier to aim for the area to the north of the park known as the **Floresta da Tijuca**. Take a bus to Alto da Boa Vista (#221 from Praça XV de Novembro; #233 or #234 from the *rodoviária*; #133 from Rua Jardim Botânico) and get off at Praça Alfonso Viseu near the

▲ Waterfall, Parque Nacional da Tijuca

**Entrada da Floresta**, with its distinctive stone columns. A few hundred metres after the entrance (where you can buy a **map**, though the main paths are well signposted) is a 35-metre-high waterfall and, further on, the **Capela do Mairynk**, built in 1860 but virtually entirely rebuilt in the 1940s. The chapel's most interesting feature is the three altar panels painted by Cândido Portinari, one of Brazil's greatest twentieth-century artists, though the originals now form part of the much-depleted collection of the Museu de Arte Moderna (see p.92) and those in the chapel are reproductions. If you have the energy for an all-day climb, you can go all the way to the **Pico do Papagaio** (975m) or **Pico da Tijuca** (1021m) – peaks in the far north of the forest, above the popular picnic spot known as **Bom Retiro**. The whole park is a good place for a picnic, in fact; come well supplied with drinks and snacks, as vendors are few and far between.

Alternatively, you can join an **organized tour** of the park. Most of those offered by hotels and travel agents involve nothing more strenuous than a short walk along a paved road, but more personal – and infinitely more rewarding – are the tours run by ★Rio Hiking (Ⓣ21/2552-9204 or mobile 9721-0594, Ⓦwww.riohiking.com.br), which take small groups of people on half- or full-day hikes along the park's many trails. Operating at weekends and on some weekdays, too, the tours are led by Denise Werneck and her son Gabriel, both of whom speak excellent English and are extremely knowledgeable about the park's biodiversity. Rio Hiking also run occasional three-day walking trips to Ilha Grande (see p.140) and Parque Nacional do Itatiaia (see p.156), and Denise and Gabriel also take groups to sample the nightlife of bohemian Lapa (see p.120).

# Eating and drinking

As one of the world's most exotic tourist resorts and with (for Brazil) a relatively large middle-class population, Rio is well served by restaurants offering a wide variety of cuisines – from traditional Brazilian to French and Japanese. In general, eating out in Rio is not cheap – and can, in fact, be very expensive – but there's no shortage of low-priced places to grab a lunchtime meal, or just a snack and a drink. *Cariocas* generally dine late, and restaurants don't start to fill up until after 9pm. Last orders are usually taken around midnight, but there are some places where you can get a meal well after 2am.

## Fast food, snacks, cakes and ice cream

There are numerous **hamburger** joints in Rio, though it's worth bearing in mind that there's a good chance that the ground beef used comes from the Amazon, where immense ranches are displacing Indians, peasants and trees at a criminal rate. You'll get better, more authentic and cheaper food at any *galeto* or *lanchonete* – there are plenty in Centro or Copacabana, though many are closed at night. You won't really need any guidance to find these; the places given below deal in more specialized fare.

If you're just peckish, then it's nice to take **tea and cakes** at ★ *Confeitaria Colombo* at Rua Gonçalves Dias 32, Centro (closed Sat at 1pm and all day Sun). Founded in 1894, the *Colombo* recalls Rio's *belle époque*, with its ornate interior and air of tradition; there's also a rather plain-looking branch in the Forte de Copacabana (see p.105). In chic Leblon, *Garcia & Rodriques*, at Av. Ataulfo de

### A note on drinking

The lists given below are for both eating and drinking. Pretty well all *botequins* (bars) serve *petiscos* (snacks) or even full meals, while lots of restaurants allow a night's drinking, too, so you should be able to find somewhere that suits you. In most regions of Brazil, **beer** comes to your table in a bottle, but in Rio draught beer – or *chopp*, pronounced "shopee" – predominates. A good place to sample Brazil's national drink, **cachaça**, is at the *Academia da Cachaça*, Rua Cde. Bernadotte 26, Leblon, a small and always crowded bar where there are 300 available brands to sample – treat the spirit with respect at all times. Also well worth considering are the bars in Lapa (see p.120), a bohemian neighbourhood known for some prime drinking-spots. A good place to start is *Antônio's Bar e Botequi*, Av. Mem de Sá 88, a place full of local colour and atmosphere.

Paiva 1251, has a wonderful bakery providing excellent sandwiches and cakes. A fine high-tea is served in the beautiful *Casa de Arte e Cultura Julieta de Serpa* in Flamengo (see opposite), but the formal eighteenth-century decor may not appeal. More modern surroundings, but arguably as good (and as expensive) a tea are offered at the *Instituto Moreira Salles* in Gávea (see p.108).

For **ice cream**, there are plenty of choices: *Chaika* at Rua Visconde de Pirajá 32 or the excellent *Felice Caffé* at Rua Gomes Carneiro 30 – both in Ipanema; *Garcia & Rodriques* (see p.113) in Leblon; or, best of all, *Mil Frutas Café*, at Rua Garcia D'Ávila 134 in Ipanema, and another near the Jardim Botânico on Rua Seabra, which boasts dozens of flavours – including exotic Brazilian fruit such as *pitanga* and *jaboticaba* – that vary according to the season.

## Centro and Lapa

The restaurants in the city centre cater largely for people working in the area, and at lunchtime the service is rushed. There are lots of cheap eating-places around Praça Tiradentes, while after work, office workers flock to the Arco de Teles area, the pedestrian zone centred on Travessa do Comércio and Rua Ouvidor, for early evening drinks and *petiscos* in the many unassuming bars. Later on, the action shifts to Lapa, one of the most important nightlife spots in Rio (see p.120).

The places listed below are marked on the map on pp.84–85.

**Albamar** Praça Marechal Âncora 186, Centro. Founded in 1933 and housed in the remaining tower of the old municipal market, this cool, green, octagonal building provides a superb view of Guanabara Bay. Stick with the moderately priced seafood, served by stern waiters in white uniforms. Lunch only; closed Sun.

**Bar Luiz** Rua Carioca 39, Centro. Near Largo da Carioca, this manic but essentially run-of-the-mill restaurant and bar, serving German-style food and ice-cold *chopp*, is considered quite an institution and has long been a popular meeting-place for journalists and intellectuals. Closed Sun.

**Bar Ocidental** Rua Miguel Couto 124, Centro. One of several bars on a small pedestrianized road near the Largo de São Francisco de Paulo. Sit at a table outside and enjoy an early evening *chopp* and a plate of fresh sardines.

**Brasserie Rosário** Rua do Rosário 34, Centro. Pasta and modern Brazilian dishes dominate the menu, with excellent-value lunch specials. The bakery is especially good, serving delicious cakes and wonderful bread and sandwiches. Mon–Fri 11am–9pm, Sat 11am–6pm.

**Cosmopolita** Travessa do Mosqueira 4, Lapa. An excellent Portuguese restaurant established in 1926 with a loyal, rather bohemian, clientele. Fish dishes – cod-based, in particular – are the firm favourites. Closed Sun.

**Penafiel** Rua Senhor dos Passos 12, Centro 1. Superb – and amazingly inexpensive – Portuguese dishes have been served here since 1912. Fish dishes and stews (such as those based on yellow wax bean, ox tongue and tripe) are specialities. Lunch only; closed Sat & Sun.

**Rio-Minho** Rua do Ouvidor 10, Centro. The *Rio-Minho* has been going strong since 1884, serving tasty Brazilian food at fair prices. The kitchen concentrates on seafood – try *badejo* fish, lobster in butter, prawn in coconut milk or the fried fish with red peppers, rice and broccoli. Lunch only; closed Sat & Sun.

## Santa Teresa

Be sure to make time for a visit up into the airy hills of Santa Teresa. There are some good restaurants here and the *bairro* is an enjoyable ten-minute tram ride from Centro. On Friday and Saturday evenings, people of all ages congregate in the bars and restaurants around Largo dos Guimarães.

The places listed below are marked on the map on pp.84–85.

**Adega do Pimenta** Rua Almirante Alexandrino 296. Most people go to this moderately priced German spot for the sausage and sauerkraut, but the duck with red cabbage is also excellent.

**Aprazível** Rua Aprazível 62 ☎21/2508-9174. Excellent and fairly expensive French-influenced Minas Gerais dishes, plus there's an attractive terrace with wonderful views across Rio. The quail, served with *jaboticaba* chutney, is a remarkable creation, while the goat is roasted to perfection. Advance booking advised. Thurs–Sat noon–midnight, Sun & public holidays 1–6pm.

**Bar do Arnaudo** Rua Almirante Alexandrino 316. Just up from the *Adega do Pimenta*, this is an excellent mid-priced place to sample traditional food from Brazil's Northeast, such as *carne do sol* (sun-dried meat), *macaxeira* (sweet manioc) and *pirão de bode* (goat-meat soup). Closed Sat & Sun from 8pm & all day Mon.

**Bar do Mineiro** Rua Paschoal Carlos Magno 99. Inexpensive and authentic country-style food in an old bar that could be in any small town in Minas Gerais. Also has good beers and an excellent range of *cachaça*.

**Espírito Santa** Largo dos Guimarães. Multi-regional Brazilian cuisine, the focus being on adaptations of flavoursome dishes of the Amazon, Bahia and Minas Gerais. The dining room has a designer-rustic look, or eat on the terrace and enjoy wonderful views of the *bairro*. Mon–Wed 11.30am–6pm, Thurs–Sat 11.30am–midnight, Sun 11.30am–7pm.

**Sobrenatural** Rua Almirante Alexandrino 432. Basically a fish restaurant, where the highlights are the *moquecas* and the catch of the day. Deliberately rustic-looking, this is an inviting place for a leisurely meal. Closed Mon.



## Flamengo

In addition to the places reviewed, there are many restaurants, *galetos* and *lanchonetes* around the Largo do Machado or wander along Rua Barão do Flamengo and try one of numerous small restaurants serving Brazilian, German, Italian, Japanese or Peruvian food.

The places listed below are marked on the map on p.102.

**Adega Real** Rua Marquês de Abrantes. No haughty *nouvelle cuisine* here, just piles of good basics – if you like decent-quality food in large quantities, this is the place, as the friendly staff serve portions sufficient for at least two people. The restaurant opens onto the street, and on Fridays you can sit at the bar and swallow *chopp* until 4am; the *bolinhas de bacalhau* (cod balls) are well worth trying.

**Alho & Óleo** Rua Barque de Macedo 13. Tasty and reasonably priced international dishes served in an upmarket atmosphere.

**Casa de Arte e Cultura Julieta de Serpa** Praia do Flamengo 340. By far the prettiest buildings in Flamengo – a mansion built in 1920 – cover several eating options including a good, but rather formal, French restaurant, a bistrot serving light meals, and a lavishly decorated tearoom attended by waiters dressed in absurdly kitsch eighteenth-century outfits.

**Lamas** Rua Marquês de Abrantes 18. This ever-popular restaurant has been serving well-prepared Brazilian food since 1874 (the Oswaldo Aranha steak – pan-fried with lots of garlic – is a staple). Always busy, with a vibrant atmosphere and clientele of artist and journalist types, *Lamas* is a good example of *carioca* middle-class tradition. Daily until 4am.

**Porcão Rio** Av. Infante Dom Henrique s/n, Aterro do Flamengo. A vast *churrascaria* offering, for R$67 per person, an abundance of red meat served *rodizio*-style, along with chicken, fish and a varied choice from the salad buffet. Although part of a chain (there's a branch in Ipanema), the food is top quality and service is always efficient. This spot is located alongside the ocean and features glorious views of Guanabara Bay and Sugar Loaf mountain.

## Botafogo, Humaitá and Urca

Botafogo hosts some of Rio's most interesting restaurants, often overlooked by tourists because they lie a bit off the beaten track, hidden away in backstreets. At the Humaitá's impressive indoor market, **Cobal**, Rua Voluntários da Pátria 446, you can take your pick of the moderately priced but excellent *lanchonetes* serving Brazilian Northeastern, Italian and Japanese food; this is a very popular lunch and evening meeting-point for local residents. Although there are few places to eat in Urca, one of Rio's quietest *bairros*, it's a pleasant place for a relaxing meal.

The places listed below are marked on the map on pp.98–99.

**Adega do Valentim** Rua da Passagem 178, Botafogo ☎21/295-2748. A comfortable restaurant (especially the front salon) serving up authentic Portuguese food. Expect to pay around R$35 per person for one of the fifteen cod dishes, roast suckling pig or goat. The smoked meats are especially good (though expensive), and there's a nice wine list, too.

**Bar e Restaurante Urca** Rua Cândido Gaffrée 205, Urca. Equally good for a cold beer and *petiscos* or a seafood meal, this traditional neighbourhood gathering-point is especially busy on Saturdays when an excellent *feijoada* is served and on Sundays when the attraction is *Cozido à Portuguesa*, a northern Portugese stew.

**Garota da Urca** Av. João Luiz Alves, Urca. Though hardly stylish, *Garota da Urca* boasts one of the best views of any Rio restaurant, looking back towards Botafogo and the Corcovado. The food – Brazilian with Italian twists – is good enough, but you can also stop by for just a drink. Try the *peixe a garota* – a delicious fish risotto that serves two for around R$35.

**Miam Miam** Rua General Góes Monteiro 34, Botafogo. Housed in a nineteenth-century house typical of Botafogo, the relaxed dining area decorated in a retro 1960s style, this treasure of a restaurant deserves going slightly out of the way for. The food is modern Brazilian at its most delicious – incorporating fresh, local ingredients and French twists. Tues–Fri lunch & dinner, Sat & public holidays dinner only.

**Yorubá** Rua Arnaldo Quintela 94, Botafogo. Friendly restaurant serving up moderately priced Afro-Bahian cooking. The beautifully presented meals always take a long time to appear, but the *bobó* (a dish based on manioc purée), *moquecas* and other Bahian specialities are well worth the wait. Sun lunch only; closed Mon & Tues.

## Copacabana and Leme

It should come as no surprise that Copacabana and adjoining Leme are riddled with restaurants, but that doesn't mean that the choice is particularly good – unless you enjoy sitting in a restaurant swamped with holiday-makers being shuttled about by tour companies. Although eating here is generally disappointing, there are a number of places that are in fact well worth trying.

The places listed below are marked on the map on p.106.

**Arab** Av. Atlântica 1936, Copacabana. At this reasonably priced Lebanese restaurant, you can enjoy a cold beer and a snack on the terrace or have a full meal inside (the *por kilo* lunch is excellent value). Though the menu is rather heavy on meat choices, vegetarians certainly won't go hungry. One of the very few good restaurants on Av. Atlântica.

**Caranguejo** Rua Barata Ribeiro 771, Copacabana. Excellent, inexpensive seafood – especially the *carangueijos* (crabs) – served in an utterly unpretentious environment packed with locals and tourists alike. Closed Mon.

**Deck** Av. Atlântica 2316, Copacabana. This always-busy restaurant serves an all-you-can-eat Brazilian buffet for just R$20 per person until 5pm, after which the offerings include *rodizio de galeto* (mouthwatering thyme-and-garlic chicken with polenta fried in palm oil) and all-you-can-eat pasta for R$15.

**La Trattoria** Rua Fernando Mendes 7, Copacabana. Cheap-and-cheerful place serving the best Italian food in in the *bairro*. Amongst the excellent range of pasta dishes, the fettuccine doused in a mixed seafood sauce is especially recommended.

**Marisqueira** Rua Barata Ribeiro 232, Copacabana. For over fifty years, this restaurant has been serving well-prepared Portuguese-style food, if perhaps a little unimaginative and a touch on the pricey side. Still, it's a good spot for seafood dishes or the Sunday special of calf's foot and white bean stew.

**Marius Crustáceos** Av. Atlântica 290, Leme ☎21/2543-6363. Rio's best-known place to come for oysters, crabs, crayfish, prawns and other seafood choices. The expensive menu is varied, though Italian–Brazilian styles dominate and the waiters have a tendency towards the brusque.

**Siri Mole e Cia** Rua Francisco Otaviano 50, Copacabana ☎21/2267-0894. A rarity in Rio – an excellent Bahian restaurant serving beautifully presented dishes (many of them spicy) in an upmarket, yet comfortable, setting. Inside, the restaurant is quite formal, but there are also a few tables outside where you can munch on *acarajé* and other Bahian snacks. There's another branch located in Centro at Av. Rio Branco 1 (☎21/2233-0107).

**Traiteurs de France** Av. Nossa Senhora de Copacabana 386, Copacabana ☎21/2548-6440. Simple cooking from one of the very few affordable and good French restaurants in Rio. Try the duck *magret* with spicy pears or one of the tasty fish dishes. Mon–Sat lunch & dinner; Sun lunch only.

# Ipanema

There's a fair selection of good (and expensive) restaurants in Ipanema. For budget eating, however, you'll generally do rather better in Copacabana, while more interesting restaurants tend to be in Leblon.

The places listed below are marked on the map on pp.98–99.

**Casa da Feijoada** Rua Prudente de Morais 10. Usually served only on Saturdays, *feijoada* is offered seven days a week here, along with other traditional, moderately priced and extremely filling Brazilian dishes.

**Fontes** Rua Visconde de Pirajá 605. Inexpensive, yet unusual vegetarian dishes such as gnocchi made with manioc. On weekends, a hearty *feijoada* is served, featuring not a shred of meat.

**Garota de Ipanema** Rua Vinícius de Morais 49. Always busy, this bar entered the folk annals of Rio de Janeiro when the song *The Girl from Ipanema* was written here one night by the composer Tom Jobim. While certainly touristy (with unexceptional and overpriced food), there are few better places in Ipanema for a beer.

**Gula Gula** Rua Henrique Dumont 57. A good choice of reasonably priced and very tasty salads, grilled dishes and desserts makes this an Ipanema favourite – and in eleven other spots around the city. The set menu is R$35.

**Livraria da Travessa** Rua Visconde de Pirajá 572. Rio's best bookshop also has an excellent bistrot serving breakfast, sandwiches and cakes as well as full meals. The food is modern Brazilian in style, with Italian and other foreign touches, and the atmosphere unhurried, making it a perfect place for a break from Ipanema's main shopping area. There's another branch of the restaurant in the Shopping Leblon (p.127). Mon–Sat 9am–11pm, Sun noon–9pm.

**Porcão Ipanema** Rua Barão da Torre 218. Part of a reliable chain of *churrascarias* (there's a branch by Flamengo beach), this huge restaurant serves a *rodizio* of high-quality cuts of meat (R$67), including choices from the *mediterrâneo* salad bar.

**Satyricon** Rua Barão de Torre 192 ⓣ21/2521-0955. Mediterranean (in particular, Italian) seafood dishes are the house speciality, though there's also a range of interesting pasta choices, too. The ingredients are as fresh as can be and the (expensive) dishes beautifully presented, but the restaurant feels excessively formal.

**Via Farme** Rua Farme de Amoedo 47. Good Italian food, with the pizzas and seafood especially worth trying. Choose from an a/c room upstairs or open-air dining downstairs. While it's not cheap, *Via Farme* is reasonable for the area.

**Zazá Bistrô Tropical** Rua Joana Angélica 40 ⓣ21/2247-9101. Light-hearted, imaginative fusion cuisine based on familiar Brazilian, Peruvian, Thai, Indian, North African and European dishes. The colourful decor of the bistro, the terrace with street-life views, and the plush cushions and divans in the relaxing, dimly lit, first-floor living room make this a popular spot with both foreign tourists and trendy locals. Around R$70 per person. Evenings only.

# Leblon

Many of Leblon's restaurants are situated along the Avenida Ataúlfo de Paiva, where you'll also find many of the late-opening bars. Another popular destination for food and drink is Baixo Leblon, the area around Rua Dias Ferreira three or four blocks back from the beach, which boasts some of Rio's most chic restaurants and gets very lively on weekends. Locals of all ages also flock to Leblon's excellent **Cobal** market, at Rua Gilberto Cardoso, where the abundant and affordable *lanchonetes* serve everything from pizza and sushi to Brazilian regional fare until late into the night.

**Antiquarius** Rua Aristides Espínola 19 ⓣ21/2294-1049. While Rio has many fine Portuguese restaurants, this is the most elegant, and arguably its best. Especially good for seafood (and not just cod), but goat and wild boar are other fine choices, as are the rich desserts. Very expensive, and definitely no shorts allowed.

**Carlota** Rua Dias Ferreira 64 ⓣ21/2540-6821. Imaginative, expensive pan-Asian cooking with a few North African influences is served in a very pleasant atmosphere. The seven kinds of spring roll are especially noteworthy. Tues–Fri & Sun dinner only, Sat lunch & dinner.

**Celeiro** Rua Dias Ferreira 199. Rio's best *por kilo* restaurant, with an extremely varied salad bar, excellent bread and delicious desserts. Well worth the sometimes long wait for a table and the price, over twice the amount you'd normally expect to pay at a *por kilo* restaurant. Mon–Sat 10am–6pm.

**Nam Thai** Rua Rainha Guilhermina 95 ⓣ21/2259-2962. Rio's top pan-Asian restaurant, although the menu is predominantly Thai-influenced. The cauliflower-coriander soup is not to be missed. Mon dinner only, Tues–Sun lunch & dinner.

**Sushi Leblon** Rua Dias Ferreira 256. Superb (but expensive) sushi, along with other Japanese-inspired dishes such as grilled squid stuffed with shiitake, are offered at this stylish restaurant – a well-known meeting point of actors, models and artists. Mon–Sat dinner only; Sun 1.30pm–midnight.

**Zuka** Rua Dias Ferreira 233 ⓣ21/3205-7154. Food is grilled in front of your eyes, then doused in amazing sauces by a chef capable of creating unforgettable fusion cuisine: one of her specialities is seared tuna in a cashew crust, served with a potato-horseradish sauce. Around R$80 per person.

## Lagoa, Jardim Botânico and Gávea

Set slightly apart from Rio's main hotel and residential neighbourhoods, these are not obvious areas for restaurants; there are, however, a few enjoyable options following a morning strolling around the botanical gardens or after a night at the races.

The places listed below are marked on the map on pp.98–99.

**Bar Lagoa** Av. Epitácio Pessoa 1674, Lagoa. Tucked into the southern shores of the lake by Ipanema, this is the cheapest and oldest (dating back to 1934) of the waterside restaurants. *Bar Lagoa* is usually full of local families, attended to by white-coated waiters delivering beer, German sausage and enormous smoked pork chops. Arrive by 9pm and grab a seat on the patio, from where there's a good view of the lake.

**Couve-Flor** Rua Pacheco Leão 724, Jardim Botânico. The range and quality of the salads and hot meals make *Couve-Flor* one of Rio's most popular *por kilo* restaurants. Brazilian dishes predominate but there's much more besides, such as roast beef, duck, pasta and sushi. Don't forget to leave room for dessert: the guava cheesecake is remarkable. Located a short walk from the side entrance of the Jardim Botânico.

**Guimas** Rua José Roberto Macedo Soares 5, Gávea. A small, intimate restaurant near the Jockey Club with a happy atmosphere, catering for an arty and intellectual crowd. The food is delicious, and, unusually, the *couvert* (wholemeal bread and paté) worth the price. Try steak in a mustard and pear sauce and leave space for the delectable chocolate and cream pudding. Though this is one of Rio's best restaurants, it's not too expensive.

**Jockey Club** Praça Santos Dumont, Gávea. Palatial surroundings of a bygone era and good, reasonably priced Brazilian and international food in this restaurant overlooking the racetrack.

**Olympe** Rua Custódio Serrão 62, Jardim Botânico ⓣ21/2539-4542. Celebrity chef Claude Trosgros makes regular expeditions to the Amazon and other remote regions in search of new ingredients and ideas. Returning to Rio, he reinvents them, fusing them with classical and *nouvelle* styles of French cuisine. Expect unusual combinations such as foie gras with baked heart of palm and a *jabuticaba* sauce, and quails stuffed with *farofa* and coriander and served with an *açа* sauce. Try the *menu confiance* (tasting menu) at R$185. Somewhere for a special occasion – or to impress. Mon–Thurs & Sat dinner only, Fri lunch & dinner.

# Nightlife and entertainment

The best way to find out what's on and where in Rio is to consult *Caderno B*, a separate section of the *Jornal do Brasil*, which lists cinema, arts events and concerts; *O Globo*, too, details sporting and cultural goings-on in the city. *Veja*, Brazil's answer to *Newsweek*, includes a weekly Rio supplement with news of local events; the magazine reaches the newsstands on Sunday. Regardless, you should never find yourself stuck: there's no end of things to do come nightfall in a city whose name is synonymous with Carnaval (see pp.123–127), samba and jazz.

## Gay Rio

If you're expecting Rio's **gay nightlife** to rival San Francisco's or Sydney's, you may well be disappointed. In general, nightlife is pretty integrated, with gay men, lesbians and heterosexuals tending to share the same venues; apart from transvestites who hang out on street corners and are visible during Carnaval, the scene is unexpectedly discreet.

A good starting-point for an evening out is Rua Visconde Silva in Botafogo, which is lined with gay- and lesbian-oriented cafés, bars and restaurants that are liveliest on Friday and Saturday nights. The classic introduction to Rio's more traditional male gay society is *Le Ball*, a bar in the Travessa Cristiano Lacorte, just off Rua Miguel Lemos, at the Ipanema end of Copacabana. Opposite this, the *Teatro Brigitte Blair* hosts a gay transvestite show from around 10pm. Also in Copacabana, the bar and nightclub *Inc* (formerly called *Encontros*), at Praça Serzedelo Correia 15, next to Rua Siquera Campos, is open nightly and very popular, although mainly with tourists.

In Lapa, at Rua Mem de Sá 25, behind a pink facade under the Aqueduto da Carioca, the *Cabaré Casanova* is Rio's oldest and most interesting gay bar. In business since 1929, the *Casanova* features drag shows, lambada and samba music, with large ceiling fans to cool down the frenetic dancers. Very different, but also wild, are the gay nights on Saturdays at the *Cine Ideal* at Rua da Carioca 62, Centro (Ⓦwww.cineideal.com.br), an informal club that always draws huge crowds. The most popular gay nightclub is undoubtedly *Le Boy* at Rua Raul Pompéia 102 in Copacabana, towards Ipanema (Ⓣ21/2513-4993, Ⓦwww.leboy.com.br). Based in a former cinema, this huge club is open nightly apart from Mondays and features dancefloors, drag shows and much more besides.

The strip of beach between Rua Farme de Amoedo and Rua Teixeira do Melo in Ipanema is the best-known daytime gay meeting-point. For Ipanema's post-beach gay crowd, there's *Bofetada*, a bar and café at Rua Farme de Amoedo 87. The beach area in front of the *Copacabana Palace Hotel* is also frequented by gay bathers, and the café next door, *Maxims*, is a fun gay place to hang out. Nearby on Avenida Atlântica at the junction with Rua Siqueira Campos, is the Gay Kiosk Rainbow, a summertime **information point** for gay visitors – ask about circuit parties, usually held in Centro.

For information about Rio's gay balls, see the "Carnaval section", pp.123–127. If it's tours highlighting Rio's gay history you're after, Carlos Roquette, a rather dapper former federal judge turned tour guide, can help you to explore (see p.74). Useful websites on gay and lesbian Rio include Ⓦwww.riogayguide.com and Ⓦwww.riogaylife.com, while Ⓦwww.arco-iris.org.br offers more political and campaigning insights, but the website is only in Portuguese.

## Samba

**Samba** shows are inevitably tourist affairs, where members of Rio's more successful samba schools perform glitzy music and dance routines. Still, some are worth catching. Every Monday night at 10pm, the Beija Flor (Ⓣ21/791-1353) school performs at the Morro da Urca, halfway up Sugar Loaf mountain; the R$75 entrance fee includes dinner (from 8pm) and a well-executed show. For a less touristy experience of a samba school, you can easily arrange to watch rehearsals held (Aug–Feb; see box, p.125), mainly at various points in the Zona Norte.

For **clubs**, you're best off heading for Lapa (see p.120), where samba, *choro* and other local rhythms play to an enthusiastic and overwhelmingly local crowd.

### Discos

Although Rio's discos attempt sophistication, the end result is generally bland and unpalatable. Too often they pump out a steady stream of British and American hits, interspersed with examples from Brazil's own dreadful pop industry. The fashionable nightclubs that attract both *cariocas* and tourists are all found in the Zona Sul, but for a more authentically local experience you'd be far better off trying some of the music venues in Lapa (see below).

**00 Zero Zero** Av. Padre Leonel Franca 240, Gávea ⓣ21/2540-8041, ⓦwww.00site.com.br. A great nightclub experience, frequented by a rich and trendy crowd, where some of Brazil's top DJs play an eclectic mix of music. Like most places, it doesn't really get going until after 11pm, though on Sunday the best time to go is 7pm, immediately after returning from the beach. Entrance R$25–50.

**Bunker** Rua Raul Pompéia 94, Copacabana ⓣ21/3813-0300. Located near Ipanema, this spot is a favourite of students, young locals and tourists alike. Music varies with nights dedicated to drum 'n' bass, hip-hop and baile funk. Entrance R$20.

**Casa da Matriz** Rua Henrique Novaes 107, Botafogo ⓣ21/2266-1014. An extremely stylish, aggressively modern club that features more Brazilian music than is typical of discos – though this varies throughout the week. Entrance R$15–20.

**Club Electro** Rua das Marrecas 38, Lapa ⓣ21/2510-3230. With three dancefloors featuring *forró*, *zouk*, samba and much more, this is a good place to end up after some Lapa bar-hopping. Located in an old house that has been renovated to convey a rustic-chic air.

**Melt** Rua Rita Ludolf 47, Leblon ⓣ21/2249-9309. A stylish, hipster haven, with a pretty good range of music, such as samba-rock on Wednesday and drum 'n' bass on Friday. Entrance R$40.

**Pista 3** Rua São João Batista 14, Botafogo ⓣ21/2266-1014. Gritty urban sounds with an emphasis on hip-hop and funk, both local and foreign. Entrance R$15.

### Jazz and bossa nova

Rio has a tradition of **jazz music** that extends well beyond *The Girl from Ipanema*. That said, if you want to hear bossa nova in its natural setting, make for *Vinicius*, Rua Vinicius de Moraes 39, a tourist-oriented bar that hosts first-rate artists. At no. 199 of the same road is *Toca do Vinicius*, a shop specializing in bossa nova records, sheet music and books, where there are also occasional performances. For live **jazz**, check out the *Allegro Bistrô* in the Modern Sound record store, Rua Barata Ribeiro 502, Copacabana, which hosts regular early evening performances. Also worth a look is *Cais do Oriente*, at Rua Visconde de Itaboraí 8, a sprawling, late nineteenth-century mansion in Centro (ⓣ21/2203-0178, ⓦwww.caisdooriente.com.br; Tues–Sat noon–midnight); it's both a spectacularly stylish (though not very good) restaurant and a jazz club on some evenings (R$20 cover) with a beautiful open patio. A more unconventional setting, if not music, is offered by the *Maze Inn* (ⓣ21/2558-5547, ⓦwww.jazzrio.info), a *pousada* (see opposite) run by a British jazz enthusiast and located in the Favela Tavares Bastos. With spectacular views across Rio, this is a unique venue for monthly jazz evenings, attracting solid local performers and an audience of Zona Sul residents able to pay the R$35 cover.

### Live music in Lapa

Live-music options abound in **Lapa**, an atmospheric district that in the early decades of the twentieth century was synonymous with music, and since the 1990s has made a comeback as one of the city's best spots for *forró*, *choro*, samba, *axé*, and other kinds of fusion and Brazilian sounds. Although tourists are visiting Lapa in increasing numbers, the clubs and bars still mainly attract locals of all ages.

A good first place to make for is Rua Joaquim da Silva, where the packed bars pull in a mix of *bairro* residents and college students – if walking, take care not to veer onto the badly lit side-streets and be alert even when walking from just one block to the next. If you feel uncomfortable going alone – or simply want company – contact Rio Hiking (see p.113), which regularly takes small groups bar-hopping in Lapa (R$100 per person, excluding drinks).

The following bars and clubs in Lapa are all well worth checking out; cover charges vary from R$15 to R$25.

**Arcos de Velha** Av. Mem de Sá 21. Bands play *fundo do quintal* style – around a table rather than on stage.

**Asa Branca** Av. Mem de Sá 17 ☎21/2224-9358. A very informal dance-hall that's been immensely popular for decades, always attracting big-name samba, *choro* and, especially, *forró* bands. Tues–Sat from 10pm, also Sat 2–9pm.

**Café Cultural Sacrilégio** Rua do 81 ☎21/3970-1461. A small, old townhouse with a great atmosphere and killer *batidas*. The place attracts some great *choro* singers who perform classical works as well as samba and fusion rock-samba artists. Tues–Sat from 6pm until early morning.

**Carioca da Gema** Av. Mem de Sá 79 ☎21/2221-0043, ⓦwww.barcariocadagema.com.br. Stop in for very reliable *choro* and samba: look out for Teresa Cristina, one of Rio's greatest female samba voices, and her regular Friday-night appearance.

**Circo Voador** Rua dos Arcos s/n ☎21/2533-5873, ⓦwww.circovoador.com.br. Whereas other Lapa clubs have a very mixed-age clientele, with its programme of rap, funk and fusion samba-punk-rock, *Circo Voador*, set in a large circus tent, is dominated by young people who come to dance and discover new bands.

**Comuna do Semente** Rua Joaquim Silva 138 ☎21/2509-3591. Friday and Saturday nights are basically reserved for young samba artists, Monday to Thursday other traditional styles of Brazilian music, in particular *choro*, are performed. Daily from 8.30pm.

**Estrela da Lapa** Av. Mem de Sá 130 ☎21/2509-9626, ⓦwww.estreladalapa.com.br. Set in a beautifully restored, late nineteenth-century house, this rather upmarket and somewhat expensive spot offers *choro*, samba and MPB.

**Rio Scenarium** Rua do Lavradio 20 ☎21/2233-3239, ⓦwww.riodcenarium.com.br. Located in an old baronial townhouse filled with antiques, this is nonetheless one of the liveliest places in Lapa. More popular for its music than its dancing, visitors can sit on one of the several landings and watch the daily shows on the stage below. While specializing in *choro*, samba and local fusions are also performed. Reservations recommended on weekends.

**Teatro Odisséia** Av. Mem de Sá 66 ☎21/2266-1014. In an old theatre, featuring an eclectic mix of recorded and live Brazilian sounds from rock to samba. Thurs–Sat.

▲ Carioca da Gema

### Other live music

The largest music venue in Rio is Citibank Hall (ⓣ0300/789-6846, ⓦwww.citibankhall.com.br) in Barra da Tijuca, attracting **Brazilian and international stars**; programmes and tickets are available at ⓦwww.ticketmaster.com.br – expect to pay from R$75. Top Brazilian artists also perform at *Canecão* (ⓣ21/2105-2000, ⓦwww.canecao.com.br; from R$60), a venue next to the Rio Sul shopping centre in Botafogo. Despite the often-superb shows, the venue feels overly formal, with up to two thousand people seated at tables served by suited waiters.

## Brazilian dancing

Brazilians can dance, no question about that. The various regionally rooted traditions in folk music remain alive and popular, and if you'd like to get into a bit of Brazilian swing, go in search of the more traditional dance-halls.

### Gafieiras

**Gafieiras** originally sprang up in the 1920s as ballrooms for the poorer classes, and today they remain popular because they are places where *cariocas* can be assured of traditional dance music. The oldest surviving of them is *Estudantina*, Praça Tiradentes 79, Centro (Thurs 8pm–1am, Fri & Sat 10pm–4am), with decor recalling its roots dating back to 1928. Attracting locals and visitors of all ages, the live bands keep up to 1500 dancers moving. Also in Centro, but smaller and more traditional in style (with less modern music and dancers wearing formal attire) is *Elite*, hidden away behind the arches of a pretty pink nineteenth-century building at Rua Frei Caneca 4 (Fri & Sat 11pm–4am, Sun 9pm–3am). If you're looking for a traditional *gafieira* in Lapa, check out *Asa Branca* (see p.121); for the most beautiful of surroundings and lively Brazilian music, try *Botanic Dancing Brazil*, in the Jardim Botânico (Thurs–Sun from 10pm). All these *gafieiras* charge around R$15 entrance.

### Forró

For some accordion-driven swing from Brazil's Northeast, look for a **forró** club. The term *forró* (pronounced "fawhaw") originates from the English "for all", a reference to the dances financed by English engineering companies for their manual labour forces, as opposed to the balls organized for the elite. As drought and poverty have forced *nordestinos* to migrate south in search of employment in Brazil's large urban centres, so the culture has followed. In recent years, *forró* has gained a following across the class divide and can often be heard in *gafieiras* and even in the glitzy Zona Sul discos, though there are still some venues dedicated purely to it. At Rua Catete 235, in the *bairro* of Catete, *Forró Forrado* (Fri–Sun 10pm–late) has an excellent band and a mixed clientele that spans Rio's social scale. On Saturday nights, there's also the *Forró da Praia*, on Avenida Nações Unidas near the Botafogo recreation ground, *Forró do Leblon* at Rua Bartolomeu Mitre 630, and *Forró do Copacabana* at Av. Nossa Senhora de Copacabana 435.

## Classical music and exhibitions

Rio is the home of the **Orquestra Sinfônica Brasileira** – the orchestra of the Theatro Municipal (see p.91), which is also home to the city's **ballet** troupe and **opera** company. The theatre serves as the venue for almost everything that happens in terms of "high culture", offering four or five major productions a year. All kinds of events attract famous names, and prices are reasonable. For musical, photographic and fine-art **exhibitions**, keep an eye on the listings in the *Jornal do Brasil* or *Veja*.

The **Centro Cultural Banco do Brasil**, Rua Primeiro de Março 66, Centro (Tues–Sun 10am–9pm; ⓣ21/3808-2020, ⓦwww.bb.com.br/cultura), puts on an especially varied programme of exhibitions, as well as films, music and plays, often free. Situated in the grand former headquarters of the Banco do Brasil, the building has several exhibition halls, a cinema, two theatres, a tearoom and a restaurant. Also particularly worth checking out are the temporary exhibitions at the Instituto Moreira Salles (see p.108), Museu Chácara do Céu (see p.93) and the Museu Nacional das Belas Artes (see p.91).

### Film

Most European and American films are quickly released in Brazil and play with their original soundtracks. **Cinemas** are quite inexpensive (R$12–20) with *Jornal do Brasil* and the Rio supplement of the weekly magazine *Veja* listing what's on and where.

Rio hosts one of Latin America's most important international film festivals, the **Festival do Rio**, which takes place over two weeks in late September and early October and screens over four hundred films from dozens of countries in cinemas all over the city. For more information, contact the organizers at Rua Arnaldo Quintela 62, Botafogo (ⓣ21/2543-4968, ⓦwww.festivaldorui.com.br).

## Carnaval

**Carnaval** is celebrated in every Brazilian city, but Rio's party is the biggest and flashiest of them all. From the Friday before Ash Wednesday to the following Thursday, the city shuts up shop and throws itself into the world's most famous manifestation of unbridled hedonism. Carnaval's greatest quality is that it has never become stale, thanks to its status as the most important celebration on the Brazilian calendar, easily outstripping either Christmas or Easter. In a city riven by poverty, Carnaval represents a moment of freedom and release, when the aspirations of *cariocas* can be expressed in music and song. And at the end of the very intense long weekend, there's a brief collective hangover before attention turns to preparing for the following year's event.

### The background

The origins of Carnaval in Rio can be traced back to a fifteenth-century tradition of Easter revelry in the Azores that caught on in Portugal and was exported to Brazil. Anarchy reigned in the streets for four days and nights, the festivities often so riotous that they were formally abolished in 1843 – this edict was ignored, however, allowing street celebrations to stand out as the most accessible and widely enjoyed feature of Carnaval ever since. In the mid-nineteenth century, **masquerade balls** were first held by members of the social elite, while processions, with carriages decorated in allegorical themes, also made an appearance, thus marking the ascendancy of the procession over the general street melee. Rio's masses, who were denied admission to the balls, had their own music – *jongo* – and they reinforced the tradition of street celebration by organizing in *Zé Pereira* bands, named after the Portuguese tambor that provided the basic musical beat. The organizational structure behind today's samba schools (*escolas da samba*) is partly a legacy of those bands sponsored by migrant Bahian port workers in the 1870s – theirs was a more disciplined approach to the Carnaval procession: marching to stringed and wind instruments, using costumes and appointing people to coordinate different aspects of the parade.

## Carnaval dates

The four days of Carnaval for the next few years are as follows:

2010 Feb 13–16
2011 March 5–8
2012 Feb 18–21
2013 Feb 9–12

Music written specifically for Carnaval emerged in the early twentieth century, by composers such as Chiquinho Gonzaga, who wrote the first recorded samba piece in 1917 (*Pelo Telefone*), and Mauro de Almeida e Donga. In the 1930s, recordings began to spread the music of Rio's Carnaval, and competition between different samba schools became institutionalized: in 1932, the Estação Primeira Mangueira school won the first prize for its performance in the Carnaval parade. The format has remained virtually unchanged since, except for the emergence in the mid-1960s of the **blocos** or **bandas**: street processions by the residents of various *bairros*, who eschew style, discipline and prizes and give themselves up to the most traditional element of Carnaval – street revelry, of which even the principal Carnaval procession in the Sambódromo is technically a part.

## The action

Rio's street celebrations centre on the **evening processions** that fill **Avenida Rio Branco** (*metrô* to Largo do Carioca or Cinelândia). Be prepared for the crowds and beware of pickpockets: even though the revellers are generally high-spirited and good-hearted, you should keep any cash you take with you in hard-to-reach places (like your shoes), wear only light clothes and leave your valuables locked up at the hotel.

Most of what's good takes place along Avenida Rio Branco. The processions include samba schools (though not the best); *Clubes de Frevo*, whose loudspeaker-laden floats blast out the frenetic dance music typical of the Recife Carnaval; and the *Blocos de Empolgacão*, including the Bafo da Onça and Cacique de Ramos clubs, between which exists a tremendous rivalry. There are also *rancho* bands playing a traditional *carioca* carnival music that predates samba. See ⓦwww.rio-carnival.net for a complete schedule of events.

### Samba schools

The **samba schools**, each representing a different neighbourhood or social club, are divided into three leagues that vie for top ranking following the annual Carnaval parades. Division 1 (the top league) schools play in the Sambódromo, Division 2 on Avenida Rio Branco and Division 3 on Avenida 28 de Setembro, near the Maracanã.

Preparations start in the year preceding Carnaval, as each school mobilizes thousands of supporters to create the various parts of their display. A theme is chosen, music written and costumes created, while the dances are choreographed by the **carnavelesco**, the school's director. By December, rehearsals have begun and, in time for Christmas, the sambas are recorded and released to record stores.

The main procession of Division 1 schools – the **Desfile** – takes place on the Sunday and Monday nights of Carnaval week in the purpose-built **Sambódromo**, further along the avenue beyond the train station; the concrete structure is 1.7km long and can accommodate 90,000 spectators. The various samba schools – involving some 50,000 people – take part in a spectacular piece of theatre: no simple parade, but a competition between schools attempting to gain points from their presentation, which is a mix of song, story, dress, dance and rhythm. The schools pass through the Passarela da Samba, the Sambódromo's parade ground, and the judges allocate points according to a number of criteria. Each school must parade for between 85 and 95 minutes, no more and no less.

Regardless of the theme adopted by an individual samba school, all include certain basic elements within their performances. The **bateria**, the percussion section, has to sustain the cadence that drives the school's song and dance; the *samba enredo* is the music, the *enredo* the accompanying story or lyric. The **harmonia** refers to the degree of synchronicity between the *bateria* and the dance by the thousands of **passistas** (samba dancers); the dancers are conducted by the **pastoras**, who lead by example. The **evolução** refers to the quality of the dance, and the choreography is marked on its spontaneity, the skill of the *pastoras* and the excitement that the display generates. The costumes, too, are judged on their originality; their colours are always the traditional ones adopted by each school. The **carros alegóricos** (no more than 10m high and 8m wide) are the gigantic, richly decorated floats, which carry some of the **Figuras de Destaque** ("prominent figures"), amongst them the **Porta-Bandeira** ("flag bearer") – a woman who carries the school's symbol, a potentially big point-scorer. The **Mestre-Sala** is the dance master, also an important symbolic figure, whose ability to sustain the rhythm of his dancers is of paramount importance. The **Comissão da Frente**, traditionally a school's "board of directors", marches at the head of the procession, a role often filled these days by invited TV stars or sports teams. The bulk of the procession behind is formed by the **alas**, the wings or blocks consisting of hundreds of costumed individuals each linked to a part of the school's theme.

## Carnaval rehearsals

If you can't make Carnaval, give the shows put on for tourists in the Zona Sul a miss and get a taste of the **samba schools** at the *ensaios* (rehearsals) below. They take place at weekends from August to February: phone to confirm times and days. After New Year, Saturday nights are packed solid with tourists and prices triple. Instead, go to one on a midweek evening or, better still, on Sunday afternoon when there's no entrance fee and locals predominate.

Most of the schools are in distant *bairros*, often in, or on the edge of, a *favela*, but there's no need to go accompanied by a guide. It's easy, safe and not too expensive to take a taxi there and back (there are always plenty waiting to take people home). Of the schools, Mangueira is certainly the most famous; it has a devoted following, a great atmosphere and includes children and old people amongst its dancers. The gay-friendly Salgueiro has a more white, middle-class fanbase.

The Cidade do Samba (see p.90), a purpose-built arena and studio complex in Centro, is an even easier way of observing Carnaval preparations. All the Division 1 schools are represented here and their daily musical and dance demonstrations are produced for the public.

**Beija-Flor** Rua Pracinha Wallace Paes Leme 1652, Nilopolis ⓣ21/2253-2860, ⓦwww.beija-flor.com.br. Founded 1948; blue and white.

**Mangueira** Rua Visconde de Niterói 1072, Mangueira ⓣ21/2567-4637, ⓦwww.mangueira.com.br. Founded 1928; green and pink.

**Moçidade Independente de Padre Miguel** Rua Cel. Tamarindo 38, Padre Miguel ⓣ21/3332-5823. Founded 1952; green and white.

**Portela** Rua Clara Nunes 81, Madureira ⓣ21/3390-0471. Founded 1923; blue and white.

**Salgueiro** Rua Silva Telles 104, Tijuca ⓣ21/2238-5564, ⓦwww.salgueiro.com.br. Founded 1953; red and white.

In addition to a parade, every school has an **Ala das Baianas** – a procession of hundreds of women dressed in the flowing white costumes and African-style headdresses typical of Salvador – in remembrance of the debt owed to the Bahian emigrants, who introduced many of the traditions of the Rio Carnaval procession.

The **parade** of schools starts at 7.30pm, with eight Division 1 schools performing on each of the two nights, and goes on until noon the following day. Two stands (7 & 9) in the Sambódromo are reserved for foreign visitors and **seats** cost over R$150 per night. Though much more expensive than other areas, the seats here are more comfortable and have good catering facilities. Other sections of the Sambódromo cost from R$15 to R$60 and there are three seating options: the high stands (*arquibancadas*), lower stands (*geral*) and ringside seats (*cadeiras de pista*) – the last being the best, consisting of a table, four chairs and full bar service.

Unless you have a very tough backside, you will find sitting through a ten-hour show an intolerable test of endurance. Most people don't turn up until 11pm, by which time the show is well under way and hotting up considerably. **Tickets** are available from the organizers online (Ⓦwww.rio-carnival.net) or at premium prices from travel agents in Rio. Book well in advance, or try local travel agents who often have tickets available for a modest commission.

## Blocos

In whatever *bairro* you're staying there will probably be a **bloco** or **banda** – a small samba school that doesn't enter an official parade – organized by the local residents; ask about them in your hotel. These schools offer a hint of what Carnaval was like before it became regulated and commercialized. Starting in mid-afternoon, they'll continue well into the small hours, the popular ones accumulating thousands of followers as they wend their way through the neighbourhood. They all have a regular starting-point, some have set routes, others wander freely; but they're easy to follow – there's always time to have a beer and catch up later.

Some of the best *blocos* are: the Banda da Glória, which sets off from near the Estação Glória *metrô* station; the Banda da Ipanema (the first to be formed, in 1965), which gathers behind Praça General Osório in Ipanema; the Banda da Vergonha do Posto 6, starting in Rua Francisco Sá in Copacabana; and the Carmelitas de Santa Teresa, which gathers in the *bairro* of the same name. There are dozens of others, including several in each *bairro* of the Zona Sul, each providing a mix of music, movement and none-too-serious cross-dressing – a tradition during Carnaval in which even the most macho of men indulge.

## Carnaval balls

It's the **Carnaval balls** (*bailes*) that really signal the start of the celebrations – warm-up sessions in clubs and hotels for rusty revellers, which are quite likely to get out of hand as inhibitions give way to a rampant eroticism. The balls start late, normally after 10pm, and the continual samba beat supplied by live bands drives the festivities into the new day. At most of the balls, *fantasia* (fancy dress) is the order of the day, with elaborate costumes brightening the already hectic proceedings; don't worry if you haven't got one, though – just dress reasonably smartly.

You'll often have to pay an awful lot to get into these affairs, as some of the more fashionable ones attract the rich and famous. There's none grander than the Magic Ball held at the *Copacabana Palace Hotel* (Ⓣ21/2545-8790; see p.80) drawing the elite from across the world. For the privilege of joining in, expect to pay well over R$1000 – black tie or an extravagant costume is obligatory.

If you've got the silly costume but a little less money, other lavish balls worth checking out include the Pão de Açúcar, on the Friday before Carnaval, halfway up the famous landmark – spectacular views, exotic company, but well over R$200 a head and very snobby (Ⓣ21/3541-3737 for details). The Hawaiian Ball, hosted by the Rio Yacht Club, opens the season on the Friday of the week before Carnaval: it takes place around the club's swimming pool, amid lavish decorations, and is popular and expensive (about R$150); tickets are available from the Yacht Club, on Avenida Pasteur, a few hundred metres before the Sugar Loaf mountain cable-car terminus. On the same Friday, other big parties take place, with the Baile de Champagne and the Baile Vermelho e Preto being amongst the most important. The latter (the "Red and Black Ball") has developed a particular reputation as a no-holds-barred affair. Named after the colours of Rio's favourite football team, Flamengo, it's a media event with TV cameras scanning the crowds for famous faces – exhibitionism is an inadequate term for the immodest goings-on. In Leblon, the Monte Libano (Ⓣ21/3239-0032 for details) hosts a number of "last days of Rome" festivities – the Baile das Gatas, Baile Fio Dental, even Bum Bum Night – sexually charged exercises all, though safe to attend and reasonable at around R$50 a ticket. In recent years, the *Rio Scala* club at Av. Afrânio de Melo Franco 292, Leblon, has become an important centre for balls, each night of Carnaval hosting a different school of samba. To reserve a table (R$300), go to the box office (Ⓣ21/2239-4448) at least five days before the event. To stand (R$50), you can simply show up on the night.

There are a number of **gay balls**, too, which attract an international audience. The Grande Gala G is an institution, usually held in the *Help* disco on Copacabana's Avenida Atlântica. Another is the Baile dos Enxutos, hosted by the *Hotel Itália* on Praça Tiradentes, Centro.

# Shopping

It's not hard to find things to buy in Rio, but it's surprisingly difficult to find much that's distinctively Brazilian. Throughout the city are shops geared to tourists (most of which sell a similar line in semiprecious stones, mounted piranha fish and T-shirts), but the best shopping area is undoubtedly Ipanema, with a wealth of boutiques lining Rua Visconde de Pirajá and its side streets. Books and CDs make good purchases – sales assistants in music stores are usually delighted to offer recommendations and you'll be able to listen before you buy. Of Rio's **markets**, the so-called Hippie Market (see p.107) in Ipanema has nowadays become very touristy; much better is the Babilônia Feira Hype in Gávea (see p.108), the Mercado das Pulgas at Largo dos Guimarães in Ipanema (second Sat of the month 2–8pm; handicrafts), or the Feira de Antiguidades at Praça Santos (Sun 9am–5pm; bric-a-brac). For arts, crafts and food from Brazil's Northeast, there's nowhere better than the **Feira Nordestina** in the Zona Norte (see p.96).

## Shopping centres

Purpose-built, air-conditioned **shopping centres** – *shoppings* – have mushroomed in Rio during the last few decades. The largest, best known and most central is Rio Sul (Mon–Sat 10am–10pm, Sun 3–9pm), before the Pasmado Tunnel at the end of Botafogo. Inside, there are department stores, a supermarket and hundreds of fashion boutiques, record stores and places to grab a snack or meal. Slightly smaller is the newer and more stylish Shopping Leblon (Mon–Sat 10am–10pm, Sun 3–9pm), at the intersection

## Crafts

**Handicraft shops** are scattered all over Rio but, in general, are disappointing. Some good places do exist – though bear in mind that the items on sale are more likely than not to be from other parts of the country. The places listed below all have good stock at reasonable prices.

**Brasil & Cia** Rua Maria Qutéria 27, Ipanema. A range of carefully chosen ceramic, paper, textile and other crafts sourced from throughout the country.

**Casa de Artesanato do Estado do Rio** Rua Real Grandeza 293, Botafogo. Crafts from around the state of Rio, but the quality is unlikely to impress. Look for occasional interesting items of basketry and embroidery.

**Feira Nordestina** (see p.96) in the Zona Norte. Stalls selling all kinds of handicrafts, handmade household items, food and drink from Brazil's Northeast.

**Loja Artíndia** Museu do Índio, Botafogo (see p.104). The best place in the city for Amerindian crafts – an excellent selection of basketry, necklaces, feather items and ceramics, with the tribes and places of origin all clearly identified.

**Raiz Forte Produtos da Terra** Av. Ataulfo de Paiva 1160, Leblon. Specializing in crafts and popular art, including lithographs from Pernambuco.

**O Sol** Rua Corcovado 213, Jardim Botânico. A non-profit outlet selling folk art including basketware, ceramics and wood carvings.

**La Vereda** Rua Almirante Alexandrino 428, Largo dos Guimarães, Santa Teresa. One of the best handicraft shops, with a varied collection from all over Brazil (including work by local artists).

of avenidas Ataulfo de Paiva and Afrânio de Melo Franco. Other *shoppings* include the compact Shopping Gávea, Rua Marquês de São Vicente (Mon–Sat 10am–10pm), and the upmarket São Conrado Fashion Mall, Estrada da Gávea 899 (Mon–Thurs 10am–9pm, Fri & Sat 10am–11pm, Sun 3–9pm). Definitely worth seeking out is Originallis, which has branches at all of Rio's *shoppings*; Brazil's answer to the Body Shop or Lush, the chain sells natural soaps infused with essential oils – the colours and smells are fantastic.

### Fashion

Although not a shopping mall, Ipanema's Rua Visconde de Pirajá has similar stores to those found in the likes of Rio Sul and Shopping Leblon, while on the side roads are some more unusual boutiques. Brightly coloured and interesting designs of bags and other accessories are the hallmark of the Brazilian designer Gilson Martins; his shop is located at Rua Visconde de Pirajá 462, Ipanema. Havaiana sandals are easily found in Rio, though there are surprisingly few shops selling the brand's complete range. One that does is Ousadiario at Rua Farme de Amoedo 76, Ipanema.

### Music and books

**CDs** are a similar price in Rio as in either Europe or North America but make great souvenirs. Many stores still have old recordings available on vinyl at bargain prices. The largest music stores in Rio include Modern Sound at Rua Barata Ribeiro 502 (near the corner of Rua Santa Clara), Copacabana, and the Saraiva Megastore, Rua do Ouvidor 98, Centro (with a branch in Rio Sul).

Ipanema's Rua Visconde de Pirajá is home to several of Rio's better bookshops, with the largest and best being the Livraria da Travessa at no. 572, with a slightly larger branch in the Shopping Leblon (see p.127). Their English-language sections are small, but the shops have an excellent stock of art and other coffee-table books on Brazilian subjects. They also have a good selection of CDs, including many by Brazilian artists, as well as an excellent restaurant (see p.117). Another great place to browse is the Livraria Argumento at Rua Dias Ferreira 417, Leblon, where, apart from a good selection of titles, there's a café serving light meals and cakes; there's a branch of the bookshop in Copacabana, at Rua Barata Ribeiro 502. In Centro, the largest bookshop is the Saraiva Megastore (see opposite), though its stock, including its English-language section, is much more limited.



# Listings

**Airlines** Aerolíneas Argentinas ⓣ21/2242-7272 or 3398-3737; Air Canada ⓣ21/2220-5343; Air France ⓣ21/3212-1845 or 3398-3490; Alitalia ⓣ21/2292-4424 or 3398-3663; American Airlines ⓣ0800/789-7778; Avianca ⓣ21/2240-4413 or 3398-3145; British Airways ⓣ0300/789-6140 or 3398-3990; Continental Airlines ⓣ21/2531-1850 or 3398-3023; Delta Airlines ⓣ21/4003-2121; Gol ⓣ0800/701-2131; Iberia ⓣ21/2282-1336 or 3398-3164; Lan Chile ⓣ21/2240-9388 or 3398-3601; Lufthansa ⓣ21/2217-6111 or 3398-3855; Pluna ⓣ21/2240-8217 or 3398-2000; TAM ⓣ21/3212-9300 or 3398-2179; TAP–Air Portugal ⓣ0800/707-7787; United Airlines ⓣ0800/162-323 or 3398-2450; Varig ⓣ21/4003-7000.

**Airports** Santos Dumont ⓣ21/3814-7070; Tom Jobim International ⓣ21/3398-4526 or 3398-4527.

**Banks and exchange** Main bank branches are concentrated in Av. Rio Branco in Centro and Av. N.S. de Copacabana in Copacabana. Note that although most banks remain open until 4.30pm, you can usually exchange money only until 3pm or 3.30pm. There are ATMs located throughout the city.

**Car rental** Most companies are represented at the international airport and, in Centro, at Santos Dumont airport. In Zona Sul, they have offices in the following locations, all on Av. Princesa Isabel in Copacabana: Avis, at no. 150 ⓣ21/2542-3392; Budget, no. 350 ⓣ21/2295-8464; Hertz, no. 500 ⓣ21/2275-3245 or 0800/701-7300; Localiza-National, no. 214 ⓣ0800/99-2000; Unidas, no. 350 ⓣ21/2275-8496. With unlimited mileage and reasonably comprehensive insurance, prices start at about R$140 per day; you'll need a credit card to rent the vehicle. It's usually cheaper to reserve and pay in advance from abroad.

**Consulates** Argentina ⓣ21/2553-1646; Canada ⓣ21/2543-3004; Peru ⓣ21/2551-9596; UK ⓣ21/2555-9600; Uruguay ⓣ21/2552-6699; US ⓣ21/3823-2000; Venezuela ⓣ21/2551-5398.

**Dentists** Dentário Rollin, Rua Cupertinho Durão 81, Leblon ⓣ21/2259-2647; Clínica de Urgência, Rua Marquês de Abrantes 27, Botafogo ⓣ21/2226-0083; Sorriclin, Rua Visconde de Pirajá 207, Ipanema ⓣ21/2522-1220.

**Health matters** If you're unlucky enough to need medical treatment in Rio, forget about the public hospitals as they're extremely crowded and the level of treatment may be poor. You can, however, get excellent medical care privately: hospitals with good reputations include Hospital Samaritano, Rua Bambina 98, Botafogo (ⓣ21/2537-9722, ⓦwww.hsamaritano.com.br), and Hospital Copa D'Or, Rua Figueiredo de Magalhães 875, Copacabana (ⓣ21/2545-3600, ⓦwww.redelabsdor.com.br). Hotels will have lists of English-speaking doctors (ask for a *médico*), and your consulate should have a list of professionals who speak English.

**Laundry** All hotels have a laundry service, but these are expensive, while most hostels have laundry facilities. Good prices for service washes and dry cleaning are offered by Lavanderia Ipanema, Rua Farme de Amoedo 55, Ipanema (Mon–Sat 7.30am–9pm), and Lavakilo, Rua Almirante Gonçalves 50, Copacabana (Mon–Fri 7.30am–7.30pm & Sat 8am–5pm).

**Newspapers and magazines** Foreign-language newspapers and magazines are available in kiosks at junctions along Av. N.S. de Copacabana, Copacabana, on Rua Visconde de Pirajá in Ipanema, and along Av. Rio Branco in Centro. The *Herald Tribune* and the *Financial Times* are the most commonly available English-language newspapers, and *Time*, *Newsweek* and the *Economist* are also easy to find.

**Police** Emergency number ⓣ190. The beach areas have police posts located at regular intervals. The special Tourist Police are located at Av. Afrânio de Melo Franco (opposite the Teatro Casa Grande), Leblon (ⓣ21/3399-7170); they are helpful, speak English and efficiently process reports of theft or other incidents (open 24hr).

**Post offices** *Correios* are open Mon–Fri 8am–6pm, Sat 8am–noon. Main post offices are at Rua Primeiro do Março (corner of Rosario) in Centro; Av. N.S. de Copacabana 540 in Copacabana; Rua Visconde de Pirajá 452, Ipanema; Av. Ataúlfo de Paiva 822, Leblon.

**Public holidays** In addition to the normal Brazilian public holidays (see p.59), most things close in Rio on January 20 (Dia de São Sebastião) and March 1 (Founding of the City).

**Visa and tourist-card renewal** If you're going to stay in Brazil for over six months and need to extend your visa or tourist card, apply in person at the Polícia Federal's Registro de Estrangeiros, Av. Venezuela 2, Centro – just behind Praça Mauá (Mon–Fri 10am–4pm; ☎21/3263-3747).



# Rio de Janeiro state

It's easy to get out of Rio city, something you'll probably want to do at some stage during your stay. There are good **bus** services to all the places mentioned below, while the easiest trips are by ferry just across the bay to the **Ilha de Paquetá** – a car-free zone popular with locals – or to **Niterói**, whose Museu de Arte Contemporânea has become an essential sight for visitors to Rio. After that, the choice is a simple one: either head east along the **Costa do Sol** to Cabo Frio and Búzios, or west along the **Costa Verde** to Ilha Grande and Paraty; both coasts offer endless good beaches and little holiday towns, developed to varying degrees. Or strike off **inland** to Petrópolis and Teresópolis, where the mountainous interior provides a welcome, cool relief from the frenetic goings-on back in Rio.

Inter-urban buses fanning out to all points in the state make getting out of the city easy. If you plan on **renting a car** (see p.129 for addresses in Rio), this is as good a state as any to brave the traffic: the coasts are an easy drive from the city and stopping off at more remote beaches is simple; additionally, having your own wheels would let you get to grips with the extraordinary scenery up in the mountains.

## Ilha de Paquetá

The **ILHA DE PAQUETÁ** is an island of one square kilometre in the north of Guanabara Bay, an easy day-trip that is very popular with *cariocas* at weekends. It was first occupied by the Portuguese in 1565 and later was a favourite resort of Dom João VI, who had the São Roque chapel built here in 1810. Nowadays, the island is almost entirely given over to tourism. About two thousand people live here, but at weekends that number is multiplied several times by visitors from the city, here for the tranquillity – the only motor vehicle allowed is an ambulance – and the beaches, which, sadly, are now heavily polluted. Still, the island makes a pleasant day's excursion – with colonial-style buildings that retain a certain shabby charm – and the trip is an attraction in itself: if possible, time your return to catch the sunset over the city as you sail back. Weekdays are best if you want to avoid the crowds, or come in August for the wildly celebrated **Festival de São Roque**.

The best way to get around Ilha de Paquetá is by **bike**, which are available to rent very cheaply from alongside the ferry terminal; you can also take a ride in a small horse-drawn cart (*charrete*) or rent one by the hour if you want to take your time and stop off along the way – not that there's a great deal to see. When you disembark, head along the road past the Yacht Club and you'll soon reach the first

**beaches**: Praia da Ribeira and Praia dos Frades. Praia da Guarda, a few hundred metres on, has the added attraction of the *Lido* restaurant and the **Parque Duque de Mattos**, with its exuberant vegetation and panoramic views from the top of the Morro da Cruz, a hill riddled with tunnels dug to extract china clay.

**Ferries** for Paquetá leave from near Rio's Praça XV de Novembro in Centro (see p.131). There's a **tourist office** on Praia José Bonifácio, near the intersection with Rua Manuel de Macedo, on the opposite side of the island from the ferry landing.



# East: Niterói and the Costa do Sol

Across the strait at the mouth of Guanabara Bay lies **Niterói**, founded in 1573, and until 1975 the capital of the old state of Guanabara. Though lacking the splendour of the city of Rio, Niterói, with a population of half a million, has a busy commercial centre, an important museum and lively nightlife.

Buses out of Niterói head east along the **Costa do Sol**, which is dominated by three large **lakes** – Maricá, Saquerema and Araruama, separated from the ocean by long, narrow stretches of white sandy beach – and flecked with small towns bearing the same names as the lakes. Approximately 10km directly south of Niterói are a number of smaller lakes, too, collectively known as the **Lagos Fluminenses**, though these aren't really worth the effort to get to as the water is polluted. However, the evil-smelling sludge that surrounds them is purported to have medicinal properties. The main lakes are also muddy, but at least the water here is clean and much used for watersports of all kinds. The brush around the lakes is full of wildlife (none of it particularly ferocious), while the fresh, salty air makes a pleasant change from the city.

## Niterói

*Cariocas* have a tendency to sneer at **NITERÓI**, typically commenting that the only good thing about the city is its views back across Guanabara Bay to Rio. While it's certainly true that the vistas are absolutely gorgeous on a clear day, Niterói has more to offer, not least for admirers of the work of the architect **Oscar Niemeyer**.

### Arrival

You can reach Niterói from Rio either by car or **bus** across the fourteen-kilometre-long Ponte Costa e Silva, the Rio–Niterói bridge (from the Menezes Cortes *rodoviária*), or, much more fun, by catching the passenger **ferry** or **hydrofoil** from the docks, close to Praça XV de Novembro (see p.131). For the centre of Niterói, take a ferry or hydrofoil for "Estação Niterói" while a crossing to the Niemeyer-designed "Estação Charitas" is best for the beaches and the **Museu de Arte Contemporânea**. At both points, there are helpful **tourist information** offices (daily 9am–6pm).

### The City and around

Most visitors to Niterói head for the Oscar Niemeyer–designed **Museu de Arte Contemporânea** (Tues–Fri 10am–6pm, Sat & Sun 10am–7pm; R$4, free on Wed; Ⓦ www.macniteroi.com.br;), or MAC as it is more commonly called. Opened in 1996, and located just south of the centre on a promontory by the Praia da Boa Viagem, the flying-saucer-shaped building offers a 360-degree perspective of Niterói and across the bay to Rio. The museum boasts a worthy,

▲ Museu de Arte Contemporânea, Niterói

though hardly exciting, permanent display of Brazilian art of the second half of the twentieth century and also hosts temporary exhibitions, although these are rarely of much interest. Instead, the real work of art is the building itself, which even hardened critics of Niemeyer find difficult to dismiss out of hand. The curved lines of the building are simply beautiful, and the views of the headland, nearby beaches and Guanabara Bay as you walk around inside it breathtaking.

The museum aside, Niterói has a few other sights worth seeing, but they are spread across the city. In the centre, almost next to the ferry terminal, Niemeyer admirers will instantly recognize the flowing lines of his 2007 creation, the **Teatro Popular** (Ⓦwww.teatropopular.com.br). Also next to the ferry terminal is the **Mercado do Peixe** (Tues–Fri 6am–4pm, Sat & Sun 6am–noon), the main fish market for Rio. As well as seeing an incredible variety of seafood, you can also eat here – there are some forty restaurants of various sizes serving delicious fish creations.

A short distance southwest of the centre, the **Ilha da Boa Viagem** (April–Dec, fourth Sun of each month, 1–5pm), connected to the mainland by a causeway leading from Vermelha and Boa Viagem beaches, offers yet more excellent views across to Rio. On the island, guarding the entrance to the bay, are the ruins of a fort, built in 1663, and opposite there's a small chapel dating from the seventeenth century.

Niteroí's beaches are every bit as good as those of Rio's Zona Sul. **Praia de Jurujuba**, long and often crowded, is reached from the centre along the beautiful bayside road by bus #33 ("via Fróes"). On the way, it's worth taking a look at the church of **São Francisco Xavier**, a pretty colonial structure said to have been built in 1572. The church is open rather irregularly, but the priest lives next door and will open it up on request.

A short distance southeast along the coast, through Jurujuba, is the **Fortaleza de Santa Cruz** (Tues–Sun 9am–4pm), dating from the sixteenth century and still in use as a military establishment. As the nearest point across the bay to Rio's Sugar Loaf mountain, the views are particularly good from here. If you have time, also check out the **Museu de Arqueologia de Itaipu** (Wed–Sun 1–5pm), in the ruined eighteenth-century Santa Teresa convent near Itaipu beach, for its collection of ceramics and other artefacts excavated from ancient burial mounds. Around here, to the east of Niterói, beyond the bay, there are numerous **restaurants, bars and hotels**, all of which fill up with *cariocas* at weekends.

### Eating

With the notable exception of the Mercado do Peixe (see opposite), Niterói cannot claim to have any particularly outstanding **places to eat**. But if fish (or a *lanchonete*) doesn't appeal, worth considering are *Coelho á Caçarola* at Av. Central 20, in Itaipu (closed Mon–Wed), which has some 25 rabbit dishes on its menu, or *Verdanna Grill* at Av. Quintino Bocaiúva 603 near the Estação Charitas ferry terminal, the best place in town to satisfy a meat craving.

## Saquarema

**SAQUAREMA**, 100km east of Rio, is a small town in a beautiful natural setting, squeezed between the sea and its sixteen-kilometre-long lagoon, retaining vestiges of its origins as a fishing village. Local anti-pollution legislation means that the environment still sustains much wildlife, including the *microleão* monkey, which you may be able to glimpse on a walk into the nearby forests. Saquarema has a healthy agricultural sector, too, based on fruit cultivation, and orchards surround the town. The main business nowadays, though, is holiday making: you'll find holiday homes, arts and crafts shops and young surfers here in abundance. Saquarema is widely rated as second only to Florianópolis (see p.652) as Brazil's surfing capital, and the **Praia de Itaúna**, 3km from town, is a favourite with surfers, who gather every year for the National Championship in mid-May. A strong undertow makes its waters potentially dangerous for the casual swimmer, so if you want to swim, head instead for the **Praia da Vila**, where the seventeenth-century church, Nossa Senhora de Nazaré (daily 8am–5pm), stands on the rocky promontory. For fishing, the **Praia de Jaconé** is a popular haunt, stretching 4km west of Saquarema.

If you're looking for somewhere to stop awhile, there's a lot to recommend Saquarema: a relaxed atmosphere, plenty of bars and restaurants, and plenty of action at the weekend. A good, inexpensive **place to stay** fairly near the centre of town is the *Casa de Nasher*, Rua Maximo Fidelis 1717, Praia de Boqeirão (Ⓣ22/9827-5141, Ⓔnasher53@gmail.com; ❸), the cheerful English owner offering simple, comfortable rooms just metres from the beach, and a large pool. For a beachside hotel, rather than a B&B, the *Maasai*, Travessa Itaúna 17, Praia de Itaúna (Ⓣ22/2651-1092, Ⓦwww.maasai.com.br; ❺), has attractive grounds (including a pool) and spacious rooms. Set amidst ten hectares of lush farmland, a twenty-minute shuttle-bus ride away from the beaches, is the *Hotel Fazenda Sítio Nosso Paraíso*, Estrada do Rio Seco 115 (Ⓣ22/9969-1969, Ⓦwww.nosso-paraiso.net; ❻ half-board); the ten rooms all have private bathroom and verandas, while meals – using the farm's produce – are taken at a communal table. Other facilities include a bar, swimming pool and sauna.

## São Pedro da Aldeia

The countryside east of Saquarema is one of Brazil's most important salt-producing regions, and the windmills that pull the saline solution up to the surface dominate the skyline. At the northeast end of the Lagoa de Araruama, the small town of **SÃO PEDRO DA ALDEIA**, on the way to Cabo Frio, is built around a Jesuit church and mission house (Mon–Fri 8am–noon & 2–5pm, Sat & Sun 8am–noon), which date back to 1617. Perched on a hill above the shores of the lake, the town provides a marvellous view over the saltpans – arranged juxtaposed like a great patchwork quilt – and surrounding area.

The cheapest **pousada** in town, located beside an attractive lagoon, is the *Aldeia dos Ventos*, Rua João Martins 160 (ⓣ22/2621-2919; ❸), with very basic rooms. It's worth paying more, however, for the colonial-style *Pousada Ponta da Peça*, 5km from town on the Praia do Sudoeste (ⓣ22/2621-1181, ⓦwww.pontadapeca.com.br; ❹), for its well-appointed rooms, pretty garden with a pool, and stunning views across the lagoon and surrounding countryside. Excellent fish dishes can be had at the *Restaurante Vovó Chica* at Av. Getúlio Vargas 32.

## Cabo Frio

During summer, and especially at weekends, **CABO FRIO** is at a pitch of holiday excitement, generated by the out-of-towners who come here to relax in the fresh sea breezes. The town was founded in the late sixteenth century, but it was only really in the twentieth century that it developed, thanks to the salt and tourist industries. Built around sand dunes, there are **beaches** everywhere in Cabo Frio – indeed, this is the only attraction, since the town is both extremely ugly and poorly planned, but it's a relaxed place and the bars are full of happy holiday-makers at night.

The closest beaches to town are the small **Praia do Forte**, near the centre, with its fort of **São Mateus** (daily 8am–6pm) built by the French in 1616 for protection against pirates, and the larger, more popular **Praia da Barra**. Six kilometres north in the direction of Búzios, near Ogivas, lies **Praia do Peró**, a good surfing spot, peaceful and deserted on weekdays, and further on is the small **Praia das Conchas**, with its sand dunes and clear, calm, blue waters.

### Practicalities

Cabo Frio has excellent **bus** connections to and from Rio, São Paulo, Belo Horizonte and Petrópolis as well as up and down the coast; it's a three-kilometre walk from the station to the centre, along Avenida Júlia Kubitschek. There are plenty of **hotels** and **pousadas** in and around town, though during summer weekends it can be impossible to find a room. The **tourist office** at Praça Cristóvão Colombo near the Praia do Forte (Mon–Fri 8am–6pm, Sat & Sun 9am–6pm; ⓣ22/2647-6227) can help find a room. The lowest-priced *pousadas*, all offering pretty basic accommodation, are in the centre on ruas Jorge Lóssio and José Bonifácio; the best ones include *Porto Fino*, on the former, at no. 160 (ⓣ22/2643-6230; ❹), and *Cochicho do Xandico* at no. 224 (ⓣ22/2643-2525; ❹). Most hotels, and the *pousadas* with better facilities, however, are concentrated along the beaches. Praia do Peró boasts Cabo Frio's most expensive hotel, the well-appointed *La Plage* (ⓣ22/2643-1746, ⓦwww.laplage.com.br; ❻), along with the more attractive *Quintais das Dunas* (ⓣ22/2643-3894; ❺). There's also a very popular **youth hostel** at Rua Goiás 266 (ⓣ22/2644-3123, ⓦwww.perohostel.com.br; ❺), charging R$40 in a dorm.

## Arraial do Cabo

Six kilometres south of Cabo Frio, **ARRAIAL DO CABO** nestles amongst more sand dunes, surrounded by hills. The **beaches** around Arraial do Cabo are some of the most beautiful in the state and are usually packed in high season. Praia dos Anjos is perfectly fine considering the area behind it is so built up, though you'd do much better by walking (15min) along a path over a steep promontory to the unspoilt Praia do Forno. A boat ride is required to reach the stunning Praia do Pontal and the **Ilha de Cabo Frio**, a small, pristine island with powdery white beaches, sand dunes and superb views from its 390-metre peak (boats leave from Praia dos Anjos and charge around R$30 per person for a four-hour excursion). Another attractive beach is Prainha, which has the advantage of shade but can get crowded as it's easily reached by car. Even so, the water is beautiful and it's easy to ignore the people around you.

Arraial do Cabo is a much more attractive place to stay than overdeveloped Cabo Frio, but has little in the way of budget **accommodation**. Your best bet is to make for Praia dos Anjos: the *Estalagem do Porto* (Ⓣ22/2622-2892, Ⓦwww.estalagemdoporto.com.br; ❺) is a comfy place with rooms sleeping up to six people; *Capitão n'Areia* (Ⓣ22/2622-2720, Ⓦwww.capitaopousada.com.br; ❹) is a similar but rather prettier *pousada*, with the added attraction of a pool. Also at Praia dos Anjos, there's an excellent **youth hostel** at Rua Bernardo Lens 145 (Ⓣ22/2622-4060, Ⓦwww.marinadosanjos.com.br), with dorms (R$40) as well as private rooms that sleep two people (members ❸, non-members ❹).

## Búzios

**ARMAÇÃO DOS BÚZIOS**, or **Búzios** as it's more commonly known, is the kind of place you either love or hate: if a crowded resort full of high-spending beautiful people is your thing, then you're sure to fall for this peninsula. Immensely scenic, it's a bit like taking a step out of Brazil and into an upscale Mediterranean resort: Armação, the main settlement, is built in a vaguely colonial style, its narrow cobbled streets are lined with restaurants, bars and chic boutiques, and even the surrounding landscape appears more at home on the Med than in Brazil. Búzios has been nicknamed "Brazil's St Tropez", and it comes as little surprise to find that it was "discovered" by none other than Brigitte Bardot, who stumbled upon it by accident while touring the area in 1964. Despite being transformed overnight from humble fishing village to playground of the rich, Búzios didn't change much until some serious property development took hold in the 1980s. Now, during high season, the population swells from 22,000 to well over 150,000, and the fishing boats that once ferried the catch back to shore take pleasure-seekers beach-hopping and scuba diving. Outside of this period, though, it's hard not to be taken in by the peninsula's sheer beauty, with March, April and May the perfect time to visit, as tourists are relatively few, prices low and the weather pretty perfect.

Direct **buses** run to Búzios from Rio at least seven times a day, or every fifteen minutes from Cabo Frio, a bumpy fifty-minute ride along a cobbled road.

### Accommodation

**Accommodation** in Búzios is fairly expensive, and in high season (Dec–Feb) reservations are essential, although the tourist offices will do their best to help you find a room in one of the resort's 300-plus hotels and *pousadas*. If nothing's available in Búzios, you might consider staying in Cabo Frio, where rooms are cheaper and usually easier to come by. The lower-priced *pousadas* can be found in or near Armação or Ossos; they're generally the nicest, too, as well as being very friendly and mainly owned and run by Argentines, who have been an important presence in Búzios since the 1960s – even today making up two-thirds of tourists.

**Búzios Central Hostel** Av. José Bento Ribeiro Dantas 1475, Armação Ⓣ22/2623-9232, Ⓦwww.buzioscentral.com.br. While the double rooms are small and the dorms (R$40) equally cramped, the pleasant common areas and general atmosphere makes this one of the best HI-affiliated youth hostels in Brazil. ❹

**Casa Búzios** Rua Morro do Humaitá, Casa 1, Armação Ⓣ22/2623-7002, Ⓦwww.respinger.jimdo.com. With just five rooms, this is more a luxurious B&B than a *pousada*. The resident French owner is very welcoming, providing breakfast at any time of the day as well as offering evening meals. Located just moments from the seafront, a 10min walk from Rua das Pedras, there's a pool, and an attractive garden with ocean view. ❺

**Hibiscus Beach** Rua 1, Praia de João Fernandes Ⓣ22/2623-6221, Ⓦwww.hibiscusbeach.com.br. Spacious bungalows, each with a small terrace and wonderful sea views, are the order of the day at this welcoming British-owned and -run *pousada*. There's a good-sized pool, and the area's best snorkelling beach is very close, while Armaçao's nightlife is a 5min taxi ride (or half-hour walk) away. 6

**Morombo** Av. José Bento Ribeiro Dantas 1242, Armação ⓣ22/2623-1532. An extremely hospitable Argentine owner, good rooms and an attractive terrace make this an appealing place to stay. Located on the waterfront road leading to Ossos. 4

**Pérola Búzios Design** Av. José Bento Ribeiro Dantas 222, Armação ⓣ22/2620-8507, ⓦwww.perolabuzios.com.br. All the facilities you'd expect of a luxury hotel, including stylish modern furniture, a fitness centre and spa, and a large, beautiful pool. Although there's no sea view, the hotel is located just metres from Rua das Pedras. 8

**Santa Fé** Praça Santos Dumont 300, Armação ⓣ22/2623-6404, ⓦwww.pousadasantafe.com. Rooms are simple and small and the staff rather unfriendly, but the lounge is attractive and it's right in the centre of Armação. Despite its flaws, it's good value and very popular thanks to its proximity to Búzios's nightlife. 5

**Solar do Peixe Vivo** Rua José Bento Ribeiro Dantas 999, Armação ⓣ22/2623-1850, ⓦwww.solardopeixevivo.com.br. At this friendly, relaxed place, the guest rooms, in cabins in the garden, are simple but spacious; there's a pool, and the beach is directly across the road. The main reception building is notable for being one of the oldest structures in Búzios. 6

## The town and beaches

Búzios consists of three main settlements, each with its own distinct character. **Manguinos**, on the isthmus, is the main service centre with a tourist office (24hr; ⓣ0800/24-9999), a medical centre, banks and petrol stations. Midway along the peninsula, linked to Manguinos by a road lined with brash hotels, is **Armação**, an attractive village where cars are banned from some of the cobbled roads. Most of Búzio's best restaurants and boutiques are concentrated here, along with some of the resort's nicest *pousadas*, and there's also a helpful tourist office on the main square, **Praça Santos Dumont** (daily 9am–8pm; ⓣ22/2623-2099). A fifteen-minute walk along the Orla Bardot that follows the coast from Armação, passing the lovely seventeenth-century **Igreja de Nossa Senhora de Sant'Ana** on the way, brings you to **Ossos**, the oldest settlement, comprised of a pretty harbour, a quiet beach (though don't swim in the polluted water) and a few bars, restaurants and several *pousadas*.

Within walking distance of all the settlements are beautiful white-sand **beaches**, 27 in total, cradled between rocky cliffs and promontories, and lapped by crystal-clear waters. A good way to get oriented is to hop on the **Búzios Trolley** (9am, noon & 3pm; 2hr; R$40 including drinks and snacks) at Praça Santos Dumont, which goes to twelve beaches and two lookout points and offers an English-language commentary on the peninsula's vegetation, micro-climate and history. The beaches are varied, with the north-facing ones having the calmest and warmest seas, while those facing the south and east have the most surf. Though the beaches at Búzios' urban centre of Armação look good, the water is polluted and swimming should be avoided; a short distance to the northeast, however, are the very clean waters of the small, rather isolated and extremely picturesque beaches of **Azeda** and **Azedinha** as well as the rather larger **João Fernandes**, the best place around here for snorkelling. Further east is **Praia Brava**, bordering a fine, horseshoe-shaped bay that's rarely over-crowded. On the north of the peninsula, to the west of Armação, is the **Praia da Tartaruga**, where the water is pristine and, apart from some bars, there are few buildings. South of Armação, the lovely bay of **Praia da Ferradura** is quite built up (and consequently crowded), but further out is the appealing **Praia de Tucuns**, a long stretch of sand that attracts surprisingly few people. Apart from walking, you can get from beach to beach by minivan (R$2) or taxi (rarely more than R$15). Once at the beaches, you can rent kayaks or *pedalos*, or indulge in a little windsurfing. Several dive operators, based in Armação, lead scuba trips to the Ilha Âncoa (R$200 for two dives) – try Casamar, based at Rua das Pedras 241 (Ⓣ22/2623-2441, Ⓦwww.casamar.com.br). Alternatively, the dive operators rent snorkelling equipment (R$15 a day) for use at Praia João Fernandes.

## Eating

With few exceptions, **restaurants** are, predictably, expensive. The best places to eat, including those listed below, are in Armação, especially along Rua das Pedras and its extension, Avenida José Bento Ribeiro Dantas. Much less expensive options include some excellent *por kilo* restaurants in the town centre, especially on Rua Manoel Turíbio de Farias, which runs immediately parallel to Rua das Pedres. Cheapest of all, and often excellent, are the beachside *barracas* selling oysters and grilled fish.

**Acquarello** Rua das Pedras 130. An elegant (and expensive) Italian restaurant, with a menu that includes some unusual dishes, such as shrimp flambéed in cognac with a tomato-curry sauce.

**Bananaland** Rua Manoel Turíbio de Farias 50. One of the best *por kilo* restaurants in Búzios, and one of the cheapest for a solid meal; the choice among the buffet of salads and hot dishes is outstanding.

**Bar do Zé** Rua Orla Bardot 382. Celebrities from Rio congregate here: the food's perfectly fine (and, naturally, very expensive) but that's hardly the point of this place to see and be seen.

**Boom** Rua Manoel Turíbio de Farias 110. A superior *por kilo* restaurant with a good range of hot Brazilian (especially from Minas Gerais) dishes, salads, grilled fish, sushi and *churrasco* served in an attractive modern setting.

**Buzin** Rua Manoel Turíbio de Farias 273. The extensive and sophisticated range of dishes at this pleasant and moderately priced *por kilo* restaurant includes salads, seafood and excellent Argentine beef.

**Chez Michou Crêperie** Rua das Pedras 90. Thanks to its open-air bar, cheap drinks and authentic crêpes, this has long been Armação's most popular hangout. Open until dawn, when it serves breakfast to the patrons pouring out of the nearby clubs.

**Da Vinci** Rua das Pedras 286. The best pizzeria in town, with wood-burning ovens and some 25 varieties of rather expensive pizzas to choose from.

**Estância Don Juan** Rua das Pedras 178. An airy Argentine restaurant serving first-rate meat to a demanding (mainly Argentine) clientele. If cuts of beef mean little to you, opt for the *bife de chorizo*, the Argentine standard.

**Mil Frutas** Orla Bardot 362. By far the best of numerous ice-cream places, offering flavours both familiar and exotic – from *jabuticaba* to "Romeu e Julieta" (guava and cream).

**Pizzeria Capricciosa** Av. José Bento Ribeiro Dantas 500. The trendiest (and most expensive) pizzeria in Búzios, with wonderful ocean views but strangely disappointing food, not least the quality of the all-important pizza dough.

**Samsara** Rua Santana Maia 684, just off Rua das Pedras. This inexpensive vegetarian restaurant offers an excellent lunch buffet of hot and cold dishes and à la carte dining in the evening, featuring interesting pasta offerings from the Italian chef that make use of fresh, organic produce.

**Sawasdee** Av. José Bento Ribeiro Dantas 422. Excellent, spicy Thai food based around vegetables and seafood. One of the best creations is "Khao Tom", a delicious spicy shellfish risotto; the steamed filet of sole in a tamarind sauce is also excellent. Although quite expensive, most of the dishes are suitable for two people.

## Nightlife

**Nightlife** gets going at around 11pm and continues until dawn and is largely limited to eating, drinking and people watching along Rua das Pedras. It's impossible to exaggerate how crowded Armação gets in January and February, but even in the off-season Rua das Pedras is quite lively at weekends at night. The *Pátio Havana*, a rather upscale restaurant and bar at Rua das Pedras 101, is well worth checking out for the first-rate **jazz** artists from Rio, São Paulo and abroad who play there.

Strangely, nightclubs have only recently reached Búzios, but there are now several along Rua das Pedras and the Orla Bardot. Open from December to March, they easily match the best in Rio, with similar funk, hip-hop, pop and occasional Brazilian offerings. Popular with *carioca* tourists is *Privilege* at Orla Bardot 500

(Fri & Sat), though, while twice as expensive, the Ibiza-based club *Pacha*, at Rua das Pedras 151 (Fri & Sat), has become the place for seriously trendy club-goers. There's an often-raucous atmosphere in *Zapata* at Orla Bardot 352 (Thurs, Fri & Sat), with dancers fuelled by the free beer until 4am.

If you're after more traditional Brazilian music, make for the *Cachaçaria do Solar* at Orla Bardot 994, where you can expect mellow guitar rhythms. Located just out of the centre of Armação, this tastfully decorated bar, in one of Búzios' very few remaining colonial-era houses, offers a vast range of *cachaças* sourced from throughout Brazil, a good choice of *cachaça*-based *batidas*, fruit juices and tasty snacks.

### Northeast to Campos

If you're not yet tired of **beaches**, you'll find more beautiful examples around the pretty colonial village of Barra de São João and Rio das Ostras, an hour or so up the coast. Near the latter, the iodized waters of the **Lagoa da Coca-Cola** (yes, really) boast more medicinal qualities – everyone must be very healthy in this neck of the woods. If you want to stay round here, you'll find *pousadas* in both these places, though there's been much uncontrolled development along this stretch of coast, leading to pretty hideous results.

The next town of any size is the extremely ugly **Macaé**, beyond which the main road heads northeast, inland through very attractive rolling countryside to **CAMPOS**, on the River Paraíba some 50km before it flows into the sea. Predominantly a sugar-cane-processing town, its primarily agro-industrial nature makes it a less than attractive target; if you're travelling from Cabo Frio or Búzios north to Espírito Santos or Bahia, your best best is to take a bus to Campos where you'll be able to pick up a connection without much delay.

## West: the Costa Verde

The mountainous littoral and calm green waters of the aptly named **Costa Verde** ("Green Coast") provide a marked contrast to the sand and surf of the coastline east of Rio. One of Brazil's truly beautiful landscapes, the Costa Verde has been made much more accessible by the **Rio–Santos BR-101 Highway** – something, however, that has led to an increase in commercial penetration of the region. The fate of this 280-kilometre stretch of lush vegetation, rolling hills and tropical beaches hangs in the balance between rational development and ecological destruction, and so far the signs augur badly. Ecologists warn that fish stocks in the Bay of Sepetiba, which covers almost half the length of the Costa Verde, are in constant danger of destruction because of pollution.

There are two ways to reach the Costa Verde from Rio. By **car**, drive through the Zona Sul by way of Barra da Tijuca, to Barra de Guaratiba; alternatively, from Rio's *rodoviária*, take one of the **buses** that leave the city by way of the Zona Norte and follow the BR-101 to Itacuruçá and beyond.

### Mangaratiba

Muddy beaches and the incongruous industrial presence of the nearby Terminal de Sepetiba put off many people stopping at **MANGARATIBA**, which lies 25km west of Itacuruçá along the BR-101. Even so, the town's immediate setting is attractive, with a mountain backdrop, a beautiful bay in front with fishing boats at anchor and a late eighteenth-century church dominating the main square.

## The "Green" Coast?

There's no doubt that the Costa Verde is one of Brazil's most beautiful stretches of coast, so it's not surprising that so many hotel and holiday-home complexes are appearing on the hillsides and in the picturesque coves. What is incredible, however, is that the coast was chosen as the location of two constructions with the potential to cause the most environmental destruction – an oil terminal and a nuclear power plant.

The Petrobrás **oil terminal** is, at least, out of sight, located 25km east of Angra dos Reis, so you only need contemplate the damage that an oil spill could wreak on this ecologically fragile stretch of coast when you pass the barrack-like housing complexes for the Petrobrás workers on the BR-101.

Perhaps more worrying are the **nuclear power plants**, Angra-1 and Angra-2, some 40km west of Angra. The project was directly managed by the Brazilian military, and it's difficult to imagine a more insane place to put a nuclear reactor. Not only would there be enormous difficulties should an emergency evacuation be necessary, as the mountains here plunge directly into the sea, but in addition the plant is in an earthquake fault zone, in a cove that local Indians call *Itaorna*, the Moving Rock.

The safety record of Angra-1 has been under particular scrutiny, and since 1985 it has been shut down for unspecified repairs over twenty times. Officials insist that there have been no radiation leaks beyond the plant, but environmentalists, who say there may be cracks in the reactor's primary container system, want the entire complex closed for good. The future, however, looks certain: it would be humiliating to abandon the project – and there would be huge problems in decommissioning the plant. In any case, the plants supply about half the electrical power used in the state of Rio de Janeiro, a figure that is set to increase greatly when work on a long-delayed third reactor (Angra-3) is completed in 2014.

Should you want to stop by the plant, the **visitors' centre** offers a predictably professional public-relations show (Mon–Fri 8.30am–4.30pm, Sat & Sun 8.30am–3pm).

Five **buses** a day run from Rio to Mangaratiba – at 5.30am, 9am, 12.30pm, 3pm and 6.45pm – and if you catch the earliest bus, you'll make the daily ferry that sails from Mangaratiba to Ilha Grande (see p.140). Nevertheless, if you do need to stay, there are a couple of **hotels** in town, such as the very basic *Rio Branco* on the main square (❸) and the air-conditioned *Pensão do Almir* on the road leading to the hospital (❹). If you head from the main square along the seashore, you'll find several good fish **restaurants**.

## Angra dos Reis

From Mangaratiba, the road continues to hug the coast as it wends its way westwards, rising and falling between towering green-clad mountains and the ocean. Roughly 60km west of Mangaratiba lies the shabby and utterly unprepossessing little town of **ANGRA DOS REIS**. The lands around here were "discovered" by the navigator André Gonçalves in 1502, though it wasn't until 1556 that a colonial settlement was established. The port first developed as an entrepôt for the exportation of agricultural produce from São Paulo and Minas Gerais in the seventeeth century. Fifteen slave-worked sugar refineries dominated the local economy, which, with the abolition of slavery at the end of the nineteenth century, suffered a dramatic collapse. The 1930s saw the economy regenerated, with the construction of a new port, and shipbuilding remains an important local trade – although today it's off-shore oil that is the mainstay of the local economy.

For those not involved in the oil industry, the main reason to come here is to get out to the thirty or so local islands in the bay. Numerous leisurely **boat and**

**fishing trips** are on offer, and most yachts have a bar at which you can fill the time between stops for swimming at beaches penned-in between clear waters and tropical forest; visiting **Gipóia** by boat, for instance, allows you a couple of hours to splash about and get something to eat in the *Luiz Rosa* bar – all together, a very relaxing excursion. Various companies offer excursions, so it's best to ask at the **tourist information office** (daily 8am–6pm; ⓣ24/3367-7855) in Largo do Lapa, right across from the bus station and next to the **Cais de Santa Luzia**, from where the boats depart. Trips can also be arranged on the quay with independent operators, but check on the noticeboard for those boat owners who have been authorized to carry tourists. Most trips leave around 10am and return in the late afternoon; on average, you'll pay around R$30 a head.

**Beaches** in the town are nothing special. Better ones are found by following the Estrada do Contorno (by car), or catching a **bus** from the bus station (hourly) to the beaches of Bonfim, Gordas, Grande, Tanguá, Tanguazinho, Ribeira or Retiro. There are other beaches within reach, too: along the main BR-101 highway, towards Rio, good spots for bathing and free camping are Garatucaia and Monsuaba.

### Practicalities

The bus station, the tourist office and the passenger ferry for Ilha Grande (see below) are all located within a few steps of each other. There's no shortage of **hotels**, but most are on the pricey side. Try the modest but comfortable *Hotel Londres*, Av. Raul Pompéia 75 (ⓣ24/3365-0044; ③); for only slightly more, you'll get a pool at the *Acrópolis Marina* on Av. das Caravelas 89 (ⓣ24/3365-2225; ④).

You'll have no trouble finding places for **eating and drinking** either, with lots of restaurants and bars to choose from: try *Cheiro Verde*, Rua Pereira Peixoto 53, which serves satisfying Lebanese cuisine, or *Taberna 33* at Av. Raul Pompéia 110, for decent pizzas.

## Ilha Grande

**ILHA GRANDE** comprises 193 square kilometres of mountainous jungle, historic ruins and beautiful beaches, excellent for some scenic tropical rambling. The entire island is a state park and the authorities have been successful at limiting development and in maintaining a ban on motor vehicles, whether owned by visitors or locals. The main drawback is the ferocity of the insects, especially during the summer, so come equipped with repellent.

### Getting to Ilha Grande

There are **boats** from both Mangaratiba and Angra dos Reis to Vila do Abraão on Ilha Grande, each taking an hour or so. From **Mangaratiba** to Abraão, the boat leaves daily at 8am (with an extra boat on Friday at 10am) and returns at 5.30pm. From **Angra dos Reis**, boats leave at 3.30pm Monday to Friday and at 1.30pm Saturday and Sunday, returning at 10am daily. Tickets cost R$6.50 during the week or R$14 Saturday, Sunday and public holidays; if you miss the ferry, you can usually count on finding a small launch to do the crossing, charging around R$25 per person and taking around one hour thirty minutes. During the summer, there's a constant flow of these launches from both mainland towns, but at other times Angra is the best bet. If you have a car, you'll have to leave it behind on the mainland, though you can get advice at the ferry terminals on where to find a secure, lock-up parking spot. Be sure to come with plenty of **cash**: changing dollars or traveller's cheques is impossible on the island, there's no ATM and not all *pousadas* and restaurants accept credit cards.

Islands like this deserve a good pirate story, and Ilha Grande is no exception. According to legend, the pirate **Jorge Grego** was heading for the Straits of Magellan when his ship was sunk by a British fleet. He managed to escape with his two daughters to Ilha Grande, where he became a successful farmer and merchant. In a fit of rage, he murdered the lover of one of his daughters, and shortly afterwards, a terrible storm destroyed all his farms and houses. From then on, Jorge Grego passed his time roaming the island, distraught, pausing only long enough to bury his treasure before his final demise. If there is any treasure today, though, it's the island's **wildlife**: parrots, exotic hummingbirds, butterflies and monkeys abound in the thick vegetation.

Ilha Grande offers lots of beautiful **walks** along well-maintained and fairly well-signposted trails, but it's sensible to take some basic precautions. Be sure to set out as early as possible and always inform people at your *pousada* where you are going – in writing if possible. Carry plenty of water with you, and remember to apply sunscreen and insect repellent at regular intervals. Darkness comes suddenly, and even on a night with a full moon the trails are likely to be pitch-black due to the canopy formed by the overhanging foliage; it's best to carry a flashlight – most *pousadas* will be happy to lend you one. Whatever you do, avoid straying from the trail: not only could you easily get hopelessly lost, but there are also rumours of booby traps primed to fire bullets, left over from the days when the island hosted a high-security prison.

## Around the island

As you approach the low-lying, whitewashed colonial port of **VILA DO ABRAÃO**, the mountains rise dramatically from the sea, and in the distance there's the curiously shaped summit of Bico do Papagaio ("Parrot's Beak"), which rises to a height of 980m and can be reached in about three hours. There's really very little to see in Abraão itself, but it's a pleasant enough base from which to explore the rest of the island. The ruins of the **Antigo Presídio** lie a half-hour walk west along the coast. Originally built as a hospital, it was converted to a prison for political prisoners in 1910 and was finally dynamited in the early 1960s. Among the ruins, you'll find the *cafofo*, the containment centre where prisoners who had failed in escape attempts were immersed in freezing water. Just fifteen minutes inland from Abraão, and overgrown with vegetation, stands the **Antigo Aqueduto** that used to channel the island's water supply. There's a fine view of the aqueduct from the **Pedra Mirante**, a hill near the centre of the island, and, close by, a waterfall provides the opportunity for a cool bathe on a hot day.

For the most part, the **beaches** – Aventureiro, Lopes Mendes, Canto, Júlia and Morcegoare to name a few – are still wild and unspoilt. They can be most easily reached by **boat**; a typical day-long excursion costs R$25–35 per person, and departure time from Abraão's jetty is at 10.30am, with stops for snorkelling (equipment provided) before continuing on to a beach, from where you'll be picked up later in the day to arrive back in Abraão at around 4.30pm. Most beaches can also be reached on **foot**, and there are some lovely quiet beaches within an hour's walk of Abraão. The hike from Abraão across the island to **Praia da Parnaioca** will take about five hours, so it's no jaunt. By the coconut-fringed *praia* is an old fishing village that was abandoned by its inhabitants because of their fear of escaped prisoners from a second prison that was built on the island. This prison closed in April 1994, though not before earning the island something of a dangerous reputation, as escapes were not infrequent. Today, the only dangers come from *borachudos*, almost invisible but vicious gnats that bite without your hearing them or, until later, feeling them. A tiny fishing community has slowly been established here, and if you need to stay over you should have little trouble finding a room to rent and something to eat. Many of the other beaches have a *barraca* or two selling snacks and cold drinks, but you should bring supplies with you.



### Accommodation

**Accommodation** is mostly around Vila do Abraão, and when you arrive you'll probably be approached by youths intent on taking you to a room in a private house (around R$35 per person) – a good option if you're on a tight budget. *Pousadas* in Abraão are mostly quite simple (though they tend to be more expensive than places of similar quality on the mainland), while those elsewhere on the island tend to be more exclusive and have greater levels of comfort. Reservations in the high season, especially at weekends, are absolutely essential; in the off-season prices are halved.

**Água Viva Abraão** ⓣ21/3361-5166, ⓦwww.ilhagrande.com.br/aguaviva. Located near the jetty amidst a busy strip of shops and restaurants, the rooms are well equipped and impeccably clean, but the general atmosphere is rather impersonal. ❹–❺

**Holandês** ⓣ24/3361-5034, ⓦwww.holandeshostel.com.br. The always popular and extremely friendly youth hostel is behind the beach, next to the Assembléia de Deus. Dorms (R$40 per person) sleep either four or eight guests, and there are chalets with a double and a single bed. The garden, with dense vegetation and sitting areas, is exceptionally attractive. ❸

**Lagamar Praia Grande de Araçatiba** ⓣ24/9221-8180, ⓦwww.pousadalagamar.com.br. The nicest of several charming little *pousadas* in this quiet fishing hamlet, offering generous seafood meals, *caipirinhas* and a wholesome breakfast served in as beautiful a setting as you could imagine. ❺

**Naturália** ⓣ24/3361-9583, ⓦwww.pousadanaturalia.net. Although set on a hillside back from the beach, all the guest rooms have breathtaking sea views from their balconies. Breakfast is always a treat, and the friendly owner is usually on hand to offer advice on hikes or boat trips. ❹

**Oásis Abraão** ⓣ24/3361-5116, ⓦwww.oasis.ilhagrande.org. In a peaceful location on the far end of the beach, a 10min walk from the jetty. Rooms are simple but cosy, and the breakfast excellent. ❹

**Sankay Praia de Bananal** ⓣ21/3365-4065, ⓦwww.pousadasankay.com.br. Rustic and very chic, with tasteful, individually furnished rooms, mostly with sea views. The stretch of coast here is a mix of rocky outcrops and sand coves. There's an excellent restaurant serving attractively presented Brazilian dishes along with Japanese ones. Included in the rate is transfer from Angra by the *pousada*'s private boat. ❼

### Eating, drinking and entertainment

**Restaurants** in Abraão, predictably, concentrate on seafood (try the *Rei dos Caldos*, which specializes in fish soups), but there are also a couple of pizzerias. Summertime **nightlife** is always lively, with the *Bar Verdinho da Ilha* bashing out some eminently danceable *forró* music. **Carnaval** is well celebrated here – much more relaxed than the Rio experience – and watch, too, for the festival of São João (Jan 20) and the Pirate Regatta, which takes place in February.

## Tarituba

Back on the mainland, the road west rises amidst the most exhilarating scenery that the whole coast has to offer. About 60km from Angra, **TARITUBA**, a charming little fishing village just off the coast road, is still relatively untouched by tourism. Any bus going along the coast will let you off at the side road that leads to the village, or there are buses several times a day from Paraty, 35km further west.

There's not much to the village – a pier along which fishing boats land their catches, a pretty church and a few *barracas* on the beach serving fried fish and cold drinks – and it's simply a place to relax in, away from the often brash commercialism of Angra and Paraty. There are a couple of decent **pousadas**, but it can be difficult to get a room in high season or even to make telephone reservations. The most comfortable place is the *Tarituba* (ⓣ24/3371-6619, ⓦwww.pousadatarituba.com.br; ⑤), where large rooms with private verandas and hammocks overlook the pool and beach beyond. The *Pousada de Carminha* (ⓣ24/3371-1120; ④), simple but very friendly, is right on the beach and offers either private or shared bathrooms. Bear in mind that here, as right along the coast, the *borachudos* and mosquitoes are murder, so bring plenty of insect repellent and mosquito coils with you.

## Paraty and around

About 300km from Rio on the BR-101 is the Costa Verde's main attraction, the town of **PARATY**. Inhabited since 1650, the centre of Paraty (or, officially, Vila de Nossa Senhora dos Remédios de Paraty) has remained fundamentally unaltered since its heyday as a staging post for the eighteenth-century trade in Brazilian gold, passing from Minas Gerais to Portugal. Before Portuguese settlement, the land had been occupied by the **Guaianá Indians**, and the gold routes followed the old Indian trails down to Paraty and its sheltered harbour. Inland raids and pirate attacks necessitated the establishment of a new route linking Minas Gerais directly with Rio, and, as trade was diverted to the bigger city, Paraty's fortunes declined.

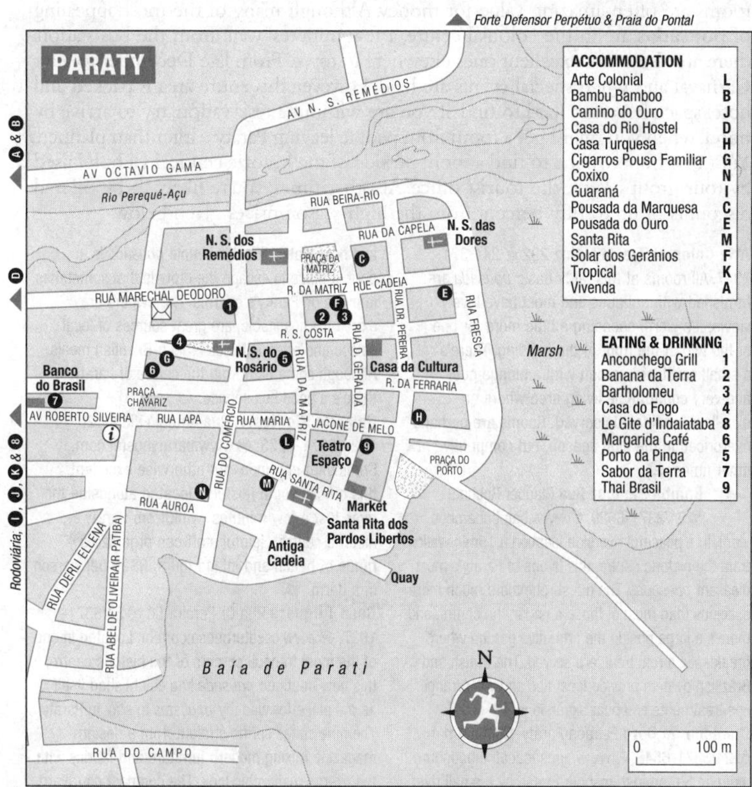

Apart from a short-lived boom in the nineteenth century of coffee shipping and the production of *cachaça*, Paraty remained hidden away off the beaten track, intact but quietly stagnating. Nowadays, however, Paraty is very much alive; UNESCO considers it one of the world's most important examples of Portuguese colonial architecture, and the entire city has the status of a national monument.

The town centre was one of Brazil's first planned urban projects, and its narrow cobbled streets, out of bounds to motorized transport, are bordered by houses built around courtyards adorned with brightly coloured flowers and teeming with hummingbirds. The cobbles of the streets are arranged in channels to drain off storm water and allow the sea to enter and wash the streets at high tides and full moon. Although businesses in Paraty's historic centre are overwhelmingly geared to tourists, the wider community has not been totally engulfed by wealthy outsiders and by and large provides a more satisfying experience than Búzios, its chic counterpart on the Costa do Sol.

## Arrival, information and accommodation

The **rodoviária** is about 500m from the old town; turn right out of the bus station and walk straight ahead. The **tourist office** is near the entrance of the historic centre, on the corner of Avenida Roberto Silveira and Praça Macedo Soares (daily 8am–7pm; ⓣ24/3371-1897), and can supply a map of the town, local bus times and a list of hotels and restaurants.

For most of the year, it's easy to find **accommodation**; the standard is high, and rooms are often amazing value for money. Although many of the most appealing of **pousadas** are in the colonial centre, a few minutes' walk from the bus station, there are also some excellent ones elsewhere in town. From late December to after Carnaval and when special events are held, however, this entire area is packed and hotel space becomes hard to find: if you are without a reservation, try to arrive by noon, when you might get a room from people leaving Paraty earlier than planned. Your best hope will be to find a room outside of the historic centre, in a hotel used by tour groups – ask the tourist office. At other times, you're likely to be offered discounts of up to fifty percent from the high-season prices given below.

**Arte Colonial** Rua da Matriz 292 ⓣ24/3371-7347. All rooms at this fairly basic *pousada* are furnished with antiques and most have lovely views; it's worth spending a little more for one of the two at the front of the building. There's a small courtyard garden with a plunge pool and very comfortable living area where an excellent breakfast is served. Rooms are perhaps overpriced in the high season, but competitive at other times. ❻

**Bambu Bamboo** Rua Glauber Rocha 9 ⓣ24/3371-8629, ⓦwww.bambubamboo.com. In a peaceful riverside location a 15min walk from the historic centre, this is one of Paraty's most pleasant *pousadas*. The guest rooms are much more spacious than most of those found in the centre, and there's a large pool in the attractive garden where breakfasts, a real treat, are served. The British and Brazilian owners provide local tips and will arrange spa treatments and boat excursions. ❻–❼

**Caminho do Ouro** Estrada Paraty–Cunha Km 4 ⓣ24/3371-6548, ⓦwww.pousadacaminhodoouro.com.br. Set amidst unspoilt forest, by a small river and near waterfalls, this simple *pousada* is a perfect place to escape the crowds that sometimes impinge on Paraty's charms. The owners are extremely hospitable, are great sources of local advice and offer delicious Franco-Brazilian meals. Although some 8km from the centre of Paraty, there's a good bus service. ❻

**Casa do Rio Hostel** Rua Antônio Vidal 120 ⓣ24/3371-2223, ⓦwww.paratyhostel.com. Somewhat cramped, but otherwise excellent, this official youth hostel is located alongside the river, just a few minutes' walk from Paraty's historic centre. Helpful staff can organize a range of beach and inland tours. R$25 per person in a dorm. ❸

**Casa Turquesa** Rua Dr Pereira 50 ⓣ24/3371-1037, ⓦwww.casaturquesa.com.br. Located in one of the most tranquil corners of the historic centre, this new boutique *pousada* has established itself as *the* place for wealthy *paulistas* to stay in Paraty. The nine suites spring straight from a design magazine mixing modern furniture and fabrics with the overall rustic-chic look. The compact courtyard (with a plunge pool) and rather small lounge and bar project a somewhat claustrophobic feel, but the service is discreet yet attentive. From R$880 per night.

**Cigarros Pouso Familiar** Largo do Rosário 7 ⓣ24/3371-1497. A lovely old house with just four simply furnished rooms. All have private bathrooms and one has a kitchenette. The atmosphere is relaxed and there are attractive views from the shared terrace. ❸

**Coxixo** Rua do Comércio 362 ⓣ24/3371-1460, ⓦwww.hotelcoxixo.com.br. Rooms are comfortable and there's a pretty garden and a good-size pool. Since this is one of the larger hotels in the historic centre, you'll have a chance of securing last-minute accommodation here. Apart from babies under 12 months, only children over the age of 15 are accepted. ❼

**Guarana** Rua Cinco 13 ⓣ24/3371-6362, ⓦwww.pousadaguarana.com.br. The 20min walk to the historic centre is compensated by having spacious, though rather basic, rooms, a pool and a lovely garden where the superb breakfast is served. The American–Brazilian owners are extremely welcoming. ❹

**Pousada da Marquesa** Rua Dona Geralda 69 ⓣ24/3371-2163, ⓦwww.pousadamarquesa.com.br. Discreet luxury *pousada* offering an attractive pool and wonderful views of the town from the bedrooms. Avoid the rooms in the annexe, as they're on the small side. ❼

**Pousada do Ouro** Rua Dr Pereira 145 ⓣ24/3371-2033, ⓦwww.pousadaouro.com.br. The least-expensive luxury *pousada* in Paraty, boasting a range of tastefully furnished rooms – spacious and light in the main building, but rather small and dark in the annexe. There's a lovely walled garden and a good-size pool, too. ❼

**Solar dos Gerânios** Praça da Matriz ⓣ24/3371-1550, ⓦwww.paraty.com.br/geranio. This beautiful and long-established *pousada* is filled with rustic furniture and curios. The rooms (including some singles) are small and spartan but impeccably kept; most have a balcony and all have a private bathroom. The *pousada* is superb value (prices remain much the same throughout the year), and the multilingual owner and her cats are extremely welcoming. Because it's popular, reservations are usually essential – request a room overlooking the *praça*. ❹

**Tropical** Rua Waldemar Mathias 38 ⓣ24/3371-2020, ⓦwww.paratytropical.com.br. Set in a residential area next to the *rodoviária*. Rooms are plain, but ask for one on the upper floor, as they're quieter and have better ventilation. ❹

**Vivenda** Rua Beija-flor s/n ⓣ24/3371-4272, ⓦwww.vivendaparaty.com. A 10min walk from the historic centre, this modern, elegant, yet immensely relaxing B&B has a double room and two spacious bungalows with kitchenettes set around a leafy patio garden and pool. The owner is a perfect host, providing local advice (and *caipirinhas*) without ever being overbearing. ❻–❼

## The Town

Paraty is a perfect place simply to wander aimlessly, each turn of the corner bringing another picturesque view. The town's small enough that there's no danger of getting lost and, no matter what time of day or night, you can feel confident about your safety. Additionally, there are several buildings worth seeking out if you don't happen to come across them.

As with most small colonial towns in Brazil, each of Paraty's churches traditionally served a different sector of the population. Dating back to 1646, **Nossa Senhora dos Remédios** (daily 9am–5pm), on the Praça da Matriz, is Paraty's main church and the town's largest building. During the late eighteenth century, the church – built for local bourgeoisie – underwent major structural reforms and the exterior, at least, has remained unchanged since. In 1800, Paraty's aristocracy had their own church built: the particularly graceful **Igreja das Dores** (daily 1–5pm), which has a small cemetery, is located three blocks from the main church, by the sea. Along Rua do Comércio is the smallest church, the **Igreja do Rosário** (Wed–Sun 9am–noon & 1.30–5pm), constructed in 1725 and used by slaves. Finally, at the southern edge of town, **Igreja de Santa Rita dos Pardos Libertos** (Wed–Sun 9am–noon & 2–5pm) is the oldest and architecturally most significant of Paraty's churches. Built in 1722 for the freed mulatto population, the structure is notable for its elaborate facade, done in Portuguese Baroque style; the small Museu de Arte Sacra, a repository of religious artefacts from Paraty's churches, is attached. Next to Santa Rita you'll find the late eighteenth-century jail, the **Antiga Cadeia**, now the public library, while opposite is the lively **fish market**. On the corner of Rua Dona Geralda and Rua Samuel Costa, the beautifully maintained **Casa da Cultura** (Mon & Wed–Sun 10am–6.30pm; R$5; ⓦwww.casadacultraparaty.org.br) is worth stopping by for the sometimes excellent, locally inspired art and photography exhibitions.

To the north of the old town, across the Rio Perequê-Açu on the Morro de Vilha Velha, is the **Forte Defensor Perpétuo**, constructed in 1703 to defend Paraty from pirates seeking to plunder gold ships leaving the port. The fort underwent restoration in 1822, and today the rudimentary structure houses the **Museu de Artes e Tradições Populares** (Wed–Sun 9am–noon & 2–5pm), which has a permanent display of fishing tools and basketware as well as handicrafts for sale.

### Beaches and islands

Keeping yourself amused while visiting Paraty should be no problem, even if you quickly exhaust the possibilities of the town itself. From the **Praia do Pontal** on the other side of the Perequê-Açu River, and from the **port quay**, schooners leave for the beaches of Paraty-Mirim, Jurumirim, Lula and Picinguaba. In fact, there are 65 islands and about two hundred beaches to choose from, and anyone can tell you which are the current favourites. Tickets for trips out to the islands, typically costing R$30 per person, leave Paraty at noon, stop at three or four islands for swimming opportunities and return at 6pm. These trips can be pretty rowdy affairs, with the larger boats capable of carrying several dozen people and usually blaring out loud music. Alternatively, for around R$250 (or R$150 in the low season) you can easily charter a small fishing boat suitable for three to five passengers.

You can reach some of the mainland beaches by road – ask at the tourist office for details of bus times. If you're really feeling energetic, you can hire a **mountain bike** for R$35 a day from Paraty Tours at Av. Roberto Silveira 11, who also supply maps marked with suggested itineraries covering beaches, mountains or forests. They can also arrange **car rental** for around R$140 a day.

▲ Paraty

## Academy of Cooking and Other Pleasures

For an unusual dining experience, drop by the **Academy of Cooking and Other Pleasures** at Rua Dona Geralda 211 (ⓣ24/3371-6468, ⓦwww.chefbrazil.com) to find out about events hosted by Yara Castro Roberts, a professional cook and restaurant consultant who has done much to encourage interest in Brazilian food through cookery classes, television segments and writing. Several evenings a week, Yara gives demonstrations in her home, alternating between menus drawn from Rio, Bahia, the Amazon and Minas Gerais, her home state. The high point of the evening comes when Yara and her guests sit around her dining-room table to enjoy food and wine and sample some fine *cachaças*, of which she is a connoisseur. The evening, which usually lasts from 7.30 to 10.30pm, costs R$130 per person, with groups limited to eight or so people.

Seventeen kilometres southwest of Paraty, including 8km along an unpaved road (which should be avoided following heavy rains), is **Paraty-Mirim**, an attractive bay with calm water ideal for swimming. There are six buses each day from Paraty, with a journey time of about 45 minutes. Although there are a couple of bars serving food, there's nowhere to stay at the beach. Roughly halfway between the beach and the main road, however, is the *Vila Volta* (ⓣ24/9815-7689, ⓦwww.vilavolta.com.br; ④), a rustic but comfortable *pousada* run by a Dutch and Brazilian couple; here you'll find a friendly reception, an extremely peaceful setting, excellent Dutch-Indonesian-Brazilian food, trails and natural swimming pools.

Some of the best beaches are near the village of **Trindade**, 21km southwest of Paraty and reached by a steep, but good, winding road (7 buses daily; 45min). Sandwiched between the ocean and Serra do Mar, Trindade has reached the physical limits of growth, the dozens of inexpensive *pousadas*, holiday homes, camping sites, bars and restaurants crammed with tourists in the peak summer season. The main beach is nice enough, but you're better off walking away from the village across the rocky outcrops to Praia Brava or Praia do Meio, where the only signs of development on what are some of the most perfect mainland beaches on this stretch of coast are simply a few bars. The best (though hardly luxurious) **place to stay** is the *Pousada do Pelé* (ⓣ24/3371-5125; ④–⑤), which is situated right on the beach and has rooms that sleep two to four people. There are numerous modest *pousadas* slightly back from the beach, all with private bathrooms: try the *Agua do Mar* (ⓣ24/3371-5210; ④), the *Pouso Trindade* (ⓣ24/3371-5121; ③), or the *Ponta da Trindade* (ⓣ24/3371-5113; ③), which also has space to pitch a tent.

### Eating

The town has a good choice of **restaurants** in all price brackets, though often the expensive-looking ones can be surprisingly reasonable, thanks to portions big enough for two people. The cheapest places to eat are outside of the historic centre, along Avenida Roberto Silveiro – while none of these are remarkable, you won't have any difficulty finding a filling meal of fish, meat, beans, rice and salad for under R$20. Predictably, fish is the local speciality.

**Anconchego Grill** Rua do Comércio 10. The best meat in town, but, in addition to the Argentine steaks (R$30–40), excellent fish dishes are on offer, as well as an assortment of salads.

**Banana da Terra** Rua Dr Samuel Costa 198. Arguably Paraty's most interesting restaurant, the *Banana da Terra* emphasizes local ingredients (such as bananas and plantains) and regional cooking. The grilled fish with garlic-herb butter and served with banana is delicious, as are the wonderful banana desserts. Expensive, at well over R$130 per person. Evenings only except Saturday & Sunday, when lunch is also served; closed Wed.

**Bartholomeu** Rua Dr Samuel Costa 176. A relatively simple but good and moderately priced menu that gives pride of place to Argentine beef filled with Roquefort and seafood *moquecas*.

**Casa do Fogo** Rua Comendador José Luiz 390. Attractively presented, immensely flavourful vegetable, seafood and other dishes, all flambéed – with local *cachaça* of course. R$60 for the three-course dinner special.

**Le Gite d'Indaiatiba** BR-101, Km 562, Graúna ⓣ24/3371-7174 or 9999-9923, ⓦwww.legitedindaiatiba.com.br. At this outstanding restaurant, the French chef serves a few classic dishes as well as his own creations based on local ingredients. Main courses are around R$80. Set inland from Paraty, the mountainside location is stunning, and it's a wonderful place to spend an afternoon – or longer, as it's also a *pousada* (❺–❻). If you don't have your own transport, phone ahead for a possible lift.

**Margarida Café** Praça Chafariz. Imaginative, well-prepared, modern Brazilian cooking is the speciality here; the desserts are a treat, none more than bananas flambéed in *cachaça*. There's a nice bar, plus remarkably good live music on most nights. Expect to pay at least R$80 per person for a full meal.

**Porto da Pinga** Rua da Matriz 12. A charmingly rustic-looking bar and restaurant boasting one of the finest collections of *cachaças* (be sure to sample Cachaça Maria Izabel, Paraty's finest) in town and serving very reasonably priced, local food prepared with a French accent.

**Sabor da Terra** Av. Roberto Silveira 180. Paraty's best *por kilo* restaurant, offering a wide variety of inexpensive hot and cold dishes that include excellent seafood.

**Thai Brasil** Rua Dona Geralda 345. Well-presented, moderately priced Thai food served in a bright and attractive setting. The German owner has created remarkably authentic dishes, with the fish being especially good.

## Drinking and entertainment

Paraty has plenty of watering holes to keep you amused into the evening, though out of season you may well find yourself drinking alone. Amongst the bars with **live music** to try are *Paraty 33*, on Rua da Lapa alongside the cathedral, and *Margarida Café* (see above). Many of the buildings in the historic centre have been converted into shops, where you can pick up clothes, artworks, *cachaça* (generally not as good as the rustic-looking bottle might suggest) and souvenirs until late at night. Otherwise, you might try the **cinema** on Avenida Roberto Silveira, which usually shows English-language films; a more novel alternative is the **puppet troupe** Grupo Contadores de Estórias (ⓦwww.ecparaty.org.br); their wordless performances nimbly leap between comedy and tragedy, exploring such adult themes as death, sex and betrayal (you must be 14 years or over to attend). Performances are every Wednesday and Saturday at 9pm at their Teatro Espaço at Rua Dona Geralda 327 (ⓣ24/3371-1575, ⓦwww.paraty.com.br/teatro.htm; R$40), which occasionally hosts other theatre, dance or music events, too.

May, June and July see frequent **festivals** celebrating local holidays, and Paraty's square comes alive during this time with folk dances – *cerandis*, *congadas* and *xibas* – showcasing the European and African influences on Brazilian culture. While such goings-on certainly demonstrate that local traditions can survive against the onslaught of tourism, they are small in scale compared with newly established events. Taking place since 2002 over the course of a week in July, the **Festa Literária Internacional de Parati** (**FLIP**) immediately established itself as Brazil's single most influential literary gathering, with panels featuring some of the most important writers from across the world. For the FLIP programme, see ⓦwww.flip.org.br.

## Inland from Paraty

Another good way to see a bit of the landscape is to drive, cycle or catch a bus from Paraty's *rodoviária*, following the Cunha road up into the Serra do Mar. The easiest place to head for is at Km 4, where there's a well-signposted side road leading 900m to the **Fazenda Murycana** (daily 10am–6pm; R$5), a farm complex that dates back to the seventeenth century. As well as a farm,

Murycana originally served as an inn for travellers on the Caminho do Ouro and also as a toll post where the royal tax of twenty percent on goods was levied. The restored buildings can be visited, the most interesting being the slightly ramshackle, yet still attractive, **casa grande**, now a museum. There's a restaurant serving typical country food (R$25 per person), and you can taste and purchase the *fazenda*'s famous, but poor-quality, *cachaça* and liquors. Horse riding is offered, as are a number of adventure sports such as canopy walking in the surrounding forest. Be sure to note, however, that this is one of the most popular excursions and the *fazenda* can get unpleasantly crowded, especially at lunchtime, with the arrival of tour groups.

Continuing up the Cunha road to Km 6, you'll spot signs pointing to the **Cachoeira das Penhas**, a waterfall up in the mountains that offers a chance to bake on the sun-scorched rocks of the river gully and then cool off in the river. From here you can descend from rock to rock for a few hundred metres before scrambling up to a road above you. About 2km along the road, just across a small bridge, you'll enter **PONTE BRANCA** where, at the far end of the village, overlooking the river, is the *Ponte Branca* restaurant, where you can take a break and enjoy a cold drink. The easy walk from the waterfall takes you through the hills and valleys, and past tropical-fruit plantations – all very pleasant. If you don't have your own transport, you'll probably manage to get a lift back to Paraty from the restaurant or you can wait by the Cunha road for a bus.

For a more rugged experience, consider hiking along a restored segment of the **Estrada Real** – the seventeenth-century mule trail that connected the port of Paraty with the gold mines of Minas Gerais. With your own transport, you can reach the trail's access point at the Centro de Informações Turísticas do Caminho do Ouro, located alongside the Cunha road. Here you can head further inland along the partially cobbled trail. Beware: the trail is very slippery after the rain, and even in dry conditions you'll need good footwear to tackle the steep and uneven terrain. The landscape, which appears pleasantly pastoral at first, grows increasingly impressive, and you'll have spectacular views of the forested mountains all around, as well as Paraty and the ocean. Be sure to bring water with you, but after about an hour you'll reach a waterfall to shower under and which is also a source of fresh drinking water.

## Inland: north to the mountains

Excellent bus services from Rio de Janeiro make the **interior** of the state easily accessible, and its mountainous wooded landscape and relatively cool climate are a pleasant contrast to the coastal heat. There's not a great deal in the way of historical interest, but the scenic beauty of the countryside, studded with small towns still bearing their colonial heritage, is an attraction in itself.

### Petrópolis

Sixty-six kilometres directly to the north of Rio de Janeiro, high in the mountains, stands the imperial city of **PETRÓPOLIS**. The route there is a busy one, with buses leaving Rio every fifteen minutes. In fine weather, the journey to Petrópolis is glorious. On the way up, sit on the left-hand side of the bus and don't be too concerned with the driver's obsession with overtaking heavy-goods vehicles on blind corners. You'll be travelling along a one-way road, bordered by naked rock on one side and a sheer drop on the other; the return to Rio is made by a slightly different route that also snakes its way through terrifying mountain passes.

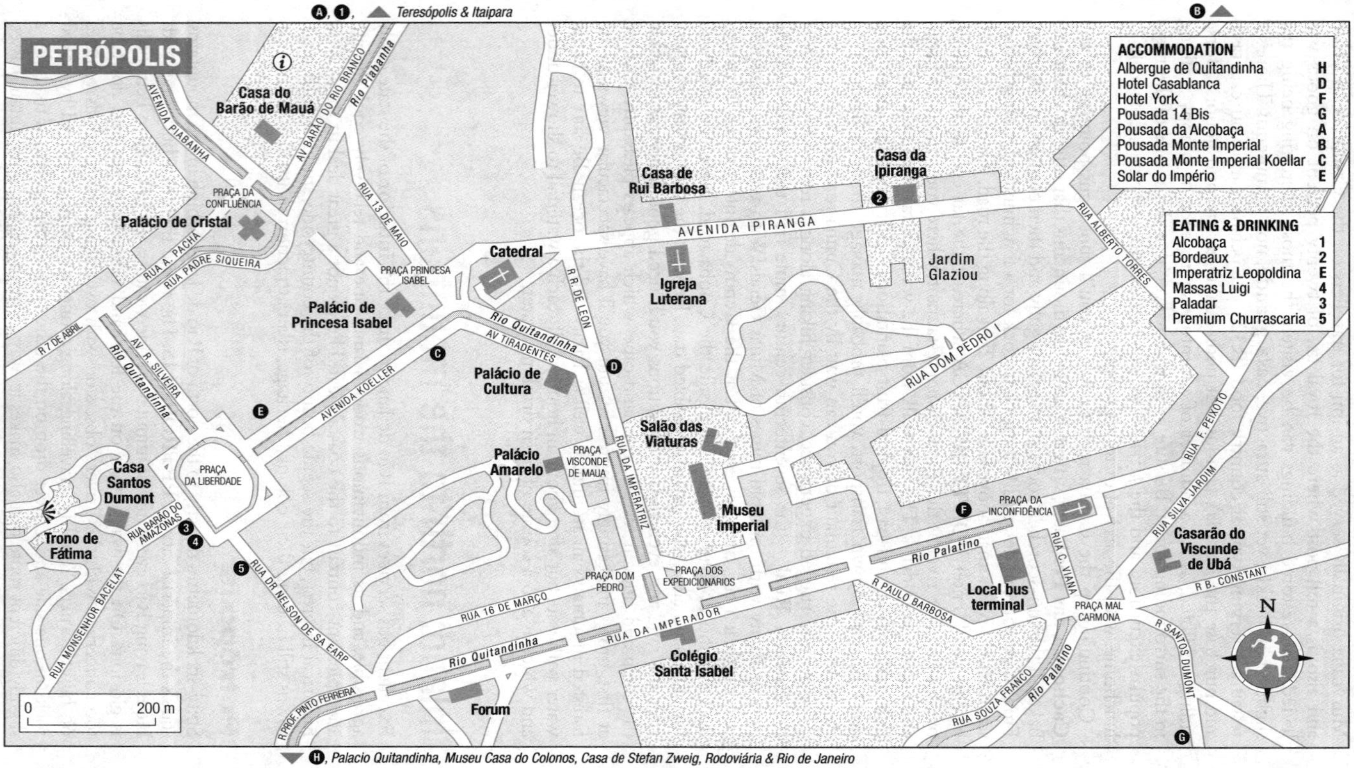

PETRÓPOLIS
A, 1, Teresópolis & Itaipara
B
ACCOMMODATION
Albergue de Quitandinha H
Hotel Casablanca D
Hotel York F
Pousada 14 Bis G
Pousada da Alcobaça A
Pousada Monte Imperial B
Pousada Monte Imperial Koellar C
Solar do Império E
EATING & DRINKING
Alcobaça 1
Bordeaux 2
Imperatriz Leopoldina E
Massas Luigi 4
Paladar 3
Premium Churrascaria 5
Casa do Barão de Mauá
Palácio de Cristal
Praça da Confluência
Casa de Rui Barbosa
Casa da Ipiranga
Catedral
Igreja Luterana
Jardim Glaziou
Palácio de Princesa Isabel
Praça Princesa Isabel
Palácio de Cultura
Salão das Viaturas
Palácio Amarelo
Praça Visconde de Maua
Museu Imperial
Casa Santos Dumont
Trono de Fátima
Praça da Liberdade
Praça Dom Pedro
Praça dos Expedicionarios
Colégio Santa Isabel
Forum
Local bus terminal
Praça da Inconfidência
Casarão do Viscunde de Ubá
Praça Mal Carmona
Avenida Ipiranga
Avenida Piabanha
Av Barão do Rio Branco
Rio Piabanha
Rua 13 de Maio
Rua A. Pacha
Rua Padre Siqueira
R 7 de Abril
Av R. Silveira
Rio Quitandinha
Avenida Koeller
Av Tiradentes
R. R. de Leon
Rua da Imperatriz
Rua Dom Pedro I
Rua Alberto Torres
Rua F. Peixoto
Rua Silva Jardim
R. B. Constant
R Santos Dumont
Rua C. Viana
Rio Palatino
R Paulo Barbosa
Rua Souza Franco
Rua da Imperador
Rua 16 de Março
Rua Dr Nelson de Sa Earp
Rua Barão do Amazonas
Rua Monsenhor Bacelat
R Prof. Pinto Ferreira
0 200 m
N
H, Palacio Quitandinha, Museu Casa do Colonos, Casa de Stefan Zweig, Rodoviária & Rio de Janeiro

The landscape is dramatic, climbing among forested slopes that give way suddenly to ravines and gullies, while clouds shroud the surrounding mountains.

In 1720, Bernardo Soares de Proença opened a trade route between Rio and Minas Gerais, and in return was conceded the area around the present site of Petrópolis as a royal land grant. Surrounded by stunning scenery, and with a gentle, alpine summer climate, it had by the nineteenth century become a favourite retreat of Rio's elite. The arrival of German immigrants contributed to the development of Petrópolis as a town, and has much to do with the curious European Gothic feel to the place. Dom Pedro II took a fancy to Petrópolis and in 1843 designated it the summer seat of his government. He also established a German agricultural colony, which failed because of the unsuitability of the soil, and then in 1849 – with an epidemic of yellow fever sweeping through Rio – the emperor and his court took refuge in the town, thus assuring Petrópolis's prosperity.

## Arrival and information

Buses from Rio, São Paulo, Belo Horizonte and Teresópolis arrive and depart from the new **rodoviária**, some 10km from town approaching from Rio. From there you can take a bus to the municipal bus terminal, a short walk from most of the sights in Petrópolis.

There's a helpful **tourist office** at the entrance to town at Quitandinha (Mon–Fri 8am–6pm, Sat 8am–7pm, Sun 8am–5pm; ⓣ0800-241-516), with branches at the *rodoviária* (daily 9am–6pm) and at Praça da Liberdade (daily 9am–6pm). Town attractions aside, Petrópolis has easy access to some lovely **hiking** country – day- and longer hikes at various scales of difficulty are organized by Serra Trekking (ⓣ24/2242-2360, ⓦwww.serratrekking.cm.br) and Trekking Petrópolis (ⓦwww.rioserra.com.br/trekking).

## Accommodation

There are some good **hotels** near the historic sights, but most people prefer staying outside of the centre where there are dozens of attractive *pousadas*, usually with beautiful gardens. These, however, are only really practical if you have a car. Prices vary considerably throughout the year, but discounts of about a third are usually given for weekday stays.

**Albergue da Quitandinha** Rua Uruguai 570, Quitandinha ⓣ24/2247-9165, ⓦwww.alberguequitandinha.com.br. Located in a pleasant residential suburb near the *rodoviária*, this secure and comfortable youth hostel offers both double rooms and beds in dorms (R$41). 4

**Hotel Casablanca** Rua da Imperatriz 286 ⓣ24/2242-6662, ⓦwww.casablancahotel.com.br. This once-stylish hotel next to the *Palácio Imperial* is somewhat institutional in character. Nevertheless, the pool, central location and clean, well-appointed rooms make this a popular city-centre choice. 5

**Pousada 14 Bis** Rua Santos Dumont 162 ⓣ24/2231-0946, ⓦwww.pousada14bis.com.br. A lovely, centrally located *pousada* with tastefully furnished bedrooms, a cosy lounge full of Santos Dumont (the Brazilian aviator) memorabilia, and relaxing gardens. 5

**Pousada da Alcobaça** Rua Dr Agostinho Goulão 298, Corrêas ⓣ24/2221-1240, ⓦwww.pousadadaalcobaca.com.br. A fairly simple yet extraordinarily comfortable *pousada* located a few kilometres from the entrance of the Parque Nacional da Serra dos Órgãos. The gardens, flowers (inside and out), superb meals (see p.154) and the owners' warm welcome make this the most delightful of Petropolis's country inns. 7–8

**Pousada Monte Imperial** Rua José Alencar 27 ⓣ24/2237-1664, ⓦwww.pousadamonteimperial.com.br. Located on a hilltop, this *pousada* has the look and air of an Alpine inn and is a stiff walk from the town's attractions. Rooms are quite small but appealing, and there's a nice garden with a pool, too; the English-speaking owner is extremely friendly. 6

**Pousada Monte Imperial Koeller** Av. Koeller 99 ⓣ24/2237-1664, ⓦwww.pousadamonteimperial.com.br. Under the same ownership as the *Monte Imperial*, this property – a relatively modest mansion built in 1875 – is on one of Petrópolis's grandest avenues, a short walk from the city's historic sites. Decorated in period style, the rooms are simple yet comfortable, with the most attractive facing the avenue. ⑥

**Solar do Império** Av. Koeller 376 ⓣ24/2103-3000, ⓦwww.solardoimperio.com.br. Set amongst the city's most elegant residences, this Neoclassical mansion dating from 1875 is now a luxurious hotel. All the rooms have been restored to their period splendour, while every modern convenience and comfort is also offered. The grounds include a small indoor pool, and there's a fine restaurant as well. ⑦–⑧

## The Town

You can easily tour Petrópolis in a day, returning to Rio in the evening (or continuing inland). For the most part, it's possible to ignore the traffic congestion and fumes of the main commercial area, as the majority of the sights are in the older, quieter part of town. And although Petrópolis is quite spread out, you can easily stroll around to pass the time, taking in plenty of elegant nineteenth-century mansions, particularly along **Avenida Koeller**, which has a tree-lined canal running up its centre, or on **Avenida Ipiranga**, where you'll also find the German **Igreja Luterana** (open only for Sun services at 9am). Most of the mansions have been converted for use as offices, but one of the most extravagant, the French-style **Casa da Ipiranga**, at Av. Ipiranga 716 (noon–6pm, closed Wed; R$5; ⓣ24/2242-5711, ⓦwww.casadaipiranga.blogspot.com) has remained virtually unchanged since being built in 1884 for a wealthy coffee merchant. The house is set in a beautiful park, designed by Emperor Dom Pedro II's gardener, and there's a good restaurant (see p.154) in the stable block.

The **Museu Imperial** on Avenida VII de Setembro (Tues–Sun 11am–5.30pm; R$8; ⓣ24/2237-8000, ⓦwww.museuimperial.gov.br) is a fine Neoclassical structure set in beautifully maintained formal gardens. Once the remarkably modest summer palace of Dom Pedro II, it now houses a fascinating collection of the royal family's bits and pieces. On entry, you're given felt overshoes with which to slide around the polished floors, and inside there's everything from Dom Pedro's crown (639 diamonds, 77 pearls, all set in 2kg of finely wrought gold) to the regal commode. In the former stables, the royal railway carriage is displayed, while other buildings in the garden serve as space for temporary exhibitions and an excellent **tearoom**. Three nights a week (Thurs–Sat 8pm; R$20) the former palace is illuminated for a **sound and light show** – well worth attending for the music alone if you don't understand the Portuguese narration.

The **Catedral São Pedro de Alcântara** (daily 8am–6pm) blends with the rest of the architecture around but is much more recent than its rather overbearing neo-Gothic style suggests – while work began in 1884, it was only finished in 1939. Inside on the walls are ten relief sculptures depicting scenes from the Crucifixion; in the mausoleum lie the tombs of Dom Pedro himself, Princess Regent Dona Isabel and several other royal personages. Other historic buildings worth tracking down are the **Palácio de Cristal**, Rua Alfredo Pacha (Tues–Sun 9am–6.30pm); **Casa Santos Dumont** at Rua do Encanto 22 (Tues–Sun 9.30am–5pm), an Alpine chalet built in 1918 and the home of the Brazilian aviator, containing personal memorabilia; the **Casa do Barão de Mauá** at Praça da Confluência 3 (Mon–Sat 9am–6.30pm, Sun 9am–5pm), featuring displays devoted to the baron, best known for his role in constructing Brazil's first railway; and the rather grand, half-timbered Norman-style **Palácio Quitandinha** on the Estrada de Quitandinha, just outside of town. Once the Quitandinha Casino, this last building stopped receiving the rich and famous when the Brazilian government prohibited gambling in 1946, and it was eventually converted into a luxury apartment building. Nearby, at

▲ Catedral São Pedro de Alcântara

Rua Cristóvão Colombo 1034, the **Museu Casa do Colono** (Tues–Sun 9.30am–5pm) is a simple house dating back to 1847 that has a small collection relating to the German immigrants who settled in and around Petrópolis in the early nineteenth century. German-speaking visitors in particular may also be interested in visiting the tomb of the Austrian-born writer **Stefan Zweig**, one of the greatest European writers of the twentieth century, who in 1942 committed suicide in Petrópolis together with his young wife, Lotte. You can take a look at the outside of his house at Rua Gonçalves Dias 34 in the suburb of Valparaiso, near the municipal cemetery; there are plans to create here a museum dedicated to the memory of refugees from Nazi Europe in Brazil (Ⓦ www.casastefanzweig.org).



## Eating

There are some good restaurants in and around town but few exceptional ones. Restaurants are usually quiet on weekdays but can get busy at weekends and during holiday periods, when reservations are recommended.

**Alcobaça** Rua Dr Agostinho Goulão 298, Corrêas ⓣ24/2221-1240. This country inn (20min by taxi or bus from the centre) is a delightful setting for a leisurely lunch or dinner. Using fresh ingredients such as local dairy produce, freshwater fish, and vegetables and herbs from the kitchen garden, food (about R$75 per person) is both unpretentious and excellent. Be sure to allow time after lunch for a gentle walk in the beautiful gardens. Reservations advisable.

**Bordeaux** Rua Ipiranga 716 ⓣ24/2242-5711. In the converted stables of one of Petrópolis's most beautiful stately homes (see p.152), the moderately priced Italian- and French-influenced offerings include local trout and salads, and there's an excellent wine list. Mon & Thurs–Sun lunch, Fri & Sat also dinner.

**Imperatriz Leopoldina** Av. Koeller 376 ⓣ24/2103-3000. Housed within the regal *Solar do Império* hotel (see p.152), the chef has given a contemporary take to dishes inspired by Empress Leopoldina's supposed love of Brazilian ingredients and flavours. The restaurant itself is surprisingly ordinary in appearance, but the food is excellent. Expect to pay around R$80 per person.

**Massas Luigi** Praça da Liberdade 185. Although considered the best Italian restaurant in town, only visit if you're desperate for a plate of pasta or a pizza (around R$20) – and are prepared for disappointment. At least the salad bar is fairly good, and there's a varied lunchtime buffet with a mix of Brazilian and Italian dishes.

**Paladar** Rua Barão do Amazonas 25. A *por kilo* buffet with a varied choice of salads and Brazilian hot dishes. Located within a nineteenth-century mansion, you can either eat indoors or on the shaded terrace overlooking Praça da Liberdade. Tues–Sun 11am–4pm.

**Premium Churrascaria** Rua Dr. Nelson de Sá Earp 297. A central location, elegant decor, quality meat (R$30 per person for the *rodizio*) and a varied salad-bar combine to make this the most popular *churrascaria* in town.

# Teresópolis

While **TERESÓPOLIS** can be reached directly from Rio by bus, the best route is from Petrópolis. It's not a long journey, no more than 40km from

### Parque Nacional da Serra dos Órgãos

One of Brazil's most beautiful mountain regions, the **Parque Nacional da Serra dos Órgãos** (Tues–Sun 9am–5pm; R$3, includes trail map; camping by advance reservation ⓣ21/2152-1119) straddles an area of highland Atlantic rainforest between Petrópolis and Teresópolis. The main features of the park are dramatic rock formations that resemble rows of organ pipes (hence the range's name), dominated by the towering **Dedo de Deus** ("God's Finger") peak. There are tremendous walking possibilities in the park, with the favourite peaks for those with mountain-goat tendencies being the Agulha do Diablo (2050m) and the Pedra do Sino (2263m); the latter has a path leading to the summit, a relatively easy three-hour trip (take refreshments). There are some campsites but no equipment for rent, so you'll need to come prepared.

Approaching from Petrópolis, take one of the frequent **buses** to Corrêas (30min; R$3) and change to a #616 "Pinheiral" bus (hourly; 35min; R$3), which will leave you near the park entrance.

## Coffee country

To many people, **coffee** and Rio de Janeiro are synonymous, a legacy of the nineteenth century when Brazil completely dominated the trade. But Rio's coffee boom was actually short-lived, getting under way in the 1820s and collapsing suddenly in 1888 as a consequence of the abolition of slavery, on which plantation owners were completely dependent. Many of the more resourceful farmers migrated south to São Paulo to take advantage of Italian and other immigrant labour and the availability of fertile, well-watered land. Furthermore, single-crop farming on the hilly terrain of the Paraiba Valley had resulted in serious levels of soil erosion, while the felling of the forest to plant coffee bushes altered the climate, causing draught. The "coffee barons" either abandoned their *fazendas* (plantations) or looked for other uses of their land. Dairy farming was eventually found to work, and today almost all the land is given over to cattle grazing – the area, some 200km west of Petrópolis, is a peaceful backwater, with the evidence of the coffee boom most clearly apparent in the **fazenda houses** that are left standing in various states of repair.

With a few days and, ideally, a car, a visit to the **Paraiba Valley** can be fascinating. The area can be reached in two hours from Rio, and is a convenient stop-off if travelling between Petrópolis and Paraty, or other points on the coast. A particularly attractive place to make for is **Rio das Flores**, a sleepy little place dotted with grand *fazenda* houses, some right alongside the approach road to town, others hidden from view off side-roads. The **tourist information office** at Rua Cesar Nillares 120 (Mon–Fri 9am–5pm; ⓣ24/2458-1162) can usually help with visiting these houses, and you can even **stay** in one, the *Fazenda Santo Antônio*, set amidst beautiful gardens some 22km southeast of town (ⓣ24/2488-2148, ⓦwww.fazendastoantonio.com.br; half-board ⑤). The six guest rooms are either in the impeccably preserved *casa grande*, or plantation house, that dates back to 1842, or in the former *senzala*, or slave quarters, and there's a pool and horses to ride. The helpful English-speaking owner and his wife can make arrangements for visits to neighbouring properties: the slightly run-down look of *Fazenda Campos Eliseos*, established in 1847, contrasts greatly with the beautifully preserved *Fazenda Santa Justa*, the detail of the period decor of the *casa grande* seemingly leaping from the pages of a coffee-table book.

Petrópolis, but the road to the highest town in the state (872m) passes through the **Serra dos Órgãos**, much of which is a national park (see opposite). Teresópolis, like Petrópolis, owed its initial development to the opening of a road between Minas Gerais and Rio during the eighteenth century. It, too, was a favoured summer retreat (for Empress Teresa Cristina, for whom the town was named), and though smaller than Petrópolis it also shares some of its Germanic characteristics, including a benevolent alpine climate. The town itself is extremely dull, centred on one main street that changes its name every couple of blocks, and the interest lies entirely in the surrounding countryside. There are, however, magnificent views from almost anywhere in town – especially from **Soberbo**, where the Rio highway enters Teresópolis, with its panoramic view of Rio and the Baixada Fluminense.

### Practicalities

Teresópolis's **tourist office** is at Praça Olimpica (Mon–Fri 8am–5pm; ⓣ21/2642-1737). Most of the numerous **hotels** are located in the picturesque hills, far from the town centre. The best of them, set in beautiful park-like gardens with several restaurants, swimming pools and an extensive network of trails is the Rosa dos Ventos, an inn some 22km from town, on the road towards Nova Friburgo (☎21/2644-8833, www.hotelrosadosventos.com.br; ⑧), that would not look out of place in the Alps. A better option near the town centre and set in attractive grounds is the very pretty *Pousada das Mansardas*, Rua Wilhelm Christian Klene 230 (☎21/3641-5102, www.mansardas.com.br; ⑤). Also fine is the *Várzea Palace Hotel*, Rua Sebastião Teixeira 41 (☎21/2742-0878; ④), a beautiful white building that was once the most elegant place to stay. Only faint traces of its former luxury remain, but the place is clean, welcoming and very inexpensive. There is also a well-equipped **youth hostel**, the *Recanto do Lord*, near the centre of town at Rua Luiza Pereira Soares 109 (☎21/2742-5586, www.teresopolishostel.com.br; R$35 per person), which has private rooms as well (③). Of the dozens of **restaurants** in and around town, only two stand out, but both are expensive: *Dona Irene*, Rua Tenente Luís Meireles 1800, Bom Retiro (☎21/2742-2901; Wed–Sat noon–midnight, Sun noon–6pm; reservations essential), serves marvellous Russian food; *Margô* at Rua Heitor de Moura Estevão 259 (closed Mon) does satisfying German cuisine.

## Parque Nacional do Itatiaia

Nestling in the northwest corner of the state, 165km from Rio, between the borders of São Paulo and Minas Gerais, the **Parque Nacional do Itatiaia** (daily 8am–5pm; R$3 entrance) is the oldest national park in Brazil, founded in 1937 and covering 120 square kilometres of the Mantigueira mountain range. People come here to climb – favourites are the **Pico das Agulhas Negras** (2787m) and the **Pico de Prateleira** (2540m) – and it is also an important nature reserve.

The park comprises waterfalls, primary forest, wildlife and orchids – but tragically a fire in 1988 ravaged some twenty percent of its area. In the sections affected by the fire, forest and pasture land were devastated, rare orchids and native conifers (*Podocarpus lamperti* and *Araucaria angustifolia*) destroyed; the fire reached areas of the Serra da Mantigueira, 2500m above sea level, wiping out 40km of mountain pathways. Also severely affected were the many natural springs and streams that combine to form the Bonito, Preto, Pirapitinga and Palmital rivers; these supply the massive hydrographic basin of the Paraíba plate, giving much-needed oxygenation to the Paraíba watercourse in one of its most polluted stretches. The situation is gradually improving, but ecologists reckon that it will still take many more years to repair this environmental disaster. For the casual walker, however, there's still plenty of unaffected park to be seen.

### Itatiaia

The town of **ITATIAIA**, on the BR-116, is surrounded by beautiful scenery and makes a good base: it has plenty of **hotels**, mainly found along Via Dutra, the two-kilometre-long road that links the town and park – take the minibus marked "Hotel Simon" from Praça São José. The *Hotel Simon* itself (☎24/3352-1122, www.hotelsimon.com.br; ⑤ full board) is extremely comfortable and in a gorgeous setting, with a wonderful orchid garden attached (daily 9–11am). Nearby and also set amidst lovely grounds is the more intimate *Pousada dos Tucanos* (☎24/9941-1659, www.pousadadostucanos.com.br; ④). In town, there's a **youth hostel** at Rua João Mauricio de Macedo Costa 352 (☎24/2352-1232; R$30 per person). You can get **information** and maps at the visitors' centre (daily 8am–5pm) and at the Museu

Regional de Fauna and Flora (Tues–Sun 10am–4pm). Tourist information on Itatiaia and the park is also available from the Secretaría de Turismo, at Rua São José 210 (Ⓣ24/2352-1660 ext 305).

### Penedo

The other possible base for visting the park is the small town of **PENEDO**, 14km away and connected to Itatiaia by regular buses. Penedo was settled in 1929 by immigrants from Finland, one of numerous Finnish utopian communities established in Latin America at about the same time. With vegetarianism and agricultural self-sufficiency being amongst the settlement's founding tenets, the Finnish community struggled to survive as they discovered that the land they occupied was unsuitable for cultivation. Those Finns who opted to remain in Penedo turned to tourism and the area gradually became popular with weekenders from São Paulo and Rio, who come for the horse riding and to buy the chocolates, jams, preserves and local liquors produced here. Much is made of this Nordic heritage, despite the fact that today only a very small minority of the population are of Finnish origin. Nevertheless, Finnish tango, polka and other dances are performed every Saturday night (9pm–1am) at the *Clube Finlândia*, and the **Museu Finlandês da Dona Eva** at Av. das Mangueiras 2601 (Wed–Sat 10am–5pm, Sun 9am–3pm) has displays of documents, photos, handicrafts and furniture relating to Finnish immigration in the region. Penedo is also a good place to visit if you like saunas, since most hotels have one.

It's usually easy to find a **place to stay** – there are dozens of hotels in and near town, though few real budget places. *Pequena Suécia* at Rua Toivo Suni 33 (Ⓣ24/3351-1275, Ⓦwww.pequenasuecia.com.br; ❼) is an excellent choice, and also features a fine Swedish restaurant; alternatively, the *Pousada A Trilha* at Estrada das Três Cachoeiras 3951 (Ⓣ24/3351-1349, Ⓦwww.penedo.com/trilha; ❺) is comfortably rustic. A more basic option is the *Rio das Pedras* at Rua Resende 39 (Ⓣ24/3351-1019; ❹). Most people eat at their hotels, but there are also a good number of decent Scandinavian- and Finnish-style restaurants in town. Especially worth trying are the delicious open sandwiches at the *Restaurante Skandinávia*, Av. das Mangueiras 2631 (daily 6–11pm), and the smorgasbord and fresh trout at *Koskenkorva*, one of the country's only Finnish restaurants, at Estrada das Três Cachoeiras 3955 (daily noon–midnight).

# Travel details



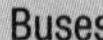

## Buses

International departures daily from Rio to Asunción (30hr), Buenos Aires (46hr), Montevideo (37hr) and Santiago de Chile (72hr).
**Paraty** to: Angra dos Reis (hourly; 2hr); Paraty-Mirim (6 daily; 45min); Rio (9 daily; 4hr 30min); São Paulo (4 daily; 5hr); São Sebastião (2 daily; 3hr); Trindade (hourly; 45min); Ubatuba (3 daily; 2hr).
**Petrópolis** to: Belo Horizonte (5 daily; 5hr); Rio (every 30min; 1hr 30min); São Paulo (2 daily; 6hr 30min); Teresópolis (4 daily; 1hr 30min).
**Rio** to: Angra dos Reis (hourly; 3hr); Belém (daily; 50hr); Belo Horizonte (20 daily; 6hr 30min); Brasília (8 daily; 17hr); Búzios (7 daily; 3hr); Cabo Frio (6 daily; 2hr 30min); Campo Grande (5 daily; 21hr); Florianópolis (3 daily; 18hr); Fortaleza (daily; 44hr); Foz do Iguaçu (6 daily; 22hr); Ouro Preto (daily; 7hr); Paraty (9 daily; 4hr 30min); Petrópolis (every 30min; 1hr 30min); Porto Seguro (3 daily; 19hr); Recife (4 daily; 38hr); Salvador (6 daily; 24hr); São Luis (daily; 51hr); São Paulo (every 15min; 6hr); Teresópolis (hourly; 2hr); Vitória (hourly; 7hr 30min).

## Planes

Frequent **domestic** flights from Sector A of Tom Jobim international airport to most state capitals and many other internal destinations.
**Rio–São Paulo** shuttle from Santos Dumont every 30min from 6.30am to 10.30pm (55min). There are also a few flights from this airport to destinations within the states of Rio and Minas Gerais.

# 2

# Minas Gerais and Espírito Santo

CHAPTER 2

# Highlights

* **Inhotim Instituto Cultural** This important contemporary art collection is set both in and out of doors, amidst Roberto Burle Marx–designed gardens and a nature reserve of Atlantic forest and *cerrado* ecosystems. See p.178

* **Historic Ouro Preto** Nowhere in the country is there a richer concentration of Baroque art and architecture than here, Brazil's eighteenth-century gold-mining centre. See p.183

* **Sculptures by Aleijadinho** Amazingly, the master sculptor of Brazilian Baroque produced his best work after leprosy deformed his hands. See p.185

* **Pedra Azul** This vast granite rock in the eponymous state park sparkles with tints of blues or greens, depending on the time of day. See p.226

▲ Facade of Matriz de Nossa Senhora do Pilar church, Ouro Preto

# 2

# Minas Gerais and Espírito Santo

Separated from the Atlantic by the small state of Espírito Santo, Minas Gerais in particular attracts visitors to its beautiful colonial-era towns, to its spa resorts created in the late nineteenth and early twentieth centuries and to **Belo Horizonte**, its thriving capital. The state's pre-eminent administrative, industrial and cultural metropolis, Belo Horizonte lies in the centre of the rich mining and agricultural hinterland that has made the state one of the economic powerhouses of Brazil, running from the coffee estates of western Minas to the mines and cattle pastures of the valley of the **Rio Doce**, in the east. The largest cities of the region apart from Belo Horizonte are Juiz de Fora in the south, Governador Valadares to the east, and Uberaba and Uberlândia in the west – all modern and unprepossessing; only Belo Horizonte can honestly be recommended as worth visiting.

All *mineiros* would agree the soul of the state lies in the rural areas, in the colonial-era hill and mountain villages and towns of its vast **interior**. North of Belo Horizonte, the grassy slopes and occasional patches of forest are swiftly replaced by the stubby trees and savanna of the Planalto Central and, in north-eastern Minas, by the cactus, rock and perennial drought of the *sertão* – as desperately poor and economically backward as anywhere in the Northeast. The northern part of the state is physically dominated by the hills and highlands of the **Serra do Espinhaço**, a range running north–south through the state like a massive dorsal fin before petering out south of Belo Horizonte. To its east, the **Rio Jequitinhonha** sustains life in the parched landscapes of the *sertão mineiro*; to the west is the flat river valley of the **Rio São Francisco**, which rises here before winding through the interior of the Northeast. The extreme west of the state is known as the **Triângulo Mineiro**, a wealthy, but for visitors uninteresting, agricultural region centred on the city of Uberlândia, with far closer economic ties with São Paulo than with the rest of Minas Gerais. In the southwest of the state, in fine mountainous scenery near the border with São Paulo, are a number of **spa towns** built around mineral-water springs including the small and quiet resorts of **São Lourenço** and **Caxambu**.

Minas Gerais' **cidades históricas**, "the historic cities", represent some of the finest examples of Portuguese colonial architecture, and are repositories of a great flowering of eighteenth-century Baroque **religious art**; *arte sacra mineira* was the finest work of its time in the Americas, and Minas Gerais can lay claim

to undisputably the greatest figure in Brazilian cultural history – the mulatto leper sculptor, **Aleijadinho**, whose magnificent work is scattered throughout the state's wonderfully preserved historic cities. The most important of the *cidades históricas* are **Ouro Preto**, **Mariana** and **Sabará**, all within easy striking distance of Belo Horizonte, the state's modern capital, and **Congonhas**, **São João del Rei**, **Tiradentes** and **Diamantina**, further afield.

**Espírito Santo** is the kind of place you rarely hear about, even within Brazil. With the exception of its coastal resorts, it's almost completely off the tourist map. This is hard to understand, as the interior of the state has some claim to being one of the most beautiful parts of Brazil. Settled mostly by Italians and Germans, it has a disconcertingly European feel – cows graze in front of German-looking farm houses, and, if it weren't for the heat, palm trees, coffee bushes and hummingbirds darting around, you might imagine yourself somewhere in the foothills of the Alps. Vast numbers of *mineiros* head for Espírito Santo for their holidays, but are only interested in the beaches, the one thing landlocked Minas lacks. This has the fortunate effect of cramming all the crowds into an easily avoidable coastal strip, leaving the interior free for you to explore.

The only places of any size in Espírito Santo are **Vitória**, a rather grimy city saved by a fine location (on an island surrounded by hills and granite outcrops) and **Vila Velha**, its equally uninspiring twin city. During colonial times, these were amongst the few spots on the coast that could be easily defended from the **Botocudo Indians**. This is one of the reasons the interior is relatively thinly settled; the other is the sheer difficulty of communications in the steep, thickly forested hills. The semi-deciduous tropical forest that once carpeted much of the southern coast of Brazil still survives relatively unscathed here – and is what southern Minas would have looked like before the gold rushes. The best way to view the region is to make the round of the towns that began as German and Italian colonies: **Santa Teresa**, **Santa Leopoldina**, **Santa Maria**, **Domingos Martins** and **Venda Nova** – the last near the remarkable sheer granite face of **Pedra Azul**, one of the least-known but most spectacular sights in the country.

### Minas Gerias: some history

The French geologist Gorceix summed up Minas Gerais 150 years ago, when he wrote the state had "a breast of iron and a heart of gold". Its hills and mountains contain the richest mineral deposits in Brazil, and led to the area being christened "General Mines" when gold and diamonds were found at the end of the seventeenth century. The gold strikes sparked a wave of migration from Rio and São Paulo, which lasted a century and shifted the centre of gravity of Brazil's economy and population from the Northeast decisively southwards. In the nineteenth century new metals, especially iron, steel and manganese, replaced gold in importance, while the uplands in the west and east proved ideal for coffee production. Land too steep for coffee bushes was converted to cattle pasture, and the luxuriant forests of southern Minas were destroyed and turned into charcoal for smelting.

In more recent times, Minas Gerais has also been at the centre of Brazilian history. *Mineiros*, who own a well-deserved reputation for political cunning, have produced the two greatest postwar Brazilian presidents: **Juscelino Kubitschek**, the builder of Brasília, and **Tancredo Neves**, midwife to the rebirth of Brazilian democracy in 1985. It was troops from Minas who put down the São Paulo revolt against Getúlio Vargas' populist regime in the brief civil war of 1932 and, less creditably, it was the army division in Minas that moved against Rio in 1964 and ensured the success of the military coup.

# Belo Horizonte

The most impressive way to approach **BELO HORIZONTE** is from the south, over the magnificent hills of the Serra do Espinhaço, on a road that winds back and forth before finally cresting a ridge where the entire city is set out before you. It's a spectacular sight, as Belo Horizonte sprawls in an enormous bowl surrounded by hills, a sea of skyscrapers, *favelas* and industrial suburbs. From the centre, the jagged, rust-coloured skyline of the Serra do Espinhaço, which gave the city its name, is always visible on the horizon – still being transformed by the mines gnawing away at the "breast of iron".

Despite its size and importance, Belo Horizonte is little more than a century old, laid out in the early 1890s on the site of the poor village of Curral del Rey – of which nothing remains – and shaped by the novel ideas of "progress" that emerged with the new Republic. Belo Horizonte was the first of Brazil's planned cities and is arguably the most successful. As late as 1945 it had only 100,000 inhabitants; now it has twenty times that number (forty times if one includes the city's metropolitan hinterland), an explosive rate of growth even by Latin American standards. While it may not be as historic as the rest of the state, it's difficult not to be impressed by the city's scale and energy. Moreover, Belo Horizonte's central location and proximity to some of the most important *cidades históricas* (Sabará is just outside the city, Ouro Preto and Mariana only two hours away by road) make it a good base for exploring Minas Gerais.

The **central zone** of Belo Horizonte is contained within the inner ring road, the **Avenida do Contorno**; the centre is laid out in a grid pattern, crossed by diagonal *avenidas*, which makes it easy to find your way around on foot. The spine of the city is the broad **Avenida Afonso Pena**, with the *rodoviária* at its northern end, in the heart of the downtown area. Just down from the *rodoviária* along Avenida Afonso Pena is the obelisk in the **Praça Sete**, the middle of the busy financial district; a few blocks further down Afonso Pena are the trees and shade of the **Parque Municipal**. A short distance south of the centre, the **Praça da Liberdade**, Belo Horizonte's main square, is dominated by a double row of imperial palms and important public buildings; the chic residential area of **Savassi**, with its restaurants, nightlife and boutiques, lies southeast.

The only places **beyond the Contorno** you're likely to visit are the artificial lake and Niemeyer buildings of **Pampulha**, to the north, the **Museu Histórico Abílio Barreto** to the southwest and the rambling nature reserve of **Mangabeiras**, on the southern boundary of the city.

## Arrival, information and city transport

The nearer of Belo Horizonte's two **airports** is Pampulha (☎31/3490-2001), 9km from the centre and connected by bus #1202. Today only flights from other parts of Minas Gerais arrive here. The much newer Aeroporto Internacional Tancredo Neves (☎31/3689-2700), usually refered to as Confins, the name of the nearby town, handles all other domestic flights as well as the city's growing number of international flights. The airport is 38km from Belo Horizonte and, due to the weight of traffic, the journey can take over an hour. Confins is linked at half-hour intervals to the city by comfortable **airport buses** (R$17) that leave you in the centre at Avenida Alvares Cabral, near the corner of Rua da Bahia. **Taxis** to the city centre from Confins cost around R$90; there are desks in the arrivals areas from where you can purchase vouchers at rates fixed according to your destination.

The **rodoviária** (☎31/3271-3000) is on Praça Rio Branco, an easy walk from the commercial centre of the city, and offers direct bus services throughout Minas Gerais and to most significant destinations in the country. Nearby is the Edwardian **train station** (☎31/3279-4366) on Praça da Estação, a significant sight in its own right (see p.169). Apart from the local *metrô* commuter line, there's now only one passenger service out of Belo Horizonte, the daily connection with Vitória on the coast. Departing at 7.30am, it's an interminably slow but fascinating ride through the industrial heartland of eastern Minas, taking about fourteen hours, much of it following the valley of the Rio Doce (see p.230 for information on departures from Belo Horizonte).

### Information

The municipal Belotur organization (☎31/3277-9777) publishes a free monthly guide, the *Guia Turística*, which contains a good map. You'll find it in most hotels and in the **tourist offices** at: Mercado Central (Mon–Sat 8am–6pm, Sun & holidays 8am–noon); Mercado das Flores, Parque Municipal (Mon–Fri

## Useful bus routes

**Yellow SCO2**: from the *rodoviária* to Praça Sete and Savassi, via Praça da Liberdade.

**Blue 1001**: from Avenida Afonso Pena (between Rua Espírito Santo and Rua Tupis) to Praça da Savassi via Praça da Liberdade.

**Blue 1202**: from Avenida Afonso Pena, down the tree-lined Avenida Amazonas and out to Pampulha airport.

**Blue 4001**: from Avenida Afonso Pena to Praça da Liberdade.

**Blue 2001**: from the Parque das Mangabeiras down Avenida Afonso Pena to Praça Sete and the *rodoviária*.

**Blue 6001**: from the northern entrance of Parque das Mangabeiras to Savassi and the centre.

8am–7pm, Sat & Sun 8am–3pm); Palácio das Artes, Av. Afonso Pena 1537 (Mon–Fri 9am–10pm, Sat & Sun 9am–4pm); Tancredo Neves (Confins) airport (daily 8am–9.30pm); and the *rodoviária* (daily 8am–10pm). The Minas Gerais state tourist office, SETUR, is at Praça Rio Branco 56 (Mon–Fri 9am–6pm; ⓣ31/3272-8585), and is worth a visit for help planning routes in the interior. For up-to-date **listings**, the *Estado de Minas* **newspaper** features a daily *Espetáculo* section, highlighting ongoing events in the city and previewing new shows.

### City transport

The **bus system** works along the same lines as elsewhere in Brazil but is colour-coded: blue buses run up and down the main *avenidas* within the city centre; yellow buses have circular routes; white buses are "express", stopping only at selected points; and red buses are radial, connecting outlying suburbs and *favelas* with the centre. Virtually all routes include a stretch along Avenida Afonso Pena, usually the most convenient place to catch a bus if you are staying in the centre, with all fares around R$2.20; see the box on this page for route details.

Otherwise, with distances being short between most points of interest in the city, **taxis** (BH Táxi ⓣ31/3215-8081; Coopertramo ⓣ3454-5757) are not very expensive. There is a city **metrô system** as well, but this was built with workers rather than tourists in mind and serves only to link the industrial suburbs with the centre.

# Accommodation

You don't need to stray far from the centre for **accommodation**, as there are scores of hotels within easy reach of the *rodoviária*. Strangely for such an important city, Belo Horizonte boasts no really great hotels. That said, there are some good options in the pleasant Savassi area, an easy taxi or bus ride (or a 20min walk) from the centre, and a few in Funcionários, midway between the two. For those on a tight budget, there are a couple of decent **youth hostels** to choose from.

As in most other business-oriented cities, mid- and upper-range hotels will often offer substantial **discounts** to the official rates indicated below; you can usually expect around thirty percent off at weekends and holiday periods.

**Brasil Palace** Rua dos Carijós 269, Centro ⓣ&ⓕ31/3273-3811. A fine 1940s building that overlooks the Praça Sete and still resembles the cinema it once was. The rooms are excellent value, with baths as well as showers, TV, *frigobar* and a/c. ③

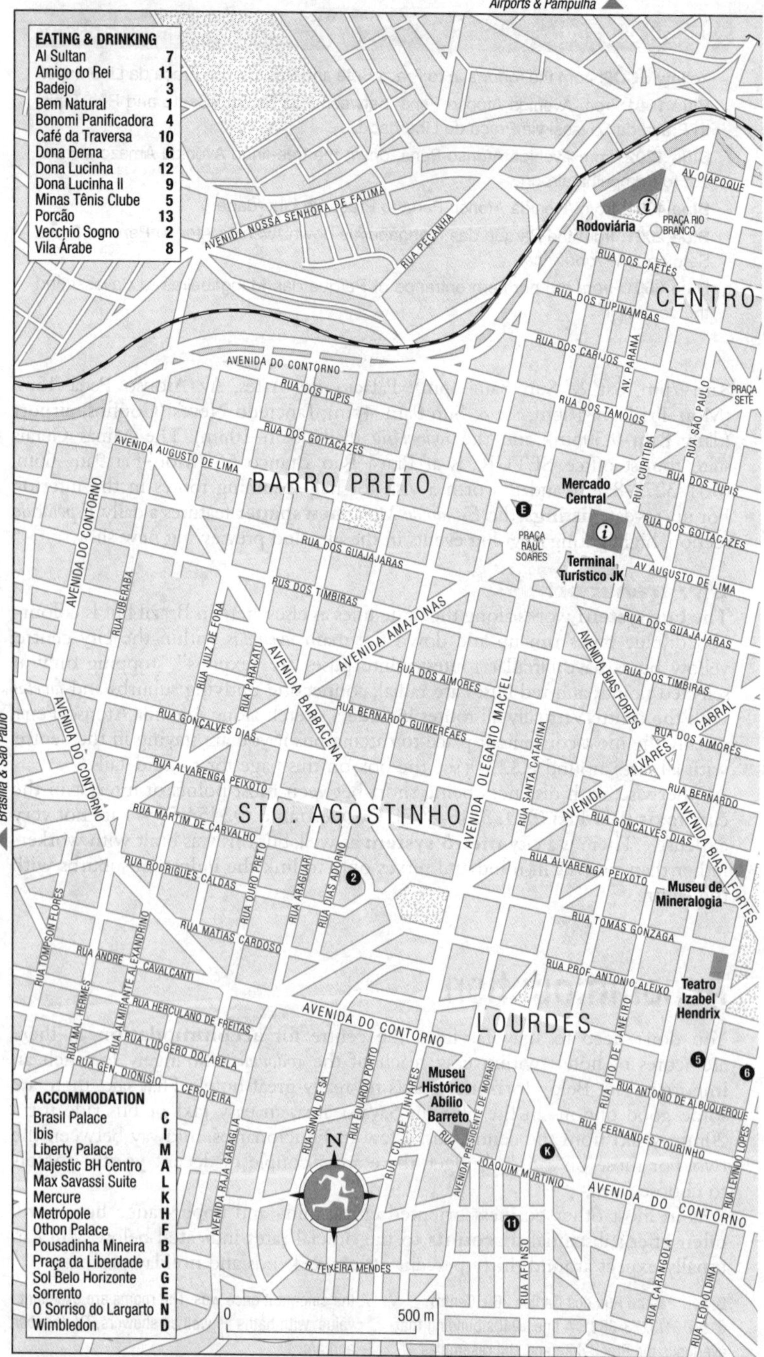
Airports & Pampulha
EATING & DRINKING
Al Sultan 7
Amigo do Rei 11
Badejo 3
Bem Natural 1
Bonomi Panificadora 4
Café da Traversa 10
Dona Derna 6
Dona Lucinha 12
Dona Lucinha II 9
Minas Tênis Clube 5
Porcão 13
Vecchio Sogno 2
Vila Árabe 8
AV OIAPOQUE
Rodoviária
PRAÇA RIO BRANCO
RUA DOS CAETÉS
CENTRO
RUA DOS TUPINAMBAS
RUA DOS CARIJOS
AV. PARANA
AVENIDA NOSSA SENHORA DE FATIMA
RUA PEÇANHA
AVENIDA DO CONTORNO
RUA DOS TUPIS
RUA DOS TAMOIOS
RUA SÃO PAULO
PRAÇA SETE
RUA DOS GOITACAZES
AVENIDA AUGUSTO DE LIMA
RUA CURITIBA
BARRO PRETO
Mercado Central
PRAÇA RAUL SOARES
Terminal Turístico JK
AV AUGUSTO DE LIMA
RUA DOS GUAJAJARAS
RUS DOS TIMBIRAS
AVENIDA AMAZONAS
RUA UBERABA
RUA JUIZ DE FORA
RUA PARACATU
AVENIDA BARBACENA
RUA DOS AIMORES
AVENIDA BIAS FORTES
RUA DOS TIMBIRAS
RUA BERNARDO GUIMERÃES
AVENIDA OLEGARIO MACIEL
RUA GONÇALVES DIAS
AVENIDA ALVARES CABRAL
Brasília & Sao Paulo
RUA ALVARENGA PEIXOTO
RUA SANTA CATARINA
RUA BERNARDO
STO. AGOSTINHO
RUA MARTIM DE CARVALHO
RUA GONCALVES DIAS
RUA RODRIGUES CALDAS
RUA ALVARENGA PEIXOTO
RUA OURO PRETO
RUA ARAGUARI
RUA DIAS ADORNO
Museu de Mineralogia
RUA TOMÁS GONZAGA
RUA MATIAS CARDOSO
RUA TOMPSON FLORES
RUA ANDRE CAVALCANTI
RUA ALMIRANTE ALEXANDRINO
RUA PROF. ANTONIO ALEIXO
Teatro Izabel Hendrix
RUA MAL. HERMES
RUA HERCULANO DE FREITAS
LOURDES
RUA LUDGERO DOLABELA
RUA GEN. DIONISIO CERQUEIRA
Museu Histórico Abílio Barreto
RUA PRESIDENTE DE MORAIS
RUA RIO DE JANEIRO
RUA ANTONIO DE ALBUQUERQUE
RUA FERNANDES TOURINHO
RUA EDUARDO PORTO
RUA SINVAL DE SÁ
RUA CD. DE LINHARES
RUA JOAQUIM MURTINHO
AVENIDA PRESIDENTE DE MORAIS
RUA LEVINDO LOPES
AVENIDA RAJA GABAGLIA
N
R. TEIXEIRA MENDES
RUA AFONSO
RUA CARANGOLA
RUA LEOPOLDINA
0 500 m
ACCOMMODATION
Brasil Palace C
Ibis I
Liberty Palace M
Majestic BH Centro A
Max Savassi Suite L
Mercure K
Metrópole H
Othon Palace F
Pousadinha Mineira B
Praça da Liberdade J
Sol Belo Horizonte G
Sorrento E
O Sorriso do Largarto N
Wimbledon D

Vitória
BELO HORIZONTE
Rio de Janeiro & Ouro Preto
Parque das Mangabeiras
Train Station & Museu de Artes e Ofícios
Igreja São José
Instituto Moreira Salles
Prefeitura
Parque Municipal
Palácio da Justica
Centro Cultural Belo Horizonte
Escola da Música
Palácio das Artes
Central Shopping
Museu Mineiro
Catedral da Boa Viagem
Edifício Niemeyer
Palácio da Liberdade
PRAÇA DA ESTAÇÃO
PRAÇA DA LIBERDADE
PRAÇA SAVASSI
STA. EFIGÊNIA
S. LUCAS
FUNCIONÁRIOS
SAVASSI
SÃO PEDRO
SION
RUA POUSO ALEGRE
RUA CÉRIO DE CASTRO
RUA GUAICURUS
AV SANTOS DUMONT
RUA RIO DE JANEIRO
R. ESPÍRITO SANTO
RUA ITAJUBÁ
AVENIDA DO CONTORNO
AVENIDA FRANCISCO SALES
AV ASSIS CHATEAUBRIAND
RUA AQUILES LOBO
AVENIDA BRANDÃO
RUA MATIAS BARBOSA
AV F. DIOS SANTOS
RUA G. MASCI
RUA BUENOPOLIS
RUA ESMALTINA
RUA ANHANGUERA
RUA PROF. GALEA VELOSO
RUA MÁRMORE
RUA EURITA
RUA BUENO BRANDÃO
RUA CRISTAL
AVENIDA DOS ANDRADAS
AL. ALVARO CELSO
RUA DOMINGOS VIEIRA
RUA ALVARES MACIEL
AV. PROF. ALFREDO BALENA
AVENIDA AFONSO PENA
RUA DA BAHIA
RUA JOÃO PINHEIRO
RUA SERGIPE
RUA ALAGOAS
RUA PERNAMBUCO
RUA PARAÍBA
RUA RIO GRANDE DO NORTE
AVENIDA BERNARDO MONTEIRO
AVENIDA BRASIL
RUA DOS OTONI
RUA GRÃO PARÁ
RUA MANAUS
AVENIDA CARANDAÍ
RUA CEARÁ
RUA PIAUÍ
RUA MARANHÃO
RUA DANTE
GUIMARÃES
RUA GONÇALVES DIAS
RUA CLAUDIO MANOEL
AVENIDA GETULIO VARGAS
RUA POUSO ALTO
RUA MONTE ALEGRE
RUA STA. RITA DURÃO
AV. CRISTOVÃO COLOMBO
RUA DOS INCONFIDENTES
RUA TOMÉ DE SOUZA
RUA PROF. ESTÊVÃO PINTO
RUA CICERO FERREIRA
RUA PALMIRA
RUA VIÇOSA
RUA PADRE ODORICO
RUA LAVRAS
AV. N.S. DO CARMO
RUA GRÃO MOGOL
RUA MINAS NOVAS
RUA FINO
RUA CALDAS
RUA ERNARDO FIGEIREDO

**Ibis** Av. João Pinheiro 602, Centro ⓣ31/2111-1500, ⓦwww.accorhotels.com.br. This efficient hotel on the edge of Funcionários is typical of the chain. Located in a renovated old house with a modern tower building behind, the no-frills rooms are small, but each has a shower and all are a/c. ④

**Liberty Palace** Rua Paraíba 1465, Savassi ⓣ31/3282-0900, ⓦwww.libertypalace.com.br. The most expensive place to stay in Savassi, with all the facilities you would expect of one of the city's top hotels (pool, business centre and decent restaurant). Many of the rooms on the sixth floor and above have panoramic views and all feature plush furnishings. ⑦

**Majestic BH Centro** Rua Espírito Santo 284, Centro ⓣ31/3222-3390, ⓕ3222-3146. Though hardly majestic, this hotel has a wide range of large, clean, basic rooms with or without private bathrooms – nothing special but well priced. ②

**Max Savassi Suite** Rua Antônio de Albuquerque 335, Savassi ⓣ31/3225-6466, ⓦwww.maxsavassi.com.br. All of the units at this good-value apartment hotel with a pool, located on a pleasant tree-lined street, have a bedroom, a living room and a kitchenette. ⑤

**Mercure** Av. do Contorno 7315, Lourdes ⓣ31/3298-4100, ⓦwww.accor.com.br. Situated on the edge of Savassi, this is the city's best-value luxury hotel. Service couldn't be more efficient, the facilities – including a pool and a fitness centre – are excellent and most of the rooms have wonderful views across the city. ⑥

**Metrópole** Rua da Bahia 1023, Centro ⓣ&ⓕ31/3273-1544. This splendid Art-Deco edifice wouldn't appear out of place in Miami's fashionable South Beach district. While its central location is convenient, the most attractive rooms (at the front of the hotel, with balconies) are very noisy during the day. The rooms have seen better days, but they're clean and well equipped, with a/c, cable TV and *frigobar*. ④

**Othon Palace** Av. Afonso Pena 1050, Centro ⓣ31/3247-0000, ⓦwww.othon.com.br. A huge and recently refurbished 1970s skyscraper with friendly and highly professional staff, well-equipped rooms and a fine rooftop pool. Be sure to request a room on one of the upper floors facing out from the front of the building – the views across the Parque Municipal and onwards to the Serra do Curral are spectacular. ⑥

**Pousadinha Mineira** Rua Espírito Santo 604, Centro ⓣ31/3273-8156. With two hundred beds, this is by far the largest youth hostel in the city. As a former hotel, it has a decidedly institutional feel, but its very central location is a plus. R$25 per person.

**Praça da Liberdade** Av. Brasil 1912, Funcionários ⓣ31/3261-1711, ⓦwww.pracadaliberdade.com.br. Located in a pleasant area filled with government offices, this mini-high-rise hotel is within easy walking distance of the city centre and Savassi. The 29 rooms, while small, are well appointed. ④

**Sol Belo Horizonte** Rua Bahia 1040, Centro ⓣ31/3274-1344, ⓦwww.solmeliabh.com.br. This four-star downtown hotel (part of the Meliá chain) has pleasant rooms, efficient though somewhat impersonal service, a pool and a sauna. Popular with business executives, the place empties at weekends. ⑥

**Sorrento** Praça Raul Soares 354, Centro ⓣ31/3272-1100, ⓦwww.hotelsorento.com.br. Clean, comfortable and efficiently run budget hotel in a pleasant downtown location on the edge of Barro Preto and its nightlife zone. The nicest rooms overlook the *praça*, but can be a little noisy. ③

**O Sorriso do Lagarto** Rua Padre Severino 285, Savassi ⓣ31/3283-9325, ⓦwww.osorrisodolagarto.com.br. A friendly and fairly small youth hostel on the edge of one of the city's most fashionable neighbourhoods. R$25 in a dorm or R$45 for a single room.

**Wimbledon** Av. Afonso Pena 772, Centro ⓣ31/3222-6160, ⓦwww.wimbledon.com.br. Good mid-range hotel in the heart of downtown. The rooms are fairly small and simply furnished, but all have cable TV, a/c and a rather ageing *frigobar*, plus there's a very small pool. Ask for one of the rooms overlooking Av. Afonso Pena, as these are much brighter. ⑤

# The City

Even the most patriotic *mineiro* would make few claims for the architecture of Belo Horizonte, dominated as it is by nondescript 1960s and 1970s high-rises. Nonetheless, there are some notable exceptions, chiefly on and around **Praça da Liberdade**. Additionally, if you stand in the heart of the city, in **Praça Sete**, and look down the broad Avenida Afonso Pena towards the Parque Municipal, or along the graceful palm-lined Avenida Amazonas, you'll notice the city has a number of attractive features.

## Praça da Estação and Praça Sete

A good place to begin wandering through downtown Belo Horizonte is the beautifully renovated **train station** on Praça da Estação, one of the city's most elegant buildings. The Neoclassical yellow-coloured edifice, which replaced Belo Horizonte's original main station in 1922, is among Brazil's finest examples of tropical Edwardiana, although these days the station's platforms are used only by passengers on the once-daily Vitória-bound service or commuters riding the city's *metrô*. Housed inside the station is the **Museu de Artes e Ofícios** (Tues, Thurs & Fri noon–7pm, Wed noon–9pm, Sat & Sun 11am–5pm; Ⓦwww.mao.com.br; R$4), which traces the history of arts and crafts in Minas Gerais. Though impressively displayed, the museum's extensive collection of handicrafts and tools provides little in the way of social or economic context, making a visit here seem somewhat pointless. You can, however, admire the craftsmanship of the hardwood staircases, stained-glass windows and iron- and plasterwork inside the building, all of which are well worth a look.

Graced on both sides by imperial palms, Avenida Amazonas, one of the city's main arteries, leads up from Praça da Estação into the **Praça Sete**. Humming with activity, Praça Sete is full of office workers (the area immediately around is the city's main financial district) and is also the main venue of street draughts tournaments, when rows of hustlers set up boards on the pavement and play all comers for money. Surrounding the square are bars and *lanchonetes*, which stay open until midnight (even later at weekends).

A ten-minute stroll beyond Praça Sete, at the intersection of Rua dos Goitacazes and Rua Santa Catarina, is the **Mercado Central** (Mon–Sat 7am–6pm, Sun 7am–1pm), a sprawling indoor market of almost four hundred stalls. There's an incredible variety of goods on offer, ranging from the usual fruit, vegetables, cheeses and meats to animals, *cachaças*, spices, medicinal herbs, kitchen equipment, rustic handicrafts, and *umbanda* and *candomblé* accessories.

## Avenida Afonso Pena and the Parque Municipal

Running southeast from Praça Sete, the broad Avenida Afonso Pena bisects Belo Horizonte and is home to some of the city's showcase buildings, as well as the **Instituto Moreira Salles**, near Praça Sete, at no. 737 (Tues–Fri 1–7pm, Sat & Sun 1–6pm; Ⓦwww.ims.com.br), a cultural centre that hosts major exhibitions of nineteenth- and twentieth-century Brazilian art and photography.

Further along the avenue, midway between Rua Tamoios and Rua Espírito Santo at the top of a flight of steps, is the **Igreja São José** (Mon–Sat 7–11am & 3–8pm and Sun 7am–noon & 3–8pm), which dates back to 1906 and was the first church in the new capital; its eclectic Manueline and Gothic style is characteristically Brazilian, and it is set in an attractive tree-filled garden. Continuing south along the avenue between Rua da Bahia and Avenida Álvares Cabral, the Art Deco–influenced **Prefeitura** (town hall) was built in the 1930s as an early boast of civic pride; just a short distance on are the imposing **Palácio da Justiça** and the **Escola da Música**, each supported by Corinthian columns. On the other side of the avenue is one of the very few large-scale areas of relief from the traffic and noise of downtown: the green and shade of the **Parque Municipal** (Tues–Sun 6am–6pm). Laid out by the French landscape artist Paul Villon, the park encompasses a boating lake, two thousand species of tree, shaded walks, aviaries, a permanent fairground and exercise yards. It also contains the main arts complex in the city, the Palácio das Artes.

### Palácio das Artes

The **Palácio das Artes** (entrance on Av. Afonso Pena 1537 ⓦwww.palaciodasartes.com.br) is one of the finest modern buildings in the city, a complex of which the citizens of Belo Horizonte are justifiably proud. The *palácio* is divided into a number of well-laid-out **galleries** (daily 9am–9pm; free), with exhibitions concentrating on modern Brazilian art, a couple of small **theatres** and one big one, the **Grande Teatro**.

Though it's hard to believe in such a large city, the *palácio* is one of the very few places in Belo Horizonte where you'll come across a good display of the state's distinctive *artesanato*. Although there's a lot of dross on sale here in the **Centro de Artesanato Mineiro** (Mon 1–6pm, Tues–Fri 9am–9pm, Sat 9am–1pm, Sun 10am–2pm), there's also some excellent pottery in the form of stubby figurines and realistic clay tableaux, the most distinctive of which comes from the valley of the Rio Jequitinhonha. Hammocks, clothes, wall hangings and rugs, roughly woven from the cotton that grows in northern Minas, are also of a high quality. Despite the sleek surroundings, the prices here are reasonable.

### Feira de Arte e Artesanato

It's worth making an effort to be in Belo Horizonte on a Sunday morning for the **Feira de Arte e Artesanato**. One of the best of its kind anywhere in the country, with buyers and sellers coming from all over Brazil, this massive market takes over the Avenida Afonso Pena bordering the Parque Municipal. It's always packed, and by mid-morning, moving through the narrow avenues between rows of stalls gets difficult; by 2pm, stallholders are packing up and leaving, and by 4pm the city's efficient street cleaners will have removed all trace of the market. An excellent place for bargains, the market is split into sections, with related stalls grouped together – jewellery, leather goods, lace, ceramics, cane furniture, clothes, food, paintings and drinks, to name but a few.

## Funcionários and Praça da Liberdade

Southwest of Avenida Afonso Pena, behind the grand public buildings, are the hilly tree-lined roads of **Funcionários**, a neighbourhood – as the name suggests – dominated by government offices.The district also contains the **Catedral da Boa Viagem**, Rua Alagoas (Mon & Sat 11am–10pm, Tues–Fri & Sun 6am–10pm), inaugurated in 1922 to mark the centenary of Brazilian independence. For a cathedral of a major city, the neo-Gothic structure is surprisingly small and plain, but the grounds are beautiful.

A short walk southwest of the cathedral, the impressive, Neoclassical **Museu Mineiro**, Av. João Pinheiro 342 (Tues–Fri 11.30am–6.30pm, Sat, Sun & holidays 10am–4pm; R$2), was one of the first buildings in Belo Horizonte, dating from 1897. The building served as the state senate from 1905 to 1930, only being converted for use as a museum much later, and today houses an unremarkable sample of the tradition of religious art in Minas. One block west from Avenida João Pinheiro is the steep Rua da Bahia where, at no. 1149, is the **Centro de Cultura Belo Horizonte** (Mon–Fri 9am–9pm, Sat & holidays 9am–6pm, Sun 2–6pm), a curious neo-Gothic structure built in 1914 as the city's legislative assembly. The inside of the building, with its wood panelling and sweeping staircase, is worth a look, and there are often small exhibitions or concerts going on. One block north down the road, the shocking-pink-and-blue *Hotel Metrópole* is one of the purest examples of Art Deco in the city.

The park-like **Praça da Liberdade** lies to the south of Funcionários. With its beautiful trees, Edwardian bandstand and fountains, the square is a wonderful place to sit and while away the time; it's especially popular on weekends when residents of neighbouring apartment buildings come out to rollerblade or sit and read in the sun. The square is dominated by the elegant Neoclassical-style **Palácio da Liberdade** (last Sun of the month 9am–5pm), built between 1895 and 1898 as the residence of the president of Minas Gerais. Today, the *palácio* remains the administrative centre of the state government, and is primarily used for state functions. Another building to look out for on the square is the **Edifício Niemeyer** apartment building, whose flowing lines architect Oscar Niemeyer designed in the 1950s; it's still one of Belo Horizonte's most prestigious residential city-centre addresses today. Directly across the *praça* from the apartment building, at Av. Bias Fortes 50, sits the ugly glass-and-steel **Museu de Mineralogia** (Tues–Sun 9am–5pm), whose extensive collection of minerals and local fossils is likely to be of interest only to geologists.

## Museu Histórico Abílio Barreto

One of the few museums in the city really worth a visit is the **Museu Histórico Abílio Barreto** (Tues–Sun 10am–5pm; Ⓦ www.amigosdomhab.org.br) at Av. Prudente de Morais 202 in Cidade Jardim. To get there, take the #5901 bus (marked "Nova Floresta/Santa Lúcia"); the most convenient stop to catch it is along Avenida Amazonas between Rua Espírito Santo and Rua dos Caetés. If you ask the conductor for the Museu Histórico, you'll be dropped on Avenida do Contorno, a block away, from where there are signs to the museum.

The museum was once a *fazenda*, built in 1883, comfortable but not luxurious, and typical of the ranches of rural Minas. Though the property has long been swamped by the burgeoning city, the *fazenda* buildings have been perfectly preserved and now house the usual collection of old furniture and mediocre paintings and, in the garden, a train from the early 1900s used in the construction of Belo Horizonte. Far better is the rustic wooden veranda at the front, where you can sit with your feet up and imagine yourself back in the 1880s.

By far the most interesting part of the museum is the **galeria de fotografias**, juxtaposing images from the sleepy village before it was obliterated – mules, mud huts and ox carts – with views of the modern city through the decades; there are a couple of well-designed maps to help you get your bearings. The last remnant of Curral del Rey, the eighteenth-century Igreja Matriz, was flattened in 1932; a few photographs and carved bits of the church piled in a shed in the garden are all that remain of the vanished community.

## Parque das Mangabeiras

Unlikely as it may seem amid the skyscrapers of Avenida Afonso Pena, the city limits are only a short bus-ride away to the south. Here, the urban sprawl is abruptly cut off by the steep hills of the **Serra do Curral**, a natural barrier that forces the city to expand in other directions. The slopes are the site of a huge nature reserve, the 600-hectare **Parque das Mangabeiras** (Tues–Sun 8am–6pm), where you can walk along forest paths that occasionally open out to reveal spectacular views of the city below. To get there, catch the blue #2001-C bus, marked "Aparecida", from Avenida Afonso Pena between Avenida Amazonas and Rua Tamóios; it's a fifteen-minute steep drive to the terminus above the park entrance. When returning to the city, you can avoid having to climb back up to the main entrance by leaving the park through the small northern gate, much lower down, and catching the #6001 bus just outside.

The park is so big it has its own **internal bus service**; buses leave every thirty minutes from the left of the entrance, and end up there again twenty minutes later after making a circuit of the park. There's an excellent view of the city from the **Mirante da Mata** viewing platform, a twenty-minute amble from the entrance; the finest walks are along the nature trails and streams of the **Parque Florestal**, a little further along.

### Mirante das Mangabeiras

The single most spectacular view of the city is from the **Mirante das Mangabeiras**, just outside the park and largely hidden by trees behind the governor's palatial official residence. Take the #2001-C bus for Mangabeiras (or the #2001-A), but get off just before at Praça do Papa and walk east up the steep Rua Bady Salum for a kilometre. The view is splendid; too high up for the grime and *favelas* to register (although pollution can obscure things on a bad day), with the city wonderful at night, when the carpet of lights below really is magnificent.

## Pampulha

Some 10km north of the centre (an hour or so by bus), the luxurious district of **Pampulha** is built around an artificial lake overlooked by some of the finest modern buildings in the city – the Museu de Arte, the modernist Igreja de São Francisco and the Casa do Baile. They are instantly recognizable as the work of architect **Oscar Niemeyer**, creator of Brasília, and landscape designer **Roberto Burle Marx** – both of whom, with their socialist ideals, were presumably horrified by the subsequent development of the area as a rich residential district.

### The Igreja de São Francisco de Assis

The construction of the **Igreja de São Francisco de Assis** (daily 8–6pm; R$2), with its striking curves, *azulejo* frontage and elegant bell tower, provides a roll call of the greatest names of Brazilian modernism: Burle Marx laid out its grounds,

▲ Igreja de São Francisco de Assis, Pampulha

Niemeyer designed the church, Cândido Portinari did the tiles and murals depicting the fourteen stations of the cross and João Ceschiatti (best known for his gravity-defying angels in Brasília's cathedral) contributed the bronze baptismal font. The church's design was decades ahead of its time and it's astonishing to realize that it dates from the early 1940s. So shocked was the intensely conservative local Catholic hierarchy by the building's daring that the archbishop refused to consecrate it and almost twenty years passed before Mass could be held there. Sunday Mass is now held at 10.30am and 6pm. To get there, take bus #2004 (marked "Bandeirantes/Olhos d'Água") from Avenida Afonso Pena, between Avenida Amazonas and Rua Tupinambás.

### The Museu de Arte (MAP) and Casa do Baile

The **Museu de Arte da Pampulha** (Tues–Sun 9am–7pm; R$4) – or MAP as it is usually called – is more difficult to reach; take the #2215 bus from Rua dos Caetés and get off when you see a sign for the *museu* to the left – you then have to walk down to the lakeside Avenida Otacílio Negrão de Lima, turn right, and the museum is on a small peninsula jutting out into the lake. It's worth the trip, although the small collection of modern art it holds isn't even faintly compelling. The structure, however, is a product of two geniuses at the height of their powers. Niemeyer created a virtuoso building, all straight lines and right angles at the front but melting into rippling curves at the back, with a marvellous use of glass; Burle Marx set the whole thing off beautifully, with a sculpture garden out back and an exquisite garden framing the building in front. It was built as a casino in 1942, but the Brazilian government abolished gambling soon after and not until 1957 was the building inaugurated as an art museum.

Directly opposite, on the other side of the lake, the **Casa do Baile** (Tues–Sun 9am–7pm), a former dance hall, is by the same duo. The building is now used as a space for temporary exhibitions of art and design that are sometimes worth a brief visit. Get there on the #1202 bus from Rua São Paulo between Avenida Amazonas and Rua dos Carijós.

### Football in Pampulha

Belo Horizonte's main football stadium, the **Mineirão** (☎31/3499-1100), is also situated in prestigious Pampulha (the #2004 bus passes by the stadium). With a capacity of 90,000, the Mineirão is a world-class stadium, but it's rarely full. One of Brazil's better teams, Atlético Mineiro, play here, and they're worth catching if you're in Belo Horizonte on a Sunday during a home game. Local derbies, especially against Cruzeiro, are torrid and very entertaining affairs, but they often end with supporters of the rival teams destroying a large number of the city's buses. Entrance costs are around R$15 for the *arquibancada* (stands), rising to R$60 for better seats.

## Eating, drinking and nightlife

You can eat well in Belo Horizonte and prices are generally quite reasonable, though outside the immediate downtown area, **restaurants** and **bars** tend to be more upmarket. Savassi has a particularly good range of options.

Belo Horizonte's chic **nightlife** is also concentrated in Savassi, but you'll find lively pockets of bars and clubs throughout the central area, as well as in the *bairros* of Barro Preto and Pampulha.

## Comida mineira

Minas Gerais' tasty (if heavy) **regional food**, *comida mineira*, is one of Brazil's most distinctive – based mainly on pork, the imaginative use of vegetables, *couve* (a green vegetable somewhat like kale), and the famous *tutu*, a thick bean sauce made by grinding uncooked beans with manioc flour and cooking the mixture. Many of the dishes originate from the early mule trains and *bandeirante* expeditions of the eighteenth century, when food had to keep for long periods (hence the use of salted pork, now usually replaced by fresh) and be easily prepared without elaborate ingredients.

*Comida mineira* is not difficult to find; outside Belo Horizonte it is rare to come across restaurants that serve anything else, and the capital itself has plenty of authentic establishments, provided you know where to look. There are also small stores everywhere serving Minas Gerais' *doces* (cakes and sweetmeats), local cheeses, made both from goats' and cows' milk, and, of course, *cachaça*, usually drunk neat here before a meal "to prepare the stomach" and then again after a meal "to settle the stomach". **Typical dishes** include:

**Carne picadinha** A straightforward, rich stew of either beef or pork, cooked for hours until tender.

**Costelinha** Stewed ribs of ham.

**Dobradinha** Tripe stew cooked with sweet potatoes. Stews (including the two above) often include the excellent Minas sausages, smoked and peppery.

**Doce de leite** A rich caramel sludge.

**Feijão tropeiro** ("Mule driver's beans"). A close relative to *tutu a mineira* (see below), with a name that betrays its eighteenth-century origins; it features everything that is in a *tutu* but also has beans fried with *farinha* (manioc flour), egg and onion thrown into the mix.

**Frango ao molho pardo** Definitely one for hardened carnivores only: essentially chicken cooked in its own blood. It's better than it sounds, but rather bitter in taste.

**Frango com quiabo** Chicken roasted with okra and served sizzling with a side plate of *anju*, a corn porridge that *mineiros* eat with almost anything.

**Tutu a mineira** Most common of all dishes, found on every menu; roasted pork served with lashings of *tutu*, garnished with steamed *couve* and *torresmo* (an excellent salted-pork crackling).

## Snacks, street food and restaurants

The best area for moderately priced meals is **downtown**, around Praça Sete and towards the train station, where many of the *lanchonetes* serve good, simple and cheap *comida mineira*. Also central, Rua Pernambuco, in **Funcionários**, is a fine place for reasonable *comida mineira por kilo* restaurants, especially popular at lunchtime with workers from nearby government offices.

**Street food** is worth trying as well. On Saturdays between 10am and 4pm, food stalls go up at the Feira Tom Jobim (a street market where antiques and bric-a-brac are sold) along Avenida Bernardo Monteiro on the corner with Avenida Brasil; the stands serve foreign and Brazilian regional food (including, of course, *mineiro*), which is often extremely good and always cheap. Similar stalls crowd the busy Sunday market on Avenida Afonso Pena. For your own supplies, head for the modern and colourful **Mercado Central** (see p.169).

### Restaurants

Oddly enough, exceptionally good **comida mineira restaurants** are not easy to find in Belo Horizonte, as the state's regional specialities (see box above) are more associated with small town and country life than city sophistication. There are, however, a good range of restaurants serving up **international cuisine**, ranging from inexpensive Lebanese to pricey French, Italian or Japanese.

**Al Sultan** Rua Tomé de Souza 1140, Savassi. Simple and inexpensive, but with a wide range of authentic Lebanese dishes. Open Mon–Sat evenings.

**Amigo do Rei** Rua Quintiliano 118, Santo Antônio ⓣ31/3296-3881. Probably the only Iranian restaurant in Brazil, serving simple but very tasty, moderately priced food in a casually elegant setting; the meat dishes (both stewed, typically with a pomegranate sauce, and grilled) are a highlight. Open Wed–Sat evenings & Sun lunch.

**Badejo** Rua Rio Grande do Norte 836, Funcionários ⓣ31/3261-2023. Lots of fish and other seafood choices are available at this restaurant, which specializes in the food of Espírito Santo. If you won't be visiting that state, at least try one of the distincive *mocquecas* – a tomato-based stew, unlike the Bahian dish of the same name which uses coconut milk. Closed Mon and also Sun evening.

**Bem Natural** Av. Afonso Pena 941, Edifício Sulacap, 2 blocks east of Praça Sete, Centro. This restaurant, which combines with a health-food shop and alternative bookstore, serves excellent vegetarian food as well as some chicken and fish dishes. Inexpensive. Open Mon–Fri; full menu at lunchtime, soup only 5–8pm.

**Bonomi Panificadora** Rua Cláudio Manoel 488, Funcionários ⓣ31/3261-3460. Located in a burgundy-coloured building without a sign on the corner of Av. Afonso Pena, this "bakery" serves excellent light meals (salads, pasta, soups and sandwiches), wonderful cakes and what may be the best bread anywhere in Brazil.

**Café da Travessa** Av. Getúlio Vargas 1405, Savassi. At Praça Savassi, within Belo Horizonte's best bookstore, the café serves tasty snacks, cakes and light meals including pasta dishes, sandwiches and excellent hamburgers. On weekdays from 6–9pm there's live music, usually jazz or bossa nova. Open Mon–Fri 8am–10pm, Sat 8am–6pm, closed Sun.

**Dona Derna** Rua Tomee de Sousa 1380, Funcionários ⓣ31/3223-6954. Very good (if rather heavy) traditional northern Italian cooking, moderately priced, with a strong emphasis on meat dishes.

**Dona Lucinha II** Rua Sergipe 811, Funcionários ⓣ31/3261-5930. This and its sister restaurant (*Dona Lucinha*, Rua Padre Odorico 38, São Pedro; ⓣ31/3227-0562) offer a very authentic *comida mineira* buffet for just R$30 per person. The vast range of meat and vegetable dishes, and the wonderful desserts, are all helpfully labelled in English, and excellent home-made *cachaça*-based liqueurs are available to sample. If you have time for just one meal in Belo Horizonte, this is the place to go. Closed Sun evening.

**Emporium Armazém Mineiro** Av. Afonso Pena 4034, Mangabeiras ⓣ31/3281-1277. Decent *comida mineira* is served amidst an attractive rustic-chic ambience. For a main dish, such as *tutu a mineira* (see opposite), suitable for two people, expect to pay about R$35. Aside from the main dining room, there's a *cachaçeria*, modelled on a typical village bar, where you can sample *cachaças* and tasty snacks. Take bus #5508 from Rua dos Caetés or #2001 from Av. Afonso Pena in the centre. Closed Sun & Mon evenings.

**Minas Tênis Clube** Rua da Bahia 2244, Lourdes ⓣ31/3516-1310. The tennis club's excellent-value (R$25 per person) lunch buffet is one of the city centre's best-kept secrets. Choose a table on the terrace overlooking the tennis courts, gardens and pool and marvel at the club's Art-Deco splendour. The food's good too – a varied selection of salads and hot dishes.

**Porcão** Rua Raja Gabaglia 2985, São Bento ⓣ31/3293-8787. Though a first rate *churrascaria*, the buffet also has a vast array of seafood dishes, pasta and salads. Located a short taxi ride a little southwest of the Contorno, the breathtaking views of the Serra do Corral and of the city are every bit as good as the food. About R$70 for *rodízio*.

**Vecchio Sogno** Rua Martim de Carvalho 75, Santo Agostinho ⓣ31/3292-5231. Widely considered to be one of the best restaurants in the city (and one of the most expensive; expect to pay around R$150 per person), *Vecchio Sogno* has made a name for itself with an imaginative mix – and sometimes fusion – of Italian, French and Brazilian recipes. Try the duck lasagna with wild mushrooms or the herb gnocchi with a prawn sauce, and don't miss the banana *tarte tatine* served with *queijo-de-minas* ice cream. Closed Sat lunch & Sun evening.

**Vila Árabe** Rua Pernambuco 781, Savassi ⓣ31/3362-1600. Moderately priced and very tasty Lebanese food is served in attractive surroundings. The buffet is good value at R$40, or you can opt for the vegetarian or mixed *mezze* at R$35 for two. The *cordeiro* (lamb) dishes are especially good.

**Xapuri** Rua Mandacaru 260, Pampulha ⓣ31/3496-6198. The superb *comida mineira* includes dishes you're unlikely to find elsewhere. The veal *osso buco* with banana is cooked to perfection and the buffet of thirty different desserts rounds off an excellent meal. *Xapuri* has a nice atmosphere too – that of a country house, the kitchen's wood-fired stoves and ovens clearly visible – and it's a good place to purchase *artesanato* as well as *doces* made on the premises.

## Nightlife and entertainment

Compared to Rio and São Paulo, Belo Horizonte's nightlife is extremely measured and discreet, but there are several areas in the central part of the city where the **bars** spring to life once it gets dark. Most days of the week, the bottom end of **Rua da Bahia** between Avenida Afonso Pena and Praça da Estação is lively; the bars put out tables under the palm trees and the action goes on until the late hours. The area around the intersection of **Rua Rio de Janeiro and Avenida Augusto de Lima** is also good, but more student-like. There are a couple of small theatres and cinemas close by, and a group of bars and restaurants – a good one is *Mateus*, serving a range of light snacks and pizzas on the corner. It's also worth checking out the bars along **Rua Guajajaras** between Rua Espírito Santo and Rua da Bahia.

The more sophisticated spots are in **Savassi** and neighbouring **Funcionários**, both pleasant places in which to spend an evening. Drinks are only marginally more expensive here than anywhere else, and the bars get very crowded at weekends. *Clube da Esquina*, Rua Sergipe 146, Funcionários (closed Sun evening) is located in a building, dating from 1902, where the first beer was produced in Minas. There's live music here most evenings and especially tasty snacks are served. There's plenty of bars in Savassi, but a good starting point is *Redentor*, Rua Fernandes Tourinho 500, for its friendly atmosphere and superior range of beers.

### Cachaça

If you want to be initiated into the wonderful world of **cachaça** (sugar-cane rum), a trip out to the *Alambique Cachaçaria*, Av. Raja Gabáglia 3200, Chalé 1, Estoril, is a must, and also offers beautiful night views of Belo Horizonte from the top of the hill. Besides the live music, the main attraction here is the *cachaça Germana*, their own brew which is available plain or infused with herbs and honey. They also serve the traditional *caipirinhas* – *cachaça* with ice, lemon and sugar – as well as straight shots. A single shot costs R$3 and a bottle begins at R$30. The easiest way to get here is to take a ten- to fifteen-minute taxi ride from the centre for about R$20.

### Discos and live music

Although Minas Gerais is considered to be one of Brazil's more conservative states, Belo Horizonte stands out for having quite a mix of nightclubs and places simply to hear live music. Big names play at *Minascentro*, Av. Augusto de Lima 785 (☎31/3201-0122), at the Palácio das Artes (☎31/3237-7333) and at the Teatro Izabela Hendrix, Rua da Bahia 2020 (☎31/3292-4405). Expect to pay around R$25 for a ticket for a lesser-known act or over R$100 for a star performer. In addition to the places listed below, there's an ever-changing clubbing scene in **Barro Preto**, where Avenida Raja Gabáglia is stuffed with gritty live-music venues, simple *mineiro* restaurants and small bars good for listening to *setaneja* (Brazilian country music) or dancing to more mainstream sounds.

**Centro Cultural Casa África** Rua Leopoldinha 48, Santo Antônio. For African dance music, this is the place to go on Fri and Sat nights.

**Mamãe já sabia** Av. do Contorno 2317, Santa Tereza ☎31/3213-9063. A bar and nightclub in the bohemian neighbourhood of Santa Tereza attracting a largely gay and lesbian crowd. DJs offer disco sounds interspersed with local bands performing an eclectic mix of Brazilian music.

**Máscaras** Rua Santa Rita Durão 667, Savassi ☎31/3261-6050. With two dancefloors, separate bars and video rooms, all kitted out in chic, modern style, this nightclub (open until 6am at weekends) is extremely popular. It operates a system similar to many of Brazil's more swish clubs, where you pay for seats at a table.

**A Obra** Rua Rio Grande do Norte 1168, Funcionários ☎31/3261-9431. Expect all forms of rock music – Brazilian and foreign – attracting a young and hip crowd to this popular basement club.

**Paco Pigalle** Rua Ouro Preto 301, Barro Preto ⓣ31/3291-0747. Plays a mix of hip-hop, reggae, salsa and disco to a young and trendy crowd.

**Parte Non** Rua Rio Grande do Norte 1470, Savassi ⓣ31/3221-9856. A glitzy club that's favoured by Scotch-drinking twenty-somethings who don't want to stray beyond their upmarket neighbourhood.

**Terra Brasilis** Rua Tomé de Souza 987, Savassi. This bar has excellent live samba.



### Cinema and theatre

There are several **art cinemas** in Belo Horizonte with imaginative programming; try the Cine Humberto Mauro (ⓣ31/3237-7234) in the Palácio das Artes (see p.170) and the Cineclube Unibanco Savassi (ⓣ31/3227-6648) at Rua Levindo Lopes in Savassi. Also well worth checking out are the films shown at the Centro Cultural Casa África at Rua Leopoldinha 48, Santo Antônio (ⓦwww.centrocultural.m2014.net); other African and Afro-Brazilian themed events are also held here such as dance performances and plays, and there's a nice bar. There are numerous **theatre** venues around town, though all productions are in Portuguese; the Palácio das Artes (ⓣ31/3201-8900) and the Teatro Izabela Hendrix both host top Brazilian companies visiting the city. The Palácio das Artes also occasionally shows opera and dance – try to catch a performance of the Grupo Corpo (ⓣ31/3221-7701, ⓦwww.grupocorpo.com.br), an internationally renowned dance company that emerged in Belo Horizonte in 1975, or watch out for the amazing puppetry of the Grupo Giramundo (ⓣ31/3421-1114, ⓦwww.giramundo.org), also based in the city.

### Shopping

The main centres for *artesanato* in the city are the Centro de Artesanato Mineiro in the Palácio das Artes (see p.170), and the Sunday market in the Parque Municipal (see p.169). Also excellent are items at Mãos de Minas at Rua Grão Mogol 678, Sion (Mon–Fri 9am–7pm & Sat 9am–1pm). Food, medicinal plants, *umbanda* and *candomblé* accessories and wickerwork can be found in the Mercado Central (see p.169). Afro-Brazilian items are sold at the Centro Cultural Casa África, Rua Leopoldina 48, Santo Antônio (Mon–Thurs 8am–noon & 2–6pm, Fri & Sat 8am–midnight). In Savassi, there's a good range of elegant boutiques to be found in BHZ Fashion Mall, Rua Paraíba 1132 (daily 9am–7pm), as well as on the streets extending off Praça da Savassi.

# Listings

**Airlines** Aerolíneas Argentinas ⓣ31/3224-7466; Air Canada ⓣ31/3344-8355; American Airlines ⓣ31/3274-3166; British Airways ⓣ31/3274-6211; Continental ⓣ31/3274-3177; Delta Airlines ⓣ31/3287-0001; Gol ⓣ31/3490-2073; Pluna ⓣ31/3291-9292; TAM ⓣ31/3689-2233; TAP-Air Portugal ⓣ31/3213-1611; United Airlines ⓣ31/3269-3939; Varig ⓣ31/3339-6000.

**Banks and exchange** Banks are concentrated downtown on Av. João Pinheiro, between Rua dos Timbiras and Av. Afonso Pena. Branches and ATMs common throughout the city.

**Bookshops** The following are reasonable for Brazilian art, history and literature: Livraria da Travessa, Av. Getúlio Vargas 1427, near Praça Savassi; the *Café com Letras*, Rua Antônio de Albuquerque 781, also near Praça Savassi; Livraria Van Damme, Rua Guarajaras 505, Centro; and Livraria UFMG (the university bookshop), Av. Afonso Pena 1534, Centro.

**Car rental** Hertz, at the airports and Av. João Pinheiro 341 ⓣ31/3224-5166 or 224-1279; Interlocadora, at the airports and Rua dos Timbiras 2229 ⓣ31/3275-4090; Localiza, at the airports and Av. Bernardo Monteiro 1567 ⓣ0800/312-121.

**Consulates** Argentina, Rua Ceará 1566, 3rd floor, Funcionários ⓣ31/3281-5288; UK, Rua dos Inconfidentes 1075, sala 1302, Savassi ⓣ31/3261-2072.

**Health matters** Hospital das Clínicas da UFMG is attached to the university, Av. Alfredo Badalena 190, Santa Efigênia ⓣ31/3239-7100.
**Police** ⓣ190. For visa or tourist permit extension, go to the Polícia Federal at Rua Nascimento Gurgel 30, Guiterrez (ⓣ31/3330-5200).
**Post office** The main post office is at Av. Afonso Pena 1270 (Mon–Fri 9am–6pm, Sat 9am–1pm).

**Tour guide** A retired school teacher with seemingly boundless energy, Daisy Quintão (ⓣ31/9135-3902, ⓔdaisyquintao@yahoo.com.br) is a registered guide with an in-depth knowledge of Belo Horizonte and the historic cities, and who speaks excellent English. She can arrange accommodation and transport.



# Around Belo Horizonte

The most popular trips out from the capital are to the *cidades históricas* (see p.180), but there are several other sites that also warrant a visit: to the southwest is **Inhotim**, a wonderful contemporary-art centre set amidst stunning landscape, while to the east, lying beyond the nearest of the *cidades históricas*, Sabará, is the beautiful **Parque Natural do Caraça**.

## Inhotim Instituto Cultural

Opened in 2006 the Inhotim Instituto Cultural (Thurs–Fri 9.30am–4.30pm, Sat & Sun 9.30am–5.30pm; R$10; ⓦwww.inhotim.org.br) is a complete contrast to what one typically associates with Minas Gerais. Here, in the heartland of a state that loudly celebrates a guilded eighteenth-century past, is one of Brazil's most important collections of contemporary art. What's more, with so much of the state's original forest cover long-since stripped away, the cultural centre is set pleasingly amidst 43 hectares of lush gardens featuring a mix of native and exotic plants and surrounded by a 600-hectare mixed *cerrado* and *mata atlântica* nature reserve.

The privately-owned collection started in the 1980s and now comprises over 350 pieces by dozens of Brazilian and international artists, covering a period from the 1960s to the present day. Of particular importance are the sculptures and installations, with fine pieces by Brazilian artists including Tunga, Amilcar de Castro, Hélio Oiticia and Cildo Meir. Although many of the works of art are undoubtedly important in their own right, what makes the collection especially remarkable is the setting. While many works are spread amongst the Centro's ten galleries, others are placed in the gardens – including areas landscape architect Roberto Burle Marx developed – where palms, orchids and other botanical treasures compete for attention with the sculptures.

Inhotim is located some 60km southwest of Belo Horizonte. There is a bus service (R$14 one-way) from the Belo Horizonte *rodoviária* direct to Inhotim on Saturdays and Sundays at 9am, returning at 4pm; on other days you can take a bus from Belo Horizonte to the nearby small town of Brumadinho (R$11 one-way) and then a local bus (R$4) or taxi (around R$15) to Inhotim. There's a good restaurant at Inhotim, serving modern Brazilian food, a café serving light meals and two snack bars.

## Parque Natural do Caraça

The striking **Parque Natural do Caraça** (daily 7am–5pm), named after the impression of a gigantic face in the surrounding mountains, lies 130km east of Belo Horizonte. The park is situated at 2400m above sea level; temperatures drop sharply on summer evenings and it can get very cold in winter. There are plenty of signed walks of varying difficulty on the tracks through the mountains – information is available from the hotel at the park entrance. The park's imposing lake provides a good opportunity for swimming from its small beaches, and there are also several natural pools by the waterfalls within the park. **Buses** from Belo Horizonte to Santa Bárbara (about 4 daily) will drop you at the entrance to the park, and a trip here makes an excellent weekend break from the city.

## Santuário do Caraça

Situated at the only entrance to the park is the **Santuário do Caraça**, a former seminary and school. The **school** was founded on the site of a hermitage and seminary in 1774, and for 150 years educated the upper classes of Minas Gerais, including generations of Brazilian politicians. In 1965 a fire destroyed much of the building, the theatre was burnt to the ground and the library lost two-thirds of its thirty thousand books.

The building was restored in 1991 and transformed into a **hotel**, the *Hospedaria do Caraça* (Ⓣ31/3837-2698, reservations essential; ❸), managed and staffed by the remaining members of the order. Some parts still remain from the original building, including rooms for private prayer, a few bedrooms and the cellar. The neo-Gothic church of Nossa Senhora Mãe dos Homens, added

### Fazenda hotels

With farming in Brazil increasingly dominated by large-scale agribusiness, small and medium-sized farms in Minas Gerais have had to look for new opportunities, and many of those set in particularly attractive countryside, or retaining a grand old *fazenda* house, have turned to tourism to generate income. Within just an hour or so of Belo Horizonte there are several superb **country hotels**, full of character and offering great facilities. If you don't have your own transport, arrangements can usually be made to be picked up locally or even from Belo Horizonte – phone ahead. Reservations are essential, particularly during summer and weekends, and rates always include full board.

**Fazenda Boa Esperança** Florestal Ⓣ31/3536-2344, Ⓦwww.fazendaboaesperanca.com.br. Set in a working 450-hectare dairy farm 45km from Belo Horizonte, the buildings are colonial-style and the guestrooms are simply but comfortably furnished. There's a large pool in the gardens that surround the main building and the property includes some 40 hectares of natural forest with trails you can explore on foot or on horseback. You certainly won't go hungry, as the meals are local cooking at its best. ❼

**Fazenda das Minhocas** Jaboticatubas Ⓣ31/3681-1161, Ⓦwww.fazendadasminhocas.com.br. A historic site in its own right, the *casa grande* dates from 1712 and there's an old Baroque chapel in the grounds as well as a sugar mill and a comfortable, if rustic, *pousada*. There are pleasant trails on the property and facilities for swimming and horse riding. ❼

**Fazenda Recanto dos Fonda** Distrito de Ravena, Sabará Ⓣ31/3672-3399, Ⓦwww.recantodosfonda.com.br. This modern *fazenda* complex, set amidst 200 hectares of lakes and woodland in pleasant walking country, 40km from Belo Horizonte, includes a swimming pool and horse-riding facilities, and serves good country food. ❺

**Pousada Altos de Minas** Município de Nova Minas Ⓣ31/9981-1930, Ⓦwww.pousadaaltodeminas. A modern but colonial-style country hotel 25km from Belo Horizonte, set in lush gardens with a pool. The restaurant offers *mineiro* food as well as international dishes. ❻

in 1883, was also spared by the fire, and has beautiful French stained-glass windows, marble and soapstone carvings and a seven-hundred-pipe organ built in the seminary itself.

A small **museum** is attached to the church and displays items rescued from the fire, including English and Chinese porcelain and furniture. One of the greatest attractions, however, is the **wolves** (*lobo-guará*) that live in the surrounding woods – there's a long-standing tradition of monks leaving food for them near the church.

# The cidades históricas

The **cidades históricas** of Minas Gerais – small enough really to be towns rather than cities – were founded within a couple of decades of each other in the early eighteenth century. Rough and violent mining camps in their early days, mineral wealth soon transformed them into treasure houses, not merely of gold, but also of Baroque art and architecture. Well preserved and carefully maintained, together the towns form one of the most impressive sets of colonial remains in the Americas, comparable only to the silver-mining towns that flourished in Mexico at roughly the same time. In Brazil, they are equalled only by the remnants of the plantation culture of the Northeast, to which they contributed much of the gold you see in the gilded churches of Olinda and Salvador.

Although they have acquired a modern urban fringe, all the historic cities have centres barely untouched by modern developers; a couple, like **Tiradentes**, look very much as they did two centuries ago. All have colonial churches (**Ouro Preto** has thirteen), at least one good museum, steep cobbled streets, ornate mansions and the atmosphere of a place soaked in history. It was in these cities that the **Inconfidência Mineira**, Brazil's first bungling attempt to throw off the Portuguese yoke, was played out in 1789. And here the great sculptor Antônio Francisco Lisboa – **Aleijadinho** or the "little cripple" – spent all his life (see box, p.185), leaving behind him a collection unmatched by any other figure working in the contemporary Baroque tradition.

## Arrival and accommodation

The nearest *cidade histórica* to Belo Horizonte is **Sabará**, only a local bus ride away; the furthest is **Diamantina**, six hours north by bus from the capital in the wild scenery of the Serra do Espinhaço. Two hours southeast from Belo Horizonte, **Ouro Preto** is the ex-capital of the state and the largest of the historic cities, with **Mariana** a short distance away. Two hours to the south of Belo Horizonte is **Congonhas**, where Aleijadinho's masterpiece, the church of Bom Jesus de Matosinhos, is located. A two-hour bus ride further south are **São João del Rei** and **Tiradentes**.

All the cities are well supplied with **places to stay**, a few of which are so inviting that you'll be tempted to linger. If you only have a little time to spare, the best option from Belo Horizonte is Ouro Preto; you can easily get there and back in a day, and – though everyone has their own favourites – it is the most classically beautiful of all.

# Sabará

**SABARÁ** is strung out over a series of hills, wound around the Rio das Velhas. Many of its cobbled streets are so steep they have to be taken slowly, but ascents are rewarded with gorgeous churches that are austere on the outside and choked with ornamentation inside. Sabará's proximity to Belo Horizonte makes it a feasible base for seeing the metropolis, but its accommodation is both limited and unexciting. Fortunately, the frequency of the **bus** link (every 15min from 4am to midnight) makes it an easy day-trip from Belo Horizonte: catch the red #5509 bus on Rua dos Caetés one block up from Avenida Afonso Pena. Start early and avoid visiting on Monday when most sights are closed.

## Arrival, information and accommodation

The nineteen-kilometre journey from Belo Horizonte takes roughly thirty minutes, though the bus station is at the far eastern end of town; ask the driver to show you the best stop for the colonial centre, from where you should easily find Praça Santa Rita. There is a rudimentary **tourist office** (Ⓣ31/3671-1403) around the corner. If in doubt, any road going uphill will invariably lead you to a church, from where it's easy to get your bearings. **Buses back to Belo Horizonte** are best caught on the main road leading out of town at the bottom of the colonial zone by the river.

If you want to **stay**, a lovely place to try, next to the Museu do Ouro, is the *Solar dos Sepúlvedas*, Rua Intendência 371 (Ⓣ31/3671-2705, Ⓦwww.pousadasolarsepulveda.com.br; ❷–❸), a restored eighteenth-century house with just seven rooms decorated with period furniture, well-tended gardens and a pool. There are several **restaurants**, which really only get busy on weekends: *Cê Qui Sabe* at Rua Mestre Caetano 56 and *Bar-ôco* at Rua Mestre Ritinha 115 both serve a reliable *comida mineira*. Cheaper places are clustered around Praça Santa Rita and dotted throughout the old centre, often in people's front rooms.

## The Town

Standing in **Praça Santa Rita**, you're in the centre not just of the oldest part of Sabará, but of the oldest inhabited streets in southern Brazil. Founded in

### Minas Baroque

There are three distinct phases of **Baroque church architecture** in Minas Gerais. The **first**, from the beginning of the eighteenth century to about 1730, was very ornate and often involved extravagant carving and gilding, but left exteriors plain; sculpture was formal, with stiff, rather crude statues. The **second phase** dominated the middle decades of the eighteenth century, with equally extravagant decorations inside, especially around the altar, and the wholesale plastering of everything with gold; the exteriors were now embellished with curlicues and panels in fine Minas soapstone, ceilings were painted and sculpture noticeably more natural, although still highly stylized. The peak was the period from 1760 to 1810, and this **third phase** of *barroco mineiro* produced stunning work: the exterior decoration was more elaborate, with fine carving in both wood and stone, but the interiors were less cluttered, with walls often left plain. By now, too, the religious sculpture, with its flowing realism, had broken the stylistic bounds that confine most Baroque art.

1674, Sabará was the first major centre of gold mining in the state, although attention shifted southwards to Ouro Preto and Mariana by the end of the seventeenth century. The city was established by Borba Gato, a typical *paulista* cut-throat who combined Catholic fervour – Sabará's original name was Vila Real de Nossa Senhora da Conceição de Sabarabuçú – with ruthlessness: his determined extermination of the local Indians made gold mining possible here.

Not until forty years after its foundation were the mud huts and stockades of the early adventurers replaced by stone buildings, and it wasn't until the second quarter of the eighteenth century, when gold production was at its peak, that serious church building began and the village acquired an air of permanence. By the beginning of the nineteenth century all the alluvial gold had been exhausted and the town entered a steep decline. Sophisticated deep-mining techniques introduced by Europeans in the nineteenth century failed to stop the slump, and Sabará became a small and grindingly poor place; today, the colonial zone is fringed by *favelas*.

### Igreja de Nossa Senhora de Ó

The very early days of Sabará are represented by the tiny **Igreja de Nossa Senhora de Ó** (Mon–Fri 8am–5pm and Sat & Sun 9am–noon & 2–5pm; R$1), one of the most unusual colonial churches in Brazil. It's a couple of kilometres from Praça Santa Rita, either via a signposted walk or a local bus marked "Esplanada", which leaves from the square. The church doesn't look in the least Portuguese: its austere, irregularly shaped exterior is topped off by an unmistakeably Chinese tower, complete with pagoda-like upturns at the corners. The cramped interior, dominated by a gilded arch over the altar, also shows distinct oriental influences, but the church is so old (construction began in 1698) that nobody knows who was responsible for its design. The most likely explanation is that the Portuguese, despairing of the local talent, imported a group of Chinese craftsmen from Macau.

### Matriz Nossa Senhora da Conceição

Sabará's main church, **Matriz Nossa Senhora da Conceição** (Mon–Fri 9am–5pm and Sat & Sun 9am–noon & 2–5pm; R$1) is on Praça Getúlio Vargas, signposted from Praça Santa Rita. Started by the Jesuits in 1720, it's a fine example of the so-called first and second phases of *barroco mineiro*. Succeeding generations added features to the original layout and inside it's extremely impressive, with a double row of heavily carved and gilded arches, a beautifully decorated ceiling and, once again, Chinese influence in the gildings and painted panels of the door leading to the sacristy.

### Nossa Senhora do Carmo

The church of **Nossa Senhora do Carmo** (Tues–Sun 9–11.30am & 1–5.30pm; R$2) on Rua do Carmo, a third-phase church, demonstrates the remarkable talents of Aleijadinho, who oversaw its construction and contributed much of the decoration between 1770 and 1783. The interior manages to be elaborate and uncluttered at the same time, with graceful curves in the gallery, largely plain walls, comparatively little gilding and a beautifully painted ceiling. Aleijadinho left his mark everywhere: the imposing soapstone and painted wood pulpits, the banister in the nave, the flowing lines of the choir, and above all in the two statues of São João da Cruz and São Simão Stock. You can tell an Aleijadinho from the faces: the remarkably lifelike one of São Simão is complete with wrinkles and transfixed by religious ecstasy.

### Nossa Senhora do Rosário dos Pretos

Despite being unfinished and open to the elements, the church of **Nossa Senhora do Rosário dos Pretos** ( Tues–Sun 9–11am & 1–5pm; R$1), fifteen minutes' signposted walk from Praça Santa Rita on Praça Melo Viana, is just as fascinating as the more ornate buildings. Slaves who worked in the gold mines built it in typical Portuguese-colonial style. Organized into lay societies called *irmandades*, the slaves paid for and built churches, but this one was begun late, in 1767, and with the decline of the mines the money ran out. Although sporadic restarts were made during the nineteenth century, it was never more than half-built, and when slavery was abolished in 1888 it was left as a memorial.

### The Museu do Ouro

The **Museu do Ouro** (Tues–Sun noon–5pm; R$1) is a short but steep signposted walk up from Praça Santa Rita on Rua da Intendência. Built in 1732, this is the only royal foundry house remaining in Brazil. When gold was discovered in Minas Gerais, the Portuguese Crown was entitled to a fifth of the output but had to collect it first. To do so, it put a military cordon around the gold mines and then built several royal foundries, where gold from the surrounding area was melted down, franked and then given accordingly to the king. The functional building that now houses the museum easily reveals its origins: it is built around an interior courtyard, overlooked by a balcony on three sides, from where the officials could keep an eagle eye on gold being melted into bars and weighed. Along with the other royal foundry in Ouro Preto, it was Brazil's most heavily guarded building.

Most of the museum is devoted to gold-mining history. **Downstairs** are rooms full of scales, weights, pans and other mining instruments, and a strongroom containing plaster-cast replicas of eighteenth-century gold bars. **Upstairs** you'll find a collection of colonial furniture and *arte sacra* as well as a very fine painted ceiling, representing the four continents known at the time it was built.

### The rest of the town

If you tire of colonial sightseeing, just wandering around the bars and cobbled streets near the Praça Santa Rita is very pleasant, too. There are a number of impressive eighteenth-century buildings, notably the **Prefeitura** (Mon–Fri 8am–5pm) on Rua Dom Pedro II, and the **Teatro Municipal** (daily 8am–noon & 1–5pm), on the same street, which was designed as an opera house and opened in 1819 just as the gold ran out. Before you leave the town, have some water from the mid-eighteenth century **Chafariz do Rosário** on Praça Melo Viana; it's believed that all those who drink from the fountain will one day come back to Sabará.

## Ouro Preto

The drive to **OURO PRETO**, 100km southeast of Belo Horizonte, begins unpromisingly with endless industrial complexes and *favelas* spread over the hills, but in its later stretches becomes spectacular as it winds around hill country 1000m above sea level and passes several valleys where patches of forest survive; imagine the entire landscape covered with it and you have an idea of what greeted the gold-seekers in the 1690s. On arrival, the first thing that strikes you is how small the town is, considering that until 1897 it was the capital of Minas (its population is still only 67,000). That said, you can see at a glance why the capital had to be shifted to Belo Horizonte: the steep hills the town is built around,

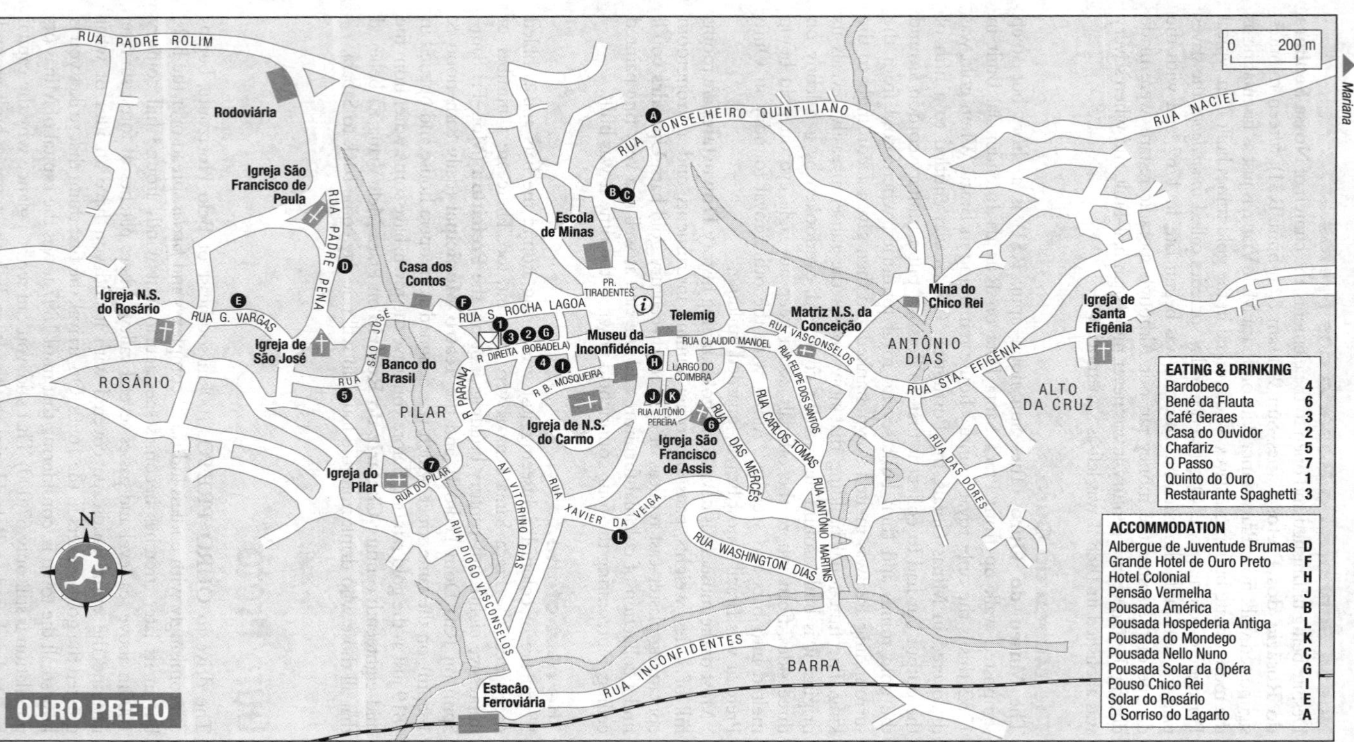
OURO PRETO
Belo Horizonte
Mariana
0 200 m
N
RUA PADRE ROLIM
Rodoviária
Igreja São Francisco de Paula
RUA PADRE PENA
Igreja N.S. do Rosário
RUA G. VARGAS
Igreja de São José
RUA SÃO JOSÉ
ROSÁRIO
Casa dos Contos
Banco do Brasil
PILAR
Igreja do Pilar
RUA DO PILAR
R PARANÁ
RUA DIOGO VASCONSELOS
AV VITORINO DIAS
Estacão Ferroviária
RUA S. ROCHA LAGOA
R DIREITA (BOBADELA)
R B. MOSQUEIRA
Escola de Minas
PR. TIRADENTES
Museu da Inconfidência
Igreja de N.S. do Carmo
RUA XAVIER DA VEIGA
RUA CONSELHEIRO QUINTILIANO
Telemig
RUA CLAUDIO MANOEL
LARGO DO COIMBRA
RUA AUTÔNIO PEREIRA
Igreja São Francisco de Assis
RUA DAS MERCÊS
RUA CARLOS TOMAS
RUA FELIPE DOS SANTOS
RUA VASCONSELOS
Matriz N.S. da Conceição
Mina do Chico Rei
ANTÔNIO DIAS
RUA ANTÔNIO MARTINS
RUA WASHINGTON DIAS
RUA INCONFIDENTES
BARRA
RUA DAS DORES
RUA STA. EFIGÊNIA
ALTO DA CRUZ
Igreja de Santa Efigênia
RUA NACIEL
EATING & DRINKING
Bardobeco 4
Bené da Flauta 6
Café Geraes 3
Casa do Ouvidor 2
Chafariz 5
O Passo 7
Quinto do Ouro 1
Restaurante Spaghetti 3
ACCOMMODATION
Albergue de Juventude Brumas D
Grande Hotel de Ouro Preto F
Hotel Colonial H
Pensão Vermelha J
Pousada América B
Pousada Hospederia Antiga L
Pousada do Mondego K
Pousada Nello Nuno C
Pousada Solar da Opéra G
Pouso Chico Rei I
Solar do Rosário E
O Sorriso do Lagarto A

straddling a network of creeks, severely limit space for expansion. Today, the hills and vertiginous streets of Ouro Preto's historic centre are vital ingredients in what is architecturally one of the loveliest towns in Brazil.

Avoid coming on Monday if you want to see the sights, as all the churches and most of the museums close for the day. Also, buy your onward ticket as soon as you arrive, as buses fill up quickly. Some people complain about Ouro Preto being touristy but they miss the point – it's precisely because there really is something to savour here that the visitors come. If you have the time, aim to spend at least a night or two so that you can enjoy the peace and quiet of the city after all the day-trippers have departed.

Ouro Preto has an extremely popular street **Carnaval** that attracts visitors from far afield, so be sure to reserve accommodation long in advance. Likewise, at

## Aleijadinho (Antônio Francisco Lisboa)

Although little is known of his life, we do know roughly what the renowned sculptor **Aleijadinho** looked like. In the Museu do Aleijadinho in Ouro Preto, a crude but vivid portrait shows an intense, aquiline man who is clearly what Brazilians call *pardo* – of mixed race. His hands are under his jacket, which seems a trivial detail unless you know what makes his achievements truly astonishing: the great sculptor of the *barroco mineiro* was presumably a leper, and produced much of his best work after he had lost the use of his hands.

Antônio Francisco Lisboa was born in Ouro Preto in 1738, the son of a Portuguese craftsman; his mother was probably a slave. For the first half of his exceptionally long life he was perfectly healthy, a womanizer and *bon viveur* despite his exclusively religious output. His prodigious talent – equally on display in wood or stone, human figures or abstract decoration – allowed him to set up a workshop with apprentices while still young, and he was much in demand. Although always based in Ouro Preto, he spent long periods in all the major historic towns (except Diamantina) working on commissions, but never travelled beyond the state. Self-taught, he was an obsessive reader of the Bible and medical textbooks (the only two obvious influences in his work), one supplying its imagery, the other underlying the anatomical detail of his human figures.

In the late 1770s, Aleijadinho's life changed utterly. He began to suffer from a progressively debilitating disease, thought to have been leprosy. As it got worse he became a recluse, only venturing outdoors in the dark, and increasingly obsessed with his work. His physical disabilities were terrible: he lost his fingers, toes and the use of his lower legs. Sometimes the pain was so bad his apprentices had to stop him hacking away at the offending part of his body with a chisel.

Yet despite all this Aleijadinho actually increased his output, working with hammer and chisel strapped to his wrists by his apprentices, who moved him about on a wooden trolley. Under these conditions he sculpted his masterpiece, the 12 massive figures of the prophets and the 64 life-size Passion figures for the **Basílica do Senhor Bom Jesus de Matosinhos** (see p.196) in Congonhas, between 1796 and 1805. The figures were his swansong; failing eyesight finally forced him to stop work and he ended his life as a hermit in a hovel on the outskirts of Ouro Preto. The death he longed for finally came on November 18, 1814; he is buried in a simple grave in the church he attended all his life, Nossa Senhora da Conceição in Ouro Preto.

Aleijadinho's prolific output would have been remarkable under any circumstances. Given his condition it was nothing short of miraculous – a triumph of the creative spirit. The bulk of his work is to be found in Ouro Preto, but there are significant items in Sabará, São João del Rei, Mariana and Congonhas. His unique achievement was to stay within the Baroque tradition, yet bring to its ornate conventions a raw physicality and unmatched technical skill.

**Easter**, the town becomes the focus of a spectacular series of plays and processions lasting for about a month before Easter Sunday; the last days of the life of Christ are played out in open-air theatres throughout town.

## Some history

Less than a decade after gold was struck at Sabará, a *paulista* adventurer called **Antônio Dias** pitched camp underneath a mountain the Indians called Itacolomi, with an unmistakeable thumb-shaped rock on its summit. Panning the streams nearby, he found "black gold" – alluvial gold mixed with iron ore – and named his camp after it. It attracted a flood of people as it became clear the deposits were the richest yet found in Minas, and so many came that they outstripped the food supply. In 1700 there was a famine and legend has it that people died of hunger with gold nuggets in their hands.

The early years were hard, made worse by a war started in 1707 between the Portuguese and *paulista bandeirantes*, who resisted the Crown's attempts to take over the area. The war, the **Guerra das Emboabas**, lasted for two years and was brutal, with ambushes and massacres the preferred tactics of both sides. Ouro Preto was the Portuguese base, and troops from here drove the *paulistas* from their headquarters at Sabará and finally annihilated them near São João del Rei. From then on, Ouro Preto was the effective **capital** of the gold-producing area of Minas, although it wasn't officially named as such until 1823. Indeed, compared to places like nearby Mariana, Ouro Preto was a late developer; all but two of its churches date from the second half of the eighteenth century, and several of its finest buildings, like the school of mining and the town hall on Praça Tiradentes, were not finished until well into the nineteenth century.

The gold gave out about the time Brazil finally became independent in 1822, but for decades the town survived as an administrative centre and university town; a school of mining – now a federal university – was founded in 1876. After the capital moved to Belo Horizonte, steady decline set in, though the populist government of Getúlio Vargas brought back the bodies of the Inconfidêntes (see box and Museu da Inconfidência on p.188) to a proper shrine, and sensitively restored the crumbling monuments.

Since the 1980s **tourism** and aluminium production have been the city's main sources of income, the latter attracting job-hungry migrants, many of whom end up living in hillside *favelas*. Indeed, for many locals Ouro Preto's architectural heritage and tourism are getting in the way of economic expansion; meanwhile hasty construction has at times threatened the city's coveted status as a UNESCO World Heritage Site, a potential embarrassment for Brazil, not least for the revenue it helps generate from tourism. Although heavy vehicle traffic has been re-routed to avoid the historic centre and there's talk of re-housing *favela* dwellers, tensions between various interest groups are proving difficult to resolve.

# Arrival and information

All buses arrive at the **rodoviária**, an easy ten minutes' walk westwards from the centre on Rua Padre Rolim. There's also a **train service** linking Ouro Preto with Mariana (see p.193), 12km to the east, which makes for a very pleasant day-trip. The train station – built in 1889 in a style that would not be out of place in northern Portugal – is located south of the city centre.

**Praça Tiradentes** is dominated by a statue of the martyr to Brazilian independence and lined with beautiful colonial buildings. On the east side at no. 41 is the **municipal tourist office** (daily 9am–6pm; ⓣ31/3559-3269). The town gets crowded at weekends and holiday periods, so it's a good idea to reserve a room in advance, while during Carnaval you'd be wise to book several weeks ahead.

## Accommodation

For a place as special as Ouro Preto, it comes as a surprise how ordinary most of its *pousadas* feel. At least room rates are competitive: the price codes below are based on weekend (Fri–Sun) and high-season prices; midweek and in low season, Ouro Preto's hotels offer discounts of around 20–30 percent.

**Albergue de Juventude Brumas** Ladeira de São Francisco de Paula 68 ⓣ31/35512944, ⓦwww.brumashostel.com.br. Part of the Hostelling International network, this place offers extremely basic dorms, kitchen and laundry facilities. Located midway between the *rodoviária* and the city centre, the hostel is reached by a steep 5min trek, but offers commanding views of Ouro Preto's historic centre. R$32 per person.

**Grande Hotel de Ouro Preto** Rua Senador Rocha Lagoa 164 ⓣ31/3551-1488, ⓦwww.hotelouropreto.com.br. Opened in 1940, this is one of Oscar Niemeyer's earliest creations – though not one of his best. The "standard" rooms at this three-star hotel are on the small side and overlook the garden but the suites have tremendous views. Offers good service and there's a nice pool in the Burle Marx–designed gardens. ❹–❺

**Hotel Colonial** Travessa Padre Camilo Veloso 26 ⓣ31/3551-3133, ⓦwww.hotelcolonial.com.br. A rather drab but convenient place located one street back from Praça Tiradentes (it's signposted), with a range of *apartamentos* sleeping up to three people, all with *frigobar*, TV, a/c and telephones. The better rooms are in the wing to the right of the entrance; some of them are on two levels. ❸

**Pensão Vermelha** Largo de Coimbra, at the corner with Rua Antônio Pereira ⓣ31/3551-1138. Quiet, family-run place with clean, simple rooms; some overlook the magnificent facade of the São Francisco church. ❷

**Pousada América** Rua Camilo de Brito 15 ⓣ31/3551-2525. Popular with international travellers, this family-run spot offers good *apartamentos* and *quartos* (both same price), though they're slightly expensive for being pretty basic. About 100m off Praça Tiradentes along Rua Barão de Camargos (the bus from Mariana passes it). ❸

**Pousada Hospederia Antiga** Rua Xavier da Veiga 1 ⓣ31/3551-2203, ⓦwww.antiga.com.br. A charming old house with simple but spacious and spotlessly clean rooms, all with private facilities. The quiet location involves a tiring, 5min, uphill walk to reach the centre. Excellent value. ❸

**Pousada do Mondego** Largo de Coimbra 38 ⓣ31/3551-2040, ⓦwww.mondego.com.br. This *should* be one of Ouro Preto's best places to stay: a grand mid-eighteenth-century building just across from the Igreja de São Francisco de Assis and decorated with period furniture and artwork. However, only seven of the twenty-seven rooms have a worthwhile view and many of the other rooms have no window at all. Noise can also be a problem – the students in the neighbouring *república* are famous for their lively parties. ❺–❻

**Pousada Nello Nuno** Rua Camilo de Brito 59 ⓣ31/3551-3375, ⓦwww.pousadanellonuno.com.br. A very pretty, small *pousada* built around a courtyard. The rooms are attractively furnished in natural woods and the artwork is mostly by the proprietor who works in her printing atelier in the same building. ❸

**Pousada Solar da Opéra** Rua Conde de Bobadela 75 ⓣ31/3551-6844, ⓦwww.hotelsolardaopera.com.br. Located moments from Praça Tiradentes along one of the main shopping streets and above a restaurant, the interior of this building has been completely modernized, and features small guest-rooms with modern furniture. ❺

**Pouso do Chico Rei** Rua Brigador Mosqueira 90 ⓣ31/3551-1274, ⓦwww.pousodochicorei.com.br. A small eighteenth-century house converted into a pleasant *pensão*, filled with a collection of eighteenth-century antiques that would do credit to a museum. There's a wonderful view from the reading room on the first floor, plus excellent breakfasts are served. There are only six rooms, so book in advance. ❹

**Solar do Rosário** Rua Getúlio Vargas 270 ⓣ31/3551-5200, ⓦwww.hotelsolardorosario.com.br. Built in 1840, this hotel remains the most luxurious in Ouro Preto, especially following its recent refurbishment. Rooms have an attractive mix of period and modern furnishings, plus there are comfortable lounges and a pool within the terraced gardens. ❼

**O Sorriso do Lagarto** Rua Conselheiro Quintiliano 271 ⓣ31/3551-4811, ⓦwww.osorrisodolagarto.com.br. Located on the road leading to Mariana, a 5min walk above Praça Tiradentes, this small hostel has all the facilities one expects, including a kitchen, laundry and internet access. Rooms are small but clean and there are panoramic views of the city. R$25 in a dorm, R$40 for a single room and R$60 for a double.

## The Inconfidência Mineira

Ouro Preto is most famous in Brazil as the birthplace of the **Inconfidência Mineira** (the Mineira Betrayal), the first attempt to free Brazil from the Portuguese. Inspired by the French Revolution, and heartily sick of the heavy taxes levied by a bankrupt Portugal, a group of twelve prominent town citizens led by **Joaquim José da Silva Xavier** began in 1789 to discuss organizing a rebellion. Xavier was a dentist, known to everyone as Tiradentes, "teeth-puller". Another of the conspirators was **Tomas Gonzaga**, whose hopeless love poems to the beautiful **Marília Dirceu**, promised by her family to another, made the couple into the Brazilian equivalent of Romeo and Juliet: "When you appear at dawn, all rumpled/like a badly wrapped parcel, no ribbons or flowers/how Nature shines, how much lovelier you seem."

The conspiracy proved a fiasco and all were betrayed and arrested before any uprising was organized. The leaders were condemned to hang, but the Portuguese, realizing they could ill afford to offend the inhabitants of a state whose taxes kept them afloat, arranged a royal reprieve, commuting the sentence to exile in Angola and Mozambique. Unfortunately the messenger arrived two days too late to save Tiradentes, marked as the first to die. He was hanged where the column now stands in the square that bears his name, his head stuck on a post and his limbs despatched to the other mining towns to serve as a warning.

## The Town

**Praça Tiradentes**, with roads leading off it to most of Ouro Preto's sights, is the best place to start a tour of the town. Given the thirteen colonial churches, seven chapels, six museums and several other places of interest, you could easily spend two or three days here.

### The Escola de Minas

Right on the Praça Tiradentes is the **Escola de Minas**, now housed in the old governor's palace. Established in 1876, it's the best mining school in the country, and its students lend a slightly bohemian air to the town. The white turrets make the building look rather like a fortress; the exterior, with a fine marble entrance, dates from the 1740s, but the inside was gutted during the nineteenth century and not improved by it. Attached to the school is the **Museu de Ciência e Técnica** (Ⓦwww.museu.em.ufop.br; Tues–Sun noon–5pm; R$5), founded in 1877 as the Museu de Mineralogia. Although most of the exhibits are of interest only to geologists, there is one fascinating room where gold and precious stones are beautifully displayed, in contrast to the chaos in the rest of the museum.

### The Paço Municipal and Museu da Inconfidência

Also in the *praça* are the old city chambers, the **Paço Municipal** (Tues–Sun noon–5.30pm), a glorious eighteenth-century building that provides a perfect example of the classical grace of Minas colonial architecture with its beautifully restored interior. Like many colonial town halls, the building was also a jail and many of the huge rooms, so well suited to the display of *arte sacra*, were once dungeons.

The Paço Municipal contains the **Museu da Inconfidência** (Ⓦwww.museuinconfidencia.com.br; Tues–Sun noon–5.30pm; R$6), with marvellously displayed relics of eighteenth-century daily life, from sedan chairs and kitchen utensils (including the seal the bishop used to stamp his coat of arms on his cakes) to horrendous instruments used to punish slaves. A ground-floor room contains the museum's highlight: four exquisite, small Aleijadinho statues that are a fitting introduction to the flowing detail of his best work.

Upstairs there's colonial furniture and more art, but the spiritual heart of the place is found at the rear of the ground floor, where the cell in which **Tiradentes** spent the last night of his life is now the **shrine to the Inconfidêntes** (see box opposite). An antechamber holds documents – including the execution order and birth and death registrations of Tiradentes – and leads into a room containing a display featuring his remains and those of his fellow conspirators, all in the vaguely Fascist style the Vargas era usually chose for its public monuments. Most of the conspirators died in Africa, some in Portugal; all but Tiradentes were exiled for the rest of their lives and never returned to Brazil.

## The Igreja de Nossa Senhora do Carmo

Next door to the Paço Municipal on Praça Tiradentes, the **Igreja de Nossa Senhora do Carmo** (Tues–Sun 1–4.45pm; R$2) is one of the finest churches in Ouro Preto. It was designed by Manoel Francisco Lisboa, Aleijadinho's father, and construction began just before his death in 1766. Aleijadinho himself then took over the building of the church and finished it six years later. He contributed the carving of the exterior and worked on the interior, on and off, for four decades. The baptismal font in the sacristy is a masterpiece, as are the carved doors leading to the pulpits. Two of the side chapels in the main church (São João and Nossa Senhora da Piedade) were among the last commissions he was able to complete, in 1809; the accounts book for the time has Aleijadinho complaining he was paid with "false gold". Of the major churches in Ouro Preto, the Igreja de Nossa Senhora do Carmo is distinctive as the only one to have *azulejo*-tiled panels, placed to make the Portuguese who patronized it feel at home.

To the side of the church is the **Museu do Oratório** (Ⓦwww.museudooratorio.org.br; daily 9.30am–5.30pm; R$2), housed in an excellently restored mansion that was once the meeting house for the lay society attached to Nossa Senhora do Carmo. On display is a high-quality collection of oratories from throughout Brazil. Although there are some glittering shrines featuring gold and silver, the most touching examples are the portable oratories carried by muleteers and other travellers to protect themselves from danger. Also fascinating are the Afro-Brazilian oratories where African gods are depicted to look like Catholic saints.

## The Igreja do Pilar

It's a lovely walk from Praça Tiradentes to Ouro Preto's oldest church. **Rua Brigador Mosqueira**, which runs downhill from the square, is one of the most beautiful streets in town, with almost every building on it worth savouring. Wander down, bear left at the bottom, and you come out onto the incredibly steep Rua do Pilar, from where you can glimpse the towers of the Igreja do Pilar well before the plunging, cobbled path deposits you in front it.

With an exterior ornate even by Baroque standards, the **Igreja do Pilar** (Tues–Sun 9–10.45am & noon–4.45pm; R$4) is the finest example anywhere of early Minas Baroque architecture. It was begun in 1711 and the interior is the opposite of the Carmo's restraint: a wild explosion of glinting Rococo, liberally plastered with gold. The best carving was done by Francisco Xavier de Brito, who worked in Minas from 1741 until his early death ten years later – and about whom nothing is known except that he was Portuguese and influenced Aleijadinho. He was responsible for the astonishing arch over the altar, where the angels supporting the Rococo pillars seem to swarm out of the wall on either side.

## The Casa dos Contos

From the Igreja do Pilar, turn right up Rua Rondolfo Bretos and round into **Rua São José** (also, confusingly, called Rua Tiradentes), whose many bars and restaurants make it a good place to take a breather. Crossing the small stone bridge, you come to the perfectly proportioned **Casa dos Contos**, the old treasury building that's now a museum (Mon 2–6pm, Tues–Sat 10–6pm, Sun 10am–4pm). Finished in 1787, it was built as a bank-cum-mansion by Ouro Preto's richest family, and in 1803 became the Fazenda Real, a foundry where the Crown extracted its fifth of the gold and assembled armed convoys to escort it down to Rio for shipment to Portugal. The collection is no more than moderately interesting – the usual mixture of *arte sacra* and furniture – but the building is terrific, a magnificent colonial mansion built when Ouro Preto was at its peak. An imposing four-storey staircase dominates the entrance hall, and the mansion is constructed around a beautiful courtyard large enough for a dozen cavalry troopers. The most interesting places radiate off the courtyard: the huge furnace for melting the gold and shaping it into bars, the slave quarters, the stables (horses were better accommodated than slaves) and even an eighteenth-century privy. Don't forget to go right up to the *mirante* on the top floor of the Casa for one of the best views of Ouro Preto.

### The Igreja de São Francisco de Assis

From Praça Tiradentes, Rua Cláudio Manoel winds downhill, lined with stores selling precious stones and jewellery that don't in fact come from Ouro Preto but from eastern Minas. Ahead, on the right, is arguably the most beautiful church in Ouro Preto, the **Igreja de São Francisco de Assis** (Tues–Sun 8.30–11.50am & 1.30–5pm; R$6). The small square that sets it off – Largo do Coimbra – plays host to a rather poor arts-and-crafts market in the afternoon.

The church was begun in 1765, and no other in Ouro Preto contains more works by Aleijadinho. The magnificent exterior soapstone panels are his, as is virtually all the virtuoso carving, in both wood and stone, inside; Aleijadinho

▲ Ceiling painting in Igreja de São Francisco de Assis, Ouro Preto

also designed the church and supervised its construction. In 1801 the church commissioners contracted the best painter of the *barroco mineiro*, **Manoel da Costa Athayde**, to decorate the ceilings. It took him nine years, using natural dyes made from plant juices and powdered iron ore, and his work has stood the test of time far better than other church paintings of the period. The squirming mass of cherubs and saints are framed within a cunning trompe l'oeil effect, which extends the real Baroque pillars on the sides of the nave into painted ones on the ceiling, making it seem like an open-air canopy through which you can glimpse clouds. There are also painted *azulejos* that look remarkably like the real thing.

### The Matriz de Nossa Senhora da Conceição and Museu do Aleijadinho

Returning to Rua Cláudio Manoel, follow the winding Rua Bernardo de Vasconcelos to the left. This is the back way down to the last of the major churches in Ouro Preto, **Matriz de Nossa Senhora da Conceição** (Tues 8am–noon & 1.30–5pm, Sun noon–5pm; R$5, including admission to the Museu Aleijadinho), and it's a steep descent. Coming this way, you're leaving the main tourist area and everything looks just as it did the day Aleijadinho died; the Matriz is famous as the church he belonged to and where he is buried. The one-time cut-throat Antônio Dias, who founded Ouro Preto and died old and rich in 1727, left his fortune to build this church on the spot of his first camp – so this is where it all began, and, with the death of Aleijadinho, where the glory days of Ouro Preto can also be said to have ended.

Despite Aleijadinho's connection with the church, he never worked on it. All the same, it is an impressive example of mid-period Minas Baroque and the painting and carving are very fine, especially the figures of saints in the side altars – note the pained expression and movement of St Sebastian, on the left of the nave. Aleijadinho is buried in a simple **tomb** on the right of the nave, marked "Antônio Francisco Lisboa", covered by nothing more elaborate than a plain wooden plank.

A side door by the main altar of the church leads to the sacristy and the fascinating **Museu do Aleijadinho**, which is worth lingering over – not so much a museum of Aleijadinho's work as of his life and times. The ground floor is taken up by an excellent collection of religious art, but the highlight is upstairs, in a room dedicated not just to Aleijadinho but to all the legendary figures of Ouro Preto's golden age. What work there is by Aleijadinho is in the basement, and is quite remarkable: don't miss the four magnificent lions that once served as supports for the plinth on which coffins were laid. Aleijadinho, never having seen a lion, drew from imagination and produced medieval monsters with the faces of monkeys.

### Igreja de Santa Efigênia

Further out from the centre is the less important but no less fascinating **Igreja de Santa Efigênia**, the church for slaves, located on the east hill some 3km from Praça Tiradentes. At the time of writing the church was closed for renovation, its reopening date uncertain. To get there, however, continue along Rua Cláudio Manoel down to the river, cross over and climb up Rua Santa Efigênia. Although plain in comparison to what you'll see in Ouro Preto's other churches, the artwork here is well worth the steep climb and the views towards town are outstanding. The altar was carved by Javier do Briton, the mentor of Aleijadinho; the interior panels are by Manoel Rabelo de Souza; and the exterior image of Nossa Senhora do Rosário is by Aleijadinho himself. Slaves contributed to its construction by smuggling gold in their teeth cavities and under their fingernails.

### Mina do Chico Rei

If you don't have time to visit the Mina da Passagem **gold mine** near Mariana (see p.195), much closer, and cheaper too, is the **Mina do Chico Rei** (guided tours daily 8am–5pm; R$10), at Rua Dom Silvério 108 in the eastern *bairro* of Antônio Dias. Founded in 1702, barely seven years after gold was first struck in Sabará, the mine continued operating until 1888. Though visually not as striking as the Mina da Passagem, it nonetheless boasts some impressive statistics, which give an idea of just how rich Ouro Preto must once have been: the mine, constructed on five levels, contains an astonishing eighty square kilometres of tunnels, vaults and passages.

## Eating and drinking

One of the nice things about Ouro Preto is the number of places where you can eat, drink or just hang out; when the students are out in force on weekend nights, it has none of the quiet atmosphere of a small interior town that you might expect.

### Restaurants

There is no shortage of **restaurants**, with the better-value ones clustered at the bottom of the hill on Rua São José. The best of these is unquestionably ✱ *Restaurante Chafariz* at no. 167; its superb *mineiro* buffet costs about R$30. Established in 1929, the restaurant has become something of a local institution, with pleasantly rustic decor and smooth service – altogether highly recommended.

More expensive places are largely grouped at the top of Rua Direita (Rua Conde de Bobadela), where you'll get good regional food in uniformly attractive surroundings for R$35 per person: a particularly appealing choice is the rather elegant *Restaurante Casa do Ouvidor*, Rua Direita 42.

If you've had your fill of *mineira* cooking, one of the few alternatives is the pizza (and wine) served at *O Passo*, Rua São José 56. Open daily from 4.30pm, there's a terrace with delightful views onto a small park and the river; expect to pay about R$25 per person. Alternatively, the excellent ✱ *Café Geraes* at Rua Direita 122 offers fairly priced sandwiches and soups, delicious cakes and wine; next door, reasonable pasta is served in the *Restaurante Spaghetti*. For a more substantial evening meal, ✱ *Bené da Flauta*, Rua Francisco de Assis 32, is a good choice for French and Italian dishes; a *mineira* buffet is served at lunch. Located right alongside the Igreja Francisco de Assis, near Praça Tiradentes, the views across town from the first-floor dining room are quite spectacular. Main courses cost about R$35.

Thankfully, for those on a tight budget, there are also several **cheap places to eat**, namely the basic *lanchonetes* on Rua Senador Rocha Lagoa (also called Rua das Flôres) just off the square (the *Vide Gula* here is good) and several on Rua Conde de Bobadela of which, at no. 76, the *Quinto do Ouro* has an excellent *por kilo* buffet for less than R$15 for a full meal.

### Drinking and nightlife

During term-time, at the weekend, the steep Rua Conde de Bobadela (also called Rua Direita), leading up to Praça Tiradentes, is packed with students spilling out of the **bars** and **cafés**, which also attract tourists and locals; there are more etsablishments in the square itself, though most of the bars there have been turned into expensive restaurants. The modern wing of the mining school on the square has a bar and a **live-music** venue (see the posters in its lobby), while the *Booze Café Concerto*, a large basement area at Rua Direita 42, attracts jazz and rock bands from as far away as Belo Horizonte. If you prefer a quiet drink without the crowds, try *Bar Sena*, a local dive on the corner outside the Igreja do Pilar. For a vast selection of *cachaças* as well as tasty snacks, try the cave-like *Bardobeco* at Travessa do Areira 15 (an alley just off Rua Direita).

# Mariana

**MARIANA** is one of the major colonial towns, and in the first half of the eighteenth century was grander by far than its younger rival 12km to the west, Ouro Preto. Mariana was the administrative centre of the gold mines of central Minas until the 1750s and the first governors of Minas had their residence here and the first bishops their palace. Yet today Mariana's churches are far less grand than its illustrious neighbour's, and it's really little more than a large village, albeit one that is steadily expanding. It does, however, have a perfectly preserved colonial centre, mercifully free of steep climbs, that is less crowded and commercialized than Ouro Preto. As Mariana is only a twenty-minute bus ride away, you might stay here if you can't find a place in Ouro Preto.

## Arrival and information

The local **buses from Ouro Preto** leave you right in the centre at Praça Tancredo Neves, opposite an excellent **tourist information post**, the Terminal Turístico (daily 8am–5pm; ⓣ31/3557-1158). If you're coming from Belo Horizonte or São Paulo, you'll arrive at the **rodoviária** (ⓣ31/3557-1122), on the main road a couple of kilometres from the centre; if you don't wish to walk into the centre, catch one of the buses from Ouro Preto, which pass through the *rodoviária* every twenty minutes or so. A much nicer way of travelling between Ouro Preto and Mariana is by **train**, with the steam engines operating Friday to Sunday, leaving Mariana at 9am and 2pm and returning from Ouro Preto at 11am and 4pm (R$18 one-way, R$30 return; ⓦwww.tremdavale.com.br). The one-hour journey is beautiful, with the narrow-gauge track gripping the sometimes terrifyingly steep mountainsides as the train winds its way to its destination. For the best views, sit on the right side of the carriage from Ouro Preto to Mariana, and on the left-hand side when travelling in the other direction.

## Accommodation

All the **places to stay** are within easy walking distance of Praça Tancredo Neves. One of the nicest is the *Solar dos Corrêa*, Rua Josafá Macedo 70 (ⓣ31/3557-2080, ⓦwww.pousadasolardoscorrea.com.br; ④), midway between the Terminal Turístico and the two churches on Praça João Pinheiro. The hotel is full of character, with fifteen very different rooms done up with mock-colonial furniture, ranging from the rather gloomy loft conversions to a gorgeous first-floor room (no. 8) with wonderful views. Similar in style and price is the *Pousada da Typographia* at Praça Gomes Freire 220 (ⓣ31/3557-1577; ④), an eighteenth-century mansion restored in period detail. The rooms are spacious and comfortable and the location especially attractive. A cheaper option is the clean and tidy *Hotel Providência*, Rua Dom Silvério 233 (ⓣ31/3577-1444, ⓦwww.hotelprovidencia.com.br; ②), along the road that leads up to the Basílica, which has use of the neighbouring school's pool when classes finish at noon.

## The Town

Orientation in Mariana is straightforward. The colonial area begins at Praça Cláudio Manoel, in front of the large Catedral Basílica; from here, Rua Frei

Durão, lined with several of the most notable eighteenth-century public buildings, leads to the exquisite Praça Gomes Freire, with its bandstand, trees and pond, lined on all sides by colonial *sobrados*, two-storey mansions. Nearby are the two finest churches in Mariana and a lovely Prefeitura building in Praça João Pinheiro, complete with *pelourinho*, the old stone whipping-post to which slaves and miscreants were tied and beaten.



## The Museu Arquidiocesano

Although it has been overshadowed by its neighbour for over two centuries, you can still get a good idea of Mariana's early flourishing in the **Museu Arquidiocesano de Arte Sacra** in the old bishop's palace on Rua Frei Durão (Tues–Fri 8.30am–noon & 1.30–5pm, Sat & Sun 8.30am–2pm; R$5).

The **building** itself is magnificent, with parts dating from the first decade of the eighteenth century, when it began life, bizarrely, as a prison for erring churchmen, some of whom were notorious for being the worst cut-throats of the *paulista* expeditions. Between 1720 and 1756 the building was extended and became the bishop's palace; the door and window frames are massive, built in beautifully worked local soapstone. Inside, the **collection** of *arte sacra* and colonial furniture is distinguished by its quality and age. It gives a vivid idea of how Mariana was thriving, with stone buildings and all the trappings of the early eighteenth-century good life, when Ouro Preto was still a collection of hovels.

On the ground floor there's a sobering collection of chains and manacles draped along the walls, but the bulk of things to see is upstairs. The stairwell is dominated by a powerful painting of *Christ's Passion* by Mariana native **Athayde**, his best-known work. The stairs lead up to a number of graceful colonial rooms, including the luxurious private quarters of the bishops, which contain an excellent collection of religious art, notably the largest number of Aleijadinho figures anywhere outside a church. The colonial furniture section, usually the dullest part of Minas museums, is actually worth seeing here: lovely writing desks and chests of drawers, all early eighteenth century and most made of jacaranda wood (there was a glut on the market at the time, as the forests were felled to get at the gold). The most unusual exhibit is a false bookcase, with wooden "books" painted to resemble leather. You can also wander around the bishop's audience room – the throne is also by Aleijadinho – and there's a separate gallery of the bishops' portraits, amongst which are three rather good, incongruously included, local landscapes by the German artist Nobauer.

## The churches

Mariana's colonial churches are smaller and less extravagant than Ouro Preto's, though most are decorated with paintings by Athayde, who is buried in the Igreja de São Francisco (see below).

The oldest church is the **Catedral de Nossa Senhora da Assunção** on Praça Cláudio Manoel (Tues–Sun 8am–6pm; R$2), begun in 1709 and choked with gilded Rococo detail. This is very much an Aleijadinho family venture: his father, Manoel Francisco Lisboa, designed and built it, while Aleijadinho contributed the carvings in the sacristy and a font. The interior is dominated by a massive German organ dating from 1701 and donated by the king of Portugal in 1751. Look closely and you can see Chinese-style decorations carved by slaves, who also worked the bellows. You can hear the organ in action, in recitals given at 11am on Fridays and at 12.15pm on Sundays.

The two churches on Praça João Pinheiro, around the corner, show how tastes had changed by the end of the century. Their ornate facades and comparatively restrained interiors are typical of the third phase of *barroco mineiro*. The **Igreja de**

**São Francisco de Assis** (Tues–Sun 9am–noon & 1–5pm; R$2), finished in 1794, has the finest paintings of any Mariana church, as befits Athayde's burial place. The numbers on the church floor are where members of the lay Franciscan brotherhood are buried; Athayde is no. 94. Inside you'll see a fine sacristy as well as an altar and pews by Aleijadinho, who, in addition, put his signature on the church in his usual way, by sculpting the sumptuous soapstone "medal" over the door. On the other side of the square, the **Igreja de Nossa Senhora do Carmo** (Tues–Sun 9–11.45am & 2–5pm), completed in 1814, with its less elaborate exterior, is disappointing in comparison. But the combination of the two churches with the equally graceful **Câmara de Vereadores** (the local government's meeting hall) makes the bare grass square an attractive place to take a break.

From here, it's a short uphill walk via the unspoilt Rua Dom Silvério to the mid-eighteenth-century **Basílica de São Pedro dos Clérigos** (Tues–Sun 9am–noon & 2–4pm) that overlooks the town, framed by groves of towering palms; you pass the strange, geometric **Igreja da Arquiconfraria** on the way. The object is not so much to check out the Basílica, but to enjoy the view of the town stretched out before you. If you follow the path along the top the views are even better.

## Mina da Passagem

Four kilometres from Mariana, amongst steep hills bearing clear traces of centuries of mining, the ancient gold mine of **Mina da Passagem** is one of the area's more unusual sights. If you don't have your own transport, take an Ouro Preto–bound bus from Mariana and get off at the stop opposite the mine.

Gold was first extracted here in 1719, making Mina da Passagem one of the oldest deep-shaft gold mines in Minas. The mine's nine faces have long since closed and the site exists today as a tourist attraction. Delightfully ramshackle but engaging **tours** operate every day from 9am until 5pm (R$24) and last about an hour.

Among the series of repair yards is probably the oldest functioning machine in Brazil – a vintage 1825 **British steam engine**, now adapted to run on compressed air. It powers a drum cable that drives railcars into and out of the mine – be careful of bumping your head once you trundle 315m into the galleries. There are other bits of nineteenth-century mining equipment knocking around, and the dripping gallery opens out into a small, crystalline floodlit lake, 120m underground. Back up on the surface, the visit is rounded off with a demonstration of gold panning, complete with real gold.

The history of the mine is a roll call of economic imperialism. The Portuguese sold it to a German enterprise in 1819, who sold it to British owners in 1854, who happily worked it with slaves at the same time the Royal Navy was intercepting slavers in the Atlantic. It was then offloaded onto the French in 1883, nationalized by Vargas in 1937, sold to a South African company in 1970, and finally ceased operations in 1985.

## Eating and drinking

Mariana has some reasonable **restaurants**, generally cheaper than those in Ouro Preto though none as good as the neighbouring city's best. Those with the nicest views look out onto Praça Gomes Freire (all open daily until midnight). *Mangiare della Mamma* does a top-notch *mineiro comida por kilo*, presented in heavy iron casseroles sizzling on a hot, wood-fired iron stove. Just up from Praça Gomes Freire at Travessa João Pinheiro 26, next to the Igreja São Francisco, is arguably the town's best *mineiro* restaurant, *Tambau*. For bargain lunches, a good place to try is the self-service *Panela de Pedra*, a restaurant attached to the Terminal Turístico.

# Congonhas

**CONGONHAS**, an ugly, modern town 72km south of Belo Horizonte, sits ill as one of the historic cities. In truth, there's only one reason for coming here: to see the Basílica do Senhor Bom Jesus de Matosinhos. It's a long way to travel just to see one thing, but this is no ordinary church; if one place represents the flowering of *barroco mineiro*, this is it – the spiritual heart of Minas Gerais.

## Arrival, accommodation and eating

**Getting to Congonhas** is easy from both Belo Horizonte (6 buses daily; 1hr) and São João del Rei (5 buses daily; 2hr). There are also two daily buses from Ouro Preto (2hr). It's possible to start out from Belo Horizonte or Ouro Preto, visit Bom Jesus in Congonhas and still get to São João del Rei in the evening (last bus 8.20pm, 10.20pm on Sun), but only if you begin your trip early. To get from Congonhas's main *rodoviária*, a couple of kilometres out of town, to Bom Jesus, catch the **local bus** marked "Basílica", which takes you all the way up the hill to the church; it's impossible to miss.

Most people visit Congonhas on a day-trip, but if you decide to **spend the night**, the most comfortable option is the *Colonial Hotel* (Ⓣ31/3731-1834, Ⓦwww.hotelcolonialcongonhas.com.br; ❸), alongside the Basílica, with its own small pool. The *Max Mazza Hotel* (Ⓣ31/3731-1970, Ⓦwww.hotelmaxmazza.com.br; ❸) at Av. Júlia Kubitschek 410, is more modern, but lacks a pool. For **food**, head to the *Cova do Daniel*, a good regional restaurant at Praça da Basílica 76, next to Bom Jesus.

## Bom Jesus de Matosinhos

Built on a hill overlooking the town, with a panoramic view of the hills around it, the **Basílica do Senhor Bom Jesus de Matosinhos** (Tues–Sun 6am–6pm) is set in a magnificent sloping **garden** studded with palms and

▲ Basílica do Senhor Bom Jesus de Matosinhos, Congonhas

what look like six tiny mosques with oriental domes. These are, in fact, small **chapels** commemorating episodes of the Passion; each is filled with life-size statues dramatizing the scene in a tableau. Looking down on them from the parapets of the extraordinary terrace leading up to the church itself are twelve towering soapstone **statues** of Old Testament prophets. Everything, the figures and the statues, was sculpted by **Aleijadinho**. His presumed leprosy was already advanced, and he could only work with chisels strapped to his wrists. The results are astonishing, a masterpiece made all the more moving by the fact it seems likely it was a conscious swan-song on Aleijadinho's part – there is no other explanation for the way a seriously ill man pushed so hard to finish such a massive undertaking whose theme was immediately relevant to his own suffering.

The whole complex is modelled on the shrine of Bom Jesus in Braga, in northern Portugal. The idea and money came from a Portuguese adventurer, **Feliciano Mendes**, who, towards the end of his life, planned to re-create the pilgrimage church of his native Braga to house an image of the dead Christ he brought with him from Portugal in 1713. Mendes died in 1756, when work had only just begun, and it was forty years before the local bishop contracted Aleijadinho to produce the figures of the Passion and the prophets. Somehow, with his apprentices filling in fine detail, Aleijadinho managed to complete everything by 1805; it almost defies belief that the finished project was executed by a man who had lost the use of his hands.

### The Passion

Start your visit at the bottom of the garden to better appreciate the deep religious mysticism that lies behind the design. The **slope** symbolizes the ascent towards the Cross and governs the sequence of tableaux, the scenes leading you up from the Garden of Gethsemane through Christ's imprisonment, trial, whipping, wearing of the crown of thorns, and carrying of the Cross to Calvary. On top, guarded by the prophets, is the church, which houses both the wooden image of Christ's body and the real body, in the Communion host; built in the shape of a cross the church represents both the Crucifixion and the Kingdom of Heaven.

Viewing of the **statues** inside the chapels isn't ideal, as there are grilles to stop people getting in, and some of the figures are difficult or impossible to see. All are sculpted from cedar and were brightly painted by Athayde, using his preferred natural paints made from ox blood, egg whites, crushed flowers and vegetable dyes. The statues are marvellously lifelike – you can see Christ's veins and individual muscles, the bulging of a soldier's cheeks as he blows a trumpet and a leering dwarf carrying a nail for Christ's crucifixion. Too savage and realistic to be Baroque art, there is nothing with which to compare it; it's as if Aleijadinho was driven to take his genius for realism to its logical conclusion, and finally shatter the restrictions of the Baroque tradition he had worked in all his life.

Things become even more interesting on the **symbolic** front when you look closely at the figures. Christ is more than once portrayed with a vivid red mark around his neck, which makes many think he also represents Tiradentes (see box, p.188). Support for the theory comes from the Roman soldiers, viciously caricatured, whom Aleijadinho gives two left feet and ankle boots – which only the Portuguese wore. Although nothing is known of Aleijadinho's politics, he was a native Brazilian and lived through the Inconfidência in Ouro Preto. He would certainly have known Tiradentes by sight, and it is more than likely that the Congonhas Christ is meant to represent him.

### The prophets and the church

If the cedar figures are outside the Baroque tradition, the statues of the **prophets** are its finest expression in all Brazil. Carved from blocks of soapstone, they dominate both the garden they look down on and the church they lead to. They are remarkably dramatic, larger than life-size, full of movement and expression; perched on the parapet, you look up at them against the backdrop of either hills or sky.

The **church** is inevitably something of an anti-climax, but still interesting. The effigy of the dead Christ that Mendes brought over from Portugal is in a glass case in the altar, and through the door to the right of the altar is the cross that carried the image. The lampholders are Chinese dragons, yet more of the Macau influence visible in Sabará and Diamantina.

Next to the church is a small building with a fascinating collection of **ex votos**. The display will be familiar to anyone who has been to other pilgrimage centres in Brazil, and the photos, pictures and messages from grateful sufferers elicit a voyeuristic fascination. This collection is remarkable for the number of really old *ex votos*, the earliest from a slave who recovered from fever in 1722. Others record in crude but vivid paintings incidents including being gored by a bull, being seriously burnt or escaping from a bus crash.

The **bus** to take you back to the *rodoviária* leaves from the parking bay behind the church.

# São João del Rei and around

**SÃO JOÃO DEL REI** is the only one of the historic cities to have adjusted successfully to life after the gold rush. It has all the usual trappings of the *cidades históricas* – gilded churches, well-stocked museums, colonial mansions – but it's also a thriving market town, easily the largest of the historic cities, with a population of just over 80,000. This modern prosperity complements the colonial atmosphere rather than compromising it, and, with its wide central thoroughfare enclosing a small stream, its stone bridges, squares and trees, São João is quite attractive. Come evening though, it's a rather dreary place and overshadowed by **Tiradentes**, its much smaller and prettier neighbour, in terms of good places to stay.

Founded in 1699 on the São João River, the town had the usual turbulent early years, but distinguished itself by successfully turning to ranching and trade when the gold ran out early in the nineteenth century. São João's carpets were once famous, and there is still a textile factory today. Among the famous names associated with São João are Tiradentes, who was born here, Aleijadinho, who worked here and, in more recent times, native son **Tancredo Neves**, the great *mineiro* politician who shepherded Brazil out of military rule when he was elected president in 1985. Tragically, Neves died before he took office and is buried in the closest thing the town has to a shrine in the cemetery of São Francisco.

### Arrival, information and orientation

The centre of town is fifteen minutes' walk southwest from the **rodoviária**, or you can take a local bus in. Local buses enter the old part of town along **Avenida Tancredo Neves**, with its small stream and grassy verges to your left. There's a **tourist office** (daily 8am–5pm; ⓣ32/3372-738), across from the Catedral, where you can pick up a tourist booklet with a helpful map.

São João is divided into two main districts, each with a colonial area, separated by a small stream – the **Córrego do Lenheiro** – which runs between the broad

Avenida Tancredo Neves, on the north side, and **Avenida Hermílio Alves**, which turns into **Avenida Eduardo Magalhães**, to the south. Relatively small and easy to find your way around, the districts are linked by a number of small bridges, including two eighteenth-century stone ones and a late nineteenth-century footbridge made of cast iron.

On the south side, the colonial zone is clustered around the beautiful **Igreja de São Francisco de Assis**, at the far western end of town. On the other side is the commercial centre, usually bustling with people, cars and the horse-drawn trailers of rural Minas. This commercial zone sprang up in the nineteenth century and shields the colonial area proper, several blocks of cobbled streets that jumble together Baroque churches, elegant mansions and the pastel fronts of humbler houses. For once you have the luxury of wandering around without losing your breath, as São João is largely flat.

## Accommodation

Finding somewhere to stay is rarely a problem as **accommodation** in São João is plentiful and good value, though hotels and *pousadas* here are not nearly as attractive as those in neighbouring Tiradentes (see p.202). Bear in mind, however, that the town is a popular spot to spend Carnaval in, and Easter celebrations also attract huge numbers of visitors; at these times advance reservations are essential.

The *Pousada Grande Hotel* (T32/3371-7475; ②) at Rua Manoel Anselmo 22, right in the centre overlooking the Lenheiro stream, is a favourite budget choice, though its basic rooms are rather noisy and lack air conditioning. Of the medium-range places, best value is the *Hotel Ponte Real*, Av. Eduardo Magalhães 254 (T32/3371-7000, W www.hotelpontereal.com.br; ④), a wonderful converted mansion near São Francisco church, with the added attraction of a small swimming pool. At a similar price, the *Quinta do Ouro*, towards the western end of

Avenida Tancredo Neves on Praça Severiano de Resende (Ⓣ32/3371-2565; ❹), has four lovely rooms, three with salons (reservations essential). Top of the range, but excellent value and with a very good pool, is the comfortable *Pousada Villa Magnólia* (Ⓣ32/3373-5065, Ⓦwww.pousadavillamagnolia.com.br; ❹–❺), just outside of the historic centre at Rua Ribeiro Bastos 2.



## The Town

São João's colonial sections are complemented by some fine buildings from more recent eras, notably the end of the nineteenth century, when the town's prosperity and self-confidence were high. The 1920s and 1930s were also good times – some of the vaguely Art-Deco buildings combine surprisingly well with the colonial ones. The main public buildings line the south bank of the stream, best viewed from Avenida Tancredo Neves on the north side; there's a sumptuous French-style **theatre** (1893), and the graceful blue **Prefeitura** with an imposing Banco do Brasil building facing it. The relaxed atmosphere is reinforced by the number of bars and restaurants.

### Igreja de São Francisco de Assis and Memorial Tancredo Neves

The most impressive of the town's colonial churches, the **Igreja de São Francisco de Assis** (daily 8am–5.30pm, Sun 9am–4pm; R$2), is one block off the western end of Avenida Eduardo Magalhães. Overlooking a square with towering palms – some more than a century old – the church, finished in 1774, is exceptionally large, with an ornately carved exterior by a pupil of Aleijadinho. The master himself contributed the intricate decorations of the side chapels, which can be seen in all their glory now the original paint and gilding has been stripped off. From the plaques, you'll see the church has been visited by some illustrious guests, including former President Mitterand of France. They came to pay homage at the **grave of Tancredo Neves**, in the cemetery behind the church. Sunday at 9.15am is an especially good time to stop in, when eighteenth-century music is played to accompany Mass.

Tancredo was a canny and pragmatic politician in the Minas tradition, but with a touch of greatness; transition to civilian rule in 1985 is unlikely to have been so smoothly achieved without his skills. He was born and spent all his life in São João, where he was loved and is still very much admired. Eerily, to some, he died on the same day of the year as Tiradentes, who was also born in São João – their statues face each other in Praça Severiano de Rezende, on the other side of the Córrego do Lenheiro. Just around the corner from the Igreja de São Francisco, on Rua José Maria Xavier at the corner with Avenida Eduardo Magalhães, is the **Memorial Tancredo Neves** (Wed–Fri 1–5pm, Sat, Sun & holidays 9am–5pm; R$2). This small nineteenth-century town house shelters a collection of personal artefacts and documents relating to the president's life, and *ex votos* used to decorate his grave, thanking him "for graces granted" – only really of interest to those Brazilians for whom Tancredo was nothing less than a modern saint.

### Museu de Arte Sacra and Rua Getúlio Vargas

Over on the other side of the stream, one block north from Avenida Tancredo Neves, lies the main street of the other colonial area, **Rua Getúlio Vargas**. The western end is formed by the small, early eighteenth-century **Igreja da Nossa Senhora do Rosário** (Tues–Sun noon–6pm; R$2), built for the town's slave population, which looks onto a cobbled square dominated by two stunning colonial mansions. The one nearest the church is the Solar dos Neves, the family home of the Neves clan for over two centuries, the place where Tancredo was born and lived.

A couple of buildings east along from the Solar dos Neves is an excellent **Museu de Arte Sacra** (Tues–Sun noon–5pm; R$2), contained within another sensitively restored house. The collection is small but very good; highlights are a finely painted St George and a remarkable figure of Christ mourned by Mary Magdalene, with rubies representing drops of blood. As you go around, you're accompanied by Baroque church music, which matches the pieces perfectly. The museum also has a small gallery for exhibitions by São João's large artistic colony.

### Catedral Basílica de Nossa Senhora de Pilar and other churches

Almost next door to the Museu de Arte Sacra on Avenida Getúlio Vargas is a magnificent early Baroque church, the **Catedral de Nossa Senhora de Pilar** (Mon 8–10.30am & 5–8pm, Tues–Fri 8–10.30am & 1–8pm, Sat & Sun 8–10.30am & 5–8pm), completed in 1721. The interior is gorgeous and only Pilar in Ouro Preto and Santo Antônio in Tiradentes are as liberally plastered with gold. The gilding is seen to best effect over the altar, a riot of Rococo pillars, angels and curlicues. The ceiling painting is all done with vegetable dyes, and there's a beautiful tiled floor.

There are further churches to visit in this part of town, if you're enthusiastic, though none of the same standard as either São Francisco or Pilar. The **Igreja de Nossa Senhora das Mercês** (Tues–Sun noon–5pm), behind Pilar, dates from 1750 and is notable for the variety and artistry of the graffiti, some of it dating back to the nineteenth century, etched into its stone steps, while the elegant facade of **Nossa Senhora do Carmo** (Mon–Fri 8am–noon & 1.30–5pm, Sat 8am–noon) dominates a beautiful triangular *praça* at the eastern end of Avenida Getúlio Vargas.

### The Museu Regional

Near the cathedral, just off Avenida Tancredo Neves on Largo Tamandaré, is the excellent **Museu Regional** (Mon–Fri noon–5.30pm, Sat & Sun 8am–1pm; R$1), housed in a magnificently restored colonial mansion. Perhaps the most fascinating pieces here are the eighteenth-century *ex votos* on the ground floor, their vivid illustrations detailing the trials both masters and slaves experienced: José Alves de Carvalho was stabbed in the chest while crossing a bridge on the way home in 1765; a slave called Antônio had his leg broken and was half-buried for hours in a mine cave-in. On the first floor, look out for the several figures of saints – crafted with a simplicty and directness that makes them stand out – made by ordinary people in the eighteenth century.

## Eating, drinking and nightlife

On the **north side** of the Lenheiro stream, on Praça Severiano de Rezende, you'll find two of the town's best **restaurants**: the *Churrascaria Ramon*, which does a good-value *churrasco*, and the *Quinta do Ouro*, whose *mineiro* food is the best in São João, though fairly expensive at around R$50 per person. On the same *praça* is the perfectly adequate and cheaper *por kilo Restaurante Rex* (11am–4pm). Alternatively, a very pleasant place for light meals and excellent afternoon teas is the *Sinhazinha* (Mon–Fri 1–6pm, Sat, Sun & holidays 8am–10pm), directly across from the Igreja de São Francisco.

The best places, however, combining good food with lively atmosphere, are on the **south side**, where tourists, young townsfolk and families flock to drink, eat and go to the cinema. Many of the **bars** have live music at weekends and get very crowded later on when people start spilling out onto the pavements. Almost all of the action is concentrated on Avenida Tiradentes, which runs parallel to Eduardo Magalhães, the avenue that runs alongside the stream. The bars are bunched both at Tiradentes' western end near São Francisco – where *Cabana do Zotti* at no. 805 (9pm onwards) is always packed and does good snacks – and halfway along Tiradentes at the junction with Rua Gabriel Passos (the road that runs in from the blue Prefeitura). For a meal, the *Restaurante Villeiros* at Rua Padré Maria Xavier 132 offers very good *comida mineira* – a *por kilo* buffet at lunch and à la carte in the evening.

## Tiradentes

Although it was founded as early as 1702, by the 1730s **TIRADENTES** had already been overshadowed by São João and is now little more than a sleepy village with a population of only 5000. The core is much as it was in the eighteenth century, straggling down the side of a hill crowned by the twin towers of the **Igreja Matriz de Santo Antônio** (daily 9am–5pm; R$3). Begun in 1710 and completed around 1730, it's one of the earliest and largest of the major Minas Baroque churches; in 1732 it began to acquire the gilding for which it is famous, becoming in the process one of the richest churches in any of the mining towns. The church was decorated with the special extravagance of the newly rich, using more gold, the locals say, than any other church in Brazil, save the Capela Dourada in Recife. Whether this is true – and Pilar in Ouro Preto is probably as rich as either – the glinting of the gold around the altar is certainly impressive. You can tell how early the altar is from the comparative crudeness of the statues and carvings: formal, stiff and with none of the movement of developed Minas Baroque. The

### The São João del Rei–Tiradentes train

If you're in São João between Friday and Sunday, don't miss the half-hour **train ride** to the colonial village of **Tiradentes**, 12km away. There are frequent buses too (8 daily from São João's *rodoviária*), but they don't compare to the trip on a nineteenth-century steam train, with immaculately maintained rolling stock from the 1930s. You may think yourself immune to the romance of steam, and be bored by the collection of old steam engines and rail equipment in São João's nineteenth-century station on Avenida Hermílio Alves – the **Estação Ferroviária** (museum open Tues–Sun 9–11am & 1–5pm) – but by the time you've bought your ticket you'll be hooked: the booking hall is right out of a 1930s movie, the train hisses and spits out cinders and as you sit down in carriages filled with excited children, it's all you can do not to run up and down the aisle with them.

Built in the 1870s, as the textile industry took off in São João, this was one of the earliest rail lines in Brazil, and the trains were immediately christened Maria-Fumaça, "Smoking Mary". The service runs only on Friday, Saturday, Sunday and holidays, when trains leave São João at 10am and 3pm, returning from Tiradentes at 1pm and 5pm (®www.city10.com.br/efom; R$25 return), or you could get one of the many local buses back to São João. Sit on the left leaving São João for the best views, and as far from the engine as you can: steam trains bring tears to your eyes in more ways than one.

The half-hour ride is very scenic, following a winding valley of the Serra de São José, which by the time it gets to Tiradentes has reared up into a series of rocky bluffs. The train travels through one of the oldest areas of gold mining in Minas Gerais, and from it you'll see clear traces of the eighteenth-century mine workings in the hills. In the foreground, the rafts on the river have pumps that suck up alluvium from the river bed, from which gold is extracted by modern *garimpeiros*, heirs to over two centuries of mining tradition.

beautifully carved soapstone panels on the facade are not by Aleijadinho, as some believe, but by his pupil, Cláudio Pereira Viana, who worked with the master on his last projects.

From the steps of the church you look down an unspoilt colonial street – the old town hall with the veranda has a restored eighteenth-century jail – framed by the crests of the hills. If you had to take one photograph to summarize Minas Gerais, this would be it. Before walking down the hill, check out the **Museu Padre Toledo** (Tues–Sun 9–11.30am & 1–4.40pm, Sat & Sun 9am–4.40pm; R$3), to the right of Santo Antônio as you're standing on the steps. Padre Toledo was one of the Inconfidêntes and built the mansion that is now the museum. He obviously didn't let being a priest stand in the way of enjoying the pleasures of life; the two-storey *sobrado* must have been very comfortable, and even though the ceiling paintings are dressed up as classical allegories, they're not the sort of thing you would expect a priest to commission, featuring, as they do, so much naked flesh. The museum comprises the usual mixture of furniture and religious art, but the interesting part is the old slave quarters in the yard out back, now converted into toilets. A more substantial reminder of the slave presence is the **Igreja da Nossa Senhora do Rosário dos Pretos** (Tues–Sun 10am–5pm; R$1), down the hill and along the first street to the right. There could be no more eloquent reminder of the harsh divisions between masters and slaves than this small chapel, built by slaves for their own worship. There is gilding even here – some colonial miners were freed blacks working on their own account – and two fine figures of the black St Benedict stand out, but overall the church is moving precisely because it is so simple and dignified.

## Arrival and information

Tiradentes might have a placid and timeless air during the week, but it gets lively at weekends, as the bars and guesthouses fill up with visitors from Rio and Belo Horizonte. For such a small place, Tiradentes is well connected to other cities, with several buses each day to both Rio and São Paulo, seven buses to Belo Horizonte and an hourly service to neighbouring São João del Rei. The efficient **tourist office** at Largo das Forras 71 (Mon–Fri 9am–12.30pm & 1.30–5.30pm, Sat & Sun 9am–5pm) provides helpful advice with accommodation, excursions and bus schedules.

## Accommodation

Finding a place to stay in Tiradentes is rarely a problem, as a good proportion of the town's population have turned their homes into *pousadas* (there are well over fifty), many of them exceptionally comfortable. During Carnaval, over Easter and in July, advanced reservations are essential, and most *pousadas* will only accept bookings of at least four nights.

**Alforria** Rua Custódio Gomes 286 ⓣ32/3355-1536, ⓦwww.pousoalforria.com.br. Unlike most *pousadas* in Tiradentes, this place is unapologetically modern. The guest rooms are spacious, and the lounge areas, garden and pool are larger than usual. The peaceful location and charming English-speaking owners compensate for the five-minute walk from the town centre. No kids under 12. ❺

**Arco-Íris** Íris Rua Frederico Ozanan 340 ⓣ32/3355-1167, ⓦwww.arcoiristiradentesmg.com.br. Basic single, double and triple rooms for just R$45 per person. The added bonus of a pool makes this one of the best budget choices in Tiradentes. ❸

**Bia** Rua Frederico Ozanan 330 ⓣ32/3355-1173, ⓦwww.pousadadabia.com.br. One of the cheapest and friendliest places to stay, with clean, simple rooms, a kitchen for guests' use and a garden with a pool. ❸

**Pousada do Largo** Largo das Forras 48 ⓣ32/3355-1166, ⓦwww.pousadadolargo.com.br. A very pleasant *pousada* with simple but comfortable guest rooms and attractive lounges with a mix of colonial-style and modern furniture. There's a small pool and a rooftop terrace. ④

**Solar da Ponte** Praça das Mercês ⓣ32/3355-1255, ⓦwww.solardaponte.com.br. Quite possibly the best *pousada* in Brazil. The gardens (which include a pool), guest rooms and lounges are as relaxing as they are beautiful, and the service is both friendly and efficient. The price includes an excellent afternoon tea, evidence of the owners' British–Brazilian background. No kids under 12. ⑦

**Villa Allegra** Travessa Pedro Lourenço da Costa 31 ⓣ32/3355-1597, ⓦwww.villaallegra.com.br. Though this modern *pousada* is a 5min walk from the town's centre and guest rooms are on the small side, the English-speaking owner could not be more welcoming; there's a nice pool and a good breakfast is served. Excellent value. ④

### Eating

Given that eating out is promoted as being one of Tiradentes' great attractions, it's surprising that few of the **restaurants** are particularly good. *Viradas do Largo*, at Rua do Moinho 11, is considered the best in town for *comida mineira* but the food and general ambience are hardly exceptional, although the price, around R$50 for a meal for two, is good. Four kilometres from the centre along the Estrada Bichinho, amidst beautiful countryside, is the *Pau de Angu*, a wonderful rustic restaurant serving *mineiro* food at its best. *Tragaluz*, at Rua Direita 52, makes a brave – and sometimes successful – attempt at modernizing *comida mineira* by producing lighter dishes; expect to pay around R$70 per person.

### Excursions

Tiradentes is surrounded by hills, but as the trails aren't marked you're best off going with a guide if you want to explore them. Caminhos e Trilhas (Rua dos Inconfidêntes 207 ⓣ32/3355-2477) lead small groups on fairly easy **hikes**, stopping at spots where there are natural pools and picnic areas and views of Tiradentes. Hikes last about four and a half hours and cost R$35 per person including a picnic. The same agency also arranges two- to three-hour **horse-riding** trips (R$35–45) and rents out **mountain bikes**.

## Diamantina and the Jequitinhonha Valley

**DIAMANTINA**, home town of Juscelino Kubitschek, the president responsible for the creation of Brasília, is the only important historic city to the north of Belo Horizonte and, at six hours by bus, is by some way the furthest from it. Yet the journey itself is one of the reasons for going there, as the road heads into the different landscapes of northern Minas on its way to the *sertão mineiro*. The second half of the 288-kilometre journey is the most spectacular, so to see it in daylight you need to catch a morning bus from Belo Horizonte.

Diamantina has a very different atmosphere to any of the other colonial towns. Still a functioning diamond-mining town, it is also the gateway to the **Jequitinhonha Valley**, the river valley that is the heart of the Minas *sertão*. The green hills that characterize so much of the southern half of Minas are utterly absent around Diamantina, which instead is set in a rocky, windswept and often cold highland zone – be sure to bring a sweater or jacket.

### The road to Diamantina

Diamantina itself, scattered down the steep side of a rocky valley, faces escarpments the colour of rust; the setting has a lunar quality you also come across in parts of the Northeast's *sertão*. In fact, at Diamantina you're not quite in the *sertão* – that begins roughly at Araçuaí, some 300km to the north – but in the uplands of the **Serra do**

**Espinhaço**, the highlands that form the spine of the state. Almost as soon as you leave Belo Horizonte, the look of the land changes to the stubby trees and savanna of the Planalto Central, the inland plateau that makes up much of central Brazil. Roughly halfway to Diamantina, the road forks – left to Brasília and the Planalto proper, right to Diamantina and the *sertão*.

You hit the highland foothills soon after the town of Curvelo, and from then on the route is very scenic. The well-maintained road winds its way up spectacularly forbidding hills, the granite outcrops enlivened by cactus, wild flowers and the bright yellow and purple *ipê* trees, until it reaches the upland plateau, 1300m above sea level. The plateau heralds yet another change: windswept moorland with few trees and strange rock formations. Look carefully on the left and you'll see traces of an old stone road, with flagstones seemingly going nowhere. This is the old slave road, which for over a century was the only communication line between southern Minas and the *sertão*.

## Arrival and information

Unless approaching by car, by far the easiest way to get to Diamantina is by one of the six buses each day from Belo Horizonte, although there is also a daily bus from São Paulo. Although the *rodoviária* is not far from the centre of town, it's on a steep hill, and the only way back to it once in the centre is by taxi (around R$10), unless you have the legs and lungs of a mountain goat. You can get **free maps** from the **tourist office**, tucked away at Praça Antônio Eulálio 53 (Mon–Fri 8am–6pm, Sat 9am–5pm, Sun 8am–noon; ⓣ38/3531-9532). You're unlikely to find anyone who speaks English, but the staff will point you towards hotels and offer advice on excursions.

## Accommodation

**Hotels** in Diamantina are plentiful and generally inexpensive. Although most are perfectly fine, none rival the atmosphere and levels of comfort that the best *pousadas* of Ouro Preto and Tiradentes offer.

**Dália** Praça JK 25 ⓣ38/3531-1477, ⓕ3531-3526. Housed in a lovely old two-storey building with creaking floors and wood panelling, this simple hotel offers excellent-value rooms and fine views over the square. ❸

**Gameleira** Rua do Rosário 209 ⓣ38/3531-1900, ⓦwww.diamantina.com.br/gameleira. One of the cheapest *pousadas* in the old part of town, this attractive choice offers clean rooms sleeping from one to four people, a comfortable lounge and a pretty courtyard garden. Many of the rooms have a balcony, but ask for one facing the Igreja do Rosário. ❷

**Garimpo** Av. da Saudade 265 ⓣ38/3531-1044, ⓦwww.pousadadogarimpo.com.br. A 10min walk from the centre on the western continuation of Rua Direita, this is the largest, priciest and most comfortable place to stay in town; it's friendly, well equipped and has a pool, yet there's a somewhat soulless feel to it. ❹

**Pouso da Chica** Rua Macau de Cima 115 ⓣ38/3531-6190, ⓦwww.pousodachica.com.br. A beautifully restored eighteenth-century property with simple guest rooms in both the historic main house and in newer outbuildings decorated with locally-made rustic furniture and textiles. ❸

**Relínquias do Tempo** Rua Macau de Baixo 104 ⓣ38/3531-1627, ⓦwww.pousadareliquiasdotempo.com.br. Located in a wonderfully converted nineteenth-century home just up from the cathedral, this simple but delightful *pousada* is filled with rustic period furnishings and decorated with handicrafts from the Jequitinhonha Valley. ❸

**Tijuco** Rua Macau do Meio 211 ⓣ38/3531-1022, ⓦwww.hoteltijuco.com.br. This 1951 Oscar Niemeyer creation has fairly spartan but perfectly adequate rooms. It's worth paying for one of the slightly more expensive "luxo" rooms, which are larger and brighter and have balconies offering wonderful views across Diamantina. ❸

### Juscelino Kubitschek

**Juscelino Kubitschek**, one of Brazil's great postwar presidents, was born in Diamantina in 1902 and spent the first seventeen years of his life in the town. His enduring monument is the capital city he built on the Planalto Central, Brasília, which fired Brazil's and the world's imagination and where his remains are interred (he was killed in a road accident in 1976). The house where he was born and his later home, Casa de Juscelino, is preserved as a shrine to his memory (Tues–Sat 8am–6pm, Sun 8am–1pm; R$2), on the steep Rua São Francisco, uphill from his statue at the bottom.

Juscelino had a meteoric political career, fuelled by his energy, imagination and uncompromising liberal instincts. You can understand his lifelong concern with the poor from the small, unpretentious house where he spent the first part of his life in poverty (Juscelino was from a poor Czech-gypsy family). Restoration has rather flattered the house, as the photos of how it was when he lived there make plain; with the exception of Lula, no Brazilian president has come from a humbler background. The photos and the simplicity of the house are very moving – a refreshing contrast to the pampered corruption of many of his successors.

Juscelino and his wife, Julia, are still sources of considerable pride for the inhabitants of the town he clearly never left in spirit. September 12, his birthday, is Diamantina's most important *festa*, featuring music of all kinds performed in the town's *praças* late into the night. Many of the bars still display photographs of him, largely dating from before he became president in 1956. And many still don't believe his death was a genuine accident, just as few *mineiros* believe Tancredo really died of natural causes. The massive turnout for Juscelino's funeral in Brasília in 1976 was one of the first times Brazilians dared to show their detestation of the military regime.

## The Town

Even if it were not set in such a striking landscape, Diamantina has a distinctive **history** that would still mark it out from the other *cidades históricas*. The Portuguese Crown had reason to feel bitter about the gold strikes in Minas Gerais, as it had been forced to expend blood and treasure in prising the gold from the hands of the *paulistas*, and when diamonds were found here in 1720 the same mistakes were not repeated. **Arraial do Tijuco**, as Diamantina was called at first, was put under strict military control. People could only come and go with royal passes and the town was isolated for almost a century. This may explain Diamantina's very distinctive atmosphere. Although it has few buildings or churches to rival the masterpieces of Ouro Preto or Congonhas, the passage of time has had little effect on the large colonial centre of the town, which is the least spoilt of any of the *cidades históricas*. The narrow stone-flagged streets, with their overhanging Chinese eaves and perfectly preserved colonial houses, are exactly as they have been for generations.

Diamantina takes the *mineiro* penchant for building on slopes to extremes. The streets are either too narrow or too steep even for Brazil's intrepid local bus drivers. Fortunately the place is small enough for you to get your bearings very quickly. The central square in the old town is **Praça Conselheiro Mota**, which has the Catedral Metropolitana de Santo Antônio built in the middle of it – everyone calls the cathedral and the square "Sé". Most of the sights and places to stay are within a stone's throw of here.

### The Museu do Diamante

The **Museu do Diamante** (Tues–Sat noon–5.30pm, Sun 9am–noon; R$1), set in a mid-eighteenth-century town house on the cathedral square, is the best place to get an idea of what *garimpagem* has meant to Diamantina. It's one of the best museums in Minas – not so much for the glories of its exhibits but for the effort it makes to give you an idea of daily life in old Diamantina.

The room behind the entrance desk is devoted to the town's mining history and is filled with old mining instruments, maps and prints. Dominating everything is an enormous cast-iron English safe, brought by ox cart all the way from Rio in the eighteenth century (it took eighteen months to get here). Inside is a genuine pile of uncut diamonds and emeralds, much as they would appear to *garimpeiros* panning; only the occasional dull glint distinguishes them from ordinary gravel. Disturbingly, there is an appalling display of whips, chains and brands used on slaves right up until the late nineteenth century.

The rest of the museum is great to wander through and stuffed with memorabilia that ranges from mouldering top hats to photos of long-dead town bandsmen; Diamantina has strong musical traditions and still supports *serestas*, small bands of accordion, guitar and flute players who stroll through the streets and hold dances around Carnaval, or on the evening of September 12, the *Dia da Seresta*.

### The Catedral and other churches

Despite the comparative ugliness of the **Catedral Metropolitana de Santo Antônio** (daily 7am–8pm), built in the 1930s on the site of an old colonial church, the cathedral square (Praça Correia Rabelo) is worth savouring. It's lined with *sobrados*, many of them with exquisite ornamental bronze and ironwork, often imported from Portugal – look closely and you'll see iron pineapples on the balconies. Most impressive of all are the serried windows of the massive Prefeitura, and the ornate Banco do Brasil building next to it – possibly unique in Brazil in that it spells the country name the old way, with a "z".

Diamantina's **other churches** are distinctive, simple but very striking, with stubby towers and Chinese eaves; street names, like Rua Macau de Meio and Rua Macau de Cima, recall the days when these streets were home to Chinese artisans the Portuguese imported during the eighteenth century. With one exception, though, the churches' exteriors are actually more interesting than the interiors.

The church most worth entering is the **Igreja de Nossa Senhora do Carmo** (Tues–Sat 8am–noon & 2–6pm, Sun 8am–noon; R$2) on Rua do Carmo. Built between 1760 and 1784, legend has it that the heir of Diamantina's richest miner made sure the tower was built at the back of the church rather than the front, as was usual, so the bells didn't disturb his wife's beauty sleep. Inside is an atypically florid interior, whose two main features are a rich, intricately carved altar screen and a gold-sheathed organ, built in Diamantina.

On the cobbled street leading down the hill from here is a local curiosity. The church at the bottom, **Igreja de Nossa Senhora do Rosário dos Pretos** (Tues–Sat 8am–noon & 2–5.30pm, Sun 8am–noon; R$2), has a tree growing in front of it; look closely and you can see a large distorted wooden cross embedded in the trunk and lower branches. The story behind this reads like something from Gabriel García Márquez, but did really happen. The year the old Sé church was knocked down, in 1932, the padre of Rosário planted a wooden cross outside his church to commemorate the chapel old Diamantina had originally been built around. A fig tree sprouted up around it so that at first the cross seemed to flower – there's a photo of it at this stage in the Museu do Diamante – and eventually, rather than knocking it down, the tree grew up around the cross and ended up absorbing it. The church itself was built in 1728 to serve Diamantina's slave population and features a marvellous Baroque altar and a simple, yet stunning, painted ceiling.

### The Mercado dos Tropeiros

Diamantina's other important economic role, besides diamond mining, is as the market town for the Jequitinhonha Valley. It's here the products of the remote *sertão* towns of northeastern Minas are shipped and stockpiled before making their way to Belo Horizonte. The old **Mercado dos Tropeiros** on Praça Barão do Guaicuí, just a block downhill from the cathedral square, is the focus of Diamantina's trade, and worth seeing for the building alone – an interesting tiled wooden structure built in 1835 as a trading station by the Brazilian army. Its frontage, a rustic but very elegant series of shallow arches, played a significant role in modern Brazilian architecture. Niemeyer, who lived in Diamantina for a few months in the 1950s to build the *Hotel do Tijuco*, was fascinated by it, and later used the shape for the striking exterior of the presidential palace in Brasília, the Palácio da Alvorada.

The market itself (Fri evening and Sat morning) has a very Northeastern feel, with its cheeses, *doces* made from sugar and fruit, blocks of salt and raw sugar, *cachaça* sold by the shot as well as by the bottle and mules and horses tied up alongside the pick-ups. The food at the stalls here is very cheap, but only for the strong-stomached: the rich *mineiro* sausages (*linguiça*) are especially worth trying. The rest of the week the market is used for exhibitions and book stalls, and on most evenings hippies from around Diamantina sell jewellery, embroidery and other simple handicrafts. From the market you have a fine vantage point of a square that is, if anything, even richer than the Praça Conselheiro Mota, a cornucopia of colonial window frames and balconies and exquisite ironwork. Most of the ground floors are still ordinary shops, open throughout the week.

The **artesanato** section of the Mercado dos Tropeiros is small and uninspiring, which is unfortunate since the most distinctive products of the Jequitinhonha Valley are its beautiful clay and pottery figures. The Casa da Cultura, however, nearby on Praça Antônio Eulálio, has a very fine collection that makes a good introduction to Jequitinhonha pottery, and has a small selection of items for sale. An excellent collection of ceramic figures are for sale at Artevale, a shop situated just across from the market. Also very reliable for items from the Jequitinhonha Valley is Relíquias do Vale, on the same street as the *Hotel do Tijuco*, at Rua Macau do Meio 401. Besides pottery, the shop also has a good stock of hammocks, rugs and wall hangings that are the other specialities of the region.

### Eating and drinking

The streets around the cathedral are the heart of the town, and there's no shortage of simple bars and *mineiro* **restaurants** here, though the food on offer is rather monotonous; the area around Diamantina is almost entirely unsuited to agriculture, so traditionally almost all food had to be brought in from afar. Local dishes include little in the way of fresh ingredients, with the staples being beans, rice, salt pork, *carne seca* and *bacalhau* (salted cod). The *Apocalipse Point*, across from the market at Praça Barão do Guaicuí 78, is a popular *por kilo* restaurant (lunch only) with a good selection of typical *mineira* dishes; expect to pay around R$10–15 per person. Opposite the cathedral, the *Restaurante Cantina do Marinho*, at Rua Direita 113 and open daily for lunch and dinner, specializes in *bacalhao* dishes but also serves quite reasonable pizza. Along Beco da Tecla (an alleyway off the Praça Barão do Guaicuí), there are a few nice places to eat and drink: at no. 39 there's the *Recanto do Antônio* (closed Mon), which has the appearance of a country tavern and serves beer, wine, sausage and *carne do sol*; at no. 31, lighter meals as well as good coffee and cakes are available at *Espaço B*, a small bookshop and internet café with a relaxed, bohemian atmosphere. This is one of the few places in town that remains open late: until midnight Monday to Thursday and 2am Friday to Sunday.

Diamantina goes to sleep early but, in addition to the *Espaço B*, there are several very popular **bars** on Boca do Mota, an alley off the cathedral square, and others on Rua Direita.

## The Jequitinhonha Valley

If you want to get a clearer idea of where the Jequitinhonha *artesanato* comes from, you have to head out into the *sertão* proper, and Diamantina is the obvious place to start your journey. Travelling into the **Jequitinhonha Valley** is not something to be undertaken lightly; it is one of the poorest and remotest parts of Brazil, the roads are bad, there are hardly any hotels except bare flophouse *dormitórios*, and you almost certainly won't find anyone able to speak English.

If you need reasons, though, you don't have to look much further than the **scenery**, which is spectacularly beautiful, albeit forbidding. The landscapes bear some resemblance to the deserts of the American Southwest, with massive granite hills and escarpments, cactus, rock, occasional wiry trees and people tough as nails speaking with the lilting accent of the interior of the Northeast. Here you're a world away from the developed sophistication of southern and central Minas.

The most accessible Jequitinhonha destination from Diamantina is **ARAÇUAÍ**, until recently just a sleepy little village but now a major processing and distribution centre for mangos. Its attraction for tourists is that it's the best place in the whole region for buying **artesanato**. A good choice of ceramic and other items is available at the producers' cooperative called Centro de Artesanato, open Tuesday to Saturday. Another attraction in town is aquamarine and, especially, **tourmaline**, as the mines around Araçuaí are the sources of some of the best in Brazil. Unless you really know your minerals, however, you'd be foolish to make any purchases here – although you won't have any trouble tracking down dealers at the market.

▲ Santa Rita church, Serro



There are two daily buses (2am & 1.30pm) from Diamantina to Araçuaí and the journey takes about five hours. As for **accommodation**, there are a couple of *dormitórios* by the bus station or, for more comfort, try the relatively luxurious *Pousada das Araras*, Rua Miguel Chalub 100 (Ⓣ33/3731-1248, Ⓦwww.pousadaras.com.br; ③). Moving on from Araçuaí, if time were no object, you could hop local buses on dusty dirt roads to **Itinga** and then on 30km to the good-quality BR-116 highway into **Bahia** state. Once you get to Vitória da Conquista there are connections to all Bahian cities, but it could well take you a couple of days to get that far. It is often quicker to take the bus that leaves every other day to Belo Horizonte and make your connections there.

# South to Serro

South of Diamantina, the main point of interest is the sleepy colonial town of Serro, a two-hour bus ride away. From Diamantina, there are two ways of getting there: on the main, asphalt-covered road or on the unpaved (but fairly good quality) road. One daily bus runs along the latter, passing through rugged, wide-open spaces with the almost lunar appearance occasionally interrupted by patches of vegetation where a stream flows through. Even in these conditions cattle can somehow graze and patches of land can be cultivated. Twenty-three kilometres from Diamantina in a lush valley there's a very simple working *fazenda* where the nineteenth-century *casa grande* has been turned into a *pousada*. The *Pousada Rural Recanto do Vale* (Ⓣ31/3271-0200, Ⓦwww.pousadarecantodovale.com.br; ③) provides an opportunity to experience everyday life well off the beaten track. While pretty basic, the rooms are perfectly comfortable and the simple meals (entirely from the *fazenda*'s produce) are delicious and of great value at R$15. Horseriding can be arranged and there are easy walks to natural swimming spots.

Nine kilometres further along the road is **SÃO GONÇALO DO RIO DAS PEDRAS**, a delightful village in an oasis-like setting of palm trees and intensely green fields. Apart from an eighteenth-century church, and a few houses and bars, there's very little to the place, but São Gonçalo's tranquillity and its natural pools and waterfalls – good for bathing – make for an enjoyable break. There are several simple but extremely nice *pousadas* here, the best of which is undoubtedly the *Refúgio dos 5 Amigos* (ⓣ38/3541-6037, ⓦwww.sgriodaspedras.com/refugio5amigos; ❸ half-board), located right in the centre of the village. While very simple, the *pousada* is tastefully furnished and impeccably maintained, and the owner, originally from Switzerland, knows every trail hereabouts. If that's full, try the *Pousada do Pequi* (ⓣ38/3541-6100, ⓦwww.pousadadopequi.com; ❸), with comfortable rooms and a friendly atmosphere.

## Serro

Situated 90km south of Diamantina, **SERRO** is set in beautiful hill country, dominated by the eighteenth-century pilgrimage church of **Santa Rita** (Sat 3–7pm) on a rise above the centre, reached by steps cut into the slope. Little visited, this is not so much a place to see and do things as it is somewhere peaceful to unwind and appreciate the leisurely pace of life in small-town Minas. There are six colonial churches, but most are closed to visitors and the rest open only for a few hours on either Saturday or Sunday; a spate of thefts has made the keyholders reluctant to let you in. Founded in 1702, when gold was discovered in the stream nearby, Serro was at one time a rather aristocratic place. Across the valley, easily recognizable from the clump of palms, is the **Chácara do Barão do Serro** (Mon–Sat noon–5pm, Sun 9am–noon), which now houses the town's Centro Cultural. The old house is a fascinating example of a nineteenth-century *casa grande*, and you are free to wander through the main building and the former slaves' quarters outside.

Just along the road from here on Praça Cristiano Otoni, the **Museu Regional** (Tues–Sat noon–5.30pm, Sun 9am–noon; R$1) has a reasonable collection of period drawings and paintings, kitchen equipment and furniture. From the front of the museum you get a good view of the finest buildings in the village, namely the enormous **Casa do Barão de Diamantina**, clinging to the hillside, beautifully restored and now a school, and the twin Chinese towers of the **Igreja da Matriz de Nossa Senhora da Conceição** (daily noon–4pm). Dating from 1713, the church forms one end of a main street that is completely unspoilt; at the other end, up an extremely steep incline, at the historic centre's highest point, is the very pretty eighteenth-century Igreja de Santa Rita from where there are fine **views** across the village and towards the surrounding countryside.

The *Pousada Vila do Príncipe*, just down from the Igreja de Santa Rita on the main street, Rua Antônio Honório Pires, at no. 38 (ⓣ38/3541-1485; ❷), is the best **place to stay**; rooms are small and simple, but the views are fantastic. Also very central is the fairly basic *Pousada Serrano*, Travessa Magalhães 55 (ⓣ38/3541-1949; ❷). There are few places to eat but try the simple *Restaurante Itacolomi* at Praça João Pinheiro 20, which has a good *por kilo* buffet of regional dishes at lunch and an à la carte menu in the evening. While here, be sure to sample the cheese, considered the best in Minas Gerais; the cooperative at Praça Ângelo Miranda 6 (Mon–Fri 7am–6pm, Sat 7am–1pm) has an excellent selection. The *rodoviária* (ⓣ38/3541-1366) is almost in the centre, so ignore the attentions of the taxi drivers and walk uphill for some thirty metres to the heart of the village.

# Southern Minas: The spa towns

The drive from Belo Horizonte **south to Rio** turns into one of the most spectacular in Brazil once you cross the state border and encounter the glorious scenery of the Serra dos Órgãos, but there is little to detain you in Minas along the way. The route passes Juiz de Fora, one of the larger interior cities, but it's an ugly industrial centre, best seen from the window of a bus.

The route **southwest towards São Paulo**, however, is altogether different. The hills rising into mountains near the state border make this one of the most attractive parts of Minas. Six or seven hours from Belo Horizonte, to the south of the main route, there's a cluster of **spa towns** – the Circuito das Águas, or "Circuit of the Waters", as the spa resorts of Cambuquira, São Lourenço and Caxambu are collectively known. They are all small, quiet and popular with older people, who flock there to take the waters and baths. Each is centred on a *parque hidromineral*, a park built around the springs, incorporating bathhouses and fountains.

### From Belo Horizonte to the Circuito das Águas

It's five hours from Belo Horizonte, or three from São João del Rei, before you hit the gateway to the Circuito das Águas. **TRÊS CORAÇÕES** is a good place for making onward bus connections and, although not a resort town itself, it is more famous, in Brazil at least, than any of the spas. This rather anonymous modern town was the birthplace of Edson Arantes do Nascimento – **Pelé**, the greatest footballer ever – and it's a holy place for any lover of the game. Keep an eye out on the left as the bus winds its way through the centre and you'll see a bronze statue of him holding aloft the World Cup, which Brazil (and Pelé) won in 1958, 1962 and 1970. If you find yourself stuck here overnight while waiting for a bus, the *Cantina Calabresa* hotel, Rua Joaquim Bento de Carvalho 65 (T35/3231-1183, W www.hotelcalabreza.com.br; 2), has good rooms and a pool.

After Três Corações the hill country begins, although it's hardly got going before you run into the first and smallest of the spas, **CAMBUQUIRA**, a pleasant enough place but nothing to compare with the other resorts. If you do want to **stay**, a good cheap option with its own pool is *Pousada Passe Fique*, 1km out on the BR-267 Lambari road (T35/3251-1587; 3); more central and upmarket, with a sauna as well as a pool, is *Hotel Santos Dumont*, Av. Virgílio de Melo Franco 400 (T35/3251-1466; 4). The thermal baths in the Parque das Águas are open daily between 6am and 7pm.

## Caxambu

Just beating São Lourenço for the title of nicest of the smaller spas, **CAXAMBU** was a favourite haunt of the Brazilian royal family in the nineteenth century. The **Parque das Águas** (7am–6pm; R$3), in the centre of town, is delightful. Built in the last decades of the nineteenth century and the early years of the twentieth, it's dotted with eleven oriental-style pavilions sheltering the actual springs and houses an ornate Turkish bathhouse that is very reasonably priced – R$15 gets you a bath in early twentieth-century opulence, and there are also various kinds of sauna (R$12) and massage (R$30–45) available. The bathhouse, which has separate facilities for men and women, is open Tuesday to Saturday 8.30am to noon and 3 to 5pm, and on Sunday 8.30am to noon.

### Arrival, information and accommodation

The *rodoviária* (Ⓣ35/3341-9063), served by direct services from Belo Horizonte, Rio and São Paulo, is on the western edge of town, but Caxambu is so small that it doesn't really matter. A **tourist information post** (Ⓣ35/3341-1298) in the terminal building hands out town maps, but, again, you don't need them to find your way around. There's just one main street, Rua Wenceslau Braz, much of which is taken up by the Parque das Águas, and around which the town is built. Although walking is easy, it's fun to get one of the **horse-drawn cabs**, or *charretes*, that seem especially appropriate to Caxambu's period charm.

For its size, Caxambu has a surprising range of **hotels**; their rates always include full board and drop by almost half in the off season. For faded, late nineteenth-century elegance, but with full facilities including pools and saunas, the best options are the *Hotel Caxambu*, Rua Penha 145 (Ⓣ35/3341-9300, Ⓦwww.hotelcaxambu.com.br; ⑤), and the *Palace Hotel*, Rua Dr Viotti 567 (Ⓣ35/3341-3341, Ⓦwww.palacehotel.com.br; ⑤).

## São Lourenço

If Caxambu is the last word in Edwardian elegance, **SÃO LOURENÇO** rivals it with its displays of Art-Deco brilliance. Its Parque das Águas is studded with striking 1940s pavilions and has a stunning bathhouse which looks more like a film set for a Hollywood high-society comedy. The most upmarket and modern-looking of the small spas, the town is popular with young and old alike.

São Lourenço is built along the shores of a beautiful lake, a large chunk of which has been incorporated into the **Parque das Águas** (Wed–Sat 8am–5.20pm; the pavilions with the mineral-water fountains are closed 11.30am–2pm, Sun 8.30am–noon), and during the day it's where everything happens. Much larger and more modern than the one in Caxambu, the park is kept to the same immaculate standard, making it a lovely place for a stroll, with its brilliant white pavilions, forested hillside and clouds of butterflies and birds – though steer clear of the ill-tempered black swans on the lake. There are **rowing boats** for rent, and an artificial island in the middle of the lake.

The **Balneário** itself offers baths (*duchas*; R$10), saunas (R$12) and massages (R$50–65), and it's worth paying for the elegant surroundings of marbled floors, mirrored walls and white-coated attendants. There are separate sections for men and women.

### Arrival, information and accommodation

The **tourist information kiosk** is on Praça Duque de Caixas in front of the *parque*. The **rodoviária** (Ⓣ35/3332-5966) served by Belo Horizonte, Rio and São Paulo buses, is just off the main street, Avenida Dom Pedro II, which is lined with bars, hotels and restaurants. There is a very large **youth hostel** at no. 468, the *Fazenda Recanto dos Caravalhos* (Ⓣ35/3799-4000, Ⓦwww.recantodoscarvalhos.com.br; ③), with accommodation in pleasant chalets. Cheaper, but very decent, is the *Pousada Normandy*, Rua Batista Luzardo 164 (Ⓣ35/3332-4724; ②), just 200m from the Parque das Águas. The luxurious *Hotel Brasil*, Alameda João Lage 87 (Ⓣ35/3332-1313, Ⓦwww.hotelbrasil.com.br; ⑤ full board), dominates the Praça Duque de Caixas and has the works, including four pools and water slides.

**Buses** to Lambari, the next town on the circuit, take about ninety minutes. Buses to Caxambu leave several times a day, or take a taxi from the post in front of the *parque*.

# Espírito Santo

**Espírito Santo**, a compact combination of mountains and beaches, is one of the smallest states in Brazil (with a population of only 2.6 million), but as Minas Gerais' main outlet to the sea it is strategically very important. More iron ore is exported through its capital, **Vitória**, than any other port in the world. Not surprisingly the preponderance of docks, rail yards and smelters limits the city's tourist potential, despite a fine natural location. To a *mineiro*, Espírito Santo means only one thing: **beaches**. During weekends and holiday seasons, people flock to take the waters, tending to concentrate on the stretch immediately south of Vitória, especially the large resort town of **Guarapari**. The best beaches, however, lie on the strip of coastline 50km south of Guarapari, and in the north of the state, heading towards Bahia.

The hinterland of Vitória, far less visited, is exceptionally beautiful – a spectacular mix of lush forest, river valleys, mountains and granite hills. It's here that the state's real pleasures lie. The soils of this central belt are fertile, and since the latter part of the nineteenth century the area has been colonized by successive waves of Italians, Poles and Germans. Their descendants live in hillside homesteads and in a number of small, very attractive country towns that combine a European look and feel with a thoroughly tropical landscape. All are easy to get to from Vitória, not more than a couple of hours over good roads, linked by frequent buses. Around the towns, the lack of mineral deposits and the sheer logistical difficulties in penetrating such a hilly area have preserved huge chunks of **Mata Atlântica**, the lush semi-deciduous forest that once covered all the coastal parts of southern Brazil. Credit should also go to the local Indians, notably the Botocudo, whose dedicated resistance pinned the Portuguese down throughout the colonial period.

## Vitória

As a city, **VITÓRIA** is vaguely reminiscent of Rio, its backdrop a combination of sea, steep hills, granite outcrops and irregularly shaped mountains on the horizon. Founded in 1551, it's one of the oldest cities in Brazil, but few traces of its past remain and nowadays most of the centre is urban sprawl. Vitória is not a tourist town, and few people visit it unless they have a very definite reason – in recent years that reason has been off-shore oil, with the city being an important supply and communications base. The heart of Vitória is an island connected to the mainland by a series of bridges, but the city has long since broken its natural bounds, spreading onto the mainland north and south. The major beach areas are on **Canto**, on the island, **Camburi**, on the mainland just to the north, and **Vila Velha** with its beach, **Praia da Costa**, to the south. While Vitória is renowned as the world capital of marlin fishing, it also has the unfortunate distinction of having the highest murder rate in Brazil. Violence is unlikely to affect the casual visitor, but appropriate care should be taken nonetheless.

### Arrival and information

The enormous, modern *rodoviária* (Ⓣ27/3222-3366) is only a kilometre from the centre and, outside, all **local buses** from the stop across the road run into town; returning from the centre, most buses from Avenida Jerônimo Monteiro pass the *rodoviária* and will have it marked as a destination on their route cards. If you're heading straight for the **beaches** on arrival, any bus that says "Aeroporto", "UFES", "Eurico Sales" or "Via Camburi" will take you to Camburi; for the southern beaches you need "P. da Costa", "Vila Velha" or "Itapoan" – all can be caught at the stops outside the *rodoviária* or in the centre. As an alternative to the buses, **taxis** are quite cheap and a good option in this small city, where the distances are relatively short.

Over in the mainland district of Cariacica, the daily **train** from Belo Horizonte pulls into the Estação Ferroviária Pedro Nolasco (ⓣ27/3226-4169), 1km west of the *rodoviária*; it's connected to the city and *rodoviária* by yellow buses marked "Terminal Itacibá" and by most of the city's orange buses, including those marked "Jardim América" and "Campo Grande".

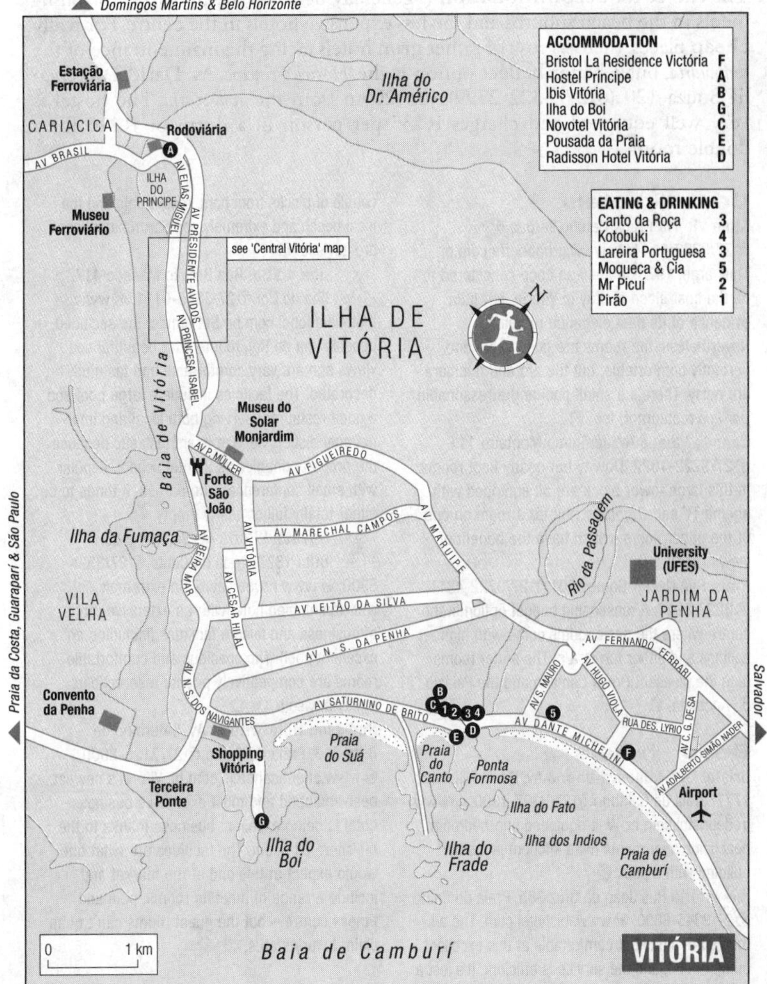

The **airport** (Aeroporto Eurico Sales; ⓣ27/3235-6300) is situated a couple of kilometres from Camburi beach, some 10km from the city centre, and is served by frequent green buses that can drop you on Avenida Beira Mar, the westward continuation of Avenida Getúlio Vargas, or at the *rodoviária*.

There are **tourist information** booths at the *rodoviária* (Mon–Fri 8am–9pm, Sat 9am–4pm) and at the airport (daily 8am–noon & 1–9pm; ⓣ27/3382-6364), both of which have lists of hotels, brochures and city maps. The central office of the state tourist company, CETUR, is at Av. Princesa Isabel 54, fourth floor (Mon–Fri 8am–6pm; ⓣ27/3322-8888). Listings for cinema, theatre, music and art exhibitions can be found in *A Gazeta*, the main local daily newspaper.

## Accommodation

The choice for **accommodation** is generally between the upmarket establishments in the beach suburbs and the less expensive hotels in the centre. For really **cheap** places, there's a row of rather grim hotels facing the main entrance of the *rodoviária*, but a better budget option is the *Hostel Príncipe*, Av. Dario Lourenço da Souza 120 (ⓣ27/3322-2799), just 200m from the *rodoviária*. The hostel is very well equipped and charges R$35 per person in a dorm or R$70 for a double room.

### Central hotels

**Alice Vitória** Praça Getúlio Vargas 5 ⓣ27/3322-1144, ⓦwww.gruponeffa.com.br. This large, 1970s hotel was once considered to be the best place to stay in Vitória, but little evidence of its past elegance remains. Nevertheless, the rooms are good value and perfectly comfortable, but the a/c and minibars are noisy. There's a small pool and a reasonable *por kilo* restaurant, too. ❸

**Cannes Palace** Av. Jerônimo Monteiro 111 ⓣ27/3222-1522. Dowdy but neatly kept rooms in this large tower block are all equipped with ageing TV and *frigobars*. Ask for a room on one of the upper floors, which have the benefit of views. ❸

**Prata** Rua Nestor Gomes 201 ⓣ27/3222-4311, ⓕ3223-0943. A reasonable budget option in the centre where the basic rooms come with high ceilings and either fan or a/c. The better rooms face the pleasant Praça Climaco and the Palácio de Anchieta. ❸

### Beach hotels

**Bristol La Residence Vitória** Av. Dante Michelini 1777, Praia de Camburí ⓣ27/3397-1300, ⓦwww.redebristol.com.br. Well-equipped one-bedroom beachside apartments (with kitchen) in a smart building with a pool. ❺

**Ibis Vitória** Rua João da Cruz 385, Praia do Canto ⓣ27/3345-8600, ⓦwww.ibishotel.com. The a/c rooms are small but comfortable at this excellent budget hotel, and the service is efficient. It's just a couple of blocks from bars, restaurants and the local beach and extremely popular; reservations are advised. ❹

**Ilha do Boi** Rua Bráulio Macedo 417, Ilha do Boi ⓣ27/3345-0111, ⓦwww.hotelilhadoboi.com.br. Set amidst the secluded, upscale Ilha do Boi, rooms offer beautiful sea views and are very comfortable and tastefully decorated. The facilities include a large pool and a good restaurant serving both local and international dishes. Service is enthusiastic because the property doubles as a hotel school. Popular with small conferences and parties, it tends to be either totally full or nearly empty. ❻

**Novotel Vitória** Av. Saturnino de Brito 1327, Praia do Canto ⓣ27/3334-5300, ⓦwww.novotel.com. An extremely well-maintained hotel with an extensive range of business and leisure facilities (including an excellent pool). The spacious and comfortable rooms are competitively priced; reservations highly advised. ❹–❺

**Radisson Hotel Vitória** Av. Saturnino de Brito 217, Praia do Canto ⓣ27/2125-8000, ⓦwww.atlanticahotels.com.br. Vitória's newest, best-equipped and most expensive business hotel is doing excellent business thanks to the off-shore oil boom. The facilities are what one would expect at this end of the market and include a range of meeting rooms, pool and fitness centre – but the guest rooms can't quite claim luxury status. ❻–❼

## The City

Vitória is built into a steep hillside overlooking the **docks** along the narrow Baía de Vitória, but the main streets are all at shore level. The name of the street that hugs the shore changes as you go eastwards from the *rodoviária*; initially called Avenida Elias Miguel, then Avenida Getúlio Vargas, Avenida Mal. de Moraes and finally Avenida Beira Mar, the whole stretch is generally known to locals as **Avenida Beira Mar**. From along here, you can catch buses to the beach districts; the yellow TRANSCOL bus #500 goes over the massive **Terceira Ponte** (third bridge) to the southern district of town, **Vila Velha**, handy for the **Praia da Costa** and site of the **Convento da Penha**, with its spectacular views over the city. From the bridge itself you can also get a good idea of Vitória's layout.

From **Avenida Jerônimo Monteiro**, the main downtown shopping street, a number of stairways (*escadarias*) lead to the Cidade Alta (the upper city), the location of the colonial Palácio de Anchieta, now the state governor's palace. Just down from here the pleasant, tree-shaded **Praça Costa Pereira** is the heart of the downtown area.

At the western end of Avenida Beira Mar, the city's oldest inhabited quarter, the **Ilha do Príncipe**, is a labyrinth of narrow paths and blind alleys. It occupies a small but very steep hill behind the *rodoviária*, and although no trace remains of the original dwellings, the atmosphere is of a bygone age, with houses constructed one on top of another, many of them propped up on stilts, complete with the stench of broken sewers and mounds of garbage. Tourists seldom venture here, but it's well worth an hour's ramble for an alternative insight into daily Vitórian life, and it harbours a few local bars should you wish to hang out a while longer. But do take care, avoid the area at night and leave valuables in your hotel.

### The centre

One of the few truly historic buildings in the centre of Vitória is the fine palace of the state governor, the **Palácio de Anchieta**, which dates from the 1650s but is almost entirely closed to visitors. The one part you can see – the **tomb of Padre Anchieta**, accessible by a side entrance (Tues–Sun noon–5pm) – is something of a curiosity. Anchieta, the first of a series of great Jesuit missionaries to Brazil, is most famous for being one of the two founders of São Paulo, building the rough chapel the town formed around in the sixteenth century and giving his name to one of that city's main avenues, the Via Anchieta. He was a stout defender of the rights of Indians, doing all he could to protect them from the ravages of the Portuguese and pleading their case several times to the Portuguese Crown; he was also the first to compile a grammar and dictionary of the Tupi language. Driven out of São Paulo by enraged Portuguese settlers, he retired to Vitória, died in 1597 and was finally canonized. The tomb is simple, set off by a small exhibition devoted to his life.

From the *palácio*, it's a short walk along winding roads to the sixteenth-century **Capela de Santa Luzia** (Mon–Fri 8am–6pm) on Rua José Marcelino, the first building to be erected in Vitória. The simple whitewashed chapel with its attractive Baroque altar would not be out of place in a Portuguese village, a vivid reminder that the coast of Espírito Santo was one of the first parts of Brazil Europeans settled. A block east of the chapel – and on an altogether different scale – is the large and unremarkable, early twentieth-century neo-Gothic **Catedral Metropolitana** (Mon–Fri 8–11am & 2–7pm, Sat & Sun 8–11am & 5–7pm). From there walk along Rua Erothildes Rosendo to the shaded Praça Costa Pereira, a busy pedestrian intersection. There are a number of distinguished-looking buildings surrounding the *praça*, the most notable being the **Teatro Carlos Gomes**, a replica of La Scala in Milan, built between 1925 and 1927. Astride a steep hillside

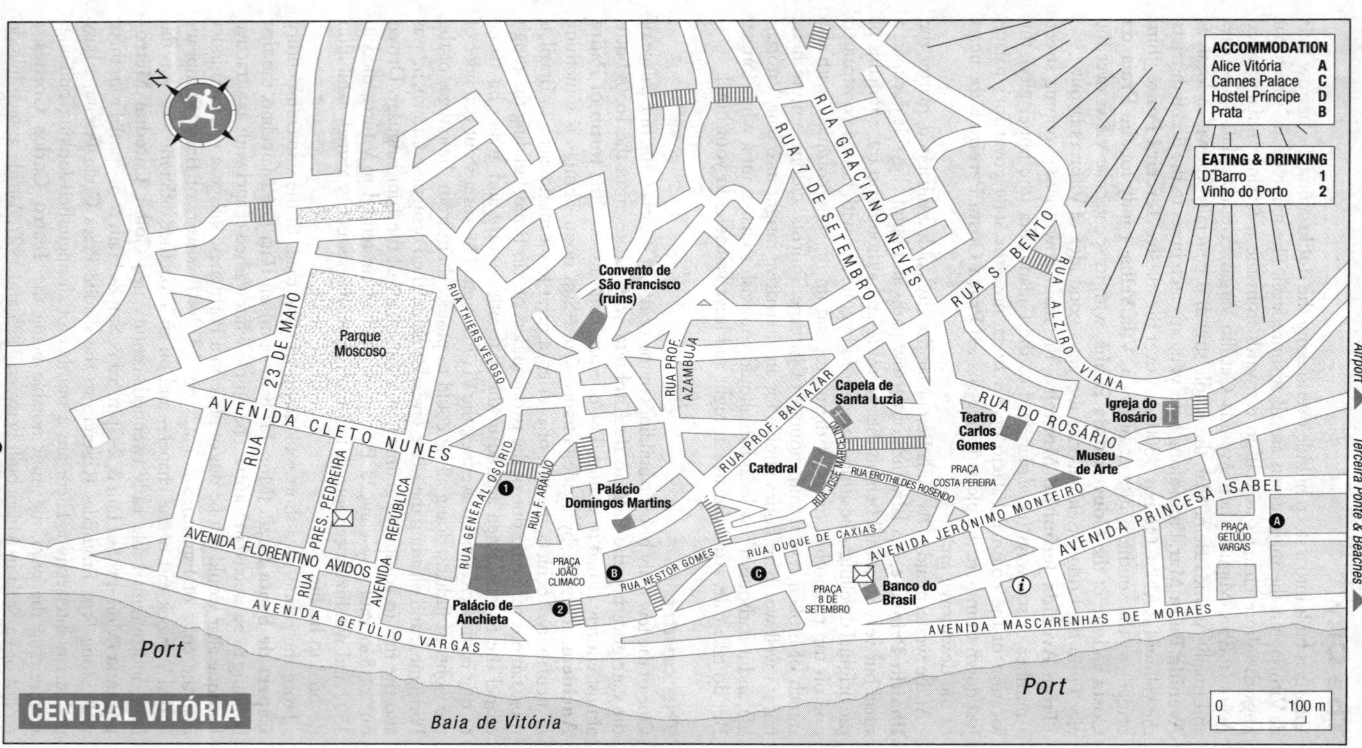
CENTRAL VITÓRIA
ACCOMMODATION
Alice Vitória A
Cannes Palace C
Hostel Príncipe D
Prata B
EATING & DRINKING
D'Barro 1
Vinho do Porto 2
Airport
Terceira Ponte & Beaches
Rodoviária & D
0 100 m
Port
Port
Baia de Vitória
RUA GRACIANO NEVES
RUA 7 DE SETEMBRO
RUA S. BENTO
RUA ALZIRO VIANA
RUA DO ROSÁRIO
Igreja do Rosário
Teatro Carlos Gomes
Museu de Arte
Capela de Santa Luzia
Catedral
RUA PROF. BALTAZAR
RUA PROF. AZAMBUJA
RUA JOSE MARCELINO
RUA EROTHILDES ROSENDO
PRAÇA COSTA PEREIRA
AVENIDA JERÔNIMO MONTEIRO
AVENIDA PRINCESA ISABEL
PRAÇA GETÚLIO VARGAS
RUA DUQUE DE CAXIAS
Banco do Brasil
PRAÇA 8 DE SETEMBRO
AVENIDA MASCARENHAS DE MORAES
Convento de São Francisco (ruins)
Palácio Domingos Martins
RUA NESTOR GOMES
PRAÇA JOÃO CLIMACO
RUA F. ARAÚJO
RUA GENERAL OSÓRIO
Palácio de Anchieta
RUA THIERS VELOSO
Parque Moscoso
RUA 23 DE MAIO
AVENIDA CLETO NUNES
RUA PRES. PEDREIRA
AVENIDA REPÚBLICA
AVENIDA FLORENTINO AVIDOS
AVENIDA GETÚLIO VARGAS
N

just behind the *praça* on Rua do Rosário, and fronted by an impressive pair of towering imperial palms, is the whitewashed **Igreja do Rosário** (Tues–Fri 8am–5pm), built in 1765 by and for local slaves; its plain interior houses a similarly impressive Baroque altar. Continuing along Rua do Rosário to the intersection with Avenida Jerônimo Monteiro, turn right and at no. 631 you'll find the **Museu de Arte do Espírito Santo** (Tues–Fri 8am–5pm), home to a sad collection of poorly displayed, uninteresting modern art.

There is, however, one museum in the city that is really worth a look – the **Museu do Solar Monjardim** (Tues–Fri 10am–4pm), on Avenida Paulino Müller, in the *bairro* of Jucutuquara to the southeast of the centre; take the bus marked "Circular Maruipe" or "Joana d'Arc" from Avenida Beira Mar. The museum is a restored nineteenth-century mansion filled with period furniture and household utensils, and it gives a good idea of the layout and domestic routines of a colonial estate. But if you're used to the fine displays of colonial artwork in the museums of Minas Gerais, you're likely to find it disappointing.

### Vitória's beach suburbs

Come evening and at weekends, downtown Vitória is pretty well deserted and the action shifts to the middle-class **beach suburbs**, where all of Vitória's best shops, hotels and restaurants are located. Both the main city beaches here look attractive, with palm trees and promenades in the best Brazilian tradition. **Praia de Camburi**, however, is overlooked by the port of Tubarão in the distance, where iron ore and bauxite from Minas are either smelted or loaded onto super-tankers, benefiting the economy but ruining the water. More exclusive, but still not recommended for swimming, is the **Praia do Canto,** where the rich flaunt themselves on the sands. To see where the city's truly wealthy live, walk across the bridge linking the Praia do Canto to the **Ilha do Frade**, an elite enclave of large, modern houses with spectacular views up and down the coast; there's also a small park in the centre of the island with the ruins of a Benedictine monastery. A short distance south of here, and joined to the mainland by a short causeway, is the **Ilha do Boi**, once used as a cattle quarantine station but now visited for its two small beaches that are popular with families and good for snorkelling. If you want to take a dip, you're better off crossing the *baía* to Vila Velha (see below) or travelling further afield for a perfect coast.

## Vila Velha

Three bridges span the narrow Baía de Vitória, linking Espírito Santo's capital with **Vila Velha**, the state's largest city. For practical purposes, the two cities are a single metropolitan area, with people commuting in both directions. Whereas Vitória is the state's administrative centre, commercially Vila Velha is of greater significance. The city is also an important transport hub, as a railway terminus and a modern port, which is highlighted in the **Museu Ferroviário**, one of Vila Velha's few tourist attractions. Vila Velha is no more attractive than Vitória, but its **beaches**, particularly the **Praia da Costa**, located just south of the **Convento da Penha**, at least allow for safe swimming.

### Museu Ferroviário

Directly across the *baía* from downtown Vitória is the fascinating **Museu Ferroviário** (Tues–Thurs 10am–6pm, Fri noon–8pm, Sat & Sun 10am–6pm). The museum was created by Vale – an international mining and industrial conglomerate hugely important to the economy of Espírito Santo – and is housed in a former train station built in 1927. Focusing on the history of the **Vitória-to-Minas railway**, constructed in the early twentieth century to carry iron ore to the coast from the interior, the exhibits include a steam engine and carriages, a model railway and maps, documents, photographs and company memorabilia relating to the 664-kilometre line. The museum is also the only public venue in either Vila Velha or Vitória where important works of **modern and contemporary art** are shown, and is noted for excellent exhibitions curated on themes loosely linked with the Brazilian mining industry, metallurgy or railways. There's also a pleasant **café**, in a converted railway carriage positioned alongside the *baía*, where snacks and full meals are served. The easiest way to get to the museum from downtown Vitória is by taxi, crossing the Ponte Florentino Avidos to the Antiga Estação Pedro Nolasco on Rua Vila Isabel. Alternatively, catch a bus marked "Vila Velha – Argolas" for the half-hour journey.

## The Convento da Penha

The most memorable reminder of Vitória's colonial past is on the southern mainland in Vila Velha: the chapel and one-time **Convento da Penha**, founded in 1558 (Mon–Sat 6am–4pm, Sun 5am–4pm). Perched on a granite outcrop towering over the city, it's worth visiting not so much for the convent itself – interesting though it is – as for the marvellous panoramic views over the entire city. It is a major pilgrimage centre and in the week after Easter thousands come to pay homage to the image of Nossa Senhora da Penha, the most devout making the climb up to the convent on their knees. It also marks the southernmost point that the Dutch managed to reach in the sugar wars of the seventeenth century; an expedition arrived here in 1649 and sacked the embryonic city, but was held off until a relief force sent from Rio drove them out – you can see how the 154m hill must have been almost impregnable.

There are a choice of **walks** up to the top. The steepest and most direct is the fork off the main road to the left, shortly after the main entrance, where a steep cobbled (and extremely treacherous) path leads up to the convent. Less direct, but considerably safer and with better views, is the winding Rua Luísa Grinalda – a very pleasant thirty-minute walk. Once at the top, the city is stretched out

▲ Convento da Penha, Vila Velha

below you, the centre to the north framed by the silhouettes of the mountains inland and, to the south, by the golden arcs of Vila Velha's beaches. The chapel's builders thoughtfully included a **viewing platform**, which you reach through a door to the left of the altar. More interesting than the chapel itself and next door to the café is the **Sala das Milagres** which houses a collection of photos, *ex votos*, artificial limbs and artefacts from grateful pilgrims.

To **get to the convent** from the centre, take the #500 bus and ask the driver to let you off at the third stop after the Terceira Ponte, which will leave you within easy walking distance of the convent. From the bus stop there are also plenty of buses to the Praia da Costa.

### Praia da Costa

Fringed by apartment buildings and a boardwalk built of granite, the **Praia da Costa** is the most popular beach hereabouts, not for any great beauty but because it's cleaner and less polluted than its counterparts on the north side of the Baía de Vitória, a couple of kilometres away. For a city beach it's not bad, though it gets packed on summer weekends. The Praia da Costa is easily reached from Vitória or any part of Vila Velha by buses marked "Praia da Costa".

## Eating, drinking and nightlife

Local cuisine, which is pretty good, is based around seafood and crab is a key ingredient for many dishes. No stay in Vitória is complete without trying the **moqueca capixaba**, the distinctive local seafood stew in which the sauce is less spicy and uses more tomatoes than the better-known Bahian variety.

**Restaurants** in the **centre of Vitória** are generally lacklustre, though there are a number of cheap *por kilo* places near the Palácio de Anchieta along the Escadaria Maria Ortiz stairway; the best, with a great selection of both *mineiro* and local dishes, is *D'Barro Restaurante* at no. 29. The only vaguely classy restaurant in the centre is the *Vinho do Porto* at Rua Nestor Gomes 152, near the Palácio Anchieta. Specializing in Portuguese dishes, and strong on seafood, this cosy spot provides a welcome contrast from the hustle and heat outside. Otherwise, even fairly humble *lanchonetes* will tend to have one or two local seafood dishes on offer beside the usual *salgados*.

For better eating, however, Vitória's beach suburbs are the places to head for. The **Praia do Canto** area is especially good, with numerous restaurants concentrated in the streets around the intersection of Rua Joaquim Lírio and Rua João da Cruz. But while most are fine, few stand out as being exceptional. Many specialize in regional dishes, such as *moqueca capixaba* and *torta capixaba* (a kind of seafood cake and an Easter speciality), though it's served at restaurants throughout the year. Of these, undoubtedly the best is *Pirão* at Rua Joaquim Lírio 753 (closed Sat & Sun evening). Other good restaurants in this area include: *Lareira Portuguesa*, at Av. Saturnino de Brito 260 (closed Sun evening), serving very authentic Portuguese dishes in a very pretty setting; *Mr Picuí*, at Rua Joaquim Lírio 813, specializing in Northeastern food; *Canto da Roça*, at Rua João da Cruz 280, offering a typical *mineiro* buffet in an attractively rustic, open-air setting; and *Kotobuki*, a good, reasonably priced Japanese restaurant at Rua Afonso Cláudio 60 (evenings only, closed Mon) that takes full advantage of the excellent seafood available here.

**Praia de Camburi** also has a fair number of restaurants (the green buses to the airport will take you past several), though they're spread out across a wide area. Authentic regional fare is available at many spots, with *Moqueca & Cia*, at Av. Dante Michelini 977, being a good, moderately priced choice.

Vitória's **nightlife** is concentrated in a couple of areas. The **Praia do Canto** (particularly the streets around Rua Joaquim Lírio and Rua João da Cruz) has loads of bars and the area attracts people from all backgrounds. There are a couple of good **live-music** venues here too: *Boca da Noite*, Rua João da Cruz 535, and *Academeia*, a few doors down on the same street, or stop by the *Oil Pub* at Rua Rômulo Samorini 33. A short taxi ride north of here, in the Santa Luzia *bairro*, is *Turk Zoo*, Rua Dr. João Carlos de Souza 472 (Wed–Sat from 10pm), with tasty Lebanese food and music ranging from local rhythms to rock that attracts students and a wider public. The **Jardim da Penha** district, with the Universidade Federal do Espírito Santo (UFES) nearby, is also lively, with bars open into the small hours of the morning. The well-established *Loft Jump Bar*, Avenida Fernando Ferrari (Thurs–Sat from 11pm), opposite the university, is the city's trendiest nightclub; to get there take the airport bus or taxi.

## Listings

**Airlines** Gol ⓣ27/3327-5364; TAM, at the airport ⓣ27/3324-1044; Varig ⓣ27/3327-0304.
**Bookshops** Books in English are virtually unavailable here. The best bookshops are Livraria da Ilha, Shopping Vitória (2nd floor), and the university bookshop on the UFES campus, which has a remarkable stock of books published by lesser-known Brazilian university presses.
**Car rental** All are based at the airport: Avis ⓣ27/3327-2348; Localiza ⓣ0800-99-2000; Unidas ⓣ27/3327-0180.
**Health matters** 24hr health care at Pronto Socorro do Coração, Av. Leitão da Silva 2351, Santa Lúcia (ⓣ27/3327-4833).
**Police** The tourist police station (open 24hr) is at Rua João Carlos de Souza 730, Barro Vermelho.
**Post office** There are post offices throughout the city, including at Praça 8 de Setembre and Rua Presidente Pedreira in the centre, Rua Sampaio 204 at Praia do Canto and in the Shopping Vitória.
**Shopping** Handicrafts are available at Artesanato Brasil at Praça Costa Pereira 226, Centro (Mon–Fri 8am–6pm), and at Mercado Capixaba de Artesanato at Av. Princesa Isabel 251, Centro (Mon–Fri 8.30am–6.30pm & Sat 8.30am–1pm); there's little distinctive on sale apart from rustic baskets and ceramics items, in particular *panelas de barro* (heavy black cooking pots used for making the *moqueca capixaba*). Shopping Vitória, at Av. Nossa Senhora dos Navegantes 1440, Enseada do Suá, is the largest shopping centre in the state.
**Trains** The Estação Ferroviária Pedro Nolasco is just over the bridge from the *rodoviária* in Cariacica (enquiries on ⓣ27/3226-4169). There are daily services to Belo Horizonte at 7.30am, taking just over 14hr.

# The coast

Espírito Santo's **coastline** is basically one long beach, some 400km in length. With the state sandwiched between Rio and Bahia, by rights the beaches should be stunning, but the reality is rather different. There's a wide coastal plain along most of the state, and with few exceptions the beaches' backdrops are hardly dramatic. Even so, if you're travelling between Rio and Bahia there are places where you could easily spend a few days enjoying little-visited stretches of sand, including **Anchieta** to the south of Vitória and **Itaúnas** to its north.

## South of Vitória

The most beautiful beaches near Vitória are around the town of **GUARAPARI**, 54km to the south of the state capital, to which it's linked by buses running every half-hour. There are dozens of hotels here, mostly white skyscrapers catering for visitors from Minas Gerais (prices are generally in the ❷–❹ bracket). If you fancy raucous nightlife and holiday-making Brazilian-style, then Guarapari is the place. On the other hand, if you need to escape to somewhere tranquil, a mere

7km to the south of Guarapari along the ES-060 is the **Praia dos Padres**, a protected area lapped by a wonderfully green sea. Just south of here, the fishing village of **Meaípe** has some excellent restaurants; the *Cantinho do Curuca* is especially recommended for its *bolinhos de aipim* and *moqueca capixaba*. Meaípe is also a good place to stay overnight. The *Pousada Enseada Verde* (Ⓣ27/3272-1376, Ⓦwww.enseadaverde.com.br; ❸), set on a hillside with views along the coast, is particularly comfortable and has a pool. For something a little more basic, try the *Pousada do Sol* (Ⓣ27/3272-0079; ❸). The beaches around here are amongst the finest in southern Espírito Santo, with a pleasant backdrop of hills covered in tropical vegetation, and they're extremely popular in the summer.

Twenty kilometres south of Guarapari, the town of **ANCHIETA** is one of the oldest settlements in the state. Of particular interest here is the imposing **Santuário Nacional Padre Anchieta** (Mon–Fri 9am–noon & 2–5pm, Sat & Sun 9am–5pm; R$2), which dominates the town from a hilltop position. Built sometime around the late sixteenth century as a Jesuit mission, the complex includes a well-kept museum commemorating the evangelical work amongst Indians of the sixteenth-century Jesuit priest José de Anchieta. An important fishing port, Anchieta is one of the few places along this stretch of coast where life isn't focused on tourism, and, as such, the hotels here are mainly grim. One exception is the *Anchieta* (Ⓣ27/3536-1258; ❷), a sprawling building dating from 1911 that still offers hints of its days as a "grand hotel". Heading south along the coast you pass a string of small beaches – some of which, like Praia dos Coqueiros, are quite pretty and not overly developed – before reaching **IRIRI**, a busy holiday resort about 10km from Anchieta with a mix of low-budget *pousadas* and holiday homes.

## North of Vitória

Considering what there is to look forward to in Bahia and elsewhere in the Northeast, most visitors heading northward from Vitória choose not to linger on Espírito Santo's **northern coast**. Indeed, the BR-101 remains far from the shore, never offering a glimpse of the ocean, and apart from the Serra do Mar far off to the west, this entire area is low-lying with a mix of cattle pasture and immense eucalyptus plantations as well as, nearer to the shore, mangrove swamps, patches of Mata Atlântica and beaches fringed with shrubs or wind-stunted coconut palms. The area does hold a few attractions, however. Coastal villages such as tiny **Regência** and **Itaúnas** remain fundamentally fishing communities, preserving traditions that have been gradually lost elsewhere, while a visit to the **Reserva Natural da Vale do Rio Doce** is a must for amateur naturalists.

Getting around these parts is usually easy, as **buses** link Vitória with Espírito Santo's northern towns along the BR-101 and beyond to southern Bahia. Onward connections to the beaches, however, can be few and far between.

### Regência

Some 35km north of Aracruz on the BR-101 is the turn-off to the village of **Regência**, a fishing community of barely 1200 inhabitants. Outside the rainy season between October and December, the unpaved, forty-kilometre road leading to Regência is always passable, but it's slow going, with buses stopping frequently at entrances to local cattle farms. As the road reaches the ocean, look out on your right for the Projeto Tamar **turtle research station** (daily 8am–5pm; Ⓦwww.projetotamar.org.br), which monitors a thirty-five-kilometre beach nearby where, between October and January, sea turtles of all kinds come to lay their eggs. If you're lucky, you'll be invited to join the scientists in the early evening as they monitor the nests of giant leatherback turtles and watch the hatchlings as they crawl into the sea between January and March. At the visitors' centre, interns guide you through exhibits explaining the turtles' life cycle and to tanks where you can view mature turtles.

The village of Regência itself holds little of interest, apart from the small **Museu Histórico de Regência** (Tues–Sun 10am–5pm), which charts local history through old photographs and artefacts. In summer, the village comes alive with young people from Belo Horizonte and Vitória. If you find the need **to stay**, there are several simple **pousadas**, including the *Pousada Careba* (Ⓣ27/3274-1089; ❷), right on the beach, and a couple of restaurants serving simple fish-based meals. When it's time to move on, you can catch a bus to Linhares (3 daily; 1hr 30min), from where you can connect with buses heading north and south.

### Reserva Natural da Vale do Rio Doce

Some 30km north of the industrial town of Linhares is the **Reserva Natural da Vale do Rio Doce** (Tues–Sun 7am–4pm; Ⓣ27/3371-9702, Ⓦwww.vale.com; R$8), home to forty percent of Espírito Santo's remaining portion of Mata Atlântica. All but a tiny fraction of the 22,000-hectare reserve is open to the public, but you'll need a couple of days to appreciate the area, which encompasses five different ecosystems ranging from tablelands forest to mangrove swamp. Although there's a wealth of flora and fauna, it's the four-hundred-odd species of bird that are the biggest draw; the best time for **birdwatching** is between September and November, when the forests are most abundant with fruit. Parrots and parakeets are easily spotted, while you may see a rare cherry-throated tanager if you're very lucky.

Any bus heading north from Linhares will drop you at the reserve's entrance, from where you can walk 500m to the **visitors' centre** and get an excellent overview (in English and Portuguese) of the region's history and ecology; there's also a *lanchonete* here. It's best to contact the reserve in advance to arrange for a guide to lead you along the forest trails, but someone's usually available and there's no charge. Without a guide, you're only allowed to wander the lightly forested, rather park-like, trails skirting the visitors' centre and hotel complex.

The reserve has its own **hotel** (Ⓣ27/3371-9797, Ⓦwww.vale.com; ❻ full board), with accommodation ranging from fairly simple rooms to chalets so luxurious they feel at odds with the forest surroundings. There's also a good restaurant and, reserved for hotel guests, a large pool.

### Conceição da Barra and Itaúnas

Some 95km further north, near the border with Bahia, is the resort town of **CONCEIÇÃO DA BARRA**. Its beaches are popular with *mineiros* in the summer and there are many reasonable **pousadas** on the attractive Praia da Guaxindiba, including the *Pousada do Sol*, Av. Atlântica 226 (Ⓣ27/3762-1412; ❸), which has a small pool, and, at no. 718, the simpler but very pleasant *Varanda da Praia* (Ⓣ27/3762-1654, Ⓦwww.varandadapraia.br; ❷). A much more enjoyable place to stay, however, is the village of **ITAÚNAS**, some 20km further north on the edge of the Parque Estadual Itaúnas, best known for its thirty-metre-high sand dunes. Beneath these dunes lies a small town that was engulfed and evacuated in the 1970s after the vegetation surrounding it had been cleared for farmland. It is said that occasionally the **dunes** shift in the wind to uncover the spire of the old church. The beaches are long and – with only low-lying vegetation – exposed, but at the height of the summer are extremely popular with students, drawn by the places's party atmosphere, where *axê* music pounds from the bars until the small hours of the morning. Very different in atmosphere to coastal settlements further south, Itaúnas is said to be where northeastern Brazil begins. Keep your ears open for **forró** music – which may owe its recent popularity in Rio and São Paulo to tourists returning from Itaúnas; dances here typically get going around midnight and continue until 10am.

There are only a few *pousadas* in Itaúnas and it's always worth calling ahead in the summer. No-frills, but friendly and blending in with the environment, is the very pretty *Pousada da Praia* (ⓣ27/3762-5028, ⓦwww.casadapraiaitaunas.com.br; ④), or for a bit more comfort (and a pool) the *Pousada das Tartarugas* (ⓣ27/9988-8155, ⓦwww.pousadatartarugas.com.br; ④) and the *Pousada dos Corais* (ⓣ27/3762-5200, ⓦwww.pousadadoscoraisitaunas.com.br; ③) are both recommended. As for **places to eat**, there are plenty of inexpensive seafood restaurants around, of which *Cipó Cravo* is famous for its desserts. When it's time to move on, catch a bus to the road leading to Conceição from where you'll be able to pick up a bus to Vitória or to Porto Seguro in Bahia.

# Inland from Vitória

In the hills and mountains inland from Vitória are several small towns surrounded by superb walking country, great for a day-trip or as a base for a relaxing few days. You can easily spot where the first immigrants came from: the houses and churches of **Santa Teresa** look as Italian as those of **Domingos Martins**, **Santa Leopoldina** or **Santa Maria** look German. The smallest of these towns, **Venda Nova**, is home to the remarkable sight of **Pedra Azul**, a grey granite outcrop almost 1000m high that's one of the unsung natural wonders of Brazil. If you're heading for Minas Gerais, Venda Nova lies on the main Vitória–Belo Horizonte highway, Domingos Martins just off it. The area is a popular destination for residents of Vitória, so if you plan to stay over a weekend – in particular in the winter dry season, when the trails can be approached most comfortably, the sky is blue and there's a chill in the air – pre-booking accommodation is advisable.

## Domingos Martins

The closest of the inland towns to Vitória is **DOMINGOS MARTINS**, 42km away on the north side of the Belo Horizonte highway. Almost completely surrounded by steep hills, Domingos Martins is high enough to be bracingly fresh by day and distinctly cold at night; it looks like a run-down German mountain village, with its triangular wooden houses modelled after alpine chalets.

Get off the bus at the first stop in the town, rather than continuing to the *rodoviária*. A few metres from here, by the immaculately manicured main square, is a wonderful inexpensive **hotel**, the imposing *Imperador*, Rua Duque de Caxias 275 (ⓣ27/3268-1115, ⓦwww.hotelimperador.tur.br; ②), built in Bavarian style. Although the place has seen better days, it's good value with very comfortable rooms and a small pool.

There's not much to Domingos Martins, just a small museum, the **Casa da Cultura** (daily 8am–5pm), almost opposite the bus stop at Av. Presidente Vargas 520, which has some old documents and artefacts dating from the colony's early days after Pomeranians founded it in 1847. Also worth a visit in the centre is the **Igreja Luterana**, dating from 1866 and said to have the first tower permitted on a Protestant place of worship in Brazil. If you're into flora, it's well worth the hassle getting to the **Reserva Kautsky** (Mon–Fri 7–10am & 2–5pm; phone in advance of visit ⓣ27/3268-1209, ⓦwww.institutokautsky.org.br), some way out of town and with the last 2km accessible only by four-wheel-drive. It has an extensive collection of orchids and camellias and a large forest reserve with trails – ask at any hotel for details. In the centre of town, near the Casa da Cultura, is a good and inexpensive *por kilo* **restaurant**, *Tia Ria*, with a buffet featuring a large variety of German- and Italian-influenced dishes, as well as more familiar Brazilian ones. For a German–Brazilian culinary experience, the *Restaurante Bigosch* (open Wed–Sun), at Ladeira Francisco dos Santos Silva 50 near the Casa da Cultura, offers unimaginative, but reasonably priced fare, while for enormous and excellent high teas, try the *Café Expresso Koeler* along Rua João Batista Wernersbach. There's a good selection of jams, preserves and biscuits on offer at the town's Prefeitura-run Casa do Artesanato, all produced by local *colonos*, or smallholders.

When it's time to **move on**, you can either return to Vitória or take any Belo Horizonte–bound bus and get off in Venda Nova.

## Venda Nova and Pedra Azul

**VENDA NOVA DO IMIGRANTE**, to give it its full name, is an Italian village some 67km further west of Domingo Martins on the Vitória–Belo Horizonte highway (the BR-262). Even by the standards of the state, the landscape in which it is set is extraordinary, a delightful mix of rich Mata Atlântica, valleys and escarpments.

Venda Nova itself is nothing more than a small village strung along the highway, with the centre based on Avenida Domingos Perim, the ES-166. The **Loja do Agroturismo** (daily 8am–5pm), an association of *colonos* (family farmers) that encourages rural tourism, is near the *Alpes Hotel* at the intersection of ES-166 and BR-262; you can pick up a very good local map there that gives the locations of the various small **farms** in the vicinity that are set up to receive visitors. There are several within a kilometre of the centre, one of the most attractive being that of the Sossai-Altoé family, south of the centre along Avenida Domingos Perim; the farm is clearly signposted and visitors are free to drop by. The Sossai-Altoé property is typical of the smallholdings hereabouts. The family, which emigrated to Brazil from the northern Italian province of Veneto in 1880, cultivate just five hectares of land, producing corn, beans, sugar cane and, most important of all commercially, coffee. Tourism has become vitally important for what are typically large families, and the Sossai-Altoés are happy to show their produce to visitors and demonstrate how they make their fruit wines and *cachaça*. All the farms have a small shop selling jams, wines and liquors, and it's only polite to make a purchase before leaving.

Ten kilometres outside the village is the most remarkable sight in Espírito Santo, a towering, bare granite mountain shaped like a thumb and almost 1000m high – the **Pedra Azul**, or "blue stone". Its peak is actually 2000m above sea level, the other thousand accounted for by the hill country from which it sprouts, an area popular with mountaineers. It's like an enormous version of the Sugar Loaf in Rio, except no vegetation grows on its bare surface, which rears up from thick forest and looks so smooth that from a distance it appears more like glass than stone. During the day sunlight does strange things to it – it really does look blue in shadow – but the time to see it is at either dawn or sunset, when it turns all kinds of colours in a spectacular natural show. The Pedra Azul forms the centrepiece of a state park, the **Parque Estadual da Pedra Azul** (Wed–Sun 9am–noon & 1.30–5.30pm; R$5 to the base or R$10 to the pools); there's a small visitors' centre at the foot of Pedra Azul with exhibits on local fauna and flora, and the park rangers will point you towards the trail leading up the stone – a tiring, but not very difficult, three-hour walk, though the area is closed when there's been heavy rain. Bring food and drink for the trek, and swimwear if you want to enjoy a refreshing dip on the way up in one of the natural pools. An excellent, very detailed map of the Pedra Azul area is sold at most local hotels.

### Arrival and accommodation

There are three direct **buses** a day from Vitória to Pedra Azul, but any bus that goes to Minas Gerais also passes by the peak as it's on the highway to Belo Horizonte. A constant flow of local buses links Venda Nova with the access road to the Parque Estadual da Pedra Azul, from where it's an easy three-kilometre hike to the park entrance.

There's a good range of **accommodation** in Venda Nova. The *Alpes Hotel* (Ⓣ27/3546-1367, Ⓦwww.alpeshotel.com.br; ❸) on the BR-262 near the centre of town is rather sterile but comfortable, with its own pool and sauna. Cheaper and far more distinctive is the *Pousada Nonno Beppi* (Ⓣ27/3546-1965; ❷), 2km from the centre of town on the BR-262 in the direction of Domingo Martins. Owned by a family of Italian descent who've farmed here since 1912, the *pousada*'s main building is a rustic farmhouse. The best (though still not very good) place to eat in town is the *Ristorante Dalla Ninna*, attached to the *Alpes Hotel*, which serves reasonably priced, Italian-inspired food.

There are also several good places to stay **nearer the park**. The *Penhazul* (Ⓣ27/3248-1206, Ⓔpenhazul@hotmail.com; ❸), at the Sítio do Bio, next to the Igreja de Fátima, is a small old farmhouse that is now a simple, but comfortable, *pousada*. Near the access road for the park at Km 88 of the BR-262 (where it meets ES-164), is the rustic-looking *Pousada Peterle* (Ⓣ27/3248-1243, Ⓦwww.pousadapeterle.com.br; ❸), consisting of several modern chalets, all with superb views and an Italian restaurant. On the continuation of the same access road, ES-164, some 6km beyond Pedra Azul, the simple, clean and friendly *Pousada Aargau* (Ⓣ27/3248-2175; ❸–❹) is located in some of the most beautiful countryside in the area. Owned and run by the son of Swiss immigrants, the *pousada* also offers an enormous *café colonial* (high tea; R$20), available every day.

## Santa Teresa

**SANTA TERESA** is only 90km northwest from Vitória but the hills between them are steep, reducing buses to a crawl for significant stretches and padding the journey out to a good two hours. The initial run up the main highway towards Bahia to the hill town of Fundão is attractive enough, but the winding road that takes you the 13km from here to Santa Teresa is something special, with great views on either side of the bus. The soils are rich, and dense forest is interspersed with coffee bushes and intensively cultivated hill farms, framed by dramatic granite cliffs and escarpments.

### Information, accommodation and eating

**Tourist information** is from the Prefeitura at Av. Jerônimo Verloet 145 (Mon–Fri 8am–6pm; Ⓣ27/3259-2268); a branch of the Banco do Brasil with an ATM is opposite the Prefeitura.

The most comfortable **place to stay**, the *Pousada Vita Verde*, 2km from the town centre along the Estrada de Aparecidinha (Ⓣ27/3259-3332, Ⓦwww.pousadavitaverde.com; ❸), is a converted farm house set amidst beautiful countryside. Slightly nearer to town, along the very pretty Estrada Lombardia, the cosy *Pousada Paradiso* (Ⓣ27/3259-3191; ❷) is set in a lovely forested valley. In town itself, the dreary looking, but extremely welcoming *Pierazzo Hotel*, Av. Getúlio Vargas 115 (Ⓣ27/3259-1233; ❷), offers excellent value. Booking ahead is essential during the Festa do Imigrante Italiano de Santa Teresa, an annual celebration of Italian culture and traditions that takes place over a four-day period coinciding with the last weekend of June.

Among **restaurants**, *Mazzolin di Fiori* on Praça Domingos Martins serves local specialities (lunchtimes only), as does *Zitu's* on Avenida Getúlio Vargas, near the *Pierazzo Hotel*.

## The Village

The closer you get to Santa Teresa, the more insistent the echoes of Europe become. The tiled hill farms look more Italian and less Brazilian, you see grape vines and when you finally pull into the sturdy village you could be arriving somewhere in the foothills of the Alps. The first Italian colonists arrived here in 1875; the last shipload of Italian immigrants docked in Vitória in 1925. Today, only the very oldest of inhabitants living in isolated smallholdings continue to speak the Italian dialects of Lombardy and Trento, although interest in the Italian heritage remains, in the form of musical bands and choirs, and with young people taking Italian evening classes.

The town has grown very little in more recent times, and is still laid out along two streets in the shape of a cross. You go right down the main artery to arrive at the **rodoviária** (☎27/3259-1300) at the far end of the village. There is a beautifully tended square, Praça Domingos Martins, full of flowers, trees and hummingbirds darting around. Along the adjacent street and at the far end, next to the school, is Santa Teresa's main attraction, the Museu Mello Leitão, a natural-history museum and nature reserve covering eighty square kilometres (see below).

From the square, steps that are cut into the hillside lead to a ridge, and a five-minute walk brings you to the unmistakeably Italian **Igreja Matriz**, complete with roundels and cupola; the names of the first colonists are engraved on a plaque on its outside wall. Rua São Lourenço, the street leading uphill from here, is the oldest in the village, now lined with solidly built houses erected in the early twentieth century by the first wave of settlers. Five hundred metres along it, you come to the surviving two-storey wattle-and-daub houses put up by the first Italian immigrants; oldest of all is the Casa de Virgílio Lambert, a farmhouse opposite the tiny chapel that was built around 1876. Also around here are numerous **cantinas** where the local wines are made and sold; the limited production from grapes is, to say the least, an acquired taste, but in any case most is made from *jabuticaba*, a berry-like fruit that grows locally on tree trunks. To taste something even stronger, carry on a further 4km along the road to Cachaça da Mata, the producer of the best **cachaça** in Espírito Santo. The best time to visit the area is during the September-to-December harvest, during which you can see every stage of the distilling process, but visitors are welcome to tastings throughout the year.

## The Museu Mello Leitão

Santa Teresa is full of flowers, and of hummingbirds feeding off them, and early this century they aroused the interest of one of the first generation of Italians to be born here, **Augusto Ruschi**. He turned a childhood fascination into a lifetime of study and became a pioneering natural scientist and ecologist decades before it was fashionable. Specializing in the study of **hummingbirds**, he became the world's leading expert in the field and, in the later years of his life, was almost single-handedly responsible for galvanizing the state government into action to protect the exceptional beauty of the interior of Espírito Santo; that so much forest remains is due in no small measure to him. He died in 1986, at the age of 71, after being poisoned by the secretions of a tree frog he collected on one of his many expeditions into the forest.

Ruschi named the **Museu Mello Leitão**, Av. José Ruschi 4 (Tues–Sun 8am–5pm; R$2), in tribute to a former teacher. It represents Ruschi's life's work, designed and laid out by him from the early 1930s. The museum contains his library and all his collections of animals, birds and insects, as well as a small zoo, a snake farm, a butterfly garden and the richest park in the state, home to thousands of species of trees, orchids, flowers and cacti – a beautiful place to wander around and a fine memorial to an extraordinary man.

## Santa Leopoldina

The drive to **SANTA LEOPOLDINA** (commonly known as just Leopoldina) from Santa Teresa is fabulous, along a country road winding through thickly forested hills and gorges. Despite the temporary look of the road and the tiny settlements you pass through – clearings in the forest uncannily like Amazon highway settlements – these are long-established communities dating from 1919, when the road was finished.

Ironically, the completion of the road to Santa Teresa meant the end of the line for Santa Leopoldina. Founded in 1857 by 160 Swiss colonists, who were followed over the next forty years by more than a thousand Luxembourgers, Saxons, Pomeranians and Austrians, Santa Leopoldina was one of the earliest European colonies in Espírito Santo and also the most successful, as coffee grew well on the hills and found a ready market on the coast. Built on the last navigable stretch of the Rio Santa Maria, inland from Vitória, Leopoldina was the main point of entry for the whole region. Once the road was finished, however, Santa Teresa swiftly outgrew it, leaving only a few streets of rather ugly houses and trading posts as a reminder of earlier prosperity. The town's German character has faded almost entirely, but the outlying parts of the *município* are still mainly inhabited by descendants of Germans, many of whom have retained the language or dialect of earlier generations.

The bus drops you at one end of the main street, **Rua do Comércio**. Nearby, on the same road, is the Prefeitura (Mon–Fri 8am–5pm), where you can pick up an excellent map of the *município*. Back along the street, the interesting **Museu do Colono** (Tues–Sun 11am–5pm), housed in the mansion of what used to be the leading German family in town, spotlights the early decades of German settlement with photographs – including some fascinating ones of the construction of the road to Santa Teresa in 1919 – along with relics and documents.

Unfortunately, there is nowhere to **stay** in town, but the *Pousada Ecológica do Tirol* (Ⓣ27/9998-0341, Ⓦwww.coloniatirol.com; ❸), about 17km south of Santa Leopoldina in the picturesque hamlet of Tirol, offers comfortable accommodation and very good Austrian–Brazilian food. There are two **buses** a day to Santa Maria and three buses covering the 28km to Santa Teresa. At a pinch, it's possible to walk to either town, but allow plenty of time, carry lots to drink and remember that the route is extremely hilly.

## Santa Maria

The road leading to **SANTA MARIA DE JETIBÁ** passes through hilly terrain, densely cultivated with coffee bushes, interspersed with pine plantations and, on the steepest of hillsides, patches of Mata Atlântica. As you enter Santa Maria – essentially one long street, the Avenida Frederico Grulke – you are greeted by a "Willkommen" sign. This is an outward expression of Santa Maria's intense pride in its German heritage, an ancestry the village is keen to promote as a tourist attraction. Virtually the entire population is descended from mid-nineteenth-century immigrants from Pomerania and today remains bound together by a common heritage based on the continued use of the *Pommersch Platt* dialect and membership in the Lutheran Church.

Santa Maria is a pleasant enough place, most of the time just a sleepy village, but the place comes to life during the periodic **festivals** (most notably the Festa do Colono, held annually over the weekend closest to July 25), celebrating Pomeranian culture. The history of the area's settlement is well covered by the **Museu da Imigração Pomerana** (Tues–Sun 9–11am & 2.30–5.30pm; R$2) in the centre of the village at Rua Dalmácio Espíndula 260.

If you want to **stay** over, the excellent-value *Pommer Haus Hotel* (☎27/3263-1718; ❷), in the centre at Av. Frederico Grulke 455 (above the Banco do Brasil), is comfortable and surprisingly large for a village of Santa Maria's size. **Food** is strangely disappointing in the village, with the only places to eat being a couple of *lanchonetes* and pizzerias on Avenida Frederico Grulke and nothing even remotely German on offer.

# Travel details

## Buses

**Belo Horizonte** to: Brasília (5 daily; 14hr); Campo Grande (3 daily; 23hr); Congonhas (hourly; 2hr); Cuiabá (4 daily; 33hr); Curitiba (2 daily; 18hr); Diamantina (6 daily; 6hr); Fortaleza (1 daily; 36hr); Goiânia (5 daily; 16hr); Mariana (hourly; 2hr); Ouro Preto (hourly; 2hr); Recife (2 daily; 40hr); Rio (20 daily; 6hr 30min); Sabará (every 15min; 30min); Salvador (5 daily; 28hr); São João del Rei (8 daily; 4hr); São Lourenço (2 daily; 6hr); São Paulo (hourly; 10hr); Vitória (4 daily; 8hr).

**Diamantina** to: Araçuaí (2 daily; 5hr); Belo Horizonte (6 daily; 6hr); São Paulo (1 daily; 16hr); Serro (1 daily; 2hr).

**Ouro Preto** to: Belo Horizonte (10 daily; 2hr); Brasília (1 daily; 11hr); Mariana (every 20min; 30min); Rio (3 daily; 7hr); São João del Rei (2 daily; 5hr); São Paulo (2 daily; 11hr).

**São João del Rei** to: Belo Horizonte (7 daily; 4hr); Caxambu (4 weekly; 3hr); Ouro Preto (2 daily; 5hr); Rio (4 daily; 4hr); São Paulo (2 daily; 8hr); Tiradentes (hourly; 30min); Três Corações (4 daily; 4hr); Vitória (1 daily; 13hr).

**Vitória** to: Belo Horizonte (6 daily; 8hr); Brasília (1 daily; 22hr); Domingos Martins (13 daily; 1hr); Fortaleza (5 weekly; 36hr); Guarapari (every 30min; 1hr); Linhares (4 daily; 3hr); Rio (hourly; 7hr 30min); Salvador (2 daily; 17hr); Santa Teresa (6 daily Mon–Sat, 3 on Sun; 2hr); São João del Rei (1 daily; 13hr); São Paulo (5 daily; 14hr); Venda Nova (hourly; 3hr).

## Trains

Calling at all stations, including Governador Valadares and Itabira:

**Belo Horizonte** to: Vitória (daily at 7.30am; 14hr).

**Vitória** to: Belo Horizonte (daily at 7.30am; 14hr).

## Tourist steam service:

**Mariana** to: Ouro Preto (Thurs–Sun at 9am & 2.30pm; 1hr 10min).

**Ouro Preto** to: Mariana (Thurs–Sun at 11am & 4.30pm; 1hr 10min).

**São João del Rei** to: Tiradentes (Fri–Sun & holidays at 10am & 3pm; 35min).

**Tiradentes** to: São João del Rei (Fri–Sun & holidays at 1pm & 5pm; 35min).

# Bahia

VENEZUELA
GUYANA
SURINAME
FRENCH GUIANA
COLOMBIA
N
5
4
3
PERU
7
6
BOLIVIA
2
8
1
PARAGUAY
CHILE
9
ARGENTINA
0
1000 km
URUGUAY

# CHAPTER 3 Highlights

* **Capoeira** Watch nimble displays of this Afro-Brazilian martial art at one of the organized *capoeira* schools. See p.244
* **Salvador's nightlife** The vibrant backstreets of Pelourinho offer the city's best live music, including samba and reggae. See p.251
* **Candomblé celebrations** The dance rituals of this religious cult can be memorable, if you're lucky enough to catch one. See p.253
* **Diogo** Relax in a stylish *pousada* cooled by ocean breezes, with vast, empty beaches just a short stroll away. See p.259
* **Boipeba** Soak up the quiet on the stunning sea and beach at Bahia's best – and least commercialized – offshore island, where there are just a few *pousadas* and absolutely no road traffic. See p.265
* **Parque Nacional da Chapada Diamantina** There's plenty of diverse terrain to keep hikers happy in this huge national park. See p.271

▲ *Capoeira* in Bahia

# 3

# Bahia



With over 1000km of coconut-fringed beaches and the most agreeable climate in the region – hot and sunny, but not as blistering as elsewhere – **Bahia** has long been one of the country's most popular destinations for foreign visitors. Constituting over a third of Northeast Brazil, it sits to the south of the area's other states. At its heart are the **Chapada Diamantina Mountains**, offering breathtaking trekking and climbing opportunities, while just north of there, the massive **São Francisco Lakes** are popular for canoeing and watersports. The countryside changes to the south of the state capital, **Salvador** (site of the first Portuguese landings in 1500), with mangrove swamps and fast-developing island resorts around the town of **Valença**, before reverting to a spectacular coastline. A string of colonial towns, including **Santo Amaro** and **Cachoeira**, also lie within striking distance of Salvador. Further south, **Ilhéus** is a thriving beach resort, as is **Porto Seguro**, whose early settlement pre-dates even Salvador's. Beyond the coastline, Bahia comprises a vast grain-producing western sector and semi-arid landscape. The Bahian **sertão** is massive, a desert-like land that supports some fascinating towns – the ex-mining bases of **Jacobina** and **Lençóis** and the river terminus of **Ibotirama** are just three.

The bay on which Salvador was built afforded its settlers a superb natural anchorage, while the surrounding lands of Bahia state were ideal country for sugar-cane and tobacco plantations. In the seventeeth century, Salvador became the centre of the **Recôncavo**, the richest plantation zone in Brazil before the arrival of coffee the following century. It was the national capital for over two centuries, before relinquishing the title to Rio in 1763.

**Carnaval** reaches a frenzied peak in Salvador every February, when the city heaves with two million people enjoying traditional tunes, from the popular and loud **Barra seaside suburb** to the more arty **Pelhourinho**.

## Getting there and around

You can reach Bahia from almost any direction, though most people will arrive first at Salvador, either by air, bus or boat. There are direct **flights** to Salvador from Europe and North America, and frequent **buses** from all parts of Brazil. **Getting around** Bahia is straightforward thanks to the region's extensive bus network. These days, Bahia's two main north–south highways are the BR-116 and BR-101 which, together with the state's extensive network of secondary paved and unpaved roads, link all the main cities and tourist destinations. The main coastal roads are in fairly good shape, but start to deteriorate away from the principal routes. Ferries, a catamaran and air service connect Salvador with some southern resorts, including Morro de São Paulo. Car hire is easy, but be aware: crazy drivers are plentiful in this part of Brazil.

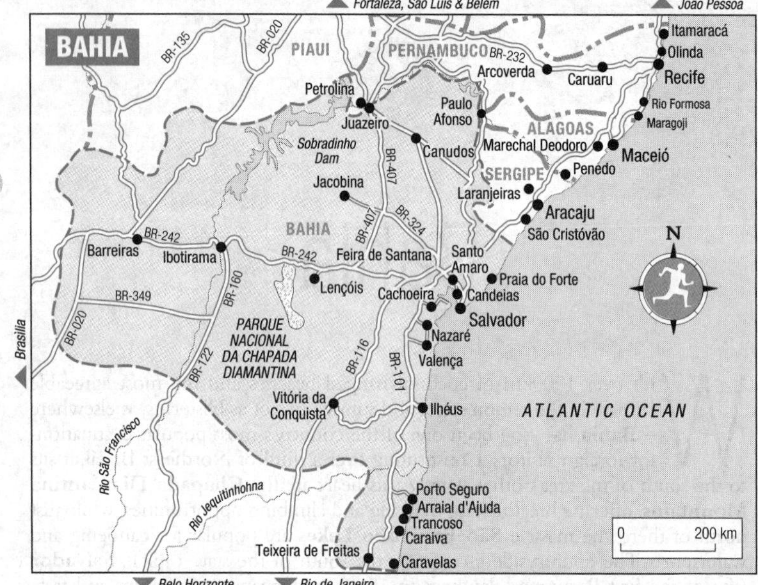


# Salvador and around

Second only to Rio in the magnificence of its natural setting, on the mouth of the enormous bay of Todos os Santos (All Saints), **SALVADOR** is one of that select band of cities that has an electric feel from the moment you arrive. The modern cloud-scraping skyline has a distinct beauty of its own, poised as it is on an undulating headland at the mouth of a deep-blue ocean bay.

Fantastic swimming beaches, the largest collection of colonial architecture in Latin America, and a vibrant modern culture – perhaps the richest living cultural mix in the country, with its multitide of Afro-Caribbean bands and performers – all combine to help make Salvador the most popular destination in the Northeast, even if it considers itself distinct from the rest of this region.

Salvador was founded in 1549 by Tomé de Sousa, who chose the city for its inaccessible perch 70m above sea level. This marked the beginning of the permanent occupation of the country by the **Portuguese**, though it wasn't easy for them. The local Caeté Indians killed and ate both the first governor and the first bishop before succumbing to superior force and steel. Salvador was also the scene of a great battle in 1624, when the Dutch destroyed the Portuguese fleet in the bay and stormed and captured the town, only to be forced out again within a year by a joint Spanish and Portuguese fleet. For the first 300 years of its existence, Salvador was the most important port and city in the South Atlantic.

Much of the plantation wealth of the **Recôncavo** was used to adorn the city with imposing public buildings, ornate squares and, above all, churches. Today, Salvador is a large, modern city, but significant chunks of it are still recognizably colonial. Taken as a whole it doesn't have the unsullied calm of, say, Olinda but many of its individual churches, monasteries and convents are magnificent.

The other factor that marks Salvador is immediately obvious – most of the population is black. Salvador was Brazil's main slave port, and the survivors of the brutal journey from the Portuguese Gold Coast and Angola were immediately packed off to city construction gangs or the plantations of the Recôncavo; today, their descendants make up the bulk of the population. **African influences** are everywhere. Salvador is the cradle of *candomblé* and *umbanda*, Afro-Brazilian religious cults that have millions of devotees across Brazil. The city has a marvellous local **cuisine**, much imitated in other parts of the country, based on traditional African ingredients like palm oil, seafood, peanuts and coconut milk. And Salvador has possibly the richest **artistic tradition** of any Brazilian city, rivalled only by Rio.

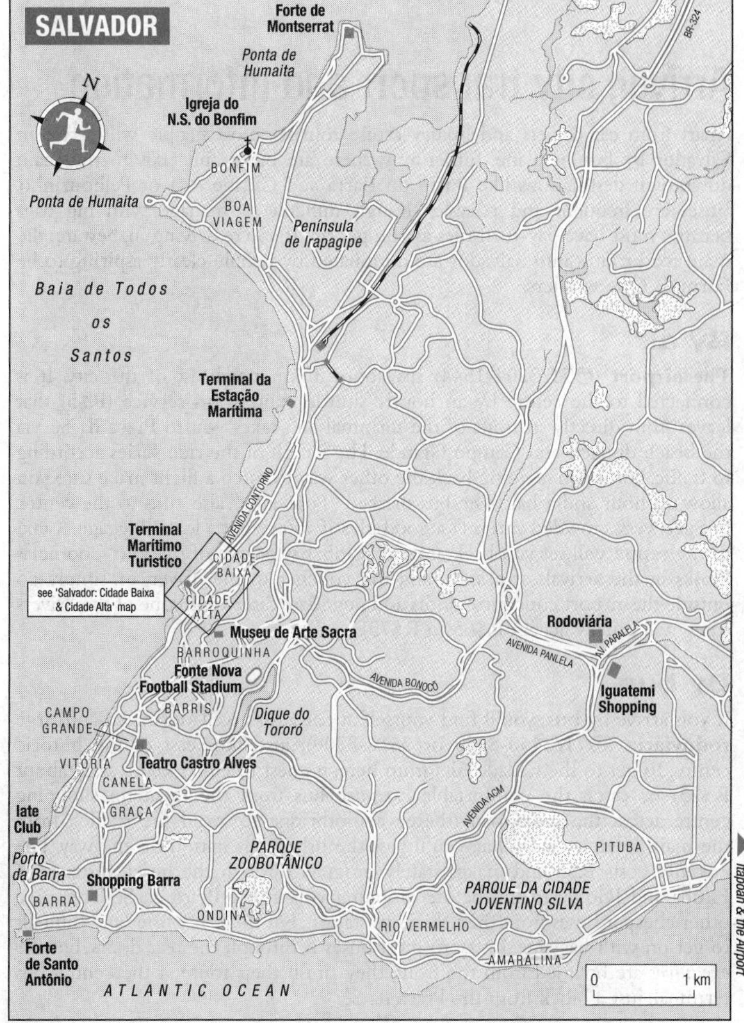

A disproportionate number of Brazil's leading **writers** and **poets** were either born in Salvador or lived there, including Jorge Amado, the most widely translated Brazilian novelist, and Vinícius de Morães, Brazil's best-known modern poet. The majority of the great names who made Brazilian **music** famous hail from the city – João Gilberto, the leading exponent, with Tom Jobim, of bossa nova; Astrud Gilberto, whose quavering version of *The Girl from Ipanema* was a global hit; Dorival Caymmi, the patriarch of Brazilian popular music; Caetano Veloso, the founder of *tropicalismo*; the singers Maria Bethânia and Gal Costa; and Gilberto Gil, who was at one time secretary of culture in the city government. Timbalada rhythms and the world-renowned black musician Carlinhos Brown are among the most recent additions to Salvador's hall of fame. The city's music is still as rich and innovative as ever, and bursts out every year in a **Carnaval** that many regard as the best in Brazil.



# Arrival, city transport and information

Apart from car drivers and luxury-cruise tourists, most people will arrive in Salvador by bus or plane. Either way, there are buses and taxis to the main downtown destinations like Porto do Barra and Cidade Alta or Pelhourinho. Buses are frequent and reliable, though difficult to manage with big bags because most have pay-turnstiles as you get on. If you're driving in, beware: the main road routes into Salvador are dominated by people clearly aspiring to be Formula One winners.

## By air

The **airport** (☎71/3204-1544) sits about 30km northeast of the city. It is connected to the centre by an hourly shuttle express bus service (R$5) that leaves from directly in front of the terminal and takes you to Praça da Sé via the beach districts and Campo Grande. The length of the ride varies according to traffic, but if you're going back the other way to catch a flight make sure you allow an hour and a half. The bus marked "Politeama" also runs to the centre, but gets very crowded and isn't a good idea if you've got a lot of luggage. A taxi to the centre will set you back around R$85; pay at one of the Taxi Coometas kiosks in the arrivals area and hand the voucher to the driver; or, simply go outside the airport concourse doors and negotiate direct with one of the drivers (they will usually accept R$65 to R$75).

## By bus

If you arrive by **bus**, you'll find yourself at Salvador's well-organized and large **rodoviária** (☎71/3460-8300 or 3616-8300), just 8km east of the historic centre. To get to the Cidade Alta from here, it's best to either take a taxi (about R$25) or catch the comfortable *executivo* bus from the Iguatemi shopping centre across the busy road (there's a footbridge to avoid the traffic), from the main intercity *rodoviária*; you'll pass the urban bus station on the way. The *executivo* costs R$5 and makes stately progress through the beach districts of Pituba and Rio Vermelho before dropping you in the Praça da Sé. There are other cheaper buses from the urban bus station, but they are busier and difficult to get on with baggage. Entry to most buses is through the rear doors, but the *executivos* are boarded from the front; they finish their route at the central bus terminal, just a block from the Praça da Sé.

## City transport

Many of the museums, churches and historic buildings in Salvador are concentrated within **walking** distance of each other in Cidade Alta. **Taxis** are also plentiful, although all the beach areas except Barra are a long ride from the centre.

There are three **local bus terminals**: Campo Grande, Estação da Lapa, and the central terminal at Praça da Sé, and the bus system is efficient and easy to use. From **Praça da Sé**, local services head to Barra and to **Campo Grande**, which has connections to the airport, *rodoviária* and Itapoan (also spelt Itapoã). The Praça da Sé bus stop is also the place to catch the *executivo* – well worth using instead of the crowded city buses for getting around the city as well as into it. There are only two routes on the *executivo* service. Buses marked "Iguatemi" run through the city to Barra, head down the coast to Rio Vermelho, and stop at the Iguatemi shopping centre, from where you can easily walk back across to the *rodoviária*; this is the fastest way to reach the *rodoviária* by public transport, though still count on at least 45 minutes in transit. The "Aeroporto" service, meanwhile, follows the same route until Rio Vermelho, before continuing along past Pituba to Itapoan, and on to the airport – cutting journey times to any of the beach areas to at least half that of a regular city bus. The third city bus terminal is **Estação da Lapa**, in Barris, which has connections to everywhere in the city; it's remarkably well laid out, with destinations clearly labelled. To reach the centre, any bus with "Sé", "C. Grande" or "Lapa" on the route card will do.

Salvador also has **ferry** services to islands in the bay and points on the mainland. There are two main ferry terminals: the **Terminal Maritimo Turístico**, behind the Mercado Modelo, clearly visible from Cidade Alta, is for launch services – *lanchas* – and excursion boats to the island of Itaparica, across the bay as well as two-hour passage direct to Morro de São Paulo (Ⓣ71/3242-4366); the **Terminal da Estação Marítima** (or Terminal São Joaquim Ⓣ71/3254-1020), to the north, past the docks and Polícia Federal offices at 1051 Av. Oscar Pontes, handles the full-size car ferries to Itaparica (every 30min during the day; 1hr) and also the less-frequent catamaran service (20min).

The quickest way to get to the ferry terminals – and Cidade Baixa in general – is to take the **Lacerda elevator** which connects Cidade Alta with the heart of Cidade Baixa. They run every few minutes from early morning to late at night (though see the box on "Personal safety", p.238), and cost only a few cents a ride.

## Information

Salvador's **tourist information** is better than anywhere else in the state. The state tourist agency, **Bahiatursa**, is used to foreigners and most of its offices have English-speakers who can provide a variety of maps and handouts on the city: the best two are the *Mapa Turístico de Salvador da Bahia* (R$10) and the free *Guia do Pelourinho*. If you're travelling on to other parts of Bahia, you should also ask for whatever material they have on the rest of the state, as elsewhere the service is nowhere near as good.

The only information office open daily is in Cidade Alta at Rua das Laranjeiras 2 (9am–9pm; Ⓣ71/3321-2463, Ⓦwww.bahia.com.br). An additional source of information is the **tourist hotline**, "Disque Turismo" – call Ⓣ71/3103-3103 and you should be able to get an English-speaker. Finally, if you need further detail, Bahiatursa's main offices are in the Centro de Convenções da Bahia, Loteamento Jardin Armação in the Avenida Simón Bolívar, first floor, Boca do Rio (Ⓣ71/3117-3000). For tourist protection matters and to report a robbery go to the **Delegacia de Proteção ao Turista**, Praça Ancieta 14, Cruzeiro do São Francisco,

### Personal safety: a warning

Salvador has more of a problem with **robberies** and **muggings** than anywhere else in Bahia.The main tourist area around Pelourinho is policed, except for the bus stop, until quite late at night and is relatively safe. However, precautions are still in order and there is an increasing crack-cocaine problem among the poor and young. Don't wander off the main drags or down ill-lit side streets at night unless you are within sight of a policeman, and don't use the Lacerda elevator (see p.237) after early evening. You should also avoid walking up and down the winding roads that connect the Cidade Alta and the Cidade Baixa and be careful about using ordinary city buses on Sundays when there are few people around; the *executivo* bus is the safest option. Give the Avenida do Contorno – the seafront road that runs north from the harbour past the marina – a miss too. It's a shame to put it out of bounds as it's a very scenic walk, but it's dangerous even in daylight as gangs lie in wait for tourists who don't know any better. If you want to go to one of the very fine restaurants here, or the Museu de Arte Moderna near them, take a taxi.

Pelhourinho (Mon–Sat 9am–6pm; ⓣ71/3322-7155). Several useful websites cover Bahia and Salvador, including ⓦwww.bahia-online.net and ⓦwww.bahia.com.br (both in English), and ⓦwww.portalsalvador.net and ⓦwww.carnaval.com.br (in Portuguese only).

One thing to bear in mind when finding your way around the city is that many **roads** have two **names**: the main seafront road, for example, is sometimes called Avenida Presidente Vargas, but more usually Avenida Oceânica. In general, we've gone for the name that actually appears on the street signs.

# Accommodation

Salvador is the second most popular tourist destination in Brazil and correspondingly full of **hotels**. Unless you want be near the beaches, the best area to head for is **Cidade Alta**, not least because of the spectacular view across the island-studded bay. The wealthy suburb of **Barra** has by far the closest of the beaches to the centre; the small but lovely Praia do Porto is especially pleasant and the best for swimming. Barra also has plenty of cafés and nightspots as well as being one of the most reasonably priced beach areas with several quality medium-priced hotels and *pousadas*. There's a **campsite**, *Camping Ecológica Stella Maris*, at Alameda da Praia (near the *farol*) in Itapoã (ⓣ71/3374-3506), which has shower and restaurant facilities, and space for motorhomes.

## City centre

**Albergue das Laranjeiras** Rua da Ordem Terceira (aka Rua Inácio Accioli) 13 ⓣ&ⓕ71/3321-1366, ⓦwww.laranjeirashostel.com.br. Excellent, lively youth hostel in the heart of the historic centre, with internet access, inexpensive laundry facilities and a trendy café. Prices range from R$25 per person in dorm without private bathroom to R$150 in high season for a double room with bath.

**Arthemis Hotel** Praça da Sé 398, Ed. Themis, 7th floor ⓣ71/3322-0724, ⓦwww.artemishotel.com.br. At the top of an office block in the middle of the city, with tremendous views, a patio bar and café. Comfortable enough for the price (❷); rooms with a view slightly more expensive (❸).

**Galeria 13** Rua da Ordem Terceira (aka Rua Inácio Accioli) 23, Pelhourinho ⓣ71/3266-5609, ⓦwww.hostelgaleria13.com. An interesting backpacker pad where English is spoken. Great breakfasts served until midday, plus luggage store, chill-out room and a pleasant garden terrace. Beds in dormitories, starting at around R$25 per person.

**Hostel Cobreu** Ladeira do Carmo 22, Pelhourinho ⓣ71/3117-1401 or 9274-6799, ⓦwww.hostelcobreu.com. A homely, colourful and very friendly hostel, with graffiti art work on many internal walls, this clean and airy place offers excellent value, has English-speaking staff and is located right on the edge of Pelhourinho. Private rooms, family rooms and dorms are available, all complemented by a chill-out space with DVD library and player. The street outside can get a bit dodgy late at night but is often the focus of live music and partying. ❶–❷

**Hotel Maridina** Av. Sete de Setembro 6 ⓣ71/3242-7176, ⓕ3452-5269. This family-run hotel just off Praça Castro Alves is mainly frequented by Brazilians and has a friendly, laid-back atmosphere. ❷

**Hotel Pelourinho** Rua das Portas do Carmo 20 ⓣ71/3322-3939 and 3243-2324, ⓦwww.hotelpelhourinho.com. Long one of the most popular hotels in Cidade Alta, comfortable and safe. It's no longer particularly cheap but is rather formal and anonymous with a large marbled lobby and shops. ❹

**Ibiza Hotel** Rua do Bispo 6-8, at Praça da Sé ⓣ71/3322-4305 & 3322-6929. Clean, well-run budget hotel with small, tiled but pleasant rooms with TV, fans or a/c and bar service; best rooms have a window onto the street. ❷–❸

**Pestana Convento do Carmo** Rua do Carmo 1, Pelhourinho ⓣ71/3327-8400, ⓦwww.pestana.com. One of the more recently converted and grandest of convents, very exclusive and centrally located. The rooms are very comfortable with all modern conveniences, but the highlights are probably the pool, bar and excellent restaurant in the courtyard and cloisters. ❽–❾

**Pousada da Praça Hotel** Rua Rui Barbosa 5, just off Praça Castro Alves ⓣ71/3321-0642, ⓦwww.pousadadapracahotel.com.br. Highly recommended budget hotel offering great service, more than adequate bedrooms, with or without private bath, and a great breakfast. ❷–❸

**Pousada do Boqueirão** Rua Direita de Santo Antônio 48, Santo Antônio ⓣ71/3241-2262, ⓦwww.pousadadoboquirao.com.br. Family-run *pousada* with excellent breakfasts and helpful staff. Pleasant decor with antique period pieces and some rooms decorated colonial style. Many of the higher-level rooms offer excellent sea views. Within walking distance of Largo do Pelhourinho. ❹–❺

**Pousada Redfish** Ladeira do Boqueiraõ 1, Santo Antônio ⓣ71/3241-0639, ⓦwww.pousadaredfish.com. A spacious, comfortable and tastefully appointed *pousada* run by an English artist and his Brazilian wife; the top two floors have terraces with hammock-swinging space. Located on a large residential street that runs between Pelourinho and Largo do San Antônio; standard and luxury rooms available. Sound advice given on trips and tours. ❺–❻

**Quilombo da Bahia** Rua Portas do Carmo 13, Pelhourinho ⓣ71/3322-4638, ⓦwww.hotelquilombodabahia.hpg.com.br. Excellent hotel in the old centre of Pelhourinho and just half a block from Terreiro de Jesus. Rooms are small but there's a good little Jamaican restaurant attached. ❸–❹

## The beaches

**Albergue do Porto** Rua Barão de Sergy 197, Barra ⓣ71/3264-6600, ⓦwww.alberguedoporto.com.br. Just a block from the seafront, this relaxed hostel has dormitories as well as double and family rooms, a snack bar, internet access, hammocks and a communal kitchen. Rooms have TV and a/c. ❸

**Âmbar Pousada** Rua Afonso Celso 485, Barra ⓣ71/3264-6956, ⓕ3264-3791, ⓦwww.ambarpousada.com.br. Friendly *pousada* near Praia do Porto da Barra. Simple but neat, cosy rooms on two storeys, with or without baths, set around an attractive courtyard. Excellent value; good breakfast included. ❸

**Bahia Othon Palace** Av. Oceânica 2294, Praia de Ondina ⓣ71/2103-7100, ⓦwww.othon.com.br. Superb luxury hotel on the seafront at the Praia Ondina. The 280 apartments, many with great views, all come with minibar and TV, and there's also a pool, sauna and an excellent restaurant. ❼

**Barra Turismo Hotel** Av. Sete de Setembro 3691, Praia do Porto da Barra ⓣ71/3264-7433, ⓕ3264-0038, ⓦwww.barraturismo.com.br. A modern hotel with a cool, spacious lobby overlooking the beach; pretty good service, a restaurant and reasonable rooms for the price. ❹

**Hotel Caramuru** Av. Sete de Setembro 2125, Vitória ⓣ71/3336-9951. Excellent value, unpretentious small hotel with a nice veranda and comfortable rooms. They can help organize *candomblé* visits and tours to Itaparica. The hotel is 35min by car from the airport and 20min from the bus station. ❹

**Hotel Catharina Paraguaçu** Rua João Gomes 128, Rio Vermelho ⓣ71/3334-0089, ⓦwww.hotelcatharinaparaguacu.com.br. One of Brazil's most elegant hotels – beautifully restored and full of character. For some reason, taxi drivers have difficulty finding it even though it's on a main road. ❺

**Hotel Porto da Barra** Av. Sete de Setembro 3783, Praia do Porto da Barra ⓣ71/3264-7711, ⓦwww.hotelportodobarra.com.br. Basic but comfortable hotel opposite the beach; all rooms have either a/c or fan. Breakfasts are OK. ❸

**Hotel Praia** Av. Sete de Setembro 3739, Praia do Porto da Barra ⓣ71/3264-7144, ⓦwww.hotelpraia.hpg.com.br. Good-value, no-frills, no-nonsense hotel right by the beach; internet access and all rooms have a/c or fan. ❷–❸

**Ibis** Rua Fonte do Boi 215, Rio Vermelho ⓣ71/3172-4100, ⓦwww.ibis.com.br. Modern, large and plain, this is a well-priced mid-range alternative located near the beach at Rio Vermelho. TV in rooms and internet access. ❹

**Pousada Azul** Rua Praguer Froes 102, Porto da Barra ⓣ71/3264-9798, ⓦwww.pousadaazul.com.br. Immaculately clean and well run with stylish rooms, internet access, a snack bar and city tours; great breakfast included. ❹

**Pousada Estrela do Mar** Rua Afonso Celso 119, Porto da Barra ⓣ71/3264-4882, ⓦwww.estreladomarsalvador.com. A pleasant *pousada*, less than two blocks from the seafront near the Farol, with a small courtyard, nice breakfast room and internet access. One room has a terrace and those with two windows are airy; TV, a/c or fan available. ❹

**Pousada Malu** Av. Sete de Setembro 3801, Porto da Barra ⓣ71/3264-4461. A small, exceptionally clean *pousada* on the seafront opposite the Forte de Santa Maria; a friendly place in a safe location. ❷–❸

**Pousada Noa Noa** Av. Sete de Setembro 4295, Porto da Barra ⓣ71/3264-1148, ⓦwww.pousadanoanoa.com. One of the more popular *pousadas* in Barra, right on the seafront, it offers safe and private rooms, a hammock area and friendly service. ❹

**Verdemar** Av. Otávio Mangabeira 513, Pituba ⓣ71/3797-4333, ⓦwww.verdemar.com.br. Comfortable hotel set in one of the cheapest of all the beach areas, Pituba, and handily close to the airport, although a little far from the centre. Special packages available for Carnaval; internet access and rooms have a/c and TV. ❺



# The City

Salvador is built around the craggy, fifty-metre-high bluff dominating the eastern side of the bay, and splits the central area into upper and lower sections. The heart of the old city, **Cidade Alta** (or simply Centro), is strung along its top, linked to the **Cidade Baixa** by precipitous streets, a funicular railway and the towering Art-Deco lift-shaft of the Carlos Lacerda elevator, the city's largest landmark. Cidade Alta is the administrative and cultural centre of the city, Cidade Baixa the financial and commercial district. Pelhourinho, the groovy old suburb with colourful and hilly winding streets is the living heart of Cidade Alta.

In the last century the city expanded into the still elegant areas of **Barris** and **Canela**, to the south of Cidade Alta, and up to the exclusive residential suburb of **Barra**, the headland at the mouth of the bay around which the city is built. From Barra, a broken coastline of coves and beaches, large and small, is linked by the twisting **Avenida Oceânica** (also known as the Av. Presidente Vargas), which runs along the shore through **Ondina**, **Rio Vermelho** and **Pituba**, the other main beach areas. Further on is the one-time fishing village of **Itapoan**, after which the city peters out.

## Cidade Alta

Most of Salvador's 26 **museums** and 34 **colonial churches** are concentrated within a short distance of each other in and around Pelhourinho in the Cidade Alta, which makes sightseeing fairly straightforward. A single meandering walk from the Praça da Sé, taking in all the highlights, but not stopping at any of them, would take about an hour; more realistically, you'll need at least two days, and possibly three, if you want to explore the city in depth.

### Praça Municipal to Terreiro de Jesus

The best spot to begin a walking tour is at the **Praça Municipal**, the square dominated by the impressive **Palácio do Rio Branco**, the old governor's palace. Burnt down and rebuilt during the Dutch wars, the building features regal plaster eagles added by nineteenth-century restorers, who turned a plain colonial mansion into an imposing palace. The fine interior is a blend of Rococo plasterwork, polished wooden floors, and painted walls and ceilings. Of lesser interest is the museum inside, the **Memorial dos Governadores** (Mon 2–7pm, Tues–Fri 9am–noon & 2–6pm, Sat 9am–5pm; free), which houses pieces from the colonial era. Also facing the square is the **Câmara Municipal**, the seventeenth-century city hall, graced by a series of elegant yet solid arches.

To the east, Rua Chile becomes Rua da Misericórdia where at number 6 you'll find the entrance to the grand and sombre **Santa Casa de Misericórdia** (Mon–Sat 10am–4pm, Sun noon–4pm; R$5), a mansion and church converted to a colonial-period art museum with an interesting contemporary art annexe. Head up to the mansion's upper rooms for breathtaking views across the bay. Originally a hospice and shelter for the sick and hungry (including abandoned children), Misericórdia's assets were built up through donations and income from property rental.

From here, the Rua da Misericórdia leads into **Praça da Sé**, the heart of Cidade Alta, near where the *executivo* buses terminate. The **Terreiro de Jesus** lies to the east in front of the plain **Catedral Basílica** (Mon–Sat daily 8.30–11.30am & 1.30–5pm; R$2), once the chapel of the largest Jesuit seminary outside Rome. Its interior is one of the most beautiful in the city, particularly the stunning panelled ceiling of carved and gilded wood, which gives the church a light, airy feel that's an effective antidote to the overwrought Rococo altar and side chapels. To the left of the altar is the tomb of **Mem de Sá**, third viceroy of Brazil from 1556 to 1570, and the most energetic and effective of all Brazil's colonial governors. It was he who supervised the first phase of building in Salvador, in the process destroying the Caeté Indians. Look in on the restored sacristy, too, while you're here – portraits of Jesuit luminaries, set into the walls and ceiling, gaze down intimidatingly on intruders.

▲ Rio Branco Palace, Salvador

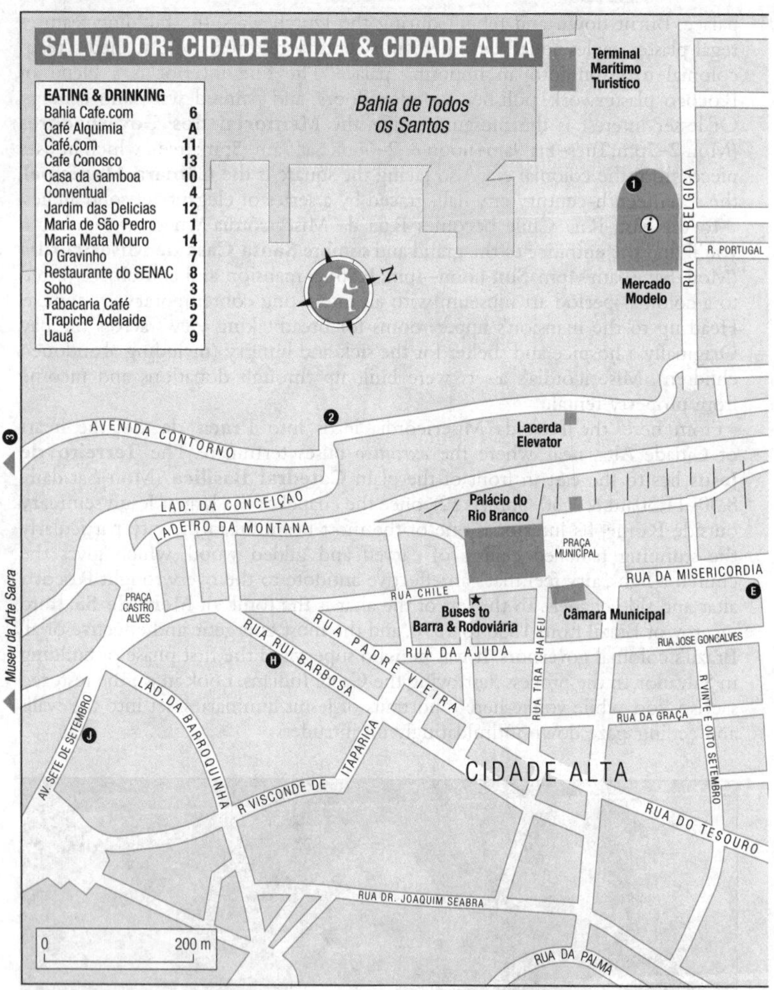


## The Museu Afro-Brasileiro

Next to the cathedral stands one of the best museums in the city, the **Museu Afro-Brasileiro** (Mon–Fri 9am–6pm, Sat & Sun 10am–5pm; R$5), contained within a large nineteenth-century building that used to be the university medical faculty; in the shady yard behind is the restored circular lecture theatre. The main building houses three different collections, one on each storey.

Largest and best is on the **ground floor**, recording and celebrating the African contribution to Brazilian culture. Four rooms are dedicated to different aspects of black culture – popular religion, *capoeira*, weaving, music and Carnaval – and everything, for once, is very well laid out. The section on *capoeira*, the balletic martial art the slaves developed (see box, p.244), is fascinating, supported by photos and old newspaper clippings. But there are other highlights, too: the gallery of large photographs of *candomblé* leaders (some dating from the nineteenth century), most

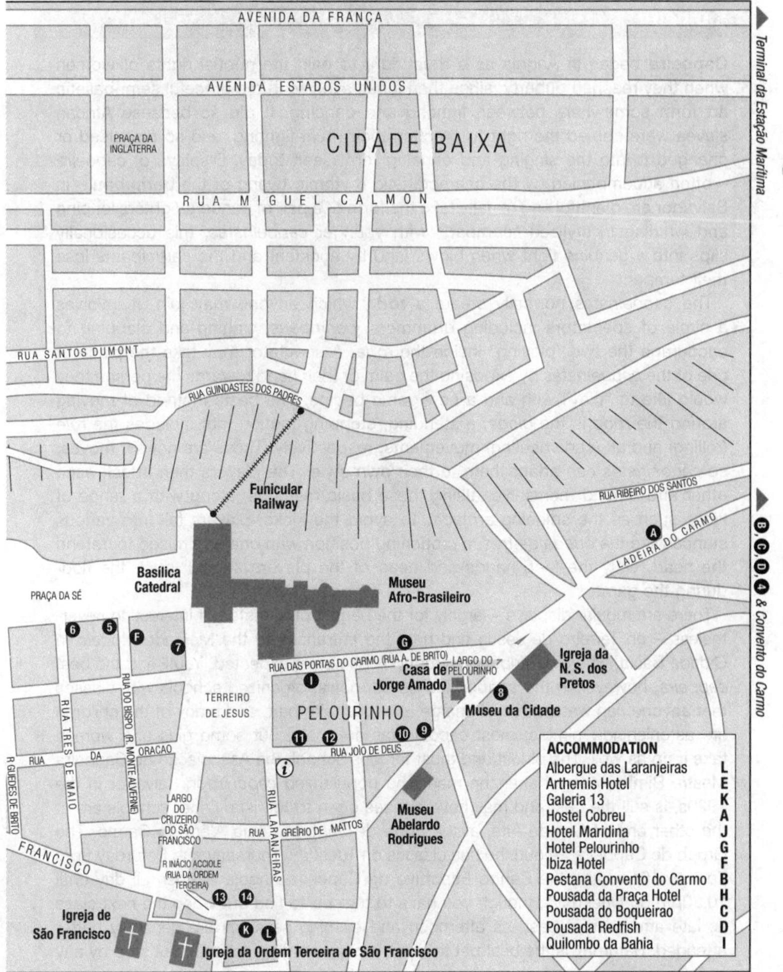


in full regalia and exuding pride and authority, and the famous carved panels by Carybé, Bahia's most famous artist, in the exhibition room past the photo gallery. Argentinian by birth, Carybé came to Salvador in 1950 to find inspiration in the city and its culture. The carved panels in the museum, imaginatively decorated with scrap metal, represent the gods and goddesses of *candomblé*.

The **first floor** houses a rather dull museum of the faculty of medicine, dominated by busts and dusty bookcases. A better idea is to look in the **basement**, at the **Museu Arqueológico e Etnológico**. Largely given over to fossils and artefacts from ancient burial sites, it also incorporates the only surviving part of the old Jesuit college, a section of the cellars, in the arched brickwork at the far end. A diagram at the entrance to the museum shows how enormous the college was, extending all the way from what is now the Praça da Sé to Largo do Pelourinho. It was from here that the conversion of the Brazilian Indians was organized, and

## Capoeira

**Capoeira** began in Angola as a ritual fight to gain the nuptial rights of women when they reached puberty; since then it has evolved into a graceful semi-balletic art form somewhere between fighting and dancing. It did so because African slaves were denied the right to practice their ritual fighting, and so disguised or changed it into the singing and dancing form seen today. Displays of *capoeira* – often accompanied by the characteristic rhythmic twang of the **berimbau** – in Salvador are plentiful and usually take the form of a pair of dancers/fighters leaping and whirling in stylized "combat"; with younger *capoeiristas*, this occasionally slips into a genuine fight when blows land by accident and the participants lose their temper.

The *capoeiristas* normally create a **roda** which anyone may join. It involves a circle of spectators including drummers, *berimbaus*, singing and clapping to encourage the two "playing" inside the *roda*. A spectator may take the place of one of the *capoeiristas* by exposing the palm of their hand towards the person they would like to "play" with and a new game begins. The basic method of moving around the *roda* is the *ginga*, a standing, stepping motion that includes the *role* (rolling) and *au* (cartwheeling) movements, respectively. These are not set moves, so *capoeiristas* can adapt them to their own style. The players then attack each other and defend themselves using these basic methods, along with a range of kicks such as the spinning *armada*. To avoid the kicks, players fall into various stances like the *queda de tres*, a crouching position with one arm raised to defend the head. Only the feet, hands and head of the players should touch the floor during the game.

There are regular displays – largely for the benefit of tourists but interesting nevertheless – on Terreiro de Jesus and near the entrances to the Mercado Modelo in Cidade Baixa, where contributions from onlookers are expected. You'll find the best *capoeira*, however, in the **academias de capoeira**, organized schools with classes that anyone can watch, free of charge. All ages take part, and many of the children are astonishingly nimble; most *capoeiristas* are male, but some girls and women take it up as well. The oldest and most famous school, the Associação de Capoeira Mestre Bimba, named after the man who popularized *capoeira* in Salvador in the 1920s, is still the best and may have classes open to tourists. Other schools are at the other end of Cidade Alta, at the Forte de Santo Antônio Além do Carmo. The Grupo de Capoeira Pelourinho has classes on Tuesday, Thursday and Saturday from 7pm to 10pm; and the Centro Esportivo de Capoeira Angola is open all day until 10.30pm on weekdays, though you have to turn up to find out when the next class is; late afternoon is best, as afternoon and evening sessions are generally better attended. Saturday is the best bet to catch a class in most schools, but stop by any early evening or late afternoon and just ask.

### Capoeira schools:

**Associação de Capoeira Mestre Bimba** Rua das Laranjeiras 1 (also known as Rua Francisco Muniz Barreto), Pelourinho ⓣ71/3322-0639, ⓦwww.capoeiramestrebimba.com.br.

**Capoeira Angola Irmaoes Gemoes e Metre Curio** Rua Gregória de Mattos 9 (upstairs), Pelourinho ⓣ71/3321-0396, ⓔmaestrecurio@yahoo.com.br.

**Escola de Capoeira Mestre Lua Rasta** Rua Inacio Acioli, Pelourinho ⓣ71/3321-6334.

**Grupo de Capoeira Angola Pelourihno** Forte de São Antônio, Barra ⓣ71/3208-1662.

**Grupo de Capoeira Lei Aurea** Rua São Jose de Lima ⓣ71/3241-9767.

**Grupo Internacional de Capoeira Topazio** Ladeira de Sautano 2, Loja 9, Edificio Marque de Moltavao ⓣ71/3521-3366

one of the many Jesuit priests who passed through its gates was Antônio Vieira, whose impassioned sermons defending Indian rights against the demands of the Portuguese slavers are generally regarded as the finest early prose in the Portuguese language. After the Jesuits were expelled in 1759, most of the college was demolished by the rich for building material for their mansions, part of the site used to found a university, and the rest parcelled out and sold for redevelopment.

### The churches of São Francisco

Terreiro de Jesus has more than its fair share of churches; there are two more fine sixteenth-century examples on the square itself. Outshining them both, however, on nearby **Largo do Cruzeiro de São Francisco** (an extension of Terreiro de Jesus sometimes known as Praça Anchieta), are the superb, carved stone facades of two ornate Baroque buildings, set in a single, large complex dedicated to St Francis: the **Igreja de São Francisco** (Mon–Sat 8.30am–5.30pm, Sun 7am–5pm; R$3) and the **Igreja da Ordem Terceira de São Francisco** (Mon–Fri 8am–5pm; R$3). Of the two the latter has the edge: it's covered with a wild profusion of saints, virgins, angels and abstract patterns. Remarkably, the facade was hidden for 150 years, until in 1936 a painter knocked off a chunk of plaster by mistake and revealed the original frontage, Brazil's only example of high-relief facade carved in ashlar (square-cut stones). It took nine years of careful chipping before the facade was returned to its original glory, and today the whole church is a strong contender for the most beautiful single building in the city. Its **reliquary**, or *ossuário*, is extraordinary; the entire room is redecorated in 1940s Art Deco style, one of the most unusual examples you're ever likely to come across. From here, there's a door onto a pleasant garden at the back.

To get into the complex, you have to go via the Igreja de São Francisco (the entrance is by a door to the right of the main doors). The small cloister in this church is decorated with one of the finest single pieces of *azulejo* (decorative glazed tiling) work in Brazil. Running the entire length of the cloister, a tiled **wall** tells the story of the marriage of the son of the king of Portugal to an Austrian princess; beginning with the panel to the right of the church entrance, which shows the princess being ferried ashore to the reception committee, it continues with the procession of the happy couple in carriages through Lisbon, passing under a series of commemorative arches set up by the city guilds, whose names you can still just read, including "The Royal Company of Bakers" and "The Worshipful Company of Sweetmakers". The vigour and realism of the incidental detail in the street scenes is remarkable: beggars and cripples display their wounds, dogs skulk, children play in the gutter; and the panoramic view of Lisbon it displays is an important historical record of how the city looked before the calamitous earthquake of 1755.

### Around Largo do Pelourinho

Heading down the narrow Rua Alfredo de Brito, next to the Museu Afro-Brasileiro, brings you to the beautiful, cobbled **Largo do Pelourinho**, still much as it was during the eighteenth century. Lined with solid colonial mansions, it's topped by the oriental-looking towers of the **Igreja de Nossa Senhora dos Pretos** (daily 9am–6pm; free), built by and for slaves and still with a largely black congregation. Across from here is the **Casa de Jorge Amado** (Mon–Sat 10am–6pm; free), a museum given over to the life and work of the hugely popular novelist, who didn't number modesty among his virtues. A number of his rich and famous friends are visible in the collection of photographs.

Next door, on the corner of Rua Gregório de Mattos, is the **Museu da Cidade** (Mon & Wed–Fri 10am–4pm; usually R$1, but free on Thurs), housed in an attractive Pelourinho mansion. The lower levels are given over to paintings and sculpture by young city artists, some startlingly good and some pretty dire, while luxuriously dressed dummies show off Carnaval costumes from years gone by. There are models of *candomblé* deities and, on the first floor, a room containing the personal belongings of the greatest Bahian poet, Castro Alves, with some fascinating photographs from the beginning of the twentieth century. Completing the constellation of museums around Pelourinho is the **Museu Abelardo Rodrigues** (Tues–Sat 1–6pm, closed Mon & Sun; R$1) at Rua Gregório de Mattos 45, which has a good collection of Catholic art from the sixteenth century onwards, well displayed in a restored seventeenth-century mansion.

From Largo do Pelourinho, a steep climb up Ladeira do Carmo rewards you with two more exceptional examples of colonial architecture: on the left is the **Convento da Ordem Primeira do Carmo** and on the right the **Igreja da Ordem Terceira de Nossa Senhora do Carmo**; both are built around large and beautiful cloisters, with a fine view across the old city at the back, but have been taken over by the *Pestana Convento do Carmo* hotel and converted into plush accommodation and a five-star restaurant. Attached to the hotel there's a sacred-art museum containing over a thousand pieces, including an expressive statue of Christ at the whipping post by Salvador's greatest colonial artist, the half-Indian slave **Francisco Manuel das Chagas**, whose powerful religious sculpture in the early eighteenth century broke the formalistic bonds of the period. Museum entry (Mon–Sat 9am–6pm, Sun 9am–1pm; R$5) also gives access to a chapel in the convent.

The rest of Cidade Alta is still largely colonial, and fascinating to wander around – although do it in daylight if you want to get off the main streets, and try to stick to where there are people around. Good streets to try are **Rua Gregório de Mattos** and the road on from the Carmo museums, **Rua Joaquim Távora**, which leads away from the heavier concentrations of tourists to the quiet Largo Cruz Pascoa and eventually ends up at the fort of **Santo Antônio Além do Carmo**, with a spectacular view across the bay. The simple bars on Largo Santo Antônio in front of the fort are a good place to rest your legs, have a drink and watch the stunning sunsets. Other good sundowner viewpoints on the edge of the bluff are the Praça da Sé itself, the bar of the *Hotel Pelourinho* (open to non-residents) and an unnamed bar on the left just after Largo Cruz Pascoa.

## ACM and the restoration of Pelourinho

The Pelourinho district is now an attractive and much visited area, but it wasn't always this way. In the early 1990s the area was virtually derelict, with many of the colonial buildings falling to pieces and tourism in decline. The neighborhood's makeover is thanks to Bahia's most famous – and controversial – politician, **Antônio Carlos Magalhães**. Widely disliked elsewhere in Brazil as an unreconstructed representative of the country's landed elite, the silver-haired **ACM** (as he's known) is popular in Bahia because of his tireless campaigns on behalf of his home state; you'll see his picture hanging up in many of the city's bars. Pelourinho's revival, which he undertook as state governor, was certainly impressive. Some of the most important colonial architecture has been restored to its original glory, the pastel pinks and blues creating a wonderfully gaudy effect. Critics point out many local residents had to be moved out and complain the area has become dominated by tourism. There is some truth to this, but you'll still see plenty of locals enjoying themselves alongside the tourists, and the economy is clearly thriving; on the whole, it's hard to argue that Pelourinho was better off as a decaying shadow of its former self. Furthermore, you only have to wander fifty metres off the beaten Pelhourinho path to find yourself in dark and sometimes dodgy backstreets.

▲ Igreja de Nossa Senhora dos Pretos



## The Museu da Arte Sacra

Despite the concentration of riches in Cidade Alta, you have to leave the old city to find one of the finest museums of Catholic art in Brazil, the **Museu da Arte Sacra** at Rua Sodré 276 (Mon–Fri 11.30am–5.30pm; R$5). It's slightly difficult to find: if you're coming into Praça Castro Alves from Rua Chile, go straight ahead and up Rua Carlos Gomes. Then take the first right down the steep

Ladeira de Santa Teresa and you'll see the museum in front of you. It's housed in the seventeenth-century Santa Teresa convent, a magnificent building with much of its original furniture and fittings still intact, and with galleries on three floors surrounding a cloister. The chapel on the ground floor is lavishly decorated with elaborate, gilded carvings, and it leads into a maze of small galleries stuffed with a remarkably rich collection of colonial art, dating from the sixteenth century. The hundreds of statues, icons, paintings and religious artefacts are enough to occupy you for hours, the only real flaw in the collection being the absence of anything by Chagas or Aleijadinho.



## Cidade Baixa

**Cidade Baixa**, the part of the city at the foot of the bluff, takes in the docks, the old harbour dominated by the circular sixteenth-century **Forte do Mar**, the ferry terminals and the main city markets. For the most part it's ugly modern urban sprawl, but for once the developers can't be blamed: the area was always the most neglected part of the city because its low-lying location deprived it of the sea breezes and cooler air of the higher ground above. Since the sixteenth century, the city's inhabitants have only ventured down into the Cidade Baixa to work, choosing to live in the more pleasant areas above and around it.

### Mercado Modelo

You are likely at least to pass through Cidade Baixa to get to the **ferry terminals**, and there is one essential stop: the **Mercado Modelo** (daily 10am–6pm; free), an old covered market set on its own by the old harbour, across the road from the foot of the Lacerda elevator. It houses a huge and very enjoyable arts and crafts market, always crowded with Bahians as well as tourists, with the best selection of *artesanato* in the city. Not everything is cheap, so it helps to have the confidence to haggle. Some of the nicest souvenirs are the painted statues of *candomblé* deities – look for signs saying *artigos religiosos*. Even if you don't buy anything the building is a joy, a spacious nineteenth-century cathedral to commerce. There is always something going on in and around the market, with displays of *capoeira* common (and donations expected). There is an **information office** sometimes staffed to the left of the front entrance, and upstairs you will find a couple of good **restaurants**.

### The Igreja do Bonfim

The Igreja do Bonfim, as everyone calls the **Igreja do Nosso Senhor do Bonfim** (Tues–Sun 6.30-11am, 1.30–6pm; free), sits on a hill overlooking the bay in the northwestern suburbs. The church is the focal point of colourful religious festivals that attract thousands of devotees from all over Brazil. To get there, take the buses marked "Bonfim" or "Ribeira" from the Estação da Lapa, or from the bottom of the Lacerda elevator.

The church – completed in 1745 with a plain white exterior and simple interior – is not, by any means, the oldest or most beautiful in the city but it's easily the most interesting. The force of popular devotion is obvious from the moment you leave the bus. The large square in front of the church is lined with stalls catering to the hundreds of pilgrims who arrive every day, and you'll be besieged by small children selling *fitas*, ribbons in white and blue (the church colours), to tie around your wrist for luck and to hang in the church when you make your requests; it's ungracious to enter without a few. It's always at least half-full of all kinds of people worshipping with almost hypnotic fervour – from middle-class matrons to uniformed military officers to peasants from the *sertão* and women from the *favelas*.

For a clearer idea of what this place means to the people of Bahia, go to the right of the nave where a wide corridor leads to the **Museu dos Ex-Votos do Senhor do Bonfim** (Tues–Sat 9am–noon & 2–5pm; R$2). An incredibly crowded antechamber gives you an idea of what to expect: it's lined to the roof with thousands of small photographs of supplicants, with notes pinned to the wall requesting intervention or giving thanks for benefits received. Every spare inch is covered with a forest of ribbons, one for each request, some almost rotted away with age. Many of the written pleas are heart-rending: for the life of a dying child, for news from a husband who emigrated south, for success in an exam – in short, a snapshot of everyday worries and hopes. Hanging from the roof are dozens of body parts – limbs, heads, even organs such as hearts and lungs – made of wood or plastic (from anxious patients asking for protection before an operation), or silver (from relieved patients giving thanks after successful surgery). Some people blessed by a particularly spectacular escape pay tribute by leaving a pictorial record of the miracle: photos of smashed cars the driver walked away from, or crude but vivid paintings of fires, sinkings and electrocutions.

Upstairs in the museum proper is the oldest material and recent offerings judged worthy of special display. The more valuable *ex votos* are displayed here in ranks of cases, classified according to the part of the body: silver heads and limbs you might expect, even silver hearts, lungs, ears, eyes and noses, but the serried ranks of silver kidneys, spleens, livers and intestines are striking. There are also football shirts (the city's two big teams always make a visit at the start of the season), models of the church, and dozens of paintings, especially of fires and shipwrecks.

### Museu Nautico da Bahia

Prominently located on the Avenida Oceânica in the wealthy suburb of Barra, the **Museu Nautico** (open Tues–Sun, 9am–9pm; R$5) sits within the lighthouse in the picturesque white Forte de Santo Antônio on the windy Barra point, where the Atlantic Ocean becomes the bay of Todos os Santos. It houses a collection of seafaring instruments, maps, model boats, art and a small amount of written historical information. Built in 1503, it was the first European fort on the Brazilian coast and meant to defend the newly founded settlement and access to the bay. There's a good book and gift shop, but most people come for the views from the internal terrace in the fort above the museum; it's a popular place to have a cocktail as the sun sets. Local buses and the *executivo* service to Barra leave from the Praça da Sé.

## Eating and drinking

**Eating out** is one of the major pleasures Salvador has to offer, and the local cuisine (*comida baiana*) is deservedly famous. There's a huge range of restaurants and, although Cidade Alta has an increasing number of stylish, expensive places, it's still quite possible to eat well for significantly less than R$25, though easier to spend R$50 plus, including drinks. You should treat yourself to at least one lavish feed before leaving the city.

If you just want a coffee, and enjoy the smell of good cigar smoke, the Tabacaria Café on the corner of Rua do Bispo and the **Praça da Se** is hard to beat for ambience, style, service and excepcional coffees, juices and snacks. The cheapest places for a sit-down meal are around **Praça Castro Alves** and in **Cidade Baixa**. Restaurants in the **Pelourinho** area and the **beach districts** are classier and tend to be more expensive. Especially at Barra and Rio Vermelho, the seafront promenade is lined with bars, cafés and restaurants, and arguably the best option is to take a bus and hop off wherever you fancy. The non-Brazilian cuisines tend to be concentrated in **Barra**, where Salvador's upper middle class lives.

## Cidade Alta

**Bahia Cafe.com** Praça da Sé 22 ☎71/3322-1266. Great café with excellent atmosphere, tasty food (from pizzas to *moquecas*), smoothies, cocktails and coffee; there's also internet access and airy windows opening onto the street.

**Café Alquimia** Ladeira do Carmo 22, Pelhourinho. This small, often crowded bar and café, located underneath the *Hostel Cobreu*, serves wonderful falafels. It's a popular meeting place where English is spoken, but it can get rowdy.

**Café Conosco** Rua da Ordem Terceira 4, Pelhourinho ☎71/3321-0481. Attractive café set in an early eighteenth-century house that doubles as a small museum; good coffee and cake, internet access and a tranquil escape from the hubbub of the streets.

**Café.com** Rua João de Deus 2, Pelhourinho. This small upstairs internet café and *creperia* also offers Skype access, international calls and good coffee.

**Casa da Gamboa** Rua João de Deus 32, Pelourinho ☎71/3321-3393. One of the district's top restaurants and worth a splurge. Serves mainly Bahian dishes; expect to pay at least R$50 per head. Closed Sun.

**Conventual** Rua do Carmo 1, Santo Antônio ☎71/3327-84000. Based in the cloisters of the exclusive *Convento do Carmo*, just a short stroll from the heart and heat of Pelourhino, this is probably the city's most expensive restaurant. It has a mainly Portuguese menu, full of excellently prepared and presented dishes, plus there's a large and fancy bar. The best reason to eat here, however, is to enjoy the ambience of the leafy and crafted stone courtyard and cloisters.

**Jardim das Delicias** Rua João de Deus 12, Pelourinho ☎71/3321-1449. Fantastic Bahian and international cuisine served both inside and out (in the lovely garden); the salads are especially good. Cover charge for gentle live music most weekend evenings.

**Maria Mata Mouro** Rua da Ordem Terceira (aka Rua Inácio Accioli) 08, Pelourinho ☎71/3321-3929. One of the finest Bahian restaurants in the district, with prices to match; whatever you choose will be divine and lovingly presented. Very busy at weekends, so it's best to book a table in advance.

**Restaurante do SENAC** Largo do Pelourinho, opposite the Casa Jorge Amado, Pelourinho ☎71/3321-5502. Municipal restaurant-school in a finely restored colonial mansion. It looks very expensive from the outside, but it's good value for what you get. You pay a set charge – about R$40 – and take as much as you want from a quality buffet of around fifty dishes, all helpfully labelled so you know what you're eating. If you go for dinner, try to finish before 10pm, when there's a rather touristy folklore show.

**Uauá** Rua Gregório de Mattos 36, Pelourinho ☎71/3321-3089. Popular restaurant specializing in Northeastern food from both the coast and the interior, with prices on the moderate to expensive side.

## Barra

**Aquarela** Av. Oceânica 141, Barra ☎71/3261-3222. Popular restaurant serving up Greek food and fish dishes. Moderately priced.

**Pereira** Av. Sete de Setembro 3959, Porto da Barra ☎71/3264-6464. Stylish spot with a cool interior and pleasant terrace overlooking the road and beach. The meals – especially the seafood and salad – and drinks are great but expensive.

**Ramma** Rua Lord Cochrane 76, Barra ☎71/3264-0044. This classic whole-food café in the backstreets of Barra provides an excellent range of tasty and healthy *comida por kilo* at lunchtimes. Get there well before 1pm to avoid the crowds.

## Other suburbs

**Aconchego da Zuzu** Rua Quintana Bocaiuva 18, Garcia ☎71/3331-5074. Enjoyably different and highly Bahian, this small family-run restaurant sits in a courtyard on a backstreet of the Garcia suburb. Choose from a wide range of local cuisine (try the *peixa au molho de camarão*); superb, traditional percussion music is sometimes performed. Open Mon–Sat lunch only.

**Chez Bernard** Rua Gamboa de Cima 11, Largo dos Aflitos ☎71/3328-1566. This French-style restaurant with a Belgian chef has attentive service and a reasonably priced menu *du jour* at lunchtime. The best tables have views towards Bahia's modern marina and below to the Museum of Modern Art and a small, waterside and well-renovated *favela*. A very fine *civet de langouste* is the most expensive à la carte dish at R$62.

**Maria de São Pedro** Mercado Modelo 1st floor, Cidade Baixa. A good Bahian restaurant, and one of the oldest, with great views across the bay – if you can get a table on the terrace. Next door, the *Camafeu de Oxóssi* offers much the same fare at moderate prices. Open Mon–Sat 11am–7pm, Sun 11am–4pm.

## Comida baiana: dishes and ingredients

The secret of Bahian cooking is twofold: a rich seafood base, and the abundance of traditional West African **ingredients** like palm oil, nuts, coconut and ferociously strong peppers. Many ingredients and dishes have African names. Most famous of all is *vatapá*, a bright yellow porridge of palm oil, coconut, shrimp and garlic, which looks vaguely unappetizing but is delicious. Other dishes to look out for are *moqueca*, seafood cooked in the inevitable palm-oil-based sauce; *caruru*, with many of the same ingredients as *vatapá* but with the vital addition of loads of okra; and *acarajé*, deep-fried bean cake stuffed with *vatapá*, salad and (optional) hot pepper. Bahian cuisine also has good **desserts**, less stickily sweet than elsewhere: *quindim* is a delicious small cake of coconut flavoured with vanilla, which often comes with a prune in the middle.

Some of the best food is also the cheapest, and even gourmets could do a lot worse than start with the street-corner *baianas*, women in traditional white dress. Be careful of the *pimenta*, the very hot pepper sauce, which newcomers should treat with respect, taking only a few drops. The *baianas* serve *quindim*, *vatapá*, slabs of maize pudding wrapped in banana leaves, fried bananas dusted with icing sugar, and fried sticks of sweet batter covered with sugar and cinnamon – all absolutely wonderful.

**Mustafa** Rua Alexandre Maia 6, Clube de Bridge da Bahia, Graça ⓣ71/3247-9884. Arabic restaurant, popular with locals and serving excellent food, including a buffet, though it's not cheap. Getting a taxi from the Barra seafront is the easiest way to get there, as the road is a little obscure. Open Mon–Sat 11.30am–3pm, Sun noon–4pm.

**Soho** Av. Contorno 1010, pier D, Bahia Marina ⓣ71/332-4554, ⓦwww.sohorestaurante.com.br. Excellent, very trendy with tables beside the ocean, they serve mainly Japanese–Bahian gourmet fusion. Valet parking, good service and a great bar; but can be very busy at weekends and holidays.

**Trapiche Adelaide** Praça dos Tupinambas 2, Av. Contorno ⓣ71/3326-2211, ⓦwww.trapicheadelaide.com.br. One of the flashiest and most exclusive restaurants in Salvador. It's right next to the sea below the Cidade Alta, close to the yachts and private jetties of the wealthy. The food, which ranges from Bahian *novo cuisine* to French, is superb, and there's also the trendy *Bar da Ponta* which serves drinks and less formal meals; the bar extends out into the sea on a glass-housed pier with flood-lit fish swimming below.

**Yemanjá** Av. Otávio Mangabeira 4655, Pituba ⓣ71/3461-9010. Highly recommended Bahian restaurant – a far better bet than the large, overpriced places at the far end of the district, but it usually closes around midnight.

# Nightlife

You'll find Salvador's most distinctive **nightlife** in **Pelourinho**. The whole area is always very lively, and there are any number of bars where you can sit and while the evening away. The Rua das Laranjeiras, Cruzeiro de São Francisco and Rua Castro Rabelo are all good places to head for, and it's local custom to start off the evening at the small, stand-up *O Gravinho* bar, Largo Terreiro de Jesus 03, for a glass of specially flavoured *cachaça*, the most traditional being made from essence of clove or ginger. This place gets busy Tuesday evenings (the busiest weekday night in Pelhourinho) and at weekends.

Bars aside, undoubtedly the biggest attraction of the area is the chance to hear **live music**. In that realm, Salvador marches to a different beat from the rest of Brazil. Instead of being connected to a single style, as Rio is to samba and Recife is to *frevo*, Salvador has spawned several, and in recent years has overtaken Rio to become the most creative centre of Brazilian music. Some of the best music in the city comes from organized cultural groups, who work in the communities that produced them, and have their own clubhouses and an *afoxé* or two – Salvador's

Africanized version of a *bloco* – for Carnaval. They are overwhelmingly black and much of their music is political. In the weeks leading up to Carnaval, their *afoxés* have public rehearsals around the clubhouses, and the music is superb (see "Carnaval", p.254). For the rest of the year, the clubhouses are used as bars and meeting places, often with music at weekends.

You can always catch live music in Pelourinho and every Sunday night at least one band plays for free at Terreiro de Jesus. Also, **pagode music** is frequently played at the Mercado Modelo from 6pm on Friday evenings. For an up-to-date list of events, ask at the tourist information office in Pelourinho. Many find it a bit claustrophobic in Cidade Alta and head for the **beaches** instead. For **dancing** into the small hours, Amaralina and Pituba are probably the liveliest areas to head for, and Friday and Saturday nights are best. Bars, too, often have **live music**, and listings appear in the local papers at weekends. Check out Ⓦwww.bahia-online.net for up-to-the-minute listings for cultural events, live music, music jamming (usually samba style) every day and night of the week. Also scan posters and local papers (under *Lazer*) or ask at the tourist office. Every Tuesday from 7 to 10pm, Gerônimo (a veteran Salvadorian songwriter) performs live music on the steps leading up to the Igreja do Passo (best viewed from the Ladeira do Carmo, around the *Café Alquimia*), supported by his band Mont Serrat, renowned for its classy horn section. Also on Tuesdays, the Orkestra Rumpilezz perform for free around 8pm, at Largo Teresa Batista in Pelourinho, playing *candomblé*-influenced Bahian jazz. Big names in Brazilian music also sometimes play the Teatro Castro Alves on Campo Grande. During the week (except Tues), the Balé Folclórico da Bahia perform athletic Afro-Brazilan dance for an hour from 8pm (R$25) at the Teatro Miguel Santana, at Rua Gregôrio de Mattos 49 (originally Rua Maciel de Baixo) in Pelourinho; it's best to buy tickets in advance from the door.The SENAC building on Largo do Pelourinho has an outdoor arena and basement theatre, used for plays, concerts and displays.

Salvador also has a lively **gay scene**. *Holmes 24th* on Rua Gamboa de Cima, opposite the Rua Banco dos Ingleses, is especially hopping on Fridays (take a taxi). *Caverna*, Rua Carlos Goma 616, Centro (Ⓣ71/3358-2410), is a popular

▲ Nightlife in Pelourinho

## Candomblé

**Candomblé**, a popular Afro-Brazilian religious cult, permeates Salvador. Its followers often dress in white and worship together in ecstatic dance rituals accompanied by lots of drumming and singing, or otherwise communicate with and make offerings to the Orixás spirits – personal protectors, guides and go-betweens for people and their creator-god Olorum.

A *candomblé* cult house, or *terreiro*, is headed by a *mãe do santo* (woman) or *pai do santo* (man), who directs the operations of dozens of novices and initiates. The usual object is to persuade the **spirits** to descend into the bodies of worshippers, which is achieved by **sacrifices** (animals are killed outside public view and usually during the day), offerings of food and drink, and above all by drumming, dancing and the invocations of the *mãe* or *pai do santo*. In a central dance area, devotees dance for hours to induce the trance that allows the spirits to enter them. Witnessing a possession can be quite frightening: sometimes people whoop and shudder, their eyes roll up, and they whirl around the floor, bouncing off the walls while other cult members try to make sure they come to no harm. The *mãe* or *pai do santo* then calms them, blows tobacco smoke over them, identifies the spirit, gives them the insignia of the deity – a pipe or a candle, for example – and lets them dance on. Each deity has its own songs, animals, colours, qualities, powers and holy day; there are different types of *candomblé*, as well as other related Afro-Brazilian religions like *umbanda*.

Many travel agencies offer tours of the city that include a visit to a *terreiro*, but no self-respecting cult house would allow itself to be used in this way – those which do are to be avoided. The best alternative is to go to the main Bahiatursa office (see p.237), which has a list of less commercialized *terreiros*, all fairly far out in the suburbs and best reached by taxi. Make sure the *terreiro* is open first; they only have ceremonies on certain days sacred to one of the pantheon of gods and goddesses, and you just have to hope you're lucky – though fortunately there's no shortage of deities.

If you go to a *terreiro*, there are certain **rules** you must observe. A *terreiro* should be respected and treated for the church it is. Clothes should be smart and modest: long trousers and a clean shirt for men, non-revealing blouse and trousers or long skirt for women. The dancing area is a sacred space and no matter how infectious you find the rhythms you should do no more than stand or sit around its edges. Don't take photographs without asking permission from the *mãe* or *pai do santo* first, or you will give offence. You may find people coming round offering drinks from jars, or items of food: it's impolite to refuse, but watch what everyone else does first – sometimes food is not for eating but for throwing over dancers, and the story of the gringos who ate the popcorn intended as a sacred offering to the spirits is guaranteed to bring a smile to any Brazilian face.

To read more on *candomblé* as practiced in Cachoeira, see the box on p.262. To make contact with *candomblé* practitioners and attend a session, either book through Lar Turismo, Rua do Passo 1, Santo Antônio (Ⓣ71/3326-0802, Ⓦwww.larturismo.com), or C&C Turismo, Rua das Portas do Carmo 28, Largo do Pelourinho (Ⓣ71/3326-6969); or approach a *terreiro* directly. It's important to call and check times, dates and terms of access (or ask the tourist information office in Pelourinho for help in booking). Below is a list of *terreiros*:

**Axé Opo Afonja** Rua Direita de São Goncalo do Retiro 557 Ⓣ71/3384-5229.

**Terreiro do Oxum** Rua Helio Machado 108, Bairro Bocado Rio Ⓣ71/3232-1460.

**Terreiro de Oxossi** Rua 6 de Janeiro 29 (by entrance to Escolinha Rosa Vermelho), Bairro Sete de Abril Ⓣ71/3393-1168.

underground spot close to Salvador's best nightlife, while *New Look Bar Holme*, Rua Gamboa de Cima 24, in Gamboa (Ⓣ71/3336-4949), is a bit more laid-back. The popular *Off Club*, Rua Dias D'Avila 33 (Ⓣ71/3267-6215) is near the Farol in Barra, itself and its beach obvious and popular meeting-spots; and there's *Beco dos Artistas*, a predominantly gay bar by the Teatro Castro Alves, on Rua Leovigildo Filgueirias (entrance beside the pizzeria). *Camarin* is a popular gay bar, close to the Teatro Castro Alves.



## Salvador's festivals

The two main **popular festivals** of the year, besides Carnaval, take place either in or near the Igreja do Bonfim. On New Year's Day the **Procissão no Mar**, the "Sea Procession", sees statues of the seafarers' protectors, Nosso Senhor dos Navegantes and Nossa Senhora da Conceição, carried in a decorated nineteenth-century boat across the bay from the old harbour to the church of Boa Viagem, on the shore down from Bonfim. The boat leaves at around 9am from Praça Cairú, next to the Mercado Modelo in Cidade Baixa, and hundreds of schooners and fishing boats wait to join the procession as the statues' boat passes: you can buy a place on the phalanx of boats that leaves with the statues, but the crowds are thick and if you want to go by sea you should get there early. On the shores of Boa Viagem, thousands wait to greet the holy images, after which there's a packed Mass in the church, and then Nossa Senhora da Conçeicão is taken back by land in another procession to her church near the foot of the Lacerda elevator. The celebrations around both churches go on

### Carnaval

Having steadfastly resisted commercialization, Carnaval in Salvador has remained a street event of mass participation. The main hubs of activity are **Cidade Alta**, especially the area around Praça Castro Alves – which turns into a seething mass of people that, once joined, is almost impossible to get out of – and, in recent years, **Porto da Barra**, equally crowded and just as enjoyable. The other focal point of Carnaval is the **northern beaches**, especially around the hotels in Rio Vermelho and Ondina, but here it's more touristy and lacks the energy of the centre. This is an expensive and very hectic time to stay in Salvador; all accommodation more than doubles in price and with added costs like paying to join a *bloco* or participate in a *camarote* (a venue with good views over the carnaval route and an organized party thrown in for the duration), you are likely to be spending in excess of R$500–600 a day.

From December onwards Carnaval groups hold **public rehearsals** and dances all over the city. The most famous are Grupo Cultural Oludum, who rehearse on Sunday nights from 6.30pm onwards in the Largo do Pelourinho itself and on Tuesdays from 7.30pm in the Teatro Miguel Santana on Rua Gregório de Mattos. On Friday night, it's the turn of Ara Ketu, who start their show at 7pm in Rua Chile, while Ilê Aiyê rehearse on Saturdays from 8pm near the fort of Santo Antônio Além do Carmo. These rehearsals get very crowded, so be careful with your belongings. One of the oldest and best loved of the *afoxés* is Filhos de Gandhi ("Sons of Gandhi"), founded in the 1940s, who have a clubhouse in Rua Gregório de Mattos, near Largo do Pelourinho, easily recognized by the large papier-mâché white elephant in the hall.

**Information** about Carnaval is published in special supplements in the local papers on Thursday and Saturday. Again, ⓦwww.bahia-online.net is great for information on and contacts for Carnaval. Bahiatursa offices also have schedules, route maps, and sometimes sell tickets for the Campo Grande grandstands. Bear in mind all-black *blocos* may be black culture groups who won't appreciate being joined by non-black Brazilians, let alone gringos, so look to see who's dancing before leaping in.

for hours, with thousands drinking and dancing the night away. The spectacle, with the bay as an enormous backdrop, is impressive enough – participating in it is exhilarating.

Soon afterwards, on the second Thursday of January, comes the **Lavagem do Bonfim**, "the washing of Bonfim", second only to Carnaval in scale. Hundreds of *baianas*, women in the traditional all-white costume of turban, lace blouse and a billowing long skirt, gather in front of the Igreja de Nossa Senhora da Conceição, and a procession follows them the 12km along the seafront to the Igreja do Bonfim, with tens of thousands more lining the route; the pace is slow, and there is no shortage of beer and music while you wait. At the church, everyone sets to scrubbing the square spotless, cleaning the church and decorating the exterior with flowers and strings of coloured lights. That evening, and every evening until Sunday, raucous celebrations go on into the wee hours, and the square is crowded with people. If you have the stamina, the focus switches on Monday to Ribeira, the headland beyond Bonfim, for a completely secular preview of Carnaval; you can freshen up after dancing in the hot sun by swimming at the excellent beaches.

## Shopping

The main place for *artesanato* is the Mercado Modelo in Cidade Baixa (see p.248). Good, cheap leatherwork is available from the street stalls of Barroquinha, the steep street leading downhill just before Praça Castro Alves; clothes and shoes can be found in the commercial area further down. For luxury items, clothes, books, CDs and food, head for either Shopping Barra or Iguatemi Shopping. For gem stones, try Agua Marina, Terreiro de Jesus 15, Pelourinho, or Kaufmann Gems at Rua Alfredo de Brito 09, Pelourinho.

## Listings

**Airlines** Air France, Rua Portugal 17, Ed. Regente Feijó, Cidade Baixa ⓣ21/3312-1818, ⓦwww.airfrance.com.br; British Airways ⓣ71/0300-789-7778, ⓦwww.british-airways.com; Lufthansa, Av. Tancredo Neves 805, sala 601, Iguatemi ⓣ71/4503-5000, ⓦwww.lufthansa.com.br; TAP Air Portugal, Av. Estados Unidos 137 (4th floor), Ed. Cidade de Ilhéus, Cidade Baixa ⓣ71/3243-6122, ⓦwww.tap-airportugal.com.br; Gol, airport desk ⓣ71/3204-1603.

**Airport** Aeroporto Deputado Luis Eduardo do Magalhães ⓣ71/3204-1544 or 3204-1010.

**Banks and exchange** There are several places where you can change money in the Pelourinho area, including Olímpio Turismo on Largo do Cruzeiro de São Francisco and Vert-Tour on Rua das Laranjeiras. Banco do Brasil has branches, all with Visa ATMs, at Av. Sete de Setembro 254 in Cidade Alta; Av. Estados Unidos 561 in Cidade Baixa; and in Shopping Barra, among many others around the city.

**Boat services** Bahia Scuba and Brazil Yacht Charter, Av. Do Contorno 1010, Bahia Marina (ⓦwww.byc.com.br), rent equipment and run boat trips, mainly by sail. Passeios de Veleros (ⓣ71/8156-5254) offer short sailboat trips in Baia de Todos Santos and to Itaparica and even Morro de São Paulo.

**Bus services** All main buses operate out of the *rodoviária* (ⓣ71/3616-8300). Real Express are good for Chapada Diamantina ⓣ71/3450-9310; Aguia Branca for Porto Seguro ⓣ71/3450-5539; Itapemirim for Recife, Fortaleza and Belem ⓣ71/3450-5644.

**Car rental** Avis Rentacar, Av. Sete de Setembro 1796 ⓣ71/3377-2276; and Localiza, based at the airport ⓣ71/3332-1999.

**Consulates** Canada, Av. Presidente Vargas 2400, sala 311, Ondina Apart Hotel, Ondina ⓣ71/3331-0064; Finland ⓣ71/3247-3312; Holland ⓣ71/3341-0410; UK, Av. Estados Unidos 4, 18-B 8th floor, Cidade Baixa ⓣ71/3243-7399; US, Rua Pernambuco 51, Pituba ⓣ71/3345-1545.

**Diving and scuba** Dive Bahia Porta da Barra, Av Sete de Setembro 3809, on the seafront

(Ⓣ71/3264-3820, Ⓦwww.divebahia.com.br) offers certification-level courses which take a few days for R$600 and they also rent out diving equipment. Bahia Scuba and Brazil Yacht Charter (see p.255) also rent out equipment.

**Football** Salvador has a couple of good teams. The biggest matches take place on Sunday afternoons in the Estádio Otávio Mangabeira, close to the centre; take the bus marked "Nazaré" from Campo Grande.

**Internet** Bahia Africa Internet Café, Rua Gregório Matos 32, Pelourinho; Cybercafe, Av. Sete de Setembro 3713, Barra (daily 8am–midnight); *Bahia Cafe.com*, Praça da Sé 22, and *Café.com*, Rua Joao de Deus 2, Pelhourinho.

**Language schools** IDIOMA, Rua Greenfeld 46, 1st & 2nd floors, Barra Ⓣ71/3267-7012, Ⓦwww.portugueseinbrazil.com.

**Laundry** Lavanderia Lavalimpo, Rua do Pilar 31, Cidade Baixa; O Casal Lavandaria, Rua Cesar Zama 20, Loja 1, Barra (English spoken); Lav–Lev, Av. Manoel Dias da Silva 2364, Pituba.

**Post office** At the airport; Marquês de Caravelas 101, Barra; Shopping Barra, 3rd floor; Av. Amaralina 908, Amaralina; Rua J. Seabra 234; the *rodoviária*; Rua Rui Barbosa 19, Cidade Alta; at the Praça da Inglaterra, Cidade Baixa. Post office open hours are Mon–Fri 8am–6pm.

**Taxis** Radio Taxi Cometas Ⓣ71/3377-6311; Chame Táxi Ⓣ71/3241-2266; Teletáxi Ⓣ71/3341-9988.

**Travel and tour companies** Ceu e Mar Turismo, Rua Fonte do Boi 12, Rio Vermelho (Ⓣ71/3334-7566, Ⓕ3335-1351, Ⓔceuemar@e-net.com.br), represents the Student Travel Bureau. LR Turismo, Rua Marques de Leao 172, Barra (Ⓣ71/3264-0999), runs several tours, from historic Bahia to boat trips to the tropical islands in the Baía de Todos os Santos. Tours Bahia, Cruzeiro de Sao Francisco 416, Pelourinho (Ⓣ71/3322-4383, Ⓦwww.toursbahia.com.br), are expensive but offer a range of good-quality services, covering city tours, airline tickets, transfers and money exchange. Privé Tur, Rua Manuel Andrade 55, sala 310, Pituba (Ⓣ71/3535-0707, Ⓦwww.privetur.com.br), organizes city tours, beach trips and schooner cruises.

# Around Salvador

Salvador looks onto the **Baía de Todos os Santos**, a bay ringed with beaches and dotted with tropical **islands**. To the **northeast** of the city a string of fishing villages lies along a beautiful coastline – in short, there's no lack of places to explore.

## The bay: Ilha de Itaparica

**Ilha de Itaparica** is always visible from Salvador, looking as if it forms the other side of the bay, but in reality it's a narrow, 35km-long island that acts as a natural breakwater. After the local Indians were driven out, it was taken over by the Jesuits in 1560, making it one of the earliest places to be settled by the Portuguese. Its main town, also called **ITAPARICA**, was briefly the capital of Bahia before the Portuguese were expelled from Salvador, though little evidence remains of these times, apart from a couple of small seventeenth-century chapels. The lovely island is now very much seen as an appendage of the city, whose inhabitants flock to its beaches at weekends, building villas by the score as they go. It's quiet enough during the week, though, and big enough to find calmer spots even at the busiest times. Itaparica is also famous for its fruit trees, especially its mangoes, which are prized throughout Bahia.

Most **ferries** (see p.237) leave you at the **Bom Despacho** terminal in Itaparica town, although some boats also go to the anchorage at **Mar Grande**, a couple of kilometres away. For **getting around** once you're there, use the *kombis* (minibuses) and buses that ply the coastline, or rent **bicycles** (rental places are easily spotted by the bikes piled up on the pavement). If you want to stay on the island, there are some reasonable hotels, but most are on the expensive side thanks to Itaparica's popularity as a resort for Salvador's middle classes, and cheaper ones are often full from December to Carnaval. Options include *Club Méditerranée*,

Estr. Praia da Conceição (ⓣ71/3681-8800, ⓦwww.clubmed.com.br; ⑧), a luxury hotel set directly on 300m of its own beachfront; *Pousada Jardim Tropical*, Estr. da Rodagem, Praia Ponta de Areia 3.5km (ⓣ71/3831-1409; ④), with a pool and a reasonable restaurant; and the more modern *Pousada Canto da Praia*, Tr. do Coqueral 20, Praia de Ponta da Areia (ⓣ71/3631-4237, ⓦwww.pousadacantodapraia.com.br; ④), on the seafront with 23 rooms and a reasonable restaurant.

To see anything of the **other islands** scattered across the bay – 31 of them, most either uninhabited or home to a few simple fishing villages – travel agents in Salvador offer day-long cruises in private schooners; the kiosks in the city's Terminal Turístico are the easiest places to buy tickets. It's less busy during the week, but crowded schooners have their advantages; if you manage to get on one full of Brazilian tourists you're likely to have a very lively time and drinks are often included in the price.

## The Coconut Coast

The coastline immediately north of Salvador, known as the Coconut Coast, is essentially a long palm-fringed sandy beach. Access to the best bathing spots and seaside facilities are limited to a few settlements, each with its own distinctive flavour. **Arembepe** has long been seen as an alternative type of place, stuffed as it is with hippy beach shops. Close by there's the plush resort of **Itacimirim**. Further north, **Praia do Forte** is slightly more conventional and famous across Brazil for the Tamar Project which works with sea turtles. Near here are the truly laid-back villages of **Imbassai** and **Diogo**, both superbly peaceful and yet with plenty of bars and cafés to enjoy in the balmy evenings.

### Arembepe

Buses from Salvador's *rodoviária* run northeast along the coastal road (Estrada do Coco or Coconut Rd) to **AREMBEPE**, 50km away, a now-gentrified former hippy hangout, though still peaceful and pretty, with a pleasant little beach sheltered by a coral reef. The journey there takes you past some fine beaches and small, friendly villages, and you can get off wherever you like. A fifteen-minute walk from town brings you to the **Aldeia Hippie**, made famous in the 1960s when Mick Jagger, Janice Joplin and other stars enjoyed its pleasures; it has vestiges of its hippie past but is now known more as a fine place to cool off in the Capivara River in the late afternoons. Arembepe lies on a well-beaten tourist track, but don't be put off by this – it's a beautiful coastline and the beaches are long enough to swallow the crowds. There are plenty of **places to stay** in Arembepe itself or close by: basic options on the seafront include the *Praia de Arembepe Hotel*, Largo São Francisco (ⓣ71/3624-1415; ②), and the *Pousada Enseada do Cabral* (ⓣ71/3624-1231; ③), the latter with a restaurant. The *Pousada Gipsy* (ⓣ71/3624-3266; ④), Rua Eduardo Pinto (Lot. Volta da Robalo), some 3km from the centre, has a pool and restaurant. More upmarket are the beachfront *Pousada Ondas do Mar* (ⓣ71/3624-1052; ⑤), a comfortable place overlooking the harbour, and the good-value *O Turbaráo Hotel*, Rua Manoel Coelho (ⓣ71/3624-1055; ④), which has a pool, and rooms and apartments facing the beach. For **food**, the main *praça* has some options, but for cold beer and the best seafood in town head for the *Restaurant Coló*, which features a shaded terrace on the beach; try the *peixes moqueca* or the *lagosta salada* (lobster salad). Close to the harbour, the small seafood **market**, Mercado do Frutas Mar (Mon–Sat mornings), sells delicious-looking *lagosta* and *carangueijo* (crab). Also on the beach, the *Mar Aberto* restaurant is well known for its memorable fresh fish dishes.

## Itacimirim

Fifteen kilometres northeast of Arembepe, is the beach resort of **ITACIMIRIM**. It is not as developed as many resorts, though there are a few hotels and lots of smart weekend residences. Out of high season and during the week, you can have this palm-fringed paradise with several natural pools to swim in more or less to yourself. If you want to **stay** over, the *Hotel Itacimirim* (ⓣ71/3626-1304, ⓕ826-1503; ③) is right on the beach, while nearby, set back from the sands, there's the modern *Hotel Beira Mar* (ⓣ71/3626-1217; ③), which has a small pool, a bar and plain but nice rooms, some with ocean views. More comfortable and with a pool, the *Pousada Mar de Luz*, Rua Praia da Espera 7 (ⓣ71/3626-1622; ⑤), has pleasant, well-appointed apartments. On the Praia da Espera, the *Pousada Jambo* (ⓣ71/3626-1091; ⑥) offers an even more delightful setting and quality accommodation with a pool, restaurant and most rooms facing the ocean.

## Praia do Forte

About 30km up the road is the hip little resort of **PRAIA DO FORTE**, 83km north of Salvador. It has a couple of exceptionally nice, if small, beaches, lots of arty craft shops and some good restaurants, but is best known for the Projecto Tamar **turtle reserve** (daily 9am–6pm; R$8, half-price for students; ⓣ71/3676-1045, ⓦwww.projetotamar.org.br). Of the seven species of sea turtle in the world, four nest off the coast of Bahia, but over fishing and the destruction of nesting sites by human activity and urban development have seriously threatened their survival. The work of the Projecto Tamar has included identifying the turtles' main nesting areas along a 1000-kilometre stretch of coastline and ensuring their protection. The local community at Praia do Forte was mainly a fishing village until ecotourism and the turtle project arrived in the mid-1990s; today most of the 2000 residents make their income from tourism. The beaches and turtle reserve are at the end of the main drag, beyond all the craft shops and stalls. Inside the reserve, you can see many turtles in large aquariums, most of them injured and unlikely to survive in the wild. The nesting season is from September to March.

You'll find several good options if you want **to stay** in Praia do Forte: the *Pousada do Forte*, Almeda do Sol 4 (ⓣ71/3676-1043; ④), offers great-value rooms, a small pool and is on the main sandy drag, while the *Pousada Ogum Marinho* (ⓣ71/3676-1165; ⑤), close to the beach at the end of the main street, Avenida ACM, has cosy rooms and a nice hammock veranda. The *Do Souza*, on the first corner of the main street as you come into town, is a popular seafood **restaurant**, its terrace shaded by a massive angelin tree. There's a small sushi bar on one of the side streets, too, and an ice-cream parlour, the *Tutti Frutti*, nearby – both are easy to find.

At the entrance to the town itself, you'll spot a **tourist information** kiosk (ⓣ71/3676-1091 and 3676-1592) standing alone on a small grassy mound. **Buses** leave regularly (four daily) from the main street for Salvador and for further north up the coast to Imbassai. For general tourist information and photos of the area, check out ⓦwww.praiadoforte.org.br.

## Imbassaí and Diogo

Increasingly popular alternatives to Arembepe and Praia do Forte are the beautiful palm-fringed beaches just 16km further north around **IMBASSAÍ**; they tend to be less busy, making it easier to find cheaper accommodation. The *Pousada Canto de Imbassaí* (ⓣ71/3677-1082, ⓦwww.cantodeimbassai.com.br; ④) sits on the beach itself and has a pool and air conditioning in all rooms. The *Pousada Agua Marina* (ⓣ71/3677-1010, ⓦwww.paguamarinha.com.br; ④) is a similar price but arguably more comfortable with bar, restaurant and pool; they also have horses to hire. Horse riding along the beach or inland towards the *mata* is a good way to explore the area; Jones Vianna (ⓣ71/3677-1111, ⓔjonesvianna@hotmail.com) is passionate about the local flora and fauna and offers an excellent horse-riding service as well as riding lessons. For eating, you'll find good seafood and even French crêpes at the *Ilha do Dende* beside the Praia Imbassaí. The *Micasa Bar* (ⓣ71/3677-1303), on the Rua das Amendoeiras, has drinks, snacks and cool music.

For an even sleepier place to stay, there are camping and *pousada* options at the village of **Diogo**. *Pousada Too Cool na Bahia* (ⓣ71/9952-2190, ⓦwww.toocoolnabahia.com; ❹) offers stylish and comfortable chalet accommodation, hearty breakfasts and the chance to swing in hammocks, relax under the shade of mango trees and canoe along the river. Heading north from Imbassaí along the Linha Verde road towards Aracaju, Diogo is accessed by a right-turn side road that turns into track by the time it reaches the village. From the village, a track crosses the river and leads through some attractive dunes before reaching a massive, usually empty, beach. The nearby fishing village of **Santo Tomas** has a few bars and rustic eating spots, or, better still, head for the *barracas* on the beach, which serve fresh fish and chilled drinks.

# The Recôncavo and Valença

The **Recôncavo**, the early Portuguese plantation zone named after the concave shape of the bay, arcs out from Salvador along 150km of coastline, before petering out in the mangrove swamps around the town of **Valença**. It's one of the most lush tropical coastlines in Brazil, with palm-covered hills breaking up the green and fertile coastal plains; it's still one of the most important agricultural areas in Bahia, supplying the state with much of its fruit and spices. Only the sugar plantations around Recife could match the wealth of the Recôncavo, but, unlike that region, the Recôncavo survived the decline of the sugar trade by diversifying into tobacco and spices – especially peppers and cloves. It was the agricultural wealth of the Recôncavo that paid for most of the fine buildings of Salvador and, until the cocoa boom in southern Bahia in the 1920s, **Cachoeira** was considered the state's second city. The beauty of the area and the richness of its colonial heritage make it one of the more rewarding parts of the region to explore.

**Access** is good, with the main highway, the BR-324, approximately following the curve of the bay, and good local roads branching off to the towns in the heart of the Recôncavo. Thirty kilometres out of Salvador, a turn-off leads to Candéias, continuing on to Santo Amaro and the twin towns of Cachoeira and São Félix. Regular buses go to all these places from the *rodoviária* in Salvador.

## Candéias and Santo Amaro

The modern market town of **CANDÉIAS** is nowhere special, but 7km outside there's a good introduction to the history of the area in the **Museu do Recôncavo** (Tues, Thurs & Sun 9am–5pm), situated in a restored plantation called the Engenho da Freguesia, where pictures and artefacts from three centuries illustrate the economic and social dimensions of plantation life. The

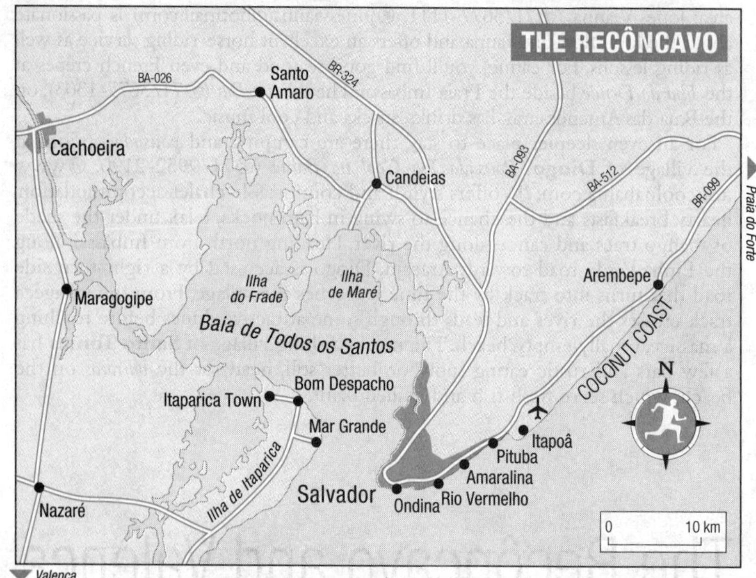




owners' mansion and the slave quarters have been impressively restored, juxtaposing the horrors of slave life – there's a fearsome array of manacles, whips and iron collars – with the elegant period furniture and fittings of the mansion. The only problem is that no bus service passes the museum; if you don't go by car you have to take a taxi from Candéias, around R$35.

**SANTO AMARO**, a further 20km from Salvador, is a lovely colonial town straddling the banks of a small river. It was the birthplace and is still the home of Caetano Veloso, one of Bahia's most famous singers and poets, who sings Santo Amaro's praises on many of his records. There's no tourist office, and the best thing to do is simply to wander around the quiet streets and squares, absorbing the atmosphere.

If you're arriving on the bus from Salvador, wait until it stops at the *rodoviária* before getting off, then turn left as you come out of the station in order to get into the centre. A few minutes' walk will bring you into the main square, the Praça da Purificação, where you'll find one of the town's most attractive sights, the **Igreja da Purificação**, a beautifully restored church sheltering a wonderfully elaborate eighteenth-century painted ceiling. Also worth a visit is the tranquil **Convento dos Humildes**, nearby on Praça Frei Bento, which has a museum attached, and plenty of friendly if slightly under-employed guides waiting to show you around. Elsewhere there are various ruined mansions that once belonged to the sugar and tobacco barons, among which is the atmospheric **Solar Araújo Pinto**, at Rua Imperador 1.

If you feel like staying, there are a few **pensões**, including the *Amarós*, on Rua Cons. Saraiva 27 (℗75/3241-1202; ③), which has a good **restaurant** at the back. The *Agua Viva Praia*, Praia Fazenda (℗75/3699-1176; ④), though 34km out of town, has well-appointed cabins and a pool, and also offers horse riding. About 18km from town, but more expensive, the *Enseada do Caeiro Eco Resort* (℗75/3264-3000; ⑥) has 32 comfortable apartments with air conditioning, restaurant, pool and horseriding.

# Cachoeira

The twin towns of **CACHOEIRA** and São Félix, two hours by bus from Salvador, are only a few kilometres apart across the Rio Paraguaçu, which an iron box-girder bridge (built by British engineers in 1885 and opened by Emperor Dom Pedro himself) spans. Cachoeira, one of the most beautiful colonial towns of Bahia, is easily the more impressive, its profusion of splendidly preserved buildings evidence of its importance in the eighteenth century. The rich sugar plantations of the **Paraguaçu Valley** supported a trading centre that rivalled Salvador in size and wealth until the beginning of the nineteenth century.

## Arrival and information

Cachoeira has no *rodoviária*, just an office by the bus stop in Rua Lauro de Freitas, so get off the bus there at the bus-company office; don't wait until it crosses the river into São Félix or you'll have to walk back across the bridge. There's a **Bahiatursa** office in Praça da Aclamação (ⓣ75/3425-1214), where you can get a map and some basic information.

## Accommodation

The nicest **place to stay** is the *Pousada do Convento* (ⓣ75/3425-1716; ③), which was a seventeenth-century convent and remains part of the Conjunto do Carmo on Praça da Aclamação; it has a pool, an attractive patio and a bar. Other options include the simple *Hotel Santo Antônio* on Praça Maciel (ⓣ75/3251-1402; ①), which is handy for the bus station but noisy at times; and the friendly, no-frills *Pousada do Guerreiro*, at Rua 13 de Maio 14 (ⓣ75/3215-1104; ②). There's also the excellent-value *Pousada do Pai Thomaz*, at Rua 25 de Junho 12 (ⓣ75/3215-1288; ④), with spotless rooms.

## The Town

A couple of blocks back along Rua Lauro de Freitas past the market you'll come to the fine Praça Doutor Milton, with its Baroque public fountain and the early eighteenth-century bulk of the **Santa Casa da Misericórdia**, which has a beautiful small garden. Leaving Praça Doutor Milton in the direction of the river, go up the narrow, cobbled Rua da Ajuda, and after a short climb you'll come to a peaceful little square that contains the **Capela de Nossa Senhora da Ajuda**, the city's oldest church. Begun in 1595 and completed eleven years later, it just about qualifies as sixteenth century, which makes it a rarity. Sadly, the simple but well-proportioned interior is often closed to visitors for fear of thieves, but if you knock on the door there might be someone around to let you in.

If you go straight down the hill as you come out of the Capela de Nossa Senhora da Ajuda, you'll find yourself in Rua 13 de Maio. On your right is the **Museu da Irmandade da Boa Morte**, which is connected with the August festival known as Nossa Senhora da Boa Morte (see box, p.262). Just a few steps in the other direction sits a renovated building that houses the small **Museu Hansen Bahia**, dedicated to the work of a German engraver who settled in the town. There's a lively tradition of **woodcarving** in Cachoeira and several sculptors have studios open to the public. One of the best is **Louco Junior**, who displays his wonderful elongated carvings in his studio on Rua 13 de Maio. The first turn on your left out of Rua 13 de Maio takes you up to Rua Ana Néri and the impressive **Igreja Matriz de Nossa Senhora do Rosário**. Again, the church has been robbed all too frequently and is sometimes shut,

### Candomblé in Cachoeira

Cachoeira is known for its **candomblé**, with some *terreiros* still conducting rituals in African dialects nobody now speaks, recognizable as variants of West African and Angolan languages. One of the best-known *candomblé* events is Cachoeira's fiesta of **Nossa Senhora da Boa Morte**, which always begins on the first Friday before August 15. It's staged by a sisterhood, the Irmandade da Boa Morte, founded by freed women slaves in the mid-nineteenth century, partly as a religious group and partly to work for the emancipation of slaves by acting as an early cooperative bank to buy people their liberty. All the local *candomblé* groups turn out with drummers and singers, and although the name of the fiesta is Catholic it's a celebration of *candomblé*, with centre stage held by the dignified matriarchs of the sisterhood. The other great day in the *candomblé* year is the **Festa de Santa Barbara**, on December 4 in São Félix, dedicated to the goddess Iansã. There are several other fiestas worth catching, like the **São João** celebrations, from June 22 to 24, while five saints' days are crammed into the last three months of the year; check with Bahiatursa for exact dates (see p.261).



but if you can get in you'll see two huge five-metre-high *azulejo* panels dating from the 1750s.

At the end of Rua Ana Néri, in the opposite direction from Praça Doutor Milton, is the finest and most spacious square in the town, **Praça da Aclamação**. On one side, it's lined with civil buildings from the golden age of Cachoeira in the eighteenth century, including the Prefeitura and the old city chambers. The other side of the square is dominated by the huge bulk of the **Conjunto do Carmo**, built in the eighteenth century and now beautifully restored in four parts: a church, a museum, a *pousada* and a conference centre. The museum contains rare seventeenth-century furniture and some fine sacred art, including carvings and statues from Macau that bring an unexpectedly Chinese flavour to the collection. The cloister leads to the church, decorated with seventeenth-century tiles and an extravagant Rococo gold-leaf interior.

If you're keen to do a bit of **shopping**, close to the bus station there is a large and colourful open-air market (closed on Sun) selling a wide variety of local produce, including some crafts.

On the stretch of waterfront nearest the old centre is Praça Teixeira de Freitas, from where you can take a launch out to the Ilha do Farol in the river, and over to **SÃO FÉLIX**. The main reason for going is the great view back across the river, with the colonial facades reflected in the water.

## Eating and drinking

For fantastic regional dishes head for the *Restaurant Gruta Azul*, Praça Manuel Vitorino 2 (daily 11am–6pm). More varied but still reasonably priced food can be found at *Beira Rio*, Rua Manuel P. Filho 19, from 9am until 11pm, daily.

# Valença and around

After Cachoeira, the coast becomes swampy and by the time you get to **VALENÇA** you're in mangrove country. Fortunately, though, instead of alligators, the swamps are dominated by shellfish of all kinds, most of them edible. Valença lies on the banks of the Rio Una, about 10km from the sea, at the point where the river widens into a delta made up of dozens of small islands, most of which support at least a couple of fishing villages. At one time the town was an industrial centre – the first cotton factory in Brazil was built here – but it has long since reverted to fishing and boat building. Today, it's also an increasingly popular destination for tourists from Salvador – mainly as a stop-off point for the nearby island resort of **Morro de São Paulo** and the pristine beaches of **Ilha de Boipeba** – but the town is not yet over-commercialized.

## Arrival and information

From Valença five daily **buses** head back to Salvador (☎75/3641-3906 for infomation), taking around five hours. Alternatively, you can travel to Salvador via Nazaré and Itaparica, thereby reducing the journey by 150km; Excursões e Turismo, on the Praça da República (☎75/3741-5305), sell combined ferry–*kombi* tickets that cut the journey time by a couple of hours.

**Tourist information** is available from an office in the old Prefeitura building, Rua Comendador Madureira 10 (☎75/3641-8673), facing the river by the Praça Admar Braga Guimarães. The best place to **change money** is the Banco do Brasil on Calle Calçado, the main pedestrianized street in the old centre. A good way of getting around the town is by **bicycle**. You can rent them cheaply all over the place: look out for signs saying "Aluga-sebicicleta".

## Accommodation

There are several hotels and *pensões* in and around Valença. The *Hotel Guaibim* on Praça da Independência (☎75/3641-1110; ③) is welcoming and good value; the *Hotel do Porto* at Av. Maconica 50 (☎75/3641-2383; ③) offers attractive rooms and spectacular views, while the *Portal Rio Una* on Rua Maestro Barrinha (☎75/3641-5050; ⑤) is a more luxurious option.

Many visitors choose to stay out of town at the beach resort of **Guaibim**, just twenty minutes' drive from Valença near the international airport. Of these, the *Aguas do Guaibim* on Avenida Taquary (☎75/3646-1047, Ⓦwww.aguasdoguaibim.com; ③) is hard to top, with its attractive apartments, pool and beach access; there's also the *Royal Praia Hotel* on the same road (☎75/3482-1131; ③), with stylish if slightly down-at-heel rooms and a beachside pool.

## The Town

Valença's **rodoviária** is close to the centre of town, which is just a few blocks' walk away along the riverside towards the market. There are a couple of colonial churches – the most interesting is the Igreja de Nossa Senhora do Amparo, built in 1757 on a hill affording beautiful views over the city and accessed from near the market. Valença is mostly the connection point for **Morro de São Paulo** and **Boipeba** islands (see p.264) or a place for walks, boat trips and lazing on beaches rather than sightseeing. By far the most absorbing thing the town has to offer is its **boatyards**, the *estaleiros*; follow the river 500m downstream from the central Praça Admar Braga Guimarães. A whole series of wooden boats is produced here, largely by hand, ranging from small fishing smacks to large schooners, and local boat-builders are renowned throughout the state for their skill. Provided you don't get in the way – try going around midday, when work stops for a couple of hours – and ask permission, people are pleased to let you take a closer look and often take pride in showing off their work.

## Eating and drinking

The **restaurants** in town are simple and reasonably priced, and serve excellent food; the combination of fresh seafood and *dendê* (palm oil) is definitely a treat. Valença is famous for its *dendê* and this stretch of Brazil is known as the Dende Coast. Try the seafood *rodizio* (all you can eat for around R$40) at the *Akuarius*, on Praça da Independência, or a plate of *moqueca* at the *Bar Kardy*, on Rua Governador Gonçalves, which has the added attraction of live music. On the relaxed Praça da República, the *Skinas Bar* is a good option for drinking or munching and, opposite, there's the very cheap *Casa do Bolo*, fine for set lunch menus. You'll find other good spots on the north side of the river, along a well-lit promenade with plenty of *barracas*, bars and restaurants, and a laid-back atmosphere on most evenings.



## Morro de São Paulo

The obvious place to head for around Valença is the island of **Tinharé** and its famous beaches at atmospheric **MORRO DE SÃO PAULO**, with reggae bars, hippy dives and great seafood restaurants. With no roads on the island, it's still relatively peaceful and undeveloped, though at the weekends, especially between December and March, it can get unbearably crowded.

### Arrival and information

Several **boats** a day (call ⓣ75/3641-3011 for information) travel from Valença to Tinharé, costing under R$10 and taking about ninety minutes to get there. There's also a faster *lancha rapida*, which takes thirty to forty minutes but costs about R$20. In high season a direct boat leaves from the Terminal Turístico in Salvador (it's also worth enquiring about it in low season, as the boat may operate on certain days then, too). It costs about R$80 for a one-way trip and takes about three hours, but the sea can be rough. There's also the occasional catamaran (R$150; 1hr).

### Accommodation

Accommodation on the island is all expensive relative to Salvador, particularly at holiday times; it's the price of being trendy. Most of the larger places are self-contained *pousadas*, with their own restaurant and bar. Nearly all places are within a stone's throw of the beautiful beaches.

#### Near the port

**O Casarão** Praça Aureliano Lima 190 ⓣ75/3652-1049, ⓕ3652-1022, ⓦwww.ocasarao.net. Based in an attractive early seventeenth-century mansion, this place offers both spacious apartments and chalets, plus a little pool. ④

**Pousada Natureza** At the top of the steps leading to the pier ⓣ75/3652-1044, ⓦwww.hotelnatureza.com. This spot has lovely rooms with hammock verandas, some apartments with jacuzzis, a patio bar set in attractive gardens and a pool. ⑤

#### The beaches

**Camping Natureza** Terceira Praia. By far the cheapest option on any of the beaches, you can put up a tent here and stay for less than R$7 per person.

**Pousada Tia Lita** Terceira Praia ⓣ75/3652-1532, ⓦwww.pousadatialita.com.br. This reasonably priced spot just 30m from the sea, offers views from some of the rooms, all of which have a/c. The building is a bit plain, but the service is good. ②–③

**Praia do Encanto** Praia do Encanto ⓣ75/3652-2000. This elegant *pousada* has some very comfortable apartments (⑦) and some less-expensive (but still comfortable) chalets (⑤), plus a good bar, restaurant and pool.

**Villa das Pedras Pousada** Segunda Praia ⓣ75/3652-1075, ⓦwww.villadaspedras.com.br. A good option, with its own beachside pool enclosed in lovely green gardens; all rooms have a/c, minibar and TV. ⑥–⑦

**Villegaignon Resort** Terceira Praia ⓣ75/3652-1010, ⓕ3652-1012. This plush resort features rooms with or without a terrace, but all have a/c, minibar and cable TV. There's a great pool, a sauna, hotel bar and beach bar. ⑥

## Beans

Regardless of region, there's no more key ingredient in Brazilian cooking than **beans** – indeed, to many people a meal is not a meal without them. Beans are served almost soup-like, refried with onion or used with pork trimmings as the basis of **feijoada**, the nearest Brazil has to a national dish. Dried beans come in numerous sizes and colours, with subtle differences in texture and flavour. *Carioquinha* (brown beans) are the most widely consumed, but they're a comparatively recent introduction to the Brazilian diet. *Feijão preto* (small black beans) are the standard in both Rio de Janeiro and Rio Grande do Sul; other regional varieties include *fradinho* beans (black-eyed peas, used in Bahia), white beans (consumed in Santa Catarina) and a red kidney bean variation (popular in Pará).

▲ *Feijoada*

▲ A juice bar in Rio

## Soft drinks

**Guaraná**, a sweet, fizzy drink based on an Amazonian berry that offers a caffeine-like kick, is consumed just about everywhere, including the most sophisticated restaurants. A far more refreshing beverage is **maté gelado**, an ice-cold, sweet infusion associated with relaxing on the beach. Its main ingredient is *erva maté*, the toasted leaf of a holly-like bush that in Rio Grande do Sul is enjoyed as **chimarrão**, a bitter-tasting drink sipped hot through a silver straw from a gourd.

Thanks to Brazil's amazing variety of fruit, you're spoilt for choice when it comes to **sucos** (juices). Look out for specialist *casas de sucos*, but even humble *lanchonetes*, or snack bars, may offer juices made from strange Amazonian fruit – such as graviola and *fruta do conde* – with tastes that defy description.

▼ *Chimarrão*

Coffee beans ▲

A night out in Santa Teresa ▼

Caipirinha ▼

## Coffee

Brazil is the world's largest producer of **coffee** and Brazilians appear to consume *cafezinhos* – tiny cups of rather bitter, and usually intensely sweet, liquid – almost constantly. Although most of the best beans are exported, quality coffee can be found at espresso bars and fine restaurants, some of which make great efforts to source their beans from the country's premier coffee plantations, concentrated in Minas Gerais.

## Alcohol

When it comes to alcohol, **beer** is very much the Brazilian drink of choice. Typically, Brazilian beer is a light, Pilsner-type brew that's rather flavourless and always demanded ice cold. Although just one company dominates the market – owning all four (very similar) leading brands (Brahma, Bohemia, Antarctica and Skol) – there are a few smaller producers: Cerpa, brewed in Belém, is pretty good, while Eisenbahn, from Blumenau, a part of Brazil settled by German immigrants, is genuinely excellent.

A uniquely Brazilian drink, however, is **cachaça**, a spirit that's made by distilling fermented sugarcane juice. The largest producers are in Ceará and São Paulo, but there are thousands of artisanal mills across the country, with the best concentrated in Minas Gerais, often using traditional methods of production.

*Cachaça* can be enjoyed neat from a small shot glass, but it's frequently used as the basis of a **batida** (cocktail). The *caipirinha* – made from lime, sugar, ice and *cachaça* – is as intrinsic to Brazil as samba and football. Its simplicity, sweetness and tangy flavour have made the drink world famous, but the *caipirinha* tastes best in Brazil, its natural habitat.

# Brazilian food and drink

**Food and drink in Brazil reflects the country's remarkable geographic and cultural diversity, and it's hardly surprising no true national cuisine has emerged. While it's easy to identify indigenous Indian, African and Portuguese influences, as well as Italian, German, Arab and Japanese ones, much of the pleasure of dining in Brazil has to do with regional cuisines. These styles have been enhanced by the country's abundance of fruit, vegetables, herbs and spices, and have increasingly taken on influences from modern European, Californian and east Asian styles of cooking.**

Comida baiana ▲

Comida amazônica ▼

Carne de sol ▼

## Bahia and Minas

There are five main regional cuisines in Brazil, and sampling them is one of the best parts of visiting the country. **Comida baiana**, from the coast of the state of Bahia, is perhaps the most exotic. With West African roots, it uses palm oil, coconut milk, fish, shellfish, coriander and chili peppers to remarkable effect.

Restaurants specializing in the food of Minas Gerais are popular across Brazil. Most **comida mineiro** recipes – even ones based on beans and fresh vegetables – include pork or bacon and have a tendency to be heavy, though a lighter touch has resulted from fusions with French *nouveau cuisine*. Desserts, in particular cheeses and fruit preserves, are specialties, and no meal is complete without a shot or two of *cachaça*.

## The far south and north

From the grasslands of Rio Grande do Sul, **comida gaúcha** has emerged as Brazil's most carnivorous cuisine – and for a country where meat is so important in the diet, that's really something. *Churrascarias* – restaurants specializing in barbecue beef and other meats – have become standard features of even small-town dining. But there's more to *comida gaúcha* than grilled meat. Rice cooked with *charque* (jerked beef), manioc and squash dishes are standard fare, but rarely reach beyond the southern ranching country.

Also a rarity outside their home regions are **comida amazônica**, based on river fish, manioc, yam, palm products and exotic fruits, and **comida do sertão**, the cuisine of the parched interior of the Brazilian Northeast. Food here is dominated by dehydrated *carne de sol*, beans and manioc – ingredients that reflect the region's agriculturally precarious conditions.

## The town and around

The small settlement of **Morro de São Paulo** sits on a hill between the port and the first of the beaches, Primeira Praia. If you don't mind being a few minutes' walk from the beach, it's a pleasant place to stay, close to the shops and restaurants. There's little of interest in town, apart from an atmospheric old fort overlooking the harbour, with a rusting canon and a Moorish-looking gun turret still standing on its crumbling battlements. To get here, follow the coastal path clockwise around the island.

The *Pizzaria Forno a Lenha* on Praça Aureliano is a good **restaurant** and one of the best places to meet people in the evenings and find out where the parties are happening. More restaurants and ice-cream parlours line the track from the square down to Primeira Praia, where *Restaurante Da Dona Elda* (Ⓣ75/3652-1041) serves excellent seafood dishes, including delicious *moqueca de peixe* and *bobó de camarão*, on its upstairs patio. There are also several shops and **tour agents** offering **money exchange** and **internet access** along this stretch; one of the best is Marlins Viagems e Turismo (Ⓣ75/3652-1242). The **tourist information office** is on Praça Aureliano Lima (Ⓣ75/3652-1104 and 3652-1083, Ⓦwww.morrosp.com.br), a short walk from the dock.

On the opposite side of the small island, 15km away, is the hamlet of **Prainha**. Here you'll find the **Casa da Sogra**, home of a local poet and sculptor who has papered the walls with his poems and decorative painted maps of the region. There are no hotels here but, if you want **to stay** for a few days of idyllic tranquillity, the locals – mainly fishing families – rent out hammock space. There is little except grilled fish and shellfish to eat, but it's a lifestyle you could easily get used to. At least one boat from Morro calls every day.

You'll find good **diving** in the clear waters surrounding the island; Companhia do Mergulho, Primeira Praia (Ⓣ75/3652-1200, Ⓦwww.ciadomergulho.com.br), offer scuba trips for certified divers both day and night (from R$100 per day) and also a six-day scuba course for beginners (from around R$500).

## The beaches

Five main beaches, all linked by paths, line the populated northwest corner of the island. The **Primeira Praia** has the widest range of accommodation, but isn't the nicest of the beaches and it's worth heading five minutes further south to **Segunda Praia**, popular with the in-crowd from all over Brazil and boasting the island's best swimming and snorkelling. **Terceira Praia** is narrow but pleasant, and more laid-back than Segunda Praia, with wooden shack bars along the lapping edge of the ocean when the tide is in. The long and quite glorious **Quarta Praia** is the least developed of the beaches and has some of the island's best restaurants. **Praia do Encanto** is little more than an extension of Quarta Praia, but has deeper natural pools.

# Ilha de Boipeba

The beaches on the island of **BOIPEBA**, separated from the Ilha de Tinharé by the Rio do Inferno, are even more beautiful than those at Morro de São Paulo, but much less developed, still possessing the tranquillity that Morro hasn't seen for over twenty years. The settlement here is small and scattered across the island, with few facilities – just a couple of restaurants and a handful of *pousadas*. The beaches are simply gorgeous, and there's good scuba diving at the coral reefs near the Ponta da Castelhauos at the southernmost point of the island.

For **accommodation**, the excellent *Pousada Lua das Aguas* on the beach (Ⓣ75/3653-6015, mobile Ⓣ9981-1012 and 3641-2238, Ⓦwww.luardasaguas .com.br; ④) has attractive bungalows with hammock verandas and a palm-thatched circular beach restaurant that serves some of the best seafood south of Fortaleza. The *Pousada do Outeiro*, Praia Tassimirim (Ⓣ&Ⓕ75/3653-1535 and 3653-6111; ④), is another good place to stay, with ten beachfront apartments. There's also a **campsite** at the Kioska Ponto do Almendeira, between the port and the beach restaurants (R$15 per person). For **food**, the *Pousada e Restaurante Santa Clara* (Ⓣ75/3653-6085, Ⓔchasbras@terra.com.br; ④) is famed for its good Bahian cooking.

Boats run to Boipeba from Valença (3hr 30min; R$40), and from Segunda Praia on the Ilha de Tinharé (2hr; R$25). You can save some time by renting a speedboat (for 4–5 people) to take you between Boipeba and Morro de São Paulo for around R$200. On the island it's possible to arrange **outdoor activities** through your *pousada*, including canoeing in the mangrove swamps, spotting wildlife in the coastal woodlands and horse riding on the beach, as well as surfing and diving.



# Inland: the Bahian sertão

The **Bahian sertão** is immense: an area considerably larger than any European country and constituting most of the land area of Bahia state. Much of it is semi-desert, with endless expanses of rock and cactus broiling in the sun. But it can be spectacular, with ranges of hills to the north and broken highlands to the west, rearing up into the tableland of the great **Planalto Central**, the plateau extending over most of the state of Goiás and parts of Minas Gerais. No part of the Bahian *sertão* is thickly populated, and most of it is positively hostile to human habitation; in some places, no rain falls for years at a stretch. Its inhabitants suffer more from drought than anywhere else in the region and in parts of the *sertão* there's still desperate poverty.

Despite its reputation, not all the *sertão* is desert. Snaking through it is the **Rio São Francisco**, which spills out into the huge hydroelectric reservoir of **Sobradinho**. River and lake support a string of towns, notably Paulo Afonso and Juazeiro. Other possible destinations to the north are **Jacobina**, in the midst of spectacular hill country, where gold and emeralds have been mined for nearly three centuries, and **Canudos**, site of a mini–civil war a hundred years ago, and a good place to get a feel for *sertão* life. By far the most popular

## Travelling in the sertão

Because the interior is not geared to tourism, travelling in the *sertão* requires some preparation. Hotels are fewer and dirtier; a **hammock** is essential, as it's the coolest and most comfortable way to sleep, much better than the grimy beds in inland hotels, all of which have hammock hooks set into the walls as a standard fitting. Buses, meanwhile, are less frequent; you often have to rely on country services that leave very early in the morning and seem to stop every few hundred yards. The towns are much smaller here than on the coast, and in most places there's little to do in the evening, as the population turns in early to be up for work at dawn. Far more people carry arms than on the coast, but in fact the *sertão* is one of the safest areas of Brazil for travellers – the guns are mainly used on animals, especially small birds, which are killed on an enormous scale. Avoid tap and stick to **bottled water**; dysentery is common, and although not dangerous these days it's extremely unpleasant. Don't let these considerations put you off, though; people in the *sertão* are intrigued by gringos and are invariably very friendly. While few *sertão* towns may have much to offer in terms of excitement or entertainment, the surrounding landscape is spectacular.

route into the *sertão*, though, is westwards along the BR-242, which eventually hits the Belém–Brasília highway in Goiás: en route you'll pass the old mining town of **Lençóis**, gateway to the breathtaking natural wonders of the **Chapada Diamantina** – one of Brazil's best and most accessible trekking areas.

## Jacobina

Nestled on the slopes of several hills with panoramic views over the **Serra da Jacobina**, the old mining town of **JACOBINA** was one of the first parts of the *sertão* the Portuguese settled in strength. The clue to what attracted them is the name of one of the two fast-flowing rivers that bisect the town – the Rio de Ouro, or "Gold River". **Gold** was first found here in the early seventeenth century, and several *bandeirante* (Brazilian conquistador) expeditions made the trip north from São Paulo to settle.

### Getting there and information

It's about a six-hour ride to Jacobina on the two daily **buses** from Salvador, which will drop you off near the centre. If you're **driving**, you'll pass through Feira de Santana – a flat and rather dull and major market town that mainly deals in automotive parts – on the BR-324, which soon strikes into the interior proper and while the scenery is uninspiring for the first couple of hours, the road eventually climbs into the highlands of the Chapada Diamantina, with rock massifs rising out of the scrub, vaguely reminiscent of the American Southwest. At the small town of Capim Grosso the BR-407 branches off on a 300-kilometre journey north to Juazeiro, but sticking with the BR-324 for another hour brings you to Jacobina. There's no tourist office here, although you might be able to get hold of a pamphlet with a street map from Bahiatursa in Salvador (see p.237). Still, it's small enough to get by without one.

### Accommodation

There are several cheap **hotels** and *pensões* in Jacobina. The *Hotel Serra do Ouro* (Ⓣ74/3621-3324, Ⓦwww.hotelserradoouro.com; ❸) is one of the best, built on a hillside on the outskirts with a magnificent view of the town and a good pool. A cheaper, less attractive, option is the *Jacobina Palace Hotel*, Rua Manoel Navares 210 (Ⓣ74/3621-2600; ❷).

### The Town

The town itself is notably friendly – they don't see many tourists and people are curious – while the altitude takes the edge off the temperature most days, which makes it a good place to walk. It's a typical example of an interior town, quiet at night save for the squares and the riverbanks, where the young congregate, especially around the *Zululândia* bar in the centre, while their parents pull chairs into the streets and gossip until the TV soaps start. **Paths** lead out of town into the surrounding hills – where there are spectacular views – in all directions, but it still gets hot during the day and some of the slopes are steep, so it's best to take water along.

Although cattle and farming are now more important than the gold that originally brought the Portuguese, mining continues: there are **emerald mines** at nearby Pindobaçu, two large **gold mines** at Canavieiras and Itapicuru, and the diamonds that gave the Chapada Diamantina its name. The last big rush was in 1948, but miners still come down from the hills every now and then to sell gold and precious stones to traders in the town – you'll notice many of them have precision scales on their counters. The *Hotel Serra do Ouro* runs trips (around R$50 per person) out to the mines of Pindobaçu, around 60km to the north, and to the mines of Canavieiras and Itapicuru. These trips can be a bit disappointing though – to the untrained eye uncut emeralds look like bits of gravel.

### Eating and drinking

Jacobina is a good place for getting acquainted with the **food** of the interior: *carne do sol com pirão de leite* is rehydrated dried meat with a delicious milk-based sauce; *bode assado* is roast goat, surprisingly tender when done well; and *buchada*, a spicy kind of haggis made from intestines, is much nicer than it sounds but not for delicate stomachs. Good **restaurants** can be found on the banks of the Rio Ouro, and you should try *doce de buriti*, a tangy, acidic-tasting paste made from the fruit of the buriti palm, sold in neat boxes made from the wood of the same tree, which keep it fresh. The favoured restaurant of locals is the *Rancho Catarinense*, at Av. N.S. da Conceição 1188, in the Tamarindo district, which specializes in meat.

## Canudos

A different route north from Feira de Santana along the bumpy BR-116 takes you to **CANUDOS**, site of Antônio Conselheiro's rebellion in the 1890s (see box below). The main reason for coming here is to get a taste of these remarkable events, but it's also a chance to sample the atmosphere of a typical small town in the *sertão*, where life is still dominated by the all-important question of rain or the lack of it. Despite the obvious poverty, it's a rewarding place to visit; everything centres on the main square, with weather-beaten *sertanejos* trudging around during the day, and the local youngsters taking over at night. If you've come from a big city, you'll certainly notice the sense of isolation provided by the *caatinga* all around.

You have to leave the town if you want to visit the **site of the Canudos war**. The valley where it all happened was flooded by a dam in the 1960s and

### Antônio Conselheiro's rebellion

The Bahian *sertão* provided the backdrop for one of the most remarkable events in Brazilian history: the 1895 **rebellion** of the messianic religious leader **Antônio Conselheiro**. Conselheiro gathered thousands of followers, built a city called Canudos, and declared war on the young republic for imposing new taxes on an already starving population. The rebels – or *sertanistas* – proved to be great guerrilla fighters with an intimate knowledge of the harsh country, and twice mauled military forces sent confidently north from Salvador; the city troops found the *sertão* as intimidating as their human enemies. A third force of over one thousand, commanded by a national hero, a general in the Paraguayan war, was sent against the rebels. In the worst shock the young republic had suffered to that point, the force was completely annihilated; the next expedition discovered the bleached skulls of the general and his staff laid out in a neat row in front of a thorn tree. A fourth expedition was sent in 1897 and Canudos finally fell, with almost all of its defenders killed. Conselheiro himself had died of fever only a few weeks before the end. One member of the force, **Euclides da Cunha**, immortalized the war in his book *Os Sertões*, generally recognized as the greatest Portuguese prose ever written by a Brazilian. It was translated into English as "Rebellion in the Backlands" and is a good introduction to the *sertão*. A more entertaining read is *The War of the End of the World* by Peruvian novelist Mario Vargas Llosa (see "Books", p.761), which gives a haunting, fictionalized account of the incredible events in Canudos.

the new Canudos is the result of a shift a few miles down the road. There is a bus that will drop you at the battlefield (ask for "Velho Canudos"), but you'll have to wait a long time to be picked up again so it may be better to arrange your own transport. Alternatively, you could walk it in a couple of hours, but it can get very hot and you should take plenty of sun protection if you decide to do so. When you get to the edge of the valley you'll see a few houses, a statue of Antônio Conselheiro and a small museum, which is usually closed. More interesting is the valley itself, where the water has sunk to such a low level that you can now see the tops of trees and houses that may have formed part of the original Canudos. It's incredible to think this valley was once a place that was thought to threaten the future of the Brazilian Republic.

Back in the new Canudos, there are two or three **places to stay**, but *Grapiuna* on Praça Monsenhor Berenguer (Ⓣ75/3275-1157; ③) is the best bet. There's a **daily bus** to Salvador and another daily service to Juazeiro, on the border with Pernambuco. The **food** isn't great; the local speciality is *bode assado*, roast goat, which is not particularly popular with outsiders, and there's a distinct lack of fresh fruit and vegetables. But there are plenty of biscuits in the shops, so you won't starve.

## The Chapada Diamantina

The route **west** into the *sertão* is along the BR-242, which skirts Feira de Santana and swings south, where a turn-off signposted to Brasília heads inland, into the heart of the *sertão*. The scenery is remarkably similar to that along the Jacobina road 200km to the north: you're still in the tablelands of the **Chapada Diamantina**, with its rock spurs and mesas forming an enormous chain of foothills to the Planalto Central.

### Lençóis

Five hours' ride down the BR-242, **LENÇÓIS** is another ex-mining town and the main tourist centre in the Chapada Diamantina region. The name of the town, meaning "sheets", derives from the camp that grew up around a diamond strike in 1844. The miners, too poor to afford tents, made do with sheets draped over branches. Lençóis is a pretty little town, set in the midst of the spectacular Parque Nacional da Chapada Diamantina (see p.271). Most of its fine old buildings date back to the second half of the nineteenth century, when the town was a prosperous mining community, attracting diamond buyers from as far afield as Europe. The **Mercado Municipal**, next to the bridge over the Rio Lençóis that runs through the centre, is where most of the diamonds were sold – it has Italian- and French-style trimmings tacked on to make the buyers feel at home. The centre of the town, between two lovely squares, Praça Otaviano Alves and Praça Horácio de Matos, is made up of cobbled streets, lined with well-proportioned two-storey nineteenth-century houses with high, arched windows. On Praça Horácio, the **Subconsulado Francês**, once the French consulate, was built with the money of the European diamond-buyers, who wanted an office to take care of export certificates.

Local **artesanato** is very good, particularly the bottles filled with coloured sand arranged into intricate patterns; get a guide to take you to the **Salão das Areias** on the outskirts of town, where you can see the sand being gathered and put into bottles by local artisans – even children do it. You can buy the finished product at Gilmar Nunes on Rua Almirante Barroso, or at Manoel Reis, Rua São Félix.

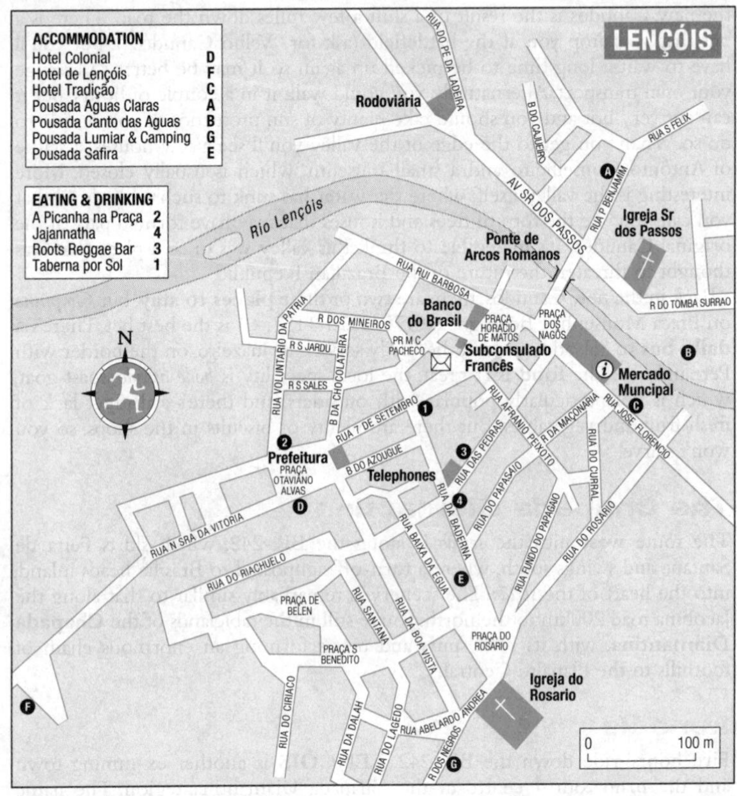


## Arrival and information

There are three **buses** a day for the six-hour journey from Salvador to Lençóis, all leaving from the main *rodoviária* (☎75/3334-1112 for information). **Tourist information** is available from an office in the old market on Praça dos Nagôs (☎75/3334-1112) beside the river bridge and from the tour agencies listed on p.272. For information on trekking in the national park try the Insituto Chico Mendes office in Palmeiras (☎75/3332-2420) or the Fundação Chapada Diamantina at Rua Pé de Ladeira 212 (☎75/3334-1305). You'll also find people offering themselves as guides to the town: at a dollar or two for an extensive tour they're not expensive, and as life is not easy around here, it might help someone out.

## Accommodation

Accommodation in Lençóis ranges from pretty luxurious and surrounded by gardens to small rooms in small houses. All seem to be run by friendly families or staff; a couple have great swimming pools. You'll find a **campsite**, *Lumiar Camping*, on the grounds of the *Pousada Lumiar* at Praça do Rosário 70 (☎75/3334-1241).

**Hotel Colonial** Praça Otaviano Alves 750 ☎75/3334-1114. Offers pleasant rooms with decent beds, well located near the centre of town. 3

**Hotel de Lençóis** Rua Altina Alves 747 ☎75/3334-1102, www.hoteldelencios.com. Located mainly in a small mansion with spacious rooms, this attractive place is set in 4 hectares of sweet-smelling gardens. ⑤

**Hotel Tradição** Rua José Florêncio ⓣ5/3334-1120, ⓦwww.hoteltradicao.com.br. A nice house-sized *pousada* with small but clean apartments. It's near the town centre, has parking, pleasant gardens and two pools – one for kids and another for adults. ②

**Pousada Aguas Claras** Rua P. Benjamin ⓣ75/3334-1471, ⓔgal700@hotmail.com. With plain but clean rooms, if you also want transport this is a good bet, since the owner is married to a reliable taxi-driver (ⓣ75/9966-1471). ③

**Pousada Canto das Aguas** ⓣ75/3334-1154, ⓦwww.lencois.com.br. Slightly more expensive and also very good, with well-kept gardens, a meditation and massage area and a beautiful riverside location; hearty breakfasts and a pool included. ⑥

**Pousada Safira** Rua do Pires ⓣ75/3334-1443. This is one of the friendliest of the basic options but with just a few small rooms, all with their own bath; it's a little hard to find in the backstreets at the heart of town. ②

### Eating and drinking

The popular *A Picanha na Praça*, Praça Otaviano Alves 153, serves mostly meat, has fast service and an open patio. The vegetarian restaurant *Jajannatha*, Rua das Pedras 133, has outside tables. For *comida por kilo* lunches it's hard to beat the extensive menu at the large, airy *Taberna por Sol* on the corner of ruas 7 de Setembro and Baderna. In the evenings, the restaurant-bars on Rua das Pedras, such as *Roots Reggae Bar*, and around Praça Horácio de Matos tend to be the focus of **nightlife**.

## Parque Nacional da Chapada Diamantina and Capão

The **Parque Nacional da Chapada Diamantina** was established in 1985 after much local campaigning and covers over 38,000 square kilometres – an area larger than the Netherlands – in the mountainous regions to the south and west of Lençóis. Its dramatic landscape incorporates swampy valleys, barren peaks and scrubby forest, punctuated by beautiful waterfalls, rivers and streams. Wildlife lovers can stop in at the unique Orquidario Pai Inacio (ⓣ71/3374-4468; open

▲ Parque Nacional da Chapada Diamantina

daily 8am–5.30pm; R$5) some 30km from Lençóis at Km 232 of the BR-242. This orchid nursery and garden has been run by a local family for decades, making it possible to see firsthand a wide range of otherwise very rare specimens.

## Capão

The Parque Nacional da Chapada Diamantina is one of Brazil's major **trekking** destinations, but also offers plenty of opportunities for canoeing, climbing and even chilling out at the hippy rural community of **Capão**. In recent years the town has attracted young people from Salvador in search of a bohemian or New Age lifestyle. There are retreats and meditation spots here, and many of the *pousadas* offer luxuries such as hot tubs and saunas – though it's hard to beat a dip in the river, as it gets very hot here in January and February. It takes three days to trek to Capão from Lençóis, or you can take a bus as far as the town of Palmeiras, which is about 15km from Capão; a taxi takes two hours to get to Capão.

Despite the poor track in from Palmeiras and the lack of general facilities, Capão, with several stores and restaurants, can make for a relaxing base while visiting Chapada. Most of the accommodation, including *Pousada Verde* (Ⓣ75/3334-1109; ④), *Pousadado Capão* (Ⓣ75/3334-1034, Ⓦwww.pousadadocapao.com.br; ③) and *Pousada Galixito* (Ⓣ75/3334-1187; ④), are scattered around Capão's undulating landscape; you should book and get confirmation far in advance and try to get someone from your accommodation to pick you up from Palmeiras or Lençóis.

### Hikes, walks and guides

Some places in the park you could just about manage without a guide, like the **Gruta do Lapão**, a remarkable grotto over a kilometre long, with a cathedral-like entrance of layered rock and stalactites. It's a short drive or a long walk (a full-day round trip) from the centre, but it's probably better to have someone take you there. The only other place within easy reach is the **Cascatas do Serrano**, a fifteen-minute walk from town, where the river flows over a rock plate forming a series of small waterfalls and pools good for swimming – very popular with the local children.

Among the most popular destinations is **Morro do Pai Inácio**, a 300-metre-high mesa formation 27km from Lençóis (don't be deceived by how near it looks). It is much more easily climbed than seems possible from a distance, and you're rewarded with quite stunning views across the tablelands and the town once you get to the top, which is covered in highland cacti, trees and shrubs. Thirty kilometres away, but with much easier road access, is **Rio Mucugezinho**, another series of small waterfalls and pools that are fun to swim in; a closer river beach is the **Praia do Rio São José**, also called Zaidã. Finally, and most spectacular of all, is the highest waterfall in Brazil, the **Cachoeira Glass**, a small stream tumbling 400m down over a mesa, becoming little more than a fine mist by the time it reaches the bottom. It's closer to town than most of the other places, and if you only feel up to one day's walking it's the best choice.

If you're planning to see sites that are as far away as some of the ones above, you'll need a proper guide, as the countryside can be difficult to negotiate. Reliable operators in Lençóis include Marimbus Ecoturismo, Praça da Coreto (Ⓣ75/3334-1292, Ⓦwww.marimbus.com), and Extreme, Av. 7 de Setembro 15 (Ⓣ75/3341-1727, Ⓦwww.extremeecoadventure.com.br). Alternatively, if you'd rather opt for an **independent guide**, contact Roy Funch (through the Fundacao Chapada Diamantina at Rua Pé de Ladeira 212; Ⓣ75/3334-1305), a resident American and author of an excellent guidebook to the region. He may not be able to guide you himself, but can certainly recommend someone and suggest places to head for. Standard rates for independent guides are between R$45 and R$80 per day. Sunglasses, a hat, sun cream and water are all essential, as it can get very hot and several of the walks are strenuous.

For **guides** from Capão, stop in at the Associação dos Conductores de Visitantes do Vale do Capão (ⓣ75/3344-1087, ⓔacv@valedocapao.com), which has an office in the valley, signposted from the main road at a cluster of huts and a shop, before the road dips down to the main settlement. The guides can take groups to most of the usual sites in and around the parks.

# South from Salvador

The BR-101 highway is the main route to the **southern Bahian coast**, a region immortalized in the much translated and filmed novels of Jorge Amado, a native of Ilhéus. From the bus window you'll see the familiar fields of sugar replaced by huge plantations of *cacau*, cocoa. Southern Bahia produces two-thirds of Brazil's cocoa, almost all of which goes for export, making this part of Bahia the richest agricultural area of the state. The *zona de cacau* seems quiet and respectable enough today, with its pleasant towns and prosperous countryside, but in the last decades of the nineteenth century and the first decades of the twentieth, it was one of the most turbulent parts of Brazil. Entrepreneurs and adventurers from all over the country carved out estates here, often violently – a process chronicled by Amado in his novel *The Violent Lands* (see "Books", p.759).

## Ilhéus and around

In literary terms **ILHÉUS**, 400km south of Salvador, is the best-known town in Brazil and the setting for Amado's most famous novel, *Gabriela, Cravo e Canela*, translated into English as "Gabriela, Clove and Cinnamon". If you haven't heard of it before visiting Ilhéus, you soon will; it seems like every other bar, hotel and restaurant is either named after the novel or one of its characters.

### Arrival and information

The **rodoviária** (ⓣ73/3634-4121 and 3251-2200) is on Praça Cairu, a little way from the centre of Ilhéus, but buses outside marked "Centro" or "Olivença" take you into town. **Buses** to Ilhéus from Salvador take around six hours. Catch the one in the morning if you want to see the pleasant countryside en route, but you'll have to book at least a day in advance. Otherwise take one of the three night departures. There are direct buses from Ilhéus, once a week, to Rio and São Paulo, but book at least two days ahead for these. The **airport** is 4km away (ⓣ73/3234-4000), connected to town by taxi (R$20) and hourly buses. There's a **tourist information** post at the *rodoviária*, with good town maps, and an Ilhéustur office near the port at Av. Soares Lopes 1741 (Mon–Sat 9am–6pm; ⓣ73/3251-3461, ⓦwww.ilheus.com.br). **Money exchange** is available at Emcamtur, Rua Dom Pedro II 116, in downtown Ilhéus (ⓣ73/3251-6535). For **internet access** try Cybercafe.com, Rua Cel. Camara 38, Centro, or Café Oclus .com on Rua Brigadeiro Eduardo Gomes. Messias Viagens (ⓣ73/3251-1949) can arrange **city tours**, while other reliable tour operators include Agua Branca Receptivo, Rua do Bonfim, Pontal 255 (ⓣ73/3231-1424), and Costa do Sol, Av. Bahia 294, Cidade Nova (ⓣ73/3231-2788).

### Accomodation

Your best bet for **accommodation** in Ilhéus is probably on one of the beaches, although there's no shortage of places in town.

*Pousada Vitóriano* (❶) is a budget option on Praça Cairu, next to the *rodoviária*. In the centre, the *Britânia*, close to the cathedral at Rua 28 de Junho 16 (Ⓣ73/3251-1722; ❸), is one of the cheapest central hotels. For beachside accommodation, there's the *Pousada Sol e Mar*, 14km from town on the Ilhéus–Olivença road (Ⓣ73/3251-1148; ❹); frequent buses run into town. If you can afford it, one of the best places to stay is the *Pousada Aldea da Mata* (Ⓣ73/3239-6041 and 3086-2999, Ⓦwww.aldeiadamata.com.br; ❻), on the edge of the Mata Atlântica roughly halfway between Ilhéus and Itacaré; look out for the partially hidden entrance at Km 31.5 on the Ilhéus–Serra Grande road. Rooms are in bungalow-style accommodation, and amenities include a terraced bar, natural hot-spring shower and even massages; the beach here is often empty and fabulous. If you want to stay in Itacaré, try the family-run *Pousada Sol e Mar*, Rua Nova Conquista (Ⓣ73/3251-2795; ❸), which is away from the beach but has well-kept rooms, some with balconies and TV. There's also the lovely *Pousada Sitio Ilha Verde*, Rua A. Setubal 234 (Ⓣ73/3251-2056, Ⓦwww.ilhaverde.com.br; ❺), set in beautiful grounds amid mango trees, with individually decorated rooms and a pool.

### The Town

The coastline around Ilhéus is broken up by five rivers and a series of lagoons, bays and waterways. Much of the town is modern but it's still an attractive place, its heart perched on a small hill overlooking one of the largest and finest-looking beaches in Bahia.

Before you head for the sands take time to look around the town. The modern cathedral, built in the 1930s with extravagant Gothic towers and pinnacles, is a useful landmark. Nearby, the oldest church in the city, the **Igreja Matriz de São Jorge**, on Praça Rui Barbosa, finished in 1556, has a religious-art museum, while the domed roof and towers of the **Igreja de Nossa Senhora de Lourdes** dominate the shoreline nearest to the centre. Domes are rare in church architecture in Brazil, and this combination of dome and towers is unique. The **Casa da Cultura**, at Rua Jorge Amado 21, is worth half an hour for a quick tour of the city's history, including interesting exhibits on the region's chocolate industry and Ilhéus's literary tradition. The house was once the home of Amado himself.

The main leisure options in Ilhéus have changed little from Amado's time: hanging around in the **bars** and squares, and heading for the beaches. The *Vezúvio*,on Praça Dom Eduardo, is the most famous bar in Brazil; in Amado's book, the hero, Nacib, owns it, a watering hole of the cocoa planters. You pay a little extra for drinks but it's a good bar renowned for its food from Arabia. Apart from the centre, you'll find the main concentration of bars along the fine beach promenade of the Avenida Atlântica – the beach itself called simply **Avenida** – though much of it is polluted and not recommended for bathing. There are other **beaches to the north**, past the port: the first is **Isidro Ramos** (bus from the centre or Avenida), followed by **Praia do Marciano** and **Praia do Norte**.

### Olivença

Most locals prefer the coastline to the south, particularly around the village of **OLIVENÇA**, served by local buses from the centre. Half an hour out of town is the beautiful beach at **Cururupe**, where there are a series of bars, some holiday homes and groves of palm trees. The main attraction is the **Balneário**, public swimming baths built around mineral water from the Rio Tororomba. The baths complex is pleasant, with an artificial waterfall, and bar and restaurant attached.

The coast between Ilhéus and Olivença is very beautiful and you can **camp** virtually anywhere along the way.

### Itacaré

The unspoiled beaches north of Ilhéus are among the best Bahia has to offer. Frequent buses run to the busiest beach town along this stretch, **ITACARÉ**, 70km from Ilhéus, and a fishing port in its own right. The town is a haven for **water-based adventure sports**, including rafting and canoeing, which you can arrange through Papaterra (☎73/3251-2252) and Hawaii Aqui, at Rua Pedro Longo 169 (☎73/3251-3050), which is also a *pousada* and internet café. There's no shortage of cafés, restaurants and bars in town, especially at the southern end of the beach.

## Porto Seguro

The most popular destination in southern Bahia is the resort area around **PORTO SEGURO**, where Cabral "discovered" Brazil in 1500. Founded in 1526, it has some claim to being the oldest town in Brazil, and buildings still survive from that period.

In 1500 **Pedro Alvares Cabral** and his men, alerted to the presence of land by the changing colour of the sea and the appearance of land birds, finally saw a mountain on the horizon, which must have been Monte Páscoal, to the south of Porto Seguro. First landfall was made on a beach to the north of Porto Seguro; the anchorage was probably the cove where the village of Santa Cruz de Cabrália now stands. Local Indians were friendly at first, though they might have been better advised, since Cabral claimed the land for the Portuguese king, thus beginning over three centuries of colonial rule.

Porto Seguro is now about as far as you can get from pre-colonial tranquillity. It's become one of the biggest holiday resorts in Brazil, and heaves with tourists throughout the year, reaching saturation point at New Year and Carnaval. You may enjoy yourself here if your main interest is nightlife – but you've got to like crowds and not expect much peace and quiet. All the same, Porto Seguro has somehow managed to retain its reputation as a fairly classy destination.

### Arrival and information

The **rodoviária** is a little way out of town, but taxis are cheap and plentiful. Three **buses** a day make the eleven-hour journey from Salvador, but one of these is an extremely expensive *leito* service, and you should book well ahead. There are also direct **flights** (airport information ☎73/3288-1880) from Rio and Salvador. There are **tourist information** offices at the *rodoviária*, the airport, and in the centre of town at the Secretaria de Turismo, Praça Visconde de Porto Seguro, in the Casa da Lenha (☎73/3288-1390 or 3288-4124). The tour agencies Pataxó Turismo, Av. dos Navegantes 333 (☎73/3288-1256), and Taípe Viagens e Turismo, Av. 22 de Abril 1077 (☎73/3288-3127), are also helpful.

### Accommodation

**Hotel** prices in Porto Seguro vary astonishingly between high and low season: a budget hotel in November can triple in price by Christmas; remember this when considering the high-season prices we've quoted.

To be in the thick of the nightlife, try the *Pousada da Orla*, at Av. Portugal 404 (☎73/3288-2434; ❸). A couple of roads back from the riverfront, in a wooden colonial-style building, is the relatively peaceful *Hotel Terra Á Vista*, Av. Getúlio Vargas 124 (☎73/3288-2035; ❹). A hotel with some real old-fashioned character is the friendly *Pousada Oásis do Pacatá*, at Rua Marechal Deodoro 286 (☎73/3288-2221; ❹), which has a swimming pool. You'll find luxury at the *Best Western*

*Shalimar Praial*, Av. Beira Mar 1500 (☎73/3288-2001, Ⓦwww.shalimar.com.br; ❻). The clean but rather noisy **youth hostel** is at Rua Cova da Moça 729 (☎73/3288-1742; from R$25 per person), while the best-equipped **campsite** is *Camping da Gringa* (☎73/3288-2076) at the edge of town.

### The Town

The colonial area, **Cidade Alta**, is built on a bluff overlooking the town, with fine views out to sea and across the Rio Buranhém. The **Igreja da Misericórdia**, begun in 1526, is one of the two oldest churches in Brazil. The **Igreja de Nossa Senhora da Pena**, nearby, dates from 1535 and has the oldest religious icon in Brazil, a St Francis of Assisi, brought over in the first serious expedition to Brazil, in 1503. There are the ruins of a Jesuit church and chapel (dating from the 1540s) and a small, early fort; the squat and thick-walled style of the churches shows their early function as fortified strongpoints in the days Indian attacks were common. Near the ruins of the Jesuit college is the **Marca do Descobrimento**, the two-metre-high column sunk to mark Portuguese sovereignty in 1503; on one side is a crude face of Christ, almost unrecognizable now, and on the other the arms of the Portuguese Crown.

**Cidade Baixa**, below the colonial area, is where the action is. The riverside Avenida 22 de Abril and its continuation, Avenida Portugal, are a mass of bars, restaurants and hotels – so much so that Avenida Portugal changes its name at night to Passarela do Álcool, or "Alcohol Street". One stretch of road – where competing stallholders urge you to try fiendishly strong cocktails – particularly merits this name.

North of town is a string of superb beaches along the Beira Mar coast road. The nearest, **Praia Curuípe**, is 3km away and has some natural pools and reefs, as well as beachside restaurants. More popular, and just a few kilometres further away, is **Praia Itacimirim**. These beaches, and others further north (notably Mundaí and Taperapuã, both good for scuba diving), are connected to Porto Seguro by regular seafront buses.

### Eating and drinking

There are a number of **places to eat** in Porto Seguro, though more sophisticated ones, like the *Cruz de Malta*, Av. Getúlio Vargas 358 (11am–midnight), specializing in Bahian seafood, tend to be quite expensive. For good pizza and beer there's *Sambuca*, Praça dos Pataxós 216 (☎73/3288-2366). Avenida Portugal is generally the liveliest area of town for **nightlife**. The bar *Area*, at Av. Portugal 246, is usually good until midnight for drinking and a fish meal.

## South of Porto Seguro

**South of Porto Seguro** are three less-developed, more relaxed beach resorts backpacking foreigners generally prefer, though there are plenty of Brazilian tourists, too. It's a good spot for beaches and nightlife, and the resorts get quieter the further south you go.

### Arraial d'Ajuda

**ARRAIAL D'AJUDA** is the closest of the three to Porto Seguro and the easiest to get to: catch the ferry from the centre of Porto Seguro for the ten-minute journey across the Rio Buranhém. From the other side, buses climb the hill and drop you in the centre of town. Don't stay on the bus after this or you'll find yourself making a very boring round-trip. In the centre and on the roads running down the hill to the beach are a number of **places to stay**. The nicest of these, the *Pousada Marambaia*, at Alameda dos Flamboyants 116 (ⓣ73/3575-1275, ⓦwww.hotelmarambaia.com.br; ④), has clean, chalet-style rooms around a peaceful courtyard, complete with swimming pool and gently jangling cowbells. The *Hotel Pousada Buganville*, at Alameda dos Flamboyants 170 (ⓣ73/3575-1007; ④), has a friendly atmosphere, while away from the centre the *Jangada*, at Estrada do Arraial 1556 (ⓣ73/3575-1255, ⓦwww.hoteljangada.com; ④), is on the Praia de Araçaipe and has a restaurant, pool and sauna.

The **beach** is lively and can become very crowded, though the further you get from the bars and the restaurants, the easier it is to find a peaceful spot. The main problem with Arraial d'Ajuda is that it's become too popular too quickly – whatever rubbish collection there is simply can't cope with the huge amounts of litter left by tourists.

### Trancoso and Caraíva

Further south is **TRANCOSO** – still peaceful, but next in the developers' sights. You can get there either **by bus** (about five a day from Arraial d'Ajuda, taking 50min) or **on foot**. It's a beautiful walk – 12km down the beach from Arraial – but you have to ford a couple of rivers so be prepared to get wet. Again, there's no shortage of **accommodation**. *Gulab Mahal* (③), on the main square, the Quadrado, is highly recommended for its hospitality. Outside of Trancoso, the *Mata Nativa Pousada* (ⓣ73/3668-1830, ⓦwww.matanativapousada.com.br; ⑤) offers lovely accommodation in tropical gardens by a river; English, Italian and French are spoken and there are four rooms with air conditioning and private baths. On the Praia dos Nativos, the *Pousada Zen Mandir* (ⓣ73/3668-1579, ⓦwww.pousadazentrancoso.com; ⑥) offers bungalow accommodation right on the beach – all very spacious, with air conditioning and a touch of zen.

If you want to get away from civilization in this part of Bahia you have to go even further south to **CARAÍVA**, which has no electricity (apart from that provided by generators) or cars. It's time-consuming to get to, as **boats** from Porto Seguro (consult a travel agent) and Trancoso take four and two hours, respectively. Two **buses** a day also leave from Trancoso, but it's a bumpy ride, ending with a boat journey across a river. Once there, you'll find superb beaches, a few rustic places to stay, some good food and plenty of peace and quiet.

## Caravelas and around

On the banks of the Rio Caravelas, in the extreme south of Bahia, lies **CARAVELAS**, an attractive colonial town that makes an ideal farewell or introduction to Bahia. Founded in 1503, it became an important trading centre in the seventeenth and eighteenth centuries. Today both the town and its nearby beach are – despite the growth of tourism – very relaxing places. Caravelas is the jumping-off point for the **Parque Nacional Marinho dos Abrolhos**, one of the best places in Brazil to see exotic marine life, including – at certain times of year – humpback whales.

Apart from organizing your trip to Abrolhos, there isn't much to do in Caravelas, but it's an agreeable place to wander around. Most of the interest lies in the streets between the river and the *rodoviária*, which is on Praça Teófilo Otoni in the centre of town. One block to your left as you come out of the *rodoviária* is the lively Praça Quinze. Another block further on and running parallel to the river is Rua Marcílio Diaz, which becomes Rua Sete de Setembro and eventually leads to the beautiful **Praça de Santo Antônio**. This is definitely the architectural highlight of Caravelas and contains the eponymous **Igreja de Santo Antônio**, which you may – if you're lucky – find open.

## Arrival and information

To get to Caravelas, you have to go first to **Teixeira de Freitas**, further inland. Águia Branca run five **buses** a day on the four-hour journey between Porto Seguro and Teixeira de Freitas. From Teixeira de Freitas, Expresso Brasileiro operates five buses a day to Caravelas, an agreeable two-hour meander through lush tropical fields. From the south, you can get there from Minas Gerais or Espírito Santo or, if you want to miss out those two states altogether, São Geraldo run a daily *executivo* service from Rio that leaves in mid-afternoon and takes fifteen hours (R$125).

## Accommodation and eating

An excellent **place to stay** near the *rodoviária* on Praça Teófilo Otoni is the cosy *Pousada Caravelense* (Ⓣ73/3297-1182; ❷), which has friendly service and a pool table. The *Pousada Liberdade*, at Rua da Baleia 333 (Ⓣ73/3297-2076, Ⓦwww.pousadaliberdade.com; ❺) has large chalets just a few minutes by car from town. There's also accommodation **on the beach**, called Praia do Graucá or Barra de Caravelas – a half-hour journey from the *rodoviária* in Caravelas and worth a visit even if you don't stay there. The *Pousada das Sereias* (Ⓣ73/3874-1033; ❸) is the obvious choice if you're on a budget, while the *Hotel Marina Porto Abrolhos* (Ⓣ73/3674-1060, Ⓦwww.marinaportoabrolhos.com.br; ❺) offers beachside luxury, including a great pool. You'll find a number of good **restaurants** in town and on the beach at Barra de Caravelas. *Muroroa Reggae Night*, which sits on the riverbank near the Praça de Santo Antônio, serves excellent *carne do sol*.

## Parque Nacional Marinho dos Abrolhos

The main reason people visit this region of Bahia is to see the extraordinary profusion of marine and bird life in the **Parque Nacional Marinho dos Abrolhos**, an archipelago of five islands lying 52km offshore. Among the clear waters and coral reefs live all kinds of rare fish, sea turtles and birds, and between July and early November the waters are home to **whales** taking refuge from the Antarctic winter.

There are two main **tour companies** in Caravelas offering trips to Abrolhos: Abrolhos Turismo, on Praça Dr Imbassay (Ⓣ73/3297-1149), and the slightly cheaper Abrolhos Viagens, at Av. das Palmeiras 2, more or less on Praça Quinze (Ⓣ73/3297-1173). Abrolhos Turismo offers a basic day-trip to the national park in a launch, leaving at 7am and returning at 5pm, for about R$280. The same sort of trip costs about R$225 at Abrolhos Viagen, though the day is shorter, starting at 8am and returning at 4pm. In either case, you can pay extra to rent snorkels, masks and more sophisticated diving equipment. Both companies also offer longer yacht trips to Abrolhos of up to three nights.

# Travel details

### Buses

**Salvador** to: Belém (4 weekly; 35hr); Brasília (6 daily; 26hr); Cachoeira (hourly; 2hr 30min); Feira de Santana (hourly; 2hr); Fortaleza (2 daily; 24hr); Ilhéus (6 daily; 6hr 30min); Jacobina (2 daily; 6hr); Lençóis (2 daily; 6hr); Porto Seguro (4 daily; 11hr); Praia do Forte (4 daily; 2hr); Recife (6 daily; 13hr); Rio (2 daily; 30hr); Santo Amaro (every 30min; 2hr); São Paulo (2 daily; 35hr); Valença (6 daily; 5hr).

### Ferries

**Salvador** to: Itaparica (every 30min; 60min).

### Flights

Salvador is connected by at least daily flights to most major Brazilian cities, including Natal.

# The Northeast



VENEZUELA
GUYANA
SURINAME
FRENCH GUIANA
COLOMBIA
N
5
4
3
PERU
7
6
2
BOLIVIA
8
1
PARAGUAY
CHILE
9
ARGENTINA
0
1000 km
URUGUAY

CHAPTER 4

# Highlights

* **Olinda** Best visited during Carnaval, when colourful parades snake through beautifully preserved colonial streets. See p.311

* **Porto de Galinhas** One of the Northeast's most active hippy beaches, this place really comes to life during high season, when sound systems and DJs from Recife's trendiest clubs move out here. See p.315

* **Fernando de Noronha** A gorgeous archipelago visited by thousands of dolphins early each morning. See p.319

* **Northeast beaches** Quintessential tropical beaches line much of the region's coast, including the idyllic Ponta Negra near Natal. See p.337

* **Jericoacoara** With some of the finest beaches and best surf and wind in Brazil, Jericoacoara attracts great crowds of young people. See p.348

* **Reggae bands** You'll hear excellent reggae throughout the region, but especially in São Luís, the reggae capital of Brazil. See p.354

▲ Swimmers in the natural pools of Fernando de Noronha

# The Northeast



The **Northeast** is one of Brazil's poorest areas, but has perhaps the most stunning coastline in South America. Despite its thriving beach scene, the area, divided politically into eight separate states, has not been spoilt by tourism. There are major cities along the coast: some, such as Recife, Olinda, São Luís and Fortaleza, have deep colonial heritage; others, such as Maceió and Natal, have developed mostly in recent decades. All have their own city **beaches** plus more idyllic and deserted resorts hidden up and down the coast (though generally accessible by bus or taxi). The **Ilha de Fernando de Noronha**, hundreds of kilometres off the coast from Natal, is one of the finest oceanic wildlife reserves in the world, an expensive destination but idyllic for ecotourism.

The semi-arid region inland, with sparse leafy vegetation but abundant cacti, is known as the **sertão**. It suffers periods of intense drought yet in the wet season is transformed for a few glorious months to a verdant green. Few people traverse the interior, except perhaps en route to Belém at the mouth of the Amazon; but if you do visit the region, there are a number of quite isolated and windswept market towns – such as Campina Grande in Paraíba state – that are worth stopping off at. Piauí boasts more than one stunningly beautiful national park, while the coast of Maranhão is known for its reggae, blisteringly hot beaches and superb cuisine.

## Some history

By the end of the sixteenth century, sugar plantations were already importing African **slaves** to the northeast of Brazil. **Olinda** was a major colonial centre and, like Salvador, developed into a relatively large town, while Rio de Janeiro remained little more than a swampy village. The Northeast quickly became Europe's main supplier of **sugar**. The merchants and plantation owners grew rich and built mansions and churches, but their very success led to their downfall. It drew the attention of the **Dutch**, who were so impressed that they destroyed the Portuguese fleet in Salvador in 1624, burnt down Olinda six years later and occupied much of the coast, paying particular attention to sugar-growing areas. It took more than two decades of vicious guerrilla warfare before the Dutch were expelled, and even then they had the last laugh: they took their new experience of sugar growing to the West Indies, which soon began to edge Brazilian sugar out of the world market.

The Dutch invasion, and the subsequent decline of the sugar trade, proved quite a fillip to the development of the interior. With much of the coast in the hands of the invaders, the **colonization** of the *sertão* and the *agreste* – a narrow, hilly zone between the *sertão* and the coastal Mata Atlântica – was stepped up. The Indians and escaped slaves already there were joined by cattlemen (*vaqueiros*), as trails were opened up into the highlands and huge ranches carved out of the

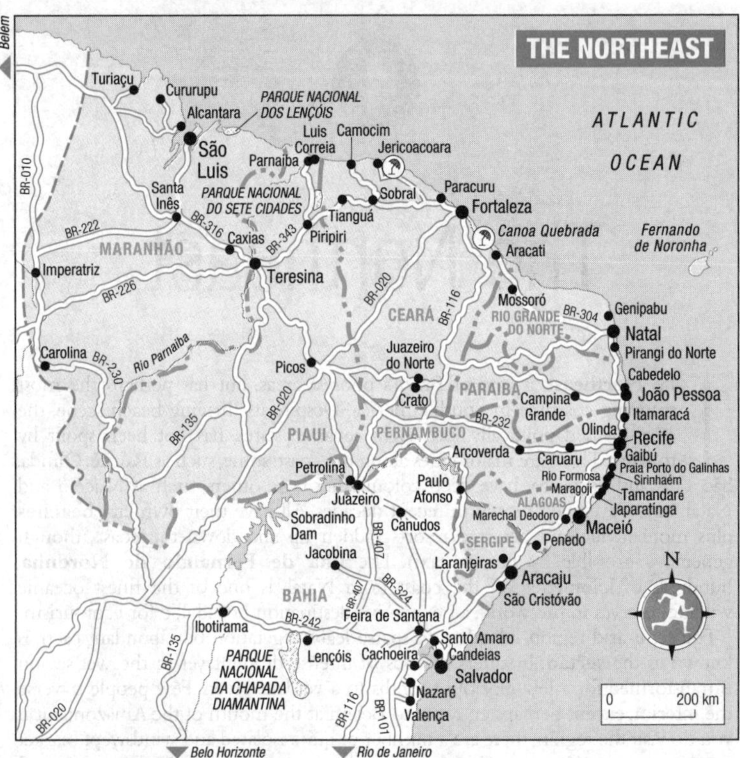


interior. Nevertheless, it took over two centuries, roughly from 1600 to 1800, before these regions were fully absorbed into the rest of Brazil. In the *agreste*, where some fruit and vegetables could be grown and cotton did well, market villages developed into towns. However, the *sertão* became, and still remains, cattle country, with an economy and society very different from the coast.

Life in the **interior** has always been hard. The landscape is dominated by cacti and dense scrub – *caatinga* – the heat is fierce, and for most of the year the countryside is parched brown. But it only requires a few drops of rain for an astonishing transformation to take place – within a few hours, the *sertão* blooms: trees bud, cacti burst into flower, shoots sprout up from the earth, and literally overnight the brown is replaced by a carpet of green. Too often, however, the rain never comes, or arrives too late, too early or in the wrong place, and the cattle begin to die. The first recorded **drought** was as early as 1710, and since then droughts have struck the *sertão* at ten- or fifteen-year intervals, sometimes lasting for years. The worst was in the early 1870s, when as many as two million people died of starvation; 1999 was also a particularly bad year. The problems caused by drought were, and still are, aggravated by the inequalities in land ownership. The fertile areas around rivers were taken over in early times by powerful cattle barons, whose descendants still dominate much of the interior. The rest of the people of the interior, pushed into less favoured areas, are regularly forced by drought to seek refuge in the coastal cities until the rains return. For centuries, periodic waves of refugees, known as *os flagelados* (the scourged ones), have poured out of the *sertão* fleeing droughts: modern Brazilian governments have been no more successful in dealing with the particular problems of the interior than the Portuguese colonizers before them.

### Regional practicalities

There are **flights** to Recife from Europe and North America, and frequent **buses** to the main northeastern cities from all parts of Brazil. From **southern and central Brazil**, buses converge upon Salvador, from where you can get to most destinations in the Northeast. **Brasília to Fortaleza** is another possible, if very long (40hr), overland route into the region. From the **Amazon**, buses from Belém run to São Luís, Teresina, Fortaleza and points east, or further south to Recife and beyond.

**Getting around** the Northeast is straightforward thanks to the region's extensive bus network. In Maranhão, the **rains** come in February, in Piauí and Ceará in March, and points east in April, and last for around three months. These are only general rules, though: Maranhão can be wet even in the dry season.

# Alagoas and Sergipe

**Alagoas** and **Sergipe** are the smallest Brazilian states. Sandwiched between Bahia to the south and Pernambuco to the north, they have traditionally been overshadowed by their neighbours and to this day still have a (not entirely fair) reputation for being something of a backwater. While it's true that there's nowhere comparable to the cosmopolitan cities of Recife or Salvador, there are the two state capitals of **Maceió** and **Aracaju**, together with some well-preserved colonial towns, and exceptional **beaches** in Alagoas, which many rate as the best in the Northeast. The harshness of the *sertão* here is much alleviated, too, by the São Francisco river valley, which forms the border between the two states.

Alagoas is very poor, as you immediately discover from the potholes in the roads and its rickety local buses, and thousands of *alagoanos* leave every year to look for work as far afield as Rio, São Paulo and Amazônia, giving the state the highest emigration rate of any in Brazil. Don't let this put you off, however; the coast is beautiful, and Maceió is a lively city, probably the best base from which to explore the neighbouring states. Sergipe was, for most of its history, in a similar position to Alagoas, but since the 1960s a minor offshore oil boom has brought some degree of affluence to parts of the coast. Brazil being what it is, this doesn't mean there's less poverty: it's simply that the rich in Aracaju tend to be richer than the rich elsewhere in the Northeast.

## Maceió

Originally founded in the seventeenth century, based around a large sugar plantation, **MACEIÓ**, the state capital of Alagoas, fronts the Atlantic Ocean with several attractive beaches; it also faces onto the Lagoa Mundaú, an inland lake accessible from the sea that offers a wide natural harbour. In the 1930s and 40s, Maceió was an elegant city of squares and houses nestling under palm trees. Today, while it is still attractive in places, the city has suffered in recent years from the attentions of planners, most notably in their wrecking of a once-famous waterfront promenade that faced the harbour and around which Maceió grew. An early nineteenth-century customs house once stood here, framed by offices and the fine houses of traders – all now gone and replaced by grimy concrete boxes.

## Arrival and information

By Brazilian standards, the **rodoviária** (Ⓣ82/3221-4615) is relatively close to the centre, though it's still well beyond walking distance for either the old town or the beach area. Buses marked "Ouro Preto" or "Serraria Mercado" connect it with the old town; to carry on to the beaches from there, take the "Ponta Verde", "Jardim Vaticano" or "Jatiúca" bus. Alternatively, a taxi direct to either the old town or the beaches will cost around R$12. The new Zumbi dos Palmares **airport** (Ⓣ82/3036-5200) is some way from the city; a taxi will set you back around R$45.

Shoals of local buses make **getting around** very simple. All routes pass through the main squares in the centre, notably Praça Deodoro and Praça Dom Pedro II, names you'll often see on route cards propped in the front windows. The Estação Ferroviária is the place to get buses for local routes south of the city, and you may use it to go to nearby Marechal Deodoro or the glorious beach of Praia do Francês.

There's a **tourist information** booth at Avenida Dr Antônio Gouveia (Mon–Fri 8am–2pm; Ⓣ82/3315-5700, 3315-1600 or 3315-1603), close to the small tourist market on the promenade of the Praia de Pajuçara, easily recognizable by the *jangada* sailboats offering trips a mile out to the reef. SEMPTUR, the Maceió tourism office, can be contacted by phone (Ⓣ82/3336-4409) for hotel and cultural events information. There are other tourist information offices at the *rodoviária* (daily 8am–11pm), the airport (until 11.30pm), and in the centre at Rua Boa Vista 453 (Mon–Fri 8am–noon & 2–6pm; Ⓣ82/3315-5700, Ⓦwww.turismo.al.gov.br). The staff are friendly and can usually provide details

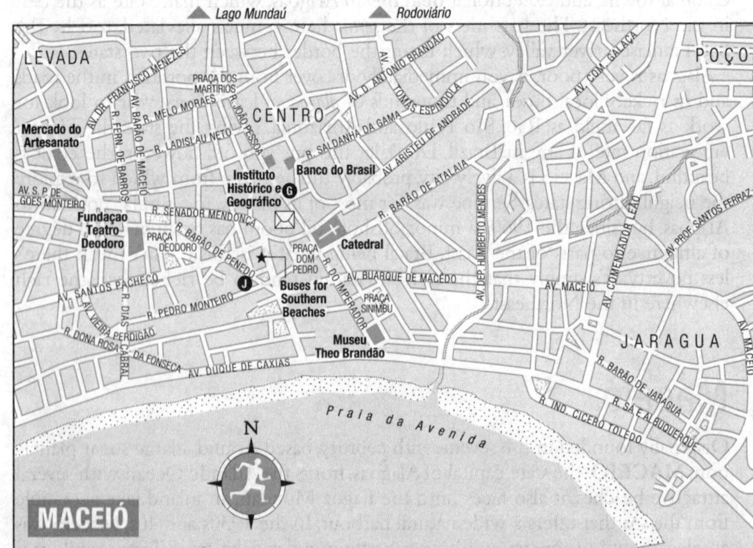

of Maceió's lively **out-of-season Carnaval** (mid-Dec) as well as maps of the city and its nearby beaches, and information on hotels and tours. If you're into diving, contact Bahia Scuba (Ⓣ71/3321-0156, Ⓦwww.bahiascuba.com.br), which sometimes operates in this area.

## Accommodation

The area around the **rodoviária** is a good bet for budget but clearly downmarket hotels. Otherwise, it's a largely one-sided choice between **Centro** and the beach districts of **Pajuçara** and **Ponta Verde**: the latter are only a short bus-ride away, and accommodation is more plentiful and of better quality. Buses there run one block in from the beach, along Avenida dos Jangadeiros Alagoanos, a road strung with a series of small hotels and *pousadas*, with more down the side streets. The beach promenade is where the luxury hotels are, and there are several good medium-priced places on Avenida Dr Antônio Gouveia, the first stretch of promenade after the centre.

**Hostal Alagamar** Rua Prof. Abdon Arroxelas 327 Ⓣ82/3231-2246, Ⓔalagamar@hostel.org.br. The local international hostel, it's located several blocks inland from the beach and offers the usual bunk-room standards from around R$25 per person. ❷

**Hotel Beiriz** Rua do Sol 290, Centro Ⓣ82/3336-6200, Ⓕ3336-6282. Clean, mid-priced hotel that's difficult to spot from the road because there's no sign; it's next to a church. ❸

**Hotel Buongiorno** Av. dos Jangadeiros Alagoanos 1437, Pajuçara Ⓣ82/3327-1530, Ⓔvapini@ig.com.br. Small, modest but attractive hotel, one block from the heart of the beach and close to most of the best restaurants. ❸

**Hotel Costamar** Rua Desportista Guimaraes 420, Ponta Verde Ⓣ82/2121-3400, Ⓦwww.hotelcostamar.com.br. A tall, thin concrete hotel with large and well-fitted rooms (though few have great views). There's a very small pool, and a decent self-service breakfast is served on the top floor, which offers excellent panoramas. ❺

**Hotel dos Palmares** Praça dos Palmares 253, Centro Ⓣ82/3223-7024. A good budget option in the city centre. Rooms are built around a courtyard, though some are a bit stuffy when it gets warm. ❷

**Hotel Pousada Dos Corais** Rua Desp. Humberto Guimaraes 80, Ponta Verde Ⓣ82/3231-9096, Ⓦwww.hotelpousadadoscorais.com.br. Very good value, but rooms – though equipped with TV, a/c,

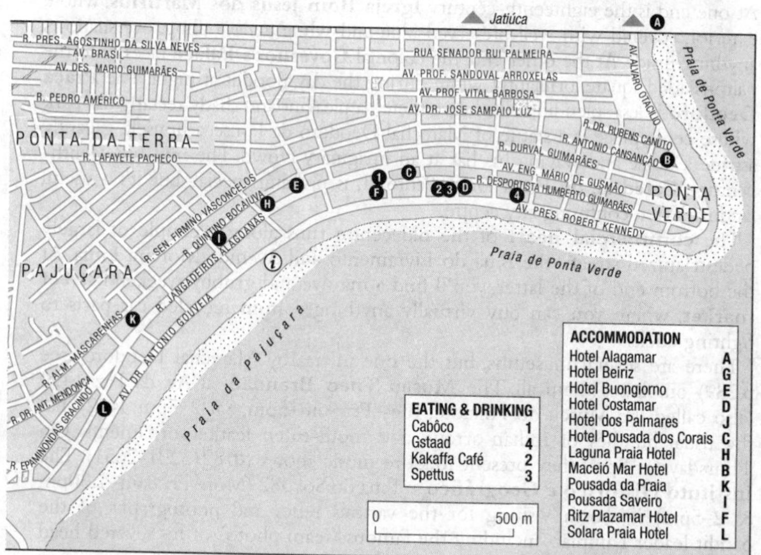

*frigobar* and private bath – are almost cell-like. Has a nice garden patio. ❸

**Laguna Praia Hotel** Av. dos Jangadeiros Alagoanas 1231, Pajuçara ⓣ82/3231-6180. More pleasant than its ugly modern exterior would suggest, with friendly staff, a/c rooms, an outstanding breakfast, parking and good discounts in the off season. ❹

**Maceió Mar Hotel** Av. Álavaro Octacílio 2991, Ponta Verde ⓣ82/2122-8000, ⓦwww.maceomarhotel.com.br. Quality hotel with very spacious and comfortable rooms, plus a bar and sauna; located close to the southern end of Praia de Ponta Verde. Offers fine views over the ocean, and is a great spot to take in December's Carnaval. ❼–❽

**Pousada da Praia** Av. dos Jangadeiros Alagoanos 545, Pajuçara ⓣ82/3231-6843. A good choice in the beach area, with reasonably cosy chalet-style rooms. You can negotiate reductions if you're staying for longer than a couple of nights. ❷–❸

**Pousada Saveiro** Av. dos Jangadeiros Alagoanos 805, Pajuçara ⓣ82/3231-9831, ⓦwww.pousadasaveiro.com.br. Very clean and friendly, this small *pousada* is one of the nicest in its range; rooms with ventilators are cheaper than those with a/c. ❸

**Ritz Plazamar Hotel** Rua Carlos Tenorio 105, Ponta Verde ⓣ82/2121-4700, ⓦwww.ritzplazamar.com.br. This big and modern place is set back a block from the beaches on a fairly quiet little square. Rooms are very comfortable and most have good views, plus there's a pool and sauna. ❹–❺

**Solara Praia Hotel** Av. Dr Antônio Gouveia 113, Pajuçara ⓣ82/3231-4371, ⓦwww.hotelsolara.com.br. Reasonable hotel close to the beach, with clean, comfortable rooms and apartments; there's a rooftop pool and terrace and service is pretty good. ❹–❺

## The City

The small **city centre** is just inland from the modest harbour, and here what remains of Maceió's past is to be found cheek by jowl with the cheap hotels and central shopping area. Quite distinct from this somewhat down-at-heel colonial heart is the modern, much larger and livelier area that starts at **Pajuçara**, a few minutes away by bus to the east, built along a spectacular beach. To the northwest, an undistinguished urban sprawl conceals the enormous lagoon of **Mundaú**. It's here that the city ends, an ideal place to watch the sunset and eat cheaply at the simple bars and restaurants that dot its banks.

The best place to get some sense of the old Maceió is **Praça dos Martírios**, the finest square in the city, and an abject lesson to those who destroyed the waterfront. At one end is the eighteenth-century **Igreja Bom Jesus dos Martírios**, whose exterior, covered with well-preserved blue-and-white *azulejo* tiling, overshadows anything inside. At the other end, the colonial **Governor's Palace** faces onto the palm-shaded square, brilliantly white during the day, floodlit at night. The **Praça Deodoro** is less splendid; at its heart, there's a pleasant and shady rectangular park whose centrepiece is a statue of Marechal Deodoro da Fonseca himself, gallantly astride a horse and waving his hat at an imaginary crowd. The mid-nineteenth-century **Catedral**, on Praça Dom Pedro II, is nothing special, but it's a useful landmark in a confusing city centre.

The **commercial heart** of the old centre runs along a couple of largely pedestrianized streets, the Rua do Livramento and Avenida Moreira Lima. At the bottom end of the latter, you'll find a massive and grubby weekend **street market**, where you can buy virtually anything – from recycled car parts to fighting cocks.

There are several museums, but the one in nearby Marechal Deodoro (see p.289) outclasses them all. The **Museu Theo Brandão**, at Av. da Paz 1490 (also called the Museu do Folclore; Tues–Fri 9am–5pm, Sat 2–5pm; R$2), has the usual bundles of Indian arrows and moth-eaten feather ornaments. On Thursdays at 8pm, they present folklore music shows (ⓣ82/3221-2651). The **Instituto Histórico e Geográfico** at Rua do Sol 382 (Mon–Fri 8am–1.30pm & 2–5pm) is worth visiting for the various relics and photographs of the bandit leader Lampião, including the famous "team photo" of his severed head

## Lampião

Lampião was born **Virgulino Ferreira da Silva** in 1897 in the northeastern state of Pernambuco. As Virgulino grew up, he and his family got involved in local feuding and they ended up on the wrong side of the law. Virgulino's father was killed in a police raid on his home, turning Virgulino, only 25 years old, into a bandit gang leader and a deadly threat to the local establishment for the next fifteen years. The **Robin Hood of Brazil** image he cultivated belies the reality of a complex, vain and brutal man. It is perhaps his boldness that made him stand out, often fighting battles when his gang was outnumbered more than three to one.

The law finally caught up with Lampião in 1938. The police detachment that shot him, his wife, Maria Bonita, and his closest lieutenants preserved their heads in alcohol so that they could be shown in market towns in the interior, the only way to convince people he really had been killed – even today, the Brazilian media occasionally publish pictures of an old man who died in 1996 and bears a striking resemblance to Lampião.

along with those of his wife and leading gang members (see box, p.287). Two other museums worth a visit if you've time on your hands are the **Fundação Teatro Deodoro** on Praça Deodoro (guided tours Mon & Tues 4–7pm; ⓣ82/3326-5252), which contains nineteenth-century furniture and fittings, and the **Museu de Arte Sacra Pierre Chalita**, Rua Loriano Peixoto 517 (Mon–Fri 8am–noon & 2–5.30pm; ⓣ82/3223-4298), which displays a number of religious paintings, statues and baroque altars.

### The beaches

The main city beach is at **Pajuçara**, whose curving road and wide mosaic promenade are studded with palm trees. The water is not always the cleanest here and many people hire *jangadas* (around R$15–20 an hour) and head 2km out to sea to swim in the natural pools that form at low tide.

The bay then curves past the yacht club into the less crowded beach of **Ponta Verde**, an easy walk from Pajuçara, with some good spots to eat – try the *Sol Maior*, which has a large palm-shaded patio and serves excellent fresh fish and crab – and wind-surfing and canoeing equipment for rent. **Diving** lessons or tours can be arranged in Ponta Verde with the Bali Hai Diving School, Av. Robert Kennedy 1473, Loja 5, Galeria 7, Coqueiros (ⓣ82/3327-3535).

Ponta Verde and the neighbouring beach of Jatiúca are the beginning of a series of fine sands to the north of Maceió. The best way to get to them is to take buses marked "Mirante" or "Fátima" from the centre, which take you along the coast as far as **Pratagi** (also called Mirante da Sereia), 13km north, where there are coral pools in the reef at low tide. You can get off the bus anywhere that takes your fancy; the main beaches, in order of appearance, are **Cruz das Almas**, **Jacarecica**, **Guaxuma**, **Garça Torta** and **Riacho Doce**, all of them less crowded than the city beaches during the week, but very popular at weekends.

Most visitors to Maceió flood north to the beaches, which leaves the coast **to the south** in relative calm, though the crowds are now beginning to make their way here, too. Hourly buses marked "Deodoro" leave from the bus stop in front of the old train station, near the harbour, passing out of the city over the Trapiche bridge into a flat, swampy coastline. Sixteen kilometres south, the road swings left to **Praia do Francês**, which even by Alagoan standards is something special. An enormous expanse of white sand, surf and thick palm forest, it even boasts a couple of small hotels; the *Hotel Cumarú* (ⓣ82/3260-1110 ③) is the best. Further afield, the large fishing village of **BARRA DE SANTO ANTÔNIO** is a popular day-trip 40km north of Maceió. Barra, which also fills up on the weekends, has a fine beach on a narrow neck of land jutting out from the coast a short canoe ride away, and good, fresh seafood is served in the cluster of small beachside hotels. The village is a stop for some Recife–Maceió interstate buses. Some 140km north of Maceió, just 15km before the border with Pernambuco state, the beautiful but sleepy beachside settlement of **MARAGOGI** has a handful of upmarket accommodation: the superb *Hotel Salinas*, Rodoviária AL101, Km124 (Ⓣ81/3296-3000 or 3296-1122, Ⓦwww.salinas.com.br; ⑦–⑨), a luxury hotel with every conceivable facility set on Maragogi beach; and the *Praia dos Sonhos*, Rodoviária AL101, Km124 (Ⓣ81/3222-4598; ⑥), on Peroba beach. If you're passing by on the road between Recife and Maceió, it's well worth stopping off here to try the local shrimps. An even more laid-back fishing and resort settlement, **JAPARATINGA**, can be found, some 40km south of Maragogi, back towards Maceió; close to here at São Bento there is accommodation with an excellent beachside restaurant, *Marazul* (Ⓣ82/3296-7228; ⑤).

## Eating, drinking and nightlife

Some of the best places to **eat and drink** in Maceió are out of the centre, at Mundaú lagoon and Pajuçara beach. From Praça dos Martírios you can take a taxi, or a local bus marked "Mundaú" or "Ponta da Barra", for the short ride to **Lagoa Mundaú**, where you can have a *caipirinha* at a waterfront bar to accompany the routinely spectacular sunset. There are simple but excellent eating places here, too, selling fish and shrimp (a town speciality), and the early evening is a good time to watch prawn fishermen at work on punts in the lagoon, their silhouetted figures throwing out nets against the sunset.

At **Pajuçara**, you'll find a series of **bars** built around thatched emplacements – *barracas* – at intervals along the beach. They mix excellent *caipirinhas* and serve cheaper food than you're likely to find in the seafront restaurants on the other side of the road. Seafood is, naturally, best: the *sopa de ostra* manages to get more oysters into a single dish than most gringos see in a lifetime; they're so common, you can even get an oyster omelette. There are one or two **cafés** in the old town centre, but more are located on the beachfront, which is also lined with *barracas* at regular intervals.

For **nightlife**, the area around Rua Sá de Albuquerque (in the Jaraguá sector) is a newly fashionable part of the city that's especially lively from Thursday to Saturday, when the main street is closed off to traffic and the bars and restaurants put their tables outside. The liveliest of Maceió's two main clubs is here, at Rua Sá de Albuquerque 588: the cavernous *Aeroporco's* (Thurs–Sat; Ⓣ82/3326-5145) has Brazilian DJs, lots of samba and a sushi bar. *Aquarela*, at Antônio Gomes de Barros 66, in Jatiúca, also has a large dancefloor, as well as reasonably good live bands playing mainly *pagode* and *forró*, and some touristy dance shows. The Fundação Teatro Deodoro on Praça Deodoro sometimes presents spectacular dance performances; check the cultural listings in the *Tribuna de Alagoas* newspaper or call Ⓣ82/3327-2727 for information.

There are a number of **gay and lesbian clubs** in Maceió, notably *Blackout* and *Heaven*, both in the Rio Uruguay sector, while *Bar Sensensura* on Rua Sá de Albuquerque has great *pagode* nights on Sundays. Stella Maris is another trendy area of town for nightlife, gay or straight.

### Restaurants

**Cabôco's** On the corner of Rua Eng. Mario de Gusmão and Rua Carlos Tenorio, just behind the *Ritz Plazamar Hotel*, Ponta Verde. Probably the best place for inexpensive lunches and *comida por kilo* self-service.

**Creperia Flor das Aguas** Av. Alvaro Otacilio 3309, Ponta Verde ☎82/3231-2335. Specializes in good waffles and, of course, crepes. Mon–Fri noon–11pm, Sat & Sun 4–11pm.
**Gstaad** Av. Roberto Kennedy (also known as Av. Carlos Luna Viana) 2167. Slightly more expensive than average, this sophisticated French restaurant is well known for its salmon dishes.
**Restaurante Carlito** Barraca 32, on the beach at Ponta Verde ☎82/3231-4029. Tasty Italian food and good service (including home or hotel delivery for pizzas).
**Restaurante Japones** Rua Senador Rui Palmeira 46, ☎82/3337-0253. Reputed to be the best Japanese restaurant in town, offering a variety of dishes including sushi.
**Spettus** Av. Roberto Kennedy (also known as Av. Carlos Luna Viana) 1911, Ponta Verde ☎82/3327-4714. This small chain offers the best steaks and *rodizios*, but they're not cheap. Daily 11.30am until late; there's another branch at Av. Alvaro Otacilio 3309.
**Sushi Bar New Hakata** Rua Eng. Paulo Brandao Nogueira 95 ☎82/3325-6160. Located in the Stella Maris suburb, this is a cheaper, but quite stylish Japanese option.

## Listings

**Airlines** TAM, Rua Epaminodas Gracindo 92, Pajuçara ☎82/3327-6400 or at airport ☎82/3214-4114 or 3214-4112; Gol Ⓦwww.voegol.com.br.
**Banks and exchange** Banco do Brasil and HSBC are both on the first block of Rua do Livramento, close to the corner with Rua Boa Vista.
**Car rental** Comercial Locadora, Rua Zeferino Rodrigues 100, Pajuçara ☎82/3327-9145; Turisauto, Antônio Cansanção 575, Loja 108, Ponta Verde ☎3033-5748.
**Internet** Many hotels and *pousadas* now offer internet. Failing that, at Ponta Verde there's a small internet café (without food or drink, however) on the second floor of the Pavilão do Artesanato shopping centre; and *Cafeconet*, Rua Emp. Carlos da Silva Nogueira 192, Loja C, in Jatiúca. *Emporio Jaragua Cybercafe*, Rua Sá de Albuquerque 378, in Jaraguá, has good food and coffee.
**Post office** The post office is at Rua João Pessoa 57 in the centre near the Asamblea building, with a branch in Shopping Centro de Artesanato Jaraguá, Rua Sá da Albuquerque 417.
**Shopping** The Pavilão do Artesanato, just over the road from Ponta Verde's beachside tourist information centre, is stuffed with local crafts such as filigree-lace bedspreads, Irish-lace tablecloths or other pieces with unusual colours and geometric or floral designs. The city's other main craft centre is the cheaper and more rustic Mercado do Artesanato, with shell ornaments, ceramics and wooden objects and utensils, located at Rua Melo Moraes 617.
**Taxis** Tele Taxi ☎82/3320-3232; Liga Taxi ☎82/3326-2121.
**Travel and tour companies** Marcão Turismo, Rua Firmino de Vasconcelos 685, Pajuçara (☎82/3327-7711, Ⓦwww.maceioturismo.com.br), offer city tours, trips to the Lagoa Mundaú and the southern and northern beaches, and excursions as far afield as Recife and Olinda. Transamerica Turismo, Av. Dr Antonio Gouveia 487 (☎82/3231-7334), run daily trips to Lagoa Mundaú and other beauty spots. For diving, contact ScuBrasil at Rua Mexihão 12, Corais do Francês, in nearby Marechal Deodoro (☎82/3260-1417).

# Marechal Deodoro

The beautifully preserved colonial town of **MARECHAL DEODORO** lies 22km south of Maceió. It's no more than a small market town, built on rising ground on the banks of a lagoon, with streets that are either dirt or cobbled, but it's immaculately kept, with not a single building that looks as if it were constructed this century. Nor is it simply preserved for tourists to gawp at: the locals spit in the streets, gossip and hang about in bars as they would anywhere else, and there's a real air of small-town tranquillity.

The bus from Maceió terminates at the end of town. You should get off a little earlier, in the manicured **Praça Pedro Paulinho**, which is dominated by the imposing facade of the Igreja de Santa Maria Magdalena, with the older **Convento de São Francisco**, finished in 1684, attached. The convent's plain exterior conceals an austere yet strikingly beautiful interior, which is now turned over to the excellent **Museu de Arte Sagrada** (Mon & Wed–Sat 9am–5pm; entrance is from the road running down towards the lake from Praça Pedro Paulinho). The convent is built around a cool courtyard, with the main galleries on the first storey. Everything on display is high Catholic religious art, with little concession made to the tropical setting save for the large number of portrayals of São Benedito, the black patron saint of the slaves who manned the *engenhos* (sugar mills) all around and built most of Marechal Deodoro itself. The highlight of the collection, extracted from churches all over the state, is the group of seventeenth- to nineteenth-century statues of saints and virgins, in the first gallery to the right. Most are no more than a foot high, made of wood or plaster, and intricately painted. Look, too, for the couple of life-size (and frighteningly lifelike) carved wooden bodies of Christ, with gruesome wounds. In comparison, the **Igreja de Santa Maria Magdalena** is not as impressive, a typical mid-eighteenth-century building, though less cloyingly Rococo than most. In front of a small side-chapel, opposite the entrance from the museum, is a concealed entrance to a secret tunnel, a relic from the original chapel that stood on the site during the Dutch wars.

Down the road curving to the right past the museum is the modest house that was the birthplace of **Marechal Deodoro**, proclaimer and first president of the Republic in 1889; it's now preserved as a **museum** (Rua Mal. Deodoro 92; Mon–Sat 8am–5pm). Deodoro, the son of an army officer, served with distinction in the Paraguayan War, and rose to become head of the armed forces with the sonorous title "Generalissimo of the Forces of Land and Sea". He was the first Brazilian to mount a military coup, unceremoniously dumping the harmless old emperor Dom Pedro II, but he proved an arrogant and inept president, the first in a depressingly long line of incompetent military authoritarians. Dissolving Congress and declaring a state of siege in 1891, he did everyone a favour by resigning when he couldn't make it stick. There's no hint, of course, of his disastrous political career in the museum, which is basically a mildly interesting collection of personal effects and period furniture.

In the streets around you'll find several **lace makers**, with goods displayed in the windows. Marechal Deodoro is famous for its lace, which you see in any sizeable market in the Northeast. It's high-quality stuff, and costs less than half the price you'll pay elsewhere when bought at source in the town. The Cooperative Artesanal in Rua Dr Ladislam Netto is a good place to look.

If you want to stay, there's a **pensão**, *Deodoré*, on Praça Pedro Paulinho (❶), but there's no sign so you'll have to ask. There's also a **campsite** (Ⓣ82/3263-1378), clean and with good facilities, half an hour's walk beyond the square; the road is marked by a sign near the small bus-company office.

# Paulo Afonso and around

Inland from Maceió, 300km to the west, the most popular destination in Alagoas is the **Cachoeira de Paulo Afonso**, once the largest waterfall on the Rio São Francisco and the third largest in Brazil, but now largely emasculated by a hydroelectric scheme that diverted most of the flow – a spectacular piece of ecological vandalism surpassed only by the destruction of the even more impressive Sete Quedas waterfall in Paraná by similar means in the early 1990s. These days, the only time a considerable amount of water passes over the falls is during the rains of January and February, but the whole surrounding area – a spectacular deep rocky gorge choked with tropical forest and declared a national park – is very scenic all year round.

You can get there by bus from Salvador, but the journey from Maceió is shorter, with two **buses** daily from its *rodoviária*. They leave you in the small river town of **PAULO AFONSO**, on the Bahian riverbank, where there is a cluster of reasonable **hotels** near the bus station; the *Belvedere*, Av. Apolônio Sales 457 (ⓣ75/3281-1814, ⓦwww.hotelbelvederepa.com.br; ④), is more upmarket than the others, but good value with a reasonable restaurant and a swimming pool.

The **waterfall** itself is some way out of town, accessible only by taxi (R$15 per hr), but the drivers do know the best spots. Alternatively, you may be able to organize something with the **tourist office** in the centre of town on Rua Apolônio Sales (Mon–Sat 9am–6pm; ⓣ75/3281-2757), which doubles up as the best place to find local guides.

## Penedo

A couple of hours, and some 168km, south of Maceió is the lively colonial town of **PENEDO**. Originally developed to control the illegal exportation of lumber by French merchant ships in the sixteenth century, it was occupied by the Dutch between 1637 and 1645, who built the original fort here. There are several colonial churches in town that are all marked on a useful map, obtainable at the **tourist office** in the main central square, the Praça Barão de Penedo (Mon–Fri 8–11am & 2–5pm; ⓣ82/3551-2727). The most attractive is the early eighteenth-century *azulejo*-decorated **Igreja de Nossa Senhora da Corrente** (closed Mon), which has a stunning gold-leaf altar inside. The **museum** in the Casa do Penedo, Rua João Pessoa 126 (Mon–Sat 9am–noon & 2–4pm; R$3), is also worth a visit for its displays of period furniture and historical photographs and documents.

Penedo is strategically placed at the mouth of the Rio São Francisco, and while the trading prosperity it might have expected as a result never quite materialized, it's still a busy little place, much of whose life revolves around the river and the waterfront. The waterfront park, with its shaded paths and kiosks selling drinks, is a good place to watch the to-ing and fro-ing of the boats. You can negotiate with boat owners to go on **cruises**: the main destinations are **Piassabussu**, a sleepy and little-visited fishing village right on the mouth of the river, and the village of **Neópolis**, opposite Penedo, where there's nothing to do except have a drink and catch the boat back – but it's a nice trip.

Penedo is served by four **buses** daily from Maceió's *rodoviária*, and for once they leave you in the centre of the town, which is well supplied with good **places to stay**: try *Pousada Colonial*, Praça 12 de Abril (ⓣ82/3551-2355; ③), which has adequate rooms and an okay restaurant plus excellent views over Penedo, or the more comfortable *São Francisco*, at Av. Floriano Peixoto 237 (ⓣ823/3551-2273, ⓦwww.hotelsaofrancisco.tur.br; ③–④) with a nice pool, both in the heart of town; nearer the **rodoviária** (ⓣ82/3551-2602) on Rua Siqueira Campos, are a number of budget hotels with prices starting at around R$30. One of the town's better **restaurants** is *Forte da Rocheira* on the seafront at Rua da Rocheira 2 (ⓣ82/3551-3273), specializing in fish dishes. Out of town, 30km east of Penedo near the town of Piaçabuçu, the *Pousada Piaçabuçu* (ⓣ82/3557-1112, ⓔroeland@sidtecnet.com.br) offers ecological tours of the surrounding countryside.

# Aracaju

From Maceió, seven buses a day run to **ARACAJU**, capital of the neighbouring state of **Sergipe**, a little-visited and rather unexceptional place. Although the Portuguese founded a colony at Aracaju in 1592, the capital of the infant state was later moved to nearby São Cristóvão. Then, in the mid-nineteenth century, there was a sudden vogue for purpose-built administrative centres (similar to the urge that led to the construction of Brasília a century later), and the core of modern Aracaju was thrown up overnight, with the city becoming the state capital again in 1855. Aracaju is – to put it mildly – something of an architectural desert, built on an American-style grid layout. Oil wealth has stimulated a lot of recent building and given the city council enough money to keep everything clean and tidy, but there is a very un-Brazilian dullness about the place. However, some of the beaches are passable and the charming colonial towns of Laranjeiras and São Cristóvão are only a short bus-ride away.

The new **rodoviária** (⊕79/3238-2900) is quite a way out of town, linked to the centre by frequent local buses; the old *rodoviária* (Terminal Velha; ⊕79/3214-2578), which serves mainly local destinations, is five blocks north of Praça Olímpia Campos. The **airport** (⊕79/3212-8500) is also out of town (12km); buses marked "Aeroporto" will get you into the centre. Sergipe's **tourist office** (⊕79/3214-1940; Mon–Sat 8am–6pm) has its headquarters at Tr. Baltazar Gois 86, in the centre, while the SEBRAE office is at the Centro de Turismo (daily 8am–8pm; ⊕79/3214-8848), in the shopping centre known as Rua 24 Horas, just next to Praça Olímpio Campos. Rua 24 Horas is actually a very pleasant place, set in a restored nineteenth-century building, with cafés, restaurants and a stage where shows are sometimes put on.

The cheaper **hotels** are as usual in the city centre, several of them near the municipal bus station, the Rodoviária Terminal Velha. For a real budget option, you could stay at the *Sergipe Hotel*, Rua Geru 205 (⊕79/3222-7898; ❷), which is perfectly adequate for the price. One comfortable mid-range hotel in the same area is the *Amado*, at Rua Laranjeiras 532 (⊕79/3211-9937; ❸).

The two main **beaches** are Atalaia Velha and Atalaia Nova. **Atalaia Velha** lies about 5km south down the road from the city centre and is the more developed of the two. It's easy to get there by bus, but the whole area is rather soulless and uninspiring. There are, however, a huge number of restaurants and **hotels**, including the *Nascimento Praia*, Av. Santos Dumont 1813 (⊕79/3255-2090; ❹), which has a small pool, and, for total luxury, the *Del Mar Hotel*, Av. Santos Dumont 1500 (⊕79/2106-9100, Ⓦwww.delmarhotel.com.br; ❼). **Atalaia Nova** lies on an island in the Rio Sergipe, accessible by boat from the *hidroviária* in the city centre (every 10min; R$1.50); you can then get a bus to Atalaia Nova from the ferry terminal. Although the beach itself isn't great, the island is a pleasant place to stay – hotels are expensive, but there are plenty of rooms for rent.

# Laranjeiras and São Cristóvão

Sergipe's main attractions are two pretty colonial towns that come as a welcome relief from Aracaju's anonymity, reminders of the time when sugar made the *sergipano* coast one of the most strategically valuable parts of Brazil. Innumerable skirmishes were fought around them during the Dutch wars, but no trace of their turbulent past survives into their tranquil present, as they slide from important market centres into rural backwaters.

Dominated by a hill crowned with the ruins of an old *engenho* chapel, the pleasantly decrepit village of **LARANJEIRAS** boasts a couple of small museums as well as the inevitable churches. The interesting **Museu Afro-Brasileiro**, Rua José do Prado Franco 70 (Tues–Sun 10am–5pm; R$2), concentrates on slave life and popular religion, while the **Centro de Cultura João Ribeiro**, Rua João Ribeiro (Mon–Fri 8am–10pm, Sat 8am–1pm, Sun 2–5pm), is mostly given over to *artesanato* and relics of plantation life. The main attraction, however, is simply wandering the winding streets, taking in the quiet squares, pastel-painted houses and small bars where locals sit around and watch the world go by. There are a couple of **pensões**, but no hotels as yet.

The other colonial town worth visiting is the old state capital of **SÃO CRISTÓVÃO**. The town was founded in 1590 and much of it hasn't changed since, as the shifting of the capital to Aracaju preserved it from the developers. Packed into its small area is the full panoply of a colonial administrative centre, including an old governor's palace, a parliament building and half a dozen period churches, together with the small **Museu de Arte Sacra e Histórico** in the Convento de São Francisco (Tues–Sun 9am–noon & 2–5.30pm). The convent contains a chapel decorated with paintings by José Teófilo de Jesus, one of the most important sacred painters from the Northeast.

**Buses** run to Laranjeiras (half-hourly; 40min) and São Cristóvão (hourly; 30min) from Aracaju's Terminal Velha.

# Pernambuco

**Recife**, capital of the state of **Pernambuco**, shares with São Luis the distinction of not having been founded by the Portuguese: when they arrived in the 1530s, they settled just to the north, building the beautiful colonial town of **Olinda** and turning most of the surrounding land over to sugar. A century later, the Dutch, under Maurice of Nassau, burned Olinda down, choosing to build a new capital, Recife, on swampy land to the south, where there was the fine natural harbour that Olinda had lacked. The Dutch, playing to their strengths, drained and reclaimed the low-lying land, and the main evidence of the Dutch presence today is not so much their few surviving churches and forts dotted up and down the coast, as the very land on which the core of Recife is built. The Portuguese first developed the coastline as far **north of Recife** as the island of **Itamaracá**, growing sugar cane on every available inch. This erstwhile fishing village still retains its Dutch fort, built to protect the new colonial power's acquisitions, but these days it's a fairly blighted weekenders' resort. Best is the **coastal route south**, where a succession of small towns and villages interrupts a glorious stretch of palm-fringed beach.

Head **inland** and the scenery changes quickly to the hot, dry and rocky landscape of the *sertão*. **Caruaru** is the obvious target, home of the largest market in the Northeast, and close by is **Alto do Moura**, centre of the highly rated Pernambucan pottery industry. If you plan to go any further inland than this, you'll need to prepare well for any kind of extended *sertão* journey, though it's straightforward enough to reach the twin river-towns of **Petrolina** and **Juazeiro**.

# Recife

The Northeast's second-largest city, **RECIFE** appears shabby and dull on first impressions, but it's lent a colonial grace and elegance by Olinda, just 6km north. Recife itself has long since burst its original colonial boundaries, and much of the centre is now given over to uninspired office blocks. But there are still a few quiet squares where an inordinate number of impressive **churches** lie cheek by jowl with the uglier urban sprawl of the past thirty years. North of the centre are some pleasant leafy suburbs, dotted with museums and parks, and to the south is the modern beachside district of **Boa Viagem**. Other beaches lie within easy reach, and there's also all the **nightlife** you'd expect from a city of nearly two million Brazilians.

## Arrival and information

The **airport** (☎81/3322-4188) is fairly close to the city centre, at the far end of Boa Viagem. A taxi to Boa Viagem itself shouldn't be more than R$25, to the neighbouring island of Santo Antônio about R$35; or take the Aeroporto bus (R$6) from right outside, which will drive through Boa Viagem and drop you in the centre. The **rodoviária** is miles out, though this is not really a problem since the **metrô** (☎81/3252-6100 for information), an overground rail link, whisks you very cheaply and efficiently into the centre, giving you a good introduction to city life as it glides through various *favelas*. It will deposit you at the old train station, called **Estação Central** (or simply "Recife"). To get to your hotel from there, you're best off taking a **taxi** – Recife is a confusing city even when you've been there a few days, and the extra money will be well spent.

The most helpful **tourist information** is the large office at the airport (daily 8am–6pm; ☎81/3462-4960), where you may find English-speaking staff and a few maps and calendars of events. They'll also ring hotels for you, but are no good for the cheapest places. There's another good little office on the corner of Praça da Independência at the end of Rua da Guia in the heart of the newly restored **Bairro do Recife** (☎81/3224-2361). In **Boa Viagem**, there's a Delegacia do Turista at Praça do Boa Viagem (8am–8pm; ☎81/3463-3621), which can help with accommodation at the beach. Alternatively, there's the **tourist hotline** (Mon–Fri 8am–6pm; ☎81/3332-8409), on which you should be able to find someone who speaks English.

For up-to-date **listings** of events in and around Recife, try the *Roteiro* section of the daily *Jornal do Comércio*, or the *Viver* section of the *Diário de Pernambuco*, also daily. Alternatively, the *Agenda Cultural do Recife* is a useful guide to museums and theatre, plus dance, music and photography events, and is available from the Casa da Cultura (see p.300) or online at Ⓦwww.recife.pe.gov.br.

## City transport

Recife's **bus network** (☎81/3452-1103) is a mess, with routes changing frequently, confusing "destination" markers on the fronts of buses, and, unlike in Rio or Salvador, no helpful signs on the side of the vehicle showing where it stops along the way. What follows is a basic guide to getting around, but you'll probably still have to ask.

Most city buses originate and terminate on the central island of **Santo Antônio**, on Avenida Dantas Barreto, either side of the **Pracinha do Diário** (also known as Praça da Independência). There are more stops nearby on Avenida

Recife is one of **Brazil's most violent cities**, an unsurprising statistic given the immediately obvious disparity of wealth and stark poverty, and the large number of homeless people on the streets. Violent muggings are common: be particularly careful with your possessions, and it's best, too, to use taxis to get home after an evening out.

Guararapes outside the main post office. To get from the city centre **to Boa Viagem**, take buses marked "Aeroporto", "Iguatemi" or "Boa Viagem", or catch the more comfortable *frescão* (an a/c bus) marked "Aeroporto", just outside the offices of the newspaper *Diário de Pernambuco*, on the Pracinha do Diário (every 20min; R$6). To get **to Olinda** from central Recife, walk south down Avenida Dantas Barreto from the Pracinha do Diário to the last of the series of bus stops, and catch the bus marked "Casa Caiada" – you'll think you're heading in the wrong direction at first, but, after half an hour or so, you'll eventually get there. Alternatively, a taxi from central Recife to Olinda will cost a few dollars and take about fifteen minutes.

**From Boa Viagem**, most buses in either direction can be caught on Avenida Engenheiro Domingos Ferreira, three blocks in from the sea. Buses marked "Dantas Barreto" will get you **to the city centre**, and so should most of those marked "Conde de Boa Vista", though it's probably best to ask. You can get directly from Boa Viagem **to Olinda** on buses marked "Rio Doce".

## Accommodation

**Hotels** are cheapest in the rather run-down centre where most Brazilian business travellers stay, and most expensive in the beach district of Boa Viagem. An obvious area to consider staying in is Olinda (see p.308), where prices fall somewhere between the two and although there's not much of a beach, it has a lot more to offer culturally. Recife's **youth hostels** are both in Boa Viagem: the *Hostel Boa Viagem*, Rua Aviador Severiano Lins 455 (Ⓣ81/3326-9572, Ⓦwww.hostleboaviagem.com.br; ❶–❸), is a good six blocks from the main beachfront but is based in a very pleasant building set in gardens with shared or independent rooms plus a small pool; the *Albergue da Juventude Maracatus do Recife*, at Rua Maria Carolina 185 (Ⓣ81/3326-1964; ❸), also has a swimming pool. Dorm beds are R$25 at both hostels.

### The centre: Boa Vista and Santo Antônio

Apart from the *Mercure Apartments*, most central hotels are concentrated around Rua do Hospício, near the bridges linking Boa Vista and Santo Antônio.

**Hotel America** Praça Maciel Pinheiro 48, Boa Vista Ⓣ81/3221-1300. Two-star hotel that's not as expensive as it looks; rooms are a bit run down but adequate and safe. ❸

**Hotel Central** Av. Manoel Borba 209, Boa Vista Ⓣ81/3423-6411. As its name suggests, this hotel has a focal location on one of Recife's quieter and more elegant streets. Does a superb breakfast. ❹

**Hotel Quatro de Outubro** Rua Floriano Peixoto 141, Santo Antônio Ⓣ81/3224-4900. Close to Recife's main *metrô* station, the hotel is run down but reasonable value; all rooms have a/c and TV. ❹

**Hotel São Domingos** Praça Maciel Pinheiro 66, Boa Vista Ⓣ81/3231-1388. Clean and modern two-star hotel just a few blocks from the beach; quite comfortable, but a little lacking in style. All rooms have private baths. ❸

**Mercure Apartments Metropolis** Rua Estado de Israel 203, Ilha do leite Ⓣ81/3087-3700, Ⓦwww.accorhotels.com.br. Located centrally, this is the only fairly luxurious hotel in Recife; it offers a pool, sauna and restaurant facilities, though most apartments also have their own kitchen. ❺

**Recife Plaza** Rua da Aurora 225, Boa Vista Ⓣ81/3231-1200. Nondescript place close to the central river bridge, the Ponte do Coelho. Rooms are reasonable, with a/c and TV, and there's a restaurant, sauna and swimming pool. ❹

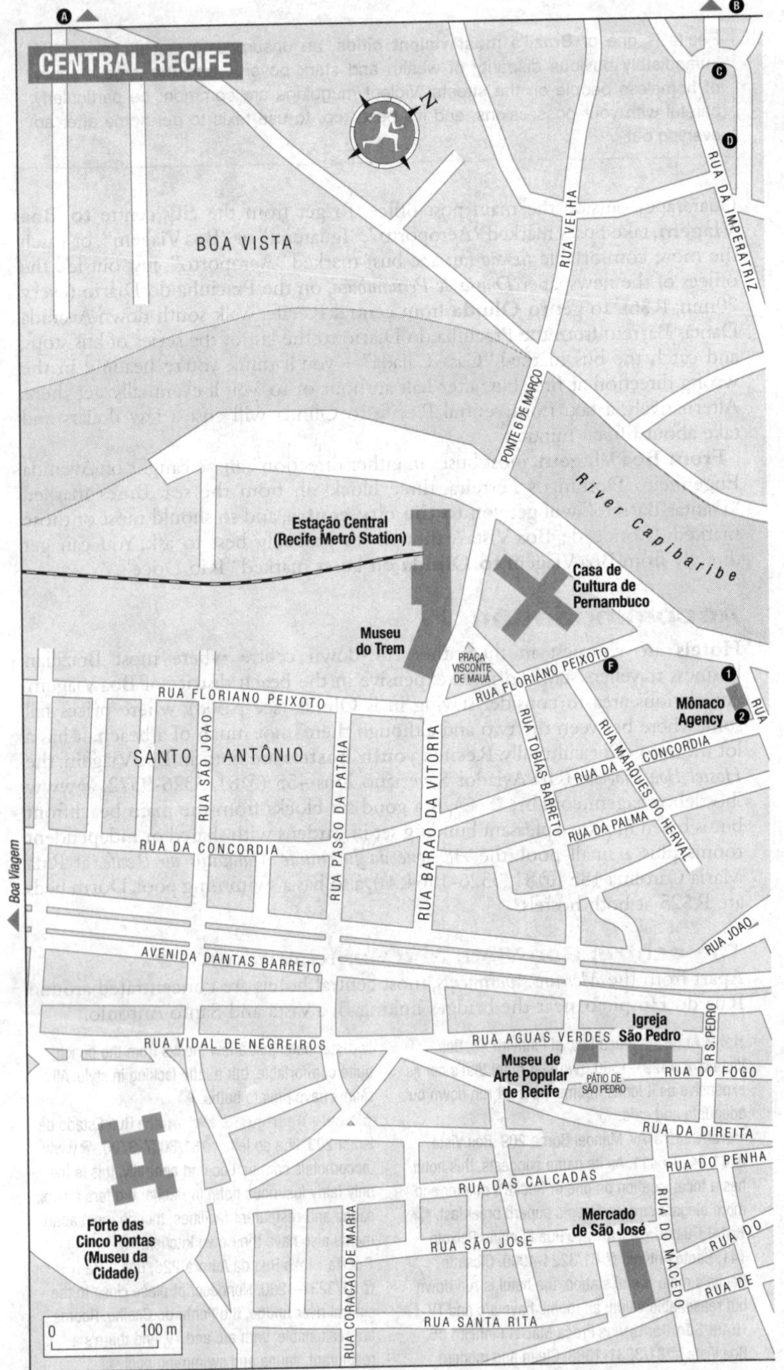
CENTRAL RECIFE
BOA VISTA
RUA VELHA
RUA DA IMPERATRIZ
PONTE 6 DE MARÇO
River Capibaribe
Estação Central
(Recife Metrô Station)
Casa de
Cultura de
Pernambuco
Museu
do Trem
PRAÇA
VISCONTE
DE MAUA
RUA FLORIANO PEIXOTO
Mônaco
Agency
SANTO ANTÔNIO
RUA SÃO JOAO
RUA PASSO DA PATRIA
RUA BARAO DA VITORIA
RUA TOBIAS BARRETO
RUA MARQUES DO HERVAL
RUA DA CONCORDIA
RUA DA PALMA
Boa Viagem
RUA JOAO
AVENIDA DANTAS BARRETO
RUA VIDAL DE NEGREIROS
RUA AGUAS VERDES
Igreja
São Pedro
R.S. PEDRO
Museu de
Arte Popular
de Recife
PÁTIO DE
SÃO PEDRO
RUA DO FOGO
RUA DA DIREITA
RUA DO PENHA
RUA DAS CALCADAS
Forte das
Cinco Pontas
(Museu da
Cidade)
Mercado
de São José
RUA DO MACEDO
RUA SÃO JOSE
RUA CORACAO DE MARIA
RUA SANTA RITA
0
100 m

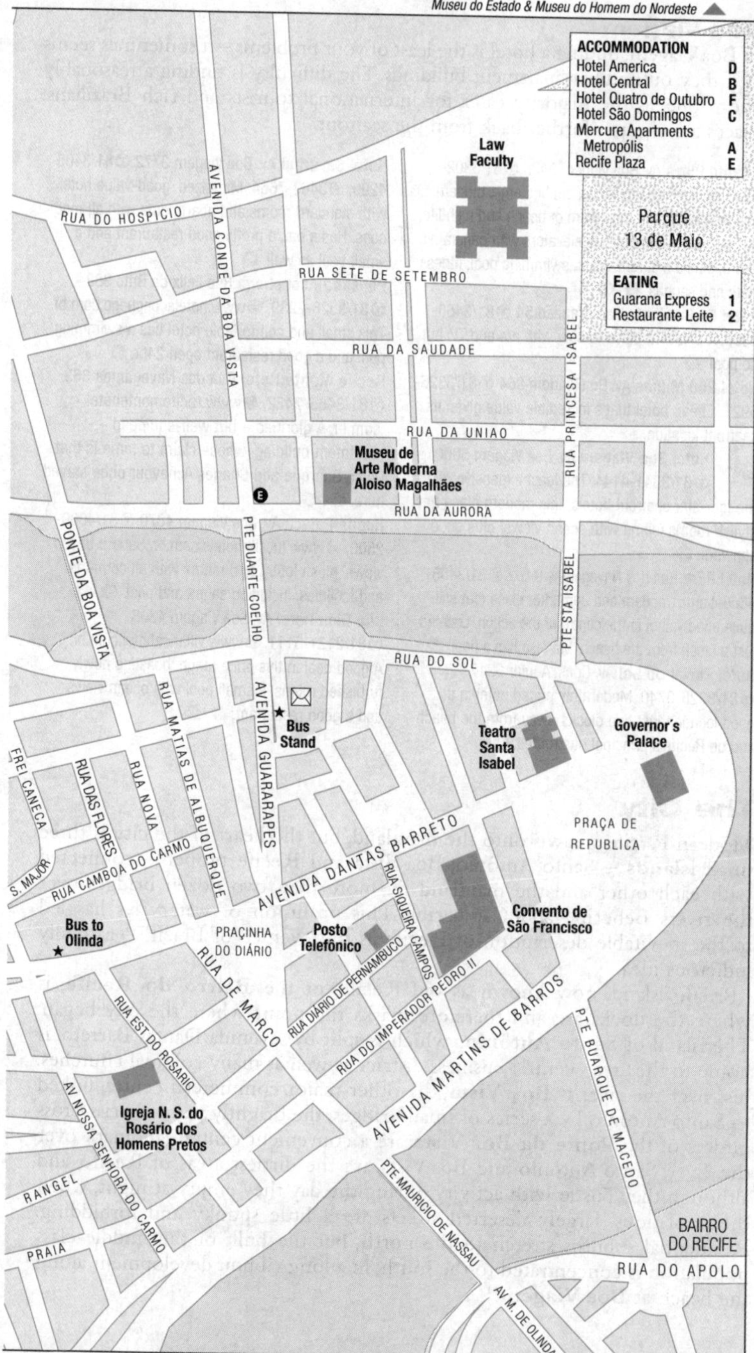
Museu do Estado & Museu do Homem do Nordeste
ACCOMMODATION
Hotel America D
Hotel Central B
Hotel Quatro de Outubro F
Hotel São Domingos C
Mercure Apartments Metropólis A
Recife Plaza E
EATING
Guarana Express 1
Restaurante Leite 2
Law Faculty
Parque 13 de Maio
RUA DO HOSPICIO
AVENIDA CONDE DA BOA VISTA
RUA SETE DE SETEMBRO
RUA DA SAUDADE
RUA PRINCESA ISABEL
RUA DA UNIAO
Museu de Arte Moderna Aloiso Magalhães
RUA DA AURORA
PONTE DA BOA VISTA
PTE DUARTE COELHO
PTE STA ISABEL
RUA DO SOL
AVENIDA GUARARAPES
Bus Stand
Teatro Santa Isabel
Governor's Palace
FREI CANECA
RUA DAS FLORES
RUA NOVA
RUA MATIAS DE ALBUQUERQUE
PRAÇA DE REPUBLICA
AVENIDA DANTAS BARRETO
RUA SIQUEIRA CAMPOS
S. MAJOR
RUA CAMBOA DO CARMO
Convento de São Francisco
Bus to Olinda
PRAÇINHA DO DIÁRIO
Posto Telefônico
RUA DE MARCO
RUA DIÁRIO DE PERNAMBUCO
RUA DO IMPERADOR PEDRO II
AVENIDA MARTINS DE BARROS
PTE BUARQUE DE MACEDO
RUA EST DO ROSARIO
Igreja N. S. do Rosário dos Homens Pretos
AV NOSSA SENHORA DO CARMO
RANGEL
PRAIA
PTE MAURICIO DE NASSAU
BAIRRO DO RECIFE
RUA DO APOLO
AV M. DE OLINDA

## Boa Viagem

In Boa Viagem, finding a hotel is the least of your problems – it sometimes seems as if they outnumber apartment buildings. The difficulty is finding a reasonably cheap one, as the majority cater for international tourists and rich Brazilians. Places are cheaper further back from the seafront.

**Atlante Plaza** Av. Boa Viagem 5426 ⓣ81/3302-3333, ⓦwww.atlanteplaza.com.br. Large, modern and well located in the centre of beach and nightlife, this upmarket hotel boasts elevators with panoramic views, plus a bar, restaurant, swimming pool, fitness suite and saunas. ⑦–⑧

**Hotel 54** Rua Prof. José Brandão 54 ⓣ81/3465-2396. A pleasant place to stay with a/c and TV, but no pool. ③

**Hotel 200 Milhas** Av. Boa Viagem 864 ⓣ81/3326-5921. Cheap hotel that's incredible value given its seafront location. ③

**Hotel Boa Viagem** Av. Boa Viagem 5000 ⓣ81/3341-4144. The least expensive of all the four-star seafront hotels, this modern place has stylish rooms (some with ocean views) plus good showers. ⑥

**Hotel Park** Rua dos Navegantes 9 ⓣ&ⓕ81/3465-4666. Large, modern and upmarket place (but still quite good value) in the centre of the action. Located just a block from the beach, but also has a pool. ④

**Hotel Portal do Sol** Av. Cons. Aguiar 3217 ⓣ81/3326-9740. Moderately priced hotel in a good location just two blocks away from the beach and on Recife's principal bus routes. ④

**Hotel Savaroni** Av. Boa Viagem 3772 ⓣ81/3465-4299, ⓕ3463-7664. Mid-sized, good-value hotel with standard rooms and apartments with all mod cons. Has a bar, a pretty good restaurant and a small pool as well. ⑦

**Pousada Aconchego** Rua Felix de Brito 382 ⓣ81/3326-2989, ⓦwww.hotelaconchego.com.br. This small and comfortable hotel has a swimming pool and a good restaurant open 24hr. ④

**Recife Monte Hotel** Rua dos Navegantes 363 ⓣ81/3465-7422, ⓦwww.recifemontehotel.com.br. A glorified – but well-equipped – apartment building, whose claim to fame is that Chico Buarque and Charles Aznavour once stayed here. ⑤–⑥

**Recife Palace** Av. Boa Viagem 4070 ⓣ81/4009-2500, ⓦwww.lucsimhoteis.com.br. Superb beach views, plush lobby, and rooms with all comforts and facilities, including sauna and pool. ⑧–⑨

**Vila Rica Hotel** Av. Boa Viagem 4308 ⓣ81/2121-5111, ⓦwww.villaricahotel.com.br. A good deal in this price range, boasting newly furbished rooms, a small pool with ocean views and a good restaurant. ⑤–⑥

# The City

Modern Recife sprawls onto the mainland, but the heart of the city is three small **islands** – Santo Antônio, Boa Vista and Recife proper – connected with each other and the mainland by more than two dozen bridges over the rivers Beberibe and Capibaribe. This profusion of waterways has led to the inevitable description of Recife as the "Venice of Brazil" – a totally ludicrous idea.

Recife island, now known as old Recife, or the **Bairro do Recife**, is where the docks are and therefore marks the point where the city began. The island of **Santo Antônio**, which is split by Avenida Dantas Barreto, is home to the area's central business district as well as many colonial churches. Just over the river is **Boa Vista**, the other major commercial centre, linked to Santo Antônio by a series of small bridges; the brightly painted criss-cross girders of the **Ponte da Boa Vista** are a convenient central landmark over the river. Santo Antônio and Boa Vista are the dirtiest areas of Recife, and although they bustle with activity during the day they empty at night, when the enormous, largely deserted streets are a little spooky and forbidding. Residential suburbs stretch to the north, but the bulk of the middle-class population is concentrated to the south, in a long ribbon development along the beach at **Boa Viagem**.

## Avenida Dantas Barreto and the Convento de São Francisco

The broad **Avenida Dantas Barreto** forms the spine of the central island of Santo Antônio. In southern Brazil, avenues like this are lined with skyscrapers, but whilst some have sprouted in Recife's financial district, generally the centre is on a human scale, with crowded, narrow lanes lined with stalls and shops opening out directly onto the streets. Dantas Barreto, the main thoroughfare, ends in the fine **Praça da República**, lined with majestic palms and surrounded by Recife's grandest public buildings – the governor's palace (not open to visitors) and an ornate theatre. One of the charms of the city, though, is the unpredictability of the streets, and even off this main boulevard you'll stumble upon old churches sandwiched between modern buildings, the cool hush inside a refuge from the noise and bustle beyond.

Perhaps the most enticing of the central buildings is the seventeenth-century Franciscan complex known as the **Santo Antônio do Convento de São Francisco**, on Rua do Imperador Pedro II – a combination of church, convent and museum. Outside, you'll be besieged by crowds of beggars, but negotiate your way through to the entrance of the museum (Mon–Fri 8–11.30am & 2–5pm, Sat 2–5pm; nominal fee) and you'll find yourself in a cool and quiet haven. Built around a beautiful small cloister, the museum contains some delicately painted statues of saints and other artwork rescued from demolished or crumbling local churches. The real highlight here, however, is the **Capela Dourada** (Golden Chapel), which has a lot in common with the churches in the old gold-towns of Minas Gerais. Like them, it's a rather vulgar demonstration of colonial prosperity. Finished in 1697, the Baroque chapel has the usual wall-to-ceiling ornamentation, except that everything is covered with gold leaf. If you look closely at the carving under the gilt, you'll see that the level of workmanship is actually quite crude, but the overall effect of so much gold is undeniably impressive. What really gilded the chapel, of course, was sugar cane: the sugar trade was at its peak when it was built, and the sugar elite were building monuments to their wealth all over the city.

## Igreja São Pedro and the Museu da Cidade

The **Igreja São Pedro** (Mon–Fri 8am–noon) is situated on the Pátio de São Pedro, just off the Avenida Dantas Barreto. The highly ornate facade is dominated by a statue of St Peter, donated to the church in 1980 by a master sculptor from the ceramics centre of Tracunhaém in the interior. Inside, there's some exquisite woodcarving and a trompe l'oeil ceiling, and on another corner of the *pátio* is

### Arts and crafts in Recife

Recife is probably the best big Brazilian city in which to find **artesanato**, and the area around Igreja São Pedro is the best place to look for it. Here, stalls coagulate into a bustling complex of winding streets, lined with beautiful but dilapidated early nineteenth-century tenements. The streets are choked with people and goods, all of which converge on the market proper, the **Mercado de São José**, an excellent place for *artesanato* (craft goods). If you can't face the crowds, there's a very good **craft shop**, Penha, on the corner of the Pátio de São Pedro, which is the main city outlet for some of Recife's excellent woodcut artists. In the same shop, you'll also find extremely inexpensive prints on both cloth and paper, known as **cordel**. Outside the shop, you can dig out *cordel* around the *mercado* or in Praça de Sebo, where the secondhand booksellers have stalls.

the **Museu de Arte Popular de Recife** (Mon–Fri 9am–7pm), which has some interesting exhibits, including pottery and wooden sculpture. If you've missed the church's opening hours, content yourself with the exterior views, best seen with a cold beer in hand from one of the several bars that set up tables in the square outside. The whole of the *pátio* has, in fact, been beautifully restored, which lends this part of the city a charm of its own.

Determined culture vultures could make the hop from here to Recife's most central museum, the **Museu da Cidade** (Mon–Sat 9am–6pm, Sun 1–5pm), in the star-shaped fort, the Forte das Cinco Pontas, off the western end of Avenida Dantas Barreto; the best view of it is coming in by bus from Boa Viagem. Built in 1630 by the Dutch, the fort was the last place they surrendered when they were expelled in 1654. The building is actually far more interesting than the museum itself, which is dedicated entirely to the history of the city, shown through old engravings and photographs.



### Estação Central and the Museu de Arte Moderna Aloísio Magalhães

Right opposite the Estação Central, now known as the Terminal Integrado do Recife (because it combines a bus station with the railway station), in Rua Floriano Peixoto, the forbidding **Casa da Cultura de Pernambuco** (Mon–Sat 9am–7pm, Sun 10am–5pm) was once the city's prison and is now an essential stop for visitors. It's cunningly designed, with three wings radiating out from a central point, so that a single warder could keep an eye on all nine corridors. The whole complex has been turned into an arts and crafts centre, the cells converted into little boutiques and one or two places for refreshment. The quality of the goods on offer here is high, but so, too, are the prices, so go to look rather than to buy. The Casa da Cultura is also the best place to get **information** on cultural events in the city, providing a monthly *Agenda Cultural* listing plays, films and other entertainments; dancing displays are often laid on, too, which are free and not at all bad.

Over in the Estação Central itself, on the busy little Praça Visconde de Mauá, the **Museu do Trem** (Mon–Sat 10am–6pm, Sun 2–6pm) is worth a look, tracing the history of the railways which played a vital role in opening up the interior of the Northeast. British visitors can get all nostalgic over the exploits of the Great Western Railway of Brazil Limited, some of whose engines and wagons decorate the forecourt between the museum and the *metrô* terminal. The fine station, lovingly restored in 1997, is a relic of the days when British companies dominated the Brazilian economy.

The **Museu de Arte Moderna Aloísio Magalhães**, located in Boa Vista just over the river at Rua da Aurora 256 (Tues–Sun noon–6pm), has prestigious changing exhibitions of mainly Brazilian modern artists, many amongst Pernambuco's best.

### Museu do Homem do Nordeste and Museu do Estado

The **Museu do Homem do Nordeste** (Mon–Fri 9am–5pm, Sat & Sun 1–5pm; ⓣ81/3441-5500), assembled by anthropologists, is one of Brazil's great museums and the best introduction there is to the history and culture of the Northeast. It's split into several galleries, each devoted to one of the great themes of Northeastern economy and society: sugar, cattle, fishing, popular religion, festivals, ceramics and so on. The museum's strongest point is its unrivalled collection of **popular art** – there are displays not just of handicrafts, but also of cigarette packets, tobacco pouches and, best of all, a superb collection of postwar bottles of *cachaça*. It's quite a way out of central Recife, in Casa Forte at Av. 17 de Agosto 2223. Take the "Dois Irmãos" bus from outside the post office or from Parque 13 de Maio, at the bottom of Rua do Hospício; there are two "Dois Irmãos" services, but the one marked "via Barbosa" is the one to get, a pleasant half-hour drive through leafy northern suburbs. The museum is not very easy to spot (on the left-hand side), so ask the driver or conductor where to get off.

The "Dois Irmãos via Barbosa" bus is also the one to take for the **Museu do Estado** (Tues–Fri 10am–5pm, Sat & Sun 2–5pm; ⓣ81/3427-9322), a fine nineteenth-century mansion at Av. Rui Barbosa 660, in Graças. It's on the right-hand side about twenty minutes after leaving the city centre, well before the Museu do Homem do Nordeste, but again difficult to spot, so you might need to ask. Here you'll find some fine engravings of Recife as it was in the early part of the last century, all of them by English artists, and upstairs there are good paintings by Teles Júnior, which give you an idea of what tropical Turners might have looked like. On the last Sunday of the month, there's also a busy little antiques fair held at the museum.

## Barrio de Recife

Until only a few years ago, the **Bairro do Recife** was a dangerous, run-down area inhabited mainly by drunks and prostitutes, but the investment of millions of dollars by the local authorities and private businesses have brought about something of a transformation in both the look and feel of the area. The brightly painted colonial buildings make the small, easily negotiable island a pleasant place to wander during the day, even though there aren't many specific things to do. The streets and *praças* are stocked with bars and cafés, which are very busy at weekends, but the main attraction is the ambience of the old-city heart around Rua da Guia and Rua do Bom Jesus.

A fascinating visit can be made to the newly restored **Sinagoga Kahal Zur Israel** also known as the **Centro Cultural Judaico** (Tues–Fri 9am–5pm, Sun 3–7pm; ⓣ81/3224-2128 or 3225-0068, ⓦwww.recife.info/centro-cultural-judaico.html) at Rua do Bom Jesus 197 (the old Rua dos Judeus). This was the first synagogue built in the whole of the Americas; it dates back to 1637 and today is the Judaic Centre for Pernambuco state, with permanent exhibitions covering the settling of Jews in the city. The walls display original seventeenth-century moulds, and upstairs you can see the well-restored and quite special synagogue itself.

The **Museu Militar** on Praça Comunidade Luso-Brasileira (Tues–Fri 9am–5pm, Sat & Sun 10am–4pm), housed in the seventeeth-century **Forte do Brum** at the northern end of the *bairro*, displays weapons, photographs, World War II artefacts and some local ethnographic pieces, but is only really of interest to military enthusiasts. The fort, a prominent, white-walled four-pointed structure, also puts on occasional modern-art exhibitions – check for details in the monthly *Agenda Cultural do Recife*.

## Instituto Ricardo Brennand

If you have the time, try and round off your sightseeing with the bizarre **Instituto Ricardo Brennand** (Tues–Sun 10am–5pm; ⓣ81/3271-1544, ⓦwww.institutoricardobrennand.org.br; R$5), an industrial estate in the northern suburbs styled after a castle (complete with working drawbridge) – there can't be anywhere more impressively offbeat in the whole of Brazil. One of three brothers who inherited a huge tile, ceramic and brickwork factory, Brennand became a very strange kind of tycoon. Although already rich beyond the dreams of avarice, he was driven to become an internationally famous ceramic artist. His factory estate, far from being an industrial wasteland, nestles in the middle of the only part of the old coastal forest (the Mata Atlântica) still surviving in the metropolitan area. It's a very beautiful piece of land, and it's sobering to think that without it, nothing at all would remain to show what the coast around Recife looked like before the arrival of the Europeans.

Past rows of workers' cottages and a brickworks, you come to the *oficina*, an enormous personal gallery containing thousands of Brennand's sculptures, decorated tiles, paintings and drawings. A lot of the work is good, and has strong erotic overtones – to say that genitals are a recurring theme is putting it mildly. Nearby, you'll find the most important collection of arms in Brazil inside the **Castle Museum**, which also has beautiful tapestries, sculpture, stained-glass windows and other curiosities from the sixteenth and seventeenth centuries.

It's a long way out, a taxi from Santo Antônio will set you back around R$30 and if you don't want to walk back you'll have to arrange for it to pick you up again, because no taxis pass anywhere near. Alternatively, take the bus marked "CDU–Várzea" from outside the post office to its terminus: once there you can either take a taxi or walk – it's not far (about 10min) but you'll need to ask the way. Make sure you stress the second syllable of "Brennand", or nobody will know what you're talking about.



## Boa Viagem

Regular buses make it easy to get down to **Boa Viagem** and the beach, an enormous skyscraper-lined arc of sand that constitutes the longest stretch of urbanized seafront in Brazil. As you'd expect of a city of islands, Recife was once studded with beaches, but they were swallowed up by industrial development, leaving only Boa Viagem within the city's limits – though there are others a short distance away to the north and south. In the seventeenth century, Boa Viagem's name was Ilha Cheiro Dinheiro, or "Smell Money Island" – as if whoever named it knew it would become the most expensive piece of real estate in the Northeast.

▲ Boa Viagem's buzzing beach

Much of Boa Viagem is only three or four blocks deep, so it's easy to find your way around. Take your bearings from one of the three main roads: the seafront **Avenida Boa Viagem**, with its posh hotels and a typically Brazilian promenade of palm trees and mosaic pavements; the broad Avenida Conselheiro Aguiar two blocks up; and Avenida Engenheiro Domingos Ferreira, one block up from the latter.

The **beach** itself is longer and (claim the locals) better even than Copacabana, with warm natural rock pools to wallow in just offshore when the tide is out. It's also rather narrow, however, and more dominated by the concrete culture around it than most in the Northeast. It gets very crowded at the weekends, but weekdays are relatively relaxed. There's a constant flow of people selling fresh coconut milk, iced beers, ready-mixed *batidas*, pineapples, shrimp, ice cream, straw hats and the like.

The heart of the action emanates from **Praça Boa Viagem**. Close to here are some of the liveliest restaurants and *choparias* (bars with draught beer and serving snacks and full meals), and at weekends there's a thriving and colourful food and craft fair in the *praça*, busiest on Sunday evenings. The usual **cautions** apply about not taking valuables to the beach or leaving things unattended while you swim. There have also been a small number of shark attacks over the years, but they have almost always involved surfers far from shore.

## Eating

The cheapest **places to eat** are the food sellers and *suco* stalls clogging the streets of **Santo Antônio**, with the usual selection of iced fruit juices (a favourite local drink is *caldo de cana*, the juice pressed from sugar cane), kebabs, cakes, sandwiches and sweet and savoury pastries. The area also has many cheap *lanchonetes* and restaurants, although as their clientele is mainly workers they tend to close in the early evening. The Bairro do Recife has plenty of restaurants, and you may want to eat there as a prelude to going on to a bar or a nightclub, but prices are relatively high and the emphasis on sophistication rather than traditional Brazilian cooking. In **Boa Viagem**, the best value is to be found at the seafood places on the promenade near the city-centre end of the beach, and in the dining rooms of the cheaper hotels, all of which are open to non-residents.

**Recifense** cuisine revolves around **fish** and **shellfish** – try *carangueijo mole*, crabs cooked in a spicy sauce until shells and legs are soft and edible, which solves the problem of digging out the meat; small crabs called *guaiamum*; and *agulhas fritas* (fried needle-fish).

### Cafés and restaurants

**Buon Gustaio** Av. Domingos Ferreira 3980, Boa Viagem. Does superb Italian food and great wines. Open until late daily, except Sundays when it shuts around 5pm.

**Gambrinus** Rua Marquês de Olinda 263, Bairro do Recife. One of the places in town where you can get some satisfying local dishes; the fish is particularly good.

**Guarana Express** Rua Frei Caneca 179, Santo Antônio. A juice café in the busy commercial area, specializing in invigorating *guaraná* drink mixes.

**O Vegetal** Av. Guararapes 210, Santo Antônio. Inexpensive lunchtime-only vegetarian restaurant. Also branches at Av. Dantas Barreto 507 and on Rua do Brum in the Bairro do Recife.

**Ponte Nova** Rua Bruno Veloso 528, Boa Viagem ☎81/3327-7226. Good Fusion restaurant, whose chef specializes in Franco-Brasilian-, Italian- and Thai-influenced creations.

**Restaurante Leite** Praça Joaquim Nabuco 147, Santo Antônio ☎81/3224-7977. Classy place serving tasty local dishes in a very stylish nineteenth-century interior.

**Sabor Antigo** Rua Vigario Tenorio 213, Bairro do Recife ☎81/3224-7321. Lunchtime regional dishes featuring chicken, steaks and seafood. Mon–Fri 11am–2.30pm.

**Soho** Av. Cons. Aguiar 1275, Boa Viagem ☎81/3325-2666. Trendy Japanese–Brazilian culinary fusion with good service and wines.

## Drinking

Most of the city-centre **bars** are in the **Bairro do Recife**, with the scene at its noisiest in and around Praça do Arsenal: Rua do Apolo's bars include places such as *Armazém da Cerveja* ("Beer Warehouse") and *Arsenal da Praça Chopp* ("Beer Arsenal"), which gives you some idea of the spirit of the place. *A Casa da Rock*, Rua Vigario Tenonrio 105, is popular and busy on weekend evenings; and there's the ritzy *Espaço Antonio Maria* on Bon Jesus 163.

The liveliest area in **Boa Viagem** is around Praça de Boa Viagem (quite a long way down the beach from the city centre, near the junction of Avenida Boa Viagem and Rua Bavão de Souza Leão); the *Lapinha* bar and restaurant is a popular meeting place, as is the *Caktos* bar, Av. Conselheiro Aguiar 2328.

Quieter and classier is the northern suburb of **Casa Forte**. Be sure to check out *Agua de Beber*, a gem of a bar at Praça de Casa Forte 661: situated in a large house with an expensive restaurant upstairs, it also has a leafy courtyard in which you can sit and drink soothing *caipirinhas*.

## Nightlife

As elsewhere in Brazil, **nightlife** in Recife starts late, after 10pm. The variety of music and dance is enormous, and the city has its own frenetic Carnaval music, the **frevo**, as well as **forró**, which you hear all over the Northeast. The dancing to *forró* can be really something, couples swivelling around the dancefloors with ball bearings for ankles. In the past couple of years, the Bairro do Recife has become the most happening place in the city centre – to get an idea of how seriously young *recifenses* take enjoying themselves, check out the *Moritzstad* club in Rua do Apolo, which frequently holds live concerts of the Mangue Beat bands, one of Pernambuco's modern musical movements.

For a taste of regional music of all types, it's worth trying out an **espaço cultural** or two. The *Espaço Nodaloshi*, at Estrada dos Remédios 1891 in Madalena (☎81/3228-3511), frequently brings together large numbers of musicians from all over Pernambuco, generally starting the shows around 10pm or later. The Espaço Cultural Alberto Cunha Melo, at Rua Leila Félix Karan 15 in Bongi (☎81/3228-6846), also runs live-music shows. These and other similar places generally promote their programmes through the *Agenda Cultural* (see p.294).

### Dancing

If you're looking to lay down a few steps, you need to head for a **casa de forró**; the best time to go is around midnight on a Friday or Saturday. In all of them you can drink and eat fairly cheaply, too. They often have rules about only letting in couples, but these are very haphazardly enforced, especially for foreigners. There's a small entry fee, usually around R$15 and you may be given a coupon as you go in for the waiters to mark down what you have – don't lose it or you'll have to pay a fine when you leave. Taxis back are rarely a problem, even in the small hours. Two good *casas de forró* are the *Belo Mar* on Avenida Bernardo Vieira de Melo, in Candeias, and the *Casa de Festejo* on Praça do Derby in the *bairro* of

### Gay Recife

*Banana República*, Rua Francisco Pesoa de Melo 260, in Candeias, and *Anjo Solto*, Rua Herculano Bandeira 513, Galeria Joanna, in D'Arc-Pina are the most popular **gay bars**, while the best-known **clubs** are *CATS*, Rua do Brum 85, in Bairro do Recife, *Butterfly*, Rua Raul Azedo 165 and *Cyborg 2000*, Av. Real de Torre 1013, Madalena.

## Carnaval

Carnaval in Recife is overshadowed by the one in Olinda, but the city affair is still worth sampling. The best place for **Carnaval information** is the tourist office, which publishes a free broadsheet with timetables and route details of all the Carnaval groups. You can also get a timetable in a free supplement to the *Diário de Pernambuco* newspaper on the Saturday of Carnaval, but it's only a very approximate guide.

The *blocos*, or **Carnaval groups**, come in all shapes and sizes: the most famous is the Galo da Madrugada; the most common are the *frevo* groups (trucks called *freviocas*, with an electric *frevo* band aboard, circulate around the centre, whipping up already frantic crowds); but most visually arresting are *caboclinhos*, who wear modern Brazilian interpetations of a traditional Amazon Indian costume – feathers, animal-tooth necklaces – and carry bows and arrows, which they use to beat out the rhythm as they dance. It's also worth trying to see a *maracatu* group, unique to Pernambuco: they're mainly black, and wear bright costumes, the music an interesting (and danceable) hybrid of African percussion and Latin brass.

In Recife, the **main events** are concentrated in Santo Antônio and Boa Vista. There are also things going on in Boa Viagem, in the area around the *Recife Palace Lucsim Hotel* on Avenida Boa Viagem, but it's too middle-class for its own good and is far inferior to what's on offer elsewhere. Carnaval officially begins with a trumpet fanfare welcoming Rei Momo, the Carnaval king and queen, on Avenida Guararapes at midnight on Friday, the cue for wild celebrations. At night, activities centre on the grand-stands on Avenida Dantas Barreto, where the *blocos* parade under the critical eyes of the judges; the other central area to head for is the Pátio de São Pedro. During the day, the *blocos* follow a **route** of sorts: beginning in Praça Manuel Pinheiro, and then via Rua do Hospício, Avenida Conde de Boa Vista, Avenida Guararapes, Praça da República and Avenida Dantas Barreto, to Pátio de São Pedro. Good places to hang around are near churches, especially Rosário dos Pretos, on Largo do Rosário, a special target for *maracatu* groups. The balconies of the *Hotel do Parque* are a good perch, too, if you can manage to get up there. Daylight hours is the best time to see the *blocos* – when the crowds are smaller and there are far more children around. At night, it's far more intense and the usual safety warnings apply.

Torre. Otherwise, look in local papers or ask at one of the many useful tourist information offices (see p.294) for details, as there are dozens of others. One place that mixes *forró* with samba is the lively *Cavalo Dourado* (Fri & Sat only), at Rua Carlos Gomes 390, in the *bairro* of Prado. More Westernized, but still good, is *Over Point Dancing* at Rua das Graças 261 in Graças.

The Bairro do Recife has a good share of **nightclubs**, though the emphasis is on Western dance music rather than *forró*, at places including *Planeta Maluco* on Rua do Apolo. The *Depois Dancing Bar*, at Av. Rio Branco 66 (8pm–late), is a nightclub with live music from Wednesday to Saturday and a reasonable restaurant. The best nights in the docks district, however, are Thursdays between October and March, when a large area along Avenida Marquês de Olinda is given over to hours of live music and open-air dancing, called – appropriately enough – **Dançando na Rua** ("Dancing in the Street").

## Listings

**Airlines** Aerolíneas Argentinas, Av. Mn. Borba 324 ⓣ81/3423-4188; Air France, Rua Sete de Setembro 42, Boa Vista ⓣ81/3231-7735; Air Portugal, Av. Conselheiro de Aguiar 1472 ⓣ81/3465-8800; Gol, Av. Conselheiro de Aguiar 456 ⓣ81/3464-4440; TAM, Praça Min. Salgado ⓣ81/3462-4466; Transbrasil, Av. Conde de Boa Vista 1546 ⓣ81/3423-2566; United Airlines, Rua Progresso 465 ⓣ81/3423-2444.

**Banks and exchange** Most banks have ATMs. The Banco do Brasil has branches at the airport (daily 10am–9pm), at Av. Dantas Barreto 541, at Av. Rio Branco 240 (4th floor), and on Rua Sete de Setembro in Boa Vista, all charging commission. Shopping centres all have ATMs, banks and money changing facilities that stay open until 9pm Monday to Saturday. The Bradesco bank on Conde de Boa Vista has an ATM that accepts most Visa cards. Don't at any time change money with people who approach you on the street.
**Car rental** Avis ⓣ81/3462-5069; Hertz, at airport ⓣ81/3800-8900.
**Consulates** UK, Av. Eng. Domingos Ferreira 4150, Boa Viagem (Mon–Fri 8–11.30am, Tues & Thurs also 2–4.30pm; ⓣ81/3325-0247); US, Rua Gonçalves Maia 163, Boa Vista (Mon–Fri 8am–5pm; ⓣ81/3421-2441).
**Internet** At Shopping Boavista, close to the Av. da Boa Vista, and Shopping Center Recife at junction of Rua Bruno Veloso and Rua Visc. De Jequitinhonha in Boa Viagem.
**Music shops** Disco 7, Rua Sete de Setembro, Boa Vista, is small, but the best record shop for Brazilian music in the Northeast (ⓣ81/3222-5932).
**Post office** The main post office is the Correio building on Av. Guararapes in Santo Antônio (Mon–Fri 9am–5pm). There's also a branch in the Bairro do Recife at Av. Marquês de Olinda.
**Taxis** Disk Taxis Recife ⓣ81/3424-5030; Teletaxi ⓣ81/3429-4242.
**Tour companies** Among the best companies in and around Recife are Evatur, Av. Cons. Aguiar 1360, Loja 14, Boa Viagem (ⓣ81/3465-1164), for city tours, Porto de Galinhas and other local tours and destinations; Martur, Rua Dr Nilo Dornelas Camara 90, Loja 02, Boa Viagem (ⓣ81/3463-3636, ⓦwww.snsweb.com.br/martur), for flights, cruises and trips to Fernando de Noronha.



# Olinda

**OLINDA** is, quite simply, one of the largest and most beautiful complexes of **colonial architecture** in Brazil: a maze of cobbled streets, hills crowned with brilliant white churches, pastel-coloured houses, Baroque fountains and graceful squares. Not surprisingly, in 1982 it was designated a World Heritage Site by UNESCO. Founded in 1535, the old city is spread across several small hills looking back towards Recife, but it belongs to a different world. In many ways, Olinda is the Greenwich Village of Recife; it's here that many of the larger city's artists, musicians and liberal professionals live, and there's a significant gay community. Olinda is most renowned, though, for its **Carnaval**, famous throughout Brazil, which attracts visitors from all over the country, as well as sizeable contingents from Europe.

A city in its own right, Olinda is far larger than it first appears. Yet despite its size, it has become effectively a neighbourhood of Recife: a high proportion of the population commutes into the city, which means that **transport links** are good, with buses leaving every few minutes. Olinda's old colonial centre is built slightly back from the sea, but arching along the seafront and spreading inland behind the old town is a modern Brazilian city of over 300,000 people – known as **Novo Olinda**, it's the usual bland collection of suburbs and main commercial drags. Like Recife, Novo Olinda has a growing reputation for robberies, but the heart of colonial Olinda is safe enough. There's a calm, almost sleepy atmosphere about the place, and wandering around at night is pretty safe. Finally, if you want to swim or enjoy a sunbathe, you'll need to head out of town, as Olinda's beach is fairly polluted and smelly.

## Arrival and information

**Buses** from Recife follow the seafront road; get off in Praça do Carmo, just by Olinda's main post office, from where it's a two-minute walk up into the old city.

A reasonable town map is available from the Secretaria de Turismo in the **Biblioteca Pública** at the foot of Rua do São Francisco near Praça do Carmo (daily 9am–5pm; ☎81/3305-1060). The **municipal tourist office** in Rua São Bento can help with information about accommodation during Carnaval, but it's not geared up for much more than this, and the information kiosk on Praça do Carmo, where the buses stop, isn't particularly useful either.

There are a huge number of teenagers and young men offering themselves as **guides** to the city, and you'll probably find yourself besieged as soon as you get off the bus. Those wearing yellow t-shirts with the words "Guia Mirim" written on the back and laminated ID Cards are official guides, but no longer receive support from the municipality. They generally do their job pretty well and depend entirely on tips. They are mostly ex-street kids and a percentage of their earnings goes towards their ongoing work with street kids, so they are well worth supporting (the recommended tip for guides is R$12–15 an hr per person), though few speak fluent English. Others, generally wearing white t-shirts and yellow caps with the acronym AGTIO, are from the Associação de Guias Turísticas Independentes, and should also have ID cards to prove this. For **internet access**, try the *Olind@.com* cybercafé opposite the *Hotel Pousada São Francisco* on Rua do Sol, Carmo. At the Telemar **phone office** on Praça Maxambomba, you can also make inter-city and and international calls. For a reliable **taxi** driver, contact Flavio on ☎81/3429-0852 or 9961-9544.

## Accommodation

It's probably cheapest **to stay** in the more modern part of the city, further north down the seafront road from Recife, but you'll be seriously missing out on the old city's atmosphere if you do, and it's worth shopping around for cheaper options in the historic area. Prices vary enormously throughout the year (March, June & Aug–Nov is cheapest). During Carnaval, it's virtually impossible to get a room unless you've booked months in advance.

If you want to stay for a while and **rent a room**, look for signs outside people's houses saying "*Aluga-se*". Alternatively, you can participate in the **Cama a café scheme**, which is a network of homes taking in guests – the programme works out to be quite cheap and gives great cultural insight; either ask at the tourist office or contact the organizer on ⓣ21/9606-0692. There's also a **campsite**, *Camping Olinda*, just inside the old city at Rua do Bom Sucesso 262, Amparo (ⓣ81/3429-1365), but do watch your valuables.

**Costeiro Olinda Hotel** Av. Ministro Marcos Freire 681, Bairro Novo ⓣ81/3429-4877. Three-star hotel in the modern part of the city; somewhat bland compared to the other places in this price range. ❻

**Hostel Olinda** Rua do Sol 233, Carmo ⓣ81/3429-1592, ⓦwww.alberguedeolinda.com.br. Excellent, very comfortable youth hostel with a nice hammock area and a small swimming pool; it's also close to the seafront, though right on a busy road. Accepts non-members at a slightly higher rate; all rooms shared. ❶–❷

**Hotel Pousada dos Milagros** Rua Manuel Borba 235 ⓣ81/3439-0392. Very friendly *pousada* close to the seafront and beach; it has a pleasant courtyard as well as a small pool. ❹

**Hotel Pousada São Francisco** Rua do Sol 127, Carmo ⓣ81/3429-2109, ⓦwww.pousadasaofrancisco.com.br. Located on the main road but quite close to the seafront; with a swimming pool and all mod cons. Prices vary with the view. ❹

**Hotel Sete Colinas** Ladeira de São Francisco 307, Carmo ⓣ81/3493-7766, ⓦwww.hotel7colinas.com.br. This fabulous hotel right in the centre of Olinda is set in beautiful gardens with modern sculpture and a fine swimming pool. There's a range of rooms, suites and luxury apartments, and a good restaurant, too. It isn't cheap, but it's still good value. ❺–❻

**Okakoaras Bungalow Hotel** Av. Cláudio J. Gueiros 10927, Praia de Maria Farinha ⓣ81/3436-1754. Set on a palm-lined beach, this peaceful hotel is a 30min bus ride from Olinda. Offers cosy, bungalow-style accommodation, a swimming pool and pleasant service. ❸

**Pousada Alquimia** Rua Prudente de Morais 292 ⓣ81/3429-1457. Cheap and cheerful, this well-located little *pension* has a front parlour full of paintings, and nice, if basic, rooms. ❷

**Pousada do Amparo** Rua do Amparo 199 ⓣ81/3439-1749, ⓦwww.pousadodoamparo.com.br. Not cheap, but a quality place set in a colonial mansion. Excellent rooms, a restaurant, a sauna, a pool and art gallery. ❺–❼

**Pousada d'Olinda** Praça João Alfredo 178 ⓣ81/3439-1163, ⓦwww.hoteldolinda.com.br. This central *pousada* is excellent value and has everything from a fine swimming pool to a good restaurant, inexpensive bungalow-style rooms and a penthouse suite. ❹

**Pousada Peter** Rua do Amparo 215 ⓣ81/3439-2171, ⓦwww.pousadapeter.com.br. Set among other art galleries, this is a comfortable gallery-cum-lodging situated in a colonial-style building. The front rooms and entry form most of the gallery, with guest rooms out back. Good value. ❸

**Pousada dos Quatro Cantos** Rua Prudente de Morais 441 ⓣ81/3429-0220, ⓦwww.pousada4cantos.com.br. Beautiful, small mansion with a leafy courtyard, right in the heart of the old city. A range of rooms and suites available; the cheapest have shared bathrooms. ❸–❺

## The Town

Olinda's hills are steep, and you'll be best rewarded by taking a leisurely stroll around town. A good spot to have a drink and plan your attack is the **Alto da Sé** (the highest square in the town), not least because of the stunning view of Recife's skyscrapers shimmering in the distance, framed in the foreground by the church towers, gardens and palm trees of Olinda. There's always an arts and crafts **market** going on here during the day, peaking in the late afternoon, but while much of what's on offer is pretty good, the large numbers of tourists have driven prices up, and there's little here you can't get cheaper in Recife or the interior.

The **churches** you see are not quite as old as they look. The Dutch burnt them all down, except one, in 1630, built none of their own, and left the Portuguese to restore them during the following centuries. There are eighteen churches dating from the seventeenth and eighteenth centuries remaining today, seemingly tucked around every corner and up every street. Very few of them have set opening times, but they're usually open during weekday mornings, and even when they're closed you can try knocking on the door and asking for the *vigia* (the watchman).

If you have time to see only one church, make it the **Convento de São Franciscano** (Mon–Fri 7am–noon & 2–5pm, Sat 7am–noon; R$2), tucked away at Rua São Francisco 280. Built in 1585, the complex of convent, chapel and church has been exquisitely restored to its former glory; particular highlights are the tiled cloister depicting the lives of Jesus and St Francis of Asissi, and the sacristy's beautiful Baroque furniture carved from jacaranda wood. In the north wing, there's an elaborate two-tiered altarpiece in gold leaf and white, and behind the convent there's a grand patio with even grander panoramas across the ocean.

Among other churches, the **Igreja da Misericórdia**, built right at the top of an exhaustingly steep hill, has a fine altar and rear walls covered in blue *azulejos*, while the **Basilica e Mosteiro de São Bento** (daily 8am–11am & 2–5pm; R$1) looks quite wonderful from the outside with palm trees swaying in the courtyard, though the interior is less striking. The **Igreja da Sé**, on the *praça* of the same name, is rather bland and austere inside – more of a museum than a living church – but worth a look if only to see the eighteenth-century sedan chair and large wooden sculptures in the small room at the northeast wing. At the back of the church is a patio from where you'll have good views of the surrounding area.

By Praça do Carmo, there's the run-down but quite splendid **Igreja do Carmo**, which sits majestically on a small hill looking down on the busy streets below, while up Rua do Amparo lies the fine eighteenth-century **Igreja do Amparo**, and within view of this the deserted ruins of the **Igreja de São João Batista dos Militares**, the one church that escaped the Dutch invaders' fires of 1630.

There's also a good sampling of religious art on display in the **Museu de Arte Sacra de Pernambuco** (Mon–Fri 8am–1pm), in the seventeenth-century bishop's palace by the Alto da Sé. The **Museu Regional** (Mon–Fri 9am–12.45pm; R$1), at Rua do Amparo 128, is well laid out, too, although the emphasis is too much on artefacts and too little on history.

There's more contemporary interest in the colourful **graffiti** in which the old city is swathed. The local council commissions artists to adorn certain streets and walls, which has the twin advantage of keeping local talent in work and ensuring Olinda has the highest-quality graffiti in Brazil. Some are political, urging people to vote for this or that candidate, some are more abstract – illustrated poems about Olinda being especially popular – but all are colourful and artistic and blend in uncannily well with the colonial architecture. One of the best places to see them is along the municipal-cemetery walls on Avenida Liberdade, but there's good graffiti all over the old city, especially during elections and Carnaval.

More serious modern art is to be found in the **Museu de Arte Contemporânea**, on Rua 13 de Maio next to the market (Tues–Fri 9am–noon & 2–5pm, Sat & Sun 2–5pm). This fine eighteenth-century building was once used as a jail by the Inquisition, though the exhibits themselves are a bit disappointing. Much more interesting is the **Museu do Mamulengo** (Tues–Fri 9am–5pm, Sat & Sun 2–5pm) at Rua do Amparo 59, which houses an excellent collection of traditional puppets.

Olinda's several markets and endless *artesanato* shops make it a good place for **shopping**. The Mercado da Ribeira, built in the sixteenth century, is at Rua Bernardo Vieira de Melo 160, and offers the usual range of craft goods, while a ten-minute walk down Rua 15 de Novembro from the governor's palace brings you to another, bigger, *artesanato* and antique market housed in the long pink building by the main road, Largo do Varadouro.

## Eating, drinking and nightlife



Olinda's relaxed atmosphere draws many *recifenses* at night, when tables and chairs are set on squares and pavements, and bars that are tucked away in courtyards amid spectacular tropical foliage make for the perfect escape. There's always plenty of music around, and, at weekends, a lot of young Brazilians out for a good time. If it's just drinks and a snack you're after, try *Bodega de Veio*, Rua do Amparo 198 (opposite *Pousada Peter*), which is occasionally the scene for live music in the evenings.

### Eating and drinking

The best place to go for crowds and serious eating and drinking is the **Alto da Sé**. The good, cheap **street food** here, cooked on charcoal fires, can't be recommended too highly; try *acarajé*, which you get from women sitting next to sizzling wok-like pots – bean-curd cake, fried in palm oil, cut open and filled with green salad, dried shrimps and *vatapá*, a yellow paste made with shrimps, coconut milk and fresh coriander. If you sit in the Alto da Sé for any length of time, you're bound to be approached by one of Olinda's many **repentistas** (see p.312), who will try to improvise a song about you. The results are sometimes wonderful, sometimes embarrassing, but they will expect a small payment, so if you don't want to shell out make it clear from the start that you're not interested.

Olinda also has countless **restaurants**. If you want to eat for around R$10 or less, try the *por kilo* places along the seafront and in the new part of town; however, for just a little bit more, you can eat far better in the old town. The streets around the Alto da Sé hold a couple of good **bars** that are well worth seeking out, including the *Cantinho da Sé*, just a few steps down the Ladeira da Sé, almost always crowded and very lively indeed at night. If it's just good coffee you're after, try the *Café Adego*, at Rua 27 de Janeiro 70.

### Cafés and restaurants

**Blues Bar** Rua do Bonfim 66 ☎81/9156-6415. Set in the garden of an old house and serving excellent, moderately priced meat dishes. Plays authentic blues music much of the time. Tues–Thurs 6pm–1am, Fri & Sat 6pm–3am, Sun 11am–8pm.

**Creperia** Praça João Alfredo 168. Does great salads as well as the crepes.

**Goya Restaurant** Rua do Amparo 157. Hard to beat for imaginative Brazilian and French cuisine; located in a lovely old house in the really arty part of town.

**Mourisco** Praça Conselheiro João Alfredo 7. Expensive, a/c place specializing in seafood; a good meal with wine will cost R$30–40.

**Oficina do Sabor** Excellent local cuisine – the shrimps in mango sauce are a highlight.

**Porta D'Italia** Rua do Bonfim. Good spot at the higher end of the price range, offering well-prepared Italian food and a good wine list.

**Restaurante Flor do Coco** Rua do Amparo 199. Has excellent regional cuisine, including both local fish dishes and great pastas.

### Nightlife

**Nightlife** in Olinda can be very hectic, especially at the end of the week – at times, the drums or bass lines carry so loudly across town that you may think they're calling out to you. Places to visit, apart from the ones along the Alto da Sé, are the seafront restaurants and bars, many of which have *forró* groups on Friday and Saturday nights; the *Acoustico Pub*, for instance, at Rua do Sol 283, has a good scene. If you get bored with *forró* – and the beat does get a bit monotonous after a while – try the more samba-like rhythms of the *Z-4 Club* or the *Clube Atlântico*, both near Praça do Carmo. Every Friday and Saturday night (from 11pm), they dance to an eclectic variety of very loud music – *frevo*, samba, *forró*, merengue, and even non-Brazilian styles like salsa and tango – either recorded or performed live by energetic groups. There are sometimes extras such as magicians and *capoeira* displays going on between, and even during, acts.

## Carnaval and other festivals

Olinda's **Carnaval**, with a massive 560 *blocos*, is generally considered to be one of the three greatest in Brazil, along with those of Rio and Salvador. It overshadows the celebrations in neighbouring Recife and attracts thousands of revellers from all over the Northeast. It's easy to see why Olinda developed into such a major Carnaval: the setting is matchless, and local traditions of art and music are very strong. Like the other two great Brazilian Carnavals, Olinda has a style and feel all its own: not quite as large and potentially intimidating as in either Rio or Salvador, the fact that much of it takes place in the winding streets and small squares of the old city makes it seem more manageable. The music, with the local beats of *frevo* and *maracatu* predominating, the costumes, and the enormous *bonecos* (papier-mâché figures of folk heroes, or savage caricatures of local and national personalities), make this celebration unique.

Carnaval actually gets going the Sunday before the **official start**, when the Virgens do Bairro Novo, a traditional *bloco* several hundred strong, parades down the seafront road followed by crowds that regularly top 200,000. By now, the old city is covered with decorations: ribbons, streamers and coloured lanterns are hung from every nook and cranny, banners are strung across streets and coloured lighting is set up in all the squares. Olinda's Carnaval is not only famous for its *bonecos*, which are first paraded around on Friday night and then at intervals during the days, but also for the decorated umbrellas that aficionados use to

▲ Olinda's famous Carnaval

dance the *frevo*. The tourist office has lists of the hundreds of groups, together with **routes** and approximate times, but there is always something going on in most places in the old city – the area around the *Pousada dos Quatro Cantos* is one of the liveliest during Carnaval. The most famous *blocos*, with mass followings, are Pitombeira and Elefantes; also try catching the daytime performances of *travestis*, transvestite groups, which have the most imaginative costumes – ask the tourist office to mark them out on the list for you.

Inevitably, with so many visitors flocking into the city, **accommodation during Carnaval** can be a problem. You might as well forget about hotels in Olinda if you haven't booked a room months in advance. Many locals, though, rent out all or part of their house for Carnaval week; the municipal tourist office has a list of places and prices, which start at around R$600 for the week, going up to as much as R$5000. If all the places on their lists are full – more than likely if you arrive less than a week before Carnaval starts – or if you fancy your chances of getting a cheaper and better deal on your own, wander round the side streets looking for signs saying "*Aluga-se quartos*"; knock on the door and bargain away.

It's easier to find a room in Recife, but, unless you dance the night away, transport back in the small hours can be difficult; buses start running at around 5am, and before then you have to rely on taxis, which means paying an exorbitant fare and running the risk of **drunken taxi drivers** – dozens of people are killed on the road during Carnaval every year, and it's best to avoid travelling by road in the small hours.

### The Torneio dos Repentistas

There are plenty of festivals other than Carnaval in Olinda, as its location and cultural traditions make it a popular venue. Definitely worth catching if you happen to be visiting in late January is the **Torneio dos Repentistas**, which is centred on and around the Praça da Preguiça and lasts for three days. A *repentista* is a Northeastern singer-poet who improvises strictly metered verses accompanied only by a guitar. Olinda's *torneio* is one of the most famous events of its kind in the region, bringing in *repentistas* from all over the Northeast who pair off and embark on singing duels while surrounded by audiences; the audiences break into spontaneous applause at particularly good rhymes or well-turned stanzas. During the rest of the year, most *repentistas* make a living singing on street corners, in squares or at markets, commenting wittily – and often obscenely – on the people going by or stopping to listen, or elaborating on themes shouted out by the audience. Even if you don't understand the lyrics, a *repentista*'s act is worth catching, especially if you can find a *cantoria*, a sing-off between two or more *repentistas*, who take alternate verses until a draw is agreed or until the audience acclaims a winner.

## North from Recife

North from Recife, the **BR-101 highway** runs a little way inland through low hills and sugar-cane fields, a scenic enough route but one that offers little reason to stop off anywhere. The **coast** north of Recife is best explored along the smaller roads that branch off the highway. Nevertheless, it's as well to bear in mind that the Pernambuco coast is thickly populated by Brazilian standards, and what seems a deserted retreat during the week can fill up quickly at weekends, with *recifenses* heading for the beaches, enlivening or destroying the rural atmosphere, depending on your point of view.

## Along the coast to Itamaracá

From Olinda, **local buses** continue 11km along the coastal road to the beautiful palm-lined beaches of **Rio Doce**, **Janga** and **Pau Amarelo**. Until recently, these were pretty much deserted, and although weekend homes are going up now, development, so far, is less obtrusive than in many places on the coast. Being close to major population centres, however, the water quality at Rio Doce and Janga is not always the best. The area gets busy at weekends, especially in Janga, when there's music and dancing in the beachside bars at night. At Pau Amarelo, you can still see one of several local star-shaped forts left behind by the Dutch in 1719.

A more popular and even more scenic route north is through the pleasantly run-down colonial village of **Igarassu** to the island of **Itamaracá**. Hourly **buses** to Igarassu, with easy connections to Itamaracá, leave from Avenida Martins de Barros on Santo Antônio in Recife, opposite the *Grande Hotel*. Another possibility is to go there **by boat**: every travel agency in Recife runs trips (R$90–100), stopping at beaches on the way.

### Igarassu

Turning off the highway past Olinda's ugly industrial suburb of Paulista, the road wends its way through a rich green landscape of rolling hills and dense palm forest. The first town on the route, 25km from Olinda, is **IGARASSU**, an old colonial settlement built on a ridge rising out of a sea of palm trees: the name means "great canoe" in the language of the Tupi Indians, the cry that went up when they first saw the Portuguese galleons. The town was founded in 1535, when during a battle with the Indians the hard-pressed Portuguese commander vowed to build a church on the spot if victorious; the **Igreja de São Cosme e Damião**, one of the oldest churches in Brazil, is still there on the ridge. Down the hill the **Convento de Santo Antônio** is almost as old, built in 1588. Both are simpler and more austere than any of the churches in Recife or Olinda.

Most of the houses in Igarassu make up the rows of tied cottages that are characteristic of the old *engenhos*, or sugar estates. You can get a good idea of what a traditional *engenho* was like at the **Engenho Monjope**, an old plantation that has been tastefully converted into a **campsite** (Ⓣ81/3543-0528). The *engenho* dates from 1756; there's a decaying mansion, a chapel, water mill, cane presses and a *senzala*, the blockhouse where slaves lived. Minibuses back to Recife from Igarassu drop you at the turn-off (ask for "*o camping*"), and the estate is an easy ten-minute walk from there. The campsite is separate from the buildings, and you can ask at the entrance to look around even if you don't want to stay. Thirteen kilometres north of Igarassu, there are a couple of more upmarket places to stay at the pleasant **Praia da Gavoa**: the *Pousada Porto Canoas*, Estr. do Ramalho 230 (Ⓣ81/3424-2845; ③), has chalets, a pool and a restaurant; and the *Hotel Gavoa Praia* (Ⓣ81/3543-7777, Ⓦwww.hotelgavoa.com.br; ⑥) offers everything you could need, including a pool and sauna. Eight kilometres further on from Praia da Gavoa at **Itapissuma**, a causeway connects the mainland to **ITAMARACÁ**. Local legend has it that the island was once the site of the Garden of Eden, and the short drive across the causeway from Itapissuma promises much, passing amongst thousands of palm trees lapped by fields of sugar cane. While the **beaches** around the island are very good – wide and lined with palms – the town of **Itamaracá** itself is something of a disappointment, crowded and increasingly scarred by hundreds of weekend homes, which spring up in ugly rashes along the beaches alongside the humble wattle huts roofed with palm leaves where the original islanders have managed to hold on. There are the usual beachside bars and restaurants on Itamaracá, and a few **hotels**, although you're probably better off staying at Gavoa and making the day-trip across.

# South from Recife

The coast south of Recife has the best **beaches** in the state and is all too quickly realizing its tourist potential – the sleepy fishing villages are unlikely to remain so for much longer. Almost all **buses** take the BR-101 highway, which runs inland through fairly dull scenery, made worse by heavy traffic. The trick is to get a bus that goes along the much more scenic **coastal road**, the PE-60, or *via litoral*; they leave from either Avenida Dantas Barreto or the Recife Rodoviária for the string of towns down the coast from Cabo, through Ipojuca, Sirinhaém, Rio Formoso to São José da Coroa Grande. Before São José, where the road starts to run alongside the beach, you may need to catch another local bus to get to the beachside villages themselves. In theory, you could hop from village to village down the coast on local buses, but only with time to spare. Services are infrequent – early morning is the usual departure time – and you might have to sleep on a beach or find somewhere to sling a hammock, as not all the villages have places to stay. As you move south, bays and promontories disappear, and walking along the beaches to the next village is often quicker than waiting for a bus.

## Gaibú and Santo Agostinho

The first stop out of Recife is the beach at **GAIBÚ**, a sizeable resort some 40km south of Boa Viagem – catch a bus to Cabo from Avenida Dantas Barreto, and then another local one to Gaibú. Gaibú sports the familiar setup – palm trees, bars and surf – and is a good base for village-hopping, with a youth hostel and a couple of cheap **pensões**: the pleasant *Pousada Aguas Marinhas* (❸) is right on the beach, run by a Belgian–Brazilian couple who serve fine breakfasts in their beach garden and have mountain bikes for rent. They can also arrange sightseeing trips in boats with local fishermen. Gaibú gets crowded at weekends, but there's a particularly beautiful stretch of coastline nearby, close enough to explore on foot.

Just before Gaibú village, a turning in the dirt road heads off to the right, leading to the cape of **São Agostinho**, a pleasant walk uphill through palms and mango trees, past the odd peasant hut in the forest. Three kilometres up is a ruined Dutch chapel, so overgrown it's almost invisible, and a path to the left leads out onto a promontory where the forest suddenly disappears and leaves you with a stunning view of the idyllic, and usually deserted, beach of **Calhetas**. You can clamber down to the beach, a ring of sand in a bay fringed with palm forest, the distant oil refinery at Suape providing the only jarring note. This beach is particularly good for surfing.

If you continue on from the ruined chapel, you'll come to the sleepy hamlet of **SANTO AGOSTINHO**. During the Dutch occupation, there was vicious guerrilla fighting here, and an infamous massacre took place when Dutch settlers were herded into a church that was then burnt down; a small chapel still stands on the spot, and there are the pulverized remains of a fort. On the cape itself are burnt-out shells of Dutch buildings from the same campaign, and there's also a plaque commemorating the Spanish conquistador Yanez Piñon, blown south by storms on his way to the Caribbean in 1500. He put in here for shelter a couple of months before Cabral "discovered" Brazil, and sailed off without knowing where he was – thus ensuring Brazil would end up speaking Portuguese rather than Spanish. The cape is crisscrossed with several walking trails, few of which are properly signposted, and a little exploring will soon bring you to the tiny village of Nazare, where there's little to keep you apart from a ruined Dutch chapel and a small bar managed by the local lighthouse-keeper.

If you find the need **to stay**, the Praia de Suape, Santo Agostinho's most southerly beach, has the delightful *Sitio Paraíso* (☎81/3522-6061; ④), a cosy *pousada* set in the middle of fruit gardens (pick your own limes for cocktails). The owner is knowledgeable about local activities and will help arrange boat trips to the Suape islands through mangrove swamps.

## Porto de Galinhas to Barra de Santo Antônio

The curious name of **PORTO DE GALINHAS** ("Chicken Port") derives from a history of slave running; tax-dodging, life-dealing smugglers would arrive to shore proclaiming they had a shipment of "Angolan chickens". Today, the port, on the southern coast of Pernambuco, has a number of very fine beaches, notably Muro Alto, Serrambi (some 5km long and particularly good for surfing) and Enseada dos Corais. In the high season, several of Recife's best clubs open shop here. As well as beautiful landscapes, the area abounds with old sugar mills and churches.

Some buses for Porto de Galinhas leave from the old Recife airport or the square near it with Real Alagoes (☎81/3452-3888). Other buses can be caught from Avenida Dantas Barreto in Recife (hourly 6.30am–7.30pm, last bus leaves Porto 5.40pm). Just 65km from Recife, Porto de Galinhas is deservedly popular – and in danger of becoming overdeveloped. From here **jangadas** will take you out to the small, natural coral pools just off the coast, and there is some excellent **surfing** here, too. Good fresh fish is to be had in the **beachside cafés**; fried needle-fish, *agulhas fritas*, is a great snack with a cold beer as you wiggle your toes in the warm sand. If you want **to stay**, there are two campsites and numerous *pousadas*, as well as an increasing number of upmarket hotels on the seafront. Right on the main beach are the luxury *Village Porto de Galinhas* (☎81/3552-4200, Ⓦwww.villageportodegalinhas.com.br; ⑦), with its own pool, and the smaller *Recanto*, Avenida Beira Mar (☎81/3552-1251; ④). The *Pousada Litoral*, just three blocks from the ocean at the corner of Rua da Esperança and Beijupira (②), has clean, simple rooms. For unbelievably tasty shrimp, lobster and local *sobremesas*, visit the excellent *Beijupirá* **restaurant** on the road of the same name (☎81/3552-2354; daily noon–midnight).

The main drag, Rua da Esperança, is where you'll find the **tourist information** office (☎81/3552-1728) and the **post office**; lines of dune buggies are at the sea end (R$45–50 for 2–3hr). If you'd rather get behind the wheel, try Buggy Tour, Rua do Colegio (☎81/3461-1902 or 3552-1400).

Four or five kilometres away – easily reached by either a forty-minute walk along the beach or a dune-buggy ride – is one of the finest beaches in the area, the **Praia de Macaripe**, where there are plenty of bars and restaurants as well as good waves, reefs and *jangada* rides on offer. The *Pousada dos Coqueiros* (☎81/3552-1294, Ⓦwww.pousadadoscoqueiros.com.br; ③) is a good place to stay, especially if you're here to surf. Another 10km further south is the beautiful **Praia da Ponta de Serrambi**, popular with windsurfers. For total luxury, *Venta Club Serrambi*, right on the beach here (☎81/3551-8800, Ⓦwww.ventaclub.com.br; ⑦), has its own pool, sauna and boats.

South again are the sleepy fishing villages of **TAMANDARÉ** and **SÃO JOSÉ DA COROA GRANDE**, where, for the time being, fishing still dominates, with *jangadas* drawn up on the beaches and men repairing nets, though even here weekend houses for city slickers are going up. In Tamandaré (served by direct bus from Recife's *rodoviária*), apart from the usual stunning beach, there are the ruins of the fort of Santo Inácio, destroyed in 1646, and a small hotel, *Marinas Tamandaré*, at

Loteamento Anaisabela, Lote 15A (☎81/3675-1388; ⑤). A little way south, in São José da Coroa Grande, where the *litoral* road finally hits the coast (also served by direct bus from Recife's *rodoviária*), there are bars, a huge beach and the overpriced *Hotel Francês*, Rua Antônia Valdemar Acioli Belo 279 (☎81/3688-1169; ④). Just offshore from here is the Ilha de Santo Aleixo – local fishermen will take you for around R$20 – where there are a couple of good beaches.



# Inland from Recife

In contrast to the gentle scenery of the coastal routes out of Recife, heading **inland** brings you abruptly into a completely different landscape, spectacular and forbidding. The people, too, look and speak differently; the typical *sertanejo* is short and wiry, with the high cheekbones and thin nose of an Indian ancestor. They converse in heavily accented Portuguese, much ridiculed elsewhere, but really one of the loveliest Brazilian inflections.

**Buses** inland all leave from the Recife *rodoviária*, and the best place to head for is the market town of **Caruaru**, 130km from Recife and the largest town in the *agreste* (frequent departures; 2hr; buy your ticket a day in advance); sit on the right-hand side of the bus for the best view.

## The route to Caruaru

The **BR-232** highway heads directly away from the sea into gentle hills covered with enormous fields of sugar cane; the size of the estates gives you some idea of the inequality of land distribution in the Northeast, and explains why this part of Pernambuco has been in the forefront of the struggle for agrarian reform in Brazil. It was here in the late 1950s that the Peasant Leagues started, a social movement pressing for land reform through direct action and one of the factors that frightened the military into launching their coup in 1964. Most of the cane is destined for the first town en route, **Vitória de Santo Antão**, where, on the left-hand side of the road, you'll see the factory that produces the most widely drunk rum in Brazil, Pitu – you can't miss the thirty-metre-high water tank cunningly camouflaged as an enormous bottle of the stuff.

After Vitória you begin to climb in earnest into the **Serra da Neblina**, threading into the hills of the *agreste* proper. Gradually the air becomes cooler, the heat drier, and highland plants replace the palms and sugar cane of the coastal strip. On a clear day, the views are stunning. You begin to see *palma* fields full of cacti; they're a foretaste of the harshness of *sertão* life: in times of drought, the cactus is chopped down and fed to cattle, thorns and all.

The next town, 50km down the road, is **GRAVATÁ**, one of several *agreste* towns that has optimistically tagged itself "The Switzerland of Pernambuco" on the strength of its cool hill climate – temperatures average around 21°C. There are lots of villas and a hotel built in Swiss-chalet style, rather incongruous in a landscape that is parched brown as often as not. **BEZERROS**, the last town before Caruaru, is the home of a famous artist and printer, **Jota Borges**, some of whose work you may have seen in the Casa da Cultura and the Penha craft shop (see p.300) in Recife. Borges has a roadside workshop on the left as you leave town. Inside, you can see the carved wooden plates he makes to manufacture the prints on paper and cloth; the smaller ones are for the covers of *cordel* (see p.299), a large library of which takes up one corner of the workshop. Borges himself is often at the market in Caruaru or delivering in Recife, but a family member is usually on hand to show visitors around. The absurdly inexpensive prints are simple but powerful depictions of peasant life.

Home of the largest market in the Northeast, **CARUARU** is also ideally placed for excursions into the *sertão*. Saturday is the main market day, but Wednesday and Friday are busy, too. People come from all over the Northeast for the **market**, which dominates the town, with stalls filling the squares and people clogging the streets. It's a slightly less traditional affair than it used to be, with Asian electronic goods playing an increasingly important part, but the atmosphere is still worth savouring.

## Alto do Moura

To explore the tradition of *figurinhas* further, it's worth making the short journey to **ALTO DO MOURA**, 6km up the road from Caruaru: take a taxi or the marked bus (departures every 2hr) from Rua 13 de Maio, one of the roads leading out of the centre towards the *rodoviária*. It's a dirt road to a small but busy village that seems entirely unremarkable, except that every other house on the only street, **Rua Mestre Vitalino**, is a potter's workshop, with kilns resembling large beehives in the yards behind. The first house on the left was Mestre Vitalino's, and is now a small museum, with his widow and grandchildren still living in the simple hut next door. There's a plaque on the adobe wall and, inside, the hut has been kept as Vitalino left it, with his leather hat and jacket hanging on a nail. The only sign that Vitalino was somebody special is the framed photos of him being feted in Rio de Janeiro and introduced to the president.

## Nova Jerusalém

In Easter Week, Caruara's market crowds are swollen with tourists and pilgrims heading for **NOVA JERUSALÉM**, in the heart of the *agreste*, 50km from the bustling town; the turn-off is on the right just after Caruaru, on the BR-104, marked "Campina Grande". After 24km, another turn-off, to the left, the PE-145, leads to the small town of **Fazenda Nova**, just outside which is the site of Nova Jerusalém.

A granite replica of the old city of Jerusalem, it was built in the early 1970s by a local entrepreneur who cashed in on the deep religious feeling of the interior by mounting a **Passion play** based on that of Oberammergau in Germany. Over the years, this *Paixão do Cristo* has become a tradition of the *agreste*, attracting thousands of spectators to watch five hundred costumed actors, mostly local amateurs, re-create the Passion and Crucifixion. The "replica" of Jerusalem is in fact a third of the size of the original, and is basically a setting for the twelve stages on which the action takes place, each representing a Station of the Cross. The Passion is performed daily from the Tuesday before Easter to Easter Sunday inclusive, taking up most of the day. The most convenient way to see it is to go on one of the day-tours that many travel agents in Recife – and other northeastern cities – run there during Holy Week. It's also easy to get there under your own steam, as there are buses to Fazenda Nova from Caruaru and a **campsite** when you get there, as well as several simple *dormitórios*. Entry to the spectacle costs about R$50.

# Into the sertão

The **Pernambucan sertão** begins after Caruaru, though there's no sudden transition; the hills simply get browner and rockier, dense thorny scrub takes over from the hill plants, and there are cacti every few yards, from tiny flowering stumps to massive tangled plants as large as trees. And, above all, it's hot, with parched winds that feel as if someone is training a hairdryer on your face.

The Pernambucan *sertão* is one of the harshest in the Northeast, a scorched landscape under relentless sun for most of the year. This is cattle country, home of the **vaqueiro**, the northeastern cowboy, and has been since the very beginning of Portuguese penetration inland in the seventeenth century; it is one of the oldest frontiers in the Americas.

The main highway that runs through the hilly Pernambucan *sertão* winds through scenery unlike any you'll have seen before – an apparently endless expanse of cactus and scrub so thick in places that cowboys have to wear leather armour to protect themselves. If you travel in the rainy season here – March to June, although rain can never be relied upon in the interior – you may be lucky enough to catch it bursting with green, punctuated by the whites, reds and purples of flowering trees and cacti. Massive electrical storms are common at this time of year, and at night the horizon can flicker with sheet lightning for hours at a stretch.

## Towards Petrolina

After Caruaru the highway passes through a number of anonymous farming towns. **ARCOVERDE**, 130km to the west, has a market on Saturdays and a reasonable **hotel**, the *Grande Majestic*, Av. Cel. Antônio Japiassu 326 (☎87/3821-1175; ❷), which doesn't quite live up to its name but is a cheap and handy place to break the journey. You may need to do just that, as the best *sertão* towns to make for are buried deep in the interior, some eight or ten hours by bus from Caruaru.

The last place that could really be called a town is **SERRA TALHADA**, some 200km west of Arcoverde. Here, the *Hotel das Palmeras*, BR-232 (☎87/3831-1625; ❸), 416km from Caruaru, is reasonable. From here on, the road passes through a succession of flyblown villages, all of which would look vaguely Mediterranean – with their whitewashed churches, cafés, dusty squares and rows of tumbledown cottages – if it weren't for the startling landscape in which they're set. Eighty kilometres beyond Serra Talhada, a turning leads north to Juazeiro do Norte (see p.328); one Petrolina bus turns south to follow an alternative route parallel to the São Francisco valley whilst the others continue for another 110km, across one of the most desolate semi-arid desert landscapes in the Northeast, before reaching **OURICURI**, a shady spot with a couple of hotels that's quite a pleasant place to break your journey; from here it's another 213km south along the BR-122 to Petrolina.

## Petrolina

After the villages that have gone before, **PETROLINA** seems like a city. Certainly, by the standards of the *sertão*, it's a large, thriving and relatively prosperous town, thanks to the river trade to places downstream. On the waterfront, you can occasionally see riverboats adorned with *carrancas*, carved wooden figureheads bolted onto the prow, brightly painted and with a grotesque monster's head, meant to frighten evil spirits lurking in wait for unwary mariners. Petrolina also has an interesting **Museu do Sertão** (Mon–Fri 10am–6pm, Sat 2–6pm, Sun 8am–noon), on Praça Santos Dumont on the road to the airstrip, about ten minutes' walk from the centre of town. Small but well put together, the museum documents *sertão* life and history through assorted relics and some fascinating photographs, including a couple of the bespectacled social bandit Lampião and his gang, popular heroes who roamed the *sertão* until they were shot dead in 1938 (see box, p.287). Lastly, Petrolina has a **market** on Friday and Saturday that brings people in from the *sertão* for miles around.

The **rodoviária** (☎87/3861-3512) is quite central. **Places to stay** include the *Petrolina Palace*, Av. Cardoso de Sá 845 (☎87/3866-3300, Ⓦwww.petrolinapalacehotel.com.br; ④), and the *Hotel Grande Rio*, Av. Pe. Fraga (☎87/3866-8050; ④–⑥); both have pools. Excellent **food** is served at *Maria do Peixe*, Av. 7 de Setembro 19, Areia Branca (☎87/3864-3982), although its speciality is fish. There are three **buses** daily to Petrolina from Recife via Caruaru.

### Juazeiro

Over the bridge, or across the river by boat, and into Bahia state lies Petrolina's poorer sister town, **JUAZEIRO**, not to be confused with Juazeiro do Norte. Many of its inhabitants had their homes flooded when dams created the enormous **Sobradinho** lake just upstream in the 1960s. Since then, the area around Juazeiro has become something of a showcase for **irrigation schemes**, and all kinds of fruit – including unlikely products such as grapes and asparagus – are grown here. The town has several **hotels**, a good choice being the *Grande Hotel do Juazeiro*, Rua José Petitinga (☎74/3612-3100; ⑤), not as grand as the name would suggest, but situated on the riverfront with a pool, bar and very good restaurant. The spotless *Rio Sol*, Rua Cel. João Evangelista 3 (☎74/3611-4481; ②) is a bearable and cheaper alternative. A nineteenth-century paddle steamer, the *Vaporzinho*, built in 1852 to ply the São Francisco river, has been restored, turned into a **restaurant** and is now moored on the riverfront. From Juazeiro you can continue south by bus along the BR-407 to Salvador (see p.234). Alternatively, if you're interested in the history of the *sertão*, you might want to make the five-hour journey southeast to Canudos (see p.268).

## Fernando de Noronha

The beautiful and environmentally protected archipelago of **FERNANDO DE NORONHA** lies in the equatorial Atlantic some 545km from Pernambuco, though it's actually nearer to Rio Grande do Norte. Access is mainly from Recife and Natal. Boasting more than sixteen very clean and stunning beaches, it's hard to beat for **scuba diving** – its clear water stretches down to a depth of 40m in places, with a white sandy sea bottom, plenty of coral, crustaceans, turtles, dolphins and a wide range of fish species and shoal types. The islands are also breeding territory for a number of tropical Atlantic birds.

European explorers first came here in 1503, and after a struggle between various powers, with the Dutch running the show from 1700 to 1736, the islands ended up under the control of the Portuguese in 1737. Lisbon considered the archipelago strategically important enough to build the **Forte dos Remédios**, of which only some remains can now be seen.

In recent years, the archipelago has become well known as an ecotourist destination. Most of it has been protected as a **marine national park**, created in 1988 in order to maintain the ecological wonders that have been preserved by the islands' isolation from the rest of Brazil. The vegetation is fairly typical northeastern *agreste*, but the wildlife is magnificent: birdwatchers will be amazed by the variety of **exotic birds**, including several types of pelican, and you'll be moved by the remarkable sight of thousands of dolphins entering the bay every day between 5am and 6am, viewed from the harbour.

The main island, **Ilha de Fernando de Noronha**, shelters plenty of stunning **beaches**. The water can sometimes be turbulent and not perfectly clear, but it is a fairly constant and very comfortable 28°C. The best **beaches** are probably

Praia da Atalaia and Cacimba do Padre, and at Mirante dos Golfinhos you can watch dolphins leaping over the waves. A number of **ecological trails** allow good birdwatching, and several companies specialize in **scuba-diving** courses and trips, including Aguas Claras (ⓣ81/3619-1225, ⓦwww.aguasclaras-fn.com.br), Atlantis (ⓣ81/3619-1371, ⓦwww.atlantisnoronha.com.br) and Noronha Divers (ⓣ81/3619-1112, ⓦwww.noronhadivers.com.br). Various companies also offer **boat trips** around the archipelago, departing from the ports at the northeastern tip of the island and from the Bahia dos Golfinhos at the island's southern end. Boat trips from the latter leave most days (R$45 per person including transport to the harbour; ⓣ81/3619-1295).



### Practicalities

All visitors to Fernando de Noronha are expected to pay the TPA **tax**, which goes toward protecting the environment, but this can be done in advance online (ⓦwww.noronha.pe.gov.br). To reach the islands, you can **fly** from either Recife or Natal with Trip (ⓣ81/3463-4610 or 3619-1379, ⓦwww.voetrip.com.br) or Varig (ⓣ0800/727-1076, ⓦwww.varig.com.br). A return flight from Natal will set you back at least R$750, one from Recife slightly more, though there are more frequent flights from the latter; tickets are available from a number of travel agents in both cities (see p.336 & p.306). Bring plenty of local currency with you as you won't be able to change money during your stay, and also bring anything else you think you may need: prices in Fernando de Noronha are high. The archipelago is best visited between August and January, when the rainfall is lowest.

The few facilities the islands have, including the **airport** (ⓣ81/3619-1633), are all on the main island. Here you'll find the **tourist information** office (ⓣ81/3619-1378) in the main settlement of **VILA DOS REMÉDIOS**, a small town in the northern part of the island, and, some 10km to the south near the airport, the **Centro de Visitantes** (daily 8am–10.30pm; ⓣ81/3619-1171).

Whilst it is possible to fly here without pre-organizing a tour, organized **tours** are the usual and preferred way to get to Fernando de Noronha. A daily ecological tax (US$36.69 per person) attempts to limit the impact of tourism on the fragile environment. Tours are generally arranged by travel agencies in Recife (p.306) or Natal (p.336); they usually include a return flight, accommodation, food and tours of the island. Prices start at around R$1400 for two nights, R$1600 for three nights and R$1800 for five nights. Ambiental Expedições (ⓣ11/3819-4600, ⓦwww.ambiental.tur.br) run good trips.

On the main island, **buggies**, **jeeps** and **motorbikes** can be rented from several operators, including Locbuggy (ⓣ81/3619-1142) and Eduardo Galvao de Brito at the *Esmeralda do Atlântico Hotel* (ⓣ81/3619-1335). Many hotels and *pousadas* rent out their own buggies, which can work out to be less expensive.

# Paraíba

**João Pessoa**, capital of the state of Paraíba, is the most attractive of the smaller northeastern cities, with some of the finest town beaches in the area, a beautiful setting on the mouth of the Rio Sanhauá, and colonial remains, including one of Brazil's most striking churches. Not enough foreign travellers make it to the city for the *pessoenses* to have become blasé about them, so you're likely to be approached by smiling kids who are anxious to practise their hard-learned English.

Out of the city, there are even nicer beaches to the north and south, while the highway inland leads to **Campina Grande**, a market town strategically placed at the entrance to the *sertão*. The main target of the interior is the fascinating pilgrim town of **Juazeiro do Norte**; while it's actually in neighbouring Ceará state (see p.340), it's covered here because it's most easily accessible from Paraíba.



# João Pessoa

**JOÃO PESSOA** is one of the oldest and also one of the poorest cities in Brazil. In the last two decades, there's been massive development along the city's two main beaches, but an air of dilapidated elegance remains around the old part of town. Of all the Northeast's city centres, this is the one least scarred by modern developers. Just a few kilometres away, the town beaches of **Cabo Branco** and **Tambaú** are well on their way to becoming much the same as most others in the Northeast, with towering skyscrapers stretching back towards the old town. There aren't enough of them yet, though, to detract from the stunning beauty of the vast white sandy beach, and, out of season, tourists are still few and far between.

## Arrival, orientation and information

The **rodoviária** (☎83/3221-9611) in João Pessoa is conveniently near the city centre. Any bus from the **local bus station**, opposite the *rodoviária*'s entrance, takes you to the city's one unmistakeable, central landmark: the circular lake of the Parque Solon de Lucena, which everybody simply calls the **Lagoa**, spectacularly bordered by tall palms imported from Portugal. All **bus routes** converge on the circular Anel Viário skirting the lake, some en route to the beach districts, others heading further afield: to the northern beaches, the neighbouring town of Cabedelo and the village of Penha to the south of the city. Buses for the beach can also be caught directly from the *rodoviária*; look for the ones marked "Tambaú".

The Presidente Castro Pinto **airport** (☎83/3041-4200) lies just 11km west of the city centre and is connected to the *rodoviária* by regular buses; taxis into town cost around R$30.

### Orientation

João Pessoa's **centre** is just to the west of the Lagoa. To the east, **Avenida Getúlio Vargas** leads out of town towards the skyscrapers and beachside *bairros* of Cabo Branco and Tambaú. At the city's core is **Praça João Pessoa**, which contains the state governor's palace and the local parliament; most of the central hotels are clustered around here. The oldest part of the city is just to the north of Praça João Pessoa, where **Rua Duque de Caxias** ends in the Baroque splendour of the **Igreja de São Francisco**. The steep Ladeira de São Francisco, leading down from here to the lower city and the bus and train stations, offers a marvellous tree-framed view of the rest of the city spread out on the banks of the **Rio Sanhauá**.

The two sweeping bays of **Cabo Branco** and **Tambaú** are separated by the futuristic, luxury *Hotel Tambaú* (see p.322) – more commonly known as the *Tropical Tambaú Center Hotel* – and the nearby Centro Turístico Tambaú shopping centre. This area is also where the highest concentration of bars and clubs can be found. The southern boundary of the city is the lighthouse on Ponta de Seixas, the cape at the far end of Cabo Branco. Locals claim it as the most easterly point of Brazil, a title disputed with the city of Natal to the north – though the *pessoenses* have geography on their side.

### Information

Official **tourist information** is available from the state tourist board, PB-Tur, at the *rodoviária* (daily 8am–6pm; ⓣ83/3222-3537), the airport (daily 9am–4pm) and in the Centro de Turismo in Tambaú, opposite the *Tropical Tambaú Center Hotel* at Av. Almirante Tamandaré 100 (daily 8am–7pm; ⓣ83/3247-0505). You can also find a post office and a *posto telefônico* here.

## Accommodation

You can find good budget and medium-range **hotels** both in the centre and on the beaches, but five-star luxury is only available by the sea. Hotels in João Pessoa rarely seem to charge the full price displayed at the reception desk, and you can get some pretty hefty discounts if you ask.

João Pessoa's beautiful **campsite**, on a promontory past the Ponta de Seixas, can be reached by taking the Penha bus from the Anel Viário or the local bus station: it passes near the campsite but only operates every couple of hours. Clean and well run, on a fine beach with a spectacular view of the city, the campsite is often full, especially from January to March, so it's advisable to book beforehand in the centre at sala 18, Rua Almeida Barreto 159 (ⓣ83/3221-4863).

### City centre

**Hotel Rio Verde** Rua Duque de Caxias 263 ⓣ83/3222-4369. Right in the middle of the old centre, this is a no-frills but clean and good-value option. ❶

**Lagoa Park Hotel** Parque Solon de Lucena 19 ⓣ83/3241-1414. Not as expensive as it looks, this hotel offers adequate rooms, some with great views over the Lagoa. ❸

**Pousada Raio de Luz** Praça Venancio Neiva 44 ⓣ83/3221-2169. An inexpensive hotel offering by far the best value in the city centre; rooms are tidy and some have private showers. ❷

### The beaches

**Hostel Manaíra** Av. Major Ciraulo 380 ⓣ83/3247-1962, ⓦwww.manairahostel.br2.net. The only youth-hostel affiliate in town, this is a well-kept house with small pool and garden just 300m from the beach at Praia de Manaíra; offering dorms beds (R$30), doubles and family spaces. The bathrooms are shared and sex-segregated. ❷–❹

**Hotel Pouso das Aguas** Av. Cabo Branco 2348 ⓣ83/3226-5103, ⓦwww.pousadadasaguas.com.br. Small but comfortable spot, right on the seafront with a garden and a pool. ❺

**Pousada Lua Cheia Mar** Av. Cabo Branco 1710 ⓣ83/3247-2470. Compact, clean and very friendly, this place is located at one of the best parts of the beach, between Tambaú and Cabo Branco. ❸

**Tropical Tambaú Center Hotel** Av. Almirante Tamandaré 229 ⓣ83/2107-1900, ⓦwww.tropicalhotel.com.br. One of the city's landmark modernist buildings (it looks a bit like a flying saucer), this luxury beachside hotel offers a sauna, pool, games room, fitness suite and classy restaurant – though the service is not really worth the money. ❺

**Victory Business Flat** Av. Almirante Tamandaré 310 ⓣ83/3041-3100, ⓦwww.victoryflat.com.br. More or less opposite the *Tropical Tambaú Center Hotel*, the *Victory* offers equally luxurious rooms at less than half the price outside high season; it also has a pool and good service. ❻

## The City

The centre of João Pessoa is dotted with **colonial churches, monasteries** and **convents**, some of which are extremely beautiful. Until 1992, they were all being allowed to fall into ruin, but, not a moment too soon, the state government and the Ministry of Culture mounted a crash restoration programme, for once using historians and archeologists to return the buildings to their original glory rather than gutting them. These days, modernization has certainly taken its toll on the city, but you can still see mule carts sitting alongside BMWs at the city's traffic lights.

### Igreja de São Francisco

João Pessoa's most spectacular church is the **Igreja de São Francisco** (Mon 2–5pm, Tues–Sun 9am–noon & 2–5pm), which sits in splendid isolation atop the hill that bears its name, at the end of Rua Duque de Caxias, and now forms part of the **Centro Cultural de São Francisco**. The exterior alone is impressive enough. A huge courtyard is flanked by high walls beautifully decorated with *azulejo* tiling, with pastoral scenes in a series of alcoves. These walls funnel you towards a large early eighteenth-century church that would do credit to Lisbon or Coimbra: its most remarkable feature is the tower topped with an oriental dome, a form that the Portuguese encountered in Goa and appropriated for their own purposes. Older than the church by a few decades is the stone cross opposite the courtyard, at the foot of which is a group of finely carved pelicans, once believed to selflessly tear flesh from their own chests to feed their young, and so commonly used to symbolize Christ. Beyond the church are the chapels and cloister of the **Convento de Santo Antônio**, and upstairs there's an excellent **museum** of popular and sacred art.

### Around São Francisco

The other places worth seeing in the centre are within a short walk of São Francisco. A little way down the steep Ladeira de São Francisco is the oldest building in town, the **Casa da Pólvora**, a relic of the times when the Dutch and Portuguese fought for control over this sugar-rich coastline. The squat, functional building was once the city arsenal, but is now the home of the **Museu Fotográfico Walfredo Rodriguez** (Mon–Fri 8–11.30am & 2–5pm), given over to a collection of enlarged photographs of the city taken in the early decades of this century.

If you go back up the Ladeira de São Francisco, turn right and right again, you'll end up on Rua General Osório. Here you'll find the cathedral, **Igreja de Nossa Senhora das Neves**, which boasts a well-proportioned interior that, for

▲ Igreja de São Francisco

once, forgoes the Rococo excesses of many colonial cathedrals. Its large, rather plain facade fronts a small square with majestic views north to the wooded river valley and, to the west, green suburbs. Further down Rua General Osório, the seventeenth-century **Mosteiro de São Bento** (Tues–Sat 2–5pm) has a simple, beautifully restored interior with a lovely curved wooden ceiling. Other colonial churches are cheek by jowl on Rua Visconde de Pelotas, two blocks to the east: the **Igreja de Nossa Senhora do Carmo** here is well worth a look, both for its ornate Baroque exterior and the gold-leaf-covered altar inside.



## The beaches

The beach areas of Tambaú and Cabo Branco are linked to the centre by frequent buses from the Anel Viário and the local bus station. The **Cabo Branco** seafront is especially stylish, with a mosaic pavement and thousands of well-tended palm trees to complement the sweep of the bay. This is best viewed from the **Ponta de Seixas lighthouse** at the southern end, where a plaque and a monument mark Brazil's easternmost point. From here, it's only 2200km to Senegal in Africa, less than half the distance to Rio Grande do Sul in the south of Brazil or the state of Roraima in the north. To get to the lighthouse, take the "Cabo Branco" bus to its terminal on the promontory at the end of the bay and walk up the hill. At the top, you'll find a park and a couple of tacky souvenir shops, but the main draw here is the **view**, which is glorious – Cabo Branco beach stretches out before you in an enormous arc, 6km long. Cabo Branco itself is one of the city's exclusive upper-class suburbs, where the rich stay hidden in their large detached houses, their high walls shutting out both the people and the view. The beach has the usual string of bars and several hotels, but they are sparser and less intrusive than on Tambaú, and during the week there's not much more at the southern end of Cabo Branco than the rustle of wind in the palm trees to disturb you.

**Tambaú** is a lot livelier, dominated by its eponymous hotel, which forms one end of a small square. Nearby, on the corner of *avenidas* Nossa Senhora dos Navegantes and Rui Carneiro, is a modern building housing the **Mercado de Artesanato Paraíbano** (Mon–Sat 9am–7pm, Sun 9am–5pm). Although not up to the standards of Pernambuco, Paraíba has distinctive *artesanato* that's worth checking out: painted plates and bowls, and striking figurines made out of sacking and wood. North of the market you encounter busier and larger clusters of beachside bars and restaurants.

## Eating, drinking and nightlife

As usual in a coastal capital, the centre tends to get deserted after dark, as people looking for a night out head for the beaches, particularly Tambaú. However, there are several **restaurants and bars** in the centre worth trying out. The more expensive restaurants (R$45–80 range) in the beach areas are in Cabo Branco. There are a few very good places on the seafront, some of which are listed below.

João Pessoa has a surprisingly rich but fluctuating **music scene** for a city of its size, concentrated at the beaches: the only nights it's difficult to catch something are Monday and Sunday. Venues open and close with bewildering frequency, so it's best to ask the tourist office for a current list, though they will direct you to the more expensive upmarket clubs unless you're persistent. Alternatively, look in the entertainment guide of the local paper, *O Norte*.

The square in front of the *Tropical Tambaú Center Hotel* is a relaxed place for a drink and some **live music**. It's surrounded by restaurants and bars, and on Friday and Saturday nights, tables and chairs are put out in the square, drink starts flowing and after about 9pm things start getting very lively. In the streets behind there are any number of small **bars and clubs**, which tend not to get going until 11pm at the earliest. There are a couple of fairly lively **gay bars**, too, in the streets behind Avenida Nossa Senhora dos Navegantes in Tambaú.

### City centre

**Bar da Pólvora** Behind the Casa da Pólvora, Ladeira São Francisco. Serves only beer, *caipirinhas* and soft drinks, from tables set out on the patio beneath the ancient walls of the arsenal against a stunning view out across the river. The best time to go is Thursday evening, when there's a show (small cover charge) with poets or singers doing spots.

**Miralha** Av. Epitácio Pessoa ⓣ83/3226-3982. Bar and *churrascaria* with a wide range of quality meats, also offering live *forró* music on Monday evenings.

**Recanto do Picuí** Rua Felicinano Dourado 198 ⓣ83/3224-1400. Serves some of the best *sertão* food in the city; the *carne do sol* here is excellent, best accompanied by green beans and *batata doce assado* (roast sweet potatoes).

**Salutte** Rua 13 de Maio 73. Good for its self-service lunches, which are hard to beat for quality and value, though it has less to offer in the evenings. Closed Sun.

### The beaches

**Apetito Trattoria** Av. Osorio Paes 35 ⓣ83/3226-6634. The best Italian in town, offering fresh pasta and seafood and a romantic ambience. Closed Mon.

**Mangai** Av. Edson Ramalho 696 ⓣ83/3226-1615. A smart place boasting a wide range of dishes, with much of the produce coming fresh from the restaurant's own ranch; this is regional cooking at its best, though it's not cheap.

**Olho de Lula** Av. Cabo Branco 2300 ⓣ83/3226-2328. Popular, if slightly exclusive, seafood restaurant; best at lunchtime.

**Tábua de Carne** Av. Rui Carneiro 648, Tambaú ⓣ83/3247-5970. Located on one of the roads running away from the beach, this is a good place for meat and *sertão* food.

## Listings

**Airlines** TAM ⓣ83/3232-2002.

**Banks and exchange** There are ATMs around the city centre and the beaches.

**Car rental** Localiza, Av. Epitácio Pessoa 4910 ⓣ83/3232-1130 or airport ⓣ0800/992-000.

**Post office** The main office is on Praça Pedro Américo, two blocks downhill from Praça João Pessoa.

**Taxis** Disk taxi ⓣ0800/83-1310; Teletaxi ⓣ0800/83-2056 or ⓣ83/3241-5656.

**Travel and tour companies** Terramar Turismo, Rua Antônio Lira Silva 299 (ⓣ83/3247-2425), and Roger Turismo, Rua Juvencio Mangueira Carneiro, Jardin Acacias (ⓣ83/3241-5332, ⓔroger@zaitek.com.br), offer a full range of tours and travel services.

# Along the coast

Like so much of Brazil, Paraíba is blessed with many wonderful **beaches** along its 140-kilometre coastline. Unlike some other parts of the Northeast, however, many of its beaches are, for the time being, largely undeveloped and many require somewhat difficult journeys by bus and then on foot or by taxi to reach them.

## South to Penha and Tambaba

Just to the **south** of João Pessoa is the fishing village of **PENHA**, served by local buses from outside the *rodoviária*. Strung out along a fine beach set in the midst of dense palm forest, Penha is distinguished from other fishing villages round about by a nineteenth-century church, the **Igreja de Nossa Senhora da Penha**, which is a pilgrimage centre and focus of much popular devotion. The beach near the church is also used by followers of *candomblé*, who identify the Virgin with Iemanjá, the goddess of the sea. According to legend, over a century ago an image of the Virgin was dredged up by fishermen in their nets, and worked so many miracles that the community adopted her as their patron saint and built the simple chapel to house her icon. Along the beach, there are several rustic **bars** where you can eat and also string a hammock for a nominal fee. Discreet camping on the beach is also possible.

**TAMBABA** is set on a volcanic outcrop some 30km to the south of João Pessoa. It's the first officially recognized nudist beach in the Northeast and is well off the beaten track. Getting here involves a bus ride from the *rodoviária* to the small seaside town of **Jacumã**, followed by an eight-kilometre walk (or a taxi ride) along a rough road. The beach is superb, and there's a small if somewhat overpriced bar here. Alternatively, and a little nearer to Jacumã, is the **Praia Coqueirinho**, which is a popular spot for the local children in the surrounding villages; again, you'll need to take a taxi. **Camping** is possible at the beach of Tabatinga, just to the north.

### North towards Cabedelo

Penha apart, most of the readily accessible **beaches** are to the **north**, off the road that leads to Cabedelo, 18km or 45 minutes by frequent local buses from the Anel Viário in João Pessoa – they get very crowded at weekends. The road runs a little inland and there are turn-offs leading to the beaches on the way: it seems to depend more on the drivers' whim than a timetable as to whether the bus takes you right to the beach, but hop on the Cabedelo bus anyway, and get off at the relevant turn-off if need be; it'll only be a short walk to the sea.

Less than 10km north of town, **POÇO** boasts a chapel, some weekend homes, a fine palm-fringed beach with the obligatory bars and several good fish restaurants. From here, you could walk the 10km along the beach to Cabedelo; otherwise, hourly buses to Cabedelo, or back to João Pessoa, leave during the day from the bus stop near the church.

**CABEDELO** itself is older than it looks. It was much fought over in the Dutch wars, and the star-shaped fort of **Santa Caterina** (Tues–Sat 8am–5pm), dating from 1585, is the major sight in the village. Unfortunately, Petrobrás have built a series of oil storage tanks right up to its ramparts, and it's difficult to get a sense of its strategic position, commanding as it does the only deep-water anchorage on this stretch of coast.

There's no reason to hang around in Cabedelo and plenty of reason to continue 20km to two superb and largely unspoilt beaches. For the more adventurous camper, there's the **Praia do Oiteiro**, a wild and beautiful beach backed by hills covered with tropical vegetation but little in the way of modern comforts. **Campina**, just north of Oiteiro, is similarly idyllic but with the addition of a small fishing settlement. You can get to both beaches on the same bus from João Pessoa via Cabedelo, or you could try renting a boat in Cabedelo as it's only half the distance along the coast.

## Inland to Campina Grande

The BR-230, a good-quality asphalt road, bisects Paraíba and leads directly into the *sertão*. The green coastal strip is quickly left behind as the road climbs into the hills and the second city of Paraíba, **CAMPINA GRANDE**, linked to João Pessoa by hourly bus (2hr). It's a large town, similar in many ways to Caruaru in Pernambuco: even the slogan you see at the city limits – "Welcome to the Gateway of the Sertão" – is the same. Like Caruaru, Campina Grande owes its existence to a strategic position between the *agreste* and the *sertão* proper. It's a market town

## Campina Grande's festivals

In June, Campina Grande hosts a month-long **festival** that uses the São João holiday – the **festas juninas** – as an excuse for a general knees-up. Streets are filled with stalls selling food and drinks, and various events are scheduled. This makes June one of the best times to visit, and the wonderfully named *forrodrómo* in the centre of town, an enormous cross between a concert hall and a *dancetaria*, is where much of the action happens.

But Campina Grande is equally well known for its out-of-season Carnaval, the **Micarande**, an event in late April that attracts some 300,000 people over a period of four days and is the largest of its kind in Brazil. The music, best described as frenetic electric, reaches fever pitch as the *trios elétricos* (Carnaval trucks), with live *frevo* bands playing on top, work their way through the crowds with their followers in train, the music lasting until dawn. Accommodation during this period is particularly scarce and expensive even for the humblest of abodes, so it's best to get in touch with one of the leading organizers, the state tourist authority (☎83/3310-6100), before setting out. A word of warning, however: although the event itself is very well policed, take care when making your way to it as the streets and buses are very crowded.

and centre of light industry, where the products of the *sertão* are stockpiled and sent down to the coast, and where the people of the *sertão* come to buy what they can't make – at a large Wednesday and Saturday **market**, you can see this process unfolding before your eyes.

You may also see evidence of the fierce competition between Campina Grande and João Pessoa. *Campinenses* proudly contrast their industries and commercial know-how with the decadence and stagnation of João Pessoa, and there is concerted pressure from the people of Campina Grande to make this the new capital of Paraíba. To the traveller, though, João Pessoa's elegance is something of a contrast with Campina Grande, which even locals admit is rather ugly. Still, it's a good place to sample the distinctive culture of the *sertão*, without having to suffer its discomforts, and also to experience some unforgettable **festivals**.

The **climate** in Campina Grande is always pleasant, as its height takes the edge off the coastal heat without making it cold, though you may need a sweater at night during the rainy season.

## The City

Although the city sprawls out into anonymous industrial suburbs, the **central layout** is compact and easy to get the hang of. The city's heart, and most useful landmark, is the obelisk in the **Parque do Açude Novo**. The park itself straddles the **Avenida Floriano Peixoto**, which bisects Campina Grande from west to east, and the stretch of the avenue from the obelisk to the cathedral is the centre proper, where most of the things to do and see are concentrated.

The highlight of Campina Grande is its **market**, held every Wednesday and Saturday. The market takes over the area around the cathedral and the municipal market behind it. Sometimes sellers of *cordel* (see p.299) recite chunks of the ballads to whet the public's appetite, and clusters of people gather around to shout comments and enjoy the story. If you miss the market, but still fancy trying to get hold of **artesanato** and **cordel**, good places are the cooperative Casa do Artesão, Rua Venâncio Neiva 85, near the Rique Palace, and Kaboclinha, nearby at Rua Vidal de Negreiros 36.

By some way, the best museum in Campina Grande is the **Museu de Arte Assis Chateaubriand** (Mon–Fri 9am–noon & 2–10pm, Sat & Sun 2–10pm), part of the complex of buildings in the Parque do Açude Novo. It's a source of justifiable civic pride, boasting a good gallery of modern art, devoted entirely to Brazilian artists, with a special emphasis on work from the Northeast. Some of Brazil's greatest modern painters are represented, notably Cândido Portinari, whose large canvasses fuse social realism with modernist technique in their depiction of workers and workplaces. The most intriguing part of the museum is the *atelier livre*, where local painters, carvers and sculptors exhibit their works in progress.

In contrast, the **Museu Histórico e Geográfico**, at Av. Floriano Peixote 825 (Mon–Fri 8am–6pm, Sat & Sun 8am–noon), is loaded with period furniture, weapons, maps and historical photos relating to the city's heritage. In a similar vein, the **Museu do Algodão** (Mon–Fri 8am–noon & 2–6pm), in the tourist centre inside the old train station, concentrates on the history of the cotton plantations of the area, including some fearsome chains, stocks, iron collars and whips used on the slaves.



## Practicalities

The **rodoviária** (☎83/3337-2305) is on the outskirts of town at Av. Sen. Argemiro de Figueiredo in Catolé; local buses marked "Centro" take you downtown. The **tourist office** is situated at Praça Clementino Procópio (Mon–Fri 8am–5pm; ☎83/3310-6100); you can get a useful city map here.

There's a good choice of **accommodation** in Campina Grande. The centrally located *Belfran*, Av. Floriano Peixoto 258 (☎83/3341-1312; ❸), is one of the best budget choices in town, with cheerful, well-kept rooms. Out of the centre, the comfortable *Hotel Village*, Rua Otacílio Nepomuceno 1285 (☎83/3310-8000, Ⓦwww.hoteisvillage.com.br; ❺), near the *rodoviária*, offers a pool and a sauna, plus a bar and decent restaurant. The best of the **restaurants** in town, *Tábua de Carne*, can be found at Av. Manoel Tavares 1040 (☎83/3341-1008); it specializes in regional cuisine and meats.

# Into the sertão

The BR-232 continues through the *sertão* past the flyblown town of Patos to **SOUSA**, an unremarkable *sertão* town five hours (445km) from João Pessoa (or 310km from Campina Grande). If you want to overnight here, try *Jardins Plaza* (Rua João Bosco Marques de Sousa ☎83/3522-4212; ❹), on the Patos road, which has a sauna, pool and restaurant. Sousa is home to one of the Northeast's more unusual sights, the **Vale dos Dinosauras**, "Dinosaur Valley", formed by the sedimentary basin of the Rio Peixe. At one time, difficult though it is to imagine in this searing semi-arid landscape, all was swamp and jungle here. Various prehistoric reptiles left their footprints, preserved in stone, at several sites in the area around the town. The only way to get to them is by battered taxi over the dusty road. The nearest site, A Ilha, is about 5km out of town – around R$35 in a taxi.

## Juazeiro do Norte

The main centre of the deep *sertão* is 500km west of Campina Grande – actually in the south of Ceará state – where a series of hill ranges, higher ground blessed with regular rainfall, provides a welcome respite. Food crops can be grown here, and every available inch of land is used to grow fruit and vegetables, or graze cattle. Here there are two towns within a few kilometres of each other, Crato and **JUAZEIRO DO NORTE**, and it was in this area that one of the most famous episodes in the history of the Northeast took place (see box below). It is still the site of a massive **pilgrimage** on July 20 each year.

### The pilgrim route

If you want to do what the pilgrims do, the first stop is Padre Cícero's **tomb** in the church of **Nossa Senhora do Perpétuo Socorro**, to the left of the square. A small monument sits outside, always decorated with *ex votos*, tokens brought by those praying for help. Inside the plain church you'll see a constant stream of *romeiros* praying intensely and queuing to kiss the marble slab by the altar; the grave itself is to the left, an unpretentious tomb covered in flowers and ribbons. The church is surrounded by souvenir shops, which specialize in the figurines of Padre Cícero with hat and walking stick that you can find all over the Northeast.

The next destination is the **statue** of Padre Cícero on the peak of the **Serra do Horto**, the hill that looks down on the town. The soft option is to take a taxi or bus for 3km along a road that winds up the hill – a route

## Miracle at Juazeiro

In 1889, Juazeiro was no more than a tiny hamlet. There was nothing unusual about its young priest, **Padre Cícero Romão Batista**, until a woman in Juazeiro claimed the wine he gave them at Communion had turned to blood in their mouths. At first, it was only people from Crato who came, and they were convinced by the woman's sanctity and the evidence of their own eyes that Padre Cícero had indeed worked a miracle. As his fame grew, the deeply religious inhabitants of the *sertão* came to hear his sermons and have him bless them. Padre Cícero came to be seen as a living saint: miraculous cures were attributed to him, things he had touched and worn were treated as relics. The Catholic Church began a formal investigation of the alleged "miracle", sent him to Rome to testify to commissions of enquiry, rejected it, sent him back to Brazil and suspended him from the priesthood – but nothing could shake the conviction of the local people that he was a saint. Juazeiro mushroomed into a large town by *sertão* standards, as people flocked to make the pilgrimage, including legendary figures such as the bandit chief Lampião.

By the end of his long life, Padre Cícero had become one of the most powerful figures in the Northeast. In 1913, his heavily armed followers caught the train to the state capital, Fortaleza, and forcibly deposed the governor, replacing him with somebody more to Padre Cícero's liking. But Padre Cícero was a deeply conservative man, who restrained his followers more often than not, deferred to the Church, and remained seemingly more preoccupied with the next world than with this. When his more revolutionary followers tried to set up a religious community nearby at Caldeirão, he didn't deter the authorities from using the air force against them, in one of the first recorded uses of aerial bombs on civilians. When he finally died, in 1934, his body had to be displayed strapped to a door from the first floor of his house, before the thousands thronging the streets would believe he was dead. Ever since, pilgrims have come to Juazeiro to pay homage, especially on the anniversary of his death on July 20; an enormous white statue of the priest looks out from a hillside over the town he created.

that can be walked if you want to see the fine views of the **valley of Cariri** unfold, with the town of Crato visible to the west. The other way is to follow the **pilgrim route**, a track from the town directly up the hill: it isn't signposted but people will willingly direct you to it if you ask for *a picada dos romeiros* or *a Via Sacra*. It's a brisk hour to the top, and at several points the pilgrims have cut steps. Thousands walk the trail on July 20, "paying the promise", that is, performing penances for help received; a few hardy souls make the journey on their knees.

Once on top, the main attractions are not so much the statue – 27m high but hardly a masterpiece – as the panoramic views and the **chapel** and **museum of ex votos** next to it. Room after room is piled high with stacks of offerings from the grateful thousands for whom Padre Cícero interceded over the decades: countless artificial limbs, wooden models of body parts, photos of disasters escaped and crashes survived, even football jerseys from victorious players, including one from Brazil's winning 1970 World Cup team. As a demonstration of the hold that religion has on the daily lives of millions of *nordestinos*, only the *ex votos* at the church of Bonfim in Salvador rival it.

The pilgrim's route finishes up at Padre Cícero's **house**, signposted from the church where he is buried, and now a cross between a museum and a shrine. It's a simple dwelling, with large rooms, a garden and glass cases displaying everything anybody could find that was even remotely connected to the great man: his glasses, underwear, hats, typewriter, bed linen, even the bed he died in.

The last act of pilgrimage is to be **photographed** to prove to the folks back home that you've made the trip. This ensures a steady flow of work for the many photographers clustered around the last church on the way to the hill, the **Igreja Matriz de Nossa Senhora das Dores**. They all have a series of props to help you pose: life-size statues of Padre Cícero, dozens of hats, toy elephants and so forth, and although the snap takes two or three hours to develop, it comes ready-mounted in a mini-viewer, far more durable than a photo proper – the ideal souvenir.

### Practicalities

When booking a ticket to Juazeiro, make sure you specify Juazeiro do Norte, or you run the risk of ending up in Juazeiro in Bahia, several hundred kilometres south. The **rodoviária** is a couple of kilometres out of the town, which is smaller than its fame suggests. There is one central square where you'll find the best and most expensive **hotel**, the *Panorama* at Rua Santo Agostinho 84 (Ⓣ88/3566-3150, Ⓦwww.panoramahotel.com.br; ❸–❹), but finding somewhere to stay is the least of your worries in a town geared to putting up pilgrims: there are small hotels and *dormitórios* everywhere. The best place **to eat** is the *Restó Jardim*, in Lagoa Seca at Av. Leão Sampaio 5460 (Ⓣ88/3571-7768; closed Tues), serving a wide variety of regional and international dishes.

**Leaving town**, seats fill up fast on the daily buses to João Pessoa, Recife and Fortaleza, so if you're staying overnight book a ticket when you arrive. Alternatively, it is usually possible to get a seat on one of the **pilgrim buses** parked around town; their drivers sell seats for the same price as on the regular bus, and groups come from all the major cities, so just pick a bus going your way.

# Rio Grande do Norte

Until the late 1980s, the small state of **Rio Grande do Norte** and its capital, **Natal**, were sleepy, conservative backwaters rarely visited by tourists. There's little of historical interest among Natal's modern hotels and office buildings, and the interior is poor and thinly populated, the only place of any size being the town of **Mossoró**. But two things have transformed Rio Grande do Norte into one of the Northeast's biggest tourist centres: **beaches** and **buggies**.

**North of Natal**, the *sertão* drives down practically to the coast, and the idyllic palm-fringed beaches give way to massive sand dunes. The landscape becomes less fertile and flatter, dedicated largely to scrawny cattle, who scratch a living alongside the people. The black Brazilian population shrinks with the sugar zone, and in Rio Grande do Norte dwindles to almost nothing.

# Natal

**NATAL** is a medium-sized city of about 600,000 people, built on the banks of the Rio Potengi and founded sixty years later than planned, after the Potiguar Indians stifled the first Portuguese landing on the coast in 1538. They continued to hold the invaders off until 1598, when the Portuguese built the star-shaped fort at the mouth of the river – the city's most enduring landmark. From Genipabu just north of Natal you can drive north in a beach buggy for 250km of uninterrupted dunes as far as Areia Branca, practically on the border with Ceará.

Natal has become a popular destination for Brazilian holiday-makers, lured by sun and sand rather than the city itself, which is mostly modern and has a sloppily developed seafront: you will look in vain for the colonial elegance of João Pessoa or Olinda. But the glorious beaches do compensate, and amid the development and hotels there are some good nightspots and *dancetarias*.

## Arrival, city transport and information

Natal's **airport**, Augusto Severo, is about 15km south of the centre on the BR-101 highway; a taxi to the centre will cost you about R$25, or you can catch the bus marked "Parnamirim–Natal". Taxis from the airport to Ponta Negra (see p.337) cost around R$35. The **rodoviária** (☎84/3232-7312) is also a long way out from the centre, at Av. Capitão Mor-Gouveia 1237 in the suburb of Cidade de Esperança, but you can get a local bus into town at the bus stop on the other side of the road, opposite the *rodoviária* entrance. Most of these buses from across the road pass through the centre: those marked "Av. Rio Branco", "Cidade Alta" and "Ribeira" are the most common. Taxis from the *rodoviária* into the centre are also plentiful and should cost around R$25.

Natal's main thoroughfare is the **Avenida Rio Branco**, which runs past the oldest part of the city, **Cidade Alta**, and terminates just to the right of a scruffy square, Praça Augusto Severo, site of the useful central bus station. The main post office is on block 5 of Avenida Rio Branco, with the Banco do Brasil next door. Cutting across the *avenida* is Rua João Pessoa, graced at its western end by the city's old cathedral. East along João Pessoa, you'll come to the small **Praça Padre João Maria**, which most days hosts a small but interesting *artesanato* market and is surrounded by some of the finest and most colourful old mansions in Natal.

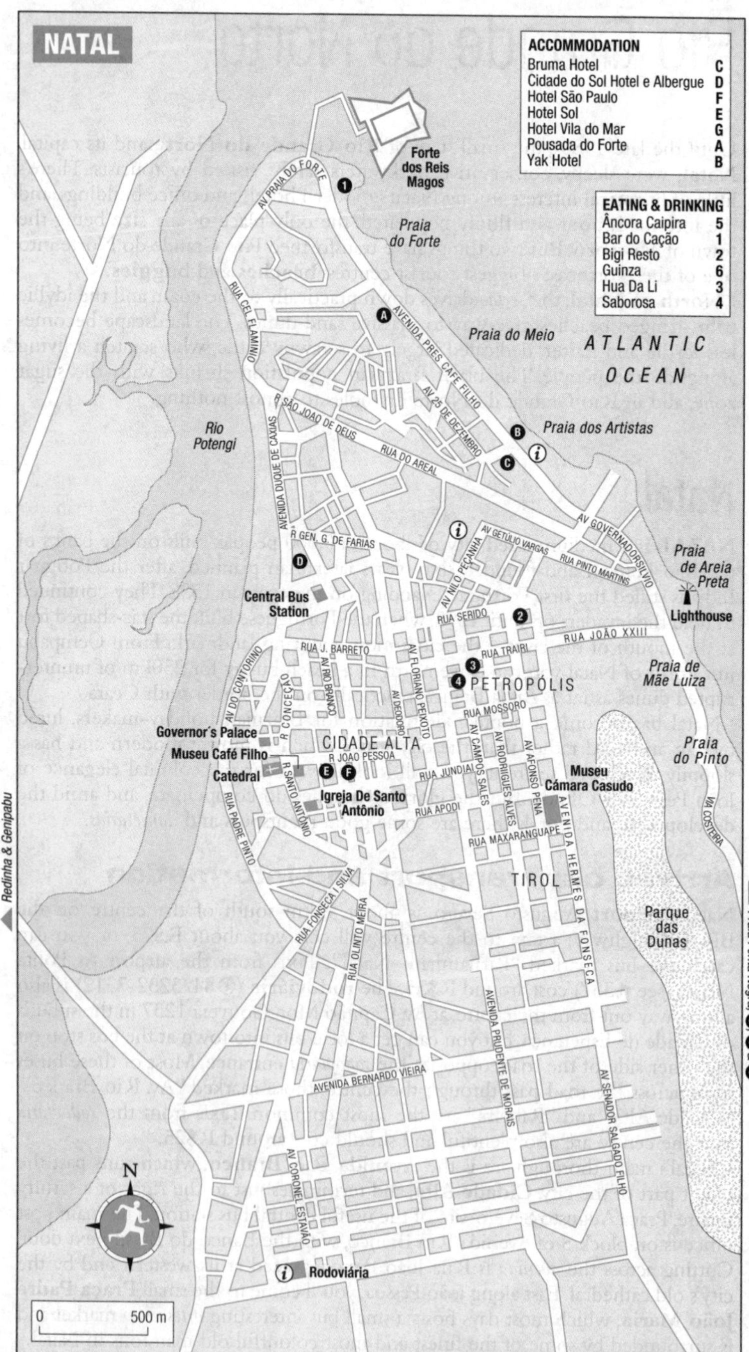
NATAL
ACCOMMODATION
Bruma Hotel C
Cidade do Sol Hotel e Albergue D
Hotel São Paulo F
Hotel Sol E
Hotel Vila do Mar G
Pousada do Forte A
Yak Hotel B
EATING & DRINKING
Âncora Caipira 5
Bar do Cação 1
Bigi Resto 2
Guinza 6
Hua Da Li 3
Saborosa 4
Forte dos Reis Magos
Praia do Forte
AV PRAIA DO FORTE
RUA CEL FLAMINIO
AVENIDA PRES CAFE FILHO
Praia do Meio
ATLANTIC OCEAN
AV 25 DE DEZEMBRO
R SÃO JOAO DE DEUS
RUA DO AREAL
Praia dos Artistas
Rio Potengi
AVENIDA DUQUE DE CAXIAS
AV GOVERNADOR SILVIO
R GEN. G. DE FARIAS
AV GETÚLIO VARGAS
RUA PINTO MARTINS
AV NILO PEÇANHA
Praia de Areia Preta
Central Bus Station
Lighthouse
RUA SERIDO
RUA JOÃO XXIII
RUA J. BARRETO
RUA TRAIRI
Praia de Mãe Luiza
AV DO CONTORINO
R CONCEÇÃO
AV RIO BRANCO
AV DEODORO
AV FLORIANO PEIXOTO
PETROPÓLIS
RUA MOSSORO
Governor's Palace
CIDADE ALTA
Museu Café Filho
R JOÃO PESSOA
Catedral
R SANTO ANTÔNIO
RUA JUNDIAI
AV CAMPOS SALES
AV RODRIGUES ALVES
AV AFONSO PENA
Museu Câmara Casudo
Praia do Pinto
Igreja De Santo Antônio
RUA APODI
RUA PADRE PINTO
RUA MAXARANGUAPE
AVENIDA HERMES DA FONSECA
VIA COSTEIRA
TIROL
Redinha & Genipabu
Praia Ponta Negra, G, 5 & 6
Parque das Dunas
RUA FONSECA I SILVA
RUA OLINTO MEIRA
AVENIDA PRUDENTE DE MORAIS
AVENIDA BERNARDO VIEIRA
AV SENADOR SALGADO FILHO
AV CORONEL ESTAVÃO
N
Rodoviária
0 500 m
Airport, Ponta Negra & Praia Shopping Centre

From Cidade Alta, roads descend straight to the **city beaches** of Praia do Forte, Praia do Meio and Praia dos Artistas, and the coastal road to the **southern beaches**. The most important of these is Ponta Negra, at 10km away just far enough from the city centre to have survived massive development. **Beaches to the north** of the city are generally less crowded and even more beautiful, but harder to get to. Just out of the centre are the quiet and pleasant grid-pattern suburbs of **Petrópolis** and the incongruously named **Tirol**, after the birthplace of the Austrian planner who laid them out in the 1930s.

## City transport

Natal's **bus system** is easy to master, and in a hot city with hills and scattered beaches it's worth spending a little time getting used to it. At the central **bus station** on Praça Augusto Severo, and from **Avenida Rio Branco**, you can catch local buses to most of the places you might want to go to: all the buses to the southern beaches, like Areia Preta and Ponta Negra, can be caught from here or the seafront; buses marked "Via Costeira" head along the southern coastal road out to Ponta Negra. Several bus routes run from the centre to the *rodoviária*, taking at least half an hour and often longer because of their circuitous routes; buses marked "Cidade de Esperança" are the most direct. **Minibuses**, acting as collective taxis, also compete with buses, stopping at all corners en route.

## Information

There are **tourist information** posts at Praia Shopping (Ⓣ84/3232-7248) and the *rodoviária* (Ⓣ84/205-1000); both have good free maps of the city and can organize accommodation for you. If you want to take a **tour** to Fernando de Noronha, one of Brazil's ecotourim jewels, a string of island wildlife and sealife havens an hour's flight from the mainland (see p.319), the Reis Magos Viagems e Turismo, at Av. Sen. Salgado Filho 1799 (Ⓣ84/3206-5888), has information on trips there.

# Accommodation

**Hotels** are plentiful in both the city centre and the beach areas. A good alternative, if you want to get away from traffic and urbanization, is to stay at one of the beaches outside the city, **Ponta Negra** being the most popular (see p.337).

### The city centre

**Cidade do Sol Hotel e Albergue** Av. Duque de Caxias 190, Ribeira Ⓣ84/3211-3233. This well-run hostel near the central bus station has decent rooms, with or without a/c, plus wi-fi access and a nice garden at the back. ❷–❹

**Hotel São Paulo** Av. Rio Branco 897 Ⓣ84/3211-8657. Refurbished budget hotel with good breakfasts. The entrance is on Rua General Osório. ❸

**Hotel Sol** Rua Heitor Carrilho 107 Ⓣ84/3201-2208. Good-value hotel in the older part of the upper city, with its own restaurant and smallish but pleasant rooms with private baths, a/c, minibar and cable TV. ❸

### The beaches

**Bruma Hotel** Av. Pres. Café Filho 1176, Praia dos Artistas Ⓣ84/3202-4303, Ⓦwww.hotelbruma.com.br. This beautifully designed building, with fine lower stone walls and an almost pagoda-style top roof, overlooks the beach and has a small pool. ❹

**Hotel Vila do Mar** Via Costeira 4233 Ⓣ84/4009-4900, Ⓦwww.viladomar.com.br. Luxury hotel close to the sea with all the facilities you'd expect, including a pool and tennis courts. ❼

**Pousada do Forte** Av. Pres. Café Filho 786, Praia do Meio Ⓣ84/3202-5050. Large, well-kept rooms with all the modern conveniences, located on the beachside opposite the statue of Iemanjá. ❹

**Yak Hotel** Av. Pres. Café Filho Ⓣ84/3202-4224, Ⓦwww.yakplaza.com.br. Located 3km from Natal's centre on the Praia do Meio, all rooms have a/c; there's also a restaurant and a large pool. ❹

## The City

For a city nearly four centuries old there is surprisingly little of historical interest in Natal itself, apart from the distinctive, whitewashed **Forte dos Reis Magos** (daily 8am–4.45pm), which dominates the river entrance. Like most of Brazil's colonial forts it looks very vulnerable, directly overlooked by the hill behind it and with thick, surprisingly low walls. There isn't much to see apart from a couple of token museums, but the city is an interesting place to wander, with stark contrasts between the old heart, the busy shopping centre and some of the swish downtown suburbs.

The oldest part of Natal is formed by the closely packed streets and small squares of Cidade Alta, but the street plan itself is one of the only things that remains from colonial times. Instead, the architecture that has survived the modern thrust for development is clustered around the administrative heart of the city, **Praça Sete de Setembro**, which is dominated by the **governor's palace**, built in tropical Victorian style in 1873. Also in the square is the **Espaço Cultural** (Mon–Fri 8am–6pm), with changing shows of mainly local artists, and the restored **Teatro Alberto Maranhão**, a Neoclassical structure built in 1898. In the neighbouring Praça Albuquerque, you'll find the **Instituto Histórico e Geográfico** (Mon–Fri 8am–noon & 2–5pm), a quaint nineteenth-century edifice housing period furniture and archives relating to the region's history, while the old **Catedral** next door (daily 4.30–6pm) was built in 1862 but is unexceptional for all that. Smaller, and rather more interesting, is the **Igreja de Santo Antônio** (Mon–Fri 8–11.30am & 2–5.30pm, Sat 8–11.30am) nearby at Rua Santo Antônio 683, a Baroque church known as the Igreja do Galo, after the eighteenth-century bronze cock crowing on top of its Moorish tower; inside you'll find a well-respected **museum of religious art** (Mon–Sat 1–6pm).

Just off Praça Sete de Setembro is the most interesting museum in a city largely bereft of them, the **Museu Café Filho** (Mon–Fri 8am–5pm, Sat 8–10am), dedicated to the only *rio grandense* to become president of Brazil – a corrupt and incompetent paternalist, despite the attempts by the museum to present him as a statesman. But he had the good taste to live in a fine two-storey mansion, at Rua da Conceição 630, which is worth seeing – more than can be said for the yellowing papers and heavy furniture of the long-dead president. Also worth a visit is the **Museu Cámara Casudo**, at Av. Hermes da Fonseca 1398, in Tirol (Tues–Fri 8–11am & 2–5pm; R$2.50), which is dedicated to local ecology, history and geology. Sponsored heavily by Petrobrás, the museum contains a large, flashy exhibit on oil drilling, but nevertheless, it's well thought out and presented, with dinosaur fossils, a *jangada* and a range of other interesting exhibits.

Located in the old prison, perched on top of a hill at Rua Aderbal de Figueiredo 980 in Petrópolis, the **Centro de Turismo** (Mon–Fri 9am–9pm; ⓣ84/3211-6149) has a lovely café, *Marenosso*, as well as scores of quality arts and crafts, with an emphasis on cotton products. On the first floor there's also an interesting gallery filled with ceramics, weavings, paintings and antiques, plus beautiful views of the beaches and city.

## The beaches

What Natal lacks in attractions for the culturally minded, it makes up for in facilities for the beach bum. There are fine **beaches** right inside the city, beginning at the fort where arcs of sand sweep along the bay to the headland and **Mãe Luiza lighthouse**, a useful point to take bearings from. Buses marked

## Beach buggies

Going to Natal without riding a **beach buggy** is a bit like going to Ireland and not drinking Guinness – you may or may not enjoy it, but you might as well try it seeing as you're there. Buggies have become a way of life in Natal, providing employment for the young drivers or *bugeiros* who race around the city and its beaches in their noisy, low-slung vehicles. After a period of explosive, unregulated growth during which unqualified cowboy *bugeiros* risked their and their passengers' necks, the buggy industry has settled down a bit, though you should still check that your driver has **accreditation** and **insurance** – most of them do.

There are two basic kinds of buggy ride. One possibility is to go on a **day-** or **half-day trip**, which involves riding either north or south down the coast, mainly along the beaches. Many firms offer a full day's outing with the *litoral norte* in the morning and the *litoral sul* in the afternoon, or vice versa. The *bugeiro* will perform a few stunts along the way, surfing the sand dunes, but it's mainly an opportunity to explore the beautiful coastline around Natal.

However, the real thrills and spills are to be found on specific beaches, especially at **Genipabu** (see p.339) to the north of Natal. Here you pay by the ride or by the hour for fairground-type stuff, with the *bugeiros* making full use of the spectacular sand dunes to push your heart through your mouth. These rides are not cheap, and you may find yourself paying over R$100 for an hour's entertainment.

Conditions inside the buggies are cramped. Most *bugeiros* will try and fit three or four people in on each trip, with two people sitting outside at the back hanging on to a metal bar. You'll need plenty of **sun protection** and an extremely tight-fitting hat. It's an exhilarating business, with the wind whipping through your hair as you bounce around the dunes.

Most hotels have deals with buggy companies, and you'll find yourself besieged by offers of rides wherever you are in Natal. Most rides cost between R$25 and R$50 per person for a day's outing. If you want to deal with the **companies** directly, try Passeio de Buggy (☎84/3219-2450, Ⓦwww.passeiodebuggy.com.br) at Rua Manoel Satíro 1, Ponta Negra.

"Mãe Luiza" transport you from the seafront to the foot of the hill crowned by the lighthouse, which you can walk up, although you'll be besieged by children offering guided tours. From the top there's a magnificent view of the **Praia do Meio**, the beach that stretches from the fort to the headland of the Ladeira do Sol, and the **Praia da Areia Preta**, curving between the headland and the lighthouse. Technically the Praia do Meio is composed of three beaches: the small Praia do Forte next to the fort, the Praia do Meio and the Praia dos Artistas, where dune buggies line up looking for customers. All the beaches are lined with stalls serving the usual array of cold drinks and food, and numerous hotels and bars are strung along the inland side of the seafront, which gets lively on weekend evenings.

On the other side of the lighthouse is another enormous beach, **Praia de Mãe Luiza**, accessible along the tourist development highway known as the Via Costeira, which takes you to Ponta Negra, 10km away. Although large, the Praia de Mãe Luiza is rarely used; much of it is rocky and much of the remainder has been taken up by brand-new concrete developments.

The beaches near the centre of town should be treated with respect: the combination of a shelving beach and rollers roaring in from the Atlantic often makes the surf dangerous, and a few tourists are drowned every year.

Some 8km south of Praia Pipa, on the way to Ponta Negra and an hour from Natal by bus, the **Barra da Cunhau** beach is breathtakingly beautiful, with miles of white sands bordered by red sandstone cliffs, and usually almost completely deserted. At the centre of the beach, fresh seafood platters including swordfish and lobster are served most days by the *Solimar* restaurant. A further 10km south from here, through sugar-cane plantations and really only accessible by buggy, you'll find the **Lagoa de Coca Cola**; this black lake, made acidic by the specific plantlife there, is part of a nature reserve where there are cashew trees as well as fragrant bark trees which are used to make some perfumes.



## Eating

Best known for its own style of tapioca and sought-after *carne de sol* (sun-dried meat) dishes, like most Brazilian cities, Natal boasts one or two excellent **restaurants**.

**Âncora Caipira** Via Costeira, most of the way along the coast road to Ponta Negra ☎84/3219-2002. A popular local restaurant within striking distance of Natal's centre, serving up superb regional dishes (a good place to try *carne de sol*).

**Bar do Cação** On the seafront near the Forte dos Reis Magos. Choose from a selection of good oyster and shellfish dishes.

**Bigi Resto** Rua Serido 720, Petrópolis ☎84/3202-5833. The best of the downtown Italian restaurants, serving good pastas and a selection of pizzas. Open most evenings until late, and for lunch on Thurs & Fri.

**Guinza** Rua Ulisses Caldas 144. Good Japanese and Brazilian food on Tuesdays and Fridays, but specializing in seafood buffet on Thursdays; always busy with locals at lunch times.

**Hua Da Li** Av. Campos Sales 454, Petrópolis ☎84/3211-2969. Easily the best Chinese in town, they also serve buffet meals by the kilo. Only open 11am–3pm.

**Saborosa** Av. Campos Sales 609, Petrópolis ☎84/3222-7338. Inexpensive restaurant serving an excellent range of regional food by the kilo.

## Nightlife

Most of Natal's nocturnal action takes place on or around the beaches rather than in the centre. One good spot to head for is **Praia dos Artistas**, the stretch of beach about halfway between the fort and the headland, which hosts plenty of live music at night, especially on weekends. *Chaplin Night and Shopping* presents mainly *forró* on Fridays and Saturdays, while the *Balada Club* next door plays a wider variety of sounds. A few hundred yards up the beach, the *Casa do Pagade*, a club inside the *Bar and Restaurant Don Pedro*, hosts plenty of good *forró* and *pagode* at weekends after 9pm.

## Listings

**Airlines** TAM, Rua Seridó 746 ☎84/3643-1624 or 3202-3385; Gol, Rua Mossoró 598 ☎84/3644-1252 or 3211-4453.

**Banks and exchange** The branch of Banco do Brasil at Av. Rio Branco 510, Cidade Alta, has ATMs.

**Car hire** Avis ☎84/3644-2500; Hertz ☎84/3207-3399; Localiza ☎84/3206-5296.

**Post office** The main branches are at Rua Princesa Isabel 711 and Av. Rio Branco 538, both in Centro.

**Shopping** The two best shopping centres are the Praia Shopping Centre, Av. Eng. Roberto Freire 8790, near Ponta Negra, and Natal Shopping, at Av. Sen. Salgado Filho 2234 in the Candelária district.

**Taxis** Radio Taxi ☎84/3221-5666 and Disk Taxi ☎84/3223-7388.

**Travel and tour companies** Casablanca Turismo (office at airport ☎85/3466-6000) books mainly flights and buses; Manary Ecoturs, based at the *Manary Praia Hotel* in Ponta Negra (see p.337) offer a range of reliable local tours.

# South of Natal

Talking of things to do and places to go around Natal boils down to talking about **beaches**. The beach *par excellence* – and the easiest southern beach to get to from Natal – is **Ponta Negra**, 10km out of town along the Via Costeira, linked by regular buses from the local bus station that you can also catch from the seafront. **Further south**, the beaches get less crowded, but access can be difficult.

## Ponta Negra

Following close on the heels of Bahia's Morro de São Paulo, **Ponta Negra** is one of the finest beaches in the Northeast. Running along a sweeping bay under steep sandy cliffs, it is magnificent, sheltered from Atlantic rollers, though still good for surfing. The resort crowds around the beach, and has expanded rapidly in recent years – it's jam-packed with places to stay and often quite crowded; bars and restaurants range from trendy beach shacks to serious seafood restaurants, and there's a constant party atmosphere. **Tours** and trips to more far-flung beaches, plus city tours, buggy rides and other excursions are also available (see p.335, and the information given in "Accommodation" below). It's a feasible day-trip from Natal, but many visitors prefer to **stay** here.

### Accommodation

**Blue Beach Pousada** Av. Beira Mar 229 ⓣ84/3641-1046, ⓦwww.bluebeach-inn.com.br. Friendly hostel, set right on the shore, with its own beach café. The front rooms are priced slightly higher for their sea views. ❹

**Lua Cheia Youth Hostal** Rua Doctor Manoel Araujo 500, Praia Ponta Negra ⓣ84/3236-3696, ⓦwww.luacheia.com.br. This is a fun place with bunk-room dorms, private doubles and family rooms. There's a lively basement tavern and the entire site is located in a castle-like folly with a lovely central courtyard. Well organized, offering airport transfers and its own souvenir shop. ❹

**Manary Praia Hotel** Rua Francisco Gurgel 9067 ⓣ84/3204-2900, ⓦwww.manary.com.br. On a relatively quiet part of the beach, just a few hundred metres from the main action, this charming, gay-friendly hotel is set in mellow garden terraces.They also operate minibus trips into the *sertão* to visit local communities, archeological sites and cave paintings. It has some rooms with hammock balconies looking over the ocean and a large beach terrace. ❹–❻

**Pousada America do Sol** Rua Erivan França 35 ⓣ84/3219-2245, ⓦwww.pousadaamericadosol.com.br. Newly built hotel in town with very comfortable rooms and great service for the price. It runs a reliable travel agency, too, organizing buggy rides, boat trips and excursions as far afield as Fernando de Noronha. ❸

**Praiamar** Rua Francisco Gurgel 33, Ponta Negra ⓣ84/3219-2230, ⓦwww.praiamarnatal.com.br. This is a spacious, modern hotel pretty close to the main beach at Ponta Negra; there's also a nice little pool. ❺

**Visual Praia Hotel** Rua Francisco Gurgel 9184 ⓣ084/3646-4646, ⓦwww.visualpraiahotel.com.br. Large, very comfortable and located right on the beach, with a pool, a big terrace and a children's play area. ❺

### Eating

There are several good **places to eat**: *Don Vincenzo* serves good pasta and seafood on a pleasant veranda overlooking the beach next to the large, pink *Ingá Praia Hotel*. Close by, at Rua Erivan França 36, the *Bar Rústico* is a trendy 24-hour bar and restaurant, catering mainly to the surfing crowd. Perhaps the best of the places on the beachfront is the *Bar Pirata*, towards the southern end, just past the *jangada* boats; this bar-restaurant plays good rock and reggae music most of the time and has live *pagode* on Saturday nights. The *Churrascaria Tereré*, Estrada de Pirangi 2316, Rota do Sol (ⓣ84/3219-4081), offers excellent *gaúcho*-influenced *rodizio de carne*, giving you the chance to try a wide range of beef cuts.

## South of Ponta Negra

The beaches **south of Ponta Negra** are more remote and consequently less crowded. The only problem is getting to them without a car, as there are usually only one or two buses a day to most of the villages from Natal's bus station. Check times with the tourist office, but they usually leave early in the morning and you may not be able to get back to Natal the same day. The villages normally have a *pousada* or two, however, and it is easy to come to an arrangement about stringing up hammocks in bars and houses. An alternative way of reaching the beaches is to take a **bus** along the main BR-101 highway to Recife from the *rodoviária*, and get off at Nízia Floresta, from where there are pick-ups, trucks and a local bus service along the dirt road to the coastal fishing villages and beaches of **BÚZIOS** and **BARRA DE TABATINGA**, 20km and 25km from Natal; the former has a few restaurants, bars and *pousadas* and is a target for fishing, surfing and windsurfing groups, the latter is a smaller, calmer bay protected by a reef and better suited to families with small children. **PIRANGI DO NORTE** is further out but more accessible, with buses running the 30km from Natal's *rodoviária*. Apart from the beach, the village's other famous attraction is the biggest **caju tree** in the world, centuries old and with branches that have spread and put down new roots. Although Brazilians know *caju* as a fruit, its seeds, once roasted, become the familiar cashew nut. It's difficult to believe this enormous (over 7000 square metres) expanse of green leaves and boughs could be a single tree; it looks more like a forest. It still bears over a ton of fruit annually, so it's not surprising that Pirangi is known for its *caju*-flavoured rum.

To get away from people, you have to travel further south to the stunning **Praia da Pipa**, 80km away, and the **Praia Sagi**, which lies almost on the border with Paraíba state, some 120km from Natal. The latter is particularly inaccessible and can only be approached by four-wheel-drive vehicles or on foot, but as a result is virtually untouched. If you want to stay, try the *Pousada Coco Fresco* (④), Rua Albacora 269, in Praia da Pipa, or the *Natal Surf & Kitesurf Camp* (Ⓦwww.nomadsurfers.com) just 15min north. The **Praia da Pipa** ("Kite Beach"), on the other hand, is set in idyllic surroundings with dolphins regularly swimming near the beach, and sports an increasing number of *pousadas* and well-established bars. Local bus services can be a bit irregular.

# North of Natal

Most of the recent hotel-building and development has been funnelled south of Natal by the building of the Via Costeira, which makes the quieter **northern beaches** an attractive option. The two main places to head for are Redinha and Genipabu.

**REDINHA**, 16km from Natal, is a small fishing village facing the city on the northern mouth of the Rio Potengi, and marks the southern end of the enormous beach that effectively makes up the state's northern coastline. The beaches are notable for their huge shifting **sand dunes**, many metres high, which cluster especially thickly to tower over Genipabu. Redinha itself (hourly buses from the local bus station in Natal) is surprisingly undeveloped for somewhere so close to the city, retaining the air of a simple fishing village, with a small chapel and beachside stalls that fry the freshly caught fish and chill the beer.

▲ A beach buggy on Genipabu's dunes

Regular buses to **GENIPABU** leave from Natal's central bus station every two hours from Monday to Saturday and hourly on Sunday. Genipabu is still a fishing village, but these days depends more on tourism for its income. Its massive, fine-particled moving dunes, just 25km from Natal itself, are spectacular and great fun to run down. A favourite local pastime is to roar up and down them in **beach buggies** – see box on p.335. **Accommodation** includes the *Pousada Caminho das Dunas* on Rua Ver Ricardo Afonso (Ⓣ84/3225-2075; ④).

# West towards Ceará

The BR-304 highway **west** to Fortaleza, capital of Ceará state, takes a dull inland route through the **interior** of Rio Grande do Norte, where plains of scrubby *caatinga* and cacti are only rarely broken up by hills or rocky escarpments. Even on a moving bus you can feel the heat, and get some idea of why this is one of the poorest and most unforgiving areas in the Northeast. From Natal three daily **buses** make the five-hundred-kilometre run to Fortaleza, taking around nine hours.

The one place you might think of stopping off at before crossing into Ceará state is **MOSSORÓ**, in many ways an archetype of the *sertão* town in which so many of the inhabitants of the northeastern interior live. Mossoró has a population of over 200,000 and is growing fast, although you wouldn't guess it from the centre, which is very much that of a small market town, with busy central market, a pleasant square and a couple of ornate 1930s public buildings as well as a range of the usual accommodation choices.

Mossoró's enduring claim to fame came in 1924 when the townspeople fought off a full-scale attack by the legendary bandit leader **Lampião** and his band. It's an event that's still celebrated every June 13 with Masses and re-enactments. On the church a plaque commemorates the event, and you can still see the walls and tower pockmarked with bullet holes, carefully preserved.

# Ceará

The state of **Ceará**, covering a vast area but with less than nine million inhabitants, has long borne the brunt of the vagaries of the northeastern climate. In the 1870s, as many as two million people may have died in a famine provoked by drought. During the 1950s and 60s the population of Fortaleza more than doubled, partly due to the city's prosperity and partly due to occasional severe droughts in the interior. As recently as the early 1980s people were reduced to eating rats.

Yet for all its problems Ceará has kept a strong sense of identity, making it a distinctive and rewarding state to visit. Its capital, **Fortaleza**, is the largest, most modern and cosmopolitan city in the Northeast after Recife and Salvador. In contrast to the city's skyscraping, futuristic architecture, the **sertão** is unforgiving to those who have to live in it, but in Ceará it rewards the traveller with some spectacular landscapes: as you travel west, the flat and rather dull plains of Rio Grande do Norte gradually give way to ranges of hills, culminating in the extreme west of the state in the highlands and lush cloud forest of the **Serra da Ibiapaba**, the only place in Brazil where you can stand in jungle and look down on desert. To the south there are the hills and fertile valleys of **Cariri**, with the pilgrim city of Juazeiro do Norte (see p.329). And the coastline boasts some of the wildest, most remote and beautiful **beaches** in Brazil.

Despite an economy based on poor soils and cattle ranching, in recent years Ceará has nevertheless developed economically as well as culturally, earning the state a reputation as one of the best governed in Brazil.

# Fortaleza

**FORTALEZA** is a sprawling city of over two million inhabitants, its centre bristling with offices and apartment blocks. It has, for well over a century, been the major commercial hub of the northern half of the Northeast. More recently it has poured resources into expanding its tourist trade, lining the fine city beaches with gleaming luxury hotels and developing the city centre. Taken together, this means that little trace remains of Fortaleza's eventful **early history**, the clue to which is in its name, which means "fortress". The first Portuguese settlers arrived in 1603 and were defeated initially by the Indians, who killed and ate the first bishop (a distinction the city shares with Belém), and then by the Dutch, who drove the Portuguese out of the area in 1637 and built the Forte Schoonenborch. In fact the Portuguese were restricted to precarious coastal settlements until well into the eighteenth century, when the Indians were finally overwhelmed by the determined blazing of cattle trails into the interior. Another fort – the Fortaleza de Nossa Senhora da Assunção – was built by the Portuguese in 1816 on the site of the earlier Dutch one.

The independence movement in northern Brazil was organized in Fortaleza, and the city was one of the few places where the Portuguese actually made a fight of it, massacring the local patriots in 1824 before being massacred themselves a few months later. Largely due to its strategic location at the very western edge of the Atlantic trade winds, the city did well in the **nineteenth century** as a port city. For decades, though, one of the city's most important exports was the people of the state: shipping lines transported *flagelados* (poor

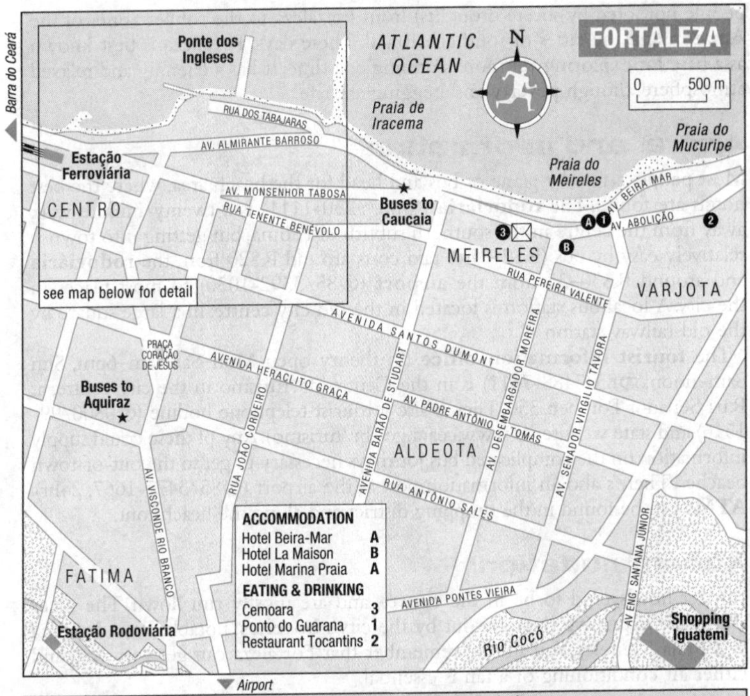

# FORTALEZA

ATLANTIC OCEAN

0 500 m

Barra do Ceará

Ponte dos Ingleses

Rua dos Tabajaras

Av. Almirante Barroso

Estação Ferroviária

Av. Monsenhor Tabosa

Rua Tenente Benévolo

CENTRO

Buses to Caucaia

Praia de Iracema

Praia do Meireles

Praia do Mucuripe

Av. Beira Mar

Av. Abolição

MEIRELES

Rua Pereira Valente

VARJOTA

see map below for detail

Avenida Santos Dumont

Praça Coração de Jesus

Avenida Heraclito Graça

Av. Padre Antônio Tomás

Buses to Aquiraz

Rua João Cordeiro

Avenida Barão de Studart

Av. Desembargador Moreira

Av. Senador Virgílio Távora

ALDEOTA

Rua Antônio Sales

Av. Visconde Rio Branco

Av. Eng. Santana Júnior

FATIMA

Avenida Pontes Vieira

Estação Rodoviária

Rio Cocó

Shopping Iguatemi

Airport

**ACCOMMODATION**

| | |
|---|---|
| Hotel Beira-Mar | A |
| Hotel La Maison | B |
| Hotel Marina Praia | A |

**EATING & DRINKING**

| | |
|---|---|
| Cemoara | 3 |
| Ponto do Guarana | 1 |
| Restaurant Tocantins | 2 |

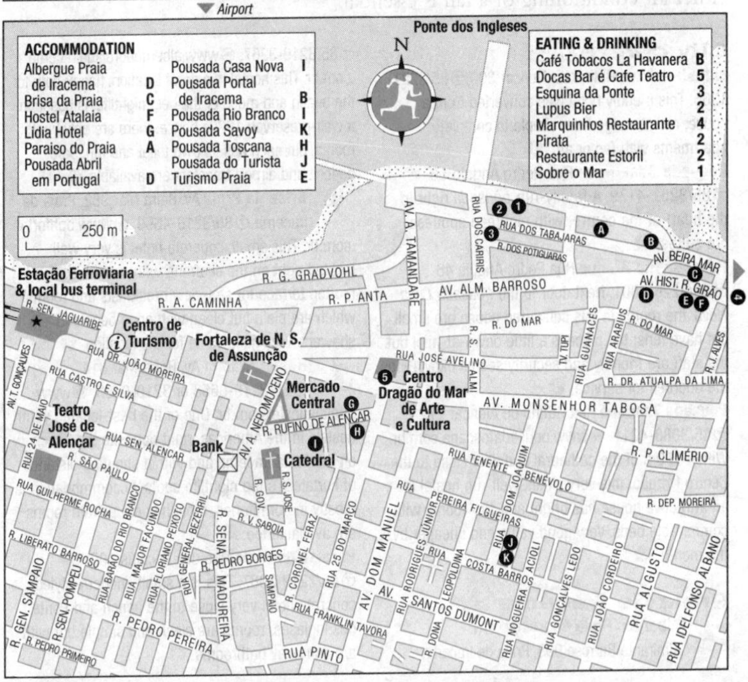

---

**ACCOMMODATION**

| | |
|---|---|
| Albergue Praia de Iracema | D |
| Brisa da Praia | C |
| Hostel Atalaia | F |
| Lidia Hotel | G |
| Paraiso do Praia | A |
| Pousada Abril em Portugal | D |
| Pousada Casa Nova | I |
| Pousada Portal de Iracema | B |
| Pousada Rio Branco | I |
| Pousada Savoy | K |
| Pousada Toscana | H |
| Pousada do Turista | J |
| Turismo Praia | E |

**EATING & DRINKING**

| | |
|---|---|
| Café Tobacos La Havanera | B |
| Docas Bar é Cafe Teatro | 5 |
| Esquina da Ponte | 3 |
| Lupus Bier | 2 |
| Marquinhos Restaurante | 4 |
| Pirata | 2 |
| Restaurante Estoril | 2 |
| Sobre o Mar | 1 |

Ponte dos Ingleses

0 250 m

Estação Ferroviaria & local bus terminal

R. G. Gradvohl

Rua dos Cariris

Rua dos Tabajaras

R. dos Potiguaras

Av. A. Tamandaré

Av. Beira Mar

Av. Hist. R. Girão

Av. Alm. Barroso

R. A. Caminha

R. P. Anta

R. Sen. Jaguaribe

Centro de Turismo

Fortaleza de N. S. de Assunção

R. do Mar

Rua José Avelino

R. S. Almi

Tv. Tupi

Rua Guanacés

Rua Ararius

R. J. Alves

R. Dr. Atualpa da Lima

Rua Dr. João Moreira

Rua Castro e Silva

Av. T. Gonçalves

Av. A. Nepomuceno

Mercado Central

Centro Dragão do Mar de Arte e Cultura

Av. Monsenhor Tabosa

Teatro José de Alencar

R. Rufino de Alencar

Rua 24 de Maio

Rua Sen. Alencar

R. São Paulo

Bank

Catedral

Rua Tenente Benévolo

R. P. Climério

Rua Guilherme Rocha

R. S. José

R. Gov. Sampaio

R. V. Saboia

Rua Pereira Filgueiras

Rua Dom Joaquim

R. Dep. Moreira

Rua Barão do Rio Branco

Rua Major Facundo

Rua Floriano Peixoto

Rua General Bezerril

R. Sena Madureira

R. Liberato Barroso

R. Pedro Borges

R. Coronel Ferraz

Rua 25 de Março

Av. Dom Manuel

Rua Rodrigues Júnior

Rua Leopoldina

Rua Costa Barros

Rua Nogueira Acioli

Rua Gonçalves Ledo

Rua João Cordeiro

Rua Algusto

Rua Idelfonso Albano

R. Gen. Sampaio

R. Sen. Pompeu

R. Pedro Pereira

R. Pedro Primeiro

Rua Franklin Tavora

Av. Santos Dumont

R. Dona

Rua Pinto

people uprooted by severe droughts) from Fortaleza to the rubber zones of the Amazon and the cities of southern Brazil. These days, Fortaleza is best known as a base for exploring yet more stunning coastline. It has a friendly and relaxed atmosphere, though poverty and begging are rife.

## Arrival and information

Most people arrive by plane or bus and head for the beach area, where the best hotels are found. The **rodoviária** (ⓣ85/3230-1111) is a twenty-minute walk away from the centre in the southern suburb of Fátima, but getting into town is relatively easy by bus (R$2–3). A taxi costs around R$20 from the **rodoviária** and around R$30–35 from the **airport** (ⓣ85/3392-1030) to most places in the city. A local bus station is located in the old city centre, in a large square by the old railway station.

The **tourist information office** (in theory open Mon–Sat 8am–6pm, Sun 8am–noon; ⓣ85/3488-7411) is in the Centro de Turismo in the city centre, at Rua Senador Pompeu 350. There's also a tourist telephone hotline (ⓣ0800/99-1516) and state website (ⓦwww.ceara.gov.br/turismo). Any of these could supply information on the complicated bus journeys necessary to get to the out-of-town beaches. There's also an information post at the airport (ⓣ85/3477-1667; 24hr). **ATMs** can be found in the shopping district and along the beachfront.

## Accommodation

Budget hotels tend to be in the **centre** and are mostly run down. The nicer and more expensive ones are out by the city's **beaches**, notably Praia Iracema and Praia Meireles. You should remember that Fortaleza can get very hot, and either air conditioning or a fan is essential.

### City centre

**Lidia Hotel** Rua Rufino de Alencar 300 ⓣ85/3221-1365. This friendly hotel was converted from a house; rooms range from simple to complete apartments with fan or a/c. ❸

**Pousada Casa Nova** Rua Pedro Ángulo 56 ⓣ85/3252-4179. A family-run *pousada* right in the heart of the centre, with eighteen spotless a/c suites. ❸

**Pousada Rio Branco** Rua Pedro Ángulo 46 ⓣ85/3226-5801. Next door to the *Pousada Casa Nova*, the rooms in this converted house are small but have fans; the place is a little down-at-heel but the staff are friendly and security seems okay. Ring the doorbell for service. ❷

**Pousada Toscana** Rua Rufino de Alencar 272 ⓣ85/3088-4011, ⓦwww.pousadatoscana.com.br. Within 100m of the cathedral and very close to the Centro Dragão, this very clean, well-run hostel in an attractive house has bright and airy rooms with comfortable beds. Very good value and cheaper by the month. ❷

### Praia de Iracema

**Albergue Praia de Iracema** Av. Almirante Barroso 998, Praia de Iracema ⓣ85/3219-3267, ⓦwww.alberguepraiadeiracema.com.br. This hostel in a great location, handy both for the beach and much of the best nightlife, is based in a well-preserved 1920s house; there are only bunk rooms, but each has its own toilet and fan. Safe deposit and airport transfers are available. ❶–❷

**Brisa da Praia** Av. Beira Mar 982, Praia de Iracema ⓣ85/3219-4699, ⓦwww.bphfortal.com.br. This small, concrete hotel is very well located right on the seafront, with a small pool, a rooftop terrace for sea-view breakfasts and rooms which are plain but clean with good beds and showers. Very good value for the location. ❹

**Hostel Atalaia** Av. Beira Mar 814 ⓣ85/3219-0658 or 3219-0755, ⓦwww.atalaiahostel.com.br. One of the best-located youth hostels in the Americas, right opposite the beach on the Praia Iracema and within shouting distance of Fortaleza's top nightlife spots. Accommodation is mostly in dormitories, though some private rooms are available too. ❷–❸

**Paraíso da Praia** Rua dos Pacajús 109 ⓣ85/3219-3387. This is a small, modern-styled concrete hotel very close to the beach and Ponte dos Ingleses; rooms are clean and simple but with a/c and okay bathrooms. ❹

**Pousada Abril em Portugal** Av. Almirante Barroso 1006, Praia de Iracema ⓣ85/3219-9509. A good-value budget hotel near the youth hostel. ❷

**Pousada Portal de Iracema** Rua dos Ararius 2, Praia de Iracema ⓣ85/3219-0066, ⓔpousada@ultranet.com.br. Well-located *pousada* very close to the sea and near the centre of the nightlife district, yet surprisingly quiet. Rooms are clean and bright and have TVs and *frigobars*; additionally, good English is spoken, service is conscientious, and the breakfasts are lovely. ❸

**Turismo Praia** Av. Beira Mar 894, Praia de Iracema ⓣ85/3219-6133. Small, good-value hotel with functional rooms, a tiny pool, and a modest restaurant. The location is great, opposite the beach. ❸

### Praia Meireles

**Hotel Beira-Mar** Av. Beira Mar (Av. Presidente Kennedy) 3130, Praia de Meireles ⓣ85/3242-5000, ⓦwww.hotelbeiramar.com.br. Luxury hotel with a pool, right next to the Praia de Meireles. ❼

**Hotel La Maison** Av. Desembarador Moreira 201 ⓣ85/3242-7017, ⓦwww.hotellamaison.com.br. This thirteen-room *pousada* is in a tastefully converted house just a few blocks from the beach; the rooms are pleasant and have TVs, telephones and a/c. French and English is spoken and parking is available. ❸

**Hotel Marina Praia** Rua Paula Barros 44 ⓣ85/3242-7734, ⓦwww.hotelmarinapraia.com.br. A small, spick-and-span hotel, little bigger than a house and less than a block from the beach in the Nautico section of Praia Meireles. It somehow fits 25 apartments into its comfortable and colourful interior, and there's also a little patio out front. Good value. ❹

**Pousada Savoy** Rua Dom Joaquim 321 ⓣ85/3226-8426. Basic, affordable hotel next door to the *Pousada do Turista*. ❷

**Pousada do Turista** Rua Dom Joaquim 351 ⓣ85/3253-7542 or 3231-6607. Budget hotel run by French-speakers, with pleasant a/c rooms. Located in a peaceful area within 10min walk of the city centre and the beaches. ❷–❸

## The City

The only visible legacy of Fortaleza's crowded history is a **gridded street pattern** laid out in the nineteenth century by a French architect, Adolphe Herbster. Herbster was contracted by the ambitious city fathers to turn Fortaleza into "the Paris of the North" – and you can only hope that they got their money back.

The **layout of the city** is easy to grasp, despite its size. The **centre**, laid out in blocks, forms the commercial, administrative and religious heart, with markets, shops, public buildings, squares and a forbiddingly ugly concrete cathedral; it's quite possible to walk and take in most of the sights in one day, though you'd probably want to take longer. To the west of the centre, undistinguished urban sprawl finally gives way to the beaches of **Barra do Ceará**, but most of the action is to the east, where the main city beaches and the chic middle-class *bairros* of **Praia de Iracema** and **Meireles** are to be found, linked by the main seafront road, **Avenida Presidente Kennedy**, usually known as **Avenida Beira Mar**. These give way to the *favelas* and docks of the port area, **Mucuripe**, the gateway to the eastern beaches, notably **Praia do Futuro**, beyond which the city peters out.

While not the most visually attractive of Brazilian city centres, there is enough going on in the heart of Fortaleza to merit more attention than it usually gets from visitors. It certainly can't be faulted for being boring: the streets are very crowded, with shops and hawkers colonizing large areas of pavement and squares, so that much of the centre often seems like a single large market. Fortaleza is an excellent place for **shopping**, and you should stock up here if you're heading west, as you won't get comparable choice until you hit Belém, 1500km away. Clothes are plentiful and cheap, there is also good *artesanato* to be had, notably lace and leather, and Fortaleza is the largest centre for the manufacture and sale of hammocks in Brazil.

## Mercado Central and around

Set right next to the grimy, neo-Gothic cathedral on Rua Conde d'Eu, the striking new **Mercado Central**, a huge complex holding hundreds of small stores, dominates the skyline. The market, along with the nearby shops on the other side of the cathedral, is the best place to buy a hammock in the city: if you're going to use one on your travels, purchase it with care (see box, p.418).

Opposite the Mercado Central, the nineteenth-century **Fortaleza de Nossa Senhora da Assunção** – the city's namesake – is easily identified by its thick, plain white walls and old black cannons. It belongs to the Tenth Military Regiment of the Brazilian army, but is open to visitors on request (Mon–Fri 9am–5pm; ⓣ85/3255-1600); visits are best organized the day before.

## The Centro Dragão do Mar de Arte e Cultura

The **Centro Dragão do Mar de Arte e Cultura**, a couple of blocks east of the market, makes a striking contrast to the rest of the city. Architecturally it's very modern, but its steel and glass curves blend sensitively with the attractive old terraced buildings over and around which it is built. The whole thing acts as a pedestrian link between the beaches and the city centre, which essentially starts on the landward side of the complex on the small Praça Municipal. Within the complex, there's a small, shiny-domed planetarium, cinemas, an auditorium, a couple of museums – one dedicated to contemporary art – an information hall and bookshop, toilets and a good coffee-bar, the *Torre do Café*, located in the tower that supports the covered walkway between the two main sections of the Centro. On the ground level there's also a shop selling quality regional *artesanato*. At weekends the bars and restaurants below the complex become a hive of eating, drinking and musical activities.

## The Centro de Turismo and the Museu de Arte e Cultura Popular

Overlooking the sea at the bottom of Rua Senador Pompeu is the **Centro de Turismo**, housed in the city's old prison – a perfect place to stop and have a beer in the bar in the one-time exercise yard, shaded by mango trees. The centre is also the location of the best museum in the city, the **Museu de Arte e Cultura Popular** (Mon–Fri 8am–6pm, Sat 8am–noon). Well laid out in a single huge gallery on the first floor, this is a comprehensive collection of *cearense artesanato* of all kinds, together with a sample of the painting and sculpture produced by the best of the state's modern artists. What distinguishes the museum is the imaginative juxtaposition of more traditional popular art with modernism. Both collections are of very high quality: the modern art is often startlingly original, as in the sculptures of bolts, nuts and scrap metal of Zé Pinto, but in style and subject matter you can see how profoundly it is rooted in the tradition of popular art all around it. In the same building, the smaller **Museu de Mineralogia** (same hours) is stuffed full of massive quartz crystals and a wide range of semi-precious stones.

## Passeio Público and Praça dos Mártires

Two blocks east from the Centro de Turismo is another survivor of nineteenth-century Fortaleza: the old municipal boulevard, the **Passeio Público**, which sits beside the pleasant shady **Praça dos Mártires**. Both are popular with children and families – as well as prostitutes. The Passeio looks out over the waterfront, and stallholders set up chairs and tables under the trees, from where they sell cold drinks and simple food. It's a good place to go in the late afternoon or early evening, when the workers stroll around after they get out of their offices, watching the variety of street entertainers and hawkers.

### Praça José de Alencar

The nerve centre of this part of the city, however, is its largest square, **Praça José de Alencar**, four blocks inland from the train station at the heart of the commercial district. In the late afternoon and early evening, the crowds here attract *capoeira* groups, street sellers of all kinds and *repentistas*. Fortaleza seems to specialize in these street poets, who with great skill and wit gather an audience by improvising a verse or two about those standing around watching, passing round a hat for you to show your appreciation. If you refuse, or give what they consider too little, the stream of innuendo and insults, in a variety of complicated metres, is unmistakeable, even if you don't understand a word.

On the square you'll also find the one truly impressive building in the city, the beautiful **Teatro José de Alencar**, named after the great nineteenth-century novelist and poet who was a native of the city. Built in the first decade of the twentieth century, the theatre's fine tropical-Edwardian exterior is in fact only an elegant facade, which leads into an open courtyard and the main body of the theatre. It is built in ornate and beautifully worked cast-iron sections, which were brought over complete from Scotland and reassembled in 1910. Surprisingly, for a building made out of iron, it is extremely cool and pleasant to be in, even when the sun is at its height: the ironwork is open and lets in the air without trapping heat, a masterly example of Scottish design in the least Scottish setting imaginable. In 1991 it was superbly restored and is now a key space for theatrical performances and concerts, with exhibitions taking place in the courtyard. Visit in the evenings or (less reliably) during the day on Saturday and Sunday, when the venue hosts *cearense* music of all varieties. Friday and Saturday are the likeliest nights to find something on: the staff can let you know what's happening, or try looking under the heading *Lazer* in the local papers.

## The city beaches

The main city beaches are the **Praia de Iracema** and the adjacent **Praia do Meireles**, both focal points for Fortaleza's nightlife. As beaches go, the Praia do Meireles wins hands down thanks to its greater expanse of sand, though the water is not as clean as the beaches out of town. The seafront boulevard is well laid out, punctuated by clumps of palm trees, and there is no shortage of watering holes. By day there are surfers on the waves and beach parties at the *barracas*, and in the early evening it seems everyone in the city turns out to stroll, jog or rollerblade down the boulevard, which has replaced the city's squares as the favoured meeting-place.

If you're a beach devotee, cleaner water, higher rollers and better seafood are to be had further out past Mucuripe at **Praia do Futuro**: take buses marked "P. Futuro" from Rua Castro e Silva in the centre. The beach *barracas* here are very good, but the ultimate surfing beaches are 6km beyond at **Porto das Dunas** and **Prainha**, 11km in combined length, and accessible on buses marked "Aquiraz" from the *rodoviária*. Porto das Dunas also has an aquatic theme-park called **Beach Park** (daily 9am–5pm; ⓣ85/4012-3000, ⓦwww.beachpark.com.br), the largest of its kind in Latin America.

## Eating, drinking and nightlife

You'll be all right in the centre during the day if you want something to eat, as there are countless places to grab a snack. However, most of what Fortaleza has to offer your palate is to be found on the beaches, especially around **Rua dos Tabajaras** on Praia de Iracema. The pier here, known as **Ponte dos Ingleses**, is very popular with couples and families in the early evenings and a lovely place to have a beer or simply watch the sunset. In two or three small streets around Rua dos Tabajaras you'll find a score of brightly coloured **bars** and **restaurants**, and glamorous young people out enjoying themselves. Whilst there are bars dotted along the beachfront of both Meireles and to a lesser extent Iracema, the busiest concentration is around the Ponte dos Ingleses and Rua dos Tabajaras; close to here, the Centro Dragão do Mar is also a hotspot at weekends and fiestas.

**Café Tobacos La Havanera** Corner of Rua dos Ararius and Av. Beira Marcuba. An interesting tobacco-themed café serving cigarettes, cigars and very good coffee.

**Cemoara** Rua Joaquim Nabuco 166, Meireles ☎85/3242-8500. Arguably the best restaurant in town; the service is superb and the *cearense* seafood even better.

**Esquina da Ponte** Rua dos Tabajaras, at the corner with Rua dos Cariris. An airy restaurant close to the Ponte dos Ingleses; excellent value and popular in the evenings when it serves up good steaks, pizzas and cheap cocktails.

**Marquinhos Restaurante** Av. Beira Mar 4566 ☎85/3263-1204. Located at the southern end of the seafront, past Praia do Futuro, this is mainly a quality seafood joint, well known for its fine skewered lobster; it's not cheap but the service is good and the restaurant open and airy.

**Ponto do Guarana** Av. Beira Mar 3127. A good *guaraná* and juice bar at Praia Meireles.

**Restaurante Estoril** Rua dos Tabajaras 397 ☎85/3219-8389. This restaurant makes the best of its beachfront setting, preparing delicious *cearense* cuisine and offering shows at weekends, plus comedy on Tuesday nights. Quite pricey.

**Restaurant Tocantins** Av. da Abolição 3210. A humble place reflected in an inexpensive menu; meat, fish and even lobster is served inside or on an outside terrace.

**Sobre o Mar** Rua dos Tremembes 2 ☎85/3219-7999. Overlooking the ocean and designed like a boat, this spacious place serves delicious lobster and a good range of wines; there's sometimes a R$2–3 cover charge for live-music shows.

### Forró: dancing and clubs

Fortaleza is justly famous for its **forró**. Nowhere is it so popular, and there is no better way to see what *cearenses* do when they want to enjoy themselves than to spend a night in a *dancetaria* here. *Pirata* at Rua dos Tabajaras 325 (☎85/4011-6161 or 3219-8030), one of the most easily accessible nightclubs in Fortaleza, has live music from Tuesday through Saturday, including *forró* but with other sounds as well; it's a great night out (cover charge around R$10). Opposite *Pirata*, there's the *Lupus Bier* club, with live music at weekends, good food and a cover charge (also around R$10). One of the best venues for live **dance shows** is *Docas Bar e Café Teatro*, beside the Centro Dragão at Rua José Avelino 491 (☎85/3219-8209), which showcases costumed dance styles every Wednesday from 9pm, among them *Afro* (slave), *Caboclinhos* (jungle) and *Maracatu* (colonial). On Fridays the same venue usually presents local pop bands, while on weekends the music tends to be more mixed, though with heavy doses of samba.

## Listings

**Airlines** TAM ☎85/3477-1945; Gol ☎85/3477-1710.

**Banks and exchange** HSBC and Bradesco have 24hr ATMs in the city centre on Rua Major Facundo, near the corner with Rua Senador Alencar. The mini-supermarket next to the *Café Tobacos La Havanera* in Irecema also has an ATM.

**Car hire** RCA ☎85/3219-7000; Localiza ☎85/3248-2900.

**Money exchange** Confidence Turismo, Shopping Iguatemi, southeast of the centre.

**Post office** The main post office is at Rua Senador Alencar 38 (Mon–Fri 8am–6pm).

**Taxis** Radio Taxi ☎85/3254-5744.

**Travel and tour companies** Ernahitur, Av. Senador Vigilio Tavora 205, 2nd floor, Room A (☎85/3533-5333, Ⓦwww.ernanitur.com.br), arrange trips to Jericoacoara, Canoa Quebrada and Lagoinha, as well as city tours. DN Turismo, Rua Bárbara de Alencar 540 (☎85/3086-8249, Ⓦwww.dnturismo.com.br), Lisatur (☎85/3219-5600, Ⓦwww.lisatur.com.br) and Enseada

Turismo (☎85/3091-2762, Ⓦwww.enseadatur.com) all have fleets of minibuses for beach transport, trips and packages. Girafa Tur (☎85/3219-3255, Ⓦwww.girafatur.com.br) tend to specialize in transport and packages to Jericoacoara beaches; you'll often find their bus looking for punters on the seafront between Iracema and Meireles beaches.

# Around Fortaleza: the beaches

The **beaches** of Ceará are what attract most visitors, and both east and west of Fortaleza they stretch unbroken for hundreds of kilometres. They are invariably superb, a mixture of mountainous sand dunes, palm trees and Atlantic breakers, wilder than the sheltered reef beaches of the southern states of the Northeast. The area has strong and predictable winds which, combined with good surf, means it's a windsurfer's paradise, and many small fishing villages now depend on the tourist dollar. Any description of the beaches becomes repetitive: they are all stunning, among the most beautiful anywhere in the world. To reach them, as a rule, you will need to get off at a town and catch a connection to the nearby coast, and the local bus network covers most places: at the better-known beaches, shoals of pick-ups and beach buggies meet the buses from Fortaleza.

## East to Canoa Quebrada

The most direct route east along the coast takes you to **ARACATI**, two hours or so from Fortaleza's *rodoviária* on the São Benedito bus (R$18). A small, once-prosperous textile town with half a dozen derelict, and a couple of functioning, eighteenth-century churches, Aracati is the jumping-off point for Ceará's best-known and most fashionable beach, **Canoa Quebrada**, half an hour further along a dirt road (when the bus doesn't go all the way, there are pick-ups, so access is no problem). Canoa Quebrada has deep green waters, very beautiful beaches and is very popular with foreigners and young Brazilians alike. The atmosphere is relaxed by day, and lively at night. Certainly, if you want company and *movimento* it's the beach to head for, and there's good buggy-riding in the sand dunes of the surrounding environmental reserve.

The road to Canoa Quebrada is flanked by dozens of boards advertising **accommodation** and **restaurants** and there's no shortage of either. The beach served directly by road from Aracati, **Majorlândia**, is less crowded and a lot quieter, its shores shared by *jangadas* and a surfing crowd, and it's just as easy to find places to stay. At Canoa Quebrada, it's hard to beat the *Pousada Fortaleza* (☎88/3421-7019, Ⓦwww.pousadafortaleza.com; ④) just 200m from the beach; this was one of the early pioneering *pousadas* here and has developed comfortable air-conditioned apartments equipped with *frigobars*, TVs and hammocks. There's also a pool and sound information on **kite-boarding**, one of the more popular beach activities. Other options include the *Pousada Lua Morena*, Rua Francisco Caraço (☎88/3421-7030, Ⓦwww.luamorena.com; ④), and the *Pousada Aruanã*, Rua dos Bugueiros (☎88/3421-7154, Ⓦwww.pousadaaruana.com.br; ④), both with pools.

## West to Jericoacoara

The choice of beaches **west of Fortaleza** is equally fabulous. Frequent buses from Fortaleza's *rodoviária* head for the beach town of **PARACURU**, 80km from Fortaleza, which gets crowded during weekends, but is less frenetic during the week. From here, you head out of Fortaleza's influence and the further west you go the less crowded the beaches become. A good place to head for, reasonably remote but not impossible to get to, is **TRAIRI**, 118km from Fortaleza, also served by direct buses from the *rodoviária*, which take around three hours. From here it's a few kilometres to the beautiful and usually deserted beaches of **Mundaú**, protected by a 100m reef, and **Fleixeiras**, more deserted still. When the tide is out, you can walk for an hour along the beach to the fishing hamlet of **GUAJIRU**, named for the indigenous local fruit that still grows abundantly in the scrubby bushes scattered around the dunes. There is no electricity or running water, but the people are friendly and the scenery marvellous.

Ceará's most famous beach, and arguably one of the world's finest, **JERICOACOARA** is a remote hangout 320km west of Fortaleza with huge dunes of fine white sand and turquoise *lagoas*. Possibly Brazil's best beach for wind and surf activities, most tour agents in Fortaleza offer packages here (see p.346). For the independent traveller, two buses a day from Fortaleza's *rodoviária* (with Redençao ⓣ85/3256-1973; R$32) cover the seven-hour journey. It's still a primitive place, but there are plenty of spots to stay as well as several outfits renting out surfboards and windsurfing equipment. **Kite-surfing** (call ⓣ88/3369-2288 and 3669-2080 for local information on this sport) is very popular here, particularly at Praia do Prea, a small fishing village some 10km down the beach (43km by road). For **accommodation**, *Pousada Wind Jeri*, Rua Forro 33 (ⓣ88/3669-2090, ⓦwww.windjeri.it; ④), has attractively rustic rooms just 50m from the beach, all with TVs, *frigobars*, air conditioning and hot showers. There's also the *Pousada Cabana*, Rua das Dunas 297 (ⓣ88/3669-2294, ⓦwww.pousadacabana.com.br; ④–⑤),

▲ Windsurfers flock to the splendid, remote beach of Jericoacoara

which offers good service and more comfort, and the *Pousada da Renata* (Ⓣ88/3669-2109; ❸–❹), close to the beach, with pleasantly decorated rooms. There are many more *pousadas* as well as endless **bars** and **restaurants** at Jericoacoara, among the best of the latter being the *Espaço Aberto*, Rua Principal 104, for superb fish and seafood, and *Nomade*, Rua da Farmácia, for wine, pizza and pasta.

## On to Piauí: the Serra da Ibiapaba

Apart from the beaches, there is little to detain you as you head west from Fortaleza, though it's a fine drive, with rocky hills and escarpments rising out of the *sertão* and the road snaking through occasional ranges of hills. You pass through the town of **SOBRAL**, an ugly industrial centre nestling in the middle of a spectacular landscape that's typical of the Northeast's interior: fiercely hot, cobalt-blue skies, flinty hills and *caatinga*. It would be very easy to sit back, enjoy the scenery and head directly west for Piauí and Maranhão in one go, but if you did you'd miss one of the finest sights Ceará state has to offer: the beautiful hills and cloud forest of the highlands that run down the border between Ceará and Piauí – the **Serra da Ibiapaba** – and the caves of **Ubajara**.

### Serra da Ibiapaba

You reach the Serra on buses arriving from either east or west, along the BR-222 highway that links Fortaleza with Teresina, capital of the neighbouring state of Piauí. You can get off at **TIANGUÁ**, a pleasant, sleepy town on the *cearense* side of the border: from here there are frequent local connections to Ubajara, 15km away (see below), also served by direct buses from Fortaleza.

Whether you approach from Teresina or Fortaleza the effect is the same. The buses drive across a bakingly hot plain, which begins to break up the nearer you get to the state border, rearing up into scattered hills and mesas covered with scrub and enormous cacti. Then on the horizon, in view hours before you actually start to climb it, all the hills seem suddenly to merge into a solid wall that rears up 900m from the parched plain below, its slopes carpeted with thick forest: the **Serra da Ibiapaba**. Everything is green and fertile: the temperature, warm but fresh with cool breezes, is an immense relief, and the contrast with the conditions only half an hour's drive away below couldn't be more marked.

### Ubajara

**UBAJARA** is a small, friendly town nestling in picturesque hills. There are a couple of simple but perfectly adequate **hotels** near the single church and quiet square, together with one or two **bars** and **restaurants**. It's a pleasant place to stay, but probably the best option is to head a couple of kilometres out of town, along the road leading away from Tianguá, to the comfortable *Neblina Park*, Estrada do Teleférico (Ⓣ88/3634-1270, Ⓦwww.pousadaneblina.com.br; ❷–❸). Standing in splendid isolation at the foot of a hill covered with palm forest, it has a restaurant and swimming pool, and is remarkable value; you can also camp here. Several buses daily connect Ubajara with Fortaleza (6hr) and Teresina (6hr).

### Parque Nacional de Ubajara

A twenty-minute walk (or 5km taxi ride) along the road from the *Neblina Park* will bring you to the gatehouse of the **Parque Nacional de Ubajara**, which ensures that the magnificent forest remains untouched. The park, nestling attractively amidst low hills, is very small (at less than six square kilometres it is in fact Brazil's smallest national park), but tourism facilities have developed rapidly in recent years and the park now has a **visitors' centre** (daily 9am–6pm; ⓣ88/3634-1388). Visits are supervised by IBAMA, the Brazilian federal environmental agency from their office at the entrance to the park; here they provide guides for the cave tour (daily 8am–5pm; entry R$1, guides extra). A cooperative of local guides (ⓣ88/3634-2365; services start at around R$45 per day) can show you round the park's eco-trails, large caves and impressive waterfalls; they are also a good source of up-to-the-minute local information.

Continuing past the gatehouse brings you to the *mirante*, a viewing platform with a small café built onto the rim of an escarpment. North and south of here the *serra* breaks into ridges covered with forest and tumbles down into the plain. From here a **chair lift** (10am–3.30pm daily; R$7) swoops down 400m to the cave complex of the **Gruta de Ubajara**. Guides prefer to start early in the morning, so you do the bulk of the walk before the heat gets up: take liquids, and wear sneakers or decent walking shoes. Going down takes a couple of hours, returning twice that, but there are streams and a small waterfall to cool off in along the way. There are also caves to explore: huge caverns with grotesque formations of stalactites and stalagmites.

# Piauí

**Piauí** is shaped like a ham, with a narrow neck of coastline 59km long that broadens out inland. Despite its size it has fewer than two million inhabitants and by far the lowest population density in the Northeast. Subject to drought, and with virtually no natural resources except the *carnaúba* palm, it is Brazil's poorest state.

Few travellers spend much time in Piauí. The capital, **Teresina**, is strategically placed for breaking the long bus journey between Fortaleza and São Luís, but it's a modern, rather ugly city where the heat can be oppressive. The southern half of the state merges into the remoter regions of Bahia and forms the harshest part of the Northeast. Much of it consists of uninhabited and largely trackless arid badlands, in the midst of which lies, ironically, the oldest inhabited prehistoric site yet found in Brazil. Cave paintings show that this desert was once jungle.

There are really only two places worth making for: the pleasant coastal town of **Parnaíba**, which has excellent beaches, and the **Parque Nacional de Sete Cidades**, good walking country with weird and striking rock formations. Strangely, this poor state has an excellent **highway** system, and the main roads between Teresina and Parnaíba and towards Ceará are very good: as the country is largely flat, the buses really fly.

Apart from cattle, the only significant industry revolves around the **carnaúba palm**, a graceful tree with fan-shaped leaves that grows in river valleys across the northern half of the state. The palm yields a wax that was an important ingredient of shellac, from which the first phonogram records were made, and for which there is still a small export market. It's also a source of cooking oil, wood, soap, charcoal and nuts, and many livelihoods depend on it.

# Teresina

People from **TERESINA** tell a joke about their city: "Why do vultures fly in circles over Teresina? Because they glide with one wing and have to fan themselves with the other!" Brazil's hottest state capital, Teresina sits far inland on the east bank of the Rio Parnaíba, where it bakes year-round in an average temperature of 40°C (which means it regularly gets hotter than that). The rains, meant to arrive in February and last for three or four months, are not to be relied upon – though twice in the last fifteen years they have actually flooded the city.

## The City

Thankfully, given the heat, most of the things worth seeing and doing are reasonably close to each other. The best place to start is the **market** that occupies most of the main square of the city, technically called Praça da Bandeira, but universally known by its old name, **Marechal Deodoro**. It's a smaller, more urbanized version of the typical northeastern market, with packed stalls forming narrow streets which fill with determined shoppers, energetic sellers, noise, loud music and plenty of *caldo de cana* kiosks, where you can slurp freshly crushed sugar cane and watch the city at work.

Overlooking the market, in one of the very few fine old buildings in the city, the **Museu do Piauí** at Marechal Deodoro 900 (Tues–Fri 8am–6pm, Sat & Sun 8am–noon) is definitely worth seeing. A governor's palace, built in 1859, it has been beautifully restored, with the exhibits well displayed in simple, elegant rooms, many with high arched windows and balconies perched just above the crowded market stalls. The collection is the usual eclectic mix, and pride of place must go to a collection of early radios, televisions and stereograms, a must for lovers of 1950s and 1960s kitsch. There are also fossils as well as fine examples of the two things that distinguish *artesanato* in Piauí: sculpture in straw and beautifully tooled leather.

### Practicalities

The **rodoviária** (☎86/3218-1514) is on the southeast outskirts of the city and has a **tourist information post** (Mon–Fri 8am–noon & 2–6pm, Sat 8am–noon; ☎86/3216-5510), where you can pick up free booklets with a city map. Frequent buses run into the centre, and there are cheap taxis, too. You will also find an information post on the corner of Magalhães Filho and Alvaro Mendes in the centre of town five blocks from the Praça da Liberdade. It's very easy to find your way around as the streets are organized in a grid pattern.

There are a number of good **hotels** opposite the *rodoviária*. The *Elite* (❷) and the *São Francisco* (❷) are no-frills options. Among those in the city centre overlooking the river is the more upmarket *Luxor Piauí*, Praça Mal. Deodoro 310 (☎86/3131-3000, Ⓦwww.luxorhoteis.com.br; ❹), with disabled access, a restaurant, quite smart rooms and a pool, while cheaper places can be found nearby around Praça Saraiva. **Restaurants** in the city are not cheap, but good seafood is served at *Camarão de Elías*, Av. Pedro Almeida 457, in the *bairro* of São Cristóvão (☎86/3232-5025). *Piauienses* excel at meat (try *paçoca*, prepared with shredded jerky and manioc meal), the best of which can be found at the lively *Favorito Grills*, Rua Prof. Mario Batista 69, São Cristóvão (☎86/3233-3333).

The city's **nightlife** lacks the focus of the coastal capitals, but there is life here after dark. The bank of the Rio Parnaíba is the best place from which to enjoy the sunset. A kilometre or so south of the centre, along the riverfront road, is **Prainha**, a series of bars and restaurants built along the riverbank, shaded by planted trees: buses run there, but are very infrequent by late afternoon – use the taxis in Teresina, which are cheap.

# Carnaúba country

The fastest and most direct route **west** from Ceará towards Amazônia follows the BR-316 highway through Teresina and on to São Luís or, a day from Teresina, to Belém and Amazônia proper. But if you have the time, there is a much more interesting and scenic route **north** up the BR-343 highway, a fine drive through a plain studded with *carnaúba* palm plantations to **Parnaíba** and the coast. From Parnaíba there is a direct bus service, over country dirt roads that get seriously difficult to travel on during the rainy season, to São Luís (see p.354), capital of neighbouring Maranhão state, where the Amazon region begins.

## Parnaíba

**PARNAÍBA**, with its attractive natural anchorage on the Rio Igaraçu, was founded in 1761, almost a centry before Teresina. For the Portuguese, it was the obvious harbour from which to ship out the dried meat and *carnaúba* (a wax derived from *carnaúba* palm) of the interior and, in the nineteenth century, it was a thriving little settlement; you can still see the chimneys of the cotton factories put up by British entrepreneurs a century ago. Then the river silted up, the port moved to Luiz Correia at the mouth of the river, and the town slipped into decline. Today, Parnaíba has a lazy feel, but is still the second largest city in the state, with around 125,000 inhabitants. Located anywhere else it would be a thriving resort town; the **beaches** nearby are excellent. There's some beach accommodation here, but it's often fully booked at busy times of year. One of the best beaches is close to **LUIZ CORREIA**, a fishing village 8km north of Paranaíba, with a small modern port attached. From here you can either walk or get the bus to the huge and popular **Praia de Atalaia**. At weekends practically the entire population of Parnaíba decamps here and the crowded bars reverberate to *forró* trios. A less crowded beach, **Coqueiro**, is 12km from here, but there are only a couple of buses there a day.

# Parque Nacional de Sete Cidades

The **Parque Nacional de Sete Cidades** comprises thirty square kilometres of nature reserve that could hardly be more different from the forest reserve of Ubajara, a couple of hundred kilometres east. Here it's the spiky, semi-arid vegetation of the high *sertão* that is preserved – cacti and stubby trees.

The really special feature of the reserve is its eroded **rock formations**, many streaked with prehistoric carvings. From the air they look like the ruins of seven towns, hence the name of the area, and their striking shapes have given rise to all sorts of theories about the area having been a Phoenician outpost in the New World. In fact the rock sculpting is the entirely natural result of erosion by wind and rain.

There are two ways of **getting to the park**, depending on whether you approach from Ceará state or elsewhere in Piauí. Coming **from Fortaleza or Ubajara**, get off the bus at the town of **Piripiri**, from where a free bus or transit van leaves at 6.45am (Tues–Fri) and takes you to the *Abrigo do Ibama* national park hostel (see below) run by the IBDF, the Brazilian forestry service. If you arrive too late, you'll have to take a taxi (R$40–50). Coming **from Teresina or Parnaíba**, get a bus to Piracuruca and take a taxi to the park – the taxi ride costs about R$50–60. There are perfectly adequate, cheap and clean **hotels** near the bus stations in both Piripiri and Piracuruca.

Despite its good facilities and its position near the main Teresina–Fortaleza highway, not as many people visit the park as you might expect. Consequently, it's the ideal place to get off the beaten track without actually venturing far from civilization.

### Into the park

There are two main **places to stay** in the park. At the entrance, the *Fazenda Sete Cidades* (Ⓣ86/3276-2222; ⑤) has a restaurant, pool and regular pick-up shuttles into the park itself, which you can use whether you stay there or not. More convenient for walking, and just as comfortable, is the cheaper *Abrigo do Ibama* (Ⓣ86/3343-1342; from R$25 per person) hostel and **campsite** in the centre of the park, again with a restaurant and bathing nearby in a natural spring.

**Walking** in Sete Cidades is not particularly difficult in physical terms, but it's important to get good local advice, as well as maps and ideally a guide before setting off. Bear in mind that the park does get extremely hot; stout walking shoes, plenty of liquid and a broad-brimmed hat are essential. Staff at the accommodation options listed above can advise you as to decent routes and the campsites dotted around the park. The **rock formations** themselves make very good landmarks and their different shapes have lent them their names: the "Map of Brazil", the "Tortoise", the "Roman Soldier", the "Three Kings", the "Elephant" and so on. Watch out for rattlesnakes.

# Maranhão

**Maranhão** is where the Northeast and Amazônia collide. Although classed as a northeastern state by Brazilians, its climate, landscape, history and capital of **São Luís** are all *amazônico* rather than *nordestino*. Maranhão is the only state in the Northeast to which more people migrate than emigrate from. Drought is not a problem here; the **climate** is equatorial – humid, hot and very wet indeed. The rainy season peaks from January to April, but most months it rains at least a little, and usually a lot – although only in concentrated, refreshing bouts for most of the year. This is one of the main rice-producing areas in Brazil.

Further west begins the tropical forest and savanna of Amazônia proper, as you hit the eastern boundary of the largest river basin in the world. The **coast** also changes character: the enormous beaches give way, from São Luís westwards, to a bewildering jumble of creeks, river estuaries, mangrove swamps and small islands, interspersed with some of the most remote beaches in Brazil – almost five hundred kilometres of largely roadless coastline with towns and villages accessible only from the sea.

Like most zones of geographical transition, Maranhão also marks a historical and cultural divide. The **people** are a striking contrast to the ethnic uniformity of the states immediately to the east: here blacks, Indians and Europeans form one of the richest cultural stews to be found in Brazil. Catch the great popular festival of **Bumba-meu-boi** in June and you'll get some idea of how different from the rest of the Northeast Maranhão really is.

The main population centres in the state are on and around the island of São Luís, and deep in the interior along the banks of the **Rio Tocantins**, a tributary of the Amazon but a mighty river in its own right. The contrast between the two regions could hardly be more stark. Only thirty years ago the Rio Tocantins was the boundary between Brazil and largely unknown Indian country. Today, as people flood into eastern Amazônia, **Imperatriz**, with 230,000 inhabitants, is the second city of the state, and dozy, historic São Luís, founded in 1612, has been transformed by docks and factories linked to the huge development projects of eastern Amazônia – the subject of much international controversy.



# São Luís

Clearly once a lovely colonial city, **SÃO LUÍS** has really been left behind by the rest of Brazil. A poor city even by Northeast standards, it's the most emphatically Third World of all the state capitals in this region. It has a huge black population, a legacy of plantation development during the eighteenth and nineteenth centuries, and responsible for the reggae music for which the city is increasingly famed. It is also far larger than it seems from the compact city centre; almost a million people live here, most of them in sprawling *favelas*, with the middle classes concentrated in the beach areas of Ponta da Areia, São Francisco and Olho d'Agua, linked to the rest of the city by a ring road and the bridge built out from the centre across the Rio Anil.

But, for all its problems, São Luís is a fascinating place. Music, street theatre, food and beaches are the city and region's main pull, along with the impressive colonial centre. Built across the junction of two rivers and the sea, on an island within the larger delta formed by the **Pindaré** and **Itapicuru** rivers, it has the umbilical connection with rivers that marks an Amazon city, but is also a seaport with ocean **beaches**. The latter are magnificent, and for the most part have been spared intrusive urban development. Above all, try to visit in June, when you can enjoy the festival for which the city is famous, **Bumba-meu-boi** (see box, p.356): here, it counts for more than Carnaval.

## Arrival and information

Both the airport and the *rodoviária* are some way from the city centre. A taxi from the **airport** (☎98/3217-6101) to the centre will cost you about R$20–25: pay at the kiosk on the left as you come out of the luggage collection area and hand the coupon to the driver. Alternatively you can

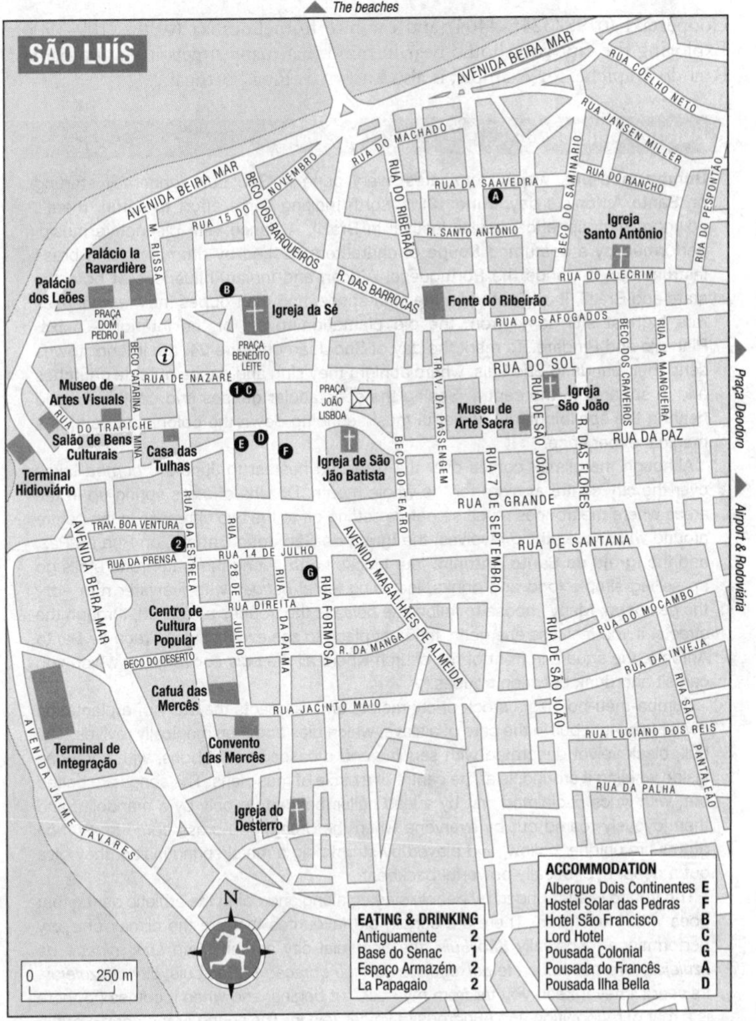




catch the bus outside marked "São Cristóvão". From the **rodoviária**, a taxi to the centre costs about R$12–15. Buses connect the *rodoviária* with the local bus station, the **Terminal de Integração** at Praia Grande, by the waterfront in the city centre. Once there you shouldn't need to use public transport very much: the area of interest is small and most things are within walking distance.

The availability of the **tourist information** office at the Praça Benedito Leite (Mon–Fri 8am–7pm, Sat & Sun 9am–5pm; ⑦98/3212-6211) is unreliable, with opening hours being more like 10am to 5pm daily. There's an ATM at the HSBC bank on Rua João Lisboa, by the Praça João Lisboa. For internet access try the Saint Louis Internet Café at Rua da Estrela 125 or the *Antiguamente Restaurant* at Rua da Estrela 220. Radio taxis are available from

Coopertaxi (☎98/3245-4404) and car hire from Localiza (☎98/2109-3900). Exploring the city, you should bear in mind that many streets have two names: Rua do Trapiche, for example, is also known as Rua Portugal.

## Bumba-meu-boi

**Bumba-meu-boi**, which dominates every June in São Luís (generally starting on Santo Antônio's day, **June 13**) is worth making some effort to catch: there's no more atmospheric popular festival in Brazil. A dance with distinctive music, performed by a costumed troupe of characters backed by drummers and brass instruments, it blends the Portuguese, African and Indian influences of both the state and Brazil. It originated on the plantations, and the troupes the *maranhenses* rate highest still come from the old plantation towns of the interior – Axixá, Pinheiro and Pindaré. To mark the day of São João on **June 24**, the interior towns send their bands to São Luís, where at night they sing and dance outside churches and in squares in the centre. Seeing the spectacular dances and costumes, and hearing the spellbindingly powerful music echoing down the colonial streets, is a magical experience.

Although the climax comes over the weekend nearest to June 24, *bumba* takes over the city centre at night for the whole month. Dozens of stalls spring up in the areas where the troupes rehearse before setting off to the two churches in the centre around which everything revolves: the **Igreja de São João Batista**, on Rua da Paz, and the **Igreja de Santo Antônio**, four blocks north. Along the waterfront, stalls go up selling simple food and drinks, including lethal *batidas* with firewater rum – try the *genipapo*. Many choose to follow the *bois*, as the troupes are called, through the streets: if you feel less energetic, the best place to see everything is Praça de Santo Antônio, the square in front of the church where all the *bois* converge, in which you can sit and drink between troupes.

Bumba-meu-boi has a stock of characters and re-enacts the story of a plantation owner leaving a bull in the care of a slave, which dies and then magically revives. The bull, black velvet decorated with sequins and a cascade of ribbons, with someone inside whirling it around, is at the centre of a circle of musicians. The songs are belted out, with lyrics declaimed first by a lead caller, backed up only by a mandolin, and then joyously roared out by everyone when the drums and brass come in. *Bumba* drums are unique: hollow, and played by strumming a metal spring inside, they give out a deep, hypnotically powerful backbeat.

The troupe is surrounded by people singing along and doing the athletic dance that goes with the rhythm. There are certain old favourites that are the climax of every performance, especially *São Luís*, the unofficial city anthem: *São Luís, cidade de azulejos, juro que nunca te deixo longe do meu coracão* – "São Luís, city of *azulejos*, I swear I'll never keep you far from my heart", it begins, and when it comes up there is a roar of recognition and hundreds of voices join in. The sound of the people of the city shouting out their song radiates from Praça de Santo Antônio across the centre, turning the narrow streets and alleys into an echo chamber.

Bumba-meu-boi starts late, the troupes not hitting the centre until 11pm at the earliest, but people start congregating, either at the waterfront or in the square, soon after dark. *Bois* don't appear every night, except during the last few days before the 24th: ask at the place where you're staying, as everyone knows when a good *boi* is on. Bumba-meu-boi troupes are organized like samba schools; towns and city *bairros* have their own, but thankfully the festival hasn't been ruined by making them compete formally against each other. Informal rivalries are intense, all the same, and *maranhenses* love comparing their merits: most would agree that Boi de Madre de Deus is the best in the city, but they are eclipsed by the troupes from the interior, Boi de Axixá and Boi de Pinheiro. The best day of all is **June 29** (St Peter's Day), when all the *bois* congregate at the Igreja de São Pedro from 10pm until dawn.

## Accommodation

Places to **stay** are mainly located in the city centre; none are particularly cheap. To get a flavour of the city's atmosphere there's no substitute for staying in the historic centre, but you should be aware that there are sometimes extremely loud reggae nights that may keep you awake.

**Albergue Dois Continentes** Rua Marcelino do Almeida 85 ⓣ3222-6286. In the *centro* area, this popular youth hostel is neat and comfortable, with shared or private rooms at reasonable prices. ❷

**Hostel Solar das Pedras** Rua da Palma 127 ⓣ3232-6694, ⓦwww.ajsolardaspedras.com.br. Another busy and cheerful youth hostel right in the heart of the action in Praia Grande, with tidy shared rooms and double rooms only. ❷

**Hotel São Francisco** Praça Dom Pedro Segundo 299 ⓣ98/3167-3200, ⓦwww.hotelvilarica.com.br. Comfortable but not as luxurious as it was a few years ago, this concrete monstrosity is well located on the edge of the historic centre, close to the tourist information office. Rooms have small balconies and there's a pool. ❻

**Hotel Sofitel** Av. Avicência ⓣ98/3216-4545, ⓔsofitel@accor.com.br. Luxury hotel set above Calhau beach some 10km from the city centre. Endowed with all possible comforts, including a sauna as well as tennis, basketball, swimming and football facilities. ❻

**Lord Hotel** Rua de Nazaré 258 ⓣ98/3221-4655. Set in a colonial building with a rather grand entrance and lobby, this slightly faded two-star hotel may be the ideal option if you want to stay just on the edge of the historic centre without spending too much money. Rooms come with or without both baths and a/c. ❸

**Pousada Colonial** Rua Afonso Pena 112 ⓣ3232-2834, ⓦwww.clickcolonial.com.br. Finely maintained mansion offering comfort and good service in pleasant surroundings. Very good value and close to the historic centre. ❸–❹

**Pousada do Francês** Rua da Saavedra 160, corner of Rua Sete de Setembro ⓣ98/3231-4844. Slightly run down (though clearly once one of the best in town), this *pousada* is on the edge of the Zona, in a poorly restored eighteenth-century mansion. ❹

**Pousada Ilha Bella** Rua da Palma 92 ⓣ98/3231-3563. One of the cleanest and least expensive of the budget hotels in the Zona. ❷

## The City

The city's central **layout** is easily grasped. Built on a headland that slopes down to rivers on two sides, the city's largest square is **Praça Deodoro**, from where the narrow but crowded Rua da Paz and Rua do Sol, each only with room for one lane of traffic and perilously tight pavements, lead down to **Praça João Lisboa**, which marks the edge of the **Zona** – the nickname for the colonial core of the city. From here steep streets lead down to the river waterfront. It's on the buildings fronting Praça João Lisboa that you will first see the lovely, glazed-tile frontages, the **azulejos**, which are the city's signature. Salvador has finer individual examples of *azulejo*, but taken as a whole the *azulejos* of colonial São Luís are unmatched for the scale of their use and their abstract beauty. Most are early nineteenth-century; some, with characteristic mustard-coloured shapes in the glazing, date back to the 1750s. Remarkably, many of the oldest tiles arrived in São Luís by accident, as ballast in cargo ships.

### The Zona

The **Zona** – also called the **Reviver** after the project to restore it – covers a small headland overlooking the confluence of the Rio Anil and the Atlantic Ocean, and though it may not look like much, a defensible harbour on this flat coastline was of some strategic importance. Now the waterfront is no more than a landing place for fishing boats and ferries, but slave ships once rode at anchor here, bringing in workers for the cotton and sugar plantations upriver. Then, the harbour was crowded with cargo boats, mostly from

Liverpool, shipping out the exports of what – from about 1780 to 1840 – was a prosperous trading centre, for the first and last time in its history.

But the Zona predates even that colonial boom. São Luís shares with Rio the distinction of having been founded by the French, and is the only city in Brazil to have been ruled by three European countries. The French, decimated by a lethal combination of malaria and Indians, were soon dislodged by the Portuguese in 1615; then the Dutch sacked the city and held the area for three years from 1641, building the small fort that now lies in ruins on a headland between Calhau and Ponta da Areia. Over the next hundred years, the original shacks were replaced by some of the finest colonial buildings in northern Brazil.

The only way to explore the Zona is on foot. A good place to begin is the Praça Benedito Leite, a small leafy square where you'll find the tourist information office along with the **Igreja da Sé**, a cream-and-white cathedral completed in 1699 and given a Neoclassical facelift in 1922. Around the corner is the **Praça Dom Pedro II**, lined by official buildings, splendidly proportioned survivors of the pre-Baroque colonial era. The oldest is the municipal hall, which dates from 1688: it still houses the Prefeitura and is called the **Palácio La Ravardière** after the French buccaneer who founded São Luís and is commemorated by a piratical bust on the pavement outside. In November 1985 the building was torched by an angry crowd, with the newly elected mayor inside, after an election acrimonious even by *maranhense* standards. Next door is the tropical Georgian elegance of the state governor's residence, the **Palácio dos Leões**, built between 1761 and 1776 and currently closed for restoration.

On the other side of the square from the Palácio dos Leões, steps lead down to the steep colonial street, **Beco Catarina Mina**, that takes you to the heart of the Zona, block after block of buildings, many restored whilst others are in an advanced state of decay. With its cobbled streets, *azulejos* and the vultures on the tile roofs, the Zona remains physically much as it was 150 years ago, although the colonial merchants and plantation owners who built it would have turned up their noses at its modern inhabitants. As economic decline bit deep, they sold up and moved on.

Beco Catarina Mina runs into the finest array of *azulejos* in the city, the tiled facades of the **Rua do Trapiche** (Rua Portugal), with the **Mercado da Praia Grande**'s gorgeous arches perfectly set off by the piercing-blue tiles and symmetrical windows and balconies. This area is the best-restored part of the Zona, given a magical feel by the brightly coloured *azulejos*, and has plenty of bars and restaurants and a lively street life at any time of day or night. The **Casa das Tulhas**, on Rua da Estrela, is an early nineteenth-century mansion now crammed with market stalls selling *artesanato*, including locally produced foods, quality cotton clothing, hammocks and tablecloths.

Many **churches** in the city have exteriors dating from the seventeenth century, though none of the interiors have survived successive restorations. The most beautiful of these is the **Igreja do Desterro**, with its Byzantine domes, at the southern end of the Zona. In these churches, over three hundred years ago, the Jesuit Padre Antônio Vieira preached sermons berating the plantation owners for enslaving and abusing Indians. Often considered the finest early Portuguese prose ever written, the sermons led directly to a new law which, while full of loopholes, prohibited their enslavement in 1655.

### Museums

There are two **museums** worth visiting on Rua do Trapiche. The **Salão de Bens Culturais** (daily 9am–9pm), at no. 303, houses an interesting collection of sacred and contemporary art, but the highlight is the display of brightly coloured cloth *bois*, or bulls, used in the festival of Bumba-meu-boi (see box, p.356). Part of this collection is also housed in the Centro de Cultura Popular Domingos Vieira Filho, Rua do Giz 221, Praia Grande (Tues–Sat 9am–7pm). Back on Rua do Trapiche at no. 273, the **Museu de Artes Visuais** (daily 9am–7pm), a gallery displays work by local artists.

Down at the southern end of the Zona is the **Cafuá das Mercês**, the old slave market, which now houses the rather depleted collection of the **Museu do Negro**. Slaves who survived the journey across from West Africa were marched up here from the harbour and kept in the holding cells until they could be auctioned off in the small square outside. One of São Luís's best museums lies outside the Zona. The **Museu de Arte Sacra**, Rua São João 500 (Tues–Fri 9am–6pm, Sat & Sun 2–6pm), houses some superb religious art from the seventeenth, eighteenth and nineteenth centuries. One of the outstanding pieces is a small wooden statue of St Paul embedded with incredibly lifelike glass eyes. There's also a statue of St John the Baptist with an incision in the neck: the space was used to hide jewels that were being smuggled out of the country.

## The beaches

São Luís is blessed with a chain of excellent **beaches**, all of which can be reached by bus from the Terminal de Integração. The surf can be dangerous and people drown every month, so take care. Swimming after sunset is not a good idea, as there are occasional attacks by sharks attracted by the kitchen waste dumped by ships offshore.

**Ponta da Areia** is the closest beach to the city centre, located by the ruins of the Forte São Marcos. Some 8km out of town, the dune beach of **Calhau** is larger and more scenic than Ponta da Areia: when the tide is out there is a lovely walk along the sands to Ponta da Areia, two hours' leisurely stroll west. After Calhau comes **Olho d'Agua**, equally fine, close to the dunes but a bit windy and well developed with houses and beach kiosks. **Araçagi**, 19km out of town, is the loveliest beach of all, an expansive stretch of sand that's also studded with bars and restaurants. It's served by hourly buses, but unless you rent a car you won't make it back the same day; there is a small hotel, though, the *Araçagi Praia* (☎98/3226-3299; ④), which offers smart rooms.

## Eating and drinking

At weekends virtually the entire city moves out to the beaches, which are large enough to swallow up the masses without getting too crowded. You will quickly discover one of the delights of this coast: the **seafood**. The seas and rivers around here teem with life, most of it edible. The beach stalls do fried fish, the prawns are the size of large fingers, and whatever they don't cook you can buy fresh from a stream of vendors – juicily tender crabs, battered open with bits of wood, or freshly gathered oysters, dirt cheap, sold by the bagful, helpfully opened for you and sprinkled with lime juice. One thing you won't find outside Maranhão is *cuxá* – a delicious dish made of crushed dried shrimp, garlic and the stewed leaves of two native plants.

This abundance makes **eating out** in town rewarding. The best seafood in São Luís is the *caldeirada de camarão* (shrimp stew) served at the *Cheiro Verde*, located in Olho d'Agua at Av. São Luís Reí de Franca 131 (☎98/3248-1641), and at the *Base do SENAC*, Rua de Nazare 242 (☎98/3232-6377), the latter a piano bar located on the Praça Benedito Leite that's also a training ground for serious apprentice chefs. Good options in the Zona are *Espaço Armazém*, at Rua da Estrela 401, with varied food and a good bar, *Antiguamente*, just down the street at Rua da Estrela 220 (Ⓣ98/232-3964), and *La Papagaio*, more or less next door, both of which have varied menus, including local seafood dishes like *file de peixe ao molho de castanhas* (fish in a nut sauce) and pastas, too; the former also puts on decent rock music. The excellent and traditional *Base do Edilson* restaurant is buried deep in the *bairro* of Vila Bessa, at Rua Alencar Campos 31; the short taxi journey from the centre is well worth the effort.

Except during Bumba-meu-boi and Carnaval, São Luís is quieter than most Brazilian cities of its size. The largest concentration of **clubs** and **bars** is just over the bridge, in the São Francisco suburb – but these are on the tacky side for the most part. In the centre, Rua da Estrela is a good bet for music and a drink, and the city's street-bars and cafés burst into life at festival times and on Wednesday nights, when **reggae** can blast out till dawn.



# Along the coast

Travel in Maranhão outside São Luís is made difficult by a road system that is limited and – given the rains – often precarious. If you want to travel **along the coast** the most practical way is by boat – an option not to be taken lightly as it's hard going, with no schedules or creature comforts, and no one who speaks English. Don't do it unless you're healthy, a good sailor, not fussy about what you eat, have at least basic Portuguese and aren't too worried about time.

The place to start is the **Estação Marítima** in São Luís, on the waterfront at the end of Praça Dom Pedro II. This is the local station for boats, which supply the nearby coastal villages and towns, take on passengers and cargo and wait for the tides. Brightly painted, these boats are built by artisans along the coast who still know how to put an ocean-going vessel together from timber.

There are sailings to the main coastal towns to the **west** about once a week. The main coastal towns, as you head west, are Guimarães (half a day away), Turiaçu (two days) and Luís Domingues and Carutapera (three days). Tour companies in São Luís who can organize itineraries for you include Simsol Turismo (Ⓣ98/3245-9655 or 3349-0260) in the suburb of Barreirinhas or Rio Ave Turismo, based at Av. Dom Pedro II 221 (Ⓣ98/3221-0238) in Praia Grande.

## São José do Ribamar

Fortunately, not all the interesting places are difficult to get to. Easiest of all are the fishing towns on the island of São Luís: Raposa, a simple village on a beach, an hour away by bus from Praça Deodoro or Rua da Paz; and the relaxing, friendly town of **SÃO JOSÉ DO RIBAMAR**, which you can reach on the bus marked "Ribamar" from Praça Deodoro.

It's 32km to São José, about an hour's drive, a lovely route through thick palm forest and small hills. The bus deposits you in the small town centre, where straggling houses on a headland have sweeping views of a fine bay; it's easy to stay over, as there are several **pensões** in the centre. São José is an important fishing town, as well as being a centre of skilled boat-building by traditional methods – you can see the yards, with the half-finished ribs of surprisingly large boats, behind the houses running inland from the small landing quay and large beach. Many of the **boats** that ply the coast both east and west drop in at

São José, and it's a convenient place to begin a boat trip. The easiest places to head for, with a fair degree of certainty that there'll be a boat back within a day or two, are Icatu, the mainland village on the other side of the bay, and Primeira Cruz on the east coast. From the latter, it's a short hop to the interior town of Humberto de Campos, where you can catch a bus back to São Luís.

### Parque Nacional dos Lençóis

From Primeira Cruz, you can also continue to what is arguably one of the most beautiful sights in Brazil, the **Parque Nacional dos Lençóis**, a desert some 370km to the east of São Luís covering around 300 square kilometres. What makes it so special is that it is composed of hundreds of massive sand dunes that reach towering heights but are subject to prolonged rainfall. The result is that the dunes are sprinkled with literally hundreds of crystal-clear freshwater lagoons. To get there either continue from the small town of Primeira Cruz, or, direct from São Luís, catch the bus to Barreirinhas from the *rodoviária* (hours variable so check beforehand), which takes about eight hours. If you wish to stay overnight here, there are some very modest *pousadas*, including the *Pousada Lins*, Av. Joaquim Sueiro de Carvalho 550 (Ⓣ98/3349-1203; ❷), which has a good restaurant, the *Pousada do Buruti*, Rua Inácio Lins (Ⓣ98/3349-1053; ❷), and the even cheaper *Pousada El Casarão*, Rua Inácio Neves 110 (Ⓣ98/3349-1078; ❷). From Barreirinhas, it's a three-hour journey down the Rio Preguiças to the dunes themselves. If you don't fancy organizing the trip for yourself then there's at least one agency in São Luís that will: Giltur, Rua Montanha Russa 22, Beiramar, Centro (Ⓣ98/3231-7065, Ⓦwww.giltur.com.br). For further information on the *parque*, contact IBAMA, the national parks authority (Ⓣ98/3231-3010, Ⓦwww.ibama.gov.br).

## Across the bay: Alcântara

Set in a wonderful tropical landscape on the other side of the bay of São Marcos from São Luís, **ALCÂNTARA** is now no more than a poor village built around the ruins of what was once the richest town in northern Brazil. São Luís had already eclipsed it by the end of the eighteenth century, and for the last two hundred years it has been left to moulder quietly away. The measure of its decline is that there are now no roads worthy of being called that going there; the only way is by sea from the Estação Marítima at the end of Praça Dom Pedro II in São Luís. The last boat back to São Luís leaves daily at 4pm, so if you want to stay for more than eight hours you'll have to spend the night in one of the few **hotels** or *pousadas*.

## Travel details

### Buses

**Fortaleza** to: João Pessoa (8 daily; 8hr); Natal (10 daily; 8hr); ); Recife (6 daily; 12hr); Salvador (daily; 23hr); São Luís (3 daily; 18hr); Teresina (2 daily; 15hr).

**João Pessoa** to: Campina Grande (hourly; 2hr); Fortaleza (8 daily; 8hr); Juazeiro do Norte (2–3 daily; 10hr); Mossoró (several daily; 4hr); Natal (10 daily; 3hr); Penha (every 2hr; 45min); Recife (10 daily; 2hr).
**Maceió** to: Aracaju (6 daily; 5hr); Recife (20 daily; 4hr); Paulo Afonso (2 daily; 4hr); Penedo (6 daily; 2hr); Salvador (daily; 9hr).

**Natal** to: Fortaleza (10 daily; 8hr); João Pessoa (10 daily; 3hr); Recife (20 daily; 4hr 30min); Salvador (daily; 20hr).
**Recife** to: Aracaju (2 daily; 8hr); Belém (5 weekly; 35hr); Belo Horizonte (3 daily; 35hr); Brasília (3 daily; 48hr); Caruaru (at least hourly; 2hr); Fortaleza (6 daily; 12hr); Goiânia (6 daily; 2hr); João Pessoa (10 daily; 2hr); Maceió (20 daily; 4hr); Natal (20 daily; 4hr 30min); Petrolina (4 daily; 12hr); Porto de Galinhas (every 30min; 1hr); Rio (2 daily; 42hr); Salvador (6 daily; 13hr); São Paulo (4 daily; 48hr).
**São Luís** to: Belém (1–2 daily; 13hr); Fortaleza (1–2 daily; 18hr).
**Teresina** to: Belém (1–2 daily; 24hr); Fortaleza (2 daily; 15hr); São Luís (several daily; 10hr).

## Flights

**Fortaleza**, **Recife**, **João Pessoa**, **Natal** and **Maceió** are all connected by at least daily flights. **Natal**, **Maceió**, **Fortaleza** and **Recife** also have daily connections to Salvador. **São Luís** links with Belém as well as some of the other main Northeast cities.

5

# The Amazon

VENEZUELA
GUYANA
SURINAME
FRENCH GUIANA
COLOMBIA
N
5
4
3
PERU
7
6
BOLIVIA
2
8
1
PARAGUAY
CHILE
9
ARGENTINA
0
1000 km
URUGUAY

CHAPTER 5

# Highlights

* **Jungle river trips** Take in the lush forest scenery, fascinating river settlements and beautiful sight of the river itself. See p.368
* **Ver-o-Peso Market** Best visited in the early morning, Belém's traditional market is a great place to watch the local trade. See p.376
* **Borboletário Márcio Ayres** A magical hummingbird and butterfly reserve in Belém's newest park. See p.379
* **Alter do Chão** Close to Santarém, this beautiful bay boasts a Caribbean combination of white sand and turquoise water that flows from the river Tapajós See p.398
* **Teatro Amazonas** A full-blown European opera house in one of the least likely locations. See p.412
* **Amazon wildlife** Make sure to spend at least a few days in the jungle if you want to spot magnificent toucans, alligators and much more. See p.421
* **Madeira–Mamoré Museu Ferroviário** This fascinating railway museum in Porto Velho will appeal to casual visitors and railroad buffs alike. See p.440

▲ Riverboat on the Amazon, near Manaus

# 5

# The Amazon



The Amazon is a vast forest – the largest on the planet – and a giant river system. It covers over half of Brazil and a large portion of South America. The forest extends into Brazil's neighbouring countries (Venezuela, Colombia, Peru and Bolivia), where the river itself begins life among thousands of different headwaters. In Brazil only the stretch between Manaus and Belém is actually known as the **Rio Amazonas**: above Manaus the river is called the **Rio Solimões** up to the border with Peru, where it once again becomes the Amazonas. It is by far the biggest river system in the world; eight of the world's twenty longest rivers are in the Amazon basin, along with a fifth of the planet's fresh water.

In its upper reaches, the Rio Solimões from Peru to Manaus, it is a muddy light brown, but at Manaus it meets the darker flow of the Rio Negro and the two mingle together at the famous "meeting of the waters" to form the Rio Amazonas. There are something like 80,000 square kilometres of **navigable river** in the Amazon system, and the Amazon itself can take ocean-going vessels virtually clean across South America, from the Atlantic coast to Iquitos in Peru.

## Ecology and development

The Amazon is far more than just a river system. The **rainforest** it sustains is a vitally important cog in the planet's biosphere and covers an area of over six million square kilometres. As rainforests in Asia and West Africa shrink in the face of development, the enormous biodiversity of the Amazon becomes more and more important, as does its future. The rainforest is an enormous carbon sink, and if it burns the implications for global warming – as well as biodiversity – hardly bear thinking about.

The region was only integrated into Brazil after independence in 1822, and even then it remained safer and quicker to sail from Rio de Janeiro to Europe than to Manaus. It was useful as a source of timber and a few exotic forest products, like rubber, but remained an economic backwater until the 1840s, when Charles Goodyear invented a process called vulcanization, giving natural rubber the strength to resist freezing temperatures and opening up a huge range of new industrial applications. The new demand for rubber coincided handily with the introduction of steamship navigation on the Amazon, beginning an unlikely economic boom as spectacular as any the world has seen. By 1900 Manaus and Belém were the two richest cities in Brazil, and out in the forest were some of the wealthiest and most powerful men in the world at that time. The rubber boom ended in 1911 as suddenly as it had begun, as rubber plantations established in the Far East (with smuggled Brazilian seeds) blew natural rubber out of world markets. The development of the region came to an almost complete halt, relying

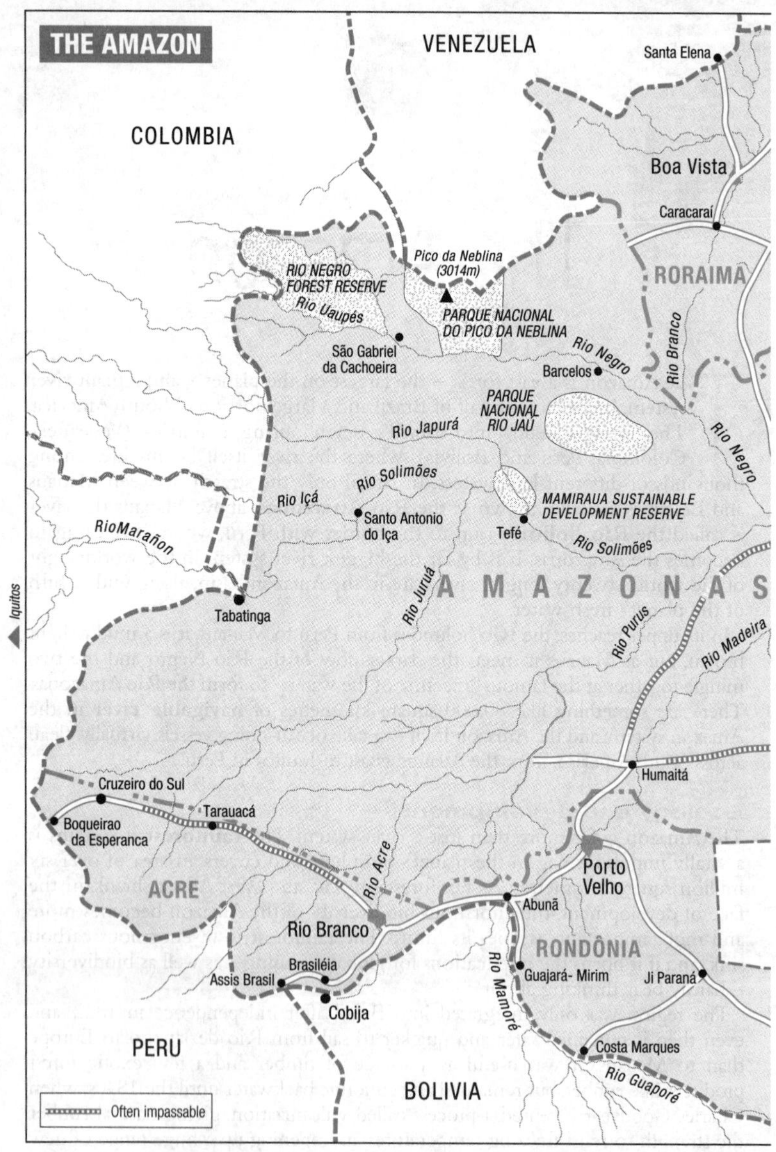


once again on the export of forest products to keep the economy going. There was a brief resurgence during World War II, when the Allies turned to natural rubber after the plantations in the Far East fell under Japanese control, but it is only in the last forty years or so that large-scale exploitation – and destruction – of the forest has really taken off (for more on this, see the section "The Amazon: A Guide to the Issues" in Contexts, p.730).

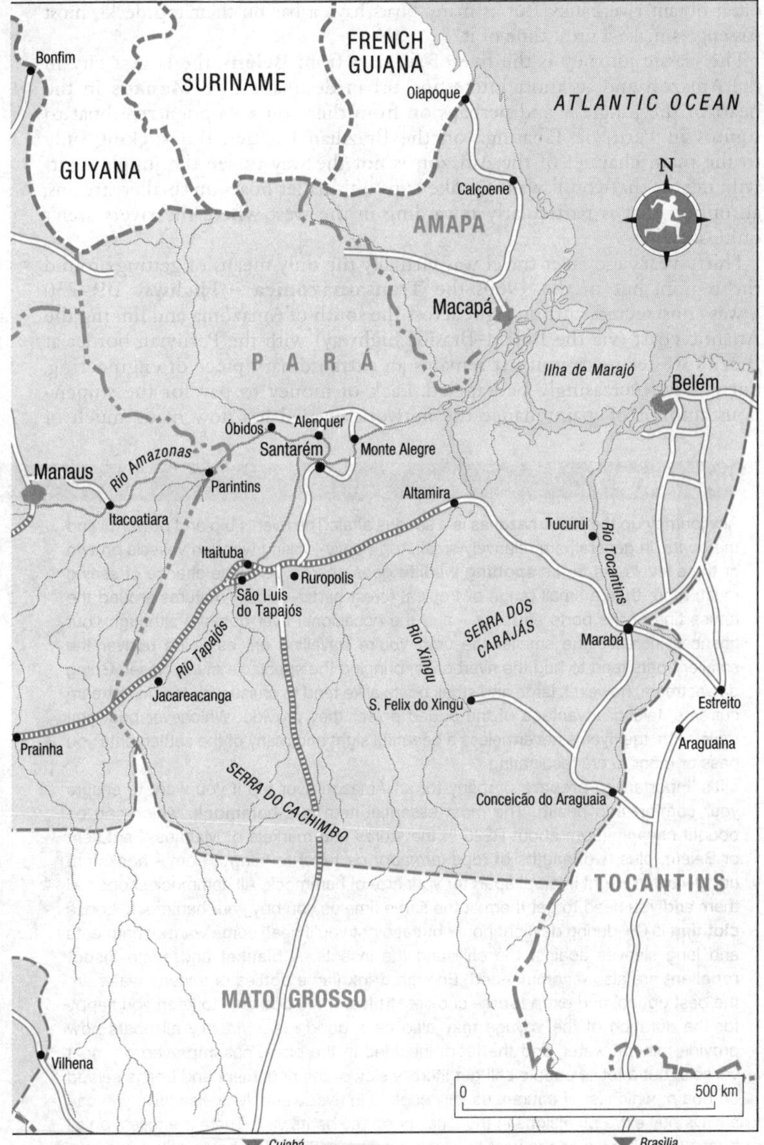


## Getting around the Amazon

Most people who visit Brazil will, at some time or other, have dreamt about taking a **boat up the Amazon** (see box, p.368). This is not hard to do, though it's not as comfortable or easy-going as daydreams might have made it seem. Given the food on some boats, the trip can be tough on the stomach, and you'll need patience or a botanical degree to appreciate the subtle changes in the forest scene on the often-distant riverbanks. But as many boats have a bar on their top decks, most passengers make a great time of it.

The classic journey is the five or six days from **Belém**, the largest city in the Amazon and its most interesting urban destination, to **Manaus** in the heart of the jungle – and perhaps on from there on a wooden riverboat to Iquitos in Peru via Tabatinga on the Brazilian frontier. But sticking only to the main channel of the Amazon is not the way to see the jungle or its wildlife: for that you'll want to take trips on smaller boats up smaller streams, an option that is particularly rewarding in the west where the rivers aren't quite so wide.



Thirty years ago river travel was virtually the only means of getting around the region, but in the 1960s the **Transamazônica** – Highway BR-230 – was constructed, cutting right across the south of Amazônia and linking the Atlantic coast (via the Belém–Brasília highway) with the Peruvian border at Brazil's western extremity. It remains an extraordinary piece of engineering, but is now increasingly bedraggled. Lack of money to pay for the stupendous amount of maintenance the network needed has now made much of

## River journeys

Any journey up the Rio Amazonas is a serious affair. The river is big and powerful and the boats, in general, are relatively small, top-heavy-looking wooden vessels on two or three levels. As far as **spotting wildlife** goes, there's very little chance of seeing much more than a small range of tropical forest birds – mostly vultures around the refuse tips of the ports en route – and the occasional river dolphin, although your chances increase the smaller the craft you're travelling on, as going upriver the smaller boats tend to hug the riverbanks, bringing the spectacle much closer. Going downstream, however, large and small boats alike tend to cruise with the mid-stream currents, taking advantage of the added power they provide. Whichever boat you travel with, the river is nevertheless a beautiful sight and many of the settlements you pass or moor at are fascinating.

It's important to **prepare** properly for an Amazon river trip if you want to ensure your comfort and health. The most essential item is a **hammock**, which can be bought cheaply (from about R$25 in the stores and markets of Manaus, Santarém or Belém, plus two lengths of rope (*armador de* rede) to hang it from – hooks are not always the right interval apart for your size of hammock. All hammock shops sell them and you need to get them at the same time as you buy your hammock. Loose **clothing** is OK during daylight hours but at night you'll need some warmer garments and long sleeves against the chill and the insects. A **blanket** and some **insect repellent** are also recommended. Enough **drink** (large bottles of mineral water are the best option) and extra **food** – cookies, fruit and the odd tin – to keep you happy for the duration of the voyage may also be a good idea. Virtually all boats now provide mineral water, and the food, included in the price, has improved on most vessels, but a lot of people still get literally sick of the rice, meat and beans served on board, which is, of course, usually cooked in river water. If all else fails, you can always buy extra provisions in the small ports the boats visit. There are toilets on all boats, though even on the best they can get filthy within a few hours of leaving port. Again, there are exceptions, but it's advisable to take your own roll of **toilet paper** just in case. **Yellow fever inoculation** checks are common on boats leaving Belém to travel upriver, and for travellers unfortunate enough not to have a valid certificate of vaccination, you risk having a compulsory injection.

There are a few things to bear in mind when choosing **which boat** to travel with, the most important being the size and degree of comfort. The size affects the length

it impassable. West of Altamira it has practically ceased to exist, apart from the Porto Velho–Rio Branco run and odd stretches where local communities find the road useful and maintain it. The same fate has met other highways like the Santarém–Cuiabá and the Porto Velho–Manaus, on which great hopes were once pinned. With the exception of the Belém–Brasília, Cuiabá–Rio Branco and the Manaus–Boa Vista highway corridors, transport in the Amazon has sensibly reverted to rivers. Access to what remains of the Transamazônica from Belém or Brasília is via Estreito, the settlement at the junction where the BR-230 turns west off the old north–south highway, the BR-153/BR-010.

Remember, there are three **time zones** in the Amazon region. Belém and eastern Pará are on the same time as the rest of the coast, except from October to February when Bahia and the states of the Southeast and the South switch to summer time, leaving Belém an hour behind. At the Rio Xingu, about halfway west across Pará, the clocks go back an hour to Manaus time. Tabatinga, Rio Branco and Acre, in the extreme west of the Amazon, are another hour behind again.



of the journey: most small wooden boats take up to seven days to cover Belém to Manaus, and the larger vessels generally make the same journey in five to six days (four to five days downriver). See the "Listings" sections for Belém, Santarém and Manaus for more on boat operators.

Better value, and usually more interesting in the degree of contact it affords among tourists, the crew and locals, is the option of taking a **wooden riverboat** carrying both cargo and passengers. There are plenty of these along the waterfront in all the main ports, and it's simply a matter of going down there and establishing which ones are getting ready to go to wherever you are heading, or else enquiring at the ticket offices; these vessels are essentially water-borne buses and stop at most towns along the way. You'll share a deck with scores of other travellers, mostly locals or other Brazilians, which will almost certainly ensure the journey never becomes too monotonous. The most organized of the wooden riverboats are the larger **three-deck vessels**, on which the Belém–Manaus trip costs US$70 for hammock space (US$50 downriver); this is negotiable if you're really stuck for cash, and will often come with a small discount if you buy your tickets two or more days before departure. The smaller **two-deck boats** are cosier, but often only cover shorter legs of the river. This is fine if you don't mind spending a day or two waiting for your next connection to load up. All of these wooden vessels tend to let passengers stay aboard a night or two before departure and after arrival, which saves on hotel costs.

There's room for debate about whether hammock space is a better bet than a **cabin** (*camarote*; currently around R$250 upriver), of which there are usually only a few. Though the cabins can be unbearably hot and stuffy during the day, they do offer security for your baggage, as well as some privacy (the cabins are shared, however, with either two or four bunks in each) and, in most cases, your own toilet (which can be a blessing, especially if you're not very well). The hammock areas get extremely crowded, so arrive early and establish your position: the best spots are near the front or the sides for the cooling breezes (it doesn't really matter which side, as the boat will alternate quite freely from one bank of the river to the other), though the bow of the boat can get rather chilly if the weather conditions turn a bit stormy. If it really gets unbearably crowded, you can always take your chances by slinging your hammock on the lower deck with the crew, though you'll also have to share your space with cargo and throbbing engine noise.

# Eastern Amazônia

Politically divided between the states of Pará and Amapá, the eastern Amazon is essentially a vast area of forest and savanna plains centred on the final seven hundred miles or so of the giant river's course. **Belém**, an Atlantic port near the mouth of the estuary which has undergone something of an urban renaissance in recent years, is the elegant capital of Pará and a worthwhile place to spend some time. The city overlooks the river and the vast **Ilha do Marajó**, a marshy island in the estuary given over mainly to cattle farming, but with a couple of good beaches.

**Pará** has always been a relatively productive region. Very little of the wealth, however, ever reached beyond a small elite, and falling prices of local commodities on the world markets have periodically produced severe hardship. Today, the state is booming once again, largely thanks to vast mining and hydroelectric projects in the south and west of the state. The landscape of southern Pará, below **Marabá** and the Tocantins-Araguaia rivers, is savanna rather than forest. Over the last twenty years some of the most controversial developments in the Amazon have been taking place here.

**Amapá**, a small state on the northern bank of the Amazon opposite Belém, is a fascinating place in its own right. A poor and little-visited area, it nevertheless offers the opportunity of an adventurous overland route to French Guiana and on into Suriname, Guyana and Venezuela – or even back to Europe via a regular Air France flight between Cayenne, capital of French Guiana, and Paris.

Apart from Belém and the area around it, the most interesting section of the eastern Amazon is the western part of Pará state, where the regional centre is **Santarém** and the neighbouring beach village of **Alter do Chão** is one of the

▲ Passengers playing dominoes on a riverboat

most beautiful spots in the Amazon. **Connections** in the region are pretty straightforward, in that you have very few choices. The main throughway between Belém and Manaus is still the Amazon, with stops at **Monte Alegre**, set amidst a stunning landscape of floodplains and flat-topped mesas housing some of South America's most important archeological sites; Santarém, at the junction of the Amazon with the most beautiful of its tributaries, the turquoise Tapajós river; and the less enticing **Óbidos**. There are good highways south from Belém towards Brasília (the BR-010) and east into the state of Maranhão (the BR-316). Across the river on the north bank of the Amazon there is just one road from **Macapá**, the capital of Amapá state, towards the border with French Guiana. It is only asphalted for the first third of its length and is often impassable in the rainy season. The BR-010 crosses the powerful Rio Tocantins near Estreito (in Maranhão) close to the start of the **Transamazônica highway**. If you're coming from the south, connections with westbound buses and other traffic are best made at Araguaina (in Tocantins) where there's a small *rodoviária* and several hotels. The first stop on the Transamazônica within Pará is **Marabá**, some 460km (12hr) by bus from Belém. Continuing from here, the Transamazônica reaches **Altamira**, on the navigable Rio Xingu, a small, relatively new city over 300km west of Marabá. With a population that's grown from 15,000 in 1970 to over 130,000 today, Altamira is at the centre of an area of rapidly vanishing jungle. Beyond here the Transamazônica becomes impassable. The Transamazônica highway and southern Pará are, it must be said, among the least attractive and most desperate places to visit in Brazil. The poverty and sheer ugliness of the region after four decades of deforestation are the best counter-arguments to the common Brazilian claim that clearing the forest is necessary for development. Pigs will fly before development comes to southern Pará on this evidence.

# Belém

Although less well known than Manaus, **BELÉM**, the only city in the Amazon that is truly old, has much more to offer: an unspoilt colonial centre, one of Brazil's most distinctive cuisines, a stunning collection of architectural survivals from the rubber boom and, to cap it all, an **urban revitalization** over the last decade that has seen new parks, imaginatively restored historic buildings and leisure complexes transform its centre and riverfront into easily the most attractive city for tourism in the Amazon.

Founded just a couple of decades later than the colonial cities of the Northeast coast, Belém at its heart looks very much like them, with the obligatory Portuguese fort, cathedral square and governor's palace. Strategically placed on the Amazon river estuary commanding the main channel, the city was settled by the Portuguese in 1616. Its original role was to protect the river mouth and establish the Portuguese claim to the region, but it rapidly became an Indian slaving port and a source of cacao, timber and spices gathered from the forests inland. In the early nineteenth century it was devastated by the Cabanagem, the bloodiest rebellion in Brazilian history (see box, p.372), before the town experienced an extraordinary revival in the Amazon rubber boom. The few decades of prosperity left an indelible architectural mark on the city. Much of the proceeds were invested in houses and palaces, most of which still survive (unlike in Manaus) and make Belém one of Brazil's top cities to walk around, despite the heat. After the rubber market crashed just before World War I the city entered a long decline, but it kept afloat on the back of Brazil nuts and the timber industry until the highways and development projects from the 1960s on, turned it into the city it is today.

## The Cabanagem Rebellion

The **Cabanagem Rebellion** ravaged the region around Belém for sixteen months between January 1835 and May 1836, in the uncertain years following Independence and the abdication of Pedro I. What started as a power struggle among Brazil's new rulers rapidly became a revolt of the poor against racial injustice: the *cabanos* were mostly black and Indian or mixed-blood settlers who lived in relative poverty in *cabaña* huts on the flood plains and riverbanks around Belém and the lower Amazon riverbanks. Following years of unrest, the pent-up hatred of generations burst in August 1835. After days of bloody fighting, the survivors of the Belém authorities fled, leaving the *cabanos* in control. In the area around the city many sugar mills and *fazendas* were destroyed, and their white owners put to death. Bands of rebels roamed throughout the region, and in most settlements their arrival was greeted by the non-white populations spontaneously joining their ranks, looting and killing.

The rebellion was doomed almost from the start, however. Although the leaders attempted to form some kind of revolutionary government, they never had any real programme, nor did they succeed in controlling their own followers. A British ship became embroiled in the rebellion in October 1835, when it arrived unwittingly with a cargo of arms the authorities had ordered before their hasty departure a couple of months previously. The crew were killed and their cargo confiscated. Five months later, a British naval force arrived demanding compensation from the rebels for the killings and the lost cargo. The leader of the *cabanos*, Eduardo Angelim, met the British captain and refused any sort of compromise; British trade was now threatened, and the squadron bombarded and blockaded Belém. In May 1836 a force of 2500 Brazilian soldiers under the command of Francisco d'Andrea drove the rebels from Belém. Mopping-up operations continued for years, and by the time the Cabanagem Rebellion was completely over and all isolated pockets of armed resistance had been eradicated, some 30,000 people are estimated to have died – almost a third of the region's population at that time.



Belém remains the economic centre of the North and the Amazon's main port. The wealth generated by the rubber boom is most evident in the downtown area, where elegant central avenues converge on two luxuriant squares: **Praça da República** and **Praça Batista Campos**. These border the old heart of the city, the harbour and colonial centre, the focus of intensive revitalization efforts in recent years, which have transformed the riverfront into the Amazon's most attractive and interesting urban space.

The first thing visitors will notice, however, is the always hot – and often wet – **climate**, which takes some getting used to by day (at night, however, it's always pleasant). The rain is torrential and the **rainy season** runs from January to May. Fortunately it falls as showers rather than persistent rain, and typically the skies clear after an hour or so of even the most intense downpour. The central zone of the city is lined by **mango trees**, over a century old and proportionately massive, which provide shade and protection from the broiling sun. When strolling around, be sure to do so slowly, and remember mangos ripen in October – keep half an eye and ear out for falling fruit or you're in for a lump on your head and some intensive shampooing.

## Arrival, orientation and information

Belém's **rodoviária** is situated some 2km from the centre at the start of Avenida Almirante Barroso, the only road out of town – the city is hemmed in by rivers in every other direction. Any bus from the stops opposite the entrance to the *rodoviária* will take you downtown. If you want Praça da República, take one with "P. Vargas" on its route card; for the port area look for "Ver-o-Peso". There are good facilities and services at the *rodoviária*, including a Parátur information office (not always open, even when it's meant to be).

### By air

If you're coming by scheduled airline, you'll arrive at Belém **airport**, 15km out of town. Tourist information is available here (see below) and there's the usual system of co-op taxis opposite the arrivals hall, for which you buy a ticket at the kiosk, but this is an expensive way of getting into town (R$30 for a 15min ride). Turn left coming out of arrivals to the far end of the terminal where you'll find the taxi stand for ordinary city cabs, which are half the price. Or you can take the "Marex Arsenal" bus from the airport to the *rodoviária* and continue into town from there, although this is definitely not recommended if you have luggage.

### By boat

**Larger riverboats** dock at the port near the town centre, from where you can walk or take a local bus up Avenida Presidente Vargas (not recommended if you have luggage or if it's late at night), or catch a taxi. **Smaller riverboats** come in at the Porto de Sal, in the old colonial area, also near the centre. (For information on boat services, see p.385.) Your best option is to take a taxi to a hotel, which will be around R$10 – at night it is unsafe to do anything else.

### Orientation

**Avenida Presidente Vargas** is the modern town's main axis, running from the Praça da República and the landmark Teatro da Paz right to the riverfront. A short walk down Avenida Serzedelo Correa takes you to Praça Batista Campos, another central landmark. Buses coming into Belém's centre from the airport and *rodoviária* travel down the dock road before turning up Vargas. Most of the hotels are along Presidente Vargas, or just off it.

### Information

**Tourist information** (patchy at best in Belém) is officially available from Parátur offices downtown at the Feira de Artesanato do Estado on Praça Maestro Waldemar Henrique, close to the junction of Presidente Vargas with the docks, but your best bet are the kiosks at the airport and bus station. The staff at Parátur are charming and anxious to help, but have little available other than pamphlets. City maps can be bought cheaply from the newspaper kiosks along Presidente Vargas, or in the foyer of the *Hilton* hotel, looming unmistakeably opposite the Teatro da Paz.

Belém is not especially dangerous, but the usual cautions apply regarding **security**. Be careful about walking the narrow streets off Presidente Vargas around Praça da República at night, as it's been a red-light district for centuries. The *Bar do Parque* on the Praça next to the Teatro da Paz is one of the loveliest places to sit and drink a beer in the city, but it's unfortunately infested by pimps, prostitutes and various low-lifes drawn like a magnet by the hope of snaring a rich tourist from the *Hilton* across the road. The whole area around Ver-o-Peso market is an essential sight, but keep a sharp eye on your pockets and be careful about cameras and bags. The riverfront street leading down from the fort to the harbour is picturesque but to be avoided at night and treated with caution even in daylight. Though bustling during the week, the whole central area empties at weekends, when you should not stray off the main streets.

There is one confusing thing about the city that's important to understand. The main riverfront focus for nightlife is "Estação das Docas". You might want to get a boat from the docks, in which case you need to head for "as docas".

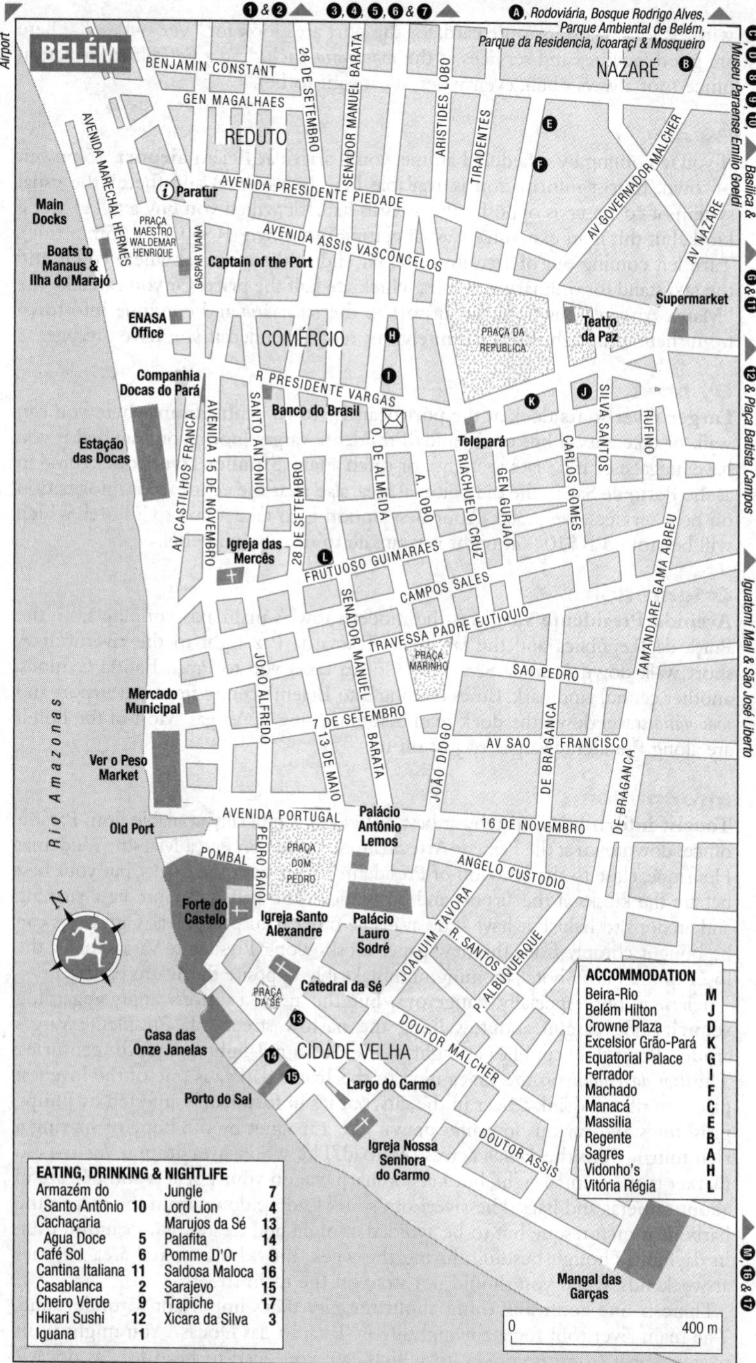

BELÉM
Airport
1 & 2
3, 4, 5, 6 & 7
A, Rodoviária, Bosque Rodrigo Alves, Parque Ambiental de Belém, Parque da Residencia, Icoaraçi & Mosqueiro
C, D, 8, 9, 10, Museu Paraense Emílio Goeldi
Basilica &
G & 11
12 & Plaça Batista Campos
Iguatemi Mall & São José Liberto
M, 16 & 17
NAZARÉ
REDUTO
COMÉRCIO
CIDADE VELHA
BENJAMIN CONSTANT
GEN MAGALHAES
28 DE SETEMBRO
SENADOR MANUEL BARATA
ARISTIDES LOBO
TIRADENTES
AV GOVERNADOR MALCHER
AV NAZARE
AVENIDA MARECHAL HERMES
AVENIDA PRESIDENTE PIEDADE
AVENIDA ASSIS VASCONCELOS
GASPAR VIANA
PRAÇA MAESTRO WALDEMAR HENRIQUE
Paratur
Main Docks
Boats to Manaus & Ilha do Marajó
Captain of the Port
ENASA Office
Supermarket
Teatro da Paz
PRAÇA DA REPUBLICA
Companhia Docas do Pará
R PRESIDENTE VARGAS
Banco do Brasil
Telepará
Estação das Docas
AV CASTILHOS FRANCA
AVENIDA 15 DE NOVEMBRO
SANTO ANTONIO
O. DE ALMEIDA
A. LOBO
RIACHUELO CRUZ
GEN GURJAO
CARLOS GOMES
SILVA SANTOS
RUFINO
TAMANDARE GAMA ABREU
Igreja das Mercês
FRUTUOSO GUIMARAES
CAMPOS SALES
SENADOR MANUEL BARATA
TRAVESSA PADRE EUTIQUIO
PRAÇA MARINHO
JOAO ALFREDO
SAO PEDRO
Mercado Municipal
7 DE SETEMBRO
13 DE MAIO
JOAO DIOGO
DE BRAGANCA
AV SAO FRANCISCO
Ver o Peso Market
Rio Amazonas
AVENIDA PORTUGAL
Palácio Antônio Lemos
16 DE NOVEMBRO
Old Port
PEDRO RAIOL
PRAÇA DOM PEDRO
POMBAL
ANGELO CUSTODIO
Forte do Castelo
Igreja Santo Alexandre
Palácio Lauro Sodré
JOAQUIM TAVORA
R. SANTOS
P. ALBUQUERQUE
Catedral da Sé
PRAÇA DA SÉ
DOUTOR MALCHER
Casa das Onze Janelas
Largo do Carmo
Porto do Sal
Igreja Nossa Senhora do Carmo
DOUTOR ASSIS
Mangal das Garças
N
0
400 m
ACCOMMODATION
Beira-Rio M
Belém Hilton J
Crowne Plaza D
Excelsior Grão-Pará K
Equatorial Palace G
Ferrador I
Machado F
Manacá C
Massilia E
Regente B
Sagres A
Vidonho's H
Vitória Régia L
EATING, DRINKING & NIGHTLIFE
Armazém do Santo Antônio 10
Cachaçaria Agua Doce 5
Café Sol 6
Cantina Italiana 11
Casablanca 2
Cheiro Verde 9
Hikari Sushi 12
Iguana 1
Jungle 7
Lord Lion 4
Marujos da Sé 13
Palafita 14
Pomme D'Or 8
Saldosa Maloca 16
Sarajevo 15
Trapiche 17
Xicara da Silva 3

The area around Avenida Souza Franco is also a likely destination, thanks to its bars and restaurants. This region is known as "Docas", without the definite article, which creates immense potential for confusion with taxi drivers.

## Accommodation

There are plenty of **hotels** in Belém, many of them overpriced, but there is adequate accommodation for every budget. Most of the more expensive and mid-priced hotels are located on Avenida Presidente Vargas; more basic hotels are in the narrow streets just off Vargas.

**Beira-Rio** Av. Bernardo Sayão 4804 ⓣ91/3249-7111. Located in the *bairro* of Guamá and reachable by bus (Guamá or UFPA) or taxi from the centre. There are great views out across the river as well as an excellent riverside restaurant, but it's a bit remote and the neighbourhood is grim; don't walk around it. The boat across to the *Saldosa Maloca* restaurant is a big plus, however. ❹

**Belém Hilton** Av. Presidente Vargas 882 ⓣ91/4006-7000, ⓦwww.amazon.com.br/hilton. Belém's best and most expensive hotel, which dominates the Praça da República, offers luxurious rooms with excellent a/c; some have superb views across the cityscape, river and forests. Radical price reductions are occasionally available at slack times of year. ❻

**Crowne Plaza** Av. Nazaré 375 ⓣ91/3202-2022, ⓦwww.crownebelem.com.br. Luxury hotel newer and better than *Hilton*, rarely full and steep 50 percent discounts often available from the eyewateringly high nominal rates if you just turn up and ask. ❺–❽

**Equatorial Palace** Av. Bras de Aguiar 621 ⓣ91/3241-2000. Overpriced but pleasant enough rooms and a small rooftop pool with a good view. ❺

**Excelsior Grão-Pará** Av. Presidente Vargas 718 ⓣ91/3242-9044. This is the best deal in town: R$65 gets you a basic but a/c room in an efficient, modernized hotel in a central downtown location. Highly recommended. ❸

**Ferrador** Rua Ó de Almeida 476 ⓣ91/3241-5999. Reasonable and very central hotel that caters mainly to a Brazilian business clientele; guest rooms are modern. *Ferrador* shares its building with *Hotel Vidonho's* (ⓣ91/3242-3109), also good value. ❸

**Machado** Rua Henrique Gurjão (next to *Massilia*) ⓣ91/4008 9800. A new, functional hotel just off Praça da República that's aimed at business travellers. Through the rooms are rather lacking in character, they're very efficient (featuring cable and broadband, for example), and are good value compared to others in this price range. ❺

**Manacá** Travessa Quintino Bocaiuva 1645 ⓣ91/3223-3335. This pleasant, quiet, family hotel is in a downtown area that's still dominated by rubber-boom buildings. Offers all modern conveniences. ❹

**Massilia** Rua Henrique Gurjão 326 ⓣ91/3222-2834. Belém's best medium-price option has a quiet central location, a small pool and a restaurant that's worth eating in even if you don't stay here. The front desk will arrange tours in the French owner's boat for cheaper than what most local tour agencies charge. Excellent value. ❹

**Regente** Av. Gov. José Malcher 485 ⓣ91/3241-1222 or 3241-1333. Newly renovated, clean and somewhat characterless but the central location is good. ❺

**Sagres** Av. Gov. José Malcher 2927 ⓣ91/3266-2222. This hotel near the *rodoviária* has a decent bar, a sauna and a pool. While the restaurant isn't worth bothering with outside of breakfast, the rooms and the views from them are fine, though overpriced. ❹

**Vidonho's** Rua Ó de Almeida 476 ⓣ91/3242-1444, ⓕ3224-7499. Good-value, modern hotel, with a/c in all rooms and good showers. Well located, if a bit noisy, just off Av. Presidente Vargas. ❸

**Vitória Régia** Rua Frutuoso Guimarães 260 ⓣ&ⓕ91/3212-3301, 3212-3628, ⓔh.v.r@uol.com.br. A cheap, clean and friendly place with a pleasant staff. R$30 gets you a room with a fan, R$40 gets you a/c; there's a 10 percent discount if you pay cash in advance. Internet access is available in the lobby, but the connection isn't very reliable. ❷

## The City

The **Praça da República**, an attractive cross between a square and a park with plenty of trees affording valuable shade, is the best place from which to get your bearings and start a walking tour of Belém's downtown and riverfront attractions. At its heart is the most obvious sign of Belém's rubber fortunes: the **Teatro da Paz**. In business since 1878 and recently restored, it's open for visits (Mon–Fri

9am–6pm; free). Although not as spectacular as the Manaus opera house, it is still a wonderful example of early rubber-boom architecture and is very much a working theatre, regularly used for plays, operas and recitals. A concert there is an unforgettable experience and a visit to the box office is always in order; tickets are subsidized to the hilt and very cheap. Dress codes are informal and the air conditioning is efficient; if there is an interval, head for the first-floor terrace and one of the best night-time views the city has to offer.

### The markets and Estação das Docas

Heading down Presidente Vargas towards the river, an old part of town lies off to the left, full of crumbling Portuguese colonial mansions and churches. This is a pleasant area to wander during business hours, and walking parallel to the river will bring you to the old harbour – always crowded with riverboats and overlooked on one side by an unmistakeably Portuguese fort and on the other by one of the most interesting traditional markets in all of South America, **Ver-o-Peso**. An essential stop, Ver-o-Peso ("see the weight") is reason enough in itself to visit Belém. There are sections devoted to fish, aromatic oils, medicinal plants and herbs and an expanding sector selling locally produced craft goods.

The market is at its most interesting from around 4am, when the boats from the interior start coming in with the two Pará products the city needs above all else: fish and *açaí*, a palm fruit from which one brews a purple mush that is a staple of Amazonian cuisine, and which no self-respecting *paraense* can get through the day without drinking straight, eating mixed with a variety of ingredients or freezing and consuming as ice cream. The fish is either sold right on the dockside or hauled into the cast-iron market overlooking the harbour (Scots reminded of home are quite right; the sections were made in Scotland in the 1890s and then assembled here). The *açaí* comes bundled up in baskets woven from the palm leaves, and is immediately pounced on by traders and customers in a hubbub of shouting and early-morning bustle. Getting there at a more realistic hour, around 8am, there is still plenty of fish to see in the old market, and stretching beyond it are, in order, an equally fascinating medicinal herbs and spices market, all grown in backyards or fresh from the forest; the colonial customs house, now restored; and a more orthodox market under modern awnings which is a good place to buy hammocks, mosquito nets, football shirts and other necessities. A little further up on the opposite side of the road is the faded but still impressive wrought-iron entrance to the **Mercado Municipal**, another rubber-boom survival that today sells an array of fascinating local products. With the iron bars above, it feels like a jail: they were added to keep the vultures away from the meat and fish the market sold when it was built.

In recent years, the once-derelict riverfront promenade both sides of Ver-o-Peso has been transformed. Where Ver-o-Peso ends, a row of old warehouses has been converted into **Estação das Docas**, a complex of restaurants, bars, stalls, exhibition spaces, shops and a cinema/theatre, where you can choose between strolling inside in the air conditioning or outside along the river (a great option at night). The designers sensibly kept everything intact and reconditioned it, rather than building anew, so you can still see the old loading cranes, now painted bright yellow. A wonderful touch is the hydraulic loading trolley, which runs beneath the warehouse roof: it has been turned into a moving stage where live music serenades the crowds every night over a poster saying "*cultura em cima de tudo*" – Culture Above All.

Estação das Docas is great at any time of day but comes into its own at night. You can stroll down and take your pick of a row of restaurants (*Lá Em Casa*

▲ Ver-o-Peso fish market

has the best regional food), there is a microbrewery with very good, locally brewed beer, the music is good, the atmosphere is lively and the river traffic is a constantly fascinating backdrop. It is also the departure point for another essential Belém activity, the **sundowner river cruise**, which leaves every day at 5pm from the end nearest Ver-o-Peso; tickets (R$30 a head) can be bought from the Valeverde Turismo office there. It may look like a cheesily tourist thing to be doing – a suspicion not exactly laid to rest by the colossally vulgar boat sporting a large, fibreglass Indian figurehead – but it's wonderful. The city is best seen close up from the river, the guides are friendly, the tourists are mainly Brazilian and, best surprise of all, the live "regional music and dancing" is in fact genuinely regional and excellent. The boat returns to its starting point two hours later, invariably with most of its passengers dancing. Drinks and light refreshments are served at reasonable prices, with *tacacá* soup (see box, p.384) the highlight.

## Cidade Velha

Across from Ver-o-Peso in the opposite direction to Estação das Docas is the **colonial heart of Belém**, Cidade Velha. The small Neoclassical building on the water's edge is the old *necrotério*, where dead bodies from villages in the interior without a priest would be landed so they could be given proper burial in the city. Behind is the bulk of the old Portuguese fort, the **Forte do Castelo**, which is mostly mid-eighteenth century, though its earliest parts date from the 1620s. There is a small, very interesting (and a/c) museum inside, open Monday to Friday 9am to 4pm (R$2). The most enjoyable thing to do, however, is walk the battlements, with views down to the harbour and across the river.

The cathedral square outside the fort, the **Praça da Sé**, looks very much as it did in the late eighteenth century; it is a wonderful place to sit at night and admire the views before moving on to the many options for eating and drinking in the neighbourhood. Next to the fort is the archbishop's palace, which houses a worthy but dull religious-art museum, the **Museu de Arte Sacra** (Tues–Fri 10am–4pm; R$2); the mid-eighteenth century cathedral known universally as the Catedral da Sé dominates the other side of the square. The exterior is classically Portuguese (although in fact built by an Italian, Antônio Landí), but the interior has been gutted by successive restorations and little of interest remains.

On the other side of the square is another essential Belém sight, the **Casa das Onze Janelas**. Dating from the early eighteenth century, it was originally the town jail and then an arsenal; today it is a cultural centre, with a mediocre restaurant downstairs, an art gallery upstairs and by far the most important feature out back: **Belém's best bar**, the *Boteco das Onze Janelas*. On a terrace behind the building, linked to the fort by a walkway and with a marvellous view of the river, the excellent beer is from the local microbrewery, and waiters circulate with trays of delicious savouries: the bean soup (*caldo de feijão*) is recommended as a stomach-liner before or after if you're getting down to serious drinking. It is a great place to arrive in the late afternoon and watch the sunset over the river – another option is to use it for drinks before heading across the square to another two excellent eating options, the *Marujos da Sé* and *Palafita* restaurants. To the side is the only non-colonial addition to the complex, a floodlit set of fountains.

To the left of the cathedral square as you exit the fort are the magnificent **palaces** of Lauro Sodré and Antônio Lemos – the former, along with the Teatro da Paz, being the finest building left in Belém by the rubber boom. Until recently the seat of the mayor and state governor respectively, and more than a little run down, they have been sensitively restored. No visit to Belém would be complete without seeing them.

The **Palácio Antônio Lemos** (Mon–Fri 9am–6pm, Sat 10am–6pm), finished in the 1890s at the height of the rubber boom, has an elegant blue-and-white Neoclassical colonnaded exterior and a series of airy, arched courtyards that are occasionally used as galleries for travelling exhibitions. Upstairs is the Salão Nobre, a huge suite of reception rooms running the entire length of the frontage and featuring crystal chandeliers, beautiful inlaid wooden floors and Art Nouveau furniture; it's marred only by a few grim paintings. A separate section of the palace houses the **Museu de Arte do Belém** (Mon–Fri 9am–6pm, Sat 10am–6pm, Sun & holidays 9am–1pm), with paintings dating back to the eighteenth century, though none worth seeing.

Next door, the dazzling white **Palácio Lauro Sodré** (Tues–Fri 9am–noon & 2–6pm, Sat 9am–1pm) was built in the 1770s by Antônio Landí, a talented emigré Italian who, as an artist, sketched the first scientifically accurate drawings of Amazonian fauna. It was here that the joint Portuguese–Spanish border commissions set out to agree the frontiers of Brazil in colonial times. Pará's independence from Portugal in 1822 and adhesion to the Republic in 1888 were declared from here, and it was on the main staircase that President Lobo de Souza was shot down on January 7, 1835, in the early hours of the Cabanagem Rebellion (see p.372). The palace later became the centre of days-long street fighting at the rebellion's height, which left hundreds dead. Today it houses the **Museu do Estado do Pará**, showcasing the usual dull historical pieces but worth seeing for the stunning (though small) collection of Art Nouveau furniture. It is the building itself, however, that is the real highlight. Apart from the magnificent central staircase, resurfaced with marble during the rubber boom, the ground floor and half of the first floor are still much as they were in the eighteenth century – uncluttered and elegant. The reception rooms overlooking the square were rebuilt at the turn of the twentieth century with no expense spared and, perhaps even more than the Manaus opera house, give an idea of what an extraordinary period the rubber boom was.

## Largo do Carmo, Mangal das Garças and São José Liberto

Back on the cathedral square, head down the narrow Rua Siqueira Mendes (easily identified by the exquisite Art-Nouveau Clube do Remo building on the corner): it is the city's oldest street. A few minutes brings you into the perfectly preserved and quite gorgeous **Largo do Carmo**, an eighteenth-century square dominated by the church of the same name (another Landí creation), which, as usual, has an exterior that's more interesting than the interior. A little further on, crossing the Avenida Almirante Tamandaré, with its unmistakeable drainage channel, swing right at another rubber-boom jewel, the local naval headquarters on the Praça do Arsenal, and you find yourself at Belém's newest and in some ways most successful urban-renewal project: the park of **Mangal das Garças** (daily 10am–6pm; the restaurant is open until midnight).

Set on the banks of the Guamá river the park is dominated by an observation tower and a large Indian-influenced wooden building with a restaurant, *Manjar das Garças* on the upper floor, best enjoyed at night, when it is cool enough to eat on the terrace looking out across the river. The ground floor is given over to a museum of Amazon boats and boatbuilding – a lot more interesting than it sounds. A wooden walkway leads out to a platform over the mudflats, where the combination of shade, river traffic and birdlife is hypnotic. But the highlights here are two striking pavilions: an **aviary** and a reserve for butterflies and hummingbirds, the **Borboletário Márcio Ayres**.

On entrance to the aviary, guides give visitors a laminated sheet that identifies all of the birds; you can then mark them off, from the easy – the spectacular scarlet ibis – to ones that are less well known but equally gorgeous when seen close up, including the tanagers. Even more compelling is the nearby *borboletário*, a combined butterfly and hummingbird sanctuary named after a pioneering Amazonian conservationist who died tragically young of cancer. As with the aviary, guides give you a laminated sheet when you enter, but the first thing you notice is the wonderful coolness of the air. This comes from pipes high above spraying water droplets to create the humidity and moisture both the hummingbirds and butterflies need. The combination of fluttering butterflies and darting hummingbirds is, quite simply, magical.

Elsewhere in the park you'll find kiosks with refreshments, a bookshop, and a small artificial lake teeming with heron and scarlet ibis. Wandering around is free but to get into the aviary, museum, *borboletário* or go up the observation tower (a great view) you need to buy tickets from a kiosk at the bottom of the observation tower: a combination ticket covering everything for R$12 is your best option. The only problem with the park is the lack of shade; although trees have been planted, Mangal das Garças was only opened in 2005 and they have not yet had time to grow.

For your final stop in Cidade Velha, take a short taxi ride (R$5; taxis are always around at the Mangal entrance) to yet another historic building imaginatively converted into a cultural centre, **São José Liberto**. Once a church and then the city prison, its often grim history has vanished without trace in an imaginative restoration and conversion: it is now a cultural complex housing exhibition space, a fascinating museum of minerals and precious stones, and a number of workshops where you can see gemcutters at work and purchase their output directly. Entrance is free and the complex is open Monday to Friday 9am to 5pm and Saturday and Sunday 3 to 8pm.

The entrance hall, a modern annexe built onto the colonial core, has a café and an excellent ice-cream stand (part of the Cairú chain) but the highlight – apart from the air conditioning – is the several stalls selling the best of local handicrafts, notably the very distinctive Indian-influenced ceramics produced at Icoaraci (see p.386). Buying here will save you a long bus ride, and it's exactly the same stuff (although rather more expensive). The space is also often used for shows and live music performances in the late afternoon and evening, especially at weekends; it's always worth asking if anything is scheduled.

The **gemology museum** and jewellery workshops are in the colonial part of the building; the workers ply their trade behind glass walls, for all the world like fish in an aquarium, with a number of bijou shops displaying the finished products nearby. The work is distinctive and cheap for what it is. Much more interesting than it sounds, the gemology museum offers a fascinating display of precious and semi-precious stones (cut and uncut) in a strongroom, but the highlight is a section of fossilized tree, against which a dinosaur might have scratched itself.

Turn right coming out of the entrance, follow the buses around the curve to the right and turn left at the light, where a four-block walk will bring you out on **Praça Batista Campos**, another gorgeous square with a cluster of rubber-boom buildings. From here, a short walk down Serzedelo Correa will take you back to Praça da República and complete the circuit.

## Avenida Nazaré: the Basílica and Museu Goeldi

Two of the most important and worthwhile sights in Belém lie about fifteen minutes' walk up from the Praça da República along Avenida Nazaré. The first is the **Basílica de Nossa Senhora de Nazaré** (daily 6.30–11.30am & 2.30–7pm) on Praça Justo Chermont. Created in 1908, and supposedly modelled on St Peter's in Rome, it rates – internally at least – with the most beautiful churches in South America. It somehow manages to be ornate and simple at the same time, its cruciform structure bearing a fine wooden ceiling and attractive Moorish designs decorating the sixteen main arches. Most importantly, however, this is home to one of the most revered images in Brazil, the small **Nossa Senhora de Nazaré** statue. There is the usual cluster of legends about the image's miraculous properties, and for *paraenses* it is something like a combination of patron saint, first port of spiritual help when trouble strikes and symbol of the city. Wherever they are, someone from Belém will do whatever they can to be back in the city in October for Brazil's most spectacular religious festival, the **Cirio de Nazaré**, when the image is paraded around in front of enormous crowds.

Two long blocks up Avenida Magalhães Barata (the continuation of Nazaré) from the Basílica, you'll find the excellent **Museu Paraense Emílio Goeldi**. (Tues–Thurs 9–11.30am & 2–5pm, Fri 9–11.30am, Sat & Sun 9am–5pm, closed Mon; botanical gardens R$4, aquarium R$3). Actually more of a botanical garden and a zoo than a museum these days, it is an essential stop: the gardens are beautiful as well as educational, and any money you spend here goes not only to the upkeep of the museum and its grounds but also to a wide programme of research in everything from anthropology to zoology. This is one of only two Brazilian research institutes in the Amazon, and it plays a vital role in developing local expertise.

A small **zoo** is set in the compact, but beautifully laid out, botanical gardens. Tapirs, manatees, big cats, huge alligators, terrapins, electric eels and an incredible selection of birds make this place an important site for anyone interested in the forest, and by Brazilian standards the animals are reasonably kept, too. The highlight is the Art Nouveau aquarium, with its selection of piranhas overmatched for sheer ugliness and menace by the (actually quite harmless) *matamata* turtle, and the incomparable pre-Columbian Marajó funeral urns in the exhibition hall, which you will see reproduced everywhere from the sides of buses to Icoaraci ceramic shops.

## Cirio de Nazaré

**Cirio** climaxes on the second Sunday of October, but for weeks beforehand the city is preparing itself for what in Belém is by far the most important time of year, easily outstripping secular rituals like Carnaval. The centre is swept and cleaned, houses and buildings on the image's route (much of the centre of town) are decorated and festooned with bunting and posters in the saint's yellow and white colours, and hotels fill up while anticipation builds. On the **Friday night** before the climax hundreds of thousands of people accompany a cortege with the image borne aloft on a flower-covered *palanque* down Avenida Nazaré from the Basílica, through Praça da República to a chapel where it spends the night. It is something to see; hundreds of thousands of people quietly and in perfect order walking along with the image, residents of buildings applauding and throwing flowers as it passes, with choirs stationed at improvised stages en route serenading it with hymns. **Saturday morning** is, in some ways, the visual highlight of the entire period. The image is put onto a decorated boat for the *procissão fluvial* and sailed around the riverfront, accompanied by dozens of boats full of devotees, so the sailors and riverboats so central to the life of the city get a chance to show their devotion too. This is best seen from the battlements of the fort or the walkway next to it, but get there no later than 10am or the places will be taken. The next part of the festivities is secular; around 1pm a riotous procession dominated by young people, with bands and drummers, wends its way through the Praça da Sé, down Rua Siqueira Mendes and ends up at the Largo do Carmo, where groups set up on stage and entertain the multitude with excellent regional music until the evening. **Sunday morning** is the climax, when the decorated *palanque* makes its way back through the centre of town and up Avenida Nazaré to the Basílica. The crowd tops a million, but is very non-intimidating: the atmosphere is saturated with devotion and everyone is very orderly – at least away from the cortege. The self-flagellating side of Catholicism is much in evidence: the image is protected on its travels by a thick anchor rope snaking around the cortege, and those with sins to pay for or favours to ask help carry the rope, where the squeeze of bodies is intense – at the end of the day the rope is stained red with blood from the hands of devotees. The especially devout follow the cortege on their hands and knees, with equally bloodstained results after several miles of crawling on asphalt. The image is usually back at the Basílica by noon, when families unite for the *paraense* equivalent of a Thanksgiving or Christmas dinner, with turkey being substituted with *pato no tucupí*, duck in *tucupí* sauce, and *maniçoba*, a fatty, smoky-tasting stew of pork and manioc leaves, which takes days to prepare. All in all, the largest and most spectacular religious festival in Brazil is worth going to some trouble to catch – but be sure to book your hotel well in advance.

Two blocks up from the museum is the **Parque da Residência**, where what used to be the official residence of the governor has been converted into a small park and cultural centre. This very pleasant spot houses one of Belém's better restaurants, the *Restô do Parque*, which does an excellent *por kilo* buffet at lunchtime. There is also a theatre, where the old governor's limo is displayed in the foyer, and, in a very *paraense* touch, an old railway wagon from the early twentieth century has been converted into an ice-cream parlour.

### The Bosque Rodrigo Alves and the Parque Ambiental

One of the surprising things about Belém is that enough patches of forest survive within the city limits to give you a real sample of the jungle all around. A taste can be had in about half an hour from the centre by any of the many buses marked "Almirante Barroso" to the **Bosque Rodrigo Alves** (Tues–Sun 8am–5pm): it's on the left and unmistakeable, an entire city block of trees as tall as a five-storey building. Though not as domesticated as the Goeldi botanical garden, it's well kept and actually better for seeing river life; you'll find hundreds of turtles, a small but very imaginative aquarium and a café by the side of an artificial lake. The highlight, however, is without doubt the Amazon manatee, the *peixe-boi* (literally, fish-cow, and up close you see why – it's *big*). These mammals are increasingly rare in the wild. As this is the only chance you will have to see one in the Amazon, you should grab it with both hands: they are astonishing creatures, combining breathtaking ugliness with sheer grace as they move through the water. The enclosure at the Bosque includes a bridge built over the water – where manatees graze on aquatic grasses – allowing you within a few feet.

For a real idea of the forest, head for the **Parque Ambiental de Belém** (Tues–Fri 9am–5pm), also known as the Parque do Utinga, after the *bairro* where it is located. Within easy reach of the centre of town, this is an area of several hundred hectares of preserved forest, protecting two lakes that provide the city's fresh water. It is astonishingly unpublicized in the city's tourist information, perhaps because officials don't understand that foreigners might actually like walking around a forest without a guide or much in the way of facilities.

The park is run by the local water company, COSANPA, and is at the very far end of Avenida 1 de Dezembro. You can get there by bus but, given that it doesn't look like a park, you are probably better off going by taxi – about R$20 from downtown but much less if you go direct from the Bosque Rodrigues Alves, which is very close. Some preparation is necessary: you will need your passport or another photo ID to get in, and there are no facilities inside, so take sunscreen, a hat and enough water and food. You will arrive at what looks like a COSANPA water-treatment plant; there is no sign and the only clue as to where you are is the forest behind. The guard will take your details and you can then just walk down the road; the forest closes in around you after about ten minutes or so. There is an extensive system of trails but, since none of them are marked and there are no maps, your best bet is probably to stay on the road, which is quite as scenic as the trails and will lead you after a couple of miles to two lakes and a visitors' centre; the centre is very basic but it's a good observation platform, with views out to the lake. There are birds all over the place, and you are likely to see monkeys, *capivara* and other wildlife. You could easily spend a day here, and getting back to the centre is easy: turn left out of the entrance, walk down a couple of hundred yards to Avenida 1 de Dezembro, and any bus heading in the same direction you are walking will take you back to the *rodoviária*. Make sure you get the bus before dark: this isn't an area to be walking around at night, although it is perfectly safe during the day.

## Eating, drinking and nightlife

Belém is a great place to eat out and get acquainted with the distinctive dishes of the Amazon region (see box, p.384). Estação das Docas and the Docas area around Avenida Visconde Souza Franco are good places to start, and they are two of the city's main focuses for nightlife as well. Belém has the best ice-cream chain in Brazil, Cairú, specializing in regional flavours; half a dozen branches across the centre are strategically placed along the walking circuit. **Street food** is also good, even for those not on a budget: fantastic roast leg of pork sandwiches (*pernil*) can be had from the stall on the corner by the Cine Olimpia, on Praça da República, and for the more adventurous palate, *tacacá* and *açaí* are safe and delicious from the stalls of Dona Miloca, in front of the Goeldi museum, and Maria do Carmo, in front of the Colégio Nazaré on Avenida Nazaré, just before the Basílica. Other cheap eating options are off Presidente Vargas but cater mainly for the lunchtime office crowd. All the restaurants listed below take major credit cards unless otherwise specified.

## Restaurants

**Amazon Beer** The microbrewery at Estação das Docas is worth visiting at any time but especially so during Sat lunch, when it serves the city's best *feijoada* – actually more of a *feijoada* buffet. Be sure to arrive hungry.

**Armazém do Santo Antônio** Travessa Quintino Bocaiúva 1696. This café attached to a bakery and deli is always a good place for snacks. It really comes into its own, however, for Sat and Sun brunch, with a buffet that includes fresh fruit, bacon, eggs and *beiju* manioc pancakes. Forget your hotel restaurant and eat breakfast here.

**Café Sol** Av. de Visconde Souza Franco 1122. Good coffee, savouries and light meals are offered alongside a panoramic view. Unfortunately, the place closes early, at 9pm, but there are plenty of other options around here for afterwards.

**Cantina Italiana** Travessa Benjamin Constant 1401. This small family restaurant, open for lunch and dinner, is the best Italian option in town. Offers excellent, moderately priced antipasti. Visa only.

**Cheiro Verde** On the corner of Brás de Aguiar and Avenida Deodoro, near the *Equatorial Palace Hotel* and the Basílica. Good cheap *comida por kilo* restaurant, with vegetarian options as well as meat and fish, and a great salad bar. Always packed, with live music performed after 9pm on Fri and Sat.

**Hikari Sushi** Av. Serzedelo Correa 220, just off Praça da República. Belém's Japanese community dates from the 1930s and this is the best of a number of good sushi places in town.

**Manjar das Garças** Mangal das Garças park. The combination of Amazonian ingredients and a chef from southern Brazil doesn't always work, but the setting, especially at night, is fantastic, and the lunch buffet is one of the best in the city. On the expensive side, but worth it – pack plastic.

**Marujos da Sé** Praça da Sé. Superb setting on the cathedral square fully matched by the food: Amazonian with international influences and arguably the best in the city. Very reasonably priced for the quality.

**Palafita** Rua Siqueira Mendes 264. Across the street from *Marujos da Sá*, wend your way through a colonial house to a wooden platform built over the river, where you'll enjoy excellent, moderately priced regional food. Try the *pastel de pato*, duck pasties served with *tucupí* to dip them in, and the *caldeiradas*, fish stews. Visa only.

**Pomme D'Or** Generalissimo Deodoro 1513. A good-quality, cheap *comida por kilo* place just off the Basílica.

**Restô do Parque** Parque da Residência, just up from the Goeldi museum. This *comida por kilo* restaurant, serving regional dishes and excellent salads, is much classier than the others in Belém. The macaws outside bite, so steer clear of them.

**Saldosa Maloca** Located on Combú island, with a fantastic view of the city, *Saldosa Maloca* is a great place to go on a weekend. The restaurant has a boat that leaves from the *Beira Rio* hotel and takes customers across for R$5 a head. Make sure you take the bigger of the two boats you'll see (located on the right as you look across the river), since a neighbouring restaurant that is not as good has a boat that leaves from the same spot. The (surprisingly cheap) food at *Saldosa Maloca* is local cuisine; recommended dishes are the *filhote na brasa* (grilled fish) and *costela de porco* (rack of pork ribs). Behind the restaurant, an elevated wooden walkway passes through *açaí* palm forest, a *casa de farinha*, where you can watch manioc flour be made, and an *açaí* pulper, where you'll see the fruit turned into deep purple juice and taken straight to the tables. Only open for lunch on Sat and Sun, unfortunately.

**Trapiche** Av. Bernardo Sayão 4906. A little further up from the *Beira Rio* hotel, this riverside restaurant has the usual good Amazonian food, but it also has a dancefloor with fine live music (regional with a touch of *brega*). It's a slightly older crowd than at the more central clubs, but you'll see some great dancing. The music isn't so loud that it interferes with the eating, if that's what you want to focus on. Moderately priced.

**Xicara da Silva** Av. Visconde Souza Franco 978. One of Belém's best restaurants is set in a surprisingly quiet and tranquil spot on a very busy street. The moderately priced food (given the quality) features local ingredients served in imaginative new ways. Highly recommended are the duck in tamarind sauce and the *escondidinho*, jerked beef served with mashed manioc. The pizza is the best in town.

## Bars and nightlife

Belém's real **nightlife** rarely begins much before 10 or 11pm, with Estação das Docas and the Docas area around Visconde de Souza Franco being the main focus in the centre. Several places cluster on Avenida Wandenkolk, one block up and parallel to Visconde de Souza Franco: *Lord Lion* at 419, *Jungle* at 800 and

*Iguana* at 247. For a more intimate, romantic setting, try *Roxy Bar* at Av. Senador Lemos 230, also in Docas. If you want to dance rather than hang out, *Casablanca* is close by at Av. Senador Lemos 175; music is loud and techno, but the club is in a beautiful old house and there is a soundproofed restaurant as well. Calmer live music (with the largest *caipirinhas* you're ever likely to see) along with a gourmet selection of *cachaça* is also close by at *Cachaçaria Agua Doce*, Rua Diogo Moiá 283. An excellent newcomer is *Club Sarajevo* in a magical setting by the Largo do Carmo square in Cidade Velha.

The other area for **live music** is the western *bairro* of **Condor**, on the banks of the Rio Guamá. There are numerous clubs to choose from, with the scene particularly lively on Thursday, Friday and Saturday, but you'll need to take a taxi there and back. *Lapinha*, Travessa Padre Eutiquio 390, is the best known and most enjoyable, though it doesn't get going much before midnight. It's not too glitzy, there's usually good food and a live band at weekends, and it may be the only club in the world that has three toilet categories – "Men", "Women" and "Gay". A similar popular destination is

## Amazon cuisine

As you might expect from the richest freshwater ecosystem in the world, **fish** takes pride of place in Amazonian cooking, and you'll come across dozens of species. There are many kinds of huge, almost boneless fish, including *pirarucu*, *tambaqui* and *filhote*, which come in dense slabs sometimes more like meat, and are delicious grilled over charcoal. Smaller, bonier fish, such as *surubim*, *curimatã*, *jaraqui*, *acari* and *tucunaré*, can be just as succulent, the latter similar to a large tasty mullet. Fish in the Amazon is commonly just barbecued or fried; its freshness and flavour need little help. It's also served *no escabeche* (in a tomato sauce), *a leite de coco* (cooked in coconut milk) or stewed in *tucupí*.

The other staple food in Amazônia is **manioc**. *Farinha*, a manioc flour consumed throughout Brazil, is supplied at the table in granulated form – in texture akin to gravel – for mixing with the meat or fish juices with most meals, and is even added to coffee. Less bland and more filling, manioc is also eaten throughout Amazônia on its own or as a side dish, either boiled or fried (known as *macaxeira* in Manaus and western Amazônia or *mandioca* elsewhere). A more exciting form of manioc, **tucupí**, is produced from its fermented juices. This delicious sauce can be used to stew fish in or to make *pato no tucupí* (duck stewed in *tucupí*). Manioc juice is also used to make *beiju* (pancakes) and *doce de tapioca*, a tasty cinnamon-flavoured tapioca pudding. A gloopy, translucent manioc sauce also forms the basis of one of Amazônia's most distinctive dishes, *tacacá*, a shrimp soup gulped from a gourd bowl and sold everywhere from chichi restaurants to street corners. Other typical regional dishes include *maniçoba*, pieces of meat and sausage stewed with manioc leaves, and *vatapá*, a North Brazil version of the Bahian shrimp dish.

Finally, no stay in the Amazon would be complete without sampling the remarkable variety of **tropical fruits** the region has to offer, which form the basis for a mouth-watering array of *sucos* and ice creams. Most have no English or even Portuguese translations. Palm fruits are among the most common; you are bound to come across *açai*, a deep purple pulp mixed with water and drunk straight, with added sugar, with tapioca or thickened with *farinha* and eaten. Other palm fruits include *taperebá*, which makes a delicious *suco*, *bacuri* and *buriti*. Also good, especially as *sucos* or ice cream, are *acerola* (originally it came over with the first Japanese settlers in the 1920s, although Amazonians swear it is regional), *peroba*, *graviola*, *ata* (also called *fruta de conde*) and, most exotic of all, *cupuaçú*, which looks like an elongated brown coconut and floods your palate with the tropical taste to end all tropical tastes.

the riverside *Palácio dos Bares*, specializing in *forró* and *brega*. *Lapinha* and the *Palácio* are large, frenetic and fun, but if it's decent music you want, the best option is *Casa do Gilson*, Travessa Padre Eutiquio 3172, with *choro* on Friday nights, samba on Saturday afternoons into the early hours, and either on Sunday evenings.

For a night at the **cinema** there is only one surviving large-screen spot, the Nazaré on the Basílica, which shows mainstream releases. There's also a good triple-screen arthouse, Cinema 1-2-3, on Travessa São Pedro behind the Iguatemi mall in Batista Campos: take any bus with an "Iguatemi" card in front, get out at the mall, and walk through it onto the street behind to reach the cinema.

## Listings

**Airlines** Varig now at the airport only; TAM, Av. Assis de Vasconcelos 265 ⓣ91/3212-2166. Air Surinam goes three times weekly to Paramaribo via Cayenne, and connections to Georgetown, and Air Caraibe three times weekly to Cayenne and the French Antilles, with Air France connections to Paris from either Cayenne or Port-au-Prince. All are best contacted via their offices in the airport.

**Banks and exchange** Banco da Amazônia, Av. Presidente Vargas; HSBC Bank, Av. Presidente Vargas 670; Banco do Brasil, 2nd floor, Av. Presidente Vargas 248. Many of the larger shops, travel agents and hotels will change dollars. Banco 24 Horas cash machines in most supermarkets and many *farmácias*, a cluster of ATMs on Praça da República by the *Hilton* is the easiest place to use your plastic.

**Boats** See also box, p.368. Boats leave Belém regularly for upstream Amazon river destinations, even as far as Porto Velho (at least one a day to Macapá, Santarém and Manaus). However, boats don't have set times of departure, as this depends on tides and river conditions, and there are a huge number of different companies, with no central place where you can get information. Any travel agent will book a ticket for you (just say when and where you want to go), or speak to the captains on the docks (try the waterfront by Armazém 3 and also 10, and the Porto do Sal terminus on Rua Siqueira Mendes in Cidade Velha). Failing that, for Santarém, Manaus and Macapá, tickets are available through the Agência Amazonas at Av. Castilho Franca 548; Amazon Star and Valeverde Turismo, below, will also book you tickets.

**Car hire** Avis, Rua Sen. Lemos 121 ⓣ91/3257-2277, and Localiza, Av. Gov. José Malcher 1365 ⓣ91/3257-1541, both also with kiosks at the airport. Better rates available from the local car-hire agency in the basement of the *Hilton*.

**Laundry** Lavanderia Marajo, Av. Bras de Aguiar 408; Lavanderia Tintuvana, Av. Presidente Vargas 762 (inside the arcade).

**Post office** The central post office (Mon–Sat 9.30am–6pm) is at Av. Presidente Vargas 498; it's often quicker to walk to the small post office at Av. Nazaré 319, three blocks beyond the Praça da República.

**Shopping** Belém is one of the best places in the world to buy hammocks (essential if you are about to go upriver) – look in the street markets between Av. Presidente Vargas and Ver-o-Peso, starting in Rua Santo Antônio. For *artesanato*, head for Casa Amazônia, Av. Presidente Vargas 512; the Loja Victoria Regia, Av. Presidente Vargas 550; or the Cantô do Uirapurú, Av. Presidente Vargas 594. Orion Perfumaria, Frutuoso Guimarães 270, produces and sells a wide range of rainforest oils, scents and cosmetic products.

**Travel and tour companies** There are two good tour agencies in Belém for foreigners, both with a reasonably priced selection of tours around Belém: Amazon Star Turismo, Rua Henrique Gurjão 208 (ⓣ91/3252-2582, ⓦwww.amazonstar.com.br), an excellent French-run agency specializing in ecotourism, and Valeverde Turismo, at Estação das Docas (ⓣ91/3212-3388) and Av. Alcindo Cacela 104 (ⓣ91/3218-7333, ⓦwww.valeverdeturismo.com.br). Packages from these two are your best bet if you want to explore the islands around Belém or spend much time in Marajó, where transport is difficult if you don't speak Portuguese. Both offer excursions to Ilha dos Papagaios, an island near Belém where tens of thousands of parrots zoom out of the trees at dawn, an unforgettable sight and cheap at R$70 a head, including pick-up from your hotel at 4.30am and a hearty breakfast. It's worth the bleary eyes. Both are used to foreign tourists and have guides who speak good German and French, as well as English.

# Around Belém

There are interesting places near Belém, although you should mostly resist the temptation to swim at the river beaches anywhere close to the city. The locals, indifferent to high fecal counts, regularly do, but it plays havoc with the unaccustomed. We've listed a number of places you can visit below but the best bet for a day at the beach, if a day is all you have, is Mosqueiro. If you have longer, head for the altogether more enticing destinations of Algodoal and Marajó – further afield but worth the effort.



## Icoaraci, Outeiro, Mosqueiro and Cotijuba

The easiest of the beaches to reach from Belém is **ICOARACI**, with local buses from anywhere downtown taking about an hour. Walk towards the river from the bus terminus and you'll hit the two things that make the trip worthwhile. One is the **ceramic workshops** on the newly paved and reconditioned riverfront, which sell distinctive pottery based on the ancient designs of the local Indians. The skill involved in shaping, engraving, painting and firing these pots is remarkable. Some of the ceramics are very large and, except to the expert eye, barely distinguishable from the relics in the Goeldi museum. They are cheap and the shops are used to crating things up for travellers; for a little extra they will deliver to your hotel the following day. The other thing justifying the trip is one of the region's best restaurants, *Na Telha*, which serves mouthwatering fresh fish and *moquecas* in the eponymous tile; one dish easily does for two people, and try if you can to get there during the week, since it's packed at the weekend.

The closest large beaches to Belém are at **OUTEIRO**, but should be avoided like the plague: they are filthy at all times and hugely crowded at the weekend, when drunk drivers by the score, fighting youths and unbelievably crowded Kombis make the whole area a danger zone. A much better bet is **MOSQUEIRO**, some 70km east of Belém but with frequent bus service from the *rodoviária* (it's about a 2hr ride). The trip to Mosqueiro is also a good excursion in a rented car; it is difficult to get lost, as Belém has only one road out of town – go up Almirante Barroso, follow the signs to the BR-316 (right fork at the Castanheira shopping centre), and keep going, turning left at the sign to Mosqueiro about 30km later. Mosqueiro is actually an island but well connected to Belém by a good road and bridge; the ride is pleasant, and a fine opportunity to see the country beyond the city. Unfortunately, the beaches close to the town are picturesque but too dirty to swim at, and you need to take a local bus from the main square to the best option, **Praia do Paraíso**, about half an hour away. Stay on the bus until the end of the line and you find yourself at a gorgeous headland, with a hotel behind you and a clean, swimmable beach in front. The *Lafaiete* restaurant serves excellent *caldeiradas* and *isca de peixe*, mouthwatering pieces of freshly fried fish. If you come this far you might as well make a night of it; the hotel is good (comfortable and with a/c) but expensive (R$80). Alternatively, there are a couple of cheap *pousadas* further back along the beach road.

Just 18km east from Belém, the island haven of **Cotijuba** is replete with beautiful beaches, rainforest and access to *igarapé* creeks. It's the perfect place for birdwatching and nature walks.

## Algodoal and further east

Your best bet for getting a sense of coastal, rural Pará is to head for another island, **Algodoal**. Reaching it is half the fun. The jumping-off point is the small town of **Marudá**, a four-hour bus ride from the Belém *rodoviária* via a Rápido Excelsior bus: several run a day (R$13 each way), but buy a ticket the day before and catch one that leaves early in the morning, to ensure you don't have to stay the night in Marudá. The bus leaves you close to the port – actually no more than a wooden jetty – where a forty-minute boat crossing (R$4; buy tickets at the booth at the jetty entrance) takes you to Algodoal island. You will be met by a number of mule-pulled carts, there being no way for cars to get to the island, or roads for them to drive if they could. You can take a cart or walk to the small village, where there are a dozen cheap *pousadas*, or take a cart to the best option, *Jardim de Eden* (Ⓦwww.algodoal-amazon-tourism.com.br, Ⓔjardimdoeden@hotmail.com), a more isolated *pousada* on Praia do Farol owned by a Brazilian–French couple, who also speak English and Spanish and are very attentive and helpful. The *Jardim* has an idyllic location, a variety of cheap to moderately priced accommodations – from camping space and hooks to sling a hammock to chalets and a bungalow – plus the best food on the island, which includes very fresh shrimp and fish. Algodoal can get moderately crowded at weekends and holidays, but nothing compared to most places on this coast. The beaches are enormous and beautiful. If you want to relax and do nothing for a few days or longer in sleepy tranquillity, this is the place to head. But take as much cash as you'll need; electricity only arrived here in 2005, and credit cards are as yet unknown.

Further east, this entire coastline is being rapidly developed. Many people from Belém head for the mainland beaches here, **Ajuriteua** and the resort of **Salinas** especially. But the truth is facilities haven't kept up with the pace of development, and the crowds that descend on places like Salinas every weekend have long since ruined it.

## Ilha do Marajó

The **Ilha do Marajó** is a vast, 40,000-square-kilometre island of largely uninhabited mangrove swamps and beaches in the Amazon river delta opposite Belém. Roughly the size of Switzerland, it is by some way the largest river island in the world. Created by the accretion of silt and sand over millions of years, it's a wet and marshy area: the western half is covered in thick jungle, the east is flat savanna, it's swampy in the wet season (Jan–June) and brown and firm in the dry season (June–Dec). Originally inhabited by the Marajoara Indians, famed for their ceramics, these days the savanna is dominated by *fazendas* where water buffalo are ranched; some 60,000 of them roam the island, and supplying meat and hides to Belém is Marajó's main trade. Among the most spectacular sights are the flocks of scarlet ibis, *guará*, which can vary in colour from flamingo pink to blood red. Common on Marajó but an endangered species in the rest of Brazil, they are born white – it is the red crabs they eat that turn their feathers red over time. Marajó has beautiful sandy beaches, and it's become a popular option for Brazilian sunseekers and ecotourists alike.

Although it was settled by Jesuits in the seventeenth century, Marajó's earliest inhabitants left behind thousand-year-old burial mounds, in which many examples of the distinctive Marajó pottery were found. The most spectacular are large funeral urns, decorated with geometric engravings and painted designs – the best examples are in the Museu Goeldi in Belém. When the Jesuits arrived and established the first cattle ranches, the island was inhabited by Aurá Indians, who lasted no more than a few decades; later its vast expanses offered haven to runaway slaves and to refugee Indians who wanted to trade with Belém without too much direct interference into their culture from white settlers. Water buffalo, ideally suited to the marshy local conditions, were imported from India during the rubber boom – or, if you believe local legend, were part of a French cargo bound for Guiana and escaped when the ship sank. River navigation around Marajó is still a tricky business, the course of the channels constantly altered by the ebb and flow of the ocean tides.

### Arrival, tours and accommodation

For such a big island there are very few anchorages, and the only **point of entry** into Marajó from Belém is the tiny port of Foz do Camará, where buses and Kombis meet all incoming boats and ferry visitors to **Soure**, **Salvaterra** and **Joanes** – the main destinations – all some 25km away. Three boats leave Belém daily. A car ferry that also takes passengers leaves from Icoaraci at 6.30am, with an additional 4am departure on Saturday. If you're renting a car, you should seriously consider a few days pottering around Marajó as an option (just make sure you leave Belém with a full tank). The ferry terminal is just to the left of the restored part of the riverfront where the Icoaraci ceramic-sellers congregate. Without a car, the Navegação Arapari ferryboat leaves daily from gates 10 and 15 of the Belém docks at 6.30am and 2.30pm; additional departures are occasionally added on holidays and weekends.

In general, you have two options when visiting Marajó: independent travel without a car basically means a beach holiday spent checking out Soure, Salvaterra and Joannes. There are few roads in Marajó, and little public transport. Alternatively, if you want to see the interior of Marajó, your best bet is to get a **package tour** through an operator in Belém who will set you up at a *hotel fazenda* – a ranch geared up to receive visitors or a specialist hotel got up to look like a ranch. These packages range in price, from moderate to expensive; Valeverde Turismo in Belém has good deals, starting at around R$100 a day but including full board and all travel. Three recommended places at the moderate end actively courting the foreign ecotourism market are *Paracauary Ecoresort* (Ⓦwww.paracauary.com.br), *Hotel Fazenda Sanjo* (the only working ranch) and *Pousada dos Guarás*. There is one luxury ecoresort, *Marajó Park Resort* (actually on Mexiana island, just off the north coast of Marajó; Ⓦwww.marajoparkresort.com.br), where prices start at around R$500 a night for a couple and include a ride in a small plane to the hotel from Belém; expensive though it may be, booking via a Belém operator will still be around twenty percent cheaper than booking it from abroad or from southern Brazil.

### Soure, Salvaterra and Joanes

A quiet town with pleasant beaches where you can relax under the shade of ancient mango trees, **SOURE** is where most visitors head for at first. The *Hotel Soure*, just a few blocks from the docks in the town centre, is very basic, while the *Hotel Marajó*, Praça Inhangaiba (Ⓣ91/3741-1396), and the *Hotel Ilha do Marajó*, Av. Assis de Vasconcelos 199 (Ⓣ91/3224-5966, Ⓦwww.dadoscon.com.br/himarajo), both offer more comfort and a pool. The best restaurant in Soure is *Delícias da Nalva*, Quarta Rua 1051, whose speciality *marajoara* banquet includes a *filé a marajoara* (buffalo meat covered with cheese), a *filhote* with crab sauce, fried shrimp and much more, all served in a beautiful, overgrown garden. In **SALVATERRA**, on the other side of the estuary and linked to Soure by a regular ferry service, is the *Beira-Mar*, on the corner of Quinta Rua with Segunda Travessa – simple, clean and starting at R$40 a night.

Both Soure and Salvaterra are occasionally noisy at night during the weekend, with partying groups over from Belém. If it's tranquillity you want, your best option is the village of **JOANES**, which has a magnificent beach, a headland with a wind turbine that supplies the town with the energy it needs and the excellent *pousada Ventania do Rio Mar* (Ⓣ91-3646-2067, Ⓔventaniapousada@hotmail.com); rates start at R$40. Run by a Belgian woman and much frequented by young Brazilian and foreign travellers, it has a range of accommodations (from beach chalets to guest rooms), good food and a splendidly panoramic bar.

On all beaches, be mindful of stingrays – they are particularly common on Marajó. Stick to places with waves and moving water, and avoid wading in rivers and streams.

# Southern Pará

The southern half of Pará, whose main towns are **Marabá** and **Altamira**, has virtually nothing to recommend it to the traveller; largely denuded of forest, it is now a jumble of unproductive ranches, poor peasants and depressing towns. When it hits the headlines it is always for the wrong reasons, such as the assassination of American nun Dorothy Stang in 2005. You are much better advised to head for western Pará and the area around Santarém, which has far more to offer. Basic details on southern Pará are given here, but our recommendation is that you avoid it unless you have good reason to go. Even then, take care.

## Marabá

**MARABÁ**, on the banks of the Rio Tocantins, almost 600km south of Belém and 400km north of Araguaina on the Belém–Brasília road, is often described as the worst of all Amazon towns. It's the market centre for the region, and also the place where the ranchers, construction workers, truckers and gold-miners come for entertainment; it has a bad reputation for theft and violent crime, and it's not a place you should (or would want to) hang around any longer than you have to.

Marabá is a city of three parts, all of them easily reached by bus from Araguaina or from Belém and linked by bridges across the river. The earliest part of town was founded on the south side of the river on ground that was prone to flooding; later settlers created the Cidade Nova on the north side, hoping to escape the waters. In the 1970s the completion of the Transamazônica led to the foundation of Nova Marabá, back on the south side.

**Buses** will drop you at the *rodoviária* at Km 4 on the Transamazônica in Nova Marabá; small local buses or taxis run from here to just about every part of town. The airport (Ⓣ94/3324-1383) is just 3km out of town near the Cidade Nova. The choice of **accommodation** is relatively small: in Nova Marabá there's the *Hotel Itacaiúnas*, Folha 30, Quadra 14, Lote 1 (Ⓣ&Ⓕ94/3322-1326; ❸–❹), and the *Hotel Vale do Tocantins*, Folha 29, Quadra Especial, Lote 1 (Ⓣ94/3322-2321, Ⓕ3322-1841; ❸–❹), both with pool, bar and restaurant and rates starting at R$60. Cheaper accommodation can be had in Cidade Nova at the *Hotel Vitória*, Av. Espírito Santo 130 (Ⓣ94/3528-1175; ❷), and the *Hotel Keyla*, Transamazônica 2427 (Ⓣ94/324-1175; ❷–❸). Nearer the *rodoviária* there's also the basic, even cheaper and somewhat noisy *Pensão Nossa Senhora do Nazaré* (❶). The town's best fish **restaurant** is *Bambu*, Travessa Pedro Carneiro 111, Cidade Nova (Ⓣ91/3324-1290), and there's a good Japanese restaurant, *Kotobuki*, at Av. Tocantins 746, Novo Horizonte (closed Tues).

# Amapá

The **state of Amapá**, north of the Amazon, is one of Brazil's poorest and least populated regions. Traditionally it was dependent primarily on rubber exports, but manganese was discovered in the 1950s and this, together with timber and other minerals, is now the main source of income. A standard-gauge rail line links the mining camps to the northwest with **Porto do Santana**, near the capital Macapá, crossing the dry, semi-forested plains of the region en route. Amapá doesn't have much going for it, other than as a transit route to **French Guiana**, and it suffers the most marked dry season in the Amazon, running from June to December, when it can get extremely hot. **Macapá** fights it out with Palmas in Tocantins for the title of dullest state capital in Brazil, but at least it's cheap.

## Macapá

On the north bank of the Amazon and right on the equator, **MACAPÁ** is the gateway to the state of Amapá and home to three-quarters of its population.

The countryside around Macapá is, like the Ilha do Marajó in the estuary, roamed by large herds of water buffalo. In town there is not a great deal to do. The one highlight is the **Fortaleza de São José do Macapá** (daily 9am–6pm, closed Mon), one of the largest colonial forts in Brazil, built in 1782 from material brought over as ballast in Portuguese ships, in response to worries that the French had designs on the north bank of the Amazon. The fort is often closed, but nobody will mind if you slip through the enormous main gates for a stroll along the battlements. There's an interesting daily artisan market nearby on Canal da Fortaleza, but the best option is to stroll along the seafront, where the breeze at least offers some relief from the heat.

### Arrival and information

If you're coming by ferry from Belém you'll actually arrive to the southwest at **Porto do Santana**, just twenty minutes by bus or an hour by boat from Macapá, though it lies on the other side of the equator. The **airport** is 4km from town on Rua Hildemar Maia (Ⓣ96/3223-2323). The **rodoviária** (Ⓣ96/3242-5193) faces the Polícia Técnica, 5km outside town on the BR-156; from there, local buses run to Praça Veiga Cabral in the centre.

For information about **boats** to the north or to Belém, the Captain of the Port, Av. FAB 427 (Ⓣ96/3223-9090 or 3223-4755), can be contacted at his offices most weekdays between 8am and 5pm. Most boat companies sell tickets through the agency Sonave at Rua São José 2145 (Ⓣ96/3223-9090). The main companies, all based at Porto do Santana, are ENAVI (Ⓣ96/3242-2167), with irregular sailings via Belém as far as Santarém, and Silnave (Ⓣ96/3223-4011) for car-carrying boats to Belém (Tues & Fri). Varig is at Rua Cândido Mendes 1039 (Ⓣ96/222-7724), but TAM (Ⓣ96/3223-2688) has a more extensive route network from Macapá, including direct flights to Brasília. For **car rental**, contact Localiza (Ⓣ96/3223-2799).

### Accommodation

For **accommodation**, the *Hotel Tropical*, Av. Antônio Coelho de Carvalho 1399 (Ⓣ96/3231-3759; ❷), is excellent value with spacious rooms. The *Hotel São Antônio* (❶) is better placed on the main *praça*, and even cheaper, but not quite as good; additionally, there's the clean and friendly *Hotel Mara* in Rua São José (Ⓣ96/3222-0859; ❷–❸). Slightly more upmarket, but still cheap is the *Hotel Centro*, Rua Tiradentes 25 (Ⓣ96/3217-2231; ❹). Out near the airport, the

*Hotel San Marino*, Av. Marcílio Dias 1395 (Ⓣ96/3223-1522, Ⓕ3223-5223; ④–⑤), offers more comfort and a pool, while top of the range for creature comforts is the *Ceta Hotel* on Rua do Matadoro 640, in the Fazendinha district (Ⓣ96/3227-3396, Ⓦwww.ecotel.com.br; ⑤–⑥). By far the best option, however, is the *Pousada Ekinox*, a short walk from the centre at Rua Jovino Dinoa 1693 (Ⓣ96/3222-4378, Ⓔjef@brasnet.online.com.br; ④–⑤). This small but lovely *pousada*, which doubles as the **French consulate**, has French–Brazilian owners, and the food is as good as that combination suggests. It's also the best place to take a tour into the surrounding country, under the competent guidance (and diplomatic protection) of Jeff, the co-owner. It's a popular place to stay, so you'll need to ring ahead and make a reservation.

### Eating, drinking and nightlife

Macapá's position as a river and sea port means there's plenty of excellent fish to be had. The *Lennon Restaurant* downtown is a popular dining spot, but greater variety can usually be found at the *Restaurante Boscão*, Rua Hamilton Silva 997. Superb fish is served at *Martinho's Peixaria*, Av. Beira-Rio 140, and at *Cantinho Baiano*, on the same street at no. 328. The coast road in either direction from the fort has the most pleasant **bars** in town, always well ventilated by the sea breeze. For unrestrained night-time entertainment, try *Rithimus*, at Rua Odilardo Silva 1489, or the *Marco Zero* **nightclub**, 5km out on Fazendinha road near the equatorial monument **Marco Zero**, for a mix of samba and mainstream sounds.

## Into French Guiana

One reason to come to Amapá is to get to **French Guiana** (or Guyane). The key road in the state connects Macapá with the town of **OIAPOQUE**, on the river of the same name that delineates the frontier. The road isn't asphalted all the way, but even where it's dirt it's usually good going in the dry season; in the wet season, however, it can take days, and you're better off flying directly to Cayenne from Belém. If you want to make it in one run, the regular buses to Oiapoque can take as little as twelve hours in the dry season. It's unfortunately a rather boring drive, largely through savanna rather than forest, with mile after mile of scrubby pine plantations blocking any view. You could break the journey in **CALÇOENE**, eight hours by bus from Macapá. A pleasant, sleepy town built around rapids on the river of the same name, Calçoene has several cheap hotels and regular bus connections on to Oiapoque. While there you may feel tempted to visit the nearby gold-mining town of Lourenço. Don't – it's dangerous and very malarial.

A more leisurely option is to go **by boat** from Macapá to Oiapoque, a journey of two days (one night); boats depart once a week or so, but there's no regular schedule. If you're interested in this option, simply go to the docks and ask around: if a boat is leaving, seek out its captain and negotiate for hammock space, which should cost no more than R$50 in either direction. The best hammock spaces are those with open sides, preferably on the middle deck. This is the Atlantic, however, and it can get rough.

If you are not a citizen of a European Union country, the US or Canada, you will need a **visa** to enter French Guiana. There is a French consulate in Macapá at the *Pousada Ekinox* (see above), though it's better to try to arrange the visa before you leave home. If you're going to travel overland, buy **euros** in Belém or Macapá. You can get them in Oiapoque but the rates are worse, and you can't depend on changing either Brazilian currency or US dollars for euros in the border settlement of Saint-Georges in Guyane.

Dug-out taxis (or canoes) are the usual means of transport between Oiapoque and Saint-Georges, about ten minutes downriver. Brazilian **exit stamps** can be obtained from the Polícia Federal at the southern road entrance into Oiapoque; on the other side you have to check in with the *gendarmes* in Saint-Georges. Buses to Cayenne take some eight hours over a good-quality asphalt highway.

# Santarém

Around 700km west of Belém – but closer to 800 as the river flows – **SANTARÉM** is the first significant stop on the journey up the Amazon, a small city of around 130,000 people, which still makes it the fourth largest in the Brazilian Amazon. Agreeable and rather laid-back, it feels more like a large town than a city – a world away from the bustle of Belém and Manaus. Even though the area around it has lately been transformed by a soy-growing boom, and the docks are now dominated by a Cargill grain terminal, this hasn't had much impact on the town's languid feel. But don't be deceived: there are plenty of things to do here, and Santarém, positioned right in the centre of a region still largely (and inexplicably) unvisited by tourists, is the perfect base for exploring some of the most beautiful river scenery the Amazon basin has to offer.

Santarém is located at the junction of the **Tapajós river** and the Amazon; the waters mix in front of the city and the contrast between the muddy waters of the Amazon and the deep blue and turquoise of the Tapajós is as spectacular as the much better known merging of the Rio Negro and the Amazon in front of Manaus. During the dry season (June–Nov) the Tapajós drops several metres, fringing the entire river system with stunning white-sand beaches. This is the time to visit **Alter do Chão**, Santarém's beach resort and certainly the most beautiful the Amazon has to offer.

## Some history

It is likely this area once supported one of the highest populations in the Americas before Europeans arrived, with towns and villages stretching for miles along the riverbanks, living off the rich stocks of fish in the river, and farming corn on even richer alluvial soils, replenished annually when the Amazon flooded. On all the distinctive flat-topped hills around Santarém, there is evidence of **prehistoric Indian occupation**, easily identified by the *terra preta do Indio* (Indian black soil), a black compost deliberately built up over generations by Indian farmers. If you

### Prehistoric finds

Thirty kilometres east of Santarém, more easily accessible by river than by road, is a nineteenth-century sugar plantation called **Taperinha**. In an excavation there in 1991, American archeologist Anna Roosevelt unearthed **decorated pottery** almost 10,000 years old – twice as old as the oldest ceramics found anywhere in the Americas. This suggests the Amazon basin was settled before the Andes, and that the Americas had been settled much earlier than previously thought. Later excavations in **Monte Alegre** confirmed the middle Amazon played an important role in the prehistory of the Americas with cave and rock paintings dotting the surrounding hills also being dated at around 10,000 years old. About two thousand years ago, Indian culture in the region entered a particularly dynamic phase, producing some superbly decorated ceramics comparable in their sophistication with Andean pottery; there are beautiful pieces in the small museum in Santarém, and even more in the Museu Goeldi in Belém (see p.380).

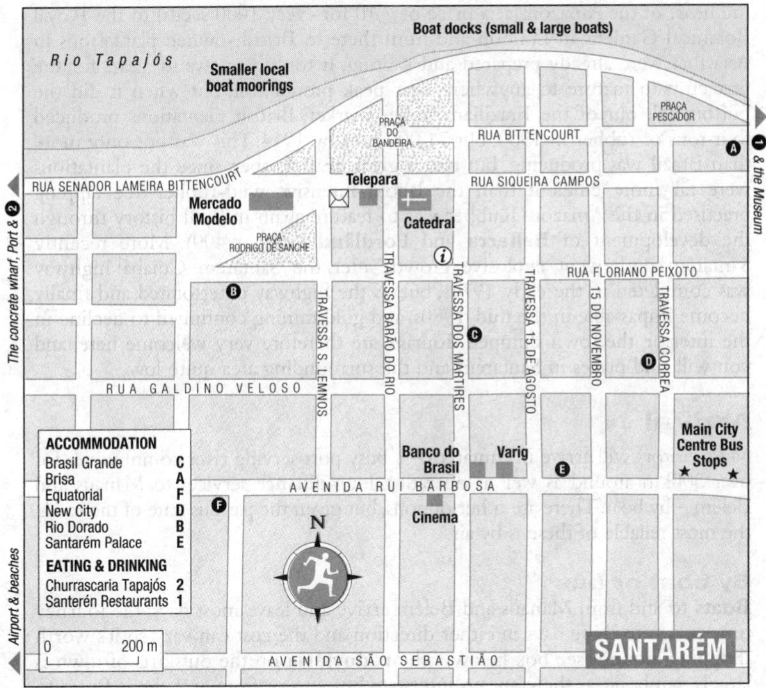


do any walking up and down these hills, especially around Belterra, keep your eyes open for ceramic shards. In recent years it has become clear Santarém and its surrounding area make up one of the most important archeological sites in the Americas.

The very first European accounts of the middle Amazon date from the early sixteenth century, and speak of swarms of canoes coming out to do battle and longhouses lining the riverbanks. The river asssumed its current, lightly populated look in the centuries after first contact, as disease and slavery wiped out the Indians or drove them upriver; as late as 1960 some two hundred Indians were massacred by settlers on a sandbank just south of Itaituba.

Santarém in its modern form began life as a Jesuit mission in the seventeenth century. The **rubber boom** proved the making of Santarém, and the town grew into an important trading centre. The region also became a refuge for two diametrically opposed groups: escaped slaves who founded communities along the Trombetas and Maicurú rivers on the Amazon's north bank, which were never conquered; and refugee Confederates, who made the big mistake of moving to Santarém under the misapprehension they could grow cotton there. By the time they realized they had been misinformed, most of them had died of malaria and yellow fever; the survivors moved into sugar and prospered, although in time their descendants intermarried with locals and adopted their language and now the only trace of them is the occasional surname like Riker, Higgins or Macdonald.

In 1874 an Englishman named **Henry Wickham** settled at Santarém with his wife and went on to be almost single-handedly responsible for the collapse of the Amazon rubber boom, smuggling quantities of valuable rubber seed from the heart of the Amazon (at a price of £10 for every 1000 seeds) to the Royal Botanical Gardens in London and from there to British-owned plantations in Asia that were already prepared and waiting. It took over twenty years for the first crop to mature to anywhere near peak production, but when it did the bottom fell out of the Brazilian rubber market. British plantations produced four tons of rubber in 1900, but 71,000 tons by 1914. This was not only more than Brazil was producing, but also a great deal cheaper, since the plantations were far more efficient than the labour-intensive wild-rubber-tree tapping practised in the Amazon. Rubber was to feature again in local history through the development of **Belterra** and **Fordlândia** (see p.400). More recently, Santarém underwent explosive growth after the Santarém–Cuiabá highway was completed in the early 1970s, but, as the highway deteriorated and finally become impassable in the mid-1980s, and gold mining continued to decline in the interior, the town slumped. Tourists are therefore very welcome here, and you will find prices in Santarém and the surrounding area quite low.



## Arrival

Most visitors will arrive in Santarém – a busy port serving river communities for over 300km around as well as operating long-distance services to Manaus and Belém – by boat. There are other options, but given the parlous state of the roads, the most reliable of these is by air.

### By boat or bus

**Boats** to and from Manaus and Belém arrive and leave most days; the journey time is two to three days in either direction and the cost can vary, so it's worth shopping around (see box below). The **rodoviária** on the outskirts of town is largely symbolic, as there are no interstate buses to or from anywhere. Buses to places within an hour or two of Santarém – notably Alter do Chão, Belterra and Fordlândia – leave from the Mercado Modelo or along Avenida Rui Barbosa, not from the *rodoviária*.

### By air

Santarém does have a useful small **airport** (Ⓣ93/3522-4328) some 14km from the centre, with a bus connection to Avenida Rui Barbosa (travelling from the town centre, take the "Aeroporto" bus, not to be confused with "Aeroporto Velho", which goes nowhere near the airport). There is also a Kombi connecting the *Hotel Amazon Park* and the airport most mornings. TAM is the only national airline that

### Boats from Santarém

Head for the docks nearer the large concrete wharves for riverboats to **Manaus** and **Belém**, where you can ask the various captains when they're leaving and how much they'll charge. Companies running boats to Manaus and Belém include Antônio Rocha, Rua 24 de Outubro 1047 Ⓣ93/3522-7947; Marquês Pinto Navegação, Rua do Imperador 746 Ⓣ93/3523-2828; and Tarcisio Lopes, Rua Galdino Veloso 290-B Ⓣ&Ⓕ93/3522-2034. Wandering along the waterfront is the best way to find boats heading to the towns between Belém and Manaus; although the larger boats stop at them as well, it's better to get one of the medium-sized boats that only ply that route, since everyone on it will be local and it will probably be less crowded. These boats usually have placards hanging from their side or set out on the concrete promenade, advertising their destinations and departure times. They are very cheap, and most serve beer and soft drinks en route, but your best bet is to take your own food.

flies there now, but nevertheless the airport is still a regional hub. Regional air companies run daily flights to Belém and Manaus considerably cheaper than TAM, and have routes to Macapá and São Luís that save you at least a day by not passing through Belém. It is even possible to get as far south as Cuiabá, with connections to southern Brazil, on three weekly flights run by Cruiser.

## City transport and information

**Local buses** in Santarém are sometimes useful, despite the small size of the city, to save you roasting yourself walking in the heat. Any bus heading left down the riverfront as you stand facing the river will take you to the Mercado Modelo, a hideous large concrete structure that houses a very useful market for stocking up on fruit and other essentials for a river journey.

For **tourist information**, most hotels have piles of a useful booklet, *Guia Turistico de Santarém*, on their reception desk. There is an excellent **tourist agency** in Santarém, run by an expatriate American, Steve Alexander, called Amazon Tours (Travessa Turiano Meira 1084; Ⓦ www.amazonriver.com, Ⓔ amazonriver@netsan.com.br). They have a private nature park, the Bosque Santa Luzia, where they run excellent tours; they are also the best option if you want to really do the archeological sites around Santarém and Monte Alegre, for which having a guide along really helps, or visit a nearby national park, the **Floresta do Tapajós**.

## Accommodation

Santarém is well supplied with **hotels** to suit every budget. Along with Manaus, this is one of the best places to take a break from a long-distance boat trip, and you could well find yourself staying a few days. Accommodation in Alter do Chão is listed separately.

**Amazon Park** Av. Mendonca Furtado 4120 Ⓣ 93/3522-3361, Ⓔ amazon@netsan.com.br. A living piece of modern Amazonian history, the military built this massive 1970s complex to enable the city to cope with the economic boom they confidently expected the highway to bring. But the boom never came and the hotel has been quietly declining ever since. Still impressive, however, are the glorious views out across the river, and, with rates starting at R$80, this place is a bargain. ❹

**Barão Center** Av. Barão do Rio Branco 352 Ⓣ 93/3523-1050. Spanking-new business hotel aimed at the soy growers and those who supply them. Has the only reliable hotel internet connection in the city as well as a reasonable restaurant with great views across the river. ❺

**Brasil Grande** Travessa 15 de Agosto 213 Ⓣ 93/3522-5660. Fine mid-range hotel right in the centre of the commercial district, with all the usual amenities including TV, a/c and *frigobar*. ❸

**Brisa** Av. Senador Bittencourt 5 Ⓣ 93/3522-1018, Ⓔ brisahotel@tap.com.br. Excellent budget option, well run by a friendly family; clean rooms have either fans or a/c. ❷

**Equatorial** corner of Av. Rui Barbosa and Silvino Pinto Ⓣ 93/3522-1135. Centrally located, no-frills hotel where you're likely to meet all sorts of travellers. Rooms are clean and airy and some have a/c. ❷

**New City** Travessa Francisco Corréa 200 Ⓣ 93/3522-3764 or 3522-4719. A clean, modern and very friendly spot. The hotel organizes river tours and airport pick-ups or boat drops. ❷

**Rio Dorado** Praça Rodrigues dos Santos 887 Ⓣ 93/3522-3814. Opposite the Mercado Modelo, this recently refurbished hotel is one of the best mid-range places around. Rooms are clean if nondescript but staff are welcoming. The location is noisy during the day, however. ❷

**Santarém Palace** Av. Rui Barbosa 726 Ⓣ 93/3523-2820, Ⓕ 3522-1779. A good mid-range hotel with tidy modern rooms in the centre of town. Also runs reasonably priced river tours. ❸

## The city and its beaches

By far the most interesting place in Santarém, at any hour of the day or night, is the **waterfront**. There are always dozens of boats tied up here, with the

## Piranhas and stingrays

One thing definitely worth bearing in mind if you are swimming anywhere in the Amazon is that **piranhas** and **stingrays** (*raia*) are common. Piranhas are actually much less of a problem than you would expect. Forget any films you have seen; they don't attack in shoals, prefer still water to currents and no death or serious injury from piranha attack is on record. Nevertheless, they can give you a nasty bite and are indeed attracted to blood. They frequent particular spots, which locals all know about and avoid, so ask for advice.

Stingrays are more of a problem. They love warm, shallow water and are so well camouflaged that they are practically invisible. If you tread on one, it will whip its sting into your ankle causing a deep gash and agonizing pain for at least 24 hours. However, stingrays really hate noise, crowds, waves and strong currents, and so are rarely found on regularly used beaches, such as Alter do Chão, near Santarém. But off the beaten track, they are an ever-present threat. You can minimize the danger by wearing canvas boots or trainers and by splashing and throwing sand and stones into shallow water if you intend to swim there.



accompanying bustle of people and cargoes being loaded and unloaded, and constant activity in the shops and outfitters by the water. You will probably have to wander along the waterfront anyway to find boats to points elsewhere, but a sunset stroll is reason enough to venture down this way. Many of the city's restaurants, bars and clubs are here, but it is especially lively during the rainy season, when the beaches are under water.

The area also boasts a surprisingly good museum, the **Centro Cultural João Foua**, a fine turn-of-the-century building constructed during the rubber boom and standing in splendid isolation on Praça Santarém, just past the *Mascotinho* restaurant (see opposite). The highlight of the collection is some stunning Indian pottery, small but elaborately decorated and around 2000 years old. The building itself is also very pleasant and the shady internal courtyard is a good spot to hide from the sun on a hot day.

### Beaches

Unlike the eastern and western reaches of the Amazon, the region around Santarém has a very distinct **dry season**, stretching from June to December. During this time, Santarém and its surroundings get extremely hot, even by Brazilian standards, with a particularly enervating dry heat. Fortunately this is also the time of year, especially between July and February, when the Tapajós drops and the region's magnificent **river beaches** are exposed.

In the city itself, the beach that forms at the waterfront in the dry season is definitely not recommended, despite the number of locals you'll see swimming there: you can count the raw sewage outlets draining directly into the water as you walk along the promenade. A much better option is to take the local bus to **Maracanã** beach on the far side of town, which is clean. There are lots of small bars and restaurants here serving delicious, freshly caught fish. The very best beach near Santarém, however, is 15km away at Alter do Chão (see p.398).

## Eating, drinking and nightlife

You'll find many of Santarém's **restaurants** along the waterfront, but the city's side streets are also a good hunting ground, as is the beach at Maracanã. As you'd expect, fish is the main cuisine. For delicious home-made **ice cream** using regional fruits, go to *Nido* on Mendonça Furtado between Assis Vasconcelos and

2 de Junho; try the *castanha*, the best brazil-nut ice cream you'll ever have. The ice cream at the *Panificadora Lucy*, on the Praça do Pescador, is also very good.

### Restaurants

**Amazonia Bar** on the waterfront. Good bar with one of the nicest atmospheres in town; it also serves great, though not cheap, food.

**Bar Mascote** Praça do Pescador 10. One of the city's popular waterfront places, with regular live music at weekends. Serves a wide range of moderately priced fish and meat dishes, and a lunchtime *comida por kilo* buffet.

**Bom Paladar** Av. Cuiabá. Regional fish any way you want it – the *caldeirada* (fish stew) is particularly recommended. Live music on Fri and Sat nights.

**Churrascaria Tapajós** Av. Tapajós. Along the waterfront, by the petrol station and just past the Mercado Modelo, this is the best option for carnivores tired of eating fish. Has a good range of salads as well.

**Mascotinho Restaurant-Bar** on the waterfront by the Praça Manoel de Jesus Moraes. The place to come for pizza and to enjoy a wonderful location – the restaurant is built out onto the river, right in the heart of town.

**Peixaria Piracatú** Av. Mendonça Furtado 174. The best fish restaurant in town. Unpretentious, with a distinctly unscenic location, this is the place to come for regional food during lunch and dinner.

**Sacy Caseiro** Rua Floriano Peixoto 521. Probably the best and busiest lunch-time *comida por kilo*.

**Uirapirú** on the waterfront opposite *Mascotinho*. The food is mediocre but the good atmosphere and great views out across the river make this a relaxing spot for a beer.

**Yacht Clube** The restaurant here serves excellent fish and is walkable from the *Amazon Park Hotel*; otherwise take a taxi and arrange for it to pick you up afterwards, as no buses pass this way. Despite its name, it's not at all exclusive, nor are you likely to come across any sailing types. The good-value food costs around R$40 for a meal for two, plus there are lovely views across the Tapajós.

### Nightlife

There's no shortage of options when it comes to **nightlife**. On Friday and Saturday nights, the *Mascote*, *Mascotinho* and other waterfront dives have live music; people start here and then head out to the serious music places. The *Yacht Clube* usually has something going on starting around midnight, and *Sygnus*, a nightclub at Av. Borges Leal 1227 (℗93/3522-4119), gets going around the same time – most local buses from the centre pass by. One of the coolest spots these days is *La Boum*, at Av. Cuiabá 694, Liberdade (℗93/3522-3632), with live Brazilian dance music until the early hours every Friday and Saturday night, or, if you want to make an all-nighter of it, *Denis Bar* on Mendonça Furtado is the place to go and, unlike the other clubs, it has no cover charge. Not far away on Mendonça is the *Babilônia*, a cavernous hangar with a stage, live music and wild crowds every weekend night. The *Bom Paladar* restaurant on Avenida Cuiabá becomes a nightclub on Friday and Saturday nights and there's good dancing here, but it's the sort of place where you might expect to see Popeye and Bluto trading blows in the corner – get under the table if you hear any shots.

## Listings

**Airlines** Tavaj, corner of Rua Floriano Peixoto with Travessa S. Lemos ℗93/3523-1600; TAM, Av. Mendonça Furtado 913 ℗93/3523-9450/9451/9453.

**Banks and exchange** None of the banks in Santarém changes foreign currency – but there are HSBC and Banco do Brasil cash machines which take foreign plastic on Mendonça Furtado in the centre.

**Car rental** Bill Car, Av. Constantino Nery 111 ℗93/3522-1705; Rede Brasil, Av. Mendonça Furtado 2449 ℗93/3522-2990.

**Health matters** Contact Fundação Esperança, Rua Coaracy Nunes 3344, an American-managed clinic and health centre. Santaremzinho, Starenzinho, Aeroporto Velho and Amparo/Conquista buses take you right to the door. Consultations cost R$5.

**Shopping** For crafts, try the Loja Regional Muiraquita, Rua Bittencourt 131, or the Casa do Artesanato, Rua Bittencourt 69.

# Around Santarém

The area around Santarém is richly rewarding, with a variety of day-trips possible out to **Alter do Chão**, **Belterra** or **Fordlândia** as well as boat journeys further afield. Due north, on the opposite bank of the Amazon, some six hours away by boat, is the town of **Alenquer**, the jumping-off point for the stunning waterfall of Véu da Noiva, on the Rio Maicurú. Similar journey times west along the Amazon will land you in **Óbidos**, east takes you to the beautiful town of **Monte Alegre**, and a slightly longer trip south up the Rio Tapajós, through gorgeous river scenery, will bring you to **Itaituba**, a classic gold-rush town 250km from Santarém. To head into less disturbed forest and consequently have better access to wildlife, your best bet is one of the tour operators in Alter do Chão. An excellent option is a visit to the **Floresta Nacional do Tapajós**, a national park some forty miles out of town down the Santarém–Cuiabá highway.

## Alter do Chão

The municipality of Santarém, which is slightly bigger than Belgium, has just 32km of asphalted road. A good two-thirds of this is accounted for by the road that leads from Santarém to its beach resort of **ALTER DO CHÃO**, and you can't fault their transport priorities. Alter do Chão is a beautiful bay in the Rio Tapajós overlooked by two easily climbable hills, one the shape of a church altar, giving the place its name. From July to November the bay is fringed by **white sand beaches**, which combine with the deep blue of the Tapajós to give it a Mediterranean look. In the dry season a sandbank in the middle of the bay is accessible either by wading or by canoe, and simple stalls provide the fried fish and chilled beer essential to the full enjoyment of the scene. During the week you'll almost have the place to yourself, unless you're unlucky enough to coincide with one of the periodic invasions by hundreds of elderly tourists from a cruise ship docked at Santarém. Weekends see the tranquillity shattered, as *santarenhos* head out en masse for the beach – be careful if you're heading back to Santarém on a weekend afternoon as many drivers on the road will be drunk. If the beach is too crowded, get a canoe to drop you on the other

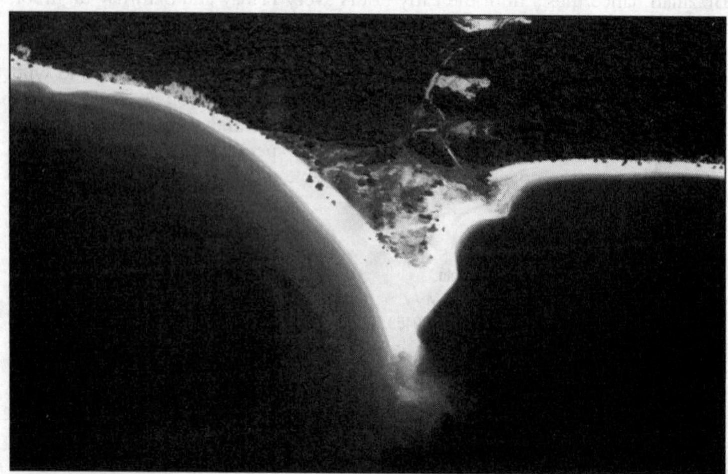

▲ Beach near Alter do Chão

side of the bay at the entrance to the path leading up to the higher conical hill. It's a half-hour walk through the forest and finally up above it to the top to a breathtaking view of the meeting of the Tapajós, Amazon and Arapiuns rivers.

In recent years Alter do Chão has become something of a cult destination on the alternative travel circuit. A couple of **tour operators** geared to this market have opened up: Vento em Popa (Ⓣ93/3527-1379, Ⓔventoempopa@netsan.com.br) on the main square, Praça 7 de Setembro, and Mãe Natureza Ecoturismo (Ⓣ93/3527-1264, Ⓔmaenatureza@hotmail.com or maenatureza@uol.com.br). They both do reasonably priced forest treks, fishing expeditions and boat trips, with a day costing around R$50 per person. They will also handle renting a house in Alter do Chão, the most economic form of accommodation if you fancy staying a week or two – which many people do, once they see the place.

Halfway along the Alter do Chão road is a signposted turn-off to **Ponto das Pedras**, some 15km along a good-quality dirt road that is easily passable in the dry season and less so in the rains (though still manageable with an ordinary car). This is another of the stunning river beaches in which the Tapajós specializes, with a row of bars and simple restaurants. Depending on what time of year you get there, the rocks that give the beach its name can be either walked or swum out to. There is one basic *pousada* here but no bus services; it's only a practical option by car.

### Arrival, accommodation and eating

At weekends there are **buses** every hour to Alter do Chão from in front of the Mercado Modelo in Santarém, with the last one returning at 7.30pm; during the week there are only three buses a day, with two daily returning to town. If you don't feel like getting the last bus back, you might as well make a night of it and stay at one of the three **pousadas** in town, all of them cheap and clean: *Pousada Alter do Chão*, on the waterfront at Rua Lauro Sodré 74 (Ⓣ93/3527-1215; ❶), which has a good restaurant open to non-residents as well; *Pousada Tia Marilda* (❶–❷) on the street leading up from the square; and *Pousada Tupaiulandia*, at Rua Pedro Teixeira 300 (Ⓣ93/3527-1157; ❷), a block further up, which is the best of the bunch. All have ranges of accommodation, starting at around R$30. Away from the beach, the town square is surrounded by **restaurants**, which are all cheap if you stick to the fish. There is also one exceptionally good hotel, with a stunning lakeside setting and rates starting at R$110: the *Hotel Belo Alter* (Ⓣ93/3527-1230, Ⓦwww.beloalter.com.br). They will pick you up from the airport if you reserve in advance.

## The Floresta do Tapajós

An essential day-trip if you can manage it is to one of the Amazon's few national parks within easy reach of a town or city, the **Floresta Nacional do Tapajós**. Some 30,000 hectares of preserved upland forest riddled by trails, it includes around 50km of Tapajós river frontage, where there are a number of small communities living within the reserve's boundaries. The forest is magnificent, climax primary rainforest towering over the secondary scrubland which the area around has been reduced to by waves of colonization over the last fifty years, with the soy growers being merely the latest of a succession of new arrivals.

There are two ways of visiting the Floresta. The first, by far the easiest, is as part of a package organized by a tour operator in Santarém or Alter do Chão. You can choose one of two points of entry: the river or one of the communities, in which case you'll be hiking up from floodplain into the uplands, or direct into the upland forest via the Santarém–Cuiabá highway. Here you will drive a few kilometres along a forest road until a clearing where there are a couple of houses belonging to park rangers, from where you hike into the forest proper. The second option is to go there independently, which can be done but only if you rent a car. You will first need to get an entry permit from the park agency IBAMA on Avenida Tapajós, on the waterfront a couple of blocks past the Mercado Modelo. The IBAMA office is actually a complex of buildings; look for the office of the Floresta Nacional on the first floor of the building on the far left as you face the entrance – the guards will point you in the right direction. You must bring your passport and pay a R$6 fee; it will take them just a few minutes to type up the permit, and there is never a queue. They will also give you useful pamphlets and maps. Then just drive some 60km down the highway and the entrance is on the right, with unmissably large placards. If you do not have the permit, the guard at the entrance will not let you in. If there is no guard, unhook the chain and drive in anyway, and eventually, if you don't get pulled over on the way, you'll run into the park rangers in the clearing the road terminates in.



## Fordlândia and Belterra

Set up by Henry Ford in the 1920s as part of a doomed attempt to guarantee rubber supplies by building massive rubber plantations, Belterra and its sister settlement Fordlândia, 120 kilometres south, are now quiet and rather beautiful towns that look bizarrely like American country villages on the wrong continent, and are well worth a visit. They mimic small-town America exactly, with whitewashed wooden houses, immaculate gardens, fire hydrants, churches and spacious tree-lined streets. The only jarring note is the potholed roads. Belterra is built on a bluff overlooking the Tapajós, with spectacular views down to the river. Fordlândia, with its water towers and the ruined hulk of the rubber-processing factory, is actually on the river and more easily accessible by boat. All boats to Itaituba stop at Fordlândia, the journey taking six to twelve hours depending on the time of year. There's no accommodation but you can probably string your hammock up in the school; and bring your own food as there isn't a restaurant. Walking around the factory, with trees growing through the roof and machinery still lying around, including 1920s bulldozers and trucks, is extraordinarily atmospheric.

A daily bus runs to Belterra from the Mercado Modelo, but the road is difficult during the rains. There is one bus a day back, but it's in the morning – again there's no accommodation – so it's not a practical proposition unless you have a car or you can get on an excursion organized by a travel agent in Santarém. Belterra is easily accessible by road from Alter do Chão in the dry season, significantly closer than Santarém, and the best way of seeing it is as a day-trip run by one of the tour operators there.

## Alenquer

Some five or six hours away from Santarém by boat, through a maze of islands and lakes on the north bank of the Amazon, is **ALENQUER**, a typical small Amazon river town rarely visited by tourists. The town is interesting enough, but wouldn't on its own detain you for more than a couple of hours. The streets are pleasant, the waterfront occasionally bustles and has a good view of the river, and there are a couple of atmospheric public buildings from the days of the rubber boom. However, the surrounding countryside is strikingly beautiful with lakes, an abundance of wildlife and the rustic tourist complex of **Vale do Paraíso**, centred around the gorgeous **waterfall** of **Véu da Noiva**, all accessible by either road or boat.



**Renting a boat** for the day costs about the same as hiring a taxi for a day – around R$80 – and, although the birdlife in the lakes surrounding Alenquer is not as rich as around Monte Alegre (see p.401), the creeks and islands you can explore are, if anything, more scenic. The lakes are actually quite heavily populated, by Amazonian standards, and your boatman is almost certain to take the chance to stop off and visit a relative somewhere on the way, giving you the opportunity to glimpse some rural life. *Botos* (river dolphins) are common but unfortunately so are piranhas, so be careful about swimming. As for supplies, you will need to take food and water for you and the boatman. You can rent a boat directly on the waterfront, if your Portuguese is up to it, or through either of the two hotels below; the trips are both well worth it.

### Arrival and accommodation

There are **boats** every day between Santarém and Alenquer, but you'll need to check on boats coming back before leaving Santarém if you are on a tight schedule – the crew of the departing boat will be able to tell you when the next one back will be. You will have a choice between the regular boats and the high-speed launch, *Vendaval*. The regular boats, which are much cheaper, take around ten hours with stops; these leave at 6pm on Monday, Wednesday and Friday and 8pm on Tuesday, Thursday and Sunday from the Santarém waterfront. *Vendaval* takes only three hours and leaves from next to the *Mascotinho* restaurant at 3pm on Monday, Friday and Sunday, and noon on Saturday. There are also boat connections from Alenquer to Belém, Manaus and Monte Alegre. In the dry season there are **buses** to Óbidos, Oriximiná and Monte Alegre, but the schedule is irregular and depends on the condition of the road, which is usually bad but passable.

There are two decent **hotels** in town, the *Hotel Cirio* (Ⓣ93/3526-1218; ❶), on the waterfront street to the right as you arrive at the quayside, and the *Pepita Hotel* (Ⓣ93/3526-0002). As tourists in Alenquer are still relatively rare, things are cheap and trips to the lake or waterfall will set you back about R$75 if you arrange them through the hotel.

### Vale do Paraíso

The best reason for visiting Alenquer is the stunning **Vale do Paraíso**, where a *pousada* and restaurant built around the gorgeous **Véu da Noiva waterfall** is on the Rio Maicurú, a couple of hours' drive from Alenquer. The best way to get there is to rent a taxi via one of the two hotels – around R$50, or call ahead to the *Pousada Vale do Paraíso* (Ⓣ93/9901-5385 or 93/3520-1284, Ⓦwww.valedoparaiso.tur.br, Ⓔvaledoparaiso@bol.com.br, only basic English; ❷–❸), who can meet boats. The taxi will drop you off at the *pousada* entrance and you have to walk the rest of the way – a beautiful stroll of a kilometre down a forested valley with occasional glimpses of river, before the path drops down right in front of the magnificent waterfall, which cascades into a glade in the forest with deep pools of deliciously cool water to swim in. Below the falls you can wade with care through shallow rapids, but watch your step on the sharp-edged rocks. It's an idyllic spot and well worth the effort involved in getting here. The staff at the *pousada* are friendly, the food at the riverside is cheap and good, and if you're looking for somewhere properly Amazonian to hang out for a few days and do nothing very much, it's perfect; there are networks of trails through the forest, and on weekdays you're likely to have the place to yourself.

## Monte Alegre

If you only have time to visit one river town in the middle Amazon, it should be **MONTE ALEGRE**. Most of the town is built along the brow of a steep hill with spectacular views out across marshes and freshwater lakes, with the

Amazon to the south and jagged hills to the north and west, the only pieces of high ground between Belém and Manaus. With its obvious strategic advantages, this was one of the first places on the Amazon to be colonized by Europeans; a small group of English and Irish adventurers settled here in the 1570s, almost fifty years before Belém was founded. The Portuguese soon expelled them, and Monte Alegre was a ranching and farming settlement, then a centre of the rubber trade before becoming the prosperous river town it is today.

However, there is a much longer history of human settlement in the region. At various points the hills behind the town are covered in spectacular **Indian rock paintings** – one of the main reasons for visiting – that range from abstract geometric patterns through stylized representations of animals and human stick figures to the most compelling images of all: palm prints of the ancient painters themselves.



### Arrival, accommodation and eating

Transport connections are good. Monte Alegre is one of the main stops on the Belém–Santarém–Manaus **boat** route, and there are also dedicated services from both Santarém and Belém that are usually less crowded. Boats from Prainha and Macapá also stop here. Leaving, you won't wait more than two days wherever you're headed.

Monte Alegre has begun to expand facilities for the still relatively small number of tourists who pass through here. The more basic **places to stay** are on the riverfront: the *Beira Rio Hospedaria* (❷) is pleasant and clean, very friendly and serves excellent food. The better options, however, are in Cidade Alta, up the hill; best of all is the *Hotel Panorama II* (❷) on the Praça Fernando Guilhon, which has a sister hotel on Rua Arnóbio Franco; another good option is the *Hotel Acapulco* (❷) – all are good value. The main square has a fabulous view out across the Amazon and the lakes, and there's a bar here, *Bar do Mirante*, conveniently situated for you to watch the sunset. **Eating options** are simple but good; *Restaurante Panorama* on Travessa Oriental has the best view, though also recommended are *Mistura Fina* on Rua João Coelho 123, and *Pontão das Aguas* on Avenida Presidente Vargas. All the hotels above have basic restaurants as well.

### Seeing the paintings

The rock paintings have been dated at just over 10,000 years old, making Monte Alegre one of the most important archeological sites in South America. Some of the paintings are on rockfaces large enough to be seen from the road, but others are hidden away, requiring a steep climb to see them, so wear good shoes. Also, whatever time of year you go, it is likely to get very hot during the day: take plenty of water, a hat and sunscreen.

You will only be able to visit the paintings by **four-wheel-drive transport** and you will need a **guide**; expect to pay around R$100 a day for the two if you arrange this in Monte Alegre. Amazon Tours in Santarém (see p.395) also does packages to Monte Alegre that take in the paintings. Depending on how many people you can get together, this trip can be very reasonable as it is an all-day expedition. Nelsi Sadeck, Rua do Jaquara 320 (Ⓣ93/3533-1430 or 3533-1215), can also arrange trips. Everyone knows him and will point you in the direction of his house. Although he only speaks Portuguese, he is used to taking parties of tourists around the hills, and if he knows people want to go he can usually rustle up a few locals interested in coming along, which will bring the price of the truck rental down. Nelsi can also arrange **boat rental** for around R$75 a day.

### Around Monte Alegre

The water world around Monte Alegre is one of the richest **bird** sites in Amazônia. All along the banks of the Amazon, huge freshwater lakes are separated from the river by narrow strips of land. Depending on the time of year, the lakes either flood over the surrounding land, become marshland or even, in places, sandy cattle pasture. The whole area is thick with birdlife: huge herons, waders of all kinds and a sprinkling of hawks and fish eagles. At sunset, thousands of birds fly in to roost in the trees at the foot of the town. The stunning waterscapes set against the dramatic backdrop of hills make a boat trip really worth doing, even if you can't tell an egret from your elbow. Take everything with you for the day, including lunch for you and the boat owner.

Finally, for a spot of relaxation, head for the **hot springs** at Aguas Sulforosas, 10km inland and reached by taxi or minibus; you can relax free of charge in the springs, and there's a bar, picnic area and pool close by.

## Óbidos

Around forty million years ago, when the Andes began to form themselves by pushing up from the earth, a vast inland sea burst through from what is now known as the main Amazon basin. The natural bursting point was more or less the site of modern-day **ÓBIDOS**. The huge sea squeezed itself through where the Guyanan shield to the north meets the Brazilian shield from the south, and cut an enormous channel through alluvial soils in its virgin route to the Atlantic. The river is some seven kilometres wide at Santarém, while at Óbidos, about 100km upstream, it has narrowed to less than two kilometres. Physically then, Óbidos is the gateway to the Amazon; there's an old fort to protect the passage, and most boats going upstream or down will stop here for an hour or two at least.

### Arrival and accommodation

**Boats** travel in and out of Óbidos every day. If you're heading to Santarém, take the smaller boats that only ply that route rather than hopping onto one of the larger Manaus–Belém boats, which tend to be slower and more expensive. If you end up **staying** try the *Braz Bello*, Rua Marios Rodrigues de Souza 86 (Ⓣ93/3547-1411), which is a reasonable mid-range hotel, while along the waterfront you'll find several decent bars and restaurants. Alternatively there's the slightly cheaper *Pousada Brasil* on Rua Correia Pinto, which offers a range of rooms.

### The town and around

Óbidos is now a pretty river-town with a very attractive **waterfront** that's little changed since the 1920s. It makes a good stopover if you feel like breaking the journey between Manaus and Santarém or Belém. The sights won't keep you more than a morning, but it is a pleasant town to stroll around. The main thing to see is the seventeenth-century **Forte Pauxis** on the Praça Coracy Nunes, which played a crucial strategic role in Amazon history. Since that era this has been the jumping-off point for the settlement of the upper Amazon, and the cannons still in position on the ramparts command the whole width of the river. Its strategic importance meant that Óbidos was the largest town on the middle Amazon during colonial times, but the fort is the only colonial relic. Elsewhere the town has some fine buildings dating from the rubber boom and identified by metal plaques giving their history (in Portuguese only). Most of them are in the commercial area just off the waterfront, constructed by trading families as emporiums on the ground floor with living quarters above. Most are still shops, selling simple hammocks and pots and pans.

The town's other attractions are river-based, as you might expect. Just 25km from Óbidos along the PA-254, you can go bathing in the beautiful **Igarapé de Curuçambá**, which is served by local buses. There are also organized trips to the narrowest of Amazon river straits with impressive forested river-cliffs and close-up views of riverbank homesteads and jungle vegetation. Ask about trips at the port or the *Braz Bello* hotel.



# Western Amazônia

An arbitrary border, a line on paper through the forest, divides the state of Pará from the western Amazon. Encompassing the states of **Amazonas**, **Rondônia**, **Acre** and **Roraima**, the western Amazon is dominated by the big river and its tributaries even more than the east. This is a remote and poorly serviced region representing the heart of the world's largest rainforest. The northern half of the forest is drained by two large rivers, the gigantic Rio Negro and its major affluent, the Rio Branco. Travelling north from Manaus the dense rainforest phases into the wooded savannas before the mysterious mountains of Roraima rise precipitously at the border with Venezuela and Guyana. To the south, the rarely visited Madeira, Purús and Juruá rivers, all huge and important in their own way, meander through the forests from the prime rubber region of Acre and the rampantly colonized state of Rondônia.

The hub of this area is undoubtedly **Manaus**, more or less at the junction of three great rivers – the Solimões/Amazonas, the Negro and the Madeira – which, between them, support the world's greatest surviving forest. There are few other settlements of any real size. In the north, **Boa Vista**, capital of Roraima, lies on an overland route to Venezuela. South of the Rio Amazonas there's **Porto Velho**, capital of Rondônia, and, further west, **Rio Branco**, the main town in the relatively unexplored rubber-growing state of Acre – where the now famous Chico Mendes lived and died, fighting for a sustainable future for the forest.

**Travel** is never easy or particularly comfortable in the western Amazon. **From Manaus** it's possible to go by **bus** to Venezuela or Boa Vista, which is just twelve hours or so on the tarmacked BR-174 through the stunning tropical forest zone of the Waimiris tribe, with over fifty rickety wooden bridges en route. You can also head east to the Amazon river settlement of Itacoatiara; but the BR-317 road from the south bank close to Manaus down to Porto Velho requires four-wheel-drive vehicles, having been repossessed by the rains and vegetation for most of its length. **From Porto Velho** the Transamazônica continues into Acre and **Rio Branco**, from where a new route has been paved all the way to Puerto Maldonado in the Peruvian Amazon, with road links on to Cusco and the Pacific coast beyond. Access is easy from here into Bolivia, too; and, from Porto Velho, the paved BR-364 offers fast roads south to Cuiabá, Mato Grosso, Brasília and the rest of Brazil.

The rivers are the traditional and still very much dominant means of travel. Entering from the east, the first places beyond Óbidos are the small ports of **Parintins** and **Itacoatiara**. The former is home to the internationally known Bio Bumbá festival every June and the latter has bus connections with Manaus if

### The western Amazon climate

The western Amazon normally receives a lot of **rain** – up to 375cm a year in the extreme west and about 175cm around Manaus. Recent **droughts**, such as in December 2005, however, left fish dying and stranded in pools as the rivers receded. Entire communities were cut off as boat-dependent island settlements were left surrounded by drying mud and rotting fish. In ordinary circumstances, the area's heaviest rains fall in January and February, with a relatively dry season from June to October. The humidity rarely falls much below eighty percent, and the temperature in the month of December can reach well above 40°C. This takes a few days to get used to; until you do it's like being stuck in a sauna with only air conditioning, shady trees, a breeze or cool drinks to help you escape.

you're really fed up with the boat, though the roads are often very hard-going in the rainy season (Dec–April). From Itacoatiara it's a matter of hours till Manaus appears near the confluence of the Negro and Solimões rivers. It takes another five to eight days by boat to reach the Peruvian frontier, and even here the river is several kilometres wide and still big enough for ocean-going ships.

# Manaus and around

**MANAUS** is the capital of Amazonas, a tropical forest state covering around one and a half million square kilometres. The city is also the commercial and physical hub of the entire Amazon region. Most visitors are surprised to learn Manaus isn't actually on the Amazon at all, but on the Rio Negro, six kilometres from the point where that river meets the Solimões to form (as far as Brazilians are concerned) the Rio Amazonas. Just a few hundred metres away from the tranquil life on the rivers, the centre of Manaus perpetually buzzes with energy: always noisy, crowded and very much alive. Escaping from the frenzy is not easy, but there is the occasional quiet corner, and the Opera House square and some of the city's museums make up for the hectic pace downtown. In the port and market areas, pigs, chickens and people selling hammocks line the streets and despite renovations in 2009, there's an atmosphere that seems unchanged in centuries.

For the Amazon hinterland, Manaus has long symbolized "civilization". Traditionally, this meant simply that it was the **trading centre**, where the hardships of life in the forest could be escaped temporarily and where manufactured commodities to make that life easier – metal pots, steel knives, machetes and the like – could be purchased. Virgin jungle seems further from the city these days (just how far really depends on what you want "virgin forest" to mean), but there are still waterways and channels within a short river journey of Manaus where you can find dolphins, alligators, kingfishers and the impression, at least, that humans have barely penetrated. Indeed, most visitors to Manaus rightly regard a **river trip** as an essential part of their stay; various **jungle tour and lodge** options are set out on pp.422–433 (see also box, p.368 for longer river journeys, and boat details under "Listings" on p.385). Even if you can't afford the time to disappear up the Amazon for days at a stretch, however, there are a number of sites around Manaus that make worthwhile day-excursions, most notably the **meeting of the waters** of the yellow Rio Solimões and the black Rio Negro, and the lily-strewn **Parque Ecólogico do Janauary**. Additionally, a six-hour bus ride will take you to Novo Aírão, where it's possible to bathe in clean rivers and watch or swim with **pink dolphins** at the port.

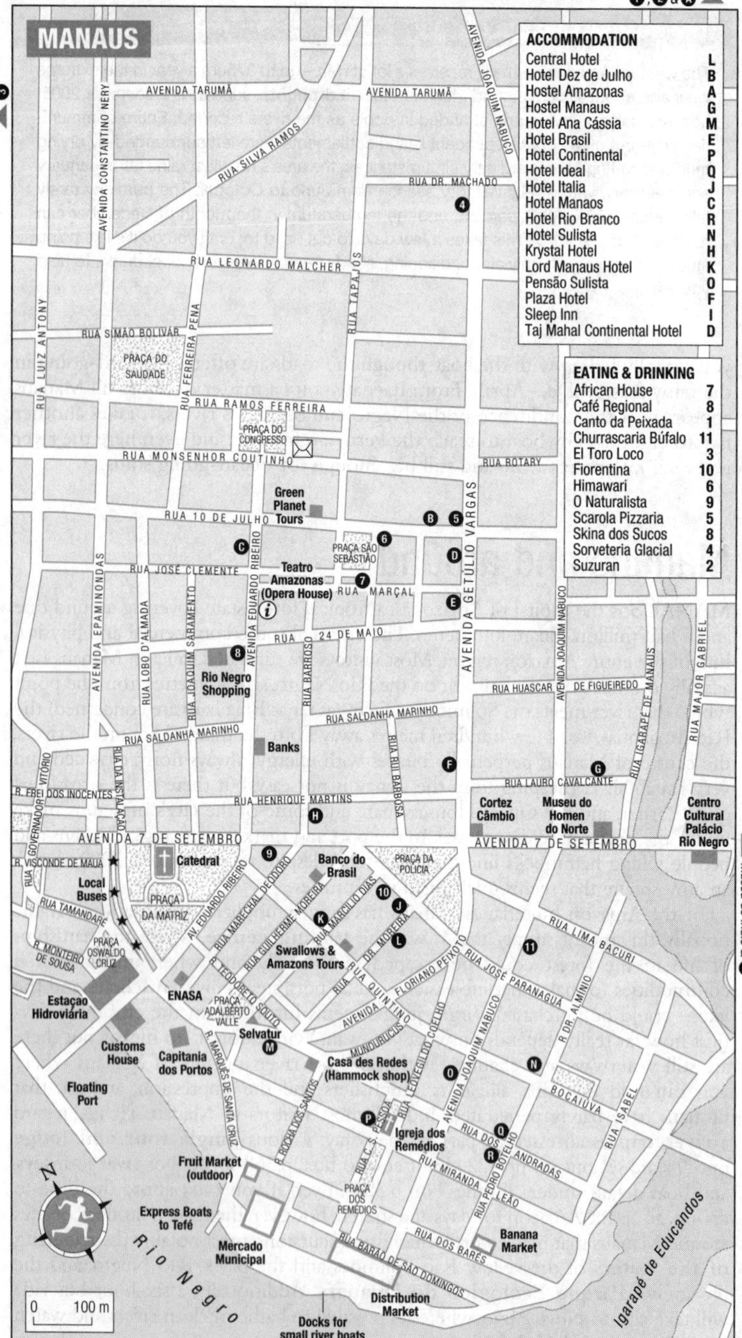


1, 2 & A
3
Museu do Indio & I

## Some history

Established as a town in 1856, the name Manaus was given for the Manaós tribe, which was encountered in this region by São Luís do Maranhão while he was exploring the area in 1616. Missionaries arrived in 1657 and a small trading settlement, originally known as São José da Barra, evolved around their presence. The city you see today is primarily a product of the **rubber boom** and in particular the child of visionary state governor **Eduardo Ribeiro**, who from 1892 transformed Manaus into a major city. Under Ribeiro the Opera House was completed, and whole streets were wiped out in the process of laying down broad Parisian-style avenues, interspersed with Italian piazzas centred on splendid fountains. In 1899 Manaus was the first Brazilian city to have trolley buses and the second to have electric lights in the streets.

At the start of the twentieth century Manaus was an opulent metropolis run by elegant people, who, despite the tropical heat, dressed and housed themselves as fashionably as their counterparts in any large European city. The rich constructed palaces and grandiose mansions and time was passed at elaborate parties, dances and concerts. But this heyday lasted barely thirty years; Ribeiro committed suicide in 1900 and by 1914 the rubber market was collapsing fast. There was a second brief boost for Brazilian rubber during World War II, but today's prosperity is largely due to the creation of a **Free Trade Zone**, the Zona Franca, in 1966. Over the following ten years the population doubled, from 250,000 to half a million, and many new industries moved in, especially electronics companies. An impressive international airport was opened in 1976 and the floating port, supported on huge metal cylinders to cope with variations of as much as 14m in the level of the river, was modernized to accommodate the new business.

Today, with over one and a half million inhabitants, Manaus is an aggressive commercial and industrial centre for an enormous region – the Hong Kong of the Amazon. It boasts one of the world's largest motorcycle assembly plants and over half of Brazil's televisions are made here. The airport is often crowded with Brazilians going home with their arms laden with TVs, hi-fis, computers and fax machines. Landless and jobless Brazilians also flock here looking for work, particularly as there are more prospects in Manaus than in many parts of the Northeast. This is Brazil's ninth biggest city and home to over ten percent of North Brazil's population.

# Arrival

Try to avoid arriving on a Sunday, when the city is very quiet and few places are open. Most visitors arrive in Manaus by air; the **airport** (Aeroporto de Eduardo Gomes; ⓣ92/3652-1212) is on Avenida Santos Dumont in the Tarumã district, 17km from town in the same direction. It is also served by bus #306 (first bus 5.30am, last bus around midnight; 40min); alternatively, take a taxi for around R$40. Many tour operators offer airport pick-up if you're booked with them; and Geraldo Mesquita of Amazon Gero Tours (ⓣ92/3232-4755 or 9983-6273, ⓦwww.amazongerotours.com) also offers a reliable airport pick-up by car or minibus.

If you arrive by river, your **boat** will dock right in the heart of the city, either at the riverside *hidroviária* near the Mercado Municipal or more likely a short distance away in the Porto Flutuante (floating port) complex, known these days as the **Estação Hidroviária** where you also need to go to buy boat tickets to most destinations. You can get a good view over the port from an indoor centre here, and there are a number of shops, cafés and lots of bars, all accessed via a walkway from Avenida Marques de Santa Cruz. If you're arriving from Peru or Colombia, don't forget to have your passport stamped at the Customs House, if you haven't already done so in Tabatinga.

## River travel to and from Manaus

There are regular passenger boat services to: Belém, Santarém and all ports along the Rio Amazonas; along the Rio Solimões to Tabatinga; and up the Rio Madeira to Porto Velho. Less frequent services go up the Rio Negro to São Gabriel da Cachoeira and up the Rio Branco to Caracaraí. Tickets for the regular services can be bought from the ticket windows inside the Estação Hidroviária Internacional. The boats are moored along the riverside near the Mercado Municipal for the days leading up to their departure, so it is possible to check them out before buying a ticket. It's best to avoid paying the captain directly, however, since tickets are now sold by the officials from the *guichês* (sales windows; open daily 6am–7pm) in the Estação Hidroviária, which are operated by the Agencia Rio Amazonas (Ⓣ92/3621-4310). It's sensible to buy tickets here days in advance and always get on your boat a good two hours or more before it's due to depart. Standard boats from Manaus to Belém can cost anything from R$150 to R$600 (depending on quality of boat and whether you want a cabin) and take three to five days, often stopping off in Santarém. Smaller boats with no regular schedules, and those serving local settlements up the Rio Negro, are found to the east of the Mercado Municipal. See also the "River journeys" box, p.368. If you are interested in a luxury boat cruise, Iberostar (Rio Ⓣ21/3325-0351, Ⓦwww.iberostar.com) have their *Grand Amazon* boat with swish accommodation for over seventy passengers, including two restaurants, two bars and two pools. For a faster speed boat to either Santarém (R$220; 13hr there, 15hr back) or Tefe (R$200; 13hr there, 10hr back) take the Expreso Barcos service from the Hidroviária near the Mercado Municipal; they leave at 6am (Tues and Fri for Santarém, Wed and Sat for Tefe).

The **rodoviária** (Ⓣ92/3642-5805) is on Avenida Recife some 10km north of the centre; #306 buses run every twenty minutes down Avenida Constantino Nery (two streets from the bus station), to Praça da Matriz in the heart of town, while taxis cost around R$25.

## Information

The most central of the **tourist offices**, the main Central de Atendimento ao Turista, operated by the state tourism company, Amazonastur, is close to the Teatro Amazonas opera house, behind and downhill from the theatre building, at Av. Eduardo Ribeiro 666 (Mon–Fri 8am–5pm, Sat 8am–midday; Ⓣ92/3622-0706, Ⓦwww.amazonastur.am.gov.br). You can also check the background of any tour operator here or lodge a complaint against one if need be. There are other tourist offices, however, at the **airport** (Ⓣ92/3652-1120; in the main arrivals hall, daily 7am–11pm); at the **Amazonas Shopping** centre, Av. Djalma Batista 482 (Ⓣ92/3236-5154; Mon–Sat 9am–10pm & Sun 3–9pm); at the **rodoviária** on Avenida Recife in the Flores district (daily 8am–5pm); and at the **Estação Hidroviária** (Ⓣ92/3233-8698; generally opens to coincide with cruise-liner arrivals).

## Accommodation

There are a number of perfectly reasonable **cheap hotels**, especially in the area around Avenida Joaquim Nabuco and Rua dos Andradas. The downtown centre is just a few blocks from here, with the docks for boats up and down the Amazon and Rio Negro also nearby. Even cheaper are the hotels along Rua José Paranaguá, two blocks north of Rua dos Andradas, though this road is particularly unsafe at night. Some streets close to the Teatro Amazonas, particularly along Rua 10 de Julho, are increasingly popular as places to stay. Business visitors may wish

# Amazon flora and fauna

**The Amazon rainforest is the largest and most biodiverse tropical forest on Earth. Its sheer abundance is overwhelming: some six thousand species of plant and nearly a thousand species of bird, not to mention numerous mammals, reptiles and hundreds of unidentified animal species, call the jungle – and often nowhere else – home. Through it all runs the mighty Amazon; while a trip on the river itself doesn't provide that many wildlife-spotting opportunities, during the rainy season in particular (Dec–April), plenty of river banks and flood plains are perfect for sightings.**

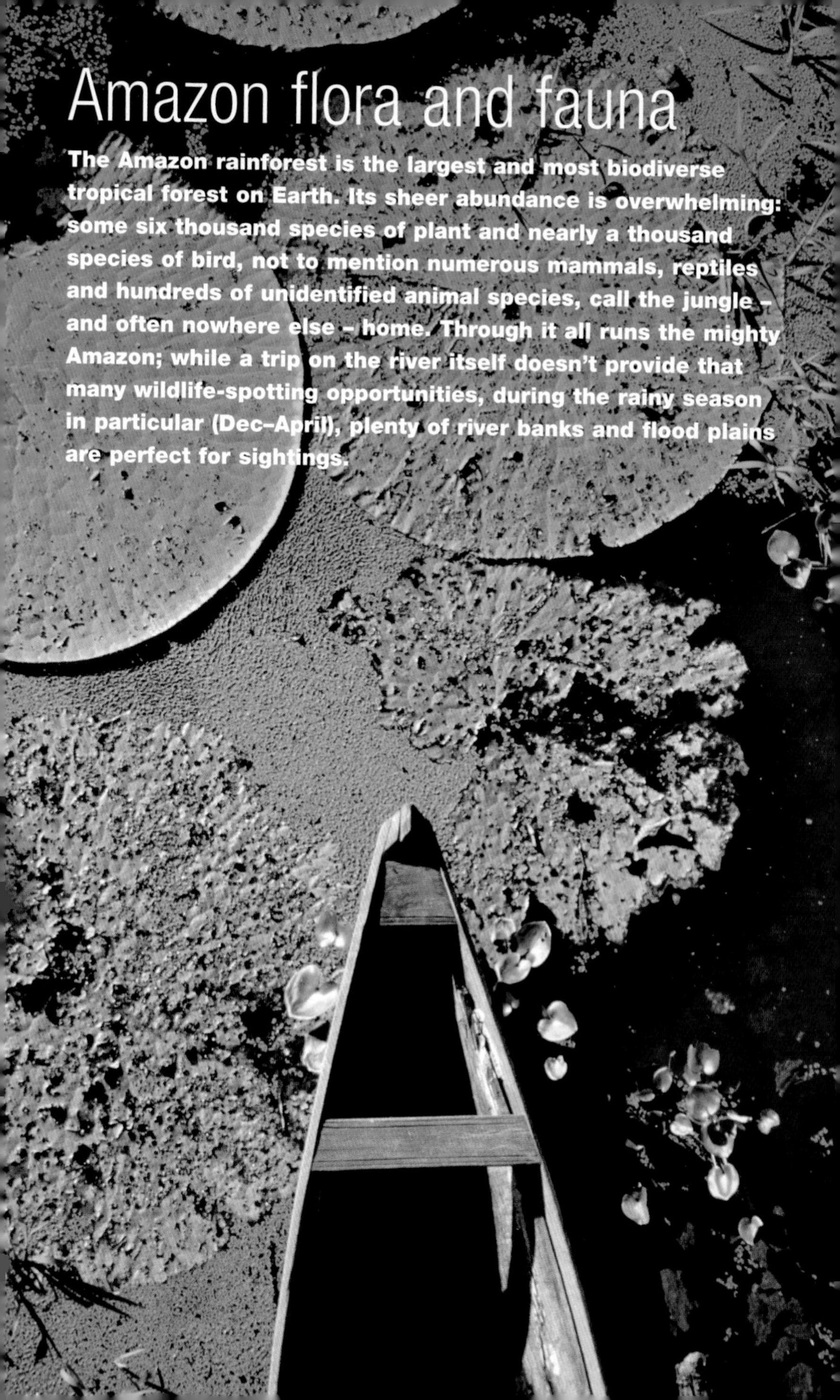

Heliconia attract hummingbirds ▲

Amazon lily ▲

A three-toed sloth peers from the undergrowth ▼

## Flora

The Amazon rainforest has well over two hundred tree species per hectare, most of them broad-leafed and evergreen. Branches and leaves are generally shed throughout the year while flowers – many with very bright red and yellow colours – are more seasonal. Many demonstrate flora and fauna interdependency, including the **heliconia**, whose brilliant flowers are pollinated by the hummingbird's perfectly designed nectar-probing beak. The region contains over 1800 species of **bromeliads**, which collect water in their leaves and can be a source of clean water for anyone unfortunate enough to be lost and parched in the forest.

Dramatic and bizarre varieties abound. The **Amazon lily** has large creamy white flowers that come out at night, become pink the next afternoon and turn a purplish red before slowly dying over the next 24 hours. Up to two metres in diameter, their ribbed leaves are exceptionally strong: small children can sometimes sit on a leaf without it sinking.

## Global resources

A few rainforest plants have provided the basis for major industries. Most of these, like the colourant **annatto** and **manioc** (cassava), are cultivated in rainforest gardens. The wild **rubber plant**, known as *seringuera* in Brazil, became an exceptional source of wealth in the early years of the twentieth century thanks to the emerging car industry, and was a vital resource for both sides in the run up to World War I. The trees' seeds were smuggled out by a British entrepreneur and rooted in Malayan plantations early last century, but rubber remains a valuable export from Brazil today.

# Birds

Exotic birds are commonplace in the Amazon. The **osprey** (fish eagle), elusive elsewhere in the world, winters in South America and is frequently spotted here. Many ibis, toucans, herons and kingfishers can be sighted in a day or two on the river. Noisy, gregarious **macaws** mate for life (which can be as long as a hundred years), and pairs can be seen flying among larger flocks.

▲ Macaws mate for life

# Reptiles and insects

Reptiles, particularly **caiman**, are easy to spot along the rivers' edges. Occasionally an **iguana** might leap from branch to ground, making a thrashing noise as it goes. **Snakes** are common, though rarely encountered, while **ants** – including the fascinating leaf-cutter and the massive bullet ant with its painful bite – are everywhere.

▲ A keel-billed toucan

▼ A leaf-cutter ant

# Mammals

Mammals are generally harder to see, though it's not unusual to come across three or more species in a three-day jungle trip. Howler and other **monkeys** make themselves visible or audible now and again. Lonesome **sloths** are frequently seen high up in the canopy, sleeping or munching leaves, while tapir, wild boar and jaguar are harder to come across. Swimming with **dolphins** – both grey and pink – is increasingly popular.

**Giant otters** are hard to spot and generally found only in remote, crystalline lakes, but some tour companies know where to look. These sleek beasts grow over 1m long, their thickish tail ending in a flattened tip. The animals live in extended family groups, with the males doing the least fishing but the most eating.

▼ Giant otters prey mainly on fish

The Amazon contains dry soil as well as jungle ▲

A caiman in the river ▼

Canoe trips ▼

## Not just jungle

The homogenous-looking canopy of the Amazon is best seen from the air, but on the ground you'll find an almost endless variety of eco-niches. The Amazon is generally thought of as flat, steamy **forest**; in fact, it has **mountains** and parts of it suffer from **droughts**. Most of the lowland is **terra firma**, where flooding doesn't regularly occur and the soil is well drained and remarkably red. *Terra firma* forests, if untouched, reach 30–50m above ground level; this is where you're more likely to find larger, slow-growing species of tree like mahogany or even cedar.

## Flooded forests

At some point most visitors will spend time in a canoe, travelling and exploring the **seasonally flooded forests** that constitute less than ten percent of the rainforest land area. The scenery here is distinctive, with the occasional flowering emergent tree standing out clearly on the bank and riverside trees dangling fruits for fish and birds to feed from. The trees are not as large as in *terra firma*, but their root systems are complex and labyrinthine, reflecting their adaptation to changing water levels.

## Endangered Amazon

The most obvious **threats** to the Amazon rainforest come from large-scale human activity – cattle ranching, logging, the production of soya and biofuels, hydro dams, gold mining and pollution from the extraction and use of fossil fuels, although there are some reasons for optimism. See p.730.

to find somewhere more modern, like the *Sleep Inn*, in the Industrial District, which, despite the name, is an area of town with plenty of new restaurants, bars and shopping facilities.

**Central Hotel** Rua Dr Moreira 202 ⓣ92/3622-2600, ⓕ3622-2609, ⓔhcentral@terra.com.br. Offers a wide choice of comfortable rooms, all with TV, *frigobar* and a/c. There's a good restaurant on-site and 24hr room service. Excellent value. ❹

**Hostel Amazonas** Rua Barao de Jaceguai 5, Parque das Laranjeiras ⓣ92/3634-6057, ⓦwww.hostelamazonas.com.br. A newly established youth hostel located away from the hubbub of the city centre and convenient for airport arrival. Rooms are mainly shared and a lovely breakfast is served on a patio with views from its hilltop location across the Cidada Nova district. There's also a pool, plus kitchen and laundry facilities. Offers free airport or port pick-up and, for travellers booking a jungle tour with Amazon Gero, there can be a free night here included in the package. ❷

**Hostel Manaus** Rua Lauro Cavalcante 231 ⓣ92/3233-4545, ⓦwww.hihostelmanaus.com. A pair of lovingly restored mansion-style houses have recently been combined and opened as a splendid downtown youth hostel. There are attractive family and private rooms available as well as shared dorms with or without a/c. There's a large and comfortable communal lounge area, a small patio garden, a rooftop terrace for breakfast with great views towards the Palácio Rio Negro, and kitchen and laundry facilities. It's probably the best place in town for meeting other travellers. Internet access and airport pick-up offered. Amazon Antonio Tours has its office inside the hostel premises.

**Hotel Ana Cássia** Rua dos Andrades 14 ⓣ92/3303-3622, ⓦwww.hotelanacassia.com.br. Located in a tall modern building close to the port, the hotel's top-floor restaurant is arguably the best place for breakfast, with its views over the river. Rooms are modern and well appointed with TV, shower, a/c and *frigobar*; there's also a rooftop pool and patio. Service is not the best, though. ❹

**Hotel Brasil** Av. Getúlio Vargas 657 ⓣ92/3233-6575, ⓔhotel-brasil@internext.com.br. Modern and busy, this mid-range hotel has a small pool inside and a bar out front by the rather noisy road. Rooms are plain, but comfortable and nice enough; service is hospitable. ❹

**Hotel Continental** Rua Coronel Sergio Pessoa 189 ⓣ92/3233-3342. Large, clean rooms, with good showers and TVs; some overlook the Rio Negro while others face onto the Praça and Igreja dos Remédios. Although the street outside is a bit dodgy, service and security seem fine in the hotel. ❷

**Hotel Dez de Julho** Rua Dez de Julho 679 ⓣ92/3232-6280, ⓦwww.hoteldezdejulho.com. This family-run hotel is located near the Opera House in a relatively pleasant and fairly safe part of the city. Rooms are modern and clean, with TVs and bathrooms. The rooms upstairs have more light, but there are also cheaper shared rooms (R$25 per person) in the basement. Breakfast is included. Amazon Gero Tours and Iguana Tours have offices inside the hotel (both offer airport pick-up) and the hotel itself operates a reliable travel agency for air and boat tickets. ❸

**Hotel Ideal** Rua dos Andradas 491 ⓣ92/3622-0038. Opposite the *Rio Branco*, the rooms here are much the same (clean and basic), though they tend to be smaller and darker. Choose between rooms with a fan or a/c and with or without minibar. ❶–❸

**Hotel Italia** Rua Guilherme Moreira 325 ⓣ92/3234-7934. Pleasant enough rooms, if small, with TV, *frigobar* and a/c. Service is friendly and a nice breakfast is included. ❸

**Hotel Manaos** Av. Eduardo Ribeiro 881 ⓣ92/3633-5744, ⓦwww.hotelmanaos.brasilcomercial.com. A modern, large, well a/c hotel very close to the Opera House. The service is cheerful and efficient, and the ambience is unpretentious. Rooms have all the modern conveniences. ❹–❺

**Hotel Rio Branco** Rua dos Andradas 474 ⓣ92/3233-4019, ⓔhotelriobranco30anos@ig.com.br. A secure well-run hotel with clean, spartan rooms (some with shared baths); a few rooms don't have windows, but ventilators or a/c available. Breakfast is served in a large communal space downstairs. ❷

**Krystal Hotel** Rua Barroso 54 ⓣ92/3233-7535, ⓦwww.krystalhotel.com.br. Located near the cathedral, this hotel is very good value for its modern, well-kept rooms; all include TV, phone and *frigobar*. ❹

**Lord Manaus Hotel** Rua Marcílio Dias 217 ⓣ92/3622-2844, ⓦwww.lordmanaus.com.br. Relatively plush for the centre, with apartments and suites; this is the best-value hotel in central Manaus. Some rooms have views over the city centre, but there is no pool. ❼

**Pensão Sulista** Av. Joaquim Nabuco 347 ⓣ92/3622-0038. A pleasant, old, colonial-style building with clean but small rooms equipped with fans. Along with the *Rio Branco*, this is the only cheap hotel that doesn't admit prostitutes. Their annexe at Rua Quintano Bocaiuva 621, the *Hotel Sulista* (ⓣ92/3234-6732), has bigger and better rooms and is only marginally more expensive. Both locations ❶–❷

**Plaza Hotel** Av. Getúlio Vargas 215 ⓣ92/3232-7766, ⓦwww.grupotajmahal.com.br. Next door to the similar but twice-as-expensive *Hotel Imperial*, the towering *Plaza* has comfortable, well-appointed rooms and a pool. It's good value, though at this price the service could be better. ④

**Sleep Inn** Av. Rodrigo Otavio 3373, Distrito Industrial ⓣ92/3321-8800, ⓦwww.atlanticahotels.com.br. A very plush and modern hotel located near the city's new convention centre. All mod cons and excellent service. ⑤–⑦

**Taj Mahal Continental Hotel** Av. Getulio Vargas 741 ⓣ92/3627-3737, ⓦwww.grupotajmahal.com.br. Arguably Manaus's grandest modern hotel, with quality rooms and adequate service, though it has seen better days. The best feature, perhaps, is the rotating restaurant, which offers the best possible views over the Opera House – though the food is not quite as splendid. Also offers an airport transfer. ⑥

**Tropical Hotel** Av. Cel. Teixeira 1320 ⓣ92/2123-5000, ⓦwww.tropicalhotel.com.br. This popular five-star resort hotel and busy convention centre lies right by the chic city beach, Praia Ponta Negra, 15km northwest of town and 8km from the airport. Facilities include a pool, tennis courts, good nightlife options, fine river beaches and even water-skiing on the Rio Negro – plus the service is excellent. The *Tropical* has its own buses from the airport; from downtown take the #120 bus from Praça da Matriz. ⑧–⑨

## Boi Bumbá in Parintins

Parintins, an otherwise unremarkable, small river-town with a population of around 100,000 lying roughly halfway between Santarém and Manaus, has become the unlikely centre of one of the largest mass events in Brazil – the **Boi Bumbá** celebrations, which take place in the last weekend of June every year.

The official name is the Festival Folclórico de Parintins, but it is often called Boi Bumbá after the name for a funny and dramatized dance concerning the death and rebirth of an ox traditionally performed at the festival. The festival's roots go back at least a hundred years, when the Cid brothers from Maranhão arrived in the area bringing with them the *Bumba-meu-boi* musical influence from the culture-rich ex-slave plantations.

Tens of thousands of visitors arrive annually at the Bumbódromo stadium, built to look like a massive stylized bull, which hosts a wild, energetic **parade** by something resembling an Amazonian version of Rio samba schools – and the resemblance is not coincidental, the organizers having consciously modelled themselves on Rio's Carnaval.

The event revolves around two schools, **Caprichoso** and **Garantido** which compete, parading through the Bumbódromo, where supporters of one school watch the opposing parade in complete silence. You thus have the strange spectacle of 20,000 people going wild while the other half of the stadium is as quiet as a funeral, with roles reversed a few hours later. Boi Bumbá has its high point with the enactment of the death of a bull, part of the legend of the slave Ma Catirina who, during her pregnancy, developed a craving for ox tongue. To satisfy her craving, her husband, Pa Francisco, slaughtered his master's bull, but the master found out and decided to arrest Pa Francisco with the help of some Indians. Legend, however, says a priest and a witch doctor managed to resuscitate the animal, thus saving Pa Francisco; with the bull alive once more, the party begins again at fever pitch, with a frenetic rhythm that pounds away well into the hot and smoke-filled night.

The parade is undeniably spectacular, and the music infectious. But if you're going to participate, remember joining in with the Caprichoso group means you mustn't wear red clothing; if you're dancing with the Garantido school, you need to avoid blue clothes. During the festival, forget about **accommodation** in any of the town's few hotels: they are booked up months in advance. Your best chance is simply to stay on a boat; in all the towns and cities of the region – notably Manaus and Santarém – you will find boats and travel agencies offering all-inclusive packages for the event, with accommodation in hammocks on the boats. Most of the riverboat companies offer three- or four-day **packages**, costing between R$200 and R$700. The trips (26hr from Manaus, 20hr from Santarém) are often booked well in advance, and are advertised from March onwards on banners tied to the boats. There is a lot of petty thieving and pickpocketing, so take extra care of anything you bring with you.

## The City

It's not hard to get used to the slightly irregular **layout** of Manaus, and, apart from the Teatro Amazonas and many of the museums, most places of interest are relatively close to the river in the older parts of town. From the Estação Hidroviária and floating port where the big ships dock, riverboat wharves extend round past the market, from one end of Rua dos Andradas to the other. The busiest commercial streets are immediately behind, extending up to the Avenida Sete de Setembro, with the cathedral marking one end of the downtown district, the leafy and popular **Praça da Polícia** the other. In some ways, Praça da Polícia is the hub of the city at the intersection of Avenida Sete de Setembro and Getúlio Vargas; the attractive park and police-academy building here are presently being restored, with the latter destined to be a home for several museum exhibitions as well as a new cultural centre.

Beyond Avenida Sete de Setembro, towards the Teatro Amazonas, it's a bit calmer, and the square at the entrance to the famous theatre is developing into an artists' quarter with bars and trendy cafés. The busy Praça da Matriz by the cathedral is the main hub of city transport, with **buses** to local points around the city and suburbs; another good connection-point for city buses and taxis is the east side of Avenida Getúlio Vargas, just north of Avenida Sete de Setembro.

The townsfolk, known as *manauanas*, are attractive and friendly. There is great ethnic variety here, but the distinctive *manauana* look comes from a genetic blending of local Indian, black and European stocks. Their hair tends to be black and wavy; they are usually short in stature, strongly built, with dark coppery skin. There are lots of young people in the population and the fact that they like to party, as much if not more than Brazilians everywhere, can be witnessed almost any night at the bars and clubs in and around the city.

### Around the docks

Since it's the docks that have created Manaus, it seems logical to start your exploration here, certainly the most atmospheric part of town. The **port** itself is an unforgettable spectacle. A constant throng of activity stretches along the riverfront, while the ships moored at the docks bob serenely up and down. Boats are getting ready to leave or, having just arrived, are busy unloading. People cook fish at stalls to sell to the hungry sailors and their passengers, or to the workers once they've finished their shift of carrying cargo from the boats to the distribution market. During the day there's no problem wandering around, and it's easy enough to find out which boats are going where just by asking. At night, however, this can be a dangerous area and is best avoided, as many of the river men carry guns.

From the Praça Adalberto Valle, the impressive **Alfândega** or Customs House (Mon–Fri 8am–1pm) stands between you and the floating docks. Erected in 1906, the building was shipped over from England in prefabricated blocks, and the tower once acted as a lighthouse guiding vessels in at night. The Porto Flutuante, or floating docks, here were built by a British company at the beginning of the twentieth century. To cope with the Rio Negro rising over a 14m range, the concrete pier is supported on pontoons that rise and fall to allow even the largest ships to dock here year-round (the highest recorded level of the river was in 1953, when it rose some 30m above sea level). The **Estação Hidroviária Internacional** is right next to the Customs House and, along with the road to the floating port is also known as the **Rodway**.

Following Rua Marquês de Santa Cruz down towards the new docks will bring you to the covered **Mercado Municipal Adolfo Lisboa** (Mon–Sat 5am–6pm, Sun 5am–noon), whose elegant Art-Nouveau roof was designed by Eiffel during the rubber boom and is a copy of the former Les Halles market in

▲ A line of boats docked at Manaus

Paris. Inaugurated in 1882 and restored in 2009, the market traditionally features an assortment of tropical fruit and vegetables, jungle herbs, scores of different fresh fish and Indian craft goods jumbled together. Just to the east of this market is the **wholesale port distribution market**, where traders buy goods and raw forest products from incoming boats and sell them on wholesale to shops, market stalls and restaurants. There are also a substantial number of retail traders here, where you can buy goods at prices only a little over wholesale. The distribution market is at its busiest first thing in the morning; by the afternoon most of the merchants have closed shop and the place looks abandoned. In the early 1990s this market was modernized, turning rat-infested wood and mayhem into concrete-based organized chaos – but it still makes for a fascinating wander.

### The commercial centre and the Opera House

Almost as busy by day as the docks themselves, Manaus's downtown commercial centre begins only metres inland from the waterfront and stretches up most of the way to the Opera House. Much of this area is little more than an electronics market. Everything from appliances to shoes can be bought here, at prices that are very cheap by Brazilian standards.

On a small hill, several blocks north away from the river lies the city's most famous symbol, the **Teatro Amazonas** or Opera House (30min guided tours only, Mon–Sat 9.30am–7pm; ⓣ92/3232-1768; R$10), which seems even more extraordinary lying in the midst of all the rampant commercialism. The whole incongruous, magnificent thing, designed in a pastiche of Italian Renaissance style by a Lisbon architectural firm, cost over R$6 million. After twelve years of building, with virtually all the materials – apart from the regional wood – brought from Europe, the Opera House was finally completed in 1896. Its main feature, the fantastic cupola, was created from 36,000 tiles imported from Alsace in France. The theatre's main curtain, painted in Paris by Brazilian artist Crispim do Amaral, represents the meeting of the waters and the local Indian water-goddess Iara. The four painted pillars on the ceiling depict the Eiffel Tower in Paris, giving visitors the impression, as they look upwards, that they are actually underneath the tower itself. The chandeliers are of Italian crystal and French bronze, and the theatre's seven hundred seats, its main columns and the balconies are all made of English cast iron. If you include the dome, into which the original curtain is pulled up in its entirety, the stage is 75m high.

Major restorations have taken place in 1929, 1960, 1974 and, most recently, in 1990, when the outside was returned from blue to its original pink. Looking over the upstairs balcony down onto the road in front of the Opera House, you can see the black driveway made from a special blend of rubber, clay and sand, originally to dampen the noise of horses and carriages as they arrived. Yet the building is not just a relic, and it hosts regular concerts, including, in April, the **Festa da Manaus**, initiated in 1997 to celebrate thirty years of the Zona Franca. There is a resident orchestra, the Amazon Philharmonic, with a high proportion of talented Russian or Eastern European musicians. The theatre can be visited only by guided tour and never within two hours of any scheduled performances; a forty-minute tour is often given at midday.

In front of the Teatro, the wavy black-and-white mosaic designs of the **Praça São Sebastião** are home to the "Monument to the Opening of the Ports", a marble-and-granite creation with four ships that represent four continents – America, Europe, Africa and Asia/Australasia – and children who symbolize the people of those continents. The Praça São Sebastião is getting trendier by the year, with a growing number of interesting shops, bars and arty cafés. Also on the *praça* is the beautiful little **Igreja Largo São Sebastião** (daily 5–9am and 3–7pm), built in 1888, and, like many other churches in Brazil, with only one tower due to the nineteenth-century tax levied on those with two towers. Nearby at Avenida Eduardo Ribeiro 833, you'll find the **Palácio da Justiça** (8am–1pm Mon–Fri), opposite the Amazonastur tourist offices. Supposedly modelled on Versailles, the Neoclassical building functions as the main state court, and, contrary to the popular image, its famous statue of the Greek goddess Themis is not blindfolded.

Some three blocks further away from the river, up Rua Tapajós, you'll find the old **Central Post Office**, another imposing reminder of the glorious years of the rubber boom. On the pavement around the back there's an ornate, much-photographed antique postbox, dated 1889.

### Along Avenida Sete de Setembro

In many ways, the Avenida Sete de Setembro is the original backbone of the city. At its heart, the **Catedral de Nossa Senhora da Conceição** (more commonly known as Igreja Matriz) on Avenida Sete de Setembro is a relatively plain building, surprisingly untouched by the orgy of adornment that struck the rest of the city – though judging by the number of people who use it, it plays a more active role in the life of the city than many showier buildings. The original cathedral, built mainly of wood and completed in 1695 by the Carmelite missionaries, was destroyed by fire in 1850, and the present building dates from 1878, with most of its materials brought from Europe, mainly Portugal. Around the cathedral are the **Praça Osvaldo Cruz** and the **Praça da Matriz**, shady parks popular with local courting couples, hustlers and sleeping drunks.

About 500m west of the cathedral, at Av. Sete de Setembro 117, is the **Instituto Geográfico e Histórico do Amazonas** (Mon–Fri 9am–noon & 1–4pm; ⓣ92/3232-7077; R$1), Rua Bernardo Ramos 117. Founded in 1917 on one of the city's oldest streets, the building is now a heritage site and has been recently restored. The institute's small museum includes a collection of ceramics from various tribes, a range of insect displays, and indigenous tools like stone axes and hunting equipment.

The **Museu do Homem do Norte** (Museum of Northern Man; Mon–Fri 9am–noon & 1–5pm; ⓣ92/3232-5373; R$2), in the opposite direction at Av. Sete de Setembro 1385, near Avenida Joaquim Nabuco, offers a quick overview of human life and ecology in the Amazon region, including exhibitions on *guaraná* and rubber production. Also worth at least a quick visit is the **Centro Cultural Palácio Rio Negro** (Tues–Fri 10am–5pm, Sat & Sun 2–6pm; free), a gorgeous colonial-period mansion housing the archives of the nineteenth-century Portuguese naturalist and scientist Alexandre Rodrigues Ferreira. The centre also hosts a wide range of exhibitions, videos, drama and events, and has a good café and bookstore; an annexe is home to two small museums – the Museu Numismatica and the Museu do Imagem e do Som – though these are expected to move to a new museum and cultural centre being prepared in the Praça da Polícia.

The excellent **Museu do Índio**, Rua Duque de Caxias 356 (ⓣ92/3635-1922; Mon–Fri 8.30–11.30am & 2–4.30pm, Sat 8.30–11.30am; R$5), lies about 500m further east along Avenida Sete de Setembro. The museum is run by the Salesian Sisters, who have long-established missions along the Rio Negro, especially with the Tukano tribe. There are excellent, carefully presented displays, with exhibits ranging from sacred ritual masks and inter-village communication drums to fine ceramics, superb palm-frond weavings and even replicas of Indian dwellings. Neatly complementing this collection is the **Museu Amazônico da Universidade do Amazonas**, to the north of the centre at Rua Ramos Ferreira 1036 (ⓣ92/3234-3242), which houses a small collection of sixteenth-century documents and engravings relating to the first explorations of the interior.

## Out of the centre

The most popular and widely touted day-trip around Manaus is to the **meeting of the waters**, some 10km downstream, where the Rio Negro and the Rio Solimões meet to form the Rio Amazonas. The alkaline Solimões absorbs the much more acid Rio Negro over several kilometres. For this distance the waters of the two rivers continue to flow separately, the muddy yellow of the former contrasting sharply with the black of the latter. Interestingly, the Rio Negro is almost always ten to fifteen degrees centigrade warmer than the Solimões. The lighter colour of the Solimões is mainly due to the high levels of soil suspended in the water, which has mostly come here as run-off from the Andes. The Rio Negro is particularly dark because most of its source streams have emerged in low-lying forests where rotting vegetation rather than heavier soil is absorbed into the river drainage system. It creates a strange sight, and one well worth experiencing. If you're going under your own steam, take the "Vila Burity" **bus** (#713) from Praça da Matriz to the end of the line at Porto de Ceasa, from where you can take a free half-hourly government ferry over the river, passing the meeting of the waters.

Most **tours** taking you there leave the docks at Manaus and pass by the shanty-town of Educandos and the Rio Negro riverside industries before heading out into the main river course. Almost all will also stop at the **Parque Ecólogico do Janauary**, an ecological park of 9000 hectares some 7km from Manaus on one of the main local tributaries of the Rio Negro. Usually you'll be transferred to smaller motorized canoes to explore its creeks (*igarapés*), flooded forest lands (*igapós*) and abundant vegetation. In the rainy season you have to explore the creeks and floodlands by boat; during the dry season – between September and January – it's possible to walk around.

One of the highlights of the area is the abundance of *Victoria Amazonica* (previously *Victoria Regia*), the extraordinary giant floating lily for which Manaus is famous. Found mostly in shallow lakes, it flourishes in the rainy months. The plant, named after Queen Victoria by an English naturalist in the nineteenth century, has huge leaves – some over a metre across – with a covering of thorns on their underside as protection from the teeth of plant-eating fish. The flowers are white on the first day of their life, rose-coloured on the second, and on the third they begin to wilt: at night the blooms close, imprisoning any insects that have wandered in, and releasing them again as they open with the morning sun.

The river beach at **Praia Ponta Negra**, about 13km northwest of Manaus near the *Hotel Tropical*, is another very popular local excursion, and at weekends is packed with locals. Once the home of the Manaós Indians, today the beach is an enjoyable spot for a swim, with plenty of bars and restaurants serving freshly cooked river fish. You can also catch music and other events at the massive modern amphitheatre nearby. The beach is at its best between September and March, when the river is low and exposes a wide expanse of sand, but even when the rains bring higher waters and the beach almost entirely disappears, plenty of people come to eat and drink. Soltur's Ponta Negra bus (#120) leaves every half-hour for the beach: catch it by the cathedral on Praça da Matriz.

The nearby military-run **CIGS Zoo** (Tues–Sun 9am–4.30pm; ⓣ3625-1966; R$4), Estrada Ponta Negra 750, is also an army jungle training centre, and many of the animals in it were captured, so they say, on military exercises out in the forest. The zoo has been recently redesigned to better cater to visitors, and you can expect to see alligators, monkeys, macaws and snakes among the more than 300 animals and 73 species kept here. To reach the zoo, take the #120, or the "Compensa" or "São Jorge" bus from the military college on Avenida Epaminondas.

The **Parque do Mindú**, out in the direction of the airport in the Parque Dez district, is the city's largest expanse of public greenery, incorporating educational trails (on which visitors can walk along suspended walkways), an *artesanato* shop and an exhibition centre. Closer to the city centre, the **Bosque da Ciência**, Alameda Cosme Ferreira 1756, Aleixo (daily 9am–4pm; ⓣ3643-3293), is an ecological park created by the Instituto Nacional de Pesquisas de Amazônia (National Institute for Amazon Research; INPA), and is home to otters, manatees, monkeys, snakes and birds. Both sites are easiest to reach by taxi, but you can also get there on buses #508, #424, #505 or #504. INPA is based at Av. A. Araújo 1756 (daily 9am–noon & 2–5pm; ⓣ92/643-3377), and runs free two-hour video screenings at weekends (10am and 2pm). A taxi ride away from here, there's more wildlife at the **Museu de Ciências Naturais da Amazônia**, Colônia Cachoeira Grande, Estrada Belém, Km 15, Aleixo (ⓣ92/3644-2799; Mon–Sat 9am–5pm; R$5), including fish such as the *piraruca* (in a 37,000-gallon aquarium), butterflies, insects and a good *artesanato* shop.

The waterfalls of **Cachoeira do Tarumã**, about 20km northwest of the city, are the last of the local beauty spots within easy reach of Manaus. Though no longer unspoiled, thanks to commercialization and weekend crowds, this is still a fun trip – there's good swimming and on busy weekends you'll often find live music in the town's bars. The cascades themselves, supplied by the Rio Negro, are relatively small whitewater affairs that more or less disappear in the rainy season (April–Aug). Soltur buses (#11) run here approximately every 20 minutes from the Praça da Matriz, taking about half an hour.

About an hour outside the town, the **Museu do Seringal Vila Paraíso** re-creates the living and working conditions of the traditional rubber-tappers from around one hundred years ago (Wed–Sun 8am–4pm; R$5). To get here, take the bus to Ponta Negra and then catch a dug-out taxi from the side of the *Tropical Hotel* at the Marina David to Igarapé São João – a tributary of the Taruma-Mirim that empties into the left bank of the Rio Negro. Tickets for the museum can be bought in advance from the tourist information offices in Manaus.

## Eating and drinking

There are very few places in Manaus where you can sit down and enjoy any peace. One advantage of the crowds is that there's **street food** everywhere, especially around the docks, the Mercado Municipal and in busy downtown locations like the Praça da Matriz, where a plate of rice and beans with a skewer of freshly grilled meat or fish costs well under R$5. One traditional dish you should definitely try here is **tacacá** – a soup that consists essentially of yellow manioc-root juice in a hot spicy dried-shrimp sauce. It's often mixed and served in traditional gourd bowls, *cuias*, and is usually sold in the late afternoons by *tacacazeiras* (street-food vendors). The following **restaurants** are closed Sundays unless otherwise stated. Be warned: prices in Manaus are relatively high.

**African House** Praça São Sebastião. A basic café opening out onto the square in front of the Opera House. Choose from light meals like burgers and grilled or fried chicken; washing it all down with juices mixed with vitamins or *guaraná* (a health supplement made from the seeds of an Amazonian bush).

**Café Regional Completo** By the corner of Av. Getúlio Vargas with Dez de Julho. This is a traditional bakery around the corner from 10 de Julho, excellent for breakfasts, juices and coffee with a/c indoor and outside patio tables.

**Canto da Peixada** Rua Emilio Moreira 1677, Praça 14 suburb ⓣ92/3234-3021. One of Manaus's best regional and river-fish restaurants, this place is not cheap, but good value nonetheless. Try the excellent *dourado* fish steaks. Usually open until 10.30pm.

**Choupana** Rua Recife 790, Adrianôpolis ⓣ92/3635-3878. Another great spot for some of the best regional cuisine on offer in or around Manaus and in a pleasant airy space; try the *tucupí* duck baked in manioc juice and *jambu* leaves with shrimps. Expensive but worth it.

**Churrascaria Búfalo** Av. Joaquim Nabuco 628A ⓣ92/3633-3773. One of the best meat restaurants in downtown Manaus, with excellent *rodízio*. It's quite cheap at around R$39 a head.

**El Toro Loco** Av. do Turismo 215, Tarumã suburb ⓣ92/3631-2557. One of the largest and most extravagant restaurants in Manaus, located under a massive ranch-style, open-sided structure. Choose from a wide range of top-quality cuisines including beef, fowl, a variety of fish dishes, pastas and cheeses; all are wonderfully presented in different corners of the restaurant. Service is difficult to beat and all for under R$60 a head (not including wine).

**Fiorentina** José Paranagua 44, Praça da Polícia, Centro ⓣ92/3215-2233. Reasonably good Italian restaurant right in the heart of town. The menu ranges from local river-fish dishes to traditional pastas and steaks. A more expensive and slightly better, sister restaurant can be found at Amazonas Shopping, on the second floor ⓣ92/3216-5240.

**Himawari** Rua 10 de Julho 618 ⓣ92/3233-2208. A spacious Japanese restaurant with tasty food and service, conveniently located on the Praça São Sebastião. Closed Mon; open until 10pm.

**Moronguêtá** Rua Jaith Chaves 31, Vila da Felicidade ⓣ92/3615-3362. Located by the riverside in the dodgy backstreets around the Porto do Ceasa this spacious restaurant looks out towards the meeting of the waters, and has a reputation as Manaus's best and freshest seafood restaurant; prices are reasonable.

**O Naturalista** Rua Sete de Setembro 752, 2nd floor. A large, clean and enjoyable vegetarian restaurant with good self-service, one block east from the cathedral. Open Mon–Fri lunch time.

**Scarola Pizzaria** Rua Dez de Julho 739. This pleasant pizzeria has a rough-and-ready patio, pretty good service and reasonably varied Italian and international food. At lunch time they have a decent and inexpensive *comida por kilo* self-service option.

**Skina dos Sucos** corner of Av. Eduardo Ribeiro with the Rio Branco Shopping Centre. Superb little café specializing almost exclusively in tropical fruit juices, served iced or pure. Service is fast.

**Sorveteria Glacial** corner of Rua Henrique Martins Calvante with Av. Getúlio Vargas. Of the several tropical-fruit ice-cream cafés around Manaus, this (and another across the road) are two of the busier ones, thanks to delicious product and kid-friendly decor.

**Suzuran** Av. Dj. Batista 3694 ⓣ92/3236-5333. This very good restaurant is worth the taxi ride to the trendy Parque 10 suburb. It's the best of the city's three Japanese dining options. Open daily.

## Nightlife

Like most large port towns, Manaus is busiest in the early mornings and again at night, with plenty of bars, clubs and other venues worth exploring if you're in town for a few days; Friday editions of *Amazonas Em Tempo* carry fairly comprehensive listings of what's going on.

The rowdiest **bars** are bunched in and around the Mercado Municipal, and along the entire length of Avenida Joaquim Nabuco south of Avenida Sete de Setembro. The usual starting place, for beer, snacks and a lively atmosphere, is the *Pizzaria Scarola* on the corner of Avenida Getúlio Vargas and Dez de Julho, with a patio that makes it a popular meeting-place in the early evenings. By the Praça da Polícia there's the busy evening *Bar do Marqinho*. Around the port, to the west of Praça da Matriz on Rua M. Sousa, a couple of even louder places – *Holanda Bar* and *Recanto da Natureza* – stay open all night, though this is a pretty dodgy area to be out late in. There are also a number of inexpensive bars around the Praça Sebastião, including the *Bar do Amandó* in front of the Opera House, which frequently has locals playing guitars and singing inside. There are several more expensive bars, some with restaurants, out at Ponta Negra. *O Laranjinha*, Estrada Ponta Negra 10675 (☎92/3658-6666; daily until 1am), is one of the most popular of the restaurant-bars; it has a large open space and stage where there are nightly performances, often including some Bio Bumbá music and dance groups. In the Aleixo district, on Avenida Constelação, there's the flashy *Haus Bier* bar, popular with Manaus's middle classes; it has its own brewery on-site and also serves very good pizzas. Out by Estudio 5 Shopping, in the Industrial District, the smart bar *Fellice's* has different music every night of the week.

The most exciting **clubs** are undoubtedly those along the Estrada Ponta Negra and around Praia Ponta Negra itself. Though their names change frequently, the music is always an enticing blend of old and modern sambas – it's worth coming just to see the formation dancing of the crowds. One of the best clubs at the moment is the rather expensive *Tucano*, near the *Tropical Hotel*. Given Manaus's prohibitive taxi fares, most of the Praia Ponta Negra clubs remain open all night, so you might as well bring a towel for a sobering early-morning dip in the river. Similarly distant is *TocToc*, a top *forró* music club located on Avenida do Turismo. Nearby, there's the *Celero Club* for great Cearense music at weekends. *Talisman* at Av. Ajurocaba 800 (☎92/3233-5520), slightly nearer the centre, is one of the best straight clubs, located out in the suburb of Cachoeirinha. The *Pagode do Almirante*, at Rua Padre Agostinho Caballeiro Martins 287 in the Santo Antônio suburb a few kilometres east of the centre, is a gay-friendly place pumping out reggae on Sundays and dance or *pagode* most other evenings.

The main cinemas include several screens at Amazonas Shopping, at Av. Djalma Batista 482, Parque 10 de Novembro; it's 4–5km from the centre by taxi or bus #306. It has hundreds of shops and cafés, plus six cinemas. The Centro Cultural dos Povos da Amazônia, on the Praça Francisco Pereira da Silva, is a massive complex including permanent exhibitions, craft goods, cafés and regular programmed music and other events (check the agenda section in local press for details).

## Shopping

The best selection of *artesanato* is at the lively Sunday-morning street market, which appears out of nowhere in the broad Avenida Eduardo Ribeira, behind the Teatro Amazonas. The Museu do Índio (see p.414) and several shops around the square in front of the Opera House also sell *artesanato*, including the Amazonas Eco Shop at Rua Dez de Julho 509. Indian crafts are sold at the Mercado Municipal. Interesting *macumba* and *umbanda* items, such as incense,

## Buying a hammock

**Cloth hammocks** are the most comfortable, but they're also heavier, bulkier and take longer to dry out if they get wet. Less comfortable in the heat, but more convenient, much lighter and more durable are **nylon hammocks**. Aesthetically, however, nylon hammocks are no match for cloth ones, which come in all colours and patterns. You should be able to get a perfectly adequate cloth hammock, which will stand up to a few weeks' travelling, from around R$25 for a single and R$50 for a double; for a nylon hammock, add R$10 to the price. If you want a more elaborate one – and some handwoven hammocks are very fine – you will pay more. Easing the path to slinging hammocks once you get home are metal *armadores*, which many hammock and most hardware shops sell; these are hooks mounted on hinges and a plate with bolts for sinking into walls. When buying a hammock you are going to use, make sure it takes your body lying horizontally across it: sleeping along the curve is bad for your back. A good hammock shop in Manaus is Casa des Redes on Rua dos Andradas.



candles, figurines and bongos, can be found at Cabana São Jorge at Rua da Instalação 36. Duty-free electronic and all kinds of other luxury items can be bought everywhere in the centre.

## Listings

**Airlines** BRA, Av. Eduardo Ribeiro 893 (☎92/3652-1507 or 3631-0007, www.voebra.com.br), offer the cheapest flights from Manaus to major destinations in Southern and Central Brazil, but they only fly a few times a week; Gol, at airport ☎92/3652-1634, www.voegol.com.br; Rico (covering Western Amazon region), Rua 24 de Maio, Loja 60-B, Edificio Cidade de Manaus ☎92/3233-1853 or 3652-1391 at airport; Tam, Rua João Valerio 123, Nosso Sra. das Gracas ☎92/3232-8833.

**Banks and exchange** Câmbio e Turismo Cortez (Mon–Fri 9am–5pm, Sat 9am–12.30pm) in Amazonas Shopping Centre, Lote 149, Av. Djalma Batista; for a better rate for larger amounts of cash try Jiboia Cambio, Floriano Peixoto 259, room 106 (2nd floor). There are several banks and ATMs on Av. Eduardo Ribeiro, just a block or two down the street from the SEC tourist offices.

**Car rental** Amore, Rua Major Gabriel 169 ☎92/3233-4539; Avis, Rua Major Gabriel 1721, 14 de Janeiro ☎92/3234-4440; Localiza, Rua Major Gabriel 1558, Centro ☎92/3233-4141; Unidas ☎92/3651-2558.

**Consulates** Bolivia, Av. Engenio Sales 2226, Quadrant B-20 ☎92/3236-9988; Colombia, Rua 24 de Maio 220, Centro Rio Negro ☎92/3234-6777; Peru, Rua A – C/19 – Conj. Aristocratico, Chapada ☎92/3656-3267 or 656-1015; UK, Rua Poraque 240 ☎92/3613-1819 or 3237-7869; US, Rua Recife 1010 – CCI – Adrianópolis ☎92/3633-4907; Venezuela, Rua Ferreira Pena 179 ☎92/3233-6004.

**Health** Instituto de Medicina Tropical, Av. Pedro Teixeira 25 ☎92/3238-7220; Hospital Tropical at Av. Pedro Teixeira 25 ☎92/3238-3192; Hospital Aventista de Manaus at Rua Gov. Danilo de Matos Areosa 139 in the Castelo Branco district. The Drogueria Nossa Senhor de Nazaré, Sete de Setembro 1333, is a reasonably well-stocked pharmacy. The emergency ambulance number is ☎192.

**Internet** Amazon Cybercafé, Av. Getúlio Vargas 625 (opposite the bottom end of Dez de Julho); Cybercity Internet, next to the Sorveteria Glacial at Av. Getúlio Vargas 188; LAN Aresenal Internet, ground floor of Centro Rio Negro quite close to both Sete de Setembro and the Opera House on Rua 24 de Maio.

**Laundry** Lavalux, at both Rua Mundurucus 77 ☎92/3233-7672 and Rua Acre 77 ☎92/3622-4262; Jo Lavanderia, at Rua Luisz Antony 503A, Centro.

**Police** ☎190.

**Post office** The main office is just off the Praça da Matriz on Rua Marechal Deodoro at the corner with Rua Teodoreto Souto (Mon–Fri 9am–5pm, Sat 8am–noon). There's a smaller branch just beyond the top of Av. Eduardo Ribeiro, on the leafy Praça do Congresso, and another in Amazonas Shopping.

**Taxis** Amazonas ☎92/3232-3005; Rádio Táxi ☎92/3633-3211; Tocantins ☎92/3656-1330.

**Travel Agents** Fontur, *Tropical Hotel*, Ponta Negra ☎92/3658-3052, www.fontur.com.br. Good for flights and city tours (will arrange free hotel pick-ups in the city centre for its city tours). Paradise

Turismo, Eduardo Ribeiro 654 (☎92/3633-8301 or 1156) and Dez de Julho Turismo, Dez de Julho 679 (☎92/3232-6280) are both good for plane tickets, the latter also for boat tickets. Tucunare Turismo, Rua Miranda Leão 194 (☎92/3234-5071, Ⓦwww.tucunareturismo.com.br), offer city tours, and trips to the meeting of the waters, fishing sites and the waterfalls of Presidente Figueiredo.

# Jungle trips from Manaus

Manaus is the obvious place in the Brazilian Amazon to find a **jungle river trip** to suit most people's needs. Although located in the heart of the world's biggest rainforest, you have to be prepared to travel for at least a few days out of Manaus if you are serious about spotting a wide range of wildlife. The city does, however, offer a range of organized tours bringing visitors into close contact with the world's largest tropical rainforest. Unfortunately, though, since Manaus has been a big city for a long time, the forest in the immediate vicinity is far from virgin. Over the last millennia it has been explored by Indians, missionaries, rubber gatherers, colonizing extractors, settlers, urban folk from Manaus and, more recently, quite a steady flow of eco-minded tourists.

## Tour planning and advice

There are scores of different **jungle tour companies** in Manaus offering very similar services and the competition is intense, which means you're likely to get hassled by touts at the airport and all over town; the sales patter can be unrelenting. Most companies have websites that give a reasonable feel for what's being offered. If possible, book in advance through one of the more established outfits registered at the Amazonastur information offices (Mon–Fri 8am–6pm, Sat 8am–1pm, Sun 8am–2pm; ☎92/3232-1998). While you may be able to bargain the price down a bit if you turn up in Manaus without a booking (groups can always get a better deal than people travelling alone), there is a surprising range of options and prices if you shop around online in advance.

You can generally get a tour cheaper if you're prepared to hang around for the operator to find others to make up a larger group. It's always a good idea to pin your tour operator down to giving you specific details of the trip on paper, preferably in the form of a written **contract**, and you should always ask about the accommodation arrangements, what the food and drink will consist of and exactly where you are going – ask to see photos and be wary of parting with wads of cash before you know exactly what you'll be getting in return. A circular trip may sound attractive, but the scenery won't change very much, whatever the name of the *rio*. You should also check that the guide speaks English, whether the operator has an environmental policy and what insurance coverage they offer (usually nil in the case of the cheaper operators). Check at the Amazonastur information office to see if the company is registered with EMBRATUR (if they are it is much easier to make a claim against them if something goes wrong). Ask what is and is not included in the price. On a more upmarket tour, you should check that binoculars and reference books are provided on the boat, if you haven't already got your own, and, on any tour, you of course have the right to expect that any promises made – regarding maximum group size, activities and so on – are kept. If not, then a promise to complain to Amazonastur may give you some leverage in obtaining redress. You can also check with Amazonastur for reports on complaints that might have been made against a particular tour operator in the past.

The most dependable and comfortable way to visit the rainforest is to take a package tour that involves a number of nights in a **jungle lodge** – though for the more adventurous traveller the experience can be a little tame. The lodges invariably offer hotel-standard accommodation, full board and a range of activities including alligator spotting, piranha fishing, trips by canoe and transport to and from Manaus. Some lodge-based tours integrate the opportunity to spend a night or two camping out in the forest. The least expensive jungle-tour options are those offering hammock-space accommodation, perhaps combined with a night in the forest; the most expensive should see visitors in at least four-star comfort. You can either book a jungle-lodge tour through a tour operator, or approach the lodge operators directly at their offices in Manaus (see box, pp.422–423); in some cases the tour operators also have their own lodges. Some of the better tour companies run their own small riverboats for more leisurely exploration, sometimes with room for up to twenty people to sleep in comfortable, if small, cabins.

If you want to forgo organized tours entirely and travel independently, **milk boats or regatão** trading boats are a very inexpensive way of getting about on the rivers around Manaus. These smaller vessels, rarely more than 20m long, spend their weeks serving the local riverine communities by delivering and transporting their produce. You can spend a whole day on one of these boats for as little as R$25, depending on what arrangement you make with the captain. The best place to look for milk boats is down on the wharves behind the distribution market. Approach the ones that are obviously loading early in the morning of the day you want to go, or late in the afternoon of the day before. Other commercial boats bound for the interior – some of them preparing for trips up to a month long – can be found at the port end by the Mercado Municipal. There are other small ports and ferry points around Manaus which also have boats travelling into the interior. In eastern Manaus, the **Porto São Raimundo** has a ferry over to the other side of the Rio Negro and sometimes boats go upriver from here. By 2011, an ambitious river-bridge project is planned to be completed, carrying the road and no doubt urbanization over onto the far side of the Rio Negro. Far west, along the Avenida Min. João Gonçalves de Araujo, there's the fruit port **Porto de Ceasa**, another ferry point. From here, it crosses the Rio Negro and enters the Solimões, passing the meeting of the waters, en route to the start of

▲ Brown-throated sloth

## Novo Airão and swimming with dolphins

**Novo Airão**, a small jungle town on the west bank of the Rio Negro, is 115km (6hr) by bus from Manaus. By boat it's around 130km (8hr). Its main attraction is the chance to feed **pink dolphins** from the floating restaurant next to the tourist information office at the town's small port. The times for seeing the dolphins are Mon–Sat 9am–noon & 3.30–5pm, and Sun 9am–noon. The owner of the restaurant who has "trained" the dolphins charges R$10 for a plate of fish to feed them. You can get in the water with the dolphins who will splash and bump into you, hoping for food. Otherwise, there's not much else to see in town.

If you decide to stay there are a couple of *pousadas* and a few restaurants, and internet access is available at a café at Rua Rui Barbosa 41. The best *pousada* is undoubtedly *Bela Vista*, at Av. Presidente Vargas 47 (☎92/3365-1023; ❸), which has small but pleasant rooms and serves delicious breakfasts on a patio overlooking the Rio Negro. If the *Bela Vista* is full, or if you want cheaper accommodation, try the *Pousada Rio Negro* (❷) on the central *praça*.

From Manaus's *rodoviária*, the bus (daily at 6am & 1pm) takes the Porto São Raimundo ferry and continues to Manacapuru before turning north and following the BR-352 to its end at the port of Novo Airão, which sits opposite the Arquipelago Anavilhanas. It's too far a distance to travel in a day, but it makes a good overnight trip from Manaus.

the BR-319, the overgrown, potholed and essentially unusable road to Porto Velho. Any expedition into protected areas of forest will require permission from the state agency IBAMA, whose offices in Manaus are at BR-319 137, Castelo Blanco district (☎92/3613-1703).

### Wildlife

The amount and kind of **wildlife** you get to see on a standard jungle tour depends mainly on how far away from Manaus you go and how long you can devote to the trip. Birds including macaws, hummingbirds, jacanas, cormorants, herons, kingfishers, hawks, chacalacas and toucans can generally be spotted – but you need luck to see hoatzins, trogons, cock-of-the-rock or blue macaws. You might see alligators, snakes, sloths, river dolphins and a few species of monkey on a three-day trip (though you can see many of these anyway at INPA or the Parque Ecólogico do Janauary; see p.414). Sightings for large mammals and cats, however, are very rare, though chances are increased on expedition-type tours of six days or more to deep-forest places like the Rio Juma. On any trip, make sure to get some time in the smaller channels in a canoe, as the sound of a motor is a sure way of scaring every living thing out of sight.

### Jungle terms

There are a few Brazilian **jungle terms** every visitor should be familiar with: a *regatão* is a travelling-boat-cum-general-store, which can provide a fascinating introduction to the interior if you can strike up an agreeable arrangement with one of their captains; an *igarapé* is a narrow river or creek flowing from the forest into one of the larger rivers (though by "narrow" around Manaus they mean less than 1km wide); an *igapó* is a patch of forest that is seasonally flooded; a *furo* is a channel joining two rivers and therefore a short cut for canoes; a *paraná*, on the other hand, is a branch of the river that leaves the main channel and returns further downstream, creating a river island. The typical deep-red earth of the Western Amazon is known as *tabatinga*, like the city on the frontier with Peru and Colombia; and regenerated forest, like secondary growth, is called *capoeira*.

## Tour itineraries

The **basic options** for jungle tours run from one-day through to three-, five- or even fifteen-day expeditions into the forest – almost all of them dominated by river travel. They usually include the services of local guides and forest

### Jungle tour operators and lodges in Manaus

Jungle lodges offer travellers the opportunity to experience the rainforest while maintaining high levels of comfort, even elegance; there are scores of lodges in and around the Manaus area, most operated by tour companies. Jungle tour operators are not difficult to find in Manaus, but it is quite hard to identify the best and most trusted operators and guides just by meeting them at the airport or in the streets of the downtown area. If you can, it's much better to book in advance on the internet. Some of the companies or agents listed below have their own lodges, riverboats and houseboats, while one or two of them select and book an appropriate lodge or boat for each tour.

#### Tour operators and lodges

**Acajatuba Jungle Lodge** Av. Sete de Setembro 1899 ⓣ92/3084-3461, ⓦwww.acajatuba.com.br. A lodge with large communal areas, spacious, clean cabins, and standard trips from one to four nights. *Acajatuba* is located in the Anavilhanas archipelago and has wooden elevated footbridges joining the various parts of the site. Night-time lighting is from battery-powered bulbs, so there's rarely any generator noise to drown out the sounds of the jungle.

**Amazon Antonio Jungle Tours** Rua lauro Cavalcante 231, Centro ⓣ92/3233-4545, mobile ⓣ9961-8314, ⓦwww.antonio-jungletours.com. This relatively new company specializes in visits to their attractive and rustic eco-lodge, which has a viewing tower right beside the Rio Negro. They also offer visits to *caboclo* families, boat-based tours and day-trips to the meeting of the waters.

**Amazonas Indian Turismo** Rua dos Andradas 311 ⓣ92/3622-0204 or 3633-5578. A basic but long-established operator, and one of the least pushy of the budget crowd. Run by Amazon Indians, it offers good jungle-trekking, lots of opportunities for spotting wildlife (mainly birds – including toucans – dolphins and alligators), canoe trips exploring *igarapés*, piranha fishing and visits to local communities. Guides vary in quality (some speak only Portuguese) but they can be good value (R$150–200 a day). Tour groups tend to be smaller than most, and more personalized itineraries are possible as well. They also operate a basic but very hospitable lodge camp around 200km from Manaus.

**Amazon Explorers** Porto do Manaus, Estação Hidroviária ⓣ92/3232-3052, ⓦwww.amazonexplorers.com.br. This reputable operator runs a reservations service for upmarket jungle lodges, luxury boat hire and fishing trips, and organizes jungle tours, with boat accommodation (from around R$230 per person a day, minimum two people for two days) and a six-hour trip to the meeting of the waters and Parque Janauary. As a travel agency, it offers a ticketing service for day-trips as well as air and boat travel.

**Amazon Gero's Tour** Dez de Julho 679, Centro ⓣ92/3232-4755, mobile ⓣ9983-6273, ⓦwww.amazongerotours.com. One of the most reliable and experienced operators, Amazon Gero's guides and other staff speak excellent English, Spanish and some other European languages. The owner Geraldo (Gero) Mesquita organizes tours mainly to the Mamori and Juma areas. Great rainforest accommodation is available in Gero's own *Ararinha Jungle Lodge*, located on the scenic and peaceful Lago Arara (see p.424) just off the Parana do Mamori. Well located in terms of peace and quiet and wildlife, it offers a range of prices and levels of comfort from family suites and standard rooms to hammock space in the round viewing platform above the circular restaurant. Gero will reliably book hotels, boats, arrange airport pick-ups (from R$40 a car) and

experts. Some offer accommodation on boats, some in hammocks in forest clearings; others offer both in the same three-day trip. The more expensive ones offer the added luxury of jungle lodges and comfortable riverboats with cabin accommodation.

also look after luggage if you have to check-out a long time in advance of travelling on. Tours include boat and canoe trips, jungle hiking and visits to native people, with accommodation in hammocks, overnight in the bush, visiting or staying at local family houses, or in luxury lodge accommodations. Gero also organizes trips elsewhere (eg to the Rio Negro) on request.

**Amazon Village Grand Amazon Turismo** Rua Ramos Ferreira 1189, sala 403 ⓣ92/3633-1444, ⓦwww.amazon-village.com.br. On Lago Puraquequara, 50km from Manaus. It's much larger than the *Amazon Lodge* (32 rooms) and has better facilities, but it's not quite as wild in terms of the surrounding forest.

**Ariaú Amazon Towers** office at Rua Leonardo Malcher 699, Manaus centre ⓣ92/2121-5000, ⓦwww.ariau.tur.br. Only 60km up the Rio Negro from Manaus (3hr by boat) by Ariaú Lake, this is one of the largest and most developed of the jungle lodges, with a helicopter pad, swimming pool, almost 100 rooms (mostly in wooden chalets) and a 35-metre viewing tower from which you get an exceptionally close and breathtaking view of the forest canopy. It's a must if your budget isn't restricted (from R$700 per person for three days and two nights). It also boasts the longest jungle walkway in the Amazon.

**Arquipelago Anavilhanas Tours** Rua Dr. Moreira 163, 1st floor, Centro ⓣ92/3231-1067, ⓦwww.arquipelagotours.com. Specializing, as the name suggests, in tours to the fantastic Anavilhanas complex of islands. This reliable and efficient operator also offers city tours, trips to the meeting of the waters and more adventurous and distant fishing or safari-type tours, including to waterfalls in the Presidente Figueiredo area.

**Dolphin Lodge** operated by Maia Expeditions, Rua Badajo 5, Parque Shangri-la, Bairro de Flores ⓣ92/3877-49247, ⓦwww.maiaexpeditions.com. A comfortable lodge with wooden double bedrooms and a pleasant circular restaurant and bar space. Based in the Parana do Mamori, there is plenty to see and do in the immediate vicinity.

**Hotel Ecológico Terra Verde** (Green Land Lodge), Rua Silva Ramos 20, sala 305 ⓣ92/3622-7305, ⓕ3622-4114, ⓔterraverde@internext.com.br. Located in a small ecological reserve on the Fazenda São Francisco, 50km from Manaus over the other side of the Rio Negro on Lago Acajatuba, this lodge has five relatively luxurious cabins, a floating swimming pool and horse-riding facilities. A comfortable and interesting place, but probably a bit tame for the adventurous traveller. From around R$350 per person for two days and night. Boats run daily to the lodge from the pier at the *Tropical Hotel* (8am & 2pm).

**Iguana** Dez de Julho 667, Centro ⓣ92/3633-6507 or (24hr) 92/9105-5660 or 9615-0480, ⓦwww.amazonbrasil.com.br. Based in the *Hotel Dez de Julho*, this company, which operates regularly in the Juma and Mamori areas, is able to organize most kinds of trips, from overnights in the forest to longer lodge- or camp-based trips. They have an attractive lodge in the Juma area which offers private wooden cabins with own shower room or shared dorms.

**Swallows and Amazons** Rua Ramos Ferreira 922 ⓣ92/3622-1246, ⓦwww.swallowsandamazonstours.com. A small company with an excellent reputation, specializing in private and small-group houseboat, riverboat, jungle lodge and rainforest adventure tours. Most trips explore the Rio Negro and the Anavilhanas archipelago, but custom tours are also possible. The company runs *Araras Lodge*, 60km from Manaus on the Rio Negro where rooms have a/c, private bathrooms and verandas with views. Rates R$200–350 per person per day.

The **one-day river trip**, usually costing around R$150 per person, generally includes inspecting the famous meeting of the waters, some 10km downriver from Manaus (see p.405). More often than not, this trip will also visit one or two fairly typical riverine settlements and take a side-trip up a narrow river channel to give at least some contact with birdlife and a tantalizing taste of the forest itself. One-day river trips usually leave port around 8 or 9am, returning before 6pm, though some last barely six hours.

The other most popular jungle river trips tend to be the **three- to five-day expeditions**. If you want to sleep in the forest, either in a lodge, riverboat or, for the more adventurous (and perhaps those on a low budget), swinging in a hammock outside in a small jungle clearing, it really is worth taking as many days as you can to get as far away from Manaus as possible. The usual price for guided jungle tours, including accommodation and food, should be between R$150 and R$300 a day per person (no matter what the sales pitch), more again if you opt for an upmarket jungle lodge or a decent riverboat. You might find it worth paying a few more dollars a day to ensure you're well looked after.

The most commonly operated tours are three-day trips combining both the **Rio Negro and Rio Solimões**, although some trips only cover the former, as it is more accessible from Manaus. Four-day trips should ideally also include both a good day's walk through the jungle and some exploring of the **Anavilhanas archipelago** opposite Novo Aírão on the Rio Negro; the second-largest freshwater archipelago in the world, it has around four hundred isles and is a fine place to see white-sand river beaches and their associated birdlife. The Rio Negro region has a very distinctive beauty influenced by the geology of the Guiana Shield where the main river sources are, and the consequent soil types and topography. The waters are very acidic and home to far fewer mosquitoes than you find in other regions. The Negro also tends to have less abundant wildlife than some of the lakes and channels around the Rio Solimões. You can still see much the same species in both regions, but the densities are lower on the Rio Negro and many of its tributaries. Plenty of tours combine both the Solimões and Negro rivers in their itineraries.

On the Solimões, some of the three- to five-day options include trips to Lago Mamori or Manacapuru. Although well visited and only half a day's travel by road and boat from Manaus, **Lago Mamori** offers reasonably well-preserved forest conditions in which you'll see plenty of birds, alligators and dolphins and have the chance to do some piranha fishing. Slightly further into the forest, the **Parana do Mamori** is a quieter river-like arm from Lago Mamori and a zone where numerous birds, sloths, pink dolphins, caiman and monkeys are easily spotted. **Lago Arara**, accessed by a pink-dolphin feeding ground of a *furo* from the Parana do Mamori, is a beautiful and relatively well-preserved corner in this area. As well as wildlife, the Parana do Mamori allows close contact with the local riverine communities of *caboclo* people (the settlers who have been here for generations and who dedicate their time to fishing, farinha making, cattle ranching and tapping rubber). From the Parana Mamori there is a large *furo* connection with the quieter **Lago Juma**; from here the **Rio Juma** region is accessible. It's remote and malarial, but excellent for wildlife, and you'll need a minimum of five or six days to make the travel time worthwhile. Much further south of Manaus, again, the **Igapó Açu** area is one of the best sites for wildlife and, despite its remoteness, it can also be easily reached from Manaus (by boat and road) in a five- or six-day trip; there are no lodges here, but it is possible to stay with locals and ideally your guide will have good contacts. West of Manaus, on the north bank of the Solimões, **Manacapuru**, also accessible by road and boat, is closer to large population centres and therefore offers more in the way of a visit to lakes and plant-familiarization walks, including access to Brazil-nut tree trails. It's also an area where visitors can make interesting excursions up smaller tributaries in search of birdlife, alligators and spectacular flora, such as the gigantic **samaumeira tree** with its buttress base (one of the tallest trees in the Amazon).

Further up the Solimões, the **Mamirauá Sustainable Development Reserve** is an area of relatively untouched, seasonally flooded *várzea*-type vegetation offering close contact with the flora and fauna, including pink dolphins. After fifteen years of intense conservation in the immediate environment, the low-impact *Uacari Floating Lodge* and a fleet of boats make it possible to explore the unspoilt surroundings from a comfortable base within the reserve. Small groups of four visitors and a guide get access to forest trails, lakes and local riverine *caboclo* communities. Access to the reserve can be organized through some Manaus tour companies or direct with the Programa de Ecoturismo (ⓣ97/3343-4160, ⓔecoturismo@mamiraua.org.br, ⓦwww.mamiraua.org.br) in Tefé (the nearest town), a one- to two-day journey (450km) upstream from Manaus. Tours tend to be costly, not least because most visitors choose to fly to Tefé. *Uacari Floating Lodge* is less than two hours by road and riverboat from the airport.

**Presidente Figueiredo** lies 100km by road north of Manaus and sits at the heart of waterfall country. There's a tourist information kiosk (ⓣ92/3324-1308) at the *rodoviária* (ⓣ92/3324-1231) there, but you can also book tours with guides from some of the tour agents in Manaus. Two hours by bus from Manaus and ten hours south of Boa Vista, there are several hotels and restaurants in town, but the *Pousada Cuca Legal*, Rua Manaus 1, Centro (ⓣ92/3324-1138, ⓦwww.pousadacucalegal.com.br; ③), offers a rural retreat with a pool and small but airy rooms and a good restaurant. The Iracema Falls are only 12km away, and, similarly, there is also Santuario (16km), Portero (19km) and the very impressive Pedra Furada (60kms) waterfalls. Closer to town there's the Water Mammal Preservation Centre (Mon–Sat 8am–noon & 2–4pm; ⓣ92/3312-1202).

Located on the west bank of the Rio Negro, just below the confluence with the Rio Branco, is Brazil's largest national park – the 23,000-square-kilometre **Parque Nacional de Jaú**, which cannot be entered alone or without official permission; it is always best to do this through a local tour operator (see p.422) who has the necessary contacts with IBAMA and the national-park offices. It takes time and money to visit the park, but this is exceptionally remote forest and well conserved; the tour operators should also be able to provide reliable guides, camping equipment and transport to the area.

### Yanomami tours: a warning

Some tourists are offered trips to the **Yanomami** or other **Indian reserves**. These are difficult to obtain these days following recent outbreaks of violence between miners and the Yanomami. Such a trip is only possible with valid permission from IBAMA (Rua Ministro João Gonçalvez de Souza, KM 1, BR-319, Distrit Industrial, ⓣ92/3613-3080 or 3613-1703, ⓦwww.ibama.gov.br), and FUNAI (Rua Maceio 224, Adrianôpolis ⓣ92/3233-7103, ⓦwww.funai.gov.br), which you have to obtain yourself. If a company says they already have permission, they're probably lying, as each visit needs a new permit. In any case, permission is generally impossible to get, so that the trips offered may actually be illegal and could land you in serious trouble. Of course, the ethics of such visits are in any case clear: isolated groups of Indians have no immunity to imported diseases, and even the common cold can kill them with devastating ease.

# The Rio Solimões and the journey to Peru

The stretch of river upstream from Manaus, as far as the pivotal frontier with **Peru** and **Colombia** at Tabatinga, is known to Brazilians as the **Rio Solimões**. Once into Peru it again becomes the Rio Amazonas. Although many Brazilian maps show it as the Rio Marañón on the Peru side, Peruvians don't call it this until the river forks into the Marañón and Ucayali headwaters, quite some distance beyond Iquitos.

From Manaus to Iquitos in Peru, the river remains navigable by large ocean-going boats, though few travel this way any more; since the collapse of the rubber market and the emergence of air travel, the river is left to smaller, more locally oriented riverboats. Many travellers do come this way, however, and, although some complain about the food and many get upset stomachs (especially on the Peruvian leg), it can be a quite pleasant way of moving around – lying in your hammock, reading and relaxing, or drinking at the bar. Against this, there are all the inherent dangers of travelling by boat on a large river, especially at night. Boats have been known to sink (though this is rare) and they do frequently break down, causing long delays; many captains seem to take great pleasure in overloading boats with both cargo and passengers. In spite of the discomforts, however, the river journey remains popular and is unarguably an experience that will stick in the memory.

The river journey is also, of course, by far the cheapest way of travelling between Brazil and Peru. There are reasonable facilities for visitors in the border town of **Tabatinga** and the adjacent Colombian town of **Leticia**. All boats have to stop at one of these ports, and most will terminate at the border whichever direction they've come from.

The boat trip from Manaus to Tabatinga – five to eight days upstream – costs from around R$200 for hammock space, inclusive of food (though bring some treats, as the fare on board, though good, does get a bit monotonous). The downstream journey, which is often very crowded, takes three to four days and costs upward of R$160. If you want to break the journey, you can do so at **Tefé**, around halfway, and visit the beautiful **Mamirauá Sustainable Development Reserve** (see p.425), a wild but accessible area of rainforest upstream from the town; if you really can't face the boat journey any longer, take one of the weekly flights from Tefé to Manaus and Tabatinga. There's also an *expresso* boat service connecting Tefé with Manaus (see "River travel to and from Manaus" box, p.408).

Several large boats currently ply the river upstream from Manaus on a regular basis, all pretty similar and with good facilities (toilets with paper, showers, mineral water and enough food). Smaller boats also occasionally do the trip, but more often terminate at Tefé, from where other small boats continue. On the other side of the border, the standard large-boat trip to Iquitos from Tabatinga costs around R$100–180 and takes three or four days; sometimes more, rarely less. Coming downstream from Iquitos to Tabatinga (R$80–100 gives you one and a half days on the river. It's advisable to take your own food and water – all normal supplies can be bought in Tabatinga. There are also more popular super-fast, sixteen-seater powerboats connecting Tabatinga and Leticia with Iquitos that cost upwards of R$180 and take roughly ten to twelve hours. Small planes also connect Iquitos with Santa Rosa, an insignificant Peruvian border settlement just a short boat-ride over the river from Tabatinga and Leticia; there is at least one flight a week operated by the Peruvian airline TANS.

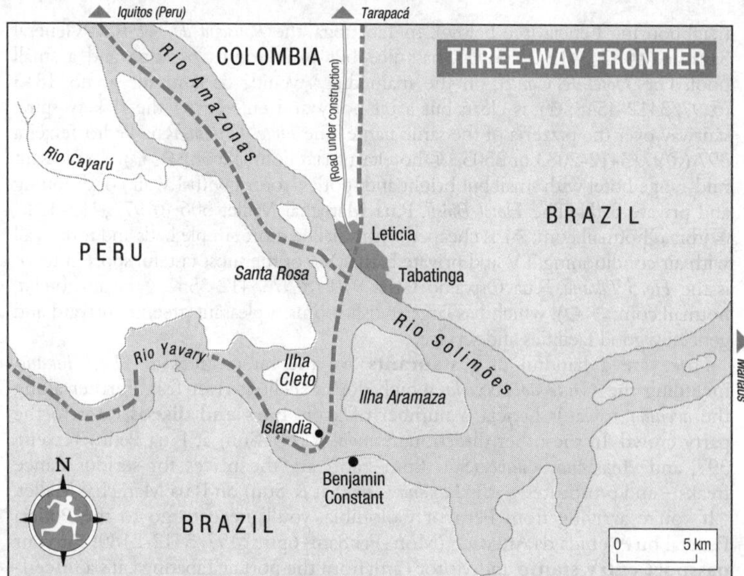


## The three-way frontier

The point where Brazil meets Peru and Colombia is known as the **three-way frontier**, and it's somewhere you may end up staying for a few days sorting out red tape or waiting for a boat. Some Brazilian boats will leave you at Benjamin Constant, across the river from **Tabatinga**, but, if you do have to hang around, then Tabatinga, or the neighbouring Colombian town of **Leticia**, are the only places with any real facilities. A fleet of motorboat taxis connects these places, and Islandia and Santa Rosa in Peru: Benjamin Constant to Tabatinga takes half an hour and costs around R$8; Tabatinga to Islandia or Santa Rosa takes fifteen minutes and costs R$6. When you're making plans, remember the three countries have differing time zones, so make sure you know which you are operating on (Tabatinga is an hour behind Manaus).

For many centuries the three-way frontier has been home to the Tikuna Indians, once large in number, but today down to a population of around 10,000. Their excellent handicrafts – mainly string bags and hammocks – can be bought in Leticia.

### Tabatinga

**TABATINGA** is not the most exciting of towns, and many people stuck here waiting for a boat or plane to Manaus or Iquitos prefer to hop over the border to Leticia for the duration of their stay, even if they don't plan on going any further into Colombia. Tabatinga is the place to complete Brazilian exit (or entry) formalities with the Polícia Federal (see p.428 for details). The town also has an airport with regular flights to Manaus. Many of the boats into Peru leave from here, and if you're coming or going the other way most downstream boats start their journeys here too (south down Rua Tamandaré, then right after the Marine base), before really filling up at Benjamin Constant.

**Accommodation** in Tabatinga isn't that great – a good reason to stay on the boat if you can or, if you really need a night of luxury, to try out the hotels in neighbouring Leticia (see below). In Tabatinga, the *Pousada do Sol*, Rua General Sampao (ⓣ97/3412-3355; ❸), has nice but plain rooms, a sauna and a small pool. The *Hotel Tè Contei*, on the main drag Avenida da Amizade at no. 1813 (ⓣ97/3412-4548; ❷), is clean but a bit noisy and entered up the rickety spiral stairway over the pizzeria of the same name. The *Hotel Taruma*, Rua Pedro Teixeira 397 (ⓣ97/3412-2083 or 3505, ⓔhoteltaruma@hotmail.com; ❸–❹), is a pleasant mid-range hotel with small but bright and spotless rooms with TV, air conditioning and private baths. The *Hotel Brasil*, Rua Marechal Mallet 306 (ⓣ97/3412-3186, ⓔjrbra@hotmail.com; ❸), is cheaper, with smaller, more simple beds and rooms, all with air conditioning, TV and private bath. One of the most tasteful spots in town is the *Hotel Takana*, Rua Oswaldo Cruz 970 (ⓣ97/3412-3557, ⓔtakanahotel@hotmail.com; ❹–❺), which has large stylish rooms, a pleasant green courtyard and generally good facilities and service.

There are a handful of **restaurants** on the same street as *Hotel Takana*, including the *Canto do Peixada*, which does excellent river fish. Further along the *avenida*, towards Leticia, a number of lively **bars and discos** cater to the party crowd. In the other direction, *Scandalo's* (Fri–Sun) at Rua Pedro Teixeira 397, and *Amazonas Clube* (Sun 8pm–5am) are the places for serious dance freaks – and prostitutes – as is *Banana Café* (Sat & Sun) on Rua Marechal Mallet.

If you're arriving from Peru or Colombia, you'll need to go to the Polícia Federal on Avenida da Amizade (Mon–Fri 8am–6pm; ⓣ97/3412-2180) for your **passport entry stamp** and visitor card; from the port at Tabatinga, it's a fifteen-minute walk straight inland to the main drag. The Polícia Federal also staff an airport entry-point meeting most planes. For **money changing**, the Banco do Brasil has an ATM, and you'll get the best deal for cash or traveller's cheques at Câmbio CNM (Mon–Fri 8am–5pm, Sat 8am–noon), at Av. da Amizade 2017; for cash exchange you're often best off crossing the border into Leticia.

### Leticia

If you are staying around for a few days then **LETICIA**, an old, more established river port – a little over twenty minutes' walk away from Tabatinga and with a steady trickle of connecting Volkswagen vans (R$3) if it's really too hot – is a more interesting place. Growing rich on tourism and contraband (mostly cocaine), it has more than a touch of the Wild West about it. There's no physical border at the port or between Leticia and Tabatinga, though people getting off boats sometimes have to go through a customs check and you should carry your passport at all times.

There are endless kiosks **changing dollars** into Brazilian, Colombian and Peruvian currency, mostly on the riverfront, but also on the boundary between Tabatinga and Leticia. Leticia is also a good place to buy hammocks, and if you're looking for a little pampering there are a couple of very good hotels in town – though they're quite expensive by Peruvian and Brazilian standards. Best of the basic **hotels** are *Residencial Monserrate* (❸) and *Residencial Leticia* (❷), but much nicer are the *Colonial*, near the port square on Carrera 10 (ⓣ0057-919/27164 from Brazil; ❺), and the swish *Anaconda* (ⓣ0057/9859-27891 or 9859-27119 from Brazil; ❼), which has a pool and a bar in an attractive jungle-style hut. The cheapest place to **eat** is at the riverside market; more upmarket are the *Bucaneer* and *La Taguara*, both on Carrera 10.

For **tours** in the region, one of the best operators is Amaturs, either in the *Hotel Anaconda* or at Carrera 11, 7–84 (ⓣ&ⓕ0057/9859-27018 from Brazil, ⓔamaturs@impsat.net.co), who run everything from two-hour trips to see the *Victoria Amazonica* water lilies at Lago Yahuaracas, to day- or week-long tours to watch river dolphins and caiman and visit Witito Indian communities; they also own a jungle lodge. The Zacambu Lodge tour company, Av. Internacional 6–25 (T 0057-819/27377 from Brazil, E amazonjungletripsZ@yahoo.com, W www.amazontrip.com), also offer a variety of tour packages and run a good jungle lodge some 70km from Leticia, up the Rio Javari. Amazons Explorers, first floor, Edificio Matiz, Carrera 10, 785, can arrange trips out to Monkey Island or visits to local Indian communities.

### Into Colombia and Peru

If you want to go further into **Colombia**, you'll need to pick up a Colombian tourist card from the DAS (Departamento Administrativo de Seguridad) office, Calle 9, 9–62 (T 098/592-7189 from Brazil; daily 24hr), just a few blocks from Leticia's port. These tourist cards are also available from the consulates at Iquitos or, coming from Brazil, Manaus. Avianca operates flights from Leticia airport to the main Colombian cities, including Bogotá, several times a week. Alternatively, an extremely adventurous option would be to cut across overland along the planned road to Tarapacá, due north of Leticia, to connect with the Rio Putumayo, where canoes to Puerto Asis meet up with the Colombian road and bus system.

Heading into **Peru**, many of the boats actually leave from Tabatinga, although Peruvian authorities and passport control are in **Santa Rosa**, a military post over the river, where all Peru-bound boats have to stop for passport and customs control. The Peruvian consulate is on the main street in Leticia (Mon–Fri 9am–3pm). Powerboats (*lanchas*) to Iquitos are run by Expresso Turístico Loreto, on Rua Marechal Mallet in Tabatinga, in one of the last shacks on the left as you walk down towards the river. Otherwise, slower boats can be found at the port in both Leticia and Tabatinga.

## Up the Rio Negro

The **Rio Negro** flows into Manaus from northwestern Amazonas, one of the least explored regions of South America. There's virtually nothing in the way of tourist facilities in this direction, but it's possible to make your way up the Rio Negro by boat from Manaus to Barcelos, from Barcelos to São Gabriel, and from there on to the virtually uncharted borders with Colombia and Venezuela. Alternatively, there are reasonably fast boats from Manaus every Friday, run by Asabranca, which call in at Barcelos (two days; R$100–200) on their way to São Gabriel (about five days up, three downriver; R$150–220). There are also daily **flights** to São Gabriel from Manaus, stopping off en route on alternate days at either Barcelos or Tefé on the Rio Solimões. To leave Brazil via these routes requires expedition-level planning and can take up to several weeks or longer, but it's an exciting trip nonetheless.

The first part of the journey, from Manaus to **Novo Aírão**, towards the middle of the Anavilhanas archipelago, is usually reached in a day; but beyond here ice and most luxury items, including foodstuffs, are pretty well impossible to find. The best part of another day or two brings you to **Moura,** a smaller river-port town with few facilities. Half a day from here the Rio Negro meets the Rio Branco and just beyond is another small town, **Carvoeiro**.

A more important settlement, **BARCELOS**, is as much as another day's boat journey up the Rio Negro from Carvoeiro. As well as the faster Asabranca boat from Manaus to Barcelos, there are ordinary boats at least twice a week (R$110), taking around sixty to eighty hours; the *Irmãos Feraes* is particularly recommended, with good, fresh river food aboard. Other boats leave fairly frequently but with no predictable regularity from the docks behind the Mercado Municipal in Manaus; look for the destination signs. Alternatively, you can hire a river taxi from the floating port to help you find a boat bound for Barcelos since they also moor to the west of the main port. Fix a price with the taxi first; it should cost no more than R$15–20. In Barcelos, the Nara family offer **accommodation** and good food to visitors who are going on their **jungle tours**. Run by Tatunca Nara, a local native, the tours take you deep into the forest where there's a better chance of spotting wildlife than there is closer to Manaus. Contact Tatunca's wife, who speaks English, in advance: Dr Anita Nara, c/o Unidade Mista, Barcelos, Amazonas 69700 (Ⓣ92/3721-1165).

At least two days further upriver, the town of **SÃO GABRIEL DA CACHOEIRA** is the next settlement of any size. Besides the Asabranca service, boats from Barcelos leave at irregular intervals, but generally several times a week; expect to pay between R$60 and R$100. It's a beautiful place where the jungle is punctuated by volcanic cones, one with a Christ figure standing high on its flank. Superb views can be had across the valley from the slopes around the town, and there's a good **pensão** and several **restaurants** here as well.

A little further upriver you reach the **Rio Negro Forest Reserve**, where local guides will take you camping from around R$50–70 a day. At present this park zone – a massive triangle between the headwaters of the Rio Negro and its important tributary the Rio Uaupés, both of which rise in Colombia – is crawling with military personnel. It's a sensitive zone, partly because of fears of narcotics smuggling, but also because it forms part of the national frontier; Venezuela, Brazil and Colombia meet here, and the Rio Negro itself serves as the border between Venezuela and Colombia for some way. There are also plans to put a highway through the park – the projected BR-210 or Perimetral Norte – which is destined to run from Macapá on the Atlantic coast to São Gabriel, passing south of Boa Vista on the way. From São Gabriel it should eventually make its way across the Amazon via Tabatinga to Cruzeiro do Sul, where it would link up with the westerly point of the Transamazônica, making it feasible to do an enormous circle by road around the Brazilian Amazon. Exactly when this will happen is anybody's guess (to date only 650km of road near Boa Vista has been built), and some of the regions that have been proposed for the road are incredibly remote.

You may also be able to get a guide to take you into the **Parque Nacional do Pico da Neblina**. The Pico da Neblina itself, Brazil's highest peak at 3014m, is on the far side of the park, hard against the Venezuelan border. You will need permission from IBAMA just for entering the protected area.

To proceed **beyond São Gabriel** by river is more difficult, particularly in the dry season from May to October. The river divides a few hours past São Gabriel. To the right, heading more or less north, the Rio Negro continues (another day by boat) to the community of Cucui on the Venezuelan border – there's also a very rough road from São Gabriel. It is possible to travel on from here **into Venezuela** and the Orinoco river system, through the territory of Yanomami Indians, but this involves a major expedition requiring boats, guides and considerable expense; cost aside, it is also potentially dangerous, and you should get a thorough update on the local situation before attempting this route (FUNAI and IBAMA in Manaus are the obvious points of reference, as well as jungle tour operators). In recent years the region has become the focus for the *garimpeiros*, who were effectively pushed out of the Yanomami territory in Roraima during the early 1990s and so moved further west into this region, which is clearly one of the last Amazonian frontiers.

The left fork in the river is the **Rio Uaupés**, where the **Araripirá waterfalls** lie a day or two upstream, just before the border settlement of Iaurete. The Uaupés continues (another day's journey) along the border to the Colombian town of Mitu. Again, this is a potentially hazardous area, home to Maku Indians and, more worryingly, to coca-growing areas and members of the Colombian underworld.

# Roraima

In the far north of Brazil, the **state of Roraima**, butting against Guiana and Venezuela, created in 1991, came to world notice in 1998 when devastating forest fires wreaked havoc on the area. It's an active frontier zone and is notable mainly for the mountains and rock formations with high table-top plateaux to the north of the region. These mountains continue into Venezuela and Guyana where they were made famous by Sir Arthur Conan Doyle's book *The Lost World*. Most of Roraima state, however, is relatively flat grassland.

## Some history

When discovered in the mid-eighteenth century, Roraima's grasslands were considered ideal cattle country. The current national borders weren't settled until the early part of the twentieth century. During the early 1990s, a massive gold rush generated an influx of 50,000 *garimpeiros*, mainly in the northwest, against the Venezuelan border in the territory of the **Yanomami Indians**, Amazonian tribal peoples living on both sides of the border.

In 1989 the plight of the Yanomami, whose lands were being invaded by prospectors, brought about an international outcry that forced the Brazilian government to announce they would evacuate all settlers from Yanomami lands. But the project was abandoned almost as soon as it began; protection of the region's valuable mineral reserves was deemed to necessitate the strengthening of the country's borders and the settlement of the area. Following the successful demarcation of Yanomami lands in 1992, and the territory's official recognition by the Federal State, things have improved, and there are now fewer *garimpeiros* prospecting in Yanomami forests.

## Up the Rio Branco

It's relatively easy to get from **Manaus to Boa Vista**, the capital of Roraima, by tarmacked road, usually taking twelve hours by **bus** (R$50). It is also possible to take a **boat** all the way from Manaus up the Rio Negro and Rio Branco as far as the waterfalls of **Caracaraí**, from where you can join the bus to Boa Vista (some boats also go from Caracaraí to Boa Vista, but they're few and far between). It isn't an easy trip and it has been known to take over two weeks, with lots of stopping and starting and depending on local river people for hospitality and food. If you can get a boat that is going direct, all the better. Expect to pay around R$200 for the trip, more if you're boat hopping. It's sometimes easier to travel first to Barcelos from where there are occasional boats bound up the Rio Branco, but it's all very much hit-and-miss once you're on the rivers.

Those who do make it up the Rio Branco are generally rewarded for their steadfastness by the sight of river dolphins, alligators and plenty of birdlife. At Caracaraí there are very few tourist facilities, but there are two very basic **hotels**, the *Hotel Márcia*, Rua Dr Zanny (Ⓣ95/232-1208; ①), and, marginally better, *Hotel Maroca*, Av. Pres. Kennedy 1140 (Ⓣ95/232-1292; ②).

## Boa Vista

**BOA VISTA** is a fast-growing city of 200,000 people, an unrelentingly hot, modern and concrete monument to its Brazilian planners who laid it out on a grand but charmless scale; traffic islands divide broad tree-lined boulevards and a vast Praça do Centro Cívico, swirling with traffic, from which streets radiate just unevenly enough to confuse the otherwise perpendicular grid. Clearly this is meant to be a fitting capital for the development of Roraima – and there are large stores full of ranching and mining equipment that reflect that growth. Busy as it is, though, Boa Vista has far to go to fulfil its ambitious designs. The huge streets seem half empty, reflecting the waning of the gold boom after the initial rush in the late 1980s and early 1990s, and many of the old hotels and gold-trading posts have closed down, or have turned into travel agencies, small-time banks and restaurants. The new layout obliterated many of the town's older buildings, which means there's little of interest to see in the city itself. Most visitors to Boa Vista are on business or travellers passing through on the overland route from Venezuela to Manaus.

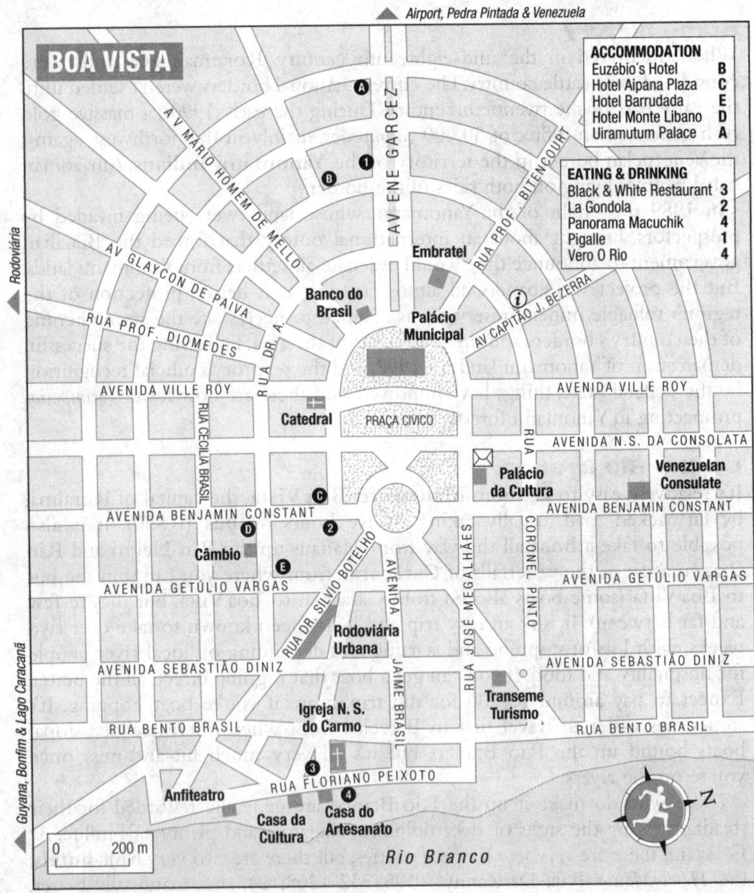

## Arrival and information

Arrival in Boa Vista (over 800km from Manaus) can be awkward because, thanks to the gold rush, international interest in the plight of the Yanomami Indians and the fact the area is increasingly used by cocaine smugglers, there are lots of military personnel about who are very suspicious of foreigners; you're likely to have your luggage taken apart and to be questioned about your motives. The best bet is probably to play the dumb tourist, and say you're heading for Venezuela or Manaus.

The city's large and modern **rodoviária** (Ⓣ95/3623-2233) is on the edge of the city, surrounded by timber yards and agricultural supply stores; it houses several stores, a *lanchonete* and a local **tourist office** (Mon–Sat 10am–5pm; Ⓣ95/3623-1238). **Taxis**, which are relatively expensive here, line up outside the station; on the main road beyond them (from the same side as the terminal) you can catch a **local bus** towards the centre. This takes something of a detour past outlying areas before heading back to near the *rodoviária*, where it turns down past the prison and heads along the broad Avenida Benjamin Constant towards the central *praça*. Buses for the *rodoviária* from town, which bear the "Joquie Clube" sign on the route card, can be caught either at the urban bus terminal (the Rodoviária Urbana) on Rua Dr Silvio Botelho, or along the Avenida Ville Roy. Coming from the **airport** (Ⓣ95/3623-0404) – where there's another tourist information office (Mon–Sat 8am–6pm, Sun 9am–1pm) – you'll have to take a taxi (R$30) for the three-kilometre ride into town.

The main tourist information spot is at the Roraima Tourism Office, Rua Coronel Pinto 241 (Mon–Fri 7.30am–1.30pm & 3.30–5.30pm; Ⓣ95/3623-1230). Further information and regional tours can be organized through Toca Turismo, Rua Dom Pedro 82 (Ⓣ95/3623-8175).

## Accommodation

Budget **accommodation** in Boa Vista, mainly along Avenida Benjamin Constant, is pretty dire; most hotels were originally designed to meet the needs of the now-ailing *garimpeiro* market, and few of them are accustomed to tourists. There are a couple of good places close to the *rodoviária*, though, while in the centre of town you'll find a handful of upmarket places, aimed at businessmen, with their own swimming pools and restaurants.

**Euzébio's Hotel** Rua Cecilia Brasil 1107 Ⓣ95/3623-0300. The most popular of the town's upmarket hotels, and often full, but not particularly central. It has a swimming pool and an expensive restaurant, yet much of its accommodation is in small, surprisingly dingy units. Make sure you get a room worth the money you're paying. ④

**Hotel Aipana Plaza** Praça do Centro Cívico 53 Ⓣ95/3224-4800, Ⓦwww.aipanaplaza.com.br. The best hotel in Boa Vista, with a pool, bar and a good restaurant – but compared to the hotels in a similar range it's overpriced. ④

**Hotel Barrudada** Rua Araújo Filho 228 Ⓣ95/2121-1700. This spot was once occupied by a charming private house of a hotel, but sadly was knocked down and replaced by a modern six-storey edifice. The staff remain helpful, however, and the rooms are still good value. ③–④

**Hotel Monte Libano** Av. Benjamin Constant 319 Ⓣ95/3224-7232. Probably has the edge over other budget hotels in the centre, as its staff are friendlier and the rooms are in slightly better condition. ①

**Hotel Três Nações** Av. Ville Roy 1885 Ⓣ95/3224-3439. Virtually opposite the *rodoviária*, this place is very clean, with pleasant rooms around an open courtyard. Because there aren't that many buses passing through, it's not as noisy as other hotels near the bus station. ②

**Itamaraty Palace** Av. N.S. da Consolata 3447 Ⓣ95/3224-9757, Ⓕ623-0977, Ⓦwww.hotelitamaraty.com.br. One of the best-value options among the mid-range hotels, this place offers a swimming pool, relatively clean and comfortable rooms, a bar, restaurant and a/c. The downside is it's located a kilometre or two from the centre. ③

**Pousada Beija Flor** Av. Nossa Senhora da Consolata Ⓣ95/3224-8241, Ⓕ224-6536. A gem of a place run by a Brazilian–Belgian couple who are tuned in to backpackers' requirements. The accommodation is basic but clean, and Néa and Jean offer a range of reasonably priced tours around Roraima, plus a wealth of information. From the *rodoviária*, walk six blocks down Av. Ville Roy, turn right at the lights and then left onto Av. Consolata; the *pousada* is two blocks further down. ❶

**Uiramutam Palace** Av. Cap. Ene Garcez 427 ⓣ95/3624-4700, ⓦwww.uiramutam.com.br. Located a few blocks from the Palácio do Governo, this place is good value with nice rooms, a pool, a/c and friendly service, though the restaurant is nothing special. ❷–❹

## The City

As capital city of one of Brazil's newest states, Boa Vista makes great efforts to establish its identity. Opposite the biggest landmark in town, the huge cylindrical concrete tube pointing towards the skies from the roof of the Embratel telephone offices on the Avenida Cap. Ene Garcez, there's a semicircular **amphitheatre** with three statues: one of a *garimpeiro* holding a shovel and a gold-panning bowl; one of a *fazendeiro* wielding a lasso; and, the central one, an Indian with a bow and arrow. Just down the road, in the centre of the Praça do Centro Cívico, there's the better-known **Monument to the Garimpeiro**, which clearly speaks more to local businessmen than it does to environmentally-minded foreign visitors.

On the south side of the *praça*, the modest-sized **Catedral** has an interesting curvaceous, airy design, with a ceiling reminiscent of the hull of a huge wooden boat. On the other side of the square is the **Palácio da Cultura** (Mon–Fri 8am–7pm, Sat 8am–1pm), with its well-stocked public library and a very smart auditorium that occasionally holds theatre and music performances. Down in the old waterfront district, connected to the *praça* by the main shopping street, Avenida Jaime Brasil, you'll find a cluster of sights, including the small Portuguese-style **Igreja Nossa Senhora do Carmo**, an open-air *anfiteatro* now used as a music venue, and the **Casa da Cultura** gallery-space – an exact replica of the city's first Prefeitura that was destroyed as part of the zealous modernization of the 1960s. Facing it is the imposing concrete **Monument to the Pioneers of Roraima**. The huge bust of a Yanomami chief dominates the sculpture, his shoulder somewhat ambiguously being trampled over by a pioneer on horseback.

The **Casa do Artesanato**, on the riverbank at Rua Floriano Peixoto 192 (Mon–Sat 8am–6pm; ⓣ95/3623-1615), is also worth a visit; its selection of handicrafts is not wide but there's some interesting stuff and it's all very cheap. There are great views from the *Restaurante Panorama Macuchik* (see below) and the riverbank near the Casa do Artesanato out across the Rio Branco, towards the large-span, modern concrete bridge and the forest stretching beyond.

## Eating and drinking

*Lanchonetes* are everywhere in Boa Vista, though more substantial **restaurants** are surprisingly scarce as well as expensive. In the centre, the *Restaurante La Gondola*, on the corner of Avenida Benjamin Constant and the Praça do Centro Cívico, is fine for *comida por kilo* and very popular. At night, *Euzébio's Hotel* restaurant serves good meals and, virtually next door, the lively *Pigalle* has good pizzas and fish, but neither place is exactly on the cheap side; both also function as bars. More reasonable, and with excellent views, are a growing number of restaurants along the riverfront. The *Restaurante Panorama Macuchik*, close to the Casa do Artesanato at Rua Floriano Peixoto 116 (ⓣ95/3623-1346), is highly recommended, as is the fish restaurant *Ver o Rio* (ⓣ95/3624-1683; closed Mon lunchtime), two buildings down on the same road. For more evening atmosphere, but without the river view, try the *Black and White Restaurant*, one road back on Rua Barreto Leite 11 (closed Mon; ⓣ95/3224-5372).

As for **bars and clubs**, *Clube ABB* near the airport is the most popular nightspot (Fri & Sat only); also well worth trying is the *Zanzibar*, corner of Avenida Sebastião Diniz and Rua Coronel Pinto, which has a good atmosphere and hosts local bands on Friday and Saturday from 9pm onwards (℡95/3224-0093). Straightforward drinking bars are surprisingly sparse, the best being *Meu Cantinho* opposite the *Panorama* and with equally good views (daily until midnight).

## Listings

**Airlines** Gol (@www.voegol.com.br) and Tam (@www.tam.com.br) are the main airlines serving Manaus, Santarém, Belém and southern Brazilian cities. To and from Manaus, planes can be solidly booked for days if not weeks ahead, especially at holiday times, though you might get lucky with the waiting list.

**Air taxis** Meta (℡95/3224-7677) is based at the airport.

**Banks and exchange** The Banco do Brasil, on the *praça* near the Palácio Municipal has an ATM, as does Bradesco at the corner of Getúlio Vargas and Brasil; there are others at the airport and *rodoviária*.

**Car rental** Localiza ℡95/3224-3933; Unidas ℡95/3224-4080.

**Post office** Praça do Centro Cívico (Mon–Fri 9am–5pm).

**Taxis** ℡95/3224-4223 or 3224-4823.

# Around Boa Vista

Situated as it is on the northern edge of the Amazon forest, where it meets the savanna of Roraima, the region around Boa Vista boasts three different forms of ecosystem: tropical rainforest, grassland savanna plains and the "Lost World"–style tepius mountain, flat plateau-like rock rising out of the savanna. Still fairly undeveloped in terms of its tourism infrastructure, the area is exceptionally beautiful, with a wealth of river beaches, and has a very pleasant climate (hot with cooling breezes). As the options for ecotourism are developed, more opportunities will no doubt emerge for visitors to explore Roraima in some depth.

Your first port of call in Boa Vista should be the tourist office, which has details of new destinations, circuits and accommodation options in the state. At present, **independent travel** in the region can be problematic, with only sketchy bus services, so you might find it easier simply to hire a car (see "Listings", above). **Organized tours**, usually dependent on enough tourists filling spaces, are operated by Baba's Home (℡95/3623-7304), Iguana Tours (℡95/3224-6576), Tocatur (℡95/3623-2597), and ECOTUR, Rua Barreto Leite 46 (℡95/3224-6010), while the agency inside *Euzébio's Hotel* deals in six-day packages for around R$1100. Much cheaper, and virtually the only outfit in town able to arrange tours for small groups, is *Pousada Beija Flor*, who combine enthusiasm with a wealth of knowledge about the state.

Places to head for include: the famous painted rock, **Pedra Pintada**, en route to Santa Elena and Venezuela; the ruined eighteenth-century **Forte São Joaquim**, two hours from Boa Vista by boat; the ecological island reserve of **Ilha do Maracá**, located on the fairly remote Rio Uraricoera; and the very pleasant **Lake Caracaranã** with its fine beaches fringed by shady cashew trees, 180km from Boa Vista in Normandia. This is currently almost the only place in the state outside Boa Vista that has adequate facilities for tourists, with fifteen chalets and ten apartments for hire, the four-bed chalets a bargain at R$150; ℡95/3262-1254 or contact Transeme Turismo in Boa Vista, Av. Sebastião Diniz 234 (℡95/3224-9409 or 3224-6271). Also of note are the **Igarape Agua Boa**, where there are islands, fine sandy beaches (R$30–40; 2–3hr from Boa Vista), and the **Serra Grande**, where you'll find more islands and beaches plus trails in the forest to the waterfall of the same name (1hr from Boa Vista).

## Into Venezuela and Guyana

It's now relatively straightforward to go from Boa Vista to Santa Elena in **Venezuela**, and beyond to Ciudad Guyana and Ciudad Bolívar, or even right on to Puerto La Cruz on the north coast if you're that anxious to escape the interior; a daily União Cascavel bus leaves Boa Vista at 7am. Santa Elena is also served by six daily Eucatur buses (3hr, plus 2hr for border formalities). The road, the BR-174, is now fully tarmacked, which means the União Cascavel bus arrives at the border in time for lunch; it stops at a very expensive restaurant, though, so bring your own lunch if you're running short on money. The journey from Boa Vista, across a vast flat savanna that is dusty in the dry season and boggy in the wet, offers very little in the way of scenery, but there is a great deal of wildlife: white egrets, storks and all sorts of waders in the rainy season, flycatchers, hawks, and the occasional large animal, such as the giant anteater. As the border approaches, the land begins to rise slightly; to the northeast, at the point where Brazil, Guyana and Venezuela meet, lies **Monte Roraima**, the fourth-highest peak in Brazil at 2875m.

Allow a couple of hours to cross the border itself (the bus waits while everyone has passports stamped and luggage checked); **SANTA ELENA DE UAIRÉN** is barely twenty minutes further. It's not necessary to spend the night here, as the União Cascavel bus continues further up into Venezuela, but if you fancy a break Santa Elena is a tiny place with the real feel of a border town in its low, corrugated-roofed houses and dusty streets. You can see the whole place in an hour's walk, but the *Hotel Frontera* also runs tours to local waterfalls and native communities. If you're staying overnight, good **hotels** include the *Frontera* (❸), the simple *Hotel Marcia* (❷), and the *Hotel Lucas* (❹), which has a casino. There's good **food** at the *Restaurante Itália* (the spaghetti is the cheapest thing to eat in a relatively expensive town). **Money** is hard to change here; various traders will accept cash US dollars or Brazilian currency – try the *Hotel Frontera*. **Leaving**, there's a 5am bus to Ciudad Bolívar (12hr), as well as the União Cascavel bus late at night, and a daily flight (2hr). If you're heading for Brazil, there are at least seven buses a day. Don't forget to get your Venezuelan exit stamp from the office next to the police station on the hill behind the bus terminal. The terminal doesn't open until 8am.

▲ Aerial view of Mount Roraima

### Visas for Venezuela and Guyana

If you're planning to enter **Venezuela** from Boa Vista and hope to get a visa in a single day, then arrive at the consulate (Av. Benjamin Constant 1675 ⓣ95/3224-2182 or 3623-9285) early. Hours are officially Mon–Fri 8.30am–1pm, but they may open later in the afternoon to give your completed visa back. You'll need to show your passport and have a photo and an onward ticket – though you may be able to get round the latter by having plenty of money and a good excuse. From the consulate they'll send you to a doctor for a cursory medical examination (R$21) and from there you go to a clinic for a free blood test, which they claim is for malaria. Having passed these you can usually go back in the afternoon, clutching the certificates, to pick up your passport and visa.

If you're heading into **Guyana**, you'll find its consulate Av. Benjamin Constant 1171 ⓣ95/9112-7071. Strict Guyanan entry regulations on the border mean there's a fair chance you may even be refused entry. All in all, if you want to go to Guyana, it's easier to fly, as the road infrastructure in Guyana is poor; there are flights from Manaus to Georgetown, but no longer any services from Boa Vista.

**Guyana** is less straightforward. It's easy enough to get to **Bonfim** on the border, just over 100km away (two daily buses with Eucatur), though the road is pretty grim, but it's much less easy to continue beyond there.

# Rondônia and Porto Velho

A large, partially deforested region in the southwest corner of the Brazilian Amazon, the **state of Rondônia** (named after the famous explorer, Indian "pacifier" and telegraph-network pioneer Marechal Cândido Rondon) has a reputation for unbridled colonization and very rapid "development". The state was only created in 1981, having evolved from an unknown and almost entirely unsettled zone (then the Territory of Guaporé) over the previous thirty years. The first phase of its environmental destruction began in the 1980s when roads and tracks, radiating like fine bones from the spinal highway BR-364, began to dissect almost the entire state, bringing in their wake hundreds of thousands of settlers and many large companies who have moved in to gobble up the rainforest. Poor landless groups are a common sight – some the surviving representatives of once-proud Indian tribes – living under plastic sheets at the side of the road.

The state is not exactly one of Brazil's major tourist attractions, but it is an interesting area in its own right, and offers a few stopping-off places between more obvious destinations. **Porto Velho**, the main city of the region, is an important rainforest market-town and pit-stop between Cuiabá and the frontier state of Acre. Rondônia also offers border crossings to Bolivia, river trips to Manaus and access to overland routes into Peru.

Given that it is such a recently settled region, the system of road **transport** is surprisingly good, and combines well with the major rivers – Madeira, Mamoré and Guaporé. The main focus of human movement these days is the BR-364, which cuts the state more or less in half and, from east to west, connects a handful of rapidly growing nodal towns: Vilhena, Pimenta Bueno, Ji-Paraná, Ouro Preto, Jaru, Ariquemes and Jamari. Ji-Paraná is the largest, having grown from a tiny roadside trading settlement to a significant sky-scraping town of 108,000 people in the last forty-odd years.

Manaus and Porto Velho are well connected by a four-day boat journey, with usually at least three leaving weekly in either direction.

## Porto Velho

The capital of Rondônia state, **PORTO VELHO** overlooks the Amazon's longest tributary, the mighty Rio Madeira. In the 1980s, settlers arrived in enormous numbers in search of land, jobs and, more specifically, the mineral wealth of the area: gold and casserite (a form of tin). As in most regions, the gold boom has bottomed out and the empty gold-buying stores are signs of the rapid decline. Seen from a distance across the river, Porto Velho looks rather more impressive than it does at close quarters, though even more than Ji-Paraná, its newest buildings are reaching for the sky and the younger generation ensures that their weekend partying helps bring a modern Brazilian vibe through music to the city. The two bell-towers and Moorish dome of the cathedral stand out strikingly above the rooftops, while alongside the river three phallic water-towers sit like waiting rockets beside a complex of military buildings. A little further downstream the modern port and the shiny cylindrical tanks of a petrochemical complex dominate the riverbank.

In the town itself, the main street – Avenida Sete de Setembro – boasts most of the shops and has a distinctive market atmosphere about it, with music stores blaring, traders shouting and stallholders chattering on about their predominantly cheap plastic goods. Every other lamppost seems to have a loudspeaker attached to it. The city has a more relaxed ambience down on the far side of the old railway sheds, where you'll find outdoor bars and cafés spread along the riverfront.

### Arrival and information

Porto Velho's **airport** (ⓣ69/3025-7450), Belmont, is 7km out of town and served by local buses and taxis (R$15–20). The **rodoviária** (ⓣ69/3222-2233), with daily connections to Guajará-Mirim and the Bolivian border, Cuiabá and Rio Branco, is also some way out on Avenida Kennedy; catch a local bus into town from here to Sete de Setembro. **Tourist information** is best from the Museu Estadual de Rondônia building on Avenida Sete de Setembro or the EMBRATUR office at Presidente Dutra 3004 (Mon–Fri 9am–5pm; ⓦwww.rondonia.com). Regular **boats** link Manaus and Porto Velho, and the docks are located just 1km west of the main waterfront area.

### Accommodation

There is plenty of accommodation to choose from in Porto Velho, as it's a settlement serving a large hinterland of farmers, prospectors, businessmen and a growing number of tourists.

**Central** Rua Tenreiro Aranha 2472 ⓣ69/3224-2099, ⓕ3224-5114, ⓦwww.enter-net.com.br/central. A good mid-range place with spacious and clean rooms, most with TV, a/c and fine views across the city. ❸–❹

**Cuiabano** Av. Sete de Setembro 1180 ⓣ69/3221-4084. A decent budget place with rooms set around a courtyard, only some of which come with a private bathroom. Can be quite noisy during the day as it's located on the main commercial drag. ❶

**Floresta** Rua Almirante Barroso 502 ⓣ69/3221-5669. This popular spot has a pool and a relatively quiet location, but is within easy walking distance of the town centre. ❸

**Rondon Palace** Av. Gov. Jorge Teixeira 491 ⓣ69/3224-2718, ⓕ3224-6160. Close to the airport and some way from the centre, this modern, soulless hotel has a pool, a bar and a quite good restaurant. ❹

**Samauma** Rua Dom Pedro II 1038 ⓣ69/3224-5300. A moderately sized and fairly modern hotel with a bar and restaurant and very reasonable rates. Rooms are adequate and all have a/c. ❷–❸

**Vila Rica** Rua Carlos Gomes 1616 ⓣ69/3224-3433, ⓦwww.hotelvilarica.com.br. As the tallest building in the town's centre, this hotel is unmissable. The luxury-class rooms are tastefully decorated, and there's a nice pool as well. Good value and hospitable. ❺–❻

**Yara** Av. General Osório 255 ⓣ69/3221-2127. Bustling modern hotel with basic and small but clean rooms with private baths, TV and a/c. The central location makes it convenient but noisy. ❸

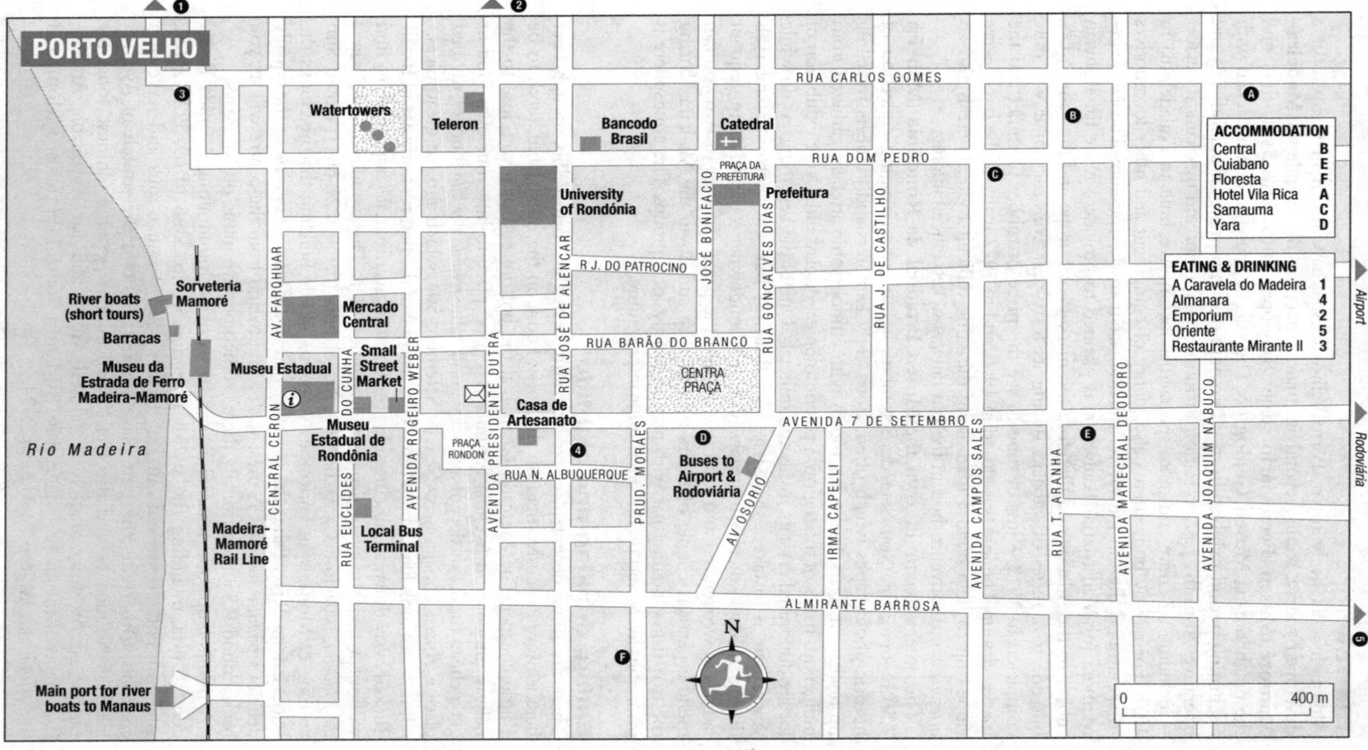
PORTO VELHO
ACCOMMODATION
Central B
Cuiabano E
Floresta F
Hotel Vila Rica A
Samauma C
Yara D
EATING & DRINKING
A Caravela do Madeira 1
Almanara 4
Emporium 2
Oriente 5
Restaurante Mirante II 3
Airport
Rodoviária
Rua Carlos Gomes
Rua Dom Pedro
R J. do Patrocino
Rua Barão do Branco
Avenida 7 de Setembro
Rua N. Albuquerque
Almirante Barrosa
Av. Farohuar
Central Ceron
Do Cunha
Rua Euclides
Avenida Rogeiro Weber
Avenida Presidente Dutra
Rua José de Alencar
José Bonifacio
Rua Goncalves Dias
Rua J. de Castilho
Prud. Moraés
Av Osorio
Irma Capelli
Avenida Campos Sales
Rua T. Aranha
Avenida Marechal Deodoro
Avenida Joaquim Nabuco
Watertowers
Teleron
Bancodo Brasil
Catedral
Praça da Prefeitura
Prefeitura
University of Rondónia
Mercado Central
Museu Estadual
Small Street Market
Museu Estadual de Rondônia
Praça Rondon
Casa de Artesanato
Centra Praça
Buses to Airport & Rodoviária
Local Bus Terminal
River boats (short tours)
Sorveteria Mamoré
Barracas
Museu da Estrada de Ferro Madeira-Mamoré
Madeira-Mamoré Rail Line
Rio Madeira
Main port for river boats to Manaus
N
0
400 m

## The Town

Although it's a lively town, Porto Velho doesn't have much in the way of a developed tourist scene beyond its main attraction, the wonderful **Madeira–Mamoré Museu Ferroviário** (daily 8am–6pm; ⓣ69/3216-5131; free) and the neighbouring **Museu Geologico**. The railway museum is jam-packed with fascinating period exhibits, from photographs of important railway officials and operatives from the past, to station furniture, equipment and mechanical devices – including an entire and quite spectacular locomotive, built in Philadelphia in 1878. For railway buffs, there's also plenty of equipment and other locomotives to see around the old railway terminal adjacent to the museum. The Madeira–Mamoré (or Mad Maria) Railway was planned to provide a route for Bolivian rubber to the Atlantic and therefore the markets of Europe and the eastern US, but due to a series of setbacks during its forty-year construction it was only completed in 1912 – just in time to see the price of rubber plummet and the market dry up. The line was closed in 1960, and in 1972 many of the tracks were ripped up to help build a road along the same difficult route. There is also an *artesanato* and souvenir shop in the old railway ticket-office building.

The other museum in town, the **Museu Estadual de Rondônia** (Mon–Fri 7.30am–6pm; free), on Sete de Setembro, has an ever-changing collection of historic photographs which often shows early explorers and pioneers travelling up uncharted rivers. It also has rooms with ethnographic artefacts gathered from indigenous tribes of the region, a paleontological display and a large exhibition of locally discovered crystals, fossils and minerals. One of the best things to do while you're here is to take a short trip on a **floating bar**. They set out at intervals during the day – there's almost always a 5pm sundowner tour and more frequent sailings at weekends – and for a few *reís* and the price of a beer or two you can spend a pleasant couple of hours travelling up and down the Madeira, sharing the two-storey floating bar with predominantly local groups. The atmosphere is invariably lively, and there's often impromptu music.

## Eating, drinking and nightlife

There are some decent places to **eat and drink** in Porto Velho, though beer here is more expensive than on the coast. Food, on the other hand, tends to be a little cheaper. The Mercado Central, at the bottom end of town close to the railway museum on Avendia Farqhua, is a good place to buy your own food or get a cheap meal. For decent and very good value *comida por kilo* lunches, the best place is *Asados & Salados*, Av. Sete de Setembro 504, which also has great juices.

It may not look like it, but Porto Velho has one of the best **restaurants** in Brazil. Tucked away down an obscure side-street on the riverfront, it's impossible to find without a taxi but every driver knows where it is. The wonderful *A Caravela do Madeira*, Rua José Camacho 104, Arigolândia (ⓣ69/3221-6641; closed Sun evening & Mon), is an enormous wooden, hillside building that overlooks the Rio Madeira. River fish is the speciality here; try *costeleta de surubim* or the equally delicious *pirarucu na brasa*. A meal with a taxi to and from the centre will set you back around R$60; additionally, there's sometimes live music on Saturdays.

A number of good restaurants and bars can be found along Avenida Presidente Dutra, including the stylish *Emporium* at no. 3366 (ⓣ69/3221-2665); tables are both inside and out and it plays good Brazilian rock and serves fun cocktails. Otherwise, the best place for restaurants is the stretch of Avenida Joaquim Nabuco behind the *Hotel Vila Rica*. For genuine Chinese food, try *Oriente*, at Av. Amazonas 1280 (closed Mon), and for reasonable Arabic–Brazilian cuisine there's the *Habibe*, Av. Lauro Sodré 1190 (closed Mon), and the *Almanara*, Av. José de Alencar 2624.

Great ice cream is available at the *Sorveteria Mamoré*, overlooking the port side of the railway sheds, and there are reasonable drinks, snacks and fish meals at the very popular *barracas* that line the riverfront promenade. Close to the military complex on the hill above the town, the *Restaurante Mirante II* has a good view over the river and often has live music on Friday evenings. As the night progresses, the *Wau Wau* **bar**, in the *Hotel Vila Rica*, generally offers good entertainment, and there are also a few **nightclubs**, notably *Amazon House* at Avenida Pinheiro Machado 753 (☎69/3223-9561); *Original*, on Rua Guanabara, which plays a range of music including *forró*, samba and *pagode*; and *Bungalo*, on the same road but closer to the centre.

## Listings

**Airlines** Ocean Air, Rico, Tavaj and TAM all have offices at the airport, though tickets can be more easily bought from travel agencies in town.
**Banks and exchange** ATM at HSBC, Av. Jorge Teixeira 1350; *câmbio* upstairs at Banco do Brasil, at the corner of José de Alencar and Dom Pedro II. Cash exchanged at the Ourominas (gold-buying) office, Rua José de Alencar; and also at the *Floresta* and the *Vila Rica*. Most banks only open between 8am and 2pm in the hottest months, between December and March.
**Boats** The main commercial port is easily located about 1km upstream from the rail yards; you'll have to go there to check out all the possibilities. For Manaus there are frequent boats offering first- and second-class passages for the four-day trip. The boats at the port generally display their destinations; otherwise it's a matter of asking the crew of each vessel and making a deal with the captain whose itinerary suits you best. Conasa (☎69/3229-4946) and Silnave (☎69/3229-3456) are among the companies operating boats up- and downriver from here. Boats for Santo Antônio (45min) leave from the riverfront close to the Praça da Madeira-Mamore and railway museum.
**Car hire** Localiza ☎69/3224-6530; Ximenes at Av. Carlos Gomes 1055, Centro ☎69/3224-5766; and Avis ☎69/3225-1011.
**Post office** The main post office is in Av. Presidente Dutra, just off Sete de Setembro (Mon–Fri 9am–5pm).
**Shopping** The well-stocked Casa do Artesanato, Av. Sete de Setembro 488, is a good place for *artesanato*; but there's also the excellent Casa da Artes close to the vegetable market and the Casa do Artesanato based in the railway museum.
**Taxi** Cooptaxi ☎69/3225-1414.

## Around Porto Velho

Despite its location on a great river and deep in the Amazon basin, it is surprisingly difficult to experience the forest around Porto Velho, as certain infrastructure – such as lodges, guides and operators – is lacking. Rondônia is home to the Parque Nacional Pacaás Novos, featuring mountains that are rarely visited but remain the source of nearly all of the state's important rivers, which fan out from it in every direction. You'll need IBAMA permission (Av. Jorge Teixeira 3559 ☎69/3223-2023) to enter the park, and the terrain is very hard going.

Going north, the BR-319 en route to Manaus is currently paved for only the first 20km and passable only with a four-wheel-drive vehicle. There are plans to pave another 260km over the next few years, and, while such an improvement may open up new areas to ecotourism in the future, for now there are only a couple of places where you can get close to the forest around Porto Velho. Undoubtedly the finest spot is *Salsalito Jungle Park*, about a forty-minute drive from Porto Velho and located at Km 43 of the BR-364 towards Ariquemes (☎69/3230-1307, Ⓦwww.junglepark.com.br; ③–④). It has several nice detached bungalows for rent and a floating restaurant in a beautiful part of the river; activities include horseriding, boat safaris, fishing trips, dolphin spotting and hikes along short forest and river-edge trails. The river is spectacularly beautiful and just upstream you'll discover the big dam serving the hydroelectric plant that feeds off the massive artificial Lago da Usina, which flooded over

74,000 hectares some twenty years ago. Nearby, at Km 673 (a 35min drive from Porto Velho), the *Tres Capelas Eco Resort* (Ⓣ69/3259-1010, Ⓔtrescapelas@uol.com.br; ④–⑤) offers bungalow accommodation, a restaurant, a bar and a swimming pool in a pleasant but not very distinctive setting. The *Pousada Rancho Grande*, c/o Haarald Schmitz, Fazenda Rancho Grande, Lote 23, Linha C20, Cacaulândia (Ⓣ69/3535-4301; ④), is a unique lodge run by a German family in the middle of rainforest and plantations. The *fazenda*, which requires advance reservations for stays, is located about 260km south of Porto Velho, about 28km off the BR-364, and is best approached from Ariquemes (if you are coming from Cuibá). They offer birdwatching, horseriding, jungle walks and a visit to the biggest tin mine in the world at Bom Futuro.



## West from Porto Velho

The backbone of modern Rondônia, the **BR-364** highway links the state more or less from north to south, connecting Porto Velho with Cuiabá, Brasília and the wealthy south-coast markets. The state's main towns are strung out along the BR-364, almost all of them – including Porto Velho itself, Ji-Paraná and Vilhena at the border with Mato Grosso – marking the points where the road crosses major waterways. There's little to stop for anywhere in this direction and you're better off heading straight through to Cuiabá.

Travelling **west from Porto Velho** is a very different matter and soon begins to feel like real pioneering. The further you go, the smaller and wilder the roads, rivers and towns become. The main attractions are **Rio Branco** and the border crossings into Peru, in the state of Acre, and **Guajará-Mirim**, where you can cross into Bolivia or undertake an adventurous visit to the Forte Príncipe da Beira. The BR-364 in this direction is asphalted, although heavy rains still have a habit of washing great sections of it away.

Most of the land beside the road between Porto Velho and Abunã has already been bought up by big companies, and much of the forest cleared. Meanwhile, many of the smaller *fazendas* have started actively producing beef cattle and other tropical cash crops. Water birds like the *garça real* (an amazing white royal heron) can frequently be spotted from the bus, fishing in the roadside streams and ditches, but the general picture is one of an alarming rate of destruction.

At **ABUNÃ** – some five hours out of Porto Velho – there are often long lines at the ferry that takes vehicles over the wide Rio Madeira into Acre. It's not a particularly pleasant town, caught at the end of a gold rush in which it expanded too fast for its own good, and the river itself is awash with wrecked gold-mining machinery half-sunk on large steel cylinders. Following the road towards Rio Branco, Bolivia lies across the Rio Abunã to your left, but if you want to cross the border the closest place to do so is Guajará-Mirim to the south. The road there turns off to the east of the ferry crossing at Abunã, following the Rio Mamoré via the small settlement of Taquaras.

### Guajará-Mirim and beyond: Bolivia and the Rio Guaporé

**GUAJARÁ-MIRIM** is easy enough to reach by bus from Porto Velho (6 daily; 5/6hr), and once you get there it's a surprisingly sophisticated place with several **hotels**, the best of which are the *Hotel Mini-Estrela*, Av. 15 de Novembro 460 (Ⓣ69/3541-2399; ③), the *Hotel Lima Palace*, on the same street at no. 1613 (Ⓣ69/3541-3421, Ⓕ3541-2122; ②), and the *Hotel Jamaica*, Av. Leopoldo de Matos 755 (Ⓣ69/3541-3721, Ⓕ3541-3722; ②). There are good restaurants here, too, including the *Oasis*, at Av. 15 de Novembro 460, which serves a varied menu at decent prices. There are, however, only two reasons you might come here – to get to Bolivia or to head up the Mamoré and Guaporé rivers on a trip to the Forte Príncipe da Beira.

The valley of the **Rio Guaporé**, around 800km in length, is an obvious destination for an adventurous break from routine town-to-town travelling. Endowed with relatively accessible rainforest, a slow-flowing river and crystal-clear creeks, it is a favourite fishing region with townspeople from Porto Velho. Likely catches include the huge *dourado*, the *tambaqui*, the *pirapitanga* and *tucunaré*. Heading towards the Guaporé, there are amazing rapids on the Rio Mamoré just south of Guajará-Mirim, close to the place where the Rio Pacaás Novas flows in.

The star-shaped **Forte Príncipe da Beira** makes a superb destination for a prolonged river trip in this region. Built in 1773 by pioneering colonists, the fort is situated on the edge of the Rio Mamoré in a remote location strategically marking the border with Bolivia. Originally this was an advanced border-post designed to mark out Portuguese territory from the Spanish lands across the water in the Bolivian jungle. By river, it will take at least three days to reach the fort from Porto Velho: the first day by bus to Guajará-Mirim, then two or three more by boat 150km to the fort itself. A road connects the fort to the small river-town of Costa Marques, some 25km away, where you'll find a hotel, restaurants and even a small airstrip. The road continues to Ji-Paraná for connection with the BR-364.

If all you want to do is see **Bolivia**, join a sightseeing tour by motor barge from Guajará-Mirim; ask at *Hotel Jamaica* (see opposite). These tours leave frequently, visiting the main sights and often stopping at the islands between Guajará-Mirim and Guayaramerin, on the Bolivian side. If you actually want to cross the border it's equally easy to get a boat over the Rio Mamoré to **GUAYARAMERIN**. This is something of a contrast to the Brazilian town – far more of a border outpost, with no roads, though there is a good air-taxi service to La Paz, Cochabamba and Santa Cruz with TAM and Lloyd Aéreo Boliviano. If you plan on travelling into Bolivia, get your passport stamped by the Bolivian consul in Guajará-Mirim, Av. Costa Marques 495 (Ⓣ69/3541-5876), and visit the Polícia Federal, Av. Presidente Dutra 70 (Ⓣ69/3541-2437), for an exit stamp before crossing the river. If you want to stay in Guayaramerin, try the *Hotel Plaza* (❸), four blocks from the port. Boats to Guayaramerin leave from the port end of Avenida 15 de Novembro. The tour operator Enaro, Avenida Beira Rios (Ⓣ69/3541-2242), can be a helpful source of information, especially for travel arrangements.

## Rio Branco

Crossing from Rondônia into the state of **Acre**, territory annexed from Bolivia during the rubber-boom days in the first years of the twentieth century, there's nowhere to stop before you reach the capital at **RIO BRANCO**. The state is a vast frontier forest zone, so it comes as a real surprise to find Rio Branco is one of Brazil's funkiest cities. It's a small but lively place with little of specific interest, perhaps best known as the home of the famous environmentalist and rubber-tree-tapper Chico Mendes (see box, p.446). Arriving at night (as you usually do) after an eight-hour journey through the desolation of what's left of the jungle between here and Porto Velho, the brightly coloured lights and animated streets can make you wonder if you've really arrived at all, or simply drifted off to sleep and are dreaming. By day Rio Branco doesn't have quite so much obvious charm, but it remains an interesting place.

Much of the reason for the liveliness is that Rio Branco is a federal **university town**, second only to Belém on the student research pecking-order for social and biological studies associated with the rainforest and development. Consequently the

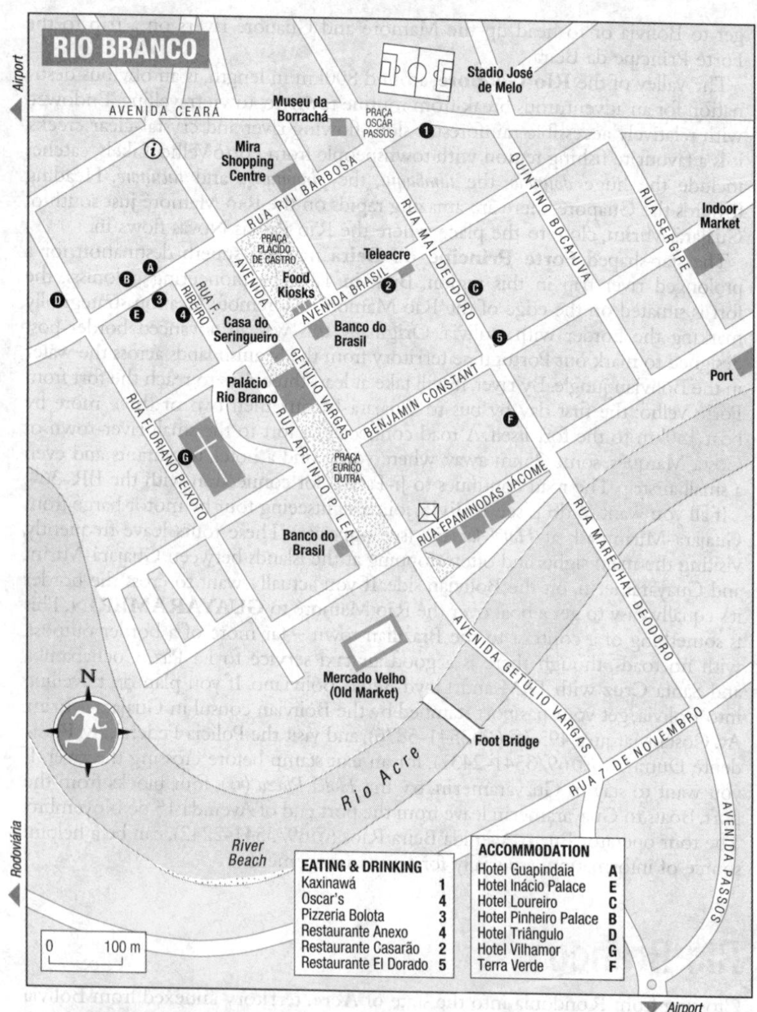




place has more than its fair share of young people – which means plenty of music and events – and of Brazilian intellectuals. On top of this, the region's burgeoning development means that Rio Branco is also a thriving and very busy market town, pivotally situated on the new road and with an active, if tiny, river port.

## Arrival and information

Rio Branco is divided in two by the **Rio Acre**, whose old Indian name was Macarinarra, or "River of Arrows", because of the arrows cut from the flowering bamboo canes found here. The commercial zone, most of the hotels and much of the nightlife are situated north of the river. In the dry season, there is a good **beach** on the curve in the river – just upstream from the bridges and on the *rodoviária* side of town.

The **rodoviária** (ⓣ68/3224-6984), 3km southwest of the river in the Cidade Nova, is just about within walking distance of the centre, or you can take a taxi; the area between the *rodoviária* and the river is considered unsafe at night. The **airport** (ⓣ68/3211-1000) is 25km northwest of town, but is well served by the green-and-white ECTA airport bus that runs more or less hourly to the centre; if you're in a hurry you'll probably want to take a taxi (R$15).

The regional **tourist office**, a kiosk below the Palácio Rio Branco on Av. Getúlio Vargas (ⓣ68/3223-3998, 3901-3029 and 0800/647-3998), in front of the main banks there, can supply maps of the town and information on hotels and travel in the region; the state web portal ⓦwww.ac.gov.br has some useful local contacts and ⓦwww.amazonlink.org is a good source of information on local social and environmental issues. If you happen to be in Rio Branco during the third week of November, don't miss the **Feira de Productos da Floresta do Acre** (Acre's Rainforest Products Fair), usually housed in the splendid SEBRAE building on Avenida Ceará (take the Conjunto Esperança bus from the central terminal and follow the signs), and accompanied by local bands.

## Accommodation

There is no shortage of **hotels** in Rio Branco, though the better ones aren't cheap. Top of the range is the *Hotel Pinheiro Palace*, Rua Rui Barbosa 450 (ⓣ68/3223-7191, ⓦwww.irmaospinheiro.com.br; ❹–❺), with swimming pool, bar and pretty comfortable rooms with all mod cons. The *Hotel Guapindaia*, Rua Rui Barbosa 193, near the corner of Avenida Getúlio Vargas (ⓣ68/3223-5747; ❹), is modern, with excellent service and TV in all rooms, and is great value. The *Hotel Inácio Palace*, on the same street at no. 469 (ⓣ68/3214-7100; ❸), is of similar standard, but the atmosphere is impersonal; guests can use the *Pinheiro*'s pool. Cheaper but still overpriced is *Hotel Triângulo*, Rua Marechal Peixoto 727 (ⓣ68/3224-4117; ❸), though some rooms overlook the river. The *Hotel Vilhamor*, at Rua Floriano Peixoto 394 (ⓣ68/223-2399; ❸), is central, modern and clean, and some rooms have views across the river valley. The *Hotel Loureiro*, Rua Marechal Deodoro 196 (ⓣ68/224-3110; ❸), also has good rooms, while just down the same road at no. 221, the much plusher *Terra Verde* (ⓣ68/3213-6000, ⓦwww.terraverdehotel.com.br; ❺) has all mod cons and decent internet access. Very close to the *rodoviária*, the *Hotel Uirapuru* (❶) is clean, with fans in most rooms and its own pool table. There is also the decent *Albergue de Juventude* at Fronteira Verde, Travessa Natanael de Albuquerque (ⓣ68/3225-7128; ❶–❷).

## The City

The real attraction of Rio Branco lies in the life of the bars, restaurants, streets and markets. The main square – the large **Praça Plácido de Castro** – is a lively and popular social-centre for the town. The newly renovated port area and **old market** (Mercado Velho) is replete with bars and cafés where music is played and the local middle-classes hang out in the evenings by the river and smart new footbridge which crosses it. Every Sunday between 5 and 10pm, the **Feira de Artesanato** takes place in the SEBRAE building on Avenida Ceará. You can find a good selection of crafts produced from sustainable rainforest products here, including jewellery made from *tagua*, an attractive palm-nut that is dense and white like ivory. There are no regular organized **boat trips** from the port, but it's often possible to travel on the rivers with traders and in *fazendeiros*' riverboats.

Other than these experiences, there's not a great deal to see in Rio Branco. Of the two main tourist attractions, the more interesting is the **Museu da Borrachá**, Av. Ceará 1177 (Tues–Fri 8am–6pm, Sat & Sun 4-7pm; free), a collection focusing

## Acre and the rubber conflict

The relaxed air of Rio Branco masks many tensions, above all to do with population movement – people are still arriving here from the east – and the conflicting claims of small rubber-tappers and multinational companies on the jungle. The tappers, who have lived here for a long time and who know how to manage the forests in a sustainable way, see the multinationals as newcomers who aim to turn the trees into pasture for beef cattle and short-term profit, destroying not only the forest but also many local livelihoods. When hired gunmen working for the cattle ranchers shot dead **Chico Mendes**, the leader of the rubber-tappers' union, in 1988, the plight of the forest peoples of Acre came to the world's attention. Today, the political situation in Acre remains uneasy, with the second- and third-generation tappers and gatherers joining forces with the native population in resisting the enormous economic and armed might of the advancing cattle-based companies.



on archeological finds, ethnographic items such as feather crafts and basketry, and a range of exhibits dealing with the rubber boom. More relevant to recent history, perhaps, though closed at the time of writing for renovations, is the **Casa do Seringueiro**, Av. Brasil 216 (Tues–Fri 8am–1pm & 2–5pm, Sun 4–7pm), near the corner with Avenida Getúlio Vargas, which houses displays about Chico Mendes and the life and times of rubber tappers in general. Nearby, the **Palácio Rio Branco** is open to visitors (Mon–Sat 9am–4pm; R$3) and is a grand example of both Art Deco and the pioneering spirit of the region.

Acre, and in particular Rio Branco, is a strong centre for some of Brazil's fastest-growing **religious cults**. A number of similar cult groups are based in the region, connected essentially by the fact that they use forest "power plants" – like the hallucinogenic vine *banisteriopsis* – to induce visionary states. These cults are deeply involved in a kind of green nature-worship that relates easily to the concept of sustainable forest management. If you want to visit a "Santo Daime" (a church blending Amazon Indian and Catholic religions and whose services involve collective consumption of the hallucinogenic plant *ayahuasca*) village, contact the travel agent Acretur (see "Listings", opposite) for details. The groups operate in a vaguely underground way, keeping their sanctuaries secret to non-participants. Interestingly, these cults have now spread to the fashionable coastal areas of Brazil where, behind closed doors in São Paulo and Rio de Janeiro, intellectuals participate in visionary ceremonies.

A short ride out from town, at Km 7.8 on Senador Guiomar, you can find the **Ambiental Chico Mendes**, an interpretive centre about the history and reality of rubber tapping in the region (Tues–Sun 7am–5pm; ⓣ68/3221-1933; free). Further afield, the state of Acre is dotted with **ancient geoglyphs** made from earthworks with spirals, circles and crescents that can only really be visited in guided groups (see "Travel and tour companies" in "Listings", opposite).

### Eating, drinking and nightlife

For **eating out** it is hard to beat the *Restaurante Casarão*, at Av. Brazil 110 (ⓣ68/3224-6479; closed Sun lunchtime), by the bottom end of the Praça Plácido de Castro, near the Teleacre office. The *comida por kilo* food is good and, at weekends, there's live music and an excellent atmosphere. On just about any evening it's also a good place to meet people, as students, musicians and poets use it as a hangout. Cheaper *comida por kilo* is available at the *Restaurante El Dorado*, at the corner of Rua Deodoro and Benjamin Constant. The *Hotel Triângulo* has a good *churrasco* restaurant, and *Oscar's*, Rua Franco Ribeiro 73, is also a popular meat-house. For a broader range of regional dishes, try the *Kaxinawá*, Rua Rui Barbosa on the corner with Avenida Ceará (closed Wed & Sun), which is also a lively club. The *Pizzeria Bolota*, Rua Rui Barbosa 62, is a relatively quiet spot, next to the *Hotel Inácio Palace*, with a patio out front and, occasionally, live music at weekends. More or less next door is the pleasant, good-value *Inácio's*. For **street food** you'll find some good kiosks at the bottom end of the **Praça Plácido de Castro** which serve a variety of regional snacks in the evenings. For quality local and international dishes the centrally located *Restaurante Anexo*, Rua Franco Ribeiro 99 (⊕69/224-1396; daily 11am–2.30pm & 7–11pm), is also very good.

A great place to meet people in the evening is the newly renovated old market (*Mercado Velho*), a trendy spot where Rio Acre is crossed by a stylish modern footbridge, with a range of pleasant bars and cafés. The small triangular Praça Oscar Passos, stuffed with chairs and tables, is served by a number of small bars under a giant mango tree; it's always very lively on weekend evenings. You might also try *Alek's Bar* on Rua Rio Grande do Sul near Rua Marechal Peixoto, which to all appearances is in someone's back garden. As for **clubs**, currently packing them in is *14 Bis*, right next to the airport (take a taxi), which has live salsa bands (Thurs to Sat, 7pm to very late). Also very popular is the *Maloca Club* out on Avenida Getúlio Vargas, open till late on Fridays and Saturdays.

## Listings

**Airlines** Tavaj, at the airport (⊕68/3211-1008), covers most of the western Amazon including Cruzeiro do Sul, São Gabriel da Cachoeira and Tabatinga. Rico also have offices at the airport but tickets are best booked with local travel agents.

**Air taxis** There are half a dozen air-taxi companies based at the airport, including Táxi-Aéreo Rio Branco ⊕68/3224-1384.

**Banks and exchange** The Banco do Brasil, Rua Arlindo P. Leal 85, set back from the Praça Eurico Dutra (Mon–Fri, *câmbio* open 8am–12.30pm), will change US dollars but arrive early as it can take around two hours; you can also change dollars at the bigger hotels.

**Car rental** Localiza ⊕69/3224-7746.

**Post office** Rua Epaminondas Jácome (Mon–Fri 9am–5pm), by the corner with Av. Getúlio Vargas.

**Shopping** Aside from the Sunday-only Feira de Artesanato, by far the best place for *artesanato* is Floresta shop on the ground floor of the Mira Shopping Centre at Rua Rui Barbosa 226. An artesan cooperative also sell wares Mon–Sat in the Parque da Maternidade. The street market along Av. Getúlio Vargas sells all the usual fruit and vegetables, and there's an indoor section for everything from machetes, fishing nets and medicinal herbs to umbrellas and cassette tapes.

**Travel and tour companies** Inacio's Tur, Rua Rui Barbosa 91, sala 100 (⊕68/3223-7191), sells mostly plane tickets. Maanaim Amazônia, Rua Santa Ines 401, Aviário (⊕68/3223-3232, ⓦwww.maanaim-amazonia.com), organizes a wide range of exciting trips to local sites, rubber-tapper and indigenous communities.

# On to Peru: Brasiléia and Cruzeiro do Sul

There are really only two onward routes from Rio Branco, and both of them end up in Peru. The fastest heads south to Brasiléia (4–5hr by bus), which is actually on the border with Bolivia. The route continues from here to Assis Brasil for the border crossing into the Peruvian jungle region of Madre de Dios. From Assis Brasil there's a road bridge crossing the river to Iñapari in Peru, whose side of the road was still being paved in 2009, but is more or less complete. This new international road links the Atlantic with the Pacific, allowing overland road travel from Salvador to Lima. Cocaine smuggling does happen on this frontier and, although it's much easier to make the crossing by public transport these days, you should not undertake this route lightly. The other, slower route travels west along the BR-364 all the way to Cruzeiro do Sul. This route is being rapidly improved from Rio Branco westwards, where it is now a proper freeway in a few sections. From Cruzeiro do Sul your options are limited still to onward connections via river or air to the jungle city of Pucallpa in Peru.

## Brasiléia and Assis Brasil

The small town of **BRASILÉIA** is 220km and six hours by bus from Rio Branco; some buses now travel all the way from Rio Branco to Puerto Maldonado (ask at the Rio Branco *rodoviária*). If you're crossing the border you can see the Polícia Federal for your exit (or entry) stamp just before the river bridge at Assis Brasil. The office (daily 8am–5pm) is just to the right of the church as you head from the international border with Bolivia, at the bus terminal just to the left. If you have to stay the night, the *Hotel Major*, Rua Salinas 326 (❶), is cheap and cheerful. Much better rooms, with air conditioning, are at *Pousada Las Palmeiras*, on Odilon Pratagi (☎68/3546-3281; ❸) or the *Kador Hotel*, Avenida Santos Dumont, Centro (☎68/3546-3206). You can change money at the Casa Castro, over the river on the road towards Assis Brasil.

**ASSIS BRASIL** is a further 110km beyond Brasiléia; from here it's a two-kilometre walk or taxi ride across the border to the small settlement of **Iñapari** in Peru and a further four hours by recently paved road to the city of Puerto Maldonado with several collective taxis daily. About twice a week there are direct buses all the way from Rio Branco to Puerto Maldonado.

# Travel details

### Buses

**Belém** to: Brasília (6 daily; 36hr); Salvador (1 daily; 32hr).
**Boa Vista** to: Bonfim (2 daily; 4hr); Manaus (6 daily; 12hr); Santa Elena (6 daily; 3hr).
**Manaus** to: Boa Vista (6 daily; 12hr).
**Porto Velho** to: Cuiabá (4 daily; 22hr); Guajará-Mirim (5 daily; 4–6hr); Rio Branco (5 daily; 8–9hr); São Paulo (2 daily; 48hr).
**Rio Branco** to: Brasiléia (3 daily; 4–6hr); Porto Velho (5 daily; 8–9hr); Puerto Maldonado (2 weekly; 9–10hr).

### Boats

**Belém** to: Macapá (several weekly; 1–2 days); Manaus (several weekly; 4–6 days); Santarém (several weekly; 2–3 days).
**Macapá** to: Belém (several weekly; 1–2 days); Oiapoque (1 weekly; 2 days); Puerto La Cruz, Venezuela (1 daily; 18hr).
**Manaus** to: Belém (several weekly; 3–5 days); Caracaraí (irregular; 4–8 days); Humaitá (4 weekly; 3–4 days); Porto Velho (3 weekly; 4–6 days); Santarém (daily; 2 days, or 11hr in speedboat); São Gabriel da Cachoeira (weekly; 5–7 days); Tabatinga (several weekly; 5 days plus upstream, 3–4 downstream); Tefé (daily; 2 days, or 11hr in speedboat).
**Porto Velho** to: Manaus (3 weekly; 3–4 days).
**Santarém** to: Belém (several weekly; 2–3 days); Macapá (several weekly; 2–3 days); Manaus (1 daily; 2–3 days, or 13hr in a speedboat).
**Tabatinga** to: Iquitos (several weekly; 3–4 days or 12hr by speedboat); Manaus (several weekly; 4–5 days).

### Planes

**Belém** to: Boa Vista (1 daily; 4hr); Brasília (1 daily; 2hr); Macapá (1 daily; 1hr); Manaus (2 daily; 2hr); Porto Velho (1 daily; 5hr); and at least once daily to all other major Brazilian cities.
**Manaus** to: Alta Floresta (1 daily; 1hr 30min); Barcelos (3 weekly; 1hr); Belém (2 daily; 2hr); Boa Vista (2 daily; 2hr 30min); Brasília (5 daily; 3hr); Cuiabá (1 weekly; 3hr); Porto Velho (1 daily; 2hr); Rio Branco (several weekly; 2hr 40min); Rio de Janeiro (3 daily; 3hr 30min); São Gabriel da Cachoeira (1 daily; 3hr); São Paulo (several daily; 4hr); Tabatinga (1 daily; 2hr 30min); Tefé (4 weekly; 1hr).
From **Porto Velho**, **Rio Branco** and **Marabá**, there are daily services to most major Brazilian cities.

6

# Brasília and the Planalto Central

# CHAPTER 6 Highlights

* **Catedral Metropolitana** Contemplate the soaring statues of St Peter and the angels from the sunken floor of this landmark cathedral. See p.465

* **Juscelino Kubitschek Memorial** Learn about the ambitious president who built the capital at this intriguing museum devoted to his life. See p.466

* **Memorial dos Povos Indígenas** Superb indigenous art is on view inside this elegant museum, itself a dazzling Niemeyer creation. See p.467

* **Salto de Itiquira** Best known for its vast waterfall, this delightful park near Formosa makes a worthwhile day-trip from Brasília. See p.473

* **Goiás Velho** A picturesque colonial town, well preserved and relatively untouched by commercialism, with fine excursions nearby. See p.481

* **Parque Nacional Chapada dos Veadeiros** The varied terrain in this national park makes it an ideal spot for hiking. See p.486

▲ Catedral Metropolitana, Brasília

6

# Brasília and the Planalto Central

The geographical heart of Brazil is the central highlands (Planalto Central), shared by the states of Goiás, Tocantins and parts of Mato Grosso. This rapidly developing and prosperous agricultural region was, as recently as fifty years ago, still largely Indian country, with a few colonial towns precariously linked by oxcart trails to the rest of the country. The founding of Brasília in the late 1950s ended that, shifting Brazil's centre of gravity from the coast to the interior and opening up an entire region of the country to settlement and development.

Love it or loathe it, Brazil's capital is like nowhere else on earth; the world's largest, most successful and in its own weird way most beautiful planned city, it remains the main reason for visiting the *planalto*. Brasília's chief attraction is its extraordinary **city architecture**, its late-1950s vision of the future now charmingly retro, even sliding over into kitsch. While the capital is no metropolis it is much more cosmopolitan than its relatively small size suggests, heaving with restaurants and bars where much of the city's business is transacted, as befits a place where politics is the main local industry. Brasília is well connected by long but good-quality **roads** to the rest of the country and is a good jumping-off point for an overland journey to the Amazon or the Northeast.

Although Brasília may be the region's main draw, it is by no means the only one. In recent years, the city has become the base for a mostly Brazilian **ecotourism** boom. People come for the emptiness and beauty of the landscape a few hours north of Brasília, as well as great **hiking** and more specialized outdoor pursuits like caving and rock climbing. The main centre, **Parque Nacional Chapada dos Veadeiros**, is an easy excursion from Brasília, and if time is limited, the spectacular waterfall of **Salto de Itiquira** is a rewarding day-trip. There is also a national park, the **Parque Nacional de Brasília**, on the city's periphery, with hiking trails. Although there are two large, modern and prosperous cities near Brasília – **Goiânia** and **Anápolis** – there is little for visitors in either of them and unless you have a specific reason for going you're better advised to stick to Brasília and the more rural parts of the Planalto.

The *planalto* itself is still at that ideal stage of tourist development where there is enough infrastructure to make it accessible and enjoyable, but not so much that you feel it is too crowded or over-commercialized. Two colonial towns in particular are worth visiting, both in Goiás: **Pirenópolis**, within easy reach of

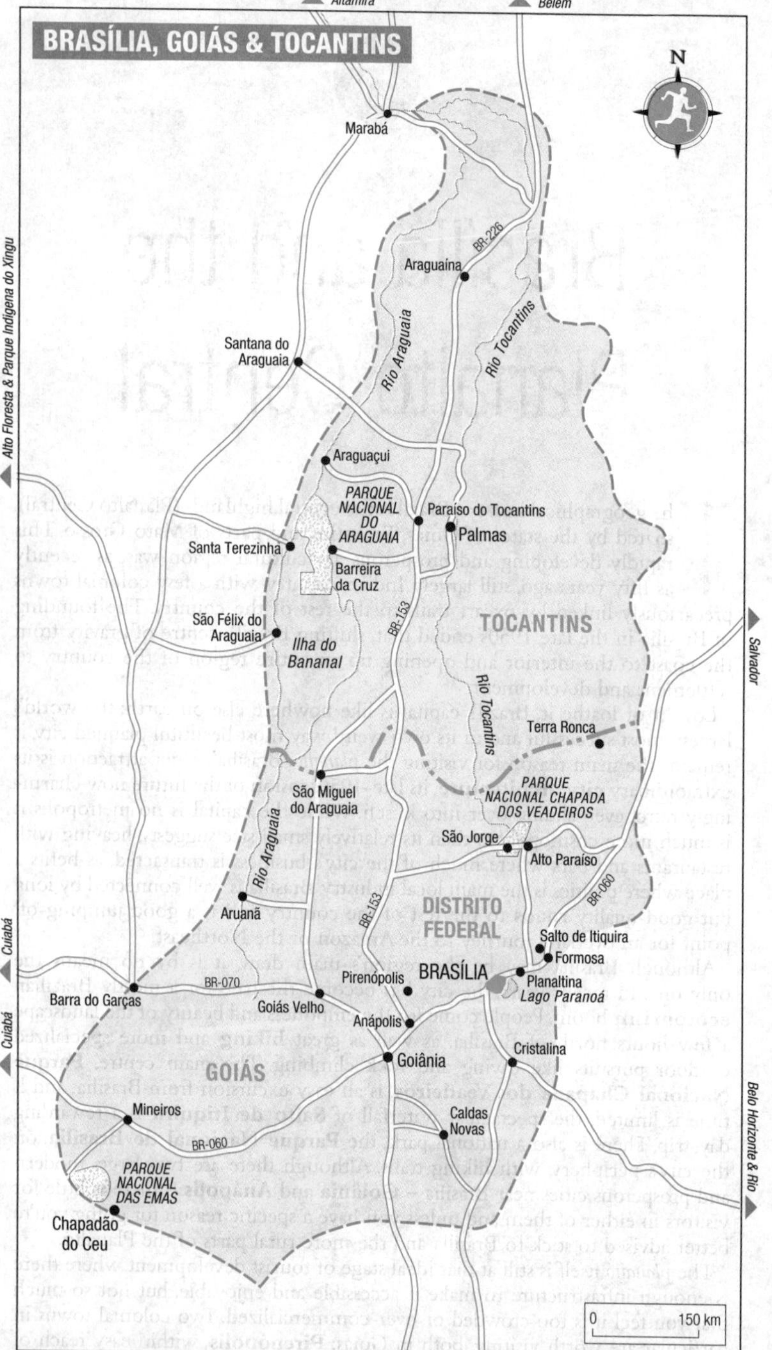
BRASÍLIA, GOIÁS & TOCANTINS
N
Altamira
Belém
Marabá
BR-226
Araguaína
Rio Tocantins
Rio Araguaia
Santana do Araguaia
Alto Floresta & Parque Indígena do Xingu
Araguaçui
PARQUE NACIONAL DO ARAGUAIA
Paraíso do Tocantins
Palmas
Santa Terezinha
Barreira da Cruz
São Félix do Araguaia
Ilha do Bananal
BR-153
TOCANTINS
Salvador
Rio Tocantins
Terra Ronca
São Miguel do Araguaia
PARQUE NACIONAL CHAPADA DOS VEADEIROS
São Jorge
Alto Paraíso
Rio Araguaia
BR-060
Aruanã
DISTRITO FEDERAL
BR-153
Cuiabá
Salto de Itiquira
Formosa
BR-070
Pirenópolis
BRASÍLIA
Planaltina
Lago Paranoá
Barra do Garças
Goiás Velho
Anápolis
Cuiabá
Cristalina
Goiânia
GOIÁS
Mineiros
Caldas Novas
BR-060
Belo Horizonte & Rio
PARQUE NACIONAL DAS EMAS
Chapadão do Ceu
0
150 km
São Paulo & Curitiba

## The planalto

The topography and ecology of the **planalto** are unique, known within Brazil as the *cerrado*, only partly translated by the word "savanna". Much of it looks startlingly African: red earth, scrubby vegetation, dusty in the dry season, missing only giraffes and zebras for the illusion to be complete. What makes it spectacular is the topography, which begins to break up the high plains into a series of hill ranges, cliffs, mesas, plateaus and moorland almost as soon as you start heading north from Brasília. This irregular landscape is situated between two enormous watersheds, the Paraná to the south and the Amazon to the north, both of which have the headwaters of major tributaries in the *planalto*. The hills and mountains are riddled with thousands of **rivers and streams**, forming spectacular waterfalls and swimholes within easy reach of Brasília.

As ecotourism grows, so too do the **threats.** Good soils and communications, and its proximity to Minas Gerais and São Paulo mean development here is far more intense than in the Amazon. The ranchers who spearheaded the early wave of settlement of the *planalto* are still there, but giving way to large-scale commercial agriculture, especially soybeans. This has underlain the development of the two largest cities in Goiás, **Goiânia**, the state capital, and **Anápolis**, and as it becomes one of the world's breadbaskets much of the *planalto* now looks like the US Midwest when you fly over it or drive through, with endless geometric fields and irrigation canals stretching to the horizon. Over sixty percent of the native vegetation has been converted to farmland or pasture, compared to fifteen percent of the Amazon, and the unique flora and fauna of the *cerrado* – the giant anteater and armadillo, the maned wolf, the glorious wildflowers that speckle the area with colour in the rainy season – are all increasingly endangered. If things continue at the present rate, within a generation the only islands of true *cerrado* left will be the national parks.

Brasília, and the old capital of Goiás state, **Goiás Velho**, a little-visited jewel that is as beautiful as any of the better known *cidades históricas* of Minas Gerais. Further north still, the **state of Tocantins** has its eastern and western frontiers defined by two of the largest tributaries of the Amazon, the **Araguaia** and **Tocantins**, but the state has little to offer the visitor and is best bypassed on the way to more interesting destinations in the North or Northeast.

# Brasília

Arriving in **BRASÍLIA**, especially at its futuristic airport, is like falling into a science-fiction novel. The entire city, and especially the central area, has a startlingly space-age feel and look, albeit with a decidedly retro twist. Originally intended for a population of half a million by the year 2000, Brasília and the area around it today has close to five million people and is the only one of Brazil's major metropolitan areas still growing quickly. Looking at the gleaming government buildings or zooming down the city's excellent roads, it really can seem Brasília is the modern heart of a new world superpower. The illusion is rapidly dispelled: drive ten minutes out of the city in any direction and you'll hit the

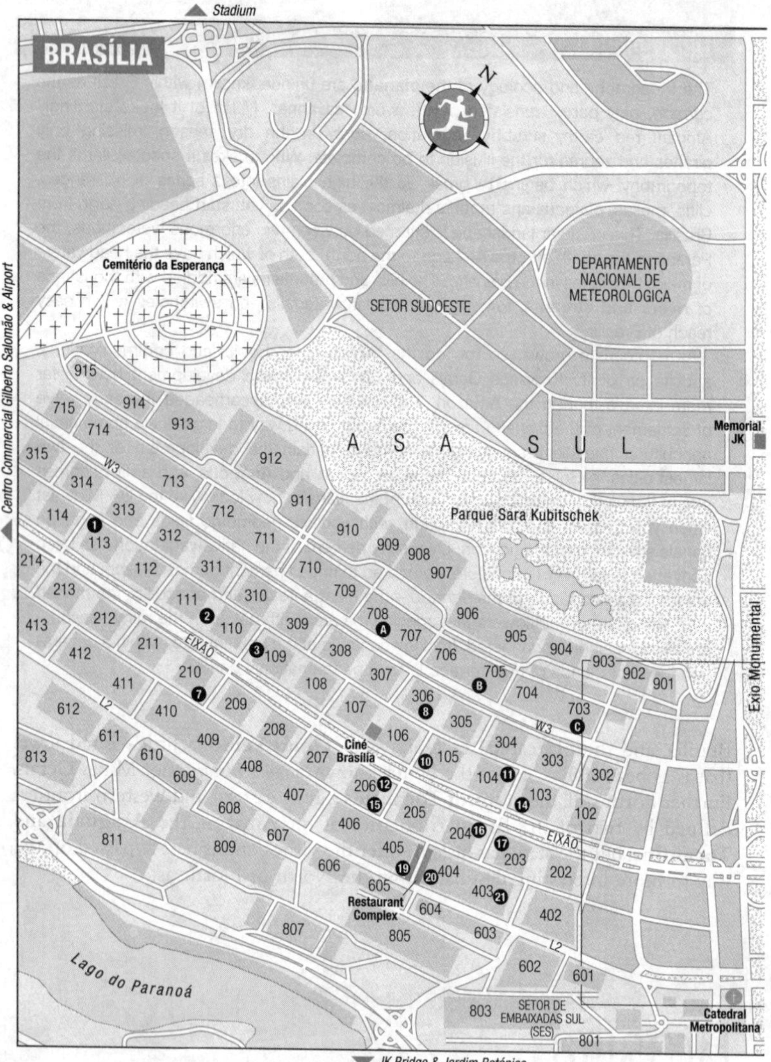


cidades satélites, poorer satellite cities that house Brasília's low-income workers, who commute into town to serve the needs of the government-employed elite. As well as being the national capital, Brasília is also the capital of its own state, the **Distrito Federal**, the Federal District, which also includes the satellite cities. The whole Federal District is in fact the perfect symbol of modern Brazil, though not in the way its creators intended: affluence close to but segregated from poverty, *favelas* over the horizon, and poor newcomers invading the countryside where the nation's elite have their walled-off weekend retreats.

Brasília's highlights are all fairly obvious **architectural** ones. Anyone with a taste for the best of 1950s and 1960s architecture will think they have died and gone to heaven, but there are other attractions, too. **Nightlife** is energetic,

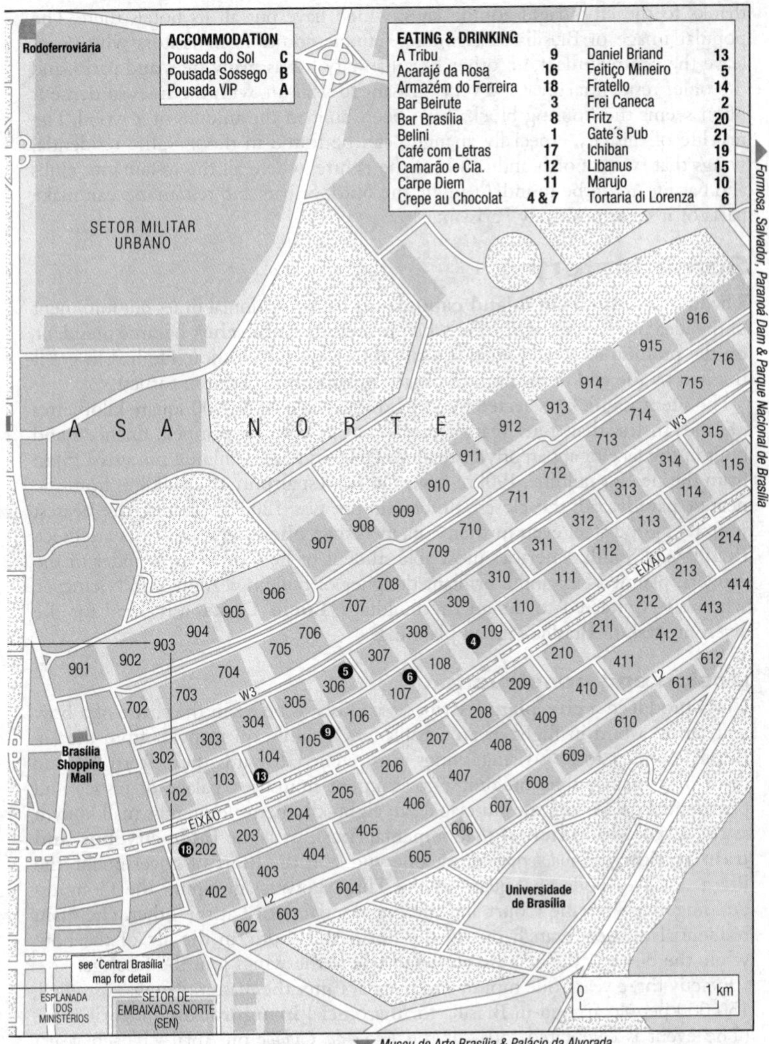


revolving around huge numbers of bars and restaurants that benefit from the city's marvellous nocturnal climate, fresh and pleasant all year round. **Cinema** is especially good here, patronized by a large local middle-class with an appetite for foreign films, and one side-benefit of the presence of the elite is the regular appearance of top-level **performing arts**.

There is a distinct New Age feel to parts of the city and environs; it has a special attraction for the wacky religious cults and UFO enthusiasts in which Brazil abounds. Some visitors find Brasília alienating, and the central part of the city can certainly seem that way, with its jumble of undistinguished skyscrapers, malls and massive empty spaces – the absence of planned gardens and parks is the centre's major design flaw. At night the centre is deserted and dead, even at weekends, thanks to the city's rigid zoning laws, which have put all its hotels there. The popular image of Brasília as a concrete jungle comes from visitors who never leave the centre; in fact, no other Brazilian city has as many trees and parks, and the older residential areas are very pleasant to walk in, with the trees so dense it often seems the housing blocks have been built in the middle of a wood. The real life of the city, especially at night, can be found in the *asas*, the residential wings that swing north and south of the centre, where all the restaurants, clubs and bar life are to be found. At night, the outdoor bars and restaurants can make parts of it seem positively Parisian.

## Some history

The idea of a **Brazilian inland capital** goes back to colonial times but fulfilment of the idea had to wait until 1956 when **Juscelino Kubitschek** became president, on the promise he would build the city if he won the election. He had to get it finished by the end of his term of office, so work soon began in earnest.

The site was quickly selected by aerial surveys of over 50,000 square kilometres of land. In less than four years a capital city had to be planned, financed and built in the face of apparently insurmountable odds: the building site was 125km from the nearest rail line, 190km from the nearest airport, over 600km from the nearest paved road; the closest timber supply was 1200km distant, the nearest source of good steel even further. Still, in **Oscar Niemeyer**, the city's architect, Brasília had South America's most able student of Le Corbusier, founder of the modern planned city and a brilliant designer of buildings. Alongside Niemeyer, who was contracted to design the buildings, **Lúcio Costa** was hired for the awesome task of Brasília's urban planning.

### Design and construction

Costa produced a **city plan** described variously as being in the shape of a bow and arrow, a bird in flight or an aeroplane. Certainly, on maps or from the air, Brasília appears to be soaring, wings outstretched, towards the eastern Atlantic coast. The main public buildings, government ministries, palace of justice and presidential palace line the "fuselage", an eight-kilometre-long grass mall known as the **Eixo Monumental** (Monumental Axis), with the **inter-city bus and train station**, the *rodoferroviária*, at one end, and the heart of government, the Praça dos Três Poderes (Square of the Three Powers) grouping the Congress building, the Supreme Court and the presidential palace at the other. The main residential districts branch out to the north and south, in the arc of the bow, while the business districts are clustered where the wings join the fuselage.

Exactly three years, one month and five days after the master plan was unveiled, 150,000 people arrived in Brasília for the official **inauguration**, in April 1960. (The event is celebrated today as the *Festa da Cidade* on April 21 each year.) It must have been a hectic time. There were only 150 first-class hotel rooms completed for the five thousand visiting dignitaries, but the celebrations went ahead anyway. In the morning it was apparent to everyone there were still years of work ahead. Road junctions were half-completed, pedestrians and apartments still had to be separated from traffic, and the accommodation units had none of their intended leafy surroundings – the flats supposedly close enough to the ground for a mother to call her child. Most poignantly, the elephant donated for the city zoo by Haile Selassie of Ethiopia had to be kept tied to a tree while its enclosure was built around it. But in time, the city slowly grew to fill in the spaces left for more organic expansion, most of the residential areas were landscaped and greened, and Brasília gradually developed some of the maladies that affect the rest of urban Brazil, including rush-hour traffic-jams.

## Growth

As Brasília developed it became apparent the original **city plans**, based on Le Corbusier's notions of urban progress through geometrical order and rectilinear planning, would have to be modified if Brazilians, the least rectilinear of people, were going to feel comfortable here. This was partly accomplished by Niemeyer's brilliant and innovative buildings, full of curves and circles. At the time of writing, Niemeyer was 101 and still working away as the city architect; he designed all Brasília's major buildings, from the angular government ministries in the 1950s to the sinuous curves of the federal prosecutor's building completed in 2003, giving the city a unique aesthetic unity. Modification was also partly accomplished by time; as the city matured, its inhabitants started to subvert its rigid zoning and building codes by adding houses and expanding leisure areas, especially in the commercial sections of the *asas*.

## Financial and environmental costs

On the face of it at least, Kubitschek lived up to his electoral campaign promise of fifty years' progress in five. What he hadn't made clear before, though, was just how much it would cost Brazil. With outstanding foreign loans of two billion dollars, the city seemed an antisocial waste of resources to many, and it was certainly responsible for letting loose inflation, a problem that would take a generation to resolve.

As it turned out, however, Brasília paid for itself many times over, and very quickly. The rapid **development of the planalto** that followed transformed the entire region into one of the most developed agricultural areas in the country, and the taxes, jobs and production generated swiftly made the decision to build Brasília seem inspired; Kubitschek's reputation has steadily climbed since his death in 1976, and he is now usually thought of as Brazil's most visionary and successful president. The costs have proved to be more environmental than financial, with the rapid conversion of much of the *planalto* to farmland and the destruction of forest along the Belém–Brasília highway corridor. As ever, those with most cause to complain were the **indigenous peoples** of the *planalto*; groups like the warlike **Xavante** did what they could to halt the tide, but it was hopeless, and by the 1970s they were all confined to reservations a fraction the size of their previous territories.

# Arrival

The **airport** (☎61/3365-1941) is 12km south of the centre, and bus #102 runs every hour from there into Brasília, dropping you at the downtown *rodoviária*. A taxi to the hotel sectors is around R$35. Inter-city and long-distance buses use

### Brasília's climate

Brasília's **climate** has marked seasonal differences you should bear in mind when timing a visit. The rainy season runs from October to March, and can be torrential. The very best time to come is the spring, from April through June, when the trees are in bloom and the climate is pleasant and mild. July through September is the height of the dry season; during the day the sun beats down hard, everything dries out and hot winds blow fine red dust over everything. The extraordinary dryness of this time of year – humidity levels are comparable with the Sahara – often causes sinus problems even among locals. If you do come during this time, drink as much as you can and don't skimp on the sunscreen. Fortunately, night always comes as a relief; temperatures drop and freshness returns all year round.

the **rodoferroviária** (☎61/3233-7200), the bus and former train station at the far western end of the Eixo Monumental. From here, the #131 bus (Platform B, stand 3) covers the 5km of the Eixo Monumental to the downtown *rodoviária*, passing the famous statue of Juscelino Kubitschek on the way. Once at the downtown *rodoviária*, go up the escalators to the second level for the shopping centres and upper roads, from where you can see most of central Brasília, and the hotel sectors are a short taxi ride. Taxis to the hotel sector from the *rodoferroviária* are about R$25.

## Information

The best place for **tourist information** is the kiosk at the airport (daily 8am–8pm; ☎61/3365-1024), which stocks a range of leaflets, maps and brochures, and also has a useful touch-screen computer terminal. There's also a helpful tourist office on the Praça dos Três Poderes (Mon 1.30–6pm, Tues–Sun 8am–6pm; ☎61/3325-5730), and in a kiosk underneath the TV Tower, with the same hours. Apart from this, you can pick up leaflets from the main hotels. By far the most detailed and useful map of Brasília is to be found at the front of telephone directories and yellow pages, which you'll find in most hotel rooms. There is an excellent listings site for Brasília at Ⓦwww.candango.com.br, unfortunately with no toggle for English, but click on Mapas. The main

### Addresses in Brasília

Most people in Brasília live in *superquadras* – massive apartment complexes, some of which you can see coming in along the Eixão from the airport. Finding out where someone lives or works can seem impossible from the **address**, but there is a perfect internal logic to the system. For example, the address

SQS 105
Bloco A – 501
70.344-040 Brasília - DF

means *superquadra* south no. 105, building A, apartment 501, postcode 70.344-040. The three-digit *superquadra* number here (105) gives the location: the first digit represents the position east or west of the Eixo Rodoviário (or Eixão), with odd numbers to the west, evens to the east, increasing the further away from the centre you get. The last two digits represent the distance north or south of the Eixo Monumental, so that, for example, SQN 208 is five *superquadras* north from SQN 203, SQS 110 five south from SQS 105. Unfortunately, addresses are rarely written out in full: you'll have to watch out for "Q" (*quadra*, and often used for *superquadra*, too), "L", "lj" or "lt" (*loja* or *lote*, meaning "lot" or "shop", used for commercial addresses), "B" or "bl" (*bloco*) and "cj" (*conjunto* meaning "compound").

A similar logic applies to main roads. Even numbers apply east of the Eixão, odd to the west, prefaced for good measure by a letter that tells you which side of the Eixão it runs, L for east (*leste*), W for west (technically *oeste*, but the planners shrank from OE). The roads that run parallel to the Eixão on either side with exits to all the *superquadras* are the ones used by the local bus services, and are universally called the Eixinhos, the "little *eixos*", Eixinho L east of the Eixão, Eixinho W west. The main commercial street, the only one that looks anything like a normal Brazilian street in the entire city, is W3, which runs the entire length of both *asas*.

The other terms you are most likely to come across are:

**Asa Norte/Asa Sul** General terms for the two "wings" (*asas*) of the city, comprising the avenues Eixo Rodoviário Norte and Eixo Rodoviário Sul, and the roads running off and parallel to them (the latter lettered "W" to the west, and "L" to the east, eg W-3 Norte, L-4 Sul).

newspaper, the *Correio Brasiliense*, publishes a daily listings supplement, the *Guia*, with comprehensive information on films, exhibitions, live music and opening hours; though in Portuguese, the details are pretty easy to work out.

## Orientation

Although initially quite confusing, Brasília is laid out with geometric precision. It is neatly divided into sectors: residential (each with its own shopping and other facilities), hotel, embassy, banking and commercial.

The residential wings are divided into *superquadras*, complexes of apartment buildings (see box below for a complete guide to Brasília's zoning system). There are sixteen in each wing, lower numbers closer to the centre, so just by looking at the address you can tell roughly how far from the centre it is. Between every *superquadra* is a **commercial area**, where local shops, bars and restaurants are found; most of Brasília's nightlife is concentrated in these, and to save confusion they are referred to here as a *comercial*, reflecting local usage; a *candango* (someone from Brasília) giving directions to a bar will say "*comercial 206 norte*", for example.

Roads, meanwhile, are numbered, rather than named, with digits representing their position and distance north or south of the **Eixo Monumental**, and east or west of the other main axis, the **Eixo Rodoviário**, universally known as

**CLN/CLS** or **SCLN/SCLS** (Setor) Comércio Local Norte/Sul. These terms describe the shopping blocks interspersed throughout the residential *superquadras* that comprise Asa Norte and Asa Sul. Their numbering follows that of the *superquadras*, so that CLN 208 is near SQN 208.

**Eixinho** The smaller, marginally slower main roads with exits to every *quadra* either side of the Eixão, the main central artery.

**EQN/EQS** Entrequadras Norte/Sul. Literally "between *quadras*", referring to the area bordering the Eixinhos.

**SBN/SBS** Setor Bancário Norte/Sul. The two banking sectors either side of the Eixo Monumental.

**SCN/SCS** Setor Comercial Norte/Sul. The two commercial-office-block areas, set back from the Conjuntos de Diversões shopping centres. Often confused with CLN/CLS (see above).

**SDN/SDS** Setor de Diversões Norte/Sul. The two shopping centres (*conjuntos*) either side of Eixo Monumental.

**SEN/SES** Setor de Embaixadas Norte/Sul. The embassy sectors, east of the bank sectors.

**SHIN/SHIS** Setor de Habitações Individuais Norte/Sul. The two peninsulas that jut into Lago Paranoá, the northern one accessible from the end of Eixo Rodoviário Norte, the southern one, also called Lago Sul, connected by bridges from Avenida das Nações.

**SHN/SHS** Setor Hoteleiro Norte/Sul. The hotel sectors either side of the Eixo Monumental, west of the *rodoviária*.

**SQN/SQS** or **SHCN/SHCS** Superquadras Norte/Sul. The individual *superquadras* in the main residential wings, Asa Norte and Asa Sul.

Although the system takes some getting used to, it's useful in pinpointing exactly where an address is located in the city – a good defence against dishonest taxi-drivers, useful when walking, and a boon if your Portuguese is too elementary for directions.

the Eixão. The different sectors are given acronyms, most fairly easy to work out (see box, p.458).

The central *rodoviária*, the urban bus and metro station, is the main hub of movement within Brasília, with the Eixo Monumental passing around it and the Eixo Rodoviário crossing over the top of it. Up above the *rodoviária*, you can see at a glance the main areas of interest. Looking east (toward the main government buildings that resemble great green dominoes) is the unmistakeable Aztec form of the **Teatro Nacional** and, a little further away to the right, the conical crown of the **Catedral Metropolitana**, itself behind the dazzling white globe of the new national library and archive, the **Biblioteca Nacional**; all are within easy walking distance. Slightly further away, but still walkable, are the striking bowls and towers of the **Congresso Nacional** complex. Immediately on either side of the *rodoviária* there are two separate, rather tacky shopping centres, the **Conjuntos de Diversões**, one to the north, another to the south. Twenty years ago these vast concrete boxes were overshadowed only by the TV Tower, but nowadays the modern towers of the nearby **Setores Hoteleiros** (hotel sectors), **Setores Comerciais** (business sectors) and **Setores das Autarquias** (government agency sectors) dominate the scene, together with the bank and government buildings on either side of the Eixo Monumental. The most distinctive is the central bank building in Setor das Autarquias Sul – black boxes hung around a central concrete framework make it look like an enormous stereo-speaker.

## Getting around

One essential point to remember is that Brasília is dominated by its **road traffic** system like no other Brazilian city; everyone, including visitors, is obliged by its enormous spaces to move around by car and bus; **walking**, like everything else in Brasília, is zoned. There are parks and residential areas specifically designed for strolling; elsewhere you should forget about walking as the city's not made for it.

It is not difficult to see most of Brasília's traditional sights in a day, though if you are foolish enough to walk after 10am it gets extremely tiring wandering around the open spaces of the centre in the heat.

### Public transport

There are two or three **city bus routes**, instead, which can save you a lot of time and energy. Details of these are given in the text, and there are also two **circular bus routes** that are very handy for a cheap overview of the city: buses #105 and #106 leave from and return to the downtown *rodoviária*, Platform A (☎61/3223-0557), after a long outer-city tour; try to avoid these routes between 4 and 6pm on weekdays when the buses are particularly crowded. Keep an eye out for pickpockets when standing in line, though once on the bus you should be all right. Bus fares vary between R$2.20 for journeys within the Plano Piloto to R$4.50 to the satellite towns.

Brasília also has a brand-new **Metro system**, with the main station underground at the *rodoviária*. Although you are unlikely to use it often, it is an excellent way to get a quick (and cheap) sense of how fast the Distrito Federal is developing, in places like Águas Claras, a new and already enormous satellite town. It has two lines, green (*Verde*) to Ceilândia and orange (*Laranja*) to Samambaia. Tickets are R$2, and the system is open from 6am to 11.30pm Monday to Friday, 7am to 7pm Saturday and Sunday. Only the first section is underground – at the end of Asa Sul trains emerge from the tunnel and the views begin. The trains are fast, air-conditioned and clean; the best route to get a sense of how the area is developing is the green line to Ceilândia, taking around 40 minutes.

## Taxi and car rental

The city has a good **taxi** service. Flag a taxi down when you want one, or pick one up at the many ranks throughout the city; every *superquadra* has at least one. Most people drive their own cars, and if you want to join them see p.472 for addresses of **car-rental** firms; it'll cost you from R$70 a day, but less if you rent over a longer period. A warning though: Brasília, uniquely among Brazilian cities, is blanketed by speed cameras. If you're caught jumping a light or speeding in a hired car, the fine will be taken off your credit card.

# Accommodation

Brasília has a vast range of accommodation to suit all budgets, contrary to its reputation as being an overpriced place to stay. The **central hotel sectors** are split into three categories, distinguishable by the height of the building, all of which post prices that are actually considerably more than they really charge if you ask for a discount. The five-star skyscrapers are the closest to the centre, offering top-range beds from around R$200 a night and upwards; smaller four- and three-star hotels are to be found either side of W3 and are more than reasonable at R$75–150; while R$50 will get you perfectly adequate accommodation at the squat one- and two-star hotels.

If you're on a tight budget, R$25–40 will get you a bed at a *pousada*; these cluster on W3 Sul, starting at *quadra* 703 to around 708. Most are squalid and none too secure; the ones recommended below are the pick of the bunch, but are still below the standards of the worst of the hotels. Staying in campsites or in the satellite cities is definitely not recommended; besides being dangerous, it costs much the same as accommodation in Brasília.

## Central hotel sectors

**Alvorada** SHS Q.4 ⓣ61/3222-7068. Cheap, central and good-value hotel, though noisy unless you get an apartment facing away from W3. ❷–❸

**Aracoara** SHN Q.5 ⓣ61/3328-9222. Comfortable mid-range hotel, very good value, but in a marginally inconvenient location with nothing in walking distance. The surrounding area is even more dead than usual for the centre at night. ❷–❸

**Aristus** SHN Q.2 ⓣ61/3328-8675, ⓕ3326-5415. One of the cheapest options in this good location, offering a choice of basement rooms at rates slightly lower than their other rooms. ❶–❷

**Bonaparte Hotel Résidence** SHS Q.2 ⓣ61/3322-2288 or 0800/619-991, ⓦwww.bonapartehotel.com.br. A top-notch hotel, with a large convention facility and all mod cons. ❹–❺

**Brasília Imperial** SHS Q.3 ⓣ61/3223-7252, ⓦwww.brasiliaimperialhotel.com.br. Excellent value and location. ❶–❷

**Bristol** SHS Q.4 ⓣ61/3321-6162, ⓕ3321-2690. Comfortable and with a rooftop swimming pool, this is a good-value hotel without being top of the range; highly recommended. ❷–❸

**Byblos** SHN Q.3 ⓣ61/3326-1570, ⓕ3326-3615. Unlike most of the hotels in SHS and SHN, this one is low-rise. Clean and spartan, but its rooms aren't as nice as the *Casablanca*'s (see below) and are slightly more expensive to boot. ❶–❷

**Carlton** SHS Q.5 ⓣ61/3226-8109, ⓦwww.carltonhotel.com.br. Older upmarket hotel, with great 1960s decor, but slightly expensive compared to similar places. ❺–❻

**Casablanca** SHN Q.3 ⓣ61/3328-8586, ⓕ3328-8273. Close to the Eixo Monumental and within sight of the TV Tower, a small and friendly hotel with excellent rooms and a nice restaurant. Good value at the lower end of this price bracket. ❶–❷

**El Pilar** SHN Q.3 ⓣ61/3326-5353. This cheap, low-rise hotel is a little spare, but the location is good and the staff friendly. ❶–❷

**Eron** SHN Q.5 ⓣ61/3329-4000. Another good-value mid-range hotel, with fine views from the upper floors and handy for the TV Tower but little else. ❷–❸

**Hotel das Américas** SHS Q.4 ⓣ61/3321-3355 or 0800/118-844, ⓦwww.hoteldasamericas.com. Comfortable and modern, with an excellent restaurant – but overpriced if you don't get a discount. ❷–❸

**Kubitschek Plaza** SHN Q.2 ⓣ61/3329-3333 or 0800/613-995, ⓦwww.kubitschek.com.br. Among the best of the five-star hotels, built in a strange blend of space-age and ancient-Egyptian styles. Everything you'd expect at this price – pool, gymnasium, sauna, plus free medical insurance throughout your stay. ❹–❺

**Manhattan** SHN Q.2 ⓣ61/3319-3060 or 0800/612-400, ⓕ3328-5683. Less extravagant than its stable-mate the *Kubitschek Plaza*, but still extremely smart, attracting a slightly younger clientele. Good Japanese restaurant attached. ❹–❺

**Metropolitan** SHN Q.2 ⓣ61/3424-3500. Swanky but reasonably priced for all the mod cons you get – along with the excellent views. ❹–❺

**Nacional** SHS Q.1 ⓣ61/3321-7575, ⓦwww.hotelnacional.com.br. The oldest of the big hotels, reflected in fine retro-1960s kitsch decor. Well run with the added advantage of having all of the major airline offices out front. ❹–❺

**Naoum Express** SHS Q.3, Bloco J ⓣ61-3212-4545. Newly opened hotel aimed at the business market but very reasonably priced and a great central location; good wi-fi in all rooms, moderately priced restaurant and free access to the fitness centre next door if you need it. ❹

**Planalto Bittar** SHS Q.3 ⓣ61/3322-217. Just about the best of the cheaper hotels, slightly more expensive but better quality than others in this market. Good location. ❷–❸

**St Paul** SHS Q.2 ⓣ61/3317-8400, ⓔstpaul@tba.com.br. Large hotel with excellent service, plus a sauna, pool, good restaurant and bar. ❹–❺

### Pousadas and pensões

**Pousada do Sol** 703 Sul, Bloco K ⓣ61/3224-9703. Along with neighbouring *Pousada JK* this is the best of a cluster of cheap places. ❶–❷

**Pousada Sossego** 705 Sul, facing W3 ⓣ61/3224-5050. Aimed at the lower end of the Brazilian business market, with clean rooms. ❶–❷

**Pousada VIP** 708 Sul, Bloco C ⓣ61/3340-8544. Doesn't quite live up to its name, but it's clean and includes basic breakfast. ❶–❷

## The City

Brasília's overriding attraction is the unique environment produced by its stunning **architecture**. The blue sky that normally hangs over the city contrasts well with the modern buildings and the deep red earth of the *planalto*. Visitors normally head straight for the downtown sites, but it's best to put them in context first on one of the circular bus routes from the *rodoviária* and a ride around on the *metrô*.

Below, the main sights in downtown Brasília are divided into three sections, following the head, body and tail concept of the bird or aeroplane the city resembles; the outlying areas of the city are dealt with later in the Guide.

### The Esplanada dos Ministérios

The focus of the Brazilian government complex, known as the **Esplanada dos Ministérios**, is the unmistakeable twin towers of the Congress building. All of the structures here are within a few minutes' walk of each other, entrance is free and they can be seen in half a day, though you can easily spend more time than this exploring. Niemeyer designed them all, and they're rightly regarded as among the best modernist buildings in the world. The combination of white marble, water pools, reflecting glass and the airy, flying buttresses on the presidential palace and supreme court make these buildings remarkably elegant. At night floodlighting and internal lights make them even more impressive; a slow walk or bus ride around the Esplanada in the early evening, when people are still working and the buildings glow like Chinese lanterns, is a must. The only

Praça dos Tres Poderes, ▼ Palácio do Planalto, Palácio da Alvorado, Congress & Itamaratí

| ACCOMMODATION | | | | | | | |
|---|---|---|---|---|---|---|---|
| Alvorada | F | Bristol | E | Eron | B | Metropolitan | Q |
| Aracoara | A | Byblos | J | Hotel das Américas | D | Nacional | O |
| Aristus | N | Carlton | C | Kubitschek Plaza | P | Naoum Express | G |
| Bonaparte Hotel Résidence | L | Casablanca | I | Manhattan | R | Planalto Bittar | H |
| | | El Pilar | K | | | St Paul | M |

blemish is the enormously ugly and vulgar flagpole at the centre of the square, mute testimony to the crassness and bad taste of the military regime that plonked it there over Niemeyer's protests.

At the centre of the complex is the **Praça dos Três Poderes** (Square of Three Powers), representing the Congress, judiciary and the presidency. The **Congresso Nacional** is the most recognizable landmark in Brasília – in a way, everything else flows from here. If you accept the analogy of the city built as a bird, then the National Congress is its beak, something it clearly resembles with its twin 28-storey towers. The two large "bowls", one on either side of the towers, house the Senate Chamber (the smaller, inverted one) and the House of Representatives, and were designed so the public could climb and play on them, though the only people allowed there now are the patrolling soldiers of the Polícia Militar. Visitors can attend debates when in session, however – something you might want to enquire about at the front entrance desk. The chambers themselves are a hoot – they come over today as retro 1960s, but haven't aged as well as that phrase implies. To see them, you must take one of the guided tours that leave every half-hour on weekdays and hourly at weekends. Most guides speak some English and there is a strict dress-code – long trousers, shirt and shoes for men, smart casual for women (Senate tours Mon–Fri 1.30–5.30pm, Sat & Sun 10am–2pm; ⓣ61/3311-2149 for information; House of Representatives tours Mon–Fri 1–5pm, Sat & Sun 9am–2pm; ⓣ61/3318-5092 for information).

The **Palácio da Justiça** (Mon–Fri 10am–noon and 3–5pm; same dress code as for Congress) is beside the Congress building, on the northern side of the Esplanada dos Ministérios. Created in 1960 with a concrete facade, the building was covered with fancy – and, to many, elitist – marble tiles by the military government during the dictatorship. With the return to democracy the tiles were removed, laying bare the concrete waterfalls between the pillars, but the water has been shut off for years as the pools proved to be a perfect breeding ground for the dengue mosquito. The structure is much less interesting inside than any of the other buildings, and without the waterfalls the exterior is more than a little bleak.

Much more worthwhile is the **Palácio Itamarati** (Mon–Fri 2–4.30pm, Sat & Sun 10am–3.30pm, no guided tours but visitors are restricted to certain areas, with same dress code as for Congress; ⓣ61/3411-6159 for information), the vast Foreign Office structure. Combining modern and classical styles, it's built around elegant courtyards, sculptures and gardens, and inside its airiness and sense of space is breathtaking, well set off by a carefully chosen selection of modern art and wall hangings. Outside, the marble *Meteor* sculpture by Bruno Giorgi is a stunning piece of work, its five parts representing the five continents.

Behind the Congresso Nacional, on the northern side, the **Palácio do Planalto** houses the president's office which can be visited only by guided tour (Sun 9.30am–1.30pm; same dress code as for Congress). Of all the Niemeyer buildings this is the most spectacular, both outside and in; the interior is dominated by sleek columns and a glorious, curving ramp leading up from the reception area. On weekdays, however, visitors will have to content themselves with a changing of the guard out front at 8.30am and 5.30pm daily. Nearby in Praça dos Três Poderes, the signposted **Museu Histórico de Brasília** (Mon–Sat 9am–1pm & 2–5pm) tells the tale of the transfer of the capital from Rio; the large-scale architectural model of the entire city, with lights for points of interest, is fun and useful to visitors. From here, you can take a **bus** to the downtown *rodoviária*, or it's a twenty-minute walk through the esplanade of ministry buildings to the cathedral and downtown commercial centre. But to complete your tour of Niemeyer gems, it's worth taking the short taxi or bus ride from here to the president's official residence two miles away, the **Palácio da Alvorada** (bus #104, leaves from stand 13 of Platform A at the *rodoviária*), which many consider the most beautiful of Niemeyer's buildings. The residence is nestled behind an emerald-green lawn and beautifully sculpted gardens, which perfectly set off the brilliant white of its exterior, with Niemeyer's signature slender buttresses and its blue-tinted glass. Somehow the fact you're only allowed to see it from fifty yards away adds to its delicateness and elegance.

If you go by taxi, make sure it waits for you in the car park to the right – taxis rarely pass by here. Guards will shout intimidatingly at you if you sit in the car in the left parking lot, the only one with the clear view, due to heightened security concerns, here as everywhere else.

On your way back, look out for Niemeyer's most recent buildings, the circular, twin mirrored-glass towers of the attorney general's headquarters, immediately behind the Praça dos Três Poderes, opened in 2003, and the Biblioteca Nacional next to the *rodoviária*, opened in 2007.

## The cathedral and commercial sectors

Between the ministries and the downtown *rodoviária*, and within walking distance of either, the **Catedral Metropolitana Nossa Senhora Aparecida** is one of Brasília's most striking edifices (daily 7am–6.30pm; no shorts allowed). Marking the spot where the city of Brasília was inaugurated in 1960, it is built in the form of an inverted chalice and crown of thorns; its sunken nave puts most of the interior floor below ground level. Some of the glass roof panels in the interior reflect rippling water from outside, adding to the sense of airiness in the cathedral, while the statues of St Peter and the angels suspended from the ceiling (the inspired gravity-defying creations of Brazilian sculptor Bruno Ceschiatti) help to highlight the feeling of elevation. Nevertheless, although some 40m in height and with a capacity of two thousand, the cathedral seems surprisingly small inside.

About ten minutes' walk away, on the northern side of the Eixo Monumental, is the **Teatro Nacional**. Built in the form of an Aztec temple, it's a marvellous, largely glass-covered pyramid set at an angle to let light into the lobby, where there are often good art exhibitions with futuristic and environmental themes. Inside are three halls: the Martins Pena, the Villa-Lobos (the largest, seating 1200) and the much smaller Alberto Nepomuceno. Most theatre productions are in Portuguese, but all three venues are also used for **concerts** – Brasília has a symphony orchestra, and popular musicians often play here as well. As the main city venue for **ballet and dance**, the theatre is always worth checking out; thanks to the presence of the government and diplomatic corps, you might luck out and catch an illustrious visitor like the Bolshoi.

The main central shopping centre, the **Conjunto Nacional**, stands on the northern side of the *rodoviária*. Contained in a huge concrete block that's

### Oscar Niemeyer

Still working at the grand old age of 101 in 2009, **Oscar Niemeyer** is the greatest architect Latin America has produced. He's best known for his unique contribution to Brasília, but during his long and highly productive life he has also left his mark on virtually all of Brazil's major cities, especially Rio and Belo Horizonte. Widely regarded as the most influential modernist architect of the twentieth century after Le Corbusier, he has also designed important buildings in Europe, notably the Serpentine Gallery in London and the Le Havre Cultural Centre in France.

Born in Rio in 1907, he was influenced as a student by Le Corbusier's geometric ideas on urban planning and design; his first major commission, the building of the Ministry of Education in Rio in 1937, now known as the Palácio Gustavo Capanema, shows this influence clearly. By the 1940s Niemeyer began to show his independence and originality with a series of buildings in the Belo Horizonte suburb of Pampulha, which gave a recognizably Brazilian twist to Le Corbusier, adding curves, ramps and buttresses to buildings decades ahead of their time. But Niemeyer's designs were **controversial**: the São Francisco church in Pampulha was completed in 1943 but not consecrated until 1959, so reluctant was the Catholic Church to endorse such a radical departure. But the germs of Brasília were clearly evident in his work in Pampulha, a decade before the new capital was begun.

After Brasília, Niemeyer became an **international star** and beyond criticism in his own country, which had its advantages: he was the only militant communist never to be troubled by the military dictatorship. He built a number of other unforgettable buildings, the most spectacular being the Museum of Modern Art in Niterói, across the bay from Rio, perched like a modernist flying-saucer over the sea. As the nation's leading architect, with major buildings spread over multiple countries, Niemeyer has made a major contribution to Brazilian culture and modern history.

covered with massive product advertisements, the flashy jewellery and furniture shops combine with restaurants and fast-food outlets, and unlike the modern shopping centres in other Latin American cities the Conjunto Nacional is not just a playground for the rich; everyone seems to shop here. The busy northern *conjunto* is much more upmarket than its neighbour across the way, the **CONIC** mall, which is increasingly run-down and now dangerous at night, when the only people moving are the prostitutes and clientele patronizing a basement complex of fleapit sex cinemas. Stuck underground between the two giant shopping blocks, the downtown **rodoviária** bus and *metrô* station is also on three levels, and here you'll find more shops, toilets, snack bars and a bus information office.

By far the most interesting place to visit within easy walking distance of the *rodoviária* can be found in the unlikely setting of the **Central Bank building**, the unmistakeable concrete-and-black-glass skyscraper in Setor das Autarquias Sul, visible from anywhere in the centre. Tucked away by the building's rear entrance is the **Museu da Moeda**, or the Museum of Money (Tues–Fri 10am–4.30pm, Sat 2–6pm; free, show your passport to get past reception), where you'll find a quirky but fascinating display of Brazilian currency from colonial times. It's very interesting as social history, but overshadowed by the second part of the display, an extraordinary exhibition behind armoured glass of the largest gold nuggets ever found in Brazil – most dating from the 1980s, when the Central Bank was buying nuggets from the Amazon gold rush. Behind the bank building is **Centro Cultural da Caixa**, the city's main art gallery, at any one time housing at least two travelling exhibitions; it's dependably high quality and free.

## The Torre de Televisão, Memorial JK and Parque Sara Kubitschek

The **Torre de Televisão** (TV Tower) on Eixo Monumental is an obvious city landmark and easily reached on foot or by bus (#131 from the *rodoviária*). The 218-metre-high tower's viewing platform (Tues–Sun 9am–9pm) is a great place from which to put Brasília into perspective, and there is no better spot to watch the sunset – though frustratingly there is no bar to watch it from. At the weekend the tower is also popular for its craft market, held around the base – a good place to pick up cheap clothes.

Further up the Eixo is the **Memorial JK (Juscelino Kubitschek)** (Tues–Sun 9am–5.45pm; R$5 entrance charge), best reached by one of the many buses heading up the Eixo, as it's too far to walk. Here, a rather Soviet-looking statue of Brasília's founder stands inside an enormous question-mark, pointing down the Eixo towards the heart of government. The museum below reverently reproduces JK's library and study, while the man himself lies upstairs in state in a black marble sarcophagus, backlit by an extraordinary combination of purple, violet and orange lights – the only thing missing is a sound system piping in "The Age of Aquarius". All around is a fascinating display of personal mementoes of JK's career and the founding and construction of the city, including photos and video clips of his funeral and the dedication of the Memorial – in turning out in their hundreds of thousands in his honour, despite the desire of the military dictatorship to keep the event low-key, the population of the Distrito Federal made the first important anti-military demonstration, one of the reasons for the subsequent slow relaxing of the military's grip on power.

A short walk from Setor Hoteleiro Sul, taking up one entire side of the Eixo, is the enormous **Parque Sara Kubitschek**, named after JK's wife (bus #152 from the *rodoviária* passes by) – a massive mosaic of playgrounds, jogging tracks, bars and restaurants, picnic grounds, artificial lakes, parklands and woods. If you want to walk or jog in Brasília, this is the place to do it. The southern entrance, a block away from the hotel sector, is where many of the attractions are concentrated, including an enjoyably tacky but perfectly safe (despite appearances) **funfair** that will appeal to young children, and a place to hire *pedalôs* – adult-sized tricycles that are harder work than they look, but great fun nonetheless. The best time to visit is Sunday morning, when the locals turn out en masse to jog, work out, sunbathe or read the paper, while dozens of kiosks and street-sellers tout everything from iced green coconuts to shiatsu massage.

## The Memorial dos Povos Indígenas

Across the road from the JK Memorial is another Niemeyer building, the white and curving **Memorial dos Povos Indígenas** (Tues–Fri 10am–4pm; free), which houses one of the best collections of **indigenous art** in Brazil, much of it from the *planalto* itself and produced by the indigenous groups who inhabit the headwaters of the Xingú river. Highlights are the extraordinary ceramic pots of the Warao, the Xingú's ceramic specialists, beautifully adorned with figures of birds and animals, and vivid, delicate featherwork. The rotating exhibits and regular travelling shows are uniformly fascinating, but the building alone is worth the visit; the gallery is set in a long, downward curve around a circular courtyard, the smoked glass set against Niemeyer's trademark brilliant white exterior. At the lower end is a **café**, virtually never open but where Indians up from the Xingú often leave artwork for the museum staff to sell for them; bargaining for these good-quality and reasonably priced items would be churlish.

Run by the chronically hard-up state government, the museum keeps opening hours that are theoretical rather than real. If you arrive on the weekend or on Monday, and find the main entrance at the top of the ramp shut, slip down to the large metal door at ground level, to the right of the ramp, and bang hard; either a security guard or one of the museum staff will let you in. It's definitely worth the effort.

## Indigenous craft market

One of Brasília's least-known – but by far most interesting – markets is the impromptu **indigenous craft market** that has grown up on the patio of the headquarters of FUNAI, the federal Indian agency, in the Setor de Rádio e Televisão Sul. The market, in its own small way, is the perfect symbol of what has changed in the relationship between Brazil's Indians and the federal government in recent years. FUNAI once controlled all the marketing of indigenous art, via its own chain of craft shops, one of which you can still find inside FUNAI's entrance hall. But too much of the revenue stayed with FUNAI rather than the producers, who have now taken matters into their own hands; every weekday, around 9am, groups of indigenous people start setting out their wares on the patio, mainly basketware and ceramics but much more besides, most of it pretty good quality and always interesting to check out. The bulk of it comes from the Xingú, far northeast of the *planalto* and the closest sizeable indigenous area to Brasília. But since Indians come to FUNAI from all over to sort out their many problems, and usually bring whatever they can stuff into a bag or two to sell and make a little money on the side, the anthropologically minded can find people and *artesanato* from all over Brazil, especially the Amazon. This is one of the rare places where the shopper often needs to pay more than asked; many sellers have only vague notions of market values and ask ridiculously low prices, US$2 or US$3 for items that are patently worth far more. Shop responsibly.

The market is a short walk from the main entrance to the Parque Sara Kubitschek, or from Setor Hoteleiro Sul along W3; go past the Pátio Brasil mall, turn right after the Assis Chateaubriand building, helpfully identified by enormous letters on its side, and the market is one block up on the other side of the road, next door to the Dom Bosco school.

## Further out: the asas, Jardim Botânico and Parque Nacional de Brasília

The residential parts of Brasília are rarely thought of as a destination for visitors, but the older areas are by far the best place for a stroll during the day. The parks and gardens between the blocks are extremely well designed, and even at the hottest times of year you can walk for hundreds of yards in certain areas without leaving the shade. The oldest *superquadras* are all in Asa Sul; 108 Sul was the first to be completed in the whole city, designed as a showpiece to make the city tolerable for those bureaucrats moving here from Rio (a miserable failure in that respect at the time, but things eventually improved as the trees grew). The adjacent blocks from 107 down to 104 were all built shortly after and make for a great **urban walk** – take a bus or walk up W3 Sul, get off at the 508 block, walk two blocks down, and then start strolling towards the centre. There are plenty of *comercials* along the way if you want to make a pit stop.

For a taste of the *cerrado* before heading deeper into the *planalto*, or just a temporary break from the city, consider venturing to the Jardim Botânico, at the far end of Asa Norte, and the Parque Nacional de Brasília, across the striking JK Bridge over Lago Paranoá in Lago Sul. Both were created in the early 1960s to preserve large green spaces within easy reach of the city – it seemed superfluous then, but the pace of development has been so fast that there would be very little native *cerrado* anywhere near the city without them. The **Jardim Botânico**, at Setor de Mansões Dom Bosco in Lago Sul (Tues–Sun 9am–5pm; R$5; taxi around R$20 from centre; bus route #147 from *rodoviária*, stands 8 & 9 at Platform A), is a calm and well-organized retreat where you can experience the flora and fauna of the *cerrado* at first hand. There's an information centre, a large display of medicinal plants of the region, a herb garden, and over forty square kilometres of nature reserve with an extensive network of trails. It's good hiking, but make sure you bring a hat and water.

The **Parque Nacional de Brasília**, the city's very own national park (daily 8am–4pm; admission R$2), at the far end of Asa Norte, is the only area of native vegetation large enough around Brasília to support proper wildlife populations.

### Getting to and from Parque Nacional de Brasília

The national park is a R$30 **taxi ride** from the centre, but you have to arrange a rendezvous to return, since very few unoccupied taxis pass by – the **bus** is a better bet, but not easy. Astonishingly, there is no bus stop at the park entrance: the closest you can get here is by picking up the W3 Norte Circular on W3 and asking the driver to drop you off as it reaches the end of W3 and turns – look hard and you can see the park entrance on the other side of the highway.

This is the one place where it is actually easier to get a **perueiro**, one of the illegal but ubiquitous and highly organized white minibuses that shadow the bus routes. Look for *perueiro* lines #82 and #84, with an orange stripe on the side: the easiest place to catch them is the car park above the *rodoviária*, opposite the Conjunto Nacional – they wait until they fill up and then go, but you'll have to tell the driver to let you off near the park entrance.

During the week, you will have the place largely to yourself, and while the park itself is enormous, visitors are restricted to its southern corner, where the main attractions are two very large **swimming holes**, Piscina Velha and Piscina Nova, both a short, well-signposted walk from either of the two entrances, and built around a stream, preserving the natural flow of the water. When there is nobody there, this is a lovely spot – especially for a picnic. You may spot capuchin monkeys leaping acrobatically through the trees, but they have become used to scavenging picnic remains so take care not to leave food lying around, and be sure to pack plastic bags away as the monkeys regularly choke on them.

Although the swimming holes get very crowded at weekends, virtually everyone sticks to the water, so if you want space and some solitude, head up the slope to a small fenced trail through a section of gallery forest and continue up the hill until you come up onto open *cerrado* savanna. Here you'll find another much longer trail, a four-mile circuit called the **Água Cristal** (crystal water trail), which lives up to its name, taking you through a number of clearwater streams before dumping you back more or less where you started. The views are beautiful, although it is frustrating you can't hike into them.

# Eating, nightlife and entertainment

One of the best things about Brasília is the wide variety of **bars and restaurants**; in fact, a combination of the government, the university and diplomats supports one of the densest concentrations of good restaurants in the country. With some deserving exceptions, the following concentrates on the best places within easy reach of the hotel sectors. Prices are more than reasonable; unless noted, a full meal with drinks averages around R$40 per head, often less. Cheaper food can be found in the street markets and stalls scattered around the *rodoviária*, Conjunto Nacional, and in the large Pátio Brasil shopping centre next to the Setor Hoteleiro Sul, dominated by *comida por kilo* places catering to lunching office workers. If you're walking, you should have no problems with safety around most places in Asa Norte and Asa Sul, but W3 and the deserted central area should be walked around with caution at night. Most restaurants close on Monday night rather than Sunday.

## Restaurants

A good place to start, especially on a weekend night, is **comercial 404/405 Sul**; some *comercials* specialize and this one, known locally as *Restaurantelândia*, is lined on both sides with at least a dozen different national cuisines from four continents, and heaves with people at weekends. Although better food is to be had elsewhere, this is a good place to bar hop and then have a range of eating options to choose from. Recommended places are all in the numbered *comercial*, unless otherwise indicated.

**A Tribu** 105 Norte. Best vegetarian food in the city, imaginative and full of flavour. Offers a lunchtime buffet, and is open at night too. The newly opened branch in Setor dos Clubes Norte, near the JK Bridge and accessible only by taxi (R$10 from centre) is even better, built in the form of an indigenous roundhouse, lit by fires at night.

**Acarajé da Rosa** 204 Sul. Cheap, unpretentious Bahian food, especially pleasant at night in the dry season, when you can sit outside beneath the trees.

**Belini** 113 Sul. Everything you need under one roof – excellent deli, good espresso bar, and classy but still reasonably priced restaurant upstairs.

**Camarão e Cia.** 206 Sul. Good seafood buffet at lunchtime, followed by Bahian food at night.

**Carpe Diem** 104 Sul. Deservedly the best-known bar/restaurant in town: great atmosphere, renowned politico hangout and very reasonably priced. Famous among locals for the best salad bar and lunch buffet in the city (you pick the salad ingredients, they whip it up for you) and the Saturday *feijoada*; food and drinks served practically 24/7, apart from a few hours in the morning.

**Crêpe au Chocolat** 109 Norte and 210 Sul. Eat elsewhere, head here for dessert and be stretchered home – not for the faint of heart.

**Don Durica** 201 Norte. Serving an excellent lunch and evening buffet of traditional, quite heavy Brazilian food, such as stewed rabbit and various dishes of lamb, pork and suckling pig. If you want something lighter, try the extremely tasty soup buffet.

**Espettus** Setor Hoteleiro Sul. Best option if you're staying in one of the nearby hotels and don't feel like going far – good, varied *churrascaria*, infinitely preferable to any of the hotel restaurants.

**Feitiço Mineiro** 306 Norte. Even without the live music at weekends (see opposite), this spot is worth patronizing for the food alone; a buffet of *comida mineira* (Minas Gerais food), heavy on the pork, bean sauce and sausages, prepared the traditional way on a wood-fired stove. Open for dinner only.

**Fratello** 103 Sul. Best pizza in town: wood-fired kiln and original ingredients. Try the eponymous Fratello, based on sweet pickled aubergine.

**Fritz** 404 Sul. This spot is known for its very German food – stodge heaven and cheap.

**Ichiban** 405 Sul. Good sushi, sashimi and whatever other Japanese food you fancy; divided into Western and Japanese seating sections, the latter can be hard on the knees if you're not used to it.

**Kosui** Academia de Tênis, Setor dos Clubes Norte. Arguably the best Japanese restaurant in the city and certainly the best located of any of them, next to the Academia's art-cinema complex – handy if you want to do dinner and a film. Good Italian and seafood restaurants are also part of the complex.

**Patu Anú** Setor dos Mansões Lago Norte (SMLN), ML12, Conjunto 1, Casa 7l, near the Paranoá dam ⓣ1/3369-2788 or 3922-8930. The very best of Brazilian cuisine, served in a fantastic lakeside location. The menu is exclusively game: wild boar, alligator, *capivara* (the largest rodent in the world, which actually tastes great) and more, cooked with mouthwatering sauces, and regional fruits and vegetables. Dinner and drinks cost about R$80 a head, plus R$60 each way for the taxi – get one via your hotel and make sure you show this address to the driver before you set out. Reservations are a good idea (English spoken), and the restaurant will get you a cab for the return trip.

**Porcão** Pier 21 Shopping Centre, Asa Sul. A short taxi ride from the centre, this spot ("big pig" in Portuguese) certainly lives up to its name as the largest and most varied *churrascaria* in Brasília, and is strictly for carnivores. Drinks are overpriced, so concentrate on the food.

**Sabor do Brasil** 302 Sul. For those on a strict budget this place offers the best meal in town – for around R$15 a head. A soup buffet with trimmings, very traditional Brazilian fare, good vegetarian options but soups for carnivores too. Open for lunch and at night. Good place to line the stomach before heading out for a night on the town, or to sober up coming back from one.

## Bars and cafés

Even discounting the hotel bars – and there are plenty of those – there's a good selection of **places to drink**, though the scene as a whole is nothing like as lively as Rio.

**Armazém do Ferreira** 202 Norte. Popular with politicians, this place is best late at night when it gets very crowded. The tables outside are very pleasant, huddled under trees; the similar *Café do Brasil* next door is also good.

**Bar Beirute** 109 Sul. Often very lively and packed at night with a young crowd, with Lebanese food that's no more than OK but cheap. There's also a playground for kids.

**Bar Brasília** 306 Sul. Successful re-creation of an old-style Rio bar, complete with surly waiters; as a bar very good, but the view out across a car park leaves something to be desired.

**Café com Letras** 203 Sul. Pleasant café above a good bookshop (with some English titles) open into the small hours. The veranda is a good spot to watch the students and young professional crowd.

**Daniel Briand** 104 Norte; side of Bloco A. This French-owned patisserie and teahouse is highly recommended (especially for a late breakfast on weekends or afternoon tea any day) and serves the best quiche and cakes in town. There's nowhere better for coffee and reading; the only problem is the early and rigidly enforced closing at 10pm – both un-French and un-Brazilian.

**Frei Caneca** Entrequadra 110/111 Sul. Large beer hall that only really gets going late at night, with good atmosphere and live music every weekend.

**Libanus** 206 Sul. Perennially crowded spot serving up excellent-value, hearty Lebanese food; the playground makes it a good place for families in the afternoons, but turns into a young and humming scene at night.

**Marujo** 105 Sul. Constantly crowded bar, where despite the terrible food, the outdoor tables under trees make it pleasant enough as a hangout.

**Tortaria di Lorenza** 107 Norte, 302 Sul. Inexpensive place for gooey, tempting cakes, espresso coffee and savouries.

## Live music

Brasília is a good place to catch **live music**. The main place to catch local and visiting bands today is *Gate's Pub* (403 Sul), much bigger than it looks from the outside, with a series of rooms and small stages – resembling in a weird way a British pub-rock venue. Thursday nights are particularly lively. Student hangout *Frei Caneca Draft*, in the Brasília Shopping mall, also often has local bands on weekend nights. *Café Cancún* in the Liberty Mall, Setor Comercial Norte, transcends its unpromising setting late on Friday and Saturday nights with live music and great DJs, Brazilian rhythms mixed with salsa.

You can see more traditional first-class Brazilian music live at *Feitiço Mineiro* (see opposite under "Restaurants"), and, especially, at the *Clube do Choro* (central strip of the Eixo Monumental, next to the convention centre – all the taxi drivers know it). Ask at your hotel or check the listings, but it's usually open at night from Thursday to Saturday, with live music on Thursdays and Fridays, turning into a *gafieira* (dance hall), on Saturday night, with its own house band and older, intimidatingly good dancers. On Thursdays and Fridays, chairs and tables are set in front of the small stage, and the house specializes in *choro*, the oldest – and arguably most beautiful – Brazilian musical genre, played here by masters young and old to an appreciative, knowledgeable audience. If you've never been in a crowd brought to its feet by a fast mandolin solo, you haven't lived. This is as good a club venue as you'll find anywhere in the country.

Visiting megastars, Brazilian and otherwise, will play either the Teatro Nacional or, more likely these days, the plush Americel Hall in the Clube de Tênis, Setor dos Clubes Sul.

## Cinema

Brasília is an excellent place to go to the cinema, with a large and appreciative audience for good films. The **Clube de Tênis** hosts the annual international film festival in October and also houses the Academia, probably the best cinema complex between São Paulo and Mexico City, with twelve screens of exclusively arthouse films to choose from year-round, not to mention several restaurants and a large bar. If you want commercial films, head for the malls. Worthy of special mention is Cine Brasília, a splendid example of early 1960s kitsch at Entrequadra 106/107 Sul, which has a huge screen. Run by the Ministry of Culture, the cinema is free to ignore commercial considerations completely and show the latest Iranian masterpiece, or classics of European and American cinema.

# Listings

**Airlines** Mostly found around the *Hotel Nacional* in various agents' shops. The main Brazilian companies are TAM, SHS 1, Galeria Hotel Nacional 61 ⓣ61/3223-5168, and at the airport ⓣ61/3365-1000; Varig, at the airport ⓣ61/3364-9583. Gol has no agencies but has phone lines and encourages on-line bookings ⓣ300/789-2121, ⓦwww.voegol.com.br. Among overseas airlines are Air France, SHS 1, Galeria Hotel Nacional 39/40 ⓣ61/3223-4152, ⓕ3223-2299; British Airways,

SHS, Galeria Hotel Nacional, Loja 18 ⓣ61/3226-4164, ⓕ3321-9016; KLM, SHS 1, Galeria Hotel Nacional 51 ⓣ61/3321-3636 or 3225-5915; Lan Chile, SCS, Q8, Bloco B-60, Ed. Venâcio ⓣ61/3226-0318; Lufthansa, SHS 1, Galeria Hotel Nacional, Loja 1 ⓣ61/3223-5002 or 3233-8202.

**Airport enquiries** ⓣ61/3365-1941, 3365-1024, 3365-1224 or 3365-1947.

**ATMs** Banco do Brasil and HSBC at the airport; Citibank at the Setor Bancário Sul opposite the Pátio Brasil mall, with another Citibank ATM tucked away at the Blockbuster video in 506 Norte; HSBC at 502 Sul, on W3, and Banco 24 Horas kiosks in many supermarkets and large *farmácias*.

**Books and newspapers** English-language papers, magazines and books at Sodiler, ground floor of the Conjunto Nacional and Millenium Revistas at 303 Sul; both bookshops also at the airport.

**Car rental** All found lining the airport road: Avis ⓣ61/3365-2991; Localiza ⓣ0800/992-000; Hertz ⓣ61/365-4747; Unidas ⓣ0800/121-121. Avoid paying a hefty surcharge at the airport by heading into town by taxi and renting from there; highly recommended is Via Rent-A-Car ⓣ61/3322-3181 or 9985-4717, SHS Q6 Cj. A, Bloco F, Loja 50, or, more comprehensibly, the side of the *Hotel Melia*.

**Embassies** For the Setor de Embaixadas Sul (SES), take a bus to Av. das Nações, or just walk. Argentina, SHIS QI 01, Cj. 01, Cs. 19 ⓣ61/3365-3000; Australia, SHIS QI 9, Cj. 16, Cs.1 ⓣ61/3248-5569; Bolivia, SHIS QL 10, Cj. 1, Cs. 6 ⓣ61/3364-3362; Canada, SES Av. das Nações 803, Lote 16, sala 130 ⓣ61/3321-2171; Colombia, SES Av. das Nações 803, Lote 10 ⓣ61/3226-8997; Ecuador, SHIS Q1 11, Cj. 09, Cs. 24 ⓣ61/3248-5560; Paraguay, SES Av. das Nações 811, Lote 42 ⓣ61/3242-3732; Peru, SES Av. das Nações 811, Lote 43 ⓣ61/3242-9435; UK, SES Av. das Nações 801 ⓣ61/3225-2710; US, SES Av. das Nações 801, Lote 3 ⓣ61/3321-7272; Venezuela, SES Av. das Nações 803, Lote 13 ⓣ61/3223-9325.

**Emergencies** Medical ⓣ192; police ⓣ197; fire brigade ⓣ193.

**Money exchange** Confidence Cambio, Unit 202, Brasília Shopping (or at airport – in either case you will need passport ID to complete exchange transaction).

**Post office** Brasília's main post office (Mon–Sat 9am–6pm) is the small, white building in the open grassy space behind the *Hotel Nacional*.

# Day-trips from Brasília

Although it is sometimes difficult to imagine in the concrete heart of Brasília, the city is at the centre of some spectacular natural scenery that is easily accessible as day-trips from the capital. We've concentrated on straight day-trips or places where an overnight stay is possible but not really worthwhile. Other destinations a little further out but still easy to get to from Brasília like **Pirenópolis** (see p.478), **Goiás Velho** (see p.481) and **Chapada dos Veadeiros**, where you can really get to grips with the *cerrado* rather than get a taste of it, are dealt with separately in the section below on Goiás state.

When out walking in the *cerrado*, remember at all times of year the sun is hot and the altitude means you will burn quickly, so a hat and lashings of sunscreen are essential. Stout sandals are a good footwear choice, allowing you to negotiate the rocky, uneven beds of the streams and swimholes. Be aware flash floods pose a danger in gorges during the rainy season. Even when the sun is shining, rain can be falling unseen in headwaters.

## Cristalina, Formosa and the Itiquira waterfall

From Brasília, an easy day-trip involves taking one of the frequent buses from the *rodoferroviária* to the town of **CRISTALINA**, a two-hour ride south of Brasília into the Goiás plateau. Indeed, the journey itself is one of the main reasons to go, as you'll pass through the distinctive rolling hills of the *planalto* along the BR-040 towards Belo Horizonte. Prospectors who came here looking for gold in the early eighteenth century came across a large quantity of rock crystal; the European market opened up over a century later, and today Cristalina is an attractive, rustic town, based around the mining, cutting, polishing and marketing of semi-precious stones. Quartz crystal and Brazilian amethyst can also be bought here at very reasonable prices, mostly from enormous warehouses on the edge of town that pull in passing motorists. If you want to stay, *Hotel Attie*, Praça José Damian 34 (Ⓣ61/3612-1252; ❷), and *Hotel Goyá*, Rua da Saudade 41 (Ⓣ61/3612-1301; ❷), are both good value. The town boasts an excellent *churrasco* restaurant, *Churrascaria Rodeio*, Rua 7 de Setembro 1237, where the Sunday lunch alone, which includes roasted game, is worth the trip.

If you only have time for one day-trip, though, your best bet is to take the two-hour bus ride to the town of **FORMOSA**, not so much for the place itself, pleasant though it is, as for the stunning waterfall and park of **Salto de Itiquira**, for which Formosa is the jumping-off point. The park, which is about 40km away, is well signposted if you are in a rented car, but buses are infrequent; haggling with a local taxi driver at the bus station should get you a return trip for around R$70. It's worth it: the drive is beautiful, with the spectacular 90-metre waterfall visible from miles away as a white line against the towering cliffs of the Serra Formosa. Surrounding the waterfall is a municipal park (admission R$7), well laid out with a series of swimholes that make it a great place to spend the day. The most spectacular of all is at the very top of the only path, where the waterfall comes plunging down. Although there is a snack bar at the car park, by far the best place to eat is the *Dom Fernando* restaurant, with an excellent buffet of local food, and freshly grilled meats to order. It's located in splendid isolation at Km 6 on the road to the waterfall, but is only open weekends and holidays – otherwise there's a restaurant to the right of the park entrance. The park is at its best during the week, when it's less crowded.

# Goiás and Tocantins states

Beyond the city and Federal District of Brasília, the hill-studded, surprisingly green *cerrado* of **Goiás state** extends towards another modern, planned city, **Goiânia**, and the historic old towns of **Pirenópolis** and **Goiás Velho**, the latter in particular worth going out of your way for. Although gold mining started there in a small way during the seventeenth century, the first genuine settlement didn't appear until 1725. These days agriculture is the main activity: ranching is important but it is soybean production that is booming, driving the conversion of the dwindling remnants of *cerrado* into enormous farms. The small rural towns are all increasingly prosperous as a result, the state road system is excellent by Brazilian standards, and it's easy to imagine most of Goiás looking like the interior of São Paulo a generation from now. Indeed, the main cities of **Goiânia** and **Anápolis**, with their rising affluence and acres of new high-rises, already look very much like the cities of the *paulista* interior – and are about as interesting to visit, which is not very.

In the north of Goiás is the heart of the *planalto*, a jumble of cliffs, spectacular valleys and mountain ranges in and around the national park of **Chapada dos Veadeiros**, excellent for hiking and a thoroughly worthwhile excursion from Brasília, although you'll need a few days to do it justice.

In the south, the thermal springs of **Caldas Novas** and **Rio Quente** bubble up into giant hotel complexes, while, over on the western border with Mato Grosso, the **Parque Nacional Emas** has less spectacular landscapes than Chapada dos Veadeiros but is wilder, a little more inaccessible (although still easily reached from Brasília), and a better place to see wildlife, in particular the large American rhea.

The Rio Araguaia with its many beautiful sandy beaches, forms the 1200-kilometre-long western frontier of both Goiás and Tocantins states. The latter, created for political rather than geographic or economic reasons in 1989, contains the huge river island, **Ilha do Bananal**, and its **Parque Nacional do Araguaia**. The main and central section (BR-153) of the 2000-kilometre-long highway from Goiânia and Brasília to Belém also runs through Tocantins. The only town of any significance is **Araguaína**, a flyblown settlement in the middle of a largely converted savanna.

# Goiânia

**GOIÂNIA** was founded in 1933, becoming the state capital four years later. Over a million strong, cheaper (and wetter and greener) than Brasília, with some good hotels and only 209km from the federal capital, the city is a good stopping-off point, since it is well connected by road to most other Brazilian cities. Goiânia earns its living as a market centre for the surrounding agricultural region, which specializes in beef and soybeans.

## Arrival and information

Both the **rodoviária** (Ⓣ62/3240-0000 and 3224-8466) and Santa Genoveva **airport** (Ⓣ62/3265-1500) lie in the northern sectors of town. The *rodoviária* is around twenty minutes by foot from Setor Central along Avenida Goiás, or a short ride by local bus. The airport is linked to the centre, 6km away, by bus (#190 or #162 "Circular Aeroporto"; R$4); a taxi to most central hotels will cost around R$25. To catch local buses in town, there are main stops on Avenida Araguaia just south of Rua 4, and along Avenida Goiás opposite *Hotel Paissandú*. There's a **tourist information** booth (daily 8am–6pm; Ⓣ62/3201-8100) at the airport, which has free maps. In the centre, the regional tourist authority, SEBRAE, has an office on Rua 30 at the Centro de Convenções (Ⓣ62/3217-2055 and 3217-1100, Ⓦwww.goiania.net) and should also be able to help.

The wide central streets are almost – but not quite – handsome in their blending of grandeur with modernist concrete and glass, offering skyscraping offices and homes for the rapidly growing middle-class population of the city. The main node of the concentric city plan is the Centro Cívico and Praça Dr Pedro Ludovico, at the head of the massive Avenida Goiás, whose broad and leafy pavement extends all the way down its middle between both directions of busy traffic. The city is divided into several sectors, the most important being the Setor Central, Setor Oeste and Setor Universitário, and many of the streets have numbers rather than names.

## Accommodation

Goiânia has a wider range of **hotels** than Brasília. As well as giving you a greater choice of accommodation, this also means that you're more likely to be able to negotiate discounts – many of the larger hotels, as a matter of course, discount their prices out of season by twenty to forty percent.

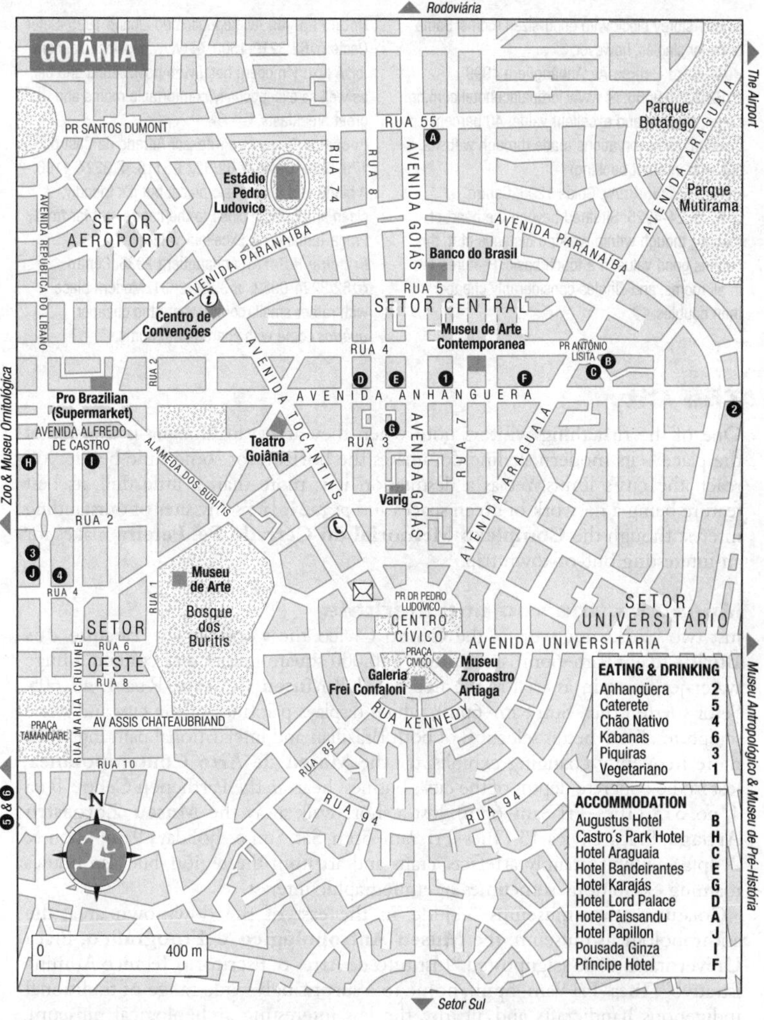


**Augustus Hotel** Av. Araguaia 702, Centro ⓣ62/3216-6600, ⓦwww.augustushotel.com.br. Located on the Praça Antônio Lisita next to the *Araguaia*, this hotel is much flashier than its neighbour, with good rooms – though a little dark – plus a pool and sauna. ④

**Castro's Park Hotel** Av. República do Líbano 1520, Setor Oeste ⓣ62/3096-2000, ⓦwww.castrospark.com.br. Luxurious hotel with immaculate service, as well as swimming pools and a superb restaurant. Outside holiday times it's a good place to try for discounted rooms. ⑥–⑦

**Hotel Araguaia** Av. Araguaia 664, Centro ⓣ&ⓕ62/3212-9800, ⓦwww.araguaiahotel.com.br. Overlooking the little Praça Antônio Lisita, this hotel has an impressive lobby, which the rooms conspicuously fail to live up to. Good value nonetheless, especially if you can negotiate a discount. ③–④

**Hotel Bandeirantes** Av. Anhangüera 3278, Centro ⓣ&ⓕ62/3224-0066. Flashy and a/c but with no pool; it's particularly worth bargaining over room prices here. ⑥

**Hotel Cabiúna** Av. Paranaíba 698 ⓣ62/3212-5001. Central location, good value, with slightly dowdy rooms but clean and efficient. ④

**Hotel Karajás** Rua 3, no. 860, Centro ⓣ62/3224-9666, ⓦwww.hotelkarajas.com.br. Very comfortable twenty-storey block with good-sized rooms. Same price for singles, however. ⑤

**Hotel Lord Palace** Av. Anhangüera 4999 ⓣ62/3224-9666, ⓦwww.lordpalacehotel.com.br. Clean, modern and excellent value; 40 percent discount for reservations made through website. ④ (③ with internet booking)

**Hotel Paissandu** Av. Goiás 1290, Centro ⓣ62/3224-4925. Situated beyond the heart of the city, though within walking distance of it, this hotel is good value, if a touch basic. Features TVs in all rooms, and singles considerably cheaper than doubles. ③

**Hotel Papillon** Av. República do Líbano 1825, Setor Oeste ⓣ62/3219-1500, ⓦwww.papillonhotel.com.br. A luxury modern hotel with pool, sauna and bar, as well as exceptionally comfortable rooms and great breakfasts. ⑤–⑥

**Pousada Ginza** Av. Professor Alfredo de Castro 179, Setor Oeste ⓣ62/3223-5118, ⓕ3224-4196. A bland and fairly basic place, but it's friendly, clean and located close to the centre, not far from Praça Tamandaré. Excellent value. ③

**Príncipe Hotel** Av. Anhangüera 2936, Centro ⓣ62/3224-0962, ⓕ3224-2831. Modern place with rather small rooms, where the cheaper *quartos* come with shared bathrooms. ②–③

## The City

One of the first things visitors note when they arrive in Goiânia is the size of the place – its modern skyline dominates the horizon for some time before you reach the city's limits. Yet as a destination it is more than a little dull, its best feature being a network of green spaces and *praças*. It lacks any sites of outstanding interest though the **Complexo Memorial do Cerrado Pe. Pereira** makes for an interesting out-of-town trip.

### Museums, the zoo and markets

Just two blocks due west of the Centro Cívico, the woods of the **Bosque dos Buritis** (daily 9am–6pm) spread over 140,000 square metres and contain a huge water-jet fountain as well as the free but dull **Museu de Arte**, Rua 1, no. 605, Setor Oeste (Tues–Sun 8am–6pm), which displays paintings of the city and stone sculptures. For a better selection of both Brazilian and international paintings with more frequently changing exhibits, try the **Museu de Arte Contemporânea**, lost in the concrete depths of the city's business heart in the Parthenon Centre, Rua 4, no. 515 (Tues–Fri 8am–6pm). Just a short walk away the **Museu Zoroastro Artiaga**, Praça Cívica 13 (Tues–Fri 9am–5pm, Sat, Sun & holidays 9am–noon & 2–4pm), exhibits mainly artefacts, crafts and art from the region, but also houses roaming exhibitions, sometimes of ethnographic interest.

Goiânia's other museums include, in the east of the downtown area, the anthropological museum, the **Museu Antropológico e Etnográfico**, Praça Universitária 1166 (signposted "Instituto de Artes & Escritorio Tecnico Administrativo"; Tues–Fri 9am–5pm), home to a surprisingly wide range of traditional indigenous handicrafts and, nearby, the less interesting archeological museum, the **Museu Goiâno de Pré-História e Arqueologia**, Praça Universitária 1440 (Mon–Fri 8–11am & 1–5pm); both museums can be reached on buses #167, #170, #164 or #162. Much less dusty and easily the most interesting museum in town even for non-birdwatchers is the **Museu Ornitológica**, Av. Para 395, Setor Campinas (daily 8am–10pm except Sun), which displays around six thousand stuffed birds.

One of the main public parks in Goiânia, **Parque Mutirama**, in the northeast of the city at the junction of *avenidas* Araguaia and Contorno (Mon–Fri 1–6pm, Sat & Sun 9am–6pm), is very popular with local kids because of its ingenious amusement centre, skating rink and planetarium (the latter open Sun 3.30pm & 4.30pm). Opposite the park, the woods of the **Parque Botafogo** (closed Mon), with their reforested native trees, help the centre of the city breathe; on the last Sunday of every month, there's also good live music here. One of the town's main outdoor features, the **Jardim Zoológico** (Tues–Sun 8am–5pm; R$4), located some nine long blocks west along Avenida Anhangüera from the Teatro Goiâno, is a pleasant and well-managed public park. At its northern end around the muddy Lago das Rosas, the park is home to a number of semi-tame monkeys, while the southern corner houses a large and well-stocked **zoo**, which is a must for anyone interested in wildlife. You'll see *emas* (rheas), *tuiuiús* (red-throated storks) and *jacarés* (alligators) closer here than you will in the wild. The **Feira Hippie** is a fascinating street market open every Sunday from early in the morning until mid-afternoon, dominating the stretch of Avenida Goiás from Rua 4 up to the Praça do Trabalhador. Originally a market for local crafts people, it has evolved to incorporate a wide range of more general alternative handicrafts, plus a global variety of socks, underwear, watches, electrical goods and all kinds of imported plastics. If you're around on a Saturday between 5 and 10pm, head for the **Feira da Lua**, which sells mainly *artesanato* in the tree-studded and lively Praça Tamandaré, a few blocks west of the Centro Cívico. Finally, the smaller **Feira do Sol**, on the Praça do Sol in the Setor Oeste, has around two hundred stalls selling crafts, antiques, foods, pets and fine arts every Sunday between 4 and 9pm.

## Complexo Memorial do Cerrado Pe. Pereira

The **Complexo Memorial do Cerrado Pe. Pereira** (daily 9am–5pm; taxi from the centre around R$35) is a large and well laid out museum, model village and eco-centre developed on the site of an old estate some 10km south of the city on the BR-153 towards São Paulo. The museum is dedicated to the evolution of the planet, with displays on geology, indigenous cultures and the wildlife and flora of the *cerrado*. There are also botanical gardens, a plant nursery with both common and endangered *cerrado* plant species and a fascinating model of a nineteenth-century *cerrado* village, including everything from the village shop and church to the bordello – an important public service in most *cerrado* settlements, which were after all just remote cowboy pit-stops.

## Eating

In Goiânia, as in Goiás Velho, the people are justly proud of their cooking. Local delicacies range from rice with *pequi* fruit through pasties (*empadões*) to roast pork with fried banana (*leitão assada com banana frita*). There are, however, a number of reasonable restaurants, *lanchonetes* and pizzerias around Praça Tamandaré, plus a few more *lanchonetes* around the cheaper hotels in Setor Centro. In general, the further south you go, the more expensive the restaurant.

**Anhangüera** Av. Anhangüera near the corner with Av. Paranaíba, Centro. Next to the Pro Brazilian supermarket, this is one of the cheapest and busiest lunchtime *comida por kilo* places.

**Árabe** Av. 83–205, Setor Sul. Goiânia has a large population of Lebanese descent and this is the best Arabic food in town, reasonably priced for the quality.

**Assoluto** Av. Cel. Eugenio Jardim 300, Setor Marista ⓣ62/3092-8281. Located in the Marista sector west of the city, this is the best place for quality Italian cuisine; it has fine wines and excellent service in a pleasant, roomy space.

**Caterete** Rua 10, Setor Oeste ⓣ62/3214-2025. Located in an outer suburb beyond the centre, this expensive restaurant is worth a taxi ride (about R$20) for its selection of the very best meat dishes including an excellent *rodizio*.

**Chão Nativo** Av. República do Líbano 1809, Setor Oeste ⓣ62/3223-5396. Located in the western sector it has the best self-service lunch spreads in the city and also serves a wide range of evening dishes, most of which are traditional *goiâno* cooking made on a wood-burning stove.

**Kabanas** Av. T-3 2693, Bueno. A little out from the centre but a very pleasant combined bar-restaurant next to a park, excellent for either eating or drinking. Very good *petiscos* – the nearest Brazil comes to tapas.

**Ki-sabor** Rua 3, no. 67, Centro. This budget-priced but very pleasant *comida por kilo* restaurant is open for lunch; get there by 1.30pm to be sure of a good choice of dishes.

**Piquiras** Av. República do Líbano 1758, Setor Oeste ⓣ62/3281-4344. One of the city's better all-round restaurants, with reliably good-quality food; you can eat inside or on a large terrace open to the road.

**Vegetariano** Rua 7, no. 475, Centro ⓣ62/3225-7290. Simple, well-presented vegetarian dishes in a small but friendly space.

### Drinking and nightlife

Goiânia has quite a lively nightlife, but most of the best **clubs** change names and venues every few months as they go in and out of fashion. Prices tend to be high, though. Praça Tamandaré is a good place to start your evening, with a number of bars and cafés and, later on, nightclubs on or near the square. The best of these is currently the terminally designer *Draft Casual Bar & Diner*, south down Avenida República do Líbano on the corner of Rua 22 and Rua 23, Setor Oeste (Tues–Sun). Nearby, on República do Líbano almost on the Praça Tamandaré, the 24-hour *Big Paint American Bar* (open daily) is another more conventional but flashy option. A little further west, *Chocolate Chic*, Av. Portugal 719, is full of the tackiness that passes as style among Goiânia's moneyed youth, but it's still a fun night out. Also fairly reliable are the *Bavária*, Rua T-51, no. 1054, Setor Bueno, and *Boate People*, Rua 7, no. 1000, Setor Oeste. As for straight drinking **bars**, there aren't that many. Very busy is *O Ceará*, on the corner of Rua 2 and Rua 8. Try also *Chopp 10*, Av. T-1, 2.215, Setor Bueno (daily 4pm until late), or the *Cervejaria Brasil* on Praça Antônio Lisita (closed Sun), which has a good range of bottled beers and cocktails.

## Listings

**Airlines** Pantanal Linhas Aéreas, Rua Dona Gercina Borges 34, Setor Sul ⓣ62/3224-4286; TAM, Av. 85, no. 944, Setor Sul ⓣ62/3207-1800; Varig, Av. Goiás 285, Centro ⓣ62/3207-1743 or 0800/997-000. Gol has no offices, but book online at ⓦwww.voegol.com.br or at the airport.

**Car rental** Hertz, Av. República do Líbano 1880, Setor Oeste ⓣ62/3223-6000; Localiza, Av. Anhangüera 3520, Setor Oeste ⓣ62/3261-7111; Unidas, Av. Caiapó, Quadra 85, Lote 123, Santa Genoveva, Setor Oeste ⓣ62/3207-1297.

**Health** Hospital Santa Helena ⓣ62/3219-9000.

**Shopping** The largest and flashiest shopping complex is Flambouyant Shopping, Av. Jamel Cecilio 3900, Jardim Goiás, Setor Pedro Ludovico, south of the city centre (daily 10am–10pm), followed closely by Bougainville, at Rua 9, no. 1855, Setor Oeste (Mon–Sat 10am–10pm).

**Travel and tour companies** SINGTUR (Sindicato dos Guias de Turismo), Alameda Progresso 511 (ⓣ62/3271-6970), is the regional tour-guide syndicate, and can provide lists of accredited guides for the Parque Nacional das Emas (see p.484). Turisplan Turismo, Rua 8-388, Centro (ⓣ62/3224-1941), speak good English and run a range of local tours; NatureTur, Av. República do Líbano 2417, Setor Oeste (ⓣ62/3215-2000, ⓕ215-2011), are especially good for visits to Caldas Novas (see p.485).

## Pirenópolis

**PIRENÓPOLIS**, a picturesque market town of about 21,000 people, straddles the Rio das Almas, 112km north of Goiânia in the scrubby mountains of the Serra dos Pireneus. Founded by *bandeirantes* in 1727 as a gold-mining settlement, it's a popular weekend retreat for residents of Brasília and often very busy during main Brazilian holidays, but well supplied with accommodation to suit all budgets.

## Arrival and information

Pirenópolis is well connected by road to the other major towns of the region. There are three direct **buses** a day from Goiânia and six from Brasília. The *rodoviária* (Ⓣ62/3331-1080) is on the eastern edge of town on Avenida Neco Mendonça, five minutes' walk from the centre. **Tourist information** is available from the Centro do Atendimento ao Turista, Rua Bonfim da Serra dos Pireneus (Mon–Sat 8am–8pm; Ⓣ62/3331-1299 and 3331-2729), and the council publishes an excellent annual *Guia do Turista* (free), available in most of the hotels and establishments mentioned below. **Internet** is available at Planeta Cybercafe, opposite the Banco do Brasil on Rua Sizenando Jaime, by the corner with Rua Benjamin Constant.

## Accommodation

A popular local resort, Pirenópolis has dozens of **hotels** and **pousadas** to choose from, many of them merely private homes with a few rooms for rent. The quality is generally well above average, and discounts are available mid-week or out of season. Camping is available at *Camping Roots*, Rua Pireneus 95 (Ⓣ62/3331-2105, Ⓦwww.campingroots.org; ❶).

**Hotel Rex** Praça Emmanoel Lopes 15 Ⓣ62/3331-1121. Located on a small square to the right of the church, this family-operated hotel has several quaint rooms, some rather small, along the edge of a traditional courtyard. ❷

**Pousada das Cavalhadas** Praça da Matriz Ⓣ&Ⓕ62/3331-1261. This is the most central hotel in town, just opposite the Igreja Nossa Senhora do Rosário. Reasonably comfortable, but its single rooms are overpriced. ❸

**Pousada Lara** Rua Direita 11 Ⓣ62/3331-1294. Small and a bit crowded, but otherwise is very clean, newly decorated and has a small pool. ❸

**Pousada dos Pireneus** Ⓣ62/3331-1028, Ⓦwww.pousadadospireneus.com.br. This is the main upmarket place in town, with its own rambling gardens, a pool, a small water-park with slides that kids will love, and horse-riding facilities – including amusing half-hour jaunts by carriage through town for a mere R$15 for four people. ❸–❺

**Pousada Walkeriana** Rua do Rosário 37, on the Praça do Rosário Ⓣ62/3331-1260, Ⓦwww.pousadawalkeriana.com.br. One of the grander places in town, with rooms set around a large and pleasant courtyard with a swimming pool. ❹

**Pouso do Sô Vigário** Rua Nova 25 Ⓣ62/3331-1206, Ⓦwww.pousadaspirenopolis.com.br. Just one road away from *Pousada Lara* is this, one of the town's nicest hotels. Housed in an old priest's residence, it has been embellished with a pool and a sauna. ❹

## The Town

The main street, **Avenida Sizenando Jayme**, is a broad, peaceful, tree-lined avenue where the old men, with their ponies and carts, and visiting *fazendeiros* hang out chatting in the shade; on Sunday mornings there's a produce market here. Just a couple of blocks down the hill is the site of the oldest church in Goiás, the **Igreja Nossa Senhora do Rosário de Meia Ponte**, once an attractive colonial edifice but tragically almost completely destroyed by fire in 2002 – although it has been rebuilt only parts of the walls are original. Opposite the church, the nineteenth-century theatre **Teatro de Pirenópolis** often has shows that cater to tourists and is always worth checking out.

The town centre's only remaining colonial church is east along the very attractive Rua Bonfim da Serra dos Pireneus. **Igreja Nosso Senhor do Bonfim**, built in the 1750s, is famous for its image of Nosso Senhor do Bonfim, originally brought here by two hundred slaves. Also in the upper part of town, at Rua Direita 39 between the remains of Rosário and the *rodoviária*, you'll find the small **Museu das Cavalhadas** (Fri–Sun 9am–5pm), located in a family's front room (knock if it appears closed). The museum contains displays of incredible carnival costumes from the Festo do Divino Espírito Santo, a lively and largely horse-mounted religious festival that takes place in the town exactly six weeks after Easter Sunday. The festival combines dances with mock battles from the Crusades, and the costumes include ornate metal armour, demonic masks and animal heads. Below the Igreja Nossa Senhora do Rosário, the town has a different atmosphere. Swimming and sunbathing spots line the river by the old stone and wood bridge, which links the main settlement with the Carmo section of town on the north bank. There's a vibrant **alternative scene** here, reflected in a handful of interesting bars, organic cafés and New Age stores; Homeostratum at Rua do Rosário 12 sells homeopathic products, natural foods, alternative magazines and *artesanato*, and Nataraja has a wide range of hippie-style clothes, crystals and alternative medicines. However, Pirenópolis is most famous in Brazil for its **silverwork**, mostly inset with semiprecious stones. The craft was introduced here just over twenty years ago by the hippies who came and stayed, and nowadays, with over two hundred artisans working in around a hundred workshops, you'll find jewellery for sale in dozens of shops, much of it inspired by Asian designs.

On the north side of the river, housed in the eighteenth-century Igreja Nossa Senhora do Carmo, the **Museu Sacro** (Mon–Sat 9am–6pm) displays an image of the town's patroness, originally brought here from Portugal.

One very worthwhile excursion into the surrounding countryside is to the **Santuário Vagafogo** (Tues–Sun 8am–5pm; R$15), a beautifully preserved patch of gallery forest with streams, swimholes, trails with walkways over the muddy patches and stairs up the steep sections, and a hammock-strung gazebo to relax in after your walks. Look hard and you can see the remains of colonial gold-mining beneath the undergrowth – part of the main trail is an eighteenth-century sluice bed. At weekends and on holidays, the small restaurant at the reserve entrance serves quite superb, very reasonably priced brunches, using home-grown ingredients: the jams and pickles using *cerrado* fruits are deliciously unusual. Eat first and walk it off down the trails. Access is a problem, since it is not well signposted and lies some 6km out of town. Your best bet is to catch a *moto-taxi* at the *rodoviária*, one of the motorbike taxis that hang out in groups at a pick-up point opposite the platforms (20min; around R$15). It is a bumpy but enjoyable ride down a dirt track, with pleasant scenery. Once there, hiking back is easy, or arrange to be picked up again.

## Eating and drinking

There are several good **restaurants** in the upper part of town, along Avenida Sizenando Jaime. Other, more expensive, restaurants can be found in the lower section, principally along Rua do Rosário and towards the river. There are several small *lanchonetes* on Avenida Sizenando Jaime and by the river opposite the police station. The liveliest bars are by the river, close to the bridge.

**Aravinda Bar and Restaurant** Rua do Rosário 25. Try the *moqueca de piexe*, curried fish, or *peixa na telha* (fish baked in an earthenware dish) at this communally-run spot, which sometimes has live music at weekends. They also serve french fries, pizza and great juices (Fri–Sun only).

**As Flor** Av. Sizenando Jaime 16. Unprepossessing in appearance but one of the best at lunchtime for regional cooking, though evening fare can dip in quality.

**Pamonharia** Just around the corner from *As Flor* on the way down to the church, this is a great spot for cheap meals.

**Restaurant Nena** Rua da Aurora 4 ⓣ62/3331-1470. Offers good self-service *comida por kilo* lunches and local dishes, including everything from pasta and steak to salads and fish.

**Trilha Zen** Rua Barbosa 23. A good bet if you want to eat on an outdoor patio, this place serves excellent crepes, salads, home-made burgers, filet mignon, along with milk shakes and *açai*.

## Tours

A number of guides and agencies offer ecological **tours** of the surrounding region, taking in sites within the Parque Estadal da Serra dos Pireneus and the Reserva Ecologica Vargem Grande. The region boasts many great trails and a host of impressive waterfalls, including the Abade, Inferno and Corumbá. Based at Rua Emílio de Carvalho 18 (Ⓣ62/3331-1392), Savanah Ecoturismo (Ⓣ62/3331-2729) runs tours leaving from the tourist information office at 10am (returning 5pm) to several destinations, including the Parque da Serra dos Pireneus and the Cachoeira dos Dragões (where there are eight waterfalls). Cerrado Ecoturismo, Rua Bonfim da Serra 46 (Ⓣ62/3331-1240), are agents for several private wildlife sanctuaries in the region. More guided tours (bicycles a speciality) are offered by Calango Expedições, Bairro do Carmo (Ⓣ62/3331-1564). For rafting try Turismo Aventura (Ⓣ62/3331-3336). The tourist office is very helpful for putting you in touch with guides, but the staff's English varies – ask for a *guia*.

# West of Goiânia

Renowned for its religious architecture and historic feel, the town of **Goiás Velho** is the main settlement west of Goiânia. But it is the huge **Rio Araguaia**, one of the Amazon's main southern tributaries, that attracts most Brazilians to Goiás. Even though most of the river now falls within the state of Tocantins, the Goiás section has hundreds of fine **sandy beaches** suitable for camping, and some well-established resorts, very popular with the residents of Goiânia and other towns in Goiás. Rich in fish, the Araguaia is particularly busy during the dry season from May to September when the water level drops, and serious anglers come from São Paulo and Goiânia to compete. The gateway to the river is **ARUANÃ**, a small town served by only a few hotels, just over 380km northwest of Goiânia.

The **best place to stay** and as comfortable as hotels come in this town, is the *Pousada Acauá*, Rua José Eufrasio de Lima 14 (Ⓣ62/3376-1294, Ⓦwww.pousadaacaua.com.br; ④), which offers fishing trips, has a pool, bar and reasonable restaurant. The *Recanto Sonhado Hotel*, Avenida Altamiro Caio Pacheco (Ⓣ62/3376-1230, reservations Ⓣ62/3212-3955; ④), is also very good, and has a pool, sauna and facilities for jet-skiing. At the same price but with less on offer (you should get a discount) is *Hotel Araguaia*, Praça Couto Magalhães 53 (Ⓣ62/3376-1251; ④), also with a pool. Cheaper still is the *SesiAruanã* (Ⓣ62/3376-1221, Ⓦwww.sesiaruana.com.br; ③). You can arrange boat trips to go fishing or rent your own boat in Aruanã. The busiest month is July, when it can be difficult to get a room.

## Goiás Velho

The historic town of **GOIÁS VELHO** – originally known as Vila Boa, and now often just called Goiás – is strung along and up a steep valley cut by the Rio Vermelho. It is one of the most beautiful colonial towns in Brazil, without the great churches and museums of the best of the *cidades históricas* in Minas but easily the equal of any of them in the calm elegance of its cobbled streets and squares, and much their superior in lack of commercialism. Its more remote location well to the north of the country's other eighteenth-century mining zones has made it the best-preserved colonial town in the country. It is simply gorgeous, fully deserving its status as a UNESCO World Heritage Site.

▲ Goiás Velho

## Arrival

Goiás Velho is 144km northwest of Goiânia, and a six-hour bus ride from Brasília. The **rodoviária** (Ⓣ62/3371-1510), which has connections to both these cities, is down by the river, and most accommodation and eating spots are close by. The best way to **get around**, other than your own two feet, are the local motorbike taxis; you'll see a stand of them in most squares, and they are usually plentiful around the bus station and its associated market – agree on price before you go.

## Accommodation

The town has several good lodging options: the *Vila Boa Hotel* (Ⓣ&Ⓕ62/3371-1000, Ⓦwww.hotelvilaboa.com.br; ④) has a decent pool and sauna; the cheaper and more central *Hotel Serrano* is also good (Ⓣ62/3371-1825; ③); the *Araguaia* (Ⓣ62/371-1462; ③) is cheaper still. Cheapest of all, but still very pleasant, is *Pousada do Sol* at Rua Americano Brasil 17 (Ⓣ62/3371-1717; ②). Highly recommended is the more upmarket *Pousada Ipê* (Ⓣ62/3371-2065; ②), on the other side of the river at Rua do Fórum 22, with essentials such as air conditioning and pool access. The best-value hotel in the centre is *Hotel Casa da Ponte* (Ⓣ62/3371/4467; ②), on Rua Moretti Foggia right in the heart of town, with air conditioning and TV in all rooms.

## The Town

Founded in 1726 as a gold-mining settlement by the *bandeirantes*, Goiás Velho remained the state capital until 1937. Nowhere else in Brazil is there a stronger sense of the colonial past, palpable in the cobbled streets and the many well-preserved eighteenth- and nineteenth-century buildings. Stone houses and quaint squares, the gaslit town centre and the occasional metallic clip-clop of mule hooves create a timeless atmosphere – one enhanced annually during the colourful, torchlit Easter Fogareu procession.

There is more than enough here to occupy you for a few days; apart from the town itself, the surrounding countryside is worth exploring, with good hiking amid the trails, waterfalls and swimholes characteristic of the *cerrado*.

In town, you'll find the usual collection of small local museums. The **Palácio Conde dos Arcos**, built in 1755 on the main Praça Dr Tasso de Camargo, was the old governor's palace and has the usual clunky period furniture; the best feature is an attractive Portuguese-style garden (Tues–Sat 8am–5pm, Sun 8am–noon; R$5). The most interesting exhibits are actually more modern, such as a nineteenth-century photo of the great-grandfather of two-term Brazilian president Fernando Henrique Cardoso, proudly pointed out by the museum guide who accompanies you, and the original application documents for their UNESCO World Heritage listing, reverently displayed in a velvet case.

The **Museu das Bandeiras**, situated up the hill on the Praça Brasil Ramos Caiado (Tues–Sat 9am–11am & 1–5pm, Sun 9am–1pm; R$2), recounts the story of the gold rush through artefacts including slave shackles and chains. A more unique feature is the building itself, which has a combined governor's office and council chamber upstairs and jail downstairs – an arrangement typical of early eighteenth-century Brazilian towns. The room to the right of the entrance desk was once part of the jail and has changed very little since it was built.

The town's **Museu de Arte Sacra da Boa Morte**, in the 1779 Igreja da Boa Morte on Praça Dr Tasso de Camargo (Tues–Fri 8am–5pm, Sat 9am–5pm, Sun 9am–1pm), is not very good; all of the local churches have had their interiors ruined by a combination of fires and misguided "improvements" – the worst example being the slave church of **Rosário dos Pretos** across the river, levelled on its bicentenary in 1934 and replaced by an incongruous Gothic structure. The other local museum worth seeing is the house of **Cora Coralina**, a local poet who never left the town in all of her 96 years of life but used it as raw material and became nationally famous. Located on the corner of Rua Dom Cândido, a colonial street overlooking the Rio Vermelho, the museum (Tues–Sat 9am–6pm, Sun 9am–4pm; R$3) is a hotchpotch of old furniture, photos and manuscripts, giving you a glimpse into small-town life.

## Exploring the countryside

If you need to cool off in the afternoon after walking the old city streets, there's a natural swimming pool out by the **Cachoeira Grande waterfalls** on the Rio Vermelho, just 7km east of town – the best (and cheapest) way to get there is on the back of one of the local motorbike taxis. The pool is pleasant when quiet, but it can get crowded at weekends. The most beautiful sight in the area is the **Cachoeira das Andorinhas** (Swallow Waterfall), 8km out of town, which makes for a wonderful day-trip. On the only road out of town, cross the Rio Vermelho, passing by the pretty church of **Igreja de Santa Bárbara**, perched on a small hill overlooking the municipal cemetery. Taking the dirt road to the left of the church (signposted *Hotel Fazenda Manduzanzan*), continue 7km through picturesque hill country until you reach a signposted trail entrance in front of the hotel (❹–❻), which has a pool and offers horse riding. The waterfall is another kilometre from here – when in doubt, always bear left. The last few hundred yards rise steeply through a forested gorge before ending at a glorious, tree-choked swimhole with a waterfall and – true to its name – swallows darting around. A highlight is a natural rock chamber that channels part of the waterfall into a cavern.

Remember Goiás is hot year-round – and baking hot in the dry season – so the usual precautions of carrying water, sunscreen and a hat applies. To save yourself some effort, consider having a motorbike taxi drop you off at the trail entrance (R$7) thereby halving the distance you need to walk, or arrange a time for a *moto-taxi* to pick you up if you don't feel like walking at all. Also consider heading out early for the trek, stopping afterward at the hotel for its excellent lunch (open to non-guests) and a doze in its hammocks, waiting until the sun starts to set and the heat lessens before heading back.

## Eating and drinking

For regional food, the *Restaurante Caseiro*, Rua Dom Cândido 31, is an inexpensive option for lunch. You can also try two excellent local restaurants. *Flor do Ipê*, at Rua Boa Vista 32 (☎62/3372-1133), which is across the small square from the *Pousada Ipê* (see p.482), serves a typical regional buffet that includes salads, pork, stewed chicken, okra and regional vegetables like *piquí*, slowly cooked on a traditional wood-fired stove; the restaurant is closed on Mondays but otherwise open for lunch and dinner. For more creative dishes based on local ingredients, the equally good *Beco do Sertão* is very central at Rua 13 de Maio 17 (☎62/3371-2459) but open only in the evenings. On a clear night the tables in the courtyard are a great place to dine.

# Parque Nacional das Emas

Down in the southwestern corner of Goiás state, the **Parque Nacional das Emas** (8am–5pm) is a *cerrado* reserve that was once the domain of zoologists and botanists but is gradually opening up to regular tourism. Located in the central Brazilian highlands near the Mato Grosso do Sul border, the park consists of some 1300 square kilometres of fairly pristine *cerrado*, mostly open grasslands pocked by thousands of termite hills, but with occasional clumps of savanna forest. While it lacks the scenic grandeur of Chapada dos Veadeiros, thanks to its relative isolation the reserve is one of the last places where you can find *cerrado* wildlife in some abundance, supporting an enormous population of **emas** (South American rheas) and also large herds of **veado-campeiro** deer, often shadowed by the solitary **lobo guará** (the maned wolf); all are more easily spotted here than anywhere else in Brazil. The Emas park is also famous for its wide range of variously coloured and extremely large **termite mounds**, which are used by *coruja-do-campo* owls as lookout posts dotted across the flat plain, and are a good source of food for *bandeira* anteaters. Due to the activity of larvae living inside them, some of the anthills glow phosphorescently green and blue – an amazing sight on a dark night, though you can only catch it in October, when conditions are right.

Within the park you are restricted to set trails – although here they traverse most of the park – and camping is not permitted. Beware of *mucuim*, irritating tiny ticks that jump onto legs and leave clumps of fantastically itchy reddish bites; wearing long trousers is your best defence, despite the heat.

## Arrival and information

It's easy to get to the area by bus from Brasília and Goiânia, but a bit of a logistical challenge once you're here: without a car distances are long, local buses are almost nonexistent, and you'll have to rely a guide's contacts to get around. As there is no **accommodation** in the park itself, you'll have to base yourself in the small towns of **MINEIROS** or **CHAPADÃO DO CÉU**, though both are a considerable distance from the park; the former, geared more to visitors and with a population of around 43,000, is unfortunately 85km away. The latter, only 27km from the park, is more rustic, and much smaller with less than 5000 inhabitants. There are direct **buses** to Mineiros from both Brasília and Goiânia, and to Chapadão from Goiânia only.

## Hiring a guide

You'll need to hire a local guide which, together with the transport they arrange, will set you back between R$100 and R$175 a day depending how many people are in your group; the more the cheaper. Both Mineiros and Chapadão do Céu have a highly organized association of **local guides**, which should be your first port of call; they will quote you a price and take care of the formalities with IBAMA, the national parks authority, such as registering entry and exit and paying the R$5 entrance fee (you have to pay your guide's entrance fee).

You will rarely be able to set out until the following day, as cars and drivers have to be found. Given the time it will take to reach the park itself, your best bet is to complete the formalities the day before and set off at dawn the next day. The association in Mineiros is located on Praça Marcelino Roque (ⓣ64/661-7153, ⓔednaldo.marelo@bol.com.br), and although the English spoken there is rudimentary, you can get by. In Chapadão do Céu, the association is at Avenida Ema, quadra 51 (ⓣ64/634-1228); ask for Sr Rubens or Sra Elaine on ⓣ62/634-1309.

## Accommodation and eating

Although there aren't many accommodation options, all are perfectly adequate and cheap. Of the **hotels in Mineiros**, the best is the *Pilões Palace* (ⓣ64/3661-1547; ④–⑤), on Praça Assis, with its own restaurant and bar. The *Dallas* at 223 Quinta Avenida (ⓣ64/3661-1534; ②–③) has quite comfortable rooms, while the *Líder* (ⓣ64/3661-1149; ③) on Rua Elias Machado and *Pinheiros* (②) on Rua Oito are serviceable if basic. **Accommodation in Chapadão do Céu** is much more basic. In town, your best options are *Hotel Ipê* (ⓣ64/3634-1722; ③), Rua Ipê 213, *Pousada das Emas* (ⓣ64/3634-1382; ③) on Rua Ipê, and *Hotel Rafael* (②) on Avenida Indaia. Out of town, the *Fazenda Santa Amelia* (ⓣ64/3634-1380; ④) has a pool, chalets and apartments, horseriding and a reasonable restaurant out at Km 65 of the GO-050 road; to find the place take the sign posted turn-off from the GR-050 for 15km (the last 5km of this is dirt track). As for **dining options**, you'll be limited to a couple of *churrascarias* in each town, plus the hotel restaurants – not *haute cuisine*, but satisfying after a day's hiking.

# Caldas Novas

More easily accessible than many of Goiás's attractions, the **thermal resorts** of **Caldas Novas**, around 185km south of Goiânia, are incredibly popular with Brazilians from beyond the state. It claims to be one of the world's largest hot-spring aquifers, a massive and very hot natural subterranean reservoir. The healing reputation and the sheer joy of relaxing in these natural spa resorts lure plenty of people from the urban sprawl of the São Paulo region. While some people do come for long, expensive courses of treatment, most visitors are simply here on holiday, relaxing, sunbathing and taking the waters for a few days or a week.

It gets crowded in the dry season from May to September, but there are thousands of hotel beds within this relatively small town of only around 40,000 people.

## Arrival and information

The bus station is just off the centre of town, a short taxi ride from the hotels. **Tourist information** is available from the SEBRAE office, on the Praça Mestre Orlando (daily 9am–6pm; ⓣ64/3454-3526), and for banking needs, head to the

Banco do Brasil at Rua Santos Dumont 55. For information on **buses**, go to the *rodoviária* or call ⓣ64/3453-3591.

## Accommodation and eating

Hotel reservations are best made in advance, usually from Goiânia. Among the better **hotels**, *Thermas di Roma*, Rua São Cristóvão 1110, Solar de Caldas, on the exit for Morrinhos (ⓣ64/3455-9393, ⓦwww.diroma.com.br; half-board ⑥), has a beautiful location out of town with panoramic views, over two hundred rooms, nine thermal pools and a sauna. On the whole, it's excellent value, as is *Taiyo Thermas*, in the town itself at Rua Presidente Castelo Branco 115 (ⓣ3455-5555, ⓦwww.hoteltaiyo.com.br; ⑤), with three pools and a sauna. As for **restaurants**, the better hotels have their own, but you could also try the *Restaurante Papas* at Praça Mestre Orlando 12, which serves a wide variety of Brazilian dishes.

# Parque Nacional Chapada dos Veadeiros

The **Parque Nacional Chapada dos Veadeiros** in the north of Goiás is the heart of the *planalto*, its stunning natural scenery among the most beautiful and distinctive in Brazil. The hundreds of square kilometres of wild and sparse vegetation, extraordinary geological formations, cave systems, waterfalls and hiking trails make this one of the best destinations for **ecotourism** in the country. A few hours north from Brasília and easily accessible by bus, the park has good local support for tourism, and apart from the occasional holidaying diplomat up from the capital, it is still remarkably unknown as a destination to foreign tourists.

## Alto Paraíso de Goiás

The main point of arrival for visitors to the park is **ALTO PARAÍSO DE GOIÁS**, a base from which to explore the surrounding countryside more than a place to hang out in itself. If you really want to explore the Chapada, your best bet is to take the bus to the village of São Jorge (see opposite), which is much closer to the national park and the best hiking.

### Arrival and information

The town is some 240km north of Brasília and connected by twice-daily buses from Brasília, or four times daily from Goiânia. Your first stop should be the very helpful **tourist information** office – the Centro de Atendimento ao Turista (Mon–Sat 9am–6pm; ⓣ62/3446-1159), close to the *rodoviária* on Avenida Ary Valadão. You can pick up maps of the park as well as the worthwhile booklet *Guia da Chapada dos Veadeiros* (R$7.50), a comprehensive listing of all the hikes and accommodation options in and around the park, organized by town, and one of the few such publications with a good English translation. Also spend a few cents on the invaluable map *O Melhor da Chapada dos Veadeiros*, which is based on a satellite image and has all the region's roads and main sights marked.

If you want to **hike on your own**, your best bet is to walk 4km up the GO-118 road north of the town, and then take the signposted dirt road right another 3km to the **Cristal waterfall**. The Cristal is at the head of a beautiful valley, where a series of swimming holes and small waterfalls have been created by a cool mountain stream as it plunges into the valley.

### Accommodation and eating

You will be spoilt for choice for **accommodation**. Most hotels are concentrated on the central Avenida Ary Valadão, the *Central* (❷) and *Tradição* (❷) being the best of the cheaper options, and there are several campgrounds located on the edge of town; the tourist office will have details on these. The most kitsch option is undoubtedly the *Camelot Inn* (GO-118 road at Km 168, about 1km from town; ⓣ62/3446-1449, ⓦwww.pousadacamelot.com.br; ❹–❻), a Monty Pythonesque fake medieval castle, opposite the exit to the town centre, which offers great value, with pool, bar, sauna and very comfortable rooms. Slightly away from the centre is the city's best hotel, the *Europa*, at Rua 1 Quadra 7, Setor Planalto, not far from the bus station (❸). Dozens of *pousadas* cater to ecotourists and weekend trippers from Brasília (all ❷–❸). Recommended are the upmarket *Pousada Alfa & Ômega*, Rua Joaquim de Almeida 15 (ⓣ62/3446-1225, ⓦwww.veadeiros.com.br; ❸–❹); the New-Agey *Aquárius* (ⓣ62/3446-1952) further up the same street at no. 326; the *Pousada Maya* (ⓣ62/3446-2062, ⓦwww.pousadamaya.com.br) at Rua Coleto Paulino 732, even more New Age but very comfortable; and *Pousada do Sol* (ⓣ62/3446-1201), Rua Gumercindo Barbosa.

**Restaurants** are equally thick on the ground, especially on Ary Valadão; all are very similar, but the lunchtime salad bar at the *Clube da Esquina* stands out and the Italian *Massas da Mamma*, Rua São Jose Operario 305 (ⓣ62/3446-1362), is pretty good for pizzas and pasta and the ambience is pleasant enough.

## São Jorge

To really get to grips with Chapada dos Veadeiros you need to head 37km further up a good-quality dirt road to the small village of **SÃO JORGE**, next to the only entrance to the national park.

### Arrival and information

From Alto Paraíso, there is one daily bus from the *rodoviária* (ⓣ62/3446-1359), Empresa São Jorge, leaving daily at 4pm, and a more irregular *kombi* run by a São Jorge tourist agency; ask at the Alto Paraíso tourist office for details. The São Jorge **tourist office** (Mon–Sat 9am–6pm; ⓣ62/3446-1090 and 3446-1159) is located in a modern pavilion at the village entrance and all restaurant and accommodation options are within five minutes of the village centre, where the bus sets you down.

As for **finding a guide**, in the unlikely event locals don't come touting for business where you're staying, let the owner know you're interested and someone should be there within a few minutes. Guides charge a daily rate of around R$25, not including the entrance fees to the national park, if you choose to hike there. If you want to go on a long hike outside the park, it's still a good idea to hire a guide to make sure you don't get lost.

### Accommodation

Despite its small size, São Jorge has no shortage of **accommodation**. At all times of the year, if you're planning to stay in one of the *pousadas*, it's a good idea to ring ahead and make a reservation – most of them have a Brasília-based reservation service. At holiday periods, especially Carnaval and the New Year, São Jorge fills up and can be noisy. A warning: at the height of the dry season (Sept), the village has been known to run out of water.

The most upmarket option, the *Pousada Casa das Flores* (reservations advisable ⓣ62/3455-1055, ⓦwww.pousadadasflores.com.br; ❺–❻), includes very high-quality breakfast and lunch in the rates, while the pool, candlelit rooms and smoochy live music in the evenings make this a great place for a romantic weekend. More reasonably priced are several very pleasant *pousadas*, including *Trilha Violeta*, Rua 12, Qd. 7, Lote 5 (Ⓣ62/3455-1088, Ⓦwww.trilhavoileta.com.br; ❷–❸), *Recanto da Paz* (Ⓣ61/646-1983; ❸) and *Pousada Palipalan* (on block 2 of Rua 2 Ⓣ62/3455-1005; ❹; reservations required). There are also a large number of campsites and rooms from R$15 and upwards in São Jorge.

### The village

Looking around São Jorge, you can see the potential that ecotourism has to protect landscapes and generate jobs and income at the same time. Before the creation of the national park in 1980, the main industry hereabouts was the mining of rock crystals. When the practice was eventually made illegal in and around the park, the parks authority, prodded and helped by the **World Wildlife Fund**, recognized the need to create jobs linked to the park and invested heavily in training local ex-miners to be guides – the perfect choice, since no one picked over every remote nook and cranny of the landscape quite like them. So there is a good reason why IBAMA, the federal parks authority, makes it compulsory for visitors to the park to be accompanied by a guide.

You can either hike into the national park from São Jorge or explore the truly spectacular countryside around the village, which is dotted with waterfalls, strange geological formations and natural swimholes; best are the otherworldly rock formations of the **Vale da Lua**, and the swimholes and waterfalls of **Raizama** and **Morada do Sol**, both a short drive or a two-hour hike away.

### Eating

The best **food** in town can be found at *Papalua*, located on Rua 12 (Block 7, Lote 8 Ⓣ62/3455-1085; open for dinner daily except Thurs). Its varied menu covers Brazilian and international dishes. For good cheap meals check out *Bar do Pelé*, in the centre; other central options include the *Casa das Flores* restaurant, which is open to non-guests, and a couple of pizzerias.

### Hiking in Parque Nacional Chapada dos Veadeiros

Visitors to the park are restricted to two **trails** in its southern corner, both 10km long and each a day's worth of exploring. Although you'll only see a fraction of the park, this area is the most spectacular, an unforgettable blend of hills and cliff-faces (mostly in the middle distance; fortunately you don't have to climb them), plunging waterfalls, swimholes and forests. You encounter the full range of *cerrado* vegetation as well: *veredas* (open moorlands lined by *buriti* palms), *floresta de galeria* (full-sized deciduous forest along watercourses) and *campo sujo* (the classic, shrubby savanna characteristic of Africa).

Of the two trails, one includes the park's main highlight – the marvellous **Salto do Rio Preto**, where two separate waterfalls plunge almost 130m into a pool 440m across. The trail's other notable sight is the **Pedreiras**, a series of natural rock pools. On the other trail, the highlight is **Salto Cariocas**, a series of falls with a sand beach at the top, and you will also pass **Canion 1 e 2**, two canyons cut by the Rio Preto and lined with granite cliffs.

Your guide's first stop will be the IBAMA office to register entry and pay the fee (R$7 a head); you are responsible for your guide's fee. Take plenty of water and enough food for a day (agree beforehand whether you will be providing your guide's food as well), and stick to the trails, taking your rubbish home with you, and, most importantly, in the dry season **do not smoke**. Fires are the worst problem the park has, and the vegetation is tinder-dry between July and October. Bringing a change of clothes and swimwear is a good idea as you'll be cooling off in swimholes between treks.

▲ Salto do Rio Preto, in Parque Nacional Chapada dos Veadeiros

### Hikes around São Jorge

Hiking options around São Jorge are less strenuous than in the national park, but still spectacular. You could easily spend a week doing a series of rewarding day-hikes without even entering the national park, and for those travelling with children, for whom the long hikes in the park are not realistic, these shorter hikes are a great family outing. All destinations are reached by heading along the road that passes the village, either west or east – that is, towards or away from Alto Paraíso.

The most striking hike around São Jorge leads to **Vale da Lua**, a forested valley where the river São Miguel has carved a narrow canyon through an extraordinary series of sculptured granite curves. To get there from the village, head to the main road and continue 4km east – in the direction of Alto Paraíso. On your right you come to a signposted trail into the Vale da Lua. There is a nominal entrance fee; you can either follow the trail directly to a swimhole, or else peel left, along a different route towards the swimhole, by walking down the valley, the best route to see its extraordinary geology. Flash floods can be a problem here in the rainy season, given the narrowness of the gorge, so exercise caution.

Back at São Jorge, heading in the opposite direction, away from Alto Paraíso, will take you, in quick succession, to **Raizama**, a beautiful gorge with a series of swimholes and waterfalls, and **Morada do Sol**, which has less-spectacular waterfalls, but more spectacular views up and down the valley. Another 5km up the main road will bring you to a private estate, **Água Quente**, where the owner has channelled a natural warm spring – tepid rather than hot – into a couple of large pools, making this a wonderful place to soak and recover from the walk. All of the above destinations charge a R$2.50–5 entrance fee.

## Tocantins

Created in 1989, the **state of Tocantins** is not an obvious geographical or cultural unit, merely a political and bureaucratic invention. Most visitors pass through the region rather than spend time around the state's hot and flyblown towns. The only attraction here is the Ilha do Bananal – but it is underdeveloped and can be an expensive, tiring headache of a place to get to, unless you're taking a guided tour; for now, we don't recommend bothering with it. Otherwise, you may end up changing buses in either **Palmas** or **Araguaiana** on your way overland through the state to the Amazon or the Northeast.

## Palmas

The state capital of **PALMAS** is a newer example of a Brazilian planned city than Brasília, started in the late 1980s and still incomplete, but with nothing approaching the imagination and stylishness that make the national capital a success. Home to almost 190,000 residents, it lies just under 1000km north of Brasília and just over 1200km south of Belém. The town itself, which has long, wide avenues and a pleasant average temperature of around 27°C, is inconveniently set back on the banks of the Rio Tocantins, some 150km by minor roads from the main Brasília–Belém highway BR-153, and there's little reason to come here. If you do get stuck in Palmas, the best **hotel** is the *Rio do Sono*, ACSUSO 10, Conj. 1, Lote 10 (Ⓣ&Ⓕ63/3219-6800, Ⓦwww.hotelriodosono.com.br; ❺), with nice bright rooms and a pool. Slightly cheaper, but also with a pool, is *Casa Grande*, Av. Joaquim Teotônio Sugurado, ACSUSO 20, Conj. 1, Lote 1 (Ⓣ&Ⓕ63/3215-1813, Ⓦwww.hotelcasagrandepalmas.cjb.net; ❹).

## Araguaína

Lying 400km north of Palmas, **ARAGUAÍNA** is many times larger, but no more attractive a place to stay. It dominates the road network in northern Tocantins, located as it is almost exactly halfway between the Araguaia and Tocantins rivers. If you do end up staying here, perhaps while changing from one bus to another, there are a few possible **places to stay**. The best is some 7km from town, the *Olyntho*, BR-153 Sul, Km 125, Gurupi exit (Ⓣ&Ⓕ63/3415-7600; ❸–❹), based on a ranch. *Araguatins*, at Av. Tocantins 250 (Ⓣ63/3415-7500; ❸–❹), is a little cheaper and beside the *rodoviária*. For **restaurants**, *Maresia's*, Rua das Mangueiras 868, has fine fish dishes; the *Estancia Gaúcha*, at Praça Pio XII 33 (Ⓣ63/3242-8731), serves good *rodizio* and specializes in meat dishes.

# Travel details

### Buses

**Brasília** to: Alto Paraíso (2 daily; 3hr); Anápolis (every 30min); Belém (2 daily; 36hr); Belo Horizonte (7 daily; 14hr); Cristalina (3 daily; 2hr); Cuiabá (6 daily; 20hr); Formosa (8 daily; 2hr); Fortaleza (1 daily; 40hr); Goiânia (every 30min; 2hr 30min); Pirenópolis (4 daily; 3hr); Recife (1 daily; 48hr); Rio (6 daily; 20hr); Salvador (1 daily; 26hr); São Paulo (7 daily; 16hr).

**Goiânia** to: Alto Paraíso: (1 daily; 6hr); Brasília (every 30min; 2hr 30min); Caldas Novas (8 daily; 3hr); Palmas (8 daily; 9hr).

### Planes

Brasília is second only to Rio and São Paulo for number and frequency of flights, although they are exclusively domestic. There are direct flights to most state capitals, and the rest are reachable after one stop. Flights to Rio and São Paulo average at least one an hour throughout the day; several flights daily to the state capitals of southern and northeastern Brazil. If you are heading to the Amazon, there are several flights daily to Belém and Manaus, but other Amazonian state capitals have fewer, mainly leaving in the evening.

7

# Mato Grosso

CHAPTER 7

# Highlights

* **Morado dos Bais** The perfect spot to enjoy live music, cold beer and good food in a pleasant courtyard setting in downtown Campo Grande. See p.502
* **Piranha fishing** Fish for your supper with a simple line and hook; the peaceful town of Coxim is a good place to arrange fishing trips, though piranha can be caught easily in pools and lakes throughout the Pantanal. See p.504
* **Aquário Natural** A spectacular river pool near the sleepy town of Bonito, offering good opportunities for snorkelling among a wide range of tropical fish. This region is also great for other adventure and eco pursuits, including whitewater rafting, caving, trekking and horseriding. See p.511
* **The Pantanal** The largest concentration of wildlife in the whole of the Americas; a terrific place to spend a few days on eco-safari to see jungle mammals, exotic birds, hundreds of caiman and quite often even a wild jaguar. See p.519
* **Chapada dos Guimarães** A breathtaking plateau with a pleasant small town, lots of trails, and the geodesic centre of South America. See p.536

▲ Tour boat on the Pantanal

7

# Mato Grosso



Very Brazilian, in both its vastness and its frontier culture, the **Mato Grosso** region is essentially an enormous plain, home to the sprawling Pantanal swamp – the best place in Brazil for seeing wildlife, and one of the world's largest wetlands – and rippled by a handful of small mountain ranges. Equally Brazilian, there's a firm political boundary, a line on a map, across the heart of the swamp, marking the competing ambitions of two mammoth states: **Mato Grosso** and **Mato Grosso do Sul**. The former state, the northern half of the region, is sparsely populated, with the only settlements of any size – Cuiabá, Rondonópolis and Cáceres – having a combined population of around one and a half million. The name Mato Grosso, which means "thick wood", is more appropriate to this northernmost state, where thorny scrubland passes into tropical rainforest and the land begins its incline towards the Amazon, interrupted only by the beautiful uplifted plateau of the Chapada dos Guimarães. By contrast, most of the state of Mato Grosso do Sul, which is marginally more populous, is either seasonal flood plain or open scrubland. To the west of Mato Grosso do Sul are Bolivian swamps and forest; the mighty rivers **Araguaia** and **Paraná** (one flowing north, the other south) form a natural rim to the east, while the **Rio Paraguai** and the country named after it complete the picture to the south.

The simple road network and the limited sprinkling of settlements make getting about within Mato Grosso fairly hard work. Distances are enormous, and although most of the buses and trunk roads are in relatively good condition, any journey is inevitably a long one. That said, the variety of landscape alone – from swamps and forests to cattle ranches, riverine villages and Indian reservations – makes the trip a unique one and, for the adventurous traveller, it's well worth the effort.

The cities of Mato Grosso are particularly deceptive. Although surprisingly modern and developed, they've only recently received the full trappings of civilization. Portuguese colonists began to settle in the region fairly late, at the time of the great **Cuiabá** gold rush of the early eighteenth century, though Cuiabá town itself remained almost completely isolated from the rest of Brazil until its first telegraph link was installed in the 1890s. Masterminded and built by a local boy made good – a down-to-earth army officer named Rondon – the telegraph lines were Mato Grosso's first real attempt to join the outside world. Since the 1980s, with the completion of Highway BR-364, Cuiabá has again become a staging post for pioneers, this time for thousands of Brazilian peasants in search of land or work in the western Amazon states of Rondônia (named after the same local boy) and Acre. While Cuiabá can't exactly claim to

MATO GROSSO
Itaituba (road currently impassable)
Marabá
Porto Velho & Rio Branco
Goiânia
N
SERRA DO CACHIMBO
Rio Xingu
Rio São Manuel
Alta Floresta
BR-163
Colídor
Ilha do Bananal
PARQUE NACIONAL DO XINGU
Rio Juruena
Sinop
BR-364
Vilhena
Rio Araguaia
MATO GROSSO
Rio Paraguai
Chapada dos Guimarães
BR-070
BR-174
Cuiabá
Águas Quentes
Sto Antônio do Leverger
Cáceres
Poconé
Barão do Melgaço
Barra do Garças

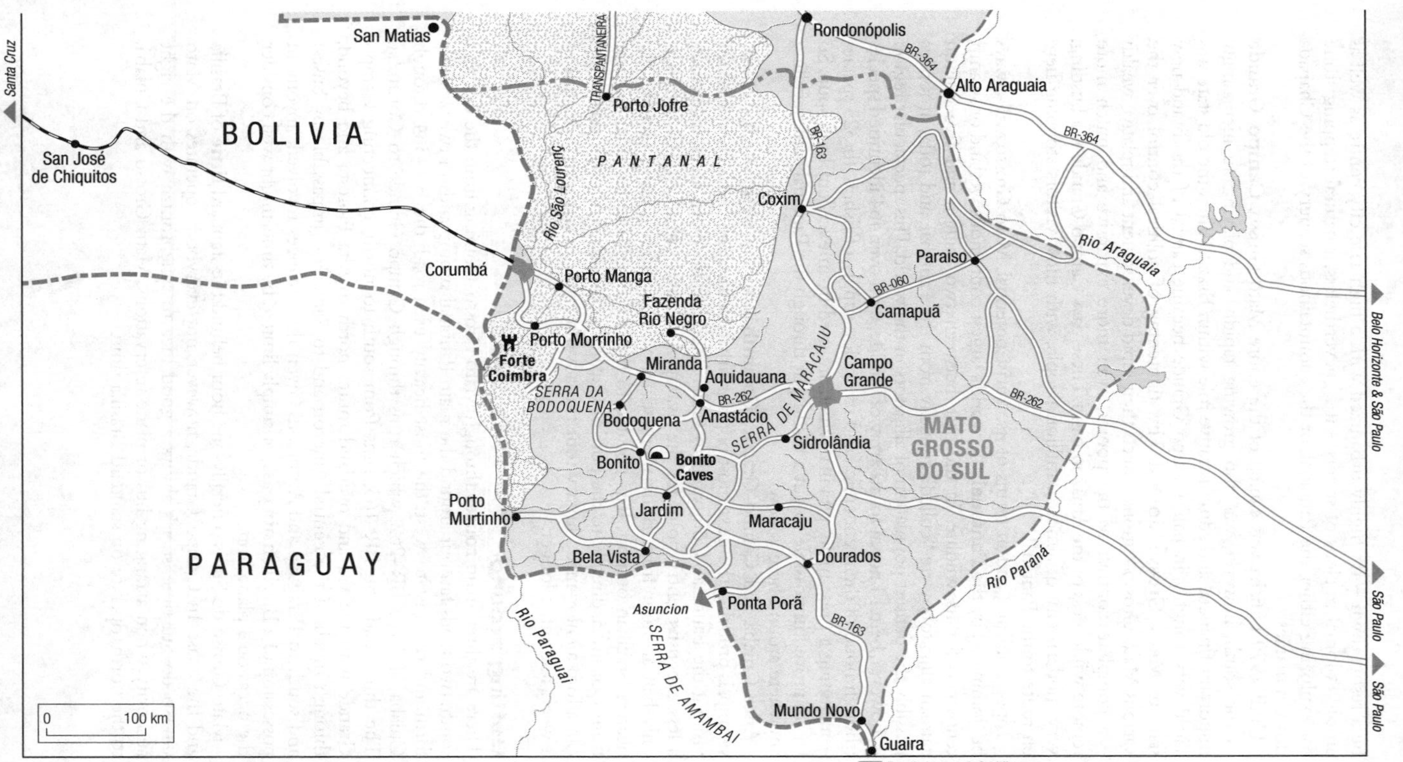
Belo Horizonte & São Paulo
São Paulo
São Paulo
Foz do Iguaçu & Curitiba
Santa Cruz
BOLIVIA
PARAGUAY
MATO GROSSO DO SUL
PANTANAL
San Matias
San José de Chiquitos
TRANSPANTANEIRA
Porto Jofre
Rio São Lourenç
Corumbá
Porto Manga
Fazenda Rio Negro
Porto Morrinho
Forte Coimbra
Miranda
Aquidauana
SERRA DA BODOQUENA
Bodoquena
Anastácio
SERRA DE MARACAJU
Bonito
Bonito Caves
Sidrolândia
Jardim
Porto Murtinho
Maracaju
Bela Vista
Dourados
Asuncion
Ponta Porã
SERRA DE AMAMBAI
Rio Paraguai
Mundo Novo
Guaira
Rondonópolis
Alto Araguaia
Coxim
Paraiso
Camapuã
Campo Grande
Rio Araguaia
Rio Paraná
BR-364
BR-163
BR-060
BR-262
0
100 km

be a resort town – it's highly urbanized with a high-rise city centre as well as an old colonial nucleus of streets – it is, nevertheless, a natural stepping stone for exploring either the Pantanal, or the mountainous scenery of the Chapada dos Guimarães.

Until 1979 Cuiabá was capital of the entire Mato Grosso. **Campo Grande** in the south, however, was also growing rapidly and playing an increasingly important financial and administrative role within Brazil. When the old state was sliced very roughly in half, Campo Grande became capital of the brand-new state of **Mato Grosso do Sul**. This tightening of political control over the various Mato Grosso regions reflects their rapid development and relative wealth – a complete contrast to the poorer, even more expansive and much more remote wilderness of the Amazon basin. These days Campo Grande is a bustling, very modern city of almost a million people, with most visitors stopping here en route to the Pantanal.

Topographically, and in terms of its tourist potential, Mato Grosso will always be dominated by the **Pantanal**, the world's largest contiguous wetland or swamp, renowned for its wildlife. In the past, between two million and five million caiman alligators were "culled" annually from the Pantanal, and today it retains possibly the densest population of alligators in the world. This spectacular region is, however, better known for its array of birdlife, with over 464 identified species (though none of them endemic), and its endless supply of fish, with 325 species – including a great many piranha, which are used in an excellent local soup. So far it's proved impossible to put a road right through the Pantanal, and travelling anywhere around here is slow.

After Cuiabá and Campo Grande, **Corumbá**, on the western edge of the swamp, is probably the next most popular urban destination and a good base for visiting the Pantanal. Compared to Cuiabá and the northern areas, it's usually a less expensive entry point for the swamp. A relatively small city, Corumbá is only half an hour from Bolivia, but seven or eight from Campo Grande, the nearest Brazilian outpost. It is possible to travel through the Pantanal by river from Corumbá, directly to the port of Cáceres near Cuiabá, though unless you can afford a tailor-made luxury tour this adventurous fluvial route takes at least a week, and often longer.

### Getting around

There are three main **routes** through Mato Grosso. Coming from the east and south, two roads fan out around the main Pantanal swamplands in tweezer-like form and run east to west: the most heavily used road, the BR-364 through Cuiabá, and the BR-262, which runs through Campo Grande to Corumbá. The third road, the BR-163, runs from south to north, connecting Campo Grande with Cuiabá and overland routes north to Alta Floresta and beyond, through much of the central Amazon and to Santarém (impassable by buses) and south to Paraguay and Asunción. Given the distances involved, anyone in possession of a Brazilian **air pass**, or simply limited by time, might well consider the occasional plane hop.

Mato Grosso do Sul is officially one hour behind the standard **time** of Brasília and the coast. In Campo Grande, however, not everybody operates on Mato Grosso do Sul time, so it's always a good idea to synchronize with the right authority when arranging bus or plane reservations. Mato Grosso and Cuiabá, to the north, operate on standard Brasília time.

# Mato Grosso do Sul

Although a relatively young state, **Mato Grosso do Sul** is nevertheless considered to be one of Brazil's better-established economic regions. It has a distinct cowboy flavour: here, close to the border with Paraguay and just a bit further from Argentinian *gaucho* territory, it's not uncommon to end up drinking *maté* sitting on a horse under the shade of a tree by day or dancing Spanish polkas through the night in some of the region's bars. Until the eighteenth century the whole region was Indian territory and was considered an inhospitable corner of the New World. A hundred and fifty years and numerous bloody battles later, Mato Grosso do Sul might now be developed and "civilized" but – thankfully – it's still a place where you can forget about industrial ravages and wonder at nature's riches. The downside is that the Brazilian Ministry of Health recommends yellow fever inoculations for this area.

The state capital, **Campo Grande**, is a useful base from which to start delving deeper into Mato Grosso do Sul or to explore one of the largest and most beautiful wetlands in the world. The road connection to Corumbá, a frontier settlement on the edge of both the swamp and Bolivia, is well served by daily buses, and one or two good tour companies operate from Campo Grande itself, so reaching the depths of the Pantanal is fairly easy. The swamp, however, is vast, so whilst you can also get a feel for what it's like from a variety of road-linked places closer to Campo Grande – like **Coxim**, north of the city, or **Aquidauana**, to the west – exposure to the flora and fauna is best off-road.

The south of the state is favoured by the beautiful hills of the **Serra da Bodoquena** and **Serra de Maracaju** and, deep in the Bodoquena hills, you can visit the spectacular cave systems, forests and rivers of the **Bonito** area, another major destination in itself. Further south, 319km from Campo Grande, **Ponta Porã** sits square on the Paraguayan border, from where there's a two-day overland route to Asunción. There are also several daily bus services from Campo Grande via **Dourados** and **Mundo Novo** to Guaira and the amazing falls of Foz do Iguaçu in the neighbouring state of Paraná.

## Campo Grande

Nicknamed the "brunette city" because of its chestnut-coloured earth, **CAMPO GRANDE** has in the last forty years been transformed from an insignificant settlement into a buzzing metropolis with a population of over 724,000. Founded in 1889, the city was only made the capital of the new state of Mato Grosso do Sul in the late 1970s, since when it has almost doubled in size, though it retains a distinctly rural flavour. Its downtown area manages to combine sky-scraping banks and apartment buildings with ranchers' general stores and poky little shops selling strange forest herbs and Catholic *ex votos*. Reminiscent in parts of quiet southern US cities, it's a relatively salubrious market centre for an enormous cattle-ranching region, as well as being an important centre of South American trade routes from Paraguay, Bolivia, Argentina and the south of Brazil. A pioneering place, many of the early twentieth-century settlers here were Arabs, who have since gone mostly into businesses such as restaurants and hotels; there is also a large Japanese section of the immigrant population, which

## The Campo Grande railroad

Look at any map of the region and you'll see a thin black line tracing the path of a long **railroad** that connects São Paulo on the Atlantic with Campo Grande, where it forks to Corumbá on the Bolivian border, and to Ponta Porã on the Paraguayan frontier. Unfortunately, the privatization of the Brazilian railways has led to the closure of all passenger lines west of Bauru, perhaps forever. This is a real shame, not least because the Corumbá line formed part of an even longer rail system, connecting with the Bolivian *Tren de los Mortes* to Santa Cruz, from where it's still possible to continue by train into Chile or via La Paz into Peru, over Lake Titicaca (by boat or around it on a bus) and on to Cuzco. There seems little chance in the immediate future of the lines being reopened (though freight trains are still running), but with ever-increasing tourist interest in the Pantanal and Mato Grosso do Sul, we can only hope that services may in the course of time resume.



has left its mark on the local culinary trade. The city has a number of splendidly planned *praças* and parks with large, leafy trees, bringing wild birds from the countryside into the modern centre.

An obvious place to break a long journey between Cuiabá or Corumbá and the coast, Campo Grande tries hard to shake off the feeling that it's a city stuck in the middle of nowhere. Apart from the *gaucho* influence, the town centre is much like that of any other medium-sized city: the people are friendly and there's little manifest poverty. The generally warm evenings inspire the locals to turn out on the streets in force. People chat over a meal or sip ice-cold beers at one of the restaurants or bars around Avenida Afonso Pena, the Praça Ari Coelho or blocks 22–23 of Rua Dom Aquino, and guitars, maracas and congas are often brought out for an impromptu music session.

## Arrival and information

The **rodoviária** (☎67/3321-8797) is a ten-minute walk west of the central Praça Ari Coelho at Rua Joaquim Nabuco 200. A surprisingly large bus terminal, it also houses six hairdressers, a cinema, bookstores and several bars. The area around the *rodoviária* is fine during the day but can be a little rough at night; despite this it boasts some reasonable hotels and the city's youth hostel. Similarly, the district south of Avenida Afonso Pena has a slightly dodgy reputation. If in doubt, take a **taxi**: there's a rank in the bus station, or phone Rádio Táxi on ☎67/3387-1414. The other point of arrival is the **airport**, Aeroporto Internacional Antônio João (☎67/3368-6000), 7km out of town on the road towards Aquidauana. Buses from the airport to the *rodoviária* cost around R$2, taxis R$20–25.

**Tourist information** is readily available at the airport (usually daily 9am–6pm; ☎67/0800-6476050 & 3318-6060) or in town at either the very helpful Morada dos Bais tourist office at Av. Noroeste 5140, on the corner with Avenida Afonso Pena (Tues–Sat 8am–7pm, Sun 9am–noon; ☎67/3324-5830 & 3382-9244), or during office hours in the Shopping Campo Grande mall (☎67/3314-3142). As well as city maps and information on attractions and accommodation, you'll find a noticeboard with details on cinema, theatre and exhibition listings in Morado dos Bais. A fun way to get to know Campo Grande, **Official City Tours**, operating from the Morada dos Bais tourist office (☎67/3321-0800), visit the main sights, including the parks and museums, on an open-topped double-decker bus.

## Accommodation

There are a few smart, comfortable **hotels** around the *rodoviária* which offer quite acceptable alternatives to the downtown options. There are reasonable budget and mid-range choices around the junction of Rua Barão do Rio Branco and Rua Allan Kardek, one street west of the *rodoviária*, though the more central *pousadas* and hotels within a few blocks of the Praça Ari Coelho are closer to the modern city's heart. For **camping**, there's the *Estancia Vovo Dede* (☎67/3321-0077), 23km from Campo Grande, which offers walking trails, horseriding, a pool and fishing; the *Estancia* is also contactable through Asteco Turismo at Rua 13 de Maio 3192.

**Alkimia** Av. Afonso Pena 1413, Centro ☎67/3324-2621. A modern, medium-sized hotel between the centre and the *rodoviária*; rooms have TVs, *frigobar* and a/c. Friendly staff. ❸

**Anache** Rua Cândido Mariano Rondon 1396 ☎67/3383-2841. A no-frills option with shared bathrooms and fans rather than a/c, but clean and safe, and in a good central location, with friendly service. ❶

**Bristol Multy Exceler Plaza** Av. Afonso Pena 444, Bairro Amambaí ☎67/3321-2800, Ⓦwww.bristolhoteis.com.br. A plush hotel where you'll be

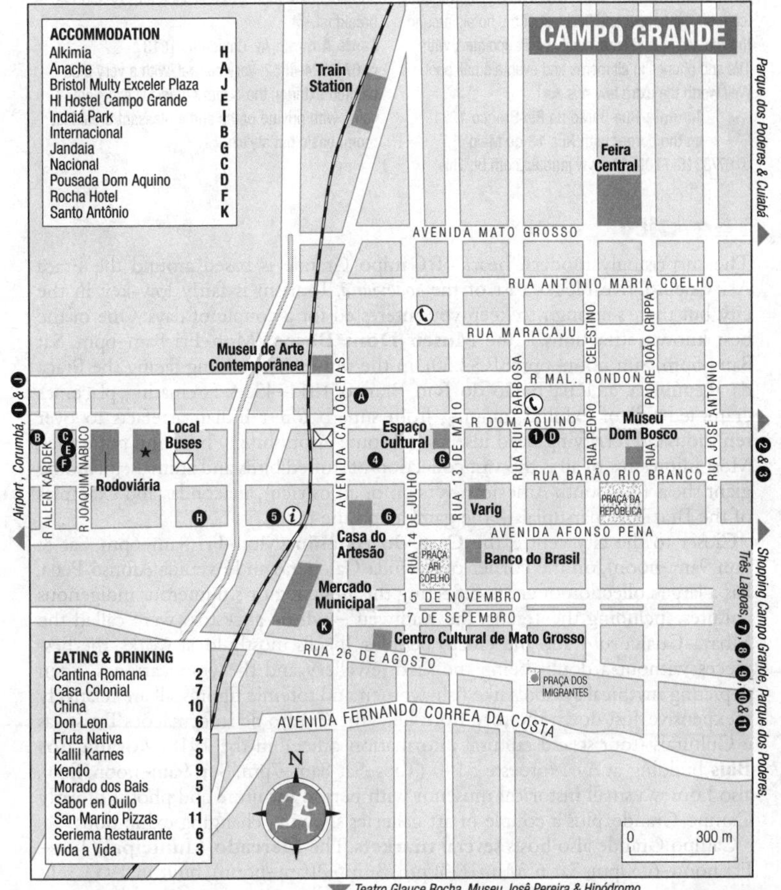

coddled and swaddled in all the usual four-star treats; includes swimming pool and sauna. 5

**HI Hostel Campo Grande** Rua Joaquim Nabuco 185 ⓣ67/3321-1022 and 3321-0505, ⓦwww.ecologicalexpeditions.com.br, ⓔcamporgrande@hostel.org.br. Close to the *rodoviária* and linked to Youth Hostelling International, with dorms, as well as single and double rooms, solar showers, some private bathrooms, plus TVs, laundry and internet facilities. Hotel staff and Ecological Expeditions (who operate from here) can provide information on trips to the Pantanal, Bonito, Bolivia, Rio and Iguazu. 1–2

**Indaiá Park** Av. Afonso Pena 354 ⓣ67/2106-1000, ⓦwww.indaia_hotel.com. A large, rather impersonal three-star hotel with internet access, pool, restaurant and piano bar; offers airport and shopping transfer. 4

**Internacional** Rua Allan Kardek 223, Bairro Amambaí ⓣ67/3384-4677, ⓦwww.hotelintermetro.com.br. The largest and flashiest of the hotels around the *rodoviária*, and surprisingly well appointed, with TVs and phones in all rooms and even a small pool. Well worth the extra few *reís*. 3

**Jandaia** Rua Barão do Rio Branco 1271, on the corner with Rua 13 de Maio ⓣ67/3316-7700, ⓦwww.jandaia.com.br. This excellent luxury hotel has a small terrace pool, internet access, gymnasium and a fine restaurant serving some delicious local dishes. 5

**Nacional** Rua Dom Aquino 610 ⓣ67/3383-2461, ⓔhotelnacional@ig.com.br. Probably the best value of the budget places around the *rodoviária*, with plenty of character and internet access. Rooms come with TV and a choice of fan or a/c. 3

**Pousada Dom Aquino** Rua Dom Aquino 1806, near the Clube Libanes ⓣ67/3382-9373, ⓔpaquino@terra.com.br. Comfortable and secure, this small hotel has a peaceful ambience, a lounge area and courtyard. Rooms are clean, airy and pleasant, and the decor is inspired by local tribes. 3

**Rocha Hotel** Rua Barão do Rio Branco 343 ⓣ67/3325-6874, ⓔajcampogrande@hotmail.com. Near the bus station and offering a good level of comfort, with parking facilities in front and adequate rooms that include a/c, TV and breakfast. 2

**Santo Antônio** Av. Calógeras 1813 ⓣ67/3324-4552. Very central, with a very blue painted exterior, the *Santo Antônio* is excellent value with private baths and a pleasant breakfast room; basic but stylish. 2

## The City

The surprisingly modern heart of Campo Grande is based around the Praça Ari Coelho, five blocks east of the *rodoviária*. Tourism is fairly low-key in the city, but there's enough to keep you interested for a couple of days. One of the best-known attractions is the **Museu Dom Bosco** (Mon–Fri 8am–6pm, Sat 8am–5pm, Sun noon–6pm; R$2.50), in the university building facing the Praça da República, at Rua Barão do Rio Branco 1811–43. A fascinating place, it's crammed full of exhibits, ranging from superb forest Indian artefacts to over ten thousand terrifying dead insects and some astonishingly beautiful butterflies. Most impressive of all is the vast collection of stuffed birds and animals, including giant rheas (the South American version of an ostrich), anacondas and examples of the Brazilian marsupials – the gamba and the quica.

Closer to the city centre, the **Casa do Artesão** (Mon–Fri 8am–6pm, Sat & Sun 9am–noon), on the corner of Avenida Calógeras and Avenida Afonso Pena, has a large collection of crafts, reflecting this huge region's numerous indigenous cultures, including the Terena, the Kadiwéu – whose ancestors were called the Mbaya-Guaicuru – and the Guato peoples. It sells mostly local works, the best pieces without a doubt being the seed jewellery and the woodcarvings, often depicting mythical symbols like fish-women and totemic figures; all are relatively inexpensive. Just down the road from here, the Centro de Informações Turisticas e Culturais (tourist and cultural information office), in the 1918 **Morada dos Bais** building at Av. Noroeste 5140 (Tues–Sat 8am–7pm, Sun 9am–noon; free), also houses a small historical museum with period furniture and photos of early Campo Grande, plus a couple of art galleries showing changing exhibitions.

Campo Grande also hosts several **markets**. The **Mercado Municipal** (Tues–Fri noon–6.30pm, Sat 6.30am–6.30pm, Sun 6.30am–noon), built in 1933, sells

▲ Pottery made by Kadiwéu indigenous people, Casa do Artesão

a good range of inexpensive souvenirs, including cow-horn trumpets, horn goblets and drinking gourds. The **Feira Indigena** (daily 6.30am–8pm), just outside the Mercado Municipal in the Praça Oshiro Takemori, devotes itself almost exclusively to market-garden produce, including lovely honey and some simple seed necklaces made from wild *mata* products. Also, the **Feira Central**, Esplanada da Ferrovia, Avenida Calogeras at the corner with 14 de Julho, takes place three times a week (Wed & Fri after 5pm, Sat from 10am), overnight until 6am, attracting a large number of forest Indians selling potions and bundles of bark, beads and leatherwork, as well as a few Paraguayans selling toys. Due to the eclectic mix of residents, there is a variety of foods on offer, ranging from *churrasquinho* to Japanese *yaki soba*.

There's good-quality *artesanato* on sale, mainly handicrafts such as cotton embroidery and leatherwork, at **Feira de Artesanato de Artistas Sul Mato Grossenses**, Praça dos Imigrantes (Mon–Fri 9am–6pm, Sat 9am–2pm), where there's also a small outdoor café. For the flip side to contemporary Mato Grosso culture, head for the **cowboy shop** at Rua Barão do Rio Branco 1296, near the *Jandaia Hotel*, which sells gun belts, holsters, saddles and boots. You can see some of this gear in action at the **horse racing**, out at the Hipódromo, run by the Jóquei Clube de Campo Grande; the Hipódromo is 5km along the BR-167, beyond the exit for Dourados. Finally, there is also the old train station, the brick Estação Ferroviária, which was built in a distinctive British style and began operating in 1914, bringing a new era of growth to the city.

Just beyond the town centre, at the eastern end of Avenida Mato Grosso, is the **Parque dos Poderes** (Mon–Fri noon–6pm). This calm ecological reserve is home to a variety of native plants and a small selection of the region's wild animals; there are a few short walking trails and the habitat is scrubby woodland. Buses for the Parque dos Poderes can be caught going east along Avenida Afonso Pena from the centre. At the entrance to Poderes there's the **Parque das Nações Indígenas**, consisting of paths serviced by cafés and toilets, plus there's a small but usually colourful modern art museum, the **Museu de Arte Contemporânea de Mato**

**Grosso do Sul (MARCO)**, Av. Maria Coelho 6000 (Tues–Fri 9am–6pm, Sat & Sun 9am–4pm; free). The MARCO houses art exhibitions from local artists as well as temporary exhibits from out-of-state artists.

Just to the south of the Parque dos Poderes (or east from the centre along Av. Joaquim Murtinho), you'll find the **Memorial de la Cultura Indígena**, Rua Terena in the Aldeia Indígena Urban (Urban Indigenous Village), Bairro Tiradentes (daily 8am–6pm; ⓣ67/3314-3589; groups by appointment only), where there is a craft workshop, visitor reception and many genuine Indian craft goods for sale, including ceramics and paintings. Inhabited by people of the Terena tribe, the surrounding brick urban settlement is a planned municipal project. The memorial building itself is an imposing traditional-looking hut with a palm-frond roof standing some 8m tall; it incorporates innovative construction techniques, such as the use of bent bamboo.

## Eating and drinking

Eating out is an important part of the local lifestyle and this is reflected in the diversity of restaurants. There are scores of **lanchonetes**, especially around the *rodoviária* and east along Rua Dom Aquino, and, during the hot afternoons, the city's many **juice bars** do brisk business: you'll find them on most street corners. This is a cattle-ranching market centre, and a lot of cows get roasted daily in Campo Grande, so if you're mad for **beef** you're in for a treat; however, there are also vegetarian options and several good oriental restaurants.

**Cantina Romana** Rua da Paz 237 ⓣ67/3324-9777. Wonderful Italian food, good atmosphere, fine wines and a/c; very fair prices.

**Casa Colonial** Av. Afonso Pena 3997, Jardin dos Estados ⓣ67/3383-3207 or 3042-3207. Primarily a *churrascaria*, this place serves excellent Brazilian *rodizio*, where you can eat meat till you drop. Expensive, but the decor is refined, quite spacious and pleasant.

**China** Rua Pedro Celestino 750 ⓣ67/3382-4476. One of the best Chinese restaurants in town, with very reasonable prices; the fried duck (*pato frito*) is particularly recommended.

**Don Leon** Av. Afonso Pena 1901 ⓣ67/3384-6520. A popular *churrascaria* and pizzeria, with scores of tables, fast friendly service and the added bonus of live music some evenings.

**Fruta Nativa** Rua Barão do Rio Branco 1097. This busy lunchtime snack bar serves light and inexpensive meals, including chips and chicken, outside at the yellow tables. Next door there's an unnamed juice bar where you can sip on *sucos de guarana* and munch on *pastels* (cakes) and *tortas* (tarts).

**Kallil Karnes** Rua Rubens Gil de Camilo 142, near Shopping Campo Grande towards the eastern end of Av. Afonso Pena in the district Chacara Cachoeira ⓣ67/3326-3715 (Mon–Sat 11am–2.30pm & 7–11pm, closed Sun evening). Meat house with a good reputation for excellent *rodizio*, but somewhat out of the way unless you're thinking of clubbing afterwards.

**Kendo** Av. Afonso Pena 4150 ⓣ67/3382-9000. The best of the town's Japanese restuarants; as well as fine fish soups, you'll also find pork and chicken soups with refined oriental spices. It's open Tues–Sun, 7pm to midnight.

**Morado dos Bais** Av. Noroeste 5140, on the corner with Av. Afonso Pena ⓣ67/3383-1227. An often-lively courtyard restaurant near the tourist information and cultural centre, serving a range of local dishes including *sopa paraguaia* (a soup with cheese and onions). Live music after 8pm most days, but best at weekends. Closed Mon.

**Sabor En Quilo** Rua Dom Aquino 1786 ⓣ67/3352-5102. An excellent Japanese-run restaurant with good self-service lunches in a spacious, cool and clean environment; the sushi is tasty, and it also serves more traditional Brazilian *feijoada*, too.

**San Marino Pizzas** Av. Afonso Pena 2716 ⓣ67/3321-5084. One of several reasonable pizzerias on Afonso Pena, with delivery service.

**Seriema Restaurante** Av. Afonso Pena 1919 ⓣ67/3721-2475. Near *Don Leon* (see above), this is a lively steak house, with cheap lunchtime *rodizio*.

**Viva a Vida** Rua Dom Aquino 1354, 1st floor ⓣ67/3384-6524 and Av. Fernando Corréa da Costa 2177 ⓣ67/3321-3208. Campo Grande's favourite vegetarian restaurant (meat also available) is self-service, and open lunchtimes only. Closed Sat.

## Nightlife

Apart from *Morado dos Bais* (see opposite), which has live and informal music sessions most evenings, most of Campo Grande's action happens at weekends, when the *churrascarias* and other large restaurants generally serve their food to the energetic sounds of Paraguayan polkas (*Don Leon*'s has them on weekdays as well). **Nightclubs** tend to change quickly, but those currently popular are *Limit*, 200m off Avenida Afonso Pena by Shopping Campo Grande; *Stones* (Ⓣ67/3326-4957), on block 21 of Avenida Ceara for rock and jazz music; and *Tango*, Rua Cândido Mariano 2181, to the east of the city centre, all offering a mix of Brazilian, European, Stateside and underground sounds. There's also *Acustic Bar*, with mainly electronic Brazilian music, at Rua 13 de Julho 945 (Ⓣ67/3385-5500).

The Glauce Rocha **theatre**, out of town in Cidade Universitária, often hosts interesting Brazilian works – call Ⓣ67/3387-3311 for details, or check the local papers *Folho do Povo* or *Correio do Estado*. *Peña Eme-Ene*, on the corner of Avenida Afonso Pena and Rua Barbosa, is a popular meeting place for artists and musicians, and has live regional music every Thursday night from 8pm – no entrance fee but you're expected to take dinner (Mon–Wed & Fri 7.30am–6pm, Thurs 7.30am–midnight, Sat noon–6pm; Ⓣ67/3383-2373).

## Listings

**Airlines** BRA, Gol, Trip, TAM, Av. Afonso Pena 1974 Ⓣ67/3368-6161 or at the airport Ⓣ67/3368-6152.

**Banks and exchange** There are ATMs by most banks, at the airport and at strategic points in the city, such as the corner of Rua 13 de Maio with Afonso Pena, by the main Praça Ari Coehlo; you can also change money in the Banco do Brasil, just off the main square at Av. Afonso Pena 133 (Mon–Fri 10am–5pm); at the HSBC bank, Rua 13 de Maio 2836; at the Câmbio, Rua 13 de Maio 2484; or at the airport bank.

**Car rental** Brascar, Rua Fernando Corréa da Costa 975 Ⓣ67/3383-1570; Lemans, Rua 7 de Setembro 334, Centro Ⓣ0800/92-5100; Localiza, Av. Afonso Pena 318 Ⓣ67/3382-8786.

**Consulates** If you're heading into either Paraguay or Bolivia from Campo Grande, you should check on border procedures and visa requirements. The Paraguayan consul is at Rua 26 de Agosto 384 (Ⓣ67/3324-4934), and the Bolivian consul at Rua João de Souza 798 (Ⓣ67/3382-2190); both are open Mon–Fri 9am–5pm.

**Hospital** The Santa Casa hospital is at Rua Eduardo Santos Pereira 88 (Ⓣ67/3322-4000).

**Internet** Blue Sky Net, Av. Calogeras 2069 (Ⓣ67/3321-0304), has efficient a/c; there's also the Sala Brasil CH@T Room Cyber Café, Rua Pedro Celestino 992 (Ⓣ67/3383-4231); and Iris Cybercafé and bar, Av. Afonso Pena 1975.

**Laundry** Planet Clean, Rua Joaquim Murtinho 135, close to the Praça dos Imigrantes.

**Pharmacy** Rua Barbosa, on the corner of the main square by Rua 14 de Julho and Av. Afonso Pena.

**Police** Emergency number Ⓣ190.

**Post offices** Av. Calógeras 2309, on the corner with Rua Dom Aquino, Mon–Fri 8am–5pm, Sat 8–11.30am; Rua Barão do Rio Branco by the *rodoviária*, 8am–6pm Mon–Fri.

**Shopping** Shopping Campo Grande, Av. Afonso Pena 4909, is a large and flashy shopping centre towards the eastern end of Av. Afonso Pena, replete with multiplex cinemas and over 170 shops. The busiest shopping streets in the town centre are mostly congregated in the square formed by Av. Calógeras, Av. Afonso Pena, Rua Cândido Mariano Rondon and Rua Pedro Celestino. A street market selling plastic goods and electronics sets up daily along Rua Barão do Rio Branco between the *rodoviária* and Av. Calógeras. The Barroarte shop at Av. Afonso Pena 4329, Jardin dos Estados, has a wide range of good local ceramics, sculptures and paintings; it's some distance from the centre, but en route to Shopping Campo Grande. For precious and semiprecious stones, the Garimpo shop, Av. Afonso Pena 2882, has many interesting items.

**Telephones** Rua Dom Aquino 1805 (daily 7am–10pm).

**Travel and tour companies** NPQ Turismo, Av. Afonso Pena 2081, on Praça Ari Coelho (Ⓣ67/3725-6789), is good for flights and some bus tickets. Ecological Expeditions (Ⓣ67/3321-0505 and 3042-0508, Ⓦwww.pantanaltrekking.com) offers a range of affordable tours (see p.525 for more information).

Impacto Turismo, Rua Padre João Crippa 1065, sala 106 (☎67/3382-5197 or 3724-3167), also runs good Pantanal tours. Also in Campo Grande, Lilian Borges Rodrigues is a very good English-speaking guide; contact her at Rua Octavio de Souza 464, Monte Libano (☎67/3742-2204).

# North from Campo Grande: Coxim

Today, **COXIM** is a quiet town of some 33,000 people, situated on the eastern edges of the Pantanal, and easily reached by bus from Campo Grande in around three to four hours (six or seven hours from Cuiabá). The scrub forest area to the east, north of Campo Grande, was formerly the territory of the **Caiapó** Indian nation, who ambushed miners along the routes to Goiás and Cuiabá from São Paulo, posing a serious threat to Portuguese expansion and development in the mid-eighteenth century. Coxim is a fantastic **fishing** centre: the fisherman Pirambero runs excellent trips into the swamp, down the Rio Taquari, to catch piranhas (ask for him at the port). If you're really serious about angling, contact IBAMA, at Rua Floriano Peoxoto 304 (☎67/3291-2310), or the Banco do Brasil for a **temporary fishing permit** (R$25) and, for more detailed local information, try the local fishing club, the Iate Clube Rio Verde, at Rua Ferreira, Bairro Piracema (☎67/3291-1246). Besides fishing, swimming in the Rio Taquari around Campo Falls is another popular pastime, in spite of the razor-toothed fish, and, nearby on the Rio Coxim, the **Palmeiras Falls** are a good place for a picnic or to set up camp. From November through to January, the two falls are the best places to see the incredible *piracema* spectacle – thousands of fish, leaping clear of the river, on their way upstream to the river's source to lay their eggs.

For more information on Coxim's attractions, you could try the **tourist information** office (☎67/3291-1143) at the bus station (☎67/3291-1552), though its opening hours are very unpredictable. The town offers plenty of **accommodation** possibilities, including the *Hotel Neves* (☎67/3291-1273; ❸) in an old brick farmhouse one block from the *rodoviária* and five minutes by bus from the town centre; the more central *Hotel Santa Ana*, Rua Miranda Reis 931 (☎67/3291-1602; ❸), with a pool and sauna; and the *Coxim*, at Km 726 on the BR-163, 4km from town (☎67/3291-1480; ❸), which also has a pool and restaurant. There are other hotels, *fazendas* and *pousadas*, mostly aimed at fishing holiday-makers, several of them 5km away in the neighbouring village of Silviolândia. When it's time to move on, it might be worth enquiring about river boats to Corumbá. The Rio Taquari has silted up considerably in recent years – the effect of land clearance for cattle grazing and agriculture, leading to huge amounts of topsoil being shifted into the river systems – and as a result, boats along the river are now rare.

# South to the Paraguayan border

There's no great draw – in fact, no draw at all – in the towns south of Campo Grande en route to the Paraguayan border at Ponta Porã. The only settlement of any size is **DOURADOS**, 225km from the state capital, a violent, rapidly expanding place which recently overtook Corumbá as Mato Grosso do Sul's second-largest city. Its name is a reminder of the fact that the spot was first settled by travellers en route to the Cuiabá gold mines. These days it's the region's most important agricultural centre, but there's little of interest to the tourist except bus connections to points further south and west (the daily bus to Bonito currently leaves at 3pm). Should you get stranded overnight, you can try three reasonable **accommodation** options: *Bahamas*, Rua João Cândido Câmara 750 (Ⓣ67/3411-3411, Ⓦwww.bahamashotel.com.br; ③), one of the most comfortable in town; *Hotel Alphonsus*, Av. Presidente Vargas 603 (Ⓣ67/3422-5211; ③–④), with pool; and cheapest of all, *Turis Hotel*, Av. Marcelino Pires 5932 (Ⓣ67/3422-1909; ②).

**MUNDO NOVO**, about eleven hours by bus from Campo Grande, is another unattractive transport terminus. From here, buses run to the crossing point for ferries to Guaira, and to Porto Frajelli and Foz do Iguaçu. The *Hotel Marajoara*, Av. Castelo Branco 93 (Ⓣ67/3474-1692; ②), has decent rooms.

## Ponta Porã

In contrast to the distinctly unthrilling towns that have gone before, **PONTA PORÃ** itself is an attractive little settlement, right on the Paraguayan border up in the Maracaju hills. The **Avenida Internacional** divides the settlement in two – on one side of the street you're in Brazil, on the other in the Paraguayan town of **Pedro Juan Caballero**. On the Paraguayan side you can polka the night away, gamble your money till dawn or, like most people there, just buy a load of imported goods at the duty-free shops, while the Brazilian side is a little more staid. There's a strange blend of language and character, and even a unique *mestizo* cuisine, making it an interesting place to spend a day or two. Ponta Porã also has a tradition as a distribution centre for *maté* – a herb brewed to make a tea-like drink.

There are plenty of **hotels** to choose from, with most of the budget places over the road from the train station. Better choices include the *Internacional*, Av. Internacional 2604 (Ⓣ67/3431-1243; ③), a mid-range hotel with regular hot water, while for a plusher stay it's hard to beat the *Pousada do Bosque*, just outside Ponta Porã at Av. Presidente Vargas 1151 (Ⓣ67/3431-1181, Ⓦwww.hotelpousadadobosque.com.br; ③), with its welcoming swimming pool.

## Bela Vista and Porto Murtinho

Two interesting destinations on the Paraguayan border are Bela Vista and Porto Murtinho, both to the west of Ponta Porã and harder to reach. While they don't serve as gateways to Paraguay (it's technically illegal to cross the frontier at these places), they are worth visiting for the splendour of their natural setting alone. Both towns are served by **bus** from Dourados (a good day's journey), and from Jardim (8hr), which in turn is connected daily with Anastácio (4hr).

### Into Paraguay from Ponta Porã

Crossing the border is a simple procedure for most non-Brazilians. An **exit stamp** must be obtained from the Polícia Federal at Rua Mal. Floriano 1483 (Ⓣ67/3431-1428) on the Brazilian side, then it's a matter of walking four or five blocks down Rua Guia Lopes to the Paraguayan customs and control. If you need a visa for Paraguay you can get this from the **consulate** on Avenida Internacional (Ⓣ67/3431-6312) on the Brazilian side. If you're pushed for time, catch a cab from the bus station to complete exit and entry formalities; the fare is about R$20, including waiting time. Once in Paraguay, there's a reasonably good road direct to Concepción, a major source of imports and contraband for Brazilians; daily buses make the five- or six-hour trip in good weather. It's another five hours from there to Asunción; there's also a direct service (8–10hr) from the bus station in Pedro Juan Caballero. There's no problem **changing money** at decent rates on Avenida Internacional, but it's impossible to change traveller's cheques on Sundays and holidays.

In **BELA VISTA** you can explore the natural delights of the Piripacu and Caracol rivers, behind which are the unspoilt peaks of the Três Cerros and Cerro Margarida. There's also the extraordinary **Nhandejara bridge**, a water-eroded underground passage over 30m long. Most Brazilians, however, come here for the opportunity to buy imported goods: over the border is the Paraguayan town of Bella Vista, which has a road connection (a day's travel) to Concepción. If you need to stay, try the *Pousada da Fronteira*, Av. Teodoro Sativa 1485 (Ⓣ67/3439-1487; ③).

Remote and tranquil, **PORTO MURTINHO** owes its foundation 453km south of Campo Grande to the thriving trade in the tea-type herb, *erva maté*. The town of 13,000 inhabitants sits on the banks of the Rio Paraguai, over 470km southwest of Campo Grande, near where the river finally leaves Brazilian territory. Well blessed with abundant wildlife and luxuriant vegetation, it marks the very southern limits of the Pantanal swamplands. You can take fairly cheap riverboat excursions from Porto Murtinho, though you might be expected to haggle over the price a little, since there are often several boatmen to choose from at the riverfront.

For **accommodation**, *Hotel Americano*, Rua Dr Corréa 430 (Ⓣ67/3287-1344; ④ full-board), has 38 large, air-conditioned rooms as well as boats for residents' use (rowing boats R$40 for 3hr, motorboats R$120 for 3hr), while 1km out of town, in the Fazenda Saladero, is the similar *Saladero Cue* (Ⓣ67/3287-1113, Ⓦwww.hotelsaladerocue.com.br; ④), with a beautiful riverside location and boats for rent. Slightly cheaper but not as nice is the *Pousada do Pantanal*, Rua Alfredo Pinto 141 (Ⓣ67/3287-1325; ③). Lastly, the *Americano* owns and runs *Hotel Nabileque* (⑤), 120km upriver on the Rio Nabileque, and primarily a base for anglers. The hotel is actually built on the river, supported on stilts, and has boats for rent. Daily boats (3hr) from the *Americano* will get you out there.

## West towards Corumbá

Several daily **buses** connect Campo Grande with Aquidauana and Anastácio (2hr) and Corumbá (7hr), the scenery becoming increasingly swamp-like the further west you travel. West of Campo Grande, the savanna becomes forested as the road approaches the first real range of hills since leaving the Atlantic coast. The **Serra de Maracaju** sticks up like a gigantic iceberg in the vast southern Mato Grosso, and beyond, interesting geological formations dominate the horizon: vast towering tors, known as *torrelones*, rise magnificently out of the scrubby savanna. Further west, around the small train station of **Camisão**, is a relatively lush valley supporting tropical fruits, sugar cane and, of course, beef cattle, and up towards the swamp's edge lies the little town of Miranda, popular for its fishing.

### Aquidauana and Anastácio

**AQUIDAUANA**, 130km from Campo Grande, is a lazy-looking place and very hot, sitting under the beating sun of the Piraputanga uplands. Since the demise of the passenger trains to Corumbá, it sweats somewhat uncomfortably some distance from the main BR-262 highway, and, though it still serves as one of several gateways into the Pantanal, it's better known for fishing and walking, with some superb views across the swamp. These days, most visitors see little more than the signpost at the crossroads where the highway bypasses the town; if you stop by here, it'll most likely be to use the highway café or toilet facilities at the junction. If you do go into town or stay over here, it's worth enquiring about two nearby but seldom visited sites: the **ruins of the Cidade de Xaraés**, founded by the Spanish in 1580 on the banks of the Rio Aquidauana; and the **Morro do Desenho**, a series of prehistoric inscriptions on the riverbank and in the nearby hills.

The river running through the town boasts some pleasant sandy **beaches**, quite clean and safe for swimming between May and October; **fishing** championships are an integral part of the annual São João August festival here. There's a reasonable choice of **hotels**, including the quiet *Hotel Pantanal* (ⓣ67/3241-1929; ❷) at Rua Estevão Alves Corréa 2611 opposite the *rodoviária*. The *Portal Pantaneiro*, Rua Pandiá Calógeras 1067 (ⓣ67/3241-4328, ⓦwww.portalpantaneiro.com.br; ❷), has a pool and very comfortable rooms; and the *Hotel Tropical*, Rua Manoel Aureliano Costa 533 (ⓣ67/3241-4113; ❸), with its smart rooms and good showers, is another of the best in town. **Aquidauana** is often the base for switching from public transport to local cars in order to reach a couple of interesting *fazendas*: the *Fazenda Pequi* (ⓣ67/3245-0949; ❺), a comfortable mid-priced lodge with a swimming pool and restaurant that offers horse, vehicle and boat expeditions; and the expensive but rather special *Fazenda Rio Negro* (ⓦwww.fazendarionegro.com.br; ❼), run by environmental NGOs. If you don't have your own car, try calling either place first and see if they will pick you up from town. One of several decent **restaurants** is the *O Casarão*, Rua Manoel Antônio Paes de Barros 533 (ⓣ67/3241-2219), which is expensive but serves delicious, though not exclusively Brazilian, dishes.

The neighbouring town of **ANASTÁCIO** – half an hour's walk on the other side of the river – has some nice beaches of its own, but is best known for the large *jaú* fish (often weighing over 75kg) that live in its river. Anastácio is the transport hub of the region, with daily bus services to Bela Vista, Bonito, Miranda and Ponta Porã, as well as Campo Grande and Corumbá. There's an infrequently taken road – you'll need your own wheels to access it – that skirts the southeastern rim of the Pantanal right up to **Rio Verde do Mato Grosso**, 200km north of Campo Grande on the way to Cuiabá; here you'll find a nice spot for bathing in the transparent waters and cascades that feed the Rio Verde.

Fifty kilometres south of Aquidauana just off the BR-419 road towards Bonito, the *Cabana do Pescador* **luxury fishing lodge** on the Rio Miranda (ⓣ67/3245-3697, ⓦwww.cabanadopescador.com.br) is a possible base from which to go fishing, horseriding or take a tour to the Bonito caves (see p.510).

## Miranda

Seventy kilometres west of Anastácio, the small town of **MIRANDA** sits straddling the BR-262 at the foot of the Serra da Bodoquena by the Rio Miranda. Once the scene of historic battles, Miranda has been somewhat ignored by visitors since the demise of the old Campo Grande to Corumbá rail service, but it's a pleasant town that is known for excellent fishing and for Terena and Kadiwéu artefacts. It's also a good base for visiting Bonito (128km) or the Pantanal swamp.

There are several reasonable **hotels**, including *Pantanal Hotel*, Av. Barão do Rio Branco 609 (ⓣ&ⓕ67/3242-1608; ❹), which has a pool; the *Hotel Roma*, a good cheap option at Praça Agenor Carrillo 356 (ⓣ67/3242-1321; ❸); and *Hotel Chalé*, just up from the *rodoviária* on Rua Barão do Rio Branco (ⓣ67/3242-1216; ❸), which is similarly good value, with clean, modern rooms, all with air conditioning. The best hotel, however, is the *Pousada Águas do Pantanal*, Av. Afonso Pena 367 (ⓣ67/3242-1242, ⓦwww.aguasdopantanal.com.br; ❹), with a pool and excellent service, which offers safaris into the Pantanal. The management here also runs the *Fazenda San Francisco*, 36km down the road to Bonito

## The Terena Indians

The **Serra de Maracaju** provided sanctuary for local **Terena Indians** during a period of Paraguayan military occupation in the 1860s. Under their highly ambitious dictator, Solano López, the Paraguayans invaded the southern Mato Grosso in 1864, a colonial adventure that resulted in the death of over half the invasion force, mostly composed of native (Paraguayan) Guaraní Indians. This was one period in Brazilian history when whites and Indians fought for the same cause, and it was in the magnificent Serra de Maracaju hills that most of the guerrilla-style resistance took place.

The late nineteenth century saw an influx of Brazilian colonists into the Aquidauana and Miranda valleys as the authorities attempted to "populate" the regions between Campo Grande and Paraguay – the war with Paraguay had only made them aware of how fertile these valleys were. Pushed off the best of the land and forced, in the main, to work for new, white landowners, the Terena tribe remained vulnerable until the appearance of **Lieutenant Rondon** (after whom the Amazonian state of Rondônia was named). Essentially an engineer, he came across the Terena in 1903 after constructing a telegraph connection – poles, lines and all – through virtually impassable swamps and jungle between Cuiabá and Corumbá. With his help, the Terena managed to establish a legal claim to some of their traditional land. Considered by FUNAI (the federal agency for Indian affairs) to be one of the most successfully "integrated" Indian groups in modern Brazil, the Terena have earned a reputation for possessing the necessary drive and ability to compete successfully in the market system – a double-edged compliment in that it could be used by the authorities to undermine their rights to land as a tribal group. They live mostly between Aquidauana and Miranda, the actual focus of their territory being the town and train station of **Taunay** – an interesting settlement with mule-drawn taxi wagons and a peaceful atmosphere. You'll find Terena handicrafts on sale in Campo Grande.

(Ⓣ67/3242-1497; ⑥), which offers lots of activities, but at a cost. The *Refúgio Ecológico Caiman* (Ⓣ67/3242-1450, reservations Ⓣ11/3706-1800, Ⓦwww.caiman.com.br; ⑧) is one of the most luxurious of all Pantanal *fazenda*-lodges, based some 40km out of town and set in 530 square kilometres of swampland. For **camping**, ask the staff at *Perqueiro Camping Lopes* around the corner from the *rodoviária* about their site 12km away. One really good **restaurant** in town is the *Cantina del Amore*, Rua Barrão do Rio Branco 515, which mainly serves standard Brazilian dishes including fresh fish.

# Bonito and around

Nestling in the Bodoquena hills, over three hours by bus from Anastácio and Miranda, and four from Campo Grande and Dourados, **BONITO** is a small, somewhat sleepy sprawl of a town, which comes to life during the main holiday seasons when it's invaded by hordes of young people from southern Brazilian cities. The dirt tracks that make up most of the region's roads conceal the fact that ever since Bonito starred as an "undiscovered" ecological paradise on TV Globo in 1993, it has become one of Brazil's major **ecotourist** destinations, with caves, rivers and nature reserves. Needless to say, visitors have been swarming to the town ever since (especially over Christmas and Easter, and in July and Aug), although the mood, out of season, is surprisingly relaxed and not at all pushy. Situated as the town is at the southern edge of the Pantanal, a visit to Bonito can happily be combined with a trip exploring the swamp; indeed, between the two locations it's possible to see a fantastic range of wildlife and several ecological centres. Culturally Bonito doesn't offer loads, but in July the Festival de Inverno showcases street theatre, art and music.

## Arrival and information

The **rodoviária** (Ⓣ67/3255-1606) is located up Rua Vicente Jacques, several blocks and a ten-minute walk from the main street Rua Cel. Pilad Rebuá, where many of the town's hotels and most of its tour operators are located. Here you'll find the SETUR **tourist information** office at no. 1780 (Mon–Sat 9am–5pm; Ⓣ67/3255-1449 and 3255-4670, Ⓦwww.bonito-ms.com.br for the local municipal site, and for a wider variety of local information, there's also Ⓦwww.portalbonito.com.br). Alternatively, the English-speaking tourist service Linha Direta con a Natureza ("Direct Line to Nature"; Ⓣ67/3255-1850) is a useful source of information and can make bookings for local tours.

**Taxis** are an easy way of getting about Bonito and its outlying areas, and there are several taxi points in town; Ponto Taxi, Rua Monte Castelo 824 (Ⓣ67/3255-1760), charges R$3–5 a ride in and around town. A cheaper alternative, particularly if you're travelling alone, is taking a **mototaxi**, or motorbike taxi (75¢ a ride in town and up to R$10 a trip to sites out of town).

Daily Cruzeiro do Sul **buses** connect Bonito with Campo Grande, Corumbá, Dourados and Ponta Porã; nevertheless, you'll need to stay two nights if you want to include even one trip to the caves or rivers (organized tours generally leave around 7.30am), though there are so many possible day- and half-day trips in the area that most people stay longer.

## Accommodation

Finding a place to stay in Bonito should be easy even in high season. Most accommodation is budget-range – there are over a dozen cheapies on Rua Cel. Pilad Rebuá, two blocks up from the *rodoviária* – but there are also a fair number of classier options, which often double up as tour agencies. Alternatively, out-of-town accommodation is available. There are more than ten **campsites** around the Bonito area; you can get their details from the travel agents in town or, in advance, from the tourist information office in Campo Grande (see p.498). The nearest to town are *Camping Boa Vista*, Rua Ari Machado (Ⓣ67/3255-1764) on the outskirts, and *Ilha do Padre* (Ⓣ67/3255-1430) about 10km further out.

### Bonito centre

**Albergue de Juventude do Ecoturismo** Rua Lício Borralho 716 Ⓣ67/3255-1022, Ⓦwww.bonitohostel.com.br. Located ten blocks north of the *rodoviária* and a 15min walk into the town centre, it has excellent facilities including pool, laundry, bar-café, kitchen and games area. They rent bikes for a couple of hours at a time and will put you in touch with local tour operators. ❶–❷

**Hotel Gemila Palace** Rua Luis da Costa Leite 2085 Ⓣ67/3255-1421. The best mid-range choice – a very friendly, family-run place with a/c rooms and a great buffet breakfast. ❹

**Paraíso das Aguas** Rua Cel. Pilad Rebuá 1884 Ⓣ67/3255-1296, Ⓦwww.paguas.com.br. The rooms at this tidy, welcoming and very central hotel with pool come with a/c, TV and *frigobar*. ❹

**Pousada Muito Bonito** Rua Cel. Pilad Rebuá 1448 Ⓣ67/3255-1645, Ⓦwww.muitobonito.com.br. One of the best backpacker options; very friendly, and with staff who speak several languages, including English. Spotless rooms, all with private bathrooms, and a pleasant terrace for breakfast. Has its own tour agency. ❷

**Pousada Olho d'Agua** Estrada Baia das Garças Ⓣ67/3255-1430, Ⓦwww.pousadaolhodagua.com.br. Set 3km from the centre on the northwestern end of town, this is no less luxurious than the *Zagaia Eco-Resort*, but arguably more personal and affordable. Offers delightful bungalow accommodation in intimate wooded surroundings, with excellent service and food, and its own tour agency. ❹

**Zagaia Eco-Resort** 2km from the centre by the airfield ⓣ67/3255-5500, ⓦwww.zagaia.com.br. Top of the range, ultra-modern complex with three swimming pools, various playing fields, horseriding, numerous restaurants and even a cabaret – popular with holiday-makers from Rio. ❼

### Surrounding area

**Pousada Bacuri** 7km away beside the Aquário Natural ⓣ67/3255-1632, or reservations in Bonito at Rua 15 de Novembro 632. This place is a little paradise run by a charming family, with a number of basic but clean dormitories, and a gorgeous stretch of the Rio Formosinho for swimming, complete with four waterfalls and virgin forest inhabited by monkeys and macaws; camping is also allowed (R$25 per person). ❹

**Projeto Vivo** ⓣ11/5561-0076 or 67/3255-3803, ⓦwww.projectovivo.com.br. Further afield, some 30km away, *Projecto Vivo* offers good-quality *fazenda*-style accommodation in a tranquil setting by the Ilha do Padre. There's a pool, and horseriding and river rafting are also on offer, but you need to book in advance through one of the local travel agents – try Natura Tour (see p.513). For more details on this place, see p.512. ❺



## Trips from Bonito

Bonito's tour companies are unusually well tuned in to the requirements of overseas visitors, and all offer identical trips at identical – and very reasonable – prices to all the places described below, plus a wide range of other options. The municipality limits the number of visitors to Bonito's natural wonders and systematically enforces a whole array of regulations intended to protect this ecologically "pure" region. Many of the sites charge for entry, and for some, such as the famous Lago Azul cave, you require both authorization and a guide to visit. Such **permits** and **guides** are arranged by the tour companies (see p.513) or hotels. Almost all the sites require transport, which makes it virtually impossible to visit them independently. Some hotels, like *Pousada Muito Bonito*, can arrange daily **car rental** for around R$70, and someone may be happy to rent you his or her bicycle for the day, but you'll still need a guide to access the main sites.

### The Gruta do Lago Azul

The **Gruta do Lago Azul** (daily 8am–2pm, holidays 7am–4pm; no children under 5; usual guide fee R$15) is a deep, large and cathedral-like cave some 20km from Bonito, out beyond the tiny municipal airstrip. It's set in forested hills rich in limestone, granite and marble, and full of minerals, as well as a growing number of mercury, uranium and phosphorus mines. Even before the mines, though, these hills, which reach up to about 800m above sea level, were full of massive caves, most of them inaccessible and on private *fazenda* land.

Rediscovered in 1924 by local Terena Indians, the entrance to the cave is quite spectacular. Surrounded by some 250,000 square metres of ecological reserve woodland, it looms like a monstrous mouth inviting you into the heart of the earth. At first you climb down a narrow path through vegetation, then deeper down into dripping stalactite territory some 100m below to the mists hovering above the cave's lake. The pre-Cambrian rocks of the cave walls are striated like the skin of an old elephant and there are weird rock formations such as the easily recognized natural Buddha. Light streams in from the semicircular cave opening, but only penetrates right to the lake level in the bottom of the cave for 45 minutes on 30 days each year.

Since 1989 a number of expeditions have attempted to fathom the depths of the lake, but with no success (70m is the deepest exploration to date). One of these, a joint French-Brazilian expedition, discovered the bones of prehistoric animals (including a sabre-toothed tiger) and even human remains. The blue waters of the lake extend into the mountain for at least another 300m and are exceptionally clear, with only shrimps and crustacea able to survive in the calcified water.

There is another spectacular cave in the area, **Nossa Senhora Aparecida**, 30km from Bonito, which can only be visited with a guide and special permission from the Prefeitura; contact SETUR (Ⓣ67/3255-4670).

### The Aquário Natural

The **Aquário Natural** complex (daily 9am–6pm; all-inclusive price for a half-day excursion is around R$125, covering transport, guide, permit, and access to snorkelling equipment and boats) is justifiably Bonito's next most popular attraction. Located at the river's source, 7km from town, the Aquário itself is a small sanctuary with water so clear and full of fish that the experience is like looking into an aquarium – something you can take advantage of by a ride in one of the glass-bottomed boats. In fact, visitors are encouraged to put on a floating jacket, mask and snorkel, and get into the water with the 35 or so species of fish, mainly *dourado* and 35cm *piripitanga* fishes – a tickling experience with no danger from piranhas who never swim this far upriver. The sanctuary is accessible by a path from the reception through a swamp and *mata* nature reserve, the **Parque Ecológico Bahia Bonita**, replete with wildlife, including white-collared peccaries, agouti and the majestic *caramugeiro* snail hawk. From the Aquário, the **Bahia Bonita**, a kilometre-long stretch of river, runs down to meet the Rio Formoso, where there's a death-slide (a pulley and rope system for exciting splashdowns into the river), and trampoline-based river fun.

The Aquário Natural is only one of several snorkelling locations in the area, though it has by far the most developed infrastructure. If you're on a tight budget, the nearby *Pousada Bacuri* (R$7 admission), 500m from the Aquário Natural, has a stretch of river all of its own, with *dourado* fish, four small waterfalls and a small forest. Tour companies also offer snorkelling trips to the **Rio Sucuri** (R$70 half day), and the **Rio da Prata** (R$140 full day). One of the best local scuba sites is the **Gruta do Mimosa** (R$250 full day); a trip here requires both a guide and permit, best obtained through either the Pousada Olho d'Agua travel agency or Ygarapé Tours (see p.513).

▲ Freshwater snorkelling near Bonito

### Ilha do Padre

Around 12km from Bonito down the Rio Formoso, there's an interesting island, the **Ilha do Padre**, which has been turned into a public nature reserve and campsite. It costs R$15 to enter (no guide or authorization is required) and R$25 per person to camp, or you can pay a little more (R$40) to use the primitive wooden chalets. **Whitewater rafting** down to Ilha do Padre (R$250 half day, sometimes done by moonlight) is one of the more exciting options available from tour agents in Bonito (see opposite). The island is surrounded by 22 waterfalls of varying sizes and covers almost 50,000 square metres. Although the Formoso is an active whitewater-rafting river, there are also delightful natural swimming spots, lots of exotic birdlife and lush vegetation. It's not quite as beautiful as the Aquário Natural at the river's source, but still very pleasant, although come prepared for the biting flies and mosquitoes. The island is annoyingly busy at peak holiday times (such as Easter).

### Fazenda da Barra Projeto Vivo

The **Fazenda da Barra Projeto Vivo**, an ecological visitors' centre 31km from Bonito at the point where the Formoso and Miranda rivers meet, provides a vivid example of how the apparently conflicting interests of ecology and business can be combined for profit, pleasure and education. The centre is one of the first of its kind in Brazil and has been very successful. Full- and half-day trips from Bonito are organized by the local travel agencies: a full day costs from R$120, a half-day from R$60 (children half-price), including transport to and from Bonito, a guided forest walk, river-rafting, horseriding and meals. There's a small eco-library for those who read Portuguese and, needless to say, it's an excellent place for children, with plenty of additional hands-on activities (painting, paper-recycling and the like) to keep them happy. You can also stay in one of their chalets sited 200m from the Rio Formoso: *Chalé das Artes* (❸) with eight beds, or *Chalé Eden* (❻) with only two. For more details, contact the *fazenda* direct (Ⓣ67/3255-3803, Ⓦwww.projectovivo.com.br), or the tour companies listed opposite.

## Eating and drinking

There is quite a range of restaurants and bars in town – some of the best are listed below – and there are plenty of ice-cream parlours on Rua Cel. Pilad Rebuá.

**Bar O Pirata** Rua 29 de Maio. Usually busy with travellers, they serve a range of cocktails and wines.

**Cantinho do Peixe** Rua 31 de Março 1918 Ⓣ67/3255-3381. This place has a great fish menu and is very popular with locals.

**Gula's Restaurante** Rua Cel. Pilad Rebuá 1626. This popular place is especially good for pizzas and inexpensive *comida por kilo* lunches.

**Pousada Muito Bonito** Rua Cel. Pilad Rebuá 1448 Ⓣ67/3255-1645, Ⓦwww.muitobonito.com.br. Good home cooking at lunchtime in pleasant surroundings.

**Pousada Olho d'Agua** Estrada Baia das Garças Ⓣ67/3255-1430. Located 3km from the centre on the northwestern end of town, the restaurant at this hotel serves high-quality meals at lunchtime and in the evenings; best to call to reserve a table in high season.

**Restaurante Tapera** Rua Cel. Pilad Rebuá 1961 Ⓣ67/3255-1110. In the centre of town, this restaurant serves excellent, if pricey, fish and other dishes in the evening and also has a good bar.

**Taboa Bar** Rua Cel. Pilad Rebuá 1841. This bar is usually quite lively from about 9pm, but only at weekends do they stay open much beyond midnight.

## Listings

**Banks and exchange** Bradesco, Rua Cel. Pilad Rebuá 1942; Banco do Brasil, Rua Luis da Costa Leite 2279, by the central square; HSBC, Rua Cel. Pilad Rebuá 680.

**Car rental** Translocar, Rua Cel. Pilad Rebuá 976 ⓣ67/3255-1391; Unidas, Rua das Flores ⓣ67/3255-1066; Yes ⓣ67/3255-1702.
**Hospital** Hospital Municipal ⓣ67/3255-3455.
**IBAMA** ⓣ67/3255-1765.
**Internet** Casa do Computador, Rua Santana do Paraíso 1760 (ⓣ67/3255-1463), offers reasonably cheap public access (R$5 per hour), or try Caffe.com, Rua Frei Mariano 635.
**Local guides** The local tour guides association is AGTB (ⓣ67/3255-1837).
**Pharmacy** Farmácia Drogacruz, Rua Cel. Pilad Rebuá 1629.
**Post office** On the main street Rua Cel. Pilad Rebua 1759 (Mon–Fri 8am–noon and 1–4.30pm).
**Travel and tour companies** Some hotels, like *Olho d'Agua* and *Muito Bonito*, have their own tour agencies, or can help you arrange a trip with one of the tour companies. Some of the better options are: Ar Bonito Tour, Rua Cel. Pilad Rebuá 1890 (ⓣ67/3255-1008, ⓦwww.agenciaar.com.br); Impacto, Rua Coronel Pilad Rebuá 1515 (ⓣ67/3255-1414, ⓦwww.impactotour.com.br); and Ygarapé Tours, Rua Cel. Pilad Rebuá 1956 (ⓣ&ⓕ67/3255-1733, ⓦwww.ygarape.com.br), who also offer scuba diving for beginners.



# Corumbá and around

Far removed from mainstream Brazil, hard by the Bolivian border and 400km west of Campo Grande, the city of **CORUMBÁ** provides a welcome stop after the long ride from either Santa Cruz (in Bolivia) or Campo Grande. As an entrance to the Pantanal, Corumbá has the edge over Cuiabá in that it is already there, stuck in the middle of a gigantic swamp, only 119m above sea level. Its name, in Tupi, means the "place of stones" and, not surprisingly, Corumbá and the Pantanal didn't start out as a great source of attraction to travellers. As early as 1543, the swamp proved an inhospitable place to an expedition of 120 large canoes on a punitive campaign against the Guaicuru tribe. Sent by the Spanish governor of Paraguay, it encountered vampire bats, stingrays, biting ants and plagues of mosquitoes. And while it doesn't seem quite so bad today, it's easy to understand why air conditioning is such big business here. It was Corumbá's unique location on the old rail link between the Andes and the Atlantic that originally brought most travellers to the town, but, ironically, the same swamp that deterred European invaders for so long has rapidly become an attraction, at the same time that the Brazilian part of the rail link has been closed down.

## Arrival and information

The **rodoviária** is close to the train station on Rua Porto Carrero (ⓣ67/3231-2033) and is served by daily buses from Campo Grande, São Paulo and even further afield. From the *rodoviária*, it's a fifteen-minute walk into town, or there are buses and taxis (R$15) plying the route. The **airport** (ⓣ67/3231-3322) is a half-hour walk or a R$30 taxi ride west of the city centre.

What little **tourist information** there is can be obtained from SETUR, Rua Manoel Cavassa 275, down at the port (Mon 1–6pm, Tues–Fri 8.30am–noon & 1.30–6pm; ⓣ67/3232-5221), or in the Casa do Artesão, Rua Dom Aquino Corréa 405 (same hours; ⓣ67/3231-2715).

## Accommodation

**Hotels** in Corumbá vary considerably but their sheer quantity means you should have no trouble finding a room, even from August to October. Out of season, especially January to Easter, there are heavy discounts all round, and prices can be bargained even lower.

The most centrally located for shops and the port, and so noisiest at night, is the clutch of cheap lodgings around **Rua Delamare**, west of Praça da República;

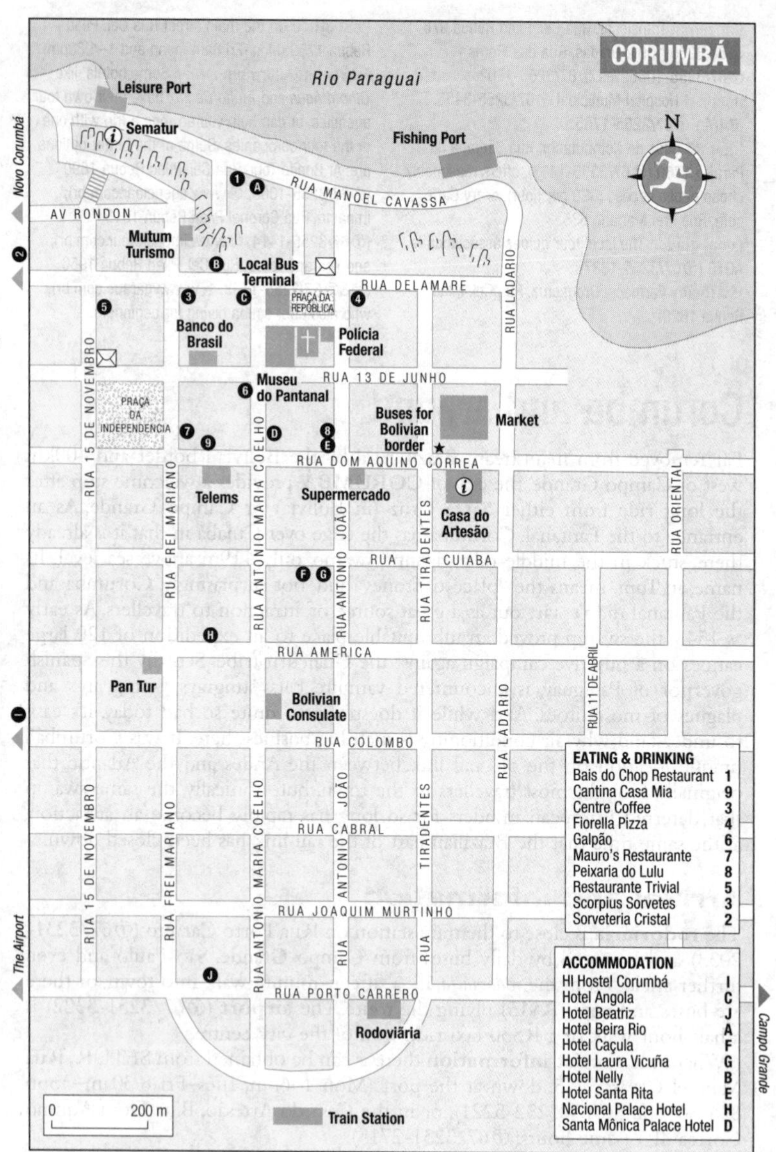


these tend to be very popular with backpackers and are good places to meet companions for trips into the Pantanal.

**HI Hostel Corumba** Rua Colombo 1419 ⓣ67/3231-1005, ⓦwww.corumbahostel.com.br. Corumbá's youth hostel with dorms and private spaces available; good service and a nice ambience. ❶–❷

**Hotel Angola** Rua Antônio Maria Coelho 124 ⓣ67/3231-7233 or 3231-7727. Safe, perfectly reasonable, with internet and cheapest of the bunch around Rua Delamare. ❸

**Hotel Beatriz** Rua Porto Carrero 896 ⓣ67/3231-7441. Facing the *rodoviária*, very cheap and pretty basic, but useful if you arrive late at night by bus and can't face the 2km hike into town. ❶

**Hotel Beira Rio** Rua Manoel Cavassa 109 ⓣ67/3231-2554. Right by the shore, with cheerful management and lots of character. Its best rooms overlook the river and the Pantanal, and there are boats for guests' use. ❷

**Hotel Caçula** Rua Cuiabá 795 ⓣ67/3231-5745, ⓕ3231-1976. Next door and better value for money than the *Laura Vicuña*, with good clean rooms, each with TV. ❷

**Hotel Laura Vicuña** Rua Cuiabá 775 ⓣ67/3231-5874, ⓕ3231-2663. A peaceful place, very neat and tidy in traditional fashion. All rooms have phone and TV. ❸

**Hotel Nelly** Rua Delamare 902 ⓣ67/3231-6001, ⓕ3231-7396. Long a favourite haunt for budget travellers and kids from Rio and São Paulo, and excellent value, if a little dank. Rooms with TV cost more. ❷

**Hotel Santa Rita** Rua Dom Aquino Corréa 860 ⓣ67/3231-5453. Rooms are clean and airy at this good-value hotel – where the more expensive ones come with a/c and TV. There's also a reasonable on-site restaurant. ❷–❸

**Nacional Palace Hotel** Rua América 936 ⓣ67/3234-6000, ⓔhnacion@brasinet.com.br. Pretty much top of the range in Corumbá. It's convenient and has a pool (non-residents can use it for R$25), but it's a bit flashy. ❹

**Santa Mônica Palace Hotel** Rua Antônio Maria Coelho 345 ⓣ67/3234-3000, ⓦwww.hsantamonica.com.br. Corumbá's largest hotel and best mid-range option, offering excellent value: rooms come with all mod cons including a/c and fridges, and the added luxuries of a pool (non-residents can use it for R$15), sauna and riverboats for hire. ❹

## The City

Commanding a fine view over the Rio Paraguai and across the swamp, the city is small (approaching 100,000 inhabitants), and is really only busy in the mornings – indeed it's one of Brazil's most laid-back towns south of the Amazon, basking in intense heat and overwhelming humidity. Even at the port nothing seems to disturb the slow-moving pool games taking place in the bars. Because of the heat, there's a very open-plan feel to the city and the people of Corumbá seem to be equally at home sitting at tables by bars and restaurants, or eating their dinners outside in front of their houses. In every street, there's at least one television blaring away on the pavement, and it's not unusual to be invited into someone's house for food, drinks or – at weekends – a party.

Corumbá's life revolves around its **port**, while its transport connections are at the other end of town around the *rodoviária* and airport; if you're intending to stay more than one night, the port end is your best bet. Within a few blocks of the riverfront you'll find the **Praça da Independência**, a large, shaded park with ponds, a children's playground and a few unusual installations dotted around: a streamroller, imported from England around 1921, whose first job was flattening Avenida General Rondon, and an antique water wheel, also English, which served in a sugar factory until 1932. Early in the day, the *praça* is alive with tropical birds, and by evening it's crowded with couples, family groups and gangs of children relaxing as the temperature begins to drop. The large but otherwise unimpressive church on this square is useful as a prominent landmark to help you get your bearings in this very flat, grid-patterned city.

A stone's throw away on the smaller **Praça da República** stands the stark late nineteenth-century Igreja Matriz Nossa Senhora da Candelária. Next door at Rua Delamare 939, facing the local bus terminal, is the fascinating **Museu do Pantanal** (Mon–Fri noon–5pm; free), which encompasses a collection of stuffed animals, artefacts from various indigenous tribes of the region, some archeological specimens, and changing exhibits of modern art. If you need advice or information about the local flora or fauna, contact the museum office. The only other thing to see is the **Casa do Artesão** at Rua Dom Aquino Corréa 405 (Mon–Fri 8–11am & 2–5pm, Sat 8–11am). It's housed in

Corumbá's most historic edifice – the old prison, dating from 1900 – and is a great place to track down some local craft work (especially wood and leather), as well as local liquors and *farinha da bocaiúva*, a flour made from palm-tree nuts and reputed to be an aphrodisiac.

## Eating, drinking and nightlife

The best restaurants in Corumbá are on Rua Frei Mariano and Rua 15 de Novembro, though there are plenty of cheap snack bars throughout town, especially on Rua Delamare west of the Praça da República, serving good set meals for less than R$15. Being a swamp city, fish is the main local delicacy, with *pacu* and *pintado* among the favoured species. For **self-catering**, there's a branch of Supermercado Ohara on the corner of Rua Dom Aquino Corréa and Rua Antônio João, and three butchers opposite. The covered market, one block east, should complete your provisions.

You'll find bars all over town, though with few exceptions they're spit-and-sawdust joints, rough-looking and a little intimidating at first. The town is not safe at night, so you do need to take care and perhaps try to avoid walking the streets after 10pm. The more relaxed bars are those down on the riverfront – where you can usually get a game of pool with your drink. **Nightlife** is best at the trendy *Bais do Chop* restaurant (☎67/3231-1079) located on the waterfront along Rua Manoel Cavassa in a lovingly restored mansion down at the port next to the *artesanato* shops; it plays good live music at weekends.

### Restaurants and cafés

**Cantina Casa Mia** Opposite the telephone office at Rua Dom Aquino Corréa 928 ☎67/3231-1327. A smart restaurant with strong local flavour; best at lunchtime. Closed Mon.

**Centre Coffee** Rua Delamare 967. This is by far the best place for good coffee and juices.

**Fiorella Pizza** On the eastern corner of Praça da República and Rua Delamare. Probably the best pizzas in town.

**Galpão** Rua 13 de Junho 797 at the corner of Rua Antônio Maria Coelho. This restaurant offers a huge choice of inexpensive meat and fish in vast portions.

**La Barca Tur** Restaurant-boat in port area ☎67/3231-3106. Created especially for those who like to cruise with their food, the restaurant-boat does 5hr lunch trips in high season, including the inevitable piranha soup, for R$80.

**Mauro's Restaurante** Rua Frei Mariano 383. This is one of the classiest and most popular eateries, particularly at lunchtimes when it has a splendid selection of surprisingly good-value self-service dishes.

**Peixaria do Lulu** Rua Antônio João 410 ☎67/3232-2142. An upmarket restaurant serving a range of quality local and international dishes.

**Restaurante Trivial** Rua 15 de Novembro 146/188. A modest place with a calm interior, it offers good self-service *comida por kilo* most lunchtimes and evenings.

**Scorpius Sorvetes** Corner of Rua Delamare and Rua Frei Mariano. This is a decent ice-cream parlour.

**Sorveteria Cristal** Corner of Rua Delamare and Rua 7 de Setembro. Another good spot for ice-cream and iced drinks.

## Listings

**Airlines** Tickets for all companies can be bought from Mutum Turismo (see opposite), or at the airport after 9.30am.

**Banks and exchange** You can change cash at the *casa de câmbio* at Rua 15 de Novembro 212 (Mon–Fri 8.30am–5pm). Otherwise, there's a host of banks including HSBC, some with ATMs, on Rua Delamare west of Praça da República (all Mon–Fri 10am–3pm), as well as the Banco do Brasil, Rua 13 de Junho 914 (10am–5pm). Out-of-hours exchange is sometimes possible at the desk in the *Nacional Palace Hotel*, Rua América 936, or ask other hotel or shop managers.

**Boats** There are plenty of boats waiting on the riverfront off Rua Manoel Cavassa that will take you into the Pantanal swamp or Bolivia; these include the *Albatroz* (☎67/3231-4858) which has eighteen cabins and does five-day trips, and the *Pira Miuna* (☎67/3232-1204), which does cheaper three-day trips and has only two cabins. See opposite for details of Pantanal operators, or ask around at the numerous offices on the waterfront. Small motorboats can be rented (two to four passengers) from *Hotel Beir Rio* and Urcabar, also on Rua Manoel Cavassa, for about R$200 a day (fuel is extra – you'll need up to 50 litres in a day). One option, a little hit or miss, is joining a cargo boat bound for Asunción. If you do find a Paraguayan trading boat, you should take care of the necessary paperwork with the Polícia Federal, Praça da República (☎67/3231-5848 or 3231-2413), and the Paraguayan consulate (see p.503) before leaving town, as well as with the Capitania dos Portos (☎67/3231-6444) at Rua Delamare 806, next to the post office.

**Car rental** Localiza is at the airport (☎67/3232-6000); Unidas, Rua Drei Mariano 633 (Mon–Sat 8am–6pm; ☎67/3231-3124), has reliable cars that can be taken out of Brazil, but must be returned to Corumbá. Both charge R$220 a day upwards.

**Consulates** Bolivia, Rua Antônio Maria Coelho 852 ☎67/3231-5605; Paraguay, Rua Cuiabá ☎67/3231-4803.

**Hospital** Clinica Samec ☎67/3231-3308.

**Laundry** There's an expensive same-day laundry service at Apae, Rua 13 de Junho 1377.

**Post office** The main post office is at Rua Delamare 708, opposite the church on Praça da República (Mon–Fri 9am–5pm, Sat 8–11.30am). A smaller office is near Praça da Independência on Rua 15 de Novembro (same hours).

**Shopping** For the Casa do Artesão and for food shopping, see opposite. Two of the shops on Praça da Independência are devoted entirely to hunting, fishing and cowboy paraphernalia, like saddles and guns, and there's a shop on Rua Antônio Maria Coelho, three blocks from the river, stuffed with garish Catholic *ex votos* and plastic icons. There are numerous photographic shops throughout town; Fotocor, Rua Delamare 871, has a good reputation.

**Taxis** Ponto Taxi ☎67/3231-4043 (taxi rank at southeast corner of Praça da Independência); Mototaxis ☎67/3231-7166.

**Travel and tour agencies** Pantur, Rua Frei Mariano 1013 (☎67/3231-2000), is a reliable air and train ticket sales agent and can also help organize comfortable *fazenda* trips into the swamp. Corumbá Tur, Rua Antônio Maria Coelho 852 (☎&Ⓕ67/3231-1532 or 1260), an upmarket operator dealing with *fazendas* and luxury angling cruises, also does half-day cruises to Puerto Suarez in Bolivia (R$40; no passport required), a good place for silverwork and tax-free goods. Green Track, Rua Antônio João 216 (☎67/3231-2258, Ⓔgreentk@terra.com.br), runs recommended packages of up to five days in the Pantanal. Mutum Turismo, Rua Frei Mariano 17 (☎67/3231-1818, Ⓦwww.mutumturismo.com.br), deals with flights and ticketing, and has a list of approved Pantanal guides. Fishing-based tours are operated by Pérola do Pantanal, Rua Manoel Cavassa 255, Porto Geral (☎67/3231-1460). Down on the riverfront there are several smaller boat tour company offices that run fishing and safari trips, including Urcabar, Rua Manoel Cavassa 181 (☎67/3231-3039), and La Barca Tour (☎67/3231-3016). See also the list of upmarket Pantanal operators on p.523. Budget Pantanal tours are run by all of the cheap hotels around Rua Delamare, whose touts will probably find you as soon as you get off the bus. Make sure you get authorized receipts for any money or valuables you deposit with a tour company or hotel; there have been reports of problems with this kind of practice in Corumbá.

## Around Corumbá

Apart from the Pantanal itself (see p.519), there isn't a great deal to visit around Corumbá. Probably the most interesting place is the ruins of the eighteenth-century **Forte de Coimbra** (daily 8.30–11.30am & 1.30–4pm), 80km to the south. Theoretically, the fort can only be visited with previous permission from the Brigada Mista in Corumbá, Av. General Rondon 1735 (☎67/3231-2861 or 3231-9866), although visitors unaware of this fact are sometimes allowed in. On the other hand, the Brigada Mista is as good a place as any to find out about transport to the fort. The fort is accessible only by water, and is most easily reached via Porto Esperança, an hour's bus ride from Corumbá (buses leave from outside *Hotel Beatriz* several times a day). The journey there is an interesting one along the edge of the swamp, and once in Porto Esperança you should have little difficulty renting a boat, or finding a guide, to take you a couple more hours downriver to the fort (it will cost at least R$50, however). It's also possible to approach the fort in traditional fashion, by following the Rio Paraguai all the way from Corumbá in a boat (from around R$35 a person, depending on the size of your group), but this takes around seven hours and involves going through a tour agency in town. One bonus of going by this route, however, is that you'll pass two little-visited natural caves, **Gruta do Inferno** and **Buraco Soturno**, sculpted with huge finger-like stalactites and stalagmites.

The Forte de Coimbra was built in 1775, three years before Corumbá's foundation, to defend this western corner of Brazilian territory and, more specifically, to protect the border against invasion from Paraguay. In 1864 it was attacked by the invading Paraguayan army, which had slipped upriver into the southern Mato Grosso. Coimbra provided the first resistance to the invaders, but it didn't last for long as the Brazilian soldiers escaped from the fort under cover of darkness, leaving the fort to the aggressors. Nearly three thousand Paraguayans continued upstream in a huge convoy of ships and, forging its way north beyond Corumbá, the armada crossed the swamps almost as far as the city of Cuiabá, which was saved only by the shallowness of its river. Nowadays the fort is a pretty dull ruin (except perhaps for military enthusiasts), and it's the journey there that's the real draw.

You may also be able to visit one of the planet's largest manganese deposits, currently being mined in the Urucum hills, just south of Corumbá off the BR-262. The hills rise more than 950m above the level of the swamp, and, although much of the area is technically out of bounds, organized visits to the **Minas do Morro do Urucum at Mineradora**, 24km from Corumbá, with their subterranean galleries (Grutas dos Belgas), can still be arranged through most tour agencies in Corumbá – or contact the company office at Av. General Rondon 1351 (☎67/3231-1661). If you decide to chance a visit unaccompanied, buses to Urucum depart from a lot next to *Hotel Beatriz* on Rua Porto Carrero.

Finally, if you're not going to have the time to get any further into the Pantanal, you can get a taste of the swamp life, without spending a lot of money, at two settlements on the Rio Paraguai. **PORTO MORRINHO** is the easier to get to, 67km or an hour by bus from Corumbá, just west of Porto Esperança on the

## Crossing the Bolivian border

Crossing into or out of Bolivia from Corumbá is a slightly disjointed procedure. **Leaving Brazil**, you should get an exit stamp from the Polícia Federal at Praça da República 51 in Corumbá (easiest before 11am or between 7pm and 9pm), before picking up a Bolivian visa (if you need one) from the consulate at Rua Antônio Maria Coelho 881 (☎67/3231-5605). After that, it's a matter of taking the bus (from the Praça Independência on Rua Dom Aquino Corréa) for the 10km to the border, checking through Bolivian immigration and receiving your passport entry stamp. **Money** can be changed at decent rates at the border.

**Train tickets for Santa Cruz** should be bought at La Brasilena train station in **Quijarro**, a few minutes by *colectivo* (a type of shuttle bus; R$5) or bus from the Bolivian immigration office. First class to Santa Cruz costs R$70, second class R$40. The first-class carriages are comfortable, with videos, but everything sways and the toilets are dirty. Limited food is available on board, and also from the trackside villages during the train's frequent stops. Insect repellent and clothes that cover your flesh are essential, as the lights of the carriages attract all manner of biting insects at night. Drinking water and a torch are also useful. As timetables vary considerably, check at the station in Corumbá or Quijarro at least a couple of days in advance. It's worth going to Quijarro the day before departure to actually make your booking.

**Entering Brazil** from Bolivia is essentially the same procedure in reverse, although US citizens should remember to pick up visas in the Brazilian consulate in Santa Cruz before leaving.

main road to Campo Grande, with ample birdlife and creeks to explore. The town has a few cheap hotels, such as the *Pousada do Pescador* (☎67/3287-1693; ②–③) and the *Hotel Tuiui* (④), the latter some 200m by *balsa* (raft) from Porto Morrinho on the banks of the river. The *Tuiui* rents out motorboats for R$100 a day and rowing boats for R$35. About the same distance from Corumbá on the old Campo Grande road (the unsurfaced MS-184/MS-228) is **PORTO MANGA**, which is renowned as a centre for wildlife-spotting and fishing on the Rio Paraguai, particularly in September. There are a couple of hotels here, including the *Pesqueiro* (☎67/3231-1987; ③), whose clean rooms have private baths, as well as some riverboats and boatmen for hire, and various potential camping locations in and around the settlement. From Porto Manga onward it's only 70km via Passo do Lontra to rejoin the BR-262.



# The Pantanal

Increasingly known worldwide as the best place for wildlife-spotting in South America, **THE PANTANAL** is fed by rivers and inhabited by rainforest bird and animal species from the Andes to the west and the Brazilian central plateau to the north. Essentially an open swampland larger than France that extends deep into the states of Mato Grosso and Mato Grosso do Sul, it is massive, running 950km north to south and averaging around 500km from east to west. This is one of those few destinations in Brazil where you're more likely to find wildlife than nightlife. Capybaras, wild boar, monkeys, and yellow anacondas (*sucuri amarela* in Portuguese or *Eunectes notaeus*) are common sights in the Pantanal, and it's probably the best place for wild mammals and exotic birds in the whole of the Americas. There are in fact 124 wild mammal species, 177 reptile species and a further 41 amphibian species in these swamps, plus over four hundred bird species. It's almost unnerving spending the afternoon on the edge of a remote lagoon in the swamp, surrounded by seemingly endless streams of flying and wading birds – toucans, parrots, red and even the endangered hyacinth macaws, blue herons, and the *tuiuiú* (giant red-necked stork). Unlike in most other areas of wilderness, the birdsong and density of wildlife here frequently lives up to the exotic soundtrack of Hollywood jungle movies, and in the middle of the swamp it's actually possible to forget that there are other people in the world – though it's difficult to forget the **mosquitoes**. (Although locals say that malaria is no longer a big problem in the Pantanal, it is advisable to check with your doctor before departure; mosquitoes, however, are abundant.) In addition to all this wildlife, it's only fair to mention that you'll still see more cattle and *jacarés* (*Caiman yacare*, alligators) than any other creature. The swamp has been a fabulous fishing-spot for thousands of years and new species of fish and vascular plants are still regularly discovered here. One of the tastiest and most popular fish – *pacu* – has been endangered by illegal over-fishing, much serving the markets of southern Brazil.

Although having only thirty percent natural forest cover, over 4.5 percent of the trees (some 6260 square kilometres) has already been destroyed by human

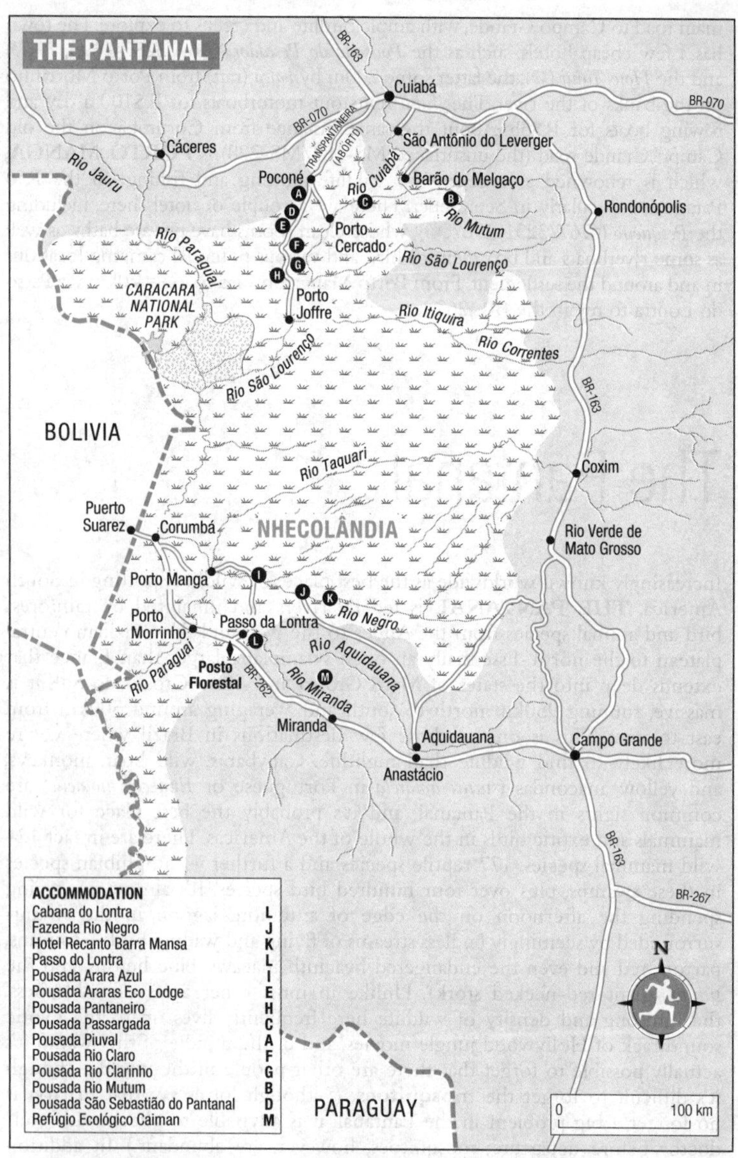


activity – mainly cattle ranching. The region is a stunning blend of swamp water with gallery forest, savanna and lakeside scrub forest. The region is dissected by around 175 rivers into roughly seventeen segments, each with its own distinctive landscape and micro-ecosytem. It was designated a UNESCO World Heritage Site in 2000 and became a Biosphere Reserve in the last few years; the protected areas of the Pantanal have expanded almost threefold since the late 1990s.

Taking off into the Pantanal is what most independent travellers have in mind when they arrive in Mato Grosso, but as no road or rail track crosses the swamp it's a tricky place to travel. The easiest and one of the best ways to experience the Pantanal is by taking an **organized tour**, perhaps spending a night or two at a **fazenda-lodge** (called **pousadas** in the northern Pantanal). The *fazenda*-lodges, mostly converted ranch-houses with decent facilities, are generally reached by jeep; those that require access by boat or plane are usually deeper into the swamp, which increases your chances of spotting the more elusive wildlife. At least one night in the swamp is essential if you want to see or do anything other than sit in a bus or jeep the whole time; three- or four-day excursions will give you a couple of full days in the swamp. Without an organized trip, unless you've got bags of money or are travelling in a large group (in which case you can hire boats to get you almost anywhere), you're dependent on local **cargo boats**, which inevitably take much longer than expected. Organized tours are also more likely to go out of their way to show you the wildlife than a captain whose boat is brimming over with livestock. **Renting a car** is also a slim possibility, though without four-wheel drive you're limited to only a few tracks on the fringes of the swamp where the wildlife makes itself scarce.

Most organized tours enter the Pantanal by road and spend a couple of days exploring in canoes, small motorboats or on horseback from a land base. The most obvious initial target is **Corumbá** in Mato Grosso do Sul. There is lots of accommodation here and no end of agencies and operators running trips into the swamp. Other routes into the swamp are from **Campo Grande** in the east or **Cuiabá**, to the north, through settlements like **Porto Jofre** and **Cáceres**. The **best time** to explore the Pantanal is probably towards the end of the rainy season, around April, when your chances of spotting wildlife are high.

## Some history

The Pantanal is known to have been inhabited for at least five thousand years. Ceramics were being produced by 1500 BC and strange mounds were created, possibly ritual sites, around the same era. These were occupied until 1000 AD,

▲ Caiman *yacare* alligators in the Pantanal

then re-utilized by various of the Pantanal's tribal groups: Paiaguá, Gutao, Terna and Mbaya-Guaicuru. At the time of early Portuguese explorations, and the first unsuccessful attempts at populating the region by the Spanish in the sixteenth century, the region was dominated by three main tribes. The horseriding **Guaicuru**, who lived to the south, adopted stray or stolen horses and cattle from the advancing white settlers, making the tribe an elite group amongst Indians. Wearing only jaguar skins as they rode into battle, they were feared by the neighbouring **Terena** (Guana) tribe, who lived much of their lives as servants to Guaicuru families. In many ways, the nature and degree of their economic and social interaction suggests that the two might once have been different castes within the same tribe. Another powerful people lived to the north – the **Paiaguá**, masters of the main rivers, lagoons and canals of the central Pantanal. Much to the chagrin of both Spanish and Portuguese expeditions into the swamps, the Paiaguá were superbly skilled with both their canoes and the bow and arrow.

In 1540, the Spaniard Alvar Nuñez Cabeza de Vaca explored some of the Pantanal. Having previously explored what is now Texas and the southeast US, he was particularly impressed here with the extraordinary fishing and healthy constitutions of the people. Some Spanish adventurers also arrived here in the late sixteenth century, bringing with them the first cattle. They were soon evicted by Brazilian *bandeirantes*, but left their cattle behind to go feral. It wasn't until the **discovery of gold** in the northern Pantanal and around Cuiabá during the early eighteenth century that any genuine settlement schemes were undertaken. A rapid influx of colonists, miners and soldiers led to several bloody battles. In June 1730 hundreds of Paiaguá warriors in 83 canoes ambushed the annual flotilla, which was carrying some 900kg of gold south through the Pantanal from Cuiabá. They spared only some of the women and a few of the stronger black rowers from the flotilla: all of the gold and most of the white men were lost. Much of the gold eventually found its way out of Brazil and into Spanish Paraguay where Cautiguacu, the Paiaguá chief, lived a life of luxury in Asunción until his death 55 years later.

The decline of the gold mines during the nineteenth century brought development in the Pantanal to a standstill and the population began to fall. The twentieth century saw the establishment of unrestricted **cattle-grazing** ranches – *fazendas* – and today over twenty million head of cattle roam the swamp. Party time here is during the bull castration period, when the local delicacy becomes readily available. Droughts and diseases ravaged the Pantanal cattle industry in the late 1960s and early 1970s, then the 1980s and 1990s saw the introduction of mechanized vehicles and light aircraft, which began to replace the labour of the traditional *gaucho* ranch worker. Thankfully, however, Brazilian cowboys still abound.

Wildlife trade and ranching were at their peak here between the late nineteenth century and the end of World War II, when the demand for beef in particular dropped off. The Pantanal, however, is still **under threat** from the illegal exploitation of skins, fish and rare birds, and even gold panning. The chemical fertilizers and pesticides used on the enormous *fazendas* to produce cash crops such as soya beans are also beginning to take their toll. **Ecotourism** has been heralded as a potential saviour for the swamp, but this will only work if sufficient money is ploughed back into conservation. The Pantanal has its own Polícia Florestal who try to enforce the environment-friendly regulations that are now being strictly applied to visitors and locals alike: no disposal of non-biodegradable rubbish, no noise pollution, no fishing without a licence (it costs R$250) or between November and January during the breeding season, no fishing with nets or explosives and no removal of rocks, wildlife or plant life.

# Visiting the Pantanal

If you talk to locals about visiting the Pantanal they will almost certainly recommend going in by road. This is usually cheaper and quicker than renting a boat or going on one of the cruises. The main problem, though, is knowing where and how to go, and which company or lodge to choose. This section gives a rough overview of the various options, together with a box listing a selection of recommended **tour operators** (see below). The following sections describe some possible **routes**, from Corumbá and from Cuiabá, together with details of **accommodation** in *fazenda*-lodges and *pousadas*. The box on pp.526–527 describes the options for **boat trips** from Cáceres and Corumbá.

If you want to go **independently** remember that the Pantanal is a difficult and dangerous place to travel in. There are very few roads and, although hundreds of tracks sneak their way into the swamp, they are used only by *fazenda* workers who know them inside out. An inexperienced driver or hiker could easily get lost. That said, there's no better way to see the wildlife than to camp or stay on a boat deep in the swamp, away from roads, tracks or *fazenda*-lodges, but to do this you will need a local **guide**; these are generally available only at lodges or in end-of-the-track settlements like Porto Jofre. Also, it's important to take all the **equipment** you need with you if you're going it alone like this in the Pantanal – food, camping gear, a first-aid kit and lots of mosquito repellent. It's possible to take **buses** and **boats** from Cuiabá and Corumbá to places such as Cáceres, Coxim, Porto Jofre or Aquidauana, and it's then a matter of finding a boat going deeper into the swamp or paying a local guide or *fazendeiro* to take you on a trip. This will cost around R$70–150 per person per day, including canoe or vehicle transport and a guide/boatman/driver. Local guides and *fazendeiros* usually prefer to use the road networks to reach *fazenda*-lodges within the swamp, and explore in canoes or on horseback from there. Cheaper still, and certainly the most unusual alternative, is to buy a passage (around R$30–60 a day; hammock essential) on one of the few **trading boats** still crossing the Pantanal between Corumbá and Cáceres, and occasionally Porto Jofre (both connected by road to Cuiabá).

## Upmarket Pantanal agents and operators

The following is a selection of the more upmarket Pantanal operators who deal with both complete packages and bookings for boats and/or lodges; for other agents and guides, see p.536 for Cuiabá, p.503 for Campo Grande and p.517 for Corumbá.

**Aguas do Pantanal** Av. Afonso Pena 367, Miranda ⓣ67/3242-1242, ⓦwww.aguasdopantanal.com.br. This company owns and runs several *pousadas* around Miranda, Passo do Lontra and Porto Morrinho on the Rio Paraguai.

**Anaconda** Av Isaac Póvoas 606, Centro, Cuiabá ⓣ65/3028-5990. Short but well-organized and comfortable tours in the Pantanal and elsewhere in the Brazilian wilderness.

**Pantanal Explorers** Rua Allan Kardek 87, Galeria Maria Auxiliadora (Sala 4), Campo Grande ⓣ67/3321-8303. Agents and operators for tours and boats around Pantanal and the Amazon.

**Pérola do Pantanal** Rua Manoel Cavassa 255, Corumbá ⓣ67/3231-1460, ⓦwww.peroladopantanal.com.br. Agents for upmarket cruises from Corumbá.

Most people, however, go on **organized tours**, entering the swamp in jeeps or trucks and following one of the few rough roads that now connect Corumbá, Aquidauana, Coxim and Cuiabá (via Poconé or Cáceres) with some of the larger *fazenda* settlements of the interior. The short **jeep trips**, often run by freelance operators, are relatively cheap (especially from Corumbá, where a hammock-and-truck tour can cost as little as R$100 a day per person; from Cuiabá, it's more like R$180 upwards), but they offer little more than a flavour of the swamp. Details of some freelance operators are given on p.538 (Cuiabá), p.503 (Campo Grande) and p.517 (Corumbá). Instead, it's better to seek out reliable and recommended companies which can offer lodge- or *fazenda*-based safaris to suit your budget. It is also possible to take **small boat trips** (around R$100–200 a day, from Corumbá, Porto Jofre or Cáceres; there are no agencies for this sort of trip, so just ask around), or a **combination of jeep and boat**, over four or five days, which would certainly give the trip a taste of adventure, and could work out cheaper if you and your companions (there's usually a minimum number of passengers needed for boats) are happy braving the mosquitoes in hammocks. Note that if you're in Campo Grande, the trips you might be offered will invariably be luxury cruises.

Swamping it in comfort is possible at one of an increasing number of **fazenda-lodges** in the Pantanal, well away from towns and main roads. However, with few exceptions these cost upwards of R$200 a night per person, and over R$500 is not uncommon. However, these prices invariably include several activities, including trips by boat or jeep, horseriding, guided walks or fishing expeditions, as well as meals. Prices are generally more reasonable in the northern Pantanal (accessible from Cuiabá) than in the south (Corumbá, Miranda and Aquidauana). Also including nights in *fazenda*-lodges are **all-inclusive package tours**, though their prices vary wildly, sometimes undercutting the official lodge price, at other times almost doubling it – it's worth shopping around and bargaining (the tour operators listed in the box on p.523 all have a selection). As a general rule, however, you'll pay less if you deal direct with a *fazenda*-lodge owner in Porto Jofre, Cáceres, Aquidauana and even Corumbá, rather than through their agents. Most of the *fazenda*-lodges are located east and northeast of Corumbá, and also on either side of the Rio Cuiabá in the north, accessible for the most part via the aborted Transpantaneira road between Poconé and Porto Jofre. At the top end of the market signing up for a **luxury cruise**, or even **hiring a boat** for a week or so, is the ideal option – see the box on pp.526–527. If you want to arrange tours from home before you leave for Brazil, see p.31.

## When to visit

The **dry season**, from April to October, with its peak normally around September, transforms the swamp into South America's most exciting natural wildlife reserve. This is the **best time** to see wildlife, when much of it is attracted to the lakes and riverbanks in search of food and water: the swamp's infamous piranha and alligator populations crowd into relatively small pools and streams, while the astonishing array of aquatic birds follows suit, forming very dense colonies known here as *viveiros*. Treeless bush savanna alternates with wet swamp, while along the banks of the major rivers grow belts of rainforest populated with colonies of monkeys (including spider monkeys and noisy black gibbons).

During the **rainy season**, from November to March, river levels rise by up to 3m, producing a vast flooded plain with islands of scrubby forest amidst oceans of floating vegetation. Deeper into the swamp, transport is necessarily dominated by the rivers, natural water channels and hundreds of well-hidden lagoons, though most of the *fazendas* are still reachable by road. The islands of vegetation created during the rains crawl with wild animals – jaguars, monkeys, tapirs, capybaras (the world's largest rodent) and wild boar living side by side with domesticated cattle. Many birds are harder to spot, nesting deeper in the forests for the breeding season; nevertheless, there are still plenty of birds and other creatures to see all year round, including hawks and kingfishers.

At other times of the year, much of the Pantanal is still very boggy though interspersed with open grassy savanna studded with small wooded islands of taller vegetation, mainly palm trees. Note, however, that the previously metronomic regularity of the seasons has become most unpredictable of late, with the onset of global warming.



# Into the swamp: routes from Corumbá and Campo Grande

**Corumbá** is well placed for getting right into the Pantanal by bus or jeep, and has a welter of guides and agencies to choose from, as well as boats for hire. Though farther from the action, Campo Grande has better hotels and communications with the rest of Brazil, so it's as likely an entry point as Corumbá. Some of the most popular *fazenda*-lodges are those in Nhecolândia, roughly speaking the area between the *rios* Negro and Taquari east of Corumbá. Many of these benefit from a well-established dirt access road, the MS-184/MS-228 (the old Campo Grande road), which loops off from the main BR-262 highway 300km from Campo Grande near Passo do Lontra (it's well signposted), and crosses through a large section of the swamp before rejoining the same road some 10km before Corumbá. The track also passes through Porto Manga (see p.519).

If you're coming from **Campo Grande**, one of the best budget options is to hook up with Ecological Expeditions, Rua Joaquim Nabuco 185 (Ⓣ67/3321-0505 or 3042-0508, Ⓦwww.ecologicalexpeditions.com.br), who offer one of the cheapest options for going deep into the swamp area by using camping facilities. They also run various tours including bush walking, horseriding, vehicle safaris, canoeing (in the wet season), piranha fishing, and wildlife-spotting. Tour prices are also reasonable, with a three-day tour at around R$400 (four days R$500 and five days R$600).

## Fazenda-lodges in the southern Pantanal

The following *fazenda*-lodges are accessible from Corumbá, Miranda or Aquidauana; they offer full-board accommodation and swamp trips, and can be booked through the addresses given below or through the upmarket Pantanal operators listed in the box on p.523.

**Cabana do Lontra** Passo do Lontra Ⓣ67/3383-4532. Situated near where the MS-184 crosses the Rio Miranda, some 100km southeast of Corumbá and 7km off the main BR-262. The *Cabana*, with over twenty rooms and its own motorboats, is located in a good spot for most wildlife; excellent for fishing. ⑤

**Fazenda Rio Negro** The main office is in Belo Horizonte Ⓣ31/3261-3889, Ⓦwww.fazendarionegro.com.br. One of the Pantanal's oldest ranches, founded in 1895 by Ciciaco and Thomázia Rondon. Located up the Rio Negro with access from Aquidauana, this is an upmarket place with boats, horses and good

## Pantanal boat tours

At present, two basic types of **cargo boat** cross the swamp between Cáceres and Corumbá on a fairly regular basis – **soya** and **cattle barges**. Neither has fixed schedules or itineraries, so it's a matter of checking on departure dates when you arrive at either town. The trip usually takes about six to ten days upstream from Corumbá, three to six downstream, with plenty of time for relaxing and looking out for wildlife. The barges, though, do tend to keep to the main channel of the Rio Paraguai, which obviously doesn't give you a good chance of spotting anything particularly shy or rare. However, if you can find space on one of these boats, then it's a very inexpensive as well as unusual way of seeing some of the Pantanal. Apart from your hammock, take some extra food (tins, biscuits, bottled drinks and the like), insect repellent and a few good books. And a bottle of whisky or good *cachaça* wouldn't go amiss with the captain.

The only other problem is that travelling on the barges hasn't been strictly legal since 1985, when the son of a naval minister accidentally died while on board one of the cement barges that used to ply the same route. Passengers have consequently been "smuggled" aboard in dinghies, under cover of darkness. However, you might find it's still possible to buy a ride simply by asking the *comandante* of Portobras, one of the barge companies – they have offices on the waterfront in both Corumbá and Cáceres (☎65/3222-1728). The cattle barge between Corumbá and Cáceres run by Serviço de Navegação da Bacia da Prata also often picks up passengers from the ports at either end, but leaves at irregular intervals. Other cattle boats leaving Corumbá are willing to take passengers on return journeys within the swamp, delivering and picking up cattle from various *fazendas*.

**Luxury fishing boats** are the other, more expensive, option, but an ideal way to encounter the swamp's wildlife on the end of a line and ultimately on your plate. Essentially floating hotels designed with the Brazilian passion for angling in mind, one of these for a week costs anything from R$1500 to R$5000 a head, though the price is full board and usually includes ample drink, food and unlimited use of their small motorboat tenders for exploring further afield. Note that for **families with small children**, any river trip is inadvisable as none of the boats currently in use has guardrails safe enough to keep a toddler from falling in.

Most of the boats are based in Corumbá, with some others in Cáceres, Barão do Melgaço and Cuiabá, and all can be booked through the upmarket agents on p.523. In high season, they tend to run pre-scheduled trips, departing and returning Sundays; routes are mentioned where they remain fixed from year to year. Out of season, they're up for rent, with a minimum number of passengers and days

guides. It's been made very famous across Brazil over recent years as the location for filming the popular soap opera *Pantanal*. Two adjacent *fazenda* areas have now also been bought and are protected, creating a total conservation area around the *fazenda* of 240 square kilometres. The *fazenda* is now a centre for research, attempting to create a much needed biodiversity corridor to link the *Fazenda Rio Negro* with the Serra de Maracaju. ❽

**Hotel Recanto Barra Mansa** Rio Negro (owned by Guilherme Rondon) ☎67/3325-6807, ⓦwww.hotelbarramansa.com.br. Further east from *Fazenda Rio Negro* (see p.525) on the north shore of the river, 130km from Aquidauana, with room for twelve guests. Specializes in game tours and fly-fishing. Daily buses run here from Corumbá. ❽

**Passo do Lontra** Some 8km into the Pantanal from the BR-262 between Campo Grande and Corumbá ☎67/3231-6569. One of the rare, relatively inexpensive options (with substantial reductions in low season), although a minimum of six guests may be required. They also allow camping. ❹

**Pousada Arara Azul** Rio Negrinho on the Estrada Parque ☎67/3389-9910 or 9987-1530, ⓦwww.pousadaararaazul.com.br. Close to the Rio Negro in Nhecolândia, 38km up the

invariably demanded, though bargaining is possible. You can find them tied up at their home ports.

### Luxury boats from Cáceres

**Cobra Grande** ⓣ65/3223-4203. A small boat with five cabins and an adequate dining room; book well in advance. R$150–250 a day per person.

**Pantanal Explorer II** ⓣ65/3682-2800. Mainly covering the Rio Paraguai, this boat is very small with only three quadruple cabins. Upwards of R$300 per person per day.

**Pantanal Vip** ⓣ11/5667-6076, ⓦwww.pantanalvip.com.br. Available for luxury fishing trips. From about R$300 a day.

**Rei do Rio and Velho do Rio** Contact Moretti Serviços Fluviais, Cuiabá ⓣ65/3361-2082, ⓕ3322-6563. A couple of Louisiana-style houseboats intended primarily as bases for fishing expeditions. R$150–250 a day per person.

### Luxury boats from Corumbá

**Arara Tur** Rua Manoel Cavassa 47, by the port, Corumbá ⓣ67/3231-4851, ⓦwww.araratur.com.br. This company runs a fine boat – the *Albatroz* – beautifully furnished with bars and cosy but very comfortable cabins. Choose from a wide range of short and longer boat tours in the Pantanal, specializing in photo safaris on the Rio Paraguai. Costs R$500 per person per day, five days minimum.

**Cabexy II** Pantanal Tours, Rua Manoel Cavassa 61, Corumbá ⓣ67/3231-1559, ⓦwww.pantanaltours.tur.br. Two two-tiered riverboats for rent, similar in style to the *Kalypso* (see below) but holding a maximum of eight passengers each, and rather more exclusive. Motorboats and fishing accessories provided. Five-day minimum period, R$500 per person per day. Reservations and R$7000 deposit required.

**Kalypso** Book direct on ⓣ67/3231-1460 or through agents, Mutum Turismo (see p.517). Brazil's answer to Nile cruisers, the *Kalypso* is a spacious three-tier affair with berths for 120 passengers, and looks for all the world like a pile of portacabins on a barge (which is what it once was). The interior is wood-panelled, the restaurant is self-service, and there's a pool on top in which to escape the mosquitoes and the heat. Originally designed as a base for fishing trips, it has a number of small motorboats and a giant fridge in which you can keep your catch. Prices start at R$300 per person per day, with a minimum stay of six nights.

**Millenium** This luxury vessel has ten cabins and can only be booked for six days at a time; bookings on ⓣ67/3231-3372 or ⓦwww.opantaneirotur.com.br. From R$180 a day per person.

MS-184 past Passo do Lontra, this *pousada* offers all the comforts you could want, plus guaranteed access to virtually all the bird and mammalian wildlife apart from the rarer jaguars and wolves. Excellent for piranha fishing, night-time *jacarés* viewing and horseriding. Camping allowed too (R$25 a night), though they may require a minimum stay of two days in the lodge. ⑤

**Refúgio Ecológico Caiman** Rio Aquidauana. Reservation centre in São Paulo where most bookings are taken (ⓣ11/3706-1800 or, locally, 67/3242-1450, ⓦwww.caiman.com.br), or book with Impacto Turismo (see p.504). The luxurious Pantanal jungle lodge experience. The *Refúgio* is located some 240km west of Campo Grande, 36km north of Miranda, and covers over 530 square kilometres. There are four *pousadas*, all with good facilities and a distinctive style to match the surroundings. Main activities include horseriding, nocturnal safaris, hikes, boat trips and cattle drives (around 70 percent of the reserve's income still derives from cattle). The *Refúgio* has its own airstrip and offers transfer services leaving from Campo Grande four times a week. Full board, all activities and bilingual guide services are included in the daily rate of R$500 per person per night in a double room.

# Into the swamp: routes from Cuiabá

One of the simplest ways into the swamp is to take a **bus** (3hr) from Cuiabá (see p.530) south to **BARÃO DO MELGAÇO**, a small, quiet village on the banks of the Rio Cuiabá. Although not quite in the true swamp, and therefore with less in the way of wildlife, Barão is perfect if you're short on time and just want a taste of the Pantanal. There's the exclusive *Pousada do Rio Mutum* just an hour away by boat, in a stunning location on the Baía de Siá Mariana near the Rio Mutum (ⓣ65/3052-7022, ⓦwww.pousadamutum.com.br; ❺). Although Barão is no longer served by regular boats from Corumbá, it might still be worth asking around should a shallow-draught vessel be covering the journey – an unforgettable experience, right through the centre of the swamp.

## Poconé and Porto Jofre

The most exploited option from Cuiabá is to follow the route south to Poconé and Porto Jofre. There are daily **buses** from Cuiabá's *rodoviária* as far as **POCONÉ** along a paved and fairly smooth 100km stretch of road. Like Barão do Melgaço, Poconé is not real Pantanal country, but it's a start and there are plenty of **hotels in town**. On the main square, Praça Rondon, the *Hotel Skala* at no. 64 (ⓣ65/3721-1407; ❸), and a couple of restaurants take most of the trade. At the southern end of town at the start of the road to Porto Jofre, the cheaper *Hotel Santa Cruz* (ⓣ65/3721-1439; ❸) is recommended for relatively clean and comfortable lodging. Cheaper still, but slightly grubby, is *Dormitório Poconé* (❶), near the *rodoviária*.

The swamp proper begins south of the town, along the aborted Transpantaneira road. In fact, it's just a bumpy track, often impassable during the rains, but you'll see plenty of wildlife from it, as well as signs marking the entrances to a number of *fazenda*-lodges and *pousadas* set back from the road around various tributaries of the Rio Cuiabá, notably the Pixaim and Rio Claro. Although pricey, they're cheaper than their counterparts in the southern Pantanal, and all have restaurants and facilities for taking wildlife day-trips into the swamp by boat, on horseback or on foot. Another track from Poconé, in an even worse state, trails off southeast to Porto Cercado on the banks of the Rio Cuiabá itself, and also has a few *pousadas*.

After 145km, having crossed around a hundred wooden bridges in varying stages of dilapidation, the track eventually arrives at **PORTO JOFRE**. Porto Jofre is a small fishing hamlet, literally the end of the road. This is as far as the Transpantaneira route has got, or ever looks like getting, thanks to technical problems and the sound advice of ecological pressure groups. As far as **accommodation in town** goes, the upmarket *Hotel Porto Jofre* (closed Nov–Feb; office at Av. São Sebastião no. 357, Cidade Alta, Cuiabá ⓣ65/3637-1593, ⓦwww.portojofre.com.br; ❻), has a monopoly and its own grassy airstrip for wealthy fishermen tourists from São Paulo. If you have a hammock or a tent, it's usually all right to sleep outside somewhere, but check with someone in authority first (ask at the port) and don't leave your valuables unattended. There are no other options unless you can get someone to invite you to their house.

From Porto Jofre, there are irregular cargo **boats** to Corumbá (sometimes on Wed; R$70–90), normally carrying soya or cattle from Cáceres; the journey takes between two and five days, depending on whether the boats sail through the night. It's also possible to arrange a day or two's excursion up the Piquiri and Cuiabá rivers from Porto Jofre. These are increasingly good places for spotting wild jaguars beside the river.

## Pousadas around Poconé and Porto Jofre

All of the following can be booked through the addresses given below or through tour or travel agents in Cuiabá; some lodges insist on advance reservations and won't let you in unannounced, but others might relent if you just drop by. All the lodges below offer full-board accommodation, with swamp trips included in the price; they're listed in loose geographical order, from northeast to southwest.

**Pousada Araras Eco Lodge** Office at Cuiabá airport, or Av. Ponce de Arruda 670, Várzea Grande ⓣ65/3682-2800, ⓦwww.araraslodge.com.br. At Km 29 of the Transpantaneira, this long-established *pousada* is an old brick ranch building, more atmospheric than most of the more modern *pousadas*, with a pool, as well as boats and horses, but its fourteen rooms are likely to be full in high season. ⑤

**Pousada Pantaneiro** Bookings through Cuiabá's travel agents. Approximately 100km south of Poconé, a small place (five rooms) and one of the more reasonably priced *pousadas* which, although not on a river itself, offers swamp trips on horseback. You should be able to camp here, too, and they have tents for rent. ③

**Pousada Passargada** Bookings through Cuiabá's travel agents, or in Rio ⓣ21/3235-2840 or São Paulo ⓣ11/3284-5434. Linked in the dry season by the Porto Cercado track, most of the year it's more easily reached by boat (1hr 30min) from Barão do Melgaço. A good place directly on the Rio Pixaim. ⑥

**Pousada Piuval** Rodovia Transpantaneira, Km 10, Poconé ⓣ65/3345-1338, ⓦwww.pousadapiuval.com.br. A comfortable spread 110km from Cuiabá with a fine pool and small but pleasant rooms. Well equipped with horses, open truck and boats for exploring deeper. ⑤–⑥

**Pousada Rio Claro** ⓣ67/3345-1054, ⓦwww.pousadarioclaro.com.br. Located at Km 41 of the Transpantaneira, it is quite large and comfortable, and has a pool. ⑥

**Pousada Rio Clarinho** ⓣ67/9998-8888, ⓦwww.pousadarioclarinho.com.br. A great little lodging based in an old family-run *fazenda* with restaurant, viewing tower, horseriding and row boats available. ⑤

**Pousada São Sebastião do Pantanal** ⓣ65/3322-0178. Situated 34km from Poconé at Km 27 of the aborted Transpantaneira road, and usually reachable even in bad weather. A first-class establishment (with pool) located close to the river in pleasant wooded surroundings, offering horse and boat safaris. Good for families. ⑥

## Cáceres

Although less frequented than the Porto Jofre route, **CÁCERES** is another good target from Cuiabá, 233km west of the city. It's a very pleasant, laid-back place, and given the prices of accommodation along the Transpantaneira, definitely deserves consideration as a base for visiting the Pantanal. It's a three- to four-hour journey by bus, several of which leave daily from the *rodoviária* in Cuiabá. On the upper reaches of the Rio Paraguai, which is still quite broad even this far upstream, Cáceres is a relatively new town, made up largely of wooden shacks, bars and pool rooms. There are lots of cheap **hotels**, the best of which is the *Santa Terezinha*, Rua Tiradentes 485 (ⓣ65/3223-4621; ②), which is clean and hospitable. More upmarket, the *Hotel Ipanema* at Rua Gen. Osorio 540 (ⓣ65/3223-1177; ④) has a pool and also has air conditioning and TV in all rooms. The **travel agency** Natureza, at Rua Coronel José Dulce 304 (ⓣ65/3223-1997), can arrange *pousada* accommodation and a number of good-value tours. Several boats operate from here, including the *Babilonia* (ⓣ67/3223-1379, ⓦwww.barcobabilonia.com.br), which has six cabins and usually goes out for seven days.

The only road to go further into the Pantanal is the track that leads on to the **Bolivian border** settlement of San Matias; from here you can fly to Santa Cruz (best to sort out exit stamp and entry visas, respectively, with the Brazilian Federal Police in Cáceres or Cuiabá and the Bolivian Consul in Cuiabá).

# Mato Grosso state

The state of Mato Grosso is dominated completely by **Cuiabá**, a city of over half a million people. Located in the very south of the political region, roads radiate from this commercial and administrative centre like tentacles, extending over the plains in every direction. The city is over 1000km from Brasília, almost 1500km from Porto Velho and more than 1700km from São Paulo: an opportune place to break a long overland haul. Beyond its strategic importance, though, Cuiabá's friendly personality and interesting city centre, combined with the breathtaking scenery of the nearby Chapada dos Guimarães, can easily lure you into staying longer than planned.

Cuiabá is as good a springboard for a trip into or through the **Pantanal** as Campo Grande or Corumbá. Furthermore, it offers long haul but simple access by bus west into the remoter Amazon region towards Bolivia and Peru, east towards Goiânia and Brasília, and north, for the more adventurous, towards Santarém and Manaus. No longer a true frontier zone, it's an established cattle-ranching and soya-producing region where cows and beans are much bigger business than tourism. Between Cuiabá and Brasília industrially farmed soya bean fields extend to every horizon.

Apart from in the mysterious and stunning **Chapada dos Guimarães**, there is relatively little tourism infrastructure outside Cuiabá and the Pantanal. The reality for most travellers will be a flight or an intrepid journey by bus (and perhaps river) to some other distant city. The most arduous of the options used to be the awful **Highway BR-163** from Cuiabá to Santarém, which, in theory, connects at Itaituba with the BR-230 Transamazônica Highway for Altamira, Marabá and Belém. However, around 400km of road has been reclaimed by jungle along the Rio Jamanxim in southern Pará, making it impassable to anything other than four-wheel-drive vehicles for the foreseeable future: the furthest north you can drive is the Serra do Cachimbo on the fringes of Pará state. The fastest road is **Highway BR-364** (known as the BR-070 in Mato Grosso) through Cuiabá, which ultimately links São Paulo with Rio Branco and Cruzeiro do Sul.

## Cuiabá

The southern gateway into the Amazon, **CUIABÁ** has always been firmly on the edge of Brazil's wilderness. Following the discovery of a gold field here in 1719 (one version of the town's name means the "river of stars"), the town mushroomed as an administrative and service centre in the middle of Indian territory, thousands of very slow, overland miles from any other Portuguese settlement. To the south lay the Pantanal and the dreaded Paiaguá people who frequently ambushed convoys of boats transporting Cuiabá gold by river to São Paulo. The fierce Bororo tribe, who dominated Mato Grosso east of Cuiabá, also regularly attacked many of the mining settlements. Northwest along a high hilly ridge – the Chapada dos Parecis, which now carries BR-364 to Porto Velho – lived the peaceful Parecis people, farmers in the watershed between the Amazon and the Pantanal. By the 1780s, however, most Indians within these groups had been either eliminated or transformed into allies: the Parecis were

CUIABÁ

ACCOMMODATION

| | |
|---|---|
| Amazon Plaza | B |
| Central | I |
| Colorado Palace | D |
| Deville | A |
| Hostel Pantanal | C |
| Mato Grosso | E |
| Mato Grosso Palace | G |
| Pousada Ecoverde | H |
| Samara | F |

EATING & DRINKING

| | |
|---|---|
| Adriana | 2 |
| Barranco Bar | 9 |
| Choppão | 4 |
| Cremilda Bar | 7 |
| Haus Bier | 6 |
| Meridiana 56 | 1 |
| Mistura Cuiabana | 10 |
| Padaria Pan Frigo | 11 |
| Presto Pizzas | 5 |
| O Regionalíssimo | 12 |
| Restaurante e Peixaria La Barca | 8 |
| Tavola Piena | 3 |

needed as slave labour for the mines; the Bororo either retreated into the forest or joined the Portuguese as mercenaries and Indian hunters; while the Paiaguá fared worst of all, almost completely wiped out by cannon and musket during a succession of punitive expeditions from Cuiabá.

The most important development came during the 1890s, when a young Brazilian army officer, Lieutenant **Cândido Rondon**, built a telegraph system from Goiás to Cuiabá through treacherous Bororo territory – assisted no doubt by the fact that he had some Bororo blood in his veins. By 1903 he had extended the telegraph from Cuiabá south to Corumbá, and in 1907 he began work to reach the Rio Madeira, to the northwest in the Amazon basin. The latter expedition earned Rondon a reputation as an important explorer and brought him into contact with the Nambikwara Indians. Since then, Cuiabá has been pushing forward the frontier of development and the city is still a stepping stone and crossroads for pioneers. Every year, thousands of hopeful settlers stream through Cuiabá on their way to a new life in the western Amazon.

The established farmlands around the city now produce abundant crops – maize, fruit, rice and soya. But the city itself thrives on the much larger surrounding **cattle-ranching region**, which contains almost a quarter of a million inhabitants. A large lead-ore deposit is being worked close to the town, and oil has been discovered at Várzea Grande; in the longer term, however, it is sustainable industries, like rubber, palm nuts and, of course, ecotourism, that may provide income. The good facilities offered in Cuiabá – in terms of hotels, restaurants and tour companies – means that ecotourism is developing rapidly and is being increasingly seen by the younger *fazenda* owners as the way forward.

## Arrival and information

Both the **BR-163** and the **BR-364** run to Cuiabá. Whether you're coming from São Paulo, Rio, Brasília or the Northeast, you'll want to take the BR-364 for travelling overland into the western Amazon.

The **rodoviária** (Ⓣ65/3621-1040 & 3621-4100), on Avenida Marechal Rondon, is a large concrete complex 3km north of the city centre. From here it's a fifteen-minute ride into Cuiabá on buses #202, #304 or #309, or ten minutes by taxi (from R$13). The **airport** (Ⓣ65/3614-2500), 8km south in Várzea Grande, is connected to the centre by the Metropolitano buses and taxis (from about R$25). From here take the bus marked "Shopping Pantanal", but remember to get off at Avenida Getúlio Vargas, for the city centre.

You'll be able to get some limited **tourist information** from the tourist office in the centre of town on Rua Voluntarios da Patria close to *Pousada Ecoverde* (see below) and on the corner with Rua Ricardo Franco (in theory, daily 8am–6pm; Ⓣ65/3613-9313).

## Accommodation

With the *rodoviária* relatively close, most people prefer to stay in or near the busy city centre, where there's a good range of places. There are also numerous two- and three-star hotels around the airport and on the way into town.

**Amazon Plaza** Av. Getúlio Vargas 600 Ⓣ65/2121-2000, Ⓦwww.hotelamazon.com.br. This is one of the smartest and most comfortable downtown options. Rooms are large with TV and a/c, and there's a small pool and garden patio-bar. Breakfasts are fantastic and the service is good. ⑥

**Central** Rua Galdino Pimentel Ⓣ65/3321-8309. A budget option in the heart of the old town, with very basic rooms, very poorly maintained and a little dodgy at night. Its neighbour *São Marcos*, on the same street (Ⓣ65/624-2300), offers much the same. ①

**Colorado Palace** Av. Jules Rimet 32 Ⓣ65/3621-3763. One of a dozen three-star hotels along the main road from the *rodoviária* into town, this one's right opposite the bus station. The rooms are predictably noisy and not particularly good value, but convenient if you're leaving by bus early the next day. ④

**Deville** Av. Isaac Póvoas 1000 Ⓣ65/3319-3000, Ⓦwww.hoteiseldorado.com.br. A five-star hotel, at the top of its range, with 182 rooms, Arctic-strength a/c, pool and decent restaurant. ⑥

**Hostel Pantanal** Av. Isaac Póvoas 655 Ⓣ65/3624-8999, Ⓦwww.portaldopantanal.com.br. Linked to Youth Hostelling International, this place has all the usual facilities, plus internet access and a communal kitchen. Rooms are mostly dorms, though some private doubles are available at a higher cost. ②

**Mato Grosso** Rua Comandante Costa 2522 Ⓣ65/3614-7777, Ⓕ3614-7053. Within three blocks of Praça da República, this place has decent breakfasts and offers excellent-value rooms with private showers. ②

**Mato Grosso Palace** Rua Joaquim Murtinho 170 Ⓣ65/3614-7000, Ⓦwww.hotelmatogrosso.com.br. Part of the Best Western chain. Situated in a grand building behind the Fundação Cultural, with excellent service and pleasant enough rooms, some with good views. No pool. ⑥

**Pousada Ecoverde** Rua Pedro Celestino 391, Centro Ⓣ65/3624-1386 and 9605-5406, Ⓦwww.ecoverdetours.com.br. This lovely *pousada* is based in a self-contained and safe colonial house with patio and rear gardens right at the heart of the old city centre. It has six rooms, all with fans. Bathrooms are shared, but there are four of them and they're kept very clean. There's also a good reference library, a rest area with shade and hammocks, laundry and cooking facilities, as well as links to one of the best Pantanal tour operators. Breakfasts are stupendous and very fresh. ②

**Samara** Rua Joaquim Murtinho 270 Ⓣ65/3322-6001. A simple but clean and friendly hotel that's a good option if other budget places are full. ①

## The City

A bustling city, Cuiabá is an exciting place to spend a few days. There's certainly a lot to see and do in the city's relatively self-contained centre, where modern skyscrapers long ago won the battle for attention with the now hidden ornate facades of crumbling, pastel-shaded colonial villas, churches and shops.

The central **Praça da República** is a hive of activity from daybreak onwards. It's the city's main meeting spot, and the cathedral, post office, the cultural foundation and university all face onto the square, while under the shade of its large trees, hippies from the Brazilian coast sell crafted jewellery and leather work. The most interesting old mansion in town, the **Paláçio da Instrução**, is on the square at no. 151. Now the **Fundação Cultural de Mato Grosso** (Mon–Fri 8.30am–4.30pm; free), it houses three excellent **museums** of history, natural history and anthropology, with exhibits spanning prehistoric to colonial times. There are some fascinating old photos of Cuiabá, along with rooms full of stuffed creatures from the once forested region and, best of all, a superb array of Indian artefacts such as feather headdresses, gourd maracas and woven fibre utensils. The **Catedral do Bom Jesus**, next door, was built in the 1960s to replace the old cathedral, a beautiful Baroque affair that was then thought old-fashioned. Constructed of pinkish concrete with a square, vaguely Moorish facade, the new cathedral has a predictably vast, rectangular interior; its main altar is overshadowed by a mural reaching from floor to ceiling that depicts a sparkling Christ floating in the air above the city of Cuiabá and the cathedral.

Sitting on the hill to the south, across the Avenida Tenente Coronel Duarte from the cathedral side of town, the early twentieth-century **Igreja de Nossa Senhora do Bom Despacho** used to dominate the cityscape before office buildings and towering hotels sprang up to dwarf it in the latter half of the twentieth century. Unfortunately, both the church and its splendid religious art collection are currently closed to visitors.

Just to the northeast of Praça da República, a few narrow central lanes – Pedro Celestino, Galdino Pimentel, Ricardo Franco and Rua 7 de Setembro – form a crowded pedestrian shopping area. It's here that you'll find the city's oldest church, the simple but run-down **Igreja Nossa Serhora do Rosário e Capela de São Benedicto**, completed in 1722, and the unusual **Museu**

▲ Bororo feather headdress, Museu do Índio Marechal Rondon

**de Pedras**, Rua Galdino Pimentel 195 (Mon–Fri 7–11am & 1–4pm; R$5). Packed tightly into just two rooms, the museum contains the marvellously eccentric collection of local man Ramis Bucair, comprising gemstones, crystals, fossils, Stone Age artefacts, stuffed animals, birds and snakes. The exhibits are a hotchpotch of genuinely fascinating pieces – rocks containing liquid and loose diamonds, and a dried catfish tongue, once used as a rasp for grating *guaraná* (a tropical berry) – mixed with some outrageous fakes, such as the inch-high carved stone purported to be a shrunken human skull from some remote Indian tribe, and a display case containing a large fossilized bone, discovered locally and boldly claimed to be that of a *Tyrannosaurus rex*. An equally dubious claim is made in Praça Moreira Cabral, along Rua Barão do Melgaço by the state assembly buildings: a small post enclosed by a tall, thin pyramid marks what was considered to be, until the advent of satellite topography, the geographical centre of the South American continent. The actual place, for what it's worth, is 67km away in the Chapada dos Guimarães. Just around the corner, and opposite the tourist office, there's the pleasant if bizarre **Museo da Imagen e do Som** (Museum of Image and Sound), located in an airy mansion offering a welcome respite from the city's unrelenting heat in its shady inner courtyard. The building houses some historic photos plus changing exhibitions relating to Cuiabá's theatrical past, some of which is more colourful than intelligible to the non-local eye.

Should you be interested in the indigenous culture, there are a couple of other museums in Cuiabá which are worth an hour or so of your time. The **ethnographic collection** belonging to the offices of FUNAI, the Foundation for Indian Affairs (☎65/3644-1850), includes feather handicraft, basketry and wooden carved objects; the foundation also has a shop around the corner from the tourist office, at Pedro Celestino 301 (☎65/3623-1675), en route to and on the same side as *Pousada Ecoverde*. Easier to find is the smaller university-run **Museu do Índio Marechal Rondon**, on Avenida Fernando Corréa da Costa (Mon–Fri 7.30–11.30am & 1.30–5.30pm, Sat & Sun 7.30–11am; free), which also focuses on local Indian culture and features more feather, fibre, ceramic and wooden objects representing the material culture of several local tribes, including the Bororo and Nambikwara. The museum is beside the university pool, 5km east of town off BR-364, in the sector known as Cidade Universitária; buses #133, #505, #513, #514 and others from Avenida Tenente Coronel Duarte will take you there. Also in the Cidade Universitária is a small **zoological garden** (Tues–Sun 7.30–11.30am & 1.30–5.20pm; ☎65/3615-8007; free) where you'll find swamp creatures including caimans, tapirs and capybaras, a small consolation if you don't have time for a Pantanal tour.

Finally, focusing mainly on work by early Republican and modern Brazilian artists, there are two **art galleries** in Cuiabá – one in the Casa da Cultura, Rua Barão do Melgaço, the other, Laila Zharan, at Av. Marechal Deodoro 504. Both are small and quiet but worth a visit for insight into local perspectives on the region's landscapes and history.

## Eating

Cuiabá has a surprising range of cuisine and some excellent **restaurants**, although you'll find almost everything closed on Sundays. Some of the best restaurants are listed below, but for **cheaper eating** and *lanches* there are plenty of places in the area around Praça Alencastro, at the north end of Travessa João Dias near Rua Comandante Costa, and in the shopping zone between Rua Pedro Celestino and Rua Galdino Pimentel. The best ice-cream parlours in Cuiabá are *Alaska*, Rua Pedro Celestino 215, *Patotinha*, Av. Generoso Ponce 761, and *Flocky's* on Avenida

Isaac Póvoas. For your own supplies, the busy **Mercado Municipal** is on Avenida Generoso Ponce (Mon–Sat 7.30am–6pm, Sun 7.30am–noon).

**Adriano** Avenida Getúlio Vargas 985 ⓣ65/3623-1664. This is a quality Italian restaurant serving great pastas and a wide range of pizzas. Open Tues–Sat 6.30pm to midnight, Sun 11.30am to 3pm.

**Barranco Bar** Rua Pedro Celestino. Inexpensive food and drinks and live Brazilian music, in a modest but inviting place – as good as any to meet the local people. One of the few inexpensive spots open Sun.

**Choppão** Praça 8 de Abril, Goiabeiras ⓣ65/3623-9101. Probably the best and most traditional restaurant-bar in the city centre. Very lively in the evening, with lots of tables in a big corner space and some outside where there is occasionally street entertainment. They serve traditional *escaldo* (egg- and fish-based soup) along with the beer and have some fascinating historical photos on the walls.

**Cremilda Bar** Rua Comandante Costa. Around the corner from *Hotel Presidente*, a gem of a *lanchonete*: cheap and delicious food with exceptionally friendly owners. Closed Sun.

**Getúlio** Avenida Getúlio Vargas 1147 ⓣ65/3624-9992. This place offers decently priced drinks and cocktails, and you can watch the cream of Cuiabá cruise by in their dream wagons in the evenings; open Tues–Fri 11.30am to 2.30pm and 5.30pm to 2am, Sat & Sun 11.30am to 4pm.

**Haus Bier** Av. Mato Grosso 764 ⓣ65/3621-1020. Five blocks down from Avenida Getúlio Vargas, one of Cuiabá's trendiest restaurant-bars and the evening focus for brash young Cuiabanos, with excellent but expensive food featuring a wide range of Brazilian and international dishes – everything from pizza to Amazon swamp fish, as well as very potent cocktails. Daily 4pm–3am.

**Meridiano 56** Av. Isaac Póvoas 1039 ⓣ65/3322-4321. Reasonably priced, fairly central and well-regarded fish restaurant. Tues–Sat evenings, Sun mornings.

**Mistura Cuiabana** Rua Pedro Celestino 8. Refreshingly cool interior of an airy colonial mansion at the heart of the city, this is a lunchtime restaurant with excellent self-service *comida por kilo*. Mon–Fri 11am–3pm.

**Padaria Pan Frigo** Rua Villa Maria 13, Centro. Just a few blocks from the tourist office and *Pousada Ecoverde*, this very busy bakery is open 7 days a week for great breakfasts and coffee; although you wouldn't think so, it attracts local celebrities, particularly on weekend mornings.

**Presto Pizzas** Av. Getúlio Vargas 1371 ⓣ65/3624-4600. Good, popular pizza restaurant with fast service; also operates a delivery service. Closed Sun.

**O Regionalíssimo** Av. Beira-Rio, Museo do Rio, Porto ⓣ65/3623-6881. Excellent, moderately priced regional dishes with a self-service option. On Wednesday they serve a speciality of beef with green bananas, and there's sometimes live music at weekends. Open for lunches only (11am–2.30pm, closed Mon).

**Restaurante e Peixaria La Barca** Located by the Ponte Nova, this floating fish restaurant gives a wonderful perspective on the city at lunchtime or at night; try a fish *rodizio* (as much as you can eat).

**Tavola Piena** Av. Getúlio Vargas 676. Another good Italian restaurant with a pleasant ambience.

## Drinking and nightlife

Although beer is twice as expensive here as it is on the coast, you'll find that **nightlife** in Cuiabá revolves mainly around the bars and restaurants in the town centre, especially along Rua Isaac Póvoas. *Haus Bier* (see above) has a good atmosphere, while beyond the downtown area, along the large Avenida CPA, there are several more bars and clubs. One of the most popular is *Deck Avenida* at number 635; *Terraço*, close by, offers live music at weekends; and *Tucano*, also on Avenida CPA, offers a diverse mix of dance music. The *Veneza Palace Hotel*, Av. Cel. Escolastico 738 in Bandeirantes (ⓣ65/3661-1480 or 3621-4847), has occasional big-name bands from Rio playing live, while the main gay venue, though not exactly a scream, is the bar under the decrepit *Hotel Presidente*.

## Listings

**Airlines** TAM, Av. Isaac Póvoas 586 ⓣ65/3682-1702; Gol ⓣ65/3682-1666. Webjet and Oceanair only have offices at the airport; the latter is the least reliable.

**Banks and exchange** Banco do Brasil, Av. Getúlio Vargas (Mon–Fri 10am–3pm). HSBC, also on Getúlio Vargas, has an ATM; dollars cash can be exchanged at good rates at the Ouro Minas office, Rua Mariano Cândido 401, or in some of the larger hotels.

**Buses** All buses run from the *rodoviária*; the most useful are probably Expresso Rubi ☎65/3621-1764 (for Porto Velho and Chapada dos Guimarães); Real Norte ☎0800-647-6666 (for Cáceres, Porto Velho, Rio Branco and Peru); and Eucatur ☎65/3901-2140 (for most major destinations to the south and east).

**Car rental** Localiza, Av. Dom Bosco 965 ☎65/3624-7979; Unidas, Praça do Aeroporto ☎65/3682-4052.

**Internet** LAN Phoenix, Av. Ten. Cel. Duarte 07, close to the centre.

**Post office** At Praça da República (Mon–Fri 9am–6pm, Sat 9am–noon).

**Shopping** Explore the streets between the Praça da República and the Igreja do Rosário or try the Casa do Artesão, corner of Rua 13 de Junho and Rua Senador Metello, or FUNAI's ArtIndia shop, Rua Pedro Celestino (close to the tourist information office) for local handicrafts. There's another good *artesanato* shop at Joaquim Murtinho 170 in the centre. For hats (essential wear for the hot Pantanal sun) the best in town is Casa do Ginete, Av. Ten. Cel. Duarte 256, in the centre. *Guaraná* drinks, seeds and tubes can be bought in the interesting shop at 27 de Dezembro 30. Homeopathic remedies can be found at Fraternidade, Rua Galdino Pimental 162 and Av Ten. Cel. Duarte 07. More curious is the magic shop on Av. Tenente Coronel Duarte, near the corner with Av. Generoso Ponce – its shelves are stacked with ceremonial swords, North American Indian ceramic figurines, incense, pots decorated with gods and demons, strings of jungle beads and seed pods. Also worth a visit is the shop Guaraná Maués, Av. Isaac Póvoas 611, which specializes in *guaraná*, grown locally in Mato Grosso state. There are two decent photographic shops on Rua Joaquim Murtinho: Cuiabá Color at no. 789, and the friendly Artcolor next door.

**Telephones** The Telemat office is at Rua Barão do Melgaço (Mon–Sat 7.30am–5.30pm).

**Travel agents** Ametur, Rua Joaquim Murtinho 242 (☎65/3624-1000), sell tickets and can arrange day-trips by boat to Barão do Melgaço. Tuiutur (☎65/3316-4680, ⓦwww.tuiutur.com.br) offer travel tickets and some local tours. See also the list of upmarket operators on p.523.

# Around Cuiabá

Although it's a major staging post for the Pantanal, there isn't a lot in terms of organized tourism in the immediate region **around Cuiabá**, and what there is is mostly aimed at local people. Nevertheless, the scenery and air of mystery around **Chapada dos Guimarães** makes for a rewarding side-trip from the city – much more of a draw than either the hot springs of **Águas Quentes** or the beach at **São Antônio do Leverger**.

## Chapada dos Guimarães

A paved road winds its way up to the scenic and increasingly popular mountain village of **CHAPADA DOS GUIMARÃES**, set on the plateau of the same name just 64km from Cuiabá. Located bang on one of the oldest tectonic plates on the planet, it also sits close to the geodesic centre of South America (the equidistant point between the Atlantic and Pacific oceans).

It is here on this plateau that the true geodesic centre of South America was pinpointed by satellite, much to the chagrin of the Cuiabanos who stick resolutely to their old 1909 mark; the actual spot, the **Mirante da Geodésia**, is located on the southern continuation of Rua Clariano Curvo from Praça Dom Wunibaldo, 8km away. Parochial disputes aside, Chapada is an interesting settlement in its own right, containing Mato Grosso's oldest church, the **Igreja de Nossa Senhora de Santana do Sacramento**, a fairly plain colonial temple built in 1779, which dominates the top end of the town's leafy Praça Dom Wunibaldo. These days, with a population nearing sixteen thousand, the town has something of a reputation as a centre for the Brazilian "New Age" movement, with crystal shops, health food stores and hippy communities springing up over the last years. If you're here in July, you're in for a treat,

## Tour operators and guides in Cuiabá

All of Cuiabá's travel agents offer trips into the Pantanal or to the closer sites, like Chapada dos Guimarães, although their primary occupation is selling flights within Brazil. For more personal service, however, you'd do better to contact one of the local **tour operators**, which tend to be smaller and offer specialist knowledge. Highly recommended is Ecoverde Tours run by the wildlife ecologist Joel Souza, a very reliable operator who speaks excellent English and German, among other languages; he often has a presence at the airport, but also has an office at Av. Getúlio Vargas 155A, as well as a base at the *Pousada Ecoverde*, Rua Pedro Celestino 391, Centro (Ⓣ65/3624-1386 or 65/9605-5406, Ⓦwww.ecoverdetours.com.br). Joel works with a number of very good guides, including Alexsander Gomez Ramos, who also speaks excellent English (Ⓣ65/9911-2231). Other operators include: Pantanal Nature (Ⓦwww.pantanalnature.com.br); Natureco, Rua Barão do Melgaço 2015 (Ⓣ&Ⓕ65/3624-5116), and Ecological Pantanal Tours, Rua Joaquim Mutinho 1134, Centro (Ⓣ65/3623-4607 and 9954-8955, Ⓔecotours@terra.com.br). Tours within the region tend to cost upwards of R$180 a day per person including transport, accommodation in *pousadas*, good food, horseriding and photo-safari outings. In low season it may be worth bargaining, particularly if there are four or more of you travelling together. Note that in low season you may also have to wait a few days for enough tourists to make up your group, unless you're happy paying more. Individual independent **guides** and the operators mentioned above tend to approach arriving passengers at the airport.

with the staging of the **Festival de Inverno** – a mix of drama, exhibitions and music, the latter ranging from traditional, sacred and Indian music to funk and rap. The Chapada is also a good place to find **artesanato shops**; these are mainly around the central square but the best is Arte Indigena at Rua Quinco Caldas 550. Artes das Tribus, Rua Cipriano Curvo 343, is another good one. There's a very professional **alternative-therapy centre** in town, Cosmus at Rua Turadentes 45 (Ⓣ65/3301-1846), which offers acupuncture, reiki and massage among other treatments.

Most of the year, however, it's not the town itself that brings most people out to Chapada. The stunning countryside, of which over three hundred square kilometres is protected as the **Parque Nacional da Chapada dos Guimarães**, consists of a grassy plateau – at 800m the highest land in Mato Grosso – scattered with low trees, a marvellous backdrop for photographing the local flora and birdlife. Within walking distance, there are waterfalls, fantastic rock formations and precipitous canyons, as well as some interesting, partially excavated archeological sites. The most spectacular of all the sights around the village is the **Véu de Noiva waterfall**, which drops over a sheer rock face for over 60m, pounding into the forested basin below. You can take a tour there with most of the operators listed above (from around R$20 a person a day, depending on how big the group is). Alternatively, you can get there by walking or perhaps hitching from the village of Buruti, on the road from Cuiabá, about 12km before Chapada dos Guimarães; Buruti is accessible by bus and only about 6km or an hour and a half's walk from the falls. Alternatively, the falls lie within a couple of kilometres of the road if you jump off the bus some 6km beyond Salgadeira (ask the driver to show you the track).

Other highlights in the park include, about 25km to the north of town, the impressive and weird rock formations of **Cidade da Pedra**, some of them up to 300m tall, the spectacular waterfalls of **Cachoeira da Martinha**, 30km further north, and a couple of interesting cave systems – the **Casa de Pedra**, not far from Véu de Noiva and, further afield, the **Caverna Aroe Jari**, the latter with cave paintings. Good views of the Cidade da Pedra can be had from **Porto do Inferno**, a viewing point some 16km from the village on the road into the Chapada from Cuiabá.

## Arrival, information and tours

Nine daily **buses** run by Expreso Rubi make the one-hour journey from Cuiabá's *rodoviária* to Chapada dos Guimarães. **Tourist information** – including details of bus times, information on campsites, contact lists for local guides and maps of the Chapada – is available from the helpful Centro de Apoio Ao Turismo on the corner of Rua Dr. P. Gomez with Rua 7 Perimetral, just a few blocks from Praça Dom Wunibaldo (Mon–Sat 9am–6pm; ⓣ65/3301-2045 & 3301-1690). Information can also be obtained from the national park office (daily 8.30am–5pm; ⓣ65/3301-1133), while the website ⓦwww.chapadadosguimaraes.com.br, run by Ecoturs, offers photos, hotel information, etc, though all in Portuguese. There are also a couple of good **tour agents** in town. Eco Turismo Cultural, Praça Dom Wunibaldo 464 (ⓣ65/3301-1393, ⓦwww.chapadadosguimaraes.com), organize good-value and reliable tours of the region and have an English-speaking guide; their prices depend on numbers but range from around R$50 per person a day, upwards. Atma, Rua Cipriano Curvo 655 (ⓣ65/3301-3391, ⓦwww.chapadaatma.com.br), specialize in adventure tours, mainly trekking and caving, and cascading, but also offer trips to the main sites in the area. Joel Souza, who operates the tour company Ecoverde from Cuiabá (see p.537), is also worth contacting to arrange a guide and/or transport for a day-trip or longer excursion here. For **changing money**, the Banco do Brasil is on the Praça Dom Wunibaldo.

## Accommodation

There's a good range of **places to stay**, both in the village and in the surrounding countryside. One of the best spots for **camping** is the *Vale da Boçátina Camping Ecológico* (ⓣ65/3301-1393, 3301-2074 or 3301-1154), 10km from the village on a beautiful site near waterfalls and streams; if you contact them in advance they'll arrange transport out there.

### In the village

**Hotel Turismo** Rua Fernando Corréa 1065 ⓣ65/3301-1176, ⓦwww.hotelturismo.com.br. It has exceptionally comfortable beds, good showers and can sometimes change dollars cash. ④

**Pousada Bom Jardim** Praça Dom Wunibaldo 641 ⓣ65/3301-2668 & 65/3301-1244. Central, clean and very friendly, serving decent breakfasts; some rooms are nicer than others. ③

**Pousada Rios** Rua Tiradentes 333 ⓣ65/3301-1126. This is one of the best basic places with TV and a/c in most rooms. ③

**Quincó** Praça Dom Wunibaldo ⓣ65/3301-1284. This is cheap but clean, and offers very reasonable service. ②

**Solar do Ingles** Rua Cipriano Curvo 142 ⓣ65/3301-1389, ⓦwww.solardoingles.com.br. Close to the main square, this *pousada* offers quaint and comfortable accommodation with pool and sauna. ⑤

### Surrounding area

**Chapada Holistica** Located just outside town at Km 63 on Rodoviária Emanuel Pinheiro ⓣ65/3301-1171, ⓔchapadaholistica@terra.com. This new-agey-style place offers an interesting mix of spacious rooms, pool, sauna and alternative therapies. ④

**Fazenda Santa Tereza** ⓣ65/3624-9197, ⓔjvalberici@hotmail.com. Smaller and very cosy, this place is set deeper into the plateau; horseriding is available. ⑤

**Pousada Chapada Aventura** Close to the southern edge of town ⓣ65/3301-2153. Similar in style to the *Fazenda Santa Tereza*, this place has three chalets beside lovely woodlands and enough room for up to thirteen visitors. ⑤

**Pousada Penhasco** On the southern precipice side of town, beyond the outskirts of the village ⓣ65/3301-1555, ⓦwww.penhasco.com.br. A large, quite plush place with great scenic views, apartments, pool and sports facilities. ⑤

### Eating and drinking

Most of Chapada dos Guimarães' best **restaurants** can be found, not surprisingly, around the Praça Dom Wunibaldo: *Felipe's*, Rua Cipriano Curvo 598 (Ⓣ65/3301-1793), is one of the most popular restaurant-bars with *comida por kilo* at lunchtime; next door, the *Trapiche* has an airy terrace and good self-service lunches; while the *Casa do Artesão* in Rua Quinco Caldas serves excellent local dishes at very reasonable prices. A busy spot in the evenings is the *Maloca* restaurant-bar, a few blocks from the *praça* at Rua Fernando Corréa 1020 (Ⓣ65/3301-3405), where you will find a range of meat dishes served in an open-sided corner space with roof cover.

## Águas Quentes and São Antônio

The hot baths of **ÁGUAS QUENTES**, 86km east of Cuiabá in the Serra de São Vicente, just off the BR-364 towards Rondonópolis, function as a weekend and honeymoon resort for locals. Apart from the baths, though, there is little of interest. The water, said to be mildly radioactive, comes in four different pools, the hottest at around 42°C, and is regarded as a cure for rheumatism, liver complaints and even conjunctivitis. There are daily **buses** to the town (1–2hr) from the *rodoviária* in Cuiabá, but be warned that the resort has only one **hotel**, the expensive hydrotherapy centre of *Hotel Águas Quentes* (Ⓣ65/3614-7500, Ⓦwww.hotelmatogrosso.com.br; ⑤).

The closest **beach** to Cuiabá is at **SÃO ANTÔNIO DO LEVERGER**, 35km south of the city on the Rio Cuiabá. It's as much fun as most of the beaches on the coast, even if it seems a little incongruous given the jungle backdrop, but the waters are now far from clean, carrying with them much of Cuiabá's effluent. The dry and relatively cool month of July is designated a beach festival. Again, there are **buses** every day from the *rodoviária* in Cuiabá.

# On from Cuiabá

Cuiabá is a central point for all sorts of long-distance trips within Brazil and a launching pad for onward travel into neighbouring countries. The two main regional highways, the **BR-163** and the **BR-364**, are accessible from the city: the BR-364 is particularly important as a link between the Amazon and almost all other regions, although parts of its westernmost sections are impassable for much of the year.

## West to Rondônia and Porto Velho

Heading **west from Cuiabá**, Porto Velho and Rio Branco are both possible destinations in their own right, or could serve as relaxing stops on the way to Manaus, Peru or Bolivia. Following Rondônia's telegraph link to Manaus in the early twentieth century, **Highway BR-364** to northern Mato Grosso and south-western Amazon was the next development to open up the region. Paving the BR-364 cost around US$600 million – partly financed by the World Bank – but construction was held up for a while when anthropologists realized that it was planned to cut straight through **Nambikwara** tribal lands. The road was eventually completed by making a large detour around these Indians, who still live in small, widely scattered groups that have very little contact with each other.

Leaving the industrial fringes of Cuiabá, the road soon enters the well-established pastoral farmlands to the west. At **Cáceres** (see p.529), three hours out of Cuiabá, the highway starts to leave the Pantanal watershed and climbs gradually towards the inhospitable but beautiful ridges of the **Chapada dos Parecis** and the state frontier with Rondônia. Here, at Vilhena, everyone usually has to pass through the **yellow fever checkpoint**: busloads of people spend half an hour either getting inoculated or showing their vaccination certificates. The Nambikwara and Sararé Indians live to the south of the Chapada escarpment, while to the north there are settlements of Parecis and various other groups. The process of occupation in this region is so recent and intense that the Indians have suffered greatly. Most of their demarcated lands have been invaded already and the situation is worsening all the time. The Indians don't generally come out to the highway, though sometimes you'll see a family or two selling crafted goods – bows and arrows, beads or carvings – beside the road at small pit stops.

The road from Cuiabá to Porto Velho passes through the humanized remains of tropical rainforest. There's the occasional tall tree left standing, but usually it's acres of cattle ranches, and the occasional burgeoning frontier town, crowded with people busy in mechanics' workshops, construction, trading or passing the time playing pool. This is **Rondônia** (see p.308), a relatively recently established jungle state, which has already, even by official reckoning, lost over fifteen percent of its original forest. **JI PARANÁ** is one of the main towns and nodal points along the BR-364, with a population that's grown from nine thousand in 1970 to over 110,000 in 2006. Now Rondônia's second-largest city, its main drag is dominated by a massive Ford showroom, while thousands of gigantic tree trunks sit in enormous piles by the roadside. Even from the bus you can hear the grating noise of circular saws, slicing the forest into manageable and marketable chunks. And on the outskirts of town, hundreds of small, new wooden huts are springing up every month. It's another five hours through decimated jungle scenery before you reach the jungle frontier town of Porto Velho (see p.438), capital of Rondônia state.

## Alta Floresta and Serra do Cachimbo

Turning west off the BR-163 some 150km before the Serra do Cachimbo, a dirt road leads to **ALTA FLORESTA**, a rapidly growing frontier town of around 43,000 people, which is increasingly tourist-friendly. Located almost 800km north of Cuiabá, it's a remote but thriving agricultural settlement with regular bus and plane connections to Cuiabá and elsewhere. The town is of little immediate interest, but has in recent years opened its doors to **ecotourism** in the form of a four-star **hotel**, the *Floresta Amazonica*, Av. Perimetral Oeste 2001 (ⓣ66/3512-7100, ⓦwww.fah.com.br; ➎), a tastefully developed place with expansive jungle grounds that serves as a base for the associated *Cristalino Jungle Lodge* (➏). The real reason for visiting this area lies close to the lodge, deeper in the forest on a tributary of the Rio Teles Pires, which ultimately flows into the Amazon. From here, there is a wide choice of trips and activities (around R$190–350 per person per day), including visits to an *escola rural productiva* where you can buy paintings and other artefacts from local Kayaby Indians. The forest around here is particularly rich in **birdlife**, and there are several set birding trails where you can also see alligators and capuchin, spider and howler monkeys. A similar but even more remote development, accessible only by air taxi, lies 140km northwest of Alta Floresta on the Rio São Benedito, on the Pará state border: *Pousada Salto Thaimaçu* (ⓣ66/3521-3587, ⓦwww.thaimacu.com.br; ➐) offers fishing and boat trips, and very pleasant chalet accommodation. You can book all of these places through Floresta Tour (Ⓣ66/3521-1396, Ⓦwww.florestatour.com.br), who organize a range of forest- and lodge-based trips. If you are trying to get to **Xingu** (one of the most important indigenous Indian reserves in Brazil, located deep in the eastern forests of the northern Mato Grosso), the staging post is the town of Sinop, but you can get there with, as well as stay at, the costly *Xingu Refúgio Amazonico* (Ⓦwww.xingurefuge.com).

Back in town, the *Grande Hotel Coroados*, Rua F-1, 118 (Ⓣ66/3521-3111; ❷), is exceptionally good value, with cosy rooms, an excellent pool and even a sauna. Difficult to find (there are few street signs in Alta Floresta), the hotel is one street back from Avenida Ludovico da Riva Nato in "Bloco F" at the end of a cul-de-sac. *Lisboa Palace Hotel*, at Av. Jaime Verissimo 251 (Ⓣ66/3521-2876, Ⓕ3531-3500; ❸), has larger rooms but no pool. A good budget option is the *Hotel e Restaurante Luz Divina*, opposite the *rodoviária* on Avenida Ludovico da Riva Nato (Ⓣ66/3521-2742 or 3521-4080; ❶), offering a wide choice of clean, modern rooms.

**Flying** is the only easy and sure option **northwards from Alta Floresta**, except if you're travelling to Serra do Cachimbo, for which there are regular buses. The **airport**, 2km northwest of Alta Floresta on the Avenida Ariosto da Riva (Ⓣ66/3521-3360; R$25 by taxi), has daily flights north to Itaituba, Santarém and Belém, and south to Cuiabá and São Paulo.

Crossing the hills to the north of Cuiabá, the BR-163 heads up towards **Serra do Cachimbo**; the 2000km continuation to the Amazon and Santarém – a bold but untenable attempt to cross what is still essentially a vast wilderness – is currently impassable. As the road climbs towards the rim of the Amazon basin, the forest becomes thicker and the climate muggier, and the road surface soon deteriorates. This transitional zone is one of the best areas south of Boa Vista for large-scale ranching, and there are plenty of open grasslands, dry enough in the dry season for ranchers to burn off the old pastures to make way for fresh shoots with the first rains. Interspersed among the grasses and tangled bamboo and creeper thickets are large expanses of cane, grown as fodder for the cows after the pasture has been burnt. It's still very much a frontier land, with small settlements of loggers and brick-firers springing up along the roads as the forest is cleared away forever.

## Colonel P.H. Fawcett

**Colonel P.H. Fawcett**, the famous British explorer, vanished somewhere in this region in 1925, on what turned out to be his last attempt to locate a lost jungle city and civilization. He'd been searching for it on and off for twenty years, as entertainingly told in his edited diaries and letters, *Exploration Fawcett* (see p.748). This last expedition was made in the company of his eldest son, Jack, and a schoolfriend of Jack's, and following their disappearance various theories were put forward as to their fate, including being kept as prisoners of a remote tribe or, more fancifully, adopted chiefs. Possibly, they were murdered out in the wilds, as were dozens of other explorers, although Fawcett had travelled for years among the Indians without coming to any harm. More likely, they merely succumbed to one of the dozens of tropical diseases that were by far the biggest killer at the time. But the fate of the colonel still remains a mystery: in 1985, the same team who had identified the body of the Nazi Josef Mengele announced that they had identified bones found in a shallow grave as those of the colonel; but in 1996 another expedition, Expedição Autan, dissatisfied with the Mengele team's evidence, set off to try to make a DNA match, but found no trace of either the colonel or his companions.

## Rondonópolis and Jatai

For those who have arrived in Cuiabá from the Amazon, the city acts as a gateway to the rest of Brazil. From the earliest times, São Paulo was the main source of settlers arriving in Mato Grosso, though until the twentieth century the route followed the river systems. These days, the **BR-364** runs all the way (over 1700km) from Cuiabá to São Paulo, with several daily buses taking around 24 hours minimum.

On the headwaters of the Pantanal's Rio São Lourenço, two to three hours from Cuiabá, the large industrial town of **RONDONÓPOLIS** with over 160,000 inhabitants also serves as a base for visiting the local **Bororo Indians**. In the present political climate, visits to Indian reservations are not always permitted, and you might consider the ethics of such visits before you decide to go. In any case, permission must be obtained first from FUNAI (see p.534), and they'll decide if, when and where you can go. There's a range of **hotels**, including the cheap but clean *Turis Hotel* on Rua Alagoas 61 (ⓣ66/3421-7487; ❷). Good mid-range hotels include the *Hotel Nacional*, right by the *rodoviária* at Av. Fernando Corréa da Costa 978 (ⓣ66/3423-3245; ❹), and the *Guatujá* at Av. Fernando Corréa da Costa 624 (ⓣ66/3423-2111; ❹). The more luxurious *Novotel* is at Rua Floriano Peixoto 711 (ⓣ66/0800-703-7000, ⓦwww.acornhotels.com.br; ❺), with pool and restaurant; and the *Vila Verde*, Av. Pres. Medici 4406 (ⓣ66/3423-2605, ⓦwww.hotelvilaverderondonopolis.com.br; ❸), offers some comfort, air conditioning and good value.

The small town of **JATAI** is almost halfway to São Paulo, about ten hours from Cuiabá in the state of Goiás. This is where many passengers will be getting off and on the bus, changing to one of the other routes which emanate from here – to Brasília, Goiânia, Belo Horizonte, Rio de Janeiro, the Northeast and Belém.

## Barra do Garças

An alternative route from Cuiabá to Goiás Velho, Goiânia and Brasília runs east via the **BR-070**. Over 500km from Cuiabá, on the frontier between Mato Grosso and Goiás states, **BARRA DO GARÇAS** is a useful and interesting point at which to break a long bus journey. This small and isolated, but still fast-growing town of some 60,000 people sits astride the Rio das Garças, one of the main headwaters of the Araguaia, underneath low-lying wooded hills. It's a surprisingly good base for a variety of nature-based hikes or relaxing in hot-water springs, and the nearest beach, the **Praia de Aragarças**, is barely 1km away. In the mountainous terrain that stretches from Barra do Garças up to the Serra do Cachimbo, the most impressive feature is the highly eroded red-rock cliff of the 700m **Serra do Roncador**, 150km due north of the town. Waterfalls and caves abound in the region; close to the limits of the town there are fourteen waterfalls in the Serra Azul alone, a range that rises to over 800m.

Much nearer, just 6km northeast of town, there are more fine river beaches and the popular natural hot baths of the **Parque Balneário das Águas Quentes** (daily 6am–9.30pm; small charge). Besides curing all the usual complaints, the waters are proudly proclaimed by the town's tourist office to have the capacity to augment one's *vitalidade sexual* – you have been warned! Nearby, too, there are the reserves of the Xavante and Bororo Indians. For information and to find out about written authorization to enter one of the reserves, contact FUNAI at Rua Muniz Mariano 3, Setor Dermat (ⓣ66/3861-2020).

### Practicalities

There is a municipal **tourist office**, FUNDATUR, on Praça Tiradentes (Mon–Sat 9am–6pm; ⓣ66/3861-2227 or 3861-2344), and there are also three **environmental organizations** in town who may be able to help with information on the region and ecotours, as well as possibilities for **rock climbing**, **potholing** and **canyoning**: CELVA, Centro Etno-Ecológico do Vale do Araguaia (ⓣ66/3861-2018); União Eco-Cultura do Vale do Araguaia, Av. Min. João Alberto 100; and the Fundação Cultura Ambiental do Centro Oeste (Caixa Postal 246). Barra do Garças also serves as a possible starting point for visits to the world's largest river island, the Ilha do Bananal, in Tocantins state (see p.489).

You can **change money** at the Banco do Brasil on Praça Tiradentes, or nearby at HSBC, Av. Min. João Alberto 528. The central **post office** is at Rua 1 de Maio 19, and **car rental** is available from Localiza (ⓣ66/3861-2140). Bus connections from the **rodoviária** on Rua Bororós (ⓣ66/3401-1217) along the BR-070 between Cuiabá and Brasília are good, and there is also an **airport**, Julio Campos, 15km out of town (ⓣ66/3401-2218), which is served by the local air-taxi service BRC (ⓣ66/3861-2140) and operates flights to Brasília, Cuiabá, Goiânia and Rondonópolis.

The swishest **place to stay** is the *Serra Azul Plaza*, at Praça dos Garimpeiros 572 (ⓣ66/3401-6663, ⓦwww.serraazulplazahotel.com.br; ❺), followed closely by *Toriuá Parque*, with a beautiful pool some 4km beyond Barra do Garças on Avenida Min. João Alberto (BR-158), Chácara Rio Araguaia (ⓣ&ⓕ66/3638-1811; ❹). In the centre, the *Hotel Presidente*, Av. Min. João Alberto 55 (ⓣ66/3861-2108; ❸), has the most comfortable rooms. There are also two **campsites**, one at the Porto Bae on the banks of the Rio Araguaia (access from Av. Marechal Rondon), and the other at the Parque das Águas Quentes, 6km from town.

There isn't a huge choice of **restaurants** in Barra do Garças, but the food is reasonably good and not particularly expensive. The *Restaurante Encontro das Águas* (ⓣ66/3401-3536), at the riverside on Avenida Min. João Alberto, is great for fish and is open for lunch and dinner every day. The *Rock Café*, Av. Rio das Garças 4 (opposite *Aquarius Pizzeria*), is a trendy place to be seen in the evenings, with a wide range of snacks and light Brazilian meals.

# Travel details

## Buses

Except on the Campo Grande–Corumbá route, which is monopolized by Andorinha, there are scores of different bus companies competing for the same routes as well as opening up new ones. Each company advertises destinations and departure times at its ticket office windows, making it relatively easy to choose a route and buy a ticket. Note that going north from Cuiabá, buses only go as far as Alta Floresta, or to Rio Branco via Porto Velho. Manaus, Itaituba, Santarém and Belém are all advertised by the bus companies, but are reachable only by enormous detours taking several days via Goiânia. Cruzeiro do Sul has no reliable road access.

**Bonito** to: Anastácio (1 daily; 4hr); Campo Grande (2 daily; 5hr); Corumbá (Mon–Sat 2 daily; 8hr); Dourados (1 daily; 5hr); Miranda (Mon–Sat 1 daily; 4hr); Ponta Porã (1 daily; 7hr).

**Campo Grande** to almost everywhere in Brazil, including: Alta Floresta (3 daily; 22hr); Anastácio/Aquidauana (8 daily; 2hr); Belo Horizonte (1 daily; 23hr); Bonito (1 daily; 5hr); Brasília (1 daily; 24hr); Corumbá (12 daily; 7hr); Coxim (4 daily; 3–4hr); Cuiabá (5 daily; 11hr); Dourados (5 daily; 4hr); Foz do Iguaçu (10 daily; 15hr); Miranda (11 daily; 3hr); Ponta Porã (4 daily; 5–6hr); Rio de Janeiro (4 daily; 22hr); São Paulo (6 daily; 14hr). There is also a weekly service to Asunción in Paraguay, leaving Sunday mornings (Amambay company).

**Corumbá** to: Campo Grande, via Anastácio/Aquidauana and Miranda (12 daily; 7hr; change in Campo Grande for most onward destinations); Rio de Janeiro (4 daily; 32hr); São Paulo (4 daily; 26hr).
**Cuiabá** to: Alta Floresta (4 daily; 12hr); Brasília (6 daily; 20hr); Campo Grande (6 daily; 11hr); Chapada dos Guimarães (9 daily; 1hr); Coxim (6 daily; 6–7hr); Goiânia (6 daily; 14hr); Porto Velho (4 daily; 23hr); Rio Branco (4 daily; 32hr); Rio de Janeiro (1 daily; 31hr); Rondonópolis (10 daily; 3hr); São Paulo (2 daily; 24hr-plus).

## Planes

**Campo Grande** Several daily flights (Gol, TAM and Pantanal Linhas Aéreas) to Brazil's main cities; also to Vilhena (halfway between Cuiabá and Porto Velho).
**Corumbá** Daily flights (TAM and Pantanal Linhas Aéreas) to Campo Grande, Rio de Janeiro and São Paulo.
**Cuiabá** Gol, Webjet and TAM cover the main cities.

# São Paulo

VENEZUELA
GUYANA
SURINAME
FRENCH GUIANA
N
COLOMBIA
5
4
3
PERU
7
6
BOLIVIA
2
8
1
PARAGUAY
CHILE
9
ARGENTINA
0
1000 km
URUGUAY

CHAPTER 8

# Highlights

* **Memorial do Imigrante museum** Explore this fascinating museum, which was once a hostel that tens of thousands of immigrants passed through upon arriving in Brazil. See p.564

* **Mercado Municipal** Look out for the lovely stained-glass windows depicting scenes of Brazilian agricultural production. See p.564

* **Avenida Paulista** A showcase for modern São Paulo, this avenue also features a few lavish mansions from bygone eras. See p.570

* **Paranapiacaba** This remarkable, late nineteenth-century British railway village is a popular base for hikes in the surrounding Mata Atlântica. See p.590

* **Fazenda Pinhal** An intriguing relic of the state's nineteenth-century coffee boom, this is one of the oldest surviving and best-preserved rural estates in the state of São Paulo. See p.594

* **Ilhabela** Protected as a state park, this island – the most beautiful spot on São Paulo's coast – remains unravaged by tourism. See p.600

▲ Stream in the Mata Atlântica, São Paulo state

# 8

# São Paulo



**São Paulo**, the country's most populous state and home to by far its biggest city, is Brazil's economic powerhouse. Home to nearly half the country's industrial output, it is also an agricultural sector that produces, among other things, more orange juice than any single nation worldwide. Its eponymous city boasts a dizzying variety of cultural centres and art galleries, and the noise from its vibrant fashion and music scenes is heard around the globe. Although most people come to the state in order to visit the city merely for business, São Paulo has numerous attractions other than the concrete jungle at its heart. The beaches north of the important port of Santos – especially on **Ilhabela** – rival Rio's best; those to the south, near **Iguape** and **Cananéia**, remain relatively unspoiled. Inland, the state is dominated by agribusiness, with seemingly endless fields of cattle pasture, sugar cane, oranges and soya interspersed with anonymous towns where the agricultural produce is processed; additionally, some impressive **fazenda houses** remain as legacies of the days when São Paulo's economy was pretty well synonymous with coffee production. To escape scorching summer temperatures, or for the novelty in tropical Brazil of a winter chill, you can head to **Campos do Jordão**, one of the country's highest settlements and a kitsch Alpine-style resort seen through a peculiarly Brazilian lens.

## Some history

São Paulo state's economic pre-eminence is a relatively recent phenomenon. In 1507 São Vicente, the second-oldest Portuguese settlement in Brazil, was founded on the coast near present-day **Santos**, but for over three hundred years the area comprising today's São Paulo state remained a backwater. The inhabitants were a hardy people, of mixed Portuguese and indigenous origin, from whom, in the seventeenth and eighteenth centuries, emerged the **bandeirantes** – frontiersmen who roamed far into the South American interior to secure the borders of the Portuguese Empire against Spanish encroachment, capturing natives as slaves and seeking out precious metals and gems as they went.

It wasn't until the mid-nineteenth century that São Paulo became rich. Cotton production received a boost with the arrival in the late 1860s of Confederate refugees from the American South, who settled around **Santa Bárbara d'Oeste**, about 140km from the then small town of **São Paulo** itself. But after disappointing results with cotton, most of these plantation owners switched their attention to coffee and, by the end of the century, the state had become firmly established as the world's foremost producer of the crop. During the same period, Brazil abolished slavery and the plantation

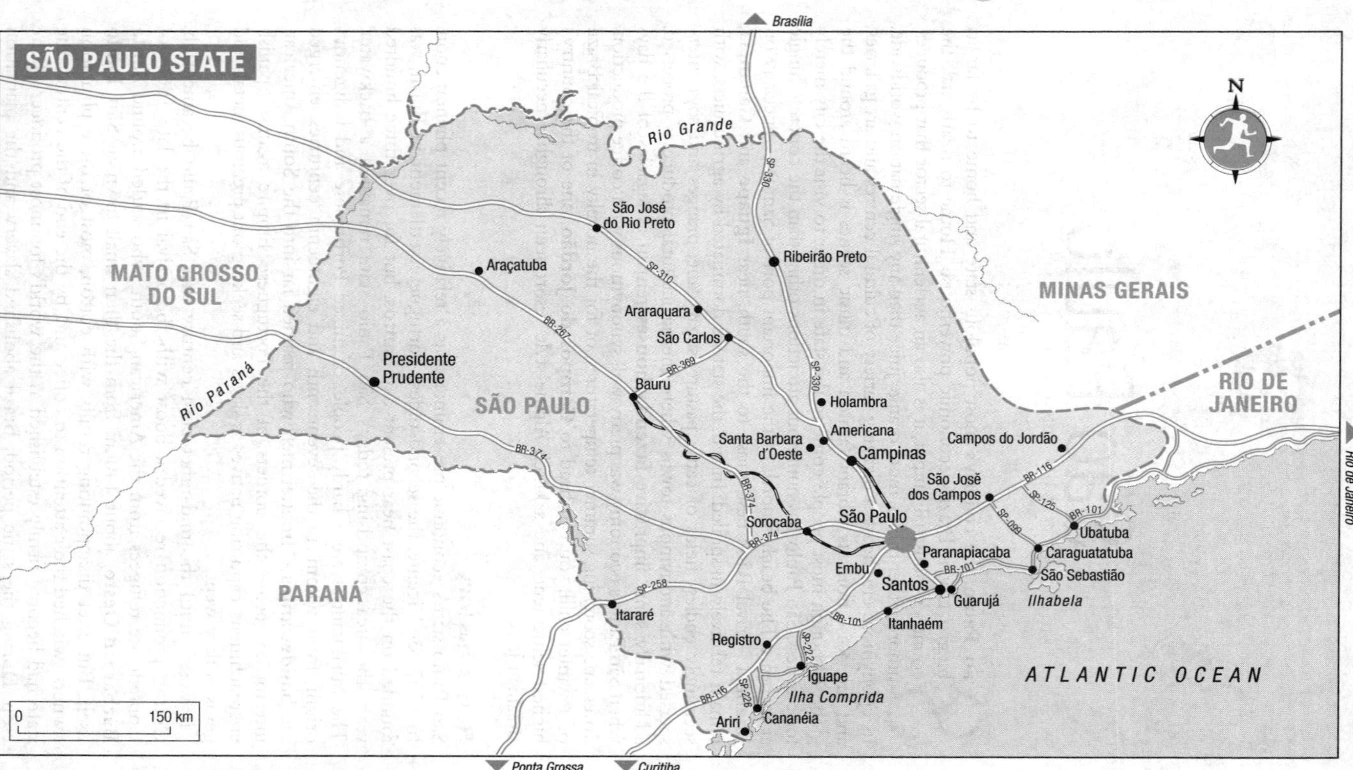
SÃO PAULO STATE
N
Brasília
Campo Grande
Campo Grande
Rio de Janeiro
Ponta Grossa
Curitiba
MATO GROSSO DO SUL
MINAS GERAIS
RIO DE JANEIRO
SÃO PAULO
PARANÁ
ATLANTIC OCEAN
Rio Grande
Rio Paraná
São José do Rio Preto
Ribeirão Preto
Araçatuba
Araraquara
São Carlos
Presidente Prudente
Bauru
Holambra
Americana
Santa Barbara d'Oeste
Campinas
Campos do Jordão
São José dos Campos
Sorocaba
São Paulo
Ubatuba
Caraguatatuba
Paranapiacaba
São Sebastião
Embu
Santos
Guarujá
Ilhabela
Itararé
Itanhaém
Registro
Iguape
Ilha Comprida
Cananéia
Ariri
SP-330
SP-310
BR-267
BR-369
BR-374
BR-116
SP-125
SP-099
BR-101
SP-258
SP-222
SP-226
0
150 km

owners recruited European and Japanese immigrants to expand production. Riding the wave of the coffee boom, foreign companies took the opportunity to invest in port facilities, rail lines and power and water supplies, while textile and other new industries emerged, too. Within a few decades, the town of São Paulo became one of Latin America's greatest commercial and cultural centres, growing from a small town into a vast metropolitan sprawl. Although the coffee bubble eventually burst, the state had the resources in place to diversify into other produce and São Paulo's prominence in Brazil's economy was assured.

# São Paulo city

**Rio is a beauty. But São Paulo – São Paulo is a city.**

Marlene Dietrich

Nicknamed "Sampa" – the title of a well-known Caetano Veloso song about the city, in which he admits that, "When I arrived here I didn't understand the hard concrete poetry of your streets and the discreet casual beauty of your girls" – São Paulo does not have an immediately appealing aesthetic. It's a place most people come for business; residents of the city, *paulistanos*, boast frequently of their work ethic, supposedly superior to what dominates the rest of Brazil, and speak contemptuously of the idleness of *cariocas* (in reply, *cariocas* joke sourly that *paulistanos* are simply incapable of enjoying anything – sex in particular).

Increasingly, though, visitors are also coming to São Paulo to play. Often described, not inaccurately, as "the New York of the tropics", the city lays claim to having surpassed Rio as Brazil's **cultural** centre, with a lively and varied programme of exhibitions and shows; its **food** is often excellent, in part thanks to immigrants from so many areas of the world and a new wave of imaginative cooks; its wide range of stores make it Latin America's best place to **shop**; and its vibrant **nightlife** has put it firmly on the international clubbing map. With over 70 museums, 120 theatres, 50 parks, dozens of cinemas – and not forgetting 15,000 bars – you certainly have no excuse for being bored in São Paulo.

## Some history

In 1554, the Jesuit priests José de Anchieta and Manuel da Nóbrega established a mission station on the banks of the Rio Tietê in an attempt to bring Christianity to the Tupi-Guarani Indians. São Paulo dos Campos de Piratininga, as the site was called, was situated 70km inland and 730m up, in the sheer, forest-covered inclines of the Serra do Mar, above the port of São Vicente. The gently undulating plateau and the proximity to the Paraná and Plata rivers facilitated traffic into the interior and, with São Paulo as their base, roaming gangs of *bandeirantes* set out in search of loot. Around the mission school, a few adobe huts were erected and the settlement soon developed into a trading post and a centre from which to secure mineral wealth. In 1681, São Paulo became a seat of regional government and, in 1711, it was made a municipality by the king of Portugal, the cool, healthy climate helping to attract settlers from the coast.

With the expansion of **coffee** plantations westwards from Rio de Janeiro, along the Paraibá Valley, in the mid-nineteenth century São Paulo's fortunes improved. The region's rich red soil – *terra roxa* – was ideally suited to coffee cultivation, and from about 1870 plantation owners took up residence in the city, which was undergoing a rapid transformation into a bustling regional centre. British, French and German merchants and hoteliers opened local operations, British-owned rail lines radiated in all directions from São Paulo, and foreign water, gas, telephone

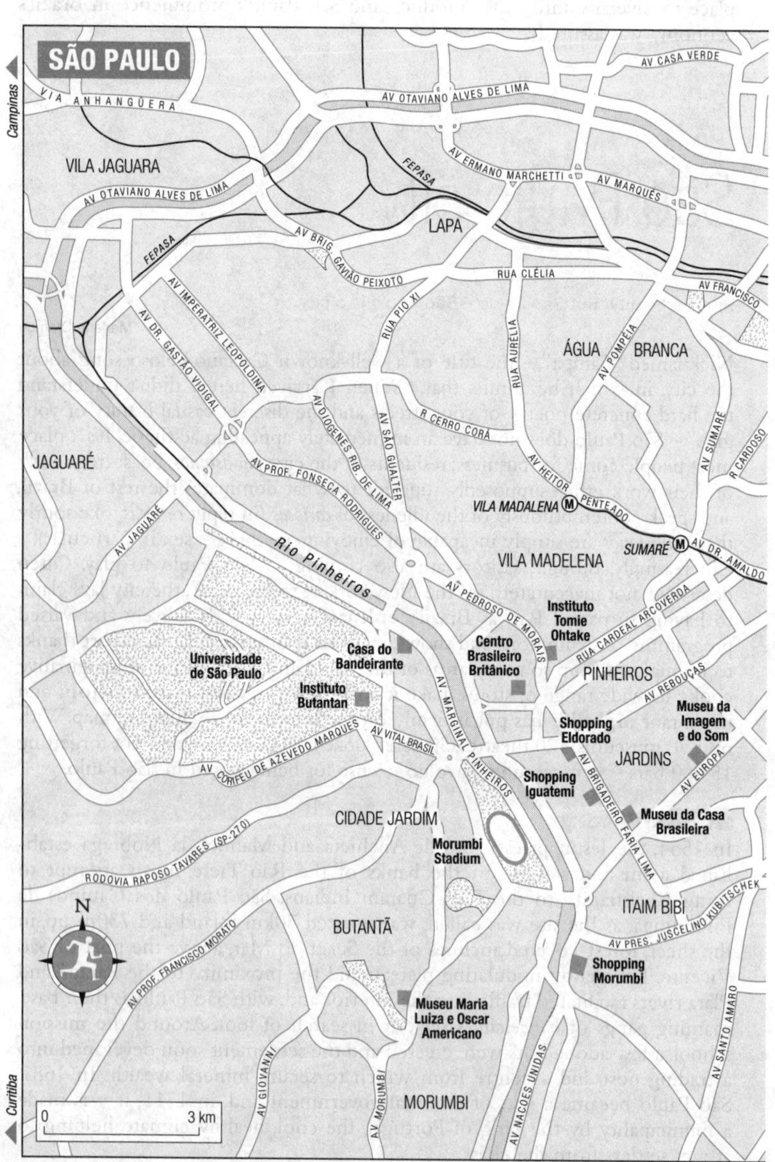

and electricity companies moved in to service the city. In the 1890s, enterprising "coffee barons" began to place some of their profits into local industry, hedging their bets against a possible fall in the price of coffee, with textile factories being a favourite area for investment.

As the local population could not meet the ever-increasing demands of plantation owners, factories looked to **immigrants** for their workforce (see box, p.568). As a result, São Paulo's **population** soared, almost tripling to 69,000 by 1890,

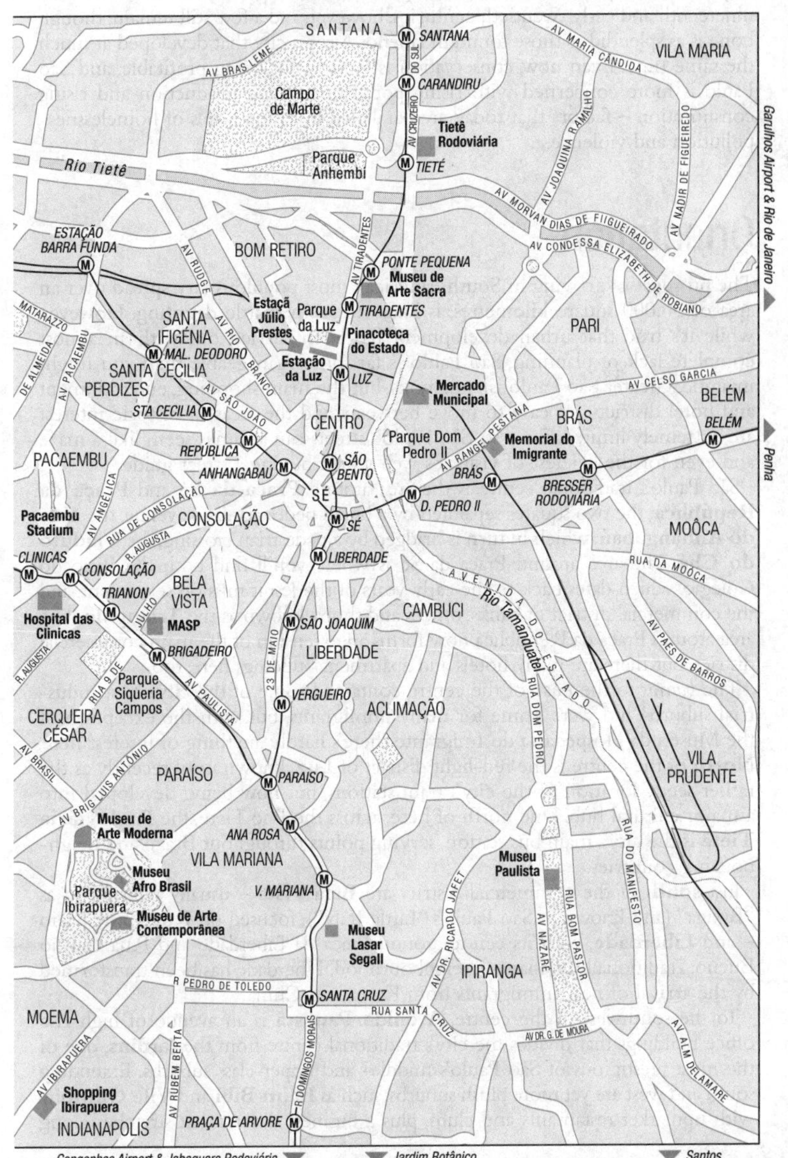

and to 239,000 by the end of the next decade. By 1950, when it had reached 2.2 million, São Paulo had clearly established its dominant role in Brazil's urbanization. Today, with a population of over twenty million, including its sprawling suburbs, São Paulo is the fifth largest city in the world.

To keep pace with the growth of industry, trade and the population, buildings were erected with little time to consider their aesthetics and, in any case, often became cramped as soon as they were built, or had to be demolished to make way for a new avenue. Some grand **public buildings** were built in the late nineteenth and early twentieth centuries, however, and a few still remain, though none is as splendid as those found in Buenos Aires, a city that developed at much the same time. Even now, conservation is seen as not being profitable, and São Paulo is more concerned with rising population, rising production and rising consumption – factors that today are paralleled by rising levels of homelessness, pollution and violence.



## Orientation

The prospect of arriving in South America's most populous city, spread over an area of 30,000 square kilometres, is likely to seem a little daunting. However, while it's true that urban development has been carried out with an almost complete lack of planning, São Paulo is far more manageable than you might imagine. Greater São Paulo is enormous, but the main shopping, entertainment and hotel districts are easy to move between, and the areas of historic interest are extremely limited. Even so, São Paulo's streets can at times seem like a maze and even for the briefest of visits it's well worth buying a street guide.

São Paulo's traditional centre is the area around **Praça da Sé** and **Praça da República**, the two squares separated by a broad pedestrianized avenue, the **Vale do Anhangabaú**, which in turn is bridged by a pedestrian crossing, the **Viaduto do Chá**. The area around Praça da Sé is where you'll find both the Pátio do Colégio, which dates back to the early years of the Jesuit mission settlement, and the commercial district of banks, offices and shops, known as the **Triângulo**. The area around Praça da República now forms an extension of the main commercial district, but there are many hotels and apartment buildings here, too.

The *bairros* to the **east** of the centre contained some of the city's first industrial suburbs and were home for many immigrants, but with the exception of the Museu da Hospedaria do Imigrante there's hardly anything of interest here. **North** of the centre is the red-light district of **Luz**, known until recently as the rather seedy location of the city's train stations, but now being developed into a major cultural hub. Due north of here, across the Rio Tietê, the **Rodoviária Tietê** is the city's main bus station, serving points throughout Brazil and neighbouring countries.

Just **south** of the commercial district are **Bela Vista** – usually referred to as "Bixiga" (and known as São Paulo's "Little Italy"), focused on Rua 13 de Maio – and **Liberdade**, with its centre around Praça da Liberdade and Rua Galvão Bueno. Traditionally a Japanese neighbourhood, Liberdade has been transformed by the arrival of new immigrants from Korea and China.

To the southwest of the centre, **Avenida Paulista** is an avenue of high-rise office buildings that divides the city's traditional centre from the **Jardins**, one of the most prestigious of São Paulo's middle- and upper-class suburbs. Extending south and west are yet more plush suburbs, such as **Itaim Bibi** and **Vila Olímpia**, with upmarket restaurants and clubs, plus a business district that stretches along

## Avoiding trouble in São Paulo

Assaults and robberies are favourite topics of conversation amongst *paulistanos*, with the city's crime statistics consistently higher than those of Rio. Nevertheless, by using a little common sense you're unlikely to encounter problems. With such a mixture of people in São Paulo, you're far less likely to be assumed to be a foreigner than in most parts of Brazil, and therefore won't make such an obvious target for pickpockets and other **petty thieves**.

At night, pay particular attention around the central red-light district of **Luz**, location of the city's main train stations and – though not as bad – around **Praça da República**. Also take care late at night in **Bixiga** (also known as Bela Vista), or if you venture into **Praça Roosevelt**. Always carry at least some money in an immediately accessible place so that, if you are accosted by a **mugger**, you can quickly hand something over before he starts getting angry or panicky. If in any doubt at all about visiting an area you don't know, don't hesitate to take a taxi.

**Avenida Brigadeiro Faria Lima**. Cutting across Avenida Paulista into the Jardins is **Rua Augusta**, which begins in the centre at Praça Franklin Roosevelt; many of São Paulo's best restaurants and shopping streets are located around here. **Vila Madalena** is west of the Jardins, and **Pinheiros** southwest of Vila Madalena – both are mainly residential neighbourhoods that are amongst the city's most fashionable nightspots. Just across the Rio Pinheiros lies the vast campus of the **Universidade de São Paulo** and the Instituto Butantan, while to the southeast lies the **Parque do Ibirapuera**, one of the city's great parks.

**Greater São Paulo** includes sprawling industrial suburbs where people are housed in a mixture of grim-looking high-rise tenements, small houses and, on just about every patch of wasteland, *favelas* – the slum homes for some two million of the city's inhabitants. The most important **industrial areas** are the so-called "A B C D" *municípios* of Santo André, São Bernardo, São Caetano and Diadema, the traditional centre of Brazil's motor vehicle industry and of the city's militantly left-wing political tradition. In the 1940s, Santo André elected Brazil's first Communist Party mayor, while from the Metal Workers' Union and the autoworkers' strikes of the late 1970s emerged Lula, the leader of the PT (the Workers' Party), inaugurated as Brazil's president in January 2003.

# Arrival and information

With trains being limited to suburban services, virtually all arrivals to São Paulo are by plane or bus. Watch your belongings at all times, as thieves thrive in the confusion of airports and stations.

## By air

São Paulo is served by two airports. Most domestic flights and all international flights use the modern **Guarulhos** airport (ⓣ11/6445-2945), 30km from the city. Just to the south of the centre, the always congested **Congonhas** (ⓣ11/5090-9000 or 5090-9032) handles services within the state of São Paulo, but also operates the shuttle service (the Ponte Aérea) to Rio, as well as some of the flights to other destinations, including Curitiba and Belo Horizonte.

On arrival at either airport, you will find desks that change cash or traveller's cheques, or you can use the airport ATMs. The city **tourist information** department has desks at terminals one and two in Guarulhos, which can provide maps and transport details (6am–10pm). **Taxis** are readily available at both airports; the fare to the centre is around R$90 from Guarulhos and R$45 from Congonhas. At both airports there are taxi desks in the arrivals halls and you pay a fixed price depending on the distance of your destination.

If you're travelling alone, it's more economical, at R$28 per person, to go for the express, air-conditioned, 24-hour airport **bus service**. This connects Congonhas and Guarulhos at roughly half-hourly intervals, less frequently at night. The buses also link Guarulhos with the western side of Praça da República and the Rodoviária Tietê, leaving at least once an hour during the day, less frequently at night; going back from the Praça da República to Guarulhos, there are no buses between 11.40pm and 5.40am. During the day (6am–11pm) there's a service from Guarulhos to the top hotels around Avenida Paulista and another service to hotels in Itaim Bibi, southwest of Jardins.

Even cheaper, but only really practical if you have little luggage, is to take a bus to Bresser *metrô* station (5am–11pm; R$2.30), from where you can catch a train into the city centre.



## By bus

Inter-city bus services arrive at one of four *rodoviárias*, all connected to the *metrô* system. Serving all state capitals as well as destinations in neighbouring countries, the major terminal is **Tietê** in the north of the city, the second largest bus terminal in the world. Don't be daunted – the exits, ticket offices, etc, are well signposted and there's a helpful information desk (*Informações*). To the south of the centre, **Jabaquara** is for buses to and from the Santos region and São Paulo's south shore as far as Peruíbe, while **Barra Funda, to the northwest of the centre** serves destinations in southern São Paulo and Paraná, and **Bresser, to the east of the centre** is for buses to Minas Gerais. For times and fares, there is a central information line (Ⓣ11/3235-0322), while Ⓦwww.socicam.com.br has the phone numbers and destinations of the individual bus companies. Bus tickets to most destinations can be bought in advance at many of the city's travel agents.

## Information

Anhembi Turismo, the city's tourism department (Ⓣ11/6224-0615, Ⓦwww.cityofsaopaulo.com), maintains several **information booths** around the city, with English-speaking staff who are especially helpful for general directions or for local transport details. Booths are located downtown in Galería Olido at Av. São João 465 (daily 9am–6pm), in the Parque da Luz (see p.565; Tues–Sun 10am–4pm), at Avenida Paulista (across from MASP; daily 9am–6pm), and at Iguatemi shopping centre (see p.587; Mon–Fri 9am–6pm & Sat–Sun noon–6pm. The state **tourist office**, at Av. São Joao 465 (Mon–Sat 8am–8pm), can provide you with colourful leaflets and answer your queries on travel within the state.

For up-to-date **listings** of what's going on in the city, the São Paulo edition of the weekly magazine *Veja* contains an excellent entertainment guide, and the daily newspaper *Folha de São Paulo* lists cultural and sporting events and, on Friday, contains an essential entertainment guide, the *Guia da Folha*. The Guia Internet São Paulo (Ⓦwww.guiasp.com.br) is a good source of up-to-the-moment information on São Paulo's culture and nightlife in Portuguese, while Ⓦwww.gringoes.com provides English-language information on living in Brazil for expats, with a particular focus on São Paulo, and featuring a weekly newsletter and lively forums.

Finding a good **map** of a city as spread out as São Paulo is not easy. The free tourist-office maps are generally poor in quality, though hotels and Anhembi Turismo sometimes offer the excellent *Mapa das Artes São Paulo*. If you're planning on staying more than a day or two in the city, it's well worth investing R$35 in the *Guia Quatro Rodas Ruas São Paulo*, an (inevitably thick) indexed street atlas, available at newsstands and book stores.

# Getting around

São Paulo's **public transport** network is extensive, but traffic congestion and a seemingly perpetual rush-hour can make travelling by bus or taxi frustratingly slow. Matters are made even worse when it rains; São Paulo's drainage system cannot cope with the summer rains and the city grinds to a halt – just take cover in a bar or *lanchonete* and sit it out. São Paulo's *metrô* network, by contrast, is fast, clean and efficient, though limited in extent.

The main difficulties of driving your own car in São Paulo are the volume of traffic and finding a parking space – you're therefore better off sticking with public transport. Roads are, however, well signposted and it's surprisingly easy to get out of the city. For a list of **car rental firms**, see p.588.

## By bus

Traffic congestion rarely allows São Paulo's **buses** (R$2.30) to be driven at the same terrifying speeds as in Rio. Despite everything, the network is remarkably efficient and includes trolley buses as well as ordinary ones.

On the downside, **bus routes** often snake confusingly through the city, and working out which bus to take can be difficult. The number of the bus is clearly marked at the front, and cards posted at the front and the entrance (towards the back) indicate the route. At **bus stops** (usually wooden posts) you'll have to flag down the buses you want – be attentive or they'll speed by. Buses run between 4am and midnight, but avoid travelling during the height of the evening rush-hour (around 5–7pm) when they are overflowing with passengers.

## By metrô

Quiet, comfortable and fast, São Paulo's **metrô** (Ⓦwww.sp.gov.br) would be by far the easiest way to move around the city were it not limited – for the moment – to just three lines. The north–south **Linha Azul** (blue line) has terminals at Tucuruvi in the far north of the city and Jabaquara *rodoviária* and also serves the Tietê *rodoviária* and Luz train station. The **Linha Vermelha** (red line) extends east–west with terminals at Corinthians–Itaquera and Barra Funda, intersecting with the

### Some useful bus routes

From Praça da República to Avenida Brigadeiro Faria Lima (via Rua Augusta): #702P

From Praça da República to Butantã (via Rua Augusta and Avenida Brigadeiro Faria Lima): #107P

From Avenida Ipiranga to Butantã and Universidade de São Paulo: #702P

From *metrô* Ana Rosa along Avenida Paulista: #875P

From Rodoviária Tietê to Rodoviária Jabaquara via Largo de São Bento and Avenida Liberdade: #501M (midnight–5am only)

Linha Azul at Praça da Sé. There's also the **Linha Verde** (green line), another east–west line that runs underneath Avenida Paulista, stopping at the Museu de Arte de São Paulo (Trianon–MASP station), then from Paraíso to Imigrantes.

Work is well under way on extending the network; by 2012, the much anticipated Linha Amarelo (yellow line) will connect Luz to Praça da República, Higienópolis, Avenida Paulista, Oscar Freire, Faria Lima, Pinheiros, Butantã, Morumbi and out to Taboão da Serra.

The *metrô* runs every day from 5am until midnight, although the ticket booths close at 10pm. **Tickets** cost R$2.40 for a one-way journey. You can also buy integrated bus and *metrô* tickets; many buses stop at the *metrô* stations, with the names of their destinations well marked.

### By taxi

São Paulo is very much a car-orientated city. Walking around it is hard work, and sooner or later you will find yourself in need of a **taxi**. Luckily, they are reliable and abundant but, given the volume of traffic and the often considerable distances involved in navigating the city, fares quickly mount. With irregular – or no – bus services at night, taxis are also really the only means of transport after midnight. There are two main types: the yellow *comuns* and the *rádiotáxis*.

The **comuns**, generally small cars that carry up to three passengers, are the cheapest and are found at taxi ranks or hailed from the street. **Rádiotáxis** are larger and more expensive, and are ordered by phone; try Coopertax (ⓣ11/6195-6000) or Ligue Táxi (ⓣ11/3866-3030). Both types of taxi have meters with two fare rates, and a flag, or *bandeira*, is displayed on the meter to indicate which fare is in operation: fare "1" is charged from 6am to 9pm Monday to Saturday; fare "2" is charged after 9pm and on Sunday and public holidays, costing twenty percent more.

## Accommodation

Finding somewhere to stay in São Paulo is rarely a problem and, as there are several areas where hotels are concentrated, you should get settled in quickly. The **prices** of hotels vary enormously throughout the year, with hefty **discounts** offered during the quieter summer months of January and February. Weekend discounts of up to fifty percent are often given, especially at the better hotels that otherwise cater largely to business executives. If making an online reservation directly with the hotel, compare the rates on the Portuguese- and the English-language versions of the website – the former often are substantially lower.

The best hotels are found in the affluent southwest of the city and, though expensive, their rooms cost less than comparative spots in Rio. With some exceptions, budget and mid-priced places are located around downtown, in parts of the city where visitors, especially women, may feel distinctly uncomfortable walking alone at night. The dangers, however, are often more imaginary than real and, by simply being alert and taking taxis late at night, you should have no problems.

### Downtown

Lots of inexpensive and mid-priced hotels are in the traditional centre of São Paulo, around Praça da República and Avenida São Luís. Budget around R$25 for a taxi each way to the restaurants and bars of Vila Madalena and surrounding neighbourhoods.

**Bourbon** Av. Viera de Carvalho 99 ⓣ11/3337-2000, ⓦwww.bourbon.com.br. One of the smartest hotels in the Praça da República area, the *Bourbon*, which is aimed at budget-oriented business travellers, has comfortable a/c rooms and extras such as a sauna and business centre. ❹

**Gávea Palace** Rua Conselheiro Nébias 445 ⓣ11/3331-7921. While not exactly a palace, this hotel on a side street full of motorbike repair shops is clean and comfortable and, not surprisingly, popular with bikers. Near Praça da República. ❷

**Marabá Palace** Av. Ipiranga 757 ⓣ11/3362-2999, ⓦwww.hotelmaraba.com.br. The city centre's newest and most stylish hotel. Attractively decorated and with a decent restaurant with an international menu, this is the most comfortable place to be safely cocooned in the area. ❺

**Marian Palace** Av. Cáspar Libero 65 ⓣ11/3228-8433, ⓦwww.marian.com.br. Though updated over the years, this Art-Deco gem retains many of its original features in its guest rooms and public areas. A nice pool and garden terrace help compensate for the neighbourhood, which can be dodgy at night. ❹

**Municipal** Av. São João 354 ⓣ11/3228-7833. This friendly hotel, located in a part of the centre that, while busy, feels safe day and night, is a protected historic monument; the functional 1940s architecture is practically antique in a city with such a rapid rate of change. Though its simple rooms have hardly been updated since it opened, they remain perfectly adequate. ❷

**Normandie Design Hotel** Av. Ipiranga 1187 ⓣ11/3311-9855, ⓦwww.normandiedesign.com.br. You'll either love or hate the general look here – everything white, black and chrome. The staff are enthusiastic, the bedrooms are comfortable (if on the small side) and the price is very reasonable. ❹

**República Park** Av. Vieira de Carvalho 32 ⓣ11/3331-5595, ⓦwww.republicaparkhotel.com.br. The chandeliers, velvet furnishings and marble bathrooms have clearly seen better days, but the hotel is comfortable and great value. Ask for a room on an upper floor with a balcony overlooking the Praça da República. ❸

**São Paulo Hostel** Rua Barão de Campinas 94 ⓣ11/3333-0844, ⓦwww.hostelsaopaulo.com.br. This city-centre hostel offers dormitory beds (R$40) and single (from R$63) and double rooms ❸. The large size and relative comfort of the single rooms make them a better deal than at most hotels. With laundry facilities and its own bar, the hostel's only drawback is its rather uninspiring and dodgy-feeling neighbourhood after dark.

## Liberdade

São Paulo's traditionally Japanese *bairro*, **Liberdade**, has a few low- and mid-priced hotels worth considering if you're on a budget – not least because the area is one of the safest parts of central São Paulo. Although the majority of people staying here are visiting Asian businessmen, other guests are made to feel just as welcome.

**Akasaka** Praça da Liberdade 149 ⓣ11/3207-1311, ⓦwww.akasakahotel.com.br. While barely recognizably Japanese, this is a good budget choice for those wanting to be in the heart of Liberdade. Rooms are spacious, with the brightest overlooking the *praça*, although bathrooms are shared. ❸

**Nikkey Palace** Rua Galvão Bueno 425 ⓣ11/3207-8511, ⓦwww.nikkeyhotel.com.br. This comfortable hotel markets itself to Japanese businessmen and is well known for its health club, which guests can use for free. Choose between standard rooms or larger, minimalist-style ones and either a continental or Japanese buffet breakfast. ❺

## Rua Augusta and around

This area offers old-fashioned five-star comfort, as well as some more affordable options, especially on Rua Augusta. The hotels here are convenient for the city centre, the international banks of Avenida Paulista and the fashionable Jardins. While the area is quite safe, walking along Rua Augusta late at night can be unpleasant, as you're likely to be accosted by men touting on behalf of sleazy nightclubs.

**Augusta Park** Rua Augusta 922 ⓣ11/3124-4400, ⓦwww.augustapark.com.br. The simple but reasonably equipped rooms all can sleep three people. There's a comfortable lounge and a small pool, and the staff are helpful with local information. ❸

**Maksoud Plaza** Alameda Campinas 150 ⓣ11/3145-8000, ⓦwww.maksoud.com.br.

For many years São Paulo's most distinguished hotel, the *Maksoud Plaza* and its luxurious rooms now seem somewhat mundane compared to the extravagance of new places like the *Unique* or *Renaissance*. Nonetheless, the staff are efficient and welcoming and there's a pool and several decent on-site restaurants. Hardly cheap, but a comparative bargain. ❺–❻

**Pergamon** Rua Frei Caneca 80 ⓣ11/3123-2021, ⓦwww.pergamon.com.br. A mid-range hotel that goes for a chic, contemporary look, with artfully placed lighting and black leather furniture. Ask for a room on one of the upper floors for a great view of downtown. ❺

**Pousada dos Franceses** Rua dos Franceses 100 ⓣ11/3262-4026, ⓦwww.pousadadosfranceses.com.br. This small youth hostel in a quiet location, just behind the *Maksoud Plaza* and a couple of blocks from both Bixiga and Av. Paulista, has been converted into a simple but very friendly *pousada*. Guests have use of the kitchen and laundry facilities, but be prepared to pay for any extras, including breakfast. Rooms – either with or without a bathroom – sleep between one and four guests. ❷

## Jardins

The south side of Avenida Paulista marks the beginnings of Jardins, a wealthy residential neighbourhood that houses some of the city's most fashionable (and expensive) shops and restaurants. It makes an excellent base as it's relatively safe by day and night, and with some excellent accommodation options.

**Caesar Business Paulista** Av. Paulista 2181 ⓣ11/2184-1600, ⓦwww.caesarbusiness.com.br. Comfortable, efficient, friendly and reasonably priced, this is an excellent business hotel situated in the heart of the Avenida Paulista's banking district, an easy stroll to excellent restaurants and moments from the *metrô* station. ❼

**Emiliano** Rua Oscar Freire 384 ⓣ11/3069-4369, ⓦwww.emiliano.com.br. With just 57 rooms, São Paulo's trendiest hotel is small compared to its other luxury spots, but the *Emiliano* prides itself on offering discreet, individual attention and lots of nice touches like free internet access, clothes pressing and even wine and massage. The light, airy rooms feature soft beds dressed in Italian linen, en-suite marble bathrooms, home cinema systems and hi-tech a/c. For an extra charge you can arrange to be transferred to and from Guarulhos airport by helicopter. ❾

**Fasano** Rua Vittório Fasano 88 ⓣ11/3896-4000, ⓦwww.fasano.com.br. A rival to the *Emiliano* for the accolade of being São Paulo's finest hotel. Decor of the lounge, bar, dining area and the 91 guest rooms could hardly be more stylish – modern (without being self-consciously hip), along with traditional accents. There's a fine rooftop pool with sweeping views across the city and on the ground floor is one of São Paulo's best Italian restaurants (see p.580). Service is impeccable – the staff all seem incredibly proud to be working here. Already expensive extras such as internet access mount up quickly, so be prepared for a final bill of eye-popping proportions. ❾

**Formule 1 São Paulo Paraíso** Rua Vergueiro 1571 ⓣ11/5085-5699, ⓦwww.accorhotels.com.br. This extremely simple, modern hotel offers a double bed (with a single bunk bed above), a shower and TV (but no telephone) in all the rather tiny rooms. A good location by the Paraíso *metrô* station and rates that are the same whether single, double or triple occupancy make this a very popular choice; reservations are always highly recommended. ❸

**Ibis Paulista** Av. Paulista 2355 ⓣ11/3523-3000, ⓦwww.ibishotel.com.br. A great location in the heart of the Avenida Paulista business district, a short walk to Bixiga's Italian restaurants and fine dining in Jardins. Well priced and very popular, this is typical Ibis property with compact guest rooms comfortably fitted with all the basics, including a shower, TV and wi-fi. ❹

**Pousada Dona Ziláh** Alameda Franca 1621 ⓣ11/3061-5413, ⓦwww.zilah.com. This pretty former home (now Jardins' only *pousada*) is one of the cheapest places to stay in the neighbourhood – although the rather small singles are still a bit overpriced. The atmosphere is friendly but unobtrusive, and there's always someone on hand to offer local advice. ❹

**Regent Park** Rua Oscar Freire 533 ⓣ11/3065-5555, ⓦwww.regent.com.br. A very good apartment-hotel with one of the neighbourhood's best addresses. Accommodation is mainly in one-bedroom units, but there are also a few two- and three-bedroom ones; all include a living room and a small but fully equipped kitchen. There's also a rooftop pool with panoramic views of the city. Rates are substantially lower for stays of a week or longer. ❻

**Renaissance** Alameda Santos 2233 ⓣ11/3069-2233, ⓦwww.marriottbrasil.com/saobr. Designed by renowned Brazilian architect Ruy Ohtake (see p.573), the burgundy-striped twin towers of *Renaissance* are not as daring as most of his other work. Part of the Marriott chain, the hotel boasts a high-tech business centre, a helipad, large, colourful and well-appointed guest rooms, a pool and a health club. 9

**Transamerica Flats International Plaza** Alameda Santos 981 ⓣ11/3146-5961, ⓦwww.transamericaflats.com.br. Self-catering one- or two-bedroom flats have kitchenettes and more space than the average hotel room. There are a dozen or so *Transamerica*s throughout the city, but this one is close to MASP and has a top-floor pool and bar with excellent views. 6

**Unique** Av. Brigadeiro Luía Antônio 4700 ⓣ11/3055-4700, ⓦwww.hotelunique.com.br. Nothing if not unique, São Paulo's most fashionable Ruy Ohtake–designed hotel looks rather like a cruise ship extraterrestrials experimented on. It's so hip there's no sign outside, nor any reception, and your cash gets you plenty of funky perks, such as a red-lit swimming pool (where you can hear the DJ's tunes perfectly underwater) and sliding hatches in rooms that allow you to watch a plasma TV from your digitally-controlled hydro-bath. The rooftop bar is open to non-guests if you want to see what all the fuss is about. 9

## Itaim Bibi and Pinheiros

The stretch along Avenida Brigadeiro Faria Lima that links Itaim Bibi with Pinheiros is a rapidly expanding business district. While the number of hotels here is increasing, they're mostly bland (but well-equipped) franchises of international chains. At night these areas offer plenty of street life, thanks to the many excellent restaurants and clubs, and walking around feels quite secure. They are also within easy reach of the bars and clubs of Vila Madalena.

**Hotel de la Rose** Praça dos Omáguas 106, Pinheiros ⓣ11/3812-9097, ⓦwww.hoteldelarose.com.br. This charming and unpretentious rose-coloured hotel offers small and simple rooms, all with private bathrooms and a/c. 3

**Radisson Faria Lima** Av. Cidade Jardim 625, Itaim Bibi ⓣ11/2133-5960, ⓦwww.radisson.com/saopaulobr.br. The most luxurious hotel in the area, located in the heart of the Faria Lima business district. The standard rooms are well-equipped and have large TVs, but on the Royal Floor you can also enjoy DVDs and breakfast in bed. In addition, the *Radisson* offers a business centre and meeting rooms, plus a sauna, fitness centre and attractive pool. 8

**Tryp Iguatemi** Rua Iguatemi 150, Itaim Bibi ⓣ11/3065-2450, ⓦwww.solmelia.com. Although a typically characterless example of the Meliá chain – which is all over São Paulo – this hotel has comfortable rooms, a fine buffet breakfast, a small rooftop pool and pleasant staff who provide helpful and efficient service. 5

# The City

For visitors and locals alike, the fact that São Paulo's history extends back over four centuries, well beyond the late nineteenth-century coffee boom, usually goes completely unnoticed. Catapulted virtually overnight from being a sleepy, provincial market-town into one of the western hemisphere's great cities, there are few places in the world that have as comprehensively turned their backs on the past as São Paulo has done. In the nineteenth century, most of colonial São Paulo was levelled and replaced by a disorganized patchwork of wide avenues and large buildings, the process repeating itself ever since; today, not only has the city's colonial architectural heritage all but vanished, there's little physical evidence of the coffee-boom decades either.

Nevertheless, a few relics have, somehow, escaped demolition and offer hints of São Paulo's bygone eras. What remains is hidden away discreetly in corners scattered throughout the city, often difficult to find but all the more thrilling when you do. There is no shortage of **museums**, some of which offer excellent insights into São Paulo's history and culture.

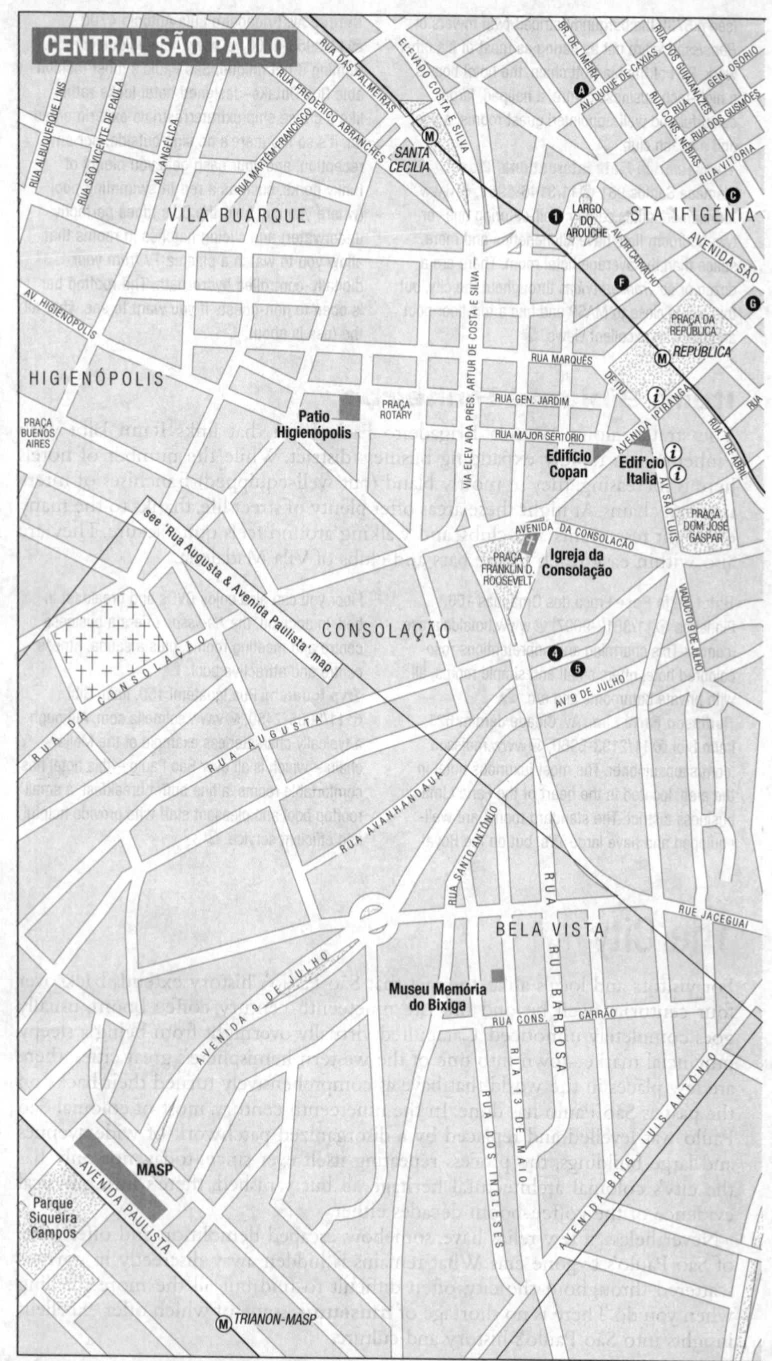
CENTRAL SÃO PAULO
RUA DAS PALMEIRAS
RUA FREDERICO ABRANCHES
ELEVADO COSTA E SILVA
BR. DE LIMEIRA
AV. DUQUE DE CAXIAS
RUA DOS GUAIANAZES
RUA GEN. OSORIO
RUA CONS. NÉBIAS
RUA DOS GUSMÕES
RUA VITORIA
RUA ALBUQUERQUE LINS
RUA SÃO VICENTE DE PAULA
AV. ANGÉLICA
RUA MARTÉM FRANCISCO
SANTA CECILIA
VILA BUARQUE
LARGO DO AROUCHE
STA IFIGÉNIA
AV. DR CARVALHO
AVENIDA SÃO
AV. HIGIENÓPOLIS
VIA ELEV ADA PRES. ARTUR DE COSTA E SILVA
PRAÇA DA REPÚBLICA
REPÚBLICA
RUA MARQUÊS DE ITU
HIGIENÓPOLIS
RUA GEN. JARDIM
IPIRANGA
RUA 7 DE ABRIL
PRAÇA BUENOS AIRES
Patio Higienópolis
PRAÇA ROTARY
RUA MAJOR SERTÓRIO
AVENIDA
Edifício Copan
Edif'cio Italia
AV SÃO LUIS
see 'Rua Augusta & Avenida Paulista' map
AVENIDA DA CONSOLAÇÃO
PRAÇA DOM JOSÉ GASPAR
PRAÇA FRANKLIN D. ROOSEVELT
Igreja da Consolação
VIADUCTO 9 DE JULHO
CONSOLAÇÃO
AV 9 DE JULHO
RUA DA CONSOLAÇÃO
RUA AUGUSTA
RUA AVANHANDAUA
RUA SANTO ANTÔNIO
RUA RUI BARBOSA
RUE JACEGUAI
BELA VISTA
AVENIDA 9 DE JULHO
Museu Memória do Bixiga
RUA CONS. CARRÃO
RUA 13 DE MAIO
RUA DOS INGLESES
AVENIDA BRIG. LUIS ANTÔNIO
MASP
AVENIDA PAULISTA
Parque Siqueira Campos
TRIANON-MASP

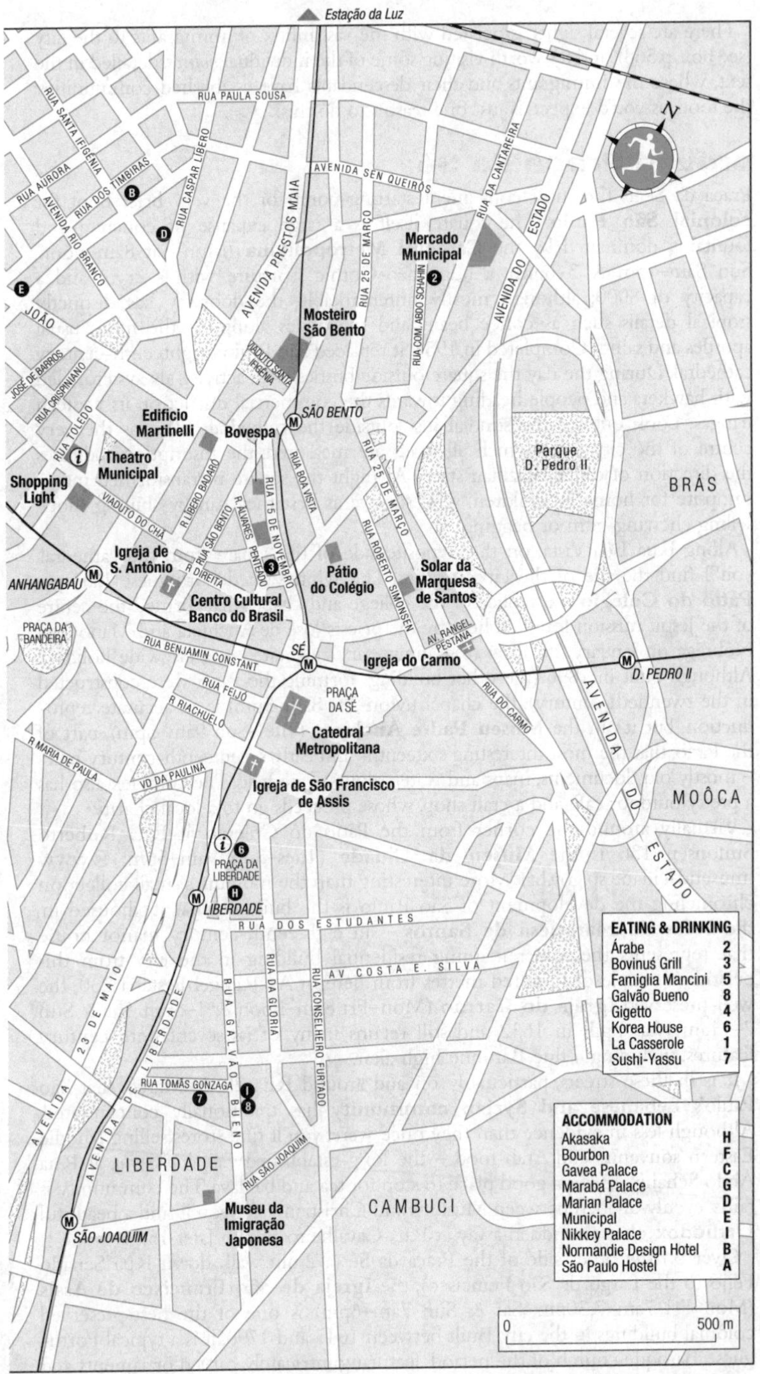
Estação da Luz
RUA PAULA SOUSA
RUA SANTA IFIGÊNIA
RUA AURORA
RUA DOS TIMBIRAS
AVENIDA RIO BRANCO
RUA CASPAR LIBERO
AVENIDA SEN QUEIRÓS
AVENIDA PRESTOS MAIA
RUA 25 DE MARÇO
RUA DA CANTAREIRA
AVENIDA DO ESTADO
Mercado Municipal
RUA COM. ABDO SCHAHIN
JOÃO
Mosteiro São Bento
VIADUTO SANTA IFIGÊNIA
JOSÉ DE BARROS
RUA CRISPINIANO
RUA TOLEDO
SÃO BENTO
Edifício Martinelli
Bovespa
Theatro Municipal
Shopping Light
RUA BOA VISTA
RUA 25 DE MARÇO
Parque D. Pedro II
BRÁS
VIADUTO DO CHÁ
R. LIBERO BADARÓ
RUA SÃO BENTO
R. ÁLVARES PENTEADO
RUA 15 DE NOVEMBRO
RUA ROBERTO SIMONSEN
Igreja de S. Antônio
R. DIREITA
Pátio do Colégio
Solar da Marquesa de Santos
ANHANGABAÚ
Centro Cultural Banco do Brasil
PRAÇA DA BANDEIRA
RUA BENJAMIN CONSTANT
AV. RANGEL PESTANA
SÉ
Igreja do Carmo
D. PEDRO II
RUA FEIJÓ
PRAÇA DA SÉ
R. RIACHUELO
RUA DO CARMO
Catedral Metropolitana
R. MARIA DE PAULA
VD. DA PAULINA
Igreja de São Francisco de Assis
MOÔCA
AVENIDA DO ESTADO
PRAÇA DA LIBERDADE
LIBERDADE
RUA DOS ESTUDANTES
AV. COSTA E. SILVA
RUA DA GLÓRIA
RUA CONSELHEIRO FURTADO
RUA GALVÃO BUENO
AVENIDA 23 DE MAIO
AVENIDA DA LIBERDADE
RUA TOMÁS GONZAGA
RUA SÃO JOAQUIM
LIBERDADE
Museu da Imigração Japonesa
CAMBUCI
SÃO JOAQUIM
EATING & DRINKING
Árabe 2
Bovinuś Grill 3
Famiglia Mancini 5
Galvão Bueno 8
Gigetto 4
Korea House 6
La Casserole 1
Sushi-Yassu 7
ACCOMMODATION
Akasaka H
Bourbon F
Gavea Palace C
Marabá Palace G
Marian Palace D
Municipal E
Nikkey Palace I
Normandie Design Hotel B
São Paulo Hostel A
0
500 m
N

There are several sights associated with the vast influx of immigrants to the city (see box, p.568), and it's worth visiting some of the individual *bairros*, detailed in the text, where the immigrants and their descendants have established communities; the food, as you'd expect, is just one reason to do this.

## Around Praça da Sé

Praça da Sé is the most convenient starting-point for the very brief hunt for **colonial São Paulo**. The square itself is a large expanse of concrete and fountains, dominated by the **Catedral Metropolitana** (Mon–Sat 8am–noon, Sun 8am–1pm & 3–6pm), a huge neo-Gothic structure with a crypt and a capacity of 8000; although mostly unremarkable, the doorway has distinctly tropical details such as coffee beans and crocodiles alongside the more usual apostles and saints. Completed in 1954, it replaced São Paulo's eighteenth-century cathedral. During the day the square outside bustles with activity, always crowded with hawkers and people heading towards the commercial district on its western fringes. Look out for the sundial just outside the cathedral, taken as the very centre of the city from which all roads are measured; the inscription indicates the direction of other Brazilian states. At night the square is transformed into a campsite for homeless children, who survive as best they can by shining shoes, selling chewing-gum or begging.

Along Rua Boa Vista, on the opposite side of the square from the cathedral, you'll find the site of the city's origins. The whitewashed Portuguese Baroque **Pátio do Colégio** is a replica of the college and chapel that formed the centre of the Jesuit mission founded here by the priests José de Anchieta and Manoel da Nóbrega on January 25, 1554 (the anniversary celebrated as a citywide holiday). Although built in 1896 (the other buildings forming the Pátio were constructed in the twentieth century), the chapel (Mon–Fri 8am–5pm) is an accurate reproduction, but it's in the **Museu Padre Anchieta** (Tues–Sun 9am–5pm), part of the Pátio, that the most interesting sixteenth- and early seventeenth-century relics – mostly old documents, maps and watercolours – are held. The complex also has a pretty outdoor café and a craft shop, whose proceeds go to a local charity.

Virtually around the corner from the Pátio do Colégio at Rua Roberto Simonsen 136 is the **Museu da Cidade** (Tues–Sun 9am–5pm; Ⓦwww.museudacidade.sp.gov.br). More interesting than the museum's small collection chronicling the development of São Paulo is the building that it's housed in, the **Solar da Marquesa de Santos** – an eighteenth-century manor house that represents the sole remaining residential building in the city from this period. A couple of hundred metres from here, at Av. Rangel Pestana 230, the well-preserved **Igreja do Carmo** (Mon–Fri 8am–noon & 1–5pm, Sat & Sun 7–11am) was built in 1632 and still retains many of its seventeenth-century features, including a fine Baroque high altar.

It is in these streets, particularly on and around Rua 25 de Março, that São Paulo's **Lebanese and Syrian community** has traditionally concentrated. Although less in evidence than they once were, you'll find stores selling Middle Eastern souvenirs and Arab food – the long-established *Empório Syrio*, at Rua Abdo Schahin 136, is a good place to stop for tea and baklava. The community is fairly evenly divided between Muslims and Christians, and you'll find a beautiful **Orthodox church** hidden away at Rua Cavalheiro Basilio Jafet 15.

Over on the other side of the Praça da Sé (a 2min walk down Rua Senado Feijó to the Largo de São Francisco), the **Igreja de São Francisco de Assis** (Mon–Fri 7am–7.30pm, Sat & Sun 7am–6pm) is one of the best-preserved colonial buildings in the city. Built between 1647 and 1790, it is a typical Portuguese Baroque church of the period, featuring intricately carved ornaments and an elaborate high altar. While here, step inside the adjoining courtyard of the Faculdade de Direito de São Paulo – the country's best and most exclusive law school, and one of its first higher-education institutions, founded in 1824 – and take a look at the huge 1930s stained-glass window depicting the Largo de São Francisco in the early nineteenth century. Before leaving this area, it's worth visiting the **Igreja de Santo Antônio**, at Praça do Patriarca, by the Viaduto do Chá (a pedestrian bridge linking the two parts of the commercial centre). Built in 1717, its yellow-and-white facade has been beautifully restored; the interior, meanwhile, has been stripped of most of its eighteenth-century accoutrements, though its simple, painted, wooden ceiling deserves a glance.

## North of Praça da Sé

The coffee boom that led to the dismantling of São Paulo's colonial buildings provided little in terms of lasting replacements. In the city's first industrial suburbs, towering brick chimneys are still to be seen, but generally the areas are now dominated by small workshops and low-income housing, and even in the city centre there are very few buildings of note, most of the area being given over to unremarkable shops and offices.

### The Triângulo

The **Triângulo**, the traditional banking district and a zone of concentrated vertical growth, lies northwest of the Praça da Sé. The city's first skyscraper, the 35-storey **Edifício Martinelli**, stands at the northern edge of the district, at Av. São João 35; it was inaugurated in 1929 and remains an important downtown landmark. Two blocks east, at Rua João Brícola 24, the similar-sized **Edifício Altino Arantes**, opened in 1947 and modelled on the Empire State Building, is home to the Banespa bank (and is often referred to as the Banespa building). You can take the elevators up to a lookout tower at the top (Mon–Fri 10am–5pm) for great views of São Paulo's intense cityscape – there's no charge, but take your passport as ID.

▲ View of São Paulo from the Banespa building

São Paulo's stock exchange, the **BOVESPA** building, is just around the corner, at Rua 15 de Novembro 275 (Ⓦwww.bovespa.com.br); next to New York's, it's the most active stock-exchange in the Americas. A tour can easily be arranged if you have official links to a foreign or Brazilian investment institution and it is open to the public one day a month (see website for details), but most of the activity happens behind computer screens these days.

The arts are hardly a driving force within the Triângulo, but a distinctive Beaux Arts–style former bank building at Rua Álvares Penteado 112 has been developed as the **Centro Cultural Banco do Brasil** (Tues–Sun 10am–9pm; Ⓦwww.bb.com.br/cultura) and is a refreshing contrast to the surrounding mammon. The temporary exhibitions on display, which are taken from the bank's own important collections of Brazilian art or those of prominent private collectors, are always worth at least a brief look. Inside, the café is a convenient place for lunch.

## São Bento

Incongruously situated just a block away from the high-rise financial district, the **Mosteiro São Bento** (Mon–Wed & Fri 6am–6.30pm, Thurs 11.30am–6.30pm, Sat & Sun 6am–noon & 4–6pm; Ⓦwww.mosteiro.org.br), on the Largo de São Bento, provides a different kind of uplifting experience. The monastery's church originally dates from 1598, but has been given a facelift five times (the last one performed in 1912). The interior is more impressive than you might expect, given the rather severe exterior; look out for fine detail such as zodiac symbols above the archway, just inside the entrance. The rest of the complex is closed to the public, however, as it still provides living quarters for Benedictine monks, who emerge in the mornings to sing Gregorian chants in the church (Mon–Fri 7am, Sat 6am, Sun 10am); Sunday's chants are, unsurprisingly, by far the best attended.

Leading off west from São Bento, the Viaduto Santa Ifigênia gives good views of the area looking south, including the new city hall with its rooftop garden. The attractive green area immediately below, the **Vale do Anhangabaú** (or Demon's Valley), stretches between this viaduct and the Viaduto do Chá.

## Mercado Municipal

About 1km to the northeast of São Bento, at Rua da Cantareira 306, you'll find the **Mercado Municipal**, an imposing, vaguely German neo-Gothic hall, completed in 1933. Apart from the phenomenal display of Brazilian and imported fruit, vegetables, cheese and other produce, the market (Mon–Sat 7am–6pm, Sun 7am–4pm; Ⓦwww.mercadomunicipal.com.br) is most noted for its enormous stained-glass windows depicting scenes of cattle raising, market gardening and coffee and banana plantations. Traditionally, Brazilians eat *pastel de bacalhau* – a salt fish and potato pie – here. If that doesn't sound very appetizing, then head up to the mezzanine, where a range of patio **restaurants** make up a food court that is considerably more colourful and authentic than the kind you find in shopping malls.

## Memorial do Imigrante

East of the Mercado Municipal, the run-down neighbourhood of Brás would have little to offer if it wasn't for the superb **Memorial do Imigrante** at Rua Visconde de Paraíba 1316 (Tues–Sun 10am–5pm; Ⓦwww.memorialdoimigrante.sp.gov.br; R$4). The hostel buildings house an immigration research centre, a basic café and one of the best museums in São Paulo.

The museum has a permanent collection of period furniture, documents and photographs, and regularly mounts temporary exhibits relating to individual immigrant nationalities. The main building itself is the most interesting feature of the complex, however, with vast dormitories and its own rail siding and platform that were used for unloading immigrants and their baggage. Near the entrance, a separate building contained the rooms where new arrivals met their prospective employers; the government provided interpreters to help the immigrants make sense of work contracts. Designed to hold four thousand people, the hostel housed as many as ten thousand at times, with immigrants being treated little better than cattle. In its early years, the place was a virtual prison. The exit ticket was securing a contract of employment and control of potential plantation-workers was considered necessary, since few people actually wanted to work in the fields and there was a large labour leakage to the city of São Paulo itself. The last immigrants were processed here in 1978.

Although the museum is only a five-minute walk from Brás *metrô* station, it is next door to a hostel for homeless men and you may feel uncomfortable walking in the area. As taxis are rarely available outside the *metrô* station, try to reassure yourself any dangers are more imagined than real. On weekends and holidays you have more interesting transport options: either a wonderful nineteenth-century train that connects the complex with Brás and Moóca stations or a tram that runs between the front entrance and Bresser *metrô* station (both R$5).

### Luz

Further north, the once affluent and still leafy *bairro* of Luz is home to São Paulo's two main train stations and, for many years, has been one of the city's seediest red-light districts. Recently, though, Luz has slowly been undergoing a renaissance, with city and state government investment aimed at transforming the area into a top-rank cultural centre.

Ascending from Luz *metrô*, you'll immediately notice the imposing **Estação da Luz**. The station was part of the British-owned rail network that contributed to São Paulo's explosive growth in the late nineteenth century. The station was built in 1901, and everything was imported from Britain for its construction – from the design of the project to the smallest of screws. Although fire destroyed the refined decoration of its chambers in 1946, interior details (iron balconies, passageways and grilles) bear witness to the majestic structure's original elegance. Until the 1940s there was a sizable British community in the area; some of the engineers and their families were housed in the **Vila Inglesa** at Rua Mauá 836, a group of 28 distinctively English-style houses built in 1924 which have long since been used as shops, offices and restaurants.

The upper floors of the **Estação da Luz** have been transformed to house the **Museu da Língua Portugesa** (Tues–Sun 10am–5pm; R$4; ⓦwww.museulinguaportuguesa.org.br), a celebration of the Portuguese language. Opened in 2006 the museum, through the display of written texts, spoken word, song and images, charts the development of the Portuguese language and explores its global variations. There are also temporary exhibitions examining individual writers such as Brazil's Machado de Assis and Clarice Lispector, and Portugal's Fernando Pessoa.

Located directly across Rua Mauá from the Estação da Luz is **Parque da Luz** (Tues–Sun 9am–6pm). Dating back to 1800, the park was São Paulo's first public garden and its intricate wrought-iron fencing, Victorian bandstands, ponds and rich foliage attest to its prominent past. Until recently, the park was considered off limits, but security is now excellent and, as one of the few centrally located patches of greenery in the city, it is popular with local residents and visitors to the surrounding cultural centres. The space includes large display panels (in English and Portuguese) on the history of the Luz district and has been developed as a sculpture park.

Adjoining the park, at Av. Tiradentes 141, is the **Pinacoteca do Estado** (Tues–Sun 10am–6pm; R$4, includes entrance to the Memorial da Resistência, see below; Ⓦwww.pinacoteca.org.br), the gallery of São Paulo state. Housed in an imposing Neoclassical building constructed in 1905 and thoroughly renovated in 1998, this is one of the finest galleries in Brazil, with an excellent permanent collection of Brazilian paintings. Pride of place in the nineteenth-century galleries goes to images of rural São Paulo by Almeida Júnior, but the work of other Brazilian landscape, portrait and historical artists of the period is also well represented. The twentieth-century galleries include Cubist-influenced engravings; important paintings by the European expressionist turned Brazilian modernist Lasar Segall (see also p.574); and works by other painters, including Emiliano di Cavalcanti, noted for his choice of Afro-Brazilian and urban themes, Cândido Portinari, whose work contained clear social and historical references, and the vibrant paintings of Tarsilla do Amaral. There is also a very pleasant café with a terrace opening onto the Parque da Luz.

One of the city's few surviving colonial churches, the **Igreja do Convento da Luz** (daily 6.30–11am & 2–5pm), is a short walk north of the Pinacoteca, by the Tiradentes *metrô* station at Av. Tiradentes 676. This rambling structure of uncharacteristic grandeur was built on the site of a sixteenth-century chapel; the former Franciscan monastery and church date back to 1774, but they've been much altered over the years. Today the site houses the **Museu de Arte Sacra** (Tues–Sun 11am–7pm), whose fine collection includes Brazilian seventeenth- and eighteenth-century wooden and terracotta religious art and liturgical pieces.

From the Parque da Luz, back along Rua Mauá, at Largo General Osório 66, there are signs of further changes to the area. The infamous Edifício DOPS, a large, anonymous-looking building that was once the headquarters of the Departamento de Ordem Política e Social, and one of the two main torture centres in São Paulo during the 1960s–1980s military dictatorships, has opened as the **Memorial da Resistência** (Tues–Sun 10am–6pm; R$4). The site serves as an exhibition centre, which commemorates its ugly past with displays charting Brazil's history of repression, from the rise of Getúlio Vargas in the 1930s to the more recent struggle for democracy. Temporary art exhibitions administered by the Pinacoteca do Estado (see above) are also held here.

Continue along the Rua Mauá, where, at the intersection of Rua Duque de Caxias, you'll find the **Estação Júlio Prestes**, built between 1926 and 1937 and drawing on late nineteenth-century French and Italian architectural forms. The building's most beautiful features are its large stained-glass windows, which depict the role of the railway in the expansion of the Brazilian economy in the early twentieth century. Although part of the building still serves as a train station for suburban lines, its Great Hall was transformed in the late 1990s into the Sala São Paulo, home of the Orquestra Sinfônica do Estado de São Paulo (Ⓦwww.osesp.art.br), and centrepiece of the **Complexo Cultural Júlio Prestes** (Ⓣ11/3337-5414). Guided tours are offered Monday to Friday at 12.30pm and 4.30pm.

Immediately to the north of here is the adjoining *bairro* of **Bom Retiro**, known for its shops selling cheap clothes and fabric. In the early 1900s the neighbourhood was predominantly Italian, with successive waves of Jewish, Greek, Korean and Bolivian immigrants becoming the most prominent ethnic groups as the century progressed. The main reason for visiting would be to sample the food; there remains a fine Jewish deli (see p.581), a Greek café (see p.582) and a rapidly growing number of Korean restaurants (see p.577).

## Around Praça da República

Praça da República is now largely an area of office buildings, hotels and shops, but it was once the site of the lavish **mansions** of the coffee-plantation owners who began to take up residence in the city from about 1870. However, no sooner had the mansions been built – constructed from British iron, Italian marble, Latvian pine, Portuguese tiles and Belgian stained glass – they were abandoned; the city centre took on the brash and commercial character of its present-day form. The Praça da República itself – once home to a bullring – has a green area with a small lake where turtles sunbathe and rows of fortune tellers throw shells and cards to part the gullible from their *reís*.

Two blocks to the east, in the direction of Praça da Sé, the **Theatro Municipal** (ⓣ11/3397-0327) is São Paulo's most distinguished public building, an eclectic mixture of Art Nouveau and Italian Renaissance styles. Work began on it in 1903, when the coffee boom was at its peak and São Paulo at its most confident. The theatre is still the city's main venue for classical music, and the auditorium, lavishly decorated and furnished with Italian marble, velvet, gold leaf and mirrors, can be viewed by attending a performance, or by contacting the theatre to arrange a free guided tour (Tues–Thurs). Outside, just down the steps leading into the Vale do Anhangabaú (see p.564), a dramatic sculpture fountain represents the characters from Carlos Gomes' opera *O Guarani*, based on the book by José de Alencar. (The opera, a story set among the Guaraní, premiered at La Scala in 1870 and was one of the first works by a New World composer to achieve success in Europe.)

On Avenida São Luís, the street leading south from the Praça da República, is the 46-storey **Edifício Itália**, built in 1965 to dwarf the Edifício Martinelli, and for many years Latin America's tallest building. On cloud- and smog-free days, the *Terraço Itália* restaurant on the 41st and 42nd floors is a good vantage point from which to view the city; unfortunately, you will either have to pay R$15 for the privilege, or else buy an expensive and poor-quality meal. In the 1940s and 1950s, **Avenida São Luís** was São Paulo's version of New York's Fifth Avenue, lined with high-class apartment buildings and offices, and, though no longer fashionable, it still retains a certain degree of elegance. Admirers of the Brazilian architect Oscar Niemeyer will immediately recognize the serpentine curves of the 1950 **Edifício Copan** (ⓦwww.copansp.com.br), on Avenida Ipiranga, just to the west of Avenida São Luís, by far the largest of the apartment and office buildings on the avenue. It's regarded as something of a social experiment in this otherwise sharply divided city, with its residents paying a wide variety of prices for the 1160 apartments that range in size from 26 to 350 square metres.

## Bela Vista and Liberdade

Since the early twentieth century, the *bairro* of **Bela Vista**, lying just southwest of downtown, has been known as "Little Italy" (it's also commonly called Bixiga). Calabrian stonemasons built their own modest houses here with leftover materials from the building sites where they worked, and the neighborhood's narrow streets are still lined with these homes today. In an otherwise ordinary house at Rua dos Ingleses 118, the **Museu Memória do Bixiga** (Wed–Sun 2–5pm) enthusiastically documents the history of the *bairro*, and has a small collection of photographs and household items. Italian **restaurants** exist throughout the city, but the greatest concentration (if not the greatest quality) can be found in Bixiga. This normally quiet neighbourhood springs to life in the evening when people throng to the central Rua 13 de Maio, and the streets

## Immigration and São Paulo

São Paulo is a city built on **immigrants**; largely due to new arrivals, São Paulo's population grew a hundred-fold in 75 years to make it the country's second-largest city by 1950. Besides sheer numbers, the mass influx of people had a tremendous impact on the character of the city, breaking up the existing social stratification and removing economic and political power from the traditional elite groups at a much earlier stage than in other Brazilian cities.

Although there had been attempts at introducing Prussian share-croppers in the 1840s, mass immigration didn't begin until the late 1870s. Initially, conditions were appalling upon arrival; many immigrants succumbed to malaria or yellow fever while waiting in Santos to be transferred inland, where they were to work on the coffee plantations. In response to criticisms, the government opened the Hospedaria dos Imigrantes in 1887, a hostel in the eastern suburb of Brás, now converted to a museum (see p.564).

Immigration to São Paulo is most closely associated with the **Italians**, who constituted 46 percent of all arrivals between 1887 and 1930. In general, soon after arriving in Brazil they would be transported to a plantation, but most slipped away within a year to seek employment in the city or to continue on south to Argentina. The rapidly expanding factories in the districts of Brás, Moóca and Belém, east of the city centre, were desperately short of labour, and well into the twentieth century the population of these *bairros* was largely Italian. But it is **Bela Vista** (or, in popular parlance, Bixiga ) where the Italian influence has been most enduring, as catalogued in the **Museu Memória do Bixiga** (see p.567). Originally home to freed slaves, Bela Vista had by the early 1900s established itself as São Paulo's "Little Italy". As immigration from Italy began to slow in the late 1890s, arrivals from other countries increased. From 1901 to 1930 **Spaniards** (especially Galicians) made up 22 percent, and **Portuguese** 23 percent, of immigrants, but their language allowed them to assimilate very quickly. Only Tatuapé developed into a largely Portuguese *bairro*.

The first 830 **Japanese** immigrants arrived in 1908 in Santos, from where they were sent on to the coffee plantations. By the mid-1950s a quarter of a million Japanese had emigrated to Brazil, most of them settling in São Paulo state. Unlike other nationalities, the rate of return migration among them has always been small: many chose to remain in agriculture, often as market gardeners, at the end of their contract. The city's large Japanese community is centred on **Liberdade**, a *bairro* just south of the Praça da Sé and home to the excellent **Museu da Imigração Japonesa** (see opposite).

São Paulo's **Arab** community is also substantial. Arabs started arriving in the early twentieth century from Syria and Lebanon and, because they originally travelled on Turkish passports, are still commonly referred to as *turcos*. Typically starting out as itinerant traders, the community was soon associated with small shops, and many Arabs become extremely successful in business. Numerous boutiques in the city's wealthy *bairros* are Arab-owned, but it's in the streets around **Rua 25 de Março**, north of Praça da Sé, that the community is concentrated (see p.562).

The **Jewish** community has prospered in São Paulo, too. Mainly of East European origin, many of the city's Jews started out as roaming pedlars before settling in **Bom Retiro**, a *bairro* near Luz train station. As they became richer, they moved to the suburbs to the south of the city, in particular to Higienópolis, but some of the businesses in the streets around Rua Correia de Melo are still Jewish-owned and there's a synagogue in the area. As the Jews moved out, **Greeks** started moving in during the 1960s, followed in larger numbers by **Koreans**. The area has long been known as a centre of the rag trade and in the Korean-owned sweatshops the latest immigrant arrivals – **Bolivians** and **Chinese** – are employed, often illegally and amid appalling work conditions.

running off it, which are lined with *cantinas*, pizzerias, bars and small theatres. During the day on Sunday there's a lively flea market, Antiguidades e Artesanato do Bixiga, at Praça Dom Orione (see p.588).

Just east of Bixiga, the *bairro* of **Liberdade** is the traditional home of the city's large Japanese community, though in recent years a number of Vietnamese, Chinese and especially Koreans have settled here. Rua Galvão Bueno and intersecting streets are devoted mostly to Japanese and other East Asian restaurants as well as shops selling semiprecious stones, Japanese food and clothes. The **Museu da Imigração Japonesa**, Rua São Joaquim 381 (7th, 8th & 9th floors; Tues–Sun 1.30–5.30pm), has a Japanese-style rooftop garden and excellent displays honouring the Japanese community in Brazil, from their arrival in 1908 to work on the coffee plantations to their transition to farming and their varied contributions to modern Brazil. On the same road, alongside drab-looking office and apartment buildings is the instantly recognizable **Templo Busshinji** at no. 285 (daily 9am–7pm), a Japanese Buddhist temple built in 1995; visitors are welcome to look around the wooden building and attend ceremonies.



## Higienópolis and Pacaembu

When, at the end of the nineteenth century, the coffee barons vacated downtown São Paulo, they moved a short distance to the west to new homes in a hilly part of the city named **Higienópolis**, so called because it was supposedly more hygienic than the spit 'n' sawdust Praça da República. While the city centre's mansions have long gone, a few still remain in Higienópolis. Completed in 1902, the Art Nouveau–influenced **Vila Penteado**, at Rua Maranhão 88 (at the intersection of Rua Sabará), is one of the finest examples and was one of the last to be built in the area; the building now forms part of the University of São Paulo's architecture faculty and visitors can enter the impressive marble-lined lobby. No sooner had the coffee barons established themselves here, they abandoned the area, replaced by families who had become rich from the business boom of the twentieth century. Higienópolis remains very wealthy, with attractive tree-lined roads, pleasant parks and large houses and luxury apartment buildings, so very different from the chaos of the city centre just a few blocks away. A large proportion of today's residents are Jewish, and there are several synagogues and Jewish community schools in the neighbourhood, as well as one of São Paulo's most innovative restaurants (see p.581).

Higienópolis merges to the west into **Pacaembu**, best known for the **Estádio do Pacaembu**, the city-owned stadium where Corinthians football team (Ⓦwww.corinthians.com.br) plays its home matches (see also p.589). Located at Praça Charles Miller (named after the Anglo-Brazilian credited with introducing to Brazil the modern game of football), Lúcio Costa (best known for his work on Brasília) designed the stadium, which was inaugurated in 1940 with a maximum capacity of 60,000 people – though 72,000 have been squeezed in. With subsequent modernization, including the introduction of seating, the stadium today can manage a crowd of 38,000.

Unless attending a match (generally held on Wed & Sat ), the best way to see the stadium is to visit the **Museu do Futebol** (Tues–Sat 10am–6pm, last entrance 5pm, closed match days; R$6; Ⓦwww.museudofutebol.org.br). Opened in 2008, this is certainly one of São Paulo's best museums and, surprisingly, the only one in the country devoted to the national sport. Although the museum is lodged in the same building that hosts Corinthians, it is careful to be completely neutral when it comes to attention paid to particular teams. While it helps to arrive with at least a mild interest in football, the museum is not merely there to pay simple homage to the sport – although there are plenty of relics, including a football kicked by **Pelé** as a child, on display. Instead, the focus of the museum is the history of twentieth-century Brazil, using football as a vehicle to explore this. Displays ranging from traditional **memorabilia** to high-tech **interactive exhibits** examine issues including the changing face of race in Brazilian football, how dictators co-opted the sport and how football affected a diverse range of writers and artists, including Cândido Portinari, Heitor Villa-Lobos and Jorge Amado. There's a great entertainment area where visitors can test their skills against a (virtual) star goalkeeper, and an excellent shop selling a range of football-related souvenirs.

## Along Avenida Paulista

By 1900, the coffee barons had moved on from Higienópolis to flaunt their wealth through new mansions set in spacious gardens stretching along the three-kilometre-long **Avenida Paulista** – then a tree-lined avenue set along a ridge 3km southwest of the city centre. (Look out for old photos – sold as postcards – showing the startlingly different avenue a century ago.) In the late 1960s, and throughout the 1970s, Avenida Paulista resembled a giant construction site, with banks and other companies competing to erect ever-taller buildings. There was little time for creativity, and along the entire length of the avenue it would be difficult to single out more than one example of decent modern architecture. There are, however, a handful of Art Nouveau and Art Deco mansions along Avenida Paulista, afforded official protection from the developers' bulldozers. Some lie empty, the subjects of legal wrangles over inheritance rights, others act as prestigious headquarters for banks.

One mansion well worth visiting is the French-style **Casa das Rosas**, Av. Paulista 37 (Tues–Sun 10am–6pm; Ⓦwww.casadasrosas.sp.gov.br), near Brigadeiro *mêtro* station at the easterly end of the *avenida*. Constructed in 1935 as a private residence, the building is set in a rose garden and has a beautiful Art Nouveau stained-glass window, making for a stunning contrast with the mirrored-glass-and-steel office building behind it. The state of São Paulo owns the Casa das Rosas, which is now a cultural centre where poetry-related exhibitions are often held. A block from here at Av. Paulista 149, the **Instituto Itaú Cultural** (Tues–Fri 10am–9pm, Sat & Sun 10am–7pm; Ⓦwww.itaucultural.org.br) features temporary exhibitions of contemporary Brazilian art.

### Museu de Arte de São Paulo (MASP)

One of the few interesting modern buildings along Avenida Paulista is the **Museu de Arte de São Paulo** at no. 1578 (Tues–Sun 11am–6pm, Thurs 11am–8pm; R$15, free Tues; Ⓦwww.masp.art.br). Designed in 1957 by the Italian-born, naturalized-Brazilian architect Lina Bo Bardi and opened in 1968, the monumental concrete structure appears to float above the ground, supported only by remarkably delicate pillars. MASP is the pride of São Paulo's art lovers, and is considered to have the most important collection of Western art in Latin America, featuring the work of great European artists from the last five hundred years on its top floor. For most North American and European visitors, notable though some of the individual works of Bosch, Rembrandt and Degas may be, the highlights of the collection are often the seventeenth- to nineteenth-century landscapes of Brazil by European artists – none more important than the small but detailed paintings by Frans Post, a painter of the Dutch Baroque school whose rich Brazil-inspired works were used as tapestry designs by the French Gobelins factory, some of which are also displayed in the museum. The museum's very reasonably priced lunchtime restaurant makes for an excellent escape from the crowds, exhaust fumes and heat of Avenida Paulista outside.

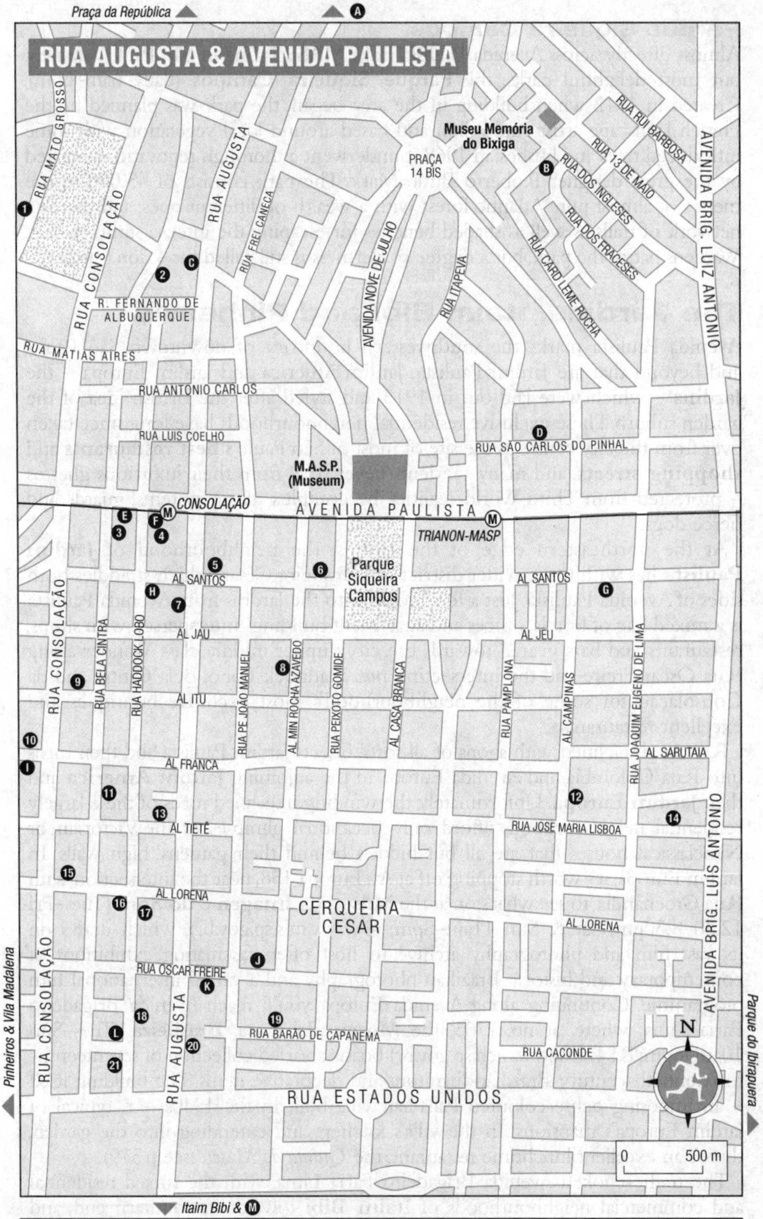

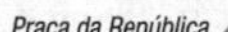


# RUA AUGUSTA & AVENIDA PAULISTA



| ACCOMMODATION | | | | EATING & DRINKING | | | | | |
|---|---|---|---|---|---|---|---|---|---|
| | | | | | | | | Le Vin Bistro | 13 |
| Augusta Park | C | Pousada Dona Ziláh | I | AK Delicatessen | 1 | East | 8 | Massimo | 6 |
| Caesar Business Paulista | F | Pousada dos Franceses | B | Antiquarius | 15 | Emporio Siriuba | 10 | Pasta e Vino | 19 |
| Emiliano | J | Regent Park | K | Arábia | 17 | Esplanada Grill | 21 | Sativa | 9 |
| Fasano | L | Renaissance | H | Asia House | 7 | Fasano | L | Subito | 4 |
| Ibis Paulista | E | Transamerica Flats | | D.O.M. | 20 | Folha de Uva | 3 | Templo da Bahia | 12 |
| Maksoud Plaza | D | Internaional Plaza | G | Deloonix | 11 | Galeto's | 5 | Tordesilhas | 2 |
| Pergamon | A | Unique | M | Dona Lucinha | 18 | Jun Sakamoto | 14 | Z-Deli | 16 |

### Parque Siqueira Campos

Almost directly across Avenida Paulista from MASP is one of São Paulo's smallest but most delightful parks, the **Parque Siqueira Campos** (daily 6am–6pm). Created in 1912 when building in the area began, the park was planned by the French landscape artist Paul Villon and based around local vegetation with some introduced trees and bushes; in 1968 it underwent a thorough renovation, directed by the great designer Roberto Burle Marx. The park consists of 45,000 square metres of almost pure Atlantic forest with a wealth of different trees, and there's a network of trails as well as shaded benches for escaping the intense summer heat. Wardens patrol the park, but a degree of alertness is still called for – don't doze off.

## The Jardins, Itaim Bibi and Pinheiros

Avenida Paulista marks the southwestern boundary of downtown São Paulo, and beyond that are Jardim Paulista, Jardim America and Jardim Europa – the **Jardins** – which were laid out in 1915 and styled after the British idea of the garden suburb. These exclusive residential neighbourhoods have long since taken over from the city centre as the site of most of São Paulo's **best restaurants** and **shopping streets**, and many residents never stray from their luxurious ghettos – protected from Third World realities by complex alarm systems, guards and fierce dogs.

At the northeastern edge of the Jardins, the neighbourhood of **Jardim Paulista** lies within the wider district of Cerqueira César, which straddles both sides of Avenida Paulista. Just a few blocks into the Jardins from Avenida Paulista is a mixed bag of hotels, offices and apartment buildings interspersed with shops, restaurants and bars geared towards the city's upper middle class. Wander along Rua Oscar Freire and the intersecting *ruas* Haddock Lobo, Bela Cintra and da Consolação for some of the neighbourhood's most exclusive boutiques and excellent restaurants.

Rua Augusta, lined with shops of all sorts, bisects Jardim Paulista and then turns into Rua Colômbia and Avenida Europa in the adjoining **Jardim America** and then **Jardim Europa**. Unfortunately, the winding tree-lined roads of these largely residential neighbourhoods afford only occasional glimpses of the Victorian or Neoclassical houses that are all but hidden behind their gardens' high walls. In Jardim Europa, it's worth stopping off at Av. Europa 158, near the intersection with Rua Groenândia, to see what's on at the **Museu da Imagen e do Som** (Tues–Fri 12.30–8.30pm, Sat & Sun 11am–8pm; Ⓦwww.mis.sp.gov.br), which draws on its vast film and photography archive to host often fascinating exhibitions of contemporary and historic Brazilian photography and a varied international film programme. Continuing along Avenida Europa you'll reach Avenida Brigadeiro Faria Lima, where, at no. 2705, the **Museu da Casa Brasileira** (Tues–Sun 10am–6pm; R$4; Ⓦwww.mcb.sp.gov.br) boasts a varied collection of seventeenth- to twentieth-century Brazilian furniture and decorative items. The building itself – an imposing ochre-coloured Palladian villa built in the 1940s – is typical of Jardim Europa's mansions. In the villa's kitchen, and extending into the garden, there's an excellent lunchtime restaurant, the *Quinta do Museu* (see p.579).

The traffic-choked Avenida Brigadeiro Faria Lima, with the mixed residential and commercial neighbourhoods of **Itaim Bibi** towards its southern end, and popular after-dark destination **Pinheiros** to the north, is the main artery of São Paulo's newest business expanse. Although the latest buildings around here have generally been constructed at a break-neck speed, leaving little time for architectural reflection, Pinheiros is not without its attractions – although you'll have to go some distance from the main concentration of office development to find them. One construction you won't fail to notice is the striking purple-and-blue office building at Av. Brigadeiro Faria Lima 201 designed by **Ruy Ohtake**, one of Brazil's most important contemporary architects (see also his hotels *Renaissance* and *Unique*, p.559). Opened in 2002, the building is notable for its curved lines and use of colour, both characteristic of Ohtake's work and a deliberate move away from the modernist tradition that has been so dominant in Brazilian architecture.

Housed on the lower floors of the building, and with its entrance on Rua Coropés, the **Instituto Tomie Ohtake** (Tues–Sun 11am–8pm; Ⓦwww.institutotomieohtake.org.br) honours the Japanese–Brazilian artist Tomie Ohtake – the architect's mother. The artist's early Brazilian work (notably landscapes) is most closely informed by her Japanese background, but this is even apparent after her shift to abstraction, in which the restrained brushstroke remains the key element. Although only a small portion of the exhibition space features her work, in rotating displays that highlight particular periods or themes, this section is always well worth a look. Otherwise the galleries are devoted to temporary exhibits of contemporary Brazilian artists or influential twentieth-century Brazilian constructivists. There's also a good gift-shop focusing on modern Brazilian art and design, as well as a restaurant (see p.574).

Four blocks west of Avenida Brigadeiro Faria Lima, at Rua Ferreira de Araújo 741, the **Centro Brasileiro Britânico** (Ⓦwww.cbb.org.br) houses the British Consulate, the British Council and various other British cultural and community organizations. Opened in 2000, the building is almost boastfully modern, its steel, plate-glass and concrete construction managing to appear both imposing and inviting. Regular (usually unremarkable) art exhibitions are held here, but most people come for the bar and restaurant, *Drake's* (see p.583).

## The Parque do Ibirapuera and around

The **Parque do Ibirapuera** (daily 5am–midnight), southeast of the Jardins, is the most famous of São Paulo's parks and the main sports centre for the city. It's a ten-minute bus ride from the bus stops on Avenida Brigadeiro Luís Antônio. Officially opened in 1954, the park was created to mark the 400th anniversary of the founding of the city of São Paulo. Oscar Niemeyer designed most of the buildings and Roberto Burle Marx produced impressive designs for landscaping.

At the park's main north entrance, in Praça Armando Salles de Oliveira, look out for the **Monumento às Bandeiras**, by Victor Brecheret. One of the city's most popular postcard sights, the 1953 sculpture shows a *bandeirante* expedition setting off, led by a Portuguese and a native on horseback. Inside the park, attractions include the peaceful and unusual **Bosque de Leitura** (reading woods) – where on Sundays (10am–4pm) you can borrow books from a small outdoor library and sit amongst the trees reading them – and several of the city's museums. The

### The São Paulo Bienal

The **São Paulo Bienal** (Ⓦwww.bienalsaopaulo.globo.com) has been held in the Parque do Ibirapuera every two years since 1951. It's widely considered to be the most important exhibition of contemporary visual art in Latin America and is only rivalled in the world by the similar event held in Venice. Each country sponsors work by its most influential contemporary artists, while a select few artists (living or dead) are also chosen by the Bienal's curators. At best, the Bienal can be an exhilarating venue to see important retrospectives and experience a wealth of innovative art, but at worst it can be little more than an embarrassing – or amusing – showing of fourth-rate global art. The Bienal is now held in October and November in even-numbered years.

▲ The Monumento às Bandeiras at Parque do Ibirapuera, São Paulo



**Museu de Arte Contemporânea** (Tues–Sun 10am–7pm; Ⓦwww.macvirtual.usp.br; free), located in the Pavilhão da Bienal in the park – and also on a larger site at Rua da Reitoria 160 (Tues–Fri 10am–7pm, Sat & Sun 10am–4pm) in the Universidade de São Paulo complex – regularly alters its displays, drawing upon its huge stored collection. Although the collection includes work by important European artists like Picasso, Modigliani, Léger and Chagall, and Brazilians such as Tarsilla do Amaral, Di Cavalcanti and Portinari, the pieces that are selected for exhibition can be disappointing. Next door to the Pavilhão da Bienal in the Marquise do Parque do Ibirapuera, the **Museu de Arte Moderna**, or MAM (Tues–Thurs, Sat & Sun 10am–6pm, Fri 10am–6pm; R$5.50, free Sun; Ⓦwww.mam.org.br), is a much smaller gallery that mainly hosts temporary exhibits of the work of Brazilian artists. There's an excellent café here serving light meals and snacks, and a good bookshop. The **Museu Afro-Brasil** (10am–5pm, closed Tues; Ⓦwww.museuafrobrasil.com.br), at the Pavilhão Manoel da Nóbrega in the northern part of the park near the lake, has temporary exhibitions of photos and artwork relating to African Brazilians, whose experience has been a neglected subject in this part of the country. The museum has yet to fully find its feet, with rather dry and poorly labelled exhibits that don't quite live up to the large, airy space or the potential of the subject matter.

If you're on the art-gallery trail, a couple of other nearby museums are well worth seeking out. The *bairro* due east of the Parque do Ibirapuera, Vila Mariana, contains the wonderful **Museu Lasar Segall** at Rua Berta 111 (Tues–Sat 2–7pm, Sun 2–6pm; Ⓦwww.museusegall.org.br; free). As most of Lasar Segall's work is contained in this museum (which served as his home and studio from 1932 until his death in 1957), the Latvian-born, naturalized-Brazilian painter is relatively little known outside Brazil. Originally a part of the German Expressionist movement at the beginning of the twentieth century, Segall settled in Brazil in 1923 and became increasingly influenced by the exuberant colours of his adopted homeland. Look out especially for the vibrant jungle green of *Boy with Gecko* and the interracial *Encounter*, an early and sensitive treatment of a complex Brazilian theme. East of here in the *bairro* of Ipiranga, the **Museu do Ipiranga** – also known as the **Museu Paulista** – (Tues–Sun 9am–4.45pm; R$4; Ⓦwww.mp.usp.br), at the intersection of *avenidas* Nazareth and Dom Pedro in the Parque da Independência, is worthwhile if you have a passing interest in Brazilian history; the museum is especially strong on the nineteenth century, featuring many paintings, pieces of furniture and other items that belonged to the Brazilian royal family. The park is also significant as the site where, in 1822, Brazilian independence was declared; in the centre of the park, at the end of Rua dos Sorocabanos, is a monument celebrating the event – a replica of the Casa do Grito, the simple house where Dom Pedro I slept – and the chapel where he and his wife were later buried.

## Butantã and Morumbi

If you've got the time, it's worth making the trek out to the *bairros* of Butantã and Morumbi, in southwest São Paulo. No houses from the colonial era remain standing in the city centre, but out here in the suburbs a few simple, whitewashed adobe **homesteads** from the time of the *bandeirantes* have been preserved. The **Casa do Bandeirante** (Wed–Sun 9am–5pm), near the huge Universidade de São Paulo campus at Praça Monteiro Lobato, Butantã, is the only one open to the public. It's a typical early eighteenth-century *paulista* dwelling containing period furniture and farm implements. This part of Butantã, where many of the university teaching staff live, is extremely pleasant to wander around – tasteful hammock-slung little houses are set amid lush foliage noisy with birdsong and cicadas.

One of the city's more popular attractions is also situated in the *bairro* of Butantã, on the university campus itself. Founded in 1901, the **Instituto Butantan**, Av. Vital Brasil 1500 (Wed–Sun 9am–4.30pm; Ⓦ www.butantan.gov.br), was one of the world's foremost research centres for the study of venomous snakes and insects and the development of antivenin serums. Despite financial cuts, it still produces over 80 percent of the country's serums and important vaccines. The highlight for visitors is the **Museu Biológico**, which showcases snakes from around Brazil – including anacondas, rattlesnakes and iridescent Amazon boas – as well as iguanas, a bizarre monkey frog and the innocuous-looking brown spider, whose painless but fatal bite makes it the country's most dangerous. Outside, there are huge snake pits with the odd, sleepy inhabitant (in the past used for venom extraction shows, now stopped for animal welfare reasons), a new museum of microbiology, a gift shop and a simple café. The campus also houses a number of other small, special-interest museums in faculties such as archeology and geoscience.

The nearest train station is Cidade Universitária, connected to Vila Madalena *metrô* station via a free bus service, the Ponte Orca. From the station, it is better to take a taxi than to try and find your way on foot around the extensive and poorly signposted campus.

### Fundação Maria Luiza e Oscar Americano

Situated in the elegant suburb of Morumbi, the **Fundação Maria Luiza e Oscar Americano**, Av. Morumbi 4077 (Tues–Fri 11am–5pm, Sat & Sun 10am–5pm; R$8; Ⓦ www.fundacaooscaramericano.org.br), is a sprawling modernist house full of eighteenth-century furniture, tapestries, religious sculptures and collections of silver, china, coins and tapestry. Amongst the most valuable works are Brazilian landscapes by the seventeenth-century Dutch artist Frans Post, and drawings and important paintings by Cândido Portinari and Emiliano di Cavalcanti. The hilltop house, designed by Oswaldo Arthur Bratke, is clearly influenced by the work of the American architect Frank Lloyd Wright, and the beautiful wooded estate, which mainly features flora native to Brazil, helps make this spot an excellent escape from the city. A superb tearoom serves English-style high teas until 6pm daily, and classical music concerts are held some Sunday mornings. Courses on music, art and architecture are offered during the week at an on-site auditorium.

## Parque do Estado and Zoo

South of the city centre, near Congonhas airport, is the largest expanse of greenery within the city: the **Parque do Estado**. The park features an extent of Mata Atlântica (the Atlantic Rainforest), with trails and picnic areas, but by far the biggest draw is the **Zoológico de São Paulo** (Tues–Sun 9am–5pm; R$13; Ⓦwww.zoologico.com.br); one of the largest zoos in the world, it houses an estimated 3200 animals from around the globe – predominantly Brazilian and African species. The reptile and monkey houses have especially important collections of the latter, while the natural habitat of the park draws several thousand migratory birds annually. The other big attraction of the park is the **Jardim Botânico** (Tues–Sun 9am–5pm; R$3; Ⓦwww.ibot.sp.gov.br), next to the zoo, featuring both native and exotic flora; its "garden of the senses" comprises plants with unusual textures or heavy scents. The easiest way to get to the park is by *metrô* to Jabaquara station, followed by a short taxi ride.



# Eating

**Eating out** is a major pastime for wealthier *paulistanos*, who take great pride in the vast number of restaurants in the city. By Latin American standards, the variety of options is certainly impressive, with chefs becoming increasingly creative with traditional Brazilian dishes, as well as adapting European and Asian ones to suit Brazilian tastes and make use of local ingredients.

## Fast food and cafés

*Paulistanos* are reputed to be always in a hurry, and on just about every block there's somewhere serving **fast food**. *Lanchonetes* do snacks and cheap, light meals in direct competition with the usual fast-food chains. The *Ponto Chic*, at Largo do Paissandu 27, Centro, claims to have invented the traditional *baurú* sandwich (made with roast beef, salad and melted cheese), while **sandwich bars** popular with a younger crowd include the *Frevo*, Rua Oscar Freire 603; the 1950s diner-style *Rockets*, serving up burgers and shakes at Alameda Lorena 2096; and *Pops*, Bela Cintra 1541, a funky café-bar that does delicious filled bagels. (All are in Jardim Paulista.) For Italian-style ice cream and fruit sorbets at their absolute best, try *Gelatería d'Arte* at Alameda Lorena 1784.

Oddly, for a city built on immigrants and coffee, São Paulo has no **café** tradition. **Coffee** is drunk endlessly in the form of the small, gooey and not very appealing *cafézinhos*. It's not usually lingered over, but if you want to take your time with something more drinkable there are an ever-increasing number of places with an espresso machine.

São Paulo has a few good **tearooms**, such as the elegant *Tatou*, at Rua Haddock Lobo 1541, at the corner of Rua Oscar Freire, serving good-quality tea and cakes in Jardim Paulista. If you have time, escape the crowds and fumes of the hectic business districts and head out to the Fundação Maria Luiza e Oscar Americano (see p.575), where superb English-style high teas are served, at R$35 a head.

## Restaurants

São Paulo's restaurants are concentrated where the money is, in the city centre and especially in the middle- and upper-class suburbs like **the Jardins**, **Itaim Bibi**, **Pinheiros** and **Vila Madalena**. You can get away with paying less than R$10 for a standard dish of rice, beans and meat at a small, side-street restaurant, while only at the most elegant places in the wealthiest neighbourhoods will you pay more than R$100 per person. There is, of course, a huge array of options between these price extremes, so you won't have any trouble finding places to suit your tastes and budget. Many moderately priced restaurants run around R$40–50 a head.

### Asian

São Paulo has many excellent **Japanese restaurants**, most of them in Liberdade, traditionally considered the city's "Japanese quarter", where good, though rather unimaginative, restaurants and sushi bars are everywhere. A much newer development has been the opening of **Korean restaurants**, with the most authentic located in the inner city *bairro* of Bom Retiro (see p.566), near the Luz cultural complexes. These simple places cater almost exclusively to the city's large Korean community, but non-Koreans will be guided through their menus.

**Asia House** Rua Augusta 1918, Jardins and Rua da Glória 86, Liberdade. The excellent-value Japanese *comida por kilo* buffet here is particularly suitable if you want to make a foray into the country's cuisine but find the thought of a Japanese–Portuguese sushi menu a little daunting.

**East** Alameda Jaú 1303, Cerqueira César. At this highly regarded Asian restaurant, dishes from China, Thailand, Vietnam, Korea, India and Japan are served with a distinctly Brazilian flair, such as beef with wasabi and manioc, or steamed *robalo* fish with Chinese greens. Expect to pay around R$60 for a three-course meal.

**Galvão Bueno** Rua Galvão Bueno 451, Liberdade. A Korean barbecue is cooked on a small grill at your table at this good-value, all-you-can-eat place; Japanese items are on the menu as well. Around R$20 per person.

**Instituto Tomie Ohtake** Av. Brigadeiro Faria Lima 201 (entrance on Rua Coropés), Pinheiros. Even if the art in the cultural centre (see p.573) leaves you cold, the restaurant is well worth a visit. This is a rare – and generally successful – attempt at fusing Brazilian dishes with pan-Asian (especially Japanese and Thai) flavours; the menu changes every three months. Tues–Sat noon–3pm, with brunch served on Sundays noon–4pm.

**Jun Sakamoto** Rua José Maria Lisboa 55, Jardim Paulista ⓣ11/3088-6019. This expensive restaurant – expect to pay at least R$70 for a meal – stands out amongst São Paulo's many Japanese restaurants, with its attractive steel-and-wood setting and a daring chef who adds modern twists to otherwise classic dishes. The sushi is creatively presented, and the tempura, in a light batter with sesame seeds, is excellent. Reservations are recommended on weekends, when the restaurant is very popular. Evenings only, closed Sun.

**Kabuki Mask** Rua Girassol 384, Vila Madalena. Good Japanese food and live Brazilian music in the evening draw a trendy crowd. Open daily for dinner and also lunch Sat & Sun.

**Korea House** Rua Galvão Bueno 43, Liberdade. This is one of only a few Korean restaurants in São Paulo. Many dishes are prepared at the table, and the inexpensive, often spicy dishes are very different from Chinese or Japanese ones.

**Seok Joung** Rua Correia de Melo 135, Bom Retiro. The most sophisticated of the increasingly numerous Korean restaurants in this *bairro*. Very authentic – and inexpensive – dishes (the speciality being *gogi gui*, or Korean barbecue) are served to largely Korean diners. Across the road at no. 142 is a slightly simpler Korean restaurant, the *Gogung*. Closed Sun.

**Sushi-Yassu** Rua Tomás Gonzaga 98A, Liberdade. Excellent, traditionally presented sushi, sashimi, noodle and other Japanese dishes are offered here – though not cheaply (about R$70 a person). Unusual for Brazil, eel (sautéed with soy sauce and sake) is regularly served, and sea urchin is frequently on the menu.

### Middle Eastern

In general, **Middle Eastern restaurants** in São Paulo are extremely reliable and excellent value. Almost all serve Lebanese or Syrian food – typically a large variety of small dishes of stuffed vegetables, salads, pastries, pulses, minced meat, spicy sausages and chicken.

**Agadir** Rua Fradique Coutinho 950, Vila Madalena. This quite simple but pleasant restaurant features moderately priced Moroccan food – in this case entirely based on couscous and served with a choice of chicken, lamb, beef or vegetable stews or tagines. Tues–Sat dinner, Sun lunch only.

**Arabe** Rua Com. Abdo Schahin 116, Centro. Though crowded at lunchtime with Lebanese diners, for the rest of the day this inexpensive restaurant mainly sees elderly local men spending hours dawdling over their coffees or mint tea.

**Arábia** Rua Haddock Lobo 1397, Cerqueira César. Excellent and moderately priced Middle Eastern food, with an emphasis on Lebanese cuisine, is served in very pleasant and spacious surroundings. The *mezze* is a good way to sample a mixture of dishes, or look for *kibe* stuffed with pine nuts and *coalhada*, a sort of sweetened yoghurt.

**Folha de Uva** Rua Bela Cintra 1435, Cerqueira César. A combination of Brazilian fast food and a buffet of Middle Eastern snacks that's popular with the lunchtime crowds. Also open Tues–Sat evening.

## Traditional Brazilian

Apart from *lanchonetes* and *churrascarías*, "typical" **regional Brazilian food**, such as *feijoadas* or *moquecas* (see p.50), are surprisingly hard to come by in São Paulo – perhaps because of the immigrant origins of so many of the city's inhabitants. However, traditional Brazilian cooking does exist, with *mineiro* cuisine being by far the most commonly found.

**Andrade** Rua Artur de Azevedo 874, Pinheiros. Northeastern food is the speciality here, with dishes including *carne do sol* (sun-dried beef) served with pumpkin, sweet potato and mandioca. Portions are moderately priced and easily serve two people. Live *forró* music is performed during Sun lunch.

**Bargaço** Rua Oscar Freire 1189, Cerquiera César. In Salvador, *Bargaço* is considered by many to be the best Bahian restaurant; it's more debatable whether this is the best *bahian* food in São Paulo, but it's certainly very good. The menu, while varied, concentrates on seafood, with *moquecas* (coconut fish stews) inevitably the biggest draw. It's an upmarket spot yet reasonably priced. Closed Mon lunch.

**Bolinha** Av. Cidade Jardim 53, Jardim Europa. Traditionally, *feijoada* (a black bean, pork and sausage stew) is served in Brazil only on Wed and Sat, but here it's the house staple every day, served as a *rodizio* along with *farofa* (toasted manioc), rice, sliced oranges and other trimmings. Choose either the traditional *feijoada* – complete with ear, nose, trotter and bacon – or the leaner "*feijoa* lite". Dishes are moderately priced.

**Capim Santo** Rua Arapiraca 152, Vila Madalena. Excellent and moderately priced food is served in an attractive patio setting, landscaped with palms and jungle fronds. The lunch buffet is a great way to experience the highlights of Bahian food, and in the evening the à la carte offerings provide a similarly wide choice of dishes; try the shrimp cooked with *banana da terra*, a variety of plantain. Tues–Sat lunch and dinner, Sun lunch only.

**Consulado Mineiro** Praça Benedito Calixto 74, Pinheiros. Authentically hearty *mineiro* food makes this a popular spot, but it's particularly bustling on weekends when Praça Benedito Calixto hosts an antiques and crafts market. Dishes are mostly meat served with all the trimmings (*farofa*, sweet potato, etc); each costs around R$45 but is easily enough for two. Closed Mon.

**Dona Lucinha** Av. Chibarás 399, Moema. The best *mineiro* food you're likely to taste in São Paulo is served here, the only other branch of Belo Horizonte's highly regarded restaurant (see p.175). Begin with a shot of *cachaça* before sampling a huge range of typical – and more unusual – vegetable and meat dishes and desserts that make up the excellent-value R$35 buffet. Tues–Sat lunch and dinner, Sun lunch only.

**Espírito Capixaba** Rua Francisco Leitão 57, Pinheiros. Unique in the city, this quiet side-street restaurant specializes in food from the overlooked state of Espírito Santo. Lots of seafood dishes are on offer – most notably distinctive *moquecas* (fish stews), cooked in tomato sauce rather than coconut milk, as in Bahia.

**O Novo Templo da Bahia** Alameda Campinas 720, Jardim Paulista. This Bahian restaurant is known for its beautifully presented – and extremely tasty – but moderately priced dishes. If you're new to Bahian food, choose one of the many *moquecas* or try a platter of *acarajé* (fried bean cakes) and *bolinhos de bacalhau* (small cod pastries).

**Restaurante Moraes – Rei do Filet** Alameda Santos 1105, Jardim Paulista. Serving customers since 1927, the house speciality of this very simple and very traditional restaurant is steak. To show how tender the meat is, the bowtie-wearing waiters cut the steaks using soup-spoons. A full meal costs around R$50. The original restaurant, still functioning, is in the city centre at Praça Júlio Mesquita 175, just off Av. São João.

**Segredos de Minas** Rua Bela Cintra 919, Cerqueira César. Tasty, inexpensive *mineiro* food that for lunch attracts office workers from nearby Avenida Paulista and in the evening attracts local residents. Sun lunch only.

## Churrasco

Grass-fed beef in a bewildering variety of cuts is at the centre of the **churrasco** (barbecue), and locals and expats agree it's in the *churrascarías* that São Paulo really comes into its own. Lamb, chicken and pork are served as well, typically alongside a huge and varied salad bar.

**Baby Beef Rubaiyat** Av. Brigadeiro Faria Lima 2954, Itaim Bibi ☎11/3078-9488. Airy, modern surroundings and meat of the highest quality have helped make this top-of-the range *churrascaría* a firm favourite among locals. The menu is bewildering, but if in doubt choose the house speciality – the exceptionally tender Baby Beef Brangus, sourced from the restaurant's own ranch. An excellent *feijoada* featuring baby boar is served on Wed and Sat, when it's advisable to reserve a table. A two-course meal with drinks is likely to set you back around R$100.

**Bovinu's Grill** Rua 15 de Novembro 250, Centro. Just off Praça da República, this excellent-value *churrascaría* and *por kilo* restaurant is always packed with local office workers. There's a huge selection of salads, Brazilian stews and other dishes, and, of course, lots of meat – various cuts of beef as well as pork, chicken and fish. Expect to spend around R$20 per person. Mon–Fri lunch only. Other branches include one at Alameda Santos 2100, Jardim Paulista, which is open in the evening and costs R$25 for all you can eat.

**Dinho's** Alameda Santos 45, Paraíso ☎11/3016-5333. One of the city's oldest *churrascarías, Dinho's* stands out for its famously high quality Wed and Sat *feijoada* buffets. Fairly expensive but consistently impressive.

**Esplanada Grill** Rua Haddock Lobo 1682, Jardim Paulista. This elegant and expensive (at least R$90) place is particularly recommended for its outstanding, thinly sliced *picanha* (rump) steak.

**Fogo de Chão** Av. Moreira Guimarães 964, Moema. A bit of a trek, but this authentic *gaúcho*-style *churrascaría* – a branch of a Porto Alegre–based chain – is rated by many *paulistanos* to have the best meat in São Paulo; this is straightforward food that relies on the sheer quality of the ingredients. Expect to pay around R$80 per person for a full meal.

**Grill da Villa** Rua Inácio Pereira da Rocha 422, Vila Madalena. Quality meat is served in this moderately priced restaurant, located in one of São Paulo's most fashionable neighbourhoods for nightlife.

**Rodeio** Rua Haddock Lobo 1498, Jardim Paulista. Overly elegant, perhaps, and certainly expensive (expect to pay at least R$100 per person), the quality of the meat is exceptional. The relaxed setting and discreet but efficient service has long made this a popular meeting-point for politicians, bankers and business executives.

## Contemporary Brazilian

A more modern, lighter cuisine has emerged on São Paulo's restaurant scene in recent years, as chefs have started to combine the enormous wealth of exotic Brazilian flavours with traditional Italian, French and Asian styles of cooking. Although a welcome addition to the city's food scene, many of the places specializing in this kind of thing are expensive and can be as popular for seeing and being seen as for the actual food.

**Cantaloup** Rua Manoel Guedes, Itaim Bibi ☎11/3078-3445. Known for placing ingredients from the tropics alongside ones from France and Italy, always with mouthwatering results. The seafood dishes are particularly good – try *namorado* fish with almond croquante and palm-heart risotto. Lush foliage and friendly, efficient service create an intimate atmosphere in this converted warehouse. Fairly expensive (main courses are around R$50) but excellent.

**Deloonix** Bela Cintra 1709, Jardim Paulista. *Deloonix* claims to be the only place in Brazil that offers "raw" cuisine (although it also does cooked) and is particularly good for vegetarians; the Brazilian, Asian and Mediterranean dishes served here have a strong emphasis on healthy and organic products. Cheaper than most contemporary places, at around R$25–30 for a main course, but still very good.

**D.O.M.** Rua Br. De Capanema 549, Jardim Paulista ☎11/3088-0761. Chef Alex Atala is considered one of the best in Brazil, and the faultless fusion cooking at *D.O.M.* is as good as you'd expect (and as expensive – expect to pay around R$80 for the main dish alone). Try the local *robalo* fish with tapioca and cassava, or the lamb with mashed *cará*, a kind of wild potato.

**Quinta do Museu** Av. Brigadeiro Faria Lima 2705, Jardim Europa. Located in the old kitchen and gardens of a 1940s villa that now houses the Museu da Casa Brasileira (see p.572), this is a wonderful place for an al fresco lunch or afternoon tea. The moderately priced cuisine is a successful blend of Brazilian and Italian that's much lighter than the standard Italo-Brazilian food – the sole with basil and roast tomato is particularly recommended. Lunch only, closed Mon.

**Santa Gula** Rua Fidalga 340, Vila Madalena ⓣ11/3812-7815. This restaurant, in the back garden of an old house, is surely one of the most beautiful in São Paulo – its sunny patios with their earthy colours, tiled floors and antique mismatched chairs evoking a rustic Mediterranean ambience. The menu, a blend of Italian and Brazilian cuisines, includes *carne seca* and pumpkin ravioli, creative risottos, grilled meats and delicious mousses made from unusual Brazilian fruit. Fairly expensive (about R$50 a head), and reservations are essential. Closed Sun evening and Mon lunch.

**Tordesilhas** Rua Bela Cintra 465, Consolação. The trailblazer of new Brazilian cuisine; traditional recipes gathered from throughout the country then adapted for a lighter touch. As well as being extremely tasty, the food is beautifully presented and served in a very attractive rustic-chic setting. There are daily three-course lunch specials for R$30 or, in the evenings, opt for the chef's tasting menu at R$100. Sun lunch only, closed Mon.



## French

**French restaurants** include some well-established places that have been serving traditional, rich French cuisine to *paulistanos* for years. The food is often excellent but always expensive – expect to pay well over R$100 a head.

**La Casserole** Largo do Arouche 346, Centro ⓣ11/3331-6283. An old favourite for a romantic evening out, with ever-reliable, classic French food. The *bouillabaisse* is particularly good. Closed Sat lunch and Mon.

**Le Coq Hardy** Rua Jerônimo da Veiga 461, Itaim Bibi ⓣ11/3079-3344. Arguably São Paulo's best traditional French restaurant, and almost certainly its most expensive. The food is well prepared and rich in a very old fashioned way – as far removed from *nouvelle cuisine* as you can get. Choices include *penne* pasta with duck ragu, or Chateaubriand in Dijon sauce; leave room for the profiteroles. On weekdays there's a comparatively good-value lunch menu. Closed Sun.

**Le Vin Bistro** Alameda Tietê 184, Jardim Paulista. Simple but attractively presented food, particularly good as a light lunch. Well known for its oysters from Cananéia, though the salmon is recommended too. Around R$70 a head.

## Italian

São Paulo has a huge number of **Italian restaurants**, ranging from family-run *cantinas* and pizzerias to elegant, expensive establishments. For the most part, the city's Italian restaurateurs are the children or grandchildren of immigrants, and they've adapted mainly northern Italian recipes to suit Brazilian tastes as well as the availability of ingredients. São Paulo's "Little Italy", Bixiga, is good for a fun night out, with countless inexpensive restaurants, but the food there is nothing special, and you'll find higher-quality dishes in other neighbourhoods.

**Braz** Rua Vupabussu 271, Pinheiros. With quite possibly the best pizzas in São Paulo, busy *Braz* strives to live up to expectations. The secret lies in the generosity of their toppings – hunks of mozzarella, roast vegetables and meat, drizzled with olive oil.

**Famiglia Mancini** Rua Avanhandava 81, Centro. The fun atmosphere is especially active late at night, when this inexpensive restaurant is crowded with young people. Long queues for a table are common, though the food is mediocre apart from the fabulous *por kilo* antipasto buffet.

**Fasano** Rua Taiarana 78, Cerqueira César ⓣ11/3062-4000. Serving without a doubt the best Italian food in São Paulo, this elegant hotel restaurant is a good choice for celebrating special occasions. Renowned for its top-quality ingredients, the chef adds his own twist to dishes from different Italian regions, with creations such as risotto with Tuscan ham, white beans and wine or polenta with gorgonzola. The atmosphere of the marble dining room is understated formality, and with wine expect a price tag over R$350 per person.

**Galeto's** Alameda Santos 2211, Jardim Paulista. Since the 1970s, this fairly inexpensive restaurant has specialized in barbecued chicken, served with salad and polenta, along the lines of the rustic food commonly found in the areas of Italian settlement in Brazil's southernmost state of Rio Grande do Sul.

**Gero** Rua Haddock Lobo 1629, Cerqueira César ☎11/3064-0005. This relaxed bistro-style restaurant with the same owners as *Fasano* has a smaller but still very good menu. The food is more moderately priced than other places like it (though it's hardly cheap), and the diners are rather trendy. Expect a wait for a table.

**Gigetto** Rua Avanhandava 63, Centro. Brazilian families crowd into this restaurant just off Rua Augusta, on a road lined with several other Italian restaurants. The food's excellent – the *cappelletti a romanesca* (alfredo, or creamy sauce with ham and peas) is a good choice – and very inexpensive.

**Jardim de Napoli** Rua Dr Martinico Prado 463, Higienópolis. A simple *cantina* where some of São Paulo's best Italian food is served at moderate prices. Justifiably famous for its giant meatballs (*polpettone*), it also does excellent pasta.

**Massimo** Alameda Santos 1826, Cerqueira César ☎11/3284-0311. Reliable pasta and polenta dishes as well as excellent main courses – including roast lamb or suckling pig – are served at this venerable spot. Fairly expensive, but the atmosphere is relaxed.

**Pasta e Vino** Rua Barão de Capanema 206, Cerqueira César. The pasta and other Italian dishes served here are adequate, but what makes this moderately priced restaurant really useful is that it's open 24hr.

**Subito** Av. Paulista 2073. Popular with nearby office workers at lunchtime, this place offers good-value risotto, pasta and salads in a small mall on Av. Paulista. Note there's no table service – you simply order, pay, and pick up your plate at the counter.

## Jewish

São Paulo's substantial Jewish population is reflected in a handful of authentic, and very good restaurants, located in the traditional Jewish *bairro* Bom Retiro (see p.566) and in Higienópolis (see p.569), the newer centre of Jewish-São Paulo life.

**AK Delicatessen** Rua Mato Grosso 450, Higienópolis. Young local chef Andrea Kaufmann takes traditional Eastern-European Jewish dishes and fuses into them Brazilian staples (for example, *varenikes*, a ravioli-like pasta usually filled with fruit) made with mandioca or with sweet potato, adding some Italian or other twists for good measure. Sometimes she's successful, and sometimes less so – but the results are always interesting, and moderately priced. Closed Mon and Sun evening.

**Shoshi Delishop** Rua Correia de Melo 206, Bom Retiro. Stop in for inexpensive Eastern-European Jewish food (such as *gefilte* fish and ox tongue accompanied by buckwheat), cheesecake and dishes incorporating contemporary Italian–Brazilian touches. Adi, the friendly English-speaking Bulgarian–Israeli owner, is a mine of local information. Day-time snacks and lunch only.

**Z-Deli** Alameda Lorena 1689, Cerqueira César. People who live or work in this trendy neighbourhood come to this small Jewish deli for *gefilte* fish, falafel, cheesecake and more. Another branch with the same hours is at Alameda Gabriel Monteiro da Silva 1350, Jardim Paulista. Mon–Fri 8am–6.30pm, Sat 8am–4pm, closed Sun.

## Portuguese

Considering the size and overall importance of the Portuguese community in São Paulo, there are surprisingly few **Portuguese restaurants**, and you get what you pay for: if it's cheap, it tends not to be very good.

**Antiquarius** Alameda Lorena 1884, Jardim Paulista ☎11/3064-8686. Excellent – but extremely expensive – Portuguese food and wine is served here. The seafood is especially good, and the desserts are fabulous, but the rustic nature of many Portuguese dishes sits uncomfortably with the formal, not to say gaudy, surroundings. Closed Mon lunch & Sun evening.

**Presidente** Rua Visconde de Parnaíba 2438, Brás. Long-running establishment offering very good food, including top-notch *bacalhau* (salted cod) and *dourada* fish, simply cooked and presented. About R$60 a head. Closes daily at 9pm; Sat & Sun lunch only.

**Rei do Bacalhau** Rua Bianchi Bertoldi 36, Pinheiros. Old-fashioned, family-style place serving traditional Portuguese dishes, many of which incorporate *bacalhau*. Good, although a little overpriced (at least R$70 a head). Closed Mon.

## Other cuisines

The cooking on offer in São Paulo increasingly includes the flavours of other **Latin American** countries, especially Mexico and Argentina. Most **European** cuisines also have at least one representative in the city. German restaurants, in particular, are popular places to go for a few drinks and some hearty if rather unimaginative food. **Seafood** tends to be incorporated on various menus rather than sold at exclusively fish restaurants, but there is a sprinkling of (mostly expensive) seafood places around town.

**Acrópoles** Rua da Graça 364, Bom Retiro. Traditional Greek food, including moussaka, is served in this long-established, popular and moderately priced restaurant.

**Bierquelle** Av. Aratus 801, Moema. A cosy place serving moderately priced German and Swiss dishes – try the delicious fried, grated potato with apple sauce.

**Don Curro** Rua Alves Guimarães 230, Pinheiros. This large, long-standing – and somewhat expensive – Spanish seafood restaurant features excellent *paellas* (serving two or three people) as well as octopus, lobster and squid.

**Drake's** Rua Ferreira de Araújo 741, Pinheiros (in the Centro Brasileiro Britânico). There's no new-wave British cooking here to match the centre's forward-looking design (see p.573); instead you'll find traditional English dishes such as shepherd's pie, alongside American-style burgers and bar food.

**Dr Tche Parrilla** Rua Franca Pinta 489, Vila Mariana. Even Brazilians admit Argentine beef is the best there is. If you won't be heading south, then dine at this authentic *parrilla* (barbecue), where you can try cuts that are hard to find outside South America, such as *vacio* (flank), served with tangy *chimichurri* condiment. Moderately priced and good value for money.

## Vegetarian

There's nowhere in Brazil where it's easier to be a **vegetarian** than in São Paulo – even *churrascarías* usually boast formidable salad bars. Fortunately, there are also a surprising number of specifically vegetarian restaurants, which have varied (and usually inexpensive) menus.

**Apfel** Rua Barão de Itapetinga 207 (1st floor), Centro. An excellent vegetarian buffet features both hot and cold dishes for around R$16 per person. Mon–Fri lunch only; another branch is in Jardim Paulista at Rua Bela Cintra 1343.

**Cheiro Verde** Rua Peixoto Gomide 1413, Jardim Paulista. Fairly sophisticated, this vegetarian restaurant serves excellent and inexpensive food. The simple menu changes with the seasons.

**Emporio Siriuba** Alameda Franca 1590, Jardim Paulista. This health-food store has its own lunchtime café at the rear, situated on an attractive outdoor patio. Slightly more upmarket and imaginative than many similar places, with the chance to try vegetarian versions of dishes such as the *bahian moqueca* (here, a shiitake and coconut stew). Expect to pay around R$20.

**Grao do Soja** Rua Girassol 602, Vila Madalena. Located on a hippyish street, with suitably bohemian decor, this place puts soya at the heart of most its dishes; there's even a soya *feijoada.*

**Sativa** Alameda Itu 1564, Jardim Paulista. In an otherwise expensive area, during the week this pleasant little restaurant serves an excellent-value lunchtime *prato del dia* (dish of the day), with freshly squeezed juice, for just R$10. In the evening there is a similarly inexpensive à la carte menu.

# Bars, nightlife and entertainment

Whether you're after "high culture", a thumping club or just a bar to hang out in, you won't encounter much of a problem in São Paulo. The city has four main centres for nightlife: **Bela Vista**, with mixed crowds and live music; **Vila Madalena** and adjoining **Pinheiros**, which host the lion's share of trendy bars, including some with a slightly bohemian feel; **Jardins**, offering both quieter, upmarket bars, popular with an older crowd, and gay bars; and **Itaim Bibi** and **Vila Olímpia**, together best known for their flashy *baladas* (clubs). For the trendy bars and clubs, be aware that Wednesday and Thursday nights are as popular, and in many ways considered more hip, than weekend nights, particularly in the summer when those who have the means tend to escape the city.

Places come and go in São Paulo continually, so on-the-spot advice is vital. Some suggestions are detailed below, but for the full picture of what's going on, consult the weekly *Veja* magazine, the daily *Folha de São Paulo* newspaper (especially its Friday supplement) and the website Ⓦwww.guiasp.com; additionally, the funky Ⓦwww.obaoba.com.br has all the essential club listings. Many places have their own websites featuring their upcoming programmes; where these exist, they are mentioned in the listing.

São Paulo has a large **gay** population but, with some exceptions, clubs and bars tend to be mixed rather than specifically gay, with the scene mainly in the Jardins area. Since 1997, the city has hosted a Carnaval-style annual **Gay Pride parade** on a Sunday in May or June, along Avenida Paulista. The first parade attracted just two thousand participants but organizers now claim well over three million revellers, making it by far the largest event of its kind in the world. For dates and other information, see Ⓦwww.paradasp.org.br.

## Bars

The liveliest bars in the city are found around Rua 13 de Maio in Bela Vista (often with live music) or in fashionable Vila Madalena and Pinheiros. A cover charge is levied in most places, making a bar crawl an expensive prospect. The amount you pay varies according to the day, time and your sex (men usually pay double the amount women do), but count on an average of about R$15.

**Astor** Rua Delfina 163, Vila Madalena. This well-established bar is one of the neighbourhood's trendiest meeting-points. Excellent beer and *petiscos* (snacks) make this a good place to start or end a night out in Vila Madalena.

**Bar Brahma** Av. São João 677 (at the corner with Av. Ipiranga), Centro. Opened in 1948, this is one of the city's oldest bars. Once a haunt for musicians, intellectuals and politicians, today it draws a post-theatre crowd to the bar and insomniacs to its 24hr café.

**Bar do Sacha** Rua Original 45, Pinheiros. Located on a hill with a pleasant garden, this is a nice place to come for a drink on a sunny day. Opens at noon daily.

**Barnaldo Lucrecia** Rua Abilio Soares 207, Paraíso Ⓦwww.barnaldolucrecia.com.br. A young crowd is drawn to this bar, located in an easy-to-spot yellow house. There is live music most evenings, but it's especially festive on Friday.

**Cachaçaria Paulista** Rua Mourato Coelho 593, Pinheiros. This is a great place for sampling *cachaça*: there are over 200 kinds here, and it's open from 6pm until the last customer leaves.

**Café do Bixiga** Rua 13 de Maio 76, Bela Vista. Excellent *chopp* and a carefully nurtured, bohemian atmosphere are the main attractions here. A good place to stop for a post-theatre drink.

**Dado Bier** Av. Juscelino Kubitschek 1203, Itaim Bibi. Arrive for an early evening drink (the club boasts one of the city's few microbreweries), stay for dinner (pizza or sushi), check out the art gallery, and then dance to techno, ska and rock music until dawn. Tues–Sun 7pm–late, happy hour 7.30–8.30pm.

**Director's Gourmet** Rua Alameda Franca 1552, Cerqueira César. An enjoyable, rather up-scale neighbourhood bar mainly attracting gay men. Weekdays are very relaxed though the place gets pretty crowded on weekends when a DJ spins 70s and 80s music.

**Drake's** Centro Brasileiro Britânico, Rua Ferreira de Araújo 741, Pinheiros Ⓦwww.drakesbar.com. Popular with a middle-aged British expat crowd, *Drake's* has an attractive outdoor decking area and is trying hard to attract younger patrons and locals with live music at the weekends.

**Empanadas** Rua Wisard 489, Vila Madalena. The simple but effective selling-point of this busy bar is that, in addition to beer, it serves *empanadas* (savoury pastries popular throughout South America but usually referred to as *empadas* in Brazil). And very good ones too – especially at 3am.

**Filial** Rua Fidalgo 254, Vila Madalena. A rather upscale place masquerading as a simple local bar. Popular with self-consciously bohemian types, 30 and over.

**Kia Ora** Dr Eduardo de Souza Aranha 377, Itaim Bibi. With its Kiwi owners, *Kia Ora* has raced into the lead as the number-one favourite pub for both young expats and *paulistanos*. It's absolutely packed to the rafters some nights – don't be surprised if there's a long wait just to get in.

**Original Beto Batata** Rua Melo Alves 769, Jardim Paulista. A light and airy bar where the food is as big an attraction as the beer. The house specialities are Swiss-style potato *rösti* and *barreado* (see p.629), a *feijoada*-like dish from the coast of Paraná. On Thursday evenings there's live Brazilian popular music.

**Posto 6** Rua Aspicuelta 644, Vila Madalena. This lively Rio-style simple corner bar, in one of the few areas of the city where bars cluster together, is a popular place for friends to meet up at the beginning (or even end) of a night.

**Pirajá** Av. Brigadeiro Faria Lima 64, Pinheiros. This attractive, mahogany bar serves tasty Spanish-style tapas and is well known for its excellent *chopp*. Packed from 8pm onwards.

**Rey Castro** Rua Min. Jesuino Cardoso 181, Vila Conceicão. It's debatable what Castro would make of this Cuban-themed bar (with its R$45 entrance fee), but its *mojitos*, cigars and waiters dressed as guerrillas – not to mention the live salsa music – go down well with *paulistanos*.

**Ritz** Alameda Franca 1088, Cerqueira César. During the day this spot is a quiet restaurant serving hamburgers and sandwiches, but at night it's a lively bar popular with the gay crowd.



## Live music

São Paulo has quite an imaginative **jazz** tradition, as well as plenty of **Brazilian music**. Check the entertainment listings in local newspapers for touring artists or, if you're feeling slightly adventurous, visit a **gafieira** – a dance hall where working-class and Bohemian chic meet. Be warned: *gafieiras* tend to be out of the centre and in poor neighbourhoods. Very much community spots, they can seem rather alien and disconcerting places if you've only just arrived in Brazil; in no time, however, you'll be made to feel welcome. Cover charges are similar to those of bars, or occasionally a little more.

**All of Jazz** Rua João Cachoeira 1366, Vila Madalena ⓦwww.allofjazz.com.br. Intimate, laid-back place with consistently excellent live jazz.

**Avenida Club** Av. Pedroso de Morães, Pinheiros ⓣ11/3814-7383. The best-known place in São Paulo for formal dancing; it features everything from ballroom to samba, *forró* and merengue.

**Bourbon Street Music Club** Rua dos Chanés 127, Moema ⓦwww.bourbonstreet.com.br. This consistently good, though expensive (R$35 upwards), jazz club hosts visiting international artists and frequent festivals.

**Café Piu-Piu** Rua 13 de Maio 134, Bela Vista ⓦwww.cafepiupiu.com.br. Although this bar has a nice neighbourhood feel to it, the wide range of Brazilian music – including live samba and MPB – draws a mixed crowd into the early hours of the morning. A lively venue for some very good jazz and *choro*.

**Carioca Club** Rua Cardeal Arcoverde 2899, Pinheiros. Live samba, *pagode* and MPB bands are interspersed with a house DJ playing a range of Brazilian disco beats. Attracts a good mix of the over-20s.

**Clube do Choro** Rua João Moura, between Rua Artur Azevedo and Rua Teodoro Sampaio, Jardim America. On Saturday and Sunday evenings the street is closed off, a stage is erected and tables and chairs are put out so you can sit and listen to some excellent music. There's a small cover charge and food and drink are available.

**Grazie a Dio!** Rua Girassol 67, Vila Madalena ⓦwww.grazieadio.com.br. This popular live-music venue showcases mainly samba-rock bands. Serves good Mediterranean food as well.

**A Lanterna** Rua Fidalga 531, Vila Madalena. A fun place to drop by that's popular with the under-25s. The house band plays music from the 1960s to the 1980s. Open 6pm–2am; closed Mon.

**Pedro Sertanejo** Rua Catumbi 183, Brás. A *gafieira* that's always packed to the rafters with migrants from the Northeast dancing to *forró*. Sat & Sun only.

**Samba** Rua Fidalga 308, Vila Madalena. As the name suggests, this is the place to head for if you want to listen to Brazil's most famous musical export. It's open daily but the best time to go is for the *roda de samba* (Tues–Fri at 9pm), when the audience joins in with the musicians.

## Clubs

São Paulo, with its own lively clubbing and musical tradition, is now a well-known spot for clubbers. Top DJs from around the globe regularly head the bill at the city's coolest hangouts, but there's plenty of homegrown talent around too, with the city particularly noted for its **drum'n'bass** DJs, considered among the best in the world. However, the scene remains fairly underground and you'll have to keep your eyes and ears open to hit the right spots. **Brazilian funk** has now come out of the *favela* and crossed over to the club scene; more traditional Brazilian music like samba and the at times execrable MPB is also often thrown into the mix. Look out also for Skolbeats, Latin America's biggest **dance festival**, which has been taking place in São Paulo each April/May since 2000. Clubs playing electronic music are considered very much the preserve of the young upper classes; they are therefore also places where English tends to be widely spoken. Cover charges again vary wildly; expect to pay normally between R$15 and R$40, sometimes with a drink or two thrown in, although if a big name is DJing at a top club you could be looking at anything up to R$100.

**Blen Blen Brasil** Rua Inácio Pereira da Rocha 520, Vila Madalena ⓦwww.blenblen.com.br. Besides being a nice place for a drink and some jazz, this fashionable yet not overly trendy club has several dancefloors with a constantly changing mix of everything from techno to *forró* to MPB.

**Canto da Ema** Av. Brigadeiro Faria Lima 364, Pinheiros ⓦwww.cantodaema.com.br. Electronic version of northeastern *forró* music that has become hugely popular amongst twenty-somethings in São Paulo. Arrive early and you can join *forró* dance lessons before the live music and DJs really get going.

**D-Edge** Alameda Olga 70, Barra Funda ⓦwww.d-edge.com.br. DJs spin everything from drum'n'bass and hip-hop to punk and heavy metal at this very eclectic and cool underground club.

**Ipsis Club** Rua Padre Garcia Velho 63, Pinheiros. This large, modern club has some great DJs and occasional live music, and it's one of the most popular gay and lesbian hangouts in the city. Thurs–Sat 11pm–5am, Sun 7pm–3am. Closed Mon–Wed.

**A Loca** Rua Frei Caneca 916, Bixiga ⓦwww.aloca.com.br. Though well-known on the gay scene, this determinedly "underground" club attracts a very diverse crowd. On Friday and Saturday it hosts nosebleed techno nights, while Thursday and Sunday see more eclectic disco and pop tunes.

**Manga Rosa** Guarapes 1754, Brooklin Novo ⓦwww.clubmangarosa.com.br. A great, well-established club for trance and progressive house. Open Wed–Sat.

**Matrix** Rua Aspicuelta 459, Vila Madalena ⓦwww.matrixbar.com.br. Popular with students, São Paulo's main "alternative" club plays indie, gothic, rock, etc. A bit watered down, but definitely a different vibe from most places.

**Show Bar Lounge** Rua Cardeal Arcoverde 1393, Pinheiros ⓦwww.showbarlounge.com.br. Though lively and fun, *Show Bar* is more down-to-earth than most Sampa clubs. It's best known for its Fri night fire-breathing shows, but in general the music is a mix of MPB, samba, house and hip-hop.

**Ultralounge** Rua da Consolação 3031, Jardim Paulista. Swanky gay club, with all-day chilled-out music on Sun.

**Vermont Itaim** Rua Pedroso Alvarenga 1192, Itaim Bibi ⓦwww.vermontitaim.com.br. This classy gay-and-lesbian club plays samba, MPB and Brazilian funk, plus there's an on-site restaurant.

## Cinema, theatre and classical music

In general, **films** arrive in São Paulo simultaneously with their release in North America and Europe and are subtitled rather than dubbed. Most cinemas, which charge around R$15, are on Avenida Paulista, but there are also several downtown on Avenida São Luís. All the shopping centres (see p.587) have cinema complexes and show the latest blockbusters. Keep a special eye out for what's on at CineSesc, Rua Augusta 2075; Espaço Unibanco de Cinema, Rua Augusta 1470 (both Cerqueira César); and the Centro Cultural de São Paulo, Rua Vergueiro 1000 (ⓦwww.centrocultural.sp.gov.br), by the Vergueiro *metrô* station – all of which are devoted to Brazilian and foreign

## Carnaval

Although São Paulo's **Carnaval** is not as spectacular or glamorous as its *carioca* sister, neither is it low-key. São Paulo has its own enthusiastically supported samba schools, which spend all year preparing for the festival and collectively form the union of *paulistano* samba schools, UESP (ⓣ11/3171-3713, ⓦwww.uesp.com.br). As in Rio, the samba competition takes the form of a massive parade, held in the Oscar Niemeyer–designed *sambódromo*, a 530m-long stadium that can accommodate around 26,000 and is part of the huge Parque Anhembi leisure complex, near the Tietê bus terminal north of the city centre. Ticket prices are cheaper than their Rio counterparts, starting at around R$15 for a bench seat up in the gods – where you'll get a flavour of the event but won't see very much – and rising to around R$1000 for a seat in a VIP box. In general, the closer you are to the ground, the better the view and the more you pay. Many local travel agents sell tickets (see p.589); alternatively, try Ticketmaster (ⓦwww.ticketmaster.com.br) or the city tourist office in Anhembi (ⓣ11/6226-0400). In the weeks leading up to Carnaval, you can sometimes attend rehearsals at the city's samba schools – one of the best to visit is Rosas de Ouro in Barra Funda (ⓣ11/3931-4555).



art-house films. Art-house films are also shown at the Belas-Artes at Rua da Consolação 2423, on the corner of Avenida Paulista.

As Brazil's theatrical centre, São Paulo boasts a busy season of classical and avant-garde productions; a visit to the **theatre** is worthwhile even without a knowledge of Portuguese. Seats are extremely cheap, starting at around R$10, and available via **ticket offices** that have details of all current productions: try the FNAC (see p.588), or Ticketmaster (ⓣ11/6846-6000, ⓦwww.ticketmaster.com.br). The Brasileiro de Comédia, Rua Major Diorgo 311, and the Teatro Sérgio Cardoso, Rua Rui Barbosa, both in Bixiga, have particularly good reputations for putting on high-quality performances.

The traditional focal-point for São Paulo's vibrant **opera** and **classical music** season is the Theatro Municipal (ⓣ11/3334-0001, ⓦwww.prefeitura.sp.gov.br/cidade/secretarias/cultura/teatromunicipal; see also p.567; tickets R$10–25), on Praça Ramos de Azevado in the city centre, where, in the 1920s, Villa-Lobos himself performed. São Paulo has always been less important than Rio when it comes to the operatic and classical music world, but now Brazilian and foreign performers divide their time between the two cities. The beautifully renovated Estação Júlio Prestes in the *bairro* of Luz is home to the world-class Orquestra Sinfônica do Estado de São Paulo and has a new 1500-seat concert hall, the Sala São Paulo (ⓣ11/3337-5414, ⓦwww.salasaopaulo.art.br; see also p.566). Concerts usually take place Fridays at 9pm, Saturdays at 4.30pm and Sundays at 5pm; seats cost between R$25 and R$80.

# Shopping

São Paulo's **shopping** possibilities are as varied as the city's restaurants. In the wealthy southwestern Jardins suburb, shops are far more impressive than those in just about any other South American city, and the quality way above par. For visitors, there are no obvious **souvenirs** of São Paulo, as such, but the city is a good place to find the things Brazil generally does well – from *cachaça* and samba records to bikinis and flip-flops. Even if you're not intent on a spree, the shopping centres and stores are worth a tour to experience the opulent surroundings, while at the other end of the spectrum the fine selection of **markets** provides exposure to both local colour and good food.

The main **shopping streets** in the centre of the city are near Praça da República, especially the roads running off Avenida Ipiranga: Rua Barão de Itapetinga, Rua 24 de Maio, and Rua do Arouche. South of the Mercado Municipal, Rua 25 de Março is another busy street, lined with hawkers selling everything from pirated CDs to Carnaval costumes. Most of the stores downtown are of the cheap'n'cheerful variety – they sell clothes, but you'll rarely find the latest fashions.

South of Avenida Paulista is where the money is – and where all the best stores are. You'll find lots of boutiques selling clothes and accessories from Brazilian, European and US designers, especially in the streets running parallel to and crossing Rua Augusta (most notably Rua Oscar Freire, Alameda Lorena, Rua Haddock Lobo, Rua Bela Cintra and Rua Dr Melo Alves). Although expensive, prices often compare well to Europe and the US. São Paulo's **shopping malls** are hugely popular amongst the city's middle-class as places to escape to and feel utterly insulated from their less-fortunate fellow citizens. Each centre tries to outdo the other, with mirrored walls and ostentatious fountains – you won't feel closer to North America than this during your stay in Brazil. Shopping centres are usually open Monday to Saturday 10am to 10pm, and Sunday after lunch to around 7pm.

## Shopping malls

**Daslu** Av. Chedid Jafet 131, Vila Olímpia. Not a shopping centre as you know it, Daslu is created to look less like a mall and more like a country mansion, complete with chandeliers, marble staircases and chaise lounges. In trying to be exclusive, it manages to be the most tasteless and vulgar paean to obscene wealth you're ever likely to come across. Go for the experience, and certainly not to pick up a bargain. Open Mon & Wed–Sat 10am–8pm, Tues 10am–10pm.

**Eldorado** Av. Rebouças 3970, Pinheiros. Though rather downmarket, Eldorado is nevertheless vast and features one of the largest ranges of shops in the city. Its crèche and play area make it popular with families.

**Ibirapuera** Av. Ibirapuera 3103, Moema. This plush shopping centre in an upmarket residential area is strong on Brazilian fashion design.

**Iguatemi** Av. Brigadeiro Faria Lima 1191, Jardim Europa. The oldest of the city's many shopping centres – and constantly being remodelled and relaunched. Well located for the Jardins area, with a mix of mid-range and boutique clothing stores.

**Patio Higienópolis** Av. Higienópolis 615. The most exclusive of the city's shopping centres until Daslu came along, this glass and wrought-iron building features lots of top-end boutiques and an above-average food hall.

**Shopping Light** Corner of Rua Xavier de Toledo and the Viaduto do Chá, Centro. While quite small, this centre is the only place downtown to find the more stylish kind of clothing store.

## Arts and crafts

**Arteindia** Rua Augusta 1371 (Galeria Ouro Velho). One of several shops around the country run by FUNAI, Brazil's protection agency for Indian interests, this is the best place in São Paulo for Amerindian crafts. There's usually an excellent selection of basketry, necklaces, feather items and ceramics with the tribes and places of origin all clearly identified.

**Espaco Brasil** Alameda Franca 1173, Jardim Paulista. Three floors showcase handicrafts, including much from Bahia, such as naïf ornaments and *berimbaus*, as well as items from elsewhere in Brazil that are, on the whole, reasonably priced.

**Galeria Arte Brasileira** Alameda Lorena 2163, Jardim Paulista. A mix of tacky souvenirs and well-chosen artisan products from throughout Brazil, especially the Amazon and the Northeast, are on sale here.

**Galeria Brasiliana** Rua Artur de Azevedo 520, Jardim America. Popular Brazilian paintings and other artwork – not cheap, but of excellent quality, with the pieces made by top craftspeople.

## Books and music

**Casa Amadeus** Av. Ipiranga 1129, Centro. Near the Praça da República, this place has a good selection of Brazilian sheet music, percussion and stringed instruments.

**Cultura** Conjunto Nacional building, Av. Paulista 2073. By far the best bookshop in São Paulo, spread over three different rooms and several floors within the same building (one specializes

in language, one in art, and the other – absolutely huge – in everything else, including CDs). There's a great café here – a perfect refuge from the Avenida Paulista crowds – and almost daily book launches to attend. Mon–Sat 9am–10pm, Sun noon–8pm.
**FNAC Centro Cultural** Av. Pedroso de Moraes 858, Pinheiros. Good range of CDs and books, including a nice array of English-language titles and high-quality Brazilian art and other coffee-table books. The area around is clustered with independent music and book shops, too. There's a smaller branch at Av. Paulista 901. Daily 10am–10pm.
**Galeria do Rock** Rua 24 de Maio 62, Centro. The place to go to buy Brazilian music, both past and present, CD and vinyl. Located just behind the Theatro Municipal.
**Livraria da Vila** Rua Fradique Coutinho 915, Vila Madalena. A charming community bookshop that, although well stocked, may not be worth going out of the way for but, as it's open late, it's certainly worth dropping by if you're spending an evening in bohemian Vila Madalena.

### Markets

**Antiguidades do MASP** Museu de Arte de São Paulo (MASP), Av. Paulista 1578 (Sun 10am–5pm). Comprising mostly medals, old letters, ceramics, etc, this is a fun place to browse, but don't expect to find much worth buying.
**Antiguidades e Artes** Praça Benedito Calixto, Pinheiros (Sat 9am–7pm). Cheaper, livelier and with a larger collection of bric-a-brac than the similar market beneath MASP (see above), you may in fact pick up the odd bargain here. Some good restaurants are located around the square and food stalls are in the market itself.
**Antiguidades e Artesanato do Bixiga** Praça Dom Orione, Bela Vista (Sun 9am–6pm). This flea market has little worth purchasing, but lots of local atmosphere.
**Casa Santa Luzia** Alameda Lorena 1471, Jardim Paulista. An amazing gourmet supermarket, this is the perfect place to stock up if you're staying in an apartment hotel in the area. Otherwise, check out the luxury Brazilian food items that include preserves, wines and liquors. Open until late daily.
**Feira Oriental** Praça da Liberdade, Liberdade (Sun 10am–7pm). Japanese horticulturalists sell house plants here and some stalls sell good Japanese meals and snacks – usually prepared and sold by kimono-clad Afro-Brazilians.
**Mercado de Flores** Largo de Arouche, Centro. A dazzling daily display of flowers (8am–4pm).
**Mercado Municipal** Rua da Cantareira 306, Centro (Mon–Sat 4am–4pm; see also p.564). About the most fantastic array of fruit, vegetables, herbs, meat, fish and dairy produce that you're likely to find anywhere in Brazil. For taking home, you'll find interesting jams, preserves, pepper sauces and other packaged items. Excellent meals and snacks are also available.
**Feira das Artes** Praça da República and Av. Veira de Carvalho, Centro (Sun 9am–5pm). Amongst the tack in this vast, tented street market, there are some interesting handicrafts, vintage records and semi-precious gems.

# Listings

**Airlines** Aerolíneas Argentinas ⓣ11/3214-4233 & 6445-3806; Air Canada ⓣ11/3254-6600; Air France ⓣ11/3049-0900 & 6445-2887; Alitalia ⓣ11/2171-7600 & 6445-5053; American Airlines ⓣ11/4502-2100 & 6445-3234; British Airways ⓣ11/4004-4440 & 6445-2142; Continental ⓣ11/2122-7500; Delta ⓣ11/4003-2121 & 6445-3926; GOL ⓣ0300/789-2121 & 11/5090-9349; Iberia ⓣ11/3257-6711 & 6445-2726; Japan Airlines (JAL) ⓣ11/3175-2270 & 6445-2040; KLM ⓣ0800/880-1818; Lan Chile ⓣ11/2121-9000 & 6445-3757; Lufthansa ⓣ11/3048-5800 & 6445-2220; Pluna ⓣ11/3231-2822 & 6445-2130; South African Airways ⓣ11/3065-5115 & 6445-4151; Swissair ⓣ11/3016-4747 & 6445-2535; TAM ⓣ0300/123-100 & 11/4002-5700; TAP ⓣ0800/070-7787 & 6445-2400; United Airlines ⓣ11/3145-4200 & 6445-3039; Varig ⓣ11/5091-7000 & 6445-3117.
**Banks and exchange** Branches are concentrated along Av. Paulista, Av. Brigadeiro Faria Lima and Rua 15 de Novembro. The best exchange rates for cash can be found at the *casas da cambio* along Av. São Luís in the centre.
**Car rental** Avis, Rua da Consolação 382, Centro ⓣ11/3259-6868; Hertz, Rua da Consolação 431, Centro ⓣ11/3258-9384; Localiza, Rua da Consolação 419, Centro ⓣ11/3231-3055.
**Consulates** Argentina, Av. Paulista 2313, Cerqueira César ⓣ11/3897-9522; Australia, Alameda Ministro Rocha Azevedo 456, Jardim Paulista ⓣ11/3085-6247; Canada, Av. das Nações Unidas 12901, 16th floor, Itaim Bibi ⓣ11/5509-4321; Ireland, Av. Paulista 2006, 5th floor, Cerqueira César ⓣ11/3287-6362; New Zealand, Alameda

Campinas 579, 15th floor, Cerqueira César ⓣ11/3148-0616; South Africa, Av. Paulista 1754, 12th floor, Cerqueira César ⓣ11/3285-0433; UK, Rua Ferreira de Araújo 741, Pinheiros ⓣ11/3094-2700; US, Rua Henri Dunant 500, Campo Belo ⓣ11/5186-7000.

**Dress** Business travellers in particular will notice a very different dress-code in São Paulo than in Brazilian cities to the north. For men, suits and ties are pretty much the order of the day, though jackets tend to be carried rather than worn. Evenings are as informal as anywhere else in Brazil.

**Football** There are two major first-division teams based in São Paulo: Corinthians, who usually play at Pacaembu, Praça Charles Miller, Consolação, near the end of Av. Paulista; and São Paulo, who play at Morumbi Stadium (bus #775P from Av. Paulista). Matches are generally held on Wed and Sat; Corinthians' fixture list can be found at ⓦwww.corinthians.com.br and São Paulo's at ⓦwww.saopaulofc.net. Ticket prices start at R$15, but plan on spending at least R$60 for a decent view of the pitch. Anyone with even the faintest interest in the sport should make time to visit the marvellous Museu do Futebol (see p.569).

**Health** The private Hospital Albert Einstein, Av. Albert Einstein 627, Morumbi (ⓣ11/3747-1233, ⓦwww.einstein) is considered to be the best hospital in Brazil. For dentistry, Dental Office Augusta, Rua Augusta 878, Cerqueira César (ⓣ11/256-3104), or Consultorio Dentario (open 24hr), Av. 9 de Julho 3446, Jardins (ⓣ11/3062-0904), are both expensive but have good reputations.

**Newspapers and magazines** Most newspaper kiosks downtown and in Jardins sell English-language newspapers: the *Financial Times*, *Miami Herald* and *International Herald Tribune* are the most widely available. Haddock Lobo Books and Magazines, Rua Haddock Lobo 1503, Cerqueira César (open until midnight), has a particularly good selection of European magazines and newspapers, as do Jardim Europa, corner of Av. Europa and Rua Groenlândia (open 24hr), and FNAC Centro Cultural at Av. Pedroso de Moraes 858, Pinheiros, open 10am–10pm.

**Police** Emergencies ⓣ190. DEATUR, a special police unit for tourists (ⓣ11/3214-0209), is located at Av. São Luís 91, one block from Praça da República.

**Post office** The main post office is downtown at Praça Correio, at the corner of Av. São João, and is open Mon–Fri 8am–10pm. Yellow-coloured postal kiosks are scattered throughout the city, including several along Av. Paulista.

**Public holidays** In addition to the normal Brazilian public holidays (see p.59), most things close in São Paulo on January 25 (Founding of the City) and on Ash Wednesday.

**Travel agents** Travel agents tend to cater towards locals trying to escape São Paulo, with city tours few and far between – though there are exceptions. Odyssey South America, Largo do Arouche 63, Centro (ⓣ11/3331-0278, ⓦwww.odysseysouthamerica.com.br), do interesting walking tours of the city centre (R$20) and can make the arrangements if you want to see a football match (R$90, minimum 4 people), as well as offering longer trips to *fazendas* (ex-coffee plantations). Graffit (ⓣ11/5549-0528, ⓦwww.graffit.com.br) offers a variety of themed tours, such as art, nightlife or religion, in and around São Paulo, while Terra Nobre, Rua Tagipuru 235, Perdizes (ⓣ11/3662-1505, ⓦwww.terranobre.com.br), also has city tours, including an all-day one.

**Visas** To extend your visa, visit the Polícia Federal, Rua Hugo D'Antola 95, 3rd floor, Lapa de Baixo (Mon–Fri 8am–2pm; ⓣ11/3616-5000). Take the *metrô* to Barra Funda and then a taxi (about R$15–20).

# Around São Paulo

What only a few years ago were clearly identifiable small towns or villages are today part of Greater São Paulo. Despite the traffic, however, escaping from the city centre is surprisingly easy, and there are even some points on the coast that can make for good excursions (see p.596).

## Embu

Founded in 1554, **EMBU** was a mere village before São Paulo's explosive growth in the twentieth century. Located just 27km west of the city, Embu has now effectively merged with its massive neighbour, and yet, surprisingly, it has managed to retain its colonial feel. Quaint buildings predominate in the town's compact centre, which is traffic-free on weekends.

▲ Art and sculpture on sale at a craft market in Embu

In the 1970s, Embu was a popular retreat for writers and artists from São Paulo, many of whom eventually set up home here. Today, the **handicraft market** (Sun 9am–6pm) in Largo dos Jesuítas, the main square, makes the town a favourite with *paulistano* day-trippers. The shops around the main square stock a similar selection to what's on offer in the market – pseudo-antiques, rustic furniture, ceramics, leather items, jewellery and home-made jams – but they are also open during the week (although many close on Mon).

Largo dos Jesuítas holds an eighteenth-century church called **Igreja Matriz Nossa Senhora do Rosário**. While its exterior is typical colonial Baroque, its interior retains almost no original features. Attached to the church is the **Museu de Arte Sacra dos Jesuítas** (Tues–Sun 9am-5pm), which houses an interesting collection of eighteenth-century religious artefacts. Otherwise, you might as well sit down and eat at one of several **restaurants** on Largo 21 de Abril and along the adjoining streets; *Patacão* at Rua Joaquim Santana 90 is a particularly good place to sample traditional regional cooking – rare in the city of São Paulo itself – or try *Orixás* at Rua Nossa Senhora do Rosário 60 for excellent Afro-Brazilian food.

For general orientation, there's a well-organized **tourist information** office on Largo 21 de Abril (9am–6pm; ⓣ11/4704-6565). To get here from São Paulo, catch the "Embu Cultural" **bus** (every 30min) from outside the Tietê Rodoviária; the ride takes less than an hour.

## Paranapiacaba

For most of its history, communications from São Paulo to the outside world were slow and difficult. In 1856 the British-owned São Paulo Railway Company was awarded the concession to operate a rail line between Santos and Jundaí, 70km north of São Paulo city, in what was then a developing coffee-growing region. The 139-kilometre line was completed in 1867, remaining under British control until 1947. Overcoming the near-vertical incline of the Serra do Mar that separates the interior of the state from the coast, the line was an engineering miracle and is gradually being restored.

**Paranapiacaba**, 40km southeast of São Paulo and the last station before the rack railway plunges down the coastal escarpment, was the administrative and engineering centre for the rail line and at one time home to four thousand workers, many of them British. Neatly laid out in the 1890s in a grid pattern, the village has remained largely unchanged over the years. All that remains of the original train station is the clock tower, said to be a replica of London's Big Ben, but the workers' cottages, locomotive sheds (which house old British-built carriages and steam engines) and funicular cable station are in an excellent state of preservation; some are even open to the public. On a hilltop overlooking the village you'll find the wooden Victorian-style Castelinho; once the residence of the chief engineer, today the building houses the **Centro Preservação da História de Paranapiacaba** (Tues–Sun 9am–4pm), which displays old maps and photographs of the rail line's early years.

You don't have to be a railway buff to appreciate Paranapiacaba, however. The village is set amidst one of the best preserved areas of Mata Atlântica in the country and most visitors use it as a starting place for fairly serious hikes into the thickly forested **Parque Estadual da Serra do Mar**, notable for its amazing orchids and bromeliads. Employing a guide is strongly advised as trails are unmarked, often very narrow and generally hard going, and poisonous snakes are common. There's an office of the association of licensed guides as you enter the settlement from the station; expect to pay around R$60 for a day and bring food, drink and sturdy footwear. The weather in this region is particularly unreliable but, as a general rule, if it's cloudy in São Paulo you can count on there being rain in Paranapiacaba.

Getting to Paranapiacaba is easy. Take a train from São Paulo's Luz station to Rio Grande da Serra (every 15min; 45min; R$2.50), where, if you're lucky, there'll be a connecting service continuing the two stops to Paranapiacaba. If there's no train, take a bus from outside the station (R$2.40), or a taxi (about R$15). Most visitors return to São Paulo the same day, but guides can point you towards villagers who charge around R$25 per person for simple **bed-and-breakfast** accommodation.

# São Paulo state

Away from São Paulo city, the state's main attraction is its coastline. **Santos**, Brazil's leading port, retains many links with the past, and a number of the **beaches** stretching north and south from the city are stunning, particularly around **Ubatuba**. The towns and cities of the state's **interior** are not so great an attraction – the rolling countryside is largely devoted to vast orange groves and fields of soya and sugar. Fortunately, good-quality roads run through this region, including major routes to the Mato Grosso and Brasília.

## The interior

Although there's not much to hold your interest inland from São Paulo, **Santa Bárbara d'Oeste** has traces of Confederate history, while more recent Dutch immigrant arrivals have had a far greater impact on nearby **Holambra**. Further into the interior is coffee country, where it's possible to visit some old *fazenda* houses. To escape the summer heat, the resort of **Campos do Jordão**, northeast of the city, offers some attractive hill scenery and hiking possibilities.

## Campinas

Around 100km northwest of São Paulo, **CAMPINAS** has been in relative decline compared to its neighbour since the nineteenth century, when it was by far the more important of the two cities. It started life as a sugar-plantation centre, produced coffee from 1870 and later made its money as a hub for agricultural processing and, more recently, high-tech industry and education. An attractive city, with a reasonably compact centre, it doesn't offer many reasons for visiting, though it's interesting enough to take a tour around Largo do Rosário, with its **Catedral** that was inaugurated in 1883. About 13km from the city centre you'll find **Unicamp**, the Universidade Estadual de São Paulo. Founded in 1969 on land belonging to Colonel Zeferino Vaz, during the worst years of military terror the university became – thanks to the protection afforded by Vaz – a refuge for left-wing teachers who would otherwise have been imprisoned or forced into exile. Unicamp rapidly acquired an international reputation and today is widely considered to be Brazil's best university, though you're only likely to visit on academic business as the campus is architecturally unremarkable. With a student population of 100,000, Campinas has a reasonably lively cultural life, centred on the **Centro de Convivência Cultural**, at Praça Imprensa Fluminense in the centre. In addition to a theatre and art galleries, the centre is home to the fine Orquestra Sinfonia.

If you have a car, one of the most interesting places to visit near Campinas is the **Fazenda Monte d'Este**, 12km from town, just off the SP-340 (the road leading to Holambra). Built during the nineteenth-century coffee boom, the beautiful *fazenda* house is open to the public and contains a small museum outlining the development of the area's former coffee-based economy. A tour of the place, which lasts two hours, costs R$45, or R$60 including an excellent lunch (bookings essential on ⓣ19/3257-1236, minimum 5 people).

### Arrival, accommodation and eating

Campinas is a major transport hub, and there are **buses** from the city to most places in the state and many beyond. The highway to São Paulo itself is one of Brazil's best, and the hourly buses from Barra Funda take an hour and a quarter. The **rodoviária** in Campinas is at Rua Barão de Itapura, a twenty-minute walk from the city centre down Rua Saldanha Marinho.

With São Paulo so close you won't necessarily need to stay in Campinas, but there is plenty of centrally located **accommodation**. The *Royal Palm Tower* at Praça Carlos Gomes (ⓣ19/3731-5900, ⓦwww.royalpalmhoteis.com.br; ❼) is a very comfortable business hotel, while the *Ermitage* at Av. Francisco Gilcério 1444 (ⓣ19/3234-7688, ⓦwww.ermitage.com.br; ❺) and the *Opala Barão* at Rua Barão de Jaguara 1136 (ⓣ19/3232-4999, ⓦwww.hoteisopala.com.br; ❹) are cheaper but perfectly decent. There is no shortage of **places to eat** in Campinas either. The three branches of *Giovanetti* in Praça Carlos Gomes and Largo do Rosário are popular student hangouts selling drinks and excellent sandwiches. The *Steiner Bar do Alemão* at Av. Benjamim Constant 1969 offers reasonable German food and cold beer amidst a sometimes raucous atmosphere, while the *Red Angus Beef* at Rua Gen. Osório 2310 is the best *churrascaria*. Excellent Japanese food is served at the *Restaurante Taka* in the *Hotel Vitória* at Av. José de Souza Campos 425.

## Santa Bárbara d'Oeste

When considering Confederate immigration to Brazil the town of Americana tends to spring to mind, but in fact it's **SANTA BÁRBARA D'OESTE**, 13km to the west, which has more Confederate associations. Whereas there are some 25 English-speaking families in Americana, Santa Bárbara, much the smaller of the two cities, is home to about 30 families of Confederate origin – most of whom still speak English with more than a touch of Dixie in their voice. Near the main square, a short walk from the *rodoviária*, the excellent **Museu da Imigração** (Tues–Fri 8–11.30am & 1–5pm, Sat 8–11.30am & 1–2.30pm; Ⓦwww.santabarbara.sp.gov.br/museu) has displays on the history of the Confederates in the area, and that of other nationalities, chiefly Italian.

About 10km from town, the **Cemitério do Campo** is a cool and shaded cemetery on a hill overlooking endless fields of sugar cane. It dates back to 1910 and all the tombstones, as well as the monument commemorating the Confederate immigrants, bear English inscriptions. There's a small chapel here, too, and a picnic area where, four times a year (the second Sun of Jan, April, July and Oct) around 250 members of the Fraternidade Descendência Americana (Ⓦwww.fdasbo.org.br) arrive from throughout Brazil to renew old ties. The cemetery is very isolated and can only be reached by car; a taxi will charge around R$50 to take you there, and will wait for you while you look around. However, as not all taxi drivers know exactly where the cemetery is, ask the museum attendant to order a taxi for you and give your driver precise directions.

As for **accommodation** in Santa Bárbara d'Oeste, there are a handful of modest hotels; try *Nosso* on Av. de Cillo 445 (Ⓣ19/3455-1106; ❷), or *Casablanca* on Rua General Osório 407 (Ⓣ19/3455-7419; ❷), both in the town centre.

## Holambra

About 50km northeast of Americana is the small town of **Holambra**, established in the nineteenth century by settlers from the Netherlands and retaining to this day a great deal of its Dutch character. Twentieth-century arrivals to Holambra (its name is a contraction of Holândia, América and Brasil) from Holland and Indonesia specialized in the cultivation of flowers, and today's residents like to

### Confederates in São Paulo

In the face of humiliation, military defeat and economic devastation, thousands of former **Confederates** from the American South resolved to "reconstruct" themselves in often distant parts of the world, forcing a wave of emigration without precedent in the history of the United States. Brazil rapidly established itself as one of the main destinations, offering cheap land, a climate suited to familiar crops, political and economic stability, religious freedom and – more sinisterly – the possibility of continued slave ownership. Just how many Confederates came is unclear; suggested numbers vary between 2000 and 20,000, and they settled all over Brazil, though it was in São Paulo that they had the greatest impact. While Iguape, on the state's southern stretch of coast, had a large Confederate population, the most concentrated area of settlement was the Santa Bárbara colony, in the area around present-day **Santa Bárbara d'Oeste**.

The region's climate and soil were ideally suited to the growing of **cotton** and the Confederates' expertise soon made Santa Bárbara d'Oeste one of Brazil's biggest producers of the crop. As demand for Brazilian cotton gradually declined, many of the immigrants switched to **sugar cane**, which remains the area's staple crop, though others, unable to adapt, moved into São Paulo city or returned to the United States. Today as many as 100,000 people claim descent from these Confederate exiles.

boast that their prosperity is based on the work ethic those immigrants brought with them. Despite the subsequent arrival of Brazilian migrants, the town's origins are played up, and the urban centre can best be described as Dutch kitsch. Most people get around by bicycle, many of the buildings have Dutch-style facades, and gardens are neatly tended and filled with flowers, while the public telephone stands are in the ludicrous shape of giant wooden clogs. The highlight of the year here is **Expoflora**, the annual spring flower festival, which takes place on most weekends throughout September; the event attracts not only commercial buyers but also ordinary individuals drawn by the colourful displays, Dutch folk-dancing, musical shows and food.

There are hourly bus services to Holambra from Campinas and several buses a day from São Paulo. One of the main reasons to visit is the **restaurants**. The *Confeitaria Martin Holandesa*, Rua Doria Vasconcelos 15, Centro, serves up tea and tasty cakes, while for meals that are more traditionally Dutch try *Old Dutch* (closed all Mon & Sun evening), 1.5km from the centre of town at *Fazenda Ribeirão*, or *Warong*, Rua Campo de Pouso 607, for Indonesian-influenced dishes. There are a handful of simple but good **hotels**, the best being *Parque Hotel das Flores* (Ⓣ19/3902-4006, Ⓦwww.phf.com.br; ③) at Rua das Dálias 100 in Jardim Holanda; at no. 57 on the appropriately named Avenida das Tulipas is the more central *Hotel Shellter* (Ⓣ19/3820-1329, Ⓦwww.shellterhotel.com.br; ②).

## Fazenda Pinhal

During the late nineteenth-century coffee boom, the interior of São Paulo state was synonymous with coffee, and the area around **São Carlos**, now a bustling university city 140km northwest of Santa Bárbara d'Oeste, was particularly productive. Today the farms around the city are largely given over to sugar cane and oranges, and little evidence remains of the area's coffee-producing past. However, the **Fazenda Pinhal**, one of the oldest surviving and best-preserved rural estates in the state of São Paulo, is well worth a visit. The *casa grande*, the main house, was built in 1831 and, typical of the period, modelled after the large, comfortable Portuguese city dwellings of the eighteenth century; it still retains its original furnishings and there are numerous outbuildings, including *senzalas*, the slave quarters. It's possible to stay the night in tasteful, country-style rooms on the estate (Ⓣ16/3375-7142, Ⓦwww.fazendapinhal.com.br; ⑦). The *fazenda* is an easy day-trip from Campinas – and, at a stretch, São Paulo – but you'll need your own transport. Located off the SP-310 highway, at Km 227 take the exit for Riberão Bonito and then turn immediately onto the much smaller Estrada da Broa. After about 4km you'll see a sign marking the *fazenda*'s entrance. It's essential to call in advance; the entrance charge is R$15, plus R$40 for an excellent two-hour tour – a fixed fee for either a large group or an individual.

There's another *fazenda* 47km to the northwest at SP-310 Km 274, just outside Araraquara, which has been developed into a superb luxury hotel, the *Fazenda Salto Grande* (Ⓦwww.hotelfazendasaltogrande.com.br; ⑥ full board). Constructed to serve as a coffee plantation in the late nineteenth century, today the estate offers two swimming pools, horseriding, very comfortable guest rooms and excellent country cooking.

## Campos do Jordão

When temperatures plunge to 15°C, São Paulo's citizens generally shiver and reach for their mothballed woollens. But to experience something approaching genuine cold weather they have to head into the highlands. East of the city, in the direction of Rio, the **Serra da Mantiqueira** boasts the lively winter resort of **CAMPOS DO JORDÃO**, 1628m above sea level. Founded by the British in the late nineteenth century, the town lies on the floor of a valley, littered with countless hotels and private homes resembling English country houses and Swiss chalets, and divided into three sections: **Abernéssia**, the older, commercial, less touristy centre and location of the *rodoviária*; and, a fifteen-minute bus ride away, **Juaguaribe** and **Capivari**, where most of the boutiques, restaurants and hotels are concentrated.

The novelty of donning sweaters and legwarmers draws the crowds in the southern winter, who spend their days filling in the hours before nightfall when they can light their fires. Day-time temperatures at this time of year are typically very pleasant, the sky is clear and the trails dry. In the summer the altitude offers relief from the searing heat of the coast – but avoid going after heavy rains, which can make walking unpleasant.

There's not much in the way of entertainment in the town itself, unless you have a thing for pastiche alpine, but in the surrounding area there are some good walks, with well-signposted trails. The **Parque Estadual Campos do Jordão** is 12km outside the town and its vegetation, including graceful *araucária* (*Paraná* pine) trees, provides a striking counterpoint to the lower-altitude Mata Atlântica. Its most accessible part, the Horto Florestal (daily 8am–7pm), can be reached by hourly buses from opposite the tourist office and has a number of short trails, the nicest being the Cachoeira trail, which leads to a waterfall. A tougher option is to climb the nearby 1950m **Pedra do Baú** peak, for which you must hire a guide (R$80) – ask at the tourist office (see below). For a less strenuous view over Campos do Jordão and the surrounding Paraíba Valley take the ski lift, the *teleferico* (daily 10am–5pm; R$8) – which whisks you up to the **Morro do Elefante**, where you can hire horses – from near the small boating lake in the centre of Capivari. Other **horse treks** in the area are possible as well, lasting between thirty minutes and four hours (R$39 per hr) and taking in hilltop viewpoints and pine forests; your hotel or the tourist office will be able to provide details. There are also a number of **tourist trains** (R$10–35) that traverse the local area. Most are short trips of about forty minutes, such as the one to the tiny village of Pindamonhangaba, surrounded by cattle and rice plantations. **Bikes** can be hired from Av. Frei Orestes Girardi 175 in Abernéssia – these are a popular choice, and useful for getting around the spread-out town, although you probably wouldn't want to take them on the rather bumpy trails.

## Information, accommodation and eating

The tourist information office (daily 8am–6pm), located by the town gate on the main road (SP-123) leading into Campos do Jordão, has maps of the resort and outlying areas and can advise you on room availability and other local interests.

Despite there being dozens of **hotels**, finding a room – especially during the winter months of June and July – is difficult, and landing an affordable one can be impossible. During this high season many places demand a minimum stay of three or even seven nights. On the other hand, during the long low-season, rates plummet. One of the more reasonably priced places is the small and pleasant *Pousada Recanto do Sossego*, Praça Benedito Albino Rodrigues (Ⓣ12/3662-4224; ❸), in Abernéssia, which offers simple rooms. Also in Abernéssia, the *Campos do Jordão Hostel*, at Rua Pereira Barreto 22 (Ⓣ12/3662-2341, Ⓦwww.camposdojordaohostel.com.br; ❹), charges R$50 for a dorm bed and resembles a rather basic hotel more than it does a traditional youth hostel; however, the staff go out of their way to be of help and it's one of the cheapest in town. Otherwise, you're best off walking along the tree-lined Avenida Macedo Soares (in Capivari), where many of the cheaper, but more comfortable, hotels are located, such as the *Nevada* at no. 27 (Ⓣ12/3663-1611, Ⓦwww.hotelnevada.com.br; ④). For something more luxurious in Capivari, the *Pousada Villa Capivary*, Av. Victor Godinho 131 (Ⓣ12/3663-1736, Ⓦwww.capivari.com.br; ⑧ full board), is a very comfortable, Swiss chalet–style hotel.

Although many people eat in their hotels, there are still plenty of pseudo-Swiss fondue **restaurants** to keep you going; the best is the expensive *Le Foyer* (Ⓣ12/3663-2767) in the *Pousada Chateau La Villette* in Vila Everest. The *Bia Kaffee*, Rua Professora Isola Orsi 33 in Capivari, is a very good and reasonably priced German restaurant serving full meals, tea and coffee. The best food, though, is found just out of town at *Harry Pisek*, Av. Pedro Paulo 857, which specializes in sausages – Harry studied sausage making in Germany. The **bar** *Baden Baden* at Djalma Forjaz 93 in Capivari is one of the town's most visited attractions, popular with the trendy set; expect a fight for a table at busy times. As well as crafting its own reasonable brew it also does very good schnitzels and potato dishes. After dark, people congregate around the terrifyingly kitsch "medieval" shopping arcade in Capivari, drinking hot mulled wine at the top of the arcade's tower or, for a really big evening out, watching the electronic thermometer.



# The coast

Despite its proximity to the city, most of the 400km of São Paulo's **coast** have, until recently, been overlooked by sun and beach fiends in favour of more glamorous Rio. But don't listen to *cariocas* who sniff that the state's beaches aren't up to par; by European or North American standards, many are pretty fabulous. Nevertheless, foreign visitors are relatively rare, and most services are aimed at Brazilians. To the northeast, following the coast up to the border with Rio state, the area is developing all too rapidly, but this part of the coast still offers great contrasts, ranging from long, wide stretches of sand at the edge of a coastal plain to idyllic-looking coves beneath a mountainous backdrop. Having the use of a car is an advantage for exploring the more isolated, less spoilt, beaches (see p.588 for car rental info); however, if it's a lively beach resort like Guarujá you're after, public transport can take you there from São Paulo in less than half a day. Southwest of Santos, tourism remains low-key, in part because the roads aren't as good, but also because the beaches simply aren't as beautiful.

## Santos

**SANTOS**, one of Portugal's first New World settlements, was founded in 1535, a few kilometres east of São Vicente. Today it is home to Latin America's largest and arguably most important port, through which a large proportion of the world's coffee, sugar and oranges pass. The city stands partly on São Vicente island, its docking facilities and old town facing landwards, with ships approaching by a narrow, but deep, channel. In a dilapidated kind of way, the compact centre retains a certain charm that the development of the enormous port complex has not yet extinguished. It's massively popular with local tourists, and, although you may want to skip the rather murky beaches, there is a good deal of historical and maritime interest around the city.

### Arrival and information

Coming from São Paulo, be sure to remember buses to Santos leave from the Jabaquara Rodoviária and not from Tietê. In Santos, there are **tourist offices** (8am–8pm) at the *rodoviária*, which is on Praça dos Andradas near the Centro, and at the corner of Avenida Ana Costa and the seafront Avenida Presidente Wilson, in a converted tram car. From outside the latter, the local tourist board runs an excellent **city tour** (Aug–Nov & March–June Sat & Sun 9am–6pm, Dec–Feb & July Tues–Sun 9am–6pm; hourly; R$15), lasting two hours. It takes in all of Santos's main sights, including the port area, and at weekends it stops at the various attractions, giving you the option of getting off and on again as many times as you like.

## Accommodation

Hotels in Santos are concentrated in the main tourist area of Gonzaga, a *bairro* of apartment buildings, restaurants and bars. For such a tatty town, they're surprisingly pricey for what you get. *Mendes Panorama*, at Rua Euclides da Cunha 15 (Ⓣ13/3208-6400, Ⓦwww.mendeshoteis.com.br; ❺), a rather hideous-looking tower block, is the best-value mid-range place around. Alternatively, try the once grand but now slightly run-down *Avenida Palace* (Ⓣ13/3289-3555, Ⓦwww.avenidapalace.com.br; ❹) at Av. Presidente Wilson 10. The *Ritz*, set back at Av. Marechal Deodoro 24 (Ⓣ13/3284-1171, Ⓦwww.hotelritz.com.br; ❸–❹) is hardly, well, the *Ritz*, being rather worn at the edges, but it's friendly, just a couple of blocks from the beach, and worth trying if you've drawn a blank elsewhere. For more comfort try the *Parque Balneário* (Ⓣ13/3289-5700, Ⓦwww.parquebalneario.com.br; ❻) at Av. Ana Costa 555, a luxurious high-rise hotel with a pool.

## The City

Arriving in Santos and getting oriented couldn't be easier. The **rodoviária** is within walking distance of the Centro, on the north side of the island; from it, walk across the square to Rua XV de Novembro, one of the main commercial streets. One block on, turn left at **Rua do Comércio**, along which you'll find the ruins of some of Santos's most distinguished buildings. Although only the facades remain of some of the nineteenth-century former **merchants' houses** that line the street, they are gradually being restored, the elaborate tiling and wrought-iron balconies offering a hint of the old town's lost grandeur. At the end of Rua do Comércio you'll find the **train station**, built between 1860 and 1867, and, while the city's claim that the station is an exact replica of London's Victoria is a bit difficult to swallow, it is true the building wouldn't look too out of place in a British town. Next to the station in Largo Marquês de Monte Alegre, the **Igreja de Santo Antônio do Valongo** (Tues–Sat 8am–6pm, Sun 8am–7pm) was built in 1641 in colonial Baroque style, but with its interior greatly altered over the following centuries; few of its original features remain. Back on Rua XV de Novembro, at no. 95, is the former **Bolsa de Café** (Tues–Sat 9am–5pm, Sun 10am–5pm; R$5; Ⓦwww.museudocafe.com.br), where coffee prices were fixed and the quality of the beans assessed; opened in 1922, the building retains its original fixtures but is now a museum charting the history of the coffee trade. At the end of the street is another Baroque building, the **Convento do Carmo** (Mon–Fri 7am–7pm, Sat & Sun 1–5pm), which is, again, seventeenth century in facade only. Running right through the historical centre, the **tourist tram** (Tues–Sun 11am–5pm; R$1) is a slightly twee but popular way to see the sights. The restored tram (*bonde*), originally brought over from Scotland in 1910, departs regularly from Praça Mauá by Rua do Comércio and takes 15 minutes to do the 1.7-kilometre trip. To get a great view over the whole of Santos, head three blocks south to Praça Correia de Mello 33, where a funicular railway (daily 8am–8pm; R$15) pulls you 150m up **Monte Serrat**; alternatively, you can save cash and climb the steps.

The city is also home to **Santos Futebol Clube**, best known as the club for whom the great Pelé played for most of his professional life (from 1956 to 1974). The stadium, the Vila Belmiro at Rua Princesa Isabel 77, is open to the public when there's no game on (Mon 1–7pm, Tues–Sun 9am–7pm; Ⓦwww.santosfc.com.br). In addition to honouring Pelé at the club's small museum, you can take an hour-long guided tour and snoop around the players' dressing rooms (R$7).

Santos's **beaches** are across town from Centro on the south side of the island, twenty minutes by bus from Praça Mauá or R$14 by taxi. The beaches are huge, stretching around the Atlantic-facing Baía de Santos, and popular in summer, but they're also fairly scruffy. Alongside the beach, facing the Baía de Santos, is **Gonzaga**. To the east, the huge **port area** is a fascinating place, with its giant elevators pouring grain into ships, and warehouses piled to the roof with sugar, but its sheer size means that you really need transport to get around it.

### Eating

There are some reasonable seafood **restaurants** in Centro; try *Café Paulista* at Praça Rui Barbosa 8, or *Rocky* at Praça dos Andradas 5. Otherwise, dining is largely limited to Gonzaga; for reliable Japanese food, there's *Tika* at Rua Bahia 93 (Fri & Sat evening & Sun lunch only), or for good Portuguese food check out *Último Gole* at Rua Carlos Afonseca 214. Alternatively, also in Gonzaga, try the excellent *Maria Farinha*, Rua Alexandre Herculano 168, which, unusually for a Brazilian vegetarian restaurant, is open for both lunch and dinner.

## Guarujá and Maresias

The very commercialized and usually crowded **GUARUJÁ** is São Paulo's most popular beach resort. Getting there is easy; there are half-hourly buses from the city's Jabaquara Rodoviária that take little more than an hour to travel the 85km to the resort. From Santos, take a bus from Gonzaga east along the beach avenue to Ponta da Praia, from where a ferry makes the ten-minute crossing of the Santos channel, and then it's a fifteen-minute bus ride on to Guarujá itself.

The resort features a set of large hotels and apartment buildings alongside lengthy, rather monotonous beaches. In the summer, finding space on the main beach, **Pitangueiras**, can be difficult and the beaches within walking distance or a short bus ride away to the northeast are little better. In fact, without a car and considerable local knowledge, Guarujá is best avoided; in any case, finding a reasonably priced **hotel** in the summer can be almost impossible. Your best bet around Praia das Pitangueiras is the small and friendly *Hotel Rio Guarujá* at Rua Rio de Janeiro 131 (Ⓣ13/3355-9281, Ⓦwww.hotelrio.com.br; ④), just a block from the sea, or at the adjoining Praia Guarujá, at the *Guarujá Praia*, Praça Brigadeiro Franco Faria Lima 137 (Ⓣ13/3386-1901; ③).

From Guarujá's *rodoviária*, buses run east as far as Ubatuba (see p.603), stopping off at points along the way. For much of the first 90km the road passes inland, but approaching Boiçucanga it again skirts the coastline, and the landscape grows increasingly mountainous as the forested Serra do Mar sweeps down towards the sea. Set on a large bay fringed by a fine beach, the once quiet resort has fallen victim to the worst excesses of uncontrolled development, and you'll find hastily built holiday homes, *pousadas* and shopping galleries occupying every square metre of land. From here the road rises steeply inland through the Serra do Mar, from which you'll catch the occasional glimpse of the distant ocean through the trees. The road eventually descends into **MARESIAS**, a resort drawing surfers and clubbers; if you want to beach it until sunset and then party until dawn, this is where to head. Accommodation here is plentiful but relatively expensive: the

*Pousada Brig a Barlavento*, set just fifty metres from the beach at Av. Francisco Loup 1158 (Ⓣ12/3865-6527, Ⓦwww.brig.com.br; ⑤), is a very attractive option with a nicely landscaped garden, a good pool and rooms of varying sizes; 2km from the beach, the *Pousada Pé da Mata*, at Rua Nova Iguaçu 1992 (Ⓣ12/3865-5019, Ⓦwww.pedamata.com; ④), also has a nice pool as well as a pretty forest setting. Alternatively, try the youth hostel, the *Pousada San Sebastian,* at Rua Sebastião Romão César 406 (Ⓣ12/3865-6612, Ⓦwww.maresiashostel.com.br; R$29 per person for a dorm bed, or R$79 for a double), which has all standard hostel facilities but with the added benefit of a pool. The reason many party-goers flock to Maresias is the fabled *Sirena* **nightclub** at Rua Sebastião Romão César 418 (Ⓣ12/3865-6681, Ⓦwww.sirena.com.br), which attracts enthusiastic clubbers from all over the state and beyond; as well as the best Brazilian DJs, it has played host to top international names. Other places, such as *Lao Bar*, opposite *Sirena*, have popped up around it to catch the overflow.

Some 10km or so further on from Maresias you'll find the much quieter and less developed **Praia Toque-Toque Pequeno** and **Praia Toque-Toque Grande** which can be reached by local bus. These are probably the prettiest beaches in the area and are armed with nothing more than a few shops and restaurants.

## São Sebastião

The bustling little town of **SÃO SEBASTIÃO** is a further 27km northeast, on the mainland, directly opposite the island of Ilhabela (see p.600). Founded in the first years of the seventeenth century, São Sebastião relied on its sugar cane and coffee farms until the eighteenth century, when the town entered a period of decline. The growth of the fishing industry and the development of a large oil refinery helped it emerge from this stagnation in the 1980s, and São Sebastião has since manged to retain many of its colonial and nineteenth-century buildings.

The narrow roads that make up the historic centre allow for pleasant wandering among the pastel-coloured, Portuguese colonial–style facades. Praça Major João Fernandes is the heart of São Sebastião and home to a slew of one-storey snack bars and stores, all dominated by the quietly impressive **Igreja Matriz**, built in 1636 and almost as old as the town (although its interior is twentieth-century plaster). The simple white construction, topped with a red-roofed bell tower, is typical of Franciscan-built churches of the period. On summer evenings, the waterfront becomes the site of a fair selling clothes and bric-a-brac, in addition to hosting free outdoor concerts. The waterfront also faces São Sebastião's visitor-centre complex, which contains fascinating displays of old photographs and scale models that chart the town's development, as well as handicrafts by Tupí-Guaraní people who live in outlying parts of the *município*. The centre also houses the **tourist office** (daily 10am–8pm; Ⓣ12/3892-1808) where you can find information on both the town and the surrounding villages and countryside (although not Ilhabela, which is in a separate *município*).

### Accommodation

Due to its proximity to Ilhabela, São Sebastião has a fair selection of simple **hotels** and **pousadas**, considerably cheaper than those on the island and, in some cases, just as nice. Transport connections to Ilhabela are good – see p.600 – though be prepared for some early starts if you're going to be touring the island.

**Hotel Porto Grande** Av. Guarda Mór Lobo Viana 1440 Ⓣ12/3892-1101, Ⓦwww.pelotastur.com.br/porto1. This pretty, whitewashed, colonial-style hotel with a pool is just a 10min walk from town and set in park-like gardens that stretch down to the beach. Rooms are spacious and well equipped, but there's considerable road noise from the adjacent coastal highway. ④

**Hotel Roma** Praça Major João Fernandes ⓣ12/3892-1016, ⓦwww.hotelroma.com.br. A good range of rooms (sleeping one to four people either with or without a private bathroom) positioned around an attractive garden are offered at this simple but tidy hotel on the city's main square. ❸

**Pousada da Ana Doce** Rua Expedecionário Brasileiro 196 ⓣ12/3892-1615, ⓦwww.pousadaanadoce.com.br. This is the prettiest, and one of the friendliest, places to stay in the town's historic centre. The small but perfectly adequate rooms, each with a thatched veranda, are set around a delightful courtyard garden. ❹

**Pousada da Sesmaria** Rua São Gonçalo 190 ⓣ12/3892-2347, ⓦwww.pousadadasesmaria.com.br. Rooms are small but comfortable at this charming, centrally located *pousada* with colonial-style furnishings. An excellent breakfast is included. ❹

### Eating and drinking

Most of the town's dining options focus on snacks and ice cream, but along the waterfront Rua da Praia there's a small cluster of places doing more substantial meals. Unsurprisingly, they primarily serve seafood; the most popular of these – and deservedly so – is *Canoa*, at no. 234, which offers particularly good dishes featuring *pejerrey*, a white fish, and shrimp. *Bombordo* at no. 68 also prepares seafood, and sometimes has live music in the evenings – the cocktails are truly dreadful, though, so stick to the beers.

## Ilhabela

Without a shadow of a doubt, **Ilhabela** is one of the most beautiful spots on the coast between Santos and Rio, though it can get rather crowded in late December and early January. Of volcanic origin, the island's startling mountainous scenery rises to 1370m and is covered in dense, tropical foliage. With 83 percent of the island protected within the boundaries of the **Parque Estadual de Ilhabela**, the dozens of waterfalls, beautiful beaches and azure seas have contributed to the island's popularity. Old or new, most of the buildings are in simple Portuguese-colonial styles, as far removed from brash Guarujá as you can get. The island is a haunt of São Paulo's rich who maintain large and discreetly located homes on the coast, many with mooring facilities for luxury yachts or with helicopter landing-pads.

### Arrival and information

**Ferries** (24hr; pedestrians free, cars Mon–Fri R$39, Sat, Sun & holidays R$59) depart from São Sebastião's waterfront every half-hour and the crossing to the island's ferry terminal at Perequê takes about twenty minutes. If you're driving, be prepared for a long queue for the ferry during the summer unless you book in advance (ⓣ0800/77-33711). On the island, buses (R$2) depart regularly from outside the Perequê terminal to **Vila Ilhabela**. There are also **launches** (R$5) that cross from São Sebastião direct to Vila Ilhabela and back again about once an hour during the day – ask at the tourist office (see below) for the current timetable.

On the waterfront at Rua do Meio, a **tourist office** (daily 9am–10pm; ⓣ12/3896-2440) offers a map of the island and can advise on transport and tours; a smaller office with similar hours can also be found at the ferry port.

### Accommodation

Yearlong, Ilhabela is the most expensive spot on São Paulo's coast, and in the summer it can be difficult to find a place to stay (reservations are essential). The island has several **campsites**, including *Canto Grande* at Praia Grande (ⓣ12/3894-9423, ⓦwww.cantogrande.com.br) and *Pedras do Sino*, 4km north of Vila Ilhabela (ⓣ12/3896-1266). Camping on beaches is forbidden, but no one cares if you pitch a tent on the island's virtually uninhabited eastern side.

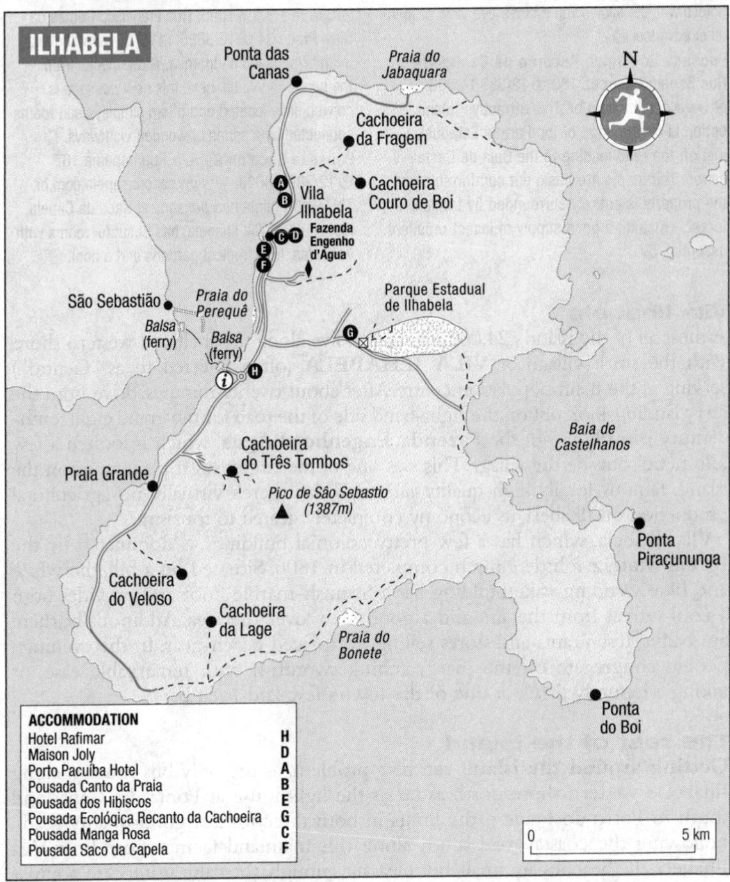


**Hotel Rafimar** Av. Faria Lima 71 ⓣ12/3896-1539, ⓦwww.rafimar.com.br. While it's not in the prettiest part of the island, this simple hotel is the area's cheapest and it has a pool. The nearby ferry landing at Perequê is convenient for reaching the mainland. ❸

**Maison Joly** Rua Antônio Lisboa Alves 278 ⓣ12/3896-1201, ⓦwww.maisonjoly.com.br. Located on a hill above the village, this is the place to go for a serious splurge. All of the hotel's luxurious but tastefully furnished rooms have private terraces with spectacular ocean views, plus it has a pool and the island's best restaurant, which is strong on seafood dishes in a mix of Brazilian and French styles. ❼–❽

**Porto Pacuíba Hotel** Av. Leonardo Reale 2392 ⓣ12/3896-2466, ⓦwwwportopacuiba.com.br. A friendly, charming hotel across the road from the Praia do Viana and a 20min walk into town. Rooms are fairly spartan but there's a nice pool surrounded by palm trees. ❺

**Pousada Canto da Praia** Av. Força Expedicionária Brasileira 793 ⓣ12/3896-1194, ⓦwww.cantodapraiailhabela.com.br. A short walk from town, this colonial-style building is one of the island's prettiest *pousadas* although the rooms' furnishings are a tad fussy. There's a fine pool and the gorgeous garden extends down to the very attractive Praia de Santa Tereza. No children under the age of 12. ❽

**Pousada dos Hibiscos** Av. Pedro Paulo de Moraes 720 ⓣ12/3896-1375, ⓦwww.pousadadoshibiscos.com.br. A reception and courtyard brimming with flowers make this one of the prettiest *pousadas* to stay in; it also has a pool. The rooms feature cool white linen, tiled floors and wooden furniture – the hotel's website allows you a bird's-eye view of them all in advance. ❺

**Pousada Ecológica Recanto da Cachoeira** Rua Benedito Garcêz 180 ⓣ12/3896-3098, ⓦwww.ecoilha.com.br. This attractive inland option is on the edge of the Parque Estadual, just off the road leading to the Baía de Castelhanos. The rooms are basic but comfortable and the property is entirely surrounded by tropical forest – making a good supply of insect repellent essential. ❹

**Pousada Manga Rosa** Rua Francisco Gomes da Silva Prado 34 ⓣ12/3896-1118, ⓦwww.ilhabela.com.br/pousadamangarosa. Three blocks from the centre of Vila Ilhabela, this new *pousada* is conveniently located and offers simple, clean rooms connected by a series of wooden walkways. ❹

**Pousada Saco da Capela** Rua Itapema 167 ⓣ12/3896-8020, ⓦwww.sacodacapela.com.br. This well-maintained *pousada* at Saco da Capela, just south of Vila Ilhabela, has beautiful rooms with verandas, lush tropical gardens and a pool. ❺

## Vila Ilhabela

Almost all of the island's 24,000 inhabitants live along the sheltered western shore, with the small village of **VILA ILHABELA** (often referred to as "Centro") serving as the main population centre. After about twenty minutes, drive from the ferry landing, look out on the right-hand side of the road for the grand eighteenth-century main house of the **Fazenda Engenho d'Agua**, which is located a few kilometres outside the village. This was one of the largest sugar plantations on the island, famous for its high-quality *cachaça*. Today there's virtually no agricultural production on Ilhabela, its economy completely geared to tourism.

Vila Ilhabela, which has a few pretty colonial buildings, is dominated by the **Igreja Matriz**, a little church completed in 1806. Situated on a hill, the white and blue wedding-cake building has a Spanish-marble floor and provides both a cool retreat from the sun and a good view over the area. Additionally, there are banks, restaurants and stores selling overpriced beach-gear. In the evenings, people congregate on the pier, catching swordfish with remarkable ease, or taking a leisurely drink at one of the town's few, laid-back bars.

## The rest of the island

**Getting around the island** can be a problem, as the only bus route is along Ilhabela's western shore north as far as the lighthouse at Ponta das Canas and south to Porto do Frade – the limits in both directions of good-quality roads. Following the coastal road south along this mainland-facing shore from Vila Ilhabela, the beaches are small, but pleasant enough, the calm waters are popular with windsurfers, and bars and restaurants dot the roadside as far as **Perequê**, the island's second biggest town, about halfway south along the island and the location of the ferry port.

There are more attractive beaches on the further-flung coasts of the island, most of which can be reached by schooner and/or jeep. Pretty beaches in coves along the northern coast, such as the **Praia do Jabaquara**, can only be reached by boat or by clambering down steep trails hidden from view from the road. It's along this stretch of coast that some of the island's most exclusive villas are located, and their owners have an interest in making sure the road remains in bad condition and that the beaches are difficult to reach. The road is also poor along the southern shore, where some of the best beaches are located; after the road ends at Borifos, it's a two-hour walk along an inland trail to the tiny fishing hamlet at **Praia do Bonete**; on the way there you'll pass an impressive waterfall, the **Cachoeira do Late**, beneath which a natural pool has formed. Just beyond both of these places lie a couple of other fine beaches.

The entire eastern half of the island falls within the **Parque Estadual da Ilhabela** and is protected from commercial tourist development. The east-coast beaches of the **Baia de Castelhanos**, 25km across the island via a steep

▲ Beach at Ilhabela

mountain road often washed out by heavy rain, have the most surf and are considered by many to be the island's most beautiful. As Castelhanos is in the park, you'll need both a permit and a jeep to visit; the easiest way round this is to book an all-day tour, costing around R$50 per person. Travel agencies that run various boat and jeep combinations exploring the island include Portal Ilhabela at Rua do Meio 38, Vila Ilhabela (☎12/3896-3086), and Lokal Adventure, Av. Princesa Isabel 171, Perequê (☎12/3896-5777). If you want to move around under your own steam, Lokal also rents out cars, jeeps, scooters, bicycles, horses and canoes.

### Eating and drinking

**Eating**, like everything else on Ilhabela, is expensive. Apart from the excellent and rather elegant seafood restaurant in the *Maison Joly* (see p.601), the other notable restaurant on the island is *Viana*, just north of the village at Av. Leonardo Reale 1560 (closed Mon–Thurs April–June & Aug–Nov), which also specializes in seafood. Cheaper options line the beach road between Vila Ilhabela and Perequê, such as the *comida por kilo* joint *Resto do Cura* at Av. Princesa Isabel 337, or, on a side road, *Paulinho* at Rua Pedro de Freitas 201. Live jazz and blues can be heard during the summer at *Jamba!*, Av. Pedro Paula de Moraes 1006.

## Ubatuba and beyond

From São Sebastião, the highway continues along the coast, passing close to isolated and deserted coves of dazzling beauty, with occasional detours through forested areas inland. Buses stop in Caraguatatuba, an extremely ugly, sprawling town with a long, gently curving beach alongside the main road, but you're better off carrying on towards **UBATUBA**. The real draw here is not the very ordinary town but the local beaches, 72 in all, on islands and curling around inlets, and reckoned by some to be among the state's best.

Ubatuba is centred on Praça 13 de Maio, a couple of blocks from the *rodoviária* on Rua Conceição. On the seafront at the end of Thomaz Gallardo there's a very helpful **tourist office** (daily 8am–6pm; ⓣ12/3833-7300), which supplies maps of the coast and whose staff will make hotel reservations for you. Also worth a visit is the local branch of the environmental organization Projeto Tamar, Rua Antônio Athanásio 273 (daily 10am–8pm Dec–Feb; 10am–6pm rest of year), which has display panels (in English and Portuguese) on their work protecting **sea turtles** (mainly loggerheads) that graze offshore, and live turtles on view in pools. Otherwise Ubatuba's main urban area has nothing going for it apart from hotels, rather uninspiring bars and restaurants, banks and other services.

## Accommodation

While not exactly a bargain, the hotels in and around Ubatuba tend to be better value for money than elsewhere along São Paulo's north coast. The town itself makes a good base if you plan to explore the surrounding beaches; accommodation here is mostly concentrated in the area around Rua Conceição. Alternatively, there are plenty of other places to stay in outlying parts.

**Itamambuca Eco Resort** Rodovia Rio-Santos Km 36, Praia de Itamambuca ⓣ12/3834-3000, ⓦwww.itamambuca.com.br. Set back amongst the trees near Itamambuca, one of the area's best beaches, this resort (about 15km north of Ubatuba) has attractive cabins of varying degrees of luxury, with its own on-site restaurants and activities for children. ❼

**Pousada da Ana Doce** Praia do Lázaro ⓣ12/3842-0102, ⓦwww.pousadaanadoce.com.br. Linked to the *pousada* in São Sebastião (see p.600), this is almost as charming, plus it has a pool. Located at Praia do Lázaro, about 20km south of Ubatuba. ❹

**Pousada da Praia** Praia do Félix ⓣ12/3845-1196, ⓦwww.praiadofelix.com.br. Simple bungalow apartments, each with a veranda and a kitchen, situated near one of the area's prettiest beaches. ❺

**Pousada das Artes** Praia das Toninhas ⓣ21/3842-0954, ⓦwww.pousadadasartes.com.br. Arty and slightly pretentious, this is nevertheless a comfy place to stay south of town. Themed guest rooms are based on different cultures, including Arabian, Japanese, and Brazilian itself. ❺

**Pousada Todas as Luas** Praia Itamambuca ⓣ12/3845-3129, ⓦwww.todasasluas.com.br. This basic *pousada* is to the north of town, near the lovely Itamambuca beach, and surrounded by lush forest. ❺

**Pousada Tribo** Rua Amoreira 71 ⓣ12/3842-0585, ⓦwww.ubatubahostel.com. A well-equipped and always popular youth hostel with beds in small dorms for R$30 per person and rooms with en-suite facilities sleeping from two to four people. The hostel is located at Praia do Lázaro, a fishing community about 15km south of town, to which it's linked by bus. ❷

## Eating and drinking

Most **restaurants** are on Avenida Iperoig, which curves alongside the town's beach, the Praia de Iperoig, and you'll find a good variety of seafood, Italian and other types to choose from. For outstanding seafood at low prices, head for *Peixe com Banana* on Ubatuba's seafront at Rua Guarani 255, which specializes in the local dish, *azul-marinho* (essentially fish stewed with green banana). Close by at no. 377, *Como se bom* is in a similar sort of vein, while *Pequim* at no. 385 offers tasty Italian food.

## Around Ubatuba

Although there's nothing wrong with the town's **Praia de Iperoig**, Ubatuba is best used as a base from which to visit some of the numerous other beaches accessible by bus or private boat. The least developed – and the most attractive – are to the **northeast** of town, with the furthest, Camburi, 46km away on the border with Rio state. To get to these beaches, take the **local bus** marked "Prumirim" from the *rodoviária* and ask the driver to stop at whichever stretch takes your fancy. One possible point to make for is the Bairro do Picinguaba, a fishing village with a couple of bars and simple restaurants set alongside a very pretty beach and connected to the main road by a three-kilometre-long narrow winding road.

The more popular beaches are to the south of Ubatuba and also easily reached by bus from the town centre, although almost all of them are fringed with hastily built condominiums as well as shopping and entertainment complexes. **Enseada**, 9km from Ubatuba, is lined with expensive beachfront hotels; nestled in a bay protected from the lively surf, its beach is popular with families, and in the summer it's always uncomfortably crowded.

Across the bay is a series of beautiful isolated beaches that draw fewer people. Walk out of Enseada on the main road for about 2km until you reach Ribeira, a yachting centre and colourful fishing port. From here, there are trips on sailing boats to the **Ilha Anchieta**, a state park on an island where only a few fisherfolk live. These will cost between R$20 and R$40, depending on the itinerary. Beyond Ribeira are sandy coves you can reach by clambering down from the trail on the cliff above the sea.

It's also easy to arrange hikes inland, in the Parque Estadual Serra do Mar, from Ubatuba; try the tour agency Belmar, at Rua Conceição 200 (Ⓣ12/3833-7422, Ⓦwww.ubatubasurfcam.com.br/belmar), which will provide transport and a guide for R$60–150, depending on the trail length.

Incidentally, if you're touring the state, you can travel between Ubatuba and Campos do Jordão by picking up a (frequent) connection in Taubaté.

## Southwest of Santos

The coastal escarpment **southwest of Santos** begins its incline 20–30km inland from the sea. Lacking the immediate mountain backdrop, and with large stretches of the coast dominated by mangrove swamp, this region was for years left more or less untouched by tourism. However, holiday development companies have been moving in recently, aiming at *paulistanos* who can't afford places further north.

Heading south from Santos, the road follows the coast as far as Peruíbe, then moves inland onto higher, firmer terrain before heading back to the coast down the Serra do Mar. The road is slow but, passing through small fishing villages, banana and sugar plantations and cattle-grazing land, you're reminded that there's more to Brazil than just beaches. Bear in mind that from São Paulo, rather than travelling via Santos, it's faster to take a direct bus to Iguape and Cananéia.

### Iguape

**IGUAPE**, roughly 180km from Santos, was founded in 1538 by the Portuguese to guard against the possibility of Spanish encroachment on the southern fringes of the empire. Its poor strategic location at the tip of an estuarine island, however, means it has forever remained a backwater – with the effect that many of its simple colonial buildings survive today in good condition. The greatest concentration of these is found around **Largo da Basílica**, Iguape's main square, which is rimmed by whitewashed and brightly coloured buildings constructed in colonial, nineteenth-century and even Art-Deco styles.

During the summer, Iguape is popular with *paulistanos* seeking a beach vacation away from the sophistication, crowds and expense of resorts further north. The nearest good beach on the mainland is **Barra do Ribeira**, frequented by surfers; it's a 15-minute boat ride to get there from Iguape, or a twenty-kilometre car ride over rough track. Facing Iguape is another island, the **Ilha Comprida**, 86km long but just 3km wide, with an interior of light forest; an uninterrupted beach stretches the entire Atlantic-facing length of the island. In the summer it gets very crowded near the access road that crosses the island, where the beginnings of urban development, including some basic hotels and snackbars, is increasing apace; if you want to be alone, just walk south for a few kilometres. Alternatively, the island can be reached from Cananéia (see below). A bridge links Iguape to the mainland, and frequent buses head inland from both the centre of the island and the **rodoviária**, located a good twenty minutes' walk (or short taxi ride) from the town centre.

Iguape has a good selection of **accommodation**, with the *Solar Colonial* at Praça da Basílica 30 (Ⓣ13/3841-1591, Ⓦwww.guiadeiguape.com.br/solarcolonialpousada; ❸) the nicest by far. The comfortable rooms in this refurbished nineteenth-century mansion are tremendous value, with the best ones overlooking the main square. A few blocks away is the *Pousada Casa Grande* at Rua Major Rebelo 768 (Ⓣ13/3841-1920; ❸) which is less atmospheric, but pleasant nonetheless. For **food**, you'll find very good fish entrées at the *Panela Velha* at Rua 15 de Novembro 190 and at the *Itacurumins* at Rua Porto do Rosário 2.

The helpful **tourist information office** is located at Largo da Basílica 272 (Ⓣ13/3841-3358; 8am–5.30pm).

### Cananéia and around

More appealing than Iguape, **CANANÉIA**, 50km further south and also on an island, lies between the mainland to which it's linked by a short bridge and the Ilha Comprida. Frequent **ferries** run between the town centre and the Ilha Comprida, from where you can either take a bus (every hour) or follow the road for 3km straight ahead by foot or bicycle to the beach (bikes are available for around R$25 per day from Silva Rent a Bike, at Av. Independência 840). Where the road hits the beach, there are a couple of very simple *pousadas* and bars. In the height of summer it gets almost crowded here, but for the rest of the year, both the town and the beaches are extremely quiet.

In the old centre of Cananéia, in particular along *ruas* Tristão Lobo, Bandeirantes and Dom João II, you'll find many ochre-coloured and whitewashed colonial and nineteenth-century buildings. Except for a few, such as the well-preserved, seventeenth-century **Igreja São João Batista** (Wed–Sun 9am–noon & 2–6pm), on Praça Martim Afonso de Souza, they're in very poor condition and for some only the facade remains. The **Museu Municipal** (Mon–Fri 9am–6pm, Sat & Sun 9.30am–6.30pm), also on the *praça*, is worth a brief look, with pride of place among its exhibits going to a preserved shark that weighed 3500kg.

To the south of Cananéia, another island, the **Ilha Cardoso**, is a protected **nature reserve**, with isolated beaches, fishing villages and some wonderful trails. Karl Beitler, a long-term German resident in Cananéia who runs the ecotourism agency Lagamar at Rua Silvino de Araújo 166 (Ⓣ13/3851-1613, Ⓦwww.cananet.com.br/lagamar), knows the area well and leads tours to the island and elsewhere. Schooner trips to Cardoso, departing from the wharf at Beira Mar in the centre of town across from the church, last five or six hours (daily Dec–Feb; R$15 per person), including a stop at a long beach – deserted except for a small café and rangers' post – and the chance to go for undemanding treks through the reserve. The waters are home to around three thousand Tucuxi dolphins, which can easily be seen from the boat and come in amazingly close to shore. If you want longer treks in the reserve, call the guide association on Ⓣ13/3851-1995, or visit their office next to the *Golfinho Plaza* hotel (see opposite).

At low tide, cars are permitted to **drive** along the beach between Iguape and Cananéia on the Atlantic-facing beach, a journey that can be completed in less than an hour; check and double-check tidal times and drive carefully, neither too near the water's edge nor too high up the beach or you risk getting stuck in the sand. Otherwise, **buses** have to take a circuitous route inland, an 80km trip that takes about two hours, with departures several times a day between the towns.

### Accommodation, eating and nightlife

There are plenty of clean and comfortable *pousadas* in the area but nothing that particularly stands out in terms of style or character. The *Pousada Recanto do Morro* (13/3851-3370, www.pousadarecantodomorro.com.br; 3–4) at Rua Profesor Besnard 420 in Morro de São João, about 500m from the town centre, is at least set in attractive gardens surrounded by lush vegetation. Otherwise Cananéia's best accommodation options are located on Avenida Independência, the main road leading into town. The *Golfinho Plaza* (13/3851-1655, www.golfinhoplazahotel.com.br; 3), at no. 885, is the best of these, and the only other local place with a pool, while the *Pousada Bom Abrigo* at no. 374 (13/3851-1546; 3) offers good-value, basic accommodation. Other simple hotels can be found along or near the waterfront in the same vicinity; the best of these is the bungalow-style *Beira-Mar*, at Av. Beira Mar 219 (13/3851-1115, www.cananet.com.br/beiramar; 3).

You can **eat** quite well in Cananéia, where, apart from pizza, the mainstays are fish, mussels, octopus and, the town's speciality, oysters. Restaurants are mainly found on Avenida Independência, and a good choice for seafood is *Bacharel*, at no. 835.

**Nightlife** is low-key here, even in summer, but several bars are located on the waterfront, alongside the *praça*, while a block away at Av. Beira Mar 71 there's the appealing *Kurt Kaffee* – a bar, restaurant and antique shop that stays open until late at night and attracts an eclectic crowd.

## On from Iguape and Cananéia

If travelling south to Paraná, you'll have to change buses in **Registro**, a bustling and rather ugly town an hour inland from both Iguape and Cananéia in the heart of Brazil's main tea-growing region. Registro's once overwhelmingly Japanese character has been greatly diluted in recent years by the arrival of migrants from other parts of the state and with a gradual exodus of young people of Japanese descent drawn to greater opportunities elsewhere. If you're unlucky with connections and need to **stay**, the most comfortable place in town is the *Lito Palace* (13/3821-1055, www.litopalacehotel.com.br; 2), at Av. Jonas Banks Leite 615.

It's also possible to reach Paraná by **boat**; three days a week there are launches from Cananéia (Mon 1pm, Wed & Thurs 8am; 13/3851-1268; R$45) that travel via a tranquil, inland waterway to Ariri (see p.635), a small fishing community just within the state of Paraná. Although the journey there takes only three hours, there is a small risk of no connecting launch if you're planning to visit Guaraqueçaba or Paranaguá. If you find yourself stuck for a night, there are several rustic *pousadas* (www.maruja.org.br; 1–2) in the fishing village of Marujá, a couple of kilometres away, which also has a great beach and wonderful forest trails leading to pristine waterfalls.

# Travel details

## Buses

**Campinas** to: Curitiba (5 daily; 6hr); São Paulo (hourly; 1hr 15min).
**Cananéia** to: Registro (6 daily; 1hr); Santos (1 daily; 5hr); São Paulo (2 daily; 4hr 30min).
**Iguape** to: Registro (13 daily; 1hr); Santos (3 daily; 4hr); São Paulo (4 daily; 4hr).
**Santos** to: Cananéia (1 daily; 5hr); São Paulo (every 15min; 1hr).
**São Paulo** to: Belo Horizonte (hourly; 12hr); Campinas (hourly; 1hr 15min); Campo Grande (8 daily; 16hr); Cananéia (2 daily; 4hr 30min); Corumbá (4 daily; 26hr); Curitiba (hourly; 6hr); Embu (every 30min; 1hr); Florianópolis (8 daily; 12hr); Guarujá (every 30min; 1hr); Holambra (6 daily; 2hr); Iguape (4 daily; 4hr); Recife (4 daily; 40hr); Rio (every 30min; 6hr); Salvador (4 daily; 30hr); Santa Bárbara d'Oeste (8 daily; 2hr); Santos (every 15min; 1hr); São Sebastião (6 daily; 3hr); Ubatuba (6 daily; 3hr 30min).
**Ubatuba** to: Parati (3 daily; 1hr 30min); Rio (2 daily; 5hr); São Paulo (6 daily; 3hr 30min).

## Trains

**São Paulo** to: Bauru (4 daily; 5hr 30min); Rio Grande da Serra (for Paranapiacaba; every 15min; 45min).

## Boats

**Cananéia** to: Ariri (3 weekly; 3hr); Ilha Comprida (frequent; 20min).
**Santos** to: Guarujá (frequent; 10min)
**São Sebastião** to: Ilhabela (every 30min; 20min).

# 9

# The South

VENEZUELA
GUYANA
SURINAME
FRENCH GUIANA
COLOMBIA
N
5
4
3
PERU
7
6
BOLIVIA
2
8
1
PARAGUAY
CHILE
9
ARGENTINA
0
1000 km
URUGUAY

CHAPTER 9

# Highlights

* **Ilha do Mel** One of Brazil's most relaxing islands, blessed with little development and no cars. See p.631

* **Iguaçu Falls** No trip to the South is complete without a visit to these breathtaking falls. See p.638

* **Old-world settlements** Head to the rural south for enduring influences of European pioneer settlers such as Ukrainions in Serra do Tigre, Germans in Pomerode and Italians in the Vale dos Vinhedos and Ukrainians in Serra do Tigre. See p.638, p.668 & p.695

* **Florianópolis beaches** Known as one of Brazil's surfing hot spots, Florianópolis offers plenty of calm swimming beaches as well. See p.656

* **Churrascarias** Choose from a staggering selection of cuts at these popular barbecue houses – two outstanding options are *Na Brasa* and *Galpão Crioulo* in Porto Alegre. See p.685

* **Rio Grande do Sul's cattle country** For a taste of *gaúcho* life the highlands around Cambará do Sul or stay at a historic *charqueada* outside Pelotas or on a working cattle *estância* near Bagé. See p.692, p.700 & p.707

* **São Miguel** The fine Jesuit ruins of São Miguel are dramatically sited in the sparsely inhabited interior of Rio Grande do Sul. See p.703

▲ Praia de Fora (beach) on the Ilha do Mel

# 9

# The South

The states forming the **South** of Brazil – **Paraná**, **Santa Catarina** and **Rio Grande do Sul** – are generally considered to be the most developed parts of the country. The smallest of Brazil's regions, the South maintains an economic influence completely out of proportion to its size. This is largely the result of two factors: the first is an agrarian structure that, to a great extent, is based on highly efficient small and medium-sized units; and the second is the economically active population that produces a per capita output considerably higher than the national average. Without widespread poverty on the scale found elsewhere in the country, the South tends to be dismissed by Brazilians as being a region that has more in common with Europe or the United States than with South America.

Superficially, at least, this view has much to substantiate it. The inhabitants are largely of European origin, and live in well-ordered cities where there's little of the obvious squalor prevalent elsewhere. Beneath the tranquil setting, however, there are tensions: due to land shortages, people are constantly forced to move vast distances – as far away as Acre in the western Amazon – to avoid being turned into mere day-labourers, and *favelas* are an increasingly common sight in Curitiba, Porto Alegre and the other large cities of the South. From time to time these tensions explode as landless peasants invade the huge, under-used *latifúndios* in the west and south of the region, and it is no coincidence that it was here that the Landless Movement (Movimento dos Sem Tera) first emerged.

For the tourist, though, the region offers a great deal. The **coast** has a subtropical climate that in the summer months (Nov to March) draws people who want to avoid the oppressive heat of the northern resorts, and a vegetation and atmosphere that feel more Mediterranean than Brazilian. Much of the Paraná's coast is still unspoilt by the ravages of mass tourism, and building development is essentially forbidden on the beautiful islands of **Paranaguá Bay**. By way of contrast, tourists have encroached along Santa Catarina's coast, but only a few places, such as **Balneário Camburiú**, have been allowed to develop into a concrete jungle. Otherwise, resorts such as most of those on the **Ilha de Santa Catarina** around **Florianópolis** remain fairly small and do not seriously detract from the region's natural beauty.

The **interior** is less frequently visited. Much of it is mountainous, the home of people whose way of life seems to have altered little since the arrival of the European pioneers in the nineteenth and early twentieth centuries. Cities in the interior that were founded by Germans (such as **Blumenau** in Santa Catarina), Italians (**Bento Gonçalves** in Rio Grande do Sul) and Ukrainians (**Prudentópolis** in Paraná) have lost much of their former ethnic

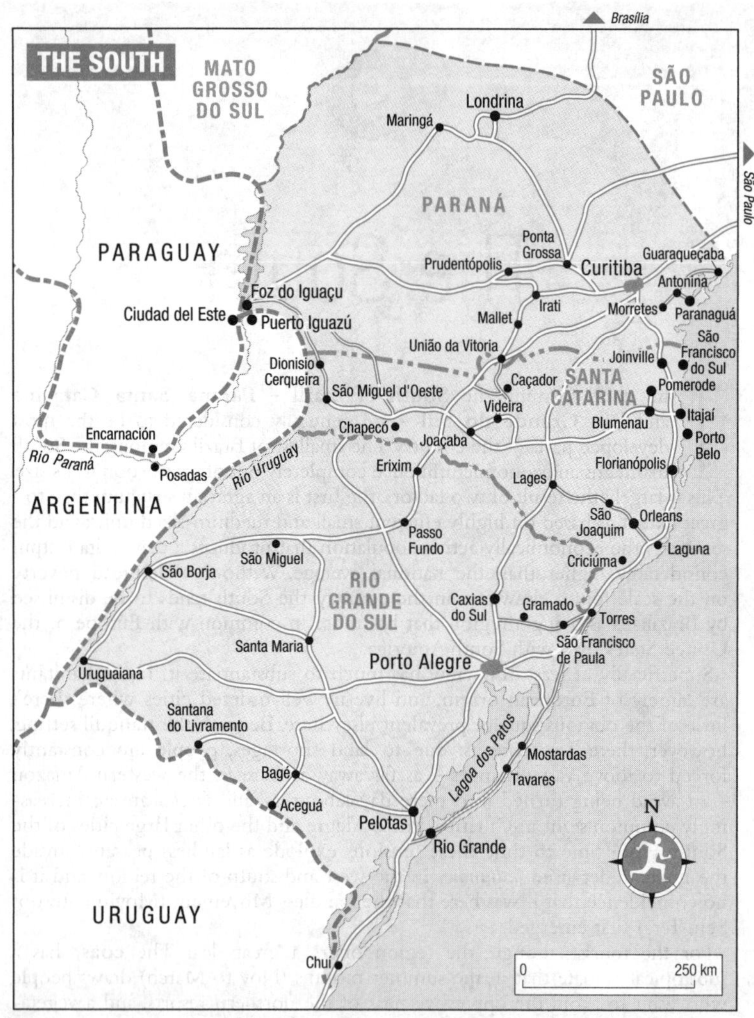


character, but only short distances from them are villages and hamlets where time appears to have stood still. The highland areas between **Lages** and **Vacaria**, and the grasslands of southern and western Rio Grande do Sul, are largely given over to vast cattle ranches, where the modern *gaúchos* (see box, p.707) keep many of the skills of their forebears alive. The region also boasts some spectacular natural features, the best known being the **Iguaçu waterfalls** on the Brazilian–Argentine frontier and the incredible canyons of the **Aparados da Serra**.

Travelling around the South is generally easy, and there's a fine **road** network. Most north–south **buses** stick to the road running near the coast, but it's easy to devise routes passing through the interior, perhaps taking in the Jesuit ruins of **São Miguel**.

# Paraná

**Paraná**, immediately to the south of São Paulo, has become one of Brazil's wealthiest and most dynamic states. Its agricultural economy is based on a mix of efficient family farms and highly capitalized, larger land holdings, while its modern industries, unlike those of so many other parts of the country, have been subject to at least limited planning and environmental controls. The state's population is ethnically extremely diverse, and largely comprised of the descendants of immigrants. All of this combines to give Paraná something of the feel of an American Midwestern state transplanted to the subtropics.

For several decades after breaking away from São Paulo in 1853, Paraná's economy remained based on pig-raising, timber extraction and *erva maté* (a bush whose leaves are used to make a tea-like beverage), and in its early years the province was only linked to the rest of Brazil by a network of trails along which cattle and mules passed between Rio Grande do Sul's grasslands and the mines and plantations of the northern provinces. Paraná was sparsely populated by Indians, Portuguese and mixed-race *caboclos*, who worked on the *latifúndios*, scratched a living as semi-nomadic subsistence farmers or, on the coast, fished.

Then, the provincial government turned to **immigration** as a means to expand Paraná's economy and open up land for settlement. The first immigrant colonies of British, French, Swiss and Icelanders were utter failures, but from the 1880s onwards, others did rather better. As mixed farmers, coffee or soya producers, Germans moved northwards from Rio Grande do Sul and Santa Catarina; Poles and Italians settled near the capital, Curitiba; Ukrainians centred themselves in the south, especially around Prudentópolis (see box, p.637); Japanese spread south from São Paulo, settling around Londrina and Maringá; and a host of smaller groups, including Dutch, Mennonites, Koreans, Russian "Old Believers" and Danube-Swabians established colonies elsewhere with varying success rates. Thanks to their isolation, the immigrants' descendants have retained many of their cultural traditions, traditions that are only gradually being eroded by the influences of television and radio, the education system and economic pressures that force migration to the cities or to new land in distant parts of Brazil. Nevertheless, this multi-ethnic blend still lends Paraná its distinct character and a special fascination.

Unless you're heading straight for the **Iguaçu** waterfalls, **Curitiba** makes a good base from which to start exploring the region. Transport services fan out in all directions from the state capital and there's plenty to keep you occupied in the city between excursions. **Paranaguá Bay** can be visited as a day-trip from Curitiba, but its islands and colonial towns could also easily take up a week or more of your time. Inland, the strange geological formations of **Vila Velha** are usually visited from Curitiba – by changing buses in Ponta Grossa, you can stop off here before heading west to the Ukrainian-dominated region around the towns of **Prudentópolis** and **Irati**, and from there head yet further west to Foz do Iguaçu.

## Curitiba

Founded in 1693 as a gold-mining camp, **CURITIBA** was of little importance until 1853 when it was made capital of Paraná. Since then, the city's population has steadily risen from a few thousand, reaching 140,000 in 1940 and some 1.8 million today. It's said that Curitiba is barely a Brazilian city at all, a view that has some basis. The inhabitants are largely descendants of Polish, German, Italian and other immigrants who settled in Curitiba and in surrounding villages that have since been engulfed by the expanding metropolis. On average, *curitibanos* enjoy Brazil's highest standard of living: the city boasts social and transport facilities that are the envy of other parts of the country. There are *favelas*, but they're well hidden and, because of the cool, damp winters, appear sturdier than those in cities to the north. As elsewhere in Brazil, the rich live secluded

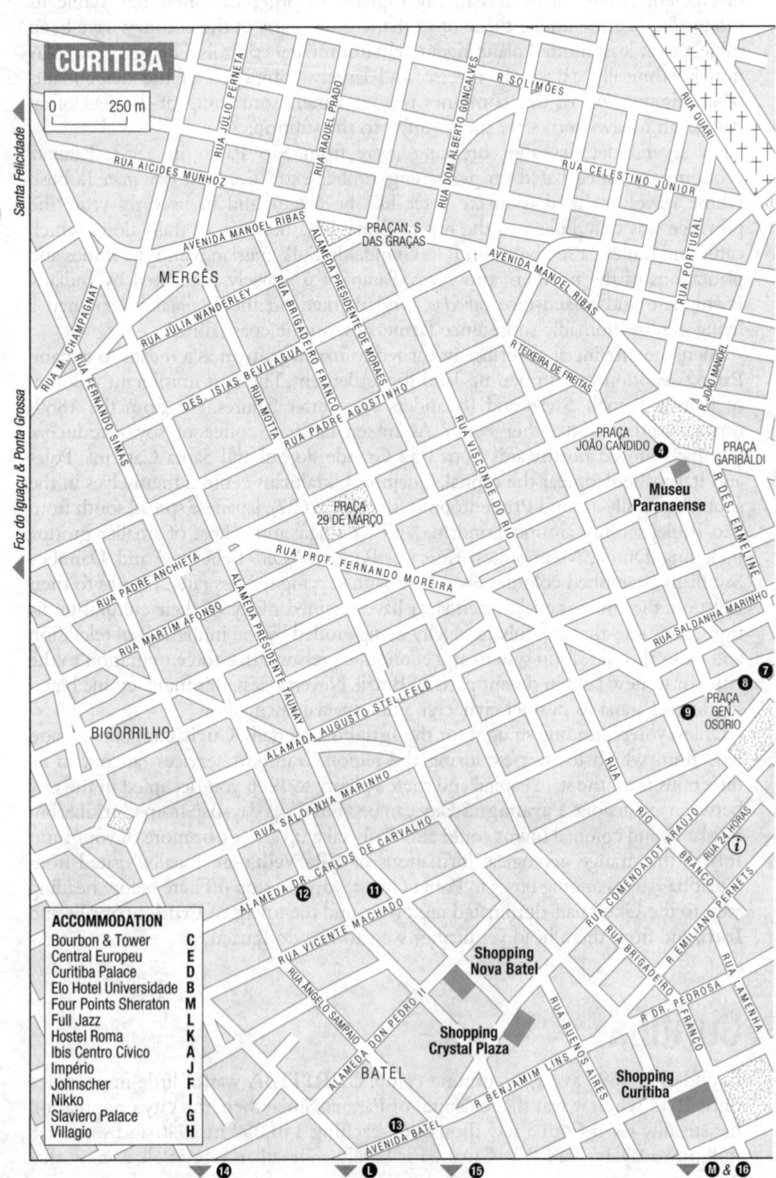

in luxury condominiums, but even these are a little less ostentatious, and need fewer security precautions, than usual.

Many nineteenth- and early twentieth-century buildings have been saved from the developers who, since the 1960s, have ravaged most Brazilian cities, and there's a clearly defined **historic quarter** where colonial and nineteenth-century buildings have been preserved. Much of the centre is closed to traffic and, in a country where the car has become a symbol of development, planners

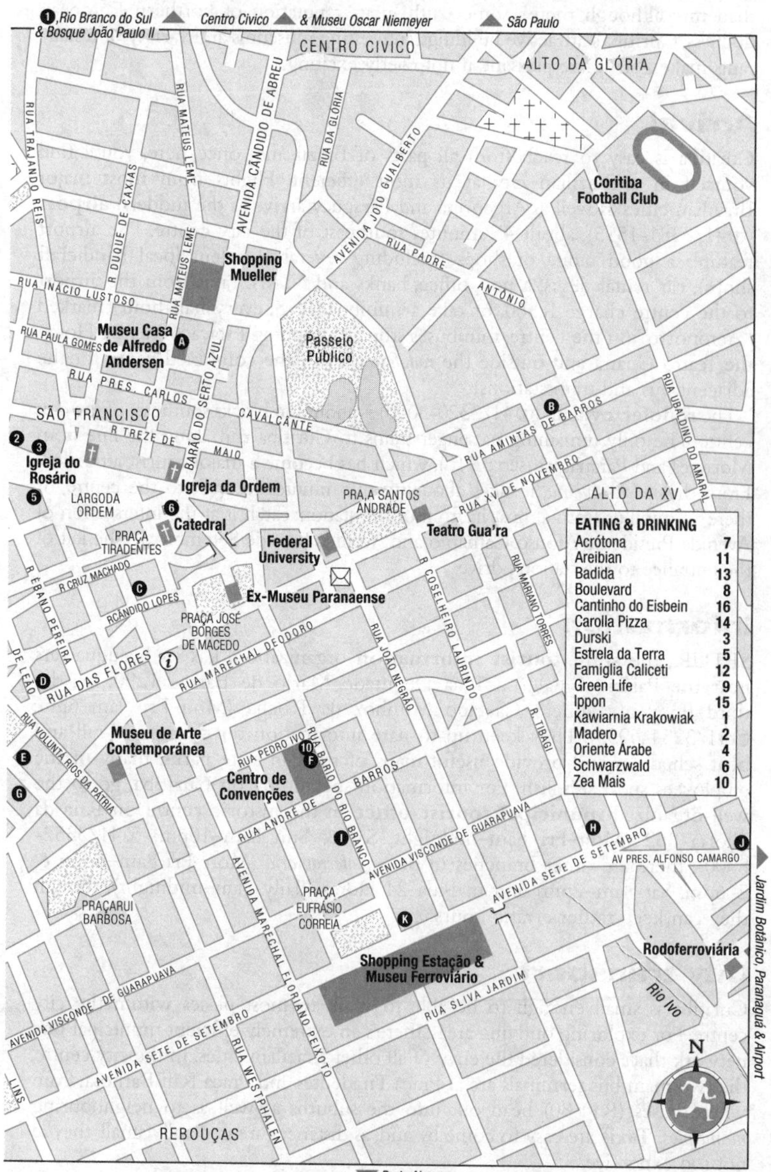

from all over the world descend on Curitiba to discover how a city can function effectively when pedestrians and buses are given priority. Thanks in part to the relative lack of traffic in the city centre, it's a pleasure just strolling around and, what's more, you can wander around the city, day or night, in safety.

One result of its being so untypical of Brazil is that few visitors bother to remain in Curitiba longer than it takes to change buses or planes. At most, they stay for a night, prior to taking the early morning train to the coast. But it deserves more than this: although there's some truth in its reputation of northern European dullness, Curitiba's attractive buildings, interesting museums and variety of restaurants make a stay here pleasant, if not overly exciting.

## Arrival

Curitiba is easy to reach from all parts of Brazil and, once here, you'll find yourself in a Brazilian city at its most efficient. Flights from most major Brazilian cities as well as Argentina and Paraguay arrive at the modern **airport** (Ⓣ41/3381-1515), about 45 minutes southeast of the city centre. The airport features a good range of shops (including several excellent local handicraft shops), car rental desks, a post office, banks and ATMs. Taxis from the airport to the centre charge R$60, or take a minibus (R$8; every half-hour) marked "Aeroporto" (in the centre, minibuses stop at Shopping Estação, Rua 24 Horas, the Teatro Guaíra and outside the *rodoferroviária* – the combined name for the adjacent bus and train stations).

The **rodoferroviária** (Ⓣ41/3320-3000) is about ten blocks southeast of the city centre. The only remaining passenger trains to Curitiba run along the line from Morretes and Paranaguá (see p.710), which has become a major tourist attraction. From the *rodoferroviária*, it takes about twenty minutes to walk to the centre, or there's a minibus from almost in front of the station: catch it at the intersection of Avenida Presidente Afonso Camargo and Avenida Sete de Setembro, to the left of the entrance to the station's drive.

## Information

SETUR, the **state tourist information** organization, has its headquarters near the Palácio Iguaçu at Rua Deputado Mário de Barros 1290, on the third floor of Edifício Caetano Munhoz da Rocha (Mon–Fri 9am–6pm; Ⓣ41/3254-6933). They keep up-to-date information on changes to rail and boat schedules and provide useful maps of trails in state parks; many of the employees speak English. For information specifically on Curitiba, go to the well-organized **municipal tourist office** in the historic centre on Rua da Glória 362 (Mon–Fri 8am–midnight, Sat & Sun 8am–10pm; Ⓣ41/3352-8000); there are other branches in the *rodoferroviária* (Mon–Fri 8am–noon & 2–6pm, Sat 8am–2pm) and in Rua 24 Horas (daily 8am–midnight), though they can keep rather erratic hours.

## City transport

Curitiba is small enough to be able to **walk** to most places within the city centre. For exploring outlying areas, there's an extremely efficient municipal **bus** network that's considered the envy of all other Brazilian cities. In the city centre, the two main bus terminals are at Praça Tiradentes and Praça Rui Barbosa, from where buses (R$1.80) head out into the suburbs as well as to neighbouring *municípios*. **Taxis** are easy to come by and, as distances are generally small, they're not too expensive.

## Linha Turismo

If you have limited time in Curitiba, an excellent way to view the city's main attractions is to take a **bus tour**. Buses of the Linha Turismo depart from Praça Tiradentes every half-hour year-round (Tues–Sun; first bus leaves here at 9am, last bus 5.30pm; R$16) and stop at 25 attractions around the city centre and suburbs. The bus takes just over two hours to complete the itinerary, but tickets allow passengers to get off at five of the stops and rejoin the tour on a later bus.

# Accommodation

If your sole reason for being in Curitiba is to catch the dawn train to the coast, you're best off staying at the youth hostel or at one of the numerous cheap and mid-range **hotels** within a few minutes' walk of the *rodoferroviária*. Otherwise, places in the centre are widely scattered but within walking distance of most downtown attractions and generally remarkable value.

**Bourbon & Tower** Rua Cândido Lopes 102 ⓣ41/3321-4600, ⓦwww.bourbon.com.br. Widely considered the best hotel in the city, with an atmosphere of traditional elegance combined with every modern facility, including a pool, business centre and very good restaurants. ❼

**Centro Europeu** Praça Osório 63 ⓣ41/3021-9900, ⓦwww.hotelcentroeuropeu.com.br. Attractively situated with the nicest rooms overlooking the tree-lined *praça*. There's a friendly atmosphere and the simply furnished rooms are good value and have the standard minibar, TV and a/c. Included in the price is a buffet dinner of soup, salads and cakes. ❹

**Curitiba Palace** Rua Ermelino de Leão 45 ⓣ41/3322-8081, ⓦwww.curitibapalace.com.br. Centrally located, long-established mid-range choice; refurbished rooms are spacious with balconies. ❺

**Elo Hotel Universidade** Rua Amintas de Barros 383 ⓣ41/3028-9400, ⓦwww.hoteiselo.com.br. Modern, rather characterless hotel with a pool, situated next to the university's main administrative building. The rooms are clean and comfortable and the staff are very helpful: excellent value and highly recommended. ❸

**Four Points Sheraton** Av. 7 de Setembro 4211 ⓣ41/3340-4000, ⓦwww.starwood.com. Located in the upmarket residential and commercial inner-city *bairro* of Batel, this is Curitiba's latest luxury hotel aimed primarily at business travellers. Offers all that you'd expect from a *Sheraton*, including a pool, business centre and multilingual staff. Rooms are all large and bright with sitting area, large-screen TV and wireless internet access. ❽

**Full Jazz** Rua Silveira Peixoto 1297 ⓣ41/3312-7000, ⓦwww.hotelslaviero.com.br. As its name suggests, the hotel is themed around jazz, with a programme of live performances, a restaurant inspired by the flavours of New Orleans and a jazz DVD and CD library. Rooms have modern furnishings and the location, in fashionable Batel, is convenient for some of Curitiba's best restaurants. ❻

**Hostel Roma** Rua Barão do Rio Branco 805 ⓣ41/3224-1212, ⓦwww.hostelroma.com.br. Curitiba's HI-affiliated youth hostel, located across from the Shopping Estação, just four blocks west of the *rodoferroviária*. Housed in what was a grand hotel when it was built in 1884, the building is slowly being refurbished so that the exterior, at least, will resemble its former glory. As well as dorms (R$22 per person), there are rooms with private bathrooms that sleep two to four people (❷).

**Ibis Centro Cívico** Rua Mateus Leme 358 ⓣ41/3324-0469, ⓦwww.ibis-brasil.com.br. The hotel's reception and dining area is in an attractive, German-style house, and small but well-appointed guest rooms are in an interlinked tower block behind. Excellent value, and its central location near the historic centre and Shopping Mueller make reservations essential. ❹

**Império** Av. Presidente Afonso Camargo 367 ⓣ41/3264-3373. One of several cheap, but perfectly respectable, hotels located virtually opposite the *rodoferroviária*, useful if you have an early morning train or bus to catch. Offers good, but small, rooms and a nice atmosphere. ❸

**Johnscher** Rua Barão do Rio Branco 354 ⓣ41/3302-9600, ⓦwww.sanjuanhoteis.com.br. The *Johnscher* opened as a luxury hotel in 1917 and established itself as a meeting point for Curitiba high society. After a long decline, it has been thoroughly renovated, recently reopening as a 24-room boutique property with a starkly modern lobby and extremely comfortable, traditionally furnished rooms. Unfortunately, only the rooms at the front of the hotel have a view, these being especially spacious. ❹–❺

**Nikko** Rua Barão do Rio Branco 546 ⓣ0800/709-1808, ⓦwww.hotelnikko.com.br. Modern hotel set behind a pretty nineteenth-century facade. The rooms are simply furnished in a contemporary Japanese style although a refit feels overdue. There's a small Japanese-style courtyard garden and pond. ❹–❺

**Slaviero Palace** Rua Senador Alencar Guimarães 830 ⓣ0800/704-3311, ⓦwww.hotelslaviero.com.br. Situated a couple of blocks from Rua das Flores, this well-established hotel is popular with business travellers. The rooms are pleasant and large and there's an excellent restaurant. ❺

**Villagio** Rua Tibagi 950 ⓣ41/3074-9100, ⓦwww.hotelslaviero.com.br. A friendly, extremely efficient new hotel located just minutes from the *rodoferroviária*. The standard rooms are very small but some can sleep three people. An excellent breakfast is served and there's a restaurant with a reasonable Italian menu. ❹

## The City

Being comparatively compact, much of Curitiba is best explored on foot and, apart from the museums – many of which are located in the central commercial district – most interest is concentrated in the historic centre, around the Largo da Ordem. The main commercial district, with Rua das Flores (part of Av. XV de Novembro) at its heart, is only a couple of blocks south of the historic quarter.

### The commercial district: Rua das Flores and around

The **Rua das Flores** – a pedestrianized precinct section of the Rua XV de Novembro lined with graceful, and carefully restored, pastel-coloured early twentieth-century buildings – is the centre's main late afternoon and early evening meeting point, its bars, tearooms and coffee shops crammed with customers. Few of the surrounding streets are especially attractive, but the **former city hall**, a magnificent Art Nouveau construction built in 1916, at Praça José Borges across from the flower market, is definitely worth a look (the inside is currently closed to the public). Just off Praça General Osório, at the far end of Rua das Flores, there's a small shopping arcade, the **Rua 24 Horas**, an attempt by city planners to keep the centre of Curitiba alive outside of office hours. As its name suggests, businesses here are open around the clock, useful if you have a 4am urge to buy a T-shirt, have a snack or get a haircut.

There are a number of other museums within the commercial centre (the tourist office has a complete list), but only two are worth a look. Of obvious interest to rail buffs, the **Museu Ferroviário**, at Praça Eufrásio Correia (daily 12.30–8.30pm), contains relics from Paraná's railway era. The building housing the museum was the original terminus of the Curitiba–Paranaguá line, and now forms the centrepiece of the **Estação Shopping**, a centre with over a hundred shops, ten cinema screens and plenty of places to eat. The **Museu de Arte Contemporânea**, at Rua Westphalen 16 (Tues–Sat 10am–7pm; ⓦwww.pr.gov.br/mac), concentrates on local artists in its permanent and temporary exhibits. A brief look round the museum's diminutive collection will be enough to recognize that Paraná has not established itself as a trendsetter in the Brazilian contemporary art scene.

A couple of blocks north from Rua das Flores is Praça Tiradentes, where the **Catedral Metropolitana** is located. Inaugurated in 1893, it's a totally unremarkable neo-Gothic construction. If you feel the need for a break from the city crowds, head east for a few blocks to the **Passeio Público**, Curitiba's oldest park. Opened in 1886, it has two large boating ponds at its centre and a network of paths to wander along, shaded by tall trees. Of particular interest here are the aviaries housing local species of brightly feathered birds.

### The historic quarter

Near the cathedral, a pedestrian tunnel leads to Curitiba's **historic quarter**, centred on Largo da Ordem and the adjoining Praça Garibaldi, an area of impeccably preserved eighteenth- and nineteenth-century architecture. The whitewashed and brightly coloured buildings of the old town are a curious mix of small-village Portugal, Poland and Germany. Today the buildings all have state preservation orders on them and do duty as bars, restaurants, art and craft galleries and cultural centres. On Sundays (9am–2pm) in the Largo da Ordem and Praça Garibaldi, the **Feira de Artesanato** sells a range of handicrafts and food representing the state's diverse ethnic traditions.

Two of Curitiba's oldest churches physically dominate the historic quarter. Dating from 1737, with the bell tower added in the late nineteenth century, the **Igreja da Ordem Terceira de São Francisco das Chagas**, on Largo da Ordem, is the city's oldest surviving building and one of the best examples of Portuguese ecclesiastical architecture in southern Brazil. Plain outside, the church is also simple within, its only decoration being typically Portuguese blue and white tiling and late Baroque altars. The church contains the **Museu de Arte Sacra** (Tues–Fri 9am–noon & 1–6pm, Sat & Sun 9am–2pm), with relics gathered from Curitiba's Roman Catholic churches. Opposite the church is the mid-eighteenth-century **Casa Romário Martins** (Tues–Fri 9am–noon & 1–6pm, Sat & Sun 9am–2pm), Curitiba's oldest surviving house, now the site of a cultural foundation and exhibition centre for artists from Paraná. A short distance uphill from here, on the same road, the church of **Nossa Senhora do Rosário** dates back to 1737, built by and for Curitiba's slave population. However, after falling into total disrepair, the church was completely reconstructed in the 1930s and remains colonial in style only.

Further up the hill is the **Museu Paranaense**, on the corner of Rua Kellers and Praça João Cândido (Tues–Fri 9.30am–5.30pm, Sat & Sun 11am–3pm; R$4; Ⓦwww.pr.gov.br/museupr), in a beautifully renovated Neoclassical-style building that once served as the state governor's residence. One of Curitiba's more interesting museums, it has an attractively displayed collection of artefacts, paintings, maps and photographs that chart in detail the history of Paraná from pre-colonial conquest into the twenty-first century.

Back down the hill, off the Largo da Ordem, there are a couple of much smaller art museums along Rua Mateus Leme that are well worth briefly visiting. At number 336 there's the well-organized **Museu Alfredo Andersen** (Mon–Fri 9am–6.30pm, Sat & Sun 10am–4pm; Ⓦwww.pr.gov.br/maa), dedicated to the work of the eponymous Norwegian-born artist and located in his former home and studio. Although a gifted painter, Andersen is hardly known in his native country, in part because the majority of his artistic output is in Brazil and because his subject matter – late nineteenth- and early twentieth-century landscapes and rural people – solely concerned Paraná.

### The outskirts

In the suburbs that ring the historic and commercial centre of Curitiba are several sights that are well worth visiting; although mostly some distance from one another, they're linked by the Linha Turismo bus (see p.617). About 3km to the north of Curitiba's old town is the **Centro Civico**, the sprawling complex of state government buildings with park-like surrounds that was created in the 1950s. The Centro Cívico itself has little architectural merit, but alongside it is the stunningly beautiful **Museu Oscar Niemeyer** (Tues–Sun 10am–8pm; R$4; Ⓣ41/3350-4400, Ⓦwww.museuoscarniemeyer.org.br), by far Curitiba's best art museum. Designed by Niemeyer in 1967 but not constructed until 2003, the building has won over even the architect's most bitter critics. Like all Niemeyer buildings, the structure is visually imposing – in this case dominated by a feature that resembles a giant eye – but it also works well as an exhibition space, something that isn't the case with Niterói's Museu de Arte Contemporânea (see p.618). Consistently excellent visiting exhibitions of Brazilian or other Latin American art are hosted here.

Adjoining the grounds behind the Museu Oscar Niemeyer is the **Bosque Papa João Paulo II** (Mon 1–6pm, Tues–Sun 9am–7.30pm), a park created to commemorate the papal visit to Curitiba in 1980. In the heart of the park, the **Memorial da Imigração Polonesa** (same hours) celebrates Polish immigration to Paraná. It's made up of several log cabins, built by Polish immigrants in the 1880s and relocated here from *colônias* Thomaz Coelho (present-day Araucária) and Muricy (the present-day São José dos Pinhais, near Curitiba's airport). The cabins contain displays of typical objects used by pioneer families, and one building has been turned into a chapel. There's a **shop** attached to the museum selling Polish handicrafts, books and vodka. On the side road as you enter the park, there's a tearoom, *Kawiarnia Krakowiak* (daily 10am–9pm), where you can get delicious home-made Polish-style cakes and light meals.

To get to both the Bosque Papa João Paulo II and Museu Oscar Niemeyer, take the Linha Turismo or a yellow bus going to Abranches from Praça Tiradentes and get off at the **Portal Polaco**, a huge concrete structure extending over the road leading north out of town. Alternatively, take any bus that goes to the Centro Cívico.

A short distance north of the park is the **Universidade Livre do Meio Ambiente** (Ⓦwww.unilivre.org.br), not a university in the traditional sense but more a park and exhibition centre promoting environmental awareness. Established in 1992 as one of the centrepieces of Curitiba's self-proclaimed status as the "environmental capital of Brazil", the grounds – a former quarry – are certainly an attractive place for a stroll. The central building (daily 7am–6pm) is visually striking – it forms an arch and aims at evoking the four elements of fire, earth, wind and water – and hosts stimulating exhibitions on themes such as the regeneration of the Atlantic forest, recycling and alternative forms of energy, as well as courses for adults and children relating to environmental studies. The easiest way to get there is with the Linha Turismo bus; alternatively catch a yellow bus marked "Bosque Zaninelli" or "Jardim Kosmos" from Praça Tiradentes. Just west of here in the Parque Tingüi, the **Memorial da Imigração Ucraniana** (Tues–Sun 10am–6pm) is a Ukrainian-style onion-domed replica church modelled on the much larger one in Serra do Tigre (see p.638) where photographs and handicrafts are displayed celebrating Paraná's Ukrainian heritage; take the Linha Turismo bus to the Parque Tingüi or catch a yellow bus marked "Raposo Tavares" from Praça Tiradentes.

On the other side of town is the **Jardim Botânico** (daily 7am–8pm; R$3), another high-profile project promoting the city's green image. Created in 1991, in the formal style of a French garden, the Jardim Botânico even now is still in its infancy, its limited attraction being its flowerbeds, gently wooded grounds, small greenhouses featuring Brazilian tropical plants and the small Museu Botânico (Mon–Fri 8am–5pm). The Linha Turismo includes the gardens as a stop, or take a red express bus from Praça Tiradentes marked "Capáo da Imbuia/Centenário".

Now completely absorbed into Curitiba, about 8km northwest of the centre, **SANTA FELICIDADE** was founded as a farming colony in 1878 by immigrants from northern Italy. Today Santa Felicidade's Italian character has virtually disappeared, with only a few buildings surviving from the early decades; the European legacy is essentially that of rustic culinary traditions. Across the road from the church there's an interesting **cemetery**, dating from 1886, but the only real reason to visit Santa Felicidade is for the **restaurants** that line the main road, Avenida Manoel Ribas.

Many of the restaurants, which compete fiercely for customers, are enormous – with one seating over four thousand diners – and are favourites of visiting tour groups and Curitiba families alike. As far as the food goes, these places offer the northern Italian food in which the local cooking is rooted, with chicken and polenta being the centrepieces of any meal. A word of warning: the "local" wine is awful, made from grapes trucked in from Rio Grande do Sul, Santa Felicidade's own production having ceased in the 1980s. Whether in a restaurant decked out to look like a pseudo-Italian palazzo, a medieval castle or somewhere less pretentious, charges remain much the same: about R$30 per person for a virtually identical *rodizio di pasta*, a continuous round of pasta, salad and chicken dishes.

Yellow **buses** to Santa Felicidade can be caught on Travessa Nestor de Castro, at the intersection of Rua do Rosário, just below Curitiba's historic quarter; the journey out along Avenida Manoel Ribas takes about thirty minutes. The Linha Turismo (see p.617) also includes Santa Felicidade on its route.

## Eating

Given Curitiba's prosperity and its inhabitants' diverse ethnic origins, it's not surprising that there's a huge range of **restaurants** here, with the historic centre and Batel, an upscale inner-city suburb, being particular areas of concentration. There's an excellent selection of produce available at the Mercado Municipal at Av. Sete de Setembro 1865. For superb cakes, it's well worth the trek out to the Bosque João Paulo II where there's an excellent Polish tearoom, the *Kawiarnia Krakowiak* (see opposite). For superb Italian-style **ice cream** as well as delicious sandwiches, cakes and coffee, try *Marcolini*, Alameda Dr Carlos de Carvalho 1181, near Praça Espanha in Batel or, a few doors away at no. 1175, *Freddo Gelateria* has equally good ice cream; both are open Sunday and Monday until 9pm and Tuesday to Saturday until 11pm.

▲ Curitiba

**Acrótona** Rua Cruz Machado 408. A cheap restaurant where the speciality is unusual Brazilian, Portuguese, Ukrainian and other soups. Evenings only.

**Areibian** Rua Presidente Taunay 435, Batel. Relatively sophisticated Lebanese dishes at very reasonable prices. The buffet offers an assortment of thirty dishes, many of them suitable for vegetarians. Closed Sun evening.

**Badida** Av. Batel 1486, Batel. A slightly upmarket *churrascaria* with a menu extending beyond beef to include other meats and salads. Good lunch specials. Closed Sun evening.

**Boulevard** Rua Voluntarios da Pátria 539 ☎41/224-8244. One of the best restaurants in Curitiba, featuring (expensive) French meals with Italian twists. The beef is superb. Closed Sat lunch & Sun.

**Cantinho do Eisbein** Av. Dos Estados 863, Água Verde. German restaurant with excellent duck and pork dishes that easily feed two people. Good value. Closed Sun evening & Mon.

**Carolla Pizza** Alameda Dom Pedro II 24, Batel. The wood-fired ovens turn out the best pizzas in Curitiba, made with buffalo mozzarella and other fine ingredients, and there's also a fine selection of pasta dishes and salads. Moderately priced. Evenings only (from 7pm).

**Durski** Rua Jaime Reis 254 ☎41/3225-7893. Curitiba's only Ukrainian restaurant, located in a renovated house in the heart of the historic centre looking onto Largo da Ordem. The food (including some Polish, Russian, Italian and Brazilian dishes) is attractively presented and very tasty but, at around R$100 per person, expensive. Lunch Sat & Sun and evenings Mon & Wed–Sat.

**Estrela da Terra** Rua Jaime Reis 176. A very good and moderately priced restaurant in the historic centre, providing *paranaense* cooking at its most varied. There's an excellent *por kilo* buffet or choose from the menu that includes *barreado* (see p.629) and *charque* (dried salted beef), as well as dishes representing the Italian, Dutch, Ukrainian and Polish immigrant traditions. Lunch only.

**Famiglia Caliceti** Alameda Dr Carlos de Carvalho 1367. Most of Curitiba's Italian restaurants are concentrated in Santa Felicidade (see p.620); this is one of the few very good ones close to the downtown area. The moderate-to-expensive menu includes *carpaccio de carne* using beef of the highest quality, and there's an outstanding choice of *tortelloni* and other filled pasta. Closed Sun evening & Tues.

**Green Life** Rua Carlos de Carvalho 271. A large, varied and inexpensive all-you-can-eat buffet drawing on produce from the restaurant's own organic farm located near Curitiba. Attached is a natural food store. Lunchtime only.

**Ippon** Rua Angelo Sampaio 161. An always-busy Japanese restaurant in Batel where you can either select from the menu or opt for the varied *rodizio* (R$48) offerings that include sushi, sashimi and hot dishes. Closed Sun.

**Kawiarnia Kwakowiak** Travessa Woellinto de Vianna 40. This small and very authentic Polish restaurant is located at the main entrance to the Bosque João Paulo II (see p.620). A meal featuring *borscht*, *bigos* and *pierogi* costs R$19, but it's the large assortment of delicious cakes that's the particular attraction. Open daily 10am–9pm.

**Madero** Rua Jaime Reis 262. Looking onto the Largo da Ordem and under the same ownership and almost next door to *Durski* (see above), the speciality here is beef. Certainly the Argentine meat is good, but their claim to serve "the best burgers in the world" is a bit excessive. The setting is elegant, the wine list is outstanding and the food is quite expensive (burgers are R$25 and huge steaks from R$35).

**Oriente Árabe** Rua Kellers 95. A good Lebanese restaurant overlooking Praça João Cândido in the historic centre. At R$16 per person, the *rodizio* is excellent value; you may also wish to try the Brazilian creation of *feijoada árabe* – *feijoada* made with lamb instead of pork. Closed Sun evening.

**Schwarzwald (Bar do Alemão)** Rua Claudino dos Santos 63. Located in the historic centre's Largo da Ordem, this always-crowded bar and restaurant is as popular for the range and quality of its beers as it is for its German food. Sausages and other pork dishes are the mainstays, but the roast duck is also excellent. Daily 5pm to late.

**Zea Mais** Rua Barão do Rio Branco 354 ☎41/3232-3988. Adjoining the *Hotel Johnscher* (see p.617), an attractively presented modern restaurant serving Mediterranean/Brazilian dishes in a contemporary setting.

## Drinking, nightlife and entertainment

During the late afternoon and early evening locals congregate in the pavement cafés at the Praça Osório end of Rua das Flores, but as the evening progresses the historic centre comes to life, its **bars, restaurants and theatres** attracting a mainly young and well-heeled crowd. On Praça Garibaldi, and the streets extending off it, there are numerous bars, many with **live music** – typically

Brazilian rock music, jazz and what seem to be parodies of country and western. Also in the historic centre, several small bars popular with students dot Rua Mateus, just off the Largo da Ordem.

The wealthy inner-city suburb of Batel also has a considerable number of bars, with a particular concentration on Alameda Presidente Taunay at the intersection of Alameda Dr Carlos de Carvalho. Especially worth checking out are *Bar Curityba* with live jazz most evenings, *Slánte Irish Pub* for live rock and the *Kaffee Bar* for more mellow piano and guitar sounds.

During the winter, the Teatro Guaíra at Praça Santos Andrade, across from the Federal University, has a varied schedule of **theatre**, **ballet** and **classical music**. With three excellent auditoriums, the Guaíra is justified in its claim to be one of the finest theatres in Latin America and is often host to companies from the rest of Brazil, and even international tours.

## Listings

**Airlines** Aerolíneas Argentinas ⓣ41/3232-9012; Gol ⓣ41/3381-1744; TAM ⓣ41/3323-5201; Varig ⓣ41/3381-1588.

**Banks and exchange** Main offices of banks are concentrated at the Praça Osório end of Rua das Flores. ATMs are found throughout the city.

**Books** For local titles, by far the best bookshop in Curitiba is the Livraria do Chain at Rua General Carneiro 441, near the intersection with Rua Amintas de Barros.

**Car rental** Avis ⓣ41/3381-1381; Hertz ⓣ41/3269-8000; Localiza ⓣ41/3253-0330; Unidas ⓣ41/3332-1080.

**Consulates** Argentina, Rua Benjamin Constant 67, 15th floor ⓣ41/3222-9589; UK, Rua Presidente Faria 51, 2nd floor ⓣ41/3094-2700.

**Hospitals** In emergencies use the Pronto-Socorro Municipal hospital at Av. São José 738 (ⓣ41/3262-1121). Otherwise, go to Nossa Senhora das Graças hospital at Rua Alcides Munhoz 433 (ⓣ41/3222-6422).

**Post office** The main office is at Rua XV de Novembro 700, by Praça Santos Andrade.

**Shopping** On Sundays (9am–2pm) the Feira de Artesanato takes over the Largo da Ordem and Praça Garibaldi, with stalls selling handicrafts produced in Curitiba and elsewhere in Paraná. Arte Nossa, on Praça Garibaldi, has a good selection of local handicrafts, while the Espaço Cooparte, nearby on Rua Mateus Leme 200, is also worth a look. For Polish and Ukrainian items, including simple embroidery and intricately painted eggs, try the shops at the Memorial da Imigração Ucraniana and in the Bosque João Paulo II (both on p.620). There's a good selection of handicrafts, T-shirts and other souvenirs available at the airport. Shopping centres include Shopping Mueller, Av. Cândido de Abreu 127, with over two hundred shops; Shopping Curitiba, Rua Brigadeiro Franco 2300; the upscale Crystal Plaza Shopping, Rua Comendador Araújo 731, Batel, which has dozens of shops as well as a cinema; and the enormous Shopping Estação, behind the old train station, which has over 130 shops, numerous restaurants, ten cinema screens and a huge bowling alley.

**Travel agent** An extremely reliable agency is Special Paraná, Edificio Tijucas, Av. Luiz Xavier 68, cj. 1314 ⓣ41/3232-1314, ⓦwww.specialparana.com. They have in-depth local knowledge and can organize general or special interest itineraries at every price range for individuals or groups.

# Around Curitiba

Apart from heading down to the coast (see p.625), there are a couple of places easily reachable by bus that are well worth seeing on day-trips from Curitiba. **Lapa**, a small colonial country town 80km southwest, is a particularly pleasant place to go for a typical *paranaense* Sunday lunch. Just under 100km west of Curitiba is **Vila Velha**, home of a strange rock formation which is the basis of a state park.

## Poles in Paraná

The ethnic group most often associated with Paraná is the **Poles**, who settled in tightly knit farming communities around Curitiba in the late nineteenth and early twentieth centuries. Poles migrated to Brazil in three main waves: the smallest number between 1869 and 1889, the largest during the period of so-called "Brazil fever" that swept Poland and the Ukraine between about 1890 and 1898, and the next-largest contribution in the years just before World War I. Most of the Poles settling in the vicinity of Curitiba arrived in the 1880s with subsequent immigrants settling further afield in south-central Paraná.

Well into the twentieth century, the Polish community was culturally isolated, but as Curitiba expanded, absorbing many of the old farming settlements, assimilation accelerated. Today the lives of most of the approximately one million *paranaenses* of Polish origin are indistinguishable from those of their non-Polish neighbours. In recent years, however, there has been a revival of interest in people's Polish heritage, and, wherever there are large concentrations of Poles, Polish language classes, folk dance and music groups are being established to preserve or revive folk traditions.



## Lapa

**LAPA** is a sleepy provincial town founded in 1731 on the trail linking Rio Grande do Sul to the once important cattle market in Sorocaba. As Lapa is one of the very few towns in Paraná's interior that has made any efforts to preserve its late eighteenth- and early nineteenth-century buildings – typical rustic Portuguese-style colonial structures – the town has become a favourite place for Sunday excursions from Curitiba.

Four blocks behind the *rodoviária*, Lapa's main church, the **Igreja Matriz de Santo Antônio** (Tues–Sun 9–11.30am & 1–5pm) dominates the principal square, Praça General Carneiro. Built between 1769 and 1784, the church is a charmingly simple Portuguese colonial structure, but its interior displays – all too typically – no original features. There are several small museums of mild interest nearby, most notably the **Museu de Epoca** (Tues–Sun 1.30–5pm), an early nineteenth-century house furnished in period style, on Rua XV de Novembro 67, opposite the Panteon dos Herois. The **Museu de Armas** (Sat & Sun 9–11.30am & 1–5pm), on the corner of Rua Barão do Rio Branco and Rua Henrique Dias, in a house of the same period, contains a poor collection of nineteenth-century weaponry.

It's the chance to sample **paranaense cooking**, rare in Curitiba itself, that makes Lapa really worth a visit; the inexpensive and excellent *Lipski Restaurante* (Ⓣ41/3622-1202; closed Sun & Mon evenings) is just a few metres uphill from the *rodoviária* at Av. Manoel Pedro 1855. *Lapeana* cooking is rooted in the early nineteenth century and the food carried by the cattle drivers who passed through the town en route from Rio Grande do Sul to São Paulo. No meal is complete without a plate of *arroz de carreteiro – charque* (jerked beef) cooked with rice, onion and tomato. There are ten **buses** a day between Curitiba and Lapa covering the 80km in less than an hour; for overnight stays modest but perfectly comfortable **accommodation** is available at the *Pousada da Lapa*, Av. Manoel Pedro 2069 (Ⓣ41/3822-1422; ❷).

## Parque Estadual de Vila Velha

Just short of 100km west of Curitiba, in the midst of the Campos Gerais, Paraná's rugged central plateau, is **Vila Velha**, the site of 23 rock pillars carved by time and nature from glacial sandstone deposits, and looking from a distance like monumental abstract sculptures. The formation is a result of sand deposited between 300 and 400 million years ago during the Carboniferous period, when the region was covered by a massive ice sheet. As the glaciers moved, the soil was affected by erosion and the ice brought with it tons of rock fragments. When the ice thawed, this material remained and, as natural erosion took its course and rivers rose, these deposits were gradually worked into their current formations.

The **Parque Estadual de Vila Velha** (Mon & Wed–Sun 8.30am–3.30pm; R$10; ⓣ42/3228-1539) is an hour and a half by **bus** from Curitiba; from the city's *rodoviária*, take a *semi-direito* bus (roughly every hour) to Ponta Grossa and ask to be let off at the park's entrance, a twenty-minute walk from the rock formations. If you're lucky, the driver may enter the park itself, leaving you only a few metres from the beginning of the area where you can wander between and above the fantastically shaped stones, around the lakes and springs and in the wooded section behind.

Facilities in the park are excellent and include a couple of modest **restaurants**. You can also stay in considerable comfort just outside the park at the *Fazenda Capão Grande* (ⓣ42/3228-1198; reservations essential; ④ half-board), which offers horseriding on trails around the *fazenda*. There are good late-afternoon bus services back to Curitiba, so there's no chance of being left stranded if you decide not to stay the night. If you're travelling on to Iguaçu, there's no need to return to Curitiba: instead, take a bus to Ponta Grossa, 20km northwest, from where you can catch an overnight bus to Foz do Iguaçu.

# Paranaguá Bay

Sweeping down from the plateau upon which Curitiba lies, the dramatic mountain range known as the **Serra do Mar** has long been a formidable barrier separating the coast of Paraná from the interior. Until 1885 only a narrow cobblestone road connected Curitiba to the coast and **Paranaguá Bay**, and it took two days for mules and carts to cover the 75km from what was, at the time, the main port, **Antonina**. In 1880, work began on the construction of a **rail line** between Curitiba and **Paranaguá**, a port capable of taking much larger vessels than Antonina could. Completed in 1885, this remains a marvel of late nineteenth-century engineering and the source of much local pride, as it is one of the country's few significant rail lines developed with Brazilian finance and technology. Sufferers of vertigo be warned: the line grips narrow mountain ridges, traverses 67 bridges and viaducts and passes through fourteen tunnels as the trains gradually wind their way down to sea level (see p.626 for details of schedules). Passing through the **Parque Estadual de Marumbi** (see p.628) on a clear day the views are absolutely spectacular, and the towering Paraná pines at the higher altitudes and the subtropical foliage at lower levels are unforgettable. The charming colonial town of **Morretes**, near the foot of the mountain range, is a good base for exploring the surrounding area.

If the fight to save the Amazon rainforest is now on, that for the **Mata Atlântica** (the Brazilian Atlantic forest), today covering barely three percent of its original area, has been all but lost. The forbidding terrain of Paraná's Serra do Mar, however, has provided limited natural protection from exploitation by farming and lumbering interests and, since 1986, legal protection for a wider area has been granted by the state government. In theory, the region's future development must serve the needs of local communities, though the regulations are being blatantly flouted, most persistently by ranchers and plantation owners in remote regions such as on the road between Antonina and **Guaraqueçaba**, the only town on the north shore of Paranaguá Bay.

It remains to be seen to what extent the Paraná's coastal zone will remain unspoilt, but at least the future of the islands seems reasonably secure. Although beautiful beaches and coastal trails attract large numbers of visitors to the **Ilha do Mel**, strict building codes limit the possibility of anything but low-key tourist development. Other islands – most notably **Superagüi** – remain even less touched by tourism, their sole inhabitants being fisherfolk and a few people running very basic *pousadas*.

Passenger **trains** (*trem convencional*) depart from Curitiba's *rodoferroviária* to the coast at 8.15am every day, arriving at Morretes at 11.15am and (Sun only) at Paranaguá at 1.15pm; the return train departs from Paranaguá at 2pm (Sun only) and Morretes at 3pm, arriving in Curitiba at 6pm. It's advisable to buy tickets in advance from the *rodoferroviária* (to Morretes/Paranaguá R$58 second class, R$85 first class; to Curitiba R$38 second class, R$56 first class). There's also an air-conditioned tourist train, the *Litorina*, which operates at weekends and holidays, stopping at scenic points along the way. It departs from Curitiba at 9.15am and arrives in Morretes at 12.15pm; on the return leg it leaves Morretes at 2.30pm to arrive in Curitiba at 5.30pm. Tickets for the *Litorina* (to Morretes R$135; to Curitiba R$100) must be purchased several days before, either

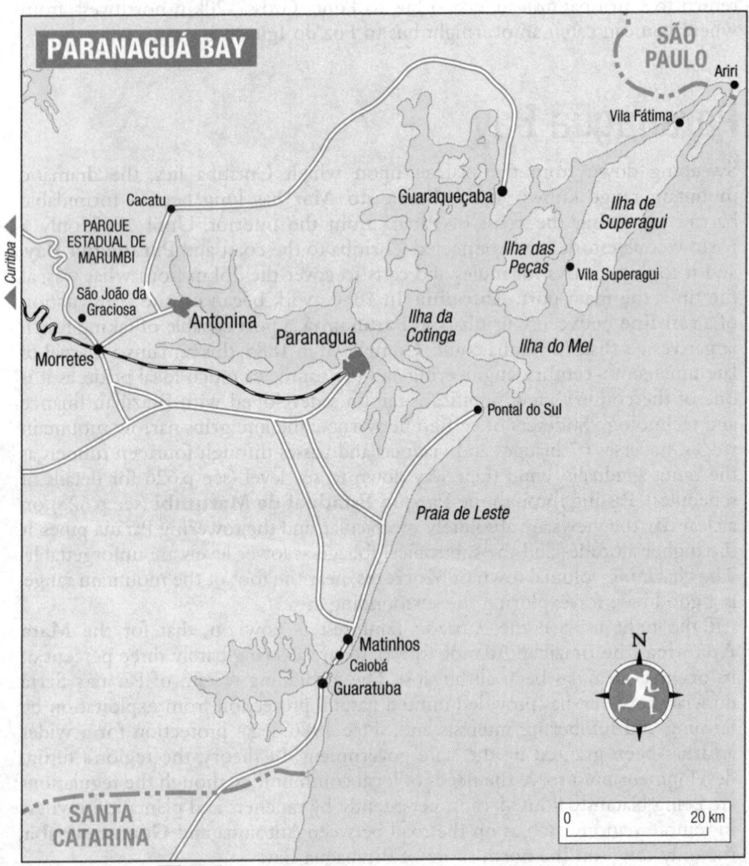

from a travel agent, or direct from the operating company, Serra Verde Express (Ⓣ41/3888-3488, Ⓦwww.serraverdeexpress.com.br) at the *rodoferroviária*. Note that only hand luggage can be carried. For the best views, sit on the left-hand side going down to the coast and on the right when returning. Avoid being persuaded on the train to buy the video of the route as it's really terrible.

If you don't have time to travel by train to the coast, take a **bus** from Curitiba that follows the **Estrada da Graciosa** (2 daily), a dramatic 28-kilometre route with 149 hairpin bends that's almost as beautiful as the train line's. There are also hourly buses between Curitiba and Morretes, Antonina and Paranaguá by the new highway (journey time approximately 1hr 30min); many people return by bus rather than on the train. Buses between Guaraqueçaba and Curitiba take six hours (2 daily), and between Guaraqueçaba and Paranaguá four hours (2 daily), both services going via Antonina. If travelling to or from Santa Catarina, Curitiba can be avoided by taking a bus between Paranaguá and Guaratuba (15 daily, most via Pontal do Sul for access to the Ilha do Mel), and another between Guaratuba and Joinville.

## Morretes

**MORRETES**, a small colonial town founded in 1721, lies 16km inland from Antonina at the headwater where the Rio Nhundiaquara meets the tidal waters of Paranaguá Bay. Buses constantly pass Morretes on their way between Curitiba and Antonina, and Antonina and Paranaguá, but it remains a sleepy little town noted mainly for its production of *cachaça*, for its *balas de banana* (chewy sweets typical of the region) and for *fandango*, a local dance introduced into the area during Spanish colonial times. Most people only stay long enough for lunch, but the cobbled streets, pretty colonial-era houses and small-town atmosphere make this an attractive spot.

Morretes is extremely compact and you just have to stroll a few hundred metres to get out of town; the Porto Morretes *cachaça* distillery is a particularly attractive destination. Located 4.5km from town along the beautiful Estrada Marumbi, an unpaved road that winds its way through lush countryside following the course of a fast-flowing river, the distillery (daily 9am–5pm; Ⓦwww.portomorretes.com.br) produces *cachaça* that rivals some of Brazil's best, thanks to the high quality of the local sugar cane and water. Continue another 3km along the road and you'll reach a grouping of eighteenth-century sugar *fazenda* buildings, including a beautifully preserved *casa grande*, water-powered mill and distillery. Although the buildings are not open to the public, you can walk freely around the sloping grounds that feature well-tended lawns studded with imperial palms, gorgeous flowering trees and bushes. There's a simple restaurant here, the *Panorâmico Ponte Velha* (March–Nov Tues–Wed & Fri–Sun 11am–4.30pm; Dec–Feb daily 11am–4.30pm), serving delicious regional farmhouse food. This 15km round trip will take a day on foot or a couple of hours by car.

Morretes can also be used as a base for visiting the Parque Estadual de Marumbi (see p.628), and Antonina is just a short bus ride away. You can get park and local information from the very helpful **tourist office** in the Casa Rocha Pombo, Largo José Pereira 43 (daily 8am–6pm; Ⓣ41/3462-1024).

There are several basic **hotels** in Morretes; the best is the *Nhundiaquara Hotel*, Rua Carneiro 13 (Ⓣ41/3462-1228; ③), picturesquely positioned on the river in the town centre. A cheaper option, 500m from the *rodoviária* at Rua 15 de Novembro 1000, is the well-kept *Pousada Vista do Marumbi* (Ⓣ41/3462-1573; ②). As well as sampling the excellent local *cachaças*, you can eat well in the town's **restaurants**, mostly specializing in seafood and the regional dish *barreado* (see p.629). For the best *barreado*, head for the the *Armazém Romanus*, at Rua Visconde do Rio Branco 141 (closed Sun & Mon evening), though the restaurant at the *Nhundiaquara Hotel* also serves good food.

## Parque Estadual de Marumbi

Occupying one of the largest and least-spoilt stretches of Mata Atlântica in the country, the **Parque Estadual de Marumbi** features a wealth of flora and fauna and a fine network of trails that, on all too rare clear days, provide stunning views across Paranaguá Bay. Among them is the original **Graciosa trail** (Caminho Colonial da Graciosa), constructed between 1646 and 1653 to link Curitiba with the coast, sections of which are slowly being reclaimed from the forest. If you're travelling by car, the Estrada da Graciosa takes you through the park, with rest areas at especially scenic spots.

From Morretes, there's a **bus** to the village of **São João de Graciosa**, a two-kilometre walk from the park's entrance; if you're coming directly from Curitiba, get off the train at the Marumbi stop, which lies within the park. At the entrance there's a **park office** (Ⓣ41/3432-2072), where you can pick up a trail map. You'll find **accommodation** either in Morretes or one of the several *pousadas* located around the small village of Porto de Cima, just off the road between Morretes and São João. Especially attractive is the *Ilha do Rio*, Estrada da Graciosa Km 7.5 (Ⓣ41/3462-1400, Ⓦwww.pousadailhadorio.com.br; ❹ half-board), with a rustic main building and cabins set within a beautiful garden with a pool. Slightly larger is the *Santuário Nhundiaquara*, Caminho do Itupava Km 2 (Ⓣ41/3462-1938, Ⓦwww.nhundiaquara.com.br; ❺), set in park-like grounds from where you can reach well-marked forest trails. In the park itself there are no places to eat, but São João sports numerous small **restaurants** and bars.

## Antonina

An important port until the 1940s, **ANTONINA** has all the atmosphere of a town that has long since become an irrelevance. As ships grew larger and access to Antonina's harbour was restricted by silt, the town abandoned its role as Paraná's main port and entered a long period of stagnation. Due to its decline, many of Antonina's eighteenth- and nineteenth-century buildings have largely been saved from the developers, leaving the town with a certain backwater charm. With neither masterpieces of colonial architecture, nor beaches immediately accessible, the town attracts few other than Sunday visitors from Curitiba. Nonetheless, along with its much smaller neighbour, Morretes, Antonina is the most pleasant of Paraná's coastal towns, and is a considerably better place to stay than Paranaguá, only a 45-minute bus ride away. It also has an important Carnaval.

The **rodoviária** is located right in the town centre. Turn right onto Rua XV de Novembro, the main commercial thoroughfare, and walk two blocks, past some rather elegant nineteenth-century merchants' houses, then one block along Rua Vale Porto to reach Antonina's very pretty main square and evening meeting point, **Praça Coronel Macedo**. This is where you'll find the town's principal church, **Nossa Senhora do Pilar**; imposing rather than interesting, it dates back to 1714 and is built in typical Portuguese colonial style. Its interior has sadly been completely remodelled and preserves no original features. Across from the church at no. 214 is Antonina's oldest house, which is of late seventeenth-century origin.

The **tourist office** is at the train station (Mon–Fri 9am–5pm, Sat & Sun 10am–5pm; Ⓣ41/3432-4134), a couple of minutes' walk from the town centre. Boats serve the otherwise inaccessible fishing hamlets across the bay from Antonina – the tourist office can provide details of departure times and destinations.

Of the places to **stay**, the *Hotel Camboa Capela* (Ⓣ41/3432-3267, Ⓦwww.hotelcamboa.com.br; ④) is the most distinctive, built amid the ruins of an eighteenth-century Jesuit mission right on the main square, and has the added attraction of a pool. Also on Praça Coronel Macedo is the *Pousada Atlante* (Ⓣ41/3432-1256; ④), with very comfortable rooms, some overlooking the *praça*, and a small pool, as well as the *Monte Castelo* (Ⓣ41/3432-1163; ②), which offers basic and much cheaper accommodation.

As for **meals**, look for a restaurant serving seafood or the regional speciality, **barreado** (see below). An especially good *barreado* (as well as fine seafood) is served at the *Restaurante Albatroz*, Travessa Marquês do Herval 14, just off the main *praça*.

## Paranaguá

Propelled since the 1980s into the position of Brazil's third most important port for exports, **PARANAGUÁ** has now lost most of its former character. Founded in 1585, it is one of Brazil's oldest cities, but only recently have measures been undertaken to preserve its colonial buildings. While both Antonina and Morretes boast less of interest than Paranaguá, they have at least remained largely intact and retain instantly accessible charm. Paranaguá doesn't, though the parts worth seeing are conveniently concentrated in quite a small area, which means you can spend a few diverting hours here between boats, trains or buses.

Both bus and train stations are only a few blocks from Paranaguá's historic centre, and in walking from one to the other you'll pass the most interesting features of the city. If you turn left out of the train station, it's three blocks or so to Rua XV de Novembro. Here, on the corner, is the **Teatro da Ordem**, housed in the very pretty former **Igreja São Francisco das Chagras**, a small and simple church built in 1741 and still containing its eighteenth-century Baroque altars. Further along is the **Mercado Municipal do Café**, an early twentieth-century building that used to serve as the city's coffee market. Today the Art Nouveau structure contains handicraft stalls and simple restaurants serving excellent and very cheap seafood.

Just beyond the market, Paranaguá's most imposing building, the fortress-like **Colégio dos Jesuítas**, overlooks the waterfront. Construction of the college began in 1698, sixteen years after the Jesuits were invited by Paranaguá's citizens to establish a school for their sons. Because it lacked a royal permit, however, the authorities promptly halted work on the college until 1738, when one was at last

### Barreado

In Paraná's coastal towns (in particular Morretes, Antonina and Paranaguá), **barreado**, the region's equivalent of *feijoada*, appears on most restaurants' menus. This speciality, a convenience dish that can provide food for several days and requires little attention while cooking, used only to be eaten by the poor during Carnaval, but is now enjoyed throughout the year. Traditionally, *barreado* is made of beef, bacon, tomatoes, onion, cumin and other spices, placed in successive layers in a large clay urn, covered and then "*barreada*" (sealed) with a paste of ash and *farinha* (manioc flour), and then slowly cooked in a wood-fired oven for twelve to fifteen hours. Today pressure cookers are sometimes used (though not by the better restaurants), and gas or electric ovens almost always substitute for wood-fired ones. *Barreado* is served with *farinha*, which you spread on a plate; place some meat and gravy on top and eat with banana and orange slices. Though tasty enough, *barreado* is very heavy and a rather more appropriate dish for a chilly winter evening than for summer and Carnaval, as originally intended.

▲ Paranaguá waterfront



granted and building recommenced. In 1755 the college finally opened, only to close four years later with the Jesuits' expulsion from Brazil. The building was then used as the headquarters of the local militia, then as a customs house, and today is home to the **Museu de Arqueologia e Etnología** (Tues–Fri 9am–noon & 1–6pm, Sat & Sun noon–6pm). The stone-built college has three floors and is divided into 28 rooms and a yard where the chapel stood, until it was destroyed by a fire in 1896. None of the museum's exhibits relate to the Jesuits, concentrating instead on prehistoric archeology, Indian culture and popular art. The displays of local artefacts are of greatest interest, and there are some fine examples of early agricultural implements and of the basketry, lace-making and fishing skills of the Tupi-Guaraní Indians, early settlers and *caboclos*.

Away from the waterfront, in the area above the Jesuit college, the remaining colonial buildings are concentrated on Largo Monsenhor Celso and the roads running off it. The square is dominated by a cathedral that dates from 1575 but which has since suffered innumerable alterations. On nearby Rua Conselheiro Sinimbu is the charming little **Igreja São Benedito**, a church built in 1784 for the use of the town's slaves, and one that is unusual for not having been renovated. Beyond the church is the **Fonte Velha** or **Fontinha**, a mid-seventeenth-century fountain, and Paranaguá's oldest monument.

## Practicalities

The **train station** is three blocks from the waterfront on Avenida Arthur de Abreu, with services limited to a Sunday train to and from Curitiba (see p.710). Inside the building is the **tourist office** (☎41/3422-6882), which has useful maps of the city and boat, bus and train information. The **rodoviária** (☎41/3423-1215) is on the waterfront, a few hundred metres beyond the Jesuit college.

Paranaguá is a departure point for **scheduled boat services** to Ilha do Mel, Ilha de Superagüi and Guaraqueçaba. Boats make the three-hour crossing to Ilha de Superagüi every Monday, Wednesday and Saturday (2pm) and charge R$20. There's a daily service to Guaraqueçaba (2hr 30min; daily 9am, also

Mon–Sat 1pm; R$15), and there are boats to Ilha do Mel (1hr 45min; Mon–Fri 9.30am & 3.30pm, Sat & Sun 9.20am & 2pm; R$24 return). Additional boat services for Ilha do Mel leave from Pontal do Sul. Keep a careful eye on the weather as storms blow up quickly (especially in Sept & Oct, the months of heaviest rainfall), making crossings uncomfortable and potentially dangerous – if travelling in a privately owned boat, check that life jackets are carried.

Essentially, Paranaguá is a place to pass through – it's worth getting details about leaving as soon as you get here, and only later setting out to explore the city. If you find you have no alternative but to spend a night, **accommodation** is rarely a problem, with several inexpensive and centrally located places to stay. Right next to the ferry landing, the excellent-value *Hostel Continente*, Rua General Carneiro 300 (T 41/3423-3224, W www.hostelcontiente.com.br; 3), has impeccably clean dorm beds and rooms, either with or without a bathroom, that sleep two to four people. For greater comfort (and a pool), the best place in the city is the *Hotel San Rafael*, Rua Júlia da Costa 185 (T 41/3721-9000; 4). There are numerous **restaurants** specializing in seafood and *barreado*, the best of which is the *Casa do Barreado* at Rua Antônio da Cruz 9 (open only Sat, Sun & holidays), which offers an excellent buffet of regional dishes at a remarkably low price. Alternatively, for lunch only, try the excellent and inexpensive seafood restaurants in the Mercado Municipal do Café.

## The Ilha do Mel and the southeast coast

To the east of Paranaguá are Paraná's main **beach resorts**, principally attracting visitors from Curitiba seeking open sea and all the familiar comforts of home. The surrounding countryside is relentlessly flat and the beaches can't really compare with those of Santa Catarina or, for that matter, most other parts of Brazil. There is, however, one notable exception, the **Ilha do Mel**, which, despite being Paraná's most beautiful island, has been protected from tourism's worst effects by being classified as an ecological protection zone – the number of visitors to the island is limited to five thousand per day, building is strictly regulated and the sale of land to outsiders is carefully controlled.

### The Ilha do Mel

Of the islands in Paranaguá Bay, **ILHA DO MEL** has the most varied landscape, the best beaches and most developed (though hardly sophisticated) tourist infrastructure. With just over a thousand permanent residents, visitors greatly outnumber locals during the peak summer months – it still has by far the largest population of any of the islands.

**ENCANTADAS** is the smaller of the island's two settlements but the one that attracts most of the day-trippers. Apart from fishermen's clapboard houses, all there is to Encantadas are a few **bars** and simple **restaurants**, some **pousadas** offering basic accommodation (3), and a police post. In a sheltered position facing the mainland with the mountains all around, it can feel rather claustrophobic, but only a few minutes' walk behind the village on the east side of the island is the **Praia de Fora**, where powerful waves roll in from Africa.

Livelier than Encantadas, but lacking the intimate fishing-village atmosphere, is **NOVA BRASÍLIA**, where the bulk of the island's inhabitants live. Stretched between two gently curving, sheltered bays on a narrow strip of land linking the flat, western section of the island to the rugged, smaller, eastern portion, this is where most tourist facilities (such as they are) are located. Close to the jetty where the passenger boats land, there's a **campsite**, an ecological station, a police, medical and telephone post, and beyond this an immense beach along which are several *pousadas*, as well as **restaurants** and **bars** that are crowded with young people in the evenings. These are not always immediately visible, as many are hidden along paths leading from the beach. For a pleasant and undemanding fifty-minute stroll, wander along the beach towards the ruins of **Fortaleza**, the Portuguese fort (built in 1769 to guard the entrance of Paranaguá Bay), in the opposite direction from the lighthouse that overlooks Nova Brasília.

The most beautiful part of the island is the series of **beaches** along its mountainous southeast side, between Encantadas' Praia de Fora and the Praia do Farol, near Nova Brasília – an area of quiet coves, rocky promontories and small waterfalls. It takes about three hours to walk between the two settlements but, because of the need to clamber over rocks separating the beaches, the journey should only be undertaken at low tide. As the tide comes in, be extremely careful on the rocks: it's easy to slip or get pulled into the ocean by a wave. Let someone where you're staying know where you're going, and carry a bottle of water (there's a clean mountain stream about halfway for a refill) and enough money to be able to return by boat if need be. If you're carrying too much luggage to walk between Encantadas and Nova Brasília, it's usually easier and cheaper to return to the mainland and pick up another boat from there rather than wait for a boat going directly between the two settlements.



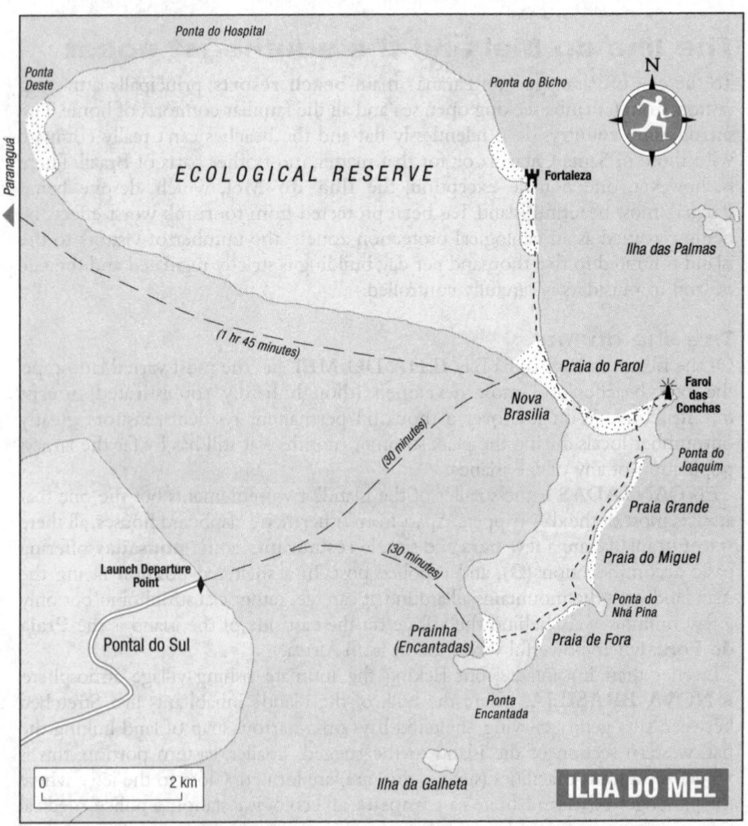

### Practicalities

The island is reached by direct boat services from Paranaguá (see p.630) or, more frequently, hourly **buses** from Paranaguá or Guaratuba to Pontal do Sul; the last bus stop is the beach, where small boats depart for the island. If travelling by car, there are private parking areas where you can safely park for a charge of R$15 per day. The **boat crossing** to Encantadas (also referred to as Prainha) or Nova Brasília, the only villages on the island, takes about thirty minutes, with boats departing hourly Monday to Friday, and every half-hour at weekends and holidays, from 8am to 6pm (R$23 return). As the few shops on the island only sell the absolute basics, it's worth coming supplied with a flashlight and candles (electric current is available for only a few hours a day), mosquito coils and repellent, and anything else you might need.

If you plan to visit in the height of summer without a reservation it's best to arrive during the week and as early as possible in the morning as **accommodation** is scarce. The island is always filled to capacity over New Year and Carnaval when reservations should be made weeks in advance and are accepted only for minimum stays of four or five nights. There's only one genuine **hotel**, complete with room service and relatively plush furnishing, the rather ugly-looking *Park Hotel Ilha do Mel* (Ⓣ41/3426-8075, Ⓦwww.parquehotelilhadomel.com.br; ❹), a 45-minute walk out towards Fortaleza – they will meet you in Nova Brasília and carry your luggage. Following the trail leading from the jetty in Nova Brasília, one of the first **pousadas** is the justly popular *Pousadinha* (Ⓣ41/3426-8026, Ⓦwww.pousadinha.com.br; ❹). The young, multilingual employees are friendly, and rooms (with or without a bathroom) are simple but comfortable. A little further along the trail, the more intimate *Pousada das Meninas* (Ⓣ41/3426-8023, Ⓦwww.pousadadasmeninas.com.br; ❺–❻) is largely built from driftwood, local stone and recycled materials and there's a lovely tree-filled garden. The owner, Suzy, speaks some English and, if you gather together a small group, her husband will take you to outlying islands in his motorboat. Towards the lighthouse, in a quieter part of the island, is the *Pousada Enseada das Conchas* (Ⓣ41/3426-8049, Ⓦwww.pousadaenseada.com.br; ❹) with just four cosy rooms. Just beyond here, at Praia Grande directly facing the Atlantic, is the island's most expensive and largest place to stay, *Grajagan Surf Resort* (Ⓣ41/3426-8043, Ⓦwww.grajagan.com.br; ❸). The rooms are very simple but a little more chic than usual for the island and most have a terrace with wonderful views of the beach. In Encantadas there's the very good HI-affiliated *Zorro Hostel* (Ⓣ41/3426-9052, Ⓦwww.hostelzorro.com.br; R$35 in a dorm or ❸); with over one hundred beds, this is the largest place to stay on the island. Alternatively try the *Ephira Pousada* (Ⓣ41/3426-9056, Ⓦwww.ephira.com.br; ❸), where the well-appointed rooms (all with private bathrooms) sleep up to five people.

**Restaurants** on the island all pretty much offer an unsophisticated menu, based on fish, prawns, rice and beans. Summer evenings are always lively, with notices advertising live music and dances in Nova Brasília's and Encantadas's bars and restaurants.

## The southern coast of Paraná

In contrast to the Ilha do Mel it's hard to find anything positive to say about the rest of the **southern coast of Paraná**, except that it's easy to get to it from Curitiba, making it a popular location for second homes for the city's inhabitants. Twenty kilometres south of Pontal do Sul is the first such resort, **PRAIA DE LESTE**, attracting families and campers. **MATINHOS**, 20km further down the coast, is Paraná's surfing capital and, during the summer months, **hotels** here are fairly expensive – though, in any case, they tend to be fully booked. If you're stuck, however, the *Casarão* and the *Beira-Mar*, both on Rua Reinoldo Schaffer, and the *Praia e Sol* on Rua União (all ❸–❹), are the cheapest hotels in town and worth a try.

Ten kilometres further south down the coastal road, and a ten-minute ferry ride from Caiobá, across the entrance of Guaratuba Bay, is **GUARATUBA** itself, Paraná's most upmarket resort. The best beaches are only accessible by car or private boat, so unless you enjoy being surrounded by luxury hotels and multi-storey apartment buildings, Guaratuba offers little but the buses going to and from Santa Catarina.

## Guaraqueçaba and its islands

North of Paranaguá, directly across the bay, lies Guaraqueçaba, Paraná's poorest and fifth-largest *município*. With 55 isolated settlements, a few poor roads and a widely scattered population of only eight thousand (including a few surviving Tupi-Guaraní Indians, sometimes seen by roadsides selling basketware), Guaraqueçaba's mountainous interior, coastal plain and low-lying islands give the authorities huge administrative headaches. The sole town, also called **GUARAQUEÇABA**, is really only visited by the most dedicated of fishing enthusiasts and people interested in the conservation zone which, in theory at least, encompasses ninety percent of the *município*. Guaraqueçaba is marked by a tremendous feeling of isolation, connected as it is to the outside world only by sea and an unpaved and severely potholed road, which winds about the interior for the convenience of the *latifúndios*. The owners – usually São Paulo-based corporations – are illegally cutting down the forest, most of which falls within the Guaraqueçaba conservation zone, for development as buffalo pasture or banana and *palmito* plantations. Isolation apart, the town's lack of beaches, and rain that seems to pause only long enough to enable mosquitoes to breed, do little to encourage visitors. The town is, however, useful as a starting point for visiting nearby islands, and is reached by a very bumpy three-and-a-half-hour bus ride from Antonina (3 daily) or a three-hour boat crossing from Paranaguá. Once in Guaraqueçaba, you'll find several **places to stay** on the waterfront with rooms that sleep up to six people: the basic, but air conditioned, *Hotel Eduardo I* (Ⓣ41/3482-1225; ❷), the characterless *Hotel Guarakessaba* (Ⓣ41/3482-1217, Ⓦwww.hotelguarakessaba.com.br; ❸), with the advantage of a pool, and the comparatively luxurious *Pousada Bambuza* (Ⓣ41/3482-1427, Ⓦwww.pousadabambuza.com.br; ❹). There are several **restaurants** serving home-style dishes, usually some sort of fish option. In town try *Guaricana* and *Thaíco*, both located in town on the waterfront.

None of Guaraqueçaba's buildings bear witness to the fact that, in the seventeenth century, the town was a more important port than Paranaguá. Nor, apart from the former banana producers' cooperative building at Rua Dr Ramos Figueira 3 (now the local headquarters for IBAMA, the national environmental protection body), do more than a few buildings remain from its heyday between 1880 and 1930 when ships sailed from here to Europe and the River Plate laden with bananas and timber. Today, a shadow of its former self, the port is used only by local fishermen and by boats belonging to the ecological station and municipal authorities, which are used to visit otherwise inaccessible parts of the *município*. Some interesting **handicrafts** are produced by local Guaraní Indians, with the best outlet being the non-profit Jagannatha, Rua Inácio Barbosa Pinto 80, and Arte Nossa, Av. Dr Agrícola da Fonseca.

### Boats and islands

From Guaraqueçaba, there are scheduled **boat services** to Paranaguá (Mon–Sat 5am & 3.30pm, Sun 3.30pm; 2hr 30min; R$15). Though rare, good weather is highly desirable for exploring this, one of the more inaccessible and least spoilt parts of Brazil's coastline; but what is absolutely essential is plenty of time, patience, mosquito repellent and anti-mosquito coils for overnight stays. You may get stuck somewhere for days if there are storms.

Boats to Paranaguá stop off at the **Ilha das Peças**, which forms part of the Parque Nacional de Superagüi and is noted for its marine and Atlantic forest birds. You can be let off on the island and collected again later in the day on the boat's return journey (though confirm that the boat will in fact collect you).

The other regular service is a fortnightly boat to **ARIRI** (first and third Thurs of the month, returning the next day), a small fishing village just within Paraná on the border with São Paulo. On this extremely rewarding trip, the boat stops off at **VILA FÁTIMA**, a tiny settlement on the northwest coast of the island of Superagüi (see below), before passing through the **Canal da Varadouro**, a long, narrow, mangrove-fringed channel. Ariri is only a very short boat trip from **ARARAPIRA**, a village just inside the state of São Paulo, from where another boat leaves the following day (though schedules are extremely fluid) for Cananéia and Iguape.

An occasional boat service also links Guaraqueçaba with the island of **Superagüi** and its village, **VILA SUPERAGÜI**, but as departures depend on the islanders' medical needs the village is more easily reached from Paranaguá either by a fishing boat or, in the summer, with a passenger boat (leaving Paranaguá Sat 10am, returning from Superagüi Sun 3pm; R$20 one way); a crossing from either Guaraqueçaba or Paranaguá takes about three hours. There are just a few basic *pousadas*: the *Sobre as Ondas* (ⓣ41/3482-7118, ⓦwww.superagui.net; ❷), the *Bella Ilha* (ⓣ41/9978-3893, ⓦwww.lol.com.br/~bellailha; ❷), *Crepúsculo* (ⓣ41/3482-7135; ❷) and *Centauro* (ⓣ41/9959-8427; ❷). All have boats that can collect you in Paranaguá and they also arrange boat trips to outlying beaches and islands. On the east side of the island, a short walk or boat ride from the village, is **Praia Deserta**, a beach stretching 34km. Here you'll see marine birds such as cormorants and frigates, and in March and April these are joined by thousands of migratory birds from North America. There are many trails on the island but only researchers working with IBAMA are allowed to venture out of the immediate area of the village or Praia Deserta.

## South-central Paraná

The hilly – and in places almost mountainous – region of **south-central Paraná** makes a good stopover between Curitiba and the Iguaçu Falls for anyone interested in European, especially **Ukrainian**, immigration. As none of the towns in the region are especially distinctive, it's better to use them more as bases from which to visit nearby villages and hamlets where the pioneering spirit of the inhabitants' immigrant forebears remains. The houses, made of wood and sometimes featuring intricately carved details, are typically painted in bright colours and are usually surrounded by flower-filled gardens. Because of the ethnic mix, even small villages contain **churches** of several denominations; most hamlets have at least a chapel with someone on hand to open it up to the rare visitor.

## Prudentópolis and around

The administrative centre of a *município* where 75 percent of the inhabitants are of Ukrainian origin, **PRUDENTÓPOLIS** is heralded as the capital city of Ukrainian Brazil. However, in common with the other regional urban centres, there's little in the city of Prudentópolis to indicate the ethnic background of most of its citizens. Blonde heads and pink noses do predominate, but if you're expecting plump, Tolstoyesque peasants wearing elaborately embroidered smocks and chatting to one another in Ukrainian, you'll be extremely disappointed.

At a glance, Prudentópolis is much like a thousand other nondescript small towns in the interior of southern Brazil. At the heart of the city is a large Roman (not Ukrainian) Catholic church set in a park-like square totally disproportionate in size to the town. The surrounding buildings are the usual mix of anonymous breeze-block and concrete-slab municipal buildings, houses, *lanchonetes* and small stores. Still, committed Ukrainophiles should not despair. A closer look around town will reveal some traces of the Ukraine: many of the older houses bear a resemblance to the peasant cottages of Eastern Europe, in particular in the style of the window frames and roofs. As throughout the region, the Ukrainian Catholic Church displays a strong presence, most visibly in the form of the **seminary**, a large mustard-coloured building next to the Ukrainian Catholic cathedral of São Josafat (masses held in Ukrainian Mon–Sat 6am & 7pm, Sun 6am, 8am, 10am & 5pm). Across the road from the seminary is the church's printing press where Ukrainian-language pamphlets are churned out on machinery that has remained unchanged since soon after the first Ukrainians arrived in Brazil. A block from here in Praça Ucrânia, the excellent **Museu do Milênio** (Mon–Sat 8–11.30am & 1.30–6pm) traces the history of Ukrainian settlement in Brazil. Amidst the photographs, documents and old farming equipment are some wonderful examples of embroidery, the most interesting being those that combine traditional Ukrainian designs with representations of Brazilian birds and flowers. A women's **handicrafts** cooperative is based at the museum with a shop selling intricately painted eggs and embroidery. The work, produced mainly in outlying parts of the *município*, is technically accomplished, but sadly most pieces are mere copies of items found in books and on the internet rather than inspired by Brazil.

There are three modest **places to stay** in town, all a couple of blocks from the main square. The best of these is the new *Elite Palace Hotel*, Rua Marechal Deodoro 1530 (Ⓣ42/3446-4838, Ⓦwww.elitehotel.com.br; ③), but the older, rather dilapidated *Hotel Mayná*, Rua Osório Guimarães 935 (Ⓣ42/3446-2091, Ⓦwww.hotelmayna.com.br; ③), is perfectly fine, with very helpful staff. If these are full, try the *Hotel Lopes*, Av. São João 2595 (Ⓣ42/3446-1476; ②), which is somewhat gloomy but adequate. Close by is the *Churrascaria do Penteado*, at Rua Domingos Luiz de Oliveira 1378, which, if you don't feel like grilled meat and can provide a few hours' notice, offers a hearty Ukrainian-style meal that includes a vast assortment of traditional dishes such as cabbage rolls, *bigos*, *borscht*, *pierogi* and *krakóvia*.

It's a fairly simple matter to reach Prudentópolis, well served by **bus** from Curitiba (4 daily), Foz do Iguaçu (3 daily) and most nearby centres. However, as one of Paraná's largest and most sparsely populated *municípios*, travelling far beyond the city without a car is difficult. To see some of the rural environs, though, you could always take a **local bus** (2 daily) about 10km northwest of town to the villages of **NOVA GALICIA**, sporting a beautiful, old domed wooden church, and **ESPERANÇA**, where there's a school staffed by Ukrainian nuns. If you're really keen, you could then turn off the road and head north for 6km to **BARRA BONITA**, another poor and overwhelmingly Ukrainian

## Ukrainians in Paraná

In the late nineteenth and early twentieth centuries, European and North American companies were contracted to construct a **rail line** linking the state of São Paulo to Rio Grande do Sul. As part payment, large tracts of land were given to the companies and, as in the United States and the Canadian West, they subdivided their new properties for sale to land-hungry immigrants who, it was hoped, would generate traffic for the rail line. Some of the largest land grants were in south-central Paraná, which the companies quickly cleared of the valuable Paraná pine trees that dominated the territory. Settlers came from many parts of Europe, but the companies were especially successful in recruiting **Ukrainians**, and between 1895 and 1898, and 1908 and 1914, over 35,000 immigrants arrived in the Ukraine's "other America". Today, there are some 300,000 Brazilians of Ukrainian extraction, of whom eighty percent live in Paraná, largely concentrated in the southern centre of the state.

As most of the immigrants came from the western Ukraine, it's the Ukrainian Catholic rather than the Orthodox Church that dominates; throughout the areas where Ukrainians and their descendants are gathered, onion-domed churches and chapels abound. While the Roman Catholic hierarchy, in general, is gradually becoming sensitive to the need to concentrate resources on social projects rather than in the building of more churches, new Ukrainian Catholic churches are proliferating in ever more lavish proportions, sometimes even replacing beautiful wooden churches built by the early immigrants. In Brazil, the **Ukrainian Catholic Church** is extremely wealthy, and its massive landholdings contrast greatly with the tiny properties from which the vast majority of the poverty-stricken local population eke out a living. Priests are often accused of attempting to block measures that will improve conditions: they are said to fear that educational attainment, modernization and increased prosperity will lessen the populace's dependence on the Church for material and spiritual comfort, so reducing their own influence.

The Ukrainians' neighbours (*caboclos*, Poles, Germans, and a few Italians and Dutch) frequently accuse them and their priests of maintaining a cultural exclusiveness. While intercommunal tensions certainly exist, the few non-Brazilian visitors to this part of Paraná are treated with the utmost civility, and if your Portuguese (or Ukrainian – the language is still universally spoken, in rural areas at least, by people of all ages) is up to it, you should have no problem finding people in the region's towns and hamlets who will be happy to talk about their traditions and way of life.

settlement. Without a guide, however, these and other villages are awkward and time-consuming to reach. Maynátur (Ⓣ42/3446-2446, Ⓦwww.maynatur.com.br), a local agency based at the *Hotel Mayná* in Prudentópolis, supplies drivers (expect to pay about R$100 for a day) and guides (R$50 a day) who know the back roads and outlying communities well. Particularly noteworthy stops are the impressive **waterfalls** hidden amidst virtually untouched forest, which require a guide to lead you along the approach trails.

## Irati, Mallet and around

Smaller, and with a greater ethnic diversity than Prudentópolis to the north, **IRATI** and **MALLET** are not especially interesting in themselves, but both are useful jumping-off points for visiting the Ukrainian villages and hamlets nearby. The two towns are very similar in character, both straddling the rail line to which they owed their existence and growth during the first decades of the twentieth century. Mallet – smaller and generally less developed – is marginally the more attractive of the two, and its small Ukrainian Catholic church is worth a visit, as is the train station that dates back to 1903.

Regular **buses** link Irati and Mallet with each other, as well as with União da Vitória, useful if you're travelling to or from Santa Catarina; there are also three buses a day to and from Prudentópolis, and two to and from Curitiba. On weekdays, finding **accommodation** in Irati can be a problem, but if the business-traveller-oriented *Hotel Colonial Palace* across from the bus station (Ⓣ42/3423-1144; ❸) is full, try the somewhat spartan *Hotel Luz*, Rua 15 de Julho 522: walk downhill to the end of the road, turn left and take the second right (Ⓣ42/3422-1015; ❷). In Mallet, there's always room at the basic *Hotel Brasil* (❷), next to the bus station. **Food** here means meat, with *churrascarias* located near the bus stations of both towns.

### Gonçalves Júnior

About 12km west of Irati, the small village of **GONÇALVES JÚNIOR** is well worth a visit if you want to get an idea of local rural traditions. Of the village's four **churches** (Lutheran, Roman Catholic, Ukrainian Catholic and Ukrainian Orthodox) the only one that deserves much attention is the Orthodox, which serves 24 local families. The small church, built in 1934, has an extremely beautiful interior featuring Orthodox icons, and a ceiling and walls bearing intricately painted traditional frescoes. From Gonçalves Júnior, take the Linha "B" road, along which there's a pretty chapel cared for by Ukrainian Catholic nuns. If you're walking to the chapel (allow at least an hour), you will no doubt come across plenty of *colonos*, Ukrainian-, Polish-, German-, Italian- and Dutch-speaking peasant farmers who live in the colourful wooden houses that front the dirt road, who will be happy to chat to you about their lives and those of their parents and grandparents.

### Serra do Tigre

Without any doubt, the most interesting and most eye-catching Ukrainian church in Paraná is in **SERRA DO TIGRE**, a small settlement south of Mallet that still retains much of its Ukrainian character. Built in 1904, **Igreja de São Miguel Arcanjo**, spectacularly positioned high upon a mountain top near the heart of the village, is the oldest Ukrainian Catholic church in Paraná. In traditional fashion, the church was constructed totally of wood – including, even, the roof tiles – and both the exterior and the elaborately painted interior frescoes are carefully maintained as a state monument.

Without your own transport, getting to Serra do Tigre is not terribly easy. Your best option is to take a bus from Mallet to the village of **DORIZZON**, 10km south, from where it takes about an hour to walk up the very steep hill to Serra do Tigre. The *Hotel Dorizzon* is a spa resort with reasonable food and a natural swimming pool (Ⓣ42/3542-1383, Ⓦwww.dorizzon.com.br; ❺ full board).

## The Iguaçu Falls and around

The **Iguaçu Falls** are, unquestionably, one of the world's great natural phenomena. To describe their beauty and power is a tall order, but for starters cast out any ideas that Iguaçu is some kind of Niagara Falls transplanted south of the equator – compared to Iguaçu, with its total of 275 falls that cascade over a precipice 3km wide, Niagara is a ripple. But it's not the falls alone that make Iguaçu so special: the vast surrounding subtropical **nature reserve** – in Brazil the Parque Nacional do Iguaçu (Ⓦwww.cataratasdoiguacu.com.br), in Argentina the Parque Nacional Iguazú (Ⓦwww.iguazuargentina.com) – is a timeless haunt that even the hordes of tourists fail to destroy.

The Iguaçu Falls are a short distance from the towns of **Foz do Iguaçu** in Brazil, **Puerto Iguazú** in Argentina and **Ciudad del Este** in Paraguay – which makes the practical details of getting in and out that bit trickier. Foz do Iguaçu and Puerto Iguazú are both about 20km northwest of the entrances to the Brazilian Parque Nacional do Iguaçu and the Argentine Parque Nacional Iguazú, while Ciudad del Este is 7km northwest of Foz do Iguaçu. Most tourists choose to stay in Foz do Iguaçu, much the largest of the three towns, though many visitors prefer the relative tranquillity and frontier atmosphere of Puerto Iguazú.

## Foz do Iguaçu

Although one of the largest cities in the south of Brazil, most visitors' experience of **FOZ DO IGUAÇU** is limited to the *rodoviária* or airport, their sights understandably entirely focused on the falls and park a short distance away. With most of the best hotels located alongside the highway connecting Foz do Iguaçu with the park, and with nothing in the urban area of particular interest to casual visitors, it's perfectly reasonable to ignore the city.

During the late nineteenth century a military outpost was established in the sensitive border area of what is now Foz do Iguaçu with the city itself only officially being created in 1914. For decades the city remained a complete backwater, only really expanding following the inauguration in 1965 of the bridge linking Brazil with Paraguay and the construction of the nearby Itaipu

▲ The Iguaçu Falls



Dam (see p.650) that attracted thousands of migrants in the 1970s and 80s. Since then, a strong urban identity has failed to emerge, with much of Foz do Iguaçu's population of over 300,000 looking outwards to express their identities. This is a pity, for as host to Brazil's second largest Chinese community – as well as large Korean, Japanese, Lebanese and Iranian populations – Foz do Iguaçu should be able to display a cosmopolitan character.

But with nothing at all of clear historic interest, unexceptional restaurants and even, due to the lower prices found across the border in Paraguay and Argentina, poor shopping options, unless you are looking for a bargain hotel, the city of Foz do Iguaçu holds few attractions.

## Arrival and information

Foz do Iguaçu's **airport** (ⓣ45/3521-4200) is served by flights from Belém, Brasília, Curitiba, Recife, Rio de Janeiro, Salvador and São Paulo. From here, regular buses (5am–midnight, Mon–Sat every 15min, Sun every 50min; R$2.10) head to the **local bus terminal** in the centre of town on Avenida Juscelino Kubitschek. If you want to go straight to Argentina, get off the bus at the *Hotel Bourbon* and then cross the road for a bus to Puerto Iguazú (R$3.50). By taxi, the fixed fare into Foz is R$40, or R$55 to Puerto Iguazú (see p.643). Arriving by bus, Foz do Iguaçu's **rodoviária** (ⓣ45/3522-3633) is located on the northern outskirts of town by the road to Curitiba and is served by buses from throughout southern Brazil, and from as far north as Rio and Mato Grosso do Sul, as well as Asunción and Buenos Aires. Buses #1, #2 and #3 link the *rodoviária* with the local bus terminal in town; taxis cost around R$20.

There are **tourist offices** at the airport (daily 9am–9pm) and at the *rodoviária* (daily 6.30am–6pm). In town, there are offices at the local bus terminal (daily 7am–6pm) opposite the cathedral on Rua Barão do Rio Branco (daily 7am–11pm), and at Rua Almirante Barroso 1300 (Mon–Sat 8am–6pm). For information by phone, call the Foz tourist office, Teletur, on ⓣ0800/45-1516.

## Accommodation

Finding **somewhere to stay** in Foz do Iguaçu is usually easy, and outside the peak tourist months of January, February and July, and over Easter, you are likely to be offered a knock-down rate at all but the top-end establishments. Many of the **hotels**, including some of the best, are located some distance from town on the road leading to the falls (p.646), and most of the cheaper ones in town (see p.639) cater largely to shoppers bound for Paraguay. Simple hotels tend to be much more pleasant in Puerto Iguazú.

**Albergue da Juventude Paudimar** Av. das Cataratas, Km 12.5 ⓣ45/3529-6061, ⓦwww.paudimar.com.br. An excellent HI-affiliated complex with superb facilities, including a large pool and an on-site travel agency offering a range of excursions. Cabins (with private bathrooms) sleep five to eight people and there are also double rooms. Lunch is available for R$6 and dinner is R$8. Although near the airport, it's a half-hour walk from the main road but regular buses pass the hostel. From the main road it's easy to flag down a bus going to Foz, the Brazilian Parque Nacional or Puerto Iguazú. R$25 per person or ③.

**Bristol Dobly Viale Cataratas** Rodovia. das Cataratas 2420 ⓣ45/2105-7200, ⓦwww.bristolhoteis.com.br. Conveniently located for access to both the Argentine and Brazilian falls, this sparkling new hotel has all the character of a rather upscale airport hotel. Rooms, though, are extremely comfortable and there's a fine pool. ⑤

**Continental Inn** Av. Paraná 1089 ⓣ45/2102-5000, ⓦwww.continentalinn.com.br. Good value for a high-quality – if somewhat anonymous – downtown hotel. The well-equipped rooms are spacious, breakfasts are ample, the staff are efficient and there's a good pool. ⑤

**Dany Palace Hotel** Av. Brasil 509 ⓣ45/3523-1530. No frills, but justifiably prides itself on cleanliness. Rooms at this centrally located spot are a/c, and some sleep three people. ③

**Hotel das Cataratas** Parque Nacional do Iguaçu ⓣ45/2102-7000, ⓦwww.hoteldascataratas.com.br. The only hotel within the Brazilian national park, located just out of sight from the falls. After years of

neglect, the hotel has finally undergone a complete renovation, with luxurious guest rooms, pleasant lounges, good dining options and beautifully landscaped gardens. Although the location is perfect for an early-morning view of the falls, it's inconvenient for visiting the Argentine park. 9

**Hotel Rafain Centro** Rua Marechal Deodoro 984 ⓣ 45/3521-3500, ⓦ www.rafaincentro.com.br. The rooms are large with balconies, and the service is friendly. Ask for a room overlooking the pool at the rear of the building. 6

**Pousada da Laura** Rua Naipi 629 ⓣ 45/3574-3628. This friendly, small B&B-style *pousada* has become a firm favourite for budget-conscious backpackers. Although the house is located in a central, pleasant residential section, care should be taken as young men from the neighbouring *favela* have been known to rob tourists. R$25 per person.

**Pousada Evelina Navarrete** Rua Kalichewski 171 ⓣ 45/3574-3817, ⓔ pousada.evelina@foznet.com.br. An extremely friendly family-run place in the city centre that mainly attracts foreign backpackers. Rooms, all of which have en-suite bathrooms, are simple but spotless; breakfasts are adequate, there's internet access and multilingual Evelina goes out of her way to be helpful. Well located for buses to the falls. 3

**San Martín** Rodovia das Cataratas, Km 17 ⓣ 45/3529-8088, ⓦ www.hotelsanmartin.com.br. Located just a few steps from both the Parque das Aves and the entrance of the Parque Nacional. Although the spacious rooms are perfectly comfortable, the garden is the hotel's best feature, offering both landscaped areas (with an attractive pool) and natural forest with nature trails. 6



## Eating and drinking

Foz do Iguaçu is certainly no gastronomic paradise, but it's possible to eat fairly well without paying too much. Most visitors eat at their hotels on the road leading to the falls, but for variety a visit to the city centre is recommended. If you're on a tight budget, try one of the numerous buffet-style *por kilo* restaurants on Rua Marechal Deodoro.

**Bier Kastell** Av. Jorge Schimmelpfeng 362. A lively beer garden where you can enjoy ice-cold *chopp* and German-style sausage and other light meals.

**Búfalo Branco** Rua Rebouças 530. Upmarket *churrascaria* with the all-you-can-eat *rodizio* system and an excellent salad bar. Around R$70 per person.

**Café Libano** Av. Jorge Schimmelpfeng 648. Excellent-value Lebanese restaurant, equally good for just a cold drink and a bowl of *hummus* and pitta bread as for a full meal.

**Clube Maringá** Porto Meira ⓣ 45/3527-3472. Justly popular among locals for its superb *rodizio de peixe* lunch and stunning views of the Iguaçu river. As well as a selection of local freshwater fish, there's an excellent salad bar and you can pay a little extra for fresh sashimi. Expect to pay R$30 per person. Take the "Porto Meira" bus and ask for directions, or take a taxi (R$10). Closed Sun evening.

**Recanto Gaúcho** Av. Cataratas, Km 15, near the turnoff to the airport ⓣ 45/3572-2358. A favourite Sunday outing for locals: the atmosphere's lively, the meat's excellent and cheap (R$15 per person for all you can eat) and the owner (who always dresses in full *gaúcho* regalia) is a real character. Turn up soon after 11am; food is served until 3pm. It's advisable to phone ahead. Closed Dec & Jan.

**Sushi Hokkai** Av. Jorge Schimmelpfeng. A fairly upscale Japanese restaurant in downtown Foz that offers reliable food and an escape from the city's bustle and often stifling heat. A varied mixed plate of sushi costs R$38; a meal of assorted tempura is R$25.

**Trigo & Cia** Rua Almirante Barroso 1750. Adjoining the *Hotel Internacional Foz*, this busy café serves tasty savoury snacks, good coffee and the best cakes in Foz. Open until 11pm.

## Listings

**Airlines** TAM ⓣ 45/3523-8500; Varig ⓣ 45/3529-6601.

**Banks and exchange** Foreign currency (cash or traveller's cheques) can be easily changed in travel agencies and banks along Av. Brasil; the latter also have ATMs.

**Car rental** Avis (ⓣ 45/3529-6160), Hertz (ⓣ 45/3529-8789), Localiza (ⓣ 45/3529-6300), and Yes (ⓣ 45/3025-4300) are all represented at the airport. Note that if you are just travelling between Foz do Iguaçu and Puerto Iguazú or the two national parks, then no special car documentation is required to cross the Brazilian/Argentine border. If, however, you intend to take your rental car to the Argentine Jesuit missions (see p.709) or anywhere else south of Puerto Iguazú, you'll need a Green Card (an extra R$45 per day is charged). You are not permitted to take a car into Paraguay.

**Consulates** Argentina, Rua Dom Pedro II 28 ⓣ45/3574-2969; Paraguay, Rua Bartolomeu de Gusmão 777 ⓣ45/5323-2898.

**Horseriding** You can ride horses at the *Recanto Gaúcho* (see opposite). Reservations are essential and the cost is R$40 per person for a two-hour ride accompanied by a guide through forested and open country trails.

**Post office** Praça Getúlio Vargas near Rua Barão do Rio Branco.

**Travel agent** Martin Travel, Travessa Goiás (ⓣ45/3523-4959, ⓦwww.martintravel.com.br), is extremely reliable for local arrangements of all kinds.

## Puerto Iguazú

In complete contrast to neighbouring Foz, **PUERTO IGUAZÚ** is sleepy, safe and small (its population is just 32,000). The town is a better place to spend time – when not visiting the park – than Foz do Iguaçu; it's less crowded here and the simpler budget hotels are more pleasant on the Argentine side of the border.

Although Puerto Iguazú is basically a relaxed place to spend an evening or two between visits to the falls, there are also a few worthwhile attractions. The **Museo Mbororé**, at the intersection of *avenidas* Misiones and Brasil (Mon–Fri 7–11am), is worth a brief look for its small exhibition relating to the indigenous Guaraní Indians. For a spectacular view towards Paraguay, across the Paraná River, and Brazil, across the Iguazú River, walk to the end of Avenida Victoria Aguirre (about 30min), or catch a bus, where you'll find the Marca de las Tres Fronteras, a monument proclaiming friendship between the three countries.

### Arrival and information

Puerto Iguazú has daily direct **flights** to and from Buenos Aires, Cordoba and Mendoza; buses (A$10) to town meet arriving flights and taxis are available (A$70 to Puerto Iguazú or A$80 to Foz do Iguaçu). The car rental companies Avis and Hertz are both represented at the airport. Aerolíneas Argentinas' office is on Avenida Victoria Aguirre (ⓣ3757/420-168). Puerto Iguazú's combined local and long-distance **bus terminal** is in the town centre, with several daily departures to Buenos Aires and Posadas, near the Jesuit ruins of San Ignacio Miní (see p.704). There's a **tourist office** at Av. Victoria Aguirre 396 (daily 8am–8pm; ⓣ3757/420-800), but only the most basic of information concerning Puerto Iguazú and the wider area is supplied.

### Accommodation

There's a good range of budget and medium-priced places to stay in Puerto Iguazú, as well as a number of more upmarket options. Unless otherwise indicated, the following places are concentrated within a few blocks of the bus station.

**Boutique Hotel de la Fonte** 1 de Mayo y Corrientes s/n ⓣ03757/420-625, ⓦwww.bhfboutiquehotel.com. This Italian-owned hotel offers six well-equipped rooms, one of which boasts an oversized jacuzzi, and an attractive garden with a pool. You can dine here too, with beautiful-looking and -tasting dishes incorporating local flavours. While in many ways excellent, the hotel provides an experience (and prices) that would be better suited to sophisticated Buenos Aires than a small frontier town. ❺–❻

**Corre Caminos** Rua Paulino Amarante 48 ⓣ03757/420-967, ⓦwww.correcaminos.com.ar. A short walk from the bus station, this is the most popular youth hostel in town. Rooms are hot and cramped but the front yard is a relaxing place to mix with other travellers. Double room with a private bathroom for A$50 (❷) or A$20 in a dorm.

**Hostel-Inn** Ruta 12, Km 5 ⓣ03757/421-823, ⓦwww.hostel-inn.com. Buses between the town and the park stop outside this flagship hostel, which is on the main road to the park. Formerly a hotel, it offers a range of rooms that sleep two to four people, an inexpensive restaurant, free internet, laundry facilities and a good-sized swimming pool. Although not quite as lively as the youth hostel across the border in Brazil, this is more comfortable and much more convenient for the parks. Double room with a private bathroom for A$120 (4) or A$25 in a dorm.

**Hostel Park** Calle Paulino Amarante 111 ⓣ0357/424-342, ⓦwww.hostelparkiguazu.com.ar. A block beyond the more popular Corre Caminos, the rooms in this friendly hostel are more spacious and there's the added bonus of a pool. A$20 in a dorm or A$45 for a double room.

**Hosteria La Cabaña** Av. Tres Fronteras 434 ⓣ0357/420-564. Opened in the early 1950s, this is the oldest guesthouse in town, the original Bavarian-style log cabin blending well with the surrounding forest. The *hosteria* is quietly located a fifteen-minute walk from the town centre and the garden (which has a pool) has spectacular views down towards the Paraná River. Rooms (which sleep between two and five people) are extremely basic, but all have en-suite bathrooms. The owner speaks excellent English and German. 2–3

**Hotel Saint George** Av. Córdoba 148 ⓣ03757/420-633, ⓦwww.hotelsaintgeorge.com. A few metres from the bus station, this is the largest and most expensive place to stay in town. Rooms are on the small side, smell of damp and are altogether rather gloomy, but there's a very nice pool and garden and the staff are efficient. 5

**Marco Polo Inn** Av. Córdoba 731 ⓣ03757/420-434. A new youth hostel directly across the road from the bus station. Accommodation available in dorms (A$35 per person) and double rooms. 3

**Orquídeas Palace Hotel** Ruta 12, Km 5 ⓣ03757/420-472, ⓦwww.orquideashotel.com. By far the most attractive and friendliest of the numerous hotels on the road between the town and the park. The rooms are perfectly comfortable, while the pool and spacious grounds are delightful. 4–5

**Panoramic Hotel Iguazu** Av. Paraguay 372 ⓣ03757/498-133, ⓦwww.panoramic-hoteliguazu.com. The only five-star hotel in town; considering the price, rooms are good rather than outstanding. Ask for a river-view room, looking across the Iguaçu to Brazil and across the Paraná towards Paraguay. 8

**Residencial King** Av. Victoria Aguirre 916 ⓣ03757/420-360. Very competitively priced for larger-than-normal rooms, all with en-suite bathrooms. There's a very attractive garden with well-cared-for lawns, flowering bushes and a small pool. 3

**Secret Garden** Los Lapachos 623 ⓣ03757/423-099, ⓦwww.secretgardeniguazu.com. This marvellous B&B has just three small but perfectly maintained rooms set around a small but verdant garden. Simple but excellent breakfasts are provided, while in the evenings drinks are offered. John Fernandes, a photojournalist originally from India but long resident in Argentina, could not be a better host. 5

**Sheraton Internacional Iguazú Resort** Parque Nacional Iguazú ⓣ3757/491-800, ⓦwww.starwoodhotels.com. Located within the Parque Nacional, this rather hideous-looking concrete structure offers spacious rooms with balconies and outstanding views of the forest or, for a bit more cash, the falls. 9

### Eating and drinking

What nightlife there is in Puerto Iguazú takes place in the "downtown" **bars** on Avenida Victoria Aguirre, where the town's two internet cafés are also located. This being Argentina, **food** means beef (although most restaurants also serve *surubí*, the local fish, and pasta) accompanied by decent wine. The best *parrillas* (grills) in town are *Acqua* and, slightly more elegant and expensive, *La Rueda*, both near the bus terminal on Avenida Córdoba. For a lighter meal, an attractive option is the *Café Jaroba* in the small, shady Plaza Pueblo on Avenida Victoria Aguirre.

## Ciudad del Este

Located on the west bank of the Paraná River and connected by bridge to Foz do Iguaçu, the Paraguayan city of **CIUDAD DEL ESTE** must rank as one of South America's more unpleasant urban areas. When it rains, the city is awash with mud and it can be dangerous to cross a road for fear of vanishing into one of the many potholes. In dry weather, the place is coated with a thick layer of red dust. Ciudad del Este has long been a magnet for Brazilian shoppers seeking out cheap electronic equipment but in recent years the city has been attempting to redefine its economy, stressing the financial services sector and, curiously, higher education – its two universities attract significant numbers of Brazilian students in fields as diverse as medicine and philosophy. But unless you're in desperate need of buying a cheap camera or are heading into Paraguay, Ciudad del Este has no great draw.

The **bus terminal** is just south of the centre, to which it is linked by local buses. If you arrive from Asunción or Encarnación (see p.706) after dark it makes sense to cross into Brazil the next morning. The frequent buses between Ciudad del Este and Foz do Iguaçu (daily 7am–8.50pm) stop on the main street, Avenida Monseñor Rodríguez, and the parallel Avenida Adrián Jara. Depending on traffic, it can take between fifteen minutes and two hours to go from city centre to centre – it's often faster to walk across the international bridge and pick up a bus heading into Foz do Iguaçu. Day and night there are taxis available for around R$25. If you're just crossing for a day you need only wave your passport at the immigration officials, but otherwise remember to be stamped in or out of the respective countries. The Brazilian **consulate** is at Tenente Coronel Pampliega 337 (Ⓣ61/31-2309).

Ciudad del Este's **tourist office** is at the Paraguayan immigration post but you can expect only the most basic assistance. Dollars, *pesos* and *reís* are all accepted in town, but if you're travelling further into Paraguay you'll need Paraguayan **guaranies**, available at similar rates in *casas de câmbio* in Foz do Iguaçu, Puerto Iguazú and, in Ciudad del Este, on Avenida Monseñor Rodríguez. The **post office** is opposite the bus station at Alejo García and Oscar Rivas Ortellado.

For **accommodation**, you can try the two good hotels sitting opposite one another on Avenida Adrián Jara, near the intersection with Alejo García. The *Mi Abuelo* (Ⓣ61/62373; ❷) is friendly, quiet and has an attractive courtyard, and the *Convair* (Ⓣ61/62349; ❹) is more impersonal but with air conditioning, TVs and minibars. Restaurants are generally poor although there are a few reasonable, but very simple, Lebanese, Chinese and Japanese places, oriented to Ciudad del Este's substantial Asian and Arab communities. Most are on Avenida Adrián Jara and the side roads, such as Calle Abay. For more traditional Paraguayan offerings, try *Mi Ranchito*, an outdoor *parrilla* at the corner of Calle Curupayty and Avenida Adrián Jara.

## Puerto Bertoni

Definitely worth the effort is a visit to **Puerto Bertoni**, 26km south of Ciudad del Este on the banks of the Paraná River. This remote spot was the home of the Swiss naturalist and ethnologist Moises Bertoni, who settled in the area in 1890, remaining until his death in 1929. Surrounded by a small jungle reserve, Bertoni's house and outbuildings are now a museum (Ⓦwww.mbertoni.org.py), housing a small botanical collection and excellent panels (in English and Spanish) describing Bertoni's life and work. A few hundred metres from the buildings is a small village inhabited by some seventy Guaraní Indians who survive by subsistence farming and the sale of simple handicrafts to visitors. Trips to Puerto Bertoni, departing twice a day (9am & 2pm), are organized by the tour operator Macuco Safari (Ⓣ45/3527-1444, Ⓦwww.macucosafari.com.br) in Foz do Iguaçu; they last about four hours and cost R$75. From the meeting point at the restaurant of the *Clube Maringá* (see p.642) in Porto Meira, you'll be led to the old Brazilian ferry landing and then taken by launch 7km downriver to the Puerto Bertoni landing. From here it's a steep fifteen-minute 2.8km walk up the river embankment and along a jungle trail to Bertoni's house and the Guaraní village beyond.

## The falls

The **Iguaçu Falls** are formed by the Rio Iguaçu, which has its source near Curitiba. Starting at an altitude of 1300m, the river snakes westward, picking up tributaries and increasing in size and power during its 1200-kilometre journey. About 15km before joining the Rio Paraná, the Iguaçu broadens out, then plunges precipitously over an eighty-metre-high cliff, the central point of the 275 interlinking cataracts that extend nearly 3km across the river. There is no "best time" to visit since the falls are impressive and spectacularly beautiful whatever the season. That said, the rainy season is during the winter months of April to July, and at this time the volume of water is at its greatest – but then the sky is usually overcast and the air, especially near the falls themselves, is quite chilly. By the end of the summer dry season, around March, the volume of water crashing over the cliffs is reduced by a third (only once, in 1977, did the falls dry up altogether), but even then there's no reduction in impact, with the added attraction of the rainbow effects from the splashing of falling water and the deep blue sky. The one time to avoid at all costs is Easter, when the area attracts vast throngs of Argentine and Brazilian tourists.

Although many people arrive at Iguaçu in the morning and depart the same evening, the falls should really be viewed from both the Brazilian and the Argentine sides of the river: at least two days are needed to do them justice and you could easily spend longer. Crossing the **frontier** to see both sides is easy, and if you're of a nationality that normally requires a visa to visit either Argentina or Brazil you won't need one just for a day-trip. If, however, you're not returning to Foz do Iguaçu or Puerto Iguazú the same day, you'll have to go through normal **immigration** formalities on either side of the **Ponte Presidente Tancredo Neves**, the bridge that crosses the Rio Iguaçu between the two towns. There are good bus services between the two cities and onwards to the falls, but consider renting a car if your time is limited; see p.642 for car rental details.

### The Brazilian side

The finest overall view of the falls is obtained from the Brazilian side, best in the morning when the light is much better for photography. You'll only need about half a day here (longer if you're also visiting the Parque das Aves), since, although the view is magnificent and it's from here that you get the clearest idea as to the size of the falls, the area from which to view them is fairly limited.

From the local bus terminal in central Foz do Iguaçu, there are **buses** every half-hour (daily 8am–7pm) to the "Parque Nacional", which cost around R$2.10 and take about 45 minutes. Buses stop at the visitors' centre at the park entrance where, after paying the R$21 entrance fee, you are encouraged to visit the exhibition on the ecology and history of the park before transferring onto an electric-powered open-top double-decker bus that takes you to the falls. Buses stop on the road beneath the renowned *Hotel das Cataratas* (see p.641), where you're only a couple of minutes' walk from the first views of the falls.

From the bus stop, there's a stairway that leads down to a 1.5-kilometre cliffside **path** near the rim of the falls. At the beginning of the path there are trails leading to a tree-walk course – a series of ropes and ladders above the forest canopy (R$80) – and to a 55-metre cliff face that you can abseil down (R$70). From spots all along the main path there are excellent views, at first across the lower river at a point where it has narrowed to channel width. At the bottom of the path, where the river widens again, there's a walkway leading out towards the falls themselves. Depending on the force of the river, the spray can be quite heavy, so if you have a camera be sure to carry a plastic bag. From here, you can either walk back up the path or take the elevator to the top of the cliff and the road leading to the hotel.

Every fifteen minutes or so you'll hear the buzzing from a **helicopter** flying overhead. It takes off just outside the park's entrance, across from the Parque das Aves, and offers ten-minute flights over the falls for US$60, or a 35-minute flight over the falls and Itaipu for US$150. In recent years the helicopter has been a consistent cause of a minor rift between Brazil and Argentina: the Argentines refuse to allow it to fly over their side of the falls as they claim it disturbs the wildlife. Whether this is in fact true is a matter of fierce debate, but certainly the view from above is spectacular and the ride exhilarating.

## The Argentine side

For more detailed views, and greater opportunities to view the local flora and fauna at close range, Argentina offers by far the best vantage points. The falls on the Argentine side are much more numerous and the viewing area more extensive and this, combined with the fact that many people only visit the Brazilian side, means that you'll rarely be overpowered by fellow tourists. With a good eye, toucans and other exotic birds can be spotted, and brilliantly coloured butterflies are seen all about in the summer months. In warm weather be sure to bring your bathing gear, as there are some idyllic river spots to cool off in.

Getting to the Argentine side of the falls from Foz do Iguaçu is straightforward enough, but if your time is very limited it makes sense to join an **excursion**, which most travel agencies and the better hotels organize (from around R$100). Otherwise, from Foz do Iguaçu's local bus terminal take a **bus to Puerto Iguazú** (R$3.50) – there are departures every forty minutes (daily 7am–6.45pm; 30min); if you miss the last bus in either direction a taxi will cost around R$40. From Puerto Iguazú's bus terminal, there are then buses every hour (daily 6.30am–7.30pm, returning 8am–8pm; A$10 return) that take thirty minutes to reach the national park's new visitors' complex where you pay an entrance fee of A$60, and where you'll be given a very useful map. Bear in mind that only Argentine currency is accepted for the entrance charge, although Brazilian *reís* and Argentine *pesos* are both accepted for the bus fare between Puerto Iguazú and the falls and for spending within the park. You should change some money at a *casa da câmbio* in Foz do Iguaçu or at the border crossing.

At the visitors' complex you'll find a large car park, souvenir shops, a café and a restaurant as well as an impressive **Centro de Interpretación de la Naturaleza** (7am–8pm). This makes a good first stop with its **museum** focusing on the region's natural history. It's here that you'll see the extremely shy, and mainly nocturnal, forest animals – though they're all stuffed. From the centre transfer to the grandly named **Tren de la Selva**, a miniature railway that winds its way through the forest between the park's entrance and the falls. The first stop is the Estación Cataratas for the *Sheraton Hotel* and the Circuito Inferior trail; the second is the Estación Garganta del Diablo.

The **Circuito Inferior** involves an easy walk that, with a few interruptions to admire the scenery, is likely to take a couple of hours – wheelchairs are available at the Centro de Interpretación. Despite not being as dramatic as the falls upriver, few parts of the park are more beautiful and the path passes by gentler waterfalls and dense vegetation. At the river shore, **boats** (9am–4pm; free) cross to the **Isla San Martín**, whose beaches are unfortunately marred by the streams of sand flies and mosquitoes present. One of the many enchanting spots on the island is **La Ventana**, a rock formation that's framed, as its name suggests, like a window. From here you can continue around the marked circuit, but, if you are at all agile, haul yourself instead across the rocks in front and behind La Ventana where, hidden from view, is a deep natural **pool** fed by a small waterfall, allowing some relaxing swimming.

The Argentine falls embrace a huge area, and the most spectacular spot is probably the **Garganta del Diablo** (Devil's Throat) at **PUERTO CANOAS**. The Garganta del Diablo marks a point where fourteen separate falls combine to form the world's most powerful single waterfall in terms of the volume of water flow per second. Catwalks lead into the middle of the river to a central viewing platform, from where it's easy to feel that you will be swallowed by the tumbling waters: be prepared to get drenched by the spray, mist and rain. From Puerto Canoas the train will take you back to the park's entrance complex from where there are frequent buses linking directly with Puerto Iguazú.

## The forest

One of the remarkable aspects of the park is that visitors can gain access to a **semi-deciduous tropical rainforest** without any difficulty and without posing a threat to people or nature. Even by keeping to the main paths around the falls, it's easy to get a taste of the jungle, in particular in the Argentine park. The forest is home to over two thousand plant varieties, four hundred bird species, dozens of types of mammal and innumerable insects and reptiles. It's essentially made up of four levels of vegetation: a nearly closed canopy reaching over 35m; a layer of trees between 3 and 10m in height; a lower layer of shrubs; and a herbaceous ground level. In reality the levels are not so pronounced, as epiphytes and other plants intertwine, at times creating a mass of matted vegetation.

Within the forest lives a rich diversity of **wildlife** species, but they are spread out over a wide area, often nocturnal and usually extremely timid. However, if you get up early, walk quietly away from other people and look up into the trees as well as towards the ground, you have a chance of seeing something. Jaguars and mountain lions have been seen in Iguaçu, but they keep so well hidden and so few remain that realistically your chances of observing them are minimal. Around the water's edge, you may occasionally see **tapirs**, large animals shaped rather like a pig with a long snout. Smaller, but also with a pig-like appearance is the **peccary**, dangerous when cornered, but shy around humans.

Far more common is the **coatimundi**, the size of a domestic cat but related to the racoon. Even on the main paths on the crowded Brazilian side of the falls, you often come face to face with coatimundi, hoping to scrounge food from tourists although feeding the animals is strictly forbidden. The *caí*, or **capuchin monkey**, is also often seen and is recognizable by its long legs and tail, small size and black skullcap mark that gives it its name. These monkeys travel the forest canopy in large groups and emit strange bird-like cries. Far bigger and with a deep voice is the **howler monkey**. You may not see any, but you're likely to hear their powerful voices emanating from the jungle. Insects, however, are always to be seen, and butterflies are one of the forest's most memorable sights, especially in the summer.

The forest is also home to a rich variety of **birdlife**, and with a good eye you should be able to see toucans, parakeets and hummingbirds even without straying from the main paths. Again, their most active hours are soon after dawn when it's cooler. For a more reliable view of local birdlife, a visit to the **Parque das Aves** (daily 8.30am–6.30pm; R$13) is highly recommended. Located just 100m from the visitors' centre of the national park on the Brazilian side of the falls, the bird park maintains both small breeding aviaries and enormous walk-through aviaries, still surrounded by dense forest. There's also a large walk-through butterfly cage – butterflies are bred throughout the year and released when mature. All the butterflies and eighty percent of the birds are Brazilian, most of them endemic to the Atlantic forests, the main exception being those in the Pantanal aviary.

**Trips** into the forest are organized in the Argentine park, and tickets are available at the offices of Iguazú Jungle Explorer (Ⓣ3757/421-600, Ⓦwww.iguazujungleexplorer.com) located at the Circuito Inferior. A typical trip lasts either one and a half hours (A$90) or two and a half hours (A$120), and involves being driven in the back of a truck along a rough road through the forest, a walk down a narrow trail to the river, and a wild boat ride down some rapids towards the Garganta del Diablo. Don't expect to see any wildlife (much of which is nocturnal), but guides may point out some of the flora. You stand a better chance of seeing some animals – or at least hearing them – at night; escorted moonlit walks take place on two or three nights a month around the time of the full moon (8–10pm; A$20). Sign up at the Visitors Centre (Centro de Visitantes).

It's also possible to rent **mountain bikes** from Iguazú Jungle Explorer; you will be given a map with which you can explore some of the trails.

## Yacutinga

About 50km east of the Parque Nacional Iguazú in Argentina, the smaller **Refugio de Vida Silvestre Yacutinga** (Ⓦwww.yacutinga.com) is an appealing place for visitors. The reserve is located on the Yacutinga peninsula, on the south bank of the Iguaçu River, and covers 5.7 square kilometres, almost all of it Mata Atlântica. As well as conducting environmental research projects, the privately run reserve works with neighbouring farming communities to encourage environmental awareness and sustainable agriculture. Expert English-speaking **guides** take you along trails within the refuge, with walks typically lasting an hour or two, while float trips on the Iguaçu River and tributaries are also offered most days. What you see, of course, varies enormously, but capuchin monkeys, deer, otters, caimans and other lizards are common sights, and there are ample bird-watching opportunities to satisfy both casual and serious birdwatchers alike. Although the longer trails require a guide, there is one short and clearly signposted trail you can take unaccompanied, and you'll also find walkways strung between trees from where you can look out for birds or animals or just take in the serenity of the rainforest.

Visits to Yacutinga must be arranged in advance through a **travel agent**; contact the reserve by email for an agent in your locality or, in Foz do Iguaçu, book through Martin Travel (Ⓣ45/3523-4959, Ⓦwww.martintravel.com.br). The cost for two nights and three days at the *Yacutinga Lodge*, with full board and the services of the local guides, is about US$350 per person. The price includes transfer by truck and river to the lodge – the road is atrocious, the three-hour drive is bone shattering, but the scenery is fascinating, at first passing through the Parque Nacional before entering a zone of smallholdings, mainly farmed by families of German descent. Accommodation is in rustic but extremely comfortable cabins, all of which have private bathrooms and a wood stove (essential for the chilly winter nights). The main lodge, which is built largely from local stone and wood from naturally fallen trees, blends remarkably unobtrusively into its forest setting, and has a lounge, bar and restaurant, while outside there's a swimming pool and an open-air bar. Meals are superb, with an emphasis on varieties of locally sourced squash, beans and other vegetables.

## Itaipu

While there's complete agreement that Iguaçu is one of the great natural wonders of Brazil, there's bitter debate as to what **Itaipu** – the world's largest hydroelectricity scheme – represents. Work on the dam, 10km north of Foz do Iguaçu, began in the early 1970s at a cost of US$25 billion, and its eighteen 700,000-kilowatt generators became fully operational in 1991. Proponents of the project argue that the rapidly growing industries of southeastern Brazil needed nothing less than Itaipu's huge electrical capacity, and that without it Brazilian development would be greatly impeded. However, critics claim that Brazil neither needs nor can afford such a massive hydroelectric scheme and that the country would have been much better served by smaller and less prestigious schemes nearer to the centres of consumption. In addition, they point to the social and environmental upheavals caused by the damming of the Rio Paraná and the creation of a 1350-square-kilometre reservoir: forty thousand families have been forced off their land; a microclimate with as yet unknown consequences has developed; and – critics say – the much-publicized animal rescue operations and financial assistance for displaced farmers barely address the complex problems.

Visiting Itaipu is easy, with hourly **buses** from Foz do Iguaçu's local bus terminal. You're dropped at the **visitors' centre** where a film about the project, in English and other languages, is shown, and from where **guided tours** of the complex depart (Mon–Sat 8 daily; 2hr; R$30; ⓦwww.itaipu.gov.br). The film is extremely slick and, until you stand on the dam and look across the massive reservoir stretching into the horizon, it's easy to be convinced by Itaipu's PR machine that the project was, at worst, no more than a slight local inconvenience.

# Santa Catarina

**Santa Catarina** shares a similar pattern of settlement with other parts of southern Brazil, the indigenous Indians having been rapidly displaced by outsiders. In the eighteenth century the state received immigrants from the Azores who settled along the coast; cattle herders from Rio Grande do Sul spread into the higher reaches of the mountainous interior around **Lages** and **São Joaquim**; and European immigrants and their descendants made new homes for themselves in the fertile river valleys. Even today, small communities on the **island of Santa Catarina**, and elsewhere on the coast, continue a way of life that has not changed markedly over the generations. Incidentally, to prevent confusion with the name of the state (though barely succeeding at times), most people call the island of Santa Catarina **Florianópolis**, which is actually the name of the state capital – also situated on the island. Elsewhere, cities such as **Blumenau** and **Joinville**, established by German immigrants, have become totally Brazilianized, but in the surrounding villages and farms many people still speak the language of their forebears in preference to Portuguese.

On the coast, tourism has become very important and facilities are excellent, though the considerable natural beauty is in danger of being eroded by the uncontrolled development that has been taking place in recent years. Inland, though, visitors rarely venture, despite the good roads and widely available hotels. Here,

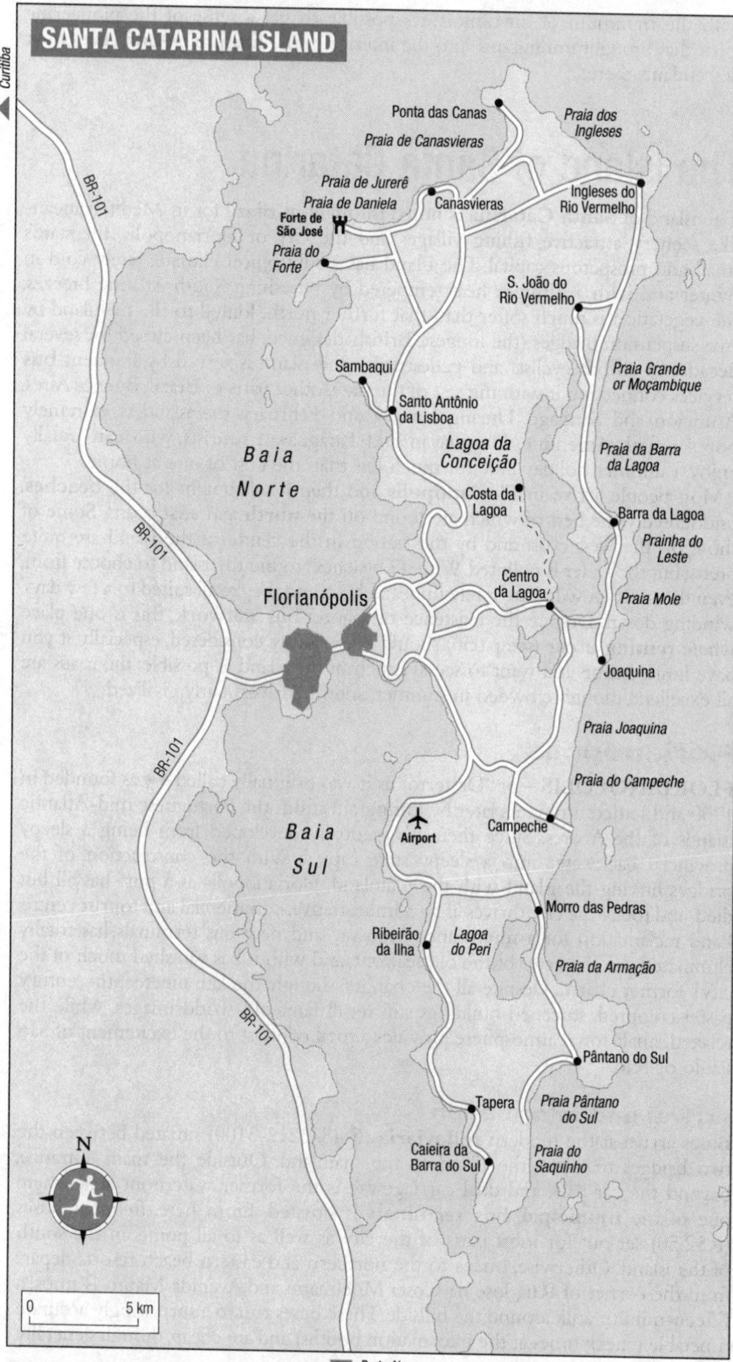
SANTA CATARINA ISLAND
Curitiba
Ponta das Canas
Praia dos Ingleses
Praia de Canasvieras
Praia de Jurerê
Praia de Daniela
Canasvieras
Ingleses do Rio Vermelho
Forte de São José
Praia do Forte
S. João do Rio Vermelho
BR-101
Sambaqui
Praia Grande or Moçambique
Santo Antônio da Lisboa
Lagoa da Conceição
Praia da Barra da Lagoa
Baia Norte
Costa da Lagoa
Barra da Lagoa
Prainha do Leste
Florianópolis
Centro da Lagoa
Praia Mole
Joaquina
Praia Joaquina
Praia do Campeche
Campeche
Airport
Baia Sul
Morro das Pedras
Ribeirão da Ilha
Lagoa do Peri
Praia da Armação
Pântano do Sul
Tapera
Praia Pântano do Sul
Caieira da Barra do Sul
Praia do Saquinho
N
0
5 km
Porto Alegre

9 THE SOUTH

with the minimum of discomfort, it's possible to get a sense of the pioneering spirit that brought immigrants into the interior in the first place – and keeps their descendants there.

## The island of Santa Catarina

The island of **Santa Catarina** is noted throughout Brazil for its Mediterranean-like scenery, attractive fishing villages and the city of Florianópolis, the state's small and prosperous capital. The island has a subtropical climate, rarely cold in winter and with a summer heat tempered by refreshing South Atlantic breezes; the vegetation is much softer than that further north. Joined to the mainland by two suspension bridges (the longest, British-designed, has been closed for several decades to all but cyclists and pedestrians), the island is served by frequent **bus** services connecting it with the rest of the state, other parts of Brazil, Buenos Aires, Asunción and Santiago. During January and February the island is extremely popular with Argentine, Uruguayan and Paraguayan tourists who can usually enjoy a summer holiday here for much less than the cost of one at home.

Most people arrive in **Florianópolis** and then head straight for the **beaches**, undoubtedly the best of which are found on the **north** and **east** coasts. Some of those on the west coast and by the lagoon in the centre of the island are quite pretty, but the water is polluted. With 42 beaches around the island to choose from, even the most crowded are rarely unbearably so, and they're all suited to a few days' winding down. Despite the existence of a good **bus network**, this is one place where **renting a car** (see p.656) should be seriously considered, especially if you have limited time and want to see as much of the island as possible: the roads are all excellent, though crowded in summer, and the drivers fairly civilized.

### Florianópolis

**FLORIANÓPOLIS** – or "Desterro" as it was originally called – was founded in 1700 and settled fifty years later by immigrants from the Portuguese mid-Atlantic islands of the Azores. Since then, it's gradually developed from being a sleepy provincial backwater into a sleepy state capital. With the construction of the bridges linking the island with the mainland, Florianópolis as a port has all but died, and today the city thrives as an administrative, commercial and tourist centre. Land reclamation for a multi-laned highway and new bus terminals has totally eliminated the character of the old seafront, and with it has vanished much of the city's former charm. Despite all the changes, though, the late nineteenth-century pastel-coloured, stuccoed buildings still recall faint old-world images, while the relaxed, small-town atmosphere provides a total contrast to the excitement of São Paulo or Rio.

#### Arrival and information

Buses arrive at the modern **rodoviária** (Ⓣ48/3212-3100) situated between the two bridges that link the island to the mainland. Outside the main entrance, beyond the car park and dual carriageway, is the former waterfront area where one of the **municipal bus terminals** is situated. From here, frequent buses (R$2.50) set out for most parts of the city as well as to all points in the south of the island. Otherwise, **buses** to the northern and eastern beach resorts depart from the corner of Rua José da Costa Moelmann and Avenida Mauro Ramos, a fifteen-minute walk around the hillside. These buses run to a surprisingly accurate timetable (check times at the information booths) and are cheap, though generally

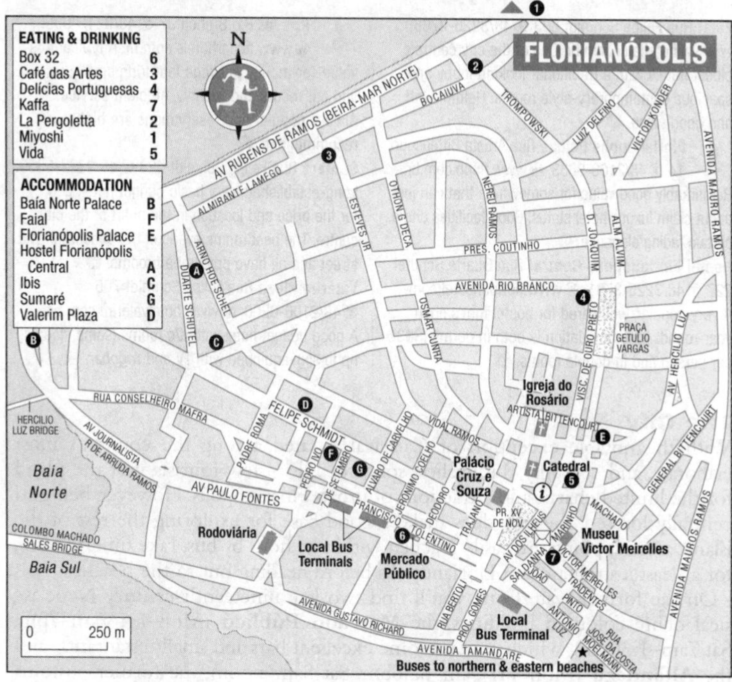


crowded. Alternatively, from both terminals there are faster, more comfortable and more expensive *executivo* minibuses (R$5) to most of the beaches.

The **airport** (☎48/3331-4000) serves São Paulo, Curitiba, Porto Alegre and Brasília as well as destinations in western Santa Catarina and Argentina. Located 12km south of the city centre, the airport is served by taxis (R$38 to the city centre or R$50 to Lagoa) and "Aeroporto" buses (R$2.50), which take about forty minutes to get to the centre.

In the city centre's Mercado Público, there's a **tourist information kiosk** (Dec–March Mon–Sat 7am–10pm, Sun 7am–7pm; April–Nov Mon–Sat 8am–6pm; ☎48/3212-3127), where very good, free maps of the island and city are available; there are also branches at the *rodoviária* (daily 8am–7pm) and at the airport (daily 8am–7pm). Listings of events in Florianópolis and elsewhere in Santa Catarina can be found in the daily newspaper *Diário Catarinense.*

## Accommodation

Most tourists choose to stay at the beaches and resorts around the island (see pp.657–660), but staying in the city centre has the benefit of a concentration of reasonably priced hotels, and direct bus services to all parts of the island. Try to arrive early in the day as **accommodation** is snapped up quickly during the peak holiday periods. Many of the cheapest **hotels** are located on, or just off, Rua Felipe Schmidt, only a few minutes from both Praça XV de Novembro and the bus terminals.

**Baía Norte Palace** Av. Beira Mar Norte ☎48/3229-3144, www.baianorte.com.br. Pleasant rooms, but be sure to ask for one facing the ocean. Although just a short walk from good bars and restaurants, it's a longer trek into the commercial centre itself. ❺

**Faial** Rua Felipe Schmidt 603 ⓣ48/3225-2766, ⓦwww.hotelfaial.com.br. One of the city centre's oldest hotels with a traditional-looking lobby and spacious contemporary-style rooms. Helpful staff and good value. ❺

**Florianópolis Palace** Rua Artista Bittencourt 14 ⓣ48/2106-9633, ⓦwww.floph.com.br. Remarkably good value for somewhere that can just about claim luxury-hotel status. Good facilities and a certain fading elegance. ❹

**Hostel Florianópolis Central** Rua Duarte Schutel 227 ⓣ48/3225-3781, ⓦwww.floripahostel.com. A very popular, well cared for hostel that's open year-round. Accommodation is both in dorms (R$37 per person and in double rooms. ❸

**Ibis** Av. Rio Branco 37 ⓣ48/3216-0000, ⓦwww.accorhotels.com.br. A typical Ibis value-for-money package featuring small, well laid out rooms and friendly, efficient service. Always popular and reservations are highly recommended. ❸

**Sumaré** Rua Felipe Schmidt 423 ⓣ48/3222-5359. Long-established, very basic budget hotel, good for the price and location in the heart of the city centre. The best rooms overlook the pedestrianized street and all have private bathrooms. ❸

**Valerim Plaza** Rua Felipe Schmidt 705 ⓣ48/2106-0200, ⓦwww.hotelvalerim.com.br. A good budget hotel with a/c rooms (some sleeping up to six), equipped with TV and *frigobar*. ❸



## The City

With the notable exception of Carnaval – rated among the country's most elaborate, and certainly the liveliest south of Rio – few tourists visit the island for the limited charm and attractions of urban Florianópolis. However, being so centrally located, the city does make a good base for exploring the rest of the island, as most points are easily reached within an hour by bus. Take time, though, for at least a stroll around Florianópolis before heading out to the beaches.

On the former waterfront, you'll find two late nineteenth-century Neoclassical ochre-coloured buildings, the **Mercado Público** (Mon–Fri 7am–7pm, Sat 7am–1.30pm), which contain some excellent bars and small restaurants, and the **Alfândega** (Mon–Fri 9am–6.30pm, Sat 8am–noon), the former customs house that has been converted for use as the Casa das Açores crafts market. From here, there's a steep walk up Rua Deodoro, past the early nineteenth-century Igreja São Francisco, to the **Rua Felipe Schmidt**, the commercial artery of the Praia de Fora, the "new town". At the end of the pedestrianized section of Rua Felipe Schmidt is the main, tree-filled square, **Praça XV de Novembro**, very much the heart of the new town. On one side of the square is the **Palácio Cruz e Souza**, an imposing pink building built between 1770 and 1780 as the seat of provincial government. It's now open to the public as the **Museu Histórico de Santa Catarina** (daily 10am–4pm; R$4) and it's worth taking a brisk walk around the building to admire the ornate nineteenth-century interior decoration, rather than to examine the unexciting collection of guns, swords and official scrolls. On the other side of the *praça* is Florianópolis's main post office and, just behind it at Rua Victor Meirelles 59, the **Museu Victor Meirelles** (Tues–Fri 1–6pm; R$2; ⓦwww.museuvictormeirelles.org.br). Meirelles was born in this building in 1832 and went on to become famous for his historically themed paintings. The museum is surprisingly interesting: sixteen of Meirelles' paintings are displayed on the first floor (most notable being the *Battle of Guararapes*, which celebrates Portugal's acquisition of north-eastern Brazil from the Dutch in 1649), while the first floor is used for visiting exhibits of other Brazilian artists.

Overlooking the square from the highest point is the utterly unremarkable **Catedral Metropolitana**; it was originally constructed between 1753 and 1773, but was enlarged and totally remodelled in 1922, so you'd be hard-pressed to identify any original features. The only church in the city centre dating back to the colonial era is the simple but charming mid-eighteenth-century **Igreja de Nossa Senhora do Rosário**, higher up from the cathedral and best approached by a flight of steep steps from Rua Marechal Guilherme.

On the campus of the Federal University (UFSC), twenty minutes by bus from the city centre, the **Museu de Antropologia** (Mon–Fri 9am–noon & 1–5pm) has a small collection of artefacts belonging to Santa Catarina's decimated Kaingang and Xokleng forest Indians and objects relating to early Azorean immigrants that's worth an hour or so on a rainy day. The **Museu de Arte de Santa Catarina** (Mon–Fri 9am–noon & 3–9pm, Sat & Sun 5–10pm), in the Centro Integrado de Cultura (reached by buses marked "Agronomica"), hosts permanent and temporary exhibitions by local and national artists of often dubious talent. The centre itself also boasts an arts cinema; a detailed programme is published in the *Diário Catarinense*.

## Eating, drinking and nightlife

In **the centre**, on the roads that run off the main square in all directions, are numerous cheap, but largely uninspiring **restaurants**. Come evening, there's very little life in the commercial centre around Praça XV de Novembro. Instead, people head for the **bars and restaurants** that spread out along the **Beira Mar Norte** (or Av. Rubens de Arruda Ramos as it is officially called), a dual carriageway that skirts the north of the city along reclaimed land starting at the Hercílio Luz bridge, or head for much more fashionable Lagoa (see p.657). Places move in and out of popularity rapidly and in summer you'll find that the bars – the first two of which are situated virtually under the bridge itself – are either packed solid with wealthy young people or, for no apparent reason, totally empty. Unfortunately the restaurants here aren't particularly good either and are generally expensive, but there is at least a fair choice, which is more than can be said for the commercial centre. Further north, in the Beira Mar Norte Shopping Center (Mon–Sat 10am–10pm), there are a dozen fast-food outlets including the usual hamburgers as well as seafood and a decent vegetarian restaurant.

**Box 32** Mercado Público. One of several excellent bars and simple restaurants in the area, serving cold beer, light meals and tasty snacks. This one is especially good and is known as a meeting point for local politicians and artists. Mon–Fri 10am–9pm, Sat 10am–3pm.

**Café das Artes** Rua Esteves Júnior 734. Located in a beautifully restored, early nineteenth-century building, delicious pasta dishes and salads are served, though the cakes and premium-quality coffee are especially recommended. Mon–Fri 11.30am–11pm, Sat & Sun 3–10pm.

**Delícias Portuguesas** Rua Visconde de Ouro Preto 559. An authentic Portuguese restaurant, predictably specializing in fish. Although meals are rather

▲ *Box 32*, Florianópolis

expensive (expect to pay around R$70 per person), you can just opt for some *petiscos* (snacks) – the *bolinhos de bacalhau* are superb. Closed Sun.

**Kaffa** Rua Victor Meirelles 184. One of the more distinctive city-centre restaurants offering huge portions of satisfying and very reasonably priced Lebanese food. Closed Sun.

**La Pergoletta** Travessa Carreirão 62. Located near the Beira Mar Norte Shopping Center (take any bus that reads "via Beira Mar Norte"), this is the best of several local Italian restaurants, all of which have similar menus featuring standard pasta, meat and fish dishes.

**Miyoshi** Av. Beira Mar Norte 1068. Florianópolis's best Asian restaurant with a choice of a *por kilo* buffet (including a good sushi selection) and an à la carte menu featuring mainly Japanese dishes, though also with a few Chinese and Thai options. Daily.

**Vida** Rua Visconde de Ouro Preto 62. A varied vegetarian *por kilo* buffet and health food store. Mon–Sat lunch only.

## Listings

**Airlines** Aerolíneas Argentinas ⓣ48/3224-7835; Gol ⓣ48/3331-4127; TAM ⓣ48/3331-4085; Varig/Pluna ⓣ48/3331-4154.

**Banks and exchange** Banks are located on Rua Felipe Schmidt and by Praça XV de Novembro.

**Books** Florianópolis's bookshops are poor, but you may find something of local interest at Livros e Livros, Rua Deodoro 191, sala 2; Lunardelli, Rua Victor Meirelles 28; Livraria Catarinense, Rua Felipe Schmidt 60, and in the Beira Mar Norte Shopping Center.

**Car rental** Avis (ⓣ48/236-1426), Hertz (ⓣ48/236-9955), Localiza (ⓣ48/236-1244), Unidas (ⓣ48/236-0607) and Yes (ⓣ48/284-4656) are all represented at the airport and can arrange delivery in the city centre. During the peak summer season advance reservations are essential.

**Consulates** Argentina, Av. Rio Branco 387, 5th floor ⓣ48/3216-8903; Uruguay, Rua Prof. Walter de Bona Castelan 559, Jardim Anchieta ⓣ48/3222-3718.

**Post office** The main post office is on Praça XV de Novembro.

**Shopping** In the centre, Rua Felipe Schmidt has a full range of shops. At the former waterfront, the Alfândega building (see p.654) is now an arts and crafts market, though the quality of the merchandise is disappointing. The Beira Mar Norte Shopping Center is on Av. Rubens de Arruda Ramos heading north from the centre. Apart from numerous surf-oriented shops, it contains all the usual Brazilian fashion brand-name shops.

## The north coast

The island's increasingly built-up **north coast** offers safe swimming in calm, warm seas and, as such, is particularly popular with families. The long, gently curving bay of **CANASVIERAS** is the most crowded of the northern resorts, largely geared towards Paulista, Argentine and Uruguayan families who own or rent houses near to the beach. Most of the bars along the beach cater to the tourists, playing Argentine and North American pop music, and serving Argentine snacks accompanied by Brazilian beer. By walking away from the concentration of bars at the centre of the beach, towards the east and Ponta das Canas, it's usually possible to find a relatively quiet spot. Unless you're renting a house for a week or more (agencies abound), finding **accommodation** is difficult, as the unappealing hotels are usually booked solid throughout the summer months. However, if you're set on staying here, by asking in the souvenir shops and restaurants you'll eventually be directed to someone with a spare **room to rent**. The local **restaurants** mostly offer the same menu of prawn dishes, pizza and hamburgers, with only the *Restaurante Tropical*, on the road that runs parallel to the beach, and its *bahian* dishes standing out as different.

Heading westwards you'll reach **JURERÊ**, another long beach that almost exclusively attracts families, and is separated from Canasvieras by a rocky promontory. Still further west, a series of coves fringed by luxuriant vegetation – reached by clambering down from the road skirting the coast, or by climbing over the rocks that separate one cove from another – link Jurerê to **DANIELA**, a smaller and less-developed beach. Though it amounts to nothing special, the turquoise waters of the nearby coves are well worth the small effort needed to reach them, and basic **rooms** (❷–❸) are available next to the *Lancheria Palheiro*. Alternatively, modern studio and one-bedroom apartments, all with kitchens, are available at the *Pousada dos Artistas* (Ⓣ48/3282-5512, Ⓦwww.pousadadosartistas.com.br; ❺). Roughly midway between Jurerê and Daniela, stunning views of the coast and across to the mainland can be appreciated from the ruins of the **Forte de São José** (usually referred to as Forte Jurerê), built in 1742 to guard the northern approaches to Desterro. Next to the fort there's a small eighteenth-century chapel.

To the east of Canasvieras, at the extreme northern tip of the island, is the almost two-kilometre-long **Praia da Lagoinha**, the prettiest beach hereabouts and with the island's warmest water. The beach has a wooded backdrop and, compared to the rest of the north coast, what development has taken place is remarkably tasteful. Located just metres from the shore is one of the most exclusive places to stay in Florianópolis, the *Pousada da Vigia*, Rua Conêgo Walmor Castro 291 (Ⓣ48/3284-1789, Ⓦwww.pousadadavigia.com.br; ❻). Once the private residence of a former state governor, the property has been turned into a *pousada* of understated luxury.

## The east coast

If you find the north coast too crowded and developed, head for the **east coast**, where Atlantic rollers scare away most of the families. Take extreme care, though, as the undercurrents here make for dangerous swimming. There are a couple of places to avoid: **PRAIA BRAVA** (the most northerly of the east-coast beaches) is dominated by huge condominium complexes that have resulted in this beautiful stretch of coast becoming the island's ugliest corner. There's been similar uncontrolled development at **INGLESES**, a little further south. Instead you're better off returning to Florianópolis and crossing the island to the Lagoa da Conceição, a large saltwater lagoon in the centre of the island.

### Lagoa da Conceição

The **Lagoa da Conceição** is very popular amongst families and others who want to swim, canoe or windsurf. **CENTRO DA LAGOA** (usually simply referred to as Lagoa), a bustling little town at the southern end of the lagoon, is a very pleasant place to stay. There are good bus services from here into Florianópolis and to the east-coast beaches, and a post office, a branch of Banco do Brasil (with an ATM), grocery stores and numerous restaurants and bars on the main road. This is one of the liveliest nightspots on the island during the summer and at weekends throughout the year, with restaurants always crowded and people overflowing into the street from the bars until the small hours of the morning. **Accommodation** is scarce, however: the nicest place by far is the *Cabanas da Gringa*, Rua das Araras 52 (Ⓣ48/3232-1181, Ⓦwww.guiafloripa.com/cabanasdagringa; ❹), a short walk from the main restaurant strip, with rooms and cabins sleeping two to four people. Alternatively, try the spartan *Pousada Águia Pequena*, a couple of minutes' walk from the bridge that crosses the lagoon, at Rua Rita Lourenço da Silveira 114 (Ⓣ48/3232-2339; ❸), or the very similar *Pousada do Grego* at Rua Antônio da Silveira 58 (Ⓣ48/3232-0734; ❸).

Lagoa's beaches are close to the centre of town: cross the small bridge on the road leaving Centro da Lagoa and it's a ten-minute walk. There are also some attractive beaches on the isolated northwest shore of the lagoon – one of the most beautiful parts of the island – around **COSTA DA LAGOA**, a charming fishing village barely touched by tourism. The area is impossible to reach by road and involves either a three-hour walk along a trail skirting the lagoon, or an hour's boat ride; boats leave every hour (7.30am–6pm; R$3) from beneath the bridge in Centro da Lagoa, stopping off at isolated houses and tiny fishing hamlets on the way. Once at Costa da Lagoa, a ten-minute walk along a rough trail will take you to a nearby waterfall, where you can take a refreshing dip in the natural pool. Back in the village there are swimming beaches and a couple of restaurants, but you'd do better to take the trail that hugs the shore of the lagoon back south towards Centro da Lagoa; a twenty-minute walk will bring you to a much more attractive beach, which has an excellent seafood **restaurant** and bar. **Rooms** are available above the restaurant here (❷), but if you don't want to stay over you can either continue back along the trail to Centro da Lagoa, or wait at the pier for the hourly boat.

**BARRA DA LAGOA**, the village at the entrance to the Lagoa da Conceição, has succeeded fairly well in allowing tourism to develop alongside the inhabitants' traditional main activity – fishing. There are beautiful cliffside walks from here, the best reached by crossing the Ponte Pêncil, a rickety suspended footbridge that leads to the very pretty **PRAINHA DO LESTE**, a small cove flanked by forbidding rock formations where beach parties are often held in summer. Barra da Lagoa has several **restaurants**, a **campsite** and plenty of **rooms** and cabins to rent. There are also several **pousadas** in Prainha, including the *Gaivota* (☎48/3232-3253; ❸), which offers no-frills bed and breakfast accommodation, and the rather more comfortable *Vipaz* (☎48/3232-3193; ❸–❹), across the Ponte Pêncil, with spacious rooms sleeping two to four people, and cooking facilities as well.

### North of Lagoa da Conceição

Stretching north for kilometres, Barra da Lagoa's beach merges into **PRAIA DA MOÇAMBIQUE** (also known as Praia Grande). This is the longest beach on the island, over 12km, and also one of the least developed, thanks to the **Reserva Florestal do Rio Vermelho**, a huge expanse of pine trees that takes up most of its hinterland. Inland from here on the Estrada Geral do Rio Vermelho – the road that leads to the village of Rio Vermelho – is one of the most outstanding, and surprising, **restaurants** on the island, well worth going out of your way for. *Chez Altamiro* (☎48/3269-7727; reservations strongly advised) is run by an islander who, despite having never set foot in France, cooks extremely good traditional French food for around R$80 a head. The restaurant is in the middle of nowhere, but is easily recognized by the tricolor that adorns the outside of the wooden building.

### South of Lagoa da Conceição

South of Barra da Lagoa, the road climbs steeply, passing mountain-sized sand dunes to the secluded **PRAIA GALHETA**, the only nudist beach on the island, and **PRAIA MOLE**, whose beautiful beach is slightly hidden beyond the sand dunes and beneath low-lying cliffs. Mole is extremely popular with young people but, rather surprisingly, commercial activity has remained low-key, probably because there's a deep drop-off right at the water's edge.

Approached by a road passing between gigantic dunes, the next beach is at **JOAQUINA**, very popular with surfers, particularly so during the Brazilian national surf championships, held annually in the last week of January. The water's cold, however, and the sea rough, only really suitable for strong swimmers. If you have the energy, climb to the top of the dunes where you'll be rewarded with the most spectacular views in all directions. The dunes are a popular location for paragliding and sandboarding – no skill is required if you sit, rather than stand, on a board as you hurtle down a dune (board rentals at the roadside for R$15 per hr). Accommodation by the beach is limited to two **hotels**, the large *Joaquina Beach* (Ⓣ48/3232-5059, Ⓦwww.joaquinabeachhotel.com.br; ⑤), usually booked solid in the summer, and the *Cris Hotel* (Ⓣ48/3232-5104, Ⓦwww.crishotel.com; ⑤) which is slightly newer and has better views along the coast. Alternatively, there's the smaller and friendlier *Pousada Bizkaia* (Ⓣ48/3232-5273, Ⓦwww.bizkaia.com.br; ④), 1.5km from the beach on the road to Lagoa.

Joaquina beach stretches 3.5km to the south, blending into **PRAIA DO CAMPECHE**, so by walking for fifteen minutes or so you can escape Joaquina's crowds and be almost alone. Campeche, which itself merges into Morro das Pedras and Armação (see below), is considered by many to be the most beautiful stretch of the island's coast, but due to the strong current and often ferocious surf fewer people are attracted here than to the beaches to the north. Consequently, there's been comparatively little building work, and only slowly are houses, bars and the like appearing, concentrated around the southern portion of the beach. One rather beautiful **hotel** complex is the *São Sebastião da Praia* at Av. Cameche 1373 (Ⓣ48/3338-2020, Ⓦwww.hotelsaosebastiao.com.br; ④). Accommodation is set within lush, landscaped grounds with a mix of lawns, native trees and flowering bushes.

Further south is the fishing village of **ARMAÇÃO**, whose lovely hilly backdrop gives it a stunning location. There's an attractive beach – though, here too, the waves and currents are unforgiving – and well-marked trails leading both inland and to more protected coves. There are some excellent **places to stay** here. The *Pousada Alemdomar* (Ⓣ48/3237-5600, Ⓦwww.alemdomar.com.br; ④), some 250m south of the village near the Lagoa do Peri, has brightly coloured rooms (all of which have either a terrace or a balcony, some with sea views) and an extremely relaxing atmosphere, while on the beach is the more exclusive *Pousada Pénaria* (Ⓣ48/3338-1616, Ⓦwww.pousadapenareia.com.br; ④–⑤). The best budget option is the well-equipped youth hostel, the *Albergue Armação* (Ⓣ48/3389-5542, Ⓔalbergue@brturbo.com; R$30 per person), but beds fill up fast; in summer reservations are essential. Armação is also the nearest point to the **Ilha do Campeche**, where the pristine white-sand beach is protected from any form of development – only four hundred visitors are permitted at any one time, along with a few people selling refreshments. Boats from Armação take about thirty minutes to complete the three-kilometre crossing (R$15 return).

Beyond here, practically at the end of the road, is **PÂNTANO DO SUL**, a rather larger fishing village at the end of a well-protected bay with a mountainous backdrop. The village itself is not at all attractive, but the water is calmer here than elsewhere on the east coast, the views of the small, uninhabited islands offshore are pleasant, and you can eat well. There are several **restaurants** right on the beach, including the *Bar do Arante*, known for serving some of the best seafood on the island, and a couple of **pousadas**, the very pleasant *Sol de Costa* (Ⓣ48/3222-5071; ③), and the *Pescador* (Ⓣ48/3237-7122, Ⓦwww.pousadadopescador.com.br; ④). Tourism has had only a minimal impact on the inhabitants' lives and Azorean traditions have remained strong, most visibly during Carnaval when brass bands wind their way through the streets and along the beach, the rhythms very different from the familiar beat of samba drums.

## The west coast

The principal places of interest on the **west coast** are **SAMBAQUI** and **SANTO ANTÔNIO DE LISBOA** to the north of Florianópolis, and **RIBEIRÃO DA ILHA** to the south. As the island's oldest, most attractive and least-spoilt settlements, the houses in these places are almost all painted white and have dark blue sash windows – in typical Azorean style – and each village has a simple colonial church. As was the case with most of the island's settlements, these villages were founded by immigrants from the Azores, and their present-day inhabitants – who still refer to themselves as being Azorean – retain many traditions of the islands from which their forefathers came. Fishing, rather than catering to the needs of tourists, remains the principal activity of the three villages, and the waters offshore from Santo Antônio and Ribeirão da Ilha are used to farm mussels and oysters, considered the best anywhere in the island. Azorean immigrants brought their lace-making skills to Santa Catarina, too, and intricately fashioned lace tablecloths, mats and other items are displayed for sale outside some of the houses in Ribeirão da Ilha – or you can buy them at the Casa Açoriana, Rua Cônego Serpa, in Santo Antônio. Local handicrafts are also on display, along with exhibits on the Azorean settlement of the island, at the **Ecomuseu** (Tues–Fri 9am–noon & 1.30–5pm, Sat, Sun & holidays noon–6pm; R$3) in Ribeirão da Ilha. Because the beaches are small and face the mainland, tourism has remained low-key, and the few visitors are usually on day-trips from resorts elsewhere on the island. They stay just long enough for a meal: especially recommended are the oyster dishes served at *Ostradamus*, on the waterfront in Ribeirão da Ilha, and the shellfish and grilled fish at the charming *Restinga Recanto*, overlooking the beach outside of Sambaqui towards Santo Antônio. In the village of Santo Antônio itself there's a bar on the beach directly in front of the church, serving fried fish and the freshest of oysters, while next to the church is the *Restaurante Açores* offering inexpensive meals.

South of Ribeirão da Ilha, hugging the steep hillside as it passes tiny, deserted coves, the dreadfully potholed road leading to Barra do Sul runs through some of the most stunning scenery on the island. The rainfall here is extremely heavy, nurturing a profusion of rich foliage, most noticeably flamboyants and bougainvillaea.

If you choose to **stay** in one of the west-coast villages, finding a room can be quite a problem, but if successful you'll be rewarded by complete tranquillity of a kind lost to most of the rest of the island over the course of the last couple of decades. Your best chance is in Santo Antônio: the *Pousada Caminho dos Açores* (T 48/3235-1363; 4) is set in a lovely garden and has an attractive pool, or there's the *Pousada Mar de Dentro* (T 48/3235-1521; 5), very similar, with a tiny pool, but right on the beach. In Ribeirão da Ilha try the modest *Pousada do Museu* (T 48/3237-8148, W www.pousadadomuseu.com.br; 3), which fronts onto the beach by the Ecomuseu.

## The north coast: to São Francisco do Sul

If you're going to travel by bus on Santa Catarina's coastal highway (the BR-101) **north of Florianópolis** in the Brazilian summer you're best off keeping your eyes firmly closed. The bumper-to-bumper traffic moves at terrifying speeds, with cars, trucks and buses constantly overtaking each other for no apparent advantage; the wrecked cars that litter the highway are enough to make you get out of the bus and walk to your destination – something that, at times, might be faster anyway. If you take a bus on this road you won't be able to stop for a dip, and will have to content yourself with the idyllic images out of the window. But if you rent a car you can stop off at the stunning beaches, some of which have remained totally devoid of buildings and people. Some of the nicest bathing and surfing beaches are found on the **Porto Belo** peninsula. The unremarkable town of **Itajaí** is Santa Catarina's most important port and you're almost certain to pass through it at some point. Much more interesting is **São Francisco do Sul**, one of southern Brazil's oldest settlements. One place you'll probably want to avoid altogether is Balneário Camboriú, Brazil's answer to the worst wall-to-wall concrete high-rise Spanish resort.

## Porto Belo

Although the stretch immediately north of Florianópolis is probably the most beautiful part of the Santa Catarina coast, during the peak summer season it is completely overrun by Argentine and *paulista* tourists. Less than two hours from Florianópolis, the peninsula and city of **PORTO BELO** is easily reached by bus, and although the local authority's claim that there are 32 beaches around Porto Belo is highly suspect, the beaches there certainly are numerous and large enough to cope with the visitors – at least outside of the peak months of January and February.

The "city" of Porto Belo is, in reality, just an overgrown village containing a tourist office (Ⓣ47/3369-5638), post office, and a few bars and restaurants, but from here frequent local buses travel to **beaches** around the peninsula, stopping along the road to pick up passengers. The most attractive beaches are **Bombas** and **Bombinhas**, 5km and 8km east of Porto Belo respectively and separated from one another by a rocky promontory. The bay in which they're found is very pretty, with rich vegetation behind, and the waves here are suitable for inexperienced surfers. South of Bombinhas, if you're looking for open sea and more powerful waves, the east-facing **Praia do Mariscal** is better, but should be braved by only the most expert of surfers. In complete contrast, the nearby **Praia do Canto** is ideal for anyone merely seeking a gentle swim.

**Hotels** in Porto Belo are generally small and fairly expensive – you're unlikely to find a room for less than R$100 a night, and you may have to pay considerably more. The best hope of finding somewhere to stay is in Bombinhas: try the Spanish colonial-style *Pousada Águas* (Ⓣ47/3340-5799; ④) or, with panoramic views and a small pool, the *Pousada das Palmeiras* (Ⓣ47/3369-2222; ④). Quite expensive, but worth every *real* is the *Pousada do Arvoredo* (Ⓣ47/3369-2355, Ⓦwww.pousadadoarvoredo.com.br; ⑤), which has attractive chalets or rooms with balconies overlooking the gardens and the ocean, and a pool. Back in Porto Belo itself, there's the *Pousada Enseada das Garoupas* (Ⓣ47/3369-4383; ⑤) or the more basic *Pousada das Vieras* (Ⓣ47/3369-4468; ④). The only inexpensive place around, at R$20 per head, is the **youth hostel** (Ⓣ47/3369-4483; open Nov–April, summer reservations essential), about ten minutes' walk from the bus terminal, at Rua José Amancio 246.

## Itajaí

Santa Catarina's most important port, **ITAJAÍ** is located at the mouth of the Rio Itajaí-Açu, 35km north of Porto Belo. Although it was founded in the early eighteenth century, Itajaí looks fairly new, with few buildings dating back to before 1950 – and with nothing of any tourist interest. However, it's an important transport centre, and it may not be possible to avoid the city altogether. Fortunately, most buses pass straight by it, with only a minority actually stopping to pick up and put down passengers in the city. And as there's a constant flow of buses to Blumenau, Joinville and Florianópolis, as well as further afield in all directions, there are few reasons actually to stay in Itajaí. One reason might be to catch an early morning plane from nearby Navegantes **airport** (Ⓣ47/3342-9200), from where you can fly to Florianópolis, Porto Alegre and São Paulo. To get to the airport, take the ferry from Avenida Argentina across the river, and then a taxi at around R$25; for slightly more, taxis will take you direct from Itajaí, via the ferry, to the airport. Should you need a **hotel**, try the convenient option clearly visible from the *rodoviária*, the *Itajaí Tur* at Rua Alberto Werner 133 (Ⓣ47/3348-4600, Ⓦwww.itajaitur.com.br; ❸), with rooms of varying levels of comfort and price. Alternatively, in Navegantes there's a reliable *Ibis* at Rua Abrahão João Francisco 567 (Ⓣ47/3249-6800, Ⓦwww.accorhotels.com.br; ❷–❸).

The city's **beaches** aren't bad, and are worth a visit if you have some time to spare. From the local bus terminal in the city centre, near the intersection of Rua Joinville and Avenida Victor Konder, buses take about twenty minutes to reach the nearest beaches, **Atalaia** and **Geremias**, or a little longer to get to the cleaner **Praia Cabecudas**.

## The Ilha de São Francisco

North of Itajaí, the highway gradually turns inland towards Joinville (see opposite), but 45km east of Joinville is the **Ilha de São Francisco**, a low-lying island separated from the mainland by a narrow strait spanned by a causeway. As Joinville's port and the site of a major Petrobras oil refinery, São Francisco may seem like a place to avoid, but both the port and refinery keep a discreet distance from the main town, São Francisco do Sul, and the beaches, while the surprisingly few sailors who are around blend perfectly with the slightly dilapidated colonial setting.

### São Francisco do Sul

The island was first visited by European sailors as early as 1504, though not until the middle of the following century was the town of **SÃO FRANCISCO DO SUL** established. It's one of the oldest settlements in the state and also one of the very few places in Santa Catarina where a concentration of colonial and nineteenth-century buildings survive. During most of its first two hundred years, São Francisco do Sul was little more than a naval outpost, its simple local economy based on fishing and sugar-cane production. In the nineteenth century, with the opening of nearby areas to immigrants from Germany, the town grew in importance as a transfer point for people and produce. Merchants established themselves in the town, building grand houses and dockside warehouses, many of which remain today – protected from demolition and gradually undergoing restoration. Dominating the city's skyline is the **Igreja Matriz**, the main church, originally built in 1665 by Indian slaves; completely reconstructed in 1884, the church has lost all of its original features. You might want to visit the **Museu Histórico** (Tues–Fri 9am–6pm, Sat & Sun 11am–6pm; R$2) on Rua Coronel Carvalho, housed in São Francisco's nineteenth-century prison building (which, incidentally, remained in use until 1968). The former cells have been converted into small exhibition halls; the most interesting exhibits are nineteenth-century photographs of the town. The **Museu Nacional do Mar** on Rua Manoel Lourenço de Andrade (Tues–Sun 10am–6pm; R$5; Ⓦwww.museunacionaldomar.com.br) has a fine collection devoted to the technology of ocean travel and the people who make their living from the sea, with an emphasis on southern Brazil.

Most of the island's visitors bypass the old town altogether and head straight for the beaches to the east, so, even in midsummer, there's rarely any difficulty in finding a **hotel** with room. Quite comfortable, and with sea views, is the *Hotel Kontiki* (Ⓣ47/3444-2232; ❸) at Rua Camacho 33 near the market or, if you want a pool, try the relatively luxurious *Hotel Zibamba* (Ⓣ47/3444-2020,

ⓦwww.hotelzibamba.com.br; ⑤) at Rua Fernandes Dias 27. Eating out holds no great excitement, with the *Hotel Zibamba*'s seafood restaurant the best of a generally poor bunch.

From the market in the town centre, there are **buses** to the *rodoviária* (ⓣ47/3444-8086) beyond the town's limits, from where there are hourly connections to Joinville as well as daily services to São Paulo and Curitiba.

### The island's beaches

The prettiest beaches, **Paulos** and **Ingleses**, are also the nearest to town, just a couple of kilometres to the east. Both are small, and have trees to provide shade, and surprisingly few people take advantage of the protected sea, ideal for a gentle swim. On the east coast, **Praia de Ubatuba** and the adjoining **Praia de Enseada**, about 15km from town, are the island's most popular beaches, with enough surf to have fun in but not enough to be dangerous. At Enseada there are a couple of **campsites** and an overpriced hotel, while Ubatuba caters mainly for families who rent or own houses that front the beach. By way of contrast, a ten-minute walk across the peninsula from the eastern end of Enseada leads to **Praia da Saúde** (also referred to as Prainha), where the waves are suitable for only the toughest surfers.

Frequent **buses** to Enseada and Ubatuba leave from the market in the town centre, with the last buses in both directions departing at about 9.30pm.

# Northeast Santa Catarina

Although the northeast of Santa Catarina is populated by people of many ethnic origins, it's an area most associated with **Germans**, who so obviously dominate both culturally and economically. **Joinville** and **Blumenau** vie with each other to be not only the economic powerhouse of the region, but also the cultural capital. However, both cities lose out in terms of tourist interest to the small towns and villages of the interior, where old dialects are still spoken. One such community is **Pomerode**, which is set in a picturesque area and does much to promote its German heritage.

## Joinville and around

An hour from São Francisco, the land on which **JOINVILLE** was settled was originally given as a dowry by Emperor Dom Pedro to his sister, who had married the Prince of Joinville, the son of Louis-Philippe of France. A deal with Hamburg timber merchants meant that, in 1851, 191 Germans, Swiss and Norwegians arrived in Santa Catarina, to exploit the fifty square kilometres of virgin forest, stake out homesteads and establish the "Colônia Dona Francisca" – later known as Joinville. As more Germans were dispatched from Hamburg, Joinville grew and prospered, developing from an agricultural backwater into the state's foremost industrial city. This economic success has diluted much of Joinville's once solidly German character, but evidence of its ethnic origins remains: the largely Germanic architecture and the impeccably clean streets produce the atmosphere of a rather dull, small town in Germany.

Shops and services are concentrated along Rua Princesa Isabel, while Rua XV de Novembro and Rua IX de Março run parallel to each other, terminating at the river. However, the points of interest associated with Joinville's German heritage are more widely scattered but still easily reached on foot. The first place to head for is the **Museu Nacional de Imigração e Colonização** at

## German Santa Catarina

In the nineteenth century, as it became more difficult to enter the United States, land-hungry European immigrants sought new destinations, many choosing Brazil as their alternative America. Thousands made their way into the forested wilderness of Santa Catarina, attempting to become independent farmers, and of all of them, it was the **Germans** who most successfully fended off assimilationist pressures. Concentrated in areas where few non-Germans lived, there was little reason for them to learn Portuguese, and, as merchants, teachers, Catholic priests and Protestant pastors arrived with the immigrants, complete communities evolved, with flourishing German cultural organizations and a varied German-language press. After Brazil's entry into World War II, restrictions on the use of German were introduced and many German organizations were proscribed, accused of being Nazi fronts. Certainly, "National Socialism" found some of its most enthusiastic followers among overseas Germans and, though the extent of **Nazi activity** in Santa Catarina is a matter of debate, for years after the collapse of the Third Reich ex-Nazis attracted sympathy in even the most isolated forest homesteads.

Later, due to the compulsory use of Portuguese in schools, the influence of radio and television and an influx of migrants from other parts of the state to work in the region's rapidly expanding industries, the German language appeared to be dying in Santa Catarina. As a result, in **Joinville** and **Blumenau** – the region's largest cities – German is now rarely heard. However, in outlying villages and farming communities such as **Pomerode**, near Blumenau, German remains very much alive, spoken everywhere but in government offices. Recently, too, the German language and Teuto-Brazilian culture have undergone a renaissance for which the German government has provided financial support. Property developers are encouraged to heed supposedly traditional **German architectural styles**, resulting in a plethora of buildings that may be appropriate for alpine conditions, but look plain silly in the Brazilian subtropics. A more positive development has been the move to protect and restore the houses of the early settlers, especially those built in the most characteristic local building style, that of **enxaimel** ("Fachwerk" in German) – exposed bricks within an exposed timber frame. These houses are seen throughout the region, concentrated most heavily in the area around Pomerode. Keen to reap benefits from the new ethnic awareness, local authorities have also initiated pseudo-German **festivals**, such as Blumenau's Munich-inspired "Oktoberfest" (see p.667) and Pomerode's more authentic "Festa Pomerana" (see p.668), both of which have rapidly become major tourist draws.

Rua Rio Branco 229, near Praça da Bandeira (Tues–Fri 9am–5pm, Sat & Sun 11am–5pm; Ⓦ www.museunacional.com.br; R$2), an excellent introduction to the history of German immigrants in Santa Catarina in general and Joinville in particular. In the main building, formerly the prince of Joinville's palace, built in 1870, there are some late nineteenth- and early twentieth-century photographs, though the museum's most interesting features are an old barn containing farm equipment used by early *colonos*, and a typical nineteenth-century *enxaimel* farmhouse with period furnishings. If you've more than a passing interest in Joinville's history, also visit the superbly organized **Arquivo Histórico** (Mon–Fri 8am–4pm), Av. Hermann August Lepper 650, where temporary, mainly photographic, exhibitions are held.

As throughout the region, Joinville's municipal authorities are making efforts to preserve the surviving **enxaimel houses**. Although scattered throughout the city, they can be seen in some concentration along the former main approach road, the cobbled **Rua XV de Novembro**. On the same road, about twenty minutes' walk from the centre, is the **Cemitério dos Imigrantes**, the final resting place of many of Joinville's pioneer settlers. Covering a hillside from which there are fine views of the city, the cemetery has been preserved as a national monument, the tombs and headstones serving as testimony to Joinville's ethnic origins. If you have some time pop into the **Mercado Público Municipal** (Mon–Fri 7am–7pm, Sat 7am–1pm) near the local bus terminal in the centre, which sells food and some handicrafts produced by local German *colonos*. On the second Saturday of each month a **handicraft market** is held in the nearby Praça Nereu Ramos.

### Practicalities

The **rodoviária** (ⓣ47/3433-2991) is 2km from the city centre, reached in five minutes by bus or in half an hour on foot by walking down Rua Ministro Calógeras and then left along Avenida Kubitschek. Bus services to neighbouring cities are excellent. The terminal for **city buses** and those to Dona Francisca (see p.666) is in the centre, at the end of Rua IX de Março. There's an **airport** (ⓣ47/3467-1000) 13km north of the city, with flights to Florianópolis, Porto Alegre and São Paulo. The **tourist information** office is at Rua XV de Novembro 4305 (daily 8am–8pm; ⓣ0800-643-5015).

Finding a comfortable, spotlessly clean and reasonably priced **hotel** is usually easy, though Joinville has become a popular place for conferences, during which accommodation is scarce. In the city centre, on Rua Jerônimo Coelho near the local bus terminal, try the *Ideal* (ⓣ47/3422-3660; ❷) at no. 98, or, if you prefer a private bathroom, the *Príncipe* (ⓣ47/3422-8555; ❸) at no. 27. Nearby is one of Joinville's priciest places to stay, the *Tannenhof* (ⓣ47/3433-8011, ⓦwww.tannenhof.com.br; ❺) at Rua Visconde de Taunay 340, with all the features you'd expect of a large, luxury hotel. Smaller but with much more character and better value is the *Anthurium Parque*, Rua São José 226 (ⓣ47/3433-6299, ⓦwww.anthurium.com.br; ❹), a curious building supposedly of "Norwegian–German" style, set in pretty grounds near the cathedral. Around the corner from here at Rua Ministro Calógeras 612 is the *Germânia* (ⓣ47/3433-9886, ⓦwww.hotelgermania.com.br; ❹), which to all appearances is just another brash tower block, but which has extremely comfortable rooms, helpful staff and very friendly owners.

▲ German farmhouse, Santa Catarina

Not surprisingly, **German restaurants** abound, but most are of the sausage, pig's knuckle, potato and sauerkraut level of sophistication. The *Bierkeller*, conveniently located at Rua XV de Novembro 497 (closed Mon), is typical, or try one of the many self-service restaurants in the Shopping Müeller, a large shopping centre next to the *Hotel Tannenhof*. For an especially good meal, head out to the suburbs (a R$15 taxi ride) to the *Sopp* (evenings only, closed Sun) at Rua Marechal Deodoro 640, the best restaurant in Joinville. The menu, based on German cooking, is varied enough for most tastes and there's an unusually good choice of beers. For **afternoon tea**, you'll get good cakes at the *Delicatesse Viktoria* at Rua Felipe Schmidt 400, near to the Shopping Müeller; alternatively, all the upmarket hotels serve a good high tea (*café colonial*).

Since 1937, the **Festa das Flores** has been held for ten days during the second half of November, the height of the orchid season – flower shows, German folk dancing, music and food are the main attractions. Pride of place in the cultural calendar goes to the annual **Festival Internacional de Dança** (ⓣ47/3423-1010, ⓦwww.festivaldedanca.com.br), the largest event of its kind in Latin America. For twelve days in late July, dance companies from around the world descend on Joinville, attracting an audience from throughout Brazil. So strong is Joinville's association with dance that in 1999 it was chosen by the Bolshoi as the location of its first ballet school outside Russia (ⓦwww.escolabolshoi.com.br).

## Around Joinville: Estrada Bonita and Estrada Dona Francisca

Although Joinville itself has developed increasingly into a rather anonymous big city, its rural, German-speaking hinterland to the west has changed little over the past few decades. There are two distinct areas to head for: the **Estrada Bonita**, with its well-organized small farms selling home-made jams, *cachaça* and biscuits, and the **Estrada Dona Francisca**, where you'll find some of the oldest and best-cared-for *enxaimel* houses in Santa Catarina. In both areas, visitors are warmly received. For Estrada Bonita's *colonos*, tourism enables them to sustain a reasonable standard of living and keep young people from moving to Joinville, while in the Dona Francisca area local awareness of the historic importance of the old buildings is high, and people are happy to show their homes to visitors. The landscape is also beautiful in this region: flat, rich farmland set against a dramatic, forested mountain backdrop.

Joinville's tourist office distributes a useful free **brochure** and **map** covering the Estrada Bonita area, as well as details of the *colonos* who are members of the Turismo Rural project and therefore happy to open their farms to visitors. The homesteads are widely scattered, however, and a car is pretty essential. In the Dona Francisca area, the most interesting houses are dispersed over a large area and often hidden in forest, and you're best off accompanied by someone who knows the area well; ask at the tourist office for the name of a taxi driver who's familiar with the area, and negotiate a price (about R$70 for a couple of hours). For overnight stays there are a couple of simple but comfortable *pousadas* along the Estrada Bonita: the *Grün Wald* at the intersection with the BR-101 highway (ⓣ47/3464-1271, ⓦwww.grunwald.com.br; ❸) and the *Vale Verde* at Km 2.5 (ⓣ47/3464-1377, ⓦwww.pvaleverde.com.br; ❹).

## Blumenau

Despite Joinville's challenge, **BLUMENAU** has succeeded in promoting itself as the "capital" of German Santa Catarina. Picturesquely located on the banks of the Rio Itajaí, Blumenau was founded in 1850 by Dr Hermann Blumenau, who served as director of the colony until his return to Germany in 1880. Blumenau always had a large Italian minority, but it was mainly settled by Germans and, as late as the 1920s, two-thirds of the population spoke German as their first language. In the surrounding rural communities an even larger proportion of the population were German speakers, many of them finding it completely unnecessary to learn Portuguese. Well into the twentieth century Blumenau was isolated, with only poor river transport connections with the rest of Brazil beyond the Itajaí valley – circumstances that meant its German character was retained for longer than in Joinville.

Today, Blumenau's municipal authority never misses an opportunity to remind the world of the city's German origins, the European links helping tourism and attracting outside investors. And, superficially at least, Blumenau certainly looks, if not feels, German. The streets are sparkling clean, parking tickets are issued by wardens dressed in a uniform that Heidi would have been comfortable in, most buildings are in German architectural styles and geranium-filled window boxes are the norm. But since German is almost never heard, and the buildings (such as the half-timbered Saxon-inspired department store and the Swiss chalet-like Prefeitura) are absurd caricatures of those found in German cities, the result is a sort of "Disneyland" interpretation of Germany.

It's easy to sneer, but tourists from São Paulo are impressed by Blumenau's old-world atmosphere and visit in large numbers, especially during the annual **Oktoberfest** (Ⓣ47/3326-6901, Ⓦwww.oktoberfestblumenau.com.br). Held, since 1984, over eighteen days in October, besides vast quantities of beer and German food, the main event attractions are the local and visiting German bands and German folk-dance troupes. Performances take place at PROEB, Blumenau's exhibition centre, located on the city's outskirts (frequent buses run during the festival period), as well as in the downtown streets and the central Biergarten. So successful has the Oktoberfest been in drawing visitors to Blumenau – a million people attended the festivities during its peak year in 1992 – that the city's authorities realized that the event's local flavour had been swamped by outsiders, and consequently they have halved attendance.

The rest of the year, local German bands perform every evening from 5pm in the **Biergarten**, the city's main meeting point, in the tree-filled Praça Hercílio Luz. In the oldest part of Blumenau, across a small bridge on the continuation of the main street, Rua XV de Novembro, the Biergarten is only a short walk from the **Museu da Família Colonial**, one of the city's few museums, at Alameda Duque de Caxias 78 (Tues–Fri 9am–5pm, Sat & Sun 10am–4pm; R$2). The museum's buildings, constructed in 1858 and 1864 for the families of Dr Blumenau's nephew and secretary-librarian, are two of the oldest surviving *enxaimel* houses in Blumenau. Exhibits include nineteenth-century furniture and household equipment, documents relating to the foundation of the city, photographs of life in the settlement during its early years, and artefacts of the Kaingang and Xokleng – the indigenous populations displaced by the German settlers. But it's in the beautiful forest-like garden that you'll find the most curious feature: a cemetery, the final resting place for the much-loved cats of a former occupant of one of the houses.

A good half-hour walk from Praça Hercílio Luz, on the river at Rua Itajaí 2195, is the **Museu de Ecologia Fritz Müller** (Mon–Fri 8am–6pm, Sat & Sun 8–11.30am & 2–5pm; R$2), built in 1867 and the former home of the eponymous German-born naturalist. Born in 1822, Müller lived in Santa Catarina between 1852 and 1897, and was a close collaborator of British naturalist Charles Darwin; the small museum is dedicated to the work of the lesser-known scientist.

## Practicalities

The **rodoviária** (☎47/3323-0690) is 7km from the city centre in the suburb of Itoupava Norte (the "Cidade Jardim" bus runs into the centre). There are hourly services to Florianópolis, Joinville and Itajaí, and frequent services to western Santa Catarina, Curitiba and São Paulo. Buses to Pomerode leave roughly hourly from Rua Paulo Zimmermann, located near the Prefeitura and Praça Victor Konder; if in doubt, ask for the bus stop of the Volkmann company.

**Tourist information offices** are found at Rua XV de Novembro 420, at the corner of Rua Nereu Ramos (daily 9am–9pm; ☎47/3326-6931), at the *rodoviária* (daily 9am–6pm), and in the Prefeitura (Mon–Fri 9am–5pm) at Praça Victor Konder.

Centrally located **hotels** are plentiful, so accommodation shouldn't pose a problem, except during the Oktoberfest. At the lower end of the price range, look no further than the wonderful *Hotel Hermann* (☎47/3322-4370, Ⓦwww.hotelhermann.com.br; ❶–❷), an early twentieth-century *enxaimel* building in the heart of the city at Rua Floriano Peixoto 213, by the intersection with Rua Sete de Setembro. More expensive, but also German in style, is the *Hotel Steinhausen Colonial*, Rua Buenos Aires 275 (☎47/3322-5276, Ⓦwww.hotelsteinhausen.com.br; ❸), with comfortable guest rooms, landscaped gardens and a pool. There's also an excellent HI-affiliated **youth hostel**, the centrally located *Pousada Grün Garten*, Rua São Paulo 2457 (☎47/3323-4332, Ⓦwww.grungarten.com.br; R$25 per person or ❷). In a well-preserved German-style house built in 1929, the hostel offers a range of dorms, and single, double and family rooms.

In general, food in Blumenau is poor and largely takes the form of **snacks** to accompany beer. There are several **German restaurants**, by far the most pleasant-looking being the *Frohsinn* (closed Sun). The food here is not particularly special (it's fairly expensive and the service is slow), but the location – on a beautiful, cool, pine-clad hill with excellent views over the city – makes the journey worthwhile. It's a bit of an effort to get there: from Praça Hercílio Luz, walk for about fifteen minutes along Rua Itajaí and turn right on Rua Gertrud Sierich – the restaurant is at the top of this very steep road.

## Pomerode

Thirty kilometres to the north of Blumenau, **POMERODE** is probably the most German "city" in Brazil. Not only are ninety percent of its 25,000 widely dispersed inhabitants descended from German immigrants, but eighty percent of the *município*'s population continue to speak the language. Unlike in Blumenau, in Pomerode German continues to thrive and is spoken just about everywhere, although in schools it takes second place to Portuguese. There are several reasons for this: almost all the immigrants – who arrived in the 1860s – came from Pomerania, and therefore did not face the problem of mixing with other immigrants speaking often mutually unintelligible dialects; as ninety percent of the population are Lutheran, German was retained for the act of worship; and, until recently, Pomerode was isolated by poor roads and communication links. This isolation has all but ended, though. The road to Blumenau is now excellent, buses are frequent, car ownership is common and televisions are universal. However, despite the changes, German looks more entrenched than ever. The language has been reintroduced into the local school curriculum, cultural groups thrive and, where the government has exerted pressure, it has been to encourage the language's survival.

Pomerode is renowned for its **festivals**, the chief of which is the **Festa Pomerana**, a celebration of local industry and culture held annually for ten days, usually from around January 7. Most of the events take place on the outskirts of town, on Rua XV de Novembro, about 1km from the tourist office, and during the day thousands of people from neighbouring cities descend on Pomerode to sample the local food, attend the song and dance performances and visit the commercial fair. By late afternoon, though, the day-trippers leave and the Festa Pomerana comes alive as the *colonos* from the surrounding areas transform the festivities into a truly popular event. Local and visiting bands play German and Brazilian music, and dancing continues long into the night. In July, Pomerode organizes the smaller, though similar, **Winterfest**.

There are more regular festivities too, as every Saturday the local hunting clubs take turns to host **dances**. Visitors are always made to feel welcome, and details of the week's venue are displayed on posters around town, or ask at the tourist office. As many of the clubs are located in the *município*'s outlying reaches, a bus is laid on, leaving from outside the post office on Rua XV de Novembro.

The main activity for visitors, other than attending the town's famous festivals and dances, is **walking**. Pomerode has Santa Catarina's greatest concentration of proudly preserved nineteenth- and early twentieth-century **enxaimel farm buildings**, the largest number found in the *município*'s Wunderwald district. To reach them, cross the bridge near the Lutheran church, turn left and continue walking along the road for about twenty minutes, then turn right just before a bridge across a small stream. If you're feeling energetic, return to the main road and cross the bridge, walk on another hundred metres or so and turn left along the Testo Alto road; about 3km up the steep valley, you'll arrive at the **Cascata Cristalina**, where you'll be able to cool off under the tiny waterfall or use the swimming pool (Oct to mid-Dec & mid-Jan to March, Sat, Sun & holidays 8am–7pm; mid-Dec to mid-Jan daily 8am–7pm; R$6).

### Practicalities

**Buses** to and from Blumenau stop outside the *Hotel Schroeder* and the Lutheran church on Rua XV de Novembro, the main street, which sprawls alongside the banks of the Rio do Testo. At no. 818 the very helpful **tourist office** (Mon–Fri 7.30am–6pm, Sat & Sun 10am–4pm; ⓣ47/3387-2627) provides a good map and details of forthcoming events, and has a small selection of local wooden and ceramic handicrafts for sale.

**Accommodation** is always easy to find, even during the Festa Pomerana. The largest hotel in town is the rather soulless *Hotel Bergblick* (ⓣ47/3387-0952, ⓦwww.bergblick.com.br; ❸–❹), on the outskirts at Rua George Zepelin 120. Just as comfortable, much more central and cheaper is the long-established *Hotel Schroeder*, Rua XV de Novembro 514 (ⓣ47/3387-0933; ❷). Much prettier, but a half-hour walk from the centre of town, is the *Pousada Mundo Antigo*, Rua Ribeirão Herdt, Km 5 (ⓣ47/3387-3143, ⓦwww.mundoantigo.com.br; ❹), housed in several early twentieth-century *enxaimel* farm buildings in a beautiful rural setting. If these are full or too expensive, the tourist office will find you a **room** with a local family.

You can **eat** well in Pomerode. There's no attempt to reproduce old-world cooking, but instead simple local dishes are prepared. Pork is, of course, ever present, but it's *marreco* (wild duck) that's considered the local speciality. The *Wunderwald* (closed Sun evening & Mon) is, without doubt, Pomerode's best restaurant, serving typical regional food at bargain prices in a perfectly preserved early twentieth-century *enxaimel* farmhouse. To get to the restaurant from the centre, cross over the bridge near the church and turn left; the *Wunderwald* is at Rua Ricardo Bahr 200, a small road to the left immediately after the hospital. Nearby, on the same street, the restaurant of the *Pousada Mundo Antigo* serves a very similar range of local dishes. For a reasonable **café colonial** try the *Torten Paradies* at Rua XV de Novembro 211.

There are almost hourly **buses** to and from Blumenau, but as the last goes to Blumenau at 6pm and returns at 10.10pm, going into the city for an evening out is only just about possible. There are also four buses each day direct to Curitiba.

# The south coast to Laguna and Criciúma

Unlike the northern stretch of coast, heading south from Florianópolis doesn't offer as many temptations to leap off the bus and into the sea. Most of this part of the BR-101 highway is too far inland to catch even a glimpse of the sea but, in any case, south of Laguna the beaches are less attractive and more exposed. Many of the coastal settlements were founded by Azorean immigrants in the late seventeenth and early eighteenth centuries, and they've retained the fishing and lace-making traditions of their ancestors. Inland, settlement is much more recent and the inhabitants are a blend of Germans, Italians and Poles, whose ancestors were drawn in the late nineteenth century by promises of fertile land and offers of work in the region's coal mines. However, apart from a handful of farms and villages where Portuguese-influenced Italian dialects are spoken, only surnames and scattered wooden and stone houses of the early settlers remain of the immigrant heritage.

## Garopaba

The first accessible spot worth stopping at is **GAROPABA**, a fishing village inhabited by people of Azorean origin, which, despite attracting more and more people every summer, has not yet been totally overwhelmed by tourism. In the 1970s, Garopaba was "discovered" by hippies from Porto Alegre, attracted to the area by the peaceful atmosphere and beautiful beaches. During the 1980s, surfers from throughout Brazil and beyond descended on the village, which fast developed a reputation for having some of the best surfing in the country.

The **beaches** are excellent, but are located a short distance from the village. The main village beach is fine, and large enough to take the summer crowds, but try to make it to the outlying beaches. Ten kilometres to the north is **Praia Siriú**, backed by huge dunes, while 6km further on, **Praia da Gambora** is a good beach for swimming, with a beautiful mountain backdrop. The best beaches for surfing are to the south, the most challenging being **Praia do Silveira** (3km from Garopaba) and **Praia do Rosa** (18km). Most visitors arrive in the summer, but between mid-June and mid-November, Garopaba is the most popular place on the Brazilian coast for **whale-watching**. With luck you should be able to spot humpback whales swimming just thirty metres from the beach, but for near-certain viewing of both adult whales and their calves it's best to take a boat excursion: the *Pousada Vida, Sol e Mar* (R$100; see below) is the most experienced operator, with boats especially designed for whale-watching.

Of the dozen or so **hotels**, amongst the cheapest is the very pretty *Pousada Casa Grande e Senzala* at Rua Dr Elmo Kiseki 444 (Ⓣ48/3254-3177; ❸), but being small, it's often full in summer. However, by asking around you can nearly always find a room in a private house. There are also plenty of places to stay around Praia do Rosa, 18km to the south, the most picturesque and least developed beach hereabouts, with several attractive *pousadas* (all ❺ and with pools) hidden amidst the hills behind the beach: try *Quinta do Bucanero* (Ⓣ48/3355-6056, Ⓦwww.bucanero.com.br), *Morada dos Bougainvilles*

(Ⓣ48/3355-6100, Ⓦwww.pousadabougainville.com.br) or the largest, the *Vida, Sol e Mar* (Ⓣ48/3355-6111, Ⓦwww.vidasolemar.com.br), with extremely comfortable guest rooms, a wonderful lounge, a pool and staff who are extremely knowledgeable about the local area. Facilities in Garopaba are mainly geared to campers and the very few **restaurants** are mainly simple places serving fried fish. Despite Garopaba's size, **bus** services are good, with buses to Florianópolis leaving from Rua Marquês Guimarães, and those destined for points south as far as Porto Alegre leaving from Praça Silveira. There are also frequent local services plying the route between Garopaba and Praia da Rosa.

## Laguna and around

**LAGUNA**, 125km from Florianópolis and the closest Santa Catarina gets to having a near-complete colonial town, is an excellent place to break your journey. Sitting at the end of a narrow peninsula, at the entrance to the Lagoa Santo Antônio, Laguna feels like two distinct towns. Facing west onto the sheltered lagoon is the old port and Laguna's historic centre, protected as a national monument. Two kilometres away, on the far side of a granite outcrop of mountainous proportions that separates the city's two parts, is the new town, facing east onto the Atlantic Ocean.

As a beach resort, Laguna's attraction is limited. The city's importance lies in its **old town**, which, even during the height of the summer tourist season, attracts few people – which is just as well, as it's quite small and could easily be overwhelmed. The one time of year that Laguna gets unbearably crowded is during Carnaval, when it hosts one of the best small-town celebrations south of Rio.

Laguna was significant as early as 1494, being the southern point of the line dividing the Americas between Spain and Portugal (the northern point was at Belém), 370 leagues west of the Cape Verde Islands. A **monument** near the *rodoviária*, a few minutes' walk from the centre, marks the exact spot. A permanent settlement wasn't established until 1676, but it rapidly became the pre-eminent port of the southern fringes of the Portuguese Empire, and a base for the exploration and colonization of what is now Rio Grande do Sul.

Not all of Laguna's old town dates from the eighteenth century, but its general aspect is that of a Portuguese colonial town. The oldest streets are those extending off **Praça Vidal Ramos**, the square that holds the **Igreja Santo Antônio dos Anjos**. Built in 1694, the church retains its late eighteenth-century Baroque altars and, though rather modest, is considered the most important surviving colonial church in Santa Catarina.

On the same square as the church is the **Casa de Anita** (daily 8am–6pm), a small museum in a modest house built in 1711 and dedicated to Anita Garibaldi, the Brazilian wife of Giuseppe Garibaldi, maverick military leader of the Italian unification movement. Garibaldi was employed as a mercenary in the Guerra dos Farrapos, between republicans and monarchists, and it was in Laguna that a short-lived republic was declared in 1839. There are some fine photographs of nineteenth-century Laguna on display, but – oddly perhaps – there's little on Anita's life and republican activities; scissors and hairbrushes that once belonged to her are typical of the exhibits. In Praça República Juliana in the former town hall and jail, built in 1747, is the **Museu Anita Garibaldi** (daily 8am–6pm), housing a rather dreary collection of local Indian artefacts and items relating to the Guerra dos Farrapos. Close by, on Praça Lauro Muller, the **Fonte da Carioca** is the oldest surviving fountain in Laguna, dating back to 1863, covered in blue and white Portuguese tiles.

### Practicalities

The **rodoviária** (Ⓣ48/3644-0208) is at Rua Arcângelo Bianchini, a couple of minutes' walk from the waterfront and the old town. Located at the official entrance to town, 3km from central Laguna on Avenida Calistralo Muller Salles is the **tourist office** (Mon–Sat 8am–6pm, Sun 8am–1pm; Ⓣ48/3644-2441), which provides excellent maps of Laguna and the surrounding area.

Most of Laguna's hotels and restaurants are in the **new town**, alongside and parallel to the **Praia do Mar Grosso**, the city's main beach. **Hotels** here tend to be large and fairly expensive, but moderately priced exceptions are the *Mar Grosso*, Av. Senador Galotti 644 (Ⓣ48/3644-0298; ❷), the *Hammerse*, Av. João Pinho 492 (Ⓣ48/3647-0598, Ⓦwww.hammers.com.br; ❸), and the *Monte Líbano*, Av. João Pinho 198 (Ⓣ48/3647-0671; ❷). There's also a youth hostel at Rua Aurélio Rótolo 497; reservations are essential from Christmas to February and in July (Ⓣ48/3647-0675, Ⓔlagunahostel@terra.com.br; ❷). The clutch of seafood **restaurants** in the middle of Avenida Senador Galotti is good, though there's little to distinguish one from another.

Apart from during Carnaval, **rooms in the old town** are easy to find. The *Hotel Farol Palace* (Ⓣ48/3644-0596; ❸), on the waterfront opposite the market, is a good choice. There are also a couple of extremely cheap *dormitórios* behind the hotel. **Restaurants** in this part of town are uninspiring, the best being two pizzerias on Praça Juliana.

### Around Laguna: the Farol Santa Marta

About 19km out of town to the south is the **Farol Santa Marta**, a lighthouse that was transported piece by piece from Scotland in 1891. The third-tallest lighthouse in the Americas, it's surrounded by bleak but beautiful scenery offering wild seas (suicidal for even the strongest of swimmers) and protected beaches. Between June and September this stretch of shore is a popular spot from which to watch the migrating **humpback whales**, which are clearly visible from shore with binoculars. There are no buses here, but if you have your own transport (most of the road is unpaved, so drive especially carefully after heavy rain) or are prepared to hitch a lift you'll discover a comfortable **hotel**, *Farol de Santa Marta* (Ⓣ48/3646-3009; ❸), complete with a heated pool, as well as the *Jurikão* (Ⓣ48/3646-7070; ❷), a basic hotel, and a couple of **restaurants**.

## Criciúma

The **coastline** between Laguna and the Rio Grande do Sul border is effectively one long beach – though it's of no great beauty and can be passed without much regret. The coastal plain, which stretches inland some 30km, provides little in the way of natural attractions, and the region's two largest towns, Tubarão and **CRICIÚMA** were founded as coal-mining centres; the area remains one of Brazil's very few producers of the mineral. Criciúma is marginally the more pleasant and less polluted of the two towns.

Killing time in Criciúma is fairly easy. The **Museu da Colonização**, Rua Cecília Daros Casagrande (Mon–Fri 9am–6pm; take the "Bairro Comerciario" bus), with its exhibits relating to Italian and German immigrants, is worth a look, but if you've only got a couple of hours to spare, a visit to the **coal mine** (daily 8–11.30am & 1–6pm; R$5), Criciúma's prime tourist attraction, is really the best idea. It's 3km from the city centre: take the "Mina Modelo" bus from the local bus terminal, which is next to the *rodoviária*. Coal seams were discovered around Criciúma in 1913, and this mine entered production in 1930, ceasing production in the late 1950s. Visitors are taken through the coal mine by retired workers from other local mines, who grind out, in exhausting detail, information about the local geological structure and mining techniques. The deepest the mine goes is just 42 metres, but the squeamish should note that it is home to huge numbers of – quite harmless – fruit bats.

The **rodoviária** is centrally located on Avenida Centenário, the main artery bisecting the town, and as there are frequent buses to all points in Santa Catarina it's unlikely you'll have to stay the night. However, if you arrive late, there are two very good **hotels**, virtually alongside the *rodoviária* – the very comfortable *Crisul* (Ⓣ48/3437-4000, Ⓦwww.crisulhotel.com.br; ③) and the somewhat basic *Turis Center* (Ⓣ48/3633-8722; ③). You'll find the **tourist office** at Praça Nereu Ramos, a five-minute walk from the back of the *rodoviária*.

# Central and western Santa Catarina

Until the road-building programme of the 1970s, mountainous **central and western Santa Catarina** was pretty much isolated from the rest of the state. Largely settled by migrants from neighbouring states, this territory has inhabitants of diverse origins including Germans and Italians in the extreme west, Austrians, Italians and Ukrainians in the central Rio do Peixe valley, and *gaúchos* – and even Japanese – in the highlands of the Serra Geral. In the more isolated areas, dominated by a single ethnic group, traditions and languages have been preserved but, as elsewhere in southern Brazil, they are under threat.

Any route taken to reach the **Serra Geral** is spectacular, but if you enter the region directly from the coast the contrasts of landscape, vegetation and climate unfold most dramatically. From the subtropical lowlands, roads have been cut into the steep escarpment and, as they slowly wind their way up into the *serra*, dense foliage emerges – protected from human destruction by its ability to cling to the most precipitous of slopes. Waterfalls can be seen in every direction until suddenly you reach the *planalto*. The graceful Paraná pine trees are fewer in number on the plateau but are much larger, their branches fanning upwards in a determined attempt to re-form the canopy that existed before the arrival of cattle and lumber interests.

For tourists, towns in the *serra* are generally places to travel towards rather than destinations in their own right. Even if it means going a considerable distance out of the way, most **bus** services from the coast to the highland town of **Lages** travel via the BR-470 – Santa Catarina's main east–west highway – before turning onto the BR-116, which cuts north–south through the state. To and from Florianópolis, for example, it's usually much faster and more comfortable for buses to travel via Blumenau; however the twice-daily services from Florianópolis direct to Lages via Alfredo Wagner are far more picturesque. From the southern coast of Santa Catarina, the *serra* can be approached by bus from Criciúma via Urussanga and Orleans on the even more spectacular road leading up to São Joaquim and on to Lages.

## Urussanga and Orleans

The route into the Serra Geral from Criciúma at first passes through a gently undulating landscape, inhabited largely by the descendants of northern Italian immigrants who settled in the region in the 1880s, before climbing the steep escarpment into the highlands. If possible choose a clear day to make the trip as the views east towards the coast are absolutely spectacular.

Some 20km from Criciúma the road passes through **URUSSANGA**, a small agricultural processing town. Urussanga and the surrounding countryside are noted for the stone farm buildings dating from the arrival of the first Italian settlers and, with federal government support, the authorities have been making tremendous efforts to restore them. A handful are located in the town itself, but to see those in outlying areas you'll need to get detailed directions from the Prefeitura. If you need somewhere **to stay**, make for the *Pousada da Vinícola Mazon* (Ⓣ48/3465-1500; ❸), some 6km from town towards the village of São Pedro. The *pousada* is set in pretty countryside, the hillsides covered in grapevine, and you can eat here too – the meals are superb examples of local Italian country cooking.

A further 20km along the road is the small town of **ORLEANS**, lying on a fairly busy crossroads, from where it's easy to pick up buses to São Joaquim, Criciúma or Laguna. If you decide to stop over, you can choose from a couple of modest **hotels**: the *São Francisco* (Ⓣ48/3666-0282; ❸), at Rua Aristiliano Ramos 120, and the *Brasil* (❷), at Rua Getúlio Vargas 9. An unremarkable little town in most ways, Orleans does boast the excellent **Museu ao Ar Livre** (Mon–Fri 9am–noon & 1.30–5.30pm, Sat & Sun 9am–5.30pm; R$5), which records early immigrant life and industry and features a water-powered sawmill and other buildings moved here from the surrounding area.

## São Joaquim

Formerly just a small highland ranching centre, **SÃO JOAQUIM**, ninety steep kilometres beyond Orleans, has only really been on the Brazilian map since the mid-1970s when apple orchards were introduced here. Within twenty years, Brazil changed from importing nearly all the apples consumed in the country to becoming a major exporter of the fruit. At an altitude of 1360m (making this the highest town in Brazil), apple trees are in their element in São Joaquim, benefiting from the very pronounced seasonal temperature variations. Temperatures in the winter regularly dip to -15°C and, as this is one of the few parts of Brazil that sees regular snowfalls, there is a surprising amount of tourism in the winter, with camping being especially popular amongst Brazilians as a way of truly experiencing the cold. Anyone with a specific interest in apples can visit the **Estação Experimental de São Joaquim**, a research centre and orchard on the outskirts of town, while for wine, a visit to the Vinícola Villa Francioni (Ⓣ49/3233-1918, Ⓦwww.villafrancioni.com.br; R$20) is a must: the production is small but arguably Brazil's finest.

The **rodoviária** (Ⓣ49/3233-0400), a couple of minutes' walk from the city centre, has good connections to Lages, Criciúma and Florianópolis. For accommodation, there's a reasonable **hotel**, the *Nevada*, on Rua Manoel Joaquim Pinto (Ⓣ49/3233-0259; ❷), as well as the newer, and more comfortable, *São Joaquim Park* at Praça João Ribeiro 58 (Ⓣ49/3233-1444, Ⓦwww.saojoaquimparkhotel.com.br; ❸). Despite the presence of some fifty Japanese apple-growing families, the only **restaurants** are a pizzeria, the *Taberna Café* on Rua João Batista Viecelli 188 (closed Mon), and the *Casa de Pedra* on Rua Manoel Joaquim Pinto 360, which offers a buffet of varied hot and cold dishes and a *rodizio de carnes*.

## Lages

Although founded in 1766, nothing remains in **LAGES** from the days when it was an important resting place for cowhands herding cattle and mules on the route northwards to the market in Sorocaba. Located 76km northwest of São Joaquim, it's now a collection of anonymous post-1950s buildings, and only the presence in town of visiting ranchers and cowhands, dressed in the characteristic baggy pantaloons, sash and poncho, reminds you of its position at the northern edge of *gaúcho* country. Because so many knife-carrying men come into town at the weekend for supplies and a good time, Lages is reputed to be the most violent town in the state. However, the general atmosphere is dull rather than menacing, and tourists are unlikely to get caught up in any trouble.

The reason to visit Lages is to get a taste of life in the *gaúcho* high country. The tourist office promotes a **turismo rural** project, which provides opportunities for people to visit typical cattle *fazendas* and catch a glimpse of life in outlying parts of the *serra* – otherwise extremely difficult for tourists to see. For day-trips, only groups are catered for, so ask at the tourist office whether you can join one that has already been formed. Alternatively, several *fazendas* accept guests, who are encouraged to participate in the everyday activities of the cattle ranches. Otherwise, the best way to get a feel for the region is to attend one of the periodic **rodeios**; again, the tourist office can provide information.

### Practicalities

The **rodoviária** (ⓣ49/3222-6710) is a half-hour walk southeast of the centre, or you can take a bus marked "Dom Pedro". The **tourist office** (Mon–Fri 8am–noon & 2–6pm; ⓣ49/3223-6206) is in the centre of town at Rua Hercílio Luz 573, and distributes a good map of Lages.

Reasonable, modestly priced **hotels** are easy to come by. The *Hotel Presidente*, Av. Presidente Vargas 106 (ⓣ49/3224-0014; ❷), is quite good and only a few minutes' walk from the cathedral and main square, Praça Waldo da Costa Avila. If you want a bit more luxury, try the *Grande Hotel Lages*, Rua João de Castro 23 (ⓣ49/3222-3522; ❸). However, to really experience *serra* life you should arrange to stay on a **cattle fazenda**, all located some distance from town. A full list and advice is available from the tourist office and if you don't have your own transport you can arrange with the *fazenda* to be picked up in town. Especially recommended are the rustic *Seriema* (ⓣ49/9986-0051; ❹ full board); *Nossa Senhora de Lourdes* (ⓣ49/3222-0798 or 9983-0809; ❺ full board), a mid-nineteenth-century *fazenda* house with period furnishings and a pool (children not accepted); and the more hotel-like *Barreiro* (ⓣ49/3222-3031, ⓦwww.fazendadobarreiro.com.br; ❻ full board), which traces its origins to the late eighteenth century, though its buildings are all of recent construction. Reservations are essential for all three. While the landscape of the *serra* is extremely rugged and the life of the highland *gaúcho* is often harsh, the *fazendas* provide comfortable accommodation, and excellent food and facilities.

## Rio do Peixe valley

Immigrants were introduced to the **Peixe valley** in around 1910 by the American-owned Brazil Railway Company. For completing the São Paulo–Rio Grande rail line, the company received land from which they could extract valuable timber and which they could divide for sale to homesteaders. Due to the region's isolation, war in Europe, anti-immigration legislation and the discovery that the soil was not as fertile as had been believed, fewer people than hoped moved into the area. Of those who did come, most were from neighbouring states, mainly Slavs from Paraná, and Germans and Italians from Rio Grande do Sul.

### Joaçaba

The region's most important town is **JOAÇABA**, 462km west of Florianópolis on the Peixe's west bank, directly across the river from the smaller town of Herval d'Oeste. Perhaps due to the narrowness of the valley, whose slopes rise precipitously along one entire side of town, Joaçaba has an oppressive, almost menacing, atmosphere. Although the population is dominated by descendants of Italian immigrants, no obvious Italian influences remain, and, as Joaçaba developed into an important centre of light industry and agribusiness, it lost any frontier charm that might have once existed. However, if you're visiting the Rio do Peixe area, Joaçaba is difficult to avoid altogether. Buses from here serve all surrounding districts and towns to the west, and there are regular departures to Blumenau, Florianópolis, São Paulo and Foz do Iguaçu.

With the **rodoviária** located just a few minutes' walk from the town centre, arriving in Joaçaba couldn't be easier. On leaving the *rodoviária*, turn right onto Avenida XV de Novembro, the road that runs alongside the river through town; turn right again on Rua Sete de Setembro and you'll find an inexpensive **hotel**, the *Comércio* (Ⓣ49/3522-2211; ❷). A few doors away is the comparatively luxurious *Hotel Jaraguá* (Ⓣ49/3522-4255, Ⓦwww.hoteljaraguareal.com.br; ❸), which has a pool and a reasonable restaurant. Also on Avenida XV de Novembro are a couple of *churrascarias* and pizzerias.

### Treze Tílias

Of the region's ethnic groups, it is one of the smallest – the Austrians – who have been most stubborn in resisting cultural assimilation. The claim of the *município* of **TREZE TÍLIAS** to be the "Brazilian Tyrol" is by no means without foundation. In 1933, 82 Tyroleans led by Andreas Thaler, a former Austrian minister of agriculture, arrived in what is now Treze Tílias. As the dense forest around the settlement was gradually cleared, more settlers joined the colony, but after Germany's annexation of Austria in 1938, immigration came to an end – as did funds to help support the pioneers during the difficult first years. With the onset of war, communications with Austria ceased altogether and, with no country to return to, abandoning the colony was not an option. During the immediate postwar years, contacts with Europe were minimal, but as Austria grew more prosperous Treze Tílias began to receive assistance. The area eventually came to specialize in dairy farming and today its milk products are sold in supermarkets throughout Santa Catarina.

Treze Tílias is only an hour north of Joaçaba and west of Videira and it's practical to use it as a base for getting to know the wider region. All buses stop right in the centre of the village outside the *Hotel Áustria* (Ⓣ49/3537-0132; ❷), the oldest, most basic and one of the friendliest of Treze Tílias's numerous **hotels**. Also in the centre, the *Hotel Tirol* (Ⓣ49/3537-0125, Ⓦwww.hoteltirol.com.br; ❸), a typical Tyrolean-style chalet, complete with geraniums hanging from every balcony, has very comfortable rooms and a pool. You'll get similar floral comforts and style at the nearby *Hotel Dreizehnlinden* (Ⓣ49/3537-0297, Ⓦwww.hotel13linden.com.br; ❸) and at the more intimate *Hotel Schneider* (Ⓣ49/3537-0184, Ⓦwww.hotelschneider.com.br; ❷). All of these hotels have good restaurants serving standard Austrian dishes at lunch, and *café colonial* in the late afternoon and evening. If you want to **eat** somewhere with more local character, make for the *Berenkamp*, right behind the Prefeitura. The food here is good, cheap and abundant, and the atmosphere is about as close as you're likely to come outside Austria to an ordinary Tyrolean pub. The best time is early evening, when elderly locals drop by to eat and chat – German speakers will be intrigued by the local Tyrolean-Brazilian dialect that has developed in Treze Tílias over the past seventy years. Other reliable options in town for Austrian food are the *Kandlerhof*, Rua Videira 80 (closed Sun), and the *Edelweiss*, Rua Dr Gaspar Coutinho 439 (evenings only, closed Mon).

But for the absence of snow-capped mountain peaks, the general appearance of Treze Tílias is not dissimilar to that of a small alpine village. **Walking** in any direction, you'll pass through peaceful pastoral landscapes; the gentle seven-kilometre walk to the chapel in the hamlet of **Babenberg** is particularly rewarding. If you decide to visit the local **waterfalls** a few kilometres outside town, get very detailed directions before setting out.

In Treze Tílias itself, try to visit some of the **woodcarvers**, several of whom have shops in the centre of the village where items, large and small, are for sale. The best woodcarvers learned their craft in Europe, and their work is in demand from churches throughout Brazil. On the main street, the **Museu do Imigrante** (Mon–Sat 9.30am–noon & 2–6pm, Sun 10am–noon & 2–5pm) features a small collection of photographs and paintings of the area in the 1930s and 1940s, as well as items brought with the immigrants from Austria. The **Tirolerfest** during the first two weeks of October is a lively display of Austrian folk traditions including singing and dancing.

## Videira

On the eastern fringes of Treze Tílias, along the Linha Pinhal road leading to the neighbouring town of **VIDEIRA**, the population is mainly of Italian origin, descended from migrants who came from Rio Grande do Sul in the 1940s, their brightly painted wooden houses instantly distinguishable from the Austrians' chalets. Vines dominate the landscape, and if you visit a *colônia* you'll probably be invited to taste their home-produced salami, *cachaça* or the wine – it's only polite to buy a bottle before leaving. In Videira itself the small, but well-organized **Museu do Vinho** (Mon–Fri 9–11.30am & 1.30–5.30pm, Sat 9am–noon) next to the main church, is worth half an hour or so. The displays relate to the local wine-making techniques in the early years of settlement.

Videira itself doesn't justify more than the briefest of pauses between buses, which are, unfortunately, far less frequent than those from Joaçaba. If you need a **hotel**, and there's no time to go to Treze Tílias, walk down the hill on Avenida Dom Pedro II from the *rodoviária* and turn right at the Shell station onto Rua Brasil (the main commercial street): the inexpensive *Savanna Hotel* (❷) and **restaurant** is the first building on the left. Alternatively, by crossing the river over the bridge at the bottom of Rua Brasil, next to the local bus terminal, you'll come to Videira's luxury *Hotel Verde Vale Palace* (Ⓣ49/3566-1622, Ⓦwww.hotelverdevale.com.br; ❸), whose reasonably priced restaurant serves the town's best food – a mix of standard Brazilian and Italian dishes.

## Caçador

The next town on the Rio do Peixe, 35km north of Videira, **CAÇADOR** is very different in character from the largely agricultural settlements to the south, with a workaday atmosphere and a landscape dominated by pine plantations. The one reason to stop is to visit the small **Museu do Contestado** (Tues–Sun 8.30–noon & 1.30–6pm), housed in the old train station. The museum commemorates the brutal war that took place in the Rio do Peixe valley from 1912 to 1916 between the Brazilian government, which was protecting the interests of the American-owned railway company that had been awarded huge land grants in the region, and the displaced native and *caboclo* population. The war eventually led to the deaths of twenty thousand people, and well-presented exhibits in the museum commemorate the lives of the local Indians and *caboclos* who fought in the conflict. Outside the station is a perfectly preserved 1907 Baldwin locomotive and passenger carriage.

There are several **hotels** within minutes of the museum, the best being the modern *Le Canard* (Ⓣ49/3563-1000, Ⓦwww.lecanard.com.br; ❷–❸). Otherwise there are good bus services to Florianópolis, União da Vitória and Curitiba from the **rodoviária** (Ⓣ49/3563-0225) across from the museum. If you're travelling north towards Paraná by car you can take one of two possible routes; the paved SC-451 road connecting to the BR-153 is the fastest, but it is much more interesting to take the road to Calmon, a village on the banks of the Rio do Peixe, and continue on north to União da Vitória. The road is absolutely appalling but the landscape is starkly dramatic, dominated by huge plantations of imported pine trees and the occasional patch of original Paraná pine.

## The extreme west

Until the 1950s, most of the population of the extreme west of Santa Catarina were Kaingang Indians and semi-nomadic *caboclos* who harvested the *erva maté* grown in the region. As land became increasingly unavailable in Rio Grande do Sul, peasant farmers moved north into Santa Catarina and the area has since become the state's foremost producer of pigs and chickens.



### Chapecó and around

Unless you have an interest in agriculture, **CHAPECÓ** – or indeed any other town in the region – is unlikely to hold your attention for longer than the time it takes to change buses. Fortunately, Chapecó is well served with **buses** to points throughout Santa Catarina and Rio Grande do Sul, to Dionísio Cerqueira (for Argentina), Curitiba and Cascavel (for connections to Foz do Iguaçu) in Paraná. If you have to stick around for a while, take one of the frequent buses from the *rodoviária*, on the city's outskirts, to the local bus terminal, which is located virtually on the main square. There are a couple of **places to stay** near the bus terminal – including the comfortable *Hotel Eston* (Ⓣ49/3323-1044, Ⓦwww.estonhotel.com.br; ❸) – and two more on the main street, Avenida Getúlio Vargas.

Chapecó's self-proclaimed status as regional capital simply means that its slaughterhouses are larger than those in the surrounding towns. If you happen to be in town during the month of August, you'll coincide with the **Festa Nacional do Frango e do Peru**, an absurdly contrived affair celebrating chicken and turkey production – almost as ridiculous as the town's **Wurstfest**, an annual jamboree in November in celebration of the sausage. One possible excursion, however, is to the **Museu Entomológico Fritz Plaumann** (Mon–Thurs & Sat 8am–noon & 1–5pm; Ⓣ49/3452-1191, Ⓦwww.museufritzplaumann.ufsc.br) in **Nova Teutônia**, an overwhelmingly German community some 45km east of Chapecó near the town of **Seara** (any bus between the two towns will drop you off there). Housed in a large 1940s wooden house typical of the region, the museum boasts what is quite possibly the most important collection of insects in Latin America. Plaumann (1902–94) arrived in Nova Teutônia from Germany in 1924 and went on to dedicate his life to entomological studies, collecting 80,000 specimens, representing 17,000 species, including 1500 that had previously been unknown. Pride of place goes to the displays of butterflies at every stage of development, but what's truly impressive is that the entire collection is supported by detailed notebooks, correspondence and other documentation representing seventy years of Plaumann's professional and personal life.

### Dionísio Cerqueira

Situated in the extreme northwest corner of Santa Catarina, **DIONÍSIO CERQUEIRA** virtually merges with the smaller town of **Barracão** in Paraná and, just across the Argentine border, **Bernardo de Irigoyen**. Dionísio

Cerqueira is an unremarkable town and you're unlikely to want to stay longer than is needed to catch a bus out. Fortunately each of the border towns is well served by **bus** companies. Dionísio Cerqueira's *rodoviária*, a few blocks back from the border, has frequent departures to all main towns in Santa Catarina, Rio Grande do Sul and Posadas in Argentina. The nearby Barracão Rodoviária serves Paraná, including Curitiba and Foz do Iguaçu. From Bernardo de Irigoyen's bus station, there are services throughout the Argentine province of Misiones, including Posadas (for the nearby Jesuit ruins, or for connections further south or west into Argentina) and Puerto Iguazú.

If you do need to stop over, you will find a **hotel** easily. The best place to stay (and eat) is the very reliable *Motel ACA* (Ⓣ751/92218; ❷) near the bus station in Bernardo de Irigoyen. In Dionísio Cerqueira there's the very basic *Hotel Iguaçu* (Ⓣ49/3844-1029; ❷), at Rua Mário Cláudio Turra 260, and only one real **restaurant**, the *Medieval* at Av. Santa Catarina 190, which serves standard Brazilian food. For those who prefer to stay in Barracão, the *Província* (Ⓣ49/3844-1261, Ⓦwww.provincia.com.br; ❷) at Rua São Paulo 411 is a perfectly comfortable hotel with a restaurant.

The **border crossing** is very relaxed and is open between 7am and 7pm. Argentine passport control is located right on the border, whereas the Brazilian Polícia Federal is two blocks back from the border on Dionísio Cerqueira's main road, at Rua República Argentina 259.



# Rio Grande do Sul

For many people the state of **Rio Grande do Sul**, bordering Argentina and Uruguay, is their first or last experience of Brazil. More than most parts of the country, it has an extremely strong regional identity – to the extent that it's the only state where the possibility of independence has been discussed. Central government's authority over Brazil's southernmost state has often been weak: in the colonial era, the territory was virtually a no-man's-land separating the Spanish and Portuguese empires. Out of this emerged a strongly independent people, mostly pioneer farmers and the descendants of European immigrants, isolated fishing communities and, best known, the *gaúchos* (see p.707), the cowboys of southern South America whose name is now used for all inhabitants of the state, whatever their origins.

The **road and bus network** is excellent and it's easy to zip through the state without stopping if need be. However, Rio Grande do Sul is as Brazilian as Bahia or Rio and it would be a shame to ignore the place. The capital, **Porto Alegre**, is southern Brazil's most important cultural and commercial centre but, like all the other cities in Rio Grande do Sul, has little to detain tourists. However, it's also the state's transportation axis and at some point you're likely to pass through the city. For a truer flavour of Rio Grande do Sul, visit the principal region of Italian and German settlement, around the towns of **Caxias do Sul**, **Bento Gonçalves** and **Nova Petrópolis**, a couple of hours north of Porto Alegre. And for the classic image, head for the cattle country of the *serra* and *campanha* where old *gaúcho* traditions still linger.

# Porto Alegre

The capital of Rio Grande do Sul, **PORTO ALEGRE**, lies on the eastern bank of the Rio Guaiba, at the point where five rivers converge to form the **Lagoa dos Patos**, a giant freshwater lagoon navigable by even the largest of ships. Founded in 1755 as a Portuguese garrison to guard against Spanish

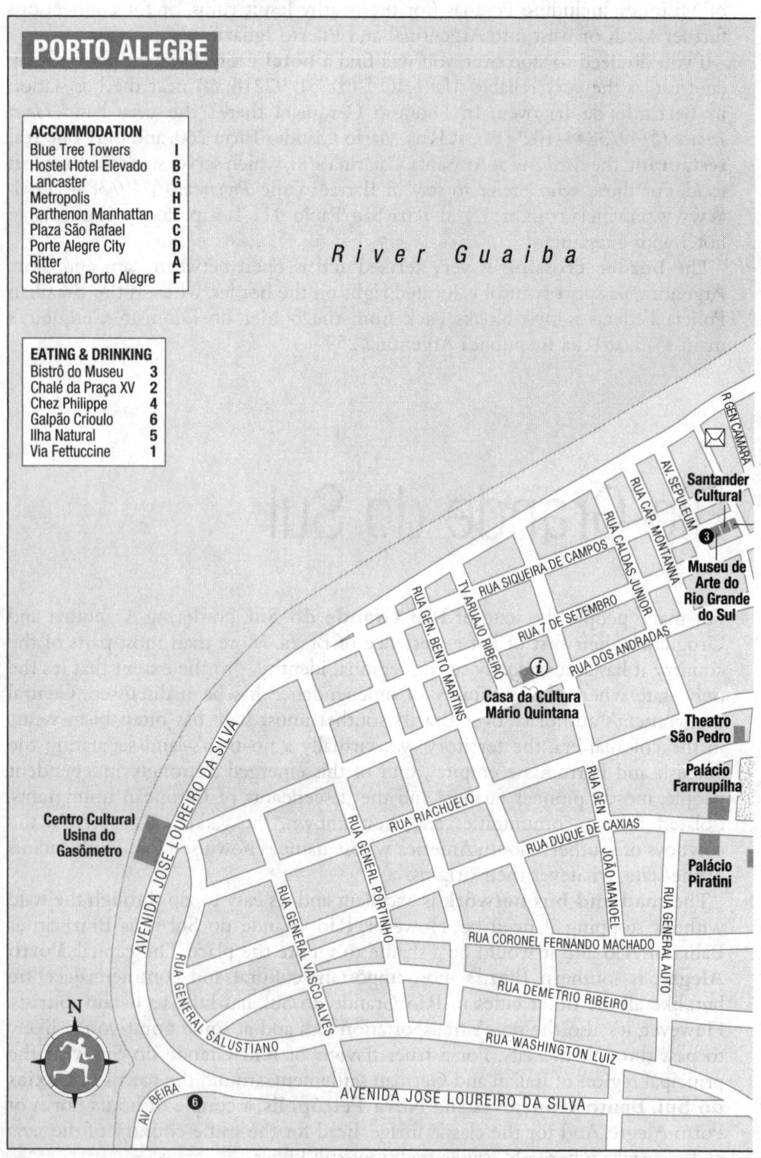

encroachment into this part of the empire, it wasn't until Porto Alegre became the port for the export of beef that it developed into Brazil's leading commercial centre south of São Paulo.

With a rather uninteresting feel to it, like a cross between a southern European and a North American city, most people will be tempted to move straight on from Porto Alegre, unless they're waiting to make a transport connection.

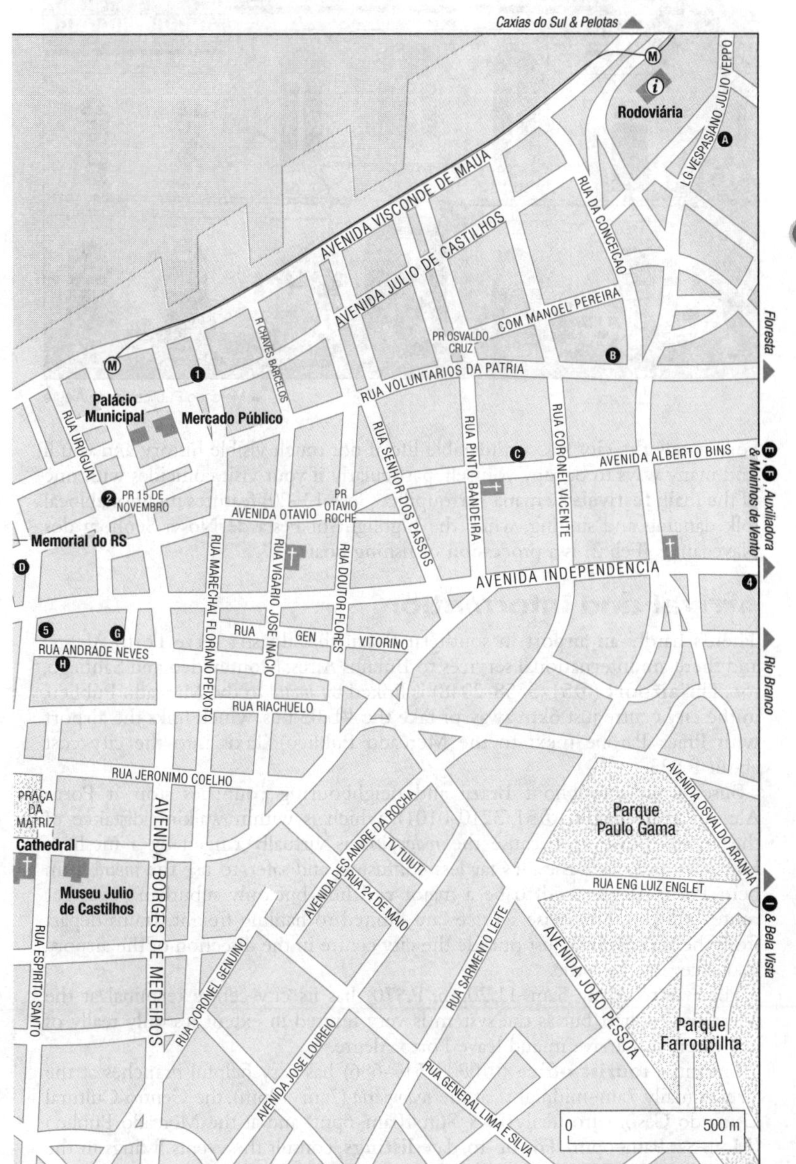

▲ Mercado Público, Porto Alegre

Fortunately the city has considerable life, if not much visible history, and you'll find many ways to occupy yourself, particularly if your visit coincides with one of the main **festivals**: Semana Farroupilha (Sept 13–20) features traditional local folk dancing and singing, while the highlight of Festa de Nossa Senhora dos Navegantes (Feb 2) is a procession of fishing boats.

## Arrival and information

There's hardly an airport in southern Brazil that doesn't serve Porto Alegre, and there are international services to Buenos Aires, Montevideo and Santiago, too. The **airport** (Ⓣ51/3358-2048) is linked by *metrô* to the Mercado Público, in the city centre just 6km away, or take the #L.05 bus, which links the airport with Praça Parobe (next to the Mercado Público). Taxis into the city cost about R$25.

Buses from throughout Brazil and neighbouring countries stop at Porto Alegre's **rodoviária** (Ⓣ51/3210-0101), which is within walking distance of the centre; however, because the *rodoviária* is virtually ringed by a mesh of highways and overpasses, it's far less confusing, and safer, to use the *metrô* from here. Porto Alegre used to be a major **rail** hub but only suburban passenger routes still run, otherwise services are limited to hauling freight. Trains depart from the **ferroviária**, just outside the city centre in the direction of the airport, also accessible by *metrô*.

The **metrô** (daily 5am–11.20pm; R$70) has its city-centre terminal at the Mercado Público, but as the system is very limited in extent it's only really of use when you arrive in and leave Porto Alegre.

The city's **tourist office** (Ⓣ0800/517-686) has very helpful branches at the airport (daily 7am–midnight), at the *rodoviária* (7am–10pm), the Centro Cultural Usina do Gasômetro (daily Tues–Sun 10am–6pm) and at the Mercado Público (Mon–Sat 9am–6pm). For up-to-date **listings**, consult the events listings in the newspaper *Zero Hora*.

## Accommodation

There's a good range of **hotels** scattered around the city centre, and as distances are small it's possible to walk to most places, although great care should be taken at night when the area tends to be eerily quiet. There are a couple of upscale options in the residential and business suburb of Moinhos de Vento, a good spot to stay in that allows for evening walks and offers a choice of bars and restaurants. Hotels are geared towards business travellers and as a consequence most offer substantial discounts at weekends. Porto Alegre can get quite cold in the winter and very hot and humid in the summer, but fortunately most hotels have central heating and air conditioning.

**Blue Tree Towers** Av. Coronel Lucas de Oliveira 995 ⓣ51/3019-8000, ⓦwww.bluetree.com.br. Excellent value for a luxury hotel in the pleasant residential district of Bela Vista. The guest rooms are tastefully furnished and the hotel has its own sushi bar. ❺

**Hostel Hotel Elevado** Av. Farropos 63 ⓣ51/3224-5250, ⓦwww.hotelelevado.com.br. This HI-affiliated hostel near the *rodoviária* offers secure accommodation and a friendly atmosphere. Single, double and triple rooms are offered with or without private bathrooms. ❶–❷

**Lancaster** Travessa Acelino de Carvalho 67 ⓣ51/3224-4737, ⓦwww.hotel-lancaster-poa.com.br. Located in one of the liveliest commercial areas downtown, this modern hotel is set behind an imposing 1940s facade. Rooms are small but well equipped, and excellent value for money. ❸

**Metropolis** Rua Andrade Neves 59 ⓣ51/3226-1800. Basic but neatly kept rooms, popular with business travellers from outlying parts of the state. The best of several places to stay on this busy road in the heart of the commercial district. ❷

**Parthenon Manhattan** Rua Miguel Tostes 30, Moinhos de Vento ⓣ51/3024-3030, ⓦwww.accor.com.br. An upmarket apartment-hotel with a pool, and well-appointed, self-catering studios and one-bedroom suites sleeping up to four people. ❺–❻

**Plaza São Rafael** Av. Alberto Bins 514 ⓣ51/3220-7000, ⓦwww.plazahoteis.com.br. Although there are now several other top-end hotels in Porto Alegre, this has a certain traditional style that's found in none of the newer establishments. Located in the city centre, rates are always competitive and are usually heavily discounted at weekends. Rooms are all spacious and very comfortable – be sure to ask for one overlooking the lagoon. ❺

**Porto Alegre City** Rua Dr José Montaury 20 ⓣ51/3212-5488, ⓦwww.cityhotel.com.br. This one-time elegant hotel is now rather frayed at the edges, but it still offers considerable comfort, as well as large rooms and helpful service. ❹

**Ritter** Largo Vespasiano Júlio Veppo 55 ⓣ51/3228-1610, ⓦwww.ritterhoteis.com.br. Across the road from the *rodoviária*, this hotel is devoid of character but is clean, efficient and serves an inexpensive buffet supper. You can use the swimming pool, sauna and other facilities of the adjoining upmarket *Porto Alegre Ritter Hotel*. ❹

**Sheraton Porto Alegre** Rua Olavo Barreto Viana 18 ⓣ51/2121-6000, ⓦwww.sheraton-poa.com.br. Located in the suburb of Moinhos de Vento, above the shopping mall of the same name, this ultra-modern hotel has lured much of the expense-account business away from the *Plaza São Rafael*. The rooms are as well appointed as you'd expect, with good fitness and business centres. ❽

## The City

Porto Alegre sprawls out over a series of hills with the centre spread between two levels, the older residential area on the higher level and the commercial area below. In the 1960s and 1970s the city centre underwent dramatic redevelopment with new urban highways, ever larger office buildings and landfill schemes to improve the docks. Despite the destruction accompanying the construction boom, many of Porto Alegre's nineteenth- and early twentieth-century buildings escaped demolition, and the city has succeeded in retaining some of its former dignity. In the city centre itself, everything is within an easy walk, and a half-day or so is enough to visit most places of interest.

The ochre-coloured **Mercado Público** (Mon–Fri 7.30am–7.30pm, Sat 7.30am–6.30pm) is at the heart of the lower town, located alongside Praça Rui

Barbosa and Praça XV de Novembro. Dating back to 1869 and said to be a replica of Lisbon's Mercado da Figueira, this imposing building, with its intricate, typically Portuguese, stuccoed detail, contains an absorbing mix of stalls selling household goods, food, a vast variety of herbs, *erva maté* of all grades of quality, items used in *Umbanda* rituals and regional handicrafts. Much of the maze of streets around the market is pedestrianized; on Praça XV de Novembro, the century-old Bavarian-style *Chalé da Praça XV* – a charming little bar and restaurant that was formerly the meeting place of the city's artists and intellectuals – is an especially good spot from which to watch the world go by. To the left of the market is the **Palácio Municipal**, the old *prefeitura*, built in Neoclassical style between 1898 and 1901, its impressive proportions an indication of civic pride and self-confidence during the period when Porto Alegre was developing from being a mere southern outpost into an important city. Between about 1880 and 1930, Porto Alegre attracted large numbers of southern and eastern European immigrants and in front of the palace is the **Talavera de la Reina**, a fountain given to the city in 1935 from its once considerable Spanish community.

The streets along the steep slope rising from the low-lying parts of the centre (Rua dos Andradas, Rua General Vitorino and Rua Andrade Neves, which becomes Av. Senador Salgado Filho) mark Porto Alegre's main **commercial district** of clothing stores, travel agents and banks. Further up the hill are Praça da Matriz (officially called Praça Marechal Deodoro) and Largo João Amorim do Albuquerque, where the former legislative assembly and some of Porto Alegre's oldest buildings are concentrated. Though the buildings in this part of the city have late eighteenth- to mid-nineteenth-century origins, they have undergone so many renovations and additions over the past couple of centuries that only a few bear any resemblance to their colonial predecessors. The foundations of the **Catedral Metropolitana** are built over those of a church that dates back to 1772; however the present Italianate structure was only begun in 1921, and wasn't completed until 1986. Work on the former legislative assembly also started in 1772 but, likewise, it has undergone innumerable renovations over the years. The **Palácio Piratini** (the state governor's residence; Mon–Fri 9–11am & 2–5pm; Ⓦwww.palaciopiratini.rs.gov.br) dates from only 1909, while across from it the **Teatro São Pedro** (Tues–Fri noon–7pm, Sat & Sun 3–9pm; Ⓣ54/3227-5100, Ⓦwww.teatrosaopaulo.rs.gov.br) was inaugurated in 1858. Surprisingly, the Neoclassical building and Portuguese Baroque-style interior has remained largely unchanged, and the theatre is an important venue for local and visiting companies. Also around the Praça da Matriz are several impressive nineteenth-century mansions, including the former **Consulado Italiano** (Italian consulate) at no. 134, whose prominent position reflects the important role Italians played in Porto Alegre and elsewhere in Rio Grande do Sul. Nearby is the **Museu Júlio de Castilhos**, Rua Duque de Caxias 1231 (Tues–Fri 10am–7pm, Sat & Sun 2–5pm; R$4), which presents a patchy and poor history of the state.

Porto Alegre's other **museums and cultural centres** are generally a poor bunch, which is somewhat surprising for a city that has long been prosperous and is the most important cultural centre south of São Paulo. One that does stand out is the **Casa de Cultura Mário Quintana**, Rua dos Andradas 736 (Tues–Fri 9am–9pm, Sat & Sun noon–9pm; Ⓦwww.ccmq.rs.gov.br), one of the city's largest cultural centres. Designed in Neoclassical style by the German architect Theo Wiederspahn in 1923, the extremely elegant rose-coloured building was a hotel until 1980 and as such was once a popular meeting point for local artists, intellectuals and politicians, including presidents Vargas and Goulart. The poet Mário Quintana was a long-time resident (hence the name), and his room is assiduously maintained as it was while he lived there. In addition to numerous exhibition galleries, the Casa de Cultura houses a library, a bookshop, a cinema, a decent restaurant and a café. Nearby, on Praça da Alfândega, are three other exhibition centres housed in imposing French-style Neoclassical buildings that are always at least worth a peek. Although the **Museu de Arte do Rio Grande do Sul** (Tues–Sun 10am–7pm; Ⓦwww.margs.org.br) has been devastated by thefts, it still has a small collection of work by *gaúcho* artists, among which the nineteenth-century landscapes deserve particular attention; it also hosts occasional special exhibitions. Alongside, the **Santander Cultural** (Mon noon–8pm, Tues–Fri 10am–7pm, Sat & Sun 11am–7pm; Ⓦwww.santandercultural.com.br) puts on temporary exhibitions of Brazilian art, often important collections first displayed in São Paulo. The building itself, a converted 1920s bank, features some remarkable stained-glass windows depicting positivist themes. Next door, the city's very grand, Neoclassical-style, former main post office building is now the **Memorial do Rio Grande do Sul** (Tues–Sat 10am–6pm; Ⓦwww.memorial.rs.gov.br). Housed here are the state archives, along with an oral history centre and various other collections preserving the history of Rio Grande do Sul.

## Eating

As you'd expect, meat dominates menus here and *churrascarias* abound. However, the city centre has only a limited selection of **restaurants** of any sort, with the best located in the suburbs – which are usually at least a R$15 taxi fare away.

Although during the daytime you can walk around most places in the city in safety, take care after dark, as Porto Alegre is developing a reputation for street crime to rival the worst of Brazilian cities. Nevertheless, it's a lively place with plenty going on until late into the evening.

**Al Dente** Rua Mata Bacelar 210, Auxiliadora Ⓣ51/3343-1841. The best of several very good Italian restaurants in the suburb of Auxiliadora, 3km northeast of the centre. Fairly expensive, northern Italian food served in attractive surroundings. Reservations advised at weekends. Evenings only, closed Sun.

**Bistô do Museu** Praça da Alfândega, Centro. In the Museu de Arte do Rio Grande do Sul and with tables on the *praça* itself, this is one of the few restaurants in the area. Food is simple – pastas, steak, salads and the like – but good. Closed Mon.

**Café do Porto** Rua Padre Chagas 293, Moinhos do Vento. Excellent light meals, sandwiches, cakes and wine are served in this very laid-back café on a fashionable side street filled with similar places.

**Chez Philippe** Av. Independência 1005, Independência Ⓣ51/3312-5333. Housed in a beautiful, early twentieth-century residence, this is arguably Porto Alegre's best restaurant and certainly its best French restaurant. The French chef is imaginative, and not afraid of combining local ingredients with traditional recipes. Although expensive, the five-course menu at R$120 per person is good value. Evenings only, closed Sun. Reservations advised.

**Chopp Stübel** Rua Quintino Bocaiúva 940, Moinhos de Vento. Hearty German food and an unusually good choice of beer are the attractions of this popular local restaurant. Pork features most prominently on the menu, but the roast duck is cooked to perfection. Prices are moderate. Evenings only, closed Sun.

**Galpão Crioulo** Parque da Harmonia, Centro. A huge and always reliable *churrascaria* in the city centre near the Centro Cultural Usina do Gasômetro, with a bewildering selection of meats in its *rodizio* and a good range of salad and vegetable offerings. In the evenings there's *gaúcho* music and traditional dance performances.

**I Puritani** Rua Hilário Ribeiro 208, Moinhos de Vento. A plush bistro serving a mix of French-, Italian- and Brazilian-influenced dishes, such as artichoke risotto, wild boar in an apricot sauce and passionfruit mousse served with a *jabuticaba* sauce.

**Ilha Natural** Rua Andrade Neves 42, 1st floor, Centro. One of Porto Alegre's rare vegetarian restaurants; the food is fairly unimaginative, but cheap. Mon–Fri lunch only.

**Koh Pee Pee** Rua Schiller 83, Rio Branco Ⓣ51/3333-5150. A brave, pricey and very successful attempt to introduce Thai food to Porto Alegre, offering authentic dishes served in appealing surroundings. Mon–Sat evenings only.

**Na Brasa** Av. Ramiro Barcelos 389, Floresta Ⓣ51/3225-2205. In the opinion of many locals, this is Porto Alegre's best *churrascaria* – quite something in a city where people appreciate meat. Located between downtown and Moinhos de

Vento, this unpretentious-looking restaurant boasts *rodizio* offerings of the highest quality and a high-quality and tremendously varied salad bar. Around R$50 per person.

**O Galo** Av. Aureliano Figueiredo Pinto 904, Cidade Baixa ⓣ51/3228-7148. Very reasonably priced, this is the best traditional Portuguese restaurant in the city centre. Specializing in seafood, the shellfish and *bacalhau* (salted cod) dishes are particularly good. Closed Mon.

**Sanduiche Voador** Praça Mauricio Cardoso 23, Moinhos de Vento. Delicious sandwiches, salads and desserts in the heart of one of Porto Alegre's most fashionable suburbs. Equally good for a light meal, afternoon tea or a cold beer on the terrace. Closed Sun evening and all Mon.

**Via Fettuccine** Largo Visconde de Cairú 17, 7th floor, Centro. An excellent-value buffet of hot and cold Brazilian and international dishes draws business diners to this anonymous downtown office block. But what's really special is the stunning view out towards the lagoon and beyond. Mon–Fri lunch only.

## Drinking, nightlife and entertainment

**Bars**, some with live music and most with a predominantly young and arty clientele, are spread out along, and just off, Avenida Osvaldo Aranha, alongside the Parque Farroupilha and near the Federal University. Favourites change constantly, but the *Ocidente*, on Avenida Osvaldo Aranha itself, is usually lively and good for dancing as well. Also try the upscale suburb of Moinhos de Vento, especially along Rua Padre Chagas and Rua Fernando Gomes, near the Moinhos de Vento shopping mall. On Rua Fernando Gomes, there's excellent beer at *Dado Pub* and good music at the *Jazz Café*, though things don't get going until around 11pm.

Porto Alegre boasts a good popular **music scene** and a considerable **theatrical** tradition. Foreign performers of all kinds usually include Porto Alegre on any Brazilian or wider South American tour. The *Sala Jazz Tom Jobim* at Rua Santo Antônio 421 (ⓣ51/3225-1229) features the city's best **jazz**, and there are live afternoon sessions at the *Café Concerto* within the Casa de Cultura (see p.684). These days *the* place to go **dancing** is the huge *Dado Bier* complex in the eastern suburb of Chácara das Pedras (take a taxi). Inauspiciously located in the Bourbon Country shopping mall, the club features top bands from all over Rio Grande do Sul.

There's a good **art-house cinema** in the Casa de Cultura, and three more screens at Espaço Unibanco, Rua dos Andradas 736 (ⓣ51/3221-7147), also showing art-house films. The Centro Cultural Usina do Gasômetro, a converted 1920s power station on the banks of the river just west of the centre is well worth a visit; there's always something going on in its cinema, theatre and galleries, and it also has a café and a good bookshop. Finally, throughout the year, Porto Alegre's numerous Centros de Tradição Gaúcha organize traditional meals, and also music and dance performances that are hugely popular with locals; for full details, contact the Movimento Tradicionalisto Gaúcho, Rua Guilherme Schell 60 (ⓣ51/3223-5194, ⓦwww.mtg.org.br).

## Listings

**Airlines** Aerolíneas Argentinas ⓣ51/3221-3300; Gol ⓣ51/3358-2028; TAP ⓣ51/3226-1211; Varig ⓣ51/3358-2595.

**Banks and exchange** Banks and *casas de câmbio* are concentrated along Rua dos Andradas and Avenida Senador Salgado Filho near Praça da Alfândega, and ATMs throughout the city.

**Boats** One-hour excursions on the Rio Guaiba leave from the Centro Cultural Usina do Gasômetro (see p.682) Tues–Sun 10.30am, 3pm, 4.30pm & 6pm (R$15).

**Consulates** Argentina, Rua Coronel Bordini 1033 ⓣ51/3321-1360; Uruguay, Av. Cristóvão Colombo 2999 ⓣ51/3325-6200; UK, Rua Antenor Lemos 57, conj. 303, Menino Deus ⓣ51/3232-1414.

**Hospital** Pronto-Socorro Municipal Hospital is on Av. Osvaldo Aranha at the intersection with Venâncio Aires (ⓣ51/3231-5900).

**Shopping** Handicrafts from throughout the state are available at Artesanato Rio Grande do Sul, Av. Senador Salgado Filho 366, and the Feira do Artesanato on Praça da Alfândega (between *ruas* da Praia and Sete de Setembro) is worth a look, too. Casa do Peão, Av. Alberto Bins 393, has a fine stock of *bombachas*, lassoes and other *gaúcho* paraphernalia. The Sunday Redenção Bric-a-Brac in the Parque Farroupilha is well worth a visit for regional handicrafts; there's a lively atmosphere, with street performers and thronging bars and restaurants.

# The Serra Gaúcha

North of Porto Alegre is the **Serra Gaúcha**, a range of hills and mountains populated mainly by the descendants of German and Italian immigrants. The Germans, who settled in Rio Grande do Sul between 1824 and 1859, spread out on fairly low-lying land, establishing small farming communities, of which **Nova Petrópolis** is just one that still retains strong elements of its ethnic origins. The Italians, who arrived between 1875 and 1915, settled on more hilly land further north and, being mainly from the hills and mountains of Veneto and Trento, they adapted well and very quickly specialized in **wine production**. **Caxias do Sul** has developed into the region's most important administrative and industrial centre, but it is in and around smaller towns, such as **Bento Gonçalves** and **Garibaldi**, that the region's – and, in fact, Brazil's – wine production is centred.

To the **east**, and at much higher altitudes, are the resort towns of **Gramado** and **Canela**, where unspoilt landscapes, mountain trails, refreshing temperatures, luxurious hotels and the *café colonial* – a vast selection of cakes, jams, cheeses, meats, wine and other drinks produced by the region's *colonos* – attract visitors from cities throughout Brazil. Beyond here lies some even more rugged terrain, this highland area largely given over to cattle ranching. What little population there is you'll find concentrated in the small towns of **São Francisco de Paula** and **Cambará do Sul**. Although both centres remain first and foremost ranching communities, they've become important jumping-off points for visiting the majestic canyons of **Parque Nacional dos Aparados da Serra**, one of southern Brazil's most impressive geological sites.

## Nova Petrópolis and around

The main road north from Porto Alegre passes **São Leopoldo** and **Nova Hamburgo** (Rio Grande do Sul's first two German settlements but now mere industrial satellites of the city) before entering more hilly terrain inhabited by peasant farmers. In most of the family farms, German-based dialects are still spoken, but in the majority of towns and villages Portuguese is the dominant language. However, in architecture and culture, the ethnic origins of the townsfolk are quite obvious, and considerable pride is taken in the German heritage.

Thoroughly unremarkable in most respects, **NOVA PETRÓPOLIS**, 100km north of Porto Alegre, makes the greatest effort in promoting its German character although here too, the language – specifically the Hunsrück dialect of the Rhineland – survives in outlying farming communities despite (or even because of) persistent attempts to teach High German in local schools. The municipal authorities encourage new building to be in "traditional" German architectural styles (which is why there's a plethora of alpine chalet-like structures around), and **festivals** take on a distinct German flavour. Principal amongst these are the Festa de Verão (weekends during Jan & Feb), the Festa do Folklore (weekends in July) and the Oktoberfest (Oct weekends), all held in the **Parque do Imigrante**.

But while clearly German-inspired, the events have little in common with the popular culture of the region's *colonos*. Indeed, of rather more interest is the Parque do Imigrante itself, where a village much like many in the region during the late nineteenth century has been created (daily 8am–6pm; R$2). The black-and-white half-timbered buildings, dating from between 1870 and 1910, were brought to the park from outlying parts of the *município* and include a Protestant chapel and cemetery, a general store with a dance hall, a credit agency (*Bauernkasse*), a school house and a smithy.

Disappointingly, given its picturesque setting, Nova Petrópolis is not a place for walks as there are no trails leading out from town. Instead, take a bus to the nearby hamlet of **LINHA IMPERIAL** and walk from there into the surrounding countryside. The scenery is hilly and pastoral and it's a good area in which to view rural life close up. There are a couple of very simple hotels here, the *Schoeler* (Ⓣ54/3298-1052; ❷) and the *Vila Verde* (Ⓣ54/3298-1161; ❸), which are remarkably comfortable for such a backwater. Just beyond here is the largely German-speaking community of **Nove Colônias** where you'll spot official notice boards indicating local farms (with English spoken at the *Recanto dos Pioneiros*) and the properties that welcome tourists Monday to Saturday; if stopping by one of these places remember that it's only polite to purchase some preserves, biscuits or other items on sale.

### Practicalities

The **rodoviária** is centrally located just off Avenida XV de Novembro, with good connections to Porto Alegre, Gramado and Caxias do Sul, as well as local buses to Linha Imperial and other outlying parts of the *município*. You'll find the helpful **tourist office** (daily 8am–6pm; Ⓣ54/3281-1398) at the entrance to the Parque do Imigrante.

As you might expect of somewhere with so much German influence, the **hotels** here are always impeccably clean. The most pleasant by far is the *Recanto Suiço*, Av. XV de Novembro 2195 (Ⓣ54/3281-1229, Ⓦwww.recantosuico.com.br; ❸), on the principal road running through town. The main building of the hotel feels like a diminutive Swiss inn, and in the extensive tree-filled gardens there's a small pool and chalets. The friendly owner speaks excellent English and, of course, German. There are several other hotels on the main road or just off it, all providing similar facilities at around the same price. Typical of the rather characterless alternatives is the *Hotel Petrópolis*, near the *rodoviária* at Rua Coronel Alfredo Steglich 81 (Ⓣ54/3281-1091, Ⓦwww.hotelpetropolis.com.br; ❹), in a modern chalet-style building with an attractive garden, pool and beautiful mountain views.

**Eating** options in town are remarkably limited. At lunchtime, *Colina Verde*, 3km from Nova Petrópolis heading towards Porto Alegre (closed Mon), serves a mix of simple German and Italian dishes typical of the local region in a beautiful hilltop location. *Opa's Kaffeehaus* at Rua João Leão 96 (R$25 per person; Tues–Fri 2–8pm) offers a good *café colonial* in a spot with spectacular views. On the main street, *Café e Cia* serves tasty (and inexpensive) soups and delicious cakes.

## Gramado

Thirty-six kilometres due east of Nova Petrópolis, along a beautiful winding road, is **GRAMADO**, Brazil's best-known mountain resort. At 825m you're unlikely to suffer from altitude sickness, but Gramado is high enough to be refreshingly cool in summer and positively chilly in winter. Architecturally, Gramado and the neighbouring resort of Canela try hard to appear Swiss, with alpine chalets and flower-filled window boxes. It's a mere affectation, though, since hardly any of the inhabitants are of Swiss origin – and only a small minority are of German extraction. The most pleasant time to visit the area is during the spring (Oct & Nov) when the parks, gardens and roadsides are covered in flowers, though the hydrangeas remain in bloom well into January. For a week in mid-August, the resort is overrun by the prestigious **Festival de Cinema** (Ⓣ54/3286-1475, Ⓦwww.festivaldegramado.net), which since 1973 has developed into one of the most important events of its kind in Brazil. In winter the festival **Natal Luz** (mid-Nov to early Jan) stirs things up with concerts, an ersatz German Christmas market, and Carnaval-style parades in December that end in an (artificial) snowstorm, but unless the kitschness of it all appeals to you, the entire event is something to avoid.

At other times there isn't much to do in town, but a stroll around the large and flower-filled **Parque Knorr** (daily 9am–6pm) and the secluded **Lago Negro**, surrounded by attractive woodland, can fill the hours between meals. The surrounding region is magnificent, but difficult to explore properly without a car, though tours taking in the back roads are available (see p.690). Just 6km from town is the beautiful **Vale do Quilombo**, where much of the original forest cover has survived intact. It's a difficult trek, though, and you'll need a local map (available from the tourist office), to identify the incredibly steep, unpaved approach road, Linha 28. For **guided tours** along the forest trails, contact the **Refúgio Família Sperry** (Ⓣ54/3504-1649, Ⓦwww.refugiosperry.com.br), an organic farm where an amazing diversity of primary forest remains. The English-speaking owner is extremely knowledgeable about the local flora and fauna and takes individuals or small groups through the forest and past dramatic waterfalls. A neighbouring family-owned vineyard, the Quinta dos Conte, offers tours of its small-scale wine and liquor production facilities, as well as the family's home, which was built by the original German owners. Arrangements to visit both properties should be made in advance and together by calling the Refúgio Família Sperry.

### Practicalities

Gramado can easily be reached by **bus** from Porto Alegre and Caxias do Sul, and in the summer from Torres. The **rodoviária** (Ⓣ54/3286-1302) is on the main street, Avenida Borges de Medeiros, a couple of minutes' walk from the town centre. The **tourist office** (Mon–Thurs 9am–6pm, Fri–Sun 9am–8pm; Ⓣ54/3286-1475) at no. 1674 is well organized and provides maps and lists of local hotels and restaurants.

Most hotels offer steep discounts outside the peak summer and winter months, especially during the week. There's an excellent **youth hostel** (Ⓣ54/3295-1020, Ⓦwww.gramadohostel.com.br) 1.5km from the centre at Avenida das Hortências 3880, towards Canela, with small dorms (R$45 per person). The lowest-priced **hotels** are the *Planalto* across from the *rodoviária*, at Av. Borges de Medeiros 554 (Ⓣ54/3286-1210; ❷), and, also in the centre, the *Dinda*, Rua Augusto Zatti 160, at the corner with Av. Borges de Medeiros (Ⓣ54/3286-2810; ❷). There are plenty of more expensive places to stay: the *Casa da Montanha* at Av. Borges de Medeiros 3166 (Ⓣ54/3286-2544, Ⓦwww.casadamontanha.com.br; ❼) has rustic-style but extremely comfortable rooms and an indoor heated pool, while smaller, but rather more luxurious, is the *Estalagem St Hubertus*, at Rua da Carriere 974, overlooking Lago Negro (Ⓣ54/3286-1273, Ⓦwww.sthubertus.com; ❼), set in attractive grounds with a heated pool. Similar in style, but much less expensive, is the long-established *Hotel das Hortênsias* at Rua Bela Vista 83 (Ⓣ54/3286-1057, Ⓦwww.hoteldashortensias.com.br; ❹).

Gramado has some reasonably good **restaurants**. Both *Belle du Valais* at Av. das Hortênsias 1432 and *Chez Pierre* at Av. Borges de Medeiros 3022 (closed Sun), in the centre, serve tasty *fondue bourguigonne* (meat fondue); though very popular, their house specialities, the cheese fondues, are disappointingly bland. For fairly authentic and reasonably priced northern Italian dishes, there's *Tarantino Ristorante*, also in the centre at Av. das Hortênsias 1522, by Praça Major Nicoleti. More intriguing are the game dishes at *La Caceria* (evenings only, closed Mon–Wed) in the *Hotel Casa da Montanha* (see p.689), which combine wild boar, venison, partridge, duck and capybara with unusual tropical fruit sauces. Rather formal and expensive, the restaurant includes some excellent and very unusual Brazilian wines on its extensive list.

For **getting around the back roads**, most of which are unpaved and treacherous following heavy rain, Casa da Montanha Adventures (ⓣ54/3286-2544) is especially recommended. The English-speaking drivers know the region well and will take you in Land Rovers to places near Gramado and further afield, such as the Parque Nacional dos Aparados da Serra (see p.691). Prices vary according to distance and whether you can join an existing group: speak to one of the drivers at their desk at the *Hotel Casa da Montanha* (see p.689).



## Canela

The resort town of **CANELA**, 8km further east down a road bordered on both sides by hydrangeas, is slightly lower, smaller and not as brashly commercialized as Gramado. Canela offers little of particular beauty within its small urban area, but it is better situated for the **Parque Estadual do Caracol** (daily 8.30am–5.30pm; R$8), 8km to the north. You can reach the park by bus – marked "Caracol Circular" (4 daily) – which leaves from Canela's *rodoviára*; get off at the information centre in the park. From here, a path leads 927 steps down to the foot of a **131-metre waterfall** from where visitors can best appreciate its power; from there you will find other small falls and the surrounding forest. A further 5km along the Caracol road is the **Parque da Ferradra** (daily 8.30am–5.30pm; R$8), a forest reserve offering panoramic views into the deep Arroio Caçador canyon and waterfall and onto a horseshoe-shaped section of the Rio Caí.

Canela's **rodoviária** (ⓣ54/3282-1375) is just behind the central main street, with regular buses from Porto Alegre and Caxias do Sul and services at least every hour to Gramado. The **tourist office**, at Largo da Fama 227 (Mon–Sat 8am–6pm, Sun 8am–1pm; ⓣ54/3282-2200), is staffed by enthusiastic students from the local tourism colleges, for which Canela has become renowned in Brazil.

There's a good **youth hostel** across the road from the *rodoviária* at Rua Ernesta Urbani 132 (ⓣ54/3282-2017; R$35 per person), but over winter weekends it can be difficult to find a bed. The cheapest **hotels** are *Bela Vista* at Av. Osvaldo Aranha 160 (ⓣ54/3282-2136; ❸) and the very similar *Turis* at Av. Oswaldo Aranha 223 (ⓣ54/3282-8436, ⓦwww.turishotel.tur.br; ❸), both centrally located but pretty basic, while there are a number of mid-range *pousadas* just outside the centre providing accommodation in comfortable but modest cabins. Try the friendly and tastefully furnished ★ *Pousada Encantos da Terra*, Rua Tenente Manoel Corrêa 282 (ⓣ54/3282-2080, ⓦwww.pousadaencantosdaterra.com.br; ❹). For more luxury, the thirteen-room *Quinta dos Marques*, Rua Gravataí 200 (ⓣ54/3282-9813, ⓦwww.quintadosmarques.com.br; ❻–❼), is the most distinctive choice available, the imposing 1930s wooden building – in typical highland style – beautifully renovated to offer rustic-chic accommodation.

Most visitors dine at their hotels, but if you'd rather **eat out**, your best bet is the *Coelho* at Av. Danton Corrêa 251, near the intersection of the main avenue, Osvaldo Aranha, which has an inexpensive *rodizio* of decent local-style Italian dishes. The town's **bars**, clustered along Avenida Osvaldo Aranha, tend to be livelier than those in Gramado, with students spilling into the street well into the night at weekends.

## Templo Budista Chagdud Khadro Ling

Just 30km south but a world away from both Canela and Gramado, is the **Templo Budista Chagdud Khadro Ling** (Mon–Fri 9am–noon & 1–5pm, Sat & Sun 9am–5pm; ⓣ51/3546-8200, ⓦwww.chagdud.org), the only Tibetan Buddhist temple complex in Latin America, attracting devotees from all over Brazil and the United States. Situated on a hilltop outside the largely German village of **Três Coroas**, the temple was founded by **Chagdud Tulku Rinpoche** (1930–2002), a high lama who left Tibet for Nepal following the Chinese invasion in 1959, settling in Brazil in 1995. On a clear day you can see the buildings – red in colour, adorned with yellow details and colourful symbols that sparkle like jewels – from far into the distance. Seen close up, the remarkable site includes a huge statue of Buddha, eight large *stupas* (holy structures representing the enlightened mind), the **temple** itself with remarkable murals depicting Buddha's life, and various other buildings erected by devotees, and artists and craftsmen from Nepal. Getting to Khadro Ling is straightforward. From Porto Alegre there are several **buses** a day to Três Caroas, while from Gramado buses to Taquara stop off in Três Caroas, where you can get a **taxi** (R$12) up to the temple. Apart from during retreats, it's not possible to stay at Khadro Ling, but there's the basic *Pousada das Águas* (ⓣ51/3501-1218; ❷) in **Três Caroas** if you don't care to stay in Gramado.

## Parque Nacional dos Aparados da Serra

The dominant physical feature of south-central Brazil is a **highland plateau**, the result of layer upon layer of ocean sediment piling up and the consequent rock formations being lifted to form the Brazilian Shield. Around 150 million years ago, lava slowly poured onto the surface of the shield, developing into a thick layer of basalt rock. At the edge of the plateau, cracks puncture the basalt and it is around the largest of these that the **Parque Nacional dos Aparados da Serra** (Wed–Sun 9am–5pm; R$6) was created.

The park lies 100km east of Canela. Approaching it from any direction, you pass through rugged cattle and sheep pasture, occasionally interrupted by the distinctive umbrella-like Paraná pine trees and solitary farm buildings. As the dirt road enters the park itself, forest patches appear, suddenly and dramatically interrupted by a canyon of breathtaking proportions, **Itaimbezinho**. Some 5800m in length, between 600m and 2000m wide and 720m deep, Itaimbezinho is a dizzying sight. The canyon and the area immediately surrounding it have two distinct climates and support very different types of vegetation. On the higher levels, with relatively little rainfall, but with fog banks moving in from the nearby Atlantic Ocean, vegetation is typical of a cloud forest, while on the canyon's floor a mass of subtropical plants flourishes. The park has abundant birdlife and is home to over 150 different species.

In the park, there's a **visitors' centre** (ⓣ54/3251-1277) with an exhibition explaining the park's history and geological structure, and a snack bar. From here, you can hire a guide to lead you down the steep trail (including a five-metre vertical incline that you must negotiate by rope) to the canyon floor. You'll need to be physically fit, have good hiking boots and be prepared for flash floods. Most visitors, however, follow the well-marked paths keeping to the top of Itaimbezinho, enjoying views either into the canyon (a 2hr 30min walk from the visitors' centre) or out towards the sea (a 45min walk).

### Visiting the park

The Parque Nacional dos Aparados da Serra can be visited throughout the year, but spring (Oct & Nov) is the best time to see flowers. In the winter, June through August, it can get very cold, though visibility tends to be clearest. Summers are warm, but heavy rainfall sometimes makes the roads and trails impassable, and fog and low-lying clouds can completely obscure the spectacular views. Avoid April, May and September, the months with the most sustained rain. As only one thousand visitors are permitted to enter the park each day, it's advisable to phone the visitors' centre in advance to reserve a place. Bring with you strong footwear and mosquito repellent.

Unless you have your own transport, **getting to the park** is quite difficult. To reach it by public transport, take a bus from Porto Alegre, Gramado or Canela to **São Francisco de Paula**, 69km from the park's entrance. From São Francisco, you need to take another bus northeast to **Cambará do Sul** and ask to be let off at the entrance to the park. From here it's a further 15km to Itaimbezinho. Buses occasionally run between São Francisco or Cambará and **Praia Grande** (which has a couple of basic hotels, one on the main square and the other at the *rodoviária*), on the Santa Catarina side of the state line. These will drop you just 3km from Itaimbezinho. In São Francisco, you may be able to join a tour group headed for the park – check with a local hotel or ask at the tourist office (see p.689). From Cambará, the park entrance is only 3km away and you should be able to get a taxi to take you. Visiting the park as a day-trip from Canela or Gramado is also feasible: Casa da Montanha Adventures (ⓣ54/3286-2544), based in the *Casa da Montanha* hotel in Gramado (see p.689) escort individuals or groups for around R$120 per person, which includes a delicious lunch.

### São Francisco de Paula and Cambará do Sul

The cattle communities of São Francisco de Paula and Cambará do Sul are both good places to use as a base for visiting the park. In **SÃO FRANCISCO DE PAULA**, the larger of the two towns, you'll pass the **tourist office** on the way into town (daily 8am–7pm; ⓣ51/244-1602), where you may be able to get advice on getting to the park. There's a wide choice of places **to stay** in and around São Francisco, much the larger though the less attractive of the two towns. Two good places to try, both a couple of kilometres from town and well signposted, are the *Pousada Pomar Cisne Branco* (ⓣ51/244-1204; ❸ including dinner) and the *Hotel Cavalinho Branco* (ⓣ51/244-1263; ❷). The best place **to eat** is the *Pomar Cisne Branco*, which serves superb, inexpensive home-style meals.

In **CAMBARÁ DO SUL**, the **tourist office** is situated in the Centro Cultural (daily 8am–6pm; ⓣ54/3251-1557), an old, bright yellow wooden building typical of the region. There are several simple but very pleasant **pousadas** in the village, including the *Favo de Mel* (ⓣ54/3251-1706; ❸), the *Paraíso* (ⓣ54/3251-1352; ❸) and the *Pindorama* (ⓣ54/3251-1225; ❸). If you want to experience highland *gaúcho* life, the *Paradouro da Fortaleza* (ⓣ54/3504-5183, ⓦwww.paradourodafortaleza.com.br; ❸) is a good option, especially if you're keen on horseriding; delicious country meals cost R$15. By far the most comfortable hotel in the area, however, is the *Parador Casa da Montanha* (ⓣ54/3504-5302 and 9973-9320, ⓦwww.paradorcasadamontanha.com.br; ❼ half-board), situated at the beginning of the road that leads to the Parque Nacional dos Aparados da Serra. Accommodation is in thermal tents, but they're secure even in the strongest of winds and have every comfort of a good hotel room. In the lodge, there's a sitting and dining area, and a terrace with views out towards a sheep-rearing *fazenda*. The food here is superb, based on local beef, mutton, squash and bean dishes, and the restaurant is open to non-guests. In Cambará itself, your **eating** options are entirely meat-based, with the *Restaurante Galpão Costaneira* especially recommended for its inexpensive, authentic local dishes served in a rustic, but attractive, setting.

## Caxias do Sul

Around 70km west of Gramado and 37km north of Nova Petrópolis is **CAXIAS DO SUL**, Rio Grande do Sul's third-largest city. Italian immigrants arrived in Caxias (as the city is known) in 1875, but the only obvious indication of the city's ethnic origins is its *adegas*, now huge companies or cooperatives that produce some of the state's poorest wine. If you're interested in the history of the region, the **Museu Casa de Pedra** (Tues–Sun 8.30am–5.30pm) at Rua Matteo Gianella 531 is well worth a look. Housed in a late nineteenth-century stone farmhouse, it contains agricultural implements, old photographs and other artefacts relating to the first Italian immigrants. The most important festival in Caxias is the **Festa Nacional da Uva**, a two-week celebration of Italian traditions, local industry and wine production. The event is held in February and March (in even-numbered years) at the Parque Exposições Centenário, on the outskirts of the city.

Caxias is a major transport centre and **buses** run to towns throughout Rio Grande do Sul, and to states to the north, from the **rodoviária** (Ⓣ54/3218-3000), seven blocks east of Praça Rui Barbosa. There's also an **airport** (Ⓣ54/3901-1219), 4km south of the city centre, with flights to Porto Alegre and São Paulo.

You'll find the **tourist office** (daily 9am–5pm; Ⓣ0800-541-1875) on the main square, Praça Dante Alighieri, along with several inexpensive **hotels** including the *Alfred*, Rua Sinimbu 2266 (Ⓣ54/3221-8655, Ⓦwww.alfredhoteis.com.br; ❸), which is particularly good value. There are plenty of more expensive options, the best being the *Reynolds International*, Rua Dr Montaury 1441 (Ⓣ54/3223-5844, Ⓦwww.reynolds.com.br; ❺), a small luxury hotel.

For authentic – and inexpensive – northern Italian **food**, try *Zanottoo*, Rua Visconde de Pelotas (closed Sun evening) and, in particular, *La Vindima*, Av. Júlio de Castilhos 962 (closed Sun and all Jan), both good for country-style chicken and polenta dishes.

## Flores da Cunha and around

Virtually all the towns and villages in the area to the north and west of Caxias do Sul were founded by northern Italian immigrants and, set amidst the mountainous landscape, **FLORES DA CUNHA** is considered to be the most Italian of Brazilian *municípios*, retaining thriving Italian folk traditions. The town itself is quite unremarkable in appearance, but the **Museu Histórico** (Mon–Fri 8–11.30am & 1–5.45pm, Sat 1–4.45pm), in the old town hall on Rua 25 de Julho, provides a good overview of the region's history. The **tourist office** (Mon–Fri 9am–5pm) is located in the same building. There are just two **hotels**: the large and impersonal *Fiório* (Ⓣ54/3292-2900, Ⓦwww.hotelfiorio.com.br; ❸) on the way into town at Av. 25 de Julho 5500 (the RS-122 road), and the slightly more comfortable *Villa Borghese Albergo* (Ⓣ54/3292-2355, Ⓦwww.hotelvillaborghese.com.br; ❸), near the centre of town at Rua John F. Kennedy 1031. The best **restaurant** in town is *L'Osteria del Gallo* at Rua Heitor Curra 2354 (closed Mon evenings), which serves reasonably priced local-style Italian food. The town is a good base from which to explore the surrounding countryside and stop off at some of the *colônias* selling their homemade cheeses, salamis, liqueurs and wine. Both in town and in the region around, there are innumerable *cantinas* that welcome visitors for tasting.

For a stronger taste of the local Italian heritage, head out to the neighbouring villages – a particularly attractive option is **OTÁVIO ROCHA**, 13km southwest of town (two buses daily). The people here are almost all of Veneto origin and still maintain their pioneer forebears' dialect and customs. The village comes alive in the last two weeks of July when the **Festo do Colono** takes place, but throughout the year the hamlet is delightful. Vines are planted on just about every patch of land, extending down to the main street itself, and the smell of fermenting grapes is remarkable. If you're looking for a good **hotel** in Otávio Rocha, try the *Dona Adélia* (ⓣ54/3292-1519; ❸); there are a couple of restaurants serving authentic *colono* food – huge meals at less than R$15 per person. A further 7km west, the village of **NOVA PÁDUA** is another good place to head for: the *Albergue Belvedere Sonda*, Travessa Mutzel (ⓣ54/3296-1200; reservations essential; ❸ half-board), is a modern guesthouse a few kilometres from the village in the direction of Nova Roma; it gives spectacular views of the Rio das Antas, and serves excellent local dishes.

Thirty-four kilometres north of Flores da Cunha, **ANTÔNIO PRADO** was founded in 1886 by another group of northern Italian immigrants. The **Museu Municipal** in Praça Garibaldi (Tues–Fri 8.30–11.30am & 1.30–5pm, Sat, Sun & public holidays 1–5pm) tells the usual story of the first pioneers, but it's Antônio Prado's wealth of well-preserved **wood and stone houses** and farm buildings that makes it particularly interesting. Until about 1940 the village and its hinterland prospered, but over the following decades the local economy stagnated and *colonos* moved as far away as the western Amazon. The town was left with dozens of disused late nineteenth- and early twentieth-century buildings, and 47 of them now have preservation orders on them – especially worth visiting are the **Casa da Neni** at Rua Luíza Bocchese 34, where local handicrafts, preserves and liquors are sold (daily 9am–noon & 1.30–6pm), and the **Farmácia Palombini** at Av. Valdomiro Bocchese 439, whose interior remains unchanged since it opened in the 1930s. For a local map, and information on the farm buildings scattered along the *município*'s back roads, ask at the helpful **tourist office** in the Prefeitura at Praça Garibaldi 57 (Mon–Fri 8.30–11.30am & 1.30–5pm; ⓣ54/3293-1500). Many of the best-preserved houses, built from a combination of wood and stone, are found along Linha 21 de Abril (off the RS-122 road, 6km in the direction of Flores da Cunha). The only place to stay in town is the functional *Hotel Piemonte* (ⓣ54/3293-1280; ❸), across from Praça Garibaldi. Much nicer is the *Pousada Colonial de Rossi* (ⓣ54/3293-1771, ⓦwww.pousadaderossi.com.br; ❺ full board), 6km from town on Linha Silva Tavares, off the RS-448 road in the direction of Nova Roma. **Places to eat** in town are disappointing, limited to a few *lanchonetes*. For local cuisine, you'll have to drive or take a taxi to *Nostra Cantina*, a few kilometres from town on the RS-122 road towards Flores da Cunha.

## Bento Gonçalves and around

Approach **BENTO GONÇALVES**, 40km west of Caxias, from any direction and there's no doubting that this is the heartland of Brazil's wine-producing region. On virtually every patch of land, no matter the gradient, vines are planted. Wine production entered a new era in the late 1970s as huge cooperatives developed, local *cantinas* expanded and foreign companies set up local operations.

The results have been somewhat mixed. In the past, the locals relied almost exclusively on North American grape varieties and produced their own distinctive wines. Gradually, though, they were encouraged to join a cooperative or agree to sell their grapes exclusively for one company. New European and, more recently, Californian vines enabled companies to produce "finer" wines of a type that until then had been imported. All this means that the *colonos* now rarely produce more than their own family's requirements, and high-tech stainless-steel vats and rigidly monitored quality control have rapidly replaced the old oaken-barrel tradition; with few exceptions, the resulting wines are, at best, mediocre.

Bento Gonçalves itself is an undistinguished-looking town whose economy, of course, totally revolves around grape and wine production. There are numerous **cantinas** in the centre of town offering free tours and tastings and a **Museu Casa do Imigrante**, at Rua Erny Hugo Dreher 127 (Tues–Fri 8–11.15am & 1.30–5.15pm, Sat 1–5pm, Sun 9am–noon), documenting the history of Italian immigration and life in the area. There's a **youth hostel**, the *Pousada Casa Mia* at Traversa Niterói 71 (Ⓣ54/3451-1215, Ⓦwww.pousadacasamia.com.br; ❷), while **hotels**, of which there is no shortage, are mainly found in the streets around the very helpful **tourist office**, Rua Marechal Deodoro 70 (Mon–Fri 8–11.45am & 1–7pm, Sat 9am–5pm; Ⓣ54/3451-1088). Very comfortable rooms are offered at *Vinocap* at Rua Barão do Rio Branco 245 (Ⓣ54/3451-1566, Ⓦwww.vinocap.com.br; ❸).

### The surrounding area

It's worth visiting the surrounding countryside and villages, where, on the surface at least, the way of life has changed little over the years. The calendar revolves around the grape, with weeding, planting, pruning and the maintenance of the characteristic stone walls – the main activities during the year – leading up to the harvest between January and late March. An excellent way to admire the beautiful countryside is to take the tourist **steam train** (year-round Wed & Sat 9am & 2pm from Bento; R$43 return; Ⓣ54/3452-6042, Ⓦwww.mfumaca.com.br) into the vine-dominated landscape. Along its 48-kilometre route (formerly part of a line extending south to Porto Alegre), the train stops at some of the more scenic spots, of which the most spectacular is the view over the **Vale do Rio das Antas** where the river's path takes the form of a horseshoe. The train continues to **GARIBALDI**, a small town mainly notable for its production of some remarkably good Champagne-style sparkling wines; if you want to stay over here, the place to head for is the *Casacurta* (Ⓣ54/3462-2166, Ⓦwww.hotelcasacurta.com.br; ❸), a stylish, early 1950s hotel which is excellent value.

Over recent years the quality of Brazilian wine has been improving greatly, with some of the most innovative producers located to the southwest of Bento Gonçalves in the very beautiful area that has become known as the **Vale dos Vinhedos**. Even more than other wine-producing areas in this part of the state, the economy and way of life here is dominated by wine, with grapes growing on every patch of farmland. The best approach is from Bento Gonçalves along the main BR-470 highway, turning off onto the RS-444, a county road called Linha Oito da Graciema (any southbound bus from Bento Gonçalves will drop you off at the intersection). Here you'll find an excellent **information centre** (daily 9am–6pm; Ⓣ54/3451-9601, Ⓦwww.valedosvinhedos.com.br) where you can pick up a map indicating wineries and other local businesses open to visitors. Basically the circuit includes Linha Oito da Graciema and Linha Leopoldina and a few well-signposted side roads. The **wineries** vary enormously in character and it's wise to settle on just a few to stop off for tastings. Miolo, probably the best of Brazil's large-scale producers, and *Casa Valduga*, the first producer to introduce modern wine-making techniques and European vines, are certainly worth visiting, but some of the smaller wineries are much more distinctive. Villaggio Laurentis is an up-and-coming producer of what pass locally as "fine wines" while Pizzato is still very much a family concern. Although not producing wine but instead excellent grape juice, the Famiglia Tasca should not be missed: located on a side road in the extreme west of the Vale dos Vinhedos, the well-maintained **wood and stone farm buildings** are some of the oldest in the area and the views across the neighbouring Aurora valley are breathtaking.

The best time to visit is January through March when the grapes are harvested, but visitors are welcomed throughout the year for tastings. There are some extremely comfortable – and quite expensive – **places to stay** including the *Casa Valduga*, Linha Leopoldina Km 6 (Ⓣ54/3453-1154, Ⓦwww.casavalduga.com.br; ⑤), and the *Borghetto Sant'Anna*, Linha Leopoldina Km 8 (Ⓣ54/3453-2355, Ⓦwww.borgettosantanna.com.br; ⑤). Dining possibilities are surprisingly limited but the *Casa Valduga* serves good, and reasonably priced, local-style Italian food.

To the immediate west of the Vale dos Vinhedos is the hilltop village of **MONTE BELO**, which wouldn't look out of place in Italy. From here there are fine views in all directions and with the basic but cheap *Bruschi Hotel* (Ⓣ54/3457-1048; ②), whose **restaurant** serves authentic *colono* food – a complete meal costs just R$15 – Monte Belo is a fine base from which to wander along the pathways and tracks between the vineyards.

# The Litoral Gaúcho

The **coast** of Rio Grande do Sul, or the Litoral Gaúcho, is a virtually unbroken 500-kilometre-long beach, dotted with a series of resorts popular with Argentines, Uruguayans and visitors from Porto Alegre and elsewhere in the state. In winter the beaches are deserted and most of the hotels closed, but between mid-November and March it's easy to believe that the state's entire population has migrated to the resorts. The attraction of this stretch of coast is essentially one of convenience: from Porto Alegre many of the resorts can be reached within two or three hours, making even day-trips possible. These resorts tend to be crowded, while – due to the influence of the powerful Rio Plate – the water is usually murky, and even in summer Antarctic currents often make for chilly bathing. Of the resorts, the only one really worth visiting is **Torres**, featuring impressive cliffs and rock formations. Further south, birdwatchers are drawn to the **Parque Nacional da Lagoa do Peixe**, while towards the Uruguayan border are the ports of **Pelotas** and **Rio Grande**, their grand nineteenth-century buildings testimony to the cities' former prosperity.

## Torres

The northernmost point on the Litoral Gaúcho, 197km from Porto Alegre, **TORRES** is the state's one beach resort that is actually worth going out of your way for. It's considered Rio Grande do Sul's most sophisticated coastal resort, and the beaches behind which the town huddles, **Praia Grande** and **Prainha**, are packed solid in the summer with *gaúcho* and Uruguayan holiday-makers. However, by walking across the Morro do Farol (a hill, identifiable by its lighthouse) and along the almost equally crowded Praia da Cal, you come to the **Parque da Guarita** (Ⓦwww.parquedaguarita.com.br), one of the most beautiful stretches of the southern Brazilian coast. The development of the park was supervised by the landscaper Roberto Burle Marx together with Brazil's pioneer environmentalist, José Lutzenberger.

The state park is centred on a huge basalt outcrop, with 35-metre-high cliffs rising straight up from the sea, from where there are superb views up and down the coast. At several points, steps lead down from the clifftop to basalt pillars and cavern-like formations, beaten out of the cliff face over the years. Although there are areas where it's both possible, and safe, to dive from the rocks, generally the sea is inaccessible and ferocious. Continue along the clifftop, and you'll eventually reach the **Praia da Guarita**, a fairly small beach that is never as crowded as those nearer town. Just beyond a further, much smaller outcrop, there's another beach, this one stretching with hardly an interruption all the way to the border with Uruguay.

### Practicalities

From the **rodoviária** (ⓣ51/3664-1787), served by buses from Porto Alegre, Florianópolis, São Paulo, Curitiba, Buenos Aires and Montevideo, walk down Avenida José Bonifácio to Avenida Barão do Rio Branco. Here, turn right for the centre and the beach (six blocks) or left (one block) for the **tourist office** (Dec–April 8am–10pm; May–Nov 8am–6pm; ⓣ51/3626-1937). Torres has dozens of **hotels**, with many of the cheaper ones located on Barão do Rio Branco and the two streets running parallel to it. Even so, in midsummer accommodation is predictably difficult to track down, so try to arrive early in the day. Hotels and *pousadas* here are an undistinguished lot and you can expect to pay at least R$100 for a double room. Worth trying are the *Farol*, Rua José Picoral 240 (ⓣ51/3664-1240, ⓦwww.farolhotel.com.br; ❸), the *Bauer*, Rua Ballino de Freitas 260 (ⓣ51/3664-1290; ❸), and the *Pousada la Barca*, Av. Beira-Mar 1020 (ⓣ51/3664-2925, ⓦwww.pousadalabarca.com.br; ❹), all of which are good value.

All the best **restaurants** are by the river, twenty to thirty minutes' walk from the centre. Either walk along Praia Grande in the opposite direction from the lighthouse or, quicker, along Rua Sete de Setembro, a couple of streets back from the beach. Especially recommended are *Gaviota* and *Anzol*, for their wide selection of seafood. In the centre, there are plenty of beachside **bars**, some serving light meals, while at Rua José Luís de Freitas 800, the *Galeto Régis* serves excellent chicken dishes (closed April–Nov).

## Parque Nacional da Lagoa do Peixe

If you're travelling south along the coast from Torres down to the Uruguayan border at Chuí, it's normally necessary to go inland via Porto Alegre. But if time isn't an issue, it is possible to take buses from village to village along the RS-101 road and the narrow peninsula that protects the Lagoa dos Patos from the sea. The road is unpaved and often in the most appalling state, while the landscape is barren and windswept, but the remote fishing communities along the way have consequently been protected from the ravages of tourism. The inhabitants, largely of Azorean stock but also descendants of shipwreck survivors and renegades fleeing other parts of Rio Grande do Sul, make a living by fishing, growing onions, raising chickens and sheep, and increasingly through tourism.

At the midpoint of the peninsula is the **Parque Nacional da Lagoa do Peixe** (daily 8am–5pm), centred on an area surrounding a long and narrow lagoon – so shallow that trucks can drive across it. The park is one of the most important **bird sanctuaries** in South America. Migrating birds stop here, attracted by the clean, brackish water rich in algae, plankton, crustacea and fish. The **best time to visit** is between September and March, when the lagoon shelters birds from the northern hemisphere winter, and then others landing on their way north from the Patagonian winter. However, bird-watching opportunities are generally good year-round, and even those with a passing interest in birds won't fail to be impressed by the pink flamingoes. The area also provides rich habitat for reptiles and mammals; in the winter months, sea lions share the sands with Malalhães penguins, and you might spot whales in the distance offshore, returning from their mating and feeding grounds.

There is no infrastructure for receiving visitors, so you'll need to track down someone with considerable local knowledge if you want to see anything of the park. It's best to head for **MOSTARDAS**, an attractive village dominated by simple Azorean-style buildings along its narrow streets. Basic **accommodation** is available at the *Hotel Mostardense*, Rua Bento Gonçalves 1020 (Ⓣ51/3673-1368; ❷), the *Hotel Municipal*, Rua Independente 761 (Ⓣ51/3673-1500; ❷), and the *Hotel Scheffer*, Rua Almirante Tamandaré (Ⓣ51/3673-1277; ❷).

On Praça Prefeito Luiz Martins, the main square, is the **Casa da Cultura** (daily 8–11.30am & 1–4.30pm), worth a visit for its display of photographs and books documenting the area; you'll also be able to pick up information on local events, such as dances, too. To find a **guide**, go to the local office of IBAMA, which administers the national parks (Mon–Fri 8am–noon & 2–5pm; Ⓣ51/3673-1464), also located on the main *praça*. You might be able to latch onto a pre-arranged group; otherwise you can hire a private guide, who won't be likely to charge more than R$60 for an early-morning or late-afternoon excursion to Barra da Lagoa do Peixe, where the greatest concentration of migratory birds is to be found. You'll need to leave plenty of time to enjoy the area, not only because of difficulties in gaining access to the park but because of the appalling state of the RS-101 – the so-called *Estrada do Inferno*, or Road of Hell – often washed out by flash floods, and because of poor bus services between the peninsula's small settlements; before heading south of Mostardas, ask at IBAMA about the current state of the road. You may find it much easier to head down the peninsula on the Atlantic beach, as the sand is hard enough to take the weight of a car, although you will have to negotiate the few streams that cut across the beach and also watch out for sudden tidal surges. Also bear in mind that the climate differs widely during the year – in the winter it can be bitterly cold, while summers are warm and perfect for mosquitoes.

## Pelotas

Rio Grande do Sul's second-largest city, **PELOTAS**, 270km to the south of Porto Alegre, is situated on the left bank of the Canal de São Gonçalo, which connects the Lagoa dos Patos with the Lagoa Mirim. Founded in 1812 as a port for the *charque* (jerked beef) producers of the surrounding region, Pelotas rapidly emerged as the wealthiest city in Rio Grande do Sul, becoming a byword for conspicuous consumption.

The first **charqueada** was established in the Pelotas area in 1780 and by the late 1820s there were two dozen producers of *charque*. Cattle were herded from *estâncias* from as far away as Bagé (see p.706) to be slaughtered, the meat salted and sundried. The *charqueadas* consisted of a long strip of land bordering the Arroio Pelotas along which *charque* was transferred to the port of Pelotas for shipment elsewhere in Brazil. Production was a brutal affair, relying almost wholly on slave labour, and when cattle were being slaughtered the river was stained bright red from the blood and waste. Evidence still remains of the *charqueadas* with several ruins on the banks of the Arroio Pelotas as well as two fine houses built by *charqueadores* that are open to visitors. The oldest, the **Charqueada São João**

(Sun 2–5pm and by arrangement; ⓣ53/3228-2425, ⓦwww.charqueadasaojoao.com.br; R$10), was established in 1810 and the house contains period furniture as well as tools. Almost alongside it is the **Charqueada Santa Rita** (ⓣ53/3228-2024, ⓦwww.charqueadasantarita.com.br), the colonial-style house built in 1826. Santa Rita now serves as a *pousada* (see p.700) but its small **Museu do Charque** is open to the public (R$8). The *charqueadas* are located about 5km northeast of the centre of Pelotas. A taxi will cost around R$15 or take any bus to "Laranjal" and get off just before the bridge that crosses the Arroio Pelotas.

With the introduction of refrigeration in the late nineteenth century, demand for beef increased, and with it Pelotas's importance as a port and commercial centre. However, by the turn of the century, Rio Grande's port, able to take larger ships, had superseded it and the local economy entered a long period of decline.

While a slowdown in investment might have been bad for the city's economy, it saved Pelotas's Neoclassical centre from the developers. **Praça Coronel Pedro Osório**, the main square, is the city's heart, and most of the very elegant, stuccoed buildings with wrought-iron balconies overlooking the square date from the nineteenth or early twentieth centuries. Buildings to look out for include the Prefeitura (completed in 1881), the Biblioteca Pública (1875), the former Grand Hotel (1928, now the city's Casa da Cultura) and the Teatro 7 de Abril (1834). Adjoining the *praça*, to the south, is the **Mercado Público** (Mon–Fri 7am–7pm, Sat 7am–1pm), a distinguished-looking building constructed in 1849, with a mix of stalls selling food and general goods.

As a railhead, port and an important commercial centre, late nineteenth-century Pelotas was home to considerable British and American communities. Bearing witness to this is the **Igreja Episcopal do Redentor**, a block from the Mercado Público on Rua XV de Novembro. Built in 1909, the ivy-covered church would go unnoticed in any English town, but in Brazil it looks completely alien. In fact, in Rio Grande do Sul such churches have become a part of the urban landscape, with some fifty others dotted around the state, although hardly any of the members of their congregations are of British origin.

Six blocks to the north of Praça Osório, on Praça José Bonifácio, is the grand **Catedral de São Francisco de Paula** (Mon–Fri 10am–noon & 1.30–7pm, Sat 2–7pm, Sun 8am–noon & 7–8pm). While its interior has undergone some alteration over the years, the exterior, crowned with a majestic dome, has not been fundamentally altered since it was built in 1853.

Scattered around the city are numerous mansions that once housed the *pelotense* aristocracy. Many of these are in a state of disrepair, but a fine example survives in the **Museu da Baronesa** (Tues–Sun 1.30–6pm; R$3) at Av. Domingos de Almeida 1490 in the suburb of Areal, about 1km northeast of the cathedral (take a bus marked "Laranjal"). The pink and white stuccoed building was built in 1863 as a wedding present to the son and daughter-in-law of a banking family, its grandeur symbolic of the wealth that was generated during the *charque* era. The museum includes a mix of family mementoes and period furniture and offers a glimpse into the lifestyle of nineteenth-century high society.

### Practicalities

The **rodoviária** (ⓣ53/3284-6700) is way out of town, with buses running into the centre every ten minutes. There are long-distance services from Rio Grande and Porto Alegre, and less frequently from Bagé, Santo Ângelo, Santa Maria, Uruguaiana and Montevideo. For tourist information, head for the **tourist office** (Mon–Fri 9am–6pm; ⓣ53/3225-3733) at Praça Coronel Pedro Osório 6. On the same square you'll find several cheap **hotels**, the best of which is the very basic *Rex* (ⓣ53/3222-1163; ❷). For more comfort, try the *Curi Palace* at Rua General Osório 719 (Ⓣ53/3227-7377, Ⓦwww.curipalacehotel.com.br; ❸). By far the most distinctive and pleasant place to stay is the *Charqueada Santa Rita* (Ⓣ53/3228-2024, Ⓦwww.charqueadasantarita.com.br; ❺), located on the outskirts of the city on the Estrada da Costa. A former *charqueada* (see p.699), the *pousada* offers unpretentious but high levels of comfort and the setting couldn't be more relaxing. There's a pool and the very helpful Anglo-Brazilian owner offers boat trips on the very pretty Arroio Pelotas, a natural canal that backs onto the property.

For a city of this size and importance, the **restaurants** are generally poor, but there are a few that are well worth seeking out. Meat – here meaning beef – is the local staple, and the quality is especially good at the moderately priced *El Paisano*, Rua Deodoro 1093 (Tues–Sat from 7pm, Sun 11am–2pm & from 7pm), a cosy Uruguayan *parrilla* (grill). Alternatively, *Lobão Galeteria*, Rua Dr Amarante, at the corner of Rua Gonçalves Chaves, offers good, inexpensive, Italian-style meals based on chicken, polenta and salad. Pelotas is famous for its intense Portuguese-style **sweets and cakes**, and the best place to try them is the *Doçaria Pelotense* at the corner of Rua Sete de Setembro and 15 de Novembro.

The city has developed a reputation as a good place to buy **antiques**, with curios and furniture items being sold by old *pelotense* families. Rua Anchieta, in the centre of town, is where the antique shops are concentrated, with Inês (at no. 2373) and Lalique (at no. 2208) being especially reliable.

## Rio Grande and around

**RIO GRANDE** was founded on the entrance to the Lagoa dos Patos in 1737, at the very southern fringe of the Portuguese Empire. With the growth of the *charque* and chilled-beef economy, Rio Grande's port took on an increasing importance from the mid-nineteenth century. Rather more spread out than Pelotas, it does not share that city's instant charm. However, you'll find some

### The Uruguayan border: Chuí

Unless you're shopping for cheap Scotch whisky or visiting the casino, there's absolutely nothing in **CHUÍ** (or "Chuy" on the Uruguayan side of the frontier) to stick around for. **Buses** entering and leaving Brazil stop at an immigration office a short distance from town for passports to be stamped. The Brazilian **rodoviária** (Ⓣ53/3265-1498; frequent services from Porto Alegre, Pelotas and Rio Grande), on Rua Venezuela, is just a couple of blocks from Avenida Brasil, which divides the Brazilian and Uruguayan sides of town; you can cross back and forth quite freely. Onda, one of Uruguay's main bus companies, stops on the Uruguayan side of Avenida Brasil and has frequent departures for Punta del Este and Montevideo. If you are travelling to or from western Uruguay and Treinta y Tres, you will have to walk 3km down Calle General Artigas (follow the signs to Montevideo) to the Uruguayan immigration post for an entry or exit stamp in your passport. If you need a **visa** to enter Brazil, you can get one from the Brazilian consulate on the Uruguayan side of town at Calle Fernández 147, while in Brazil the Uruguayan consulate is at Rua Venezuela 311.

**Changing money** is easy: either use a Uruguayan *casa da câmbio* or bank before travelling on into Brazil where you'll receive the equivalent of the best rates available in Brazilian cities, or wait until you cross into Chuí where there are ATMs. If you can, try to avoid **staying** in Chuí as hotels are overpriced and unpleasant; as a rule, those on the Brazilian side of the common avenue are cheaper, those on the Uruguayan side cleaner and more comfortable. **Restaurants**, even the simplest ones, are better on the Uruguayan side of the avenue.

distinguished-looking nineteenth-century buildings in the area around Rua Floriano Peixoto and **Praça Tamandaré** (the main square), which is almost next to Largo Dr Pio and the much-renovated eighteenth-century **Catedral de São Pedro**. Among the city's museums, you'll want to visit the **Museu Oceanográfico** at Rua Reito Perdigão 10 (daily 9–11am & 1.30–5.30pm; R$5), perhaps the most important of its kind in Latin America and stuffed with fossils and preserved sea creatures. Also worthwhile is the **Museu Histórico da Cidade do Rio Grande** on Rua Riachuelo (Tues–Sun 9–11.30am & 2–5.30pm), whose photographic archive and objects trace the city's history. The museum is housed in the old customs house (*alfândega*), a Neoclassical building built in 1879.

Just a stone's throw from the cathedral, the **waterfront** is always busy with ocean-going ships, fishing vessels and smaller boats. From here boats cross the mouth of the Lagoa dos Patos to the small village of **São José do Norte**, one of the oldest settlements in the state, where there's a simple church, **Nossa Senhora dos Navegantes**, built in 1795.

As far as **beaches** are concerned, though, you'll need to go to **Cassino**, a resort facing the Atlantic that's very popular with Uruguayans, 25km south of Rio Grande and served by buses from Praça Tamandaré. Like most of the rest of the Litoral Gaúcho, the beaches here are long, low and straight and only merit a visit if you have time between buses.

### Practicalities

A few blocks from Praça Tamandaré is Rio Grande's **rodoviária** (Ⓣ53/3232-8444), served by buses from most cities in Rio Grande do Sul, and from cities as far north as Rio de Janeiro.

Built in 1826, the *Paris Hotel*, on the waterfront at Rua Marechal Floriano 112 (Ⓣ53/3231-3866, Ⓦwww.hotelvillamoura.com.br; ③), was once the place **to stay** in Rio Grande and, after decades of neglect, much of its former "Grand Hotel" feel and fabric have been restored, making it an important sight in its own right. There's a wood-panelled breakfast room and an extremely pretty courtyard with a central fountain, and while most of the bedrooms are fairly basic, some have period furnishings and offer amazing value. For **eating**, try the *Pescal*, Rua Mal. Andrea 269 (closed Sun), which specializes in fish, or the *Angola*, Rua Benjamin Constant 163 (closed Mon), for Portuguese specialities.

## The Jesuit missions

For much of the seventeenth and eighteenth centuries, the **Guaraní Indians** of what is now northeastern Argentina, southeastern Paraguay and north-western Rio Grande do Sul were only nominally within the domain of the Spanish and Portuguese empires, and instead were ruled – or protected – by the Society of Jesus, the **Jesuits**. The first **redução** – a self-governing Indian settlement based around a Jesuit mission – was established in 1610 and, within a hundred years, thirty such places were in existence. With a total population of 150,000, these mini-cities became centres of some importance, with *erva maté* and cattle the mainstay of economic activity, though spinning, weaving and metallurgical cottage industries were also pursued. As the seventeenth century progressed, Spain and Portugal grew increasingly concerned over the Jesuits' power, and Rome feared that the religious order was becoming too independent of papal authority. Finally, in 1756, Spanish and Portuguese forces

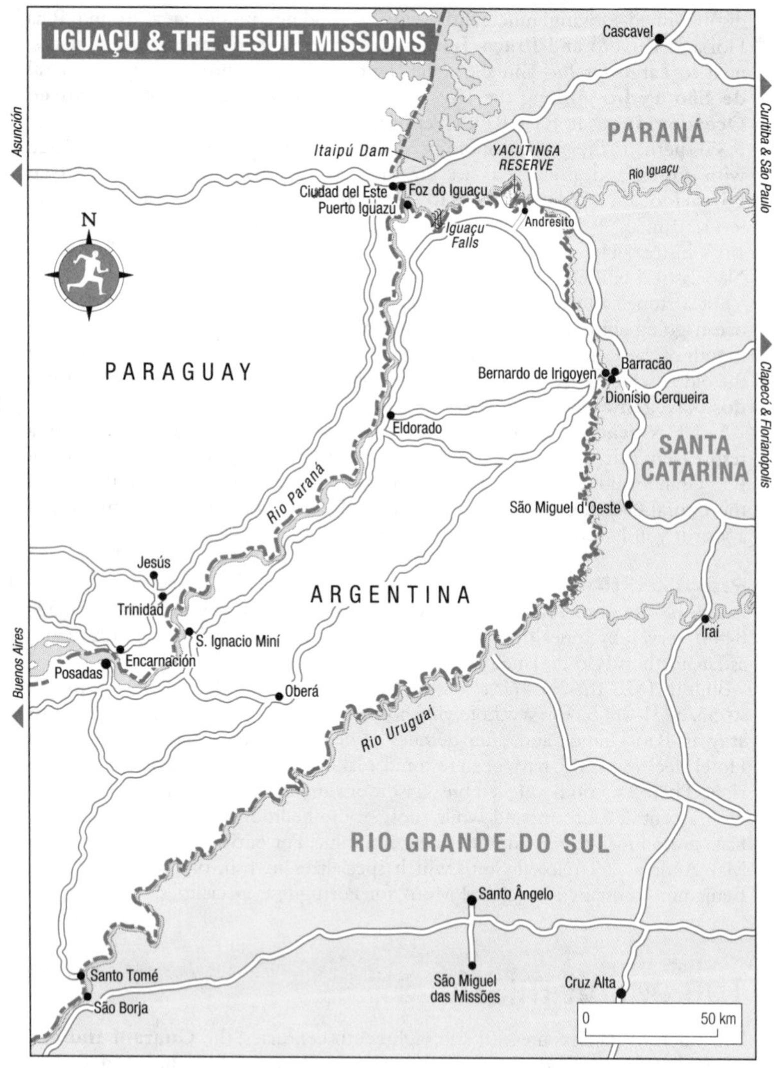




attacked the missions, the Jesuits were expelled and many Indians killed. The missions themselves were dissolved, either razed to the ground or abandoned to nature, surviving only as ruins. Of the thirty former Guaraní mission towns, sixteen were in present-day Argentina, seven in Paraguay and seven were situated in what is now Brazil.

There are direct bus services every day between **Santo Ângelo**, which serves the **São Miguel** site in Brazil, and Posadas in Argentina, crossing the border at São Borja (see p.709). Posadas is a short distance from Argentina's **San Ignacio Miní** ruins and Paraguay's **Trinidad and Jesús**. Alternatively, these last three missions are a fairly easy side-trip from the Iguaçu Falls.

## Santo Ângelo

The town of **SANTO ÂNGELO**, set in a farming region inhabited predominantly by people of German origin, is a good point from which to catch buses to the missions. Santo Ângelo is served by buses from throughout Rio Grande do Sul as well as from Curitiba, São Paulo and Rio. If you're planning on visiting the Jesuit ruins in Argentina and Paraguay, you can take the daily **bus** to Posadas, or take a bus to the border town of São Borja and change there. The **rodoviária** (Ⓣ55/3313-2618) is within a few blocks of Praça Pinheiro Machado; there are four buses a day to and from São Miguel, with the last going to the ruins at 5pm and returning at 7pm.

There's not much to see in the town itself, although the **Catedral** (daily 8.30am–5pm), on the main square, Praça Pinheiro Machado, is worth a look as it's a fair replica of São Miguel's church. The best cheap hotel in Santo Ângelo is the *Santo Ângelo Turis* (Ⓣ55/3312-4055; ❷), just off the main square at Rua Antônio Manoel 726, or for more comfort try the *Maerkil* at Av. Brasil 1000 (Ⓣ55/3313-2127; ❹). The best restaurant in town is a *churrascaria*, the *Chico*, at Rua Antônio Manoel 1421.

## São Miguel

The one mission site in Brazil that was not completely levelled is **SÃO MIGUEL** (daily 9am–noon & 2–6pm or to 8pm in the summer; R$5), not to be compared in extent and significance to San Ignacio Miní in neighbouring Argentina, but still of considerable visual interest, particularly for its dramatic location on a treeless fertile plain. Despite vandalism and centuries of neglect, São Miguel's ruins offer ample evidence of the sophistication of Guaraní Baroque architecture, and of *redução* life generally. Founded in 1632, to the west of the Rio Uruguai, São Miguel moved only a few years later to escape *paulista* slavers, and then a few years after that it was destroyed by a violent windstorm. After being rebuilt, its population increased rapidly and in 1687 it was relocated across the river to its present site.

▲ São Miguel Jesuit mission

The initial priority was to provide housing, so not until 1700 did work begin on the **church**, designed by the Milanese Jesuit architect Giovanni Baptista Prímoli, the ruins of which still stand. The facade is a handsome example of colonial architecture. One of the church's two towers is missing, but otherwise its stone structure is reasonably complete, the lack of a vault or dome explained by the fact that these would have been finished with wood. Other aspects of the ruins are of less interest, but the outline of the *redução*'s **walls** provides a guide to the former extent of São Miguel which, at its peak, was home to over four thousand people. The **museum** has an excellent collection of stone and wood sculptures, which are beautifully displayed in Jesuit-influenced but stylistically modernist buildings designed by Lúcio Costa, the urban planner of Brasília. Every evening (7pm in winter, 9pm in summer; R$5) there's a **sound and light show**, which, even if you don't understand the Portuguese narrative, is well worth staying for. You can actually **stay** in the quiet village here, which will give you an ideal opportunity to wander round the ruins early in the day before most of the other tourists arrive. In any case, if you're attending the sound and light show, there are no late buses returning to Santo Ângelo. Right next to the ruins, there's the excellent *Pousada das Missões* (ⓣ55/3381-1202, ⓦwww.pousadatematica.com.br; ❸) and the *Wilson Park* (ⓣ55/3381-2000, ⓦwww.wilsonparkhotel.com.br; ❹), a comfortable, modern hotel with a pool. There are a couple of basic **restaurants** next to the ruins, or you can eat at the *Wilson Park*.



## San Ignacio Miní (Argentina)

Like many of the missions, **SAN IGNACIO MINÍ** was initially established on another site and later relocated for safety. Consecrated in 1609 as San Ignacio-guazú across the Rio Paraná in present-day Paraguay, the mission was moved to the Rio Yabebiry in 1632 due to constant attacks by slave-hunting *bandeirantes*. This site proved unsuitable and in 1695 the mission was moved a short distance to its present location, developing into one of the largest of the *reducciones* (*redução* in Portuguese) with, at its peak, an Indian population of over four thousand. Following the Jesuits' expulsion from South America, San Ignacio Miní fell into decline, its ruins not discovered until 1897.

Of all the mission ruins, those of San Ignacio Miní (daily 7am–7pm; A$8) are the largest in area and feature some of the most interesting museum displays. Throughout the site the buildings, trees and bushes are labelled in Spanish. As you enter the site, be sure not to miss the **Centro de Interpretación Regional**, its elaborate stage-prop-style displays depicting an idyllic pre-Hispanic past, the voyages of "discovery", the clash of cultures and the enslavement of the Guaraní, and finally the rise and fall of the Jesuit *reducciones*.

The mission is centred around the **Plaza de Armas**, dominated by the church. Visitors can wander into the ruins of the red sandstone buildings flanking the plaza: these served as workshops, schools, cloisters and living quarters for the Indians and missionaries. Completed in 1724, and designed by the Italian architect Giovanni Brazanelli, the huge Baroque church was, and still is, the focal point of the mission, although only part of the facade and a few other parts of the structure remain standing. The church, like many of the other buildings, is decorated with delicate, mainly floral designs, bas-relief sculptures by Guaraní artisans. Near the exit from the ruins is a small **museum** where sculptures excavated over the years are displayed.



### Practicalities

San Ignacio Miní is located 60km north of the city of Posadas, just off the main highway to Puerto Iguazú. There's a constant flow of buses between Puerto Iguazú (see p.643) and Posadas, most of which stop off at the sleepy little village of **SAN IGNACIO** (3hr 30min from Puerto Iguazú, 1hr from Posadas), adjoining the ruins, which is a pleasant place to spend a night. If travelling from São Miguel, the best option is a bus from Santo Ângelo to São Borja from where you can catch a bus to Posadas and another to San Ignacio. There are two good **accommodation** options in San Ignacio. On the village's central plaza is the comfortable, air conditioned *Hotel San Ignacio* (☎752/470047; ❸), while near the ruins' entrance is the friendly and very clean *Hospedaje Los Alemanes* (☎752/470362; ❷). Nearby there are numerous **restaurants**, with little to differentiate them, except that *La Carpa Azul* has a swimming pool, wonderful on a hot summer afternoon. Argentine *pesos* are available from an **ATM** located next to the church.

## Trinidad and Jesús (Paraguay)

Of the three best-preserved Jesuit mission ruins, those of **TRINIDAD and JESÚS** (Mon–Sat 7.30–11.30am & 1.30–5.30pm, Sun 1.30–5.30pm) in Paraguay are the least visited. Founded in 1706, Trinidad was one of the last *reducciones*, but it grew quickly and by 1728 it had a Guaraní population of over four thousand. The mission was designed by the Milanese architect Giovanni Baptista Prímoli, and the work wasn't completed until 1760, just a few years before the Jesuits' expulsion from South America. Trinidad prospered, developing *maté* plantations, cattle *estâncias* and a sugar plantation and mill, and its Guaraní artisans became famous for the manufacture of organs, harps and other musical instruments, bells and statues, exported throughout the Rio Plate region and beyond. One of the most grandiose of the missions, Trinidad is thought to have been the regional centre for Jesuit activity in Paraguay. Following the departure of the Jesuits, the community fell into rapid and terminal decline, the final blow coming in 1816 when Paraguay's dictator, José Gaspar Rodríguez de Francia, ordered the destruction of all Indian villages as part of his infamous scorched-earth policy.

Trinidad is Paraguay's best-restored Jesuit ruin and there is intense local pride in its status as a UNESCO World Heritage Site. Occupying a hilltop position surrounded by soya fields and cattle pasture, the site is not as extensive and the church not as large nor as complete as at San Ignacio Miní and São Miguel. Even so, much of the **church** remains in remarkable condition, including the elaborate pulpit and some of the most beautiful and intricate of **Guaraní Baroque frescoes**. Especially charming is the procession of little angels carved in sandstone that has somehow survived the centuries. Behind the ruins of the church is a small chapel: ask the guard to let you in as it contains yet more stunning wood and stone statues of angels. For an excellent view of the entire mission site and across the surrounding countryside climb the church's bell tower.

Ten kilometres to the north lies the Jesuit mission of **Jesús**. Not strictly ruins as such, Jesús (same hours and fees as Trinidad), founded in 1685 but only settled in 1763, is really an unfinished construction site, the large **church** half built when the Jesuits were ordered out of South America. What exists of the church has been restored, its beautiful arched portals resembling shamrocks, and it has an enormous part-erected guardian tower. Lacking the wealth of other missions, Jesús was not such a target of treasure seekers and remained relatively intact.

### Practicalities

Trinidad is located 28km (45min) northeast of Paraguay's third-largest city, Encarnación. There aren't many facilities in Trinidad (and there are even fewer in Jesús) and most visitors stay in Encarnación or in Posadas. There are frequent buses between the two cities and also good bus services from Ciudad del Este (4hr; see p.644) for Iguaçu. Inexpensive and comfortable **hotels** are easy to find in

**Encarnación.** An excellent budget choice is the *Viena* (☎71/3486; ❷), a couple of blocks behind the bus terminal at Calle P.J. Caballero 568. Near Plaza Artigas the *Cristal* at Av. Estigarribia 1157 (☎71/2371; ❹) is the best hotel in town.

There are some good **parrillas** (grills): on Avenida Mariscal Estigarribia near Plaza Artigas is the excellent *Rancho Grande*, while the *Cuarajhyon*, on Plaza Artigas, is also reasonable. Meat, of course, dominates menus, but vegetarians can enjoy huge salads and should try *sopa paraguaya*, a national staple that is not, as its name suggests, soup but corn bread made with onion and cheese.

# The border towns: gaúcho country

Apart from Chuí (see p.700), the most commonly used **border crossing** into **Uruguay** is at **Santana do Livramento**. While most buses cross into **Argentina** via **Uruguaiana**, you may find **São Borja** quicker if you're travelling between Jesuit mission sites or making your way north to the Iguaçu Falls. Alternatively, use a smaller border crossing point, like **Aceguá**, near **Bagé**, where at least your first impressions of Uruguay or Brazil will be of cattle and ranch hands rather than duty-free shops and casinos. Rarely do people remain in the border towns longer than it takes to go through immigration formalities, but, if you're trying to get a taste of *gaúcho* life, check to see if there's a *rodeio* about to be held somewhere around or, to witness the everyday working life of the pampas close up, you could arrange to stay at an *estância* – a cattle ranch.

## Bagé and Aceguá

Of all the towns on or very near Rio Grande do Sul's border with Argentina and Uruguay, **BAGÉ** is the only one with genuine charm, full of stately late nineteenth- and early twentieth-century buildings and a place that remains first and foremost a cattle and commercial centre, rather than a transit point. Like all towns in the *campanha*, Bagé has its own lively events, which attract people from the surrounding *estâncias*. The most important **festival**, held in January in odd-numbered years, is the **Semana Crioula Internacional**, but the Semana de Bagé (a folklore festival held annually from July 10 to 17), or even the Exposição (first half of Oct), will give you a taste of the *campanha*. For details of these and other events ask at the **tourist office** at Praça Silveira Martins (Mon–Fri 8am–6pm, Sat 9am–7pm). For an understanding of the region's history, a visit to the **Museu Dom Diogo de Souza**, Av. Emílio Guilayn 759 (Tues–Sun 2–6pm), is a must.

Arriving in Bagé from the Uruguayan border (Melo is the nearest Uruguayan town), ask to be let off at the **Polícia Federal** at Rua Barão do Trunfo 1572, a few blocks from the main square, Praça General Osório. It's here, not at Aceguá (see p.708), that you'll need to have your passport stamped. Arriving in Bagé from elsewhere, take a "Santa Tecla" bus into the centre from the main road next to the **rodoviária** (☎53/3242-7433; buses from Santa Maria and Porto Alegre, Santo Ângelo and, via Curitiba, São Paulo).

### Passport control

If you're leaving Brazil, have your passport stamped; failing to report to the Polícia Federal here will mean that you're likely to have difficulties entering or leaving Brazil later on.

## Gaúchos

During the colonial era and well into the nineteenth century, Rio Grande do Sul's southern and western frontiers were ill-defined, with Portugal and Spain, and then independent Brazil, Argentina and Uruguay, maintaining garrisons to assert their claims to the region. Frontier clashes were frequent, with central government presence weak or nonexistent. If anyone could maintain some measure of control over these border territories it was the **gaúchos**, the fabled horsemen of southern South America. The product of miscegenation between Spanish, Portuguese, Indians and escaped slaves, the *gaúchos* wandered the region on horseback, either individually or in small bands, making a living by hunting wild cattle for their hides. Alliances were formed in support of local *caudilhos* (chiefs), who fought for control of the territory on behalf of the flag of one or other competing power. With a reputation for being tough and fearless, the *gaúcho* was also said to be supremely callous – displaying the same indifference in slitting a human or a bullock's throat.

As the nineteenth century ended, so too did the *gaúcho*'s traditional way of life. International boundaries were accepted, and landowners were better able to exert control over their properties. Finally, as fencing was introduced and rail lines arrived, cattle turned into an industry, with the animals raised rather than hunted. Gradually *gaúchos* were made redundant, reduced to the status of mere *peões* or cattle hands.

Still, more in Rio Grande do Sul than in Argentina, some *gaúcho* traditions persist, though for a visitor to get much of a picture of the present-day way of life is difficult. In general, the cities and towns of the state's interior are fairly characterless, though travelling between towns still brings echoes of former times, especially if you get off the beaten track. Here, in the small villages, horses are not only a tool used to herd cattle, but remain an essential means of transport. While women are no differently dressed than in the rest of Brazil, men appear in much the same way as their *gaúcho* predecessors: in *bombachas* (baggy trousers), linen shirt, kerchief, poncho and felt-rimmed hat, shod in pleated boots and fancy spurs. Also associated with the interior of Rio Grande do Sul is *chimarrão* (sugarless *maté* tea), which is sipped through a *bomba* (a silver straw) from a *cuia* (a gourd). In the towns themselves, cattlemen are always to be seen, purchasing supplies or hanging out in bars. But undoubtedly your best chance of getting a feel of the interior is to attend a **rodeio**, held regularly in towns and villages throughout *gaúcho* country. Branches of the state tourist office, CRTur, will have information about when and where *rodeios* are due to take place.

**Hotels** in Bagé are plentiful, with the *City Hotel* (Ⓣ53/3242-8455, Ⓦwww.bagecityhotel.com.br; ❸), right in the centre at Av. Sete de Setembro 1052 offering modern comforts. With much more character, however, there's the *Pousada do Sobrado* (Ⓣ53/3242-2713, Ⓦwww.pousadadosobrado.com.br; ❹), 5km from the town centre along the Rua São João. The three guest rooms (all with period furniture) are in a beautiful *estância* house built in 1820, and there is a large pool in the grounds.

Ideally, though, you should **stay at a working estância** in the surrounding pampas. The owners of the *Estância Retiro* (Ⓣ53/3242-8002, Ⓦwww.estanciaretiro.com.br; R$150 per person, full board) have opened their 13-square-kilometre property, 25km from town, to paying guests and delight in receiving visitors. Built in 1834, the main house is one of the oldest around and guests stay either in one of its very comfortable bedrooms or a converted barn. You can spend your time joining the owner and his workers on horseback in their day-to-day duties minding the thousand head of cattle on the property or learn about the very distinctive local cooking. There's a swimming pool and streams for cooling off in on hot summer days, while the open fires are essential features for the often bitterly cold winter evenings. Reservations are crucial and you can arrange to be collected from town.

**ACEGUÁ**, 60km south and the actual frontier crossing point, is very much a back door into Brazil and Uruguay, with only a Uruguayan immigration post (remember to be stamped in or out of the country) and a few houses and stores – certainly not a place to spend a night. However, as the four buses a day in each direction between Bagé and Aceguá connect with others to and from Melo (Uruguay), this shouldn't be a problem – but check bus times carefully before setting out.

## Santana do Livramento and around

Few people stay in **SANTANA DO LIVRAMENTO** for long apart from Brazilians attracted to the casino and the duty-free shopping in **Rivera**, the Uruguayan border town into which Livramento (as it's usually known) merges. Unless you're in pursuit of *gaúchos* and intent upon taking local buses to outlying villages, the only time when Livramento is actually worth visiting in its own right is when there's a livestock exhibition, *rodeio* or cultural event on. The most important of these **events** are the Charqueada da Poesia Crioula (last two weeks in April), the Exposição Internacional do Corriedale (March 5–12) and the Exposição Agropecuária (last two weeks in Sept), but check with the **tourist office** at Rua Tamandaré (Mon–Sat 7am–1pm & 3–6pm, Sun 3–8pm) to see if there are any other smaller events due, in or around the town.

Otherwise, the only possible reason not to move straight on would be a visit to the surrounding *campanha*, the rolling countryside traditionally given over to raising cattle and, to a lesser extent, sheep. For a more authentic *gaúcho* experience, visit the *Fazenda Palomas* (Ⓣ55/3242-2551, Ⓦwww.fazendapalomas.com), located 20km from Livramento with the access road at Km 480 of BR-158 in the direction of Porto Alegre. Founded in 1897, the 10-square-kilometre *fazenda* receives visitors during the daytime for horseriding or to participate in cattle round-ups and other daily activities (around R$40 per person). It's possible to stay the night in one of the three comfortable guest rooms (❺ full board).

### Practicalities

Livramento's **rodoviária** (Ⓣ55/3242-5322), at Rua Sen. Salgado Filho 335, serves most points in Rio Grande do Sul, while **from Rivera** there are several departures a day for Montevideo from the bus terminal.

**Hotels** are cheapest in Livramento. The *Laçador* (❷) near the park at Rua Uruguai 1227 is a very basic option, or there is also the *Livramento*, opposite the *rodoviária* (Ⓣ55/3242-5444; ❷). For more comfort, a good alternative is the *Jandaia* at Rua Uruguai 1452 (Ⓣ55/3242-2288, Ⓦwww.jandaiah.com.br; ❸). **Restaurants** are better in Rivera: the best is *La Picanha*, Calle Sarandi 825.

Before **leaving** Livramento and Rivera, you'll need a Brazilian exit (or entry) passport stamp from the Polícia Federal, Rua Uruguai 1177, near the central park, and a stamp from Uruguay's Dirección Nacional de Migración, Calle Suarez 516 (three blocks from Plaza General José Artigas, Rivera's main square). In the case of any problems, you can visit Brazil's Rivera **consulate** at Calle Caballos 1159 (Ⓣ622/244-3278), and Uruguay's Livramento consulate at Av. Tamandaré 2110 (Ⓣ55/3242-1416). **Change money** at a *casa da câmbio* or bank in Rivera, where exchange rates are as good as you'll find in Brazil and the process much faster, or use a Brazilian ATM.

## Uruguaiana

The busiest crossing point on Rio Grande do Sul's border with Argentina, **URUGUAIANA** is also one of the state's most important cattle centres. However, unless you're around while there's a livestock show or folklore festival, there's little incentive to remain here: ask about festival dates at the **tourist office** (Mon–Fri 8.30am–6pm) in the Prefeitura, Praça Barão do Rio Branco. The most important annual events are the Campeira Internacional (a festival of regional folklore) held in the first half of March, Semana Farroupilha (another folklore festival) held September 13–20, and a huge livestock show, the Expo-feira Agropecuária, held in the first half of November. Otherwise, the **Museu Crioulo, Histórico e Artístico** (Mon–Fri 8.30am–noon & 2–5.30pm), in the cultural centre on the corner of *ruas* Santana and Duque de Caxias (by the main square), is worth a look for its interesting collection of *gaúcho*-related items.

**Bus** services from Uruguaiana are excellent, and you can get to or from most of the important centres, from Rio southwards. From Paso de los Libres, there are equally good services to points within Argentina, including Buenos Aires, Posadas and Puerto Iguazú. There are also daily **air services** from Uruguaiana to Porto Alegre and from Paso de los Libres to Buenos Aires.

Uruguaiana is connected to Argentina and the town of **Paso de los Libres** by a 1400-metre-long bridge spanning the Rio Uruguai. Frequent **local buses** connect the train and bus stations, and the centres of each city, and **immigration** formalities take place on either side of the bridge. If you have problems entering Argentina, the **consulate** in Uruguaiana is at Rua Santana 2496 (Ⓣ55/3412-1925). The Brazilian consulate in Paso de los Libres is at Calle Mitre 918. The modest hotels in Uruguaiana include the *Wamosy* (Ⓣ55/3412-1326; ❷) and *Mazza Tur* (Ⓣ55/3412-3404; ❸), at Rua Sete de Setembro, nos. 1973 and 1088 respectively. For more luxury head for the new *Presidente* at Av. Presidente Vargas 4070 (Ⓣ55/3411-3160; ❹). **Restaurants** (for carnivores only) are better over the border in Argentina; however, in Uruguaiana, the *Casa d'Itália* at Rua Dr Maia 3112 has a varied menu to choose from.

## São Borja

Today a fairly major border crossing point and regional trading centre, **SÃO BORJA** is best known in the rest of Brazil as the birthplace of two of the country's most controversial presidents: **Getúlio Vargas** and **João Goulart**. In São Borja, if nowhere else in Brazil, the populist Vargas remains a venerated figure, and his former home at Av. Presidente Vargas 1772 is now open to the public as the **Museu Getúlio Vargas** (Tues–Sat 9am–1pm & 2–5pm, Sun 8am–noon), containing his library, personal objects and furniture. Goulart, whose incompetent presidency led to the military's seizure of power in 1964 followed by 25 years of often ruthless rule, is someone that São Borja tries to forget.

As a **border crossing**, São Borja is most useful when travelling between the Brazilian Jesuit mission of São Miguel and those in Argentina and Paraguay. São Borja has good **bus** connections with Santo Ângelo (for São Miguel), most other important towns in Rio Grande do Sul, Curitiba, São Paulo and, across the bridge that links Brazil with Argentina, the Argentine town of Santo Tomé. From Santo Tomé there are several bus services a day to Posadas, Puerto Iguazú, Buenos Aires and other towns in Argentina.

The cheapest **hotel** in São Borja is the *Itaipu* at Rua Aparício Mariense 1167 (Ⓣ55/3431-1577; ❷), while the newer *Village* at Rua Cândido Falcão 1014 (Ⓣ55/3431-3316; ❸) offers greater comfort.

# Travel details

## Buses

**Antonina** to: Curitiba (9 daily; 2hr); Guaraqueçaba (3 daily; 3hr 30min); Morretes (hourly; 30min); Paranaguá (hourly; 45min).
**Blumenau** to: Florianópolis (6 daily; 3hr); Itajaí (hourly; 2hr); Joinville (hourly; 2hr); Pomerode (hourly; 45min).
**Curitiba** to: Antonina (9 daily; 2hr); Blumenau (10 daily; 4hr); Buenos Aires (2 daily; 37hr); Florianópolis (14 daily; 5hr); Foz do Iguaçu (14 daily; 12hr); Guaraqueçaba (2 daily; 6hr); Joinville (hourly; 2hr 30min); Paranaguá (hourly; 2hr); Pomerode (4 daily; 3hr); Porto Alegre (10 daily; 11hr); Prudentópolis (4 daily; 3hr 30min); Rio (9 daily; 11hr); São Paulo (hourly; 6hr).
**Florianópolis** to: Blumenau (6 daily; 3hr); Buenos Aires (2 daily; 30hr); Curitiba (14 daily; 5hr); Foz do Iguaçu (2 daily; 16hr); Joinville (hourly; 3hr); Porto Alegre (10 daily; 7hr); Rio (8 daily; 18hr); Santo Amaro da Imperatriz (4 daily; 1hr); São Paulo (10 daily; 12hr).
**Foz do Iguaçu** to: Curitiba (14 daily; 12hr); Florianópolis (2 daily; 16hr); Itaipu (hourly; 1hr); Prudentópolis (3 daily; 7hr); Rio (4 daily; 22hr); São Paulo (7 daily; 18hr).
**Joinville** to: Blumenau (hourly; 2hr); Curitiba (hourly; 2hr 30min); Florianópolis (hourly; 3hr); Porto Alegre (2 daily; 10hr); Rio (1 daily; 15hr); São Francisco do Sul (hourly; 1hr); São Paulo (7 daily; 9hr); Vila Dona Francesca (hourly; 45min).
**Pelotas** to: Montevideo (2 daily; 8hr); Porto Alegre (hourly; 3hr); Rio Grande (hourly; 1hr).
**Pomerode** to: Blumenau (hourly; 45min); Curitiba (4 daily; 3hr).
**Porto Alegre** to: Buenos Aires (2 daily; 22hr); Curitiba (10 daily; 11hr); Florianópolis (10 daily; 7hr); Livramento (4 daily; 7hr); Montevideo (3 daily; 12hr); Pelotas (hourly; 3hr); Rio (6 daily; 26hr); Rio Grande (hourly; 1hr); Santo Ângelo (6 daily; 6hr 30min); São Paulo (8 daily; 18hr).
**Prudentópolis** to: Curitiba (4 daily; 3hr 30min); Foz do Iguaçu (3 daily; 8hr); São Paulo (3 daily; 10hr).

## Trains

**Curitiba** to: Morretes (1–2 daily; 3hr); Paranaguá (2 weekly; 4hr).

## Boats

**Guaraqueçaba** to: Ariri (2 weekly; 10hr); Paranaguá (2 daily; 4hr).

# Contexts

# Contexts

# History

Brazil's recorded history begins with the arrival of the Portuguese in 1500, although it had been discovered, and settled, by Indians for millenia. The importation of millions of African slaves over the next four centuries completed the rich blend of European, Indian and African influences that formed modern Brazil and its people. Achieving independence from Portugal in 1822, Brazil's enormous wealth in land and natural resources underpinned a boom-and-bust cycle of economic development that continues to the present day. Industrialization turned Brazil into the economic giant of South America, but sharpened social divisions. After a twenty-year interlude of military rule, the civilian "New Republic" has struggled, with some success, against deep-rooted economic and social problems. Although social divisions remain, democracy is now fully consolidated and competent leadership during the presidencies of Fernando Henrique Cardoso and Lula means the outlook is the best it has been for a generation.

## Early history

Very little is known about the thousands of years during which Brazil was inhabited exclusively by **Indians**. The first chroniclers who arrived with the Portuguese – Pedro Vaz da Caminha in 1500 and Gaspar Carvajal in 1540 – saw large villages, but nothing resembling the huge Aztec and Inca cities the Spanish encountered. The oldest ceramics yet found in the Americas were discovered near Santarém in the 1990s, however, suggesting the Amazon was colonized before the Andes in remote prehistory. But the fragile, material traces Brazil's earliest inhabitants left have for the most part not survived. The few exceptions – such as the exquisitely worked, glazed ceramic jars unearthed on Marajó island in the Amazon – come from cultures that have vanished so completely that not even a name records their passing.

The Indians fascinated the Portuguese, and many of the first Europeans to visit Brazil sent lengthy reports home. **Hans Staden**, a German mercenary who spent three nervous years among the cannibal **Tupi** after being captured in 1552, penned the most vivid account. He tells how they tied his legs together, "… and I was forced to hop through the huts, at which they made merry, saying 'Here comes our food hopping towards us.'" Understandably, his memoirs were one of the first bestsellers in European history, and contained much accurate description of an Indian culture still largely untouched by the colonists. The work of Staden and the first explorers and missionaries offers a brief snapshot of Indian Brazil in the sixteenth century, a blurred photograph of a way of life soon to be horribly transformed.

It was unfortunate the Portuguese first landed in the only part of Brazil where ritualized cannibalism was practised on a large scale; away from the Tupi areas it was rare. Nowhere was stone used for building. There was no use of metal or the wheel, and no centralized, state-like civilizations on the scale of Spanish America. There are arguments about how large the Indian population was: Carvajal described taking several days to pass through the large towns of the Omagua tribe on the Amazon in 1542 but, away from the abundant food sources on the coast and the banks of large rivers, **population** densities were much lower. The total number of Indians was probably around five million. Today there are around 350,000 in Brazil.

## Conquest

The Portuguese discovery of Brazil, when **Pedro Alvares Cabral** landed in southern Bahia on April 23, 1500, was an accident: Cabral was blown off course as he steered far to the west to avoid the African doldrums on his way to India. After a week exploring the coast he continued to the Philippines, where he drowned in a shipwreck a few months later. King Manuel I sent **Amerigo Vespucci** to explore further in 1501. Reserving the name of the continent for himself, he spent several months sailing along the coast, calendar in hand, baptizing places after the names of saints' days: entering Guanabara Bay on New Year's Day 1502, he called it Rio de Janeiro. The land was called Terra do Brasil, after a tropical redwood that was its first export; the scarlet dye it yielded was called *brasa*, "a glowing coal".

Portugal, preoccupied with the lucrative Far East spice trade, neglected this new addition to its empire for a few decades; apart from some lumber camps they made no attempt at settlement. Other European countries were not slow to move in, with French and English privateers in the lead. Finally, in 1532, King João III was provoked into action. He divided up the coastline into **sesmarias**, captaincies fifty leagues wide and extending indefinitely inland, distributing them to aristocrats and courtiers in return for undertakings to found settlements. It was hardly a roaring success: Pernambuco, where sugar took hold, and São Vicente, gateway to the Jesuit mission station of São Paulo, were the only securely held areas.

Irritated by the lack of progress, King João repossessed the captaincies in 1548 and brought Brazil under direct royal control, sending out the first governor-general, **Tomé de Sousa**, to the newly designated **capital** at Salvador in 1549. The first few governors successfully rooted out the European privateers, and – where sugar could grow – wiped out Indian resistance. By the closing decades of the century increasing numbers of Portuguese settlers were flowing in. Slaves began to be imported from the Portuguese outposts on the African coast, as **sugar plantations** sprang up around Salvador and Olinda. Brazil, no longer seen merely as a possible staging-point on the way to the Far East, became an increasingly important piece of the far-flung Portuguese Empire. When Europe's taste for sugar took off in the early seventeenth century, the northeast of Brazil quickly became very valuable real-estate – and a tempting target for the expanding maritime powers of northern Europe, jealous of the Iberian monopoly in the New World.

## War with the Dutch

The **Dutch**, with naval bases in the Caribbean and a powerful fleet, were the best placed to move against Brazil. A mixture of greed and political self-interest lay behind the Dutch decision. From 1580 to 1640 Portugal was united with Spain, against whom the Dutch had fought a bitter war of independence; the continuing Spanish presence in Flanders still menaced them. Anything that distracted Spain from further designs on the fledgling United Provinces seemed like a good idea. As it turned out, neither the Spanish nor the Portuguese crowns played much of a role in the war: it was fought out between the Dutch, in the mercantile shape of the Dutch West India Company, and the Portuguese settlers already in Brazil, with Indian and *mameluco* (mixed race) backing, in a war made vicious by the Catholic–Protestant divide that underlay it.

In 1624 a Dutch fleet appeared off Salvador and took the city by storm. But they were pinned down by enraged settlers and expelled in 1625 by a hastily assembled combined Spanish and Portuguese fleet – the only direct intervention made by either country in the conflict. When a Dutch force was once more repulsed from Salvador in 1627, they shifted their attention further north and found the going much easier. Olinda was taken in 1630, the rich sugar zones of Pernambuco were occupied, and Dutch control extended up to the mouth of the Amazon by 1641. With settlers moving in and a fleet more powerful than Portugal's, Dutch control of the northeast threatened to become permanent.

**Maurice of Nassau** was sent out as governor of the new Dutch possessions in Brazil in 1630, as the Dutch founded a new capital in Pernambuco, Mauritzstaadt, now Recife. His enlightened policies of allowing the Portuguese freedom to practise their religion, and including them in the colonial government, would probably have resulted in a Dutch Brazil had it not been for the stupidity of the Dutch West India Company. They insisted on Calvinism and heavy taxes, and when Maurice resigned in disgust and returned to Holland in 1644 the settlers rose. After five years of ambushes, plantation burnings and massacres, the Brazilians pushed the Dutch back into an enclave around Recife. The Dutch poured in reinforcements by sea, but two climactic battles in 1648 and 1649 at **Guararapes**, just outside Recife, where the Dutch were routed and their military power broken, decided their fate. Although they held on to Recife until 1654 the dream of a Dutch empire in the Americas was over, and Portuguese control was not to be threatened again until the nineteenth century.

## The bandeirantes: gold and God

The expulsion of the Dutch demonstrated the toughness of the early Brazilians, which was also very evident in the penetration and settling of **the interior** during the seventeenth and eighteenth centuries. Every few months expeditions set out, following rumours of gold and looking for Indians to enslave. They carried an identifying banner, a *bandeira*, which gave the name **bandeirantes** to the adventurers; they became the Brazilian version of the Spanish *conquistadores*. São Paulo became the main *bandeirante* centre thanks to its position on the Rio Tietê, one of the few natural highways that flowed east–west into the deep interior.

The average *bandeira* would be made up of a mixed crew of people, reflecting the many – and often conflicting – motives underlying the expedition. None travelled without a priest or two (*bandeirantes* may have been cut-throats, but they were devout Catholic cut-throats); Jesuits and Franciscans – in their drive to found missions and baptize the heathen – backed many *bandeiras*. The majority combined exploration with plundering and could last for years, with occasional stops to plant and harvest crops, before returning to São Paulo – if they ever did: many towns on the Planalto Central or Mato Grosso have their origins in the remnants of a *bandeira*.

The journeys *bandeiras* made were often epic in scale, covering immense distances and overcoming natural obstacles as formidable as the many hostile Indian tribes they encountered. It was the *bandeirantes* who pushed the borders of Brazil far inland, and also supplied the geographical knowledge that now began to fill in the blanks on the maps. But the most important way they shaped the future of Brazil was by locating the Holy Grail of the New World: gold.

*Bandeirantes* first found **gold** in 1695, at the spot that is now Sabará, in Minas Gerais. As towns sprang up around further gold strikes in Minas, gold was also discovered around Cuiabá, in Mato Grosso, adding fresh impetus to the opening-up of the interior. The 3500-kilometre journey to Cuiabá, down five separate river systems, took six months at the best of times; from São Paulo it was easier to travel to Europe. Along the way the *bandeirantes* had to fight off the Paiaguá Indians, who attacked in canoes and were excellent swimmers, and then the Guaicuru, who had taken to the horse with the same enthusiasm the Plains Indians of North America were later to show. They annihilated entire *bandeiras*; others following observed "rotting belongings and dead bodies on the riverbanks, and hammocks slung with their owners in them, dead. Not a single person reached Cuiabá that year."

But the *paulista* hunger for riches was equal even to these appalling difficulties. By the mid-eighteenth century, the flow of gold from Brazil was keeping the Portuguese Crown afloat, temporarily halting its long slide down the league table of European powers. In Brazil the rush of migrants to the gold areas changed the regional balance, as the new interior communities drew population away from the northeast. The gateways to the interior, Rio de Janeiro and São Paulo, grew rapidly. The shift was recognized in 1763, when the capital was transferred to Rio from Salvador, and what was then a filthy, disease-ridden port began its slow transformation into one of the great cities of the world.

## The Jesuits

Apart from the *bandeirantes*, the most important agents of the colonization of the interior were the **Jesuits**. The first Jesuit missionaries arrived in Brazil in 1549 and, thanks to the influence they held over successive Portuguese kings, they acquired power in Brazil second only to that of the Crown itself. In Salvador they built the largest Jesuit college outside Rome, and set in motion a crusade to convert the Indian population. The usual method was to congregate the Indians in **missions**, where they worked under the supervision of Jesuit fathers. From 1600 onwards, dozens of missions were founded in the interior, especially in the Amazon and in the grasslands of the southeast.

The role the Jesuits played in the conversion of the Indians was ambiguous. Mission Indians were often released by Jesuits to work for settlers, where they died like flies, and the missionaries' intrepid penetration of remote areas resulted in the spread of diseases that wiped out entire tribes. Yet many Jesuits distinguished themselves in protecting Indians against the settlers, a theological as well as a secular struggle, for many Portuguese argued the native population had no souls and could therefore be treated like animals.

The most remarkable defender of the Indians was **Antônio Vieira**, who abandoned his privileged position as chief adviser to the king in Lisbon to become a missionary in Brazil in 1653. Basing himself in São Luís, he struggled to implement the more enlightened Indian laws that his influence over João IV had secured, to the disgust of settlers clamouring for slaves. Vieira denied them for years, preaching a series of sermons along the way that became famous throughout Europe, as well as Brazil. He didn't mince his words: "An Indian will be your slave for the few days he lives, but your soul will be enslaved for as long as God is God. All of you are in mortal sin, all of you live in a state of condemnation, and all of you are going directly to Hell!" he thundered to settlers from the pulpit in 1654. So high did feelings run that in 1661 settlers forced Vieira onto a ship bound for Portugal, standing in the surf and shouting "Out! Out!"

But Vieira returned, with renewed support from the Crown, and Jesuit power in Brazil grew. It reached a peak in the remarkable theocracy of the **Guaraní missions**, where Spanish and Portuguese Jesuits founded over a dozen missions on the pampas along the Uruguayan border. Left alone for fifty years they effectively became a Jesuit state, until the Treaty of Madrid in 1752 divided up the land between Spain and Portugal; the treaty ordered the missions abandoned so settlers could move in. The Guaraní rebelled immediately. The Jesuit hierarchy made half-hearted efforts to get them to move but most of the priests stayed with their Guaraní flocks. Resistance was heroic but hopeless: the superior fire-power of a joint Spanish–Portuguese military expedition decimated both Guaraní and Jesuits in 1756.

Jesuit involvement in the Guaraní war lent added force to the long-standing settler demands to expel them from the colony. The rise to power of the **Marquês de Pombal**, who became the power behind the Portuguese throne for much of the eighteenth century, helped them; he seized upon the Guaraní wars as an excuse to expel the Order from Brazil in 1760. The Jesuits may have been imperfect protectors but from this time on the Indians were denied even that.

## Independence

Brazil – uniquely among South American countries – achieved a peaceful transition to independence, although the odds seemed against it at one point. Brazilian resentment at exclusion from government and at the Portuguese monopoly of foreign trade grew steadily during the eighteenth century. It culminated in 1789 with the **Inconfidência Mineira**, a plot hatched by twelve prominent citizens of Ouro Preto to proclaim Brazilian independence. But the rebels were betrayed before they started; their leader, **Tiradentes**, was executed and the rest exiled. Then, just as the tension seemed to be becoming dangerous, events in Europe took a hand in shaping Brazil's future.

In 1807 **Napoleon** invaded Portugal. With the French army poised to take Lisbon, the British navy hurriedly evacuated **King João VI** to Rio, which was declared the temporary capital of the Portuguese Empire and seat of the government-in-exile. While **Wellington** set about driving the French from Portugal, the British were able to force the opening-up of Brazil's ports to non-Portuguese shipping, and the economic growth that followed reinforced Brazil's increasing self-confidence. João was entranced by his tropical kingdom, unable to pull himself away even after Napoleon's defeat. Finally, in 1821, he was faced with a liberal revolt in Portugal and was unable to delay his return any longer. In April 1822 he appointed his son, **Dom Pedro**, as prince regent and governor of Brazil; when he sailed home his last words to his son were, "Get your hands on this kingdom before some adventurer does."

Pedro, young and headstrong, grew increasingly irritated by the strident demands of the Cortês, the Portuguese parliament, that he return home to his father and allow Brazil to be ruled from Portugal once again. On September 7, 1822, Pedro was out riding on the plain of Ypiranga, near São Paulo. Buttoning himself up after an attack of diarrhoea, he was surprised by a messenger with a bundle of letters from Lisbon. Reading the usual demands for him to return his patience snapped, and he declared Brazil independent with the cry "Independence or death!" With overwhelming popular support he had himself crowned **Dom Pedro I**, Emperor of Brazil, on December 1, 1822. The Portuguese, preoccupied by political crises at home, put up little resistance. Apart from an ugly massacre of Brazilian patriots in Fortaleza, and some fighting in Bahia and Belém, the Portuguese withdrawal was peaceful and by the end of 1823 none of its forces remained.

## Early empire: revolt in the regions

The early decades of independence proved much more difficult than the break with Portugal. Dom Pedro became increasingly estranged from his subjects, devoting more attention to scandalous romances than affairs of state. In April 1831 he abdicated in a fit of petulance and returned to Portugal. His son and heir, **Dom Pedro II**, would later prove an enlightened ruler but, as he was only five at the time, his capacity to influence events was limited. With a power vacuum at the centre of the political system, tensions in the provinces erupted into revolt.

There were common threads in all the **rebellions** in the provinces: slaves rebelling against masters, Indian and mixed-race resentment of white domination, Brazilians settling scores with Portuguese and the poor rising against the rich. The first and most serious conflagration was the **Cabanagem Rebellion** in Pará, where a mass revolt of the dispossessed began in 1835. The rebels took Belém, killing the governor of Pará and many of the town's elite; the uprising spread through the Amazon like wildfire and took a decade to put down. A parallel revolt, the **Balaiada**, began in Maranhão in 1838. Here the rebels took Caxias, the second city of the state, and held out for three years against the army. Similar risings in Pernambuco, Bahia and Rio Grande do Sul punctuated the 1830s and 1840s; the disruption was immense, with large areas ravaged by fighting that threatened to tear the country apart.

The crisis led to Dom Pedro II being declared emperor four years early, in 1840, when he was only fourteen. He was a sensible, scholarly man, completely unlike his father. His instincts were conservative, but he also had a modernizing streak and was respected even by republicans. With government authority restored, the provincial rebellions had by 1850 either blown themselves out or been put down. With **coffee** beginning to be planted on a large scale in Rio, São Paulo and Minas, and the flow of European immigrants rising from a trickle to a flood, the economy of southern Brazil began to take off in earnest.



## The War of the Triple Alliance

With the rebellions in the provinces, the **army** became increasingly important in Brazilian political life. Pedro insisted it stay out of domestic politics but his policy of diverting the generals by allowing adventures abroad ultimately led to the disaster of the war with Paraguay (1864–70). Although Brazil emerged victorious, it was at dreadful cost. The **War of the Triple Alliance** is one of history's forgotten conflicts, but it was the bloodiest war in South American history, with a casualty list almost as long as that of the American Civil War: Brazil alone suffered over 100,000 casualties.

It pitted in unequal struggle the landlocked republic of Paraguay, under the dictator **Francisco Lopez**, against the combined forces of Brazil, Argentina and Uruguay. Although the Paraguayans started the war by invading Mato Grosso in 1864, Brazil had sorely provoked them. The generals in Rio, with no more rebels to fight within Brazil, wanted to incorporate Uruguay into the empire; Paraguay saw Brazil blocking its access to the sea and invaded to pre-empt a Brazilian takeover, dragging Argentina reluctantly into the conflict through a mutual defence pact with Brazil.

The Brazilian army and navy were confident of victory as the Paraguayans were heavily outnumbered and outgunned. Yet the Paraguayans, for the first time, demonstrated the military prowess that would mark their history. Under the able leadership of Lopez the Paraguayan army proved disciplined and brave, always defeated by numbers but terribly mauling the opposition. It turned into a war of extermination and six bloody years were only ended when Lopez was killed in 1870; by this time the male adult population of Paraguay was reduced (by disease and starvation as well as war) to under twenty thousand, from over a million in 1864.

## The end of slavery

From the seventeenth to the nineteenth century around ten million Africans were transported to Brazil as **slaves** – ten times as many as were shipped to the United States – yet the death rate in Brazil was so great that in 1860 Brazil's slave population was half the size of that in the US. Slavery was always contested. Slaves fled from the cities and plantations to form refugee communities called *quilombos*; the largest, **Palmares**, in the interior of the northeastern state of Alagoas, was several thousand strong and stayed independent for almost a century.

But it was not until the nineteenth century that slavery was seriously challenged. The initial impetus came from Britain, where the abolitionist movement became influential just when Portugal was most dependent on British capital and naval protection. Large landowners in Brazil regarded abolition with horror, and a combination of racism and fear of economic dislocation led to a determined rearguard action to preserve slavery. A complicated diplomatic waltz began between Britain and Brazil, as slavery laws were tinkered with *para inglês ver* – "for the English to see" – a phrase that survives in Portuguese to this day, meaning to do something merely for show. The object was to make the British believe slavery would soon be abolished, while ensuring the letter of the law kept it legal.

British abolitionists were not deceived, and from 1832 to 1854 the Royal Navy maintained a squadron off Brazil, intercepting and confiscating slave ships, and occasionally entering Brazilian ports to seize slavers and burn their ships – one of history's more positive examples of gunboat diplomacy. The slave trade was finally **abolished** in 1854 but slavery itself remained legal. British power had its limits and ultimately it was a passionate campaign within Brazil itself, led by the fiery lawyer **Joaquim Nabuco**, that finished slavery off. The growing liberal movement, increasingly republican and anti-monarchist, squared off against the landowners, with Dom Pedro hovering indecisively somewhere in-between. Slavery became the dominant issue in Brazilian politics for twenty years. By the time full **emancipation** came, in the "Golden Law" of May 13, 1888, Brazil had achieved the shameful distinction of being the last country in the Americas to abolish slavery.



## From empire to republic

The end of slavery was also the death knell of the monarchy. Since the 1870s the intelligentsia, deeply influenced by French liberalism, had turned against the emperor and agitated for a republic. By the 1880s they had been joined by the officer corps, who blamed Dom Pedro for lack of backing during the Paraguayan war. When the large landowners withdrew their support, furious that the emperor had not prevented emancipation, the **monarchy collapsed** very suddenly in 1889.

Once again, Brazil managed a bloodless transition. The push came from the army, detachments led by **Deodoro da Fonseca** meeting no resistance when they occupied Rio on November 15, 1889. They invited the royal family to remain, but Dom Pedro insisted on exile, boarding a ship to France where he died two years later. Deodoro, meanwhile, began a Brazilian tradition of hamfisted military autocracy. Ignoring the clamour for a liberal republic he declared himself dictator in 1891, but was forced to resign three weeks later when even the army refused to support him. His deputy, **Floriano de Peixoto**, took over, but proved even more incompetent; Rio was actually shelled in 1893 by rebellious warships demanding his resignation. Finally, in 1894, popular pressure led to Peixoto stepping down in favour of the first elected civilian president, **Prudente de Morais**.

## Coffee with milk – and sugar

The years from 1890 to 1930 were politically undistinguished but saw large-scale **immigration** from Europe and Japan rapidly transform Brazil. They were decades of swift growth and swelling cities, which saw a very Brazilian combination of a boom-bust-boom economy and corrupt pork-barrel politics.

**Coffee** and **rubber**, at opposite ends of the country, led the boom. They had very different labour forces. Millions of *nordestinos* moved into the Amazon to tap rubber, but the coffee workers swarming into São Paulo in their hundreds of thousands came chiefly from Italy. Between 1890 and 1930 over four million migrants arrived from Europe and another two hundred thousand from Japan. Most went to work on the coffee estates of southern Brazil, but enough remained to turn São Paulo into the fastest-growing city in the Americas. Urban industrialization appeared in Brazil for the first time, taking root in São Paulo to supply the voracious markets of the young cities springing up in the *paulista* interior. By 1930 São Paulo had displaced Rio as the leading industrial centre.

More improbable was the transformation of **Manaus** into the largest city of the Amazon. Rubber turned it from a muddy village into a rich trading city within a couple of decades. The peak of the **rubber boom**, from the 1870s to the outbreak of World War I, financed its metamorphosis into a tropical *belle époque* outpost, complete with opera house. Rubber exports were second only to coffee, but proved much more vulnerable to competition. Seeds smuggled out of Amazônia by Victorian adventurer Henry Wickham in 1876 ended up in Sri Lanka and Malaysia, and the resulting plantation-rubber pushed wild Amazon rubber out of world markets. The region returned to an isolation it maintained until the late 1960s.

Political development did not accompany economic growth. Although not all the early presidents were incompetent – **Rodrigues Alves** (1902–06), for example, rebuilt Rio complete with a public-health system, finally eradicating the epidemics that had stunted its growth – the majority were corrupt political bosses relying on a network of patron–client relationships, whose main ambition was to bleed the public coffers dry. Power was concentrated in the two most populous states of São Paulo and Minas Gerais, which struck a convenient deal to alternate the presidency between them.

This way of ensuring both sets of snouts could slurp away in the trough uninterrupted was called "**café com leite**" by its opponents: coffee from São Paulo and milk from the *mineiro* dairy herds. In fact, it was coffee with milk and sugar: the developing national habit of the sweet *cafézinho* in the burgeoning cities of the south provided a new domestic market for sugar, which ensured support from the plantation oligarchs of the Northeast. In a pattern that would repeat itself in more modern times, the economy forged ahead while politics went backwards. The saying "Brazil grows in the dark, while politicians sleep" made its first appearance around this time.

## The revolution of 1930

The revolution of 1930 that brought the populist **Getúlio Vargas** to power was a critical event. Vargas dominated Brazilian politics for the next quarter-century, and these years were a time of radical change, marking a decisive break with the past. Vargas had much in common with his Argentinian contemporary, Juan Perón: both were charismatic but also cunning and ruthless, and created new power bases in their countries rooted in the urban working class.

It was the **working class**, combined with disillusion in the junior ranks of the military, that swept Vargas to power. Younger officers, accustomed to seeing the armed forces as the guardian of the national conscience, were disgusted by the corruption of the military hierarchy. When the **Great Depression** hit, the government spent millions protecting coffee growers by buying crops at a guaranteed price; the coffee was then burnt, as the export market had collapsed. Workers in the cities and countryside were appalled, seeing themselves frozen out while vast sums were spent on landowners, and as the economic outlook worsened the pressure started building up from other states to end the São Paulo and Minas grip on power. This time the transition was violent.

In 1926, **Washington Luís** was made president without a proper election, as the elite contrived an unopposed nomination. When Luis appeared set to do the same thing in 1930, an unstoppable **mass revolution** developed, first in Vargas's home state of Rio Grande do Sul, then in Rio, then in the northeast. There was some resistance in São Paulo but the worst fighting was in the Northeast, where street battles left scores dead. The shock troops of the revolution were the young army officers who led their units against the *ancien régime* in Minas and Rio, and the gaúcho cavalry who accompanied Vargas on his triumphant procession to Rio. Although São Paulo rose briefly against Vargas in 1932 the revolt was swiftly crushed and Getúlio, as Brazilians affectionately knew him, embarked on the longest and most spectacular political career in modern Brazilian history.

## Vargas and the Estado Novo

It was not just Vargas who took power in 1930, but a new generation of young, energetic administrators who set about transforming the economy and the political system. Vargas played the nationalist card with great success, nationalizing the oil, electricity and steel industries, and setting up a health and social welfare system that earned him unwavering working-class support even after his death. Vargas's very Latin-American style of top-down, state-led development influences Brazilian politics to this day.

Reforms this fundamental could not be carried out under the old constitutional framework. Vargas simplified things by declaring himself **dictator** in 1937 and imprisoning political opponents – most of whom were in the trade union movement, the Communist Party or the *Integralistas*, the Brazilian Fascists. He called his regime the "New State", the **Estado Novo**, and certainly its reforming energy was something new. Although he cracked down hard on dissent Vargas was never a totalitarian dictator. He was highly popular and his political talents enabled him to outflank most opponents.

The result was both political and economic success. The ruinous coffee subsidy was abolished, industry encouraged and agriculture diversified; by 1945 São Paulo had become the largest industrial centre in South America. With the federal government increasing its powers at the expense of the states, power in the regions was wrested out of the hands of the oligarchs for the first time.

It took **World War II** to bring Vargas down. At first Brazil stayed neutral, reaping the benefits of increased exports, but when the United States offered massive aid in return for bases and Brazilian entry into the war, Vargas joined the Allies. Outraged by German submarine attacks on Brazilian shipping, Brazil was the only country in South America to play an active part in the war. A **Brazilian Expeditionary Force** fought in Italy from 1944. When it returned, the military High Command was able to exploit the renewed prestige of the army, forcing Vargas to stand down. They argued the armed forces could hardly fight for democracy abroad and return home to a dictatorship, and, in any case, after fifteen years a leadership change was overdue. In the election that followed in 1945 Vargas grudgingly endorsed army general **Eurico Dutra**, who duly won – but Getúlio, brooding on his ranch, was not yet finished with the presidency.

## The death of Vargas

Dutra proved a colourless figure, and when Vargas ran for the presidency in 1950 he won a crushing victory, the old dictator "returning on the arm of the people", as he wrote later. But he had powerful enemies in the armed forces and on the right, and his second stint in power was turbulent. Dutra had allowed inflation to climb, and Vargas proposed to raise the minimum wage and increase taxation of the middle classes. In the charged climate of the Cold War, the right denounced this as veering towards communism, and vitriolic attacks on Vargas and his government were made in the press, notably by a slippery, ambitious Rio journalist named **Carlos Lacerda**.

Vargas's supporters reacted angrily and argument turned into crisis in 1954, when shots were fired at Lacerda, missing their target but killing an air-force officer guarding him. The attempt was traced to one of Vargas's bodyguards, and the press campaign rose to a crescendo. Finally, on August 25, 1954, the military High Command demanded his resignation. Vargas received the news calmly, went into his bedroom in the Palácio de Catete in Rio, and shot himself through the heart.

He left an emotional suicide note to the Brazilian people: "I choose this means to be with you always... I gave you my life; now I offer my death. Nothing remains. Serenely I take the first step on the road to eternity, as I leave life and enter history." When it was published, the initial stunned popular reaction gave way to fury and Vargas's supporters turned on the forces that had hounded him to death, burning the newspaper offices, driving the army back into barracks and forcing Lacerda to flee the country. Eighteen months of tension followed, as an interim government marked time until the next election.

## JK and Brasília

**Juscelino Kubitschek** – "JK" to Brazilians – was president from 1956 to 1961, and proved just the man to fix Brazil's attention on the future rather than the past. He combined energy and imagination with integrity and political skill, acquired in the hard school of Minas Gerais, one of the main nurseries of political talent in Brazil. Although the tensions in the political system were still there – constitutionalists in the armed forces had to stage a pre-emptive coup to allow him to take office – Kubitschek was able to serve out his full term. He left a permanent reminder of the most successful post-war presidency in the form of the country's **new capital**, Brasília, deep in the Planalto Central.

"Fifty years in five!" was his election slogan, and his economic programme lived up to its ambitious billing. His term saw a spurt in growth rates that was the platform for the "economic miracle" of the next decade; the economic boom led to wider prosperity and renewed national confidence. Kubitschek drew on both in the flight of inspired imagination that led to **the building of Brasília**.

It could so easily have been an expensive disaster: a purpose-built capital miles from anywhere, the personal brainchild of a president anxious to make his mark. But Kubitschek implanted the idea in the national imagination by portraying it as a renewed statement of faith in the interior, a symbol of national integration and a better future for all Brazilians, not just those in the South. He brought it off with great panache, bringing in the extravagantly talented **Lúcio Costa**, whose brief was to come up with a revolutionary city layout, and the great architect **Oscar Niemeyer** to design the buildings to go with it. Kubitschek spent almost every weekend on the huge building site that became the city, consulted on the smallest details, and had the satisfaction of handing over to his successor, **Jânio Quadros**, in the newly inaugurated capital.

## 1964: the road to military rule

At the time, the **military coup of 1964** was considered a temporary hiccup in Brazil's post-war democracy, but it lasted 21 years and left a very bitter taste. The first period of military rule saw the famous economic miracle, when the economy grew at an astonishing average annual rate of ten percent for a decade, only to come to a juddering halt after 1974, when oil price rises and the increasing burden of debt repayment pushed it off the rails. But most depressing was the effective end of democracy for over a decade, and a time – from 1969 to 1974 – when terror was used against opponents by military hardliners. Brazil, where the *desaparecidos* numbered a few hundred rather than the tens of thousands butchered in Argentina and Chile, was not the worst military regime on the continent. But it is difficult to overestimate the shock even limited repression caused. It was the first time Brazilians experienced systematic brutality by a government, and even in the years of economic success the military governments were loathed across the political spectrum.

The coup was years in the brewing. It had two root causes: a constitutional crisis and the deepening divides in Brazilian society. In the developed South relations between trade unions and employers went from bad to worse, as workers struggled to protect their wages against rising inflation. But it was in the Northeast that tension was greatest, as a result of the **Peasant Leagues** movement. Despite industrial modernization, the rural region was still stuck in a time-warped land-tenure system, moulded in the colonial period and in many ways unchanged since then. Peasants, under the charismatic leadership of **Francisco Julião** and the governor of Pernambuco, **Miguel Arrães**, began forming cooperatives and occupying estates to press their claim for agrarian reform; the estate owners cried communism and openly agitated for a military coup.

The crisis might still have been avoided by a more skilful president, but Kubitschek's immediate successors were not of his calibre. Quadros resigned after only six months, in August 1961, on the anniversary of Vargas's suicide. He apparently wanted popular reaction to sweep him back into office, but the masses stayed home and the vice-president, **João Goulart**, took over.

Goulart's accession was viewed with horror by the right. He had a reputation as a leftist firebrand, having been a minister of labour under Vargas, and his position was weakened by the fact that he had not succeeded by direct popular vote. As political infighting began to get out of control, with the country polarizing between left and right, Goulart decided to throw himself behind the trade unions and the Peasant Leagues; his nationalist rhetoric rang alarm bells in Washington and the army began to plot his downfall, with tacit American backing.

The coup was swift and bloodless. On March 31, 1964, troops from Minas Gerais moved on Rio; when the military commanders there refused to oppose them, the game was up for Goulart. After futile efforts to rally resistance in Rio Grande do Sul he fled into exile in Uruguay, and the first in a long line of generals, **Humberto Castelo Branco**, became president.

## Military rule

The military moved swiftly to dismantle democracy. Congress was dissolved, and those representatives not to military taste were removed. It then reconvened with only two parties, an official government and an official opposition ("The difference," ran a joke at the time, "is that one says 'Yes', and the other, 'Yes Sir!'"). All other parties were banned. The Peasant Leagues and trade unions were repressed, with many of their leaders tortured and imprisoned, and even prominent national politicians like Arrães were thrown into jail. The ferocity of the military took aback even those on the right who had agitated for a coup. Ironically, many of them were hoist with their own petard when they voiced criticism, and found themselves gagged by the same measures they had urged against the left. Even Lacerda was imprisoned.

The political climate worsened steadily during the 1960s. An **urban guerrilla campaign** took off in the cities – its most spectacular success was the kidnapping of the American ambassador in 1969, released unharmed in return for over a hundred political detainees – but it only served as an excuse for the hardliners to crack down even further. General **Emílio Garrastazú Médici**, leader of the hardliners, took over the presidency in 1969 and the worst period of military rule began. Torture became routine, censorship was strict and thousands were driven into exile; this dark chapter in Brazilian history lasted for five agonizing years, until Médici gave way to **Ernesto Geisel** in 1974. The scars Médici left behind him, literally and metaphorically, have still not completely healed.

## The economic miracle

Despite the cold winds blowing on the political front, the Brazilian economy forged ahead from the mid-1960s to 1974, the years of the **economic miracle** – and the combination of high growth and low inflation indeed seemed miraculous to later governments. The military welcomed foreign investment, and the large pool of cheap but skilled labour was irresistible. Investment poured in, both from Brazil and abroad, and the boom was the longest and largest in Brazilian history. Cities swelled, industry grew, and by the mid-1970s Brazil was the economic giant of South America; São Paulo state alone had a GNP higher than any South American country, a distinction it maintains to this day.

The problem was uneven development. Even miraculous growth rates could not provide enough jobs for the hordes migrating to the cities, and the squalid **favelas** expanded even faster than the economy. The problem was worst in the Northeast and the Amazon, where industry was less developed, and drought combined with land conflict to push the people of the interior into the cities. It was also the miracle years that saw the origins of the **debt crisis**, a millstone around the neck of the Brazilian economy in the 1980s and early 1990s.

After 1974 petrodollars were sloshing around the world banking system, thanks to oil price rises. Anxious to set this new capital to work, international banks and South American military regimes fell over themselves in their eagerness to organize deals. Brazil had a good credit rating – its wealth of natural resources and jailed labour leaders saw to that. The military needed money for a series of huge development projects central to its trickle-down economic policy, like the **Itaipú dam**, the **Carajás** mining projects in eastern Amazônia, and a **nuclear power programme**. By the end of the 1970s the debt was at $50 billion; by 1990 it had risen to $120 billion, and the interest payments were crippling the economy.

## Opening up the Amazon

Kubitschek, who built a dirt highway linking Brasília to Belém, took the first step towards opening up the vast interior of the **Amazon**. But things really got going in 1970, when Médici realized the Amazon could be used as a huge safety valve, releasing the pressure for agrarian reform in the Northeast. "Land without people for people without land!" became the slogan, and an ambitious programme of highway construction began that was to transform Amazônia. The main links were the **Transamazônica**, running west to the Peruvian border, the **Cuiabá–Santarém** highway into central Amazônia, and the **Cuiabá–Porto Velho/Rio Branco** highway, opening access to western Amazônia.

For the military, the Amazon was empty space, overdue for filling, and a national resource to be developed. They set up an elaborate network of tax breaks and incentives to encourage Brazilian and multinational firms to invest in the region, who also saw it as empty space and proceeded either to speculate with land or cut down forest to graze cattle. The one group that didn't perceive the Amazon this way was, naturally enough, the millions of people who already lived there. The immediate result was a spiralling land conflict, as ranchers, rubber tappers, Brazil-nut harvesters, gold-miners, smallholders, Indians, multinationals and Brazilian companies all tried to press their claims. The result was chaos.

By the 1980s the situation in the Amazon was becoming an international controversy, with the uncontrolled destruction of forest in huge annual burnings, and the invasion of Indian lands. Less internationally known was the **land crisis**, although a hundred people or more were dying in land conflicts in Amazônia every year. It took the assassination in 1988 of **Chico Mendes**, leader of the rubber-tappers' union and eloquent defender of the forest, to bring it home. (See "The Amazon: a guide to the issues", p.730.)



## Democracy returns: the abertura

Growing popular resentment of the military could not be contained indefinitely, especially when the economy turned sour. By the late 1970s debt, rising inflation and unemployment were turning the economy from a success story into a joke, and the military were further embarrassed by an unsavoury chain of corruption scandals. Geisel was the first military president to plan for a return to civilian rule, in a slow relaxing of the military grip called *abertura*, the "opening-up". Yet again Brazil managed a bloodless – albeit fiendishly complicated – transition. Slow though the process was, the return to democracy would have been delayed even longer had it not been for two events along the way: the **strikes** in São Paulo in 1977 and the mass **campaign for direct elections** in 1983–84.

The strikes – led by unions that were still illegal, and the charismatic young factory worker **Lula (Luís Inácio da Silva)** – began in the car industry and soon spread throughout the industrial belt of São Paulo, in a movement bearing many parallels with Solidarity in Poland. There was a tense stand-off between army and strikers, until the military realized having São Paulo on strike would be worse for the economy than conceding the right to free trade unions. This dramatic re-emergence of organized labour was a sign the military could not control the situation for much longer.

**Reforms** in the early 1980s lifted censorship, brought the exiles home and allowed normal political life to resume. But the military came up with an ingenious attempt to determine the succession: their control of Congress allowed them to pass a resolution that the president due to take office in 1985 would be elected not by direct vote, but by an electoral college made up of congressmen and senators, where the military party had the advantage.

The democratic opposition responded with a counter-amendment proposing a direct election. It needed a two-thirds majority in Congress to be passed, and a campaign began for **diretas-já**, "direct elections now". Even the opposition was surprised by the response, as the Brazilian people, thoroughly sick of the generals, took to the streets in their millions. The campaign culminated in huge rallies of over a million people in Rio and São Paulo, and opinion polls showed over ninety percent in favour; but when the vote came in March 1984 the amendment just failed. The military still nominated a third of Senate seats, and this proved decisive.

It looked like defeat; in fact it turned into victory. The moment found the man in **Tancredo Neves**, ex-minister of justice under Vargas, ex-prime minister, and a wise old *mineiro* fox respected across the political spectrum, who put himself forward as opposition candidate in the electoral college. By now it was clear what the public wanted, and Tancredo's unrivalled political skills enabled him to stitch together an alliance that included dissidents from the military's own party. In January 1985 he romped home in the electoral college, to great national rejoicing, and military rule came to an end. Tancredo proclaimed the civilian **Nova República** – the "New Republic".

## The New Republic: crisis and corruption

Tragically, the New Republic was orphaned at birth. The night before his inauguration Tancredo was rushed to hospital for an emergency operation on a bleeding stomach tumour; it proved benign, but in hospital he picked up an infection and six weeks later died of septicaemia. His funeral was the largest mass event in Brazilian history; a crowd of two million followed his coffin from the hospital where he had died in São Paulo to Guarulhos airport. The vice-president, **José Sarney**, a second-league politician from Maranhão who had been fobbed off with a ceremonial post, suddenly found himself serving a full presidential term.

His administration was disastrous, though not all of it was his own fault: he was saddled with a ministerial team he had not chosen, and a newly powerful Congress that would have given any president a rough ride. But Sarney made matters worse by a lack of decisiveness, and wasn't helped by the sleaze that hung like a fog around his government, with **corruption** institutionalized on a massive scale. No progress was made on the economic front either. By 1990 inflation accelerated into **hyperinflation** proper, and, despite spending almost $40 billion repaying interest on the foreign debt, the principal had swollen to $120 billion. The high hopes of 1985 had evaporated – Sarney had brought the whole notion of civilian politics into disrepute and achieved the near-impossible: making the military look good.

## Collor and Franco: marking time

Despite everything, Brazil still managed to begin the next decade on a hopeful note, with the inauguration in 1990 of **Fernando Collor de Melo**, the first properly elected president for thirty years, after a heated but peaceful campaign had managed to consolidate democracy at a difficult economic moment.

The campaign had passed the torch to a new generation of Brazilians, as the young Collor, playboy scion of one of Brazil's oldest and richest families, had squared off against **Lula**, who had come a long way since the São Paulo strikes. Now a respected – and feared – national politician, head of the Workers' Party that the strike movement had evolved into, Lula took most of the cities but Collor's conservative rural support was enough to secure a narrow victory.

His presidency began promisingly enough, as he pushed for a long-overdue opening-up of the economy and implemented the most draconian currency stabilization plan yet, the infamous **Plano Collor**, hated by the middle classes because it temporarily froze their bank accounts. But the economy resisted all attempts at surgery and inflation began to climb again. The only bright spot was the ending of the debt crisis by an American-led restructuring. Collor became even more unstable than the economy; he was increasingly erratic in public and rumours grew about dark goings-on behind the scenes. Thanks to fine journalism and a denunciation by Collor's own brother (apparently angry that Fernando had made a pass at his wife) it became clear a web of **corrupt dealings** masterminded by Collor's campaign treasurer, **P.C. Farias**, had set up what was effectively a parallel government. Billions of dollars had been skimmed from the government's coffers in a scam breathtaking even by Brazilian standards.

**Impeachment** proceedings were begun in Congress but few politicians expected them to get anywhere. But then demonstrations began to take off in the big cities, led initially by students but soon spreading to the rest of the population. It rapidly became clear that if Congress did not vote impeachment through, there would be hell to pay. In September 1992 Collor was duly impeached and **Itamar Franco**, the vice-president, replaced him. Farias was jailed, dying later in mysterious circumstances – he was allegedly murdered by a girlfriend who then committed suicide but the full story of his death will never be known. Collor, who probably knows more than most about the murder, is still active in politics. Corruption charges failed and his continued liberty is eloquent testimony to the weakness of the Brazilian legal system.

Franco, like Sarney before him, proved a buffoon left minding the shop. The real power in his government was the finance minister, **Fernando Henrique Cardoso**, who staked his claim to the succession by implementing the **Plano Real** in 1994. This finally tamed inflation and stabilized the economy, for the first time in twenty years. A grateful public duly gave him an overwhelming first-round victory against Lula in the presidential election later that year.

## Cardoso: stability and reform

Cardoso, a donnish ex-academic from São Paulo universally known by his initials, FHC, proved able and effective. Ironically, before he became a politician he was one of the world's most respected left-wing theorists of economic development. His political career, however, moved along a different track, as his government opened up the Brazilian economy and pushed through important **political reforms**.

Cardoso entered office with a clear vision of Brazil's economic and political problems and how to cure them. On the economic front he built on the Plano Real by pushing through a privatization programme in the teeth of fierce nationalist opposition, cutting tariff barriers, opening up the economy to competition and making Brazil the dominant member of **Mercosul**, a regional trade organization that includes Argentina, Uruguay and Paraguay. During his first term the result was healthy growth, falling unemployment and low inflation, an achievement without precedent in modern Brazilian history. Politically, he steered a skilful middle course between dinosaurs of right and left, corrupt *caudilhos* and their patron–client politics on the one hand, and time-warped nationalists still clinging to protectionism and suspicious of the outside world on the other. In a steady if unspectacular process, a series of constitutional amendments was passed reducing the role of the state and reforming the political system.

The stabilization of the economy Cardoso achieved was not forgotten by the poor, who were the most affected by hyperinflation; he was **re-elected** in 1998, again beating Lula, and providing a much-needed period of stability at the top. His second term proved more difficult, however. The Asian financial collapse of 1998 brought down much of Latin America with it, including Brazil. Yet despite devaluations of the *real*, foreign investment kept coming and inflation remained low, an important break with earlier economic patterns, and a sign that at least some of Cardoso's reforms were working. Aerospace, telecommunications and agriculture grew to become internationally competitive, and good administration in health and education led to significant improvements in life expectancy, literacy and child mortality.

Cardoso's legacy was not all roses, however. Corruption, social inequality and regional imbalances still plagued Brazil. Cardoso's reliance on a broad centrist coalition limited his ability to deal with rural inequalities or really get to grips with environmental issues.

## Lula: left turn?

Historic is an over-used word, but there was no question it was the only one to describe the **2002 election of Lula** to the presidency of Brazil, at the fourth attempt. The outcome represented the final consolidation and maturing of Brazilian democracy, as the generation that had been tear-gassed by the military and opted for armed struggle suited up and became ministers (there were four ex-guerrilla ministers in Lula's first government, and its dominant figure, **José Dirceu**, had plastic surgery in Cuba and lived underground for five years). **Lula** himself is a truly historic figure – the first Brazilian president not to be a member of the country's elite.

Born in desperate poverty in the Pernambuco *sertão*, like millions of North-easterners he made the journey as a child to São Paulo on the back of a truck. He worked as a shoeshine boy before becoming a factory worker at a car plant, eventually rising to leadership of the strike movement in the early 1980s and founding the PT (Partido dos Trabalhadores, or Workers' Party), which allied the union movement to the liberal middle class. With FHC's retirement no other Brazilian politician was able to match Lula's charisma. The PT, learning from earlier defeats, moderated its policies to bring it closer to the centre, where Brazilian elections are won.

Lula proved adept at keeping his party happy with tub-thumping rhetoric and playing up his image as a reformist on the international conference circuit, but in fact his first government bore a distinct resemblance to that of his predecessor. **Antonio Palocci**, a quiet but competent finance minister, kept the economy open and inflation down – which was just as well, since politically the government rapidly ran into deep trouble.

## Corruption again

Lula had been elected in large part because the Brazilian electorate believed his PT was, uniquely among Brazilian political parties, largely untouched by corruption. They were rapidly disabused. From 2004 Brazilian journalism yet again proved itself the healthiest part of the body politic by revealing a series of large-scale scams and rackets commanded by Lula's political enforcer, **José Dirceu**. Although it was clear Lula was at least aware of what was happening, he managed to avoid impeachment by firing Dirceu and convincing the opposition, by now fancying its chances in the 2006 election, that the national interest would be best served by having the government finish its term.

Lula won the election as Brazilians, who have low expectations of their politicans, drew a distinction between him and his shady ministers and credited Lula for the increasing economic prosperity and stability of his first term. Lula has presided over higher economic growth, combined with a continuing reduction of income inequality and improvement in social indicators – most famously in a programme called **Bolsa Família**, the family grant, where poor families receive cash payments in return for keeping children in school, getting them vaccinated, and so forth. It has proven extremely effective and become a model for many parts of the developing world. Economically and socially

Brazil is on the right track. A series of major **oil discoveries** in the seas off Rio was the icing on the cake, with Brazil becoming self-sufficient in oil in 2006 and set to replace Venezuela before too long as South America's biggest oil producer.

## Looking ahead

The **financial crisis of 2008** in some ways showed how far Brazil has come in recent years. While it would have led to instant economic collapse prior to the second FHC government, Brazil came through the first phase of the crisis well and has large currency reserves, a well-regulated banking sector and an economy driven more by the domestic market than exports to help it weather the storm. But there are still problems.

Short term, there is the uncertainty of **Lula's succession**. No Brazilian politician matches his charisma or has anything like his record, and although Lula is pushing his lieutenant **Djilma Roussef** to be Brazil's first female president, his endorsement alone may not be enough against powerful challenges including that of her most formidable rival, **Aécio Neves**, grandson of Tancredo, the founder of the New Republic. Either way Lula's going will mark the end of an era, as the last of the leading figures of the opposition to the dictatorship leaves the stage and a new generation takes over.

Longer term, **structural problems** continue to plague Brazil. As it becomes in many ways a more modern and successful country, the dysfunctional nature of its politics is increasingly a drag on its development. **Corruption** is institutionalized, reinforced by a legal system incapable of jailing even the most blatantly thieving politician. The public finances remain perennially in deficit because of a bloated pensions system extraordinarily resistant to reform (among those who benefit from it most directly are politicians and judges). The legal system – equally resistant to reform – is weak and underlies the frightening level of **violence in Brazilian society**, since those using it know they will almost certainly not be brought to book. Brazil's rise as an oil power may even make all this worse rather than better.

Brazil has been lucky that a succession of competent presidents and finance ministers has managed to insulate the economy from the worst effects of political mismanagement, but this may not last forever. Brazil's dysfunctional politics and incompetent political class stands in sharp contrast to the dynamism and self-confidence of Brazilian culture and parts of its economy. Brazil often gets a bad press abroad, but burning rainforests and urban drug wars are only part of the country's story. Now a stable and consolidated democracy, Brazil has grown and matured as many of its neighbours have gone backwards, limping from crisis to crisis. Few developing countries are better placed to benefit from globalization.

All the same, a national report-card would read "Could do better". Brazil is best compared with other large, populous countries like India and China, but its growth rates are mediocre in comparison, despite Brazil having much greater natural resources than either. With a decent political system and functioning courts, Brazil might already be a developed country rather than somewhere that has made enough progress to lie somewhere between the First and the Third worlds. Economic success, and thus continued progress on reducing inequality, depends upon ending the **culture of impunity** that has allowed Brazilian politicians to get away with so much for so long. But at least in the short term there is no prospect of the serious political and legal reforms that would entail.

# The Amazon: a guide to the issues

The Amazon rainforest is the largest and most biodiverse tropical forest on Earth. It is culturally diverse too: home to over 300,000 Indians, some still isolated, speaking over two hundred languages. Many Brazilians react with outrage at being lectured on the preservation of the Amazon and the protection of native peoples by North Americans and Europeans. Justifiable as Brazilian accusations of hypocrisy may be, they cannot hide the fact that there is a real environmental crisis in the Amazon. It has increasingly high visibility as an issue inside Brazil as well as abroad, and as climate change moves up political agendas in Brazil as elsewhere, there is now real momentum for reform – and some grounds for hope.

## Amazon ecology

The Amazon contains one fifth of the world's fresh water, sustaining the world's largest rainforest – over six million square kilometres – which in turn supports millions of animal and plant species, many of them still unknown. At the heart of the forest, the Amazon River is a staggering 6500km from source to mouth. About seventeen percent of the Brazilian Amazon has been deforested, mostly in the last thirty years, and at least as much again has been affected by selective cutting of trees and other environmental stresses, like over-hunting. With global warming promising to increase drought and hence susceptibility to fire, over the course of this century there is real long-term danger to the integrity of this extraordinary complex of ecosystems.

## Lands and rivers

The Amazon is generally thought of as flat, steamy, equatorial forest. This is misleading – it has mountains, parts of it suffer droughts, and by no means all of it is jungle. Around 25 percent of the Amazon is actually savanna, known in Brazil as **cerrado**, and concentrated in a vertical band through the central Amazon from Roraima to southern Mato Grosso, where soil and rain conditions are markedly dry. Between five and ten percent of the Amazon, depending on the time of year, is **várzea** (flood plain), a zone of marshes, lakes, wetlands and annually flooded forest (*igapó*) that is the most varied and among the most biodiverse of the Amazon's ecosystems; it's also one of the most threatened, since for historical reasons all of the Amazon's larger cities and most of its human population are concentrated on the flood plain. But the bulk of Amazonian forests are **terra firme** (upland) that never flood; upland forest topography is typically made up of gentle hills and occasional steep escarpments. The Amazon also has a long **coastline**, where mangroves alternate with sand dunes, and the largest and most ecologically complex river estuary in the world.

**Amazonian rivers** are equally varied. There are three main river types, classified by the nature of the area they drain. The Amazon itself is a deep brown river, the sediments scoured from the Andes giving it the colour of milky tea or coffee; other rivers of this type include the Madeira, Juruá and Purus. **Blackwater** rivers drain granite uplands with few sediments, and are stained black by chemicals released by decomposing vegetation; they are much poorer in nutrients and have much less aquatic biodiversity as a result, but have the side-benefit of being blessedly free of insects in general. Rivers of this type in the Amazon include, as the name suggests, the Rio Negro, but many other smaller rivers, like the Arapiuns near Santarém. The third type of river drains areas between these two extremes and is the most beautiful of all, with a blueish-green colour; the Tapajós is the largest river of this type.

## Flora and fauna

The most distinctive attribute of the Amazon basin is the overwhelming abundance of plant and animal species. Over six thousand species of plant have been reported from one square kilometre tract of forest, and there are close to a thousand species of bird (the Amazon contains one in five of all the birds in the world) spread about the forest. The rainforest has enormous structural diversity, with layers of vegetation from the forest floor to the canopy 30m above providing a vast number of habitats. With the rainforest being more stable over longer periods of time than temperate areas (there was no Ice Age here, nor any prolonged period of drought), the fauna has also had freedom to evolve, and to adapt to often very specialized local conditions. This is the foundation of the Amazon's biodiversity.

Most of the **trees** found in the Amazon floodplain are tropical palms, scattered between which are the various species of larger, emergent trees. Those plants which are found growing on the forest floor are mostly tree **saplings**, **herbs** (frequently with medicinal applications) and **woody shrubs**. The best-known of all Amazon trees are concentrated on the upland *terra firme*, which never floods; here can be found the **rubber tree** (*Hevea brasiliensis*), known as *seringueira* in Brazil and the **Brazil nut tree** (*Bertholletia excelsa*), which grows to 30m and takes over ten years to reach nut-bearing maturity; once this is reached, a single specimen can produce over 450kg of nuts every year.

## The endangered forest

Advances in satellite imagery over the last twenty years have radically improved our knowledge of what is actually happening in the Amazon, how far deforestation has gone and what the trends are over time. So far, about seventeen percent of the Brazilian Amazon has been deforested. About the same amount has suffered some fragmentation of forest cover. The amount deforested varies from year to year because of a number of factors, especially climate. In El Niño years, such as 1998, the Amazon is much drier than usual, fires start more easily, and deforestation is greater. Thus many models of climate change over the next few decades, which suggest longer dry seasons and a drier forest in many parts of the Amazon, are a cause for concern. What matters is not a deforestation spike in one year or another, but general trends over time. These show deforestation increased alarmingly in the 1970s and 1980s, fell back in the 1990s, and then rose again in the early twenty-first century. Much deforested land is abandoned and re-grows over time; although it usually does not return to the level of ecological complexity it had, deforested land can re-acquire some of its biodiversity value.

In other words, all is not lost; the bulk of the Amazon is intact, and even the damaged areas need not be written off. The other thing to remember is that the frontier period of Amazonian development is largely over. The Amazon's population is stable, and rapidly urbanizing; almost seventy percent of the Amazon's population lives in cities. There are no longer waves of migrants flooding to the region, or a growing rural population putting pressure on the forest. Policy makers and Amazonians themselves are realizing it makes more sense to concentrate development efforts into degraded areas, where there are already roads and people living, intensifying development instead of extending it. This is unfortunate for the environmental integrity of the 25 percent or so of the Amazon in this position, but it offers the real prospect that pressure on the remaining 75 percent will diminish.

Forest clearance generally follows **road building**. When a road reached into new territories in the glory days of highway building into the Amazon in the 1970s and 1980s, it brought with it the financial backing and interests of big agricultural and industrial companies, plus an onslaught of land-seeking settlers. Historically, the great villain in the deforestation piece has been **ranching** – the latest research suggests around eighty percent of forest cleared was turned into pasture, dwarfing the deforestation caused by smallholders, commercial agriculture and logging. Although much has been written recently about **soy farming** as a cause of deforestation, most soy planting takes place on land that has already been cleared, and it remains a very minor cause of deforestation. Forest **fires** are a major threat, generally caused by colonizing farmers and ranchers, often exacerbated by the process of selective **logging**, which opens up the forest canopy and leaves debris ripe for lighting.

Until roads opened up the Amazon, many areas were inhabited and exploited only by **indigenous peoples**. The indigenous Indians and many of the modern forest-dwellers – including rubber tappers, nut collectors and, increasingly, even peasant settlers – view the forest as something which, like an ocean, can be harvested regularly if it is not overtaxed. **Chico Mendes**, the Brazilian rubber-tappers' union leader, was the best-known voice on the side of those arguing for a more sustainable approach. Hired gunmen killed him outside his house in Acre state in 1988, but his ideas lived on. In time, Acre became the showpiece state of the Brazilian environmental movement from 1998, when a PT government, led by **Jorge Viana** and dominated by old friends and colleagues of Chico Mendes, implemented an environmental programme, including a rubber subsidy to help rubber tappers remain in the forest, and a series of innovative initiatives for marketing forest products. Over twenty years, the environmental movement in Acre has moved to the centre of Brazilian political life: Viana was triumphantly re-elected in 2002 and went on to become an adviser to Lula; and a close friend, **Marina da Silva**, an ex–rubber tapper from Acre who had been a colleague of Mendes in the rubber-tapper union movement, was Minister of the Environment from 2003 to 2008.

## Deforestation: regional and global consequences

The most serious effects of the destruction of the Amazon rainforest are related to global warming.

• **Local climate change**: There is now hard scientific evidence from the deforested highway corridors that removing forest reduces rainfall, creates dry seasons where there were none, and extends them where they already existed. This has obvious implications for crops, soils, flora and fauna.

• **Global climate change**: The Amazon is a vital link in maintaining regional rainfall and it is clear that continuing large-scale deforestation would change weather patterns in the rest of the hemisphere, including the US. The destruction of the forest has two effects on the earth's atmosphere. The carbon in the smoke released by forest clearances makes a significant direct contribution to the **greenhouse effect**; tropical deforestation as a whole accounts for around twenty percent of global carbon emissions. The exact percentage contributed by Amazonian deforestation is controversial. Few experts accept a figure of less than five percent of global emissions, but the Brazilian government fiercely contests this. Less immediately, the fewer trees there are to absorb carbon dioxide, the faster the planet will warm.

## Forces driving deforestation

The blame for deforestation is often wrongly attributed. The following are some popular, but mistaken, explanations:

• **Population and land pressures**: Perhaps the most popular theory of all, certainly in Brazil, is that an unstoppable tide of humanity is swamping the forest. While there was something to this between the 1960s and the early 1990s, the rural Amazon has been losing population for a decade, and the region as a whole has a stable population with, according to the 2001 census, a small net migration to other parts of Brazil.
• **Debt**: Brazil's foreign debt is another popular scapegoat, but this is even less convincing. The bulk of the capital Brazil borrowed to create the debt was invested in southern Brazil. The need to make interest payments has not been a driver of economic policy in Brazil since the debt was restructured in the early 1990s. Most of the borrowed capital invested in the Amazon went into the mineral sector and into building dams, neither of which were significant causes of deforestation compared to ranching and agriculture.
• **The logging industry**: Virtually no deforestation can be directly attributed to logging. The biodiversity of the Amazon means that economically useful trees are jumbled together with valueless ones. As a result, clearcutting – removing forest tracts for timber – is almost unknown in the Amazon. Logging is more selective, resulting in the fragmentation of forest cover – degradation rather than deforestation. One often hears that logging trails open up areas into which deforesters later move, but just as often it is the loggers who head down the trails made by others.
• **"Big business"**: It is certainly true most of the deforestation in the grim decades of the 1970s and 1980s was driven directly by big business, specifically the tax breaks that attracted large companies to the region, and the ignorance and arrogance that led them to think megalomaniac development projects in the jungle would make money. But when the tax breaks were withdrawn in the early 1990s, most of the large companies left. The big companies remaining in the Amazon – mainly in mining and commercial agriculture – work in areas degraded long ago, and are not drivers of much new deforestation.
• **Soy and biofuels**: Despite the headlines soy is not and never has been an important driver of Amazon deforestation. Only two percent of cleared land in the Amazon is commercially farmed; ranching and smallholder agriculture account for the rest. Although there are grain terminals in the Amazon almost all the soy they ship is grown outside the Amazon. A ban on buying soy from deforested land has been in place since 2006 and is enforced. Biofuels are equally unimportant as a driver of deforestation. Little sugar-cane is grown in the Amazon, and although palm oil may be an important Amazonian product in the near future, it will be grown on land cleared decades ago in the eastern Amazon, where costs are lowest and ports are close.

A number of reasons are put forward for the continuing destruction of the rainforest. A complete answer would include the following three major factors:

• **The Brazilian economy**: Save for minerals and soy, the vast bulk of what the Amazon produces is consumed within the Amazon, or goes elsewhere in Brazil. For every cubic metre of tropical hardwood exported, for example, two cubic metres are consumed in Brazil, largely by the furniture and construction industries. The export of Amazonian timber is highly regulated; educated consumers in the US and EU demand proof that Amazon timber in products they buy has been sustainably produced – non-certified Amazon timber is barred from the EU, for example. There is no such demand among the vast majority of Brazilian consumers and, until there is, the domestic economy will be the single biggest driver of deforestation. Within the domestic economy itself, the biggest problem is **ranching**, which accounts for four out of every five units of land cleared in the Amazon.

• **Government policy**: Regional development policy is one of the most unreconstructed areas of the federal government, and run by old-fashioned politicians who equate development with dams and power plants. Corruption, in the form of loosely monitored federal contracts and regional development funds that operate as slush funds for politicians of every ideological complexion, hangs like a fog over everything the government does in the Amazon.

• **Amazonian state governments**: With a couple of exceptions – most notably Acre – Amazonian states tend to be run by old-style oligarchs, ignorant, provincial and deeply hostile to an environmental agenda they feel is threatening to "development". As far as they can – which fortunately is not very far, given their limited resources – they tend to back policies harmful to the forest. Recent examples include the Rondônia state government's sale of chunks of the state park system, and the attempt by the Roraima state government to block the declaration of indigenous reserves and hand the land over to farmers.

## Possible solutions

Deforestation happens because it makes economic sense for the person cutting the tree down; the **key to preserving the forest** is to ensure it makes more economic sense to keep it standing. A perfect example of the latter is the case of Belém; the largest city in the Amazon is surrounded by extensive areas of intact flood-plain forest. This is because there is massive demand for *açaí*, a palm fruit central to Amazonian cuisine, and palm heart. Both are locally consumed in large quantities, but also preserved, packed and exported to the rest of Brazil and the world. Both products come from flood-plain palm forests and, as a result, without subsidies or development projects, vast areas of flood-plain forest are preserved. Because gathering these forest products can never be mechanized, tens of thousands of livelihoods are assured, and the industry is sustainable. Overharvesting does not happen because everyone knows the level of production the ecosystem can sustain, and that they would shortly be out of a job if they went beyond it.

But this is only half the story. Gathering palm products is a living, but there is not much money in it – or wasn't. A few years ago, DaimlerBenz was looking for a way to reassure its German shareholders of its environmental responsibility. The R&D department discovered compressed fibres from Amazon palms could be used to stuff upholstery and also to make a material from which sunshields could be manufactured. They hooked up with the local university in Belém, which brokered a series of contracts with cooperatives in Marajó to supply and process palm fibre, creating what by local standards are scores of well-paid jobs. Everybody won: the local people, the local university (which gets a cut of each contract), the foreign corporation, the Brazilian consumer in southern Brazil driving the car, and, most of all, the environment. The Marajó villagers are now going to the university for help in reforesting deforested areas – because it makes economic sense.

So far these are isolated success stories, but they are part of a trend. Other companies looking to the Amazon to source products include Pirelli, which is producing tyres in southern Brazil with Acrean rubber, and Hermès, the French luxury-goods firm, which is using *couro vegetal*, a form of latex treated to look and feel like leather, to make handbags and briefcases. A number of venture-capital firms have sprung up in São Paulo, looking to finance environmentally sound but also profitable projects in the Amazon, including ecotourism, organic agriculture, sustainable production of certified timber, furniture making and fruit-pulp processing. Even big companies investing in the Amazon, like **Cargill** and **Alcoa**, are looking to minimize potential damage to their reputations by setting up compensation funds and managing their supply chains to reduce environmental impact. NGOs like **Greenpeace** are watchful, and increasingly effective in reining in corporate misbehaviour.

The principles underlying this sea-change are clear. First, long-term success usually lies in satisfying local and regional demand, not the export market. Brazilian ecotourism grew in the aftermath of September 11, 2001, for example, because the growing number of Brazilian ecotourists compensated for the drop in international, especially American, travellers. Second, interventions are often necessary: partly the removal of subsidies that reward destruction, now largely accomplished, but also incentives to encourage more environmentally friendly land use. A recent example is the national credit programme for family farms, PRONAF, which established a credit line for small Amazonian farmers who want to do agro-forestry, rather than straight farming, with subsidized rates of repayment. Thousands have so far taken it up. If this can be increased to tens or hundreds of thousands, it could transform the scene in the rural Amazon.

The other principles are more controversial, and are still not widely accepted by the international environmental movement, which lags far behind Brazilian environmentalism in its understanding of what needs to be done. First, it is always going to make economic sense for certain parts of the Amazon to be **dedicated to production**, not conservation. No country refuses to develop rich mineral deposits, or blocks investments in commercial agriculture with high rates of return. The choice is not whether to develop, but where development takes place and whether the environmental movement has any influence in channelling and controlling it. Looking at the broader picture, it makes better political and economic sense to accept the more controllable form of development – capitalism – in areas already degraded, and thus ensure the frontier fills out rather than moves on to new areas where the damage would be much greater.

Finally, it needs to be recognized that many parts of the Amazon, because of their remoteness or lack of marketable resources, are never going to be able to generate income or jobs. These areas do however provide valuable **environmental services**: their forests remove carbon from the atmosphere, reducing global warming, and keeping forests intact also protects watersheds and soil quality beyond the areas themselves. As things stand neither the Brazilian government nor the inhabitants of these areas receive any compensation for this, although perhaps in the future new markets in carbon and environmental services will fill the gap. In the meantime they should be protected, and the international community should be willing to pay most of the costs toward this, which to an extent is already happening. But much more needs to be done, especially for indigenous areas.

## The future

It is actually possible to feel optimistic about the future of the Amazon, especially when comparing the situation now to that of twenty years ago. Deforestation, while still a problem to be watched closely, is at a manageable level. Crucial players, like the Brazilian president, the ministry of the environment, the World Bank and the scientific community inside and outside Brazil, are stressing environmental safeguards and the importance of reconciling conservation with development, the opposite of their positions a generation ago. Increasing areas of the Amazon are being put under strict or partial protection, and, astonishingly, 22 percent of it has been demarcated and ratified as indigenous reserves. Perhaps most encouraging, a state government – Acre – running on an explicitly environmentalist platform has been wildly successful in attracting investment and resources to a remote part of the western Amazon. In Brasília, people who were persecuted union leaders or dissident academics twenty years ago are now running government departments or representing Brazil at international conferences. What had been a dangerous set of opinions, for which people like Chico Mendes and many others had died, is becoming, in the jargon of the bureaucrats, "mainstreamed".

Still, there is some way to go. The **murder of American missionary Dorothy Stang** in 2005 was a salutary reminder that going up against ranchers and illegal loggers in much of the Amazon is still potentially lethal. Stang was killed because she was trying to protect local smallholders from ranchers by forming them into an association and pressing for the creation of a sustainable development reserve. The international outcry at her murder forced the Brazilian government to act, and her killers, including – unprecedentedly – the rancher who commissioned the murder, were eventually tried and convicted a few months later. But Stang's death was an indication of how far there is still to go when only the international spotlight could make the justice system deliver.

It is still too early to say whether all this will be enough in the long term. Even if Brazil gets its act together, the fate of the Amazon is not only determined within Brazil. Global climate change is already having an impact in the Amazon. Even without further ill-judged development the area of dry forest vulnerable to fire will expand whatever Brazil, and Amazonians, do on their own. But if things come as far in the next twenty years as they have in the last twenty, and if the pressure is kept up, the satellite images may in the future be showing recovery, as well as loss.

## Indigenous peoples

Today, there are around 330,000 Indians in Brazil, spread between more than two hundred tribes speaking a hundred and eighty languages or dialects. When the Portuguese first arrived in the sixteenth century, there were probably over five million indigenous inhabitants.

The opening up of first the centre-west region in the 1950s with the construction of Brasília, and then the Amazon from the 1960s, was an unmitigated disaster for Brazil's indigenous peoples. They were dispossessed of their lands, and one of the consequences of the chaotic settlement of new frontiers was the spread of diseases, which brought many groups to the verge of extinction. The military regime regarded Indians with open racism: the Indian Code, which the military drew up in 1973 (and is still technically in force today, although widely ignored), explicitly said it was a transitional set of legal regulations to be enforced until Indians were assimilated, and indistinguishable from other Brazilians. In the

Amazon especially, many non-indigenous people in the areas around indigenous reserves are still openly racist, a sad legacy of their forebears who migrated there a generation ago.

Within Brazil indigenous peoples have always had defenders, notably in the Catholic Church, in the universities, and even in more liberal circles in the Brazilian military and FUNAI (the federal Indian agency), where some individuals were able to make a difference. The best examples were the brothers **Claudio and Orlando Vilas-Boas**, who were able to create **the Xingú indigenous park** in southern Mato Grosso in the 1960s, which turned out to be crucial in assuring the eventual survival of many indigenous groups of the southern Amazon. But these were isolated actions in the midst of what is best described as genocide by negligence.

The beginnings of change came in the darkest days of military repression and unrestrained road building in the late 1960s, when a combination of embarrassing international media coverage, foreign pressure and lobbying by the Catholic Church forced the military to curb the worst excesses of development in indigenous areas, and provide emergency medical assistance – too late in many cases. With the fall of the military regime the situation gradually improved; the **1988 Constitution** guaranteed indigenous land rights and protection of indigenous languages and culture. Although enforcing it has been problematic, it at least provided a legal basis for effective protection of indigenous lands.

The situation now is incomparably better than it was a generation ago. The presidencies of Fernando Collor and Fernando Henrique Cardoso, whatever their other shortcomings, were quite sound on indigenous issues. **Ruth Cardoso**, Fernando Henrique's wife, was an anthropology professor and a very effective advocate for indigenous peoples behind the scenes. During the 1990s most of the outstanding issues to do with the demarcation and full legalization of indigenous areas were resolved. A remarkable 22 percent of the Brazilian Amazon is now officially indigenous land – an area more than twice the size of France. While there are still occasional invasions of indigenous lands, the combination of a free press, more responsive policing and political will at the highest levels of the Brazilian government means invasions are much less of a problem than they once were.

Perhaps the greatest grounds for hope in the future is the strength of the **indigenous movement**. Born out of the patient organizational and educational work of the Catholic Church from the 1960s, the movement rapidly outgrew its religious roots to become an important secular force, founding local associations and regional confederations, and learning from their non-indigenous colleagues in the rural-union and rubber-tapper movements. Prominent national leaders like **Mário Juruna**, elected federal deputy for Rio in the 1980s despite being from Mato Grosso, were important in getting the movement off the ground. Juruna died in 2002, but an able new generation of younger indigenous leaders – **Daví Yanomami**, **Gerson Baniwa**, **Escrawen Sompre**, **Ailton Krenak**, the late **Jorge Terena** and others – have taken up the torch.

### For further information contact:

Survival, 6 Charterhouse Buildings, London EC1M 7ET, UK Ⓣ020/7687-8700, Ⓕ020/7687-8701, Ⓦwww.survival-international.org.

Also check out Ⓦwww.socioambiental.org and the Brazil & Amazon Resources and Links site at Ⓦwww.geocities.com/RainForest/Canopy/1316 for information and news on the Amazon, environmental issues, NGOs working in the region, maps and other more general travel and political links.

# Race in Brazilian society

The significance of **race** in Brazilian society has long been a controversial topic in Brazil. Until recently, despite the country's ethnic and racial diversity, official thinking refused to acknowledge the existence of minority groups, promoting the concept of the Brazilian "racial democracy" and denying absolutely the existence of racism or racial discrimination. If, in a country where blacks and mulattoes form at least half of the population, there are few dark-skinned people at the upper levels of society – so the theory runs – this simply reflects past disadvantages, in particular poverty and lack of education.

## Myth...

No one contributed more to the consolidation of this myth of racial brotherhood than the anthropologist **Gilberto Freyre**. In the early 1930s he advanced the view that somehow the Portuguese colonizers were immune to racial prejudice, that they intermingled freely with Indians and blacks. If **Brazilian slavery** was a not entirely benevolent patriarchy, as some people liked to believe, the mulatto offspring of the sexual contact between master and slave was the personification of this ideal. The **mulatto** was the archetypal social climber, transcending class boundaries, and was upheld as a symbol of Brazil and the integration of the nation's cultures and ethnic roots. "Every Brazilian, even the light-skinned and fair-haired one," wrote Freyre in his seminal work, *Casa Grande e Senzala*, "carries about him in his soul, when not in soul and body alike, the shadow or even birthmark, of the aborigine or negro. The influence of the African, either direct or remote, is everything that is a sincere reflection of our lives. We, almost all of us, bear the mark of that influence." The myth has endured, even in the minds of those who are also prepared to admit its flaws: "I believe in our illusion of racial harmony," said the (white) singer Caetano Veloso, in an interview in early 2000.

Accepted with, if anything, even less questioning outside Brazil than within, the concept of a racial paradise in South America was eagerly grasped. For those outside Brazil struggling against the Nazis or segregation and racial violence in the US, it was a belief too good to pass up. "Whereas our old world is more than ever ruled by the insane attempt to breed people racially pure, like race horses or dogs," wrote the Austrian writer Stefan Zweig in exile in Brazil, "the Brazilian nation for centuries has been built upon the principle of a free and unsuppressed miscegenation, the complete equalization of black and white, brown and yellow" (*Brazil – Land of the Future*, 1942). Brazil was awarded an international stamp of approval – and its **international image** is still very much that of the happy, unprejudiced melting-pot.

Anomalies were easily explained away. A romanticized image of the self-sufficient **Indian** could be incorporated into Brazilian nationalism as, deep in the forested interior and numbering only a quarter of a million, they posed no threat. Picturesque Indian names – Yara and Iraçema for girls, Tibiriça and Caramuru for boys – were given to children, their white parents seeing them as representing Brazil in its purest form. Afro-Brazilian religion, folklore and art became safe areas of interest. **Candomblé**, practised primarily in the north-eastern state of Bahia and perhaps the purest of African rituals, could be seen as a quaint remnant from the past, while syncretist cults, most notably **umbanda**, combining elements of Indian, African and European religion and which have attracted mass followings in Rio, São Paulo and the South, have been taken to demonstrate the happy fusion of cultures.

## ... and reality

Many visitors to Brazil still arrive believing in the melting pot, and many leave without questioning it. It is undeniable that Brazil has remarkably little in the way of obvious **racial tension**; there are no legal forms of racial discrimination – indeed *anti*-discrimination is enshrined in the constitution – and on the beach the races do seem to mix freely. But it is equally undeniable that race is a key factor in determining social position. Institutional racism, born of prejudice and stereotyping, affects access to education, employment opportunities and the treatment of black people within the criminal-justice system, manifested most notably in day-to-day harassment and violence from the police.

To say this in Brazil, even now, is to risk being attacked as "un-Brazilian". Nevertheless, the idea that race has had no significant effect on social mobility and that socioeconomic differentials of a century ago explain current differences between races is increasingly discredited. It is true Brazil has a rigidly stratified society within which upward mobility is difficult for anyone. But the lighter your skin, the easier it appears to be. Clear evidence has been produced that, although in general blacks and mulattoes (because of the continuing cycle of poverty) have lower education levels than whites, even when they do have equal levels of education and experience whites still enjoy substantial economic benefits. The **average income** of white Brazilians is twice that of black, and while there is a growing black Brazilian middle class, it is concentrated in the arts, music and sports – black people are still hugely under-represented in the middle and upper ranks of politics, business and industry.

Perhaps the most surprising realization is that, except amongst politically developed intellectuals and progressive sectors of the Church, there seems little awareness or resentment of the link between colour and class. The black-consciousness movement has made slow progress in Brazil – although grassroots community groups and national coalitions of organizations representing black people have emerged over the past decade or two – and most people continue to acquiesce before the national myth that this is the New World's fortunate land, where there's no need to organize for improved status.

# Music

Brazil's talent for music is so great it amounts to a national genius. Out of a rich stew of African, European and Indian influences it has produced one of the strongest and most diverse musical cultures in the world.

Most people have heard of **samba** and **bossa nova** but they are only the tip of a very large iceberg of genres, styles and individual talents. Music is a constant backdrop to social life in Brazil, and Brazilians are a very musical people. Instruments help but aren't essential: matchboxes shaken to a syncopated beat, forks tapped on glasses and hands slapped on tabletops are all that is required. Accompanying the music is some of the most stunning dancing you are ever likely to see. In Brazil, no one looks twice at a couple who would clear any European and most American dancefloors. You don't need to be an expert, or even understand the words, to enjoy Brazilian popular music, but you may appreciate it better – and find it easier to ask for the type of music you want – if you know a little about its history.

## Roots: Rio and the regions

The bedrock of Brazilian music is the apparently inexhaustible fund of "traditional" **popular music**. There are dozens of genres, most of them associated with a specific region of the country, which you can find in raw uncut form played on local radio stations, at popular festivals – Carnaval is merely the best known – impromptu recitals in squares and on street corners, and in bars and *dancetarias*, the dance halls Brazilians flock to at the weekend. The two main centres are Rio and Salvador. There's little argument that the best Brazilian music comes from Rio, the Northeast and parts of Amazônia, with São Paulo and southern Brazil lagging a little behind.

## Samba

Brazil's best-known music, **samba**, began in the early years of the twentieth century, in the poorer parts of Rio as Carnaval music. Over the decades it has developed several variations. The deafening **samba de enredo** is the setpiece of Carnaval, with one or two singers declaiming a verse joined by hundreds or even thousands of voices and drums for the chorus, as the *bloco*, the full samba school, backs up the lead singers. A *bloco* in action during Carnaval is the loudest music you'll ever hear, and it's all done without the aid of amplifiers – the massed noise of the drums vibrates every part of your body. No recording technology yet devised comes close to conveying the sound, and recorded songs and music often seem repetitive. Still, every year the main Rio samba schools make a compilation record of the music selected for the parade, and any CD or DVD with the words *Samba de Enredo* or *Escola de Samba* will contain this mass Carnaval music.

On a more intimate scale, and musically more inventive, is **samba-canção**, which is produced by one singer and a small back-up band, who play around with basic samba rhythms to produce anything from a (relatively) quiet love song to frenetic dance numbers. This style transfers more effectively to recordings than *samba de enredo*, and in Brazil its more laid-back pace makes it especially popular with the middle-aged. Reliably high-quality *samba-canção* is anything by **Beth Carvalho**, acknowledged queen of the genre, **Alcione**, the late, great **Clara Nunes**, and the even greater **Paulinho da Viola**, who always puts at least a couple of excellent sambas on every record he makes. You can get a taste of the older samba styles that dominated Rio in the 1960s and 1970s in the recordings of old-school greats like **Cartola**, **Bezerra da Silva** and **Velha Guarda de Mangueira**.

## Choro

Much less known, **choro** (literally "crying") appeared in Rio around the time of World War I, and by the 1930s had evolved into one of the most intricate and enjoyable of all Brazilian forms of music. Unlike samba, which developed variations, *choro* has remained remarkably constant over the decades. It's one of the few Brazilian genres that owes anything to Spanish-speaking America, as it is clearly related to the Argentinian tango (the real River Plate versions, that is, rather than the sequined ballroom distortions that get passed off as tango outside South America). *Choro* is mainly instrumental, played by a small group; the backbone of the combo is a guitar, picked quickly and jazzily, with notes sliding all over the place, which is played off against a flute, or occasionally a clarinet or recorder, with drums and/or maracas as an optional extra. It is as quiet and intimate as samba is loud and public, and of all Brazilian popular music is probably the most delicate. You often find it being played as background music in bars and cafés; local papers advertise such places. The loveliest *choros* on record are by **Paulinho da Viola**, especially on the album *Chorando*. After years of neglect during the post-war decades *choro* is now undergoing something of a revival, and it shouldn't be too difficult to catch a *conjunto de choro* in Rio or São Paulo. The eponymous *Casa de Choro* in Brasília is another outpost.

## North by Northeast

A full list of other "traditional" musical genres would have hundreds of entries and could be elaborated on indefinitely. Some of the best known are **forró**, **maracatú**, **repentismo** and **frevo**, described at greater length in the "Northeast" chapter; you'll find them all over the Northeast but especially around Recife. **Baião** is a Bahian style that bears a striking resemblance to the hard acoustic blues of the American Deep South, with hoarse vocals over a guitar singing of things like drought and migration. **Axé**, also from Bahia, is a samba-and-reggae mix that is the basis of inescapable and rather repetitive, light Brazilian pop in Salvador and elsewhere. **Carimbó** is an enjoyable, lilting rhythm and dance found all over northern Brazil but especially around Belém; a souped-up and heavily commercialized version of *carimbó* enjoyed a brief international vogue as **lambada** in the 1990s. **Bumba-meu-boi**, the haunting music of Maranhão, is one of the strangest and most powerful of all Brazilian genres.

A good place to start is with one of the dozens of CDs and DVDs by the late **Luiz Gonzaga**, also known as **Gonzagão**, which have extremely tacky covers but are musically very good. They have authentic renderings of at least two or three northeastern genres per record. His version of a beautiful song called *Asa Branca* is one of the best loved of all Brazilian tunes, a national standard, and guaranteed to reduce any homesick Northeasterner to tears immediately.

## The golden age: 1930–60 and the radio stars

It was the growth of radio during the 1930s that created the popular-music industry in Brazil, with home-grown stars idolized by millions. The best known was **Carmen Miranda**, spotted by a Hollywood producer singing in the famous Urca casino in Rio and whisked off to film stardom in the 1930s.

Although her hats made her immortal, she deserves to be remembered more as the fine singer she was. She was one of a number of singers and groups loved by older Brazilians, including **Francisco Alves**, **Ismael Silva**, **Mário Reis**, **Ataulfo Alves**, **Trio de Ouro** and **Joel e Gaúcho**. Two great songwriters, **Ary Barroso** and **Pixinguinha**, provided the raw material.

Brazilians call these early decades *a época de ouro*, and that it really was a golden age is proved by the surviving recordings. It is slower and jazzier than modern Brazilian music, but with similar rhythms and beautiful, crooning vocals. Even in Brazil it used to be difficult to get hold of **records** of this era but after years of neglect there is now a widely available series of reissues called *Revivendo*.

## International success: bossa nova

With this wealth of raw material to work with it was only a matter of time before Brazilian music burst its national boundaries, something that duly happened in the late 1950s with the phenomenon of **bossa nova**. Several factors led to its development. The classically trained **Antônio Carlos ("Tom") Jobim**, equally in love with Brazilian popular music and American jazz, met up with fine Bahian guitarist **João Gilberto** and his wife **Astrud Gilberto**. The growth in the Brazilian record and communications industries allowed bossa nova to sweep Brazil and come to the attention of people like **Stan Getz** in the United States; and, above all, there was a new market for a sophisticated urban sound among the newly burgeoning middle-class in Rio, who found Jobim's and Gilberto's slowing down and breaking up of what was still basically a samba rhythm an exciting departure. It rapidly became an international craze, and Astrud Gilberto's quavering version of one of the earliest Jobim numbers, *A Garota de Ipanema*, became the most famous of all Brazilian songs, *The Girl from Ipanema* – although the English lyric is considerably less suggestive than the Brazilian original.

Over the next few years the craze eventually peaked and fell away, leaving most people with the entirely wrong impression that bossa nova is a mediocre brand of muzak well suited to lifts and airports. Tom Jobim would later talk of being haunted by innumerable cover versions murdering *The Girl From Ipanema*. In North America, bossa nova sank under the massed strings of studio producers but in Brazil it never lost its much more delicate touch, usually with a single guitar and a crooner holding sway. Early bossa nova still stands as one of the crowning glories of Brazilian music, and all the classics – you may not know the names of tunes like *Corcovado*, *Isaura*, *Chega de Saudade* and *Desafinado* but you'll recognize the melodies – are all easily available on the various Jobim and Gilberto compilation recordings. But for the best bossa-nova album of all time, look for *Elís e Tom*, the incomparable collaboration between Elís Regina and Tom Jobim when both were at their peak in the early 1970s.

The great Brazilian guitarist **Luiz Bonfá** also made some fine bossa-nova records – the ones where he accompanies Stan Getz are superb. The bossa-nova records of **Stan Getz** and **Charlie Byrd** are one of the happiest examples of inter-American cooperation, and as they're easy to find in European and American shops they make a fine introduction to Brazilian music. They had the sense to surround themselves with Brazilian musicians, notably Jobim, the Gilbertos and Bonfá, and the interplay between their jazz and the equally skilful Brazilian response is often brilliant. **Live bossa nova** is rare these days, restricted to the odd bar or hotel lobby, unless you're lucky enough to catch one of the great names in concert – although Tom Jobim, sadly, died far too young in 1995. But then bossa nova always lent itself more to recordings than live performance.

## Tropicalismo

The military coup in 1964 was a crucial event in Brazil. Just as the shock waves of the cultural upheavals of the 1960s were reaching Brazilian youth, the lid went on in a big way: censorship was introduced for all song lyrics; radio and television were put under military control; and some songwriters and musicians were tortured and imprisoned for speaking and singing out – although fame was at least some insurance against being killed. The result was the opposite of what the generals had intended. A movement known as **tropicalismo** developed, calling itself cultural but in fact almost exclusively a musical movement, led by a young and extravagantly talented group of musicians. Prominent amongst them were **Caetano Veloso** and **Gilberto Gil** from Bahia and **Chico Buarque** from Rio. They used traditional popular music as a base, picking and mixing genres in a way no one had thought of doing before – stirring in a few outside influences like the Beatles and occasional electric instruments, and topping it all off with lyrics that often stood alone as poetry – and delighted in teasing the censors. Oblique images and comments were ostensibly about one thing, but everyone knew what they really meant.

Caetano, Gil and Chico – all of Brazil is on first-name terms with them – spent a few years in exile in the late 1960s and early 1970s, Caetano and Gil in London (both still speak fluent English with immaculate BBC accents) and Chico in Rome, before returning in triumph as the military regime wound down. They have made dozens of records between them and are still, in their sixties, the leading figures of Brazilian music. Gilberto Gil's stint as **Minister of Culture** in Lula's government, while thin on political achievements, at least meant Brazil could boast unquestionably the coolest government minister on the planet. Chico Buarque's dense lyrics and hauntingly beautiful melodies are still flowing, although he produces recordings more rarely now, devoting more of his time to novel-writing and theatre. Pride of place, however, has to go to **Caetano Veloso**. Good though he was in the 1960s and 1970s, he is improving with age, and his records over the last fifteen years have been his best: mature, innovative, lyrical and original as ever. His continuing originality has kept him at the leading edge of Brazilian popular music, acknowledged everywhere from the *favelas* of Rio to Carnegie Hall as the finest modern Brazilian musician.

## Female singers

Brazilian music has a strong tradition of producing excellent female singers. The great **Elis Regina** was something of a Brazilian Edith Piaf: her magnificent voice was tragically stilled in 1984, when she was at the peak of her career, by a drug overdose. She interpreted everything, and whatever Brazilian genre she touched she invariably cut the definitive version. Two of her songs in particular became classics, *Águas de Março* and *Carinhoso*, the latter being arguably the most beautiful Brazilian song of all. After her death the mantle fell on **Gal Costa**, a very fine singer although without the extraordinary depth of emotion Elis could project. More recently, **Marisa Monte** has emerged as a worthy heir to Elis; the classic *Cor de Rosa e Carvão* is the best introduction to her enormous talent, and 2008's *Universo Ao Meu Redor* is the best samba record of recent years.

Other good younger singers include **Silvia Torres**, **Belô Veloso** (a niece of Caetano) and **Fernanda Porto**, whose musical style is a fusion of samba and drum 'n' bass. More recently, younger singers – like Brazilian footballers – have been heading abroad much earlier and carving careers in the US and Europe as much as at home. Rio and New York are developing particularly close musical links, best represented by the eclectic, fusion sound and occasional English lyrics of **Céu**, a superb singer whose ability to mix influences from all over and still remain unmistakeably Brazilian is a sign Brazilian music will surf globalization rather than be swamped by it – to everyone's benefit.

## Fifty of the best: a selected discography

For **back catalogues**, armed with the names of recommended artists in the sections above, go to a Brazilian music store and look for series called *A Arte de...*, *O Talento de...*, *A Personalidade de....* Below, we've picked out both the historically essential and our take on the best of the rest. Putumayo (in the US) and Globestyle (in the UK) regularly produce good Brazilian compilations and are a good starting-point, given their availability outside Brazil. The list – as in Brazilian music stores – is by first name of the artist.

**Belô Veloso**
*Belô Veloso*
**Bezerra da Silva**
*Se Não Fosse o Samba*
*É Isso Aí o Homem*
**Caetano Veloso**
*Velô*
*Estrangeiro*
*Circuladô Vivo*
*Fina Estampa*
*Um Outro Som*
**Caetano Veloso and Roberto Carlos**
*A Música de Tom Jobim*
**Carlinhos Brown**
*Timbalada*
**Cartola**
*Cartola*
*Céu*
**Chico Buarque**
*Ópera do Malandro*
*Vida*
*Para Todos*
*Uma Palavra*
**Daniela Mercury**
*Daniela*
**Dorival Caymmi**
*A música de Caymmi*
**Elís Regina and Tom Jobim**
*Elís e Tom*
**Fernanda Porto**
*Fernanda Porto*
**Gal Costa**
*Aquarela do Brasil*
**Gilberto Gil**
*Parabolicamera*
*Unplugged*
*O Sol de Oslo*
**Gilberto Gil and Caetano Veloso**
*Tropicalia 2*
**João Gilberto**
*Voz e Violão*
**Jorge Ben Jor**
*Acústico*
*Ao Vivo*
*Kid Abelha*
*Acústico*
*Luiz Gonzaga*
*Maiores Sucessos*
**Maria Bethânia**
*Ambar*
**Marisa Monte**
*M*
*Cor de Rosa e Carvão*
*Barulhinho Bom*
*Memórias, Crônicas e Declarações de Amor*
*Universo Ao Meu Redor*
**Milton Nascimento**
*Clube da Esquina*
**Paulinho da Viola**
*Cantando*
*Chorando*
*Eu canto samba*
*Bebado samba*
**Seu Jorge**
*Cru*
*América Brasil*
*Tim Maia*
*In Concert*
**Tom Jobim**
*Wave*
**Tribalistas**
*Tribalistas*
**Various**
*Eu Tu Eles* (film soundtrack)
**Velha Guarda da Mangueira**
*E Convidados*
**Zeca Baleiro**
*Por onde andará Stephen Fry?*
*Líricas*

## The Bahian sound

Although Rio is the traditional capital of Brazilian music, for some years now it has been rivalled by **Salvador**, the capital of Bahia. Bahia in general, and Salvador in particular, has always produced a disproportionate number of Brazil's leading musicians including Caetano Veloso and his sister, **Maria Bethânia**. The main reason for this is the extraordinary musical blend provided by deep African roots, Caribbean and Hispanic influences coming in through the city's port, and a local record industry that quickly realized the money-making potential of Bahian music.

The Bahian sound has two dimensions. Bahian pop is, at its best, an enjoyable blend of Brazilian and Caribbean rhythms, exemplified by groups including **Reflexus**, and singers such as **Luis Caldas**, **Margareth Menezes**, **Ivete Sangalo** and **Daniela Mercury**. But Bahia also has a much funkier, rootsy and percussive side, much rougher and rawer than Bahia's more poppy singers. Its guiding light is the percussionist and producer **Carlinhos Brown**; a great performer and songwriter in his own right, he is also the *éminence grise* behind the rise of other prominent artists like Marisa Monte, with whom he joined forces, together with the punk singer **Arnaldo Antunes**, to create the **Tribalistas** group.

## Other singers and musicians

The number of high-quality singers and musicians in Brazilian music besides these leading figures is enormous. **Milton Nascimento** has a talent that can only be compared with the founders of *tropicalismo*, with a remarkable soaring voice, a genius for composing stirring anthems and a passion for charting both the experience of blacks in Brazil and the traditions of his native Minas Gerais. **Fagner**, **Morães Moreira**, **Zé Ramalho**, **Elba Ramalho** and **Alceu Valença** are leading modern interpreters of northeastern music and strikingly original singers. **Chico Science e Nação Zumbi** is the best younger northeastern star, reinterpreting the region's genres and mixing them with a range of other influences, from jazz to rap. **Renato Borghetti**, from Rio Grande do Sul, has done much to popularize gaúcho-influenced music through his skill on the accordion and his adaptations of traditional tunes. **Jorge Ben** is arguably the most danceable of all Brazilian musicians, although the late, great **Tim Maia**, heavily influenced by US funk and soul (although Brazilian to every last inch of his enormous girth), runs a close second.

**Vinícius de Morães** and **Toquinho** are (or were, in the case of Vinícius) a good singer-and-guitarist team, and **Dorival Caymmi**, who died in 2008, was the grand old man of Bahian music. Whilst all these figures have been going strongly for decades now, the best recent arrivals are **Zeca Baleiro** from Maranhão, with a *bumba-meu-boi-* and reggae-influenced style, and **Seu Jorge**, born Jorge Mário da Silva and raised in a Rio *favela*. He is no mean actor too, and can be seen basically playing himself in the superb film *Cidade de Deus* (City of God) (see "Cinema", p.765).

# Live music and recordings

If you want to see or hear **live music**, look for suggestions in this book, buy local papers with weekend listings headed *Lazer*, which should have a list of bars with music, concerts and *dancetarias*, or ask a tourist office for advice. If sampling live music is high on your list of priorities for your trip, route yourself through Rio, Salvador and/or São Paulo; while the latter has far less of a musical tradition it's where the money is, and thus where everyone plays.

**Local radio** is often worth listening to and there are also local TV stations that often have **MPB** (Música Popular Brasileira) programmes; the TVE, Televisão Educativa, network is especially worth checking – if you see the initials FUNARTE, it might well be a music programme.

Finally, a word about **buying CDs and DVDs**. The price varies according to how well known the recording artist is. Recordings even by leading artists are less expensive than in the US or Europe, and those by more obscure artists and regional music are cheaper still. At the upper end of the scale, but dependably high quality, are the *A Arte de…*, *O Talento de…* or *A Personalidade de…* series, often double albums, which are basically "Greatest Hits" compilations of the best-known singers and musicians. The best place to buy any music, no matter how regional, is São Paulo, then Rio, with cities like Recife, Salvador, Belo Horizonte and Porto Alegre a long way behind. If time is an issue, any mall will have a music shop where you will be able to get at least some worthwhile material. You will see pirated CDs being sold on street corners and stalls everywhere – while the rip-offs of major artists will be terrible quality, in places like Salvador this is a good way of buying local music, since many local musicians use streetsellers to make extra money even if they have a record contract. Vendors are happy to play you sample tracks.

# Books

Surprisingly, perhaps, Brazil is spottily covered by **books** in English. The riches of Brazilian literature lie largely untranslated and too many books on Brazilian politics tell you more about the political leanings of their authors than Brazil. Still, a large number of distinguished visitors, from Charles Darwin on, have generated a rich "impressions of Brazil" genre. An encouraging trend in recent years has been for Brazilian authors to be translated into English, allowing foreigners access to their inevitably more nuanced takes on their own country.

## The best introductions

**Elizabeth Bishop** *One Art* (Farrar, Straus and Giroux). One of the best American poets of the twentieth century spent much of her adult life in Brazil, living in the hills behind Petrópolis from 1951 to 1969 but travelling widely. This selection from her letters and diaries is an intimate, sharp-eyed chronicle of Brazil in those years, and much else. Her *Collected Poems* (Farrar, Straus and Giroux) is equally essential – she is one of the greatest poets of place in English, and her talent is unforgettably unleashed on Rio, Minas Gerais and the Amazon.

**Fernando Henrique Cardoso** *The Accidental President of Brazil: A Memoir* (PublicAffairs). This is that rarest of political memoirs – a well-written, funny, fair-minded and often moving book by Brazil's most urbane and cosmopolitan president. There's material about his fascinating life before he became president, and the usual vignettes of the famous – including a memorable account of being upstaged at Buckingham Palace by the Brazilian football team. Fascinating introduction to the country by somebody who did more than anyone to modernize Brazil.

**Charles Darwin** *The Beagle Diaries* (Penguin). Although this edited collection of extracts includes Darwin's travels all over South America, Brazil, where he spent more time on land than anywhere else, figures heavily, especially Rio and what were then the forests around it. Fresh and interesting in his descriptions of the natural world, Darwin was also a shrewd observer of Brazilian society; his contempt for slavery in action is memorably expressed.

**Boris Fausto** *A Concise History of Brazil* (Cambridge UP). The best single-volume introductory history of Brazil, written by an eminent historian from São Paulo. Fausto shows very effectively how Brazil has changed dramatically over time, despite the temptation to see it as a prisoner of its own history.

**Annette Haddad and Scott Doggett** (eds) *Travelers' Tales: Brazil* (Travelers' Tales). A superb anthology of extracts from books and magazine articles by journalists, anthropologists, historians and other travellers to Brazil, which will make you want to search out the publications they're drawn from. Although a great read, it's a pity more wasn't done to include the work of Brazilian authors.

**D. Hess and R. DaMatta** *The Brazilian Puzzle* (Columbia UP). A riveting collection of Brazilian perspectives on Brazilian culture; sociologists and anthropologists contribute essays of variable quality on a variety of topics – race, gender, politics, the courts, sex – but a valuable chance to see the country through Brazilian eyes.

**Ruth Landes** *The City of Women* (New Mexico UP). New edition of a classic first published in 1947: an American woman remembers her time in Bahia studying *candomblé* and Afro-Brazilian culture. Written for the general reader, and over sixty years on still the best introduction there is to both the Northeast and racial issues in Brazil.

**Claude Lévi-Strauss** *Tristes Tropiques* (Picador; Penguin). The great French anthropologist describes four years spent in 1930s Brazil – arguably the best book ever written about the country by a foreigner. There are famous descriptions of sojourns with Nambikwara and Tupi-Kawahib Indians, epic journeys, and a remarkable eyewitness account of São Paulo exploding into a metropolis. *Saudades do Brasil: A Photographic Memoir* (Washington UP) is a beautifully produced collection that makes a wonderful companion to *Tristes Tropiques*, featuring some of the thousands of photographs Lévi-Strauss took.

**Robert M. Levine and John J. Crocitti** (eds) *The Brazil Reader: History, Culture, Politics* (Latin America Bureau; Duke UP). The breadth of subject matter in this thoughtful anthology is impressive, covering Brazil from colonial times to the present, using book and article extracts, original documents and historical photographs. If it wasn't for the volume's sheer weight, it would be the perfect travel companion.

**Roberto da Matta** *Carnival, Rogues and Heroes* (Notre Dame UP). A collection of essays by one of Brazil's leading anthropologists, who also teaches in the US. They include some very stimulating – and entertaining – dissections of Carnaval.

**Thomas E. Skidmore** *Brazil: Five Centuries of Change* (Oxford UP). Very readable account of the emergence of Brazilian national identity, from the first European contact to the present day. The author, a renowned US "Brazilianist", made important contributions to the discussion of racial ideology and the analysis of twentieth-century Brazilian political development, and this book is an excellent synthesis of his work and that of other Brazilian and foreign scholars.

# Regions: travel and history

## The Amazon

**Henry Bates** *The Naturalist on the River Amazon* (o/p but easy to find). A Victorian botanist describes his years spent collecting in the Amazon, in an obscure but wonderful book. Bates's boyish scientific excitement illuminates every page. A sympathetic, very English eye cast over the Amazon and its people. No better book for a river trip.

**Alan Campbell** *Getting to Know Waiwai: An Amazonian Ethnography* (Routledge). Superbly written and wrenching book. A Scottish anthropologist writes of two years among the Wayapí of Amapá, as they try to come to terms with Brazilian society.

**Colonel P. H. Fawcett** *Exploration Fawcett* (o/p). Fawcett carries his stiff upper lip in and out of some of the most disease-infested, dangerous and downright frightening parts of interior Brazil. It's a rattling good read, compiled by his son from Fawcett's diaries and letters after his disappearance. Readily available in secondhand bookshops. For more on Fawcett, see p.541.

**Colin McEwan, Cristiana Barreto and Eduardo Neves** (eds.) *Unknown Amazon: Culture in Nature in Ancient Brazil* (British Museum). Fantastically illustrated and photographed companion volume to a 2001 exhibition at the British Museum, revealing revolutionary discoveries on the scale and complexity of late prehistoric indigenous cultures in the Amazon.

**Candace Millard** *The River of Doubt* (Scribner). Historian with a talent for writing for a general audience tells the fascinating and forgotten story of Teddy Roosevelt's journey to the Amazon after renouncing the presidency of the US in the early twentieth century. It was close to being a complete disaster, almost killed him at the time, and Roosevelt's health never recovered.

**Stephen Nugent** *Big Mouth: The Amazon Speaks* (Fourth Estate, o/p; Brown Trout Publications). Intelligent and hilarious antidote to the gooey rainforest literature. Jaundiced anthropologist returns to old haunts in Belém and Santarém, debunking as he goes. There is no better guide to the complexities of modern Amazônia; convincing and depressing at the same time.

**Hugh Raffles** *In Amazonia: A Natural History* (Princeton UP). Superbly written mixture of history, anthropology and geography, exploring the gap between the way outsiders and Amazonians think about the region and its landscapes, and periodically very moving in its interweaving of personal memory with wider concerns.

**Peter Rivière** *Absent-Minded Imperialism: Britain and the Expansion of Empire in Nineteenth-Century Brazil* (Tauris). Hilarious, dryly written account of how the border between Brazil and what was then British Guiana came to be drawn, an extraordinary and forgotten story of fanatical missionaries, mutual misunderstanding between British and Brazilian officials, and bewildered Indians stuck in the middle unaware of the diplomatic problems they were causing. A minor classic.

**Candace Slater** *Dance of the Dolphins* (Chicago UP). Interesting compendium of the many legends and folk tales centring on river dolphins, beautifully translated. There is a clumsy academic subtext linking the stories with environmental destruction in the Amazon, but you can skip those bits. There is no better book for giving you a feel for the popular imagination in the small towns you pass through on a river trip.

**Anthony Smith** *Explorers of the Amazon* (Chicago UP). A chapter devoted to each of the main explorers of the Amazon from the sixteenth to the nineteenth centuries, written for the general reader and showing that truth can be stranger than fiction; those who remember Klaus Kinski's demented portrayal of Aguirre in the film *Aguirre, Wrath of God* will be shocked to realize he actually played down the extent of the conquistador's madness.

**Nigel Smith** *The Amazon River Forest: A Natural History of Plants, Animals and People* (Oxford UP). An expert with the rare knack of writing clearly and interestingly for the general public tells you all you need to know about the flood plain from the year dot to the present. A great book for a long river journey, and many fine photos too.

## Minas, Mato Grosso and Brasília

**Glenn Alan Cheney** *Journey on the Estrada Real: Encounters in the Mountains of Brazil* (Academy Chicago, US). A beautiful account of a walk tracing the northern section of the Estrada Real (the Royal Road, also known as the Caminho do Ouro) from Mariana to Diamantina. Cheney offers descriptions of hamlets and villages way off the beaten track – where, for better or worse, life appears to have stood still for generations – and meditations on how communities such as these can survive "development" and the impact of globalization.

**Richard Gott** *Land Without Evil: Utopian Journeys Across the South American Watershed* (Verso). Although the subject matter is centred on eastern Bolivia, this is an important look at the swampland between the rivers Plate and Amazon, exploring the region through the adventures of missionaries and explorers and through the travels of the author himself.

**Alex Shoumatoff** *The Capital of Hope: Brasília and its People* (Vintage). The author talked with government officials and settlers – rich and poor – to weave a very readable account of the first 25 years of the Brazilian capital.

## The Northeast

**Billy Jaynes Chandler** *The Bandit King: Lampião of Brazil* (Texas UP, US). Compulsive reading that seems like fiction but is well-documented fact. Based on original sources and interviews with participants and witnesses, an American historian with a talent for snappy writing reconstructs the action-packed (and myth-encrusted) life of the famous social bandit, complete with fascinating photographs.

**Euclides da Cunha** *Rebellion in the Backlands* (Picador; Chicago UP). Also known by its Portuguese title *Os Sertões*, this remains perhaps Brazil's greatest historical account. An epic tale of Antônio Conselheiro's short-lived holy city, the Canudos Rebellion and its brutal suppression that left some 15,000 dead, the book is also a powerful meditation on Brazilian civilization.

**Gilberto Freyre** *The Masters and the Slaves* (California UP). Classic history of plantation life in the Northeast, with a wealth of detail (includes index headings like "Smutty Stories and Expressions" and "Priests, Bastards of"). Very readable, and there is passionate debate in Brazil over his take on race and national identity to this day.

**Robert M. Levine** *Vale of Tears: Revisiting the Canudos Massacre in Northeastern Brazil 1893–1897* (California UP). A vivid portrait of backland life and a detailed examination of the myths behind Canudos. Shocking but utterly compelling reading, especially when read in conjunction with da Cunha's classic.

**João José Reis** *Slave Rebellion in Brazil: The Muslim Uprising of 1835 in Bahia* (Johns Hopkins UP). The last major slave rebellion in Brazil began in Salvador on January 24, 1835. This is a unique portrait of urban slavery: an absorbing account of the most important urban slave rebellion in the Americas and the only one where Islam played a major role, detailing the background of the conspiracy and the brutal repression and punishment of Africans that followed.

**Peter Robb** *A Death in Brazil* (Bloomsbury, UK; John Macrae Books, US). Sporadically vivid travel writing focused mainly on Recife and Alagoas, interspersed with analysis of the Collor years. Those coming to this from Robb's brilliant *Midnight in Sicily* will be disappointed with his much more superficial knowledge of Brazil. But the quality of his writing still makes this a good introduction to the Northeast.

## Rio and around

**Ruy Castro** *Rio de Janeiro* (Bloomsbury). Ruy Castro, a renowned journalist, offers a historical and cultural overview of Rio and, far more importantly, captures his fellow *cariocas'* soul. Leaving aside Castro's sometimes irritating generalizations, this book provides an alluring entry into Rio life.

**Warren Dean** *With Brandaxe and Firestorm* (California UP). Brilliant and very readable environmental history that tells the story of the almost complete destruction of the Mata Atlântica, the coastal rainforest around Rio and points north and south, from colonial times to the twentieth century.

**Alma Guillermoprieto** *Samba* (Bloomsbury; Vintage). The author, a trained dancer and a well-known journalist, describes a year she spent in Rio's Mangueira *favela* preparing with its inhabitants for Carnaval. Riveting, superbly written and the best account in English of *favela* life.

**Eduardo Silva** *Prince of the People: The Life and Times of a Brazilian Free Man of Colour* (Verso). Was Dom Obá II d'Africa a genuine prince, or was he merely an unbalanced son of slaves with delusions? Whatever the truth, Dom Obá was revered by the poor around him; his story sheds light on the life of slaves and people of colour in Rio, and on popular thought during the final decades of slavery.

**Stanley Stein** *Vassouras: A Brazilian Coffee County, 1850–1900* (Princeton UP). Re-edition of a 1940s classic that improves with age. On the surface, a straightforward reconstruction of the rise and fall of the coffee plantation system in a town in the interior of Rio. Look closer and you see a devastating indictment of slavery, based on archive work but also, uniquely, on the memories of the last generation to have been born as slaves. Includes a fascinating selection of photos.

## The South

**Cyrus and James Dawsey** (eds) *The Confederados: Old South Immigrants in Brazil* (Alabama UP). An extremely readable collection of essays by US and Brazilian scholars looking at different aspects of the experience of immigrants from the former Confederacy and their descendants. Contributions discuss the history of the agricultural settlements as well as the cultural (in particular religious) influence of the immigrants on the wider society and linguistic change.

**Todd Diacon** *Millennarian Vision, Capitalist Reality: Brazil's Contestado Rebellion 1912–1916* (Duke UP). Fascinating analysis of the Contestado Rebellion in Paraná. The rebels attacked train stations, sawmills and immigrant colonies in Santa Catarina and Paraná but were ultimately outnumbered and outgunned.

**Alexander Leonard** *The Valley of the Latin Bear* (o/p). A delightful account of everyday life in an isolated German village in Santa Catarina. Although written some forty years ago, the account remains very recognizable and it's still worth seeking out.

**Guy Walmisley-Dresser** *Brazilian Paradise* (o/p). Romantic reminiscences of growing up on a cattle ranch in Rio Grande do Sul in the late nineteenth century. The anecdotes are both amusing and full of insight and describe a part of Brazil that, although distinctive in character, is all but ignored by travel writers.

# Brazil: history

**Gilberto Freyre** *The Mansions and the Shanties* (California UP). Brazil's most famous – and still most controversial historian decades after his death – looks at the origins of Brazilian urbanism and city life; deliberately provocative conclusions and brilliantly written.

**John Hemming** *Red Gold: The Conquest of the Brazilian Indians* (o/p). The definitive history of the topic, well written and thoroughly researched. Both passionate and scholarly, it's a basic book for anyone interested in the Indian question in Brazil. Companion volumes, *Amazon Frontier: The Defeat of the Brazilian Indian* (Pan) and *Die if You Must: The Brazilian Indians in the Twentieth Century* (Pan), bring the depressing story up to date.

**Stephen Lone** *The Japanese Community in Brazil, 1908–1940* (Palgrave). This is a welcome introduction to the history of Brazil's important Japanese community, drawing largely from Japanese sources. The author argues against the uniqueness of the Japanese community, suggesting they were not particularly the subject of racism or hostility and that the hardships they overcame were no greater – and sometimes less – than those of other immigrant groups.

**Frederick C. Luebke** *Germans in Brazil: A Comparative History of Cultural Conflict During World War I* (Louisiana State UP). One of the very few studies in English on Germans in Brazil. Despite the title, this social history covers the period 1818–1918, though the focus is World War I, when Brazilians of German origin began to accept they could not remain foreigners in their own country.

**Oliver Marshall** *English, Irish and Irish-American Pioneer Settlers in Nineteenth-Century Brazil* (Centre for Brazilian Studies, University of Oxford). In the 1860s and 1870s, several thousand people were recruited in England and New York for agricultural settlements in southern Brazil. This book discusses what motivated the organizers of this venture and vividly describes the grim fate of the immigrants.

**Katia M. de Queiros Mattoso** *To be a Slave in Brazil, 1550–1888* (Rutgers UP, US). A history of slavery in Brazil, unusually written from the perspective of the slave. Writing for the general reader, the author divides her excellent study into three themes: the process of enslavement, life in slavery and escape from it.

**Joseph A. Page** *The Brazilians* (Addison-Wesley). A cultural history of Brazil in a clear if eclectic style, drawing on sources ranging from economics and political psychology to film and literature. The author is a law professor at Georgetown University in Washington, DC.

**Patrick Wilcken** *Empire Adrift: The Portuguese Court in Rio de Janeiro 1808–1821* (Bloomsbury). In 1807 the Portuguese royal family, accompanied by 10,000 aristocrats, servants, government officials and priests, fled Lisbon in advance of Napoleon's invading army, which was sweeping across the Iberian Peninsula. In this wonderfully lively account, the author brings to life the incredible atmosphere in Lisbon and Rio during this key episode in Brazilian history.

## National politics and society

**Sue Branford and Bernardo Kucinski** *Politics Transformed: Lula and the Workers' Party in Brazil* (Latin America Bureau). An impassioned if rather starry-eyed look at the rise of the PT, charting its development from trade-union resistance to the military regime in São Paulo to Lula's election in 2002.

**Gilberto Dimenstein** *Brazil: War on Children* (Latin America Bureau; Monthly Review, o/p). A grim but compelling picture of life for the street children of São Paulo, but true also for most Brazilian cities. The children, living in constant fear of death squads made up of off-duty police and other vigilantes, survive as best they can as petty criminals, beggars and prostitutes, supporting one another in small gangs.

**Tobias Hecht** *At Home in the Street* (Cambridge UP). Excellent study of street children and those who deal with them, from death squads to social workers. Based on work in Recife, but equally applicable to any large Brazilian city.

**Dan Linger** *Nobody Home: Brazilian Selves Remade in Brazil* (Stanford UP). Brazil has the largest Japanese population outside Japan and many Brazilians move back and forth between the two countries doing the work the Japanese prefer to leave to others. This is a sensitive, accessible study of their lives, problems and dreams.

**Maxine L. Margolis** *Little Brazil: An Ethnography of Brazilian Immigrants in New York City* (Princeton UP). Since the early 1980s, there's been considerable migration from Brazil, especially to Europe and the US. The greatest concentration of expatriate Brazilians – especially educated middle-classes from Minas Gerais – is in the New York City area, with most living in Long Island, Manhattan and Astoria. The community's heart is Little Brazil, a one-block stretch of Manhattan's West 46th Street, and this is a thoroughly readable exploration of community life.

**Ruben Oliven** *Tradition Matters: Modern Gaúcho Identity* (Columbia UP). This is not about the life of "cowboys" in southern Brazil, but rather an examination of the predominantly urban, middle-class social movement that prizes an idealized rural lifestyle of which it has no real experience. Oliven points up the apparent paradox in Brazil (as elsewhere) of ever-increasing cultural globalization and the strengthening of regional identity. An important study illuminating a part of Brazil largely ignored by outsiders – Brazilian as well as foreign.

**Nancy Scheper-Hughes** *Death Without Weeping: The Violence of*

*Everyday Life in Brazil* (California UP). An often shocking, ultimately depressing anthropological study of *favela* women, and in particular of childbirth, motherhood and infant death. Although over-long – judicious skipping is in order – it is very accessible to the general reader, interesting, and often moving.

**Thomas Skidmore** *Politics in Brazil 1930–1964; The Politics of Military Rule in Brazil 1964–85* (Oxford UP). The former is the standard work on Brazilian politics from the rise of Vargas until the 1964 military takeover. The latter continues the story to the resumption of Brazil's shaky democracy.

## Gender and sexuality

**Caipora Women's Group** *Women in Brazil* (Latin America Bureau). Articles, poems and interviews about life for women on farms, in fishing communities and in *favelas*. The issues repeat themselves: racism, machismo, legal rights, religious and feminist beliefs. A welcome relief from published doctoral dissertations, this is both important and highly readable, both depressing and uplifting.

**Herbert Daniel and Richard Parker** *Sexuality, Politics and AIDS in Brazil* (Falmer Press, US). Excellent, clearly written history of AIDS in Brazil, covering the way the epidemic has developed in relation to popular culture at one end and government policy at the other. There are bright spots – Brazilian TV health-education slots on AIDS may be the best in the world, completely frank, and often screamingly funny – but this book will help you understand how this coexisted with a scandalous lack of supervision of blood banks.

**Richard Parker** *Bodies, Pleasures and Passions* (Beacon Press, US). A provocative analysis of the erotic in Brazilian history and popular culture. Tremendous subject matter and some fascinating insights into sexual behaviour, combining insider and outsider perspectives.

**Daphne Patai** *Brazilian Women Speak: Contemporary Life Stories* (Rutgers UP, US). Oral testimony forms the core of this very readable work that lets ordinary women from the Northeast and Rio speak for themselves to describe the struggles, constraints and hopes of their lives.

**João Trevisan** *Perverts in Paradise* (GMP, US). This is a fascinating survey of Brazilian gay life ranging from the papal inquisition to pop idols, transvestite *macumba* priests and guerrilla idols.

## Race

**George Reid Andrews** *Blacks and Whites in São Paulo 1888–1988* (Wisconsin UP). Why is the notion of a racial democracy still so widely accepted while at the same time people are fully aware that for all practical purposes it's a complete myth? For large proportions of Brazilians, racism is a fact of life and this is an interesting examination of how the state has long encouraged myths of black inferiority and perpetuates racial stereotypes.

**Darién J. Davis** *Afro-Brazilians: Time for Recognition* (Minority Rights Group, UK). A valuable introduction focusing on Afro-Brazilians in national culture and the human-rights struggle. Produced for a respected British-based NGO, the report is scholarly, impassioned and essential reading for anyone wanting to understand the often contradictory nature of Brazilian racial ideology and politics.

**Thomas E. Skidmore** *Black into White: Race and Nationality in Brazilian Thought* (Duke UP). First published in 1974, this new edition has a preface that brings the book up to date. A landmark in the intellectual history of Brazilian racial ideology, examining scientific racism and the Brazilian intellectual elite's supposed belief in assimilation and the ideal of whitening.

**Frances W. Twine** *Racism in a Racial Democracy* (Rutgers UP). Fascinating ethnography of racism in a small Brazilian town, by a black American sociologist interested in the differences between Brazilian and American racial politics.

## Amazon politics and society

**Warren Dean** *Brazil and the Struggle for Rubber* (Cambridge UP). Good environmental history of the rubber boom and subsequent failed attempts to set up rubber plantations in the Amazon.

**Susanna Hecht and Alexander Cockburn** *The Fate of the Forest* (Penguin; Verso). Excellently written and researched, this is as good an introduction to the problem as you will find. Very strong on Amazonian history, too – essential to understanding what's going on, but often ignored by Amazon commentators.

**Chico Mendes and Tony Gross** *Fight for the Forest: Chico Mendes in His Own Words* (Latin America Bureau; Inland Book Co). Long, moving passages from a series of interviews the rubber-tappers' union leader gave shortly before his assassination in 1988. Well translated and with useful notes giving background to the issues raised.

**Marianne Schmink and Charles Wood** *Contested Frontiers in Amazonia* (Columbia UP). The best of the more recent academic books on modern Amazônia; examines southern Pará before, during and after the construction of the highway network. Clearly written and very interesting, especially in its description of how the Kayapó Indians adapted to a gold rush.

**Charles Wagley** *Amazon Town* (o/p). Classic anthropological study of an interior Amazon town during the 1940s that inspired generations of students. Written with incisive style and complete command of the material.

# Birdwatching, wildlife and hiking

**Balthasar Dubs** *Birds of Southwestern Brazil* (Beltrona, Switzerland). Essential reading if you're heading for the Pantanal. The main body of the book is a comprehensive annotated and illustrated list of species in the region.

**David L. Pearson and Les Beletsky** *Brazil: Amazon and Pantanal – The Ecotravellers' Wildlife Guide* (Academic Press). The main body of this book examines the regions' ecosystems and the threats they face before moving on to chapters discussing insects, amphibians, reptiles, birds, mammals and fish. Richly illustrated and clearly written, the book will enrich any visit to the Amazon or Pantanal.

**Ber van Perlo** *A Field Guide to the Birds of Brazil* (Oxford UP). The only single-volume field guide for birding in Brazil that fits easily into a bag (although not a pocket); heavily illustrated and a special focus on Brazil's 218 endemic species.

**Philips Guides** (Horizonte Geografico). An excellent Brazilian series of English-language guides aimed at the ecotourist. So far, titles include the *Amazon*, *Pantanal*, *National Parks of Brazil*, *Northeast* and *South*, and all are full of practical information, good maps and photos. Especially useful for hikers, nature-lovers and beach bums. Impossible to get hold of outside Brazil, but easy to find in good Brazilian book-chains like Sodiler and Saraiva.

**Helmut Sick** *Birds in Brazil* (Princeton UP). An English translation of an encyclopedic Brazilian work. The illustrations are superb, but it's too hefty to travel with. More portable guides include Hilty and Brown's *A Guide to the Birds of Colombia* (Princeton UP), and Schaunsee's *Birds of Venezuela* (Princeton UP), which both have considerable overlap for Brazil's western and northern Amazônia, while Narosky and Yzuriea's *Birds of Argentina and Uruguay: A Field Guide* (Vazques Mazzini) is valuable for southern Brazil. See also van Perlo, above.

**Deotado Souza** *All the Birds of Brazil: An Identification Guide* (DALL, Brazil). This handbook clearly describes birds that are found in Brazil, and includes location maps and fairly good colour illustrations. Although published in Brazil, don't expect to stumble across a copy there; instead purchase one from a specialist bookseller before leaving home. An essential companion for any remotely serious Brazil-bound birdwatcher.

# Arts and leisure

## Architecture

**Lauro Cavalcanti** *When Brazil Was Modern: Guide to Architecture, 1928–1960* (Princeton Architectural Press, US). This valuable guide to Brazil's unique contribution to modernist architecture discusses the work of over thirty architects, with sections on specific sites such as Brasília, Pampulha (Belo Horizonte) and the Ministry of Health and Education building in Rio. Compact, but well illustrated, the book makes a perfect travel companion for modernist junkies.

**Deutsches Architektur Museum** (ed) *Oscar Niemeyer: A Legend of Modernism* (Birkhäuser). This sumptuously produced book is a concise survey of Niemeyer's work from his first commissions in Rio in the early 1930s, through Pampulha and Brasília in the 1940s to 1960s, to Niterói's Museu de Arte Contemporânia of the late 1990s. Included are essays by architectural critics which, although at times overly fawning, help illuminate Niemeyer's architectural legacy.

**Marta Iris Montero** *Burle Marx: The Lyrical Landscape* (Thames & Hudson; California UP). A beautifully illustrated book celebrating the life and work of one of the twentieth century's foremost landscape architects, who designed many of Brazil's prominent parks, gardens and other urban spaces (the most famous of which are probably the flowing mosaics alongside Copacabana and Flamengo beaches).

**Styliane Philippou** *Oscar Niemeyer: Curves of Irreverence* (Yale UP). Good biography-cum-assessment of Niemeyer, well illustrated and especially strong on the cultural context of Niemeyer's rise to prominence in the 1940s and 1950s.

**Fernando Tasso Fracaso Pires** *Fazenda: The Great Houses and Plantations of Brazil* (Abbeville Press). A lavish coffee-table book, richly illustrated with photographs of coffee, sugar and cattle *fazenda* houses. There's a useful historical introduction discussing the importance of the *casa grande* in Brazilian society, followed by a look at individual houses, mainly in rural Rio de Janeiro and São Paulo, but also Minas Gerais, Pernambuco, Bahia and Rio Grande do Sul.

## Art and photography

**Gilberto Ferrez** *Photography in Brazil 1840–1900* (New Mexico UP, US, o/p). One of the little-known facts about Brazil is that the first-ever non-portrait photograph was taken of the Paço da Cidade in Rio in 1840, by a Frenchman hot off a ship with the new-fangled Daguerrotype. This is a fascinating compendium of the pioneering work of early photographers in Brazil, including material from all over the country, although the stunning panoramas of Rio from the 1860s onward are the highlight.

**Daniel Levine** (ed) *The Brazilian Photographs of Genevieve Naylor, 1940–1942* (Duke UP). Recently uncovered photographs by a young American photographer, mainly of Rio, Salvador and the small towns of the interior. They are a revelation: Naylor was a great photographer, interested in people and street scenes, not landscapes, and this is a unique visual record of Brazil and its people during the Vargas years.

**Edward Lucie-Smith** *Latin American Art of the Twentieth Century* (Thames & Hudson). It's a pity there aren't volumes on other periods in Latin American art in this excellent and easy-to-obtain series. Still, this is valuable as a look at the Brazilian scene in the context of Latin American art in general.

**Edward J. Sullivan** (ed) *Brazil Body & Soul* (Guggenheim Museum, US). Remarkably, there is still no thorough overview of Brazilian art history, but this lavishly illustrated catalogue to the 2001/2002 New York and Bilbao exhibition is a pretty good starting-point. The catalogue offers glimpses of the art of indigenous cultures and the paintings of Frans Post and Albert Eckhout, two seventeenth-century Dutch visitors, before moving on to discuss in greater detail Baroque art and architecture, Afro-Brazilian art, and twentieth-century artistic movements.

## Music, dance and capoeira

**Bira Almeida** *Capoeira – a Brazilian Art Form* (North Atlantic Books). A *capoeira mestre* (master) explains the history and philosophy behind this African–Brazilian martial art/dance form. The book offers valuable background information for those who practice *capoeira* and for those who are merely interested.

**Ruy Castro** *Bossa Nova – The Story of the Brazilian Music That Seduced the World* (A Capella). A welcome translation of an excellent book by a Brazilian journalist and biographer. This is basically an oral history of bossa nova, packed with incidental detail on Rio nightlife and city culture of the 1950s and early 1960s. A very good read.

**Chris McGowan and Ricardo Pessanha** *The Brazilian Sound: Samba, Bossa Nova and the Popular Music of Brazil* (Temple UP). An easy-to-flick-through and well-written basic manual on modern Brazilian music and musicians. Good to carry with you if you're planning on doing some serious music-buying. There's also a useful bibliography and a good discography.

**Claus Schreiner** *Musica Brasileira* (Marion Boyars, US). Detailed coverage of all aspects of Brazilian music from colonial times through to the present within the broader context of the country's culture and history. One for the specialist.

**Caetano Veloso** *Tropical Truth: A Story of Music and Revolution in Brazil* (Bloomsbury; Knopf). The maestro's account of *tropicalismo* and his early career, including exile, from the 1960s to the early 1970s. Veloso is as good a writer as you would expect, a little over-anxious to show off his learning sometimes, but this is a fascinating despatch from the culture wars of the 1960s.

## Cuisine

**Michael Bateman** *Street Café Brazil* (Conran Octopus; Contemporary Books). The title is rather deceptive, as you're unlikely to come across many of these recipes on Brazilian street stalls, but they are authentic, and the lavish pictures are enough to inspire you to attempt to reproduce them at home.

**Christopher Idone** *Brazil: A Cook's Tour* (Pavilion; Clarkson Potter). A region-by-region look at Brazilian cooking, its origins and influences, with a few recipes thrown in as well. The colour photos of ingredients, markets and dishes are mouthwatering and the text lively and informative. It's good to see São Paulo and the Amazon being discussed separately and at length (when it comes to cookbooks usually only Rio and Bahia get a look in), but the South is completely ignored.

**Joan and David Peterson** *Eat Smart in Brazil: How to Decipher the Menu, Know the Market Foods & Embark on a Tasting Adventure* (Ginkgo Press). The title says it all: a guide for selecting food, both in shops and markets and off a menu, in Brazil. The book is divided into three main sections: a region-by-region account of food ingredients and cooking styles, with some recipes and listings of Brazilian ingredients and dishes. A must for any foodie who needs to know the difference between *pimenta malagueta, pimenta-do-cheiro* and *pimenta-do-reino*.

## Football

**Alex Bellos** *Futebol: The Brazilian Way of Life* (Bloomsbury). Accessible and engaging analysis of Brazilian football, from its early history to its present compulsive mixture of world-class players on the pitch and equally world class levels of corruption off it. Written by a journalist with an eye for original stories: homesick Brazilians playing in the Faroe Islands, tactics for transvestites, and much more. Essential reading.

**Josh Lacey** *God is Brazilian: Charles Miller, the Man Who Brought Football to Brazil* (Tempus, UK). A well-researched and entertaining account of the life and times of Charles Miller, the Anglo-Brazilian who is credited with introducing modern football to Brazil. Football apart, the book offers fascinating observations regarding late Victorian and Edwardian British society both in England and São Paulo.

**Pelé** *Pelé – The Autobiography* (Simon & Schuster, UK). Published to coincide with the 2006 World Cup, this ghost-written "autobiography" of the world's most famous Brazilian is as wooden and formulaic as this type of book alway is, but hey – it's Pelé, and therefore compulsive reading for any football fan.

**Chris Taylor** *The Beautiful Game: A Journey Through Latin American Football* (Latin America Bureau; Perennial). Pinching Pelé's catch-phrase for the title, this is a journalistic report on football subcultures in Brazil and other Latin American countries, often linked to both big business and drug trafficking. Interesting enough, but the author unfortunately forgets to say much about the football.

# Fiction

## Works by Brazilian authors

**Jorge Amado** *Gabriela, Clove and Cinnamon*; *Tereza Batista* (both Abacus, o/p; Avon); *Dona Flor and Her Two Husbands* (Serpent's Tail; Avon); *The Violent Lands* (Collins; Avon). Amado is the proverbial rollicking good read, a fine choice for the beach or on long bus journeys. He's by far the best-known Brazilian writer abroad – there is even a French wine named after him. Purists rightly quibble that the local colour is laid on with a trowel, but Amado's blend of the erotic and exotic has him laughing all the way to the bank.

**Mário de Andrade** *Macunaíma* (Quartet Books, UK). First published in 1928, *Macunaíma* is considered one of the greatest works of Brazilian literature. In this comic tale of the adventures of a popular hero, Macunaíma, a figure from the jungle interior, Andrade presents his typical wealth of exotic images, myths and legends.

**Machado de Assis** *Posthumous Memoirs of Brás Cubas* (Oxford UP). The most important work by the finest novelist Brazil has yet produced. Told by one of the most remarkable characters in fiction, this is an often-hilarious tale of absurd schemes to cure the world of melancholy and half-hearted political ambitions unleashed from beyond the grave. For good translations of Machado's great short stories, *The Devil's Church and Other Stories* (Texas UP, US, o/p) and *Helena* (California UP) are worth going to some trouble to get hold of. His cool, ferociously ironic style veers between black comedy and sardonic analysis of the human condition.

**Patrícia Galvão (Pagu)** *Industrial Park: A Proletarian Novel* (Nebraska UP). An avant-garde novel first published in 1933. Set in the rapidly changing São Paulo factory district of Brás, this remarkable novel captures the sense of time and place, reproducing the voice of a city in the midst of rapid change.

**Luiz Afredo Garcia-Roza** *The Silence of the Rain* (Picador; Henry Holt). A police-procedural thriller by one of Brazil's bestselling writers. Inspector Espinosa is the unorthodox detective who solves a complex web of crime – murder, robbery and fraud – against the backdrop of the sometimes seedy, sometimes exotic, setting of Rio. The inspector returns in the equally compulsive mysteries *December Heat* and *Pursuit*.

**Milton Hatoum** *The Brothers* (Bloomsbury). Set in late nineteenth-century Manaus, this is a family saga based on Lebanese twin brothers and their relationship with their mother. Filled with local colour, this is one of the best Brazilian novels in translation to emerge in recent years.

**Paulo Lins** *City of God* (Bloomsbury; Grove Press). The author, who went on to become a photojournalist, was brought up in Rio's *Cidade de Deus* housing project and uses his knowledge of drug trafficking and gang warfare as the basis of this remarkable novel, the book behind the internationally acclaimed film.

**Clarice Lispector** *The Hour of the Star* (New Direction, US). The most instantly approachable translation of this work by the important Ukrainian-born writer. Her short stories are carefully constructed but, as an author to whom the existence of plot doesn't seem to matter, her books can be difficult. Other translated titles include *Family Ties* (Carcanet, o/p; Texas UP) and *The Foreign Legion* (New Direction, US).

**Patrícia Melo** *Inferno* (Bloomsbury, UK). A thriller set in a *favela* in Rio, this is a powerful story of an 11-year-old boy who becomes a local gang leader. Though his story's often grim, the central character is a complex figure in terms of his relationships with other gang members and his family.

**Antônio Olinto** *The Water House* (Carroll & Graf, US). A wonderful story about an African matriarch and her progeny over a seventy-year period, and the story of her return to West Africa from Bahia after the abolition of slavery. The family saga continues in the *King of Ketu* (R. Collings, US).

**Graciliano Ramos** *Barren Lives* (Texas UP). Masterpiece of the northeastern novelist who introduced social realism into modern Brazilian fiction. The heavy use of regional northeastern Portuguese in the original makes it fiendishly difficult to translate, but it gives you a sense of his great talent.

**João Ubaldo Ribeiro** *An Invincible Memory* (Faber; HarperCollins, o/p). A family saga spanning a 400-year period from the arrival of the Portuguese in Brazil to the present day, featuring anecdotes, history and myths narrated through the experiences of two Bahian families, one aristocratic, the other enslaved. The book was wildly popular when published in Brazil and is considered a national epic.

**Darlene J. Sadlier** (ed) *One Hundred Years After Tomorrow* (Indiana UP). An excellent anthology of short stories introducing the work of twenty twentieth-century Brazilian women, some famous and others less well known.

**Moacyr Scliar** *The Collected Stories of Moacyr Scliar* (New Mexico UP). Scliar, who hails from Porto Alegre, is Brazil's most distinguished Jewish writer. This anthology includes haunting, comic and bleak stories that proclaim Scliar as a master of the short story.

**Márcio Souza** *Mad Maria* (Avon, US, o/p). A comic drama set against the backdrop of the absurdity of rail construction in nineteenth-century Amazônia. Souza's excellent *The Emperor of the Amazon* (Abacus, o/p;

Avon, o/p) is another humorous and powerful description of the decadence that characterized late nineteenth-century Amazonian society.

**Antônio Torres** *The Land* (Readers International). Set in a decaying town in the parched interior of the northeast, this is a grim tale of people trapped and people trying to get away. In *Blues for a Lost Childhood* (Readers International), Torres continues with the same theme, but this time focusing on a journalist who makes it to Rio but finds life there to be a living nightmare.

## Works set in Brazil

**Mario Vargas Llosa** *The War of the End of the World* (Faber; Penguin). Goes well with da Cunha. The Peruvian writer produced this haunting novel, based on the events of Canudos, in the 1970s. The translation is good and the book is easy to obtain.

**Jean-Christophe Rufin** *Brazil Red* (Picador; W.W. Norton). The winner of France's prestigious Goncourt literary award, this action-packed historical novel is set against France's ill-fated attempt to conquer Brazil in the sixteenth century as well as questions about the nature of civilization and culture, religion and freedom.

**John Updike** *Brazil* (Picador). Unfortunately, it has to be admitted this is probably the worst novel the great Updike ever wrote, as he transposes the Tristan and Isolde myth to Brazil. While appreciating the thanks he gives to *RG Brazil* in his acknowledgements, we dissociate ourselves from the result.

**Karen Tei Yamashita** *Brazil-Maru* (Coffee House Press, US). The story of Brazil's Japanese immigrant population is told through a multi-generational saga involving conflicts between family members seeking individual freedom in their adopted country and those striving to maintain community cohesion.

## Children's literature set in Brazil

**Josua Doder** *Grk and the Pelotti Gang* (Andersen Press). Along with his dog Grk, Tim, a brave (and foolhardy) British child finds himself in the mean streets of Rio in search of the notorious Pelotti gang. Fast-paced and funny and with lots of local colour, Tim and Grk survive being kidnapped and being held in a Rio *favela* as well as jungle adventures. Suitable for 8- to 12-year-olds.

**Eva Ibbotson** *Journey to the River Sea* (Macmillan; Puffin). Set at the turn of the twentieth century in Manaus amidst the Amazon rubber boom, this old-fashioned adventure story unfolds in an environment that its host of amusing characters either cherishes or feels nothing but contempt for. A great book to give kids to read, especially girls; 9 years up.

# Brazilian cinema

Brazil and Mexico are the only Latin American countries with strong **national cinemas**, and the best Brazilian directors, like the best Mexican ones, now work outside Brazil on international productions. Brazil has produced excellent films since the 1950s, many of them widely available abroad, and a few nights in front of the DVD player before departure is a good investment in getting the most out of your trip.

## Two-way traffic

Brazil, for understandable reasons, has long attracted foreign filmmakers looking for exotic scenery – from James Bond fight sequences on the Pão de Açúcar cable car to *Blame It on Rio*, the lowest moment of Michael Caine's distinguished career. Fred Astaire and Ginger Rogers danced together for the first time in *Flying Down to Rio*, in which 1930s Copacabana, complete with a half-built *Copacabana Palace Hotel*, can be glimpsed below the legs of the dancing girls on the top wing of the biplane in the climactic dance sequence – all of which took place on a Hollywood film set.

But other foreigners made a more serious cultural contribution. **Orson Welles** spent many months filming in Brazil immediately after *Citizen Kane* had made him a star. Although he was, characteristically, never able to finish the project, the footage was later put together into a documentary film called *It's All True*, an invaluable record of Rio and Carnaval in the early 1940s. Two decades later, French director Marcel Camus filmed *Orfeu Negro* ("Black Orpheus") in Rio with a largely amateur cast, resetting the Orpheus myth during the Rio Carnaval and putting it to an unforgettable soundtrack by Tom Jobim. *Pixote*, a searing 1982 film about street children in Rio that also used amateurs was directed by Hector Babenco, an Argentinian.

More recently, Brazilians have been moving the other way. Sônia Braga traded in success in Brazilian films in the 1970s for a career in US independent cinema from the 1980s on, but the country's most distinguished cinematic exports have been directors, most notably **Walter Salles**, who caught international attention with *Central Station* in 1998 and the underestimated, beautifully filmed biopic of Che Guevara's early life, *Motorcycle Diaries*, and **Fernando Meirelles**, whose brilliant *City of God* in 2003 led to *The Constant Gardener* (2005), the first international Hollywood hit directed by a Brazilian. His success outside Brazil, with four Oscar nominations so far, is an indication of how Brazilian talent can be a shot in the arm for international cinema.

But Brazilian cinema's recent international success was built on decades of hard work, establishing a national cinema industry and somehow keeping it going in the face of intense competition from television on the one hand and Hollywood on the other. Along the way Brazil has created a national cinema like no other South American country, returning again and again to its history for inspiration.

## The early years: chanchadas and cinema novo

The history of Brazilian cinema goes right back to the earliest years of the medium: the first cinematograph arrived in Brazil in 1897 and there were already 22 cinemas registered in Rio by 1910. But the first decades of cinema in Brazil were dominated by American and European silent films, and it was not until the early years of sound that the first Brazilian features were made. The first Brazilian film studio, Cinedia, based in Rio, was making Carnaval films and slapstick comedies, nicknamed *chanchadas*, from the early 1930s – **Carmen Miranda** was the major star of the period, making her film debut in *A Voz do Carnaval* ("The Voice of Carnaval") in 1932. But in an indication of the low quality of the Brazilian film industry in those years it was not her films that led to her discovery by Hollywood, but the fact a Hollywood producer saw her sing and dance in the legendary Urca casino in the late 1930s and took her home for a screen test.

Serious cinema in Brazil really began in the early 1950s when Assis Chateaubriand, a Brazilian press baron and early media entrepreneur, put up the money to create Vera Cruz Studios and hired director **Lima Barreto** to make *O Cangaçeiro* ("The Outlaw"). Very loosely based on the true life story of Lampião in the northeastern *sertão*, it was by far the most expensive Brazilian film made up to that point. It was shot on location in the Northeast, and Barreto, heavily influenced by John Ford, made what was basically a Brazilian Western, with the landscape just as much a character as any of the actors – which was just as well, since the acting was pretty dire. But the film, shot in luminous black and white, looked fabulous and was a minor sensation in Europe, winning Brazilian cinema's first international award for best adventure film at Cannes in 1952.

*O Cangaçeiro* was a forerunner of what by the late 1950s was being called *cinema novo*: heavily influenced by the Italian neorealism of masters like Vittorio Da Sica, young Brazilian directors took a hard look at the trials and tribulations of daily life in Brazil. The Northeast loomed large in *cinema novo*; the two classics of the genre, *Vidas Secas* ("Barren Lives"), directed by Nelson Pereira dos Santos in 1963, and *O Pagador de Promessas* ("The Promise Keeper"), directed by **Anselmo Duarte** in 1963, are both set in the region and were both banned by the military after the 1964 coup for their unflinching portrayal of poverty and rural desperation.

## Cinema under dictatorship

The military had a paradoxical effect on Brazilian cinema. On the surface they were every bit as repressive as one would expect: films and scripts were subject to rigid censorship and regularly banned, and anything that could be considered unpatriotic – such as the portrayal of poverty or social problems – was off limits. Italian neorealism, for example, was definitely out. On the other hand, the military did believe a flourishing film industry was a form of building national prestige, and in 1969 set up a state film production and financing company, **Embrafilme**, still going today and without which the modern Brazilian film industry would not exist. As a channel for (modest) government subsidy towards the film industry, it allowed a generation of Brazilian filmmakers to hone their talents without having to spend all their time chasing commercial work, and with expanding television networks supplying increasing numbers of professional actors to the film industry, the 1960s and 1970s saw a sharp rise in the number of films produced in Brazil.

In cinema, as in music, this was a time of great inventiveness in Brazil. Filmmakers reacted to military censorship in a number of ways. One was diverting political comment into genres the authorities usually didn't bother to monitor, such as erotic films, where the usual scenes of rumpy-pumpy would be punctuated by political soliloquies as the characters smoked cigarettes in bed together afterwards. Another was to make dramas that faithfully portrayed episodes of Brazilian history, but in a way pregnant with meaning for the present. This was a style one of the masters of *cinema novo*, the director **Nelson Pereira dos Santos**, made his own with two superb films during the dictatorship. *Como Era Gostoso o Meu Francês* ("How Delicious Was My Frenchman"), released in

1971, went so far as to be shot largely in Tupi and French instead of Portuguese. It was a faithful historical reconstruction of the earliest days of Brazil but also a hilarious political allegory. *Memórias do Cárcere* ("Memories of Jail"), produced in 1984, was based on Graciliano Ramos's prison diaries during his various incarcerations by Getúlio Vargas in the 1930s and 1940s. Another example of the genre was **Joaquim Pedro de Andrade**'s *Os Inconfidentes* ("The Conspirators"), released in 1974 at the peak of the dictatorship. An uncensorable reconstruction of the national hero Tiradentes' eighteenth-century conspiracy against the Portuguese Crown, so well researched that much of the dialogue is taken from court transcripts of the period, its portrayal of the brutal repression of dissent by the colonial authorities was a brilliantly subversive use of a national myth to make contemporary political points.

The other response was to make films so elliptical and packed with symbolism that nobody outside film schools could understand them. The influence of 1960s French filmmakers, especially Godard, was overwhelming in the main exponent of this genre, **Glauber Rocha**. Still widely admired by the Brazilian intelligentsia, his films created a stir on the European art-house circuit of their time, but his best-known works, *Terra em Transe* ("Land In Trance", 1967) and *Antônio das Mortes* (1969), are unwatchable today, save for their historical interest.

## Modern Brazilian cinema

As the military dictatorship wound down, realism returned to Brazilian cinema, notably with Leon Hirszman's portrayal of the São Paulo car-factory strikes in *Eles Não Usam Black Tie* ("They Don't Wear Dinner Jackets", 1981) and Cacá Diegues's excellent *Bye Bye Brazil* (1979), which followed a tawdry group of circus perfomers through the country's hinterland against a marvellous soundtrack by Chico Buarque. Hector Babenco's *Pixote* (1982) became the best-known film abroad from this period, but *Bye Bye Brazil* is the real classic.

It was not until the consolidation of democracy in the 1990s that Brazilian filmmakers could relax, put politics in its proper place as part of life rather than the crux of everything and start producing the kind of films that could catch the attention of international audiences in a way Brazilian cinema in previous decades – often fascinating but ultimately a little parochial – was never quite capable of doing.

There were indications of new directorial talent well before the hits came. Female directors emerged for the first time, with **Carla Camaruti** producing a highly entertaining take on early Brazilian history in *Carlota Joaquina* (1994), and **Helen Solberg**'s intelligent and thought-provoking exploration of Carmen Miranda's life and myth in the drama-documentary *Carmen Miranda – Bananas Is My Business* (1994). Young directors also emerged; **Andrushka Waddington** was all of 30 when he directed *Eu Tu Eles* ("Me You Them") in 2002, a reworking of the old *cinema novo* theme of life in the northeastern *sertão*, but this time with the central character a woman choosing from a variety of husbands rather than the other way around, and with yet another superb soundtrack, this time by Gilberto Gil.

But three films in particular catapulted Brazilian cinema to international attention. *O Que É Isso Companheiro* (literally "What's Up Comrade", but sensibly renamed "Four Days in September" for English-speaking audiences), released in 1997, is a taut, beautifully done thriller directed by Bruno Barreto, re-creating very accurately the kidnapping of the American ambassador in 1969 and featuring Alan Arkin in a cameo role as the ambassador. It was a hit internationally, but not as big a hit as two later films by the young and extravagantly talented directors **Walter Salles** and **Fernando Meirelles**.

Salles's *Estação Central* ("Central Station"), released in 1998, tells the story of the developing relationship between a young boy and an old woman thrown together by chance, as they travel by bus from Rio into, inevitably, the interior of the Northeast, where all Brazilian filmmakers seem to head when they need a metaphor for the national condition. The plot, which could easily have turned sentimental and mawkish in less assured hands, is excellently acted and directed and becomes almost unbearably moving at the end.

*Cidade de Deus* ("City of God"), Fernando Meirelles's stunning directorial debut released in 2003, tells the story of a real Rio *favela* from its early days in the 1960s to the mid-1980s. It is a remarkable film. The cast is largely amateur, drawn from Cidade de Deus itself, with a few professional actors thrown in (including the mesmerizing Matheus Nachtergaele as a gunrunning gangster, also to be seen in an almost equally memorable performance as a cold-blooded terrorist in *Four Days in September*). Meirelles came to cinema from shooting mainly commercials and music videos for television, and it shows, with his jumpy editing and distinctive, stylish use of colour and sound. The novel on which it is based is – it should be stressed – a novel rather than a memoir, but in its unflinching portrayal of the descent into urban hell drug wars have produced in many of Rio's *favelas*, there is more truth in the film than in most documentaries.

Brazil's next international hit, *Tropa de Elite* ("Elite Troop"), directed by **José Padilha** in 2008, had the same theme. Its extremely violent portrayal of Rio's elite anti-narcotics police unit was mistakenly criticized as fascistic by some reviewers, but the film is in fact ethnographically accurate in its portrayal of police corruption, the nexus between violence, politics and organized crime in Rio, and the complex, intimate yet distant relationship between Rio's middle and working classes, sharing the same urban space but in wholly different ways. After winning the Golden Bear in Berlin's 2008 biennial, it looks set to emulate the success of *City of God* once it goes on general release.

In their different ways – *Estação Central*'s quiet building of character and atmosphere, *Cidade de Deus*'s pyrotechnic brilliance – Salles and Meirelles are examples of the heights to which Brazilian cinema can now reach. Yet as they would be the first to admit, they stand on the shoulders of predecessors who for over fifty years struggled to create what is now the liveliest and most innovative national cinema in South America. With the best of Brazilian cinema now easily available on DVD everywhere, investing a little time in your living room is a quick, painless and above all entertaining way to get to know Brazil, wherever and whenever you go.

# Football

Far more than just a game, **football** is a central part of popular culture, with all Brazilians fiercely proud of the country's record of being the only country to have qualified for all World Cups – and to have won more of them than any other nation. Brazilian fans are the most demanding in the world; it is not enough to win, Brazilians insist on winning in style, on the untranslatable but self-explanatory *futebol-arte*. Even though the Brazilian leagues are now effectively feeder leagues for Europe, and the best now head directly for Europe as teenagers rather than serving an apprenticeship at home, there are such reserves of talent in the country that very high quality football is still the rule in most of the big cities. And everywhere you find that compulsive mix of brilliant attack and fragile defending that makes the Brazilian national team the most charismatic side in the world, win or lose. **Brazil's hosting of the 2014 World Cup** is already eagerly anticipated and work on the stadiums has already begun.



## Early days

British railway engineers introduced football to Brazil in the 1890s, and, as in Argentina, the British influence is still visible in football vocabulary (*futebol, pênalti*) and in the names of some of Brazil's oldest teams, like São Paulo's Coríntians. Brazilians took to football like a duck to water, and by the 1920s the Rio and São Paulo state leagues which still largely dominate Brazilian football were up and running. Brazil became the first South American country to send a team to compete in Europe, to Italy in 1934, and already by then Brazilians had realized that football was far too important for race to get in the way: Brazil's first World Cup star, **Leônidas**, who fascinated Europeans in the 1930s with his outlandish skills, was Afro-Brazilian.

Getúlio Vargas was the first in a long line of Brazilian presidents to make political capital out of the game, building the gorgeous Art-Deco Pacaembu stadium in São Paulo in the 1930s, and then bringing the **1950 World Cup** to Brazil by constructing what has become one of the game's great global temples, the **Maracanã** in Rio. In that competition, Brazil had what many of the older generation still think was the greatest Brazilian side ever; the team hammered everyone, then came up against Uruguay in the final, where a draw would have been enough to secure Brazil's first *Copa*. Brazil went in at half-time ahead 1-0 but the Uruguayans hadn't read the script and won 2-1, a national trauma that still haunts popular memory sixty years on – most notably in a serious argument over whether to play the final of the 2014 World Cup in the Maracanã, on the grounds it may be jinxed.

## Greatness

But success was not long in coming. A series of great teams, all with the incomparable **Pelé** as playmaker, won the World Cup in Sweden in 1958 (still the only World Cup a South American team has won in Europe), and then retained it in Chile in 1962, even with Pelé injured. His place as heart of the team was taken by probably the greatest winger in football history, **Mané Garrincha**, an alcoholic all his adult life, including his footballing years, who died tragically young in a life that transfixed Brazilians then and now. Then, most memorably, Brazil **won the 1970 World Cup in Mexico** with what is universally regarded as the greatest team in the history of the game, with Pelé surrounded by such great names as **Gerson**, **Rivelino**, **Tostão** and **Carlos Alberto**. Brazil got to keep the Jules Rimet trophy as the World Cup's first three-time winners. Embarrassingly, but rather typically, bandits stole the historic cup from the headquarters of the Brazilian football association in Rio a few years later; it was never seen again.

After an interlude during the 1970s, Brazil flirted with greatness again in the 1980s, when a new generation of *craques* (the wonderful Portuguese word for crack players), led by **Zico** in attack but also including an extraordinary midfield made up of **Falcão**, **Sócrates**, **Éder** and **Cerezo**, failed to win the World Cups of 1982 and 1986; they played some of the best football in the tournament's history in the process, losing to Italy in 1982 and France in 1986 in matches that have become legendary.

## Good but not great: modern Brazilian football

It took Brazil until **1994** to reclaim the World Cup, when they beat Italy on penalties in one of the worst finals on record. This was a triumph built on such un-Brazilian virtues as a combative rather than a creative midfield and a solid defence; a team whose only endearing features were the comically dependable incompetence of its goalkeeper, **Taffarel**, maintaining a great Brazilian tradition of fragility between the sticks, and the quality of the attack, where the brilliance of **Romário** found the perfect foil in **Bebeto**.

But there was uneasiness in Brazil at the workmanlike way they had won, an uneasiness that crystallized into scandal four years later in France when, despite the presence of the young prodigy **Ronaldo** leading the attack, they had an unconvincing campaign. They were lucky to get to the final, where a French side that looked inferior on paper beat them 3-0. There was strong suspicion that Ronaldo, who suffered a seizure before the game, only played at the insistence of the team's sponsor, Nike. This symbolized a widespread feeling in Brazil that the game was on the wrong track: club owners selling out to commercial interests; stars making their living in Europe and forgetting their obligation to the national team; and a duller, more European-style emphasis on fitness and teamwork banishing the individual skill that lies at the heart of *futebol-arte* as a result.

There was and is something to this; unprecedented amounts of money flowed into Brazilian football in the 1990s, and it would certainly have been unthinkable to the national sides of 1970 and the 1980s that Brazil could play two finals of a World Cup without scoring a goal in open play. The malaise seemed to deepen in the run-up to the 2002 World Cup: corruption scandals roiled the game; Ronaldo was sidelined by career-threatening injuries; and the team struggled for the first time ever to qualify for the competition, coming close to the indignity of having to play Australia in a play-off to get there at all.

So when Brazil won the competition that year it was a heartening surprise. There were several factors behind it, most importantly Ronaldo's recovery from injury and shrewd manager **Felipe Scolari**'s ability to pull together a settled, solid side just when it mattered most. Brazil played some fantastic football on their way to a final with a fairytale ending, where Ronaldo crowned his comeback with both goals in a 2-0 victory against Germany. The only negative aspect was that victory took the pressure off the sleazy figures in the boardrooms – but frankly, against the Germans, it seems a price worth paying.

The year **2006**, was a disappointment, as traditional bugbears France beat an overhyped but underperforming Brazil side. It is too early to say how Brazil will measure up against their storied history in **South Africa in 2010**, but one thing is sure: the *favelas* and small towns of the interior from where most of Brazil's greatest players – Pelé, Garrincha, Romário, Ronaldo – have come are a permanent conveyor-belt of talent, as football offers a glittering exit-route out of poverty. Playing at home, as they will in 2014, it's a brave person who would bet against them.

# Language

# Language

# Portuguese

Learning some Portuguese before you go to Brazil is an extremely good idea. Although many well-educated Brazilians speak English, and it's now the main second language taught in schools, this hasn't filtered through to most of the population. If you know Spanish you're halfway there: there are obvious similarities in the grammar and vocabulary, so you should be able to make yourself understood if you speak slowly, and reading won't present you with too many problems. However, Portuguese pronunciation is utterly different and much less straightforward than Spanish, so unless you take the trouble to learn a bit about it you won't have a clue what Brazilians are talking about.

Unfortunately, far too many people – especially Spanish-speakers – are put off going to Brazil precisely by the language, but in reality this should be one of your main reasons for going. Brazilian Portuguese is a colourful, sensual language full of wonderfully rude and exotic vowel sounds, swooping intonation and hilarious idiomatic expressions. You'll also find that Brazilians will greatly appreciate even your most rudimentary efforts, and every small improvement in your Portuguese will make your stay in Brazil ten times more enjoyable.

People who have learned their Portuguese **in Portugal or in Lusophone Africa** won't have any real problems with the language in Brazil, but there are some quite big differences. There are many variations in vocabulary, and Brazilians take more liberties with the language, but the most notable differences are in pronunciation: Brazilian Portuguese is spoken more slowly and clearly; the neutral vowels so characteristic of European Portuguese tend to be sounded in full; in much of Brazil outside Rio the slushy "sh" sound doesn't exist; and the "de" and "te" endings of words like *cidade* and *diferente* are palatalized so they end up sounding like "sidadgee" and "djiferentchee".

The best **dictionary** currently available is the *Collins Portuguese Dictionary*. There is a pocket edition, but you might consider taking the fuller, larger version, which concentrates on the way the language is spoken today and gives plenty of specifically Brazilian vocabulary. For a **phrasebook**, look no further than *The Rough Guide to Portuguese*, with useful two-way glossaries, basic grammar and more.

## Pronunciation

The rules of **pronunciation** are complicated, but the secret is to throw yourself wholeheartedly into this explosive linguistic jacuzzi.

### Non-nasal vowels

**A** shouldn't present you with too many problems. It's usually somewhere between the "**a**" sound of "b**a**t" and that of "f**a**ther".

**E** has three possible pronunciations. When it occurs at the beginning or in the middle of a word, it will usually sound either a bit like the "**e**" in "b**e**t"– eg *ferro* (iron) and *miséria* (poverty) – or like the "**ay**" in "h**ay**"– eg *mesa* (table) and *pêlo* (hair). However, the difference can be quite subtle and it's not something you should worry about too much at the start. The third pronunciation is radically different from the other two: at the end of a word, "**e**" sounds like "**y**" in "happ**y**", eg *fome* ("fommy", hunger) and *se* (if), which actually sounds like the Spanish "si".

**I** is straightforward. It's always an "**ee**" sound like the "**i**" in "pol**i**ce", eg *isto* (this).

**O** is another letter with three possible pronunciations. At the beginning or in the middle of a word, it normally sounds either the way it does in "d**o**g" – eg *loja* (shop) and *pó* (powder) – or the way it does in "g**o**"– eg *homem* (man) and *pôquer* (poker). At the end of a word "**o**" sounds like the "**oo**" in "b**oo**t", so *obrigado* (thank you) is pronounced "obri-GA-doo". And the definite article "**o**" as in *o homem* (the man) is pronounced "**oo**".

**U** is always pronounced like "**oo**" in "b**oo**t", eg *cruz* (cross).

There are also a variety of vowel combinations or diphthongs that sound pretty much the way you would expect them to. They are **ai** (pronounced like "i" in "ride"); **au** (pronounced as in "sh**out**"); **ei** (pronounced as in "h**ay**"); and **oi** (pronounced as in "b**oy**"). The only one that has an unexpected pronunciation is **ou**, which sounds like "o" in "r**o**se".

## Nasal vowels

The fun really starts when you get into the **nasal vowel sounds**. Generally speaking, each "normal" vowel has its nasal equivalent. The trick in pronouncing these is to be completely uninhibited. To take one example, the word **pão** (bread). First of all, just say "pow" to yourself. Then say it again, but this time half close your mouth and shove the vowel really hard through your nose. Try it again, even more vigorously. It should sound something like "powng", but much more nasal and without really sounding the final "g".

There are two main ways in which Portuguese indicates a nasal vowel. One is through the use of the **tilde**, as in *pão*. The other is the use of the letters **m** or **n** after the vowel. As a general rule, whenever you see a vowel followed by "m" or "n" and then another consonant, the vowel will be nasal – eg *gente*. The same thing applies when the vowel is followed by "m" at the end of a word, eg *tem*, *bom* – in these cases, the "m" is not pronounced, it just nasalizes the vowel.

Below are some of the main nasal vowels and examples of words that use them. However, it must be emphasized that the phonetic versions of the nasal sounds we've given are only approximate.

**Ã, and -am or -an followed by a consonant** indicate nasal "**a**" – eg *maçã* (apple), *campo* (field), *samba*.

**-ão or -am at the end of a word** indicate the "**owng**" sound, as explained above in *pão*. Other examples are in *estação* (station), *mão* (hand), *falam* ("FA-lowng"; they talk).

**-em or -en followed by a consonant** indicate a nasalized "**e**" sound – eg *tempo* (weather), *entre* (between), *gente* (people).

**-em or -ens at the end of a word** indicate an "**eyng**" sound – eg *tem* ("teyng"; you have or there is), *viagens* ("vee-A-zheyngs"; journeys).

**-im or -in at the end of a word** or followed by a consonant are simply a nasal "**ee**" sound, so *capim* (grass) sounds a bit like "ca-PEENG".

**-om or -on at the end of a word** or followed by a consonant indicate nasal "**o**". An obvious example is *bom* (good), which sounds pretty similar to "bon" in French.

**-um or -un at the end of a word** or followed by a consonant indicate nasal "**u**"– eg *um* (one).

**-ãe** sounds a bit like "**eyeing**" said quickly and explosively – eg *mãe* (mother).

**-õe** sounds like "**oing**". Most words ending in "-ão" make their plural like this, with an "s" (which is pronounced) at the end – eg *estação* (station) becomes *estações* (stations).

## Consonants

Brazilian **consonants** are more straightforward than the vowels, but there are a few little oddities you'll need to learn. We've only listed the consonants where they differ from their English counterparts.

**C** is generally pronounced hard, as in "**c**at" (eg *campo*). However, when followed by "i" or "e", it's pronounced softly, as in "**c**eiling"(eg *cidade*, city). It's also pronounced softly whenever it's written with a cedilla (eg *estação*).

**CH** is pronounced like English "**sh**", so *chá* (tea) is said "sha".

**D** is generally pronounced as in English. However, in most parts of Brazil it's palatalized to sound like "**dj**" whenever it comes before an "i" or final "e". So *difícil* (difficult) is pronounced "djee-FEE-siw", and the ubiquitous preposition *de* (of) sounds like "djee".

**G** is generally pronounced hard as in English "**g**od" (eg *gosto*, I like). But before "e" or "i" it's pronounced like the "**s**" in English "vi**s**ion" or "mea**s**ure" – eg *geral* (general) and *gíria* (slang).

**H** is always silent (eg *hora*, hour).

**J** is pronounced like the "**s**" in English "vi**s**ion" or "mea**s**ure"– eg *jogo* (game) and *janeiro* (January).

**L** is usually pronounced as in English. But at the end of a word, it takes on a peculiar, almost Cockney pronunciation, becoming a bit like a "**w**". So Brasil is pronounced "bra-ZEEW". When followed by "h", it's pronounced "**ly**" as in "million"; so *ilha* (island) comes out as "EE-lya".

**N** is normally pronounced as in English, but when it's followed by "h" it becomes "**ny**". So *sonho* (dream) sounds like "SON-yoo".

**Q** always comes before "u" and is pronounced either "**k**" or, more usually, "**kw**". So *cinquenta* (fifty) is pronounced "sin-KWEN-ta", but *quero* (I want) is pronounced "KE-roo".

**R** is usually as in English. However, at the beginning of a word it's pronounced like an English "**h**". So "Rio" is actually pronounced "HEE-oo", and *rádio* (radio) is pronounced "HA-djee-oo".

**RR** is always pronounced like an English "**h**". So *ferro* is pronounced "FE-hoo".

**S** is normally pronounced like an English "**s**", and in São Paulo and the South this never changes. But in Rio and many places to the north, "**s**" sounds like English "**sh**" when it comes before a consonant and at the end of a word (*estação*, "esh-ta-SOWNG").

**T** is normally pronounced as in English but, like "d", it changes before "i" and final "e". So *sorte* (luck) is pronounced "SOR-chee", and the great hero of Brazilian history, Tiradentes, is pronounced "chee-ra-DEN-chees".

**X** is pronounced like an English "**sh**" at the beginning of a word, and elsewhere like an English "**x**" or "**z**". So *xadrez* (chess) is pronounced "sha-DREYZ", while *exército* (army) is pronounced "e-ZER-si-too".

## Stress

Any word that has an accent of any kind, including a tilde, is stressed on that syllable, so *miséria* (poverty) is pronounced "mi-ZE-ree-a". If there is no accent, the following rules generally apply (the syllables to be stressed are in capitals):

• Words that end with the vowels a, e and o are stressed on the penultimate syllable. So *entre* (between) sounds like "EN-tree", and *compro* (I buy) "KOM-proo". This also applies when these vowels are followed by -m, -s or -ns: *falam* is stressed "FA-lowng".

• Words that end with the vowels i and u are stressed on the final syllable: *abacaxi* (pineapple) is pronounced "a-ba-ka-ZEE". This also applies when i and u are followed by -m, -s or -ns, so *capim* is pronounced "ka-PEENG".

• Words ending in consonants are usually stressed on the final syllable, eg *rapaz* (boy), stressed "ha-PAZ".

Some useful examples:

**Rio de Janeiro** HEE-oo djee zha-NEY-roo
**Belo Horizonte** BE-loo o-ri-ZON-chee
**Rio Grande do Sul** HEE-oo GRAN-djee doo Soow
**Recife** he-SEE-fee
**rodoviária** ho-do-vee-A-ree-a
**onde** (where) ON-djee
**não entende** (he doesn't understand) now en-TEN-djee
**sim** (yes) SEENG (but hardly sound the final "g")
**ruim** (bad) hoo-WEENG (again hardly sound the "g")
**vinte** (twenty) VEEN-chee
**correio** (post office) co-HAY-oo

# Brazilian Portuguese words and phrases

## Basic expressions

| | | | |
|---|---|---|---|
| **Yes, No** | Sim, Não | **Good, Bad** | Bom, Ruim |
| **Please** | Por favor | **Big, Small** | Grande, Pequeno |
| **Thank you** | Obrigado (men)/ Obrigada (women) | **A little, A lot** | Um pouco, Muito |
| | | **More, Less** | Mais, Menos |
| **Where, When** | Onde, Quando | **Another** | Outro/a |
| **What, How much** | Que, Quanto | **Today, Tomorrow** | Hoje, Amanhã |
| **This, These** | Este | **Yesterday** | Ontem |
| **That one, Those** | Aquele | **But** | Mas (pronounced like "mice") |
| **Now, Later** | Agora, Mais tarde | | |
| **Open, Closed** | Aberto/a, Fechado/a | **And** | E (pronounced like "ee" in "seek") |
| **Entrance, Exit** | Entrada, Saída | | |
| **Pull, Push** | Puxe, Empurre | **Something, Nothing** | Alguma coisa, Nada |
| **With, Without** | Com, Sem | **Sometimes** | Ás vezes |
| **For** | Para | | |

## Greetings and responses

| | | | |
|---|---|---|---|
| **Hello, Goodbye** | Oi, Tchau (like the Italian "ciao") | **Excuse me** | Com licença |
| | | **How are you?** | Como vai? |
| **Good morning** | Bom dia | **Fine** | Bem |
| **Good afternoon** | Boa tarde | **Congratulations** | Parabéns |
| **Good night** | Boa noite | **Cheers** | Saúde |
| **Sorry** | Desculpa | | |

## Useful phrases and colloquial expressions

| | | | |
|---|---|---|---|
| **Do you speak English?** | Você fala inglês? | **What's your name?** | Como se chama? |
| **I don't understand** | Não entendo | **I am English** | Sou inglês/inglesa |
| **I don't speak Portuguese** | Não falo português | **...Scottish** | ...escocês/escocesa |
| | | **...Welsh** | ...galês/galesa |
| **What's the Portuguese for this?** | Como se diz em português? | **...Irish** | ...irlandês/irlandesa |
| | | **...American** | ...estaduidense |
| | | **...Canadian** | ...canadense |
| **What did you say?** | O que você disse? | **...Australian** | ...australiano/a |
| **My name is...** | Meu nome é... | | |

| | |
|---|---|
| …New Zealander | …neozelandês/ neozelandesa |
| …South African | …sul-african/a |
| Do you have…? | Você tem…? |
| the time? | as horas? |
| Everything's fine | Tudo bem |
| OK | Tá bom |
| I'm hungry | Estou com fome |
| I'm thirsty | Estou com sede |
| I feel ill | Me sinto mal |
| I want to see a doctor | Quero ver um medico |
| What's the matter? | Qual é o problema? |
| There is (is there?) | Há…(?) |
| I want, I'd like… | Quero… |
| I can… | Posso... |
| I can't… | Não posso… |
| I don't know | Não sei |
| It's hot | Está quente |
| It's cold | Está frio |
| It's great | Está legal |
| It's boring | É chato |
| I'm bored, annoyed | Estou chateado |
| I've had it up to here | Estou de saco cheio |
| There's no way | Não tem jeito |
| Crazy | Louco/a, maluco/a |
| Tired | Cansado/a |

## Asking directions, getting around

| | |
|---|---|
| Where is…? | Onde fica…? |
| the bus station | a rodoviária |
| the bus stop | a parada de ônibus |
| the nearest hotel | o hotel mais próximo |
| the toilet | o banheiro/sanitário |
| Left, right, straight on | Esquerda, Direita, Direto |
| Go straight on and turn left | Vai direto e dobra à esquerda |
| Where does the bus to…leave? | De onde sai o ônibus para…? |
| Is this the bus to Rio? | É esse o ônibus para Rio? |
| Do you go to…? | Você vai para…? |
| I'd like a (return) ticket to... | Quero uma pasagem (ida e volta) para… |
| What time does it leave (arrive)? | Que horas sai (chega) |
| Far, Near | Longe, Perto |
| Slowly, Quickly | Devagar, Rápido |

## Accommodation

| | |
|---|---|
| Do you have a room? | Você tem um quarto? |
| with two beds/ double bed | com duas camas/ cama de casal |
| It's for one person/ two people | É para uma pessoa/ duas pessoas |
| It's fine, how much is it? | Está bom, quanto é? |
| It's too expensive | É caro demais |
| Do you have anything cheaper? | Tem algo mais barato? |
| Is there a hotel/ campsite nearby? | Tem um hotel/ camping por aqui? |

## Numbers

| | |
|---|---|
| 1 | Um, Uma |
| 2 | Dois, Duas |
| 3 | Três |
| 4 | Quatro |
| 5 | Cinco |
| 6 | Seis |
| 7 | Sete |
| 8 | Oito |
| 9 | Nove |
| 10 | Dez |
| 11 | Onze |
| 12 | Doze |
| 13 | Treze |
| 14 | Quatorze |
| 15 | Quinze |
| 16 | Dezesseis |
| 17 | Dezessete |
| 18 | Dezoito |

| | |
|---|---|
| 19 | Dezenove |
| 20 | Vinte |
| 21 | Vinte e um |
| 30 | Trinta |
| 40 | Quarenta |
| 50 | Cinquenta |
| 60 | Sesenta |
| 70 | Setenta |
| 80 | Oitenta |
| 90 | Noventa |
| 100 | Cem |
| 200 | Duzentos |
| 300 | Trezentos |
| 500 | Quinhentos |
| 1000 | Mil |
| 2000 | Dois mil |
| 5000 | Cinco mil |
| Million/s | Milhão/milhões |

## Days and months

| | |
|---|---|
| Monday | Segunda-feira (or Segunda) |
| Tuesday | Terça-feira (or Terça) |
| Wednesday | Quarta-Feira (or Quarta) |
| Thursday | Quinta-feira (or Quinta) |
| Friday | Sexta-feira (or Sexta) |
| Saturday | Sábado |
| Sunday | Domingo |
| January | Janeiro |
| February | Fevereiro |
| March | Março |
| April | Abril |
| May | Maio |
| June | Junho |
| July | Julho |
| August | Agosto |
| September | Setembro |
| October | Outubro |
| November | Novembro |
| December | Dezembro |

# A Brazilian menu reader

## Basics

| | |
|---|---|
| Açúcar | Sugar |
| Alho e óleo | Garlic and olive-oil sauce |
| Almoço | Lunch |
| Arroz | Rice |
| Azeite | Olive oil |
| Café colonial | High tea |
| Café de manhã | Breakfast |
| Cardápio | Menu |
| Carne | Meat |
| Colher | Spoon |
| Conta/Nota | Bill |
| Copo | Glass |
| Entrada | Hors d'oeuvre |
| Faca | Knife |
| Farinha | Dried manioc flour |
| Garçom | Waiter |
| Garfo | Fork |
| Garrafa | Bottle |
| Jantar | Dinner, to have dinner |
| Legumes/Verduras | Vegetables |
| Manteiga | Butter |
| Mariscos | Seafood |
| Molho | Sauce |
| Ovos | Eggs |
| Pão | Bread |
| Peixe | Fish |
| Pimenta | Pepper |
| Prato | Plate |
| Queijo | Cheese |
| Sal | Salt |
| Sobremesa | Dessert |
| Sopa/Caldo | Soup |
| Sorvete | Ice cream |
| Taxa de serviço | Service charge |
| Tucupi | Fermented manioc and chicory sauce used in Amazonian cuisine |

## Cooking terms

| | |
|---|---|
| **Assado** | Roasted |
| **Bem gelado** | Well chilled |
| **Churrasco** | Barbecue |
| **Cozido** | Boiled, Steamed |
| **Cozinhar** | To cook |
| **Grelhado** | Grilled |
| **Mal passado/ Bem passado** | Rare/Well done (Meat) |
| **Médio** | Medium grilled |
| **Milanesa** | Breaded |
| **Na chapa/Na brasa** | Charcoal grilled |

## Seafood (frutos do mar)

| | |
|---|---|
| **Acarajé** | Fried bean cake stuffed with *vatapá* (see below) |
| **Agulha** | Needle fish |
| **Atum** | Tuna |
| **Camarão** | Prawn, Shrimp |
| **Caranguejo** | Large crab |
| **Filhote** | Amazon river fish |
| **Lagosta** | Lobster |
| **Lula** | Squid |
| **Mariscos** | Shellfish |
| **Moqueca** | Seafood stewed in palm oil and coconut sauce |
| **Ostra** | Oyster |
| **Pescada** | Seafood stew, or hake |
| **Pirarucu** | Amazon river fish |
| **Pitu** | Crayfish |
| **Polvo** | Octopus |
| **Siri** | Small crab |
| **Sururu** | A type of mussel |
| **Vatapá** | Bahian shrimp dish, cooked with palm oil, skinned tomato and coconut milk, served with fresh coriander and hot peppers |

## Meat and poultry (carne e aves)

| | |
|---|---|
| **Bife** | Steak |
| **Bife a cavalo** | Steak with egg and *farinha* |
| **Cabrito** | Kid |
| **Carne de porco** | Pork |
| **Carneiro** | Lamb |
| **Costela** | Ribs |
| **Costeleta** | Chop |
| **Feijoada** | Black bean, pork and sausage stew |
| **Fígado** | Liver |
| **Frango** | Chicken |
| **Leitão** | Suckling pig |
| **Lingüiça** | Sausage |
| **Pato** | Duck |
| **Peru** | Turkey |
| **Peito** | Breast |
| **Perna** | Leg |
| **Picadinha** | Stew |
| **Salsicha** | Hot dog |
| **Veado** | Venison |
| **Vitela** | Veal |

## Fruit (frutas)

| | |
|---|---|
| **Abacate** | Avocado |
| **Abacaxi** | Pineapple |
| **Ameixa** | Plum, Prune |
| **Caju** | Cashew fruit |
| **Carambola** | Star fruit |
| **Cerejas** | Cherries |
| **Côco** | Coconut |
| **Fruta do conde** | Custard apple (also *ata*) |
| **Goiaba** | Guava |

| | |
|---|---|
| **Graviola** | Cherimoya, custard apple |
| **Laranja** | Orange |
| **Limão** | Lime |
| **Maçã** | Apple |
| **Mamão** | Papaya |
| **Manga** | Mango |
| **Maracujá** | Passion fruit |
| **Melancia** | Watermelon |
| **Melão** | Melon |
| **Morango** | Strawberry |
| **Pera** | Pear |
| **Pêssego** | Peach |
| **Uvas** | Grapes |

## Vegetables and spices (legumes e temperos)

| | |
|---|---|
| **Alface** | Lettuce |
| **Alho** | Garlic |
| **Arroz e feijão** | Rice and beans |
| **Azeitonas** | Olives |
| **Batatas** | Potatoes |
| **Canela** | Cinnamon |
| **Cebola** | Onion |
| **Cenoura** | Carrot |
| **Cheiro verde** | Fresh coriander/ cilantro |
| **Coentro** | Parsley |
| **Cravo** | Clove |
| **Dendê** | Palm oil |
| **Ervilhas** | Peas |
| **Espinafre** | Spinach |
| **Macaxeira** | Roasted manioc |
| **Malagueta** | Very hot pepper, looks like red or yellow cherry |
| **Mandioca** | Manioc/Cassava/ Yuca |
| **Milho** | Corn |
| **Palmito** | Palm heart |
| **Pepinho** | Cucumber |
| **Repolho** | Cabbage |
| **Tomate** | Tomato |

## Drinks

| | |
|---|---|
| **Água mineral** | Mineral water |
| **Batida** | Fresh fruit juice with *cachaça* |
| **Cachaça** | Sugar-cane rum |
| **Café com leite** | Coffee with hot milk |
| **Cafézinho** | Small black coffee |
| **Caipirinha** | Rum and lime cocktail |
| **Cerveja** | Bottled beer |
| **Chopp** | Draught beer |
| **Com gás/Sem gás** | Sparkling/Still |
| **Suco** | Fruit juice |
| **Vinho** | Wine |
| **Vitamina** | Fruit juice made with milk |

# Glossary

**Agreste** In the Northeast, the intermediate zone between the coast and the *sertão*

**Aldeia** Originally a mission where Indians were converted, now any isolated hamlet

**Alfândega** Customs

**Amazônia** The Amazon region

**Artesanato** Craft goods

**Azulejo** Decorative glazed tiling

**Baile funk** Afro-Brazilian hip-hop rhythms

**Bairro** Neighbourhood within town or city

**Bandeirante** Member of a group that marched under a *bandeira* (banner or flag) in early missions to open up the interior; Brazilian conquistador

**Barraca** Beach hut

**Batucada** Literally, a drumming session – music-making in general, especially impromptu

**Bloco** Large Carnaval group

**Bolsa** Ferry

**Bosque** Wood

**Bossa nova** literally "new trend"; a jazz form that evolved from samba

**Caatinga** Scrub vegetation of the interior of the Northeast

**Caboclo** Backwoodsman/woman, often of mixed race

**Candomblé** African-Brazilian religion

**Cangaceiro** Outlaws from the interior of the Northeast who flourished in the early twentieth century; the most famous was Lampião

**Capoeira** African-Brazilian martial art/dance form

**Carimbó** Music and dance style from the north

**Carioca** Someone or something from Rio de Janeiro

**Carnaval** Carnival

**Cerrado** Scrubland

**Choro** Musical style, largely instrumental

**Convento** Convent

**Correio** Postal service/post office

**Correio electrónico** Email

**CUT/CGT** Brazilian trades union organizations

**Dancetaria** Nightspot where the emphasis is on dancing

**Engenho** Sugar mill or plantation

**Estado Novo** The period when Getúlio Vargas was effectively dictator, from the mid-1930s to 1945

**EUA** USA

**Ex voto** Thank-offering to saint for intercession

**Favela** Shantytown, slum

**Fazenda** Country estate, ranch house

**Feira** Country market

**Ferroviária** Train station

**Forró** Dance and type of music from the Northeast

**Frescão** Air-conditioned bus

**Frevo** Frenetic musical style and dance from Recife

**FUNAI** Government organization intended to protect the interests of Brazilian Indians; seriously underfunded and with a history of corruption

**Garimpeiro** Prospector or miner

**Gaúcho** Person or thing from Rio Grande do Sul; also southern cowboy

**Gringo/a** Foreigner, Westerner (not derogatory)

**Ibama** Government organization for preservation of the environment; runs national parks and nature reserves

**Iemanjá** Goddess of the sea in candomblé

**Igreja** Church

**Jangada** Raft

**Largo** Small square

**Latifúndios** Large agricultural estates

**Leito** Luxury express bus

**Literatura de cordel** Literally "string literature" – printed ballads, most common in the Northeast but also found elsewhere, named after the string they are suspended from in country markets

**Litoral** Coast, coastal zone

**Louro/a** Fair-haired/blonde – Westerners in general

**Maconha** Marijuana

**Macumba** African-Brazilian religion, usually thought of as more authentically "African" than *candomblé*; most common in the North

**Marginal** Petty thief, outlaw

**Mata** Jungle, remote interior

**Mata Atlântica** Atlantic forest – the native jungle that once covered most of coastal Brazil and its immediate hinterland, but is now restricted to the South

**Mercado** Market

**Mineiro** Person or thing from Minas Gerais

**Mirante** Viewing point

**Mosteiro** Monastery

**Movimentado** Lively, where the action is

**MPB** Música Popular Brasileira, common shorthand for Brazilian music

**Nordeste** Northeastern Brazil

**Nordestino/a** Inhabitant thereof

**Nova República** The New Republic – the period since the return to civilian democracy in 1985

**Paulista** Person or thing from São Paulo state

**Paulistano** Inhabitant of the city of São Paulo

**Pelourinho** Pillory or whipping post, common in colonial town squares

**Planalto Central** Vast interior tablelands of central Brazil

**Posto** Highway service station, often with basic accommodation popular with truckers

**Pousada** Inn

**Praça** Square

**Praia** Beach

**Prefeitura** Town hall, and by extension city governments in general

**PT** Partido dos Trabalhadores or Workers' Party, the largest left-wing party in Brazil, led by Lula

**Quebrado** Out of order

**Rodovia** Highway

**Rodoviária** Bus station

**Samba** Type of music most associated with Carnaval in Rio

**Selva** Jungle

**Senzala** Slave quarters

**Sertanejo** Inhabitant of *sertão*

**Sertão** Arid, drought-ridden interior of the Northeast

**Sesmaria** Royal Portuguese land grant to early settlers

**Sobrado** Two-storey colonial mansion

**Terreiro** House where *candomblé* or *umbanda* rituals and ceremonies take place

**Umbanda** African-Brazilian religion especially common in urban areas of the South and Southeast

**Vaqueiro** Cowboy in the North

**Visto** Visa

# Small print and

# Index

## A Rough Guide to Rough Guides

Published in 1982, the first Rough Guide – to Greece – was a student scheme that became a publishing phenomenon. Mark Ellingham, a recent graduate in English from Bristol University, had been travelling in Greece the previous summer and couldn't find the right guidebook. With a small group of friends he wrote his own guide, combining a highly contemporary, journalistic style with a thoroughly practical approach to travellers' needs.

The immediate success of the book spawned a series that rapidly covered dozens of destinations. And, in addition to impecunious backpackers, Rough Guides soon acquired a much broader and older readership that relished the guides' wit and inquisitiveness as much as their enthusiastic, critical approach and value-for-money ethos.

These days, Rough Guides include recommendations from shoestring to luxury and cover more than 200 destinations around the globe, including almost every country in the Americas and Europe, more than half of Africa and most of Asia and Australasia. Our ever-growing team of authors and photographers is spread all over the world, particularly in Europe, the US and Australia.

In the early 1990s, Rough Guides branched out of travel, with the publication of Rough Guides to World Music, Classical Music and the Internet. All three have become benchmark titles in their fields, spearheading the publication of a wide range of books under the Rough Guide name.

Including the travel series, Rough Guides now number more than 350 titles, covering: phrasebooks, waterproof maps, music guides from Opera to Heavy Metal, reference works as diverse as Conspiracy Theories and Shakespeare, and popular culture books from iPods to Poker. Rough Guides also produce a series of more than 120 World Music CDs in partnership with World Music Network.

Visit www.roughguides.com to see our latest publications.

Rough Guide travel images are available for commercial licensing at www.roughguidespictures.com

## Acknowledgements

**Dilwyn Jenkins**: Tess Jenkins, Cecilia McCallum, Ann Tatham, Joel Souza, Alex Gero Mesquita, also Max, Pedro and George of the Caves from the Hotel Dez de Julho in Manaus) and João of Maanaim Amazônia (Rio Branco).

**Oliver Marshall**: Karin Hanta, Leslie Bethell, Eduardo Silva, Graça Salgado and Isaura in Rio, Ben Berry in Paraty, Alicia and Kevan Prior in Búzios, Jo Marcos and Virginio Mello in Petrópolis, Bibiana Schappel in Curitiba, Silvana Nascimento and Daisy Quintão in Minas Gerais, John Fernandes in Puerto Iguazú, Cleverson Gonzalez of the ICVB in Foz do Iguaçu, Dona Margarida of the always wonderful Hotel Pousada Recanto Suiço in Nova Petrópolis and our editors at Rough Guides.

## Readers' letters

Thanks to all the readers who have taken the time to write in with comments and suggestions (and apologies if we've inadvertently omitted or misspelt anyone's name):

Priscilla Adey, Marjolijn Bens, Miriam Dolgos, Oliva & Edvan Coutinho van Eeghem, Peter Elford, Macdara Ferris, Jerry Fisher, Nicholas Goodyer, Daniël en Hester, Simon Hillyard, Barnaby Hodgson, Maeve Hosea, Diana & Tom John, Thomas Jonsson, Tanya Jordan, Magds van Kinderen, Lila Koumandou, Cathy Larson, Gregg & Janet Lewis, Julia MacKenzie, Clare Martin, Sharlene Matsuhara, Fernando Mattoso, Noel McDermott, Jaime Miranda, Pedro Novak, Rebekah Parker, Billy Rawcliffe, Mark Rickards, Hester van Santen, Henk Segaert, Garry Telford, Martin Vegoda, Franz Aichinger Vienna, Sandra & Terry Wall, Dr Richard Williams, Eugene Zelikman.

## Rough Guide credits

**Text editors**: Keith Drew, Lara Kavanagh, James Smart, Harry Wilson
**Layout**: Nikhil Agarwal
**Cartography**: Rajesh Chhibber, Deshpal Dabas
**Picture editor**: Sarah Cummins
**Production**: Rebecca Short
**Proofreader**: Diane Margolis
**Cover design**: Chloë Roberts
**Photographers**: Demetrio Carrasco, Roger d'Olivere Mapp, Alex Robinson
**Editorial**: Ruth Blackmore, Andy Turner, Edward Aves, Alice Park, Lucy White, Jo Kirby, Natasha Foges, Róisín Cameron, Emma Traynor, Emma Gibbs, Kathryn Lane, Christina Valhouli, Monica Woods, Mani Ramaswamy, Lucy Cowie, Helen Ochyra, Amanda Howard, Alison Roberts, Joe Staines, Peter Buckley, Matthew Milton, Tracy Hopkins, Ruth Tidball; **Delhi** Madhavi Singh, Karen D'Souza, Lubna Shaheen
**Design & Pictures: London** Scott Stickland, Dan May, Diana Jarvis, Mark Thomas, Nicole Newman, Emily Taylor; **Delhi** Umesh Aggarwal, Ajay Verma, Jessica Subramanian, Ankur Guha, Pradeep Thapliyal, Sachin Tanwar, Anita Singh, Sachin Gupta
**Production**: Vicky Baldwin
**Cartography: London** Maxine Repath, Ed Wright, Katie Lloyd-Jones; **Delhi** Ashutosh Bharti, Rajesh Mishra, Animesh Pathak, Jasbir Sandhu, Karobi Gogoi, Alakananda Bhattacharya, Swati Handoo
**Online: London** George Atwell, Faye Hellon, Jeanette Angell, Fergus Day, Justine Bright, Clare Bryson, Aine Fearon, Adrian Low, Ezgi Celebi, Amber Bloomfield; **Delhi** Amit Verma, Rahul Kumar, Narender Kumar, Ravi Yadav, Debojit Borah, Rakesh Kumar, Ganesh Sharma, Shisir Basumatari
**Marketing & Publicity: London** Liz Statham, Niki Hanmer, Louise Maher, Jess Carter, Vanessa Godden, Vivienne Watton, Anna Paynton, Rachel Sprackett, Libby Jellie, Laura Vipond, Vanessa McDonald; **New York** Katy Ball, Judi Powers, Nancy Lambert; **Delhi** Ragini Govind
**Manager India**: Punita Singh
**Reference Director**: Andrew Lockett
**Operations Manager**: Helen Phillips
**PA to Publishing Director**: Nicola Henderson
**Publishing Director**: Martin Dunford
**Commercial Manager**: Gino Magnotta
**Managing Director**: John Duhigg

ROUGH GUIDES

SMALL PRINT

## Publishing information

This seventh edition published October 2009 by **Rough Guides Ltd**,
80 Strand, London WC2R 0RL
14 Local Shopping Centre, Panchsheel Park, New Delhi 110017, India
**Distributed by the Penguin Group**
Penguin Books Ltd,
80 Strand, London WC2R 0RL
Penguin Group (USA)
375 Hudson Street, NY 10014, USA
Penguin Group (Australia)
250 Camberwell Road, Camberwell, Victoria 3124, Australia
Penguin Group (Canada)
195 Harry Walker Parkway N, Newmarket, ON, L3Y 7B3 Canada
Penguin Group (NZ)
67 Apollo Drive, Mairangi Bay, Auckland 1310, New Zealand
Cover concept by Peter Dyer.
Typeset in Bembo and Helvetica to an original design by Henry Iles.
Printed in Italy by L.E.G.O. S.p.A, Lavis (TN)

792pp includes index
A catalogue record for this book is available from the British Library
ISBN: 978-1-84836-189-8

1 3 5 7 9 8 6 4 2

## Help us update

We've gone to a lot of effort to ensure that the seventh edition of **The Rough Guide to Brazil** is accurate and up-to-date. However, things change – places get "discovered", opening hours are notoriously fickle, restaurants and rooms raise prices or lower standards. If you feel we've got it wrong or left something out, we'd like to know, and if you can remember the address, the price, the hours, the phone number, so much the better.

Please send your comments with the subject line **"Rough Guide Brazil Update"** to ©mail@roughguides.com. We'll credit all contributions and send a copy of the next edition (or any other Rough Guide if you prefer) for the very best emails.

Have your questions answered and tell others about your trip at
ⓦcommunity.roughguides.com

## Photo credits

All photos © Rough Guides except the following:

### Title page

Pernambuco State, Olinda © Derwal Fred/ Photolibrary

### Introduction

Carnival, Olinda © Vittorio Sciosia/Alamy
Candomble priestess sitting with child, Salvador © Annie Belt/Corbis
Rio carnival © Jon Arnold Images Ltd/Alamy
Fernando de Noronha © Herve Collart/Sygma/ Corbis

### Things not to miss

**02** Capoeira, Salvador © Paul Nevin/ Photolibrary.com
**03** Buying codfish at the Mercado Municipal de Sao Paulo © Paulo Fridman/Corbis
**06** Reggae band in Salvador's Pelourinho square © Ricardo Azoury/Corbis
**07** Avenida Paulista, Sao Paulo © David R Frazier Photolibrary Inc/Alamy
**08** Fazenda Pinhal © Francesco Venturi/Corbis
**09** Morro do Pai Inacio, Chapada Diamantina © FAN travelstock/Alamy
**10** Street scene, Olinda © TTL Images/Alamy
**11** Churrasco, Brazil © Photolibrary
**13** Candomblé dance, Sao Paulo © Gianni Muratore/Alamy
**17** Ouro Preto © WottoWotto/Photolibrary
**18** Traditional sailboat © Photolibrary
**21** Teatro Nacional © VIEW pictures Ltd/Alamy
**22** Jabaquara beach at Ilhabela © Cristiano Burmester/Alamy
**23** Rio nightlife © Steve J Benbow/Phot290/Axiom
**25** Amazon Ecopark, Manaus © Alfio Garozzo/ Photolibrary
**26** Glória church © Andrew Holt/Alamy
**27** Snorkeller in natural freshwater spring, Bonito © Andre Seale/Alamy
**28** Promenade, Ipanema Beach © Kordcom Kordcom/Photolibrary
**30** Teatro Amazonas © Tips Images
**31** Rio de Janeiro Carnaval Marcelo © Sayao/ epa/Corbis

### Black and whites

**p.90** Cathedral, Rio de Janeiro © Arco Images GmbH/Alamy
**p.121** Nightlife in Lapa District © IML Image Group Ltd/Alamy
**p.210** Minas Gerais © Photolibrary
**p.220** Convento da Penha, Espirito Santo © Andre Seale/Alamy
**p.232** Capoeira © Vittorio Sciosia/Alamy
**p.241** Rio Branco Palace © GM Photo Images/ Alamy
**p.247** Nossa Senhora do Rosario © Arco Images GmbH/Alamy
**p.252** Pelourinho © Peter Turnley/Corbis
**p.271** Chapada Diamantina National Park © John Loggins/www.DanitaDelmont.com
**p.280** Baia dos Porcos © Robert Harding Picture Library Ltd/Alamy
**p.302** Recife beach © Rolf Richardson/Alamy
**p.311** Street carnival, Olinda © Stefano Paterna/ Alamy
**p.323** São Francisco © SPP Images/Alamy
**p.339** Dune buggy, Natal © GM Photo Images/ Alamy
**p.348** Windsurfer, Jericoacoara © Silvan wick water-sports/Alamy
**p.364** Small riverboat, Manaus © Worldwide Picture Library/Alamy
**p.370** Passengers on a ship from Santarem to Belem © Good Look/Corbis
**p.377** Fish market in the Para Belem province © Good Look/Corbis
**p.398** Alter do Chao © Douglas Engle/Corbis
**p.412** Cargo and passenger boats at Manaus, Amazonas © Stephanie Maze/Corbis
**p.420** Brown throated three-toed sloth, Amazon river basin © Tom Brakefield/Corbis
**p.436** Aerial view of Mount Roraima © Yann Arthus-Bertrand/Corbis
**p.511** Freshwater snorkelling in Bonito © Cristiano Burmester/Alamy
**p.590** Craft market, Embu © Gavin Mather/Alamy
**p.603** Beach at Ilhabela © Cristiano Burmester/ Alamy
**p.665** Farmhouse in the German immigrant region of Brazil © Michael Fritzen/Alamy

### Brazilian food and drink colour section

Assorted chillies in bags at spice market, Brazil © Guy Moberly/Photolibrary
Bahian food stalls © Owen Franken/Corbis
Daily life in Amazonian rainforest villages © Colin McPherson/Corbis
Carne de sol © KUBA/Corbis
Juice shop, Rio © Ricardo Azoury/Corbis
Chimarrao drinker, Rio Grande do Sul © AGB Photo/Alamy
Coffee sack © Ryman Cabannes/photocuisine/ Corbis

### Amazon flora and fauna colour section

Waterlily, Amazon river © Danita Delimont/Alamy
Amazon lily © Kevin Schafer/CORBIS
Leaf cutting ants © Keren Su/Corbis
Giant river otter eating fish © Theo Allofs/Corbis
Three vehicles on rough terrain © Daniel Beltra/ Getty
Dwarf caiman © Visuals Unlimited/Corbis
Tourists taking Amazon river tour © Ricardo Azoury/CORBIS

# Index

Map entries are in colour.



ROUGH GUIDES

SMALL PRINT

# O



# P



# R

## S

## T



## U



## V



## W



## X



## Y

# Map symbols

maps are listed in the full index using coloured text

- International border
- Chapter division boundary
- State border
- Major road
- Minor road
- Steps
- Path
- Railway
- Metro station & line
- Ferry route
- Waterway
- Funicular
- Cable car
- Bridge/tunnel
- Mountain peak
- Cave
- Marsh
- Waterfall
- Cliffs
- Hill shading
- Point of interest
- Gate
- Viewpoint
- Lighthouse
- Fort
- Airport
- Bus stop
- Tourist office
- Post office
- Telephone office
- Statue/memorial
- Church (regional)
- Church (town)
- Building
- Market
- Stadium
- Cemetery
- Park or reserve
- Beach